MULE AND BLACK-TAILED DEER
OF NORTH AMERICA

MULE AND
BLACK-TAILED

DEER OF NORTH AMERICA

A WILDLIFE MANAGEMENT INSTITUTE BOOK

Developed in cooperation with
U.S. DEPARTMENT OF AGRICULTURE, FOREST SERVICE

Compiled and Edited by

Olof C. Wallmo

Illustrated by

Dean Rocky Barrick

Technical Editors

Richard E. McCabe and Laurence R. Jahn

University of Nebraska Press • Lincoln and London

University of Nebraska Press
901 North 17th Street
Lincoln NE 68588

Library of Congress Cataloging in Publication Data
Main entry under title:
Mule and black-tailed deer of North America.

"A Wildlife Management Institute book." Includes bib-
liographical references and index. 1. Mule deer.   2.
Mammals—North America.
    I.   Wallmo, Olof C.
QL737.U55M84   599.73'57   80–20128
ISBN 0–8032–4715–X

3 9, 4/9

Design and layout by Dick McCabe and Ken Sabol

CONTENTS

FIGURES

TABLES

FOREWORD

Perhaps the most recognizable of the mule deer's unique characteristics is its stiff-legged, bounding gait, known as stotting. The gait is an adaptation to the sometimes rugged terrain of western North America and a behavior used to escape pursuing predators. But, while advantageous in the deer's natural world, such adaptations and defensive strategies offer the mulie and the blacktail no protection against man's incursions into that world.

Because of man's growing numbers, spreading settlements, and technological capabilities, his life-style threatens the very foundation of the deer's well-being—its habitat. During the past half century, in fact, man's reach has spread increasingly into the deer's domain, occupying lush valleys and key ranges, blocking or curtailing migration routes, altering vegetational cover, and in other ways reducing the acreage as well as the amount and quality of forage available to the animals.

Historically, mule and black-tailed deer populations have undergone gradual buildups and relatively abrupt declines. In recent decades, with no definite geographic pattern whatever, most populations have trended downward. Wildlife scientists have investigated the apparent causes of local declines, which have ranged from predation to forage shortages, to weather conditions on winter ranges, to drought, to diseases and parasites and other factors including, in some cases, too-liberal hunting regulations. Yet, while the animals have coped with such situations over the millennia, and undoubtedly will again, one factor that grows more troublesome and unmanageable is the effect of an ever-enlarging human population on the animals' habitat base.

In 1956 the Wildlife Management Institute produced *The Deer of North America,* edited by Walter P. Taylor. That book was "a consolidation of available information, both new and old" that gave "a complete picture of deer management as it is understood today." It served the emerging science of wildlife management well, but much of what then was known of mule and black-tailed deer ecology has since been either discarded or revised, updated, and supplemented. What then was known of mule and black-tailed deer management was to large extent in the trial-and-error stage. Although scientific wildlife management still is relatively young, a wealth of new information has been uncovered, and techniques of management are considerably more refined than they were in 1956 or, for that matter, a decade ago.

Mule deer and blacktails, along with white-tailed deer, collectively are considered North America's premier big game species. For the deer to retain that lofty position, both in fact and opinion, scientific management must keep pace. This book was prepared to provide a new and formidable base for understanding and managing mule and black-tailed deer and, of course, their habitats. By gathering in a single volume the most recent and most pertinent information about these interesting and valuable animals, the Institute seeks to provide the information and understanding that will lead to further refinement in management practices.

This comprehensive work can serve research, applied management, and policy-and decision-making in the best interest of the resource. Besides historical background, data, techniques, and advice, the book offers a sense of optimism—optimism that deer and their necessary habitats, through scientific wildlife management, can continue to be an integral and important part of the North American landscape.

Daniel A. Poole, President
Wildlife Management Institute

PREFACE

The genus of deer *Odocoileus* evolved in North America long before *Homo sapiens* invaded the continent. Over the many centuries since man arrived, he may have helped exterminate several large mammal species. Deer, however, were too swift, alert, elusive, and well adapted to the landscape to be significantly affected by man's primitive predatory activity. As man himself evolved and gravitated to a sedentary lifestyle in the New World, deer actually prospered in the new or revitalized habitats made available by the ever-increasing scope of human settlement.

Today, when the daily affairs of most North American citizens are conducted in an environment of high-rise buildings, superhighways, fast-food restaurants, urban and suburban sprawl, corporate farming, and supersonic aviation, deer are a reminder of wilderness heritage. At the very least, these animals symbolize a fundamental ecological value.

Each year, more than twelve million hunters in the United States go afield in pursuit of deer during regulated hunting seasons. But this does not account for all the people to whom deer are a valued resource. Some seek to witness and perhaps record the grace and beauty of the animal; some want to experience the atavistic role of the predator; some wish to supplement their larders; and some endeavor primarily to enjoy the sanctity and beauty of field and forest. All share appreciation for a resource that represents the pristine conditions that "civilization" and "progress" tend to overshadow.

I am certain that deer would rank at or very near the top of any poll of popular and desirable North American wildlife. Precisely for that reason, management of deer, of one sort or another, is inevitable. Social pressures are exerted, political forces enlisted, legislative decisions made, and administrative mandates issued in behalf of deer. Public demands may be altruistic, selfish, ill-conceived, conflicting, or even impossible to fulfill, but still they can be assigned as management goals.

Of course, this accommodation of public demand poses a frustrating responsibility for administrators and a staggering challenge to wildlife biologists and resource managers. They must seek both philosophical and technical solutions. This book offers neither. Solutions to such problems seldom are found in books; they usually are decided in social and political arenas. But this book does provide a scientific base from which management alternatives can be generated, decisions made, and results appraised.

This book deals with a number of kinds of deer that are similar enough taxonomically to be considered members of the species *Odocoileus hemionus*. There is no universally accepted common name for the collection of subspecies throughout their combined range in Mexico, Canada, and the United States, but there are two major groups, referred to as mule deer and black-tailed deer. It must be kept in mind, however, that, like other "mule" deer, black-tailed deer or blacktails are merely distinctive subspecies of *Odocoileus hemionus*.

This book reviews the scientific literature, research, and insights—particularly those of the last quarter century—that contribute to our understanding of mule and black-tailed deer and their interactions with their environments. It is a synthesis of current knowledge about the species and its habitats. Admittedly, however, the information provided here is but a small fraction of the data that can and should be obtained in order to manage populations of the species most effectively in their many and varied habitats. Perhaps the ultimate value of the book is not necessarily in what it synthesizes for use in management today, but rather in what it does not and cannot *yet* say about management of mule and black-tailed deer tomorrow. By virtue of this unavoidable deficiency, it gives clue to further opportunities for enhancing management expertise and hence the well-being of the species and its habitats.

This book is directed primarily to wildlife resource biologists, managers, educators, students, researchers, and administrators. It is their professional performance, for better or worse, that will continue to shape attitudes toward and priorities for and among natural resources in both social and political arenas. In addition, *Mule and Black-tailed Deer of North America* is designed to be of interest and use to outdoor enthusiasts and all others interested in improved management of mule deer, black-tailed deer, and deer habitats. It is these individuals who ultimately determine the values of these resources and the amount of attention given to maintaining them. Therefore, although this book is oriented toward the professional wildlife community, it has been prepared in a manner to encourage greater public understanding of the species and greater appreciation of the need for the role of sound scientific management.

O. C. Wallmo

ACKNOWLEDGMENTS

Foremost among those to be recognized for cooperation in developing this book is the United States Department of Agriculture, Forest Service. Personnel of this agency helped provide the foresight, insights, and persistence required to develop the form and substance of this publication.

The authors and editors of *Mule and Black-tailed Deer of North America* also gratefully acknowledge the important contributions and assistance of the following individuals in completing this book.

E. O. Allen, Montana Fish and Game Department

J. W. Banks, Colorado State University

C. Barette, Laval University, Quebec

E. Beltran, Instituto Mexicano de Recursos Naturales Renovables

R. W. Brown, United States Forest Service

E. H. Bruns, Alberta Recreation, Parks, and Wildlife

R. A. Carlson, Minnesota Department of Natural Resources

G. C. Christensen, Nevada Department of Fish and Game

R. M. Corsi, Wyoming Game and Fish Department

I. McT. Cowan, University of British Columbia

J. Crawford, United States Bureau of Land Management

J. Crenshaw, New Mexico Department of Fish and Game

D. Daughtry, Arizona Game and Fish Department

R. Denney, The Wildlife Society, Washington, D.C.

D. Domenick, Colorado Division of Wildlife

W. R. Dwyer, United States Fish and Wildlife Service

D. L. Eaton, United States Fish and Wildlife Service

P. N. Ebert, Oregon Department of Fish and Wildlife

J. L. Egan, Montana Fish and Game Department

M. Egbert, Utah State University

R. Ferguson, Wyoming Game and Fish Department

R. Fowler, South Dakota Department of Game, Fish, and Parks

S. Gallizioli, Arizona Game and Fish Department

R. B. Gill, Colorado Division of Wildlife

J. Gladson, Oregon Fish and Wildlife Department

J. R. Gross, United States Fish and Wildlife Service

M. Haderlie, United States Fish and Wildlife Service

P. F. Haley, British Columbia Fish and Wildlife Branch

D. R. Halladay, British Columbia Fish and Wildlife Branch

N. V. Hancock, Utah Division of Wildlife Resources

K. W. Harmon, Wildlife Management Institute, Firth, Nebraska

W. G. Hauser, United States Forest Service

D. Hebert, British Columbia Fish and Wildlife Branch

M. Hershkopf, Colorado Division of Wildlife

M. Hoefs, Yukon Game Branch

M. Hornocker, Idaho Cooperative Wildlife Research Unit

E. G. Hunt, California Department of Fish and Game

F. H. Jacot, United States National Park Service

R. T. John, Utah Division of Wildlife Resources

J. F. Johnson, New Mexico Department of Game and Fish

L. Johnson, Alaska Fish and Game Department

D. A. Jones, United States Forest Service

M. Kaschke, United States Fish and Wildlife Service

D. R. Klein, Alaska Cooperative Wildlife Research Unit

F. F. Knowlton, United States Fish and Wildlife Service

P. R. Krausman, University of Arizona

R. Kuhn, Oregon Department of Fish and Wildlife

E. J. Larson, United States Soil Conservation Service

A. S. Leopold, University of California at Berkeley

W. M. Longhurst, University of California at Davis

C. M. Loveless, United States Forest Service

T. R. McCabe, Utah State University

S. McColloum, United States Fish and Wildlife Service

C. Y. McCulloch, Arizona Game and Fish Department

W. G. MacGregor, British Columbia Fish and Wildlife Branch

J. V. McKenzie, North Dakota Game and Fish Department

D. E. McKnight, Alaska Fish and Game Department

R. R. MacLennan, Saskatchewan Department of Tourism and Renewable Resources

C. T. Mason, Jr., University of Arizona at Tucson

L. D. Mech, United States Fish and Wildlife Service

K. Menzel, Nebraska Game and Parks Commission

B. Miller, Texas Parks and Wildlife Department

M. A. Miller, Montana Fish and Game Department

C. H. Nellis, Idaho Department of Fish and Game

L. Nelson, Jr., University of California at Davis

R. D. Nelson, United States Forest Service

B. W. O'Gara, Montana Cooperative Wildlife Research Unit

L. D. Parsons, Washington Department of Game

C. M. Paul, Englewood, Colorado

W. C. Peabody, Kansas Forestry, Fish, and Game Commission

T. M. Pojar, Colorado Division of Wildlife

D. A. Poole, Wildlife Management Institute, Washington, D.C.

R. Pratt, freelance graphic artist, Washington, D.C.

W. V. Reaves, Texas Parks and Wildlife Department

W. L. Robinette, United States Fish and Wildlife Service (retired)

R. D. Roughton, United States Fish and Wildlife Service

G. Ruiz, Lomas Bozares, Mexico

K. J. Sabol, Wildlife Management Institute, Washington, D.C.

R. M. F. S. Sadleir, Simon Fraser University, Burnaby, British Columbia

D. E. Samuel, West Virginia University

H. Shaw, Arizona Game and Fish Department

S. G. Shetler, Smithsonian Institution, Washington, D.C.

V. C. Simpson, California Department of Fish and Game

J. W. Skene, Saskatchewan Department of Tourism and Natural Resources

D. R. Smith, United States Forest Service

R. H. Smith, Arizona Game and Fish Department

D. Strickland, Wyoming Game and Fish Department

D. Strode, United States Forest Service

L. H. Suring, Colorado State University

T. C. Telfer, Hawaii Department of Land and Natural Resources

J. Thiessen, Idaho Department of Fish and Game

C. Trainer, Oregon Department of Fish and Wildlife

G. Tsukamoto, Nevada Department of Fish and Game

P. B. Uzzell, Texas Parks and Wildlife Department

M. T. Walton, Wildlife Management Institute, Dripping Springs, Texas

J. Warburton, United States Bureau of Land Management

R. H. Wauer, United States National Park Service

P. M. Webb, Arizona Game and Fish Department

J. Weis, Utah Division of Wildlife Resources

A. Whittaker, Colorado Division of Wildlife

J. E. Williams, New Mexico Game and Fish Department

M. Williams, Idaho Fish and Game Department

L. L. Williamson, Wildlife Management Institute, Washington, D.C.

L. Wilson, United States Bureau of Land Management

E. R. Wiltse, Saskatchewan Department of Tourism and Renewable Resources

C. K. Winkler, Texas Parks and Wildlife Department

J. D. Yoakum, United States Bureau of Land Management

For their assistance in expediting the draft manuscripts for this publication, the editors extend their thanks to C. E. Wallmo, B. S. Gutierrez, L. B. Baumann, D. Gore, E. J. Walters, C. A. Urlass, D. A. Taylor, and C. J. Peddicord.

Chapter 1

MULE AND BLACK-TAILED DEER DISTRIBUTION AND HABITATS

Olof C. Wallmo
Principal Wildlife Biologist
United States Forest Service
Juneau, Alaska

Mule deer and black-tailed deer, along with white-tailed deer, constitute a genus called *Odocoileus*—one of seventeen worldwide genera of the deer family, Cervidae. Including such diverse animals as moose, elk, caribou, and many other Eurasian, South American, northwest African, and Pacific island genera, this family belongs to the ruminant suborder Ruminantia of the large and varied order of even-toed hoofed mammals, Artiodactyla.

Cervids differ most conspicuously from other Ruminantia in that the males—and female caribou—grow bony antlers that are shed each year. This contrasts with sheep, cattle, pronghorn, antelope, and other ruminants that have permanent horns with a keratin or hair-derived sheath over a bony core. Members of the genus *Odocoileus* cannot be described well in terms of unique characteristics; they simply are medium-sized deer with a combination of characterisitics that none of the other genera possess in total.

Leaving a more explicit definition to other texts, such as *Mammals of the World* (Walker 1975), we can proceed to other considerations of mule and black-tailed deer. Paleontologists believe the genus evolved in the Old World, where it no longer is represented, and arrived in North America more than two million years ago. Fossil remains from mid- to late-Pliocene deposits have some characteristics similar to those of modern-day *O. hemionus,* the mule and black-tailed deer (Fry and Gustafson 1974; Opdyke et al. 1977). The fossil record is poor, however, and how the earliest genetic stock resulted in the two species and many subspecies known today is open to speculation.

Although mule and black-tailed deer interbreed with white-tailed deer, *O. virginianus,* the two species are clearly distinct: they maintain their separate identities in the extensive areas where their ranges overlap. And, though mule and black-tailed deer intergrade in some areas to form hybrid populations, they are different enough to have prompted Cowan (1956*b*, p. 339) to speculate that blacktails (*O. h. columbianus* and *O. h. sitkensis*) represent "a species in the making."

Columbian and Sitka blacktails differ only in slight degree, as do the several subspecies referred to generally as mule deer. With respect to recent evolution, Cowan (1956*b*, p. 339) observed that one subspecies, the Rocky Mountain mule deer, occurs in a large area that was covered by ice during the Pleistocene, whereas "in the southern quarter of mule deer range, where the tenure of deer residence has probably continued uninterrupted from the ages preceding the continental glaciation, the mule deer has diversified into eight recognizable races." It might be added that the Pacific Northwest domain of the black-tailed deer also escaped major glaciation in the Pleistocene (Waring and Franklin 1979). Northern areas of the Pacific coastal region were extremely glaciated, however, but presumably were not occupied by deer in the Pleistocene. Subsequently, then, deer invaded north coastal British Columbia and Alaska and have become what is considered a separate subspecies—Sitka black-tailed deer (Alaska Department of Fish and Game 1973).

Additional hypotheses on the evolution of subspecies might be generated from the influences of topographic, climatic, and vegetational factors associated with their distribution. But they would only be hypotheses. Still, it should be understood that differences recognized by taxonomists in naming subspecies *might* be accompanied by differences in behavior or physiology that reflect unique adaptations to different environments. The content of this book will reveal that such inquiry has been neglected despite its potential ecological significance.

Indeed, little effort has been applied to discriminating between phenotypic and genotypic variation. For example, specimens from Sierra Seri, Sonora, differed slightly in coloration from desert mule deer (*O. h. crooki*), and so they were called burro deer (*O. h. eremicus*) and given a geographic range. Subsequent specimens from within the range were found to be more typical of *O. h. crooki* (Hoffmeister 1962). Such information justifies the examination of extensive series of specimens collected over a range of space and span of time adequate to determine whether the populations of one area are consistently different from those of another area. This remains a challenge to deer biologists and taxonomists.

Subspecies are not totally distinct entities with ranges enclosed by lines on which taxonomists agree for all time. Mayr (1949, p. 106) noted: "It is, in many cases, entirely dependent upon the judgement of the individual taxonomist how many . . . populations are to be included in one subspecies. The limits of most subspecies, therefore, are subjective as we

can give only empirical definition for this taxonomic category. . . . Subspecies intergrade almost unnoticeably in nearly all cases in which there is distributional continuity." Distributional continuity is a conspicuous feature of this species—a fact that makes designating subspecies more difficult and less subject to universal agreement.

The classification presented by Cowan (1956*a*) has been reconsidered in minor respects. He recognized eleven subspecies of mule and black-tailed deer, including the burro deer (*O. h. eremicus*) of southwestern Arizona, southeastern California, and adjacent Mexico, and the Inyo mule deer (*O. h. inyoensis*) of eastern California. Hoffmeister (1962) disposed of the name *O. h. eremicus,* and included this group with desert mule deer (*O. h. crooki*). I. McT. Cowan (pers. comm., December 1975) wrote: "I have misgivings about the validity of *O. h. inyoensis.*" A. S. Leopold (pers. comm., October 1977) also did not consider it "a very valid subspecies." W. G. MacGregor (pers. comm., November 1977) expressed the same judgment.

Two other subspecies—*O. h. sheldoni,* the mule deer of Tiburon Island, Mexico, and *O. h. cerrosensis* of Cedros Island—also might be questioned. Cowan and Leopold revealed in their personal communications that, despite earlier concern that these two subspecies may have been extirpated, some deer apparently continue to exist on both islands. Cowan felt there was no alternative to indicating their presence on the map (fig. 1). The Cedros Island deer is the only subspecies of *O. hemionus* regarded as under threat of extinction (Cowan and Halloway 1978).

Cedros Island is separated from the west coast of Baja California off Punta Santa Eugenia, and specimens examined by Cowan (1956*a*) were quite different from the mainland deer. He learned there still were "50+ deer on the remote S.W. part of the island" (pers. comm., November 1977). Tiburon Island is separated from the coast of Sonora by about 2.5 kilometers (1.5 miles). Leopold (pers. comm., October 1977) learned that deer still were there ten years before. Cowan (1956*a*, p. 353) de-

Figure 1. Geographic range of (1) Rocky Mountain mule deer, (2) desert mule deer, (2*a*) Tiburon Island mule deer, (3) California mule deer, (4) Southern mule deer, (4*a*) Cedros Island mule deer, (5) peninsula mule deer, (6) Columbian black-tailed deer, and (7) Sitka black-tailed deer.

scribed them as "closely similar to the burro deer" that Hoffmeister (1962) incorporated into the desert mule deer subspecies.

Subspecies arise because of partial or complete geographic and, consequently, genetic isolation from the remainder of a species and because of genetic selection imposed by different environments. From this it follows logically that a subspecies is better adapted to its own habitat and less well equipped to exist in the habitat of other subspecies. With mule deer and blacktails, such an assumption becomes perplexing, however, when it is recognized that one subspecies may occupy a wide diversity of habitats, some of which are characteristically used by another subspecies. Columbian

On one of the earliest official expeditions into the western United States—led by Major Stephen H. Long—Titian Ramsay Peale made what has long been believed to be the first non-Indian painting of a black-tailed deer. In fact, it was made 1 August 1820, of a deer killed by another member of the expedition, in the valley of Ute Creek near present-day Buegeros, Harding County, New Mexico (Tucker 1963). The animal likely was a Rocky Mountain mule deer, and probably not of either blacktail subspecies. The animal was called "black tail" to distinguish it from "common deer"—whitetails—and because the expeditioners had no frame of reference except the Lewis and Clark journals, which referred to the species interchangeably as "mule deer" and "black-tailed deer" (James 1823, pp. 88–89). While Peale's painting is not necessarily the first modern rendering of the black-tailed deer, it may have been the first definitive illustration of a mule deer, and therefore, of the entire species. Photograph courtesy of the American Philosophical Society.

black-tailed deer, California mule deer, Southern mule deer, and desert mule deer all occur in chaparral habitats. Each also occurs in other habitats that structurally are quite different from chaparral. It would be difficult to attribute the differences between these subspecies (races) to structural characteristics of the different environments.

Moreover, deer from one geographic subspecies may be successfully transplanted to unfamiliar habitat in the range of another subspecies. Rocky Mountain mule deer have been introduced in several habitats of desert mule deer and apparently have mixed with the lo-

Dr. Edgar A. Mearns, the naturalist who was credited with collecting and classifying two mule deer type specimens (burro and desert mule deer), is shown skinning a Rocky Mountain mule deer in 1887 at his camp on San Francisco Mountain in Arizona. Photograph courtesy of the Smithsonian Institution, Division of Mammalogy.

cal populations (McCulloch 1955, 1967*b*). Through transplants, desert mule deer from the Trans-Pecos region of Texas have replaced Rocky Mountain mule deer where the latter formerly occurred in the Panhandle (C. K. Winkler, pers. comm. to K. E. Severson, January 1976). Though habitats of subspecies can be described from several standpoints—climate, nutrition, topography, structure, and so on—one cannot infer that the deer from each habitat are unique genotypic or phenotypic products of those environments (see chap. 5).

In Tennessee, indigenous whitetails were permitted to breed with imported Columbian blacktails (Nichols and Murray 1973). All possible combinations, including double hybrids, produced viable offspring. This was an interesting experiment in genetics and perhaps a dangerous one in ecology (see chap. 4).

DISTRIBUTION

Information about currently accepted geographic ranges of the subspecies was obtained by canvassing authorities from states and provinces throughout North America, with emphasis on the periphery of the species' range. No new information was obtained from Mexico. For reasons discussed previously, and because of limitations of the information received, only the following subspecies of mule and black-tailed deer are considered here:

Odocoileus hemionus hemionus	Rocky Mountain mule deer
O. h. crooki	Desert mule deer
O. h. fuliginatus	Southern mule deer
O. h. peninsulae	Peninsula mule deer
O. h. californicus	California mule deer
O. h. columbianus	Columbian black-tailed deer
O. h. sitkensis	Sitka black-tailed deer

In the absence of information from Mexico, nothing of substance can be added to or subtracted from Cowan's (1956*a*) identification of southern range limits. Accounts of desert, Southern, and peninsula mule deer are incomplete. Distributions presented here for those three subspecies are the products of information from regional authorities. Where the information was contradictory in detail—mostly minor—figure 1 presents an arbitrary compromise. Following is a resume of the information on which it is based.

Alaska

Sitka black-tailed deer occur naturally throughout coastal islands of southeastern Alaska (the Alexander Archipelago) and in a narrow strip along the adjacent mainland. The precipitous Coast Mountains with extensive ice fields constitute a barrier to the east. Continental, subarctic climate terminates northern distribution above Juneau. Sitka deer were transplanted to several rain forest areas along the Gulf of Alaska between 1917 and 1934 (Elkins and Nelson 1954) and have established persistent populations around Yakutat, Prince William Sound, and Afognak and Kodiak is-

lands. Because of topographic and climatic barriers, they cannot be expected to spread farther.

Yukon Territory

Information from M. Hoefs (pers. comm., July 1978) extends the range of mule deer from northwestern British Columbia into southern Yukon Territory, as shown in figure 1. Hoefs reported that the "continuous range" in the Yukon Territory was limited, however, to a smaller area roughly between Whitehorse and Haines Junction. He wrote, "It appears that Mule deer have moved into the Yukon during recent decades; or at least they have extended their range and become more numerous and therefore more obvious recently. . . . Mule deer are now widely distributed over the southern half of the Yukon with resident, even though small, populations reported for the following

Sitka black-tailed deer on the open beach of Montague Island, Alaska. Photograph by Loyal J. Johnson; courtesy of the Alaska Department of Fish and Game.

localities: Takhini River area west of Whitehorse, Atlin Road, Marsh Lake, Lake LaBerge, Carmacks, Pelly farm, Ross River, Stewart Crossing/Mayo Road area, Champagne, Haines Junction, Kluane Lake, Rancheria River, and Frances/Liard Rivers. . . . Deer appear to be concentrated in habitats with successional vegetation, usually on sites of recent burns."

British Columbia

Cowan and Guiguet (1975) provided an adequate description of distribution in British Columbia. Sitka blacktails introduced to Graham Island in the Queen Charlotte Islands (Cowan 1956a) remain abundant throughout that island group. Southward, the range of Sitka blacktails is confluent in some areas with that of Rocky Mountain mule deer. Cowan and Guiguet (1975) did not discuss mixing of these subspecies, but they reported that Sitka blacktails intergrade imperceptibly with Columbian blacktails to the south. A line between the two ranges is purely arbitrary. However, Columbian blacktails are said to interbreed with mule deer, giving rise to populations of mixed character.

In the far north of British Columbia, the range of mule deer now is shown as extending westward to the Telegraph Creek area on the Stikine River (131 degrees longitude), which flows into Alaska, and to the Dease River area (129 degrees longitude) near the Yukon border.

Alberta

E. Bruns (pers. comm. to K. E. Severson, January 1976) showed the range of mule deer extending across the northern part of Alberta from about 57 degrees north latitude on the west to 58 degrees on the east, incorporating a large northeastern segment that was excluded by Cowan (1956a). Although isolated sightings occur in the Northwest Territories, the Territories are not considered to be within the normal range of the species.

Saskatchewan

Whereas Bruns extended the mule deer range in Alberta to the Saskatchewan border at about 58 degrees north latitude, J. W. Skene picked up the line on the Alberta border just north of 51 degrees (pers. comm., January 1976). He showed only the extreme southwestern corner of Saskatchewan as an area with "huntable mule deer populations," but he reported isolated deer or small populations as far north as 55–56 degrees on the west side of the province. Skene added, "There are other locations at which mule deer are said to have existed, but we do not have recent personal corroboration. Since we are experiencing habitat reduction and alteration on a massive scale we may no longer have these populations. . . . In so far as we know, there are no longer any mule deer on the east side of the province, except, perhaps, in the northern forest area . . . the map, on page 334 of *The Deer of North America* [Taylor 1956], does not fit any situation as far back as current members of the staff have any knowledge of it."

North Dakota

Current distribution in North Dakota was considered to be described adequately by Cowan's (1956a) map (J. V. McKenzie, pers. comm., January 1977). McKenzie outlined primary mule deer range (0.8–2.3 deer per square kilometer: 2–6 per square mile) in the southwestern corner of the state and secondary range (fewer than 0.8 deer per square kilometer: 2 per square mile) in a peripheral area extending to the Missouri River, both constituting the southwestern fourth of North Dakota. Occasional observations of single deer or small breeding colonies are reported throughout the state.

South Dakota

Information obtained from South Dakota makes it difficult to draw a range boundary that is consistent with lines drawn for North Dakota and Nebraska. Richardson and Petersen (1974, p. 5) divided South Dakota into three major habitat units—East River habitat, West River Prairies habitat (east and west of the Missouri River, respectively), and Black Hills habitat. The mule deer is reported to be dominant in the West River Prairies, but "by 1969 there had been at least one mule deer killed in each East River county."

Connecting the arbitrary range boundary in southern North Dakota to the arbitrary boundary in northern Nebraska, with a line just east of the Missouri River in South Dakota, is merely a convenience.

Nebraska

A distribution map supplied by K. Menzel (pers. comm., November 1975) depicts mule deer range as all but the eastern fourth of Nebraska. Numerous occurrences have been recorded to the eastern border. Iowa and Missouri both have several records of mule deer. This contrasts strongly to Cowan's map (1956*a*), in which the limit of mule deer range is delineated as the extreme northwestern corner of Nebraska.

Kansas

W. C. Peabody (pers. comm. to K. E. Severson, November 1975) wrote, "Mule deer are found primarily in the western one-third of the state. . . . Densities are greatest in the northwest one-quarter of Kansas." Reference should be made to Severson's account (see chap. 12) of the westward shrinkage and subsequent eastward expansion of mule deer range during the past century.

Minnesota, Iowa, and Missouri

Minnesota, Iowa, and Missouri are excluded arbitrarily as "normally" occupied range for

A Rocky Mountain mule deer exits a livestock pasture on the plains of Kansas. Photograph by Ken Stiebben; courtesy of the Kansas Fish and Game Commission.

mule deer. In Minnesota, twenty-three widely scattered kills or sightings from 1953 through 1974 suggest that mule deer appear sporadically or occur in very small numbers west and south of a southeast-northwest line bisecting the state (R. A. Carlson, pers. comm. to K. E. Severson, November 1975). Iowa and Missouri both have several records, but these document unusual occurrences rather than normal range. In eastern Nebraska and Kansas, such records are not included in delineation of principal mule deer range.

Texas and Oklahoma

Cowan (1956*a*) showed the range of Rocky Mountain mule deer cutting across the extreme northwest corner of the Texas Panhandle and the western tip of the Oklahoma Panhandle. However, more recent information from Texas reveals that its Panhandle population results from transplants of desert mule deer from the Trans-Pecos region. The transplants have generated huntable populations in the Palo Duro Canyon area and southeastward to Mottley and Cottle counties (C. K. Winkler, pers. comm. to K. E. Severson, January 1976). The remaining range of desert mule deer, from the vicinity of the Pecos River westward, is the same as shown by Cowan (1956*a*).

No information was obtained from Oklahoma; so, for the the present report, a line is drawn from the Panhandle of Texas to join the line in Kansas.

Colorado

Mule deer range is discontinuous in eastern Colorado, but viable populations occur throughout the state (Crouch 1961; and see chap. 12).

New Mexico

The distribution shown by Lang (1957) excludes only a rectangular area in the southeastern corner of New Mexico and conforms with boundaries in Texas. The southern third of this range is considered arbitrarily to be the domain of desert mule deer. The remainder is that of Rocky Mountain mule deer.

Arizona

The distribution of Rocky Mountain and desert mule deer is shown by Hoffmeister (1962) as continuous throughout Arizona except for the extreme southwestern corner. These subspecies merge along a line extending from Lake Mead in the northwestern corner southeastward to New Mexico. However, Arizona Game and Fish Department personnel consider a large part of the northeastern portion of Arizona to be devoid of deer. New Mexico Department of Game and Fish personnel consider this area to extend into the northwestern corner of their state. Most of the area consists of Indian reservations where, to a great extent, excessive livestock grazing and the absence of effective restrictions on hunting have eliminated deer.

The gap between desert mule deer and Rocky Mountain mule deer range depicted by Cowan (1956*a*) should be considered unrealistic. Furthermore, the existence and range of the burro deer can be deleted. For lack of more definitive information, the western edge of the range of desert mule deer is shown by Hoffmeister (1962) as extending into southeastern California but is modified there to conform with the distribution of burro deer shown by Dasmann (1958), as revised by W. G. MacGregor in 1975.

Nevada

Personnel of the Nevada Department of Fish and Game consider mule deer to be distributed throughout the state, including the very southern tip (G. C. Christenson, pers. comm., January 1976). It is understandable that the department's personnel do not make distinctions among subspecies, because, on the basis of other information, deer in the southern part of the state would be expected to show characteristics of Rocky Mountain, desert, burro, and Inyo mule deer if the latter two are accepted subspecies.

California

A complex distribution pattern was presented by MacGregor's 1975 revision of Dasmann (1958). It has been simplified somewhat in figure 1 by drawing arbitrary lines rather than zones of intergradation among subspecies.

Oregon and Washington

The zone of intergradation for Rocky Mountain mule deer and Columbian blacktails shown by Cowan (1956*a*) is accepted as representative of the situation today. Populations of mixed characteristics occur along this zone in Oregon (P. Ebert, pers. comm., February 1976) and British Columbia (Cowan and Guiguet 1975), so the same should be true of Washington.

Mexico

Several inquiries yielded no new information from Mexico. Baker (1956) was pessimistic about the survival of the mule deer in Coahuila, assuming that because of uncontrolled hunting it would slowly disappear from much of the range he depicted at that time. A. S. Leopold (pers. comm., October 1977) wrote, "I think the ranges of Baja California are adequate [as shown in fig. 1] but I share with Rollin Baker the idea that the desert mule deer probably is eliminated from a very substantial part of its original range in the central highlands of Mexico. This conviction is not however backed up by any solid data. . . . I think what I would do . . . is show the total range as it is with a big question mark toward the southern edge of the range of *crooki*." The range of desert mule deer (fig. 1) simply is copied from Cowan

(1956*a*), with the addition of Leopold's question mark.

HABITATS

Mule and black-tailed deer are remarkably adaptable. Of at least sixty types of "potential natural vegetation" identified by K̈uchler (1964, p. 1) west of the 100th meridian in the United States, all but possibly two or three are or once were occupied by blacktails or mule deer or both. The species inhabits several additional vegetation types in Canada and in Mexico as well. The Mexican types of vegetation, for the most part, are similar to types occurring in the United States, but with many distinctive species of the same dominant genera. However, the tropical deciduous vegetation at the tip of Baja California is unique (Leopold 1950*b*). In Canada, mule deer occupy at least five boreal forest types that do not occur in the United States (Rowe 1972).

The multitudinous habitats of the mule and black-tailed deer subspecies are so diverse as to defy generalization. Rocky Mountain mule deer occur in the entire gamut of vegetation types, from tallgrass prairies on the eastern side of their range, westward across shortgrass plains and all shrublands, woodlands, and forest types of the Rocky Mountain region, to desert scrub of the Great Basin. The southern end of their range is hot, arid desert land; the northern end is underlain by permafrost.

Of Rocky Mountain mule deer, Cowan (1956*a*, p. 346) said, "its climatic tolerance has few parallels among mammals." Considering the range of climates tolerated by other subspecies, their tolerance might not seem so remarkable. Climate is composed of many factors, only two of which are graphed in figure 2 for five mule and black-tailed deer subspecies. Monthly mean temperature was plotted against monthly precipitation for several stations within the ranges of the subspecies. Obviously, adaptability or climatic "tolerance" of both Columbian blacktails and Rocky Mountain mule deer encompasses a wide range of conditions.

The simple climatographs of figure 2 do not adequately describe the environment of deer, but climate must be considered the basic determinant of habitat. Climates of the western half of North America are a product of five major air masses plus ocean currents that contribute moisture, and of the location and topography of the land in relation to them. Within

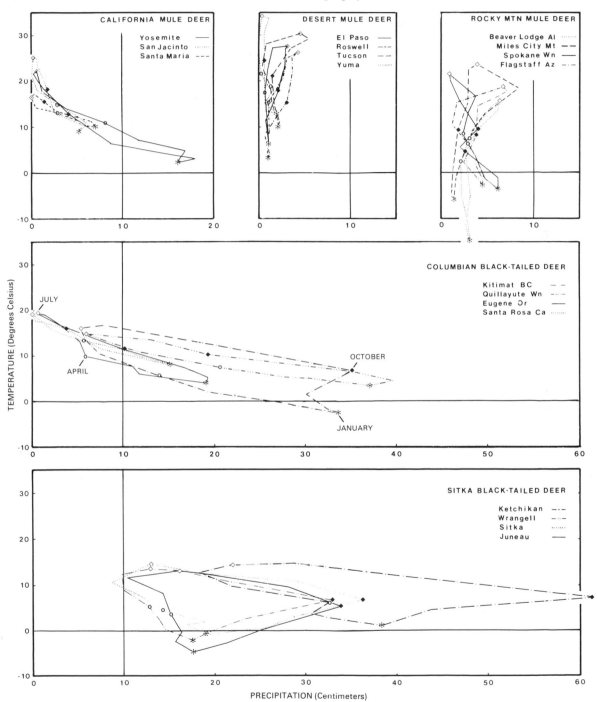

Figure 2. Climatographs of localities within the ranges of California, desert, and Rocky Mountain mule deer and of Columbian and Sitka black-tailed deer.

the range of mule and black-tailed deer, eleven general climates result (fig. 3). Diverse vegetation communities of the region also are products of climate. Soil characteristics account for lesser variations in the vegetation. Küchler's (1964) delineation of vegetation types indicates patterns that correspond closely to the generalized climatic zones.

These patterns permit a logical grouping of vegetation types into "habitat provinces" of black-tailed and mule deer (fig. 4 and table 1). The climates, vegetation types, and terrain types of the "provinces" constitute environments, or habitats, of the subspecies that occur there. In the following discussion of the provinces, information on vegetation types is

Figure 4. Habitat provinces of mule and black-tailed deer (see table 1).

Table 1. Mule and Black-tailed Deer Habitat Provinces, corresponding with figure 4

Province	Subspecies

1. Coastal rain forest	Sitka
	    black-tailed deer
	Columbian
	    black-tailed deer

2. California woodland
    chaparral
	Columbian
	    black-tailed deer
	California mule deer
	Southern mule deer

3. Mojave Sonoran desert	Peninsula mule deer Desert mule deer
4. Interior semidesert shrub woodland	Desert mule deer
5. Great Plains	Rocky Mountain mule deer

6. Colorado Plateau
    shrubland and forest
	Rocky Mountain
	    mule deer

7. Great Basin	Rocky Mountain mule deer
8. Sagebrush steppe	Rocky Mountain mule deer
9. Northern mountain	Rocky Mountain mule deer
10. Canadian boreal forest	Rocky mountain mule deer

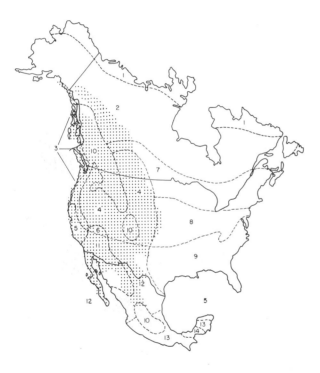

Figure 3. Major climatic regions of North America (after Critchfield 1966), and the range (screened) of mule and black-tailed deer. Climates dominated by polar and arctic air masses: (1) tundra; (2) taiga. Climates dominated by tropical and polar air masses: (3) marine; (4) midlatitude semiarid; (5) dry summer tropics; (6) midlatitude arid; (7) humid continental cool summer; (8) humid continental warm summer; (9) humid subtropics. Climates dominated by altitude: (10) highland. Climates dominated by equatorial and tropical air masses: (11) tropical arid; (12) tropical semiarid; (13) wet and dry tropics; (14) rainy tropics.

drawn from Küchler (1964), Leopold (1950*b*), and Rowe (1972). Information on climates is taken largely from Critchfield (1966) and is supported by various sources of local weather data.

Coastal Rain Forest Province

The west coast of North America from northern California through southeastern Alaska is dominated by a marine climate, with cloudy days from nearly half to more than two-thirds of the year, normally cool temperatures year-round, high precipitation from autumn to spring, and a relatively short summer dry season. Tall, dense coniferous forests are characteristic. Redwood forest mixed with Douglas fir and grand fir predominates in northern California. Northward in Oregon, dominance changes to Sitka spruce, western red cedar, and western hemlock. These three species characterize the mature forest throughout coastal Washington, British Columbia, and Alaska, with cedar becoming less common to the north. At the far northwestern extreme of the province, where Sitka blacktails have colonized small areas along the Gulf of Alaska, only Sitka spruce has become established since the glacial retreat. The marine climate there is restricted to a narrow coastal fringe.

In inland California, there is a transition to the California mixed evergreen forest, a mixture of needleleaf and broadleaf evergreens with some broadleaf deciduous trees, oaks, Douglas fir and madrone predominating. Farther north in California, Oregon, Washington, and British Columbia, the transition is to cedar/hemlock/Douglas fir, then, approaching the Coast Range, to Douglas fir and silver fir. Along the mainland of northern British Columbia and Alaska, hemlock/spruce forest terminates abruptly in alpine tundra and permanent glaciers.

"The blacktail lives in a geographic region that features hundreds of square miles of unbroken forest," wrote Cowan (1956*b*, p. 615). Today, less than three decades later, there are very few 259-square kilometer (100-square mile) areas of unbroken mature forest. The

A Columbian black-tailed buck in coastal rain forest habitat. Photograph by Joseph S. Dixon; courtesy of the United States National Park Service.

A Sitka black-tailed doe in British Columbia. A Wildlife Management Institute photograph; by H. W. Terhune.

forest has been broken up by logging except in some portions of Alaska, and even there few low-elevation areas have not been logged to some degree in the past 150 years.

The southern three-quarters of this province is inhabited by Columbian blacktails and the northern quarter by Sitka blacktails. Though black-tailed deer often are presumed to be particularly adapted to the dense, high-canopied conifer forests, several workers—notably Brown (1961), Cowan (1945*a*), and Hines (1973)—have contended that early stages of secondary succession following logging or fire are more conducive to proliferation of the deer in Oregon, Washington, and British Columbia. Farther north this may not be true because in winter—the only period when food availability is critical—snow accumulations in openings are deep enough to preclude use by deer. Even in summer the vegetation of early successional stages is too dense to be used by deer, and midsuccessional stages have improverished understories that are poor deer habitat at best (see chap. 11, part 2). In any case, in this region of high timber values, habitat management is inextricably involved with forest management.

California Woodland/Chaparral Province

The dry summer, subtropical climate of the southern California coast and the Great Central Valley also is referred to as a Mediterranean climate. Its "chief features . . . are a hot, dry summer and a mild, rainier winter" (Critchfield 1966, p. 179). In terms of deer habitat, the province consists mainly of two intergrading vegetation types, California oakwoods and chaparral, bordering all sides of the Great Central Valley. Chaparral extends southward west of the Mojave and Sonoran deserts to Baja California. The oakwoods terminate short of Mexico, but a somewhat similar type—the Oregon oakwoods—occurs in a small area in southwestern Oregon.

Küchler (1964, p. 30) described the California oakwoods as "medium tall or low broadleaf evergreen or semideciduous forests with an admixture of low to medium tall needleleaf evergreen trees." The dominants include coast live, canyon live, blue, valley, and interior live oaks, and digger and Coulter pines. Many shrub species occur in the type, and small grassy openings are common. Chaparral is dense shrub vegetation with chamise, manzanita, and ceanothus dominating in this province.

Mild, rainy winters are conducive to the development of a seasonal bloom of ephemeral herbaceous vegetation that provides a large fuel source for wildfires in summer. Dry chaparral also carries fire well. Periodic fires are characteristic of the type, and their value to deer depends on their setting back or opening up dense, mature stands (see chap. 9, part 2). The oakwoods are more resistant to fire.

Columbian blacktails occur in the western portion of this province, intermixing with California mule deer southeast of Monterey

Columbian blacktails at the western edge of the California woodland/chaparral province. Photograph by R. N. McIntyre.

Bay. In the northern half of the east side of the province, blacktails extend into the northern end of California mule deer range. California mule deer range southward along both sides of the province to east of the Los Angeles area, where they intergrade with Southern mule deer, which occupy the extension of the province into Baja California (Dasmann 1958, as revised by W. G. MacGregor in 1975).

The Great Central Valley, originally grassland with extensive tule marshes along major drainages, now is densely settled, farmed, and essentially devoid of deer.

Mojave/Sonoran Desert Province

The tropical arid climate of this province is hot in summer and warm in winter. It is characterized by low, erratic precipitation in all seasons, mostly from brief thunderstorms falling on largely bare soil, resulting in rapid runoff with little moisture retained in the soil. To the west, the climate grades into the Mediterranean climate of southern California and northern Baja.

The extreme desert areas of southeastern California, extreme southern Nevada, and southwestern Arizona are not deer habitat. Areas between the sparse shrubs—mainly creosote bush and white bursage, which are of little or no value to deer—essentially are bare except during infrequent moist periods in late winter or early spring. Another area of true desert that is largely devoid of deer lies west of the Great Salt Lake.

Peripheral to the desert on the west, north, and east there is more varied topography and a more diverse shrub-dominated flora, including numerous species that are of use to deer (such as cat's-claw, paloverde, dalea, ocotillo, matrimony vine, prickly pear, and numerous forbs). Still, it is relatively inhospitable deer habitat, with adequate supplies of succulent forage occurring too infrequently to maintain significant deer population densities. It is a relatively stable ecosystem, resistant to manipulation. The development of watering places is the only common management practice.

Southern mule deer occur on the western edge of the Imperial Valley where desert grades into chaparral and woodland. Desert mule deer occur on the east where the climate grades toward tropical semiarid (interior semidesert/shrub/woodland province), and intergrade with Rocky Mountain mule deer to the north where the climatic gradient is toward midlatitude arid (Southern Great Basin desert scrub/pygmy forest province).

Interior Semidesert/Shrub/Woodland Province

The transitional area between the tropical arid climate of the preceding province and the humid subtropical climate along the shores of the Gulf of Mexico is classified as tropical semiarid. The province is dominated in summer by a continental tropical air mass originating over this region. In winter this air mass tends to be dissipated by the continental polar air mass. Moisture comes both in winter and in summer, with a pronounced rainy period in late summer as a result of moisture from the marine tropical air mass from the Gulf of Mexico being lifted by surface heat, causing convection storms. Small mountain ranges add an orographic effect and receive sufficient moisture to support shrubland, woodland, and limited forest.

This province includes southeastern Arizona, southern New Mexico (except the extreme southeast), Texas west of the Pecos River, and the central highlands of Mexico. It presents a mosaic of elevational intergradations of vegetational types—from desert shrub at the lowest elevations, through semidesert/shrub/grassland, chaparral of sorts, mountain shrub, woodland, and some forest at the highest elevations. Although an extensive area of dense scerophyllous shrubs is called chaparral, with both winter and summer rainy periods, it has some attributes that do not conform with the usual definition of that type. In Mexico the vegetational zones involved are referred to by Leopold (1950b) as boreal forest, pine/oak forest, chaparral, and mesquite/grassland.

Desert mule deer and Coues white-tailed deer occur throughout the province, with the

Desert mule deer in the interior semidesert/shrub/woodland habitat province. Photograph courtesy of the New Mexico Department of Game and Fish.

feathergrass, and squirreltail. The climate essentially is semiarid, but predominantly humid weather may move westward or semiarid weather eastward for periods of time, sometimes years (Critchfield 1966). Severson (see chap. 12) discusses the westward shrinkage and eastward expansion of mule deer range under the influence of shifting climates accentuated by human land use.

The midlatitude, semiarid climate is strongly influenced by mountains to the west that cast a rain shadow eastward. Annual precipitation is highly variable. In winter it normally is meager, with blizzards accompanying bursts of polar air. In summer it comes as scattered thundershowers and violent cloudbursts.

It is not the near-uniform plains per se, but the breaks in topography and accompanying trees and shrubs that provide habitable areas for mule deer in this province. This is discussed in detail in chapter 12. Dakota and Texas whitetails also occur in this province, most commonly in heavily wooded bottomlands.

former dominating the lower elevations and the latter claiming the wooded and forested mountains. East of the Pecos River, desert mule deer give way abruptly to Texas whitetails, and in central Arizona and New Mexico—in the transition to the Colorado Plateau province and a highland climate—they intergrade with Rocky Mountain mule deer.

Mule deer populations have fluctuated radically within the province. A series of relatively wet years can produce good forage supplies; and a series of dry years can produce very marginal forage.

Great Plains Province

The eastern boundary of normally occupied mule deer range coincides closely with the western boundary of the humid continental and subtropical climates. West of that vicinity there is a fairly abrupt transition from tallgrass prairie to shortgrass prairie types, with characteristically western dryland genera generally taking over, such as wheatgrass, grama,

Colorado Plateau Shrubland and Forest Province

A circle drawn to include northern Arizona, eastern Utah, southern Wyoming, western Colorado, and northern New Mexico encompasses the area of highest general elevation in North America. Most of it is more than 1,500 meters (approximately 5,000 feet) above sea level, and mountain ranges throughout rise to more than 3,000 meters (approximately 10,000 feet). It has a highland climate, somewhat comparable to that of the northern Rockies, but is isolated by an intervening strip of midlatitude semiarid climate in Wyoming. Because of its elevation, the area intercepts residual moisture in eastward-moving air masses. Local relief results in a great diversity of local climates. Precipitation is distributed rather evenly throughout the year, with variations reflecting proximity to surrounding climatic regions. Increased precipitation occurs at high elevations owing to the effects of mountainous topography.

Migrating Rocky Mountain mule deer at the western edge of the Wasatch Mountain Range in northern Utah. Photograph by Paul S. Bieler; courtesy of the United States Forest Service.

In winter, high elevations usually accumulate snow to depths that preclude deer use. Seasonal migrations of varying distances are necessary for deer to take advantage of nutrient-rich forage supplies in the mountains in summer and to escape deep snow in winter. But low elevations are hot and arid, with herbaceous vegetation largely dried out by later summer, leaving poor-quality forage for wintering deer. Also, many winter ranges are subject to cold air drainage and very low winter temperatures.

The province includes a profusion of vegetation types, with five general forms most significant to deer and habitat management. They are sagebrush, juniper/piñon woodland, mountain shrub, montane forest, and subalpine forest. At lower elevations, big sagebrush, juniper (one-seeded, Utah, alligator, and Rocky Mountain juniper) and piñon occur in combinations varying from sagebrush alone to predominantly juniper woodland. The mountain mahogany/oak scrub type (curl-leaf mountain mahogany/Gambel oak) and a variety of pine (ponderosa pine is the most common pine) and Douglas fir types occur at mid elevations. In the higher subalpine forests, cork-bark fir, blue spruce, and Englemann spruce are more prevalent to the south, and lodgepole pine, subalpine fir, and Engelmann spruce are more prevalent to the north. Quaking aspen stands are conspicuous in the montane and lower subalpine zones.

Despite a long period of submarginal nutrition in most winters and periodic die-offs of massive proportions, deer populations in this province have been remarkably prolific. Habitat management technology, or at least philosophy, is relatively advanced. Reviewed in depth in later chapters, management consists basically of modifying the continuity of sagebrush, woodland, mountain shrub, and forest stands and encouraging the development of other forage. Other than a scattering of Northwest and Dakota whitetails, the province is occupied only by Rocky Mountain mule deer.

Great Basin Province

The Great Basin, between the Wasatch Range of Utah and the Sierra Nevada mountain range, is a region of midlatitude arid and semiarid climates, largely as a result of its low elevation in the rain shadow of the Sierra Nevada. On the south it grades into tropical arid climate. Topographically, it is characterized by extensive, largely level lowlands, interrupted by isolated mountains that are oriented mainly north to south. The saltbrush/greasewood type and the Great Basin sagebrush type cover most of the lowlands. Juniper/piñon woodlands (one-seeded juniper, Utah juniper, and piñon) and pine forests (ponderosa, bristlecone, and limber pines)—the latter at higher elevations—characterize plateaus and mountains.

Rocky Mountain mule deer occur throughout the province but are increasingly uncommon or absent away from the mountains. In general, the province receives less than half the amount of precipitation that is received by the Colorado Plateau province. Aridity of the lowlands makes for poor winter range, but lesser snow depths permit deer to use more of the mountain slopes than in the preceding province. High-elevation habitat is not extensive, and summer ranges often are overused, especially where there is competition with domestic sheep. Manipulation of juniper/piñon woodland to improve it for livestock, deer, or both is a major habitat management practice.

Sagebrush Steppe Province

The most extensive vegetation type in western United States, exceeded in area only by boreal forest in western North America (Rowe 1972), is the sagebrush steppe (Küchler 1964).

It extends some 1,200 kilometers (746 miles) east to west from central Wyoming to western California, Oregon, and Washington, with extensions northward to north-central Washington and southward into northern Colorado. This region has a midlatitude semiarid climate with cold-dry winters and hot-dry summers. The Coast Range intercepts most of the Pacific moisture. In winter the region is swept by waves of dry polar continental air.

The vegetation of the province is relatively uniform. In the absence of excessive livestock use, numerous cool-season grasses (such as bluebunch wheatgrass, Idaho fescue, Indian ricegrass, and several species of bluegrass and feathergrass) may occupy more of the ground than sagebrush. While big sagebrush is dominant over much of the area, black sagebrush is the common dominant to the west and small sagebrush to the east.

Mule deer on winter range in sagebrush-steppe province. Photograph by William S. Keller; courtesy of the United States National Park Service.

Of significance to deer, bitterbrush and snowberry are abundant or dominant in many areas. Both are browsed by Rocky Mountain mule deer, but bitterbrush is one of the most widely used foods of this subspecies (Kufeld et al. 1973) and generally is rated as one of its most valuable winter foods. Although sagebrush is used extensively in winter, its nutritional value is questionable.

Some areas of the states in this province support large mule deer populations year round. In Idaho, Oregon, and Washington, much of the land has been converted to agriculture. Nearly all of the remainder is used to graze livestock. Overgrazing is believed to be a major cause of increasing densities of sagebrush at the expense of grasses, forbs, and other shrubs. Large areas have been treated chemically and mechanically in the effort to restore them to grass/shrub or grass types (see chap. 10, part 2, and chap. 13).

Northern Mountain Province

As mule deer habitat, the northern mountain province differs from the Colorado Plateau province more in degree than in kind. It has a highland climate with somewhat more precipitation than the Colorado Plateau and is influenced locally by similar factors—elevation, slope, and aspect. The northern mountain province has more continuous forest cover and less shrub or woodland vegetation. Forest types on the east and south are similar to those in Utah and Colorado, but to the west and north different species often are dominant (such as grand fir, western larch, western white pine, western red cedar, and western hemlock). Valleys and piedmonts have grassland or parklike ponderosa pine forest. This province includes an extension of the highland climate southward along the Cascade/Sierra Nevada ranges with their own complex of forest types

Mule deer in the northern mountain province. Photograph courtesy of the Idaho Fish and Game Department.

(Küchler 1964). These forest types include silver fir/Douglas fir, subalpine fir/mountain hemlock, and ponderosa shrub forest in Washington and Oregon, and, mixed conifer (white fir, incense cedar, sugar and ponderosa pines, and Douglas fir), red fir forest, and lodgepole pine subalpine forest (lodgepole, whitebark and foxtail pine, and mountain hemlock) in California.

The mule deer of this province are strongly migratory, as are those of the Colorado Plateau. The northern mountain province is lower in elevation and closer to the coast than is the Colorado Plateau, so winters of the former generally are not as cold, but deep snow does occur in high mountainous areas. Although the northern mountain is primarily a forest province, mule deer are presumed to thrive best in disclimax conditions caused by fire or logging (Lyon 1969; Pengelly 1963). However, Edwards (1956) considered snow depth—as it influences winter forage supplies—to be the primary regulator of deer populations in the Canadian portion of the province.

Kellogg's (1956) map of Northwest white-tailed deer range may characterize the northern mountain province more accurately. However, in contrast to Rocky Mountain mule deer, which occur generally in the province, whitetails are restricted largely to bottomlands with heavy, dense vegetation (Krämer 1972; Mundinger 1976; Prescott 1974).

In habitat management for mule deer in this province, much emphasis is placed on maintaining significant areas of forest in early stages of secondary succession. Since most of the forest land is devoted to timber production, cooperation with forest managers is necessary. Comprehensive guidelines for deer habitat management in forests of the Blue Mountains of Oregon and Washington have been provided by Black et al. (1975).

Canadian Boreal Forest Province

Boreal forest, as classified by Rowe (1972), covers most of Canada south of the arctic tundra with the exception of deciduous forests in the southeast, montane, and coast forests in the southwest, and grasslands of southern Alberta and Saskatchewan. The province is characterized by two climatic zones: a taiga climate across the north from Alaska to Newfoundland and a humid continental, cool summer climate from central Alberta and Saskatchewan eastward across southeastern Canada.

The northern zone (taiga climate) is a partial source of polar air masses, and its weather is dominated by cold-dry, stable air during winter and summer (Critchfield 1966). At this high latitude, important aspects of climate are long winters with short days, little effective insolation, extremely low temperatures, and short summers with long days. The southern zone (humid, continental, cool summer climate) also is dominated by polar air in winter, but it receives incursions of tropical continental and tropical maritime air in summer and consequently has more summer precipitation.

In the Northwest Territories and northern Saskatchewan, boreal forest grades into open subarctic woodland. This transition roughly marks the northern limits of mule deer range. Below, within the range of mule deer, four major forest types or "sections" were recognized by Rowe (1972).

The aspen grove section occurs as a belt, varying from about 60 to 250 kilometers (38–155 miles) in width, encircling the north edge of the grasslands of southern Alberta and Saskatchewan. It has generally rolling terrain with occasional rough, broken land. As described by Rowe (1972), trembling aspen is abundant, balsam poplar occurs frequently in moist lowlands and occasionally is prominent on uplands after fire, and white birch occurs sporadically, usually on rough, broken land. Interspersed prairie and meadow patches largely have been taken over by agriculture.

The mixed-wood section—some 1,500 kilometers (930 miles) long from Manitoba to British Columbia and as much as 500 kilometers (310 miles) wide in Alberta—contains "a mixture in varying proportions of trembling aspen and balsam poplar, white and Alaska

Mule deer in Canadian boreal forest province habitat. Note the browse line on shrubs and trees from the preceding winter. Photograph by E. S. Shipp.

birches, white spruce and balsam fir, the last two species especially prominent in old stands" (Rowe 1972, p. 36). Rolling terrain predominates but, approaching the Rockies, higher rounded hills and plateaus occur. Small areas of aspen grove forest occur within this section near the Alberta/British Columbia border.

The lower foothills and northern foothill sections of the boreal region flank the Rocky Mountains. The former is characterized by lodgepole pine, trembling aspen, and balsam fir, with white and black spruce in older stands. The northern foothill section was considered comparable, as a vegetational zone, to subalpine forest farther south, lacking Engelmann spruce, however, and having extensive areas of the "black spruce–white spruce–pine type"

(Rowe 1972, p. 39). Alpine fir is a common associate, increasing in abundance with elevation. White birch is scattered in upland stands; trembling aspen is found on south-facing slopes; and balsam poplar occurs on lowland alluvium.

Mule deer, whitetails, moose, and caribou occur in the Canadian boreal forest province, with snow being a major factor governing distribution of the mule and white-tailed deer (Prescott 1974). A number of Prescott's observations help in understanding mule deer's habitat choices: (1) they prefer open grassland/parkland types; (2) they range farther north and higher in elevation than do whitetails and apparently can tolerate longer and more severe winters; (3) whitetails tend to winter in dense, continuous coniferous forest types; (4) mule deer use the subalpine zone in winter and whitetails do not; (5) mule deer are forced out by settlement and agriculture while whitetails adapt and exploit agricultural crops for winter food; (6) mule deer have expanded northward, and their southern range is being occupied by whitetails. Krämer (1972, p. 33) suggested that northward and altitudinal movements of whitetails are inhibited by winter severity, and that westward movements are restricted by lack of cover. He did not know what prevented eastward spread of mule deer, though "wet conditions and heavy cover may have something to do with it" (see also chap. 5).

In this province, mean annual minimum temperatures range from −37 degrees Celsius (−36 degrees Fahrenheit) in the south to −45 degrees Celsius (−57 degrees Fahrenheit) in the north. Continuous snow cover ranges from an average of less than one month in the south to more than four months in the north. Median midwinter snow depth varies from about 30 to 76 centimeters (12–30 inches) south to north, and by the end of March there usually is no snow on the ground in the south whereas the north still has an average median snow depth of 40 centimeters (16 inches) (Krämer 1972). Although reasons for the southern (in Mexico) and eastern limits of mule deer distribution may remain uncertain, it seems clear that winter conditions are a major factor in defining the northern and northwestern limits.

FACTORS LIMITING DISTRIBUTION

Food and water, climate, and cover logically can be considered three general groups of factors that determine where mule deer and blacktails can exist. Food of suitable quality must be available in adequate quantity in one or more seasons to enable them to survive seasons of nutritional stress. Also, the body's water balance must be maintained. Climate must be within the range of physiological tolerance, or, at the extremes, vegetational cover or terrain must provide microclimates that permit deer to exist in generally adverse climate, espe-

cially during periods of potential malnutrition. There must be vegetational cover or terrain that provides opportunities for escape from predators (see chap. 5).

Mule and black-tailed deer occur in climates with average temperatures ranging from −15 degrees Celsius (5 degrees Fahrenheit) or less in January in northern British Columbia to more than 30 degrees Celsius (86 degrees Fahrenheit) in July on the hot deserts. Extreme temperatures range from below−60 degrees Celsius (−76 degrees Fahrenheit) to above 50 degrees Celsius (122 degrees Fahrenheit). Mean annual precipitation ranges from less than 10 centimeters (approximately 4 inches) in the Mojave Desert, with many years having essentially none, to more than 500 centimeters (approximately 200 inches) in some areas of the Pacific Northwest, with the "driest" months commonly receiving more precipitation than falls in an entire year in the southwestern deserts.

Granting that cover—in the form of vegetation, terrain, or both—can provide more favorable microclimates, it still is remarkable that desert mule deer can tolerate ambient temperatures in limited shade more than 10 degrees Celsius (50 degrees Fahrenheit) above their body temperature daily for much of the summer. Yet populations apparently grow or decline not in relation to hot-season temperatures, but in relation to forage quality, governed by precipitation in cooler seasons. It is equally remarkable that Rocky Mountain mule deer can endure wind-chill temperature equivalents commonly 75–100 degrees Celsius (approximately 100–150 degrees Fahrenheit) or more below their normal body temperature. However, as with whitetails in northern climates (Severinghaus 1947), extensive mule deer mortality occurs in winters of deep snow when little forage is available, irrespective of temperatures, whereas little mortality occurs in cold-dry winters when nutritious forage is generally available. So far, the only information on differences in thermoregulatory adaptations among subspecies seems to be about the thicker hair coat on Sitka blacktails measured by Cowan and Raddi (1972) (see chap. 2).

Successful evolution of mule and black-tailed deer has required adaptation to the many and extreme conditions of habitat and weather, and to the influences of man. Photograph courtesy of the Wyoming Department of Game and Fish.

It often is suggested that certain kinds of vegetational cover or terrain are important to mule deer in providing thermal cover (see Loveless 1967; Moen 1973; Black et al. 1975). Testing such a hypothesis, however, demands consideration of the alternative—that special kinds of thermal cover are unimportant if available forage provides sufficient metabolizable energy.

Alternative hypotheses can be argued, but they remain untested. Though some workers have been interested in the subject for many years, it is fair to say that research on the thermal tolerance of deer has only begun (see also Moen 1973). Several studies suggest that heat loss in cold climates can constitute a significant energy drain, but other evidence indicates that well-nourished deer do not succumb solely to extreme temperatures (Severinghaus 1947; Baker 1976; Wallmo et al. 1977). Thermoregulatory problems at the high end of the scale have been given little attention, although the work of Holter et al. (1975) suggested an appreciable increase in the energy expenditure of whitetails at higher temperatures. Perhaps deer can endure this extreme if adequate quantities of easily digestible forage are available. But can they endure heat without such forage, as may occur in the Southwest?

The availability of drinking water clearly influences the local distribution of deer in the Southwest (see chap. 9, part 1, and chap. 13). Is it a factor in geographic distribution? Succulent forage can provide enough water to meet metabolic needs seasonally on most ranges, but free water is required at other times of year. In Montana the distribution of deer appears to have no relationship to the distribution of water (Mackie 1970), but it does in southwestern deserts. Yet the most arid areas of mule deer range—in the Mojave/Sonoran desert province—would support few or no deer even if drinking water were made available; the inadequacy or undependability of palatable and digestible forage would still be limiting.

In the interior North, available water usually is frozen for much of the winter, so mule deer obtain water by eating snow. After ingestion, melting the snow and raising the water to stomach temperature involves a significant energy expenditure. That energy cost is a matter of practical interest to range livestock nutritionists, because it can influence growth and gain in livestock. Over long periods in northern winters, mule deer take in less energy daily than they expend, and consequently they lose weight (Baker 1976; Wallmo et al. 1977). At the very northern end of mule deer range—where the mean temperature is below 0 degrees Celsius (32 degrees Fahrenheit) for nearly half the year and snow cover often is of equal duration—the energy cost of eating snow, added to costs of thermoregulation and activity on an energy-deficient diet, might be important. At least it seems to be a factor that warrants more consideration.

Successful evolution of mule deer and blacktails required adaptation to habitats that permitted sufficient numbers to escape predators. Likewise, successful deer predators were those that developed the ability to capture some deer despite protective cover. Severson (see chap. 12) concluded that habitability of the plains environment for mule deer is governed basically by "security cover," with forage—conditioned by drought, snow, and livestock grazing—being a secondary determinant of habitat quality. In tropical arid climates, security cover may be equally important. But, at the margins of habitat suitability, food and water probably become critical before cover does. In the Great Central Valley of California and in most extensive agricultural areas, cover unquestionably has a significant influence on the distribution of mule deer.

Predators, except man, apparently have not regulated the geographic distribution of mule deer and blacktails. A continuing predator/prey relationship requires coexistence. This does not mean that predators wisely ration their food supply. It only suggests that, within recent times, regional distribution has not been affected by even the most specialized deer predators—mountain lions and wolves—although deer populations may be influenced by them.

Diseases may be a contributing factor in determining where deer do and do not exist. Again, current knowledge comes from areas where populations wax and wane but persist with their diseases. When introduced to foreign ranges, deer may encounter new diseases that can be devastating (see chap. 4). This, however, is not prima facie evidence that those diseases prevented the deer's natural occurrence there.

It seems reasonable to suggest that single factors do not limit distribution at any margin of deer range. Effective combinations of factors are different in each area, and expansions and contractions of range are due to somewhat different combinations of causes each time they occur. Furthermore, the time frame in which deer distribution is conceptualized is so brief (less than two-hundred years) and so influenced by changes that man has imposed on habitat, thereby masking the effects of "natural" events, that a convincing analysis of the causes of distribution is unlikely to be devised.

From a larger perspective, North American cervids—caribou, moose, elk, white-tailed deer, black-tailed deer, and mule deer—occupy distinct but widely overlapping zones of the continent with characteristics that may suggest adaptive limitations. Caribou exist in the tundra and boreal forest. Moose are primarily boreal, extending into locally suitable areas of the tundra and montane zones. Elk, once with a transcontinental midlatitude distribution, now occur mainly in the Rockies from northern Arizona and New Mexico to central British Columbia and Alberta and in a coastal strip from northern California to Vancouver Island. Whitetails extend from the midboreal of Canada to the equatorial tropics, overlapping most of the range of mule and black-tailed deer except the most arid-warm, wet-cool, and cold regions. Mule deer and blacktail range extends well beyond that of whitetails in the arid-cold and wet-cool North and in the arid-warm Southwest but stops short of the humid-cool and humid-warm climates to the east and south. Within these ranges and climates, the complexity of habitats used is bewildering (see chap. 13). If there is some common denominator, it has not yet been described.

The degree to which mule deer and whitetails may limit each other's distribution remains largely hypothetical, but it seems to be initiated by habitat changes in which one of the species is favored at the expense of the other. While whitetails have expanded northward and westward into mule deer ranges in Saskatchewan and Alberta, along with the spread of agriculture, mule deer in Arizona may be expanding into whitetail range with the expansion of desert scrub habitat and shrinkage of woodland habitat resulting from more arid climate, overgrazing, and the absence of fire (Anthony and Smith 1977). Meanwhile, the Columbian white-tailed deer of western Oregon and Washington has recently been classified as an endangered subspecies. Presumably because of clearing and agricultural development on brushlands in river valleys and lower foothills, few if any remain outside of a small area along the lower Columbia River in western Washington. Columbian black-tailed deer, whose range has not changed significantly over time, frequently occupy that area along with whitetails (Suring and Vohs 1979).

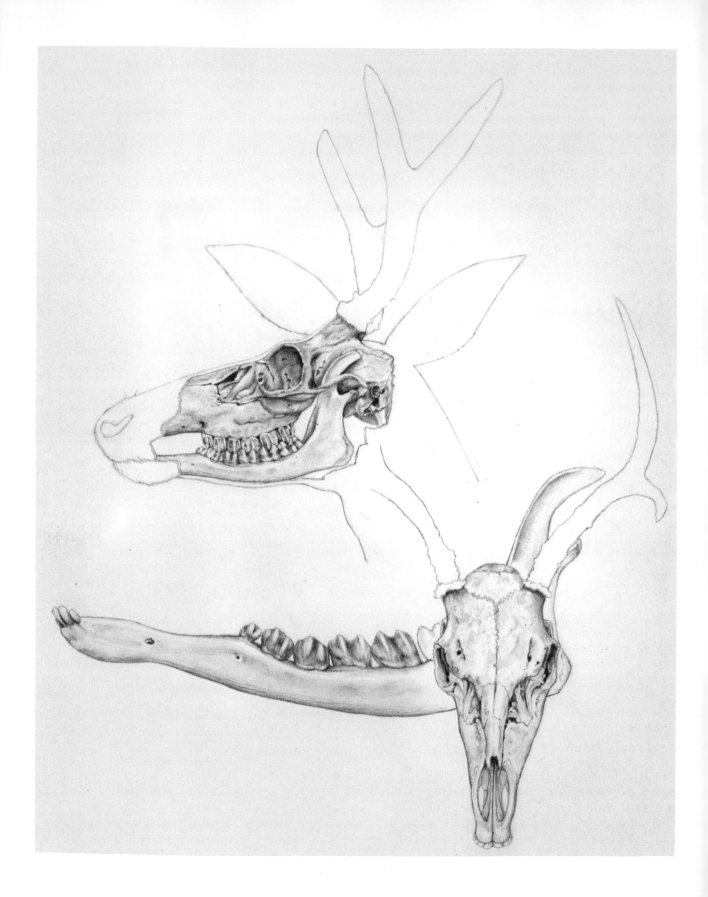

Chapter 2

MORPHOLOGICAL AND PHYSIOLOGICAL CHARACTERISTICS

Allen E. Anderson
Wildlife Researcher
Colorado Division of Wildlife
Fort Collins, Colorado

As used in this review, morphology is concerned with some features of form, structure, and selected parts of deer—mule and black-tailed deer in particular. Physiology includes a few functional properties of presumably healthy deer. Where possible, inferences are made from selected morphological and physiological measurements to the deer-environment system and to their relevance to deer management.

Many tissue, organ, and whole-body characteristics of black-tailed and mule deer have been used as potential indicators of conditions that might be relevant to management: eyes, teeth, bones, blood, testes, sperm, ovaries, fetuses, adrenal glands, thyroid glands, fat, antlers, hair, body weight, body size, and so on. In most cases they have been used and interpreted without adequate understanding of implications of the measurements obtained. In fact, the necessary background information usually was not available. It still is not complete, of course, but this chapter reviews the knowledge that exists today.

Wildlife managers are interested in maintaining healthy and productive deer. Various environmental conditions that influence health and productivity may be manifested grossly or subtly in many tissues and organs. Some measurements used in the past apparently have little relationship to environmental conditions that interest managers, but others appear to be potentially useful.

The technical terminology used here may intimidate some readers, but it is not possible to convey the information exactly without using precise words for the structures, substances, and processes involved. Without them, the reader who might make use of the information would be incapable of making accurate interpretations.

BODY COMPOSITION

The body composition considered here consists of water, fat, protein, bone, teeth, muscle, and blood. Ambient temperature is an important factor in the dynamics of body composition (Hafez 1968*a*).

Water and Fat

Total body water content of ruminants varies inversely with total body fat and the variable amounts of water within the extracellular spaces and gut, ranging from 50 to 85 percent of total body weight (MacFarlane 1968). Water intake of cattle is so closely related to the type of ration (Yousef et al. 1968) that it has been studied as an estimator of forage intake and quality (Hyder et al. 1968; Hyder 1970). There are few published data on water kinetics of mule, black-tailed, and white-tailed deer. Knox et al. (1969) suggested that water kinetics of mule deer essentially were similar to those of other mammals, though Longhurst et al. (1970) documented several important differences between certain aspects of the rates of change in water systems of Columbian black-tailed deer and domestic sheep. Estimates of total body water of deer (table 2), based on the tritiated water (TOH) technique, are known to exceed actual values by 1–3 percent (MacFarlane 1968). Total body water estimates obtained by TOH in mule and black-tailed deer (table 2) are within the range of chemically determined values of the ingesta-free carcasses of 8 male and 15 female white-tailed deer, 2 weeks to 42 months of age, killed June through September (fawns) and 24–27 October (adults) (Robbins 1973; Robbins et al. 1974).

In these deer, percentages of fat ranged from 1.1 to 17.7. Female fawns were higher in fat and energy than were male fawns, but at about 25 kilograms (55 pounds) male and female carcasses were similar in mean levels of both water and fat. Water (X) and fat (Y) were negatively correlated: $r=-0.977$ to $r=-0.983$. In contrast, similarly derived percentage fat values of the ingesta-free carcasses of 19 male and 32 female white-tailed deer, 10 weeks to 7 months of estimated age, ranged from 6.5 to 12.4 (Urbston 1976). Both season (autumn versus

Table 2. Estimates of Total Body Water and Water Kinetics in Mule and Black-tailed Deer

Subspecies	No.	Dates	Sex	Age	Body Weight in Kilograms (Range or Mean)	Water Percentage of Body Weight (Mean, ±SE)	Half-Time Days[a] (Mean, ±SE)	Water Intake, Milliliters per Kilogram per Day
Rocky Mountain mule deer	2	Sept.–Oct.	F	105–120 days	18.5–23.2	70.3	2.3	216
	9	Jan.–Apr.	F	211–305 days	30.0–42.5	67.1 ± 3.4	6.5 ±1.0	57[c]
	1	Jan. and July	F	Adult				31, 25 (Jan.) 79, 65 (Jul.)
	6	21 Dec.–10 Jan.	F	1–7 years	28.6–38.6	63.4	8.5	53
	6	10 June–15 July	F	2–5 years	25.0–38.6	73.5	4.9	104
Desert mule deer	28	July–Aug.	Not given	Most Adult	56.8[b]			105

[a]Time for one-half of total body water to exchange.
[b]Based on ocular estimates.
[c]Based on five trials, 17–105 days in length, with four deer.

winter) and habitat (swamp versus upland) had a significant ($p<0.05$) effect on mean percentage fat values, but sex did not. The mean ($\pm$SE) percentage of fat in selected muscle tissue of 5 Columbian black-tailed deer fawns from each of two habitats was 2.79$\pm$0.73 and 2.24$\pm$0.50 at 5 months of age, and 4.10$\pm$0.80 and 2.00$\pm$0.14 at 11 months of age (Mansfield 1974). Mean percentage of fat in the ham and loin muscle tissue of 5 male adult mule deer shot per month for fourteen months ranged from less than 1.0 (January) to 4.5 (August) in California (Cook et al. 1949). The ether-extractable percentage of fat mean ($\pm$SD) for the skinned, eviscerated carcasses of 8 male and 10 female Colorado mule deer 7–128 months in estimated age and shot from 15 December to 27 April was 5.54$\pm$1.19 (Anderson et al. 1969). As estimated by densitometry,

(Table 2.)

Conditions	Source
In 0.9 by 1.5 meter cages. Temperature maintained at 18.3–23.9 degrees Celsius. Tritiated water used to obtain water values.	Knox et al. (1969)
In 4.6 by 1.5 meter rooms. Temperature maintained at 18.3–23.9 degrees Celsius. Tritiated water used to obtain water values.	Knox et al. (1969)
In large pens, southern Arizona. Intake measured Jan. and July in two years.	Nichol (1938)
In large pens. Mean daily ambient temperature: −5 to 16 degrees Celsius. Deer 2+ months pregnant. Tritiated water used.	Longhurst et al. (1970)
In large pens. Mean daily ambient temperature: 5 to 35 degrees Celsius. Tritiated water used.	Longhurst et al. (1970)
Wild. Sonoran Desert, Arizona.	Elder (1954)

using underwater weighing, mean ($\pm$SD) fat percentages of the weights of the skinned, eviscerated carcasses of mule deer about 18 months and older ranged from 5.4$\pm$1.7 (winter) to 16.9$\pm$7.1 (summer) in males and from 6.9$\pm$3.1 (spring) to 12.5$\pm$3.2 (autumn) in females (Anderson et al. 1972a).

The caloric content of body fat was estimated by Robbins et al. (1974) as 9.49 kilocalories per gram. They described the body caloric content of white-tailed deer as a positive curvilinear function of both body weight and age in years.

The biochemistry of fat storage and use in animals in general has been reviewed by Allen (1976). However, properties of fat in cervids have received little attention. Densities of internal, subcutaneous, and bone marrow fat from 9 Colorado mule deer were measured as a function of their temperature (10–35 degrees Celsius; 50–95 degrees Fahrenheit) (Whicker 1964). This author noted that the melting points of these fats ranged from 45 to 50 degrees Celsius (113–122 degrees Fahrenheit). As in most mammals, the iodine number melting point of saturation of the fatty acids of the adipose tissue decreased distally in the limbs of a caribou (Meng et al. 1969) and of caribou, elk, moose, and white-tailed deer (Garton et al. 1971). This might seem to represent an adaptation to extremely cold temperatures, but Young (1976) noted that the same phenomenon occurs in tropical mammals.

Protein

Robbins et al. (1974) reported that in white-tailed deer the mean ($\pm$SE) percentages of major carcass components were: protein, 20.5$\pm$0.3 for males and 20.2$\pm$0.7 for females; ash, 4.6$\pm$0.9 for males and 4.7$\pm$0.7 for females. Computed daily changes in grams of protein and fat of 5 white-tailed deer fawns over a fifteen-month period ranged from −15 to 64 for protein and −39 to 92 for fat (Holter et al. 1977). These changes correlated poorly with each other and with gains in body weight.

Bone and Muscle Tissue

According to Banks (1974*a*), skeletal bone furnishes support and locomotion for the body and, as an extremely vascular tissue, also provides a dynamic store of calcium and phosphorus. Although the gross morphology of bone changes little throughout life, internal characteristics constantly change by the process of internal remodeling. There are two types of bone—the lamellar or mature, and the woven or immature. Immature bone is the first type of bone that develops in ossification centers of the fetus.

Total bone in 3 near-term mule deer fetuses averaged 17.7 percent of their body weight (Hakonson and Whicker 1971*b*). Corrected for weight of bone marrow, total bone constituted 17.7 percent of the body weight of a 22-day-old fawn, 9.6 percent of a 4–5-month-old female, 11.9 percent of a 4–5-year-old female, and about 10 percent in 2 males 2–3 years old (Hakonson and Whicker 1971*a*) and 2 mature females (Hakonson and Whicker 1971*b*). Long bones of this sample constituted 49 percent of the total skeletal weight. Hakonson and Whicker (1971*a*) calculated a skeleton-to-body weight ratio for male and female mule deer of 0.103.

The carcasses of 3 female Rocky Mountain mule deer, 22 days to 4–5 years of age, contained 35.4–44.8 percent muscle. Two carcasses of male Rocky Mountain mule deer, 2 to 3 years old, contained 47.2 and 52.4 percent muscle (Hakonson and Whicker 1971*a*).

Teeth

Subspecies of mule and black-tailed deer have a heterodont dentition consisting of incisors, canines, premolars, and molars. Molars are permanent. Upper incisors, canines, and the upper and lower first premolars are missing. The permanent dental formula (Riney 1951) is: incisor $\frac{0=0=0}{1=2=3}$, canines $\frac{0}{1}$,

premolars $\frac{0=2=3=4}{0=2=3=4}$, molars $\frac{1=2=3}{1=2=3}$.

The histologic development of Rocky Mountain mule deer dentition resembles that of other mammalian species (Rees et al. 1966*a*). Because matrix formation and mineralization in enamel and dentin are disturbed by pathologic and physiologic stresses, a permanent record of their occurrence is found in the mineralized dental tissue. These include daily and weekly incremental lines on the enamel, believed to represent each day's growth and a weekly physiologic cycle. Unlike the high-crowned, short-rooted molars of domestic sheep, the short-crowned, long-rooted molars of cervids do not grow continuously (Rees et al. 1966*a*). The annular structure of dental cementum in incisiform teeth has been investigated in relation to age of Rocky Mountain mule deer (Low and Cowan 1963; Erickson and Seliger 1969).

Blood

With increased frequency, blood is being examined for clues to the nutritional condition of deer in relation to their environment. The volume of blood in mammals approximates 7–10 percent of total body weight and is about 8 percent higher in males than in females (Bell et al. 1959). Blood has many functions, but primary are transport of oxygen and nutrients to all cells of the body and removal of carbon dioxide and other waste materials. Thus, measurements of metabolites and other constituents may be indicators of nutritional status if the range of baseline, or "normal," values is known. Detection and investigation of blood abnormality are useful aids in diagnosing disease only if the normal ranges of blood variables are known and if information is available on "the physiological and technical limitations or complications which may alter the interpretation" (Benjamin 1961, p. 65). The term "normal" is employed here in the sense that the mean health condition is partial illness, not perfect health, as is frequently implied in the medical literature (Simpson et al. 1960). This section is mainly a description of blood values in mule and black-tailed deer and may be regarded as a study in variations associated with method, laboratory technicians, laboratory equipment, sample size, age, subspecies, sex, season, year, environmental stresses, nutritive status, circadian rhythms, parasitic load, diseases, and other factors. Blood as a diagnostic aid in the detection and investigation of parasites and diseases is not treated here. Where possible, reference will be made to blood values presumably affected by nutritional status or environmental stresses.

The available literature on blood cellular constituents in mule and black-tailed deer is summarized in table 3. There has been some apparent limited response of blood cellular values to nutritional status. For example, in a population sample of adult Inyo mule deer believed to be starving on winter range, significant ($p < 0.05$) correlation coefficients of intact carcass weight versus erythrocyte numbers and hemoglobin were $r = 0.53$ and $r = 0.44$, respectively. Similar responses were not detected in 5 other less severely stressed mule and black-tailed deer populations on winter range (Rosen and Bischoff 1952). Kitts et al. (1956a) cited experimental evidence in Columbian black-tailed deer and theorized that starvation to the point of death may occur in growing black-tailed deer without significant alteration of packed cell volume. Percentage of femur marrow fat—as one index of relative fatness (Anderson et al. 1972a)—accounted for only 4 to 7 percent of the variation (R^2) in some erythrocytic values of Rocky Mountain mule deer (Anderson et al. 1970). They also found that mean numbers of erythrocytes and mean weights of eviscerated female carcasses decreased significantly ($p < 0.01$), and that mean packed cell volumes and mean hemoglobin of adult deer of both sexes remained stable while the neutrophil-lymphocyte ratio increased, suggesting noninfectious or infectious stress (Schalm 1965), during a four-year period of drought. Among 19 blood cell variables sampled from 177 deer, there were 76 instances of extreme cellular values. Cursory and incomplete necropsies revealed that only 22 abnormal values from 15 individual deer had any possible pathological explanation (Anderson et al. 1970). Interpretation of blood cellular values must be tempered by the rapid, sequential changes in blood cellular values typical of both health and disease (Schalm 1965).

Fifteen chemical constituents of blood sampled from the serum or plasma of mule and black-tailed deer subspecies are listed in table 4. Alkaline phosphatase and lactic dehydrogenase (LDH) values have been reported by Anderson (1976), Pederson (1970), and Smith (1976a). In addition to these two enzymes, serum glutamic oxaloacetic transaminase (SGOT) also was listed by Dhindsa et al. (1975), Pederson (1970), and Smith (1976a). The values for these enzymes have not been tabulated here because they were reported in different units of measurement that apparently

Table 3. Some Cellular Constituents of Blood from Mule and Black-tailed Deer

Constituents	Literature Sources[a]	Subspecies[b]	Range of Mean Values
Hemoglobin	1, 3, 4, 5, 6, 7, 9	a, c, d	9.8–20.5 g/100 ml
Packed cell volume	1, 2, 3, 4, 5, 6, 7, 8, 9	a, b, c, d	30.6–58.2 percent
Sedimentation rate	7, 9	a, c, d	0.4–9.9 mm/hr
Erythrocytes	1, 2, 3, 5, 7	a, b, c, d	4.6–14.2 $10^6/mm^3$
Leukocytes	1, 3, 5, 7	a, c, d	3.0–5.8 $10^3/mm^3$
Total neutrophils	3, 5, 7	a, c, d	34.0–72.8 percent
Lymphocytes	3, 5, 7	a, c, d	23.0–60.0 percent
Monocytes	3, 5, 7	a, c, d	1.4–15.8 percent
Eosinophils	3, 5, 7	a, c, d	0.0–8.3 percent
Basophils	3, 5, 7	a, c, d	0.2–0.8 percent

[a]1, Browman and Sears (1955); 2, Rosen and Bischoff (1952); 3, Anderson et al. (1970); 4, Halford (1974); 5, Anderson (1976); 6, Rohwer (1970); 7, Cowan and Bandy (1969); 8, Mansfield (1974); 9, Kitts et al. (1956a).
[b]a, Rocky Mountain mule deer; b, California mule deer; c, Columbian black-tailed deer; d, Sitka black-tailed deer.

Table 4. Some Chemical Constituents of Blood from Mule and Black-tailed Deer

Constituents	Literature Sources[a]	Subspecies[b]	Range of Mean Values
Total protein	2, 5, 6, 7, 8, 9, 10, 11, 13	a, b, c	4.6–8.5 g/100 ml
Albumin	7, 8, 9, 11, 13	a, c, d	1.6–4.4 g/100 ml
Total globulin	9, 13	a, c, d	1.8–5.1 g/100 ml
Glucose	5, 9, 11, 13	a, c, d	37.2–161.1 mg/100 ml
Cholesterol	5, 7, 8, 9, 11	a, d	70.2–111.9 mg/100 ml
Total bilirubin	9, 11	a, d	0.5–1.1 mg/100 ml
Uric acid	9, 11	a, d	0.4–2.2 mg/100 ml
Blood urea nitrogen	9, 11, 12	a, c, d	7.4–29.8 mg/100 ml
Inorganic phosphorus	1, 3, 5, 6, 7, 8, 9, 11	a, d	5.2–11.2 mg/100 ml
Calcium	1, 3, 5, 7, 8, 9, 11	a, d	9.1–12.8 mg/100 ml
Calcium	1, 3, 5, 7, 8, 9, 11	a, d	4.6–6.4 meq/1
Magnesium	3, 7, 8	a	2.2–4.0 mg/100 ml
Magnesium	3, 7, 8	a	1.9–3.3 meq/l
Vitamin A	4, 7, 8	a	45.6–110.3]/100ml
Vitamin A	4, 7, 8	a	151.9–367.7 IU/100 ml

[a]1, Murphy (1969); 2, Anderson et al. (1972*b*); 3, Anderson et al. (1972*c*); 4, Anderson et al. (1972*d*); 5, Halford (1974); 6, Anderson (1976); 7, Rohwer (1970); 8, Hunter (1973); 9, Smith (1976*a*); 10, Taber et al. (1959); 11, Pederson (1970); 12, Mansfield (1974); 13, Bandy et al. (1957).

[b]a, Rocky Mountain mule deer; b, California mule deer; c, black-tailed deer; d, desert mule deer.

cannot be readily converted to one common unit, thus precluding comparisons.

The following discussion briefly outlines the function and significance of tabulated values for each chemical constituent, based on information in Harrow and Mazur (1958), Benjamin (1961), Schalm (1965), and Cornelius and Kaneko (1963). Examination of large differences among tabulated means in tables 3 and 4 suggests, however, that methodological and temporal differences among investigations greatly reduce their usefulness as comparative baseline values. These values can best be obtained by controlled experiments with large numbers of mule and black-tailed deer of both sexes on different dietary regimes from birth to middle age.

Blood serum or plasma protein largely are synthesized by the liver from food proteins (amino acids) and interact constantly with body proteins and diets. Decreased levels of total serum protein have been associated with malnutrition, pregnancy, lactation, wounds, and renal and liver disease. Shock, infections, dehydration, and certain neoplasms have been related to increased total serum protein. Tabulated means range from 4.6 to 8.5 grams per 100 milliliters. Anderson et al. (1972*b*) found no significant differences between sexes and no significant increases with age. However, among mature males there was significantly higher mean total serum protein during summer, and mature males had significantly higher mean total serum protein than did females during that season.

Albumin is the most important component of total serum protein and generally reflects its concentration. Extreme albumin values range from 0.2 to 4.0 grams per 100 milliliters. It is a useful interpretative supplement to total serum protein.

Globulin is composed of twenty-two proteins, most of which have separate functions. Their measurement may improve diagnosis of disease (Seal and Erickson 1969). Beta globulin increased with relative fatness in moose (Franzmann et al. 1976). Among mule and black-tailed deer, alpha, beta, and gamma globulin proteins are known only from wild Rocky Mountain mule deer blood plasma sampled during January and February in Nevada (Rohwer 1970; Hunter 1973). Total globulin was measured during summer in captive Columbian black-tailed deer (Bandy et al. 1957) and during autumn in wild Rocky Mountain mule deer (Smith 1976*a*).

Blood glucose is primarily a product of propionic acid, one of the volatile fatty acids

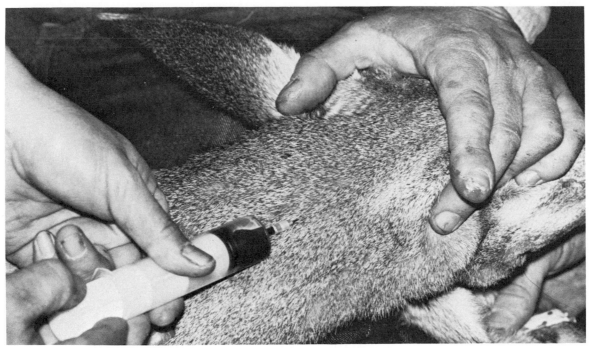

A blood sample is drawn from the jugular vein of a Columbian black-tailed deer. Analyses of the sample may be used to evaluate nutritional status, disease, parasite conditions or environmental stresses. Photograph by Guy E. Connolly.

(VFA) produced by rumen fermentation. In ruminants, only relatively small amounts of dietary glucose are absorbed. The major function of glucose is to provide a source of cellular energy. Because glucose increases with body temperature and is extremely unstable in stressed animals, it is a poor indicator of nutritive stress.

Cholesterol levels fluctuate with dietary intake of saturated fatty acid, and minimal levels occur during starvation. The maximum value (119 milligrams per 100 milliliters) was from a captive nursing fawn (Halford 1974). Cholesterol may be a useful adjunct indicator of nutrition. Coblentz (1975) reported a significant ($p<0.05$) decrease in mean serum cholesterol concentration, 8 October to 23 January, among 31 white-tailed deer of unstated age and sex. The total mean cholesterol concentration of this postmortem sample was 77.0 milligrams per 100 milliliters.

Bilirubin is a hemoglobin-derived bile pigment. High levels are often associated with hemolytic breakdown. Relative amounts of

bilirubin form the basis for various tests of liver function.

Uric acid is produced by purine metabolism. Blood serum contains small amounts. Increases in uric acid may be associated with tissue protein turnover, reduced renal excretion, or increased glucogenesis.

Blood urea nitrogen (BUN) fluctuates with seasonal levels of average dietary protein intake and absorption. However, these changes also may reflect protein catabolism in a starving animal. Hence, BUN may be unreliable as a single indicator of nutritive status if the point between dietary protein intake and protein catabolism cannot be defined.

Inorganic phosphorus levels generally exist in balance with those of calcium and reflect changes in absorption, withdrawal, deposition in bone, and excretion. Absorption may be increased by pregnancy and lactation and may be decreased by increasing age. An excess of either phosphorus or calcium usually suppresses the other element. Seasonal variation is believed to be associated with vitamin D and lactation. Mature male and female Rocky Mountain mule deer had larger mean phosphorus levels during winter, however, when vitamin D—the "sunshine" vitamin—probably was minimal (Anderson et al. 1972*c*). Significant ($p<0.05$) decreases in mean phosphorus occurred with age in both sexes (Anderson et al. 1972*c*; Hunter et al. 1972). Among mature females, mean annual phosphorus decreased significantly during an extended period of drought (Anderson et al. 1972*c*). A twofold difference among their tabulated mean phosphorus values (5.2–11.2 milligrams per 100 cubic centimeters) suggests extreme variation. Hunter et al. (1972) reported that mean phosphorus values of mature female mule deer differed significantly by location and year, and Rohwer et al. (1971) noted minimal mean phosphorus levels in pregnant mule deer. Phosphorus levels also may increase as a result of excitment associated with venipuncture in the living experimental animal (Gartner et al. 1965) or shock from gunshot wound (Wilber and Robinson 1958). Speculatively, excitement also may be present in a wild deer stalked and shot on open range or may occur as an auditory response to rifle shot.

Calcium is found almost entirely in bone and, of the little found in serum, about half is bound to protein. Dietary intake and vitamin D are the main regulators of absorption, whereas mobilization is regulated by the parathyroid hormone, which releases calcium, and by thyrocalcitonin, which controls release. Among female Rocky Mountain mule deer, mean calcium levels decreased significantly with age but inexplicably increased annually during a four-year period of drought (Anderson et al. 1972*c*).

Magnesium, like calcium, is stored largely in the skeleton. Metabolically, it appears to resemble calcium; and, next to potassium, magnesium is the major metal cell cation. Goats (Fowle and Church 1969) and domestic sheep (Christian and Williams 1960) both have shown a decrease in magnesium during experimentally induced starvation. The latter authors suggested that, under those conditions, inclement weather may increase magnesium

requirements. Among 101 Rocky Mountain mule deer, serum magnesium did not show significant ($p<0.05$) variation associated with sex, age, season, or year (Anderson et al. 1972*c*). Low levels of magnesium have been associated with grass tetany in cattle (Scotto et al. 1971). Tetany is a condition of mineral imbalance characterized by intermittent spasms of the voluntary muscles. However, nutritional diseases related to magnesium deficiency apparently have not been reported for mule or black-tailed deer.

Because serum sodium and serum potassium values in mule and black-tailed deer have been reported from only one study, those values have not been tabulated. Relevant findings from that study, however, are discussed next.

Sodium, the chief cation of extracellular water and of intestinal secretions, aids in maintaining homeostasis in the body. Like calcium, serum sodium increased significantly ($p<0.05$) and inexplicably in both sexes of mature Rocky Mountain mule deer over a four-year period of drought (Anderson et al. 1972*c*). High levels of serum sodium often are indicative of liver, heart, kidney, or adrenal malfunction.

Potassium is the predominant intracellular ion and, along with sodium, is important in maintaining the homeostatic equilibrium of the body. Acute water loss may induce potassium deficiency and subsequent muscular paralysis. Potassium deficiencies were believed to have been a factor in mass mortality of sika deer (Christian 1964). Like phosphorus, potassium values may increase as a result of excitement (Gartner et al. 1965) or shock (Wilber and Robinson 1958), depending on the method of blood sampling.

Vitamin A has an essential role in growth, reproduction, lactation, vision, and maintenance of normal epithelial tissue. This role was reviewed by Moore (1957) and by Maynard and Loosli (1969). Tabulated means from serum of Rocky Mountain mule deer of both sexes collected yearlong in Colorado (Anderson et al. 1972*d*) are well below total plasma means in blood collected by Rohwer (1970) and Hunter (1973) in Nevada during January and February. Neither the Colorado data nor the Nevada data were affected by age or sex. Significant ($p<0.01$) seasonal variations in blood serum vitamin A of Colorado mule deer were high values in late spring and low values in autumn 1963, with later summer high values and low values in winter 1964. Small amounts of carotene were detected in blood serum of 10 of 52 male and 13 of 61 female mule deer. Significantly more ($p<0.01$) blood serum carotene was found in deer collected from upper elevational strata than in those collected at lower elevations (Anderson et al. 1972d). In that study, means of liver carotene and vitamin A values also were presented, and their relationships to their counterparts in blood serum were described.

Blood and Some Influents

Franzmann et al. (1976) related blood chemistry and hematology of Alaskan moose classified by sex and age to season, pregnancy, lactation, location, condition, and excitability. "Condition" was assessed by slight modification of the procedure developed by Robinson (1960) for captive white-tailed deer fawns. The method involved examining body contours and behavioral patterns and assigning animals to one of ten categories of relative fatness ranging from 10 (fat) to 4 (emaciation) and 3 to 1 (mainly stereotyped posture and behavior patterns associated with a decreasing gradient of weakness). Each classification was evaluated as a source of variation. These authors found that—based on 1,506 serum samples and 1,235 whole blood samples analyzed for seventeen blood parameters—serum calcium, phosphorus, total protein, albumin, beta globulin, hemoglobin, and packed cell volume increased with improved condition (relative fatness), but hemoglobin and packed cell volume were most useful in "condition" evaluation. The authors listed specific values for each of these blood variables for moose in average or better condition.

Criteria were developed and applied for bighorn sheep (Franzmann and Thorne 1970;

Franzmann 1972) and Alaskan moose (Franzmann et al. 1976) for quantifying excitability in individual animals, identifying blood values so affected. These criteria included heart rate, respiratory rate, rectal temperature, and amount of struggling before and during handling. Franzmann et al. (1975) also found that serum corticoid levels adequately reflected relative amounts of handling stress in Alaskan moose.

Anderson et al. (1970) assigned behavior scores from the written record of mule deer behavior before, during, and after shooting, plus the time in minutes from the impact of the bullet to death and from death to blood sampling to evaluate the effects of shooting on blood constituents in wild Rocky Mountain mule deer. Regression analyses of nineteen blood cellular variables estimated that the elapsed time (minutes) from death to blood sampling accounted for about 16 percent of the variation (R^2) in the percentage of lymphocytes of females (Anderson et al. 1970) and, among five serum electrolytes, for only about 10 percent of the variation (R^2) in serum inorganic phosphorus in males (Anderson et al. 1972c).

Drug immobilization is widely used in the capture and handling of both captive and wild deer for various purposes, including blood sampling. Seal et al. (1972a) immobilized white-tailed deer with phencyclidine and promazine and assessed the effects of those drugs on selected serum and cellular constituents. They documented significant decreases related to drug treatment in mean hemoglobin, erythrocytes, packed cell volume, total serum protein, and fibrinogen, and an increase in glucose among 3 males and 8 pregnant females. Mean cholesterol and serum phosphorus levels also decreased in females. Delayed effects of handling without drugs were apparent in 2 pregnant and 2 unbred females twenty-four hours later. These included a decrease in hemoglobin, packed cell volume, erythrocyte count, and total serum protein, and an increase in fibrinogen. Seal et al. (1972a, p. 1039) expressed the opinion that "final determination of base line values in deer perhaps will require biotelemetry using sensors not yet available." They refer to studies of Farrell et al. (1970), in which automatic blood-aspirating devices have monitored blood and ruminal fluids of grazing sheep as a potential solution.

Presidente et al. (1973) found that the effects of etorphine and xylazine on hematologic values of 8 white-tailed deer fawns generally were similar to those described by Seal et al. (1972a) for phencyclidine and promazine. Hematologic values of physically restrained fawns were similar to those reported in the literature for that species and age group. Thus the accepted "normal" values from captive experimental deer may reflect rather uniformly the variation associated with physical restraint involved in blood sampling.

"Field immobilization is a method of rendering wild animals tractable while using a minimum of restraint. This may be done with paralyzing drugs, narcotic or anesthetic drugs, or tranquilizers" (Harthoorn 1965, p. 9). Like other specialized techniques, use of a Cap-chur gun requires considerable skill and experience. Blindfolds often are used to decrease the animals' level of excitement and, consequently, trauma. Photograph courtesy of the Arizona Department of Game and Fish.

Blood and Taxonomy

To assess the technique's value as a taxonomic criterion, starch-gel electrophoresis of blood serum proteins of three mule and black-tailed deer subspecies and two white-tailed subspecies were carried out by Cowan and Johnston (1962) and by van Tets and Cowan (1966), and similar tests of the serum protein lipid fraction were done by van Tets and Cowan (1967). The general conclusion was that serum differences exist among these forms, but other influences negate their value as a useful taxonomic criterion. Preliminary work with the serum protein lipid fraction suggests that additional research is warranted. According to Urbston (1976, p. 17), electrophoretic analysis of the polymorphic proteins of white-tailed deer has made it "possible to identify local populations on the basis of their genetic makeup."

BODY TEMPERATURE

Bianca (1968) generalized that the range of normal body temperature of mammals is similar in both sexes. It decreases with age and approximates 36–40 degrees Celsius (96–104 degrees Fahrenheit). Elevated temperatures in health may be caused by feeding, exercise, estrus, and terminal stages of pregnancy. Depressed temperatures result from starvation. Body temperatures may fluctuate diurnally and seasonally, being minimal in early morning and synchronized with seasonal variation in environmental temperatures and the reproductive cycle. Bianca also noted a 1–3 degree (Celsius) variation in body temperature during a twenty-four-hour period for several species of unrestrained domestic ruminants. Thermal gradients exist from trunk core to periphery and from trunk to extremities, with the body surface serving as a thermal buffer. Rectal temperature is considered a good general index of deep body or body core temperature for most purposes, even though rumen temperatures are 2 degrees (Celsius) greater and brain, liver, and heart temperatures are 1–2 degrees

Two Sitka blacktail fawns, both suffering from malnutrition, exhibit piloerection. This thermoregulatory mechanism is an aid to survival during winter. Photograph by Loyal L. Johnson; courtesy of the Alaska Department of Fish and Game.

(Celsius) greater than rectal temperature. Carotid blood may be 0.2 degree (Celsius) lower. Folk (1966), however, considered a single body core temperature measurement as unsatisfactory for calculations of heat loss from the mammalian body.

Thermoregulation

Thermoregulation in mammals is believed to be controlled by the central nervous system, with the anterior hypothalamus being the sensory receptor organ (Whittow 1971). Nearly all thermoregulation is achieved by physical or physiological mechanisms such as shivering and voluntary behavioral adjustments, including changes in food intake and increasing depth of pelage by piloerection. Holter et al. (1975) emphasized the importance of postural changes in the thermoregulation of white-tailed deer.

Body Core Temperatures

There apparently are no published data on body temperature of free-ranging mule, black-tailed, and white-tailed deer. Nearly all information on body temperature of deer has been obtained from repeated measurement of small numbers of captive, usually restrained deer (table 5). Knowledge of the body temperature of unrestrained mule and black-tailed deer is based on only two captive animals (Thorne 1975). He indicated that for yearling

Table 5. Body Core Temperatures of Mule and Black-tailed Deer

Subspecies	Sex	Age	Characteristics	Number	Date	Number of Readings	Ambient Temperature[a]	Site and Method
California mule deer	M	Fawns	Live-trapped	8	Nov.–Apr.	8		Rectal, thermometer
	M	Yearlings	Live-trapped	3	Nov.–Apr.	3		Rectal, thermometer
	M	Adults	Live-trapped	11	Nov.–Apr.	11		Rectal, thermometer
	F	Fawns	Live-trapped	4	Nov.–Apr.	4		Rectal, thermometer
	F	Yearlings	Live-trapped	5	Nov.–Apr.	5		Rectal, thermometer
Columbian black-tailed deer	M	Fawns	Very tame, captive	2	Autumn (one month)	45	0.6–20.3	Rectal, thermometer
	F	Adults	Very tame, captive	2	Autumn (one month)	45	0.6–20.3	Intrauterine, thermometer
Rocky Mountain mule deer	M	Yearling	Semitame, captive	1	20–27 Aug.	159	11.7–30.5	Under musculature of right paralumbar fossa on upper flank of abdominal cavity, telemetry
	F	Yearling	Semitame, captive	1	20–27 Aug.	159	11.7–30.5	Under musculature of right paralumbar fossa on upper flank of abdominal cavity, telemetry

[a]In degrees Celsius.

Rocky Mountain mule deer time of day had no significant effect on mean body temperature.

Lethal body temperature generally is regarded as the body core temperature at which 50 percent of experimental animals die (Bianca 1968). Bianca stated that the lower lethal body temperature in most mammalian species lies between about 15 and 20 degrees Celsius (59–68 degrees Fahrenheit), and that it is about 25 degrees Celsius (77 degrees Fahrenheit) for humans. Lethal body temperatures have not been established for mule, black-tailed, and white-tailed deer. Moen (1967) recorded a rectal temperature of 26.4 degrees Celsius (79.5 degrees Fahrenheit) in a wild adult male white-tailed deer about 1.5 hours following immersion for an unknown period of time in water that approximated 0.4–2.0 degrees Celsius (32.7–35.6 degrees Fahrenheit). Inside a heated building, the rectal temperature of this initially helpless deer rose to 39.5 degrees Celsius (103 degrees Fahrenheit) within 10.5 hours and fluctuated from 38.0 to 38.6 degrees Celsius (100–102 degrees Fahrenheit) following an apparently complete recovery.

Body Surface Temperatures

Exchange of energy between a deer and its environment occurs by conduction, evaporation, convection, and radiation. Moen (1973) and Moen and Jacobsen (1975) discussed these thermal exchange processes as applied to white-tailed deer. From 12 Rocky Mountain mule deer, Parker and Driscoll (1972) obtained a mean of 23.4 degrees Celsius (74 degrees Fahrenheit) and a range of 21–26 degrees Celsius (70–79 degrees Fahrenheit) for

(Table 5.)

Mean Temperature[a]	Temperature range[a]	Reference
40.0	38.9–41.1	Leopold et al. (1951)
40.6	40.0–41.1	Leopold et al. (1951)
40.6	38.9–41.7	Leopold et al. (1951)
40.6	37.8–42.8	Leopold et al. (1951)
40.0	39.5–41.1	Leopold et al. (1951)
38.9	38.4–39.8	Cowan and Wood (1955b)
38.3	37.8–39.3	Cowan and Wood (1955b)
37.1	36.3–42.1	Thorne (1975)
38.1	36.2–41.7	Thorne (1975)

1969) and energy balance calculations (Moen 1973). Experiments by Parker and Harlan (1972) with a tanned, furred hide of Rocky Mountain mule deer showed a decline of 18.3 degrees (Celsius) in 120 seconds after shading from solar radiation. Moen (1974) described relationships among radiant temperature and air temperature as linear and those among radiant temperature and wind velocities as nonlinear. He used the equation of Stevens (1972) to predict radiant temperature from wind velocity and air temperature and found that the winter pelage of mule and white-tailed deer yielded nearly identical regression equations for predicting radiant temperature from air temperature. Moen and Jacobsen (1974) stated that the magnitude of change in radiant temperature is somewhat less for wind effects than for direct-beam solar radiation. Although Parker (1972) believed that infrared detection (thermal scanning) had potential as a method of censusing big game—given proper equipment, ambient thermal conditions and habitats—Moen (1974, p. 403) concluded that "the feasibility of thermal scanning for censusing purposes is doubtful in all but the simplest of habitats."

radiant surface temperature. The ambient air temperature was 13.3 degrees Celsius (56 degrees Fahrenheit) under calm, overcast conditions. With similar conditions and an ambient air temperature of 15 degrees Celsius (59 degrees Fahrenheit), radiant surface temperatures of a red deer were 17, 25, and 28–30 degrees Celsius (62, 77, and 82–85 degrees Fahrenheit) for the body, head, and antlers, respectively (Gates 1969). At −4 degrees Celsius (24.8 degrees Fahrenheit) ambient air temperature with mild wind and high overcast conditions, radiant surface temperatures of white-tailed deer averaged about 7 degrees greater than that from the snow background (McCullough et al. 1969).

Measurement of infrared radiation from deer surfaces has received considerable attention because of its apparent potential for deer census (Croon et al. 1968; McCullough et al.

HEARTBEAT RATE

Heartbeat rate is a function associated with heat production (Moen 1973). Probably the first attempt to obtain information on the heartbeat rate of wild mule deer was that of Leopold et al. (1951). They found that over approximately ten months, mean pulse rates (beats per minute) of live-trapped male and female California mule deer were 189–250 in summer fawns, 109–250 in winter fawns, 105–121 in yearlings, and 119 and 115 in adults. These values are presumed to be greatly elevated because of capture and handling procedures. Folk (1968, p. 339) noted the "profound effect of restraint upon physiological measurements." Only recently has the use of telemetric techniques—similar to those described by Skutt et al. (1973) and Cupal et al.

(1974)—permitted the collection of data on heartbeat rate without physically handling the deer. Apparently there are no published telemetric data on the heartbeat rate of mule and black-tailed deer.

Seasonal Effects

Telemetric measurements of mean heartbeat rate of 3 male and 3 female adult white-tailed deer in twenty respiration chamber trials covering nine different calendar months over a four-year period revealed a mean ($\pm$SE) heartbeat rate of 60.1 ± 1 beats per minute and a mean ($\pm$SE) metabolic rate of 137.5 ± 1.9 kilocalories per kilogram of body weight $^{0.75}$ (Holter et al. 1976). Mean heartbeat rate accounted for 78 percent of the variation (r^2) in metabolic rate. Seasonally, r^2 values of heartbeat rate versus metabolic rate ranged from 0.55 (winter) to 0.94 (summer). Jacobsen (1973) telemetrically monitored the heartbeat rates of one female for thirteen months and one male white-tailed deer for six months. The approximate mean heartbeat rates per minute obtained seasonally were 69 in summer, 60 in winter, and 62 in spring. Seasonal differences in posture and activity may account for some of the seasonal variation in mean heartbeat rate.

Seasonal Postural Interactions

Based on yearlong telemetric readings, the mean ($\pm$SE) heartbeat rates of 3 adult male and 3 adult female white-tailed deer at ambient temperatures ranging from -20 to 37 degrees Celsius (-4 to 99 degrees Fahrenheit) were 74 ± 2, standing; 53 ± 1, bedded; and 60 ± 1 overall (Holter et al. 1975). The authors hypothesized that low heartbeat rate in the bedded position may conserve energy at very low temperatures, because the heartbeat rate of bedded deer was constant regardless of ambient temperature, whereas the heartbeat rates of deer in a standing posture increased as ambient temperature decreased. It also was found that, during winter, spring, and summer, ambi-

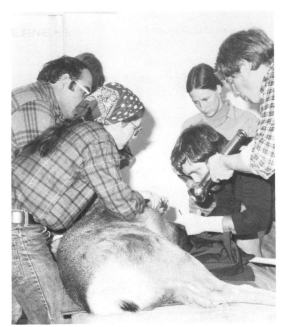

Surgery is conducted to implant a transmitter so that heart rate can be measured telemetrically. Photograph by Paul F. Gilbert; courtesy of the Colorado Division of Wildlife.

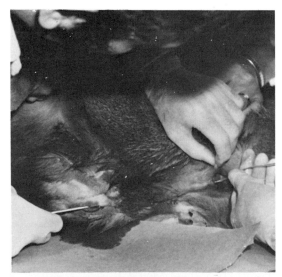

In surgery to implant a heart-rate telemetry transmitter, the transmitter package *(at right)* is placed subcutaneously at the base of the deer's neck, while electrodes are fed through a catheter and located subcutaneously along the sternum. Photograph by F. Waugh; courtesy of the Colorado Division of Wildlife.

ent temperature decreases were accompanied by increased heartbeat rate and energy expenditure. During autumn, however, variation in ambient temperature had no effect on heartbeat rate or energy expenditures.

Age and Behavioral Effects

Heartbeat rate of newborn white-tailed deer decreased exponentially from 200–300 beats per minute at approximately 3 kilograms (6.6 pounds) to about 60–100 beats per minute at 8–12 kilograms (17.6–26.5 pounds), just after weaning (Jacobsen 1973). Jacobsen also observed alarm brachycardia in three white-tailed deer fawns up to 14 days of age. Heartbeat rate decreased by 30–80 percent of the previous rate. Among adult white-tailed deer, peak heart rates of about 250 beats per minute were elicited by alarm situations where the deer ran or bounded away. Heart rates of 72–189 beats per minute were measured telemetrically during tarsal gland rub-urination posture. The usual urination posture had little effect on heart rate (Jacobsen 1973; see also chap. 5).

REPRODUCTION

Reproduction in Females

Only in the last decade has much effort been directed to the experimental study of the reproductive biology of mule, black-tailed, and white-tailed deer.

Female deer in the temperate zone breed during autumn and may release more than one ovum in an estrous period. They may complete several estrous cycles if conception does not occur (Asdell 1964). The estrous cycle in captive female Columbian black-tailed deer lasted approximately 22–28 days, and the period of estrus was 24–36 hours (West 1968). Perhaps these data approximate those for does of other mule and black-tailed deer subspecies as well. Selected information on chronology of the breeding season is listed for mule and black-tailed deer in figure 5. Extreme values are as-

sociated, in part, with the wide range of environments represented. For example, in Utah, Robinette et al. (1977) calculated that a 304.9 meter (1,000 foot) rise in elevation was associated with a seven-day delay in the fawning period.

The pioneer investigation of Cheatum (1949a) on ovary structure of white-tailed deer showed that quantitative indexes of productivity could be obtained macroscopically by counting the corpora lutea in the hand-sectioned ovary. Corpora lutea are endocrine glands within the ovary that develop from the Graafian follicles after ovulation and that, during the gestation period, provide information on ovulation rates. From deer killed during the autumn hunting season, counts of regressed corpora lutea residual from the previous breeding season (corpora albicantia) provide a gross estimate of the number of prenatal young produced during that season. Error with the technique occurs when other pigmented structures are mistaken for the corpora albicantia of corpora lutea of pregnancy (Golley 1957a) or simply corpora albicantia (Nalbandov 1964). This factor, plus loss of ova and intrauterine mortality, suggests that most counts of corpora albicantia probably are overestimates of the number of neonates produced. Golley detected an 18 percent error in macroscopic identification of the corpora albicantia of corpora lutea of pregnancy. Brown (1961), however, suggested that this error was about 10 percent. The macroscopic technique has never been subjected to rigorous tests involving mule or black-tailed deer of known breeding history. Thomas (1970) noted that quantitative relationships among corpora lutea and fetuses and among corpora lutea and corpus luteum scars were poorly understood.

The count of corpora lutea can be useful, however, in gross comparisons of deer productivity in regions or areas having large habitat variations. This is particularly true in those regions where few data are available on fetal rates, such as Arizona, New Mexico, and western Texas. Comparison of counts of corpora albicantia from selected populations of mule and black-tailed deer occupying the

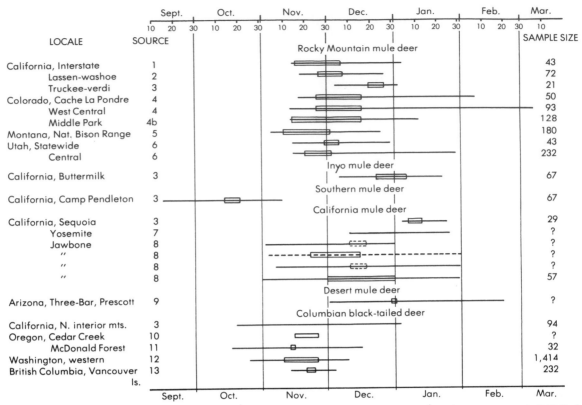

Figure 5. Estimated breeding seasons in mule and black-tailed deer. Sources: 1, Chattin (1948); 2, Lassen et al. (1952); 3, Bischoff (1957); 4, Anderson and Medin (1967); 4b, Gill (1972b); 5, Hudson and Browman (1959); 6, Robinette and Gashwiler (1950); 7, Dixon (1934); 8, Leopold et al. (1951); 9, Swank (1958); 10, Hines (1975); 11, Jordan and Vohs (1976); 12, Brown (1961); 13, Thomas (1970). The rectangles and horizontal lines represent the inferred periods of maximum and minimum breeding activity, respectively.

southwestern and northern portions of the United States, for example, suggests that deer productivity tends to be lower in xeric habitats (table 6).

Thomas (1970) and Thomas and Cowan (1975) have described the ovarian cycle in the Columbian black-tailed deer. Based on detailed histological studies of ovaries of 444 deer killed during November and December, they determined that cyclic development and degeneration occurred in single follicles of ovulatory age several weeks before ovulation. Immediately before the breeding season, a second or third follicle developed in each cycle, but, in nearly half the adult females, follicles were at different stages of maturation. First ovulation occurred during November, but implantation never occurred then, even though spermatozoa penetrated ova. They suggest that insufficient progesterone may have been a

factor. Second ovulation occurred 6 to 9 days later and lasted for about 7 to 8 days in nearly half the adult females. About 96 percent of the females conceived at second ovulation. If conception does not occur during the second ovulation, follicular cycles 8–9 days in length may occur, with estrus occurring every second or third follicular cycle, or every 23–29 days. In cases of persistent conception failure, a doe may experience at least five periods of estrus. Corpora lutea of pregnancy, which equaled the number of fetuses implanted, developed into distinctive scars that persisted for the life of the doe. The regression relating the average number of scars of corpora lutea of pregnancy on the estimated age of females during the previous breeding season showed a correlation coefficient (r) of 0.998; 28 and 27 such scars were counted in the ovaries of females estimated to be 17.0 and 18.5 years of age, re-

Table 6. Counts of Corpora Albicantia from Mule Deer in Mesic and Xeric Habitats

Habitat	State	Herd and Years	Number of Deer	Mean Corpora Albicantia per Deer	Percentage of Deer with Corpora Albicantia	Reference
Mesic	Idaho	Cassia, 1952–53	177	1.56	88.5	McConnell (1957)
	Colorado	Cache la Poudre, 1961–64	204	1.68	90.7	Anderson and Medin (1965)
Xeric	Texas	Black Gap, 1958–61	254	1.43	79.5	Anderson et al. (1970)
	New Mexico	Guadalupe, 1957–58	301	1.30	79.7	Anderson et al. (1970)

Note: Deer were about 27+ months of age at time of death. Conception was estimated to have occurred 10–12 months earlier. Ovaries were obtained at check station during autumn hunting seasons.

spectively. Based on mean ovulation rates, fertility within the younger age classes of Columbian black-tailed deer was directly and significantly related to body size. Accessory corpora lutea occurred in 47 percent of Columbian blacktail females between the first and second ovulation, and in 36 percent of these deer during pregnancy. Accessory corpora lutea were found in large and small unruptured follicles, small ruptured follicles, and regressing corpora lutea (Thomas 1970).

Differences between corpora lutea of pregnancy and fetal counts indicate loss of fertilized ova during gestation. A minimum loss of ova of 8.3 percent occurred in females that produced corpora lutea, and the loss was 4.3 percent in pregnant females. Moribund fetuses accounted for a 3.4 percent loss of ova in these pregnant females (Thomas 1970). Robinette et al. (1955) found a 10.5 percent loss of ova in 482 Rocky Mountain mule deer. Excluding yearlings, Medin (1976) recorded a 7.6 percent loss of ova in 41 does of that subspecies.

Gonadotrophic levels in the pituitary were not obviously related over time to numbers of ovarian follicles in Rocky Mountain mule deer. Bioassays of the pituitary glands from 20 female fawns, 19 female yearlings, and 22 adult females indicated that pituitaries of fawns had maximal gonadotrophic potency during summer and minimal potency during winter. In adults, gonadotrophic potency was high by late November and early December and low in February and March. The mean numbers of ovarian follicles for all age classes were maximal in August-September and minimal during January-February (Grieser and Browman 1956). In Columbian black-tailed deer, the number, size, and appearance of follicles exceeding 10 cubic millimeters (0.00061 cubic inches) provided a crude estimate of the number of follicles that ruptured and therefore an estimate of female reproductive status before the breeding season (Thomas 1970).

Research on ovarian hormones in North American deer has been limited to whitetails. Estrone and estradiol increased six- or seven-fold from the third to the seventh (last) month of pregnancy but dropped to very low levels after birth (Harder and Woolf 1976).

Weight of ovaries increased significantly ($p < 0.01$) with age of doe. This weight did not vary seasonally. Ovarian weight also was larger in does 1–5 months old than in does 6–11 months old (A. E. Anderson et al. 1974). The same phenomenon has been described in Columbian black-tailed deer (Thomas 1970). This possibly could be associated with the decrease in gonadotrophic potency of Rocky Mountain mule deer during February and March (Grieser and Browman 1956).

The literature on fetal rates in mule and black-tailed deer is summarized in the form of age-specific and non-age-specific rates of prenatal young in tables 7 and 8. Obviously, the relative numbers of younger deer, particularly yearlings, have a strong influence on the calculated mean rates. Because many authors do not make this clear, the tabulated values may not be accurate or comparable. Data in table 7

Table 7. Frequency of Occurrence of Fetuses in Mule and Black-tailed Deer Does by Age Class

Subspecies	Locale (Reference)[a]	Year Class	Number of Fetuses								Total Number of Fetuses	Total Number of Does	Percentage and Total Number Pregnant Does		Fetuses per Doe	Fetuses per Pregnant Doe	Sampling Period (if Given)
			0 %	0 No.	1 %	1 No.	2 %	2 No.	3 %	3 No.			%	No.			
Rocky Mountain mule deer	Raft River Mountains, Utah (1)	1	80.0	4	20.0	1		0		0	1	5	20.0	1	0.20	1.00	Jan. (1 deer
		2		0	57.1	4	42.9	3		0	10	7	100.0	7	1.43	1.43	July
		3		0		0	100.0	1		0	2	1	100.0	1	2.00	2.00	
		4		0		0	100.0	1		0	2	1	100.0	1	2.00	2.00	
		5–9		0		0	87.5	7	12.5	1	17	8	100.0	8	2.13	2.13	
		>9		0		0	75.0	3	25.0	1	9	4	100.0	4	2.25	2.25	
		Uncl.	25.0	1	25.0	1	25.0	1	25.0	1	6	4	75.0	3	1.50	2.00	
		$\bar{X}, \Sigma$	16.7	5	20.0	6	53.3	16	10.0	3	47	30	83.3	25	1.57	1.88	
	Cache la Poudre, Colorado (2)	2		0	77.7	7	22.2	2		0	11	9	100.0	9	1.22	1.22	Jan.–June
		3		0		0	100.0	5		0	10	5	100.0	5	2.00	2.00	
		4–8		0	23.8	5	76.2	16		0	37	21	100.0	21	1.76	1.76	
		9+		0	20.0	3	73.3	11	06.6	1	28	15	100.0	15	1.87	1.87	
		$\bar{X}, \Sigma$		0	30.0	15	68.0	34	02.0	1	86	50	100.0	50	1.72	1.72	
	Utah, mostly Wasatch Front[b] (3)	<2	59.5	47	35.4	28	05.1	4		0	36	79	40.5	32	0.46	1.13	Jan.
		3	05.5	2	41.7	15	52.8	19		0	53	36	94.4	34	1.47	1.56	
		4–8	07.6	7	25.0	23	64.1	59	03.3	3	150	92	92.4	85	1.63	1.75	
		>8	11.8	8	42.6	29	45.6	31		0	91	68	88.2	60	1.34	1.52	
		Uncl.	05.4	2	51.4	19	43.2	16		0	51	37	94.6	35	1.38	1.46	
		$\bar{X}, \Sigma$	21.2	66	36.5	114	41.3	129	01.0	3	381	312	78.8	246	1.22	1.55	
	Utah, mostly Wasatch Front[b] (4)	<2	24.7	54	58.0	127	17.4	38		0	203	219	75.3	165	0.93	1.23	Jan.
		3	01.3	1	22.4	17	76.3	58		0	133	76	98.7	75	1.75	1.77	
		4–8	06.3	14	19.5	43	72.4	160	01.8	4	375	221	93.7	207	1.70	1.81	
		>8	10.8	13	16.7	20	70.0	84	02.5	3	197	120	89.2	107	1.64	1.84	
		Uncl.	05.3	1	31.6	6	63.2	12		0	30	19	94.7	18	1.58	1.67	
		$\bar{X}, \Sigma$	12.7	83	32.5	213	53.7	352	01.1	7	938	655	87.3	572	1.43	1.64	
	Antimony Unit, Utah (5)	2									5	8	62.5	5	0.63	1.00	
		3+									27	19			1.42		
		$\bar{X}, \Sigma$									32	27			1.19		
	Sublett Unit, Utah (5)	2									14	9	100.0	9	1.56	1.56	
		3+									47	24			1.96		
		$\bar{X}, \Sigma$									61	33			1.85		
	Lassen-Washoe 1951	2		0	100.0	2		0		0	2	2	100.0	2	1.00	1.00	Dec.
		3+	08.7	2	34.8	8	56.5	13		0	34	23	91.3	21	1.48	1.62	
	1956	3+		0	35.7	10	64.3	18		0	46	28	100.0	28	1.64	1.64	

	Truckee-Verdi (6)	3+	05.0	1	40.0	8	55.0	11		0	30	20	95.0	19	1.50	1.58	Jan.
		$\bar{X}$, Σ	04.1	3	38.4	28	57.5	42		0	112	73	95.9	70	1.53	1.60	
	Colorado, 1969–71 (7)	1	100.0	13		0		0		0	0	13		0	0.00		Jan.–June
		2+	3.4	4	41.0	48	53.0	62	02.6	3	181	117	96.6	113	1.55	1.60	
		$\bar{X}$, Σ	13.1	17	36.9	48	47.7	62	02.3	3	181	130	86.9	113	1.39	1.60	
Columbian black-tailed deer	California, six populations combined (6)	2	63.6	5	36.4	3		0		0	3	8	37.5	4	0.38	0.75	Nov.
		3+	00.9	3	41.9	50	53.8	63	03.4	4	188	120	99.1	117	1.57	1.61	
		$\bar{X}$, Σ	06.2	8	41.4	53	49.2	63	03.1	4	191	128	93.8	120	1.49	1.59	
	Vancouver Island, British Columbia, 1963–66 (8)	2									12	13	84.6	11	0.92	1.09	
		3									16	12	91.7	11		1.45	
		4									8	6	100.0	6	1.33	1.33	
		5									15	9	100.0	9	1.67	1.67	
		6									12	6	100.0	6	2.00	2.00	
		7									11	6	83.3	5	1.83	2.20	
		9									4	2	100.0	2	2.00	2.00	
		10									8	5	100.0	5	1.60	1.60	
		13									2	1	100.0	1	2.00	2.00	
		14									1	1	100.0	1	1.00	1.00	
		$\bar{X}$, Σ									89	61	93.4	57	1.46	1.56	
	McDonald State Forest, Oregon (9)	1									0	4			0.00		Mar.–May
		2									7	8			0.88		
		3+									45	28			1.61		
		$\bar{X}$, Σ, all does									52	40			1.30		
		$\bar{X}$, Σ, excluding fawns									52	36			1.44		
	Washington (10)	2	54.6	12	45.4	10		0		0	10	22	45.4	10	0.45	1.00	Jan.–May
		3–6	08.2	6	46.6	34	45.2	33		0	100	73	91.8	67	1.37	1.49	
		7+	33.3	5	26.7	4	40.0	6		0	16	15	66.7	10	1.07	1.60	
		Uncl.		0	100.0	4		0		0	4	4	100.0	4	1.00	1.00	
		$\bar{X}$, Σ	20.2	23	45.6	52	34.2	39		0	130	114	79.8	91	1.14	1.43	
Inyo mule deer	California (6)	2	75.0	3	25.0	1		0		0	1	4	25.0	1	0.25	1.00	Feb.
		3+		0	34.3	12	65.7	23		0	58	35	100.0	35	1.66	1.66	
		$\bar{X}$, Σ	07.7	3	33.3	13	59.0	23		0	59	39	92.3	36	1.51	1.64	
Southern mule deer	California (6)	2	28.6	4	71.4	10		0		0	10	14	71.4	10	0.71	1.00	Nov.
		3+	05.9	4	35.3	24	58.8	40		0	104	68	94.1	64	1.53	1.63	Nov.
		$\bar{X}$, Σ	09.8	8	41.5	34	48.8	40		0	114	82	90.2	74	1.39	1.54	
California mule deer	California (6)	2+		0	24.0	6	76.0	19		0	44	25	100.0	25	1.76	1.76	May

[a]References: 1, Jensen and Robinette (1955); 2, Medin (1976); 3, Robinette and Gashwiler (1950); 4, Robinette et al. (1955); 5, Julander et al. (1961); 6, Bischoff (1958); 7, Reed and Pojar (1977); 8, Thomas (1970); 9, Jordan and Vohs (1976); 10, Brown (1961).

[b]Data from an additional 382 Utah mule deer are listed in table 52 of Robinette et al. (1977).

Table 8. Frequency of Occurrence of Fetuses in Mule and Black-tailed Deer Does of Unspecified Age

Subspecies	Locale (Reference)[a]	Year	Number of Fetuses							
			0		1		2		3	
			%	No.	%	No.	%	No.	%	No.
Rocky Mountain mule deer	National (1)	1953–54	08.6	6	38.6	27	50.0	35	01.4	1
	Bison (2)	1957		0	28.6	2	71.4	5		0
	Range, (3)	1955–56	16.7	10	30.0	18	48.3	29	05.0	3
	Montana (4)	1963		0	21.4	3	78.6	11		0
		$\bar{X}, \Sigma$	10.6	16	33.1	50	53.0	80	02.6	4
	Middle Park, Colorado (5)	1969		0	24.4	10	61.0	25	12.2	5
		1970	11.9	5	16.7	7	66.7	28	04.8	2
		1971	02.0	1	37.3	19	58.8	30	02.0	1
		$\bar{X}, \Sigma$	04.5	6	26.9	36	61.9	83	06.0	8
	Interstate Deer Herd, California (6)	1946		0	33.3	4	66.7	8		0
		1947	02.7	1	27.0	10	64.9	24	05.4	2
		$\bar{X}, \Sigma$	02.0	1	28.6	14	65.3	32	04.1	2
	Utah (7)		13.6	8	23.7	14	62.7	37		0
	Oregon (8)		02.3	2	28.7	25	64.6	56	04.6	4
	Washington (9)		07.6	6	34.2	27	58.2	46		0
	Gunnison, Colorado (10)		27.3	39	07.7	11	65.0	93		0
	Lassen County, California Washoe County, Nevada (11)	1948–49 1949–50 1950–51 $\bar{X}, \Sigma$								
Columbian black-tailed deer	North-central California (12)	$\bar{X}, \Sigma$								
	Washington (13)		08.0	11	49.3	68	42.0	58	00.7	1

[a]1, Sears (1955); Sears and Browman (1955); 2, Nellis (1968); 3, Hudson (1959); 4, Nellis (1968); 5, Gill (1972b); 6, Chattin (1948); 13, Lauckhart (1948).

support the general assumption that fawns (about 1 year old) and yearlings (about 2 years old) produce fewer young than do older mule and black-tailed deer females. Also, there may be little change in average productivity of age classes from years 3 through perhaps 9, but there are too few age-specific samples beyond 9 years to estimate an age or age-range of declining productivity.

The most common litter size in adult Rocky Mountain mule deer is two, with fawns and yearlings (aged 1 and 2 years at parturition) most frequently producing singletons. In the limited data available, triplets mainly were born to females more than 4 years old (table 7).

Reproduction in Males

The testes of mule deer older than about 7 years showed histological evidence of atrophy (Markwald et al. 1971). During April, spermatogenesis for a sexually mature buck began with increased nuclear volume and associated histochemical changes in the Leydig cells. The

(Table 8.)

4 %	4 No.	Number of Fetuses	Number of Does	Percentage and Total Number Pregnant Does %	Percentage and Total Number Pregnant Does No.	Fetuses per Doe	Fetuses per Pregnant Doe	Sampling Period (if given)
01.4	1	104	70	91.4	64	1.49	1.63	early Dec.
	0	12	7	100.0	7	1.71	1.71	Jan.
	0	85	60	83.3	50	1.42	1.70	early Dec.
	0	25	14	100.0	14	1.79	1.79	Jan.-May
00.7	1	226	151	89.4	135	1.50	1.67	
02.4	1	79	41	100.0	41	1.93	1.93	mid-Jan./May
	0	69	42	88.1	37	1.64	1.86	mid-Jan./May
	0	82	51	98.0	50	1.61	1.64	mid-Jan./May
00.7	1	230	134	95.6	128	1.72	1.80	
	0	20	12	100.0	12	1.67	1.67	
	0	64	37	97.3	36	1.73	1.78	
	0	84	49	98.0	48	1.71	1.75	
	0	88	59	86.5	51	1.49	1.73	
	0	149	87	97.7	85	1.71	1.75	
	0	119	79	92.4	73	1.51	1.63	Mar.-May
	0	197	143	72.7	104	1.38	1.89	
		54	39	92.3	36	1.38	1.50	Dec.
		35	33	78.8	26	1.06	1.34	Dec.
		21	17	82.4	14	1.23	1.50	
		110	89	85.4	76	1.24	1.45	
		20	13			1.54		
		16	13			1.23		
		11	12			0.92		
		47	38			1.24		
	0	187	138	92.0	127	1.36	1.47	Mar.–May

7, Robinette and Olsen (1944); 8, McKean (1947); 9, Lauckhart (1948); 10, Tolman (1950); 11, Lassen et al. (1952); 12, Taber (1953;

Triplets are a rarity, and most are born to does 4 years old or older. Photograph by Harry H. French; courtesy of the United States Forest Service.

glandular epithelium of seminal vesicles began activity three to four weeks after the initial Leydig cell activity, as indicated by shifts in enzyme focal points and other histochemical changes. Leydig cell activity was maximal during late September, began decreasing during November, and was minimal by January.

Mean volume of the testes and serum testosterone and sperm production levels were maximal in 6–16 captive and 25 wild Columbian black-tailed deer during November (West and Nordan 1976a). Minimum values of these parameters were attained during February and March. By domestic animal standards, sperm concentration and semen quality were judged adequate for successful breeding between September and January. Some males produced sperm yearlong. West and Nordan reported that sperm, although of low viability and motility, increased briefly in concentration during spring when antlers began growth, then decreased to postbreeding levels. Mean weights of the testes of 51 mature Rocky Mountain mule deer were maximal during November and minimal during May (A. E. Anderson et al. 1974). Mature sperm was present in the seminiferous tubules of some mature Rocky Mountain mule deer during each month of the year (Anderson and Medin 1964).

GROWTH AND MORPHOLOGY

According to Hafez (1968a, p. 76), "growth is a complex set of metabolic events, which are environmentally and genetically controlled." Rates of prenatal, preweaning, and postweaning growth are influenced, for example, by temperature, humidity, air movement, and radiation. These in turn affect the amount of food and water intake, energy available in ingested forage, the heat production mechanism, and net energy available for productivity and body composition. In theory, there are three phases of postnatal growth: (1) from birth to near the end of weaning, when growth is accelerating; (2) from weaning to sexual maturity, when growth is slowing rapidly; and (3) during sexual maturity, when growth—as mea-

sured by weight changes—may be slightly negative (Moen 1973).

Fetal Development

Ambient temperature probably is the most important climatic variable affecting prenatal growth (Hafez 1968a). Huggett and Widdas (1951) noted that the range of variation in fetal growth rates among mammalian orders approximated 1,000. Fetal growth curves for estimating age of deer—based on body weight, forehead-rump length, or length of hind foot singly or on various body weight–body dimension ratios—have been published by Cheatum and Morton (1946), Armstrong (1950), Hudson and Browman (1959), Verme (1963a), Short (1970), Thomas (1970), and Robbins and Moen (1975), based on groups of 12, 12, 5, 21, 21, 2, and 26 prenatal young of known age. The first three authors did not provide prediction equations. Robinette et al. (1977) provided constants for the formula of Huggett and Widdas (1951) to estimate the ages of Rocky Mountain mule deer singletons, twins, and triplets based on body weight.

Body weight does not seem to be the best predictor of age in prenatal young. Short (1970) computed three linear prediction equations based on 21 white-tailed deer fetuses of known age, in which oven-dried weight of paired eye lenses, length of hind foot, and forehead-rump length were correlated more strongly ($r=0.99$) with gestation age than with body weight. Forehead-rump length on mean gestation age yielded an r of 0.99 in Columbian black-tailed fetuses (Thomas 1970). Studies of relative growth in the prenatal young of Columbian black-tailed deer (Ommundsen and Cowan 1970) indicated that, among eighteen morphologic attributes, body weight had the fastest growth rate in relation to forehead-rump length and length of hind foot.

Experimental evidence is in conflict on the effects of the maternal diet on birth weight of mule, black-tailed, and white-tailed deer. In Colorado mule deer, nutritional levels of the pregnant mothers had no detectable effect on the birth weight of their fawns (Robinette et al. 1973). Verme (1963*a*, p. 436), however, found that malnutrition of the white-tailed deer dam reduced fetal weights 46 percent, and that "surviving fawns averaged 6.4 pounds [2.9 kilograms] at birth, over 2 pounds [0.9 kilograms] heavier than those that died."

Fetal skeletons of 42 Rocky Mountain mule deer and 20 white-tailed deer were studied by whole-body x rays (Short 1970). In 20 white-tailed fetuses of known age, ossification centered in long-bone shafts, spine, and ribs at 50–69 days; in the scapula, sternum, pelvic girdle, and two-three rows of phalanges, it was present by 70–79 days. Neural spines and the tuber calcis ossified at 80–89 days; tarsal bones and neural spines on thoracic vertebrae were present at 120–39 days; and carpals and patellas appeared at 140–69 days. Essentially the entire skeleton was ossified by 180–89 days. In red deer fetuses, ossification of bone also began during the seventh week of intrauterine life (Pantić and Brna 1967).

In 20 white-tailed deer fetuses of known age, gum-swelling occurred in the cheek and incisiform gums by 58 and 79 days after conception, respectively (Short 1970). The incisiform teeth erupted at about 180 days. In 15 Rocky Mountain mule deer fetuses, mineralization of the first incisor and the third and fourth premolars began at age 99 days, and that of the second and first molars, incisors, canines, and second premolars began at 130 days (Rees et al. 1966*b*). Mineralization of the roots of these mandibular teeth began at about 150–55 days of gestation. According to Rees et al., the crown of the first molar is developing at parturition.

There are few published data on the absolute fresh or fixed weights of fetal organs and glands in mule and black-tailed deer. Short (1970) expressed fixed weights of heart, liver, spleen, kidneys, and lungs of 10 known-age white-tailed deer and 44 approximately aged Rocky Mountain mule deer fetuses as percentage of total weight of the organs sampled. For both

A drugged, pregnant doe is x-rayed to determine by skull count the number of fawns she carries. Photograph courtesy of the Utah Division of Wildlife Resources.

species, total fixed weight of each organ thus expressed decreased with age. Fixed weight of paired eyeballs and oven-dried weight of paired eye lenses of known-age white-tailed deer fetuses were correlated strongly ($r=0.97$; $r=0.99$) and linearly with age.

Short also noted that, unlike the situation in adults of each sex, the two lobes of the thymus gland were not connected in either white-tailed or mule deer fetuses. In 14 Columbian black-tailed deer fetuses, weight of the paired ovaries increased from 4.8 milligrams (0.00017 ounces) at 64 days of gestation to 42.7 milligrams (0.0015 ounces) at 204 days, then decreased to 28.0 milligrams (0.00099 ounces) at 1–2 days postpartum in one fawn (Thomas 1970). He also described oogenesis in the fetal ovary.

Mean (±2 SE) percentage of total body mass of eleven organs and four glands of 3 near-term Rocky Mountain mule deer fetuses, averaging 3.26 kilograms (7.2 pounds) in body weight, ranged from 5.60±0.39 (lungs), 2.53±0.34 (liver), 1.01±0.04 (stomach tissue), and 0.87±0.08 (heart) to 0.02±0.007 (adrenals) and 0.02±0.007 (thyroid) (Hakonson and Whicker 1971*a*).

Based on 65 sets of known dates of conception and birth in mule and black-tailed deer, mean gestation periods approximated 200–208 days, with a range of 183–218 days (table 9).

Fetal growth curves for Rocky Mountain mule deer of Hudson and Browman (1959) and a mean gestation period of 203 days were used to calculate peak fawning periods of 19–20 June in Utah (Robinette et al. 1977)

and 16 June to 6 July in Colorado (Anderson and Medin 1967), with extreme dates of 16 May to early October in Utah and 4 June to 25 September in Coloardo. In both states, about 85 percent of the fawns were born within a thirty-day period. Fawning periods for other mule and black-tailed deer populations can be approximated from the estimated breeding seasons (fig. 5) and gestation periods (table 9).

Males generally predominate in fetal sex ratios of both mule deer—64:100 to 25:100 (Bischoff 1958); 91:100 to 112:100 (Robinette et al. 1957*a*); 113:100 to 144:100 (Robinette et al. 1977); 115:100 (Medin 1976)—and black-tailed deer—80:100 to 177:100 (Bischoff 1958). There was a tendency for male Rocky Mountain mule deer fetuses to decrease in number with increased litter sizes (Robinette et al. 1957*a*).

Postnatal Development

Based on 329 birth weights of Rocky Mountain mule deer from nine studies of penned deer and two studies of wild deer, mean birth weights ranged from 2.74 to 3.99 kilograms (6.04–8.80 pounds), with individual fawns weighing 2.27–5.0 kilograms (5–11 pounds) (table 10). Based on 79 birth weights obtained in four studies of penned and wild Columbian blacktails, means ranged from 2.97 to 3.29 kilograms (6.5–7.3 pounds). Weights of individual fawns ranged from 2.04 to 4.54 kilograms (4.5–10.0 pounds) (table 10).

Is there a sex difference in the mean birth weights of mule and black-tailed deer? There

Table 9. Gestation Period (Days) in Mule and Black-tailed Deer

Subspecies	Number of Deer	Arithmetic Mean	Standard Error of Mean	Median	Standard Error of Median	Number of Days Minimum	Maximum	Reference
Rocky Mountain mule deer	5	207.60	0.84	208	1.33	205	210	Dixon (1934)
	9	199.67	1.44	201	1.81	193	205	Nichol (1938)
	36	203.10	0.89			189	218	Robinette et al. (1973)
Columbian black-tailed deer	5	203.00	1.27	203	1.58	199	207	Golley (1957*b*)
	10					183	212	Cowan (1956*a*)

Table 10. Birth Weights of Mule and Black-tailed Deer

Subspecies	Sex	Number of Fawns	Litter Sizes	Birth Weight[a]			
				Mean	Standard Error	Minimum	Maximum
Rocky Mountain mule deer	M and F	9[b]	1 singleton, 5 twins[d]	3.39	0.16	3.22	3.72
	?	66[c]	All twins[e]	3.27		2.27	4.49
	M	14	All twins[f]	3.99	0.06	3.72	4.45
	F	15	All twins[f]	3.65	0.08	3.18	4.09
	M and F	172[a]	25 singletons, 139 twins, 8 triplets[f]	3.69		2.70	5.00
	M and F	44[c]	13 singletons, 30 twins, 1 unknown[g]	3.70	0.07	2.72	4.76
	M and F	9	Not given[h]	2.74	0.39		
	M and F	6	Not given[h]	2.97	0.49		
	M and F	23	Not given[i]	3.33	0.11		
Columbian black-tailed deer	M and F	11	2 singletons, 4 twins,	2.97	0.13	2.04	3.63
		1	unclassified[j]				
	M and F	11	5 singletons, 3 twins[k]	3.21	0.77	2.49	4.54
	M and F	49[c]	Not given[l]	2.99		2.31	3.22
	M and F	8[c]	Not given[m]	3.29		2.95	3.99

[a] In kilograms.
[b] Number of fawns did not include all individuals from the litters.
[c] Wild deer.
[d] Nichol (1938).
[e] Robinette and Olsen (1944).
[f] Robinette et al. (1973).
[g] Robinette et al. (1977).
[h] Halford (1974).
[i] Baker (1976).
[j] Cowan and Wood (1955a).
[k] Golley (1957b).
[l] Brown (1961).
[m] Cowan (1956a).

are not enough data to give an unequivocal answer. Among twins, mean birth weights of males were significantly ($p<0.01$) greater than those of females (Robinette et al. 1973). But, among 13 singletons and 30 twins, there was no significant difference among sexes in mean birth weight (Robinette et al. 1977). Baker (1976) found no significant ($p<0.05$) sex difference in the mean birth weight of 23 mule deer fawns from litters of unstated composition. The sex composition of litters sampled may be an important consideration in assessing sex differences in birth weights of mule and black-tailed deer. Robinette et al. (1973,

Postpartum examinations have shown that single fawns tend to weigh significantly more than fawns from multiple births. Photograph by Harold Jensen; courtesy of the United States Forest Service.

1977) noted that single fawns weighed significantly ($p<0.01$) more than those from multiple litters.

Prediction equations are available for estimating age of twin Rocky Mountain mule deer fawns by employing (1) body weight as the predictor from birth to 150 days of age; (2) length of hind foot to 75 days; and (3) new

hoof growth to about 90 days (Robinette et al. 1973).

Gross estimates of weight increase rates in mule and black-tailed deer members less than one year old are listed in table 11. Cowan and Wood (1955a) calculated instantaneous percentage growth rates per day by the method of Brody (1945) for 10 dam-raised Columbian

Table 11. Growth in Weight of Mule and Black-tailed Deer Fawns

| Subspecies | Number by Sex | | | Age (Days)[a] | Initial Body Weight[b] | | | |
	Male	Female	Not Given		Mean	Standard Error	Minimum	Maximum
Rocky Mountain deer			8	0–?[c]				
	1			0–200				
	14			0–150				
		15		0–150				
	14	15		0–12				
	14	15		13–75				
	14	15		76–150				
	6	3		0	2.97	0.49		
				70	17.74	0.68		
	9	6		0	2.74	0.39		
				70	14.16	0.47		
	9			0–90				
		9			14.12	0.48		
	9			91–180				
		9						
	6			0–90	3.30	0.11		
		6			17.10	0.83		
	6			91–180				
		6						
California mule deer	1			2–3			3.01	3.40
	1			3–4			3.40	3.46
			1	2–3			2.83	3.06
Columbian black-tailed deer	9			0–100			2.7	30.0
			49	0–21			2.31	
	1			0–200				

	Male	Female		Male	Female		
	6	6		28	30	5	
				67	70	10	
				98	106	15	
				126	137	20	
				153	166	25	

[a] "0" indicates data obtained at birth or within twenty-four hours of birth; values are approximations in most cases.
[b] In kilograms.
[c] Terminal age not stated.

black-tailed deer: 1–6 days, 10; 7–21 days, 5; and 22–100 days, 1.5. Not all fawns, however, exhibited the first phase. Bandy et al. (1970) reported instantaneous percentage growth rate per day in 22 100-day-old dam-raised, male Columbian black-tailed deer, Rocky Mountain mule deer, and Sitka deer as 1.60, 1.64, and 1.42, respectively, and 1.58 for 1 female Sitka

deer. These percentage rates of prepubertal gain are much higher than in hand-raised fawns of these subspecies (Wood et al. 1962).

Nordan et al. (1970) noted cumulative changes in body weight for 2 male and 2 female Columbian black-tailed deer from birth to about 310 days of age as 18.16 kilograms (40 pounds) and 17.25 kilograms (38 pounds)

(Table 11.)

Daily Gain[b]		Hand-Raised	Dam-Raised	Comments	References
Mean	Standard Error				
0.227		X			Nichol (1936)
0.091		X		Values are extremes of daily gains	Bandy et al. (1970)
0.499					
0.220		X			Robinette et al. (1973)
0.210		X			
0.290		X			
0.220		X			
0.190		X			
			X		Halford (1974)
0.220			X		
		X			
0.167		X			
0.155	0.012	X		Preweaning 1974	Baker (1976)
0.135	0.011	X			
0.213	0.009	X		Postweaning 1974	
0.183	0.009	X			
0.169	0.012	X		Preweaning 1975	
0.149	0.011	X			
0.184	0.010	X		Postweaning 1975	
0.188	0.012	X			
0.195			X	Wild fawns	Dixon (1934)
0.030			X		
0.115			X		
0.200		X		Calculated from tabular data in pounds	Cowan and Wood (1955a)
0.200			X	Wild fawns	Brown (1961)
0.045		X		Values are extremes of daily gains	Bandy et al. (1970)
0.272		X			
Male Female					
0.102 0.115		X		Fawns were captured in the wild at birth	Nordan et al. (1970)
0.148 0.132		X			
0.171 0.148		X			
0.182 0.164		X			
0.186 0.178		X			

body weight, respectively. To about 10 kilograms (22 pounds) body weight, females grew faster and consumed more food than did males. Males grew faster thereafter (table 11), and, based on the daily food consumption of high nutritional value, Sitka deer probably had a greater daily intake of digestible nutrients (Bandy et al. 1970).

Brown (1961) published the first growth-in-body-weight curve of mature Columbian black-tailed deer, based on sequential weighings of one male and one female Columbian black-tailed deer from 12 to 54 months of age. These curves reflected seasonal changes in weight and continuing growth until maturity. As used herein, a mature deer is one that has "attained the normal peak of natural growth and development" (Gove 1961, p. 1394). Wood et al. (1962) and Bandy et al. (1970) analyzed and compared growth curves based on sequential weighings of a few individual Rocky Mountain mule deer (most of which were male), two stocks of Columbian black-tailed deer, and Sitka deer. These deer were fed a highly nutritious diet ad libitum until at least 3 years of age. Data from a few deer deemed "representative" of their subspecies were selected for publication. Wood et al. (1962) noted the complexity of growth among subspecies and employed four curves to describe the course of growth: prepubertal growth; actual weight changes through an annual cycle; maximum annual weight reached; and minimum annual weights reached. Periods of weight gain fit the equation of Brody (1945): $W=Ae^{kt}$, where W is the body weight in pounds at time t in days from birth, A is an integration constant, k is the gain in weight per unit weight per unit time (percent per day), and e is the base of natural logarithms. Periods of the postinflection portion of each seasonally sigmoid growth and the accelerating phase of effective growth fit the equation: $W=A-Be^{-kt}$, where W represents body weight at time t in days from birth, A is the calculated asymptotic weight, B is an integration constant, e is the base of natural logarithms, and $-k$ is the instantaneous relative decline in growth rate (Brody 1945). The use of these equations re-

quired identification of the inflection point and an estimate of the asymptotic or "mature" weight. The data were fitted to the equation by the method of least squares. Interracial differences in growth in weight rate and pattern were so documented. For example, during the first year of life, instantaneous percentage growth rates per day were: Rocky Mountain mule deer, 1.72; Sitka deer, 1.58; Vancouver Island black-tailed deer, 1.47; and California black-tailed deer, 1.16. On the average and throughout life each subspecies retained its relative rate of growth (Bandy et al. 1970). Thus, Rocky Mountain mule deer had the greatest capacity for growth, followed by the Sitka, Vancouver Island, and California subspecies. During the deer's first year, distinctly different patterns of growth were detected among subspecies, but over the first three years of life these patterns developed in approximate synchrony. Bandy et al. also found that males declined in weight during winter twice as fast as did females but generally reached the point of inflection about twenty days later and at higher body weight. It is interesting to note that, though the Sitka blacktail exhibited a relatively high growth rate, in its native habitat it may be the smallest of mule and black-tailed deer subspecies. More extensive weight data for age and sex classes are needed to substantiate that inference.

In both sexes of each subspecies, postpubertal weight fluctuated seasonally during each year of life. Weight was gained in summer and early autumn and lost during late autumn and winter despite an abundance of highly nutritious food. Weight losses presumably were due to losses of fat associated with reproductive activity and loss of appetite, especially in males. The growth-in-weight curve of a male Rocky Mountain mule deer on a high nutritional plane estimated a winter weight loss of about 18.2 kilograms (40 pounds) or 20 percent of its peak weight during the second year of life, and about 22.7 kilograms (50 pounds) or 22 percent of its peak during the third year (Wood et al. 1962). Similar magnitudes of change in body weight have been documented for both wild white-tailed deer (Hoffman and Robinson 1966) and confined whitetails (French et al. 1956; Silver and Colovos 1957).

Over a four-year period, biweekly collection of Rocky Mountain mule deer ($N=192$) of each sex and from 17 days to 162 months of age, from a portion of the Cache la Poudre River drainage in north-central Colorado, permitted fitting predictive growth curves to both bled (intact) and eviscerated carcass weights. Multiple regression techniques were used, with $\log_e Y$ (weight) as the dependent variable and (1/age+10), estimated age, and collection day as independent (X) variables that also might occur in polynomial terms (A. E. Anderson et al. 1974). Bled carcass weight was strongly correlated with the independent variables for 85 male ($R^2=0.928$) and 113 female ($R^2=0.815$) deer (fig. 6). The predictive ability of the male curve has been verified experimentally (Schreckhise and Whicker 1976).

Eviscerated carcass weight also was strongly correlated with the independent variables for 83 male ($R^2=0.926$) deer and 111 female ($R^2=0.776$) deer. Estimated growth-in-weight curves exhibited a strong seasonal response in approximate synchrony with reproductive phenology and seasonal temperatures generally similar to those described by Wood et al. (1962) and Bandy et al. (1970) from individual deer of this subspecies. Among mature males, the predicted curve of bled carcass weight peaked during October and troughed during March. Among mature females the predicted curves of bled carcass weight had two peaks and two troughs each year of the deer's lives. A major peak occurred during October and a minor peak during January, and a major trough occurred during April and a minor trough during December. It is not clear whether the minor peaks and troughs are biological or mathematical in origin. As approximated from estimated curves, the magnitude of annual changes in average bled carcass weight approximated 18.1 kilograms (39.9 pounds) or 19 percent of predicted peak weight of males, and 16.2 kilograms (35.7 pounds) or 22 percent of predicted peak weight of females. The predictive curves of eviscerated carcass weight yielded the same general pattern of predicted

peaks and troughs as did those for bled carcass weight.

It is probable that courses of predictive curves of body weight are influenced by the phenomenon of "compensatory growth," or increased growth rates during normal nutrition following periods of malnutrition (Wilson and Osbourn 1960). As Wilson and Osbourn noted, compensatory growth allows an animal that has suffered from malnutrition to reach normal body size and conformation at a later stage of growth as long as the malnutrition is not prolonged.

Predictive growth curves of bled carcass weight (fig. 6) of Rocky Mountain mule deer indicate that males continue to gain weight and presumably to grow throughout life, whereas females achieve their maximum weight at about 8 years of age (A. E. Anderson et al. 1974). Other estimates of ages at which mule and black-tailed deer subspecies cease to gain body weight and presumably cease to grow are: male and female Rocky Mountain mule deer, 7.5 and 2.5 years, respectively (Mackie 1964); male California mule deer, at least 8 years (Mankins and Baker 1956); male and female California mule deer, less than 30 months (Leopold et al. 1951); and male Sitka and Columbian black-tailed deer, 12 years (Bandy et al. 1970). These apparent differences in ages of growth cessation may be associated more with procedural and analytical method than with actual differences.

McEwan (1975) used the concepts and equations of Brody (1945), involving prepubertal and minimal curves of body weight, plus appropriate values in the literature to calculate growth curves for captive arctic caribou, reindeer, Rocky Mountain bighorn sheep, and musk-oxen. He also calculated minimal winter weight curves for bison and elk. The various curves were compared with those of Wood et al. (1962) depicting growth in mule and black-tailed deer. Prepubertal instantaneous relative growth rates of Rocky Mountain bighorn sheep and Rocky Mountain mule deer resemble each other more than do those of Rocky Mountain mule deer and either Columbian or Sitka blacktails.

Most of the interpretable information on body weights of mule and black-tailed deer seems to be from Rocky Mountain mule deer. In this subspecies the mature buck was about 20 percent heavier than the average mature doe. Autumn weights of mature males were about twice as variable as those of mature does (A. E. Anderson et al. 1964, 1974). Maximum bled carcass weights of Rocky Mountain mule deer include a wild buck at 112.3 kilograms (247.6 pounds) and two wild does at 75.2 kilograms (165.8 pounds) (A. E. Anderson et al. 1974) and 76.9 kilograms (170 pounds) (Taber et al. 1959). Maximum live weights include a 159.1 kilogram (351 pound) tame buck, an 86.4 kilogram (190 pound) tame doe (Wood et al. 1962), a 108.6 kilogram (240 pound) wild buck and a 62.0 kilogram (137 pound) wild doe (Robinette et al. 1977). Maximum eviscerated carcass weights of wild bucks of this subspecies are 172 kilograms (380 pounds), 158.4 kilograms (350 pounds) (Hunter 1924), and 153.9 kilograms (340 pounds) (Mackie 1964). Statistical descriptions of mature Rocky Mountain mule deer are listed in table 12, including bled carcass weight less stomach, bled carcass weight less weight of gravid reproductive tract, eviscerated carcass weight, and skinned eviscerated carcass weight in one Rocky Mountain mule deer population (A. E. Anderson et al. 1974). Mean eviscerated carcass weights are listed by fifteen year classes for male and female Rocky Mountain mule deer killed during October (Robinette et al. 1977).

When plotted on a double logarithmic scale, bled carcass weights of Rocky Mountain mule deer of either sex can be predicted ($R^2 = 0.941$) from chest girth. Predicted weights, with 95 percent confidence intervals, have been tabulated for each of 81 deer (40-120 centimeters: 15.7–47.2 inches of chest girth) (A. E. Anderson et al. 1974).

Postnatal Growth of Skeleton

It has been suggested that, during winter, growth of skeletal tissue ceases in deer of northern latitudes (Klein 1964). However, predictive growth curves of body length (fig. 7), head length, cranial breadth, head length by cranial breadth, shoulder height, left hind foot length, left front hoof length, and left rear hoof length of mule deer from a Colorado population did not support this conclusion (A. E. Anderson et al. 1974). The curves showed that (1) growth of the eight variables was more rapid in males than in females; (2) age of males accounted for the largest proportion of the varia-

Table 12. Weights (in Kilograms) of Carcass Components of Rocky Mountain Mule Deer about 18+ Months of Age, Shot Yearlong over a Four-Year Period

Component	Sex	Number of Deer	Mean	Standard Error	Minimum	Maximum
Bled carcass weight[a]	M	51	74.04	2.41	43.1	112.3
	F	91	58.99	0.78	43.9	75.2
Bled carcass weight less stomach weight	M	47	66.64	2.36	37.5	100.4
	F	75	52.64	0.75	39.1	68.9
Bled carcass weight less weight of gravid reproductive tract	F	50	54.55	1.02	42.7	68.3
Eviscerated carcass weight[b]	M	50	55.20	1.85	31.6	86.0
	F	89	41.83	0.56	31.6	54.2
Skinned, eviscerated carcass weight[c]	M	45	48.78	1.71	28.0	76.3
	F	71	37.87	0.58	28.2	48.0

Source: A. E. Anderson et al. (1974).
[a] Bled carcass weight is the completely intact carcass less the blood and tissue loss from gunshot wounds.
[b] Eviscerated carcass weight is the completely intact carcass less all viscera (except esophagus) and blood and tissue loss from gunshot wounds.
[c] Less the weight of the antlers, viscera, and hide, but with the subcutaneous fat intact.

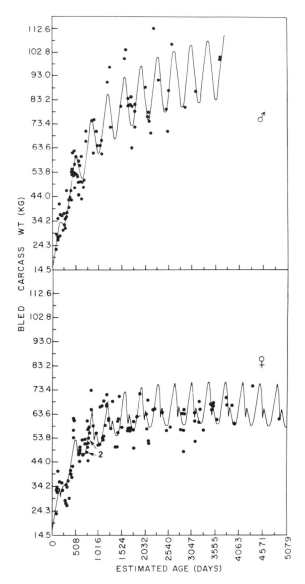

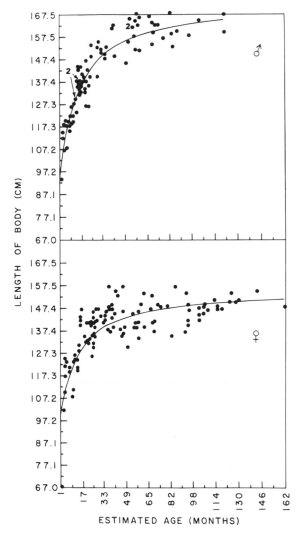

Figure 6. Growth curves for the bled carcasses of 85 male and 113 female Rocky Mountain mule deer collected yearlong, 1961–65; R^2 = 0.928 for males and 0.815 for females (A. E. Anderson et al. 1974).

Figure 7. Growth curves for the length of the body (excluding tail) in 85 male and 113 female Rocky Mountain mule deer collected yearlong, 1961–65; R^2 = 0.887 for males and 0.659 for females (A. E. Anderson et al. 1974).

tion (R^2); and (3) most rapid growth occurred before about 25 months of age. Also, cessation of significant growth of most skeletal variables seemed to occur at about age 48 months in males and at about 36 months in females (A. E. Anderson et al. 1974). Further analysis revealed a lack of significant linear growth among the eight skeletal variables in male deer 49 or more months of age. Among female deer about 37 or more months of age, significant

growth occurred only in body length and shoulder height. The precise age of growth cessation could not be identified for any of the eight skeletal variables (A. E. Anderson et al. 1974). Mean length of hind foot, girth, and shoulder height for thirteen year classes of male and female Rocky Mountain mule deer killed during October are listed by Robinette et al. (1977).

Scatter diagrams of adult deer with means (±SE) depicted for lengths of head and hind foot in male and female California mule deer suggested that only the length of head in males continued growth beyond about 36 months of age (Leopold et al. 1951). Leopold et al. mentioned a "mature" male California deer whose head length increased 3 percent but whose hind foot length remained unchanged over 11.5 months. Graphical depiction of the mean (±95 percent confidence interval) length of hind foot for eight year classes among 292 female Columbian black-tailed deer collected during November and December indicated that growth of this skeletal variable ceased between 30 and 42 months of age (Thomas 1970). Factor analysis of 446 male California mule deer killed during autumn hunting seasons showed that length of body did not increase beyond 6 years (Mankins and Baker 1956). The order of epiphyseal closure in the long bones of 24 male and 10 female mule and black-tailed deer of known age indicated that males, and perhaps females, may increase in height up to 3 years of age (Lewall and Cowan 1963). Observed differences in the approximate age of growth cessation among sexes and among and within subspecies probably are associated, in part, with sample sizes and with methods of sampling and analyses.

Skeletal and other external carcass measurements of male and female Rocky Mountain mule deer are given in table 13. Significant ($p<0.05$) sexual dimorphism within age classes did not occur among most skeletal features of Rocky Mountain mule deer until about 18 months of age, when all skeletal structures of males were larger (A. E. Anderson et al. 1974). Extreme values of left mandible length in male and female deer 1–11 months of age did not overlap with those of deer 19 months and older, so mandibular length can be used to segregate those age classes.

Head length and hind foot length averaged greater in males and increased in successive age classes of California mule deer (Leopold et al. 1951). Although these measurements tended to overlap slightly even among adult deer, mean lengths of hind foot increased with age in two adjacent populations of mule deer in New Mexico until at least 27 months and were greater and slightly more variable among males (Anderson et al. 1964). Significant sexual di-

morphism in mean length of hoofs was limited to mature males in both Columbian blacktails (McCullough 1965) and Rocky Mountain mule deer (A. E. Anderson et al. 1974).

Sexually dimorphic morphological characteristics of the pelvic girdle in Columbian black-tailed deer and white-tailed deer can be used to distinguish the sex of individual skeletons of mature animals (Taber 1956a). These characteristics are the relatively thick, blunt, pubic symphysis of the male, the presence (male) or absence (female) of the suspensory tuberosity on the interischial bone, and the symphysis depth/pubis length ratio.

There are few data on the interrelationships of skeletal components or among dimensions of the external carcasses of mule and black-tailed deer. Correlation matrixes of sixteen variables—ten of which were skeletal—were presented for each sex and all ages in Rocky Mountain mule deer. Most simple correlation coefficients (r) were large and differed significantly ($p<0.001$) from zero correlation, suggesting fairly synchronous growth of skeletal components. Among males, the r values of head length versus mandible length, body length versus head length, body length versus mandible length, and hind foot length versus metacarpal length all were equal to or greater than 0.96. Among females, the largest (r) value, 0.93, was derived from head length versus mandible length and hind foot length versus metacarpal length (A. E. Anderson et al. 1974). In general, measurements of skeletal elements that probably had similar sequences of growth—such as the skull, hind foot, and metacarpal (Pálsson 1955)—were most strongly correlated with each other.

Klein (1964) employed a skeletal ratio (mean length of the femur:mean length of hind foot) to detect differences in skeletal growth between two insular populations of Sitka deer. Klein claimed that skeletal ratios are influenced less by genetic factors than by carcass weight or body length and thus are especially suitable when sample sizes are small.

Rocky Mountain mule deer probably have the largest skeleton among subspecies of mule and black-tailed deer. This is suggested by

Table 13. External Carcass Measurements of Rocky Mountain Mule Deer about 18+ Months of Age, Shot Yearlong over a Four-Year Period

Measurement	Sex	Number	Mean	Standard Error	Minimum	Maximum
Chest girth	M	52	96.62	1.24	80	117
	F	89	88.72	0.48	78	97
Neck circumference[a]	M	52	42.42	1.17	30	65
	F	89	31.40	0.27	26	38
Neck circumference[b]	M	52	54.67	1.24	40	80
	F	89	43.13	0.47	32	56
Body length	M	51	152.29	1.54	126.0	167.5
	F	90	142.37	0.72	125.0	156.0
Tail length	M	51	17.98	0.26	13.5	22.0
	F	89	17.18	0.22	12.0	22.0
Ear length	M	51	21.01	0.17	16.5	23.0
	F	89	20.30	0.09	17.5	22.0
Head length	M	51	31.68	0.28	27.5	35.3
	F	91	25.59	0.12	26.8	32.6
Cranial breadth	M	51	13.71	0.16	11.0	15.6
	F	89	12.23	0.07	10.2	13.6
Shoulder height	M	52	96.58	0.76	84	106
	F	91	90.80	0.39	80	100
Hind foot length, left	M	50	48.70	0.27	44.8	53.0
	F	88	46.47	0.16	41.8	50.0
Hind foot length, right	M	51	48.66	0.27	44.4	53.0
	F	91	46.52	0.16	41.9	50.0
Metacarpal length	M	46	21.52	0.12	19.5	23.3
	F	77	20.70	0.09	18.1	23.0
Metacarpal width	M	46	1.91	0.02	1.66	2.18
	F	77	1.73	0.01	1.50	1.89
Fresh metacarpal weight	M	46	112.43	2.02	85	141
	F	77	89.45	1.01	67	112
Mandible length, left	M	50	23.16	0.20	19.7	25.8
	F	86	22.01	0.09	19.5	23.5
Metatarsal gland length, left	M	50	15.4	0.20	12.0	20.0
	F	89	15.0	0.18	12.0	23.5
Metatarsal gland length, right	M	50	15.6	0.21	11.5	20.0
	F	91	15.1	0.18	12.0	23.5
Metatarsal gland width, left	M	50	4.6	0.08	3.0	6.0
	F	89	4.6	0.06	3.0	6.0
Tarsal gland width, left	M	50	4.9	0.11	3.0	7.0
	F	89	4.8	0.08	3.0	7.0

Source: A. E. Anderson et al. (1974).

Note: All units are in centimeters except metacarpal weight (in grams).

[a] Measured 15 centimeters posterior to the occiput.

[b] Measured at the extreme lower base of neck.

comparing measurements of skeletal criteria (A. E. Anderson et al. 1974, 1964; Leopold et al. 1951; Rees 1971a; Robinette et al. 1977).

Teeth

Among 7 newborn Rocky Mountain mule deer, incisors and canines were fully erupted 10 days after birth. Tooth eruption and minerali-zation were complete for the second, third, and fourth deciduous premolars at about 2.5–3 months in estimated age (Rees et al. 1966b). Rees et al. tabulated estimated ages at which incisal or cusp and root mineralization and tooth eruption began, when mineralization reached the apex of the root, and when erup-tion was completed for most deciduous and permanent teeth based on 133 wild Rocky Mountain mule deer ranging in estimated age from birth to 33 months.

The chronology of tooth replacement and wear has been studied in mule and black-tailed deer by Cowan (1936), McLean (1936), Hunter (1947), Robinette and Jensen (1950), Leopold et al. (1951), Moreland (1953), Jones (1954), Robinette et al. (1957b), Taber and Dasmann (1958), Brown (1961), Erickson et al. (1970), and Thomas and Bandy (1973, 1975). Most of these authors did not have specimens whose ages were known precisely or even approximately. Thus their studies were concerned primarily with the general chronology of tooth replacement. The most complete records are listed in Robinette et al. (1957b) and Rees et al. (1966b). Robinette et al. noted that malnutrition may delay eruption of permanent incisiform teeth in wild yearling mule deer, and that most incisor and premolar replacement and eruption of M_1 and M_2 occurred during late spring, summer, and early autumn periods of relatively abundant forage. An age/nutrition/tooth eruption interaction is implied in their observation that mean eviscerated weights of 915 male and 236 female yearling mule deer increased with an increase in the number of erupted, permanent incisiform teeth. Although average increase was about 0.91 kilograms (2 pounds) per tooth, the increases were not tested for statistical significance. However, there was no significant ($p<0.05$) between-sex difference in the mean number of erupted, permanent incisiform teeth.

Lengths of the mandibular and maxillary cheek-tooth rows in male Rocky Mountain mule deer were strongly and positively correlated ($r^2=0.88$) with estimated age until about 25 months, and weakly and negatively correlated ($r^2=-0.28$) in older deer (A. E. Anderson et al. 1974). Rees (1971b) reported the same phenomenon in mandibular cheek teeth in both sexes of white-tailed deer. Histological evidence in Rocky Mountain mule deer indicated that the observed decreases probably occurred because of dental tissue wear between teeth and between the teeth and tongue (Rees et al. 1966a).

Rees (1971a) compared fourteen mandibular variables of 24 adult male Rocky Mountain mule deer, 24 adult male Columbian blacktails, and 15–26 adult males of three white-tailed deer subspecies. Samples from mule and black-tailed deer possessed relatively shorter diastemata and narrower third molars than did those of the white-tailed deer. Mean widths of all molariform teeth in Rocky Mountain mule deer were larger than their counterparts in Columbian black-tailed deer.

The first objective measure of molariform tooth wear applied to mule and black-tailed deer was the molar tooth ratio (Robinette et al. 1957b). This value was obtained by measuring the width of the buccal crests and the lingual height of each molariform tooth plus the posterior crown of M_3 of one mandibular tooth row. The sum of the seven buccal width values then was divided by the sum of the seven lingual heights. The resultant molar tooth ratio was compared with the mean molar tooth ratios (±95 percent confidence interval) derived for four year classes from 36 jaws of known age. Brown (1961) described a similar procedure with six year classes developed from 76 jaws of known age in Columbian black-tailed deer. Erickson et al. (1970) reported molar tooth ratios of 72 Rocky Mountain mule deer whose ages had been estimated with the dental cementum technique (Erickson and Seliger 1969). Molar tooth ratios of four year classes from each of the three studies are listed in table 14. The ratios suggest that tooth wear is highly variable and may differ between the two subspecies. It was speculated that the amount and kind of soil ingested with forage (Robinette et al. 1957b) or the type of forage (Flook 1970) may affect the rate of cervid tooth wear. Accelerated tooth wear resulting from fluorosis was recorded in a Utah mule deer population (Robinette et al. 1957b). Studies of tooth wear in 859 Columbian black-tailed deer indicated that male teeth wear at a faster rate than do the teeth of females, but additional study was recommended (Thomas and Bandy 1975).

Not surprisingly, estimates of age based on tooth wear in mature black-tailed and mule deer generally have been found to be grossly inaccurate (Brown 1961; Erickson et al. 1970). Robinette et al. (1977, p. 41) presented a re-

Table 14. Age-Specific Molar Tooth Ratios of Mule and Black-tailed Deer

| | Rocky Mountain Mule Deer | | | | | | Columbian Black-tailed Deer | | |
| | Utah and Colorado[a] | | | Colorado[b] | | | Washington[c] | | |
Age in Years	Number	Mean	95 Percent Confidence[d]	Number	Mean	95 Percent Confidence	Number	Mean	95 Percent Confidence
2	23	0.34	0.11–0.45	19	0.36	0.34–0.38	38	0.29	0.22–0.37
3	6	0.39	0.19–0.61	20	0.41	0.40–0.42	18	0.34	0.27–0.40
4	5	0.46	0.29–0.61	19	0.46	0.44–0.48	8	0.38	0.27–0.49
5	2	0.50	0.23–0.77	14	0.54	0.49–0.60	8	0.43	0.26–0.60

Note: The molar tooth ratio is the sum of occlusal widths of buccal crowns divided by the sum of lingual crown heights (Robinette et al. 1957b).
[a] From Robinette et al. (1957b). Ages known: 2 years 4 months, 3 years 4 months, etc.
[b] From Erickson et al. (1970). Ages estimated from cementum annuli.
[c] From Brown (1961). Ages known: each class includes entire year.
[d] Approximated, because calculated for 7, 1, and 1 fewer deer in the 2, 3, and 4 year classes, respectively. Means are corrected for the additional deer.

gression equation of age in months (Y) on molar tooth ratios (X) based on 109 deer of known age from 2.3 to 14.75 years. Although the correlation coefficient was 0.887, only "55 percent of the deer used in deriving this equation would have been aged correctly." However, Thomas and Bandy (1975, p. 678) concluded that the wear-age technique "was sufficiently accurate in black-tailed deer especially if sex-specific series of mandibles, aged from dental annulations, are used comparatively." Low and Cowan (1963) and Erickson and Seliger (1969) reported completely accurate age estimations from cementum annuli counts in small samples of known-age mule deer. But a test with 55 known-age white-tailed deer revealed a 16 percent error (Sauer 1971). In another test involving 166 estimates of age, two observers made a 51 percent error using incisor sections from 49 Rocky Mountain mule deer 3–14 years in known age (Robinette et al. 1977).

The method chosen for estimating age of mule and black-tailed deer would depend on considerations of budget, personnel, and equipment as well as on study objectives. If maximum accuracy is required and other considerations are secondary, then cementum annuli counts should be used. However, as Erickson (1967) and Robinette et al. (1977) have pointed out, the cementum annuli technique is fairly subjective and, therefore, those doing the counts should train on known-age

material. Studies of variation among trained persons doing the counts have not been published. Additional research also needs to be done to improve further the histological techniques currently employed.

Organs

Most of the available measurements of internal organs of mule and black-tailed deer come from work by A. E. Anderson et al. (1974) on Rocky Mountain mule deer in northern Colorado. Their data revealed that body organs grew more rapidly in males and that the most rapid growth for both sexes occurred during the first 25 months of postnatal life. Most organs of males, except the brain and spleen, continued to grow indefinitely, but at a much slower rate after 25 months of age. Growth of the brain and spleen in males and females slowed abruptly at about 35 months, and continued growth was barely perceptible. Growth of all organs in females essentially was complete at 5 to 6 years of age and thereafter was either extremely slow (kidneys) or perhaps even slightly negative (heart, liver, and lungs) (A. E. Anderson et al. 1974). Fresh weights of brain, spleen, heart, lungs, kidneys, and liver from mature Rocky Mountain mule deer of both sexes are described statistically in table 15.

Except for the brain, spleen, and eye lens, fresh weights of individual organs vary season-

Table 15. Fresh Weights (in Grams) of Organs of Rocky Mountain Mule Deer about 18+ Months of Age, Shot Yearlong over Four-Year Period

	Sex	Number of Deer	Mean	Standard Error	Minimum	Maximum
Brain	M	50	197.7	2.7	143	243
	F	89	189.3	1.8	160	242
Spleen	M	49	198.2	8.2	96	347
	F	84	160.7	5.0	98	337
Heart	M	49	581.5	14.7	359	782
	F	83	487.2	8.1	322	687
Right lung	M	37	772.8	50.6	318	1,710
	F	62	636.6	21.2	380	1,250
Left Lung	M	38	479.5	28.0	204	1,020
	F	62	408.5	12.0	190	660
Right kidney	M	51	117.9	4.4	56.8	179.2
	F	90	94.8	2.0	56.3	150.1
Left kidney	M	51	119.8	4.4	61.1	185.4
	F	89	95.9	2.0	56.8	144.5
Liver	M	49	1,546.4	57.0	777	2,510
	F	86	1,193.6	21.8	798	1,760

Source: A. E. Anderson et al. (1974).

ally, frequently being greater during summer and early autumn than during winter and early spring. Variation in weight of the organs of 5-year-old mule deer throughout the year is rather large. The variations approximate 16 percent (male) and 15 percent (female) of peak heart weight, 37 percent (male) and 32 percent (female) of peak lung weight, 23 percent (male) and 28 percent (female) of peak total kidney weight, and 22 percent (male) and 24 percent (female) of peak liver weight. Interrelationships of growth chronology of these organs and other attributes of mule deer that exhibit annual, cyclic changes are related to selected phenological events in figure 8 (A. E. Anderson et al. 1974).

The October maximum and March-April minimum carcass weights shown in figure 8 are presumed to reflect voluntary reduction in food intake and the subsequent loss of weight during winter (Wood et al. 1962; Bandy et al. 1970; Holter et al. 1977), fat accretion during late summer and early autumn, and the November-December breeding season (Anderson et al. 1972a). Organs of mule deer also may gain and lose lipids seasonally, as has been shown for the liver in elk (Flook 1970) and several organs of hibernating mammals (Kayser 1965). Organs showing significant sea-

sonal variation in fresh weight (A. E. Anderson et al. 1974) include heart, lungs, kidney, and liver.

Heart

The heart of mammals is a four-chambered pump that receives blood from the veins and pumps it through the arteries. The maximum weight of the male heart occurred during December, and the minimum weight occurred during January (A. E. Anderson et al. 1974). Since increased work increases heart mass (Fuller 1969), the December peak weight may in part reflect the increased activity of the November-December breeding season, while the minimal January weight may reflect both a rapid depletion of heart fat and cessation of breeding-season activity. The September maximum and April minimum heart weights of female deer are in general synchrony with fluctuations in carcass weights, which may reflect fat levels in heart tissue as well. Minimal heartbeat rates (Jacobsen 1973) and metabolic rates (Silver et al. 1969; Holter et al. 1976) occurred during winter and also could be a factor in minimum heart weights recorded during January in male mule deer and in April

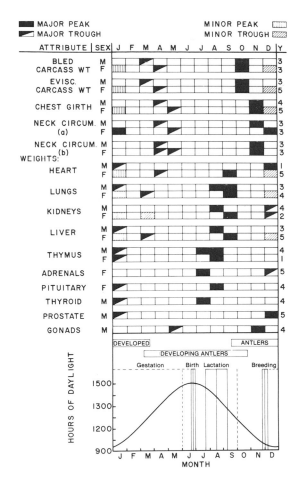

Figure 8. Chronological summary of the peaks and troughs of growth curves of those attributes that exhibited significant annual periodicity related to photoperiodicity, reproductive phenology, estimated age, and seasonal range elevation of collected Rocky Mountain mule deer (A. E. Anderson et al. 1974). The numbers under the Y are estimated ages (years) beyond which the predicted annual periodicity did not vary. The broken vertical lines represent the period when deer were collected on summer range or above 2,591 meters (8,500 feet) elevation.

in female mule deer. Heart weights of male Rocky Mountain mule deer were significantly ($p < 0.01$) greater than those of female deer (A. E. Anderson et al. 1974). Heart tissue of mature Rocky Mountain mule deer constituted 0.79 percent of mean bled carcass weight for males and 0.83 percent for females. Thus, the heart of a mule deer is almost twice as large in relation to body weight as that of humans (0.40–0.43 percent) (Bell et al. 1959).

Lungs

The lung may be considered a compound tubuloalveolar, highly elastic gland with its excretory product, carbon dioxide, "secreted" across the alveolar surface in exchange for uptake of oxygen. It consists of two half-lungs (Banks 1974a), here referred to as left and right lungs, and each divided into lobes that are readily apparent in deer. Maximum total lung weights occurred during August-September in males and during September in females. Minimal lung weights occurred during January in male mule deer and during March in females. As with the heart, months of maximum weight approximate the autumn period of maximum reserve of carcass fat, while months of minimal weight include the postbreeding and gestation periods when fat reserves are decreasing or minimal (Anderson et al. 1972a). Wallace (1948) reviewed the literature on relationships among nutrition and lung weight and concluded that the mammalian lung seems to lose weight at about the same rate as the rest of the body. Hence, fluctuations of lung weight in mule deer may be related to gains and losses of fat in lung tissue. Mean weights of both lungs of male deer were significantly greater than those of female deer, and the right lung of both sexes was significantly ($p < 0.001$) heavier than the left lung. Both lungs in mature Rocky Mountain mule deer averaged about 1.7 percent of the mean bled carcass weight (A. E. Anderson et al. 1974).

Kidney

Kidneys and associated urinary passages "filter the blood, remove waste materials, recover useful metabolites, store the fluid waste and eventually transport the waste products to the exterior of the body" (Banks 1974a, p. 198). The kidney also functions as an endocrine organ and is thought to be implicated in the metabolism of vitamin D. Kidney weights were maximal in male mule deer during August and in female mule deer during September. In both sexes, kidney weights were minimal during the December breeding season. Thus, as with heart and lungs, maximum and minimum kidney weights were in general synchrony with increasing and decreasing levels of carcass fat (Anderson et al. 1972*a*). Kidney weights also varied seasonally in red deer (Batcheler and Clarke 1970) and in caribou (Dauphine 1975). Growth curves of total kidney weights, presented as generally representative of other organs, are show in figure 9.

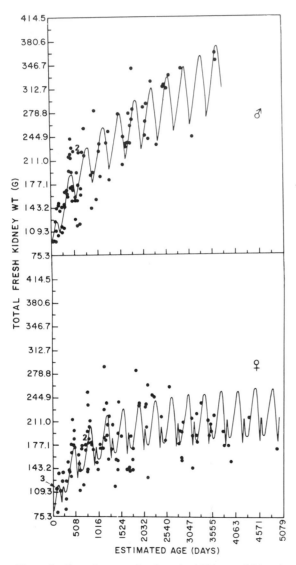

Figure 9. Growth curves for the paired kidneys of 84 male and 111 female Rocky Mountain mule deer collected yearlong, 1961–65; R^2 = 0.801 for males and 0.582 for females (A. E. Anderson et al. 1974).

Fresh weights of the two kidneys were significantly ($p<0.001$) larger in mature male Rocky Mountain mule deer than in females (A. E. Anderson et al. 1974). For mature females, the mean fresh weight of the left kidney was significantly ($p<0.01$) greater than that of the right—a difference that did not occur for mature males. Fresh weight of both kidneys of mature mule deer averaged about 0.32 percent of the mean bled carcass weight in each sex.

Liver

The largest single organ in vertebrates, the liver, is functionally an exocrine and endocrine gland. In contrast to most internal organs, the liver can regenerate itself to some degree. Banks (1974*a*) reported that up to one-third of the entire liver tissue can be regenerated. Among other functions, the liver synthesizes protein, metabolizes fat, detoxifies foreign substances, produces vitamins, and synthesizes hemoglobin (Banks 1974*a*). Maximum liver weights also occurred during August in male mule deer and during September in female mule deer, and minimum liver weights occurred during January for males and March for females. The same inferences about possible influences on seasonal variations in weight mentioned for the heart, lungs, and kidneys also apply to the liver. Liver weight also varied seasonally in red deer (Mitchell 1971). The mean fresh weight of livers in mature male Rocky Mountain mule deer was significantly ($p<0.001$) greater than that for mature females. The liver of mature Rocky Mountain mule deer constituted about 2 percent of the mean bled carcass weight (A. E. Anderson et al. 1974). Weights of livers in Rocky Mountain mule deer seemed relatively larger than values reported for some white-tailed deer (Robinson 1966).

I know of no evidence that seasonal variation occurs in weights of eye lens, brain, or spleen of deer.

Eye Lens

The weight of the eye lens of deer and many other vertebrates has been considered a possible indicator of age. Changes in weight of the eye lens of Rocky Mountain mule deer and Columbian black-tailed deer have been measured over time. The age (nearest year) of individual deer could not be predicted reliably solely on the basis of eye lens weights after age 24 months of either black-tailed or mule deer (Connolly et al. 1969), or after 16 months for mule deer (Erickson et al. 1970; Robinette et al. 1977). Connolly et al. (1969) found that Rocky Mountain mule deer had a significantly higher lens weight than Columbian black-tailed deer, but the same growth rate.

Brain

Brain weight has been related functionally to basal metabolic rate, number of brain nerve cells, and life span (Brody and Kibler 1941; Shock 1962; Sacher 1970). Fresh weights of brains in mature Rocky Mountain mule deer males were significantly $(p<0.025)$ greater than those of females. The mean fresh brain weight of mule deer made up 0.27 percent of the mean bled carcass weight of males and 0.32 percent in females (A. E. Anderson et al. 1974).

Spleen

The spleen is the largest mass of lymphatic tissue in the body, but it is not essential for life (Banks 1974*a*). Among its many functions, the spleen forms blood cells, metabolizes hemoglobin and iron, destroys red blood cells, and filters and stores blood. Fresh weights of mature male Rocky Mountain mule deer spleens were significantly $(p<0.001)$ heavier than those of females (A. E. Anderson et al. 1974), although splenic weight was rather variable. The variability may have been caused by the collection method (shooting), since exercise and hemorrhage in some animals causes the spleen to contract (Bell et al. 1959). Mean splenic weight of mature Rocky Mountain mule deer constituted about 0.27 percent of mean bled carcass weight (A. E. Anderson ct al. 1974).

Stomach

The ruminant stomach consists of four chambers—the rumen, reticulum, omasum, and abomasum. The first three chambers promote digestion of plant material through action of their microorganisms, while the abomasum is glandular and similar to the simple stomach of nonruminant animals (Banks 1974*a*). In the neonate deer, milk passing through the esophageal groove bypasses the rumen and is digested in the abomasum (Nagy 1970). Functions and anatomy of the stomach are discussed further in chapter 3.

The water-filled capacity of the entire gastrointestinal tract of a Columbian black-tailed deer and a domestic sheep of approximately equal weight totaled 7.79 and 13.87 liters (8.23 and 14.66 quarts), respectively (Longhurst and Douglas 1953). The mean total length of the alimentary canal of 7 Rocky Mountain mule deer was 24.1 meters (79 feet), with a range of 22–26 meters (72–86 feet) (Browman and Sears 1955). The volume of the mule deer rumen-reticulum averaged 6.18 liters (6.53 quarts) for males and 5.17 liters (5.46 quarts) for females. The weight of ruminoreticular contents averaged 4.6 kilograms (10.14 pounds) in males and 4.08 kilograms (8.99 pounds) in females. Fresh ruminoreticular tissue weight averaged 1.05 kilograms (2.31 pounds) for males and 0.93 kilograms (2.05 pounds) for females, as determined from 14 male and 16 female Rocky Mountain mule deer 4–143 months of age (Short et al. 1965). Ruminoreticular volume was about 10 percent of bled carcass weight, and according to Short et al. a mule deer has a small ruminoreticular volume in proportion to body weight compared with a cow. The significance of this relatively small ruminoreticular volume in deer also is explained in chapter 3.

Stomach tissue made up 1.21 ± 0.09 percent (mean $\pm2SE$) of total carcass weight in 6 adult Rocky Mountain mule deer (Hakonson and Whicker 1971*a*). A. E. Anderson et al. (1974) calculated mean weight of the intact stomach as constituting about 10.0 of mean bled carcass weight in male mule deer and 10.8 percent in females. Weight of the intact stomach of these same deer showed significant ($p<0.01$) seasonal variation (Anderson et al. 1975).

Glands

Glands of internal secretion are termed *endocrine glands*. Endocrine glands secrete from one to several hormones that are either released immediately or temporarily stored. Once in the bloodstream, hormones may affect an entire organism, selected organs, or one specific organ. An organ or group of organs may have a low threshold of response to hormonal stimulation, and these are called *target organs* (Banks 1974*a*).

Fresh weights of adrenals, pituitary, and thyroid of mature Rocky Mountain mule deer frequently vary throughout the year, apparently being greater in summer than in winter. Variations in weight are pronounced for different glands and also between the sexes. The adrenal and pituitary glands of female, the thyroid gland of male, and the thymus glands of male and female Rocky Mountain mule deer also show significant seasonal variation in fresh weights (A. E. Anderson et al. 1974). In deer 5 years old and older, these changes approximate 17 percent of peak adrenal weight in females, 42 percent of peak pituitary weight in females, 36 percent of peak thyroid weight in males, and 84 percent of peak weight of the thymus in males and females. These seasonal sex-specific variations are related chronologically to organs and selected phenological events in figure 8. Fresh weights of the adrenal, pituitary, thyroid, and thymus glands of mature male and female Rocky Mountain mule deer are described statistically in table 16.

Adrenal or Suprarenal Glands

The adrenal or suprarenal glands are located adjacent to the kidneys. The adrenal cortex secretes hormones essential to many bodily processes such as electrolyte and water balance, protein catabolism, and initial immune response. Although not essential for life, the adrenal medulla synthesizes and releases epinephrine, the "fight or flight" hormone (Banks 1974*a*).

Lack of annual cyclic changes in fresh absolute weight of adrenals in male Colorado mule deer is different from the pattern for male and female white-tailed deer (Hoffman and Robinson 1966). Fresh absolute weight of the adrenal in female mule deer in Colorado was relatively heavy in July and light in December (A. E. Anderson et al. 1974). Growth curves of male and female adrenals, presented as generally representative of the endocrine glands of mule deer, are shown in figure 10. Browman and Sears (1956) did not detect seasonal changes in average adrenal weight of 70 female

Table 16. Fresh Weights (in Grams) of Endocrine Glands of Rocky Mountain Mule Deer about 18+ Months of Age, Shot Yearlong over a Four-Year Period

	Sex	Number Deer	Mean	Standard Error	Minimum	Maximum
Left adrenal	M	51	2.94	0.10	1.56	5.51
	F	87	2.52	0.06	1.52	4.34
Pituitary	M	50	0.71	0.04	0.12	1.37
	F	89	0.64	0.02	0.28	1.45
Left lobe of thyroid	M	50	2.65	0.16	1.17	6.22
	F	85	2.16	0.08	1.06	4.66
Left ovary	F	88	1.14	0.05	0.33	2.67
Left lobe of thymus	M	50	1.44	0.30	0.00	10.32
	F	88	2.37	0.38	0.00	14.00
Right lobe of thymus	M	50	0.96	0.28	0.00	9.91
	F	88	1.74	0.28	0.00	12.04

Source: A. E. Anderson et al. (1974).

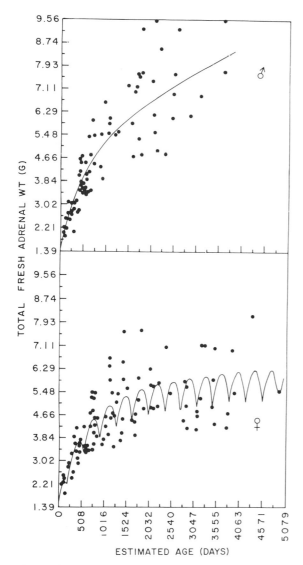

Figure 10. Growth curves for the paired adrenals of 78 male and 100 female Rocky Mountain mule deer collected yearlong, 1961–65; $R^2 = 0.827$ for males and 0.691 for females (A. E. Anderson et al. 1974).

mule deer. Relative adrenal weight may respond to apparent changes in population density of wild white-tailed deer (Welch 1962). It may increase as population density increases (Christian and Davis 1964). In a migratory mule deer population sampled on its seasonal ranges by Anderson et al. (1971), deer densities were minimal on summer range during summer and maximal on winter range during winter and early spring. Thus it is unlikely that seasonal deer densities were a factor in the July

peaks and December troughs predicted for female mule deer by A. E. Anderson et al. (1974). It may be that these relatively high and low values of the adrenal are related to the reproductive cycle, since estrogens enlarge adrenal glands (Gorbman and Bern 1962). And, in some mammals, variation in adrenal weight is related to the estrous cycle (Bourne and Jayne 1961) and to gestation and birth (Parkes 1945). Lack of significant temporal variation in the male adrenal is inexplicable, since androgen may have an antiadrenal action (Gorbman and Bern 1962).

Pituitary Gland

The pituitary gland, situated at the base of the brain, consists of a glandular lobe (adenohypophysis) and a neural lobe (neurohypophysis). The glandular lobe secretes twelve hormones essential to many bodily processes and is regulated by a negative feedback system involving the hypothalamic region of the brain. The neural lobe is associated functionally with the hormones oxytocin and vasopressin, essential for some reproductive and antidiuretic processes, respectively (Banks 1974a).

There was no detectable seasonal variation in fresh weight of the male pituitary in mature Rocky Mountain mule deer. Pituitary weight in female Rocky Mountain mule deer was greater during August and smaller during January in both Colorado (A. E. Anderson et al. 1974) and Montana (Grieser and Browman 1956) populations. Greiser and Browman found that pituitary gonadotrophic potency was greater during August and September and was reduced during January and February. Weight of the female pituitary increased during gestation periods for both mule deer (A. E. Anderson et al. 1974; Grieser and Browman 1956) and white-tailed deer (Hoffman and Robinson 1966). Increases in pituitary weight possibly are a function of estrogen (Lisk 1969), since ovarian follicles—a source of estrogen (Hafez 1968b)—increased in average number during gestation in mule deer (Greiser and Browman

1956). In male white-tailed deer, secretion of all testicular hormones and pituitary gonadrotrophins occurred during the breeding season (Robinson and Thomas 1966). Mean pituitary weight in mature Rocky Mountain mule deer in Colorado averaged about 0.001 percent of bled carcass weight (A. E. Anderson et al. 1974).

Thyroid Gland

The thyroid gland consists of two lobes situated along the trachea near the larynx. Its structural unit is the thyroid follicle. The follicles contain a gellike material (colloid) that is the storage form of secretory products (Banks 1974a). The mechanisms of secretion are extremely complex: iodide is oxidized to iodine, and several hormones, including thyroxine and calcitonin, are produced. Thyroxine is essential in maintaining body temperature in homeotherms, and in water balance, protein metabolism, and fat mobilization and degradation. Calcitonin tends to reduce blood calcium levels (Banks 1974a).

The thyroid gland of mature male Rocky Mountain mule deer was relatively heavy in July and light in January. There was no detectable seasonal variation in thyroids of females (A. E. Anderson et al. 1974). However, Browman (1957) reported annual changes in mean relative and absolute thyroid weights (May-June peaks and January-February troughs) for female Rocky Mountain mule deer in Montana. Seal et al. (1972b) suggested that "the thyroids of pregnant and poorly nourished white-tailed deer would weigh less than in reproductively quiescent and well-nourished female deer." Seasonal changes in thyroid gland weights of male mule deer during each year of life also might be related to seasonal changes in metabolic rate demonstrated for adult white-tailed deer of both sexes (Silver et al. 1969).

Only for mature Rocky Mountain mule deer did mean thyroid weight differ between sexes. In mature deer, mean weight was significantly greater among males than among females. Significant between-sex difference in the mean

fixed thyroid weight was not detected in a study of white-tailed deer (Hoffman and Robinson 1966). The mean fresh weight of the thyroid of mule deer in Colorado approximated 0.0072 percent of mean bled carcass weight in both sexes (A. E. Anderson et al. 1974).

Thymus Gland

The thymus, a bilobed gland situated in the thorax just above the heart, may be related more closely to the endocrine system than to the lymphatic system (Banks 1974a). However, most evidence indicates that the function of the thymus is immunological, particularly until the age of puberty. Involution of the thymus begins at this time and continues through old age. The thymus produces lymphocytes in early postnatal life and thymic corpuscles until old age. The latter structures are rich in gamma globulins, but their immunological role is not clear (Banks 1974a).

In mature Rocky Mountain mule deer, the thymus of males is relatively heavy in July and light in January, whereas the thymus of females is heavy in August but also light in January (A. E. Anderson et al. 1974). Mean fresh weight of thymus glands of deer 12–17 months of age was significantly greater than that of mature deer, although the thymus varied widely in weight throughout the year. Frequently, thymic tissue is so diffuse or exists in such small quantitites that it is not readily visible in some mule deer. The left lobe of the thymus in mature male deer weighed significantly ($p < 0.01$) more than the right lobe. The mean weight of the thymus constituted 0.27 percent of male and 0.31 percent of female mean bled carcass weights of 12–17-month-old male deer. It also constituted 0.0032 percent of the mean bled carcass weight of mature male mule deer and 0.0070 percent of that of females.

Some Influences of Postnatal Development of Organs and Glands

The more complex (two maxima and two minima per year) growth curves of carcass, heart, lungs, kidneys, and liver of females (figure 8) probably reflect a longer and perhaps more stressful reproductive cycle, than do the growth curves of males. The apparent lack of seasonal variation in weights of male adrenal and pituitary glands and the female thyroid may indicate either unidentified sex-specific influences on endocrine gland function or inability to detect changes of relatively small magnitude. Leathem (1961, p. 667) noted that hormones "influence the metabolic pool by affecting appetite as well as absorption, utilization and excretion of foods."

The chronological sequence of maximum and minimum weights of organs and glands in figure 8 suggest that light-mediated endocrine glands influence metabolism as well as regulating the reproductive cycle. It should be emphasized that effects of light and temperature on these physiological processes are confounded, since the curve of light generally is synchronous with that of temperature. In general, weights of organs were minimal during winter and spring with increasing daylight following the winter solstice (22 December) and breeding season. Weights of organs were maximal during summer and autumn with decreasing daylight following the summer solstice (22 June) and birth of fawns when levels of dietary energy probably were maximal (A. E. Anderson et al. 1974).

The general pattern of maximum carcass and organ weights during late summer and autumn, and of minimum carcass and organ weights during winter and spring, appears to be characteristic of mule, black-tailed, and white-tailed deer in temperate regions. This differs from the usual pattern for mammals in that exposure to low temperatures elevates the metabolic rate and thus (1) increases the work, hence the size, of heart and lungs; and (2) increases food intake, hence the size of liver and kidneys (Fuller 1969).

Mule deer, blacktails, and whitetails possess several skin glands (forehead, tail, interdigital, tarsal, and metatarsal) whose pheromones, often in conjunction with urine, are important in communication (Müller-Schwarze 1967, 1969, 1971; Brownlee et al. 1969; Quay and Müller-Schwarze 1970) and whose histology may change with age (Quay and Müller-Schwarze 1971). Of these glands, the metatarsal (on the middle outside portion of the hind foot) and the tarsal (inside the hind foot at the hock joint) are most conspicuous by virtue of their characteristic hair tufts. Since the relative length of the metatarsal gland may have some taxonomic value (Cowan 1956b; Anderson et al. 1964), the maximum dimensions of their circumglandular hair tuft outlines are described statistically in table 13. Mature male and female Rocky Mountain deer had significantly

The tarsal gland of a calm Columbian black-tailed deer. Photograph by Guy E. Connolly.

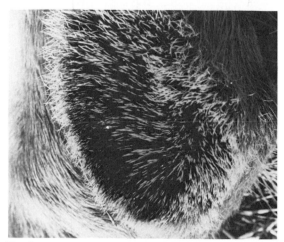

During excitation, hairs surrounding the tarsal gland are erect when scent chemicals are emitted. Photograph by Guy E. Connolly.

($p<0.05$) larger metatarsal and tarsal glands than did younger deer. There were no significant ($p<0.05$) differences between sexes in mean dimensions of metatarsal and tarsal glands (A. E. Anderson et al. 1974).

Seasonal Aspects of Physiology and Morphology

Seasonal variation in fresh weights of organs and glands is a subtle phenomenon. Seasonal fatness, molting, reproduction, neck enlargement, and the growth and loss of antlers in the male are familiar phenomena that will be shown here to be in general synchrony with seasonal changes in organ and gland weights, certain other physical characteristics of deer, and selected environmental factors.

Fat

The role of lipids in the life histories of mammals was reviewed by Young (1976, p. 699), who stated, "The food and energy storage levels are especially important in allowing the animal to survive food shortages and stresses associated with competition for mates, territorial defense, gestation, and lactation and to accomplish migrations." Physical condition, physiological condition, and simply "condition" are somewhat ambiguous concepts that frequently refer to the general state of health of a deer, apparently inferred from its relative fatness.

Harris (1945) and Rausch (1950) qualitatively described the depletion of fat deposits in starving deer. Rausch also discussed gross and microscopic pathological symptoms of malnutrition in starving deer during winter. Fatness can be quantified as a single entity or with reference to body weight, organ weight, or a linear or circumferential skeletal measurement.

Riney (1955, p. 431) stated, in reference to ruminants, that "fat can be taken as a direct measure of the condition reflecting the metabolic level or goodness of physiologic adjustment of an animal with its environment."

In the view of Franzmann et al. (1976, p. 5), whose categories of condition were based largely on relative fatness, "condition is relative and is simply the state in which an animal is at a particular time." Yet there are disease states in which relative fatness of a deer may not be appreciably affected but in which potentially fatal lesions exist. Some examples, primarily associated with white-tailed deer, are anthrax, bluetongue, epizootic hermorrhagic disease, blackleg, and malignant catarrhal fever (C. P. Hibler and W. Lance, pers. comm., September 1977). These diseases are described for mule deer, blacktails, and white-tailed deer in Davis et al. (1970) (*see* chap. 3). In addition, capture myopathy may occur in deer after pursuit, capture, or restraint (Barsch et al. 1977). The following discussion therefore reviews various indexes of relative fatness, recognizing that some diseased deer may be average or above average in relative fatness according to age, sex, and season.

Each of the following indexes of carcass fat—percentage of femur marrow fat, kidney fat, carcass density, percentage of carcass fat, depth of back fat, bled and eviscerated carcass weights—showed significant ($p<0.01$) seasonal variation. In general, maximum values of relative fatness approximated the inferred breeding season in both sexes, and minimum values approximated the period of minimum testicular weight in male Rocky Mountain mule deer and the period of birth and early lactation in females (Anderson et al. 1972a).

The percentage of ether-extractable fat in the femur marrow was related to color and consistency of marrow in an approximation of the state of malnutrition (Cheatum 1949b). Intended primarily as a field technique to detect or absolve malnutrition as a probable cause of death in studies of winter deer mortality, assessing the percentage of fat, color, or consistency of femur marrow also has been employed in studies of predator-cervid interaction (Hornocker 1970; Kolenosky 1972; Franzmann and Arneson 1976). The conceptual basis for using marrow as an index of nutritive adequacy was challenged by Christian et al. (1960, p. 94), who stated, "The value of the marrow as a specific diagnosis of malnutrition is open to serious question, unless one defines malnutrition in terms of basic anabolic-catabolic balances rather than in terms of food intake."

Bischoff (1954) found that the percentage of femur marrow fat was not well correlated with other fat depots ($r = 0.55$) or femur marrow color ($r = 0.53$) but was strongly correlated with visual estimate of marrow consistency ($r = 0.87$). Harris (1945) suggested that fat depots are used in the sequence of subcutaneous, visceral, and femur marrow fat. Thus, strong correlations among fat depots would be unexpected, particularly if samples were obtained from deer killed during a short portion of the annual fat cycle. Riney (1955), working with red deer, and Ransom (1965), working with white-tailed deer, both believed that the percentage of femur marrow fat was most useful at the very lower and upper portions of its percentage scale. Anderson et al. (1972a) presented data about the percentage of femur marrow fat measure that revealed highly disparate frequency distributions among male and female Rocky Mountain mule deer.

Chemical analyses of the percentage of fat in tibia marrow of mule deer (Trout and Thiessen 1968) and of the tissue within the mandibular bone cavity of white-tailed deer (Baker and Leuth 1967) also have been used as indexes of carcass fat. The alcohol or petroleum ether-extraction method of measuring percentage of fat in bone marrow on a fresh weight basis furnished the most potentially accurate data. But, because of time and facility requirements, simpler and faster methods have been developed, including compression (Greer 1968), dry weight (Nieland 1970), and the reagent–dry assay (Verme and Holland 1973). The modified Babcock acid-digestion procedure (Salwin et al. 1955) was reported as somewhat less accurate but faster (thirty minutes per sample) than the ether-extraction procedure and more accurate but slower than the compression procedure (Mansfield 1974). The necessary number of femurs from individual Rocky Mountain mule deer—to estimate percentage of femur marrow fat by the petroleum

ether-extractable procedure to be within 10 percent of the true mean at the 95 percent confidence level—ranged from 2 (summer) to 19 (spring) for males and 2 (winter) to 66 (summer) for females (Anderson et al. 1972a). It should be emphasized that these and following estimates of sample size requirements are from rather small samples of a population subject to a similar environment. They do not apply if samples came from deer of various ecological backgrounds.

Since its introduction by Riney (1955), the "kidney fat index" perhaps has been the most widely used measure of cervid carcass fat. This measure correlated adequately with percentage of femur marrow fat, carcass density and weight, percentage of carcass fat, and depth of rump fat in about 192 male and female Rocky Mountain mule deer collected yearlong at approximately weekly intervals from 1961 to 1965 (Anderson et al. 1972a). However, the measure of kidney fat is highly variable and consequently requires a large sample size.

In addition, the kidney fat index—based on one kidney—is not very comparable to indexes using both kidneys. Also, a series using left kidneys would not be comparable to a series using right kidneys. The required numbers of mature deer—to be within 10 percent of the true mean of the kidney fat index at the 95 percent confidence level—ranged by season from 88 (winter) to 221 (summer) for males and 114 (winter) to 532 (summer) for females (Anderson et al. 1972a).

The measurement and use of carcass density to estimate carcass fat has been reviewed critically by Jones et al. (1978). Density (grams per milliliter) of the skinned, eviscerated deer carcass has been reported only from Rocky Mountain mule deer (Anderson et al. 1972a). This method uses the weight of the carcass in air and submerged in water with the carcass at or near the water temperature, and the tabulated value of the relative density of water (grams per milliliter) at its recorded temperature (Lange and Forker 1956). Density of the carcass is calculated from these measurements using the expression of Goldman and Buskirk (1961). Higher density values indicate relatively low levels of carcass fat. This index of relative fatness is remarkable for its extremely low variability. Only two deer of each sex per season would be required to be within 10 percent of the true mean carcass density at the 95 percent confidence level (Anderson et al. 1972a).

Percentage of carcass fat can be calculated by using the carcass density, the theoretical density (1.1 grams per milliliter) of the fat-free carcass (Behnke 1961), and the expression of Morales et al. (1945). This densitometric estimate of the carcass fat percentage for 18 skinned and eviscerated mule deer shot from December through April was compared with the percentages of carcass fat obtained by petroleum ether extraction from the same 18 entire, intact eviscerated carcasses examined by Anderson et al. (1969). The mean (±SD) percentage fat of 5.45±2.34 for the densitometric and 5.54±1.19 for the petroleum ether extraction did not differ significantly ($p < 0.05$). Estimated by the two procedures, however, percentages of fat of total skinned and eviscerated carcass were not highly correlated ($r = 0.66$), thus precluding prediction of the inherently more precise and time-consuming chemical determination from the densitometric estimate. This is not surprising, since Jones et al. (1978, p. 1153) cited four recent studies of carcass fat in cattle that suggested that "density becomes a less reliable estimator of carcass fat in carcasses containing less than 12 percent fat." The required number of mature deer carcasses—to provide an estimate of carcass fat using the densitometric procedure within 10 percent of the true mean at the 95 percent confidence level—ranged by season from 46 (winter) to 194 (spring) for males and 33 (autumn) to 100 (spring) for females (Anderson et al. 1972a).

Densitometric estimates of the percentage of fat in skinned and eviscerated carcasses of 40 male and 55 female Rocky Mountain mule deer, about 18 months of age and older, shot yearlong from 1961 to 1965, ranged from 1.3 to 26.0 percent in males and 2.6 to 19.7 percent in females (Anderson et al. 1972a). Peaks of significant ($p < 0.01$) polynomial curves of percentage of carcass fat (Y) versus collection date (X) of those deer approximated the initiation of the breeding season in both sexes. Troughs approximated the periods of minimum testicular volume in males and of parturition and early lactation in females. Female deer appeared to lag about one month behind males in the peaks and troughs of the percentage of carcass fat curves. However, if one assumes that annual fluctuations in carcass weight of both sexes of mature Colorado mule deer shown by predictive growth curves (A. E. Anderson et al. 1974) were due largely to gains and losses in body fat, females lagged behind males only during troughs, which were March for males and April for females. The predicted peak of the weight curve (and presumably the peak of fatness) occurred in both sexes during October or just before the breeding season. The magnitude of predicted annual losses of weight and, presumably, body fat increased with age. And, as read from the predicted curves for 5-year-old mule deer, these predicted losses approximated 17.2 kilograms (37.9 pounds) or 19 percent of the predicted peak weight of males and 16.0 kilograms (35.2 pounds) or 22 percent of the predicted peak weight of females.

About 65 percent of male and 52 percent of female mature Rocky Mountain mule deer collected yearlong had no measurable back (subcutaneous) fat (Anderson et al. 1972a). None of the 14 mature males collected during the winter had measurable back fat. The required number of mature deer—to provide an estimate of depth of back fat within 10 percent of the true mean at the 95 percent confidence level—ranged by season from 381 (summer) to 2,595 (spring) for males and 383 (winter) to 2,192 (summer) for females.

Body weight has been used as an index of nutritional status of mule and black-tailed deer in both field (Cook et al. 1949; Leopold et al. 1951; Taber and Dasmann 1958; Browning and Lauppe 1964; Anderson et al. 1972a) and experimental studies (Bissell et al. 1955; Brown 1961; Wood et al. 1962). Experimental studies generally have shown that adequately nourished deer of both sexes voluntarily reduce their feed intake and lose weight appreciably during winter. Field studies of both sexes of

Tranquilized and secured to a stretcher, a deer is tagged and weighed as part of assessing immediate, seasonal, or cyclical levels of body fat. Photograph courtesy of the Oregon Department of Fish and Wildlife.

Rocky Mountain mule deer have demonstrated annual cyclic changes among several indexes of relative fatness, including weight of the eviscerated carcass (Anderson et al. 1972a). Apparently the only field study of mule or black-tailed deer that seems to show a lack of seasonal variation in body or carcass weight is that of Browning and Lauppe (1964), which was a study of adult female Columbian black-tailed deer in a redwood/Douglas fir forest. However, Browning and Lauppe did not discuss the possibility that seasonal age distribution of the shot sample may have affected seasonal carcass weight. Relatively few mature Rocky Mountain mule deer had to be sampled to provide an estimate within 10 percent of true mean eviscerated carcass weight at the 95 percent confidence level. The number ranged by season from 9 (spring) to 33 (autumn) for males and from 2 (autumn) to 7 (winter and summer) for females (Anderson et al. 1972a).

The choice of a suitable index of relative fatness may be influenced as much by sex of deer, time and manpower available, physical facilities, and constraints on collecting procedures as by expected variation associated with a given index. Thus, for female deer, eviscerated carcass weight may be the best choice, but this may not necessarily be so for males, because the strong age-weight (eviscerated) relationship may complicate its use. If data about both sexes of deer were desired, estimation of carcass density would require minimum sample sizes. Both the kidney fat index and femur marrow fat may be useful in combination if the collection method (highway, hunter, predation, etc.) involves large numbers of damaged or incomplete carcasses. Migratory mule deer populations may best be compared by using the procedure requiring the smallest sample during seasons of primary research interest. Clearly, however, measurement of back fat depth in Rocky Mountain mule deer has very limited usefulness because of extreme variability and the large proportion of mature deer with zero values during all seasons.

Relative fatness also has been assessed by comparing the hind foot length with the chest girth of deer less than 24 months of age that were fed a nutritionally adequate diet ad libitum, with similar relationships derived from wild deer of the same age and sex (Bandy et al. 1956; Wood and Cowan 1968).

Relative fatness of two deer populations also has been compared, with small sample sizes, by the regression of body weight (X) (Robinson 1960) or eviscerated carcass weight (X) (Anderson et al. 1965) on length of hind foot (Y). Means and slopes of the regression lines may be tested for statistically significant differences by analysis of covariance, and the data may be conveniently expressed in terms of a measure of weight per centimeter of hind foot length. This method is useful only when the sex, mean age, and sampling season of the two population samples are similar.

These predicted annual fluctuations in carcass fat probably are associated with the voluntary reduction in feed intake and activity during winter that was observed experimentally by Wood et al. (1962), Silver et al. (1969), Ullrey et al. (1970), and Seal et al. (1972b). Taylor (1959) found that there was a lower intake of food in cattle maintained on a high level of nutrition and postulated that food intake may be decreased by some function of physiological maturity, thereby reducing body fat. Some other probable influences are: (1) an autumn response to the higher energy levels theoretically available during summer (Short et al. 1966); (2) breeding season activity, including the possibility that testosterone may aid in mobilizing fat (Laron and Kowaldo 1963); (3) gestation; (4) lactation; and (5) ambient temperature. Peak daily energy and nitrogen requirements of lactation in white-tailed deer, for example, were estimated to increase sevenfold over early lactation levels (Robbins 1973). Relative amounts of body fat may vary with ambient temperature, and some deposits such as subcutaneous fat may serve both as food storage and as an insulator (Hensel 1968). However, as I mentioned, subcutaneous fat was entirely lacking in mature males and near minimal in mature females during winter (Anderson et al. 1972a). Hence body maintenance, not insulation, probably was the primary function of subcutaneous fat in that population at 40 degrees 40 minutes north latitude.

Wallmo et al. (1977) estimated that the body energy deficit of a 70 kilogram (154.3 pound) male Colorado mule deer in winter is 1,749 kilocalories. Wallmo et al. calculated various estimates of body fat, including net usable caloric yield in catabolized stored fat of 6 kilocalories per gram (Mautz et al. 1976), stored fat deposits totaling 8–9 kilograms (17.6–19.8 pounds) (Anderson et al. 1972a; Robbins et al. 1974), and a stored catabolization rate of 292 grams (10.3 ounces), and concluded that fat stores would be depleted in about 30 days. However, if protein was catabolized, as suggested for mule deer fawns by de Calesta et al. (1975), its caloric content (5.41 kilocalories per gram) (Robbins et al. 1974) would extend survival much beyond 30 days. Indeed, penned mule deer survived up to 64 days without food (de Calesta et al. 1975). These authors noted that weight loss was significantly ($p < 0.01$) faster in fawns, and mean loss of weight of 4 starved fawns was about 30 percent of the prestarvation weight.

In an evolutionary sense, the annual cycle of body fat may represent a homeostatic adaptation of deer populations to complex seasonal interactions of biotic and abiotic factors characteristic of temperate regions.

Pelage and Molt

Hair is nonliving material, and pelage is the coat of hair that functions primarily as insulation, regulating dissipation of heat from the skin surface and absorption of heat from the environment (Vaughan 1972). Moen and Jacobsen (1975, p. 513) stated: "The overall conductance of the hair layer and of the entire thermal boundary region is a dynamic property that is an integration of the radiation conductance, conduction conductance, covection conductance, and evaporation effects. Each of these is dynamic depending on the interaction between energy flux in the hair layer and energy flux in the ambient atmosphere." Cowan (1956a) gave a concise qualitative account of pelage and molt in mule deer. Silver et al. (1969) cited instances of controlling molt in white-tailed deer by changing the photoperiod.

Raddi (1967) described ontogeny of black-tailed deer pelage and distinguished anatomical characteristics that separate this pelage form from that of common domestic ruminants. Cowan and Raddi (1972) recognized and described the natal, juvenile, adult summer, and adult winter pelages and six types of hair as well as the annual cycle of follicles producing the four types of adult hair. These hair types are termed the large guard, intermediate guard, mane type, and woolly underhairs. Among adult deer, two hair cycles are completed annually, alternating between a summer pelage for five months and a winter pelage for seven months. Among adult black-tailed deer, autumnal molt begins on the outer ear pinnae and proceeds caudad to the head, neck, shoulders, flanks, and outer thighs to the abdomen, margins of the rump patch, and the legs and leg gland areas from August to October. The tail sheds throughout summer. The spring molt sequence occurs from April to late June, and is the approximate reverse of the autumnal molt. All follicles shed hair during autumn, but during spring only guard follicles shed hair, and the undercoat hair is shed by breakage. Ryder and Kay (1973) and Ryder (1977) found that in red deer all follicles shed hair during spring.

A sensory function has been ascribed to the long guard hairs that emerge simultaneously on all parts of the body (Cowan and Raddi 1972). Diameter of guard hairs was found to increase with age, while guard hair lengths and densities varied more with specific body sites than did other types of hair. When lengths and diameters of guard hairs were compared, it was determined that Sitka deer had the thickest hair, while the guard hairs of the California stock of black-tailed deer were shorter and thinner.

According to Cowan and Raddi, each hair commonly has four color zones from tip to base: black, yellow, gray or reddish yellow, and unpigmented. At birth, fawns have hair with three color zones. Among adults, the winter and summer pelages have guard hairs with four and with three zones of pigment. The apparent pelage color depends on relative proportions of the various bands as well as on quantity of exposed surface hair. Contrasts between winter and summer pelages are due largely to the density of woolly underfur. The distinctly different summer and winter hairs presumably arise from the same hair follicles.

Cowan (1956b, p. 342) furnished a narrative description of pelage color in mule and black-tailed deer and noted that, in Rocky Mountain mule deer, "seasonal bleaching is one of the outstanding causes of color change." He characterized the apparent seasonal variation in pelage colors among several subspecies as follows: Rocky Mountain mule deer (winter) grayish brown, (summer) reddish brown; Columbian black-tailed deer (winter) warm brown to gray-brown, (summer) redder than mule deer; Sitka black-tailed deer, (winter) more reddish brown than Columbian black-tailed deer, (summer) less red than the Columbian black-tailed deer. Cowan did not describe seasonal variation in the pelage color of southern,

peninsula, Inyo, burro, and Tiburon Island mule deer. The meager material available permitted the following generalizations. Pelage color of Inyo mule deer is intermediate between Rocky Mountain mule deer and California mule deer, while the southern mule deer has relatively dark pelage, and the peninsula mule deer, desert mule deer, burro mule deer, Tiburon Island mule deer, and Cedros Island deer have relatively light pelage in contrast to Rocky Mountain mule deer. Cowan also described subtle-to-obvious differences in the characteristic coloration and patterns of the brow, back, rump, and tail pelages of mule and black-tailed deer. Quantitative methods (Bowers 1956; Miller 1958; Nickerson 1946) apparently have not been used to describe pelage color in North American deer.

Among fawns, pelage replacement began in July and was completed by October (Cowan and Raddi 1972). For fawns of known age, Robinette et al. (1977) recorded that faint spots were readily visible until 77–78 days of age. Spots disappeared at 83–87 days, and pelage was gray at 92–98 days. Among adults, the growth of summer coats occurred from March to mid-June, the woolly undercoat grew from September to late December, and the winter coat grew from early June to November (Cowan and Raddi 1972). The winter coat and the woolly undercoat were shed during May and June, and the summer coat was shed from mid-August through October. Robinette et al. (1977) graphed pelage changes during autumn, from field observations of about 7,800 Rocky Mountain mule deer in Utah and Nevada. Robinette et al. noted that about half of the observed deer had changed from summer to winter pelage by 2–3 September (fawns), 7 September (does), 4 September (yearling bucks), and 26–27 August (mature bucks). The physiologic status of a deer can affect the phenology of molting. Nonpregnant does molt earlier than pregnant does, and deer in poor physical condition have a prolonged molt. In male Rocky Mountain mule deer, molting precedes shedding of antler velvet by 9 days for yearlings and 10–11 days for mature bucks (Robinette et al. 1977).

Reproductive Phenomena

Seasonal changes in the testes of deer have been described in various ways by Cheatum and Morton (1946), Wislocki (1943), Illige (1951), Robinson et al. (1965), and Anderson and Medin (1971). Most of these references consider only seasonal means of the testes of "mature" deer. A growth in weight curve of testes of 86 Rocky Mountain mule deer bucks estimated maximal weights during November for each year of life, and minimal weights during March for the first year, April-May for the second and third years, and May after the fourth year (A. E. Anderson et al. 1974). The November peak in testes weight included the early portion of the breeding season of that population (Anderson and Medin 1967). Variation in fresh weight of testes throughout the year approximated 21.3 grams (0.75 ounce) or 44 percent of peak curve weight during the second year and 57.3 grams (2.02 ounces) or 67 percent of peak curve weight during the fifth year. The predicted curve suggested a marked regression in fresh weight of testes after year six.

Relatively little research has been conducted on the prostate gland in deer. Predicted growth of the prostate gland generally approximated that estimated for testicular weight (A. E. Anderson et al. 1974). West and Nordan (1976a) used histological and cytological criteria to define glandular activity for the bulbourethral and prostate glands in mature Columbia black-tailed deer, and they noted approximate snychrony with testes functional activity.

Comparative anatomy of bulbourethral and prostate glands in cervids is worthy of investigation since there are differences of opinion on gross morphology and identification. For example, bulbourethral glands were reported as disseminate in white-tailed deer (Wislocki 1943) and red deer (Aughey 1969; Lincoln 1971), while the prostate gland of red deer was seen as disseminate by Aughey (1969) and as discrete and bilobed by Lincoln (1971). According to West and Nordan (1976a, p. 1622) bulbourethral glands of Columbian black-tailed deer are "ovoid, compound tubular glands that are partially embedded in, and extend laterally from, the urethral muscle as it curves around the pelvic outlet." One duct from each gland enters the pelvic urethra. West and Nordan (1976a, p. 1622) characterized the disseminate prostate gland as "simple branched tubules organized into lobules embedded within a stroma of smooth muscle and fibrous connective tissue surrounding the pelvic urethra. Tubules open separately into the urethra along 5 to 6 cm [1.97–2.36 inches] of its length." As Wislocki (1943) found in white-tailed deer, West and Nordan (1976a) noted that there was little evidence of seasonal variation in the histology of the prostate gland.

The length, width, and height of the scrotum increased significantly ($p < 0.01$) by age class from about 6 months to 12–17 months. Mean length of prepuce of mature deer was significantly ($p < 0.01$) greater than in each of the three younger age classes (A. E. Anderson et al. 1974).

Neck enlargement and regression associated with the breeding season of temperate-region male cervids is a commonly observed but rarely quantified secondary sexual characteristic. Rate of growth in neck circumference (15 centimeters [5.9 inches] posterior of occiput) of Rocky Mountain mule deer shows maximum values during March of the first year and during April after the second year. Average annual changes in neck circumference (fig. 11) approximated 8.9 centimeters (3.5 inches) or 21 percent of maximum circumference during the second year of life and 13 centimeters (5.1 inches) or 24 percent of maximum circumference during the fifth year. Similar approximations of females' neck circumference predicted that neck circumference peaked during January of the first year of life and during December-January after the second year. Predicted low values occurred during April of the first year, during April-May of the second year, and during May thereafter. Neck circumference of female deer may vary by about 6 percent (1.9 centimeters: 0.75 inches) of maximum during the second year of life and 10 percent (3.4 centimeters: 1.34 inches) of maximum during the fifth year.

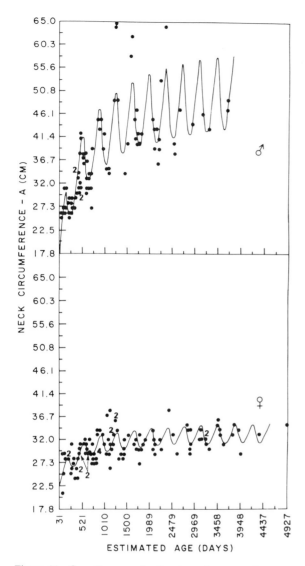

Figure 11. Growth curves for the circumferences of necks measured 15 centimeters posterior to the occiput of 85 male and 110 female Rocky Mountain mule deer; R^2 = 0.860 for males and 0.519 for females (A. E. Anderson et al. 1974).

Lyposomes, generally involved in protein turnover and measured by a lyposomal proteolytic enzyme, were found to decrease in muscle cells of the enlarging neck of male reindeer during breeding season (Lund-Larsen 1977). Proteolytic activity increased in neck muscle after a decrease in testosterone and regression of neck muscles. Since these changes in lyposomal activity did not parallel changes in forage intake or nutritional levels, it was inferred that lyposomal proteolytic activity of neck muscles of male reindeer may be controlled partly by steroid hormones. Verification in reindeer and applicability of this mechanism to mule, black-tailed, and white-tailed deer require additional investigation.

Seasonal changes in depths of subcutaneous fat and pelage mass were associated in a correlative manner with cyclic changes in neck circumferences of both male and female Rocky Mountain mule deer in Colorado (A. E. Anderson et al. 1974).

In female mule deer, characteristics such as length of the third caruncle, length of mammary gland, length of left front nipple, and basal diameter of the left rear nipple show significant ($p<0.01$) seasonal variation and approximate synchrony with the annual reproductive cycle. Mean ($\pm$SD) seasonal weights (kilograms) of the mature female reproductive tract without prenatal young were: 0.119±0.056 (autumn); 1.619±1.074 (winter); 2.824±1.326 (spring); and 0.267±0.498 mer). Weights of gravid female reproductive tracts were predictable from estimated age (Hudson and Browman 1959) of their prenatal young (A. E. Anderson et al. 1974).

Antlers

True deer evolved from the Palaeomerycidae, which appeared during the Miocene and early Pliocene epochs of the Cenozoic era in Eurasia about 11–25 million years ago (Romer 1966). The Palaeomerycidae are believed to have had permanent bony, skin-covered structures resembling the pedicels of modern cervids. True deer (Cervidae) with deciduous antlers arose later in the Miocene

ment of the neck in male deer during the breeding season have received little attention. In male red deer, Lincoln (1971) found that the neck of the castrated male did not swell during breeding season. Later experiments with male red deer revealed that testosterone implants into castrated deer stimulated and maintained neck enlargement as long as testosterone was present (Lincoln et al. 1972).

epoch of the same era. They were characterized by generally well-branched antlers arising from numerous, relatively long pedicels that grew from various sites on the skull (Bubenik 1971). Cervids probably reached North America during the lower Miocene epoch (Walker 1975).

In North America, the Pleistocene ice ages displaced and isolated deer populations and perhaps increased the rate of evolutionary change (Cowan 1956b). Cowan noted that, where glaciation was most extensive, only the Rocky Mountain mule deer still exists. But where glaciation was not extensive or did not occur, mule deer have separated into eight geography-specific races. Mature mule deer of some of these subspecies typically bear antlers of distinctive size and shape, particularly Rocky Mountain mule deer, Columbian black-tailed deer, and Sitka deer (Cowan 1936; see also chap. 5).

In mature mule, black-tailed, and white-tailed deer, shedding of antler velvet is synchronized with increasing levels of blood serum testosterone during early summer (McMillin et al. 1974; West and Nordan 1976a). Relative aggressiveness in cervids probably is related to the amount of testosterone secreted (Lincoln et al. 1972). Masturbatory behavior involving fully developed antlers has been observed in red deer (Darling 1937) and moose (Denniston 1956), but apparently not in white-tailed deer (Marchinton and Moore 1971) and only rarely in Rocky Mountain mule deer (see chap. 5).

In several subspecies of deer, use of the antler points against an opponent typically is preceded by several stereotyped acts of aggressive behavior (Cowan and Geist 1961). Cowan and Geist described how the antler points of captive mule deer in rut occasionally penetrated a 0.64-centimeter (0.25-inch) fir plywood shield used by observers for protection. In contests among mature bucks, the terminal forks make contact, and each deer attempts to twist the neck of his adversary, presumably to force the antler points to his head or neck (Dixon 1934). Most contests are of short duration, from a few seconds to 2–3 minutes, but the sources for this generalization timed one contest at 17 minutes (Dixon 1934) and another at about 30 minutes (Linsdale and Tomich 1953). Linsdale and Tomich described 25 contests and concluded that injuries to combatants were rare. They categorized contests as (1) struggles without injury, (2) struggles resulting in injury or death, (3) sparring or pushing, and (4) "bluffing" with presumably little or no antler contact (see also chap. 5). In addition, they interpreted some contests essentially as play behavior for one or both participants. Antlers may become locked together, resulting in the death of both combatants. The Boone and Crockett Club (1964) illustrated locked antlers of two mule deer, of a mule deer and a white-tailed deer, and of two white-tailed deer antlers locked in reverse. In the last case, one buck apparently had thrown the other over its head.

Bubenik (1968) generalized that antlers provide the major visual stimulus for social interaction. Thus Bailey (1960) observed that, in groups of mule deer bucks, those animals that had shed their antlers were dominated by smaller bucks that retained their antlers. Once all bucks had shed their antlers, the social hierarchy returned to that prevailing before antler shedding.

Wika and Krog (1971) noted a minor thermoregulatory effect in growing antlers of reindeer. Preliminary work by Jackson (1971) with growing antlers in white-tailed deer indicated their potential to dissipate heat even though antler velvet of this species lacks sweat glands (Billingham et al. 1959). Stonehouse (1968) hypothesized that developing antlers in most male cervids evolved as thermoregulatory organs, which necessitates their annual renewal. Geist (1968a) agreed that growing antlers may dissipate body heat, but argued convincingly that antlers evolved not as thermoregulatory organs but as social adaptations associated with the reproductive success of individuals.

Antlers are true bone. Banks (1974a, p. 60) defined bone as "a very specialized connective tissue which consists of a few cells embedded with a gellike substance which becomes mineralized to varying degrees, and . . . the mineral phase of the matrix makes bone distinct from the other connective tissue." Ac-

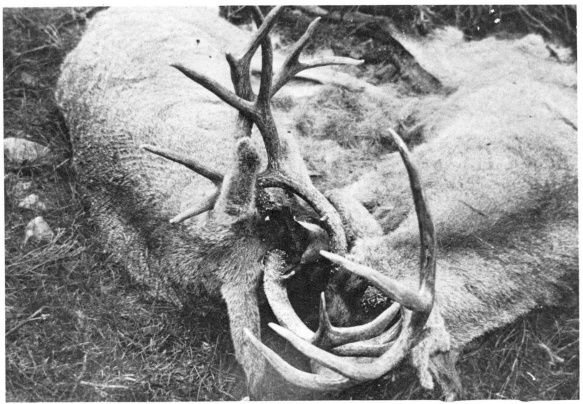

Locking horns, though infrequent, usually results in the death of the combatants. Photograph courtesy of the Wyoming Department of Game and Fish.

cording to Banks, antler bone "develops by a modified type of endochondral ossification." Bubenik (1971) and Chapman (1975) summarized much of the international literature on ossification of antlers.

Banks (1974*b*) studied ossification of the developing antler in white-tailed deer by routine and special histological techniques. A complex series of changes originated with reserve mesenchymal tissue. Chondroitin 4- and 6-sulfates, hyaluronic acid, and sialic acid characterized the reserve mesenchyme (Frasier et al. 1975). According to Banks (1974*b*, p. 257), the series continued "through the differentiation of a cartilaginous supportive tissue and culminated in the total osseous replacement of the cartilage and woven bone." He stated that remodeling and removal of the mineralized cartilage and woven bone were accomplished by chondroclasia and osteoclasia and that "subsequent oseogenesis resulted in

lamellar cancellous and compact, bone deposition." He further stated, "Specifically, antler cartilage differentiates, matures, undergoes mineralization and is replaced subsequently by bone." Frasier et al. (1975, p. 273) defined "some of the mucosubstance constituents involved in the chondrogenic and calcification process" and established the "cartilaginous nature of the developing antler." Newbrey and Banks (1975) characterized the ultrastructure of the developing antler cartilage matrix in white-tailed deer.

The completely ossified (mature) antler consists of a thick sheath and a base of hard, compact bone around a core of spongy bone at its anterior portion. This core of spongy bone grades into coarser spongy bone near its posterior portion (Modell 1969).

According to Hudson and Browman (1959), the dark-colored antler (pedicel) primordia of Rocky Mountain mule deer first appear 73–83 days after conception. Presumably, the antler (pedicel) primordia in Rocky Mountain mule deer and Columbian black-tailed deer occur at the same general stage of development and are visible in both sexes of the Columbian deer and possibly in mule deer (Hudson and Browman 1959; Ommundsen and Cowan 1970).

Davis (1962, p. 62) noted that, among Rocky Mountain mule deer male fawns, the "first discernible growth appeared as a somewhat diamond-shaped placode on the frontal crest" at about 3 months of age, and Robinette et al. (1977) reported that pedicels were detectable at 80–93 days of age. Pedicels were first observed at about 2–3 months of age in Columbian black-tailed deer (Brown 1961) and 3–3.5 months of age in Pacific Coast mule and black-tailed deer (Cowan 1936).

Removing skin from the future pedicel area in 2- to 4-month-old white-tailed deer retarded but did not stop pedicel growth (Goss et al. 1964). Goss et al. found that removing pedicels with or without the overlying skin terminated pedicel growth. Bubenik (1966) concluded that testosterone is necessary to initiate and ensure growth of the pedicel. This implies that testosterone is secreted at about 3 months of age. I know of no published experimental evidence that male mule deer secrete testosterone at that age.

The diameter of the pedicel increases with age. Annuli, macroscopically visible in the sagittal section, can be used to estimate age in caribou (Banfield 1960). Concentric rings also can be seen macroscopically in sagittal sections of the mule deer pedicel, but their value as an estimator of age in mule, black-tailed, and white-tailed deer has not been established. In red deer, mean diameter of the pedicel increased and mean length of the pedicel decreased with age (Isaković 1969).

Structure of the pedicel is dynamic, according to stage of the antler cycle. Just before shedding, the antler is attached by osseous trabeculae in a circular intermediate zone (Goss 1963). Goss indicated that osteoclastic erosion of the haversian lamellae at the line of demarcation causes the shedding. After shedding, the concave surface of the pedicel bleeds

and a scab is formed. In some species, a fibrocellular tissue forms between this scab and the bony pedicel and is the blastema for the next antler.

Velvet is a modified extension of normal skin of the head and pedicels that envelops the growing antler and is shed after normal growth ceases (Bubenik 1971). Billingham (1958) and Billingham et al. (1959) discussed some of the major modifications of cervine skin that characterize antler velvet: (1) the velvet apical region is characterized by "germinal caps" that strongly resemble the blastemas from which amputated limbs regenerate in lower vertebrates; (2) pigmented hairs emerge at right angles to the skin surface and over the entire velvet sheath but are relatively sparse in the apical region; (3) velvet lacks the fatty subcutaneous layer of loose connective tissue, and its inner portion unites invisibly with the fibrous portion of the periosteum of the antler; (4) velvet is thicker and more heavily pigmented than skin of the head region; and (5) pilosebaceous glands lack arrectores pilorum muscles. Also, sweat glands are absent in antler velvet of white-tailed deer (Billingham et al. 1959) and Rocky Mountain mule deer (Davis 1962).

Extremely rapid ossification of the antler and consequent changes in its blood supply certainly are linked to the necrosis and shedding of the velvet, but specific causal mechanisms are not known. It has been suggested that testosterone might cause closure of the blood vessels (Wislocki 1942). In mule deer, testosterone levels may increase during velvet shedding (Markwald et al. 1971). Recent work with captive Columbian black-tailed deer showed that a serum testosterone level of 1.5 milligrams per milliliter usually initiated velvet shedding, and the rate of shedding was greater at higher levels of serum testosterone. When testosterone levels increased rapidly, the velvet was stripped before the blood supply was completely stopped (West and Nordan 1976a). One captive mule deer, which lived to be about 18 years of age, shed its antler velvet slightly later each successive year and failed to shed it completely during the "last few years"

Velvet that envelops the growing antler is a modified extension of normal skin of the head and pedicels. Photograph by Joseph S. Dixon; courtesy of the United States National Park Service.

of life (Steinhoff 1957, p. 29).

Periods of time estimated for individual deer to shed velvet were: one and three hours (Cowan 1956*a*); one day (Linsdale and Tomich 1953); about four days (Dixon 1934); and "days and even weeks" (Graf 1956, p. 167). Nutritional levels of deer may be associated with the timing of velvet shedding in mule, black-tailed, and white-tailed deer (Long et al. 1959; Robinette et al. 1973). Captive black-tailed deer were observed to eat the velvet as it was stripped (Cowan 1956*a*).

Davis (1962) observed two different types of antler growth that occurred in captive mule deer at about 5 months of age. In the first type, velvet was removed by rubbing and exposing 1 or 2 centimeters (0.39 or 0.79 inch) of hard antler, which was shed four to six weeks later. Dixon (1934) also reported 2 wild mule deer fawns with hard antlers free of velvet and 2.54 centimeters (1 inch) long on 30 January. In the second common type, skin-covered antlers grow very slowly, reaching a height of about 2.54 centimeter (1 inch) in March. From 3 of 17 wild mule deer fawns examined in a labo-

ratory, a third type was observed, wherein bony tips were attached to skin-covered antlers (Anderson and Medin 1971). Cowan (1936) referred to the second type of fawn antler as frontal growth, which includes both the pedicel and the base of the yearling antler beam. Length of the second type of fawn antler ranged from 3.5 centimeters (1.38 inches) in September to 8 centimeters (3.15 inches) in March in individual Rocky Mountain mule deer (Anderson and Medin 1971) and from about 1.9 centimeters (0.75 inch) to 2.54 centimeters (1 inch) during September in coastal black-tailed deer (Linsdale and Tomich 1953).

The extreme dates of antler growth, velvet drying and shedding, mature development, and shedding are given in table 17 for mature mule and black-tailed deer in North America. Only extreme dates are tabulated, because available data are too meager to calculate means or frequency distributions.

The blood supply of mule deer and black-tailed deer antlers has not been studied. In white-tailed deer, blood is supplied to pedicels via the vascular supply of frontal bones.

Table 17. Antler Phenology in Mule and Black-tailed Deer

Subspecies	State	Growth	Velvet Drying-Shedding	Fully Developed	Antler Shedding	References
			Beginning and Ending Dates or Periods			
Rocky Mountain mule deer	Arizona	25 Mar.[a] 16 July	15 Sept.– 7 Oct.	1 Sept.– 20 Apr.	1Feb.– 15 Feb.[c] 22 Feb.– 20 Apr.[d]	Swank (1958)
	Colorado	6 Mar.– 22 Oct.	17 Aug.– 27 Oct.	18 Sept.– 11 Mar.	17 Dec.– 10 Apr.	Anderson and Medin (1971)
	Colorado		5 Sept.– 1 Oct.	5 Sept.– 17 Apr.	23 Feb.– 17 Apr.[e] 24 Oct.[f]	Robinette et al. (1973)
	Utah– Nevada	Apr.	25 Aug.– 24 Sept. 29 Oct.[b]		20 Oct.– late Mar.	Robinette et al. (1977)
	Wyoming				6 Jan.– 28 Mar.[g]	Skinner (1921)
Not given	California	2 Mar.– 14 Sept.				Dixon (1934)
California mule deer	California	12 Apr.– early Aug.	early Apr.– 15 Oct.	Late Aug.– early Apr.	mid-Jan.– early Apr.	Leopold et al. (1951)
Columbian black-tailed deer	California	23 Feb.– 28 July	9 July– 17 Nov.	20 July– 2 Mar.	2 Dec.– 2 Mar.	Linsdale and Tomich (1953)
	California	Late Mar.– July	20 July– 10 Aug.	Aug.– mid-Dec.	mid-Dec.– 28 Feb.	Dasmann and Taber (1956a); Taber and Dasmann (1958)
	Washington	1 Apr.– 31 July	1 Aug.– Oct.	24 Aug.– 10 Mar.	4 Dec.– 11 Mar.	Brown (1961)
	Pacific Coast	Early May– Sept.	mid-July– Sept.	Late Aug.– 25 Mar.	9 Dec.– 25 Mar.	Cowan (1956a)

[a] Reported beginning growth—25 March in old deer, 15 July in young deer.
[b] Mean date recorded at checking station for yearlings.
[c] Adults.
[d] Young.
[e] Mean shedding date—17 March.
[f] Inferred from one hunter-killed buck (Robinette et al. 1977).
[g] Mean shedding date—4 February.

Branches of superficial temporal arteries supply the growing antler via lateral and medial coronal artery branches. Each of these branches into twelve arteries that ascend the velvet. One vein is associated with the lateral artery and one with the medial coronal artery, and both join to form the superficial temporal vein (Wislocki 1942; Waldo et al. 1949). These external arteries supply velvet, cartilage, and bone at all stages of growth. During early stages of antler growth, blood also enters and drains from the antler via the pedicel. Later ossification of the antler base greatly reduces but does not completely stop passage of blood from the pedicel to the antler (Wislocki 1942; Waldo et al. 1949). These authors noted that external arteries supply both the velvet and the antler via numerous arterioles, while the antler core is drained by thin-walled medullary sinuses.

Waldo et al. (1949) pointed out that the external arteries have thick walls composed of interwoven muscular fibers with small lumina. They speculated that these unique structural features facilitate rapid arterial constriction and prevent blood loss when velvet is shed or in the event of injury.

The vascular layer of white-tailed deer velvet contains supraorbital and temporal branches of the trigeminal nerve. Both nerves follow the lateral and medial coronal arteries (Wislocki and Singer 1946). The growing antler is extremely rich in nerve fibers (Bubenik 1971).

There are few data on the chemical composition or specific gravity of mule deer antlers. Specific gravity (grams per cubic centimeter) of mule deer antlers has been measured as 1.53 (Bernard 1963), 1.52 (White 1958), 1.55 (Robinette et al. 1977), and 1.67 (French et al. 1956) for white-tailed deer. The mineral components of bone are amorphous calcium phosphate and hydroxyapatite crystals (Banks 1974a). Chapman (1975) generalized that values for calcium, ash, phosphorus, and strontium in antlers are very similar to those described for skeletal bone of deer. If this is true for mule deer, the average percentage composition of ash of the mule deer rib may approximate that for the antlers. Banks et al. (1968b) reported average rib ash percentages for 3 mule deer during the antler cycle as: calcium, 37.71; magnesium, 0.56; and phosphorus, 15.7. They also reported mean molar calcium-phosphorus ratios for the rib ash as 1.86, with little variability during the antler cycle. Bubenik (1971), however, generalized that the calcium-phosphorus ratio resembles that of skeletal bone apatite only in the central portion of the antler. He asserted that antler tips have maximum calcium-phosphorus ratios and are the focal point for iron, manganese, silicon, and traces of bismuth, tin, antimony, titanium, and gold. Chapman (1975) listed amounts of sodium, potassium, strontium, and barium in antlers of red deer and mentioned sources of information on the amounts of trace elements in red deer and roe deer. Because calcium values of antlers were less variable when expressed as a percentage of the ash, he believed there are specific differences in amounts of organic materials in their antlers. Some properties of antlers are useful in assessing levels of radioactive fallout (Longhurst et

al. 1968b). Geilmann (1968) found that levels of strontium 90 in shed antlers provided a crude estimate of the year of antler growth in red deer. Erythropoietic properties have been ascribed to extracts derived from growing deer antlers (Song 1970). A gonadotrophic effect was associated with the lipid fraction of the growing deer antler (Elyakov et al. 1971).

Mechanical properties of antlers—such as tensile strength, impact test, and modulus of elasticity—apparently have not been quantified for mule, black-tailed, or white-tailed deer. Chapman (1975) listed values for these properties measured from a single red deer antler.

According to Banks et al. (1968b, p. 405), osteoporosis is "the reduction in bone mass per unit volume without changes in the quality of bone." It has been estimated that the rate of antler growth is three to seven times that of skeletal growth (Rerábek and Bubenik 1963). These values suggest that the mineral requirements of antler growth may exceed mineral requirements available in forage. Banks et al. (1968a) investigated the role of skeletal mineral in the rib (costa compacta) in antler growth of 2 mature mule deer. Despite large quantities of dietary minerals, internal cortical bone was mobilized during antler growth and replaced after growth. Bone densities and the amount of ash per unit volume showed that bone mineral was mobilized during periods of antler growth, but calcium-phosphorus ratios remained constant while the amount of bone resorption exceeded bone formation in this cyclic physiological osteoporosis (Banks et al. 1968b). This process also was described for mule deer in the trabecular bone in sternebrae (McIntosh 1969) and in the rib, tibia, metacarpal and metatarsal bones (Hillman et al. 1973). Hillman et al. found that internal modeling of these bones was maximal during the peak period of antler growth, and they described as did Banks et al. (1968a), a thickening of the rib cortex and long bones during antler growth and a constant bone mineral composition throughout the remodeling cycle. Experiments with radioactive isotopes of calcium 45 and strontium 80 seemed to corroborate mineral mobilization and storage after antler growth and removal in 4 white-tailed deer (Cowan et al. 1968). Both storage and removal of these isotopes were maximal in younger deer.

Chapman (1975, p. 143) stated that, "in general, most of the minerals required by growing antlers are probably obtained direct from the food but that a certain amount is obtained from the skeleton. The skeletal contribution may be more important in cases where the diet is inadequate." Banks et al. (1968*b*, p. 405) said that demonstration of a *cyclic physiological process* indicates that deer possess "complex control mechanisms for calcium metabolism" and would mobilize mineral deposits despite the dietary excesses (W. J. Banks, pers. comm., July 1977).

One theory of antler growth suggests that each pedicel and its frontal bone have an independent growth center. The centers are situated in the central nervous system, either in the diencephalon or in the hypothalamus of the brain, and are activated by testosterone during the prepubertal period. Metabolic control of pedicels and antlers is believed to be effected through the efferent sympathetic nerves. The centers have a "growth memory" and the necessary information for individual and specific patterns of antler growth. Thus the response to a stimulus can be observed through several sequential antler cycles, with the most intensive response occurring in the cycle following the cycle in which the stimulus was applied. Light triggers the neurohumoral activation of the centers, but the precise mode of action in this "triggering" is not well understood (Bubenik 1966).

Detectable antler growth in individual mule deer and blacktails may begin about two weeks (Linsdale and Tomich 1953), two to four weeks (Dixon 1934), "a month or so" (Cowan 1956*a*, p. 544), or about two months (Leopold et al. 1951) after antler shedding. According to Modell (1969, p. 117), the antler "is far and away the fastest growing postnatal bone known," and linear growth occurs at the tips only. Goss (1963, p. 339) generalized that antler growth "may exceed 0.39 inch (1 centimeter) per day, a growth rate probably un-

equaled elsewhere in the animal kingdom." Banks et al. (1968*a*) graphed monthly increments of antler growth for 2 captive, 3-year-old mule deer bucks from January 1965 to January 1966. As approximated from their parabolic curves, antler growths were: April, 1.27 centimeters (0.5 inch); May, 2.54 centimeters (1 inch); June, 7.87 centimeters (3.1 inches); July, 27.69 centimeters (10.9 inches); August, 5.08 centimeters (2 inches); September, 0.25 centimeter (0.1 inch) for one deer; and April, 2.54 centimeters (1 inch); May, 5.84 centimeters (2.3 inches); June, 15.75 centimeters (6.2 inches); July, 25.65 centimeters (10.1 inches); August, 3.3 centimeters (1.3 inches); and September, 0.0 centimeters for the other deer.

Developing antlers of individual wild mule deer in Colorado ranged in total beam length from 2.8 centimeters (1.1 inches) on 27 March to 116 centimeters (45.67 inches) on 30 July. Total fresh beam weights ranged from 40 grams (1.41 ounces) on 9 May to 4,330 grams (152.74 ounces) on 30 July (Anderson and Medin 1969). Fresh weight of developing antlers may vary greatly among mule deer of the same estimated age and among proximate dates of collection from the same population. For example, total beam weights were 397 grams (14 ounces) and 80 grams (2.82 ounces) from yearling bucks shot 17 August and 29 September, and 275 grams (9.07 ounces) and 666 grams (23.49 ounces) from two 24-month-old deer shot 13 June and 20 June (Anderson and Medin 1971).

Increased testosterone secretion at the time of the rut is involved in vascular constriction, shedding of velvet, hardening of bone, and death of the antler (Goss 1963). Nicolls (1969, p. 123) postulated the following antler-shedding mechanism for mule deer: "The reduced testosterone levels probably slow protein anabolism between the antler and pedicel, first by direct action and second by indirect action on the pars distalis acidophils, which produce protein anabolic hormones. The reduced testosterone levels also enhance resorption of osseus material. The reduced protein anabolism and increased bone resorption at the antler-pedicel union would be the two activities which prepare the antler for shedding." Alkaline phosphatase is an enzyme that provides a catalyst necessary for production of inorganic phosphate, hence calcification and probably antler ossification. In Columbian black-tailed deer, serum alkaline phosphatase was two to ten times higher during antler growth than in the mature antler (West and Nordan 1976*a*). Mollelo (1960) hypothesized that, with a lack of alkaline phosphatase in the mature (dead) antler, fluids of the pedicel erode the union between the pedicel and antler until the antler falls off. Detailed histological changes in the pedicel of mule, black-tailed, and white-tailed deer before shedding have not been described.

Different subspecies of deer in the same geographical area will shed their antlers at different times (Goss 1963). Antler shedding dates observed among individual mule deer of the same subspecies from the same geographical area spanned 114 days (Anderson and Medin 1971). Such variation presumably involves genetic factors superimposed on such interacting variables as (1) age—mature bucks generally shed antlers earlier than yearling bucks (Dixon 1934; Leopold et al. 1951; Cowan 1956*a*; Brown 1961; Behrend and McDowell 1967; Robinette et al. 1973); (2) diet—poorly nourished males may shed antlers earlier (Severinghaus and Cheatum 1956); (3) physical condition—poor physical condition may cause early (Hawkins et al. 1968; Robinette et al. 1977) or late (Taber and Dasmann 1958) loss of antlers; (4) injury—also may cause early loss of antlers (Cowan 1956*a*); and (5) social stresses—may delay antler shedding (Topinski 1975).

Both antler beams rarely are shed at the same time. Documented maximum differences in shedding dates between antler beams of individual bucks range from 9 days (Robinette et al. 1977) to 19 days (Brown 1961).

Because the pituitary exerts a regulating and controlling influence on other endocrine glands and directly or indirectly affects most body functions (Purves 1961), it may have a role in the antler cycle. This hypothesis has been strengthened by observations that castrated

deer grow antlers (Goss 1963) and that a hypophysectomized fawn did not (Hall et al. 1966). Histochemical staining techniques indicated the presence of seven cell types in the anterior pituitary, most of which underwent cyclic changes that may be related to hormonal regulation of reproduction and the antler cycle (West and Nordan 1976*c*).

The importance of light in the antler cycle of deer has been demonstrated experimentally by subjecting white-tailed deer (French et al. 1960) and sika deer (Goss 1969*a*, *b*) to artificial photoperiods. However, Goss found that neither inherent cyclic rhythms nor changing photoperiods explained all observed effects on the antler cycle. With changed frequency of light, sika deer grew as many as four sets of antlers per calendar year when the simulated "year" was of three months' duration (Goss 1969*a*).

The antler cycle might be mediated by light acting on the hypothalamus (Nicolls 1971), presumably through the eyes. However, other receptors may be operative, since the antler cycle of a captive blind elk apparently was normal over several years (Adcock et al. 1965). However, optic stimuli still can reach the hypothalamus in certain types of blindness (W. J. Banks, pers. comm., July 1977).

Nicolls (1971) established an apparent relationship between photoperiod, size of the acidophils in pars distalis of the anterior pituitary of adult mule deer, and the antler cycle. Based on his research and that of Banks et al. (1968*a*, *b*) and Markwald (1968), Nicolls (1971, p. 324) hypothesized that acidophils—influenced by rate of change in day length—secrete "proteinaceous growth stimulating hormones which act primarily on the antler and incidentally on the testes." He suggested that antler hardening, shedding, and the rutting period are controlled by decreasing photoperiod through action of the gonadotrophins on Leydig cells, thus producing testosterone. Testosterone stimulates both acidophil cells and absorption of bone mineral in the antler. These cells affect resorption of bone mineral from the skeleton and maintain elements of connective tissue at the junction of the pedicel and antler base. However, there is no physiological evidence for anterior pituitary control of bone mineral (W. J. Banks, pers. comm., July 1977).

McMillin et al. (1974) showed that antler growth began in white-tailed deer when serum testosterone levels began to rise. Antlers were shed several weeks after a decrease in serum testosterone. Volumes of testes were minimal when levels of serum testosterone were low. Generally, similar changes were described for Columbian black-tailed deer by West and Nordan (1976a, p. 1617), who concluded that "the maturation of antlers, shedding of the velvet, and the maintenance of antlers in the hard, functional condition are dependent on testosterone." West and Nordan (1976b) also applied methallibure, a nonsteroidal inhibitor of gonadotrophic secretion, during April and June. Antler growth was arrested and reproduction inhibited. These responses supported "the hypothesis that a gonadotrophin is responsible for stimulating antler growth" (West and Nordan 1976b, p. 1637).

Markwald et al. (1971) presented indirect evidence of increased testicular secretion of an unknown trophin as antler growth began in Rocky Mountain mule deer. However, testosterone is not an equally important component of the antler cycle of all cervids. For example, Bubenik (1966) hypothesized that testosterone is critically important in the antler cycles of roe deer; important but probably not essential in the antler cycles of mule, white-tailed, and black-tailed deer, elk, and red deer; and probably not essential in caribou. In caribou, the essential antler cycle components probably are the products of the adrenal cortex. Recent experiments tentatively have suggested, moreover, that adrenal androgens also may be important in the antler growth and mineralization processes of roe deer (Bubenik et al. 1976).

Bubenik (1966) suggested that both the testes and the adrenal gland are important regulators of the antler cycle in mule, black-tailed, and white-tailed deer, red deer, and American elk. Chapman (1975) reviewed the international literature on cervid adrenal, pituitary, pineal, thyroid, and parathyroid glands in rela-

tion to the antler cycle. He implied that there is much conflicting and inconclusive information because most studies have not attempted to relate attributes of these glands to the antler cycles of individual deer. For example, the functional role of the thyroid can be inferred reasonably from some but not all studies of the thyroid gland and the antler cycle in mule deer, whitetails, and blacktails. Referring to their unpublished histometrical studies of mule deer endocrine glands, Markwald et al. (1971, p. 277) mentioned male thyroid and adrenal glands in which "no clearcut evidence of increased activity was apparent during the initiation of antler growth." A. E. Anderson et al. (1974) found no evidence of annually cyclic variation in absolute fresh weight of adrenal and pituitary glands of male mule deer. The growth curve of absolute fresh weight of the male thyroid gland, however, peaked during July—as did antler growth (Banks et al. 1968a)—and troughed during January when antlers were being shed (Anderson and Medin 1971). This temporal variation approximates that of the relative thyroid weight in male white-tailed deer (Hoffman and Robinson 1966). While changes in average weight of endocrine glands are not necessarily indicative of changes in hormonal secretion, the temporal variations described are suggestive in that calcitonin—a thyroid hormone that lowers blood calcium and inhibits bone resorption—was high during periods of rapid antler growth in red deer (Phillippo et al. 1972). Also, blood serum calcium decreased with increased volume of growing antlers in 24 wild mule deer shot from April through September (Murphy 1969).

The pineal (epiphysis cerebri) is a light-sensitive endocrine gland. One of its secretory products, melatonin, has an inhibitory effect on gonadal development. Its functional role is not completely understood, but it may be the biological clock associated with circadian rhythms and seasonal breeding of some species (Banks 1974a). Even though the gland is situated at the base of the brain (diencephalon), pinealectomy has been performed successfully on several male white-tailed deer

(Mazur 1973). The main effects were to place their antler and pelage cycles out of phase with those of normal deer. Owing to the small number of animals, experimental results were inconclusive.

West and Nordan (1976a, p. 1630) listed four effects of testosterone on the antler cycle of Columbian black-tailed deer: "(1) it induces secondary ossification of the antler, and by accelerating the maturation process it terminates antler growth; (2) it induces behavioral changes that result in velvet shedding; (3) the continued production of testosterone aids in the maintenance of osteoblasts and osteocytes to ensure that the antlers are retained in the hard, functional condition throughout the breeding season; and (4) the withdrawal of testosterone at the end of the breeding season permits the resorption of bone at the base of the antlers, and they are cast off." Silberberg and Silberberg (1971) noted that small amounts of testosterone may stimulate bone growth, while large amounts often are inhibitory.

Antlers of mule deer are typically dichotomous—that is, with repeated bifurcation or forking as opposed to the somewhat suppressed dichotomy of white-tailed deer. In addition, the brow tine (basal snag) of adult mule deer typically is relatively short, circular rather than elliptical in cross section, and directed dorsally rather than dorsomedially as contrasted to that of white-tailed deer. Subadults of the two subspecies, however, may bear antlers of similar form and forking (Cowan 1936).

According to Cowan (1936, p. 208), none of the antlers of mule and black-tailed deer subspecies have "constant characters of racial significance," but they possess "certain peculiarities of form useful in interspecific comparison." The following descriptions of typical antler form among mature adults for nine subspecies are paraphrased from Cowan (1936).

1. Rocky Mountain mule deer—similar to Columbian black-tailed deer antlers but much larger, with a higher proportion of perfectly

A California mule deer exhibits antlers of almost perfect symmetry. Photograph by Joseph S. Dixon; courtesy of the United States National Park Service.

dichotomous antlers and a higher proportion of brow tines.

2. California mule deer—intermediate in size and incidence of brow tines, compared with Columbian mule deer antlers.

3. Columbian black-tailed deer—the perfectly dichotomous antler; brow tines are rare.

4. Sitka black-tailed deer—large brow tines; secondary beams are thick relative to length and conformation; resemble antlers of white-tailed deer.

5. Inyo mule deer—probably similar to antlers of California mule deer.

6. Southern mule deer—antlers similar to those of California mule deer.

7. Peninsula mule deer—brow tines rare but otherwise similar to California mule deer antlers.

8. Desert mule deer—similar to Rocky Mountain mule deer antlers.

9. Cedros Island mule deer—very small antlers, probably without brow tines.

Based on allometric considerations, the comments by Cowan (1956*b*) on variation in body size among Pacific Coast mule deer suggest that southern coastal Columbian blacktails may have smaller average antlers than their counterparts of the interior mountains or northern coastal areas.

For many years, mule deer antlers have routinely been measured and related to age classes at hunter check stations. In general, the objectives of measuring antlers have been unstated, but apparently they were mainly descriptive. One exception was the study reported by Hunter (1947), which attempted to use antler measurements as one of several sets of variables to estimate age empirically and thus obtain an estimate of age structure of the annual kill and perhaps the residual population.

Working with white-tailed deer, French et al. (1956) and Long et al. (1959) suggested a relationship among nutritional levels and antler development. Also, the field studies of Severinghaus et al. (1950) indicated regional differences among mean antler development that apparently were a product of deer population density relative to available forage. This information probably provided the impetus for workers on mule deer to use mean antler development of specific age classes, particularly yearlings, as an index of forage adequacy on winter ranges (Taber 1958). The comment by Long et al. (1959), that nutritional levels during the late summer stage of antler growth were most crucial to final antler development—a concept particularly important to migratory mule deer—went unheeded.

Documented changes in antler development of mule deer as related to environmental factors have been most dramatic in the arid southwestern United States. Thus, 52 percent of an unstated number of yearling mule deer bucks from the Kaibab North, Arizona, had "spikes" after a summer of "critical range conditions," compared with 12 percent of an un-

stated number of "spike" bucks when summer conditions were less rigorous (Swank 1958). Similarly, Snyder (1959) recorded that, among yearling bucks from the Guadalupe Mountains in New Mexico, "spikes" decreased from 64.4 percent to 25.7 percent when total annual precipitation increased twofold. From data presented by Snyder, I calculated a simultaneous and significant increase ($p<0.01$) in mean ($\pm$SD) antler beam diameter of yearlings (from 1.42 ± 0.33 centimeters: 0.56 ± 0.13 inch [N=179] to 1.77 ± 0.37 centimeters: 0.70 ± 0.15 inch [N=287]). These improvements in antler development accompanied both increased deer weight and an inferred change in yearlong diet from predominantly browse to predominantly forbs after exceptional rainfall (Anderson et al. 1965). After heavy rainfall markedly improved forage conditions in the Big Bend area of west Texas, the percentage of "spikes" among yearling mule deer bucks decreased from about 52 percent to 21 percent, accompanied by significant increases in the field-dressed weights of mature bucks (Wallmo 1960). Annual fluctuations in forage abundance and average antler development also have been correlated in Columbian black-tailed deer (Taber and Dasmann 1958) and in a Rocky Mountain mule deer population (Robinette et al. 1977). By contrast, the mean antler development of Colorado mule deer did not change significantly ($p<0.05$) over a five-year period when precipitation decreased, browse yields decreased, and carcass fat and mean carcass weight decreased (Anderson and Medin 1969; Anderson et al. 1970, 1972*a*).

French et al. (1956) and Long et al. (1959) regarded their conclusions on nutrition and antler development in white-tailed deer as tentative, primarily because of necessarily small sample sizes. Similar or expanded studies on mule deer have not yet been published. Thus the necessary information is not available to interpret adequately the apparent lack of measurable response to the seemingly drastic environmental changes documented in the Colorado study. I suggest, however, that one or both of two possibilities may have been operative: (1) the probable inclusion of both migratory and resident deer in the sample introduces a confounding variable, since these groups subsisted on different dietary regimes; (2) mean antler development indicated by linear measurements may be a relatively insensitive indicator of changes in moister environments. However, the presence of significantly ($p<0.01$) smaller antler measurements of 1960 (Anderson and Medin 1969) before measurement of environmental variables suggests that mean antler development indeed was responsive to some unidentified environmental factor(s).

Linsdale and Tomich (1953) tabulated antler measurements for Columbian black-tailed deer, as did Robinette et al. (1977) and Anderson and Medin (1969) for mule deer. Anderson and Medin statistically described and demonstrated symmetry among mean left and right antler beam diameters, lengths, and number of points in 1,200 bucks segregated into two broad age classes. Regression analysis showed singly or in combination that Rocky Mountain mule deer beam diameter, beam length, and number of points within the two age classes were related significantly ($p<0.05$) to weight of antler beams.

Lengths of brow tines also were correlated ($r=0.80$) significantly ($p<0.01$) with the weights of 25 single mature antler beams from deer 16–121 months in estimated age (Anderson and Medin 1969). Cowan (1936) concluded from his study of Rocky Mountain mule deer on the Pacific Coast that brow tines were absent from the antlers of yearling bucks but occurred in 99 percent of adult buck antlers. In a six-year Colorado study of 1,706 Rocky Mountain mule deer, brow tines occurred on 6 percent of the yearling buck antlers, 43 percent of the 28–30-month-old bucks, and 77 percent of bucks 40 months old and older (Anderson and Medin 1969).

Of 820 yearling mule deer bucks examined, 78.8 percent had even numbers of points 2.54 centimeters (1 inch) or more in length, 19.8 percent bore uneven numbers, and 1.4 percent were abnormal in various ways (Anderson and Medin 1969). In that population, symmetry of antler points decreased to 67.1 percent in 372

deer 28–30 months of age and to 69.1 percent in deer of about 40 months and older. Jaczewski et al. (1962) postulated that asymmetry in antlers may be controlled by a unilateral change in blood supply to the growing antler. Speculatively, then, the foregoing data on symmetry suggest a relatively stable blood supply to both antler beams of yearling bucks.

The role of genetics in antler morphometry has not been demonstrated experimentally. According to Taber and Dasmann (1958), antler shape is due largely to genetic factors, whereas relative antler mass is related to nutritional levels. However, ongoing studies have shown that some individual yearling whitetail bucks will have spike antlers regardless of nutritional level (Baxter et al. 1977). Improved nutritional levels of "spike" yearlings improved the development of subsequent sets of antlers, but not to the extent achieved by forked-antlered yearlings. Rocky Mountain mule deer fawns born singly had significantly ($p\cong0.03$) larger antlers as yearlings than did twins (Robinette et al. 1977). Some types of antler malformation may be controlled genetically, since some individual black-tailed bucks have been known to produce successive sets of antlers with similar malformations (Cowan 1956a).

Eviscerated carcass weight was related positively and nonlinearly to—and accounted for 72 percent of the variation (r^2) in—total antler weight in 23 mule deer (fig. 12). Estimated age was related positively and linearly to and accounted for 88 percent of the variation (r^2) in total antler weight in 23 mule deer (fig. 13) (Anderson and Medin 1969). Comparable curves apparently have not been published for black-tailed and white-tailed deer.

One very old mule deer with two normal antler beams had a small deciduous, branched, polished beam about 5.7 centimeters (2.25 inches) in height growing from a normal-appearing pedicel derived from the nasal bones. The skull was bilaterally imperfect, so the pedicels of the two normal antler beams were not in the same relative position (Dixon 1934). A presumably younger buck in the same vicinity also had two normal antler beams plus

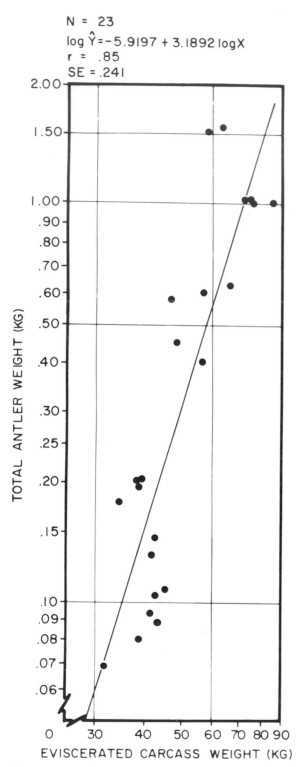

$$N = 23$$
$$\log \hat{Y} = -5.9197 + 3.1892 \log X$$
$$r = .85$$
$$SE = .241$$

Figure 12. Relationship of eviscerated carcass weight of Rocky Mountain mule deer to total weight of the mature (hard) antler (Anderson and Medin 1969).

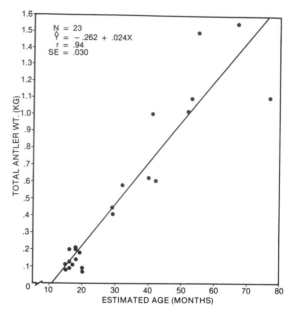

$$N = 23$$
$$\hat{Y} = -.262 + .024X$$
$$r = .94$$
$$SE = .030$$

Figure 13. Relationship of estimated age of Rocky Mountain mule deer to the total weight of the mature (hard) antler (Anderson and Medin 1969).

a third polished beam about 3.2 centimeters (1.25 inches) in height growing between the eyes.

Robinette and Gashwiler (1955) and Robinette and Jones (1959) reported a total of 14 mule deer bucks from the Oak Creek drainage in Utah missing one or both antlers. In most of these bucks, small bony protuberances replaced the normal structure. Six of the 14 exhibited normal neck enlargement and testes of normal size during the rut. In contrast, only 1 of 1,674 mule deer bucks examined from a Colorado drainage (1960–66) lacked an antler and a pedicel (Anderson and Medin 1969). Anderson and Medin also showed that 2.7 percent of their sample animals had abnormal antler development, 1.4 percent of the entire sample being yearlings. In most cases these abnormalities consisted of apparent beam rudiments flattened or enlarged around the pedicels.

Three types of testicular pathology have been described for deer that result in a gross appearance that might be confused with that of castration: genital hypoplasia (Marburger et al. 1967); testicular degeneration (Murphy and

Mule deer bucks missing one or both antlers as a result of injury or physical abnormality are not uncommon. Photograph courtesy of the Wyoming Department of Game and Fish.

Clugston 1971); and testicular atrophy (Taylor et al. 1964; DeMartini and Connolly 1975). Only in the last condition, however, is antler development affected so that mineralization is incomplete and the velvet persists.

Castration may occur in the wild and, according to Cowan (1936), always results in malformed antlers with persistent velvet. Cowan offered generalizations about the effects of castration on antler development in relation to age classes and stage of the antler cycle when castration occurs: (1) young fawn, no antler development; (2) older fawn, a knoblike permanent antler; (3) adult, with the first one-half to two-thirds antler growth completed, permanent antlers; (4) adult, last half to two-thirds growth completed, antlers shed within a few weeks and replaced by permanent antlers; and (5) adult, mature antlers, shed and not replaced.

A malignant bone tumor of the skull was thought to have caused deformed or "cactus" antlers in a Columbian black-tailed buck (Cowan 1956*a*). A mule deer with a corkscrew type of antlers was recorded in Colorado (Harrah 1971). A similar phenomenon, common in localized populations of roe deer, was tentatively ascribed to faulty calcium metabolism (Hemmer 1964). Parasitic infections also have been suggested as causing abnormal antlers, but there is no substantial experimental evidence (Dunn 1969). One mule deer buck shed one antler with a piece of frontal bone 2.54 centimeters by 3.81–centimeters (1.0 inch by 1.5 inches) attached (Cowan 1936). This might be indicative of a metabolic deficiency. Antlers often are injured during growth. According to Robinette et al. (1977, p. 35), "an osseous ring, enlargement, or sharp angle often marks the point of injury in the matured antler."

The relationship between body injury and antler malformation has been described by Robinette and Jones (1959) and Robinette et al. (1977) for mule deer and has been studied

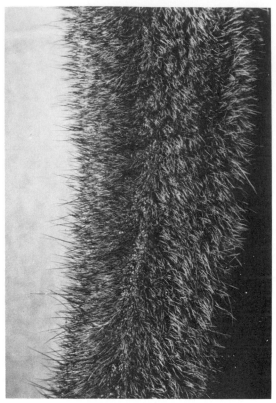

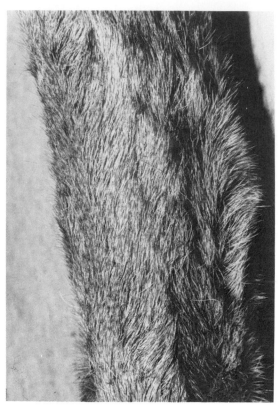

"Normal" velvet on this antler—of a healthy 2-year-old spike buck in Douglas fir habitat of northern California—would have been shed one month after the photograph was taken on 23 June 1973. Photograph by Guy E. Connolly.

An antler beam with persistent velvet, from a buck with degenerative testicles. Such disability could occur to a deer at any age, and the same effect could be caused by castration. Photograph by Guy E. Connolly.

experimentally by Marburger et al. (1972) for white-tailed deer. The experimental data suggest a cause-and-effect relationship between antler malformation and rear leg injury. They showed that amputation or neurectomy of a rear leg during antler growth resulted in a contralateral antler malformation in each of four bucks treated. Marburger et al. (1972, p. 314) speculated that "complex neural relationships" are involved. A possible mechanical explanation for the contralateral case is that if a deer turns to lick a wound on the left side, for example, the growing antler on the right side is most likely to be injured by striking a solid object (Morrison-Scott 1960).

Except for caribou and reindeer, female cervids normally do not bear antlers, but antlered females occasionally do occur in other genera,

particularly in roe deer and mule, black-tailed, and white-tailed deer (Wislocki 1956). Available data on antlered deer believed to be females of the various mule and black-tailed deer subspecies are summarized in table 18. Of this sample, all but two had antlers in velvet and 6 were with fawns, had fetuses, or were lactating. The velvet antlers of the 6 generally were poorly developed and were apparently deciduous in only one deer—a doe with a normal chromosomal complement and histologically normal endocrine glands, including the adrenals (Mierau 1972). Based on the studies of Donaldson and Doutt (1965) and Crispens and Doutt (1973) of antlered "female" white-tailed deer, some of the deer in table 18 may have been cryptorchid males or hermaphrodites rather than functional females.

Antler anomalies are thought to be associated primarily with hormonal imbalance, faulty mineral metabolism, or damage to primordial tissue. Photograph courtesy of the Wyoming Department of Game and Fish.

An antlered, captive doe about 3 years of age, immediately after shedding one antler beam. Each year until it died late in its third year, this female grew and shed antlers in the same chronological sequence as did bucks. Although penned with bucks, the doe did not exhibit reproductive behavior, though, except for rudimentary ovaries, her reproductive organs were of normal size and appearance. Photograph by A. W. Alldredge.

RADIONUCLIDES

Radionuclides have entered the environment by fallout from nuclear weapons testing and effluents from nuclear reactors, chemical processing plants, waste disposal, warfare, and technology involving radioactive materials such as that in the Plowshare Program (Wolfe 1963). According to Whicker et al. (1967, p. 622), strontium 90, cesium 137, and iodine 131 are "among the more biologically hazardous radionuclides produced by nuclear explosions. Although each of these nuclides enters food chains and becomes incorporated into living tissues, unique problems are associated with each isotope." Many other nuclides are of current concern, because they may be equally or more biologically hazardous. These include hydrogen 3, plutonium 239, radium 226, and radon 222 and daughters. The latter two nuclides occur naturally (F. W. Whicker, pers. comm., September 1978).

Concentrations in Deer and Their Environments

Studies of radionuclide concentrations in North American deer apparently began in 1950 with measurements of strontium 90 accumulations in mandibles (with teeth) of 85 yearling Columbian black-tailed deer collected sequentially in Mendocino County, California, through 1967 (Schultz and Longhurst 1963; Longhurst et al. 1968b). Strontium 90 levels in yearling mandibles generally were correlated

Table 18. Description of Antlers and Other Characteristics of Some Mule Deer Believed to Be Female

Subspecies	Location	Estimated Age[a]	Velvet Yes	Velvet No	Beam Length[b] Left	Beam Length[b] Right	Spread[b]	Description[b]	References
Rocky Mountain mule deer	Alberta	6	X					12 June. Spike on left; no antler right; well-developed corona. Reproductive tract, ovaries, mammary glands normal. Two fetuses.	Cowan (1946a)
	Arizona	5–6	X		1.27	5.84		15 Nov. Right antler base malformed from trap injury; horizontal projections ≤ 2 millimeters. Velvet apparently persistent. Twin fawns. Lactating.	Diem (1958)
	Arizona	Mature	X					Large antlers, four well-developed points plus brow tines on each side (from photo and caption).	Swank (1958)
	California	"Old"	X		45.60	86.36		14 Sept. Malformed antlers, four points left, five points right beam. Dressed weight 72.6 kilograms. Genitalia normal.	Dixon (1927, 1934) Cowan (1936)
	California	Mature		X		24.76		29 Sept. Symmetrical antlers with brow tines. Dressed weight 68.0 kilograms.	Dixon (1927, 1934) Cowan (1936)
	California	Mature		X		29.21		10 Oct. Forked symmetrical antler.	Dixon (1927, 1934) Cowan (1936)
	Colorado	5–7	X				10.00	Antler measured 7 May 1968. Bore and lost twins 1967; adopted fawn. Bore twins 1968.	Mierau (1972)
			X		0.79	13.00		Antlers measured 30 Sept. 1968 and 23 May 1970. Small corona. Twin fetuses.	
			X		4.10	4.30			
	Colorado	10	X		1.27			7 Apr. Left pedicel 2.54 centimeters long. "Bony protuberance" 0.64 centimeter long beneath skin on right. Twin fetuses. "Two fully developed corpora lutea in one ovary and corpora albicantia in the other."	Robinette et al. (1977, p. 35)

(Table 18.)

Subspecies	Location	Estimated Age[a]	Velvet		Beam Length[b]		Spread[b]	Description	References
			Yes	No	Left	Right			
	Idaho	7–9	X					7 Oct. Antlers large, symmetrical, seven points each beam; left one-third velvet-covered, right no velvet. No evidence of lactation or previous pregnancy. Uterus, ovaries, and oviduct appeared normal.	Buss (1959)
	Idaho	Mature	X		7.0	11.43		Oct. Spike antlers, no corona. With fawn, lactating. Normal ovaries, one regressing corpus luteum.	Wislocki (1956)
	Montana	5–7	X		15.90	16.00		Spike antlers from pedicels 2.2 centimeters long.	McCann (1973)
	Washington	10+	X		6.35	21.59		21 Oct. Left beam slightly branched, right beam not branched. Lactating.	Buechner (1957)
California mule deer	California	2	X					June. Antlers with several pencil-sized branches near base. Nursing a fawn.	Berry (1932)
Unspecified[c]	California		X				66.04	Autumn. Apparently without fawns.	Cronemiller (1932)
	California		X				71.12	Autumn. Apparently without fawns.	Cronemiller (1932)
	California						27.94	Dressed weight 42 kilograms.	Ellsworth (1930)
	California	Mature					48.26	3 Oct. Three-point antlers. Observed with a buck.	Bullard (1926)

Note: Only the deer described by Mierau (1972) was subjected to chromosome analysis; this revealed a normal female karyotype.

[a] Numbers refer to age in years.

[b] Measurements taken in inches and pounds were converted to centimeters and kilograms. Refer to sources for original standard measures.

[c] Subspecies not specified by authors. Based on locale, the deer may have been California mule deer, Columbian black-tailed deer, or intermediate.

positively with atmospheric testing, fallout deposition, and precipitation.

In white-tailed deer, it was found that strontium 90 concentration did not vary appreciably with sampling location of the antler (Schultz 1964) and that the antler is not a reliable indicator of strontium 90 consumed during antler growth regardless of age (Schultz 1965). Schultz and Flyger (1965) concluded from extensive studies of strontium 90 concentration in mandibles (with teeth) of 68 white-tailed deer that mandibular strontium 90 was correlated with year of birth, annual strontium 90 increment, and total strontium 90 in soil. There was a significant difference in mean concentrations between age classes. Male and female deer mandibles had similar concentrations of strontium 90 regardless of age.

Concentrations of strontium 90 in the long bones (Farris et al. 1967, 1969), iodine 131 in the thyroid (Hanson et al. 1963; Whicker et al. 1967), and cesium 137 in muscle (Whicker et al. 1965, 1967) and in the liver (Whicker et al. 1967) were measured in a Colorado Rocky Mountain mule deer population sampled from 1961 through 1965. Concentrations of cesium 137 in air, precipitation, soils, and twelve forage species were measured over a three-year period from the yearlong range of this migratory population. Because of soil factors, tissues of white-tailed deer from the lower coastal plain of the southeastern United States were very high in cesium 137 (Jenkins and Fendley 1968). Some were 100 times higher than tissues of Colorado mule deer. Dietary differences in two adjacent populations of Columbian black-tailed deer occupying a chaparral and an oak/woodland habitat were believed to account for the higher concentrations of cesium 137 in the rumen contents and muscle of deer from the oak/woodland habitat (Book et al. 1972). Those deer occupying the oak/woodland habitat ate large amounts of lichens yearlong, and cesium 137 activity was up to 140 times higher in lichens than in other forage. Unpublished studies have shown that cesium 137 may differ 200–300 percent among deer from adjacent habitats (G. E. Connolly to R. E. McCabe, pers. comm., April 1978). Further, Whicker et al. (1967, p. 631) stated that, in Colorado mule deer, "the distribution patterns indicated that a small percentage of the population, which happened to be exposed to certain ecological circumstances, could accumulate radionuclide body-burdens several times greater than those of the majority of individuals."

Information gained from studies of wild deer on natural range provided necessary background for experimental studies of radionuclide dynamics in captive mule deer. Hakonson and Whicker (1971b) described the distribution of cesium 134 in tissues of 2 captive adult mule deer and their 3 fetuses. Gist and Whicker (1971) described retention and uptake of iodine 131 by the thyroid; and Schreckhise and Whicker (1976) made predictions of strontium 90 kinetics in mule deer. Except for iodine 131 in thyroids, levels of radionuclides measured in deer were extremely low, in the subpicocurie per gram range (F. W. Whicker, pers. comm., September 1978).

The role of Rocky Mountain mule deer as a plutonium transport vector was studied at the Rocky Flats nuclear weapons plant of the United States Department of Energy near Denver, Colorado. This investigation involved estimation of plutonium intake and dispersal by mule deer (Arthur 1977; Hiatt 1977).

Concentrations in Venison and in Humans

Cesium 137 was believed to be the most important radionuclide from a human dietary standpoint, since its concentrations in venison were thirteen and eleven times higher than in beef and in pork (Whicker et al. 1968). However, Whicker et al. (1968, p. 1106) concluded that "levels of ^{137}Cs [cesium 137] would have to be increased by several orders of magnitude to produce somatic effects in deer or in humans." humans."

The deer liver accumulates cerium 144, cesium 137, magnesium 54, and ruthenium 106 in measurable but insignificant amounts from worldwide fallout. Since the thyroid of deer usually is not eaten by humans, and since iodine 131 has a short radioactive half-life, the thyroid is not a likely vector for iodine 131 in the human diet.

Whicker et al. (1968, p. 1109) generalized that "radiation doses to deer from fallout radionuclides during this study have been orders of magnitude lower than those required to produce somatic damage in other mammals." However, doses received by deer are much higher than those received by most humans. Whicker et al. believed that strontium 90 may be the most potentially harmful radionuclide and stated that "during 1963, ^{90}Sr [strontium 90] concentrations and radiation doses in the bones of yearling deer were higher by a factor of 35 than 0–20-year-old humans from New York, Chicago, and San Francisco."

Some Applications

Deer tissues are considered useful and often sensitive indicators of environmental contamination by cerium 144, cesium 137, iodine 131, magnesium 54, ruthenium 106, and strontium 90 (Whicker et al. 1968). For example, the two major peaks of iodine 131 concentration in Colorado mule deer thyroids occurred four days after nuclear weapons tests in China in 1964, and one month after such tests in China in 1965 (Whicker et al. 1966).

Forage intake rates were calculated with an intake function and a retention function of cesium 137 concentration in 87 Rocky Mountain mule deer and their diet, inferred from botanical analyses of rumen content samples (Alldredge et al. 1974). The calculated mean forage intake values were in approximate agreement with those in the literature derived from feeding trials.

CONCLUSIONS

Data are fragmentary or lacking for most aspects of body composition, body temperature, and heartbeat rate in mule and black-tailed deer. Current information is somewhat better on development and growth, particularly for such seasonal phenomena as body fat accumulation and antler growth. However, in most cases small sample sizes limit reliable interpretation. In the future, greater emphasis on controlled experiments involving adequate numbers of deer of both sexes and various age classes, and utilizing telemetric or other appropriate techniques to reduce handling stress, may yield more usable information applicable to wild mule and black-tailed deer populations and their management.

Chapter 3

NUTRITION AND METABOLISM

Henry L. Short
Terrestrial Ecologist
United States Fish and Wildlife Service
Fort Collins, Colorado

The nutrition and metabolism of mule and black-tailed deer can be treated in a variety of ways. It is addressed in this chapter about midway in the continuum between exceedingly general and exceedingly specific detail. This treatment of the subject is general in that I do not paraphrase biochemical and physiological texts. It is specific in that I present an overview of how deer depend on the environment to fulfill their needs for sustenance and production. The reader is invited to supplement this account with readings in general texts on ruminant nutrition and physiology and in texts on biochemistry, range science, soil science, animal behavior, forest science, and wildlife science. Information sifted from all these disciplines will help explain how deer are able to survive in wildlands in close proximity to man.

Mule deer are small ruminants with limited ability to digest highly fibrous roughage. They are physiologically adapted to enter the winter season of food scarcity in maintenance status and to be in a productive condition during the warm seasons when forage frequently is abundant, green, and lush. Deer have physical, behavioral, and physiological adaptations that allow them to feed on vegetation as varied as that found in alpine meadows and in the Sonoran desert, to exist in habitats as different as wilderness and city suburbs, and to cope with climates ranging from the severe winters of the northern Rocky Mountains to the sweltering summers of southwestern deserts. This chapter describes how mule deer digest available foods and how they use energy and nutrients produced from those foods for maintenance and production.

THE DIGESTIVE PROCESS

The Mechanics of Eating

Deer utilize foodstuffs selectively. Foods actually eaten by mule deer in different geographical regions are described in chapter 9, part 1. Foods seem to be selected largely on the basis of smell, although selection also is affected by sweet, sour, and bitter tastes (Church 1971) and by appearance and touch (for example, the presence or absence of spines on the surface of the foodstuff).

Whereas the cow's broad, flat muzzle enables it to clip a swath of grass close to the ground, the deer's relatively long, pointed face seems to be useful in eating small individual forbs, selecting leaves from brushy shrubs, and picking up individual food items like acorns from the ground. A row of chisel-shaped incisor and canine teeth on the front portion of the mandible enables deer to nip or tear selected food items by pressing the teeth against the dental pad lining the base of the maxilla. A deer can strip a twig of its leaves

A mule deer grasps a fern that it will tear away by pressing its lower canine teeth against the dental pad lining its maxilla. Photograph by Leonard Lee Rue III.

close to a woody stem or cut a succulent forb near the ground. Its mobile tongue pushes food back to the cheek teeth or molariform teeth present on both upper and lower jaws. Both premolars and molars have ridges of alternating hard enamel and softer dentin. This highly abrasive and irregular grinding surface allows the normal lateral chewing motion to fragment food items before they are swallowed.

As foods are chewed, they are mixed with saliva from glands in the cheeks, underneath the tongue, and behind the cheek teeth. Saliva aids formation of a soft food mass called a bolus and coats the bolus with mucus so it is more easily swallowed. Saliva also contains enzymes that aid in digesting foods, nutrients and minerals for rumen microorganisms, and salts that aid in maintaining the acid content of the stomach at levels beneficial to rumen microorganisms (Church 1969).

Biting, formation of boluses, and swallowing constitute a rapid process. Two or three bites of coarse foods, such as leaves of gray oak or alligator juniper, may be chewed together for 5–10 seconds and then swallowed. When deer feed on more delicate foods, such as leaves of

The pointed faces of mule deer allow them to select and grasp individual food items or portions of plants, such as balsamorrhiza leaves, as shown here, pawed free from snow. Photograph by Valerius Geist.

mountain mahogany or succulent forbs, there is more constant motion. A bite is clipped, chewed briefly, and swallowed while the deer prepares to take the next bite. A bolus then is formed from each individual bite, and boluses may be swallowed as rapidly as every three seconds. Mule deer can eat and swallow a quantity of food quickly and minimize the length of time they are obvious and vulnerable. The digestive process then is continued at a more leisurely pace in a protected spot. The amount of time spent feeding and the hours when feeding occurs depend on the quantity and quality of foods available, seasonal food requirements, disruptions (such as the activities of man), climatic conditions, and deer behavior, such as the rut.

Ruminant Digestion

Different food habits in animals are associated with different digestive systems. Vegetation with high sugar or fat content (fleshy fruits and some nuts, seeds, or fleshy fungi) can be digested readily by mule deer as well as by fox, coyote, or man. Vegetation, however, generally contains cellulose, which is impervious to digestive enzymes and acids in the gastrointestinal tract of omnivores and carnivores. Cellulose represents energy potentially available only to animals with very specialized digestive systems. The digestive tract of herbivores (such as cows, horses, rabbits, and deer) contains great quantities of bacteria and protozoa that, by fermentation, reduce cellulose to nutritionally useful metabolites. The herbivore has a constant need for these metabolites, and, since fermentation is relatively slow, its digestive tract is greatly expanded to accommodate large quantities of vegetation.

The gastrointestinal tract of herbivores is very different from those of other mammals. Omnivores and carnivores have simple stomachs and absorptive small and large intestinal tracts with relatively little specialization (fig. 14). The volume of a pig's stomach may be 30 percent of the volume of its total gastrointestinal tract. Although some fermentation

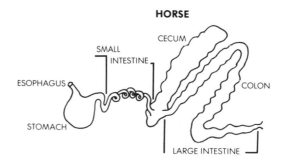

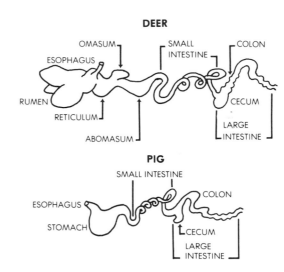

Figure 14. Comparison of digestive tracts of horse, mule deer, and pig (after Ensminger 1969).

may occur in the colon, the cecum generally is so small that it contributes little to digestion of foods. The more fully carnivorous the animal, the less bulky is the total digestive tract and the smaller are absorptive organs (such as intestines). Intestines of dogs and cats, for example, are only four to six times longer than their bodies, while those of horses are twelve times greater and those of sheep and goats are more than twenty-five times their body length (Dukes 1955). In contrast, the intestines of a deer are about fifteen times as long as the body (Longhurst and Douglas 1953).

Two different types of specialization occur in herbivores such as the horse and the deer. The stomach and small intestine of a horse are not highly specialized. The volume of its simple stomach may represent less than 10 percent of the volume of the gastrointestinal tract. The rear gut, however, is highly modified, with the cecum and large intestine representing more than 60 percent of the gastrointestinal tract's total volume (fig. 14). Extensive fermentation, some vitamin synthesis, and nutrient absorption occur in both the cecum and the colon. Fermentation within the large intestine is not as efficient as is rumen fermentation, since only about 30 percent of the cellulose in foodstuffs is digested, and synthesis of vitamins and protein is limited (Ensminger 1969). Because of these limitations in digestive efficiency, the diet of a horse must contain relatively more protein and vitamins than that of a ruminant.

Herbivory has attained great efficiency and specialization in ruminants such as mule deer. The ruminant stomach is like a fermentation vat in which extensive microbial fermentation occurs before enzymatic processes normal in the mammalian stomach. The swallowed food bolus stops at the anterior or cardiac portion of the rumen (the largest compartment of the ruminant stomach; fig. 15). The relative size of the rumen can be appreciated by realizing that the rumen, if filled with water, would weigh about 10 percent of the body weight of an adult mule deer. Rumen volume is nearly 60 percent of the total volume, and rumen weight with contents may be nearly 75 percent of total gastrointestinal tract weight in a well-fed deer. The rumen is a relatively thick-walled chamber with a muscular middle layer that provides rhythmic contractions that knead the contents. The rumen's inner surface is covered with papillae (fig. 15) about 1 centimeter (0.4 inch) long and 2 millimeters (0.08 inch) wide. Papillae provide a great amount of surface area for absorbing nutrients from the contents of the rumen.

The swallowed bolus is added to the total rumen content, which consists of material from several meals, water, saliva, and innumerable rumen microorganisms. Rumen contents frequently constitute 70–75 percent of the rumen capacity before spilling over into the reticulum—a small, thin-walled sac immediately anterior to the rumen. The absorptive surface of the deer's reticulum is not as highly modified as that of the rumen (fig. 15). Relatively large

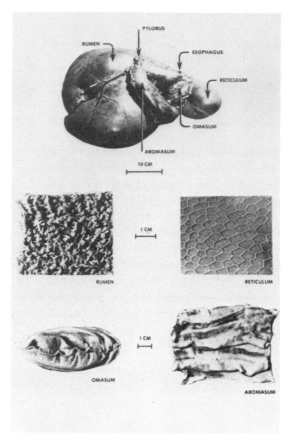

Figure 15. The compound stomach of the mule deer, and the appearance of internal tissue surfaces from each stomach compartment.

food materials from the reticulum may be returned, by a complex regurgitation process, to the mouth for remastication (cud-chewing), a characteristic trait of ruminants. Rechewing of food reduces particle size, increases food surface exposed to microbial fermentation, and allows reswallowed foods to pass from the rumen-reticulum to other portions of the digestive tract.

Fluidlike digesta, consisting of small soaked particles, periodically pass from the reticulum to the omasum. The omasum is a rather rigidly structured compartment that contains long folds or leaves (10 centimeters: 4 inches long; 5 centimeters: 2 inches wide) of muscular and vascular tissue (fig. 15). These leaves run most of the omasum length and have small granular papillae on their surfaces. They provide a

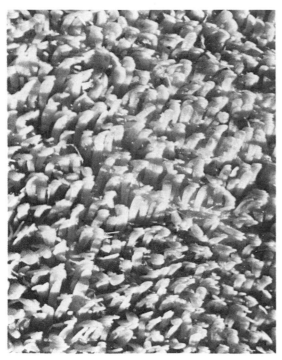

A close-up view of rumen papillae from a healthy black-tailed deer. The papillae greatly expand surface area to enhance the absorption of metabolites produced in the rumen. Photograph by Guy E. Connolly.

Fresh rumen contents of a deer browsing on chaparral vegetation. The leaf *(right center)* is from buckbrush. Identification of rumen materials has been the basis of many efforts to determine the foods eaten by deer. Photograph by Guy E. Connolly.

relatively large absorptive area, and much of the water content of digesta is absorbed in the omasum. Food particles then are passed to the abomasum, a rather flaccid organ that has the same function for the ruminant as does the simple stomach in omnivores and carnivores. Extensive secretion of gastric juice in the abomasum renders food material very acidic. Some acid-pepsin digestion of food proteins and microorganisms occurs before food remnants pass into the small intestine.

The small intestine in adult deer is about 1 centimeter (0.4 inch) in diameter and 15 meters (49 feet) long (about eleven times body length) and represents about 25 percent of the gastrointestinal tract volume. In contrast, the small intestine of sheep may be 28 meters (92 feet) long (Longhurst and Douglas 1953). The semifluid materials flowing from the abomasum into the small intestine contain inorganic salts, many organic substances representing products of digestion, and undigested food residues. Juices from the pancreas are secreted into the small intestine. These secretions are basic in pH and contain enzymes that convert plant and microbial proteins into peptides and amino acids, hydrolize fats to fatty acids and glycerol, and hydrolize starches and dextrins to glucose. Other secretions from glands within the intestinal wall provide salts to neutralize the acidic semifluid mass from the abomasum and supply enzymes to further digestive processes. Bile from the liver also is secreted into the small intestine, and substances in the bile enhance the activity of some enzymes and aid in the absorption of long-chain fatty acids and fat-soluble vitamins from the small intestine. The small intestine is the major site of absorption of digested nutrients essential to deer metabolism. The small intestine's mucous membrane is modified into villi that provide a large absorptive surface and contain lymphatic and blood capillaries. Fatty acids and glycerol that have been hydrolized from fats become soluble in the presence of bile and are absorbed into lymph capillaries of the villi. Peptides, amino acids, and monosaccharides produced by enzymatic digestion of proteins and carbohydrates are absorbed through the villi into blood capillaries (Dukes 1955).

The cecum is a muscular pouch about 20 centimeters (8 inches) long and 3–4 centimeters (about 1.5 inches) in diameter, with a volume equal to only about 2 percent of that of the total gastrointestinal tract. Some microbial fermentation may occur within, and some absorption of volatile fatty acids may occur from the cecum.

The large intestine of adult deer is about 5 meters (16 feet) long—four times the length of the body (Longhurst and Douglas 1953). The large intestine is about 2–3 centimeters (about 1 inch) in diameter and may, with its contents, represent about 8 percent of the weight of the gastrointestinal tract. Volume of the large intestine (when filled with water) represents about 10 percent of the total volume of the gastrointestinal tract (Longhurst and Douglas 1953). Water is absorbed from food residues, resulting in the formation of fecal pellets. Fecal pellets also contain cellular materials scraped from the gut's wall and residues from glandular secretions in the tract. Dead and living microbes from the gastrointestinal tract also are present in large numbers. Fecal pellets often are used as evidence of deer population density and distribution (see chap. 8). Although this is based on the regularity of passage of food residues over long periods of time, it is known that the rate varies to some degree among deer and with type of forage, but the variability has not been well defined.

The ruminant stomach develops from embryonic stomach tissue. In newborn deer the rumen is small and flaccid. The internal surface has a texture similar to fine-grained sandpaper because rumen papillae are undeveloped. An "esophageal groove" exists between the area where the esophagus enters the cardia of the rumen and the reticulo-omasal opening into the omasum. This groove is well developed in newborn deer even though the rumen is small. The groove is closed, apparently in response to sucking, so that ingested milk bypasses the rumen and goes from the esophagus directly through the esophageal groove into the omasum and abomasum (Dukes 1955). The abomasum of a newborn deer is anatomically and functionally well developed. Milk is coagulated in the abomasum, and pepsin begins to act on the increased surface area of coagulated milk to convert milk proteins into proteoses and peptones (Dukes 1955). Further digestion and absorption of digestible solids occurs in the small intestine.

Colostrum, the first milk secreted by does, contains antibodies that provide disease immunity for fawns until their own antibody-producing systems begin to function efficiently. Milk from deer contains more ash, fats, and proteins and less water than ordinary cow's milk (Silver 1961). The relatively high fat content of the milk of mule deer may have survival benefit to the fawn. Fawns obtain sufficient energy per feeding so that relatively long intervals can occur between feedings (Mueller and Sadleir 1977). Very young fawns, with a monogastric type of digestion, utilize doe's milk with very high efficiency. A few days after birth, fawns begin to eat leaves and grasses, and by 15 days of age some fermentation activity occurs within the rumen (Short 1964). By this time, rumen-reticular tissue weights have tripled since birth, while the weights of the omasum and abomasum have only doubled. This trend in the development of a young deer's digestive tract—increasing differentiation of the ruminant stomach and an increased reliance on products of rumen metabolism—continues until the deer is about 4 months of age. Fawns obtain much of their nutrition from their dams until 5 weeks of age, and if the doe dies within this early period of life the fawn is likely to starve, since the rumen is not sufficiently developed to provide the necessary fermentation products. When fawns are about 5 weeks of age and weigh about 10 kilograms (22 pounds) (Moen 1973), the volume of their rumen-reticulum equals that of the omasum-abomasum, and weaning begins. Dependence of the fawn on its dam continues to decline as the ruminant function increases, and weaning is completed by 4 months of age. At this time, only traces of milk still occur in the abomasum, and the relative volumes, appearance, and functions of the four stomach compartments are the same as in adult deer.

Rumen Microbes in Deer

Proper management of deer requires an appreciation of the digestive adequacy of available range forage and the competition for digestible foods that occurs among herbivores. These factors are understood better with a knowledge of the great populations of microbes that live symbiotically within the rumen, fermenting plant material and producing useful digestive products.

Gases of fermentation within the rumen consist of carbon dioxide, methane, and nitrogen. Gases, such as methane, are a metabolic waste product whose energy value is lost to the animal. Rumen contents are liquid (averaging about 85 percent fluid), warm (39 degrees Cesius: 102 degrees Fahrenheit), buffered but acidic (pH about 6.0–6.5), and reducing in reaction. The rumen is a highly dynamic and open system: food materials, saliva, and water are added frequently; products of fermentation (such as volatile fatty acids) are absorbed; gases are belched from the rumen; and fermented foods and microbes are passed to the omasum and then to the lower digestive tract.

The microbial population within the rumen is immense. Thirteen types of bacteria, varying in physical appearance (such as gram stain characteristics, size, and shape), were isolated from the rumen of weaned mule deer in Utah (Pearson 1969). In that study, the number of bacteria found in the rumen of free-ranging mule deer averaged about 12 billion per milliliter of rumen fluids in late autumn and winter, when rumen contents are driest, and about 11 billion per milliliter in spring, when deer ate succulent foods and rumen contents were more liquid. The presence of grasses, forbs, woody twigs, seeds, or fruit in the diet also affects the number and kinds of bacteria within the rumen. Both newly weaned and adult deer have similar quantities of microbes per unit of rumen contents.

Ciliate protozoa of the genus *Entodinium* also were found in the rumens of wild deer in Utah (Pearson 1969). The number of protozoa ranged from about 730,000 per milliliter of rumen fluid in late summer to as low as 160,000 per milliliter of rumen fluid in winter. The number of protozoa present was associated with forage availability and food quality and increased as the quality of the diet improved. Different kinds of microbes coexist at different relative levels of abundance within the rumen, and specific types of microbes may become more dominant as diet quality and pH of the rumen vary.

Protozoa within the rumen help digest cellulose, proteins, and polysaccharides (Annison and Lewis 1959). In addition, protein in protozoa that pass on from the rumen is digestible and useful to the deer.

Bacterial fermentations within the rumen are very complex. Streptococci produce lactic acid from starch and glucose. Lactobacilli produce lactic acid and some acetic acid from a variety of carbohydrates. Several types of cellulolytic bacteria digest cellulose, cellobiose, and some sugars and yield carbon dioxide, methane, and large quantities of volatile fatty acids (acetic, butyric, and propionic). Selenomonads ferment glucose and yield acetic, propionic, and lactic acids. Other organisms reduce sulfates to sulfides and digest a varied series of carbohydrates (Annison and Lewis 1959).

Carbohydrate Digestion in the Rumen

Carbohydrates are found extensively in plant tissues. Microbes within the deer rumen ferment plant carbohydrates and produce several different shortchain volatile fatty acids (VFAs). These VFAs are absorbed through the rumen wall and provide essential energy to deer. Different carbohydrates vary in composition and in the ease and completeness with which they are degraded within the rumen.

Cellulose—a structural carbohydrate found in plant cell walls—is readily attacked by a variety of rumen microbes, but its extensive digestion requires a lengthy fermentation period, and little or no digestion of cellulose occurs beyond the rumen. Acetic acid constitutes a high proportion—perhaps as much as 70 percent of molar composition—of volatile fatty acids produced from fermentation of cellulose. When deer eat leaves and mast (such as acorns) that contain the more easily digested nonstructural carbohydrates, microorganisms adapted to fermenting these foodstuffs bloom at the expense of cellulolytic microbes, and cellulose digestion of other foods within the rumen is reduced. Cellulose and hemicelluloses, especially when combined with lignin, are the most difficult of plant carbohydrates to ferment.

Starches—a prominent carbohydrate reserve in seeds and plant-storage organs—are fermented readily within the rumen and produce a lower acetic-propionic acid ratio (relatively more propionic acid) per unit of food than does cellulose digestion. Increased production of propionic or butyric acids in fermentation products means more calories to deer because acetic acid has a heat of combustion only about 59 percent that of propionic acid and only about 42 percent that of butyric acid. Unlike cellulose digestion, which is restricted to the rumen-reticulum, starch digestion can also occur within the small intestine of deer, and starch granules stored in rumen protozoa may be digested when protozoa pass into the small intestine.

Other carbohydrates vary in their utility to deer. Pentosans, an important constituent of mature grass, and fructosan, a constituent of immature grasses, both are fermented readily within the rumen. Simple sugars—available as photosynthetic products and as metabolites in the rumen digestion of starches, hemicelluloses, and fructosans—also occur as substrates for bacterial and protozoan fermentation. Glucose, fructose, and sucrose generally are fermented more quickly than are maltose, lactose, and galactose. The digestion of sugars and starches yields more propionic acid and therefore more calories to deer than is realized from the digestion of cellulose. This increased energy yield is important both for the metabolism of deer and for the growth of rumen microbes that synthesize other important nutrients deer require.

Relative amounts of the various volatile fatty acids within the rumen vary depending on the type of plant carbohydrate eaten and digested. Relative concentration of fermentation products within the rumen of a deer at any particular time is a rough index of fermentation rate within the rumen. Some measure of the quality of a deer's diet and therefore the quality of its environment is indicated by fermentation products in the deer's stomach. Total concentration of VFAs is greatest when easily fermentable foodstuffs are eaten and when a high population of healthy rumen microbes is present. Rumen contents under these conditions are thick and heavy. Deer utilizing less desirable foodstuffs, as often occurs during winter, have a diminished ruminoreticular fill, and the rumen contents are drier while the liquid phase of contents may be watery. The VFA concentrations and energy represented by rumen VFAs are reduced.

Mule deer increase the energy potentially available to them by selecting foods carefully. Cellulose in mature grasses or twigs, for example, is fermented slowly and yields mostly acetic acid with its reduced caloric equivalence. Mast or mushrooms are fermented quickly and yield more total VFAs per food unit and more propionic and higher acids with increased caloric values. Mule deer ranges in western North America normally undergo a transition from good quality forage during the growing season to fair or poor quality forage when vegetation is dormant during cold and/or dry seasons. For example, mule deer feeding on good quality winter range in north-central Colorado ate dried weeds, leaves, and twigs of browse species such as bitterbrush, mountain mahogany, and other mature forages of little succulence. The ruminoreticular contents were relatively dry (15.6 percent dry matter), and the molar percentages of the VFAs of fermentation were 68 percent acetic acid, 20 percent propionic acid, and 12 percent butyric and

Mule deer buck in velvet exhibits selective browsing. Photograph by Leonard Lee Rue III.

Forage quality as well as availability within most mule and black-tailed deer habitats changes from season to season, and the deer must adjust either by movement or by altered feeding habits. Photographs from a subalpine forest in southern Alberta; taken by Valerius Geist.

higher acids. During late spring and summer, when the mule deer were feeding on succulent vegetation of high protein content on high-altitude summer range, the rumen dry matter content was 13.6 percent and the VFAs were 63 percent acetic acid, 22 percent propionic acid, and 15 percent butyric and higher acids (Short et al. 1966).

The physiology of the rumen of a healthy deer, with an abundant population of rumen microbes, changes throughout the day. After a deer eats, the more easily fermented foodstuffs are digested quickly, producing a fermentation "bloom." The more refractory food materials that require an extended fermentation time are digested later. Products of rumen fermentation, such as gases and volatile fatty acids, vary in rate of formation according to time since food was consumed. Rumen dry matter increases during eating and gradually diminishes as digestion occurs. Gases and volatile fatty acids are produced at high rates when available sugars and starches are digested quickly after a meal. Later, after the easily digested carbohydrates are digested, fermentation rate slows. Periodic feeding of quality rations maintains relatively steady fermentation rates. At any time, the rumen may contain food residues from several meals. Portions of a particular meal may be retained in the rumen of deer from many hours to several days. Irregular feeding reduces the frequency of fermentation "blooms," and foodstuffs with few readily digestible carbohydrates reduce the extent of these "blooms."

Lipid Digestion in the Rumen

The crude fat content of vegetation eaten by mule deer varies. Blades and stems of tufted hair grass from high-altitude mountain meadows may contain only 1 percent crude fat, leaves of mountain mahogany contain about 3 percent, and leaves of Rocky Mountain juniper during the winter contain about 19 percent. When the crude fat of foods is highly digestible, it provides readily available energy to deer because fats have more than twice the caloric value of carbohydrates.

Crude fats in plants are mainly glycerides but also may include waxes, sterols, and phospholipids (Church 1969). Glycerides mainly contain unsaturated fatty acids, and linolenic acid often is most abundant.

The nature of dietary fats has little effect on the composition of fat deposits in deer. Fat deposits of many ruminants contain a high proportion of saturated fatty acids. For white-tailed deer and presumably mule deer, stearic and palmitic acids predominate (Garton et al. 1971). The hydrogenation of many unsaturated fatty acids and some phospholipids is accomplished by both bacteria and protozoa within the rumen. Some hydrogenation also may occur in the lower gastrointestinal tract. Other fatty acids are synthesized within the rumen from both plant lipids and carbohydrates.

During late summer to midautumn, deer synthesize lipids and deposit saturated fats under their skin and around many internal organs. The high energy values of these fat stores—which may amount to 15 percent of body weight (Wallmo et al. 1977)—help deer survive the winter season. Lipids are not deposited extensively earlier in the year, presumably because of metabolic demands involving recovery of condition from the previous winter, fetal development, milk production, and antler development.

The Role of Nitrogen

Omnivores and carnivores, with relatively unspecialized gastrointestinal tracts, must consume enough protein to provide necessary amino acids. Food proteins digested within the stomach and small intestine are absorbed as peptides or amino acids. For deer and other ruminants, food protein is extensively digested by rumen microbes that then use the available nitrogen to synthesize amino acids and microbial proteins later digested in the abomasum and small intestine.

An advantage of ruminant digestion is that, whereas forage protein varies in quality throughout the year, microbial protein synthesized within the rumen remains of good quality and digestibility. Still, the quantity of nitrogen in the foods consumed is important. Optimum growth and production has been reported for diets of 16 percent protein, but deer develop slowly, and reproductive success is low on diets of 7 percent protein or less (Verme and Ullrey 1972).

A portion of dietary protein is degraded to peptides and amino acids by action of microbes in the rumen. The nature of dietary protein determines the extent of digestion in the rumen. Presence of inhibitors, such as tannins, may affect the amount of dietary protein actually converted to microbial protein (Church 1969). Peptides and amino acids are digestion products that may be reduced further to ammonia or synthesized into nitrogen compounds within rumen microbes. Volatile fatty acids, carbon dioxide, and ammonia are products of the degradation of amino acids. Ammonia is transported through the portal vein to the liver, where it is converted to urea. Some urea is excreted later in urine, and some is secreted through the rumen wall or as part of saliva that is returned to the rumen. Plant proteins that yield large quantities of ammonia may be used with less efficiency than proteins that are degraded more slowly in the rumen or lower gastrointestinal tract.

A variety of nitrogen compounds are available for synthesis of microbial proteins within the rumen. These include ammonia, proteins, nucleotides, peptides, and some free amino acids. When ruminants are fed diets low in protein content, or when they are starved, urea is secreted through the rumen walls to supply nitrogen to rumen microbes and maintain a viable rumen microbial population. When deer are unable to maintain a healthy, though diminished, supply of rumen microbes during a period of severe environmental conditions, they are unable to digest food when it is next available. They then starve. Ruminants generally do not require specific nitrogen compounds in the rumen. Microbes constantly die and add various nitrogenous compounds in the

rumen. Sometimes, however, microbial productivity of domestic ruminants is improved by providing specific amino acids in their diets (Fontenot 1971). This suggests that microbial synthesis of nitrogenous compounds does not completely satisfy amino acid requirements. Easily digested foodstuffs—such as mast, succulent and immature grasses and forbs, and browse leaves—provide more energy for rumen metabolism and microbial nitrogen synthesis than do diets high in cellulose, such as mature grasses and forbs or woody twigs (table 19). Products of rumen fermentation are formed at higher rates when easily digested foodstuffs are eaten.

The amount of microbial protein synthesized within the rumen and subsequently digested by mule deer is not known but undoubtedly is several grams per day. Rumen microbes contain high levels of readily digestible crude protein relatively rich in amino acids. The daily yield of microbial protein varies considerably in relation to the composition of food and the rate of food consumption. Plants are high in protein and low in fiber content during the season of rapid vegetational growth. When mature, these same plants are relatively high in fiber and low in protein. The protein present in mature perennial forages is largely restricted to buds and leaf chloroplasts. Proteins in dead vegetation

Table 19. Cell Wall Contents and Estimated Digestibility of Some Different Types of Forage

Food	Cell-Wall Content as Percentage of Dry Matter	Lignin as Percentage of Lignocellulose Content	Estimated Digestibility (percentage)	
			True Digestibility[a]	Nylon Bag Dry Matter Digestibility[b]
Immature grasses	37	10	87	94
Mature grasses	85	18	56	20
Immature forbs	44	25	71	69
Mature forbs	75	24	53	27
Leaves	31	41	73	71
Fallen and weathered leaves	49	54	50	45
Immature woody twigs	36	33	73	75
Mature woody twigs	62	37	52	40
Acorns	40	48	65	68
Fleshy fruits	41	49	64	69
Legume seeds	40	21	78	87
Mushrooms	39	6	93	95

[a] Estimated true digestibility (Goering and Van Soest 1970).

[b] Nylon bag dry matter digestibility: forty-eight hours of incubation (Short et al. 1974; Short et al. 1975; Short and Epps 1976).

may be degraded and leached from plant tissues by rain. Therefore dead plant tissues will not satisfy the nitrogen requirements of deer. Seeds (especially those of legumes), mushrooms, and actively photosythesizing green leaves are relatively high in protein content, while mature grasses and mature woody twigs are relatively low. The changing rate of food consumption by deer throughout the year coincides with differences in food abundance at different seasons. Even when captive deer are offered unlimited amounts of adequate rations, they consume more food during seasons when native food sources are succulent and abundant and less during seasons when range foods are dormant and less digestible (Bandy et al. 1970).

Ranges that provide deer with sufficient dietary protein in all seasons seem to be superior to those where forage protein occasionally is deficient. Diets that provide 15–16 percent protein during seasons of production when growth, fattening, pregnancy, and lactation occur, and about 10 percent protein during seasons of maintenance, probably are adequate for deer.

VITAMIN REQUIREMENTS

Most vitamin requirements of an unweaned fawn are supplied by its lactating dam. Most potential vitamin-related problems disappear as the fawn becomes a functional ruminant.

Carotene is common in green vegetation, and animals can store enough of vitamin A or its precursors to overcome periods of dietary scarcity. More carotene, for example, was present in the liver of mule deer from north-central Colorado during late spring, summer, and early autumn than during other months (Anderson et al. 1972*b*). Vitamin D—important in metabolism of calcium and phosphorus—has a precursor in the body that is activated by radiant solar energy. Adequate levels of vitamin E are attained through consumption of green forage and efficient storage of the vitamin within the body. Ruminants have no dietary need for vitamin C. Vitamin K,

thiamine, riboflavin, nicotinamide, vitamin B_6, pantothenic acid, biotin, folic acid, and vitamin B_{12} are synthesized within the rumen (Maynard and Loosli 1956). Nutritional deficiencies encountered by mule deer can be traced to energy, nitrogen, or minerals, but apparently not to vitamins.

WATER REQUIREMENTS

A large portion of the body of an adult mule deer is water. The proportion is even greater in fetuses and fawns. The amount of body water in adult deer varies as the amount of carcass fat changes throughout the year. Water within body cells may be nearly 50 percent of mature deer weight. In blood plasma and outside the body cells, water may account for nearly another 20 percent of body weight. It acts as a lubricant, a solvent for biochemical reactions, a medium for transporting nutrients to and wastes from cells, and a buffer in temperature regulation. Water also is important in maintaining the electrolyte and acid-base balances of the body. Body water is dynamic, and several environmental factors—such as temperature, humidity, forage succulence, and rate of food consumption—affect the water content of body tissues.

Foods vary in succulence. The moisture content of mushrooms may be 95 percent, of berries and fruits 80 percent, of succulent leaves 70 percent, of mature leaves 55 percent, of succulent woody twigs 80 percent, and of mature woody twigs less than 45 percent. Mature, weathered, and field-dried herbaceous materials have very low moisture levels. Changing food habits provide differing amounts of forage water to deer. The moisture content of the rumen-reticulum of mule deer is greater in summer when succulent foods are eaten than during winter when range forages are dry and fibrous (Short et al. 1966). Metabolic water derived from biochemical reactions within cells also supplies some water to mule deer. Free water presumably is the most important source for maintaining a favorable water balance. The attraction of free water to deer is especially evident in desert habitats.

Free water sources are particularly important for deer in habitats where succulent vegetation is at a premium and where the water is critical in temperature regulation. Photograph courtesy of the United States Forest Service.

Deer that consume succulent forage require less free water. Captive white-tailed deer fed a pelleted dry ration drank about 2.9 kilograms (6.4 pounds) of water for each kilogram (2.2 pounds) of food eaten. The deer drank only about 0.5 kilogram (1.1 pounds) of water per kilogram (2.2 pounds) of food when fed fresh succulent browse (Verme and Ullrey 1972). During winter, deer utilize snow as a source of free water. Water intake by deer seems related to dry matter intake (Church 1971), so that water requirements probably are greater in late spring, summer, and early autumn when food consumption is greatest. Succulent forage can provide some of the water required during seasons when the water needed for temperature regulation increases. Pregnant mule deer have significantly increased water requirements during late gestation, and water requirements are great during lactation.

Water is lost in urine, fecal excretion, and sweat and from the lungs. When the water balance is upset, so that more water is lost than gained, dehydration normally will cause reduced food intake, reduced urinary excretion, drier fecal pellets, and losses in plasma and intra- and extracellular body water with a resulting upset in blood chemistry and electrolyte balance. Fawns, with a greater relative metabolic rate, probably are more sensitive to water deprivation and consequently succumb more quickly to this form of stress than do adult deer.

MINERAL REQUIREMENTS

Minerals are necessary for growth, development, and metabolism of mule deer. Calcium, besides being the major mineral constituent of bones and teeth, also has a role in blood clotting, in maintaining neuromuscular irritability, and in the acid-base equilibrium of the body. Fawns absorb calcium from milk with great efficiency, but the efficiency with which weaned deer absorb calcium from digested vegetation is considerably reduced. Calcium can be mobilized and transported from the skeleton during periods when body demands are large and when calcium intake is inadequate, such as during early antler development (Cowan et al. 1968), pregnancy and lactation (Maynard and Loosli 1956).

Calcium probably is at adequate levels in vegetation on western ranges, and nutritional problems that occur there usually are related to high calcium levels in vegetation combined with very low phosphorus values. Dietary calcium at a level of 0.40 percent of dietary dry matter in the presence of 0.25–0.27 percent phosphorus is adequate for postweaning fawns (Ullrey et al. 1973). Levels of calcium and phosphorus somewhat higher than these values (0.59 percent calcium and 0.54 percent phosphorus) produce the best antler growth in mature white-tailed bucks (Magruder et al. 1957). A useful recommendation for deer management is that phosphorus levels should be about 0.20–0.25 percent of the diet, and calcium should be no more than one to five times the phosphorus level.

Phosphorus is an important constituent of bones, teeth, and red blood cells. This mineral is important in the absorption and transport of nutrients throughout the body. Phosphorus also is important in the process of oxidative phosphorylation, in high energy pyrophosphate bonds, nucleic acids, and the buffering of body fluids. Phosphorus content of range vegetation may be deficient seasonally or commonly throughout many western mule deer ranges, and this deficiency may affect the well-being of deer inhabiting those ranges. When ruminants feed on phosphorus-deficient forage, they experience a decrease in inorganic blood phosphorus level, depletion of the mineral content of bones, diminished rates of weight gain and milk production, and a possible reduction in fertility (Church 1971). Future management of mule deer may require supplements on some ranges to correct dietary inadequacies of this important mineral.

Much of the sodium in the body of mule deer is confined to extracellular fluids, where it affects the regulation of pH and the maintenance of osmotic gradients, and is functional in buffer systems. Sodium also plays a role in the transmission of nerve impulses. Mule deer use natural salt licks or mineral blocks supplied for domestic livestock, and they may drink brackish surface water when vegetation is inadequate in sodium. Many types of forage on a mule deer range in north-central Colorado were low in sodium content (Short et al. 1966).

Most of the potassium in deer occurs in body cells. This mineral aids in transmission of nerve impulses in muscle contraction, and enhances the function of some enzyme systems (Church 1971). Many range plants probably have enough potassium to supply the metabolic requirements of deer. Leaves of juniper, rabbitbrush, sagebrush, aspen, and willow on a deer range in north-central Colorado contained at least 0.5 percent potassium—a level that would provide more than the estimated minimum dietary requirement.

Chlorine occurs in body fluids, where it helps regulate osmotic pressure and maintain tissue pH values (Church 1971). Foodstuffs available to mule deer apparently provide sufficient dietary chlorine for normal body requirements.

Magnesium is found in skeletal tissues, some soft tissues, muscles, and blood serum. Magnesium also is an important constituent of many enzyme systems. Magnesium levels in many types of forage available to mule deer are 0.15 percent or more of dry matter, which seems adequate for normal body requirements.

Sulfur is present in some amino acids, vitamins, and peptides. The sulfur content of common range plants apparently is adequate for mule deer.

Iron is found in hemoglobin, myoglobin, and blood serum. This mineral functions in oxygen transport and in some enzyme systems. Although grasses sometimes are deficient in iron, it seems probable that forage eaten by mule deer contains sufficient iron.

Iodine is concentrated in the thyroid gland. Reduced thyroid hormone levels result in a diminished basal metabolic rate and reproductive failure. Iodine requirements of mule deer are greatest during late spring, summer, and early autumn, when mule deer are in production status. Iodine deficiencies have been reported in domestic livestock grazing vegetation in eastern Montana, North Dakota, the Pacific Northwest, British Columbia, and other scattered areas within the general range of mule deer (Dukes 1955). There could be areas where forage iodine deficiencies affect mule deer herds. Providing iodized salt might be a useful management practice in these instances.

Copper is important in several enzyme systems. Copper deficiencies can occur because of either low dietary intake of copper or excessive amounts of molybdenum or sulfates in the diet. Copper poisoning can occur if copper intake is normal but molybdenum ingestion is very low. Mule deer probably do not encounter difficulties in copper metabolism when eating vegetation growing on western soils.

Other trace minerals, such as cobalt, zinc, and manganese, probably occur at adequate levels in plants on mule deer range.

Selenium is required at very low dietary levels. The absence of selenium from the diet, as sometimes occurs on soils of volcanic origin, may cause nutritional muscular dystrophy, which is debilitating to the animal. Selenium occurs at high levels in soils of the northern Great Plains and northern and central Rocky Mountain states, where it may be toxic to range animals grazing certain plants. When ingested at rates above trace requirements, selenium may cause alkali disease, which can be fatal to cattle and sheep (Church 1971). Mule deer throughout the West encounter forage deficient in selenium as well as forage with excessive selenium. It is not known if mule deer on western ranges are affected by either nutritional muscular dystrophy or alkali disease.

INTAKE AND PASSAGE OF FOODSTUFFS

Forage Digestibility

Forage varies in nutrient composition at different stages of maturity. Vegetation that is green and growing is more useful to animals than is either mature or weathered plant tissue. Intelligent husbandry of domestic ruminants includes harvesting forage while nutrient quality is high and storing it to be used in seasons when wild foods are of low quality. Livestock also are selected for their ability to maintain relatively high production levels even during seasons when wild forage is mature and of reduced digestibility. Mule deer, however, voluntarily reduce food consumption during late autumn and winter and remain in a maintenance state rather than a production state at this time.

Forage quality can be expressed in terms of chemical solubility of plant tissues. Results from digestion trials where mule deer were fed rations compounded from bitterbrush, mountain mahogany and big sagebrush or were fed fresh bitterbrush or fresh mountain mahogany indicated that cell contents (sugars, starches, fructosans, organic acids, lipids, and protein and nonprotein nitrogen) were 98 percent digestible (Short and Reagor 1970). Cell-wall contents (lignin, hemicellulose, and cellulose) vary in quantity among plants and are of limited digestibility to deer. Hemicellulose and cellulose are digested only by microbial action, and lignin is considered indigestible.

Different foodstuffs have various cell-content/cell-wall ratios and different cell-wall components. Proportions of hemicellulose, cellulose, and lignin are variable, and lignin differs in chemical composition among plant tissues. Grasses characteristically have a high cell-wall content compared with other types of forage but have a relatively small amount of lignin in cell walls (table 19). Forbs such as alfalfa and many broad-leaved weeds characteristically have a lower total cell-wall content but a higher lignin content. Whether they develop from seeds or perennial roots, grasses and forbs sequentially develop leaves for photosynthesis, produce flower stalks, and develop buds, flowers, and seeds. Leaf tissues, stems, flowers, or fruit each may be the dominant plant tissue at some time during the growing season. The different tissues vary in composition so that foods available to mule deer throughout the growing season vary in nutrient content. As grasses and forbs develop beyond leafy and succulent stages, they increase substantially in cell-wall components, have somewhat more lignin in their cell walls, contain fewer cell contents, and become less digestible (table 19).

Mule deer frequently browse leaves and twigs of trees and shrubs. Green leaves are very succulent and, except for epidermal tissue and structural ribs, consist largely of easily digestible cell contents. The low cell-wall content of leaves, however, is characterized by a high lignin-lignocellulose proportion. Even when mature, leaves of most broad-leaved plants are fairly succulent, with good levels of cell contents. As long as photosynthesis continues, they remain good-quality deer forage. Nutrients in deciduous leaves frequently are transferred back into woody twigs before leaf fall. Dead and weathered leaves have little protein and high cell-wall values and frequently are of very low digestibility (table 19).

Woody twigs of perennial trees and shrubs develop from buds produced during the previous year. Twig elongation occurs only during a relatively brief portion of the total growing season. During rapid growth, cell-wall components and digestibility of succulent twigs are similar to that of green leaf tissue. After twig elongation has ceased, the twig matures, hardens, and becomes woody in appearance. At this time twigs are low in digestibility, with cell-wall components frequently greater than 60 percent of dry matter and with lignin-lignocellulose ratios greater than those of grasses and forbs (table 19).

Mule deer also eat acorns, legume seeds, and fleshy fruits, including berries and drupes, that have moderate cell-wall levels and are easily digested (table 19). Mushrooms and other fungi have low fiber levels and are highly digestible.

The goal of range management should be to provide deer with foods of high cell content and low lignocellulose levels. Seasonal ranges that provide only mature woody twigs, dead and weathered leaves, and dormant grasses as deer food will present nutritional problems that, in turn, result in reduced productivity (see also chap. 9, part 1, and chap. 10, part 1).

Food Passage Rates

The quantity of food eaten by mule deer varies. The rate of flow of foodstuffs through the gastrointestinal tract is increased when food consumption rates are high. Lowered retention time of food within the digestive tract

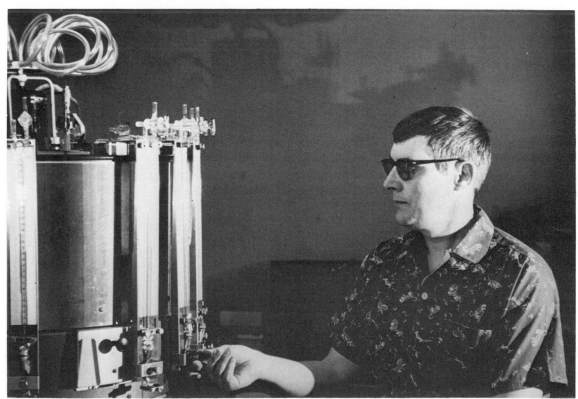

This Warburg apparatus was used at the Hopland Field Station in California to measure the rate of fermentation of various forage species by deer rumen microbes. Flasks (in a controlled-temperature water bath) contained mixtures of plant samples and fresh deer rumen fluid. Fermentation produced gas, whose internal pressure was measured on mercury columns. Serial readings gave information about rates of fermentation activity over twenty-four and forty-eight-hour periods. Such studies suggested that deer tend to prefer plants and plant parts that are easily digested by their rumen microbes (Longhurst et al. 1968). Photograph by Guy E. Connolly.

occurs during seasons when immature, succulent, and easily digested plant foods are eaten. High food consumption rates and easily digested food stuffs produce abundant digestible nutrients during late spring, summer, and early autumn, in contrast to diminished levels in late autumn and winter. Products of rumen fermentation during the plant growth seasons often are of increased energy values to deer.

The length of time foods are retained within the ruminant digestive tract depends on the quality and kind of food eaten and the species of ruminant. Mule deer, with a rumen-reticulum that is relatively small compared with that of the cow, for example, are very selective feeders who thoroughly masticate their food. They frequently retain foodstuffs in their rumen for less than a day. Retention time of several wild foods fed to white-tailed deer varied from 14 to 28 hours (Mautz and Petrides 1971). Deer benefit from foodstuffs that are digested quickly and yield abundant fermentation products within normal retention times.

Food and Energy Intake

Deer depend on their ability to maintain a positive energy balance over an extended period. Their every action can be expressed in terms of energy. Seeking food, eating, microbial fermentation within the rumen, belching fermentation gases, intestinal digestion of microbial rumen fermentation products, absorption of digested nutrients, and excretion of waste products require energy and are negative functions associated with digestion. Maintenance of muscle tone, pumping blood, production of body fluids, growth of hair, deposition of bone, protein, and fat, pregnancy and fetal growth, lactation, development of antlers, and other processes of maintenance and production require additional expenditures of energy. Balanced against these demands is the energy value of the products of digestion. Over an extended period, an animal loses or gains weight depending on whether its energy intake is deficient or in excess of energy expenditures.

Mule deer eat foods that vary drastically in composition and ease of digestion throughout the year. The gross energy of a foodstuff (total calories measured in a bomb calorimeter under prescribed conditions so that combustion is complete) might not vary greatly among stages of growth, but the energy required for digestion may vary considerably because of differences in plant composition. The return of digestible energy to deer from 10 grams (0.35 ounces) of dry matter of a mature forb thus is less than that from 10 grams (0.35 ounces) of dry matter of the same forb when succulent and immature.

The amount of food consumed by black-tailed deer varies throughout the year, even when they have access to unlimited supplies of quality food (fig. 16). Gross energy intake for deer also varies among seasons. Generally, maximum rates of food and energy intake for bucks occur during summer. Food and gross energy intake diminish, and bucks become very active after antlers mature. Consequently, they lose weight (fig. 17). The relative weight loss in late autumn and winter apparently is greater for older males. A very abrupt drop in food and gross energy intake (fig. 16) is characteristic of

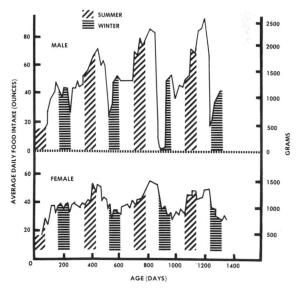

Figure 16. Food consumption rates of black-tailed deer of designated ages are high in summer and reduced in winter (after Bandy et al. 1970). Each 20-ounce unit equals about 0.57 kilograms.

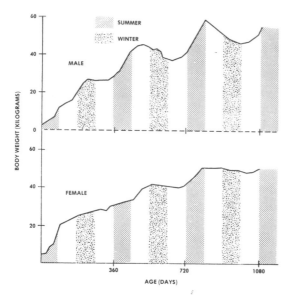

Figure 17. Black-tailed deer—even with unlimited quantities of quality rations available at all times—gain weight in summer and lose weight during winter (after Nordan et al. 1970). Each 20-kilogram unit equals about 44 pounds.

bucks during the rut (Bandy et al. 1970). Throughout the remainder of winter, food and gross energy intake increases to an intermediate level, and body weight stabilizes. As food and gross energy intake for male deer increases during spring and summer, weight loss is recovered, antler growth is initiated, and further body growth occurs. Food consumption during summer in the Sonoran desert of the Southwest may be affected by heat stress, so that the pattern of food consumption may differ somewhat throughout the mule deer range.

Does also reduce food and gross energy intake during late autumn and winter, but they do not duplicate the fasting level characteristic of bucks during the rut (Bandy et al. 1970). Food and gross energy intake is increased during spring. Does in late pregnancy are in a production state, and additional metabolic demands are met by increased energy intake at this time. Bandy et al. (1970) suggested that the prolonged and feverish rutting behavior in bucks—as opposed to the brief, discontinuous, and quiescent heat periods of the doe—may account for differences in their respective rates of energy intake during autumn and winter. Reduced gross energy intake of mule deer

during late autumn and winter may be a response to normal environmental stresses during these seasons. Increased energy intake in spring and summer, when wild forage is more available and digestible, also seems to be a physiological adaptation by deer to the seasonal quality of their environment.

The length of the daylight period may be the external stimulus that influences seasonal changes in rates of food intake. Light-mediated endocrine glands, through secretions, affect the central nervous system and may stimulate deer to eat at higher rates during summer than during winter. The concentration of tissue metabolites, or a feeling of fullness in the gastrointestinal tract, may be the internal stimulus that determines feeding behavior throughout the day (Church 1971).

ENERGY METABOLISM

Cellular Metabolism

The total energy demands of mule deer depend on energy requirements of individual cells, tissues, and organs. Some compounds absorbed from the gastrointestinal tract are carried by the portal vein to the liver, where they are removed and eventually excreted in urine. Other compounds, such as the volatile fatty acids, amino acids, and long-chain fatty acids, are absorbed into the bloodstream and transported to individual cells, where they are used both as sources of energy and as building blocks in the synthesis of other body tissues.

Metabolites transported in arterial blood are oxidized within body tissues, such as muscles, to yield carbon dioxide, water, and energy for tissue work. The actual oxidation of food materials occurs along the "final metabolic pathway" (tricarboxylic acid cycle), where compounds like acetic acid, propionic acid, blood glucose, fatty acids from fats, and amino acids from proteins are oxidized. Much energy from these oxidations results in formation of the terminal pyrophosphate bond of adenosine triphosphate (ATP) from adenosine diphosphate (ADP) through a process called "oxidative phosphorylation." The energy available in the pyrophosphate bonds of ATP is a large portion of the energy obtained from the actual oxidation of foodstuffs. ATP has been termed the "energy currency" of the body (Blaxter 1962) because it provides energy for such diverse functions as synthesis of peptide bonds in protein formation, muscular contraction, absorption of substances such as food metabolites across cell membranes so cell metabolism can continue, oxidation in the tricarboxylic cycle, and conduction of nerve impulses. Enzyme systems required for the complex tricarboxylic acid cycle and oxidative phosphorylation exist in the mitochondria that occur as numerous small inclusions within the cytoplasm of individual cells (Blaxter 1962).

Metabolic Rate

Basal metabolism in mule deer represents the amount of energy necessary to keep an animal alive. It is the energy cost of blood circulation, respiration, nerve impulses, manufacture of secretions, maintenance of muscle tone, and even production of pyrophosphate bonds in cellular respiration. Basal metabolic measurements do not include energy costs of digestion; they are performed after foods have been digested and absorbed from the gastrointestinal tract. Fasting metabolic rates, rather than basal metabolic rates, usually are measured in metabolic chambers because deer do not remain motionless in the chambers. Fasting values are slightly greater than basal values.

The basal metabolism of mule deer is accounted for mainly by the metabolic demands of individual tissues and organs. Metabolic demands increase when animals become active, because tissues and organs require more energy for increased function. Tissues and organs of fawns are both functioning and growing, and the basal metabolic rate of young deer per unit of body weight is relatively greater than that measured for mature deer.

Indirect respiration calorimeter chambers are used to measure fasting metabolic rate in deer. Photograph by Haven Hayes.

Most warm-blooded animals have a body temperature near 38 degrees Celsius (100 degrees Fahrenheit), with a heat loss that is proportional to the radiating surface area of the body. They have a basal metabolic rate that approximates 70 kilocalories per kilogram of body weight $^{0.75}$. The metabolic rate of mule deer may be slightly higher than that rate during midwinter, and it is substantially higher during spring and summer. This is assumed from the fasting metabolic rate of white-tailed bucks, which is about 20 percent greater than the interspecific mean value of 70 kilocalories per kilogram of body weight $^{0.75}$ during winter and 70 percent greater during summer (Silver et al. 1971). The lower fasting metabolic rate in winter corresponds to a period when food consumption is decreased, whereas the high summer rate occurs at a time when the rate of food consumption is high (fig. 16). It is interesting that light-mediated endocrine glands—such as the pituitary and thyroid, which are associated with appetite regulation, growth, and metabolism—generally are smaller in mule deer during winter, when daylight length is reduced, and are larger during summer, when daylight length is greatest (A. E. Anderson et al. 1974).

Ambient temperatures, wind velocities, and relative humidity may affect the ability of mule deer to maintain heat production near the fasting metabolic level. Behavior is important, since deer can voluntarily avoid some unpleasant environmental circumstance such as intense summer heat or light on deserts of the Southwest and exposed sites on wet, cold, and windy days in the Northwest. The insulating capacity of a deer's coat is especially important during winter. Body hair of increased length and thickness with more insulative value grows in response to shortened daylight length. When temperatures dropped to −9 degrees Celsius (18 degrees Fahrenheit), heat production of buck white-tailed deer increased 91 percent from that measured at thermoneutrality (Silver et al. 1971). Thermoneutrality is the environmental temperature that is moderate enough so it does not cause an increase in the animal's metabolism. A buck whose hair had been clipped had to increase heat production to 500

percent above basal metabolic rates to balance body heat loss. The role of body hair in modifying heat loss is discussed further by Moen (1973).

Receptors within the deer detect deep body temperature, while those on the skin detect air temperature. In response to these stimuli, heat loss is reduced or increased by a regulation of temperature in peripheral tissues. In winter, a mule deer may curl up, fluff its hair, and, through involuntary muscular reactions, shiver and constrict muscles around blood vessels, thereby limiting blood supply to the skin. These actions all help reduce heat loss through radiation, convection, and conduction. Extremities such as large ears and long legs undergo cyclical changes of rapid heating and slow cooling by regulation of blood flow rate through the skin that helps keep legs and ears from freezing in cold weather (Blaxter 1962). There is a critical temperature that varies because of the animal's insulation and below which the restriction of blood flow to the skin of deer is ineffective in reducing heat loss from the body. Mechanisms such as shivering and metabolism of body fats then become neces-

Mule deer fawns exhibit physiological and behavioral responses to reduce heat loss in cold winter weather. Both deer show piloerection. The standing fawn shows a thick winter coat; the other fawn rests in a curled position. Photograph courtesy of the Wyoming Department of Game and Fish.

sary for increasing body heat. During hot weather, deer can stretch out to maximize their radiating surface area. They usually limit heat-generating activities during the hottest hours. During this season they have a lighter coat that provides less insulation so they are able to increase heat loss from the skin.

Mule deer inhabiting hot, dry habitats in the southwestern United States encounter environmental conditions that cause heat stress and lowered food consumption in domestic livestock. Months of greatest heat stress for deer are those when late gestation, parturition, and lactation occur. This stress may contribute to low fawn crops observed in these hot, dry habitats.

Energy Costs for Activity

Results from calorimetric studies on other animals (Blaxter 1962) suggest that mule deer might require 10–15 percent more energy if they stand rather than remain in a reclining position for 24 hours. A mule deer might increase its fasting energy expenditure by 1 percent for every five or six times it stands up or lies down. Play, climbing, and running also increase energy expenditures. A calf at play may require 10 percent more energy, a cow on range may require 15 percent more energy, and a sheep on range may require 20 percent more energy than their respective fasting metabolic levels (Blaxter 1962). Normal activity in a mule deer may require energy at a rate about 25–50 percent above fasting energy metabolism. Extremely vigorous activity, such as escape actions, may require energy at a rate 50–100 percent above fasting energy expenditures.

If some form of vigorous activity required an energy expenditure 50 percent above the fasting energy expenditures, then mature deer would be expending energy at a rate about 2.6 times the interspecific mean metabolic rate during the production season, and at a rate about 1.8 times the mean interspecific metabolic rate during the maintenance season.

During a period of high temperature, a mule deer buck (in velvet) and doe rest in stretched-out positions to maximize their radiating surfaces. They also are maintaining close proximity to free water and minimizing heat-generating activity. Photograph by Olaus J. Murie; courtesy of the United States National Archives.

Unusually strenuous activity in periods of nutritional stress can dramatically increase energy expenditures and contribute directly to deer mortality. Photograph by Geoff Tischbein; courtesy of the Colorado Division of Wildlife.

During winter, when digestible energy intake is reduced severely and may not even equal the fasting metabolic rate, activities such as dog or snowmobile chases quickly deplete energy reserves and contribute directly to deer mortality.

The energy required by activities comes from products of digestion and stored reserves. If a foodstuff is 50 percent digestible, its apparent digestible energy may be half its gross energy. Other energy losses can occur before any energy is available for maintenance or production. The gases resulting from microbial fermentation represent one source of energy lost to deer. Heat generated by the fermentation process also is a loss, although this heat may be useful to deer during cold weather. Every kilocalorie of energy available for maintenance or production requires about 1.7 kilocalories of apparently digested energy (Blaxter 1962). Only about 30 percent of the gross energy of a foodstuff that is 50 percent digestible actually may be available to mule deer for maintenance and production. Extreme exertion and adverse environmental conditions can cause energy expenditure in excess of net energy intake.

Mule deer encounter foodstuffs that vary greatly in quantity, quality, and digestibility

Indirect respiration calorimetry using a face mask enables measurement of energy expenditure for different activities and a variety of environmental conditions (Mautz 1978). Photograph by William Seitz.

throughout the year. Stress is encountered when foodstuffs are unavailable or of high fiber content and low digestibility so that net energy does not equal the requirements for fasting metabolism or normal foraging behavior. Malnutrition for long periods is more serious for young deer because body proteins are utilized more quickly and more thoroughly than they are in older animals with greater fat reserves. Adult female mule deer, originally in good physical condition, have been starved during midwinter for about nine weeks (deCalesta et al. 1975). When fed, most does readily recovered their approximately 30 percent loss in body weight. One-third of a group of fawns, housed under similar conditions and starved for about five weeks, exhausted fat reserves, began to metabolize body proteins extensively, and died (deCalesta et al. 1975). When fed, surviving does and fawns readily became functional ruminants, indicating that some populations of rumen microbes survived the fasting period. These experimental deer were housed under conditions that produced few demands beyond fasting metabolic requirements.

Adaptations by mule deer during winter include reduced demands for growth and production, restricted activities (except during the rut), and a lowered fasting metabolic rate demanding fewer nutrients to sustain life.

Energy Costs for Production

Gross energy intake and fasting metabolic rates of mule deer increase during spring and early summer, presumably because of the influence of increased daylight length on those endocrine glands that affect deer metabolism. These changes occur at a time when new and succulent forage is growing on many mule deer ranges. Easily and quickly digested types of forage are eaten at high rates; metabolites are readily absorbed; and the net energy available to deer is greatly increased.

Quality nutrition is essential for reproduction in mule deer. If nutrition is suitable only for maintenance, then productive functions suffer. Reduced body weights, small antlers, and low reproductive success occur. A main

Malnutrition affects fawns more seriously than older deer because fawns lack abundant energy reserves and yet have relatively large metabolic demands per unit of body weight. The fawn shown here is much weaker than the accompanying does. Photograph courtesy of the Oregon Department of Fish and Wildlife.

function of deer management is to provide range conditions that allow quality production to occur in the herd.

Much of the research identifying effects of nutrition on reproductive performance in deer has been accomplished with whitetails. Research in northern Michigan has shown that fawn losses are associated with the nutritional plane of their does: (1) well-nourished does lost only about 5 percent of their fawns; (2) does fed deficient diets during winter lost about 33 percent; and (3) does underfed throughout their pregnancy lost 90 percent (Verme 1962). Some fawns from underfed does were stillborn, and many live-born fawns quickly perished owing to insufficient energy reserves. Poorly nourished does often produce fawns that are too weak to nurse, and the does may not have sufficient milk to feed fawns successfully. Blaxter (1962) studied sheep and noted that lambs of poorly nourished ewes may not even have sufficient energy reserves to dry themselves following birth, so that they quickly die of exposure.

When range conditions become marginal, they affect the nutrition of does and the reproductive success of mule deer. The nutritional quality of summer range is especially important. If relatively few nutrients are available, owing to overgrazing or seasonal drought, high metabolic requirements during summer will not be met, and requirements for reproduction will not be satisfied. Yearling whitetail does require abundant nutrients and energy for growth and will not conceive fawns if summer and autumn nutrition is inadequate (Verme 1967). Verme also indicated that whitetail does on poor range that lose fawns at birth are relieved of the strain of lactation so that their metabolic requirements are met during summer and autumn. They enter the autumn breeding season in good condition and may conceive and rear fawns successfully during the second year. A doe may be in such poor shape during the autumn breeding season after successfully rearing fawns that she may not produce viable fawns the following spring. In effect, deer on marginal habitats may reproduce successfully only biennially, so that overall recruitment is reduced.

On good-quality range, whitetail doe fawns in excellent physical condition will breed and occasionally produce twin fawns. Mule deer may breed only occasionally as fawns; they usually breed first as yearlings (Zwank 1976). As with whitetail deer, the ovulation rate and number of fetuses per mule deer doe vary with range quality. The rates on depleted range in central Utah were only 67 and 64 percent, respectively, of the corresponding measurements on good-quality summer range in Idaho (Julander et al. 1961).

Deer productivity on ranges providing only marginal nutrition and energy may be lower than on ranges of good quality. Deer managers therefore must understand the impact of nutrition on deer productivity and, in turn, the impact of herd productivity on herd management.

The metabolic rate of young fawns is very high, at least twice the interspecific mean metabolic rate. During the first month after birth, the resting metabolic rate and rate of weight gain of female fawns are greater than those of male fawns. Thereafter, males produce body tissue at a more rapid rate (Nordan et al. 1970). Growth in young fawns depends on the quantity and quality of doe's milk. If a doe's diet is of marginal quality, her milk may be high in fat and low in protein. The milk may supply adequate energy but be deficient in the protein required for growth. As previously indicated, poor nutrition at this early stage may result in poor growth or death of fawns. When milk is of good nutrient quality, fawns use the available energy with great efficiency once maintenance needs have been satisified.

For optimum growth to occur, the food of newly weaned fawns should contain at least 16–17 percent protein (Verme and Ullrey 1972). White-tailed deer fawns grow more rapidly on diets containing 20 percent protein than on diets with less protein (Ullrey et al. 1967). Mushrooms, many seeds (especially legumes), palatable and succulent twigs in early developmental stages, new leaves, and immature grasses and forbs on summer range provide protein levels sufficient for good growth. Newly weaned fawns require more digestible protein per unit of energy in summer than in winter, when growth and heat production rates are reduced. When digestible protein is limited during summer, protein intake may limit the growth rate of fawns, production in lactating does, and consequently herd recruitment. This seems more likely to occur on ranges with substantial summer drought than in the Rocky Mountains and Pacific Northwest, where summer climate, habitat diversity, or both on summer range normally provide adequate quantities of succulent forage.

Nutrients available beyond those needed for maintenance, normal activity, and bone and protein synthesis are converted to fat. Fawns, however, may not accumulate abundant reserves of subcutaneous, intramuscular, and intraabdominal fat, and the lack of such reserves reduces their resistance to nutritional inadequacies of winter.

Metabolism of growth in adult deer is correlated with increased endocrine function and increased length of daylight. When range resources are adequate, mule deer quickly reestablish good condition during late spring or summer (Fig. 17). Demands for maintenance and recovery are the first fulfilled by digestive products. Body growth in bucks, for instance, takes precedence over antler development (French et al. 1955).

The efficiency with which yearling deer convert food to flesh is similar to that of cows and sheep. The efficiency of conversion by older bucks is much reduced. Yearlings attain about two-thirds of their mature weight by early in their second autumn. They retain or may actually lose some of this body weight by late spring, when body weight again increases. Mature bucks gain weight for half the year and merely maintain themselves the other half. After a deer's first year, ingested nutrients are used for maintenance, some body growth, antler production, and recovery of weight lost over the winter. Weight gain per unit of food and energy intake obviously decreases from youth to maturity, since a mature animal ceases to grow, though it continues to eat. Each kilogram of flesh gained after weaning on a two-year-old buck resulted from ingestion of about

50 percent more high-quality food than did each kilogram of flesh gained after weaning by yearling deer (Short 1972). Older bucks require proportionally more nutrients. Conversion efficiencies for middle-aged does are somewhat better, since the does generally lose less weight in winter. In addition, they continue to yield fawns annually, which represent a net gain to the deer herd. These relationships are useful in understanding the efficient use of range resources.

If deer are to be harvested in a manner that maximizes the efficiency with which they utilize range to produce venison, it should be done at 2 or 3 years of age. If trophies such as large body size or large antlers are a goal, then deer must be retained in the herd for longer periods (perhaps up to 5 or 6 years of age), and their energy and nutrient intakes are large.

The amount of carcass fat in mule deer is greatest in autumn, declines in winter, and is lowest in early spring for bucks and in late spring/early summer for does, when parturition and early lactation occur (Anderson et al. 1972a). Most body fat is deposited during summer and early autumn, after many production demands have been met. At that time, net energy exceeding metabolic requirements can go for fat production. Range vegetation is used with greater efficiency for fat production during summer and early autumn because succulent and starchy foods yield increased levels of propionic acid during rumen fermentation, and this favors fat synthesis. Foods of high fiber content yield proportionally high levels of acetic acid during rumen fermentation, and this acid is used with low efficiency in the production of body fat (Blaxter 1962). Deer on poor range with limited amounts of easily digested foods do not develop extensive fat deposits. Mule deer became lean when three successive years of drought reduced browse and other useful foods in north-central Colorado (Anderson et al. 1972a).

Energy requirements during lactation frequently are greater than those of any other reproductive activity—they may reach 2.3 times basal metabolic rates at the peak of lactation (Wallmo et al. 1977). Milk of mule deer and blacktails contains about 25 percent total solids, including 1.4 percent ash, 5.4 percent lactose, 7.6 percent protein and 10.9 percent fat (Jenness and Sloan 1970). Energy content of mule deer milk is about 1,650 kilocalories per kilogram (227.4 kilocalories per ounce). Colostrum—the first product of the mammary gland following parturition—contains more total solids, total ash, proteins, vitamins and minerals, but less lactose than milk does. The lactoglobulin fraction in colostrum contains antibodies that provide passive disease immunity to fawns until their antibody-producing system becomes functional. Mule deer milk contains more fat, protein, ash, and total solids than does cow's milk. The nutritional value of deer's milk is twice that of cow's milk, and this

Lactation places a heavy nutritional stress on the doe, whose diet must include abundant sources of readily digestible foodstuffs that allow for nutrient intake sufficient to maintain the doe and also nourish the fawn. Photograph by William Finley; courtesy of the Oregon Department of Fish and Wildlife.

increased quality largely accounts for the very rapid growth rate of fawns (Kitts et al. 1956*b*).

The secretion of protein, energy, and minerals in milk places great nutritional stress on the doe. Protein requirements include normal maintenance demands of the doe and protein secreted in milk. Diets that have inadequate protein reduce milk production. Calcium and phosphorus account for about 50 percent of the ash of milk, and during heavy lactation there is a depletion of mineral reserves in the doe's body. Fawns must attain self-sufficiency quickly so that does can replenish their skeletal calcium and phosphorus before winter, when food intake is on a maintenance rather than a production level. Verme and Ullrey (1972) suggested that diets containing 0.45 percent calcium and 0.35 percent phosphorus satisfy the normal requirements of deer. As I indicated previously, vegetation of many western deer ranges does not provide adequate phosphorus, and this deficiency also may adversely affect the productivity of mule deer in some locations.

Abundant sources of readily digestible foodstuffs must be available to allow a doe to nurse her fawns successfully. Foods that yield molar percentages of 50–60 percent acetic acid and about 20 percent propionic acid upon fermentation may be used with great efficiency in milk production. Energy generally is used with greater efficiency in milk fat production than in body fat production, because many of the direct precursors of milk solids already are present in the blood. Amino acids in the blood are precursors of milk protein; blood glucose is the precursor of milk lactose; acetic and butyric acids are precursors of the fatty acids of milk fat, while higher fatty acids—molecules having sixteen or more carbon atoms arranged in long chains—are derived from long-chain fatty acids in the blood (Blaxter 1962).

If a doe is in poor nutritional condition when parturition occurs, lactation demands weaken both the doe and her fawn(s). Inadequate lactation capabilities among mule deer does, because of nutritional stress, may be a major cause of postnatal mortality among fawns.

NUTRITION, METABOLISM, AND MANAGEMENT

Deer tend to accumulate body fat during summer and autumn, after productive functions—such as recovery of overwinter weight loss, antler growth, pregnancy, lactation, and body growth—generally have been satisfied. Some productive functions may be curtailed in favor of fat production during autumn. For example, when digestible energy is deficient, growth of fawns may cease, but some fat production will occur (Verme and Ullrey 1972). Major fat stores are deposited if digestible energy intake is adequate, and rates of digestible food intake will remain high through October if range conditions are favorable. If deer cannot obtain high levels of quality foods on summer and intermediate ranges during early autumn, production of body fat will be diminished.

Voluntary food consumption is reduced from November through March so that the intake of digestible energy only equals a sum slightly above the winter season fasting metabolic rate. Consequently, slight weight losses may occur even in the presence of abundant rations. Deer rely on their stored energy reserves at this time to supplement digestible energy available from winter range. Digestible energy intake will be reduced severely if (1) forage on winter ranges is of poor quality because of drought during the growing season, (2) overgrazing by domestic livestock occurred during summer or autumn, (3) overcrowding occurs on deer winter range, or (4) winter conditions are particularly severe. Fat stores then act as fundamental rather than supplemental energy sources. Deer with limited fat stores, such as fawns or animals from poor-quality summer and intermediate ranges, will deplete reserves quickly and will succumb

Artificial feeding programs are viewed by many wildlife biologists and managers as a last resort. Often, by the time such measures are begun, the physiological condition of many deer has deteriorated irrevocably, so such programs often fail. Photograph courtesy of the Oregon Department of Fish and Wildlife.

when insufficient energy is present for maintaining body temperatures and normal body functions.

Artificial feeding programs usually are proposed and may be initiated when body fat reserves are exhausted and body proteins are being catabolized. Frequently, dried grasses in the form of hay are used. These foods, with high cell-wall contents, are not particularly palatable and are digested slowly, so they add few nutrients to a body demanding good nutrition. Animals dying of malnourishment during periods of artificial feeding frequently have impacted rumens—evidence of man's lack of understanding of the digestive physiology of deer. Other foods used in feeding programs, such as alfalfa hay, may be picked over and the leaves consumed and digested by deer. Stems frequently remain uneaten. When alfalfa leaves

or palatable and digestible evergreen forage are provided before extensive body deterioration has occurred, artificial feeding during winter may succeed in providing digestible energy sufficient to supplement body stores. The secret to keeping a deer alive during winter is twofold: (1) body energy stores going into the winter must be substantial; and (2) foods yielding adequate digestible energy must be provided throughout the stress period so that a condition of irreversible undernourishment is not reached.

Both deer and domestic herbivores consume a wide variety of foods, so there frequently is some diet overlap among animals occupying the same range. On well-stocked ranges, different herbivore species generally can select the types of forage that best fulfill their nutritional needs. In addition, grass can become

A biologist examines the carcass of a mule deer that died of starvation after gorging itself at haystacks on Colorado ranches. It and several hundred other deer died in the same area at a time when severe winter weather precluded foraging for more digestible foodstuffs. An emergency feeding program, using a nutritious pelleted food, prevented even greater losses to the local deer population and even greater damage to crops. Photograph by Don Domenick; courtesy of the Colorado Division of Wildlife.

dense enough to cause shrub stands to deteriorate, and a dense grass cover can carry fire onto browse slopes and destroy perennial woody species useful to deer. Thus, grazing by domestic livestock that does not cause deterioration of grasslands and does not extensively use browse tissues required by deer is compatible with deer management. On overstocked ranges, severe competition for desirable forage may exist. In these instances, heavy overgrazing by domestic livestock can deplete food sources and adversely affect deer productivity, production of fat stores necessary for winter survival, or digestible energy required by deer during winter.

Appreciation of the digestive abilities of deer is important to their management. Summer forage should allow adequate milk production by does and permit all deer to achieve adequate growth and fat storage. Autumn forage should be abundant and of good quality to delay the depletion of fat stores. Winter range should provide forage that minimizes energy deficits and fat depletion. Spring range should offer feed that permits early recovery from stresses of winter. Thus, all ranges are important to deer and must be managed carefully to provide quality nutrition in order to maintain healthy and productive deer populations.

Chapter 4

DISEASES

Charles P. Hibler
Director
Wild Animal Disease Center
Colorado State University
Fort Collins, Colorado

Infectious, parasitic, and nutritional diseases, competition, predation, and adverse environmental conditions can act alone or in combination to the detriment of a wildlife population. An infectious or parasitic disease can be a primary mortality factor or the consequence of another "predisposing factor," such as adverse environmental conditions or stress from competing animal populations. Generally, several interdependent factors must be considered.

Sometimes disease is an excellent indicator of the "predisposing factor." Gastrointestinal parasitism by nematodes is an example. Severe burdens of gastrointestinal parasites generally are an indication of crowding and competition, within and among deer populations, resulting in inadequate nutrition. Although gastrointestinal parasitism must be blamed as the cause of death, these parasites were only the final insult. Unfortunately, wildlife biologists, managers, and disease specialists seldom look back far enough into the proverbial forest; they see only the trees.

There are, however, some notable exceptions to the "predisposing factors." Viruses such as bluetongue and epizootic hemorrhagic disease can wreak havoc with susceptible deer and pronghorn populations. The arterial nematode *Elaeophora schneideri,* normally a parasite of mule deer, can severely limit populations of North American elk. The meningeal worm of white-tailed deer, *Parelaphostrongylus tenuis,* is quite capable of killing all other

wild North American ruminants. The lungworm *Protostrongylus stilesi,* by virtue of its ability to cross the placenta and infect fetuses of Rocky Mountain bighorn sheep, can virtually eliminate populations of this species.

Evaluating the impact of disease on a wild population is much easier proposed than done. Unlike man and his domesticated species, free-ranging wild animals are not amenable to hospitalization or confinement. Indeed, when confinement has been attempted, the stress of captive conditions frequently initiates diseases that tend to mask the real problem, leading the well-intentioned investigator to an inaccurate conclusion. Thus, to determine the impact of a disease on a free-ranging wildlife population, the investigator must go where the disease is occurring. This is not an easy job, for it is well known that most sick and weak animals are quickly eliminated in their natural habitats.

VIRAL DISEASES

Bluetongue

Bluetongue is an infectious, noncontagious viral disease of both domestic and wild ruminants. Infection is manifested by mucoid inflammation of mucous membranes, nose, and gastrointestinal tract. Coronary bands and laminae of hooves also may be affected. After exposure, the first indication of infection is a rise in body temperature that begins in four to six days and reaches a maximum six to seven days later. Depressed appetite and increased respiratory rate usually accompany the fever (Trainer 1970). Signs of bluetongue are reddening of lips, muzzle, and ears. The tongue swells and is a bluish purple color. This often is accompanied by excessive salivation. A mucoid nasal exudate develops in fatal cases, and this discharge may form crusts about the nostrils. Lameness and hemorrhages around the coronary band will develop in protracted cases (Vosdingh et al. 1968; Stair et al. 1968; Trainer 1970).

Lesions usually seen in deer with bluetongue are crusting of membranes of the mouth, lips, and tongue. Mucosal lining of the rumen may have widespread hemorrhages or be hyperemic. Hemorrhagic enteritis or cecitis is not unusual, and hemorrhages on the serosal surface of the viscera frequently are evident. The liver, lymph nodes, and spleen may be enlarged, and the latter two may be congested and hemorrhagic. Hemorrhages generally occur on outer and inner surfaces of the heart wall as well as in the heart muscle. Hemorrhages and fluids often are present in intermuscular connective tissue and fascia of the skeletal musculature.

Bluetongue is an arthropod-borne virus; its primary vectors are species of *Culicoides* (blood-sucking gnats). Although species in this genus are proved biological vectors, there is a good possibility that some other blood-sucking arthropod may be a better vector, primarily because most species of *Culicoides* prefer birds as a source of blood. Since an arthropod is the vector, bluetongue is a seasonal disease and occurs from midsummer to early autumn, but it may be more pronounced during wet seasons or a long "Indian summer."

Bluetongue is a disease of domestic sheep, and all breeds are susceptible (Howell 1963). While cattle generally are latent carriers and infections usually are not apparent, clinical disease can occur (Bowne et al. 1966; Prestwood et al. 1974).

Unfortunately, most of our knowledge regarding bluetongue in deer is based on serologic evidence. Negative serologic results are misleading because immune animals often will not show a serologic titer unless recently exposed. Also, exposure may have been to a less pathogenic serotype, which may not confer immunity to another serotype.

Several cases of bluetongue have been recorded that attest to susceptibility of captive mule deer. Serologic titers obtained from mule deer in northern New Mexico indicate exposure to the virus (Hibler, n.d. [1970–78]). However, susceptibility of mule deer in natural settings is unknown. Pronghorn are highly susceptible, and an outbreak during autumn 1977 killed several thousand in the western United States, especially in Wyoming (E. T. Thorne, pers. comm., October 1976; Hibler, n.d.).

In 1977, 8 captive mule deer at Colorado State University developed severe lameness. Some showed excessive salivation and lesions of the tongue and palate, and one showed crusting of the muzzle. The condition was transient, however, and the animals recovered in about four days. Bluetongue virus was isolated from 3 of these animals.

Therefore, mule deer will show signs of clinical disease, and, while some serotypes are only slightly pathogenic, others are highly pathogenic.

Epizootic Hemorrhagic Disease

This infectious, noncontagious viral disease of wild ruminants occurs principally in white-tailed deer, but on occasion mule deer and pronghorn have succumbed (Chalmers et al. 1964). Initial clinical signs are loss of appetite and loss of fear of man. Deer often salivate excessively and have difficult or labored respiration and an accelerated heart rate. Hemorrhages occur around the eyes and mouth and give the mucosa a rosy or blue appearance. Sometimes the feces and urine are spotted with blood. Within thirty-six hours after these signs develop, animals become comatose and die.

Gross and microscopic lesions are characterized by hemorrhage. These range from pinhead size to rather large and confluent areas. Organs generally involved are the lungs, heart, liver, spleen, kidneys, and intestines. Hemorrhage is caused by derangement of the blood-clotting mechanism and degenerative changes in blood-vessel walls (Karstad et al. 1961). As a result of blood changes, edema is present throughout the connective tissues of the subcutaneous and intermuscular areas. Pleural edema and pulmonary edema also are present.

The disease was recognized first by Shope et al. (1955) during an outbreak in New Jersey where about 200 whitetails died. Later in 1955 an outbreak occurred in Michigan. Following these initial epizootics, the disease has occurred in white-tailed deer in North Dakota, South Dakota, Wyoming, and Alberta, Canada. Suspected outbreaks were reported in Nebraska, Missouri, Iowa, Washington, and British Columbia (Trainer and Karstad 1970).

The epizootic characteristically involves a considerable number of deer, and mortality is very high. Thereafter the disease apparently does not recur. However, in some areas such as Nebraska and South Dakota, mortalities involving small numbers of deer occur year after year, indicating that the virus might be enzootic in these regions.

As in bluetongue, the virus is transmitted by species of *Culicoides* (Jones et al. 1977). Experimentally, it can be transmitted by oral, intravenous, subcutaneous, or intramuscular administration. Because the virus is arthropod-borne, epizootics occur in late summer and early autumn.

Although mule and black-tailed deer and pronghorn have been exposed to this virus and are susceptible to it, no outbreaks or suspected outbreaks have been reported in the western United States. But, since both mule deer and pronghorn have succumbed during outbreaks in white-tailed deer herds as far west as Nebraska and Wyoming, the possibility that the disease can occur must be considered. During the 1962 epizootic in Alberta, 440 whitetails, 18 mule deer, and 13 pronghorn were found to be infected (Chalmers et al. 1964). Unfortunately, little is known about the susceptibility of these species to the virus. Serologic evidence from mule deer in northern New Mexico indicated that they may have been exposed to this virus. Of 42 animals examined, 3 had a low (1:10) titer (Hibler, n.d. [1976]).

Foot-and-Mouth Disease

Foot-and-mouth disease is caused by a highly contagious picornavirus that is infectious for all cloven-hooved domestic and wild mammals. Clinically, infection is characterized by blisters in the mouth and above the hooves and between their digits. Initial clinical signs are a period of high fever, 40–41 degrees Celsius (104–106 degrees Fahrenheit), and loss of appetite. Shortly thereafter, acute inflammation develops, and excessive salivation occurs. Small vesicles develop on the tongue, dental pad, and oral mucosa. Almost simultaneously, blisters arise in the skin near the hooves. When these rupture they cause extreme pain. Lameness develops, and swelling occurs around the coronary band.

Ingestion is considered to be the route of infection. The virus is present in all excretions of sick animals. These include urine, feces, saliva, milk, and semen. Animals can be viremic (and shedding the virus) before clinical signs occur.

Foot-and-mouth disease was eradicated from the United States nearly sixty years ago (Fletch 1970). The only known outbreak occurred during 1924 among cattle, swine, and deer in California. The disease originally was discovered in dairy herds near Oakland and Berkeley. Intensive investigation revealed that infection was present in sixteen of California's fifty-eight counties. When cattle introduced the disease to the Stanislaus National Forest in Tuolumne County, California, the virus soon spread to deer on two different ranges, and a campaign was initiated to eradicate it from deer herds. As a result, more than 22,000 deer were killed. Active or healed lesions were present in 2,214 deer examined.

Elsewhere in North America, there was a foot-and-mouth outbreak in Canada in 1952. It was eradicated the same year. Another outbreak occurred in Mexico in 1946 and lasted until 1952. It erupted again in 1953 and was eradicated in 1954 (J. S. Smith, pers. comm. to L. L. Williamson, August 1978).

Malignant Catarrhal Fever

This virus is infectious to both domestic and wild ruminants. The disease characteristically induces high and prolonged fever with temperatures of 40–41 degrees Celsius (104–106 degrees Fahrenheit) for two to seven days. Fever is accompanied by tissue destruction in the upper respiratory tract, with discharges of mucus or pus. There is a mucopurulent eye and nasal discharge, cloudiness of the cornea, and erosion and crusting of mucous membranes of nose and mouth. Erosion of skin may occur on feet and teats. Early clinical signs are dullness, loss of appetite, swelling of lips, profuse salivation, licking of lips, and sensitivity to or fear of

An eye examination is made of a neck-banded mule deer doe. Photograph courtesy of the Wyoming Department of Game and Fish.

light. Small ulcers occur on mucous membranes of the mouth and nose and on the conjunctiva. Cracks may occur in the area between the digits of the hoof. In peracute cases, animals generally die quickly, before development of many clinical signs. Mode of transmission is unknown. Since infection in cattle frequently is related to contact with seemingly normal domestic sheep, this latter species may be a carrier. Sheep, however, do not develop clinical disease.

At postmortem examination, there is inflammation and superficial necrosis of the muzzle, mouth, and tongue and of the rumen and omasum. Hemorrhagic inflammation can occur in the abomasum and intestines. Lymph nodes are enlarged, congested, and often hemorrhagic. Diagnosis is based on lesions and results of transmission to calves and rabbits. Inoculum of blood and tissues must be fresh and must be introduced intravenously or into lymph nodes.

Malignant catarrhal fever has a long incubation period of 18–48 days and in this respect is different from many other diseases with clinicopathologic similarities. Bluetongue and epizootic hemorrhagic disease have an incubation period of five to seven days. Mucosal disease, however, is more difficult to diagnose. Virologic as well as immunologic studies often are necessary.

Very little information is available on malignant catarrhal fever in free-ranging deer, and published accounts of this disease have not been substantiated by animal inoculation. The only outbreak in mule deer reportedly occurred among captive animals in Colorado Division of Wildlife holding facilities in Fort Collins during early autumn 1972. These deer had fever and hemorrhagic diarrhea; 17 of 20 animals died within three to five days (Pierson et al. 1974). My opinion, after reviewing postmortem records of these deer, is that they probably died of bluetongue or epizootic hemorrhagic disease.

Diagnosis of any of the aforementioned viral diseases in a wild population can involve many difficulties. Karstad (1970, p. 167) best summed up these diseases in ruminants when he said, "In comparing the clinical and pathologic descriptions of epizootic hemorrhagic disease, bluetongue, malignant catarrhal fever, mucosal disease and rinderpest, one is impressed by the difficulty, if not impossibility, of making a differential diagnosis on the basis of clinical and pathologic features alone. Whenever possible, therefore, attempts to isolate and identify the causative viruses must be made."

Bovine Virus Diarrhea/Mucosal Disease Complex

This viral disease of wild and domestic ruminants is manifest by acute mucoid inflammation of mucous membranes in gastrointestinal and upper respiratory tracts. Clinical signs in experimentally and naturally infected deer are weakness, dehydration, and emaciation. Vision and hearing sometimes are impaired. Fecal matter frequently contains large amounts of stringy mucus and flecks of blood. Gross changes seen at necropsy are mucosal erosions of the abomasum and intestines. Mucoid or bloody inflammation of trachea, lungs, abomasum, and intestines also occurs, as well as inflammation of kidneys and necrosis of the liver. Widespread hemorrhages frequently are found in turbinates, sinuses, pharynx, trachea, and gastrointestinal tract.

Richard et al. (1956) observed white-tailed deer and mule deer with lesions and inflammation similar to those in mucosal disease of cattle. Clinical signs in deer were similar in many respects to those in mucosal disease of cattle and were different in others. Diagnosis was based on similarity of signs and lesions to those of bovine mucosal disease and on transmissions from deer to deer and deer to cattle. Incubation periods in experimental deer ranged from 10 to 24 days. Transmission of the virus from deer to cattle produced inconclusive results. Therefore one must conclude that, though it appears to be mucosal disease, unequivocal proof is lacking (Karstad 1970).

The virus causing bovine viral diarrhea crosses the placenta in cattle to infect the fetus. This may result in cerebellar hypoplasia and ocular defects. A mule deer fawn from northern New Mexico, found dead a few hours after birth, was observed to be extremely light in weight (2.3 kilograms: 5.0 pounds). No body fat was evident, and the thymus was atrophied. The only organism isolated was bovine viral diarrhea virus; hypoplasia of the cerebellum was not evident.

BACTERIAL DISEASES

Pasteurellosis

Pasteurellosis is an infectious bacterial disease of both wild and domestic animals, generally caused by *Pasteurella multocida*. Clinical signs range from those of generalized hemorrhagic septicemia to those of pneumonia, arthritis, meningitis, and mastitis. Occasional epizootics have been responsible for severe mortality in wild populations of many species. Some of the wild ruminant populations decimated by bacterial epizootics have been black-tailed deer (Rosen 1952; Brunetti 1952), mule deer (Quortrup 1942), white-tailed deer (Fenstermacher et al. 1943; Erickson et al. 1961), bison (Gochenour 1924; Carter and Bain 1960), elk (Murie 1951), and bighorn sheep (Honess and Frost 1942; Honess and Winter 1956; Spraker and Hibler, in press).

Pasteurellosis characteristically strikes quickly, especially in acute or peracute forms of the disease. Healthy-appearing animals are found dead or near death. The most common form of pasteurellosis in wild ruminants appears to be the pneumonic form, resulting in a pleuropneumonia and often followed by a septicemia. Clinical signs are nasal discharge and rapid, shallow (painful) respiration.

Pasteurella is an obligate parasite of the upper respiratory tract that is transmitted by contact. It is not considered a primary invader and must rely on some predisposing factor to initiate disease. This can be inclement weather, malnutrition, parasitism, and so forth. Stress often is considered to be the predisposing factor and no doubt plays a role. However, stress is difficult to measure and evaluate.

Classic examples of pasteurellosis in deer were reported for black-tailed deer in California (Rosen 1952; see Longhurst et al. 1952). Quortrup (1942) reported a major epizootic in Tooele County, Utah, in September 1940. The disease appeared to have caused 50 percent mortality. The majority of dead deer were yearlings, but older animals also were affected.

Mortality from pasteurellosis probably occurs more frequently than is reported, primarily because onset of the disease is so sudden that signs rarely are observed. The disease may induce a pneumonia, a septicemia, or both. But, before *Pasteurella* can be considered the cause or even a contributor, it must be isolated from the lungs as well as the blood and then identified.

Brucellosis

Bacteria in the genus *Brucella* are responsible for a highly contagious infection in many animals. Usually the infection is initiated as a bacteremia and later establishes in lymph nodes, reproductive organs, spleen, joints, and tendon sheaths, where it can exist for long periods. Clinical signs vary among species. In ruminant animals, *Brucella* induces abortion during the second half of gestation. The strains or species generally considered responsible are *Br. abortus, Br. suis, Br. melitensis, and Br. neotomae.* Abortions are seen most commonly during first pregnancy of young ruminants and during a population's first exposure to the disease. Young animals may be born immature or weak, and the placenta often is retained. These specific signs, attributable to brucellosis, have been observed in deer, moose, caribou, and elk. Cattle often show metritis along with excessive vaginal discharge, resulting in reproductive failure or breeding difficulties. They also show lameness when their bursae, tarsal joints, and carpal joints are swollen and abscessed.

Brucella usually is transmitted by oral exposure but can be transmitted by genital contact, contamination of eyes, and through wounds. Milk, aborted fetuses, vaginal discharges, the placenta, and joint or bursal abscesses are other likely means of transmission.

Although brucellosis has been found in most ruminants in the United States and Canada, the results of several thorough and important surveys have shown that it is uncommon in deer (Trainer and Hanson 1960). However, moose, bison, elk, and caribou are susceptible (Tunnicliff and Marsh 1935; Neiland et al. 1968; Honess and Winter 1956; Thorne et al. 1978). Honess and Winter (1956) believed that brucellosis in Yellowstone National Park, Wyoming, was brought in by domestic cattle and spread to bison, then from bison to elk.

Once *Brucella* gains entrance to the host, it invades the circulatory system and localizes in various organs. In pregnant animals, the endometrium and associated chorionic tissues are edematous, intercotyledonary membranes thicken and become leathery, fetal circulation decreases, and abortion occurs.

Necrobacillosis

Fusibacterium (Spherophorus) necrophorus is a pyogenic bacterium responsible for abscesses in the mouth, esophagus, rumen, and reticulum or on one or more feet in wild and domestic ruminants (Marsh 1944). In young captive deer, lesions first appear in the mouth and esophagus. The jawbone often is affected, giving the appearance of "lumpy jaw." Animals go off feed, become weak, and usually die. Ulcers in the rumen and reticulum may perforate, resulting in death from peritonitis. On occasion young deer become lame, as from arthritis or injury, but lesions typical of "foot rot" in cattle have not been seen in captive fawns (Hibler, n.d. [1976]).

Gross lesions of necrobacillosis are purulent abscesses, often greenish, with an extremely foul odor. Ulcerations frequently occur around the teeth, on the inner part of the cheeks, on the tongue, larynx, and pharynx, and in the esophagus. Large, often perforating ulcerations are common in the rumen and reticulum. Captive deer born on contaminated soil frequently have an infection of the navel ("navel ill").

Diagnosis must be based on recovery and identification of the organism; however, lesions are good presumptive evidence.

Several epizootics of necrobacillosis have been reported throughout North America in elk (Murie 1930; Allred et al. 1944), caribou (King 1963), white-tailed deer (Shillinger 1937), and mule and black-tailed deer (McLean 1940; Herman and Rosen 1949; Rosen et al. 1951; Honess and Winter 1956). Outbreaks are reported to be associated with crowding, either for winter feed, as in the Yellowstone outbreak in elk (Murie 1930; Allred et al. 1944), or during dry periods when deer congregate around water holes (anonymous 1924; McLean 1940). Epizootics of necrobacillosis usually occur among deer in California during late summer and early autumn. If the preceding spring has been unusually dry, it is possible to predict foot rot, particularly on overcrowded ranges in dry parts of the state (Rosen 1970). According to Longhurst et al. (1952), foot rot ranks second only to gastrointestinal nematodes as a mortality factor in California, especially when deer are crowded and browse is sparse.

Some investigators feel that *F. necrophorus* is not a primary invader and needs a lesion to become established (Allred et al. 1944). Recent research with captive mule deer fawns at Colorado State University has shown that this is not true (Nelson 1974). Mule deer fawn mortality in captive herds often is 70–80 percent if young are left with dams on contaminated areas. Bottle-fed fawns seldom contract the disease.

Actinomycosis

Actinomycosis is an infectious but usually chronic disease manifested by suppurative granulomatous lesions generally localizing in the mandible, maxillae, or other bony tissues of the head. Most wild and domestic ruminants are susceptible. *Actinomyces bovis* is a filamentous bacterium that forms branched mycelia. The bacteria can be found in oral cavities of healthy animals; the portal of entry into tissues is through abrasions in the mouth, generally caused by rough feed. Actinomycosis of the mandible and maxilla is characterized by swelling, abscesses, fistulous tracts, extensive fibrosis, osteitis, and granuloma. Teeth become loose so that eating is difficult; swelling of the nasal cavity causes difficult breathing (dyspnea); and emaciation gradually develops. A history of slowly developing swelling on the maxilla or mandible with abscesses or fistulous tracts suggests actinomycosis. These fistulous tracts extend through the skin, discharge pus for a short time, and then harden, leaving indented fibrotic scars in the skin. Bone generally is destroyed by this necrotizing infection, and then is replaced by a granulomatous mass.

The disease commonly occurs among captive deer in western North America and frequently is seen among free-ranging animals. However, the actual detrimental effect is very difficult to evaluate because infected animals in natural environments succumb quickly. It often is seen among captive mule deer, especially among fawns.

Blackleg and Malignant Edema

Blackleg is caused by *Clostridium chauvei*, and malignant edema is caused by *Cl. septicum*. Both are common soil contaminants and common inhabitants of the gastrointestinal tract. Both diseases are acute, febrile, and noncontagious in wild and domestic ruminants and are characterized by sudden onset, fever, and emphysematous swelling.

Clinical signs of the two diseases are similar. In blackleg, lameness, high fever, and depression frequently occur. Crepitant swellings appear about the shoulders, neck, back, thighs, and legs. Malignant edema is characterized by edematous swellings in the subcutaneous tissues. Local lesions generally are soft, but they leave pits when pressurized and extend rapidly owing to the formation of large quantities of exudate that infiltrate subcutaneous and intramuscular connective tissues in infected areas.

Blackleg is characterized by crepitant swellings of the heavy musculature. The affected muscle is dark red to black, dry and spongy, has a sweetish odor, and is infiltrated with small bubbles of gas, but with little edema. With malignant edema, edema is pronounced in skin and the subcutaneous regions. Hemorrhagic areas of emphysema occur under the skin and between muscle layers of extremities. Accumulations of gas are uncommon in malignant edema. However, it must be noted that the two diseases are so similar that any differentiation made at necropsy must be considered unreliable; diagnosis by laboratory confirmation is the only certain procedure.

Armstrong and MacNamee (1950) reported at least 400 of an estimated 2,500 white-tailed deer died in late summer and early autumn of 1949 as a result of blackleg. LeDune and Volkmar (1934) reported that white-tailed deer in the Roosevelt Game Preserve, Ohio, had been dying of a "septicemic condition" for several years. Most were found near water holes and creek beds.

Most reports of these diseases in mule and black-tailed deer have been incidental and of a suggestive nature (Howe 1966). In 1970, when New Mexico Department of Game and Fish personnel tranquilized free-ranging mule deer with the aid of a "Capchur gun," 5 of 7 deer died three to five days after capture, all with clinical signs and postmortem changes compatible with malignant edema. The cause was traced to darts that had not been properly sterilized (Hibler, pers. files).

Caseous Lymphadenitis

Caseous lymphadenitis is a chronic but sometimes acute disease of wild and domestic ruminants, horses, and rabbits, caused by *Corynebacterium ovis* (*C. pseudotuberculosis*) and *C. pyogenes*. Since infection usually is benign, clinical signs rarely are observed. If infection is acute, gradual emaciation develops, followed by general weakness and death. Generally, however, lesions are discovered during postmortem examination. Superficial lymph nodes, particularly the precrural and prescapular nodes, usually are primary sites for lesions. Later, other lymph nodes may become involved, especially the mediastinal, bronchial, and sublumbar nodes. Lesions may occur in lungs, liver, kidneys, and spleen. Lymph nodes and many of the visceral organs—especially lungs, liver, spleen, and mesentery—contain rather large abscesses filled with caseous, greenish yellow, odorless pus. In old chronic lesions, pus becomes dry and firm and usually is arranged in concentric layers within a thick fibrous capsule.

In Oregon, Shaw et al. (1934) were the first to report this disease in deer. Hammersland and Joneschild (1937) found the disease among mule deer in Montana. Seghetti and McKenney (1941), noting that reports of diseased deer had been frequent for several years, examined 4 animals. They commented that this disease in deer apparently is benign and becomes fatal only if disseminated. Humphreys and Gibbons (1942) also studied 4 cases in British Columbia. Rosen and Holden (1961) examined 24 infected deer in California over a period of thirteen years. The latter authors noted that many deer killed during hunting seasons were abandoned when found to contain multiple purulent abscesses. Because of such abandonment, they felt the actual prevalence of the disease was unknown. In my experience, caseous lymphadenitis is a much more prevalent disease of mule deer than heretofore reported; most cases go undetected. Examination of deer at hunter check stations, and deer collected for scientific purposes in Arizona, Colorado, and New Mexico, indicates infection is widespread but generally benign.

Anthrax

Anthrax is an acute, infectious, febrile disease that has a rapidly fatal course. The disease is caused by *Bacillus anthracis*, a gram positive, spore-forming bacterium of relatively large size. *B. anthracis* is highly virulent and, when it gains access to the animal, multiplies rapidly, invading the blood and producing a rapidly fatal septicemia. The incubation period is variable, and experimental evidence indicates that it may vary from twenty-four hours to five days or longer. The disease is manifest in several forms, generally referred to as peracute, acute, and subacute. The peracute form is characterized by a sudden onset and a rapidly fatal course. Infected animals generally stagger, have labored respiration, appear to tremble, and collapse. In the acute and subacute forms, there initially is a rise in body temperature followed by a period of excitement, then depression, stupor, spasms, respiratory or cardiac distress, a staggering type of convulsion, and death. In these two forms, bloody discharges may emanate from the natural body openings; moreover, swellings may appear in different parts of the body. In the peracute form of the disease, death can occur without any noticeable signs of illness.

Most animals, including man, are susceptible to this disease to some degree. This includes rodents, lagomorphs, carnivores, swine, and most domestic and wild ruminants. Man generally acquires the disease by handling contaminated hides, wool, hair, or other material (industrial anthrax). Man also can acquire the disease by skinning, butchering, and making postmortem examinations of infected carcasses. Animals usually contract the disease after ingesting contaminated food or water. Direct infection also is possible.

If animals are sick, the clinical signs given above are at least suggestive of anthrax. Bloating, together with putrefaction, is rapid in carcasses of diseased animals. Dark blood or bloodstained fluid oozes from the natural body openings; in some species the skin often exudes bloodstained fluid. Although these gross changes are indicative of anthrax, such changes are not restricted to this disease. Incomplete or nonexistent rigor mortis and swelling in various parts of the body are suggestive of anthrax. At necropsy, the blood is dark and fails to clot. A yellowish serous fluid generally is present in the body cavity. Blood-tinged, clear, or even gelatinous exudates are present at the sites of swellings. More often than not, the spleen is dark, greatly enlarged, soft, and semiliquid. Frequently, the spleen in this condition is referred to as "raspberry jam" in consistency and

color. Lymph nodes are greatly enlarged and hemorrhagic; the intestinal mucosa are hemorrhagic and thickened; and the lungs, liver, pancreas, kidneys, and urinary bladder usually are congested and swollen.

If anthrax is suspected as the cause of death in an animal, postmortem examination is not advised. Not only will examination spread the spores, but the examiner—being highly susceptible to the disease—also can become infected. Examination should be done only by a qualified pathologist.

Actually, postmortem examination generally is not necessary. Blood smears usually contain considerable numbers of bacteria that, in a qualified laboratory, are readily identifiable as *B. anthracis*. Moreover, blood may be absorbed on a small piece of filter paper or a sterile cotton swab and allowed to dry. Since these bacteria are spore formers, they are readily cultured in a diagnostic laboratory.

Since the spores of *B. anthracis* are resistant to environmental conditions, control of anthrax necessitates rapid and effective disposal of dead animals. This generally is done by incineration or by burial (at least 1.8 meters: 6 feet deep) under a layer of quicklime. Carcasses should be buried where they are found. Those working with anthrax should wear protective clothing that can be disposed of as soon as all carcasses have been destroyed. All equipment that is not expendable should be thoroughly sterilized.

Although anthrax is found throughout the world, and though the number of animals reported to be susceptible includes most species of wild and domestic animals, documented reports of anthrax in native free-ranging animals in North America are tenuous at best. Grinnell (1928) suggested that the disappearance of bighorn sheep from the Bear Paw Mountains of Montana was due to anthrax introduced by domestic sheep. Stein (1955) reported that anthrax had been found in deer in California, Florida, Louisiana, and Texas. These reports, however, were not otherwise documented. Good (1956) reported that 58 cattle and 18 moose had died of anthrax in the mountains of Wyoming. More than 900 bison died of anthrax in Canada in 1963, 1964, and 1967 (Novakowski et al. 1963; Choquette 1970). D.

E. Harmel and R. M. Robinson (pers. comm., 1980) reported an anthrax outbreak in white-tailed deer from an endemic area in Texas in summer 1979. The outbreak was controlled by burning the carcasses.

Although outbreaks among wild ruminants in North America are not well documented, the highly infectious nature of *B. anthracis* and the fact that most animals are susceptible are sufficient to indicate that, if an outbreak does occur, it will involve the free-ranging wild species as well as the domestics. Mule and black-tailed deer probably are as susceptible as any other ruminant.

PARASITIC DISEASES

Elaeophorosis

Elaeophora schneideri is an intraarterial nematode commonly found in mule deer, black-tailed deer, and, on occasion, white-tailed deer in western North America. Recently the parasite was reported in white-tailed deer of the southeastern United States (Prestwood and Ridgeway 1972). The parasite uses deer as a normal definitive host, and, with the possible exception of white-tailed deer, disease does not occur in these species. Elaeophorosis commonly occurs in North American elk (Adcock 1967; Hibler and Adcock 1970), moose (Worley 1975), domestic sheep (Kemper 1938; Jensen and Seghetti 1955; Hibler n.d. [1970]), and domestic goats (Hibler, n.d. [1970]). Since this chapter considers diseases of mule and Columbian black-tailed deer, and since these deer rarely if ever develop elaeophorosis, the attributes of the disease in the abnormal host will be mentioned only briefly. For detailed description of other species' responses to this disease, see the references cited.

E. schneideri usually occurs in the common carotid and internal maxillary arteries of deer. However, on occasion the parasites will occupy the lumen of any artery large enough to accommodate them. Female parasites are 60–120 millimeters (2.4–4.7 inches) long by 0.6–0.9 millimeter (0.02–0.035 inch) thick. Adult males are 55–85 millimeters (2.1–3.3 inches) long by 0.4–0.7 millimeter (0.015–0.027 inch) thick. Microfilariae are 239–79 microns long by 17–18 microns thick. Microfilariae usually are found in arterioles, capillaries, or venules supplying the skin of the poll, forehead, and facial region of deer.

E. schneideri is a common parasite of mule deer in New Mexico, Colorado, Wyoming, Arizona, California, Utah, and British Columbia (Hibler and Adcock 1970; Herman 1945*b;* Longhurst et al. 1952; Cowan 1946*b*). Prevalence of infection in mule deer in both Arizona and New Mexico, generally is about 90 percent of the adult population where the animals reside at 1,524 meters (5,000 feet) above sea level or higher. Prevalence of infection varies considerably in Colorado, Wyoming, Utah, and California. In Colorado it varies from about 10 percent in mountainous regions west of Denver to approximately 50 percent near Durango. In California the parasite is found commonly in both mule and black-tailed deer. Prevalence varies from 4 percent in Tehama County, to 44 percent in Inyo County, to as high as 78 percent in a Mendocino County herd (Weinmann et al. 1973).

Adult parasites in the cephalic arterial circulation produce microfilariae that are distributed in the dermal region about the poll, forehead, and face. Species of horseflies in the genera *Hybomitra* and *Tabanus* (especially the former) are intermediate hosts. Examination of horseflies captured in forests of New Mexico and Arizona revealed that 17–25 percent of those collected at random were infected with an average of 25 larvae (with a range of 1–500) of *E. schneideri*. In these forests, horseflies emerge about 1 June and die about 10 July. Horseflies frequently are so numerous that 100 per hour may feed on animals during the ten hours or more of daylight during the last two weeks of June. For some unknown reason, horseflies prefer to feed on the facial region of deer. After two weeks of development in the horsefly, infective larvae of *E. schneideri* migrate into the head and mouthparts. If the infective stage (third-stage larvae) is introduced into deer, it migrates into the venous circulation, to the heart and lungs, and back to the heart, then (by some unknown means) enters the carotid arteries and is swept into the leptomeninges. Here the larvae begin development from the third to fifth (adult) stage.

In mule deer (and probably Columbian black-tailed deer), development occurs very rapidly. The nematode develops to the fourth stage within one week and to the immature fifth stage after two weeks. As development progresses in deer, the nematode migrates upstream toward the heart. Consequently, it does not interfere with cephalic circulation. By 3.5 weeks after infection, the young adult parasite returns to the common carotid artery. It continues to grow and develop, reaching sexual maturity about 5 to 5.5 months later.

In the abnormal host, disease occurs as a result of an extended period of development in leptomeningeal arteries. Whereas larvae migrate upstream as they develop in deer, in the abnormal host they spend an abnormally long period of time (five to eight weeks) in these small arteries. As a result, they cause ischemic necrosis of tissue in the brain or other organs (eyes, ears, muzzle, and tongue) supplied via the cephalic circulation. This ultimately results in blindness, brain damage, and necrosis of ears, tongue, and external nares.

Clinical signs of elaeophorosis in elk are blindness, brain damage, "cropped" ears, necrosis of the muzzle, and abnormal antler development in bulls that survive infection (Hibler and Adcock 1970). Domestic sheep and goats and also moose develop almost identical signs (Hibler, pers. files; Worley 1975). Elk calves and other abnormal hosts do not seem to have any resistance to extremely heavy infections of *E. schneideri*. As a result, it is not unusual to find more than 100 parasites in an animal (deer usually have 5–33 parasites). When extremely heavy infections occur, clinical signs generally are compatible with listerosis or enterotoxemia in domestic sheep. When mule deer or Columbian black-tailed deer occupy the same habitat as the North American elk and when horseflies are extremely common, it is not unusual for

elaeophorosis to be a severe limiting factor on the elk. For a detailed description of elaeophorosis in North American elk, see Hibler and Adcock (1970).

Setaria

The abdominal worm, *Setaria yehi,* commonly occurs in white-tailed deer, mule deer, Columbian blacktails, moose, and caribou. The adult parasites generally are found lying free in the abdominal cavity of the host; their microfilariae circulate in the blood. Adult parasites are quite large—adult females measure 18–25 centimeters (7.1–9.8 inches) long, and adult males measure 12–18 centimeters (4.7–7.1 inches) long. They are the only nematodes known to occur freely in body cavities of wild North American ruminants. The sheathed microfilariae have an inner body and measure 240–60 microns long by 7–8 microns thick. Microfilariae circulate in the blood, but their periodicity, if any, is unknown.

S. yehi is widely distributed in cervids throughout North America. However, information on the prevalence of this parasite in deer is somewhat sketchy and no doubt inaccurate despite their large size, because discovery necessitates a careful examination of abdominal viscera. Fortunately, two rather thorough studies have been published. Weinmann et al. (1973) found that 67 percent of 186 fawns, 42 percent of 112 yearlings, and 11 percent of 190 adult Columbian black-tailed deer in California were infected. Prestwood and Pursglove (1977) found that 27 percent of 1,045 white-tailed deer from thirteen of seventeen southeastern states were infected. *S. yehi* has been found in mule deer in Arizona, Colorado, and New Mexico (Hibler, pers. files). However, discovery of these parasites was incidental to other studies, and no concerted effort was made to determine prevalence.

All known species of *Setaria* use mosquitoes as intermediate hosts, and, though the biological cycle for several species has been elucidated, very little information is available on *S. yehi*. Weinmann et al. (1973) determined that *Aedes sierrensis* was the mosquito primarily responsible for transmitting this parasite to Columbian black-tailed deer in California. Like other filarioid nematodes, mosquitoes feeding on blood of the host ingest microfilariae, and these microfilariae then develop to the infective stage somewhere in the arthropod's body tissues.

Weinmann et al. (1973) noted that *S. yehi* were likely to be more numerous in debilitated deer, but this appeared to be a secondary effect. Relatively few infected deer had more than 30 abdominal worms, the heaviest worm burden encountered being 88. They also noted that burdens in excess of 50 worms occurred infrequently. I have found that infected animals in the southwestern United States generally harbored 1 to 5 adult parasites (Hibler, pers. files). However, as I indicated previously, thor-

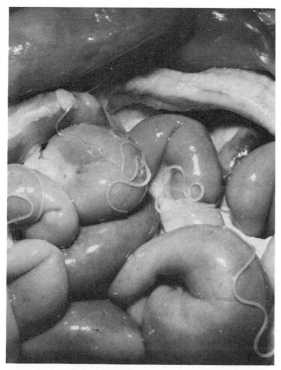

Adult nematodes (hairlike worms) of the genus *Setaria* in the viscera of a mule deer. These are commonly found in the abdominal cavities of wild North American ruminants. Photograph by Guy E. Connolly.

ough examinations rarely were made. Prestwood and Pursglove (1977) indicated that mild fibrous peritonitis was common in white-tailed deer in the Southeast. In most instances this condition was associated with *S. yehi* infections, but deposits of fibrin on serosal surfaces occasionally were noted when filarial worms were not found. Fibrinous tags were most obvious on the serosal surface of the diaphragm and on Glisson's capsule of the liver. Hibler and Adcock (pers. files) noted a similar mild peritonitis associated with this infection in mule deer in the western and southwestern United States.

Parelaphostrongylosis

Cervids in western North America face a potentially hazardous parasite if white-tailed deer continue to expand their range westward. White-tailed deer frequently are infected with the meningeal worm, *Parelaphostrongylus tenuis*. The adult of this parasite inhabits the cranial venous sinuses and the subdural space. Eggs generally are deposited in venous blood and carried to the lungs, where they hatch into first-stage larvae. These larvae pass up the respiratory tract, enter the mouth, are swallowed, then are eliminated with feces. Larvae must penetrate the foot of terrestrial molluscans (which are common on most deer ranges), to develop to the infective stage (three to four weeks in summer).

White-tailed deer become infected by accidentally ingesting snails carrying infective larvae. Once ingested, larvae are released, migrate to the spinal cord, and develop to the young adult stage in dorsal horns of gray matter. They migrate from the neural parenchyma into the spinal subdural space, and from there move to the cranium. The entire life cycle in white-tailed deer—from infective larvae to appearance of first-stage larvae in feces—is almost exactly three months. White-tailed deer tolerate the nematode well; apparently only two cases of clinical disease have been reported (Prestwood 1970; Eckroades et al. 1970).

In moose, woodland caribou, elk, reindeer, mule deer, black-tailed deer, fallow deer, and probably other exotic cervids, the meningeal worm causes excessive trauma to the central nervous system. Even small numbers may result in neurologic disease, often leading to paraplegia and death. All the forenamed mammalian species seem unusually susceptible to neural invasion and show little resistance to infection.

Currently, the meningeal worm has not been reported in western North America. However, because agricultural and forestry practices favor white-tailed deer, this animal is moving westward. While vanguards may not be infected, some of the animals that follow undoubtedly will carry the infection and, if a suitable snail intermediate host is present, westward expansion of this parasite problem will occur. Unfortunately, *Discus cronkhitei* serves as an intermediate host for the meningeal worm, and this terrestrial mollusk is found in Colorado and, no doubt, in other geographic regions of the West. It would not be surprising if other species of terrestrial molluscans serve equally well.

Anderson (1972) remarked that there is concern in North America about the introduction of exotic species. But he also said there is insufficient concern about the dangers of relocating native animals. Two classic examples supporting this statement are transplants of elk to Pennsylvania and black-tailed deer to Tennessee. Elk imported to Rachelwood Wildlife Preserve, Pennsylvania, share their range with white-tailed deer and as a consequence have suffered morbidity and mortality from meningeal worm (Woolf et al. 1977). Black-tailed deer were sent to Tennessee from Oregon during 1966 and 1967. The objective was to determine if these deer would thrive in urbanized areas of east Tennessee where restocking with white-tailed deer had failed. The animals were released in a large enclosure. The population increased but hybridized with local whitetails. In early 1973 the first instance of neurologic disease was observed. In subsequent years, despite good reproduction, the blacktail population steadily declined while the white-tailed deer population increased (Nettles et al. 1977).

Another example is that of fallow deer imported to a game ranch in Georgia, where they were maintained in captivity for three years. White-tailed deer, together with other wild and domestic species, also were present in the enclosure. During autumn 1971, two mature male fallow deer developed neurologic disease. Postmortem examination confirmed that the meningeal worm was responsible (Kistner et al. 1977).

Considerable concern has been voiced by parasitologists and wildlife biologists in western North America over the potential invasion of white-tailed deer, especially the possibility that the meningeal worm will accompany the whitetails' encroachment on the Rocky Mountain region. Consequently, an experiment was initiated at Colorado State University to determine if mule deer were susceptible to infection with this parasite. Of 8 deer experimentally infected at low levels, 7 succumbed, showing classic signs of this disease. In addition, one pronghorn was infected experimentally, and it too succumbed to meningeal worm infection (Tyler 1977).

R. C. Anderson's report, "The Ecological Relationships of Meningeal Worm and Native Cervids in North America" (1972) should be required reading for every student of wildlife biology in North America. It is especially valuable for those students studying movements of native or exotic wildlife across the continent.

Gastrointestinal Parasitism by Nematodes

Wild and domestic ruminants throughout the world are parasitized by a myriad of gastrointestinal nematodes; cervids in western North America are no exception. Throughout their ranges, mule and Columbian black-tailed deer frequently are infected with a number of nematode species in the genera *Haemonchus, Ostertagia, Trichostrongylus, Nematodirus, Nematodierella, Trichuris, Capillaria,* and possibly *Marshallagia.* It would be unusual to find a deer that was not parasitized by several species in one or more of those genera. However, parasitism by gastrointestinal nematodes does not necessarily indicate that the animal is suffering detrimental effects. Unfortunately, parasitologists are prone to interpret the presence of parasites as the cause of morbidity or mortality. Clinical parasitism (disease) results from a combination of several factors:

1. *Age.* Owing primarily to lack of exposure to gastrointestinal nematodes, young animals are much more apt to develop clinical signs when exposed to high levels of infection than are older animals. Older animals are more likely to have been previously exposed to parasites and thus to have developed some degree of immunity.

2. *Nutritional status.* Despite previous experience with gastrointestinal nematodes, undernourished animals are more prone to disease because they are not in good enough condition to develop immune responses.

3. *Crowding* (of all age groups). Species of parasites of the aforementioned genera have direct life cycles; that is, they have eggs or larvae that enter the environment with feces, undergo a free-living existence, and depend on ingestion by a susceptible host to complete their biological cycle. As a result, crowding of hosts promotes high levels of exposure. When young, susceptible host animals are present, they can be predisposed to levels of parasitism capable of causing disease.

4. *Environmental conditions.* For clinical parasitism (disease) to occur, environmental conditions must be suitable for development of free-living larval stages. The larval stages of most nematodes require a certain amount of warmth and moisture. If these conditions are met, the parasite can perpetuate itself. However, the degree of availability of these two conditions determines the number of successful parasites.

5. *Interspecific competition.* This category, at least in part, can be considered a factor determining the nutritional status of the host animal. Use of wild ruminant range by parasitized domestic ruminants leads to competition for both nutrition and space, resulting in clinical parasitism.

Clinical signs of severe gastrointestinal parasitism generally are loss of body condition, rough hair coat, diarrhea, and anemia. However, infections with bacterial or viral agents often are responsible for similar clinical signs. Therefore, if gastrointestinal parasitism is to be blamed as the cause of morbidity, this must be confirmed by recovery of nematodes from intestinal contents in numbers sufficient to cause the observed signs and lesions.

According to my observations, high levels of gastrointestinal parasitism are excellent indicators that a deer population has been subject to crowding, competition, and inadequate nutrition, and that parasites may be the final insult. Healthy, well-nourished deer seldom harbor large numbers of gastrointestinal nematodes.

Lungworms

Five species of lungworms have been reported in deer of western North America: *Dictyocaulus viviparus, D. filaria, D. hadweni, Protostrongylus macrotis,* and *Parelaphostrongylus odocoilei.* However, the validity of some of these *Dictyocaulus* species is questionable. For convenience, all five are lumped together even though their biologic cycles are different. *Dictyocaulus* spp. have a simple, direct cycle, while the other two genera use terrestrial molluscans as intermediate hosts. Species of *Dictyocaulus* are rather long, white nematodes commonly found in larger air passages (trachea and bronchi) of their host. *P. macrotis* is a long, slender, reddish brown nematode generally found in smaller air passages (bronchioles) of the host. The primary location of *P. odocoilei* is open to question. Brunetti (1969) found these parasites in lymphatics and blood vessels of the skeletal musculature in many parts of the body. Some were present in blood vessels of the lungs.

Species of *Dictyocaulus* have been reported from many geographic regions in western North America (Cowan 1951; Hall 1925; Honess and Winter 1956; Shaw et al. 1934). *Dictyocaulus* spp. require a certain amount of warmth and moisture for development of larval stages. The climates of much mule and Colum-

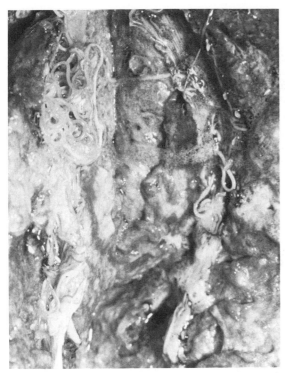

Lungworms in the lung of a Columbian black-tailed deer. Photograph by Guy E. Connolly.

bian black-tailed deer range do not provide conditions suitable for severe infections.

P. macrotis has been reported in Wyoming (Honess and Winter 1956) and commonly occurs in deer in western and northwestern Colorado (Hibler, n.d.). In my experience, however, seldom are more than 8–10 nematodes encountered in an animal. Examination of deer throughout New Mexico revealed that a small percentage are infected with a nematode that produces a larva (found in the feces) compatible with a species of *Protostrongylus*. All infections thus far encountered have been of low intensity.

Foot Worm or Leg Worm

Onchocerca cervipedis (Wehrdikmansia cervipedis), the foot worm of deer, probably is one of the most widespread and common filarial nematodes of mule and Columbian black-tailed deer in western North America (Herman and Bischoff 1946; Yuill et al. 1961; Hibler 1965). This long, slender, almost transparent filarial nematode generally is found in subcutaneous tissues of lower legs, but it also occurs along the brisket and has been reported in subcutaneous tissues overlying the pelvic region. It appears to be an innocuous parasite. On occasion, deer are infected so heavily that adult nematodes are found in intermuscular fascia, often to the extent that the meat is unsightly and the carcass unfit for human consumption (Herman and Bischoff 1946; Hibler, n.d.).

The biological cycle of this parasite currently is unknown, but Weinmann et al. (1973) showed that species of black flies *(Simulium)* are intermediate hosts. Hibler (1965), working on *Elaeophora* in Arizona, discovered that microfilariae of *O. cervipedis* congregate in the dermis of the ears—a preferred feeding site for some species of *Simulium*. Thousands of microfilariae often accumulate here in heavily infected deer. Moreover, examination of several deer revealed a considerable number of male parasites together with gravid female parasites congregated at the base of the ear. Possibly this is the preferred site, because females without males usually are the only parasites found in legs.

Yuill et al. (1961) examined 126 mule deer killed in Utah during the 1958 hunting season. All animals were infected with foot worm. Intensity of infection increased with age. Weinmann et al. (1973) showed that, in California, 86 percent of the deer more than 3 years of age were infected. Every mule deer older than 6 months of age that I examined (200+) in Arizona, Colorado, and New Mexico was infected with this parasite.

Eye Worm

Thelazia californiensis is a small nematode parasite that occurs under the third eyelid of deer in parts of California, Oregon, and Nevada (Parmelee et al. 1956; Dixon and Herman 1945; Herman 1944). The parasite also is found commonly in coyotes, dogs, cats,

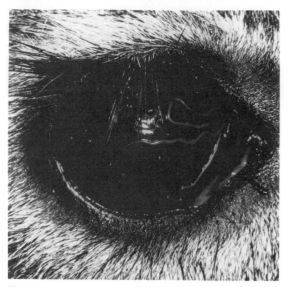

Eyeworms *(Thelazia californiensis),* which normally remain under the third eyelid, are common in deer in parts of California, Oregon, and Nevada. Photograph by Guy E. Connolly.

black bears, foxes, rabbits, and occasionally man (Stewart 1940; Herman 1945*b*, 1949; Douglas 1939). Weinmann et al. (1974) reported that, between 1964 and 1968, approximately 60 percent of the deer and 30 percent of the jackrabbits at a field station north of San Francisco were infected with eyeworm; thereafter, the prevalence of infection decreased for an unknown reason. It also has been reported from a single mule deer in New Mexico (Schad and Raught 1958). This small, white nematode measures from 7 to 18 millimeters (0.27–0.71 inch) in length. Generally, little or no pathogenicity is associated with light infections. But, when the parasites are numerous, conjunctivitis, lachrymation, and possibly photophobia may be present.

Tapeworms

Mule and Columbian black-tailed deer in western North America commonly are infected with the larval stages of *Taenia hydatigena* and *T. krabbei,* and with adult *Moneizia* spp. and

Thysanosoma actinioides. Moreover, it is not unusual for both mule and Columbian black-tailed deer to be infected with *Echinococcus granulosus,* especially in parts of California and Canada. Larval and adult tapeworms generally are not detrimental to their hosts.

Moneizia expansa is a rather large tapeworm that may reach 4.0 meters (157.5 inches) in length. The parasite commonly occurs in the small intestine of its host and is much more common in young animals up to 6 months of age than in adults, but it is not at all unusual to encounter this species in adult deer. The life cycle is indirect, and eggs must be ingested by one of several species of free-living mites in the family Oribatidae. Once the larva (cysticercoid) is mature—at 4 to 6 months of age, depending on environmental temperature—the host animal becomes infected by accidental ingestion of the infected mite. Sexual maturity within the host occurs in about 6 weeks, and longevity of the tapeworms is 2 to 6 months, after which they are immediately eliminated. Extremely heavy infections of 25–50 individual tapeworms are occasionally encountered, but light infections of no more than 5 tapeworms per animal is the general rule (Longhurst and Douglas 1953).

Thysanosoma actinioides, the "fringed tapeworm," occurs in bile ducts, pancreatic ducts, and small intestines of domestic sheep, mule deer, Columbian black-tailed deer, and elk in western North America. The parasite is not found east of the Mississippi River. A relatively small tapeworm, it measures 15–40 centimeters (5.9–15.7 inches) in length. While it normally inhabits the host's small intestine, the parasite frequently moves into liver bile ducts via the common bile duct. The complete life cycle is not known. The cysticercoid stage has been found in small, primitive insects of the family Psocidae, but investigators have been unable to complete the cycle in the definitive host, domestic sheep.

All three species of tapeworms are distributed widely among deer in western North America. Their prevalence depends on proximity of cattle and domestic sheep populations or their competition for forage and space. Infected deer have been found in Colorado (Hibler, n.d.), Wyoming (Honess and Winter

1956), New Mexico and Arizona (Hibler, pers. files), California (Longhurst and Douglas 1953; Herman 1945*b*), and Canada (Cowan 1951).

Despite reports to the contrary, species of *Moneizia* have not been proved detrimental to hosts, nor has the fringed tapeworm. But the fringed tapeworm's movement into the liver from the small intestine does on occasion cause hyperplasia of the bile duct epithelium, resulting in a thickening of the common bile duct. This lesion is not detrimental to the host's welfare.

Larval stages of *Taenia hydatigena (Cysticercus tenuicollis)* and *T. krabbei (Cysticercus tarandi)* probably are the most common parasites found in mule and Columbian black-tailed deer in western North America (Honess and Winter 1956; Cowan 1951; Hanson and McCulloch 1955; Olsen and Williams 1959; Shaw 1947; Stelfox 1962; Rosen 1951; Doman and Rasmussen 1944). Larval stages of *T. hydatigena* often measure 2–3 centimeters (0.78–1.18 inches) in diameter and occur in mesenteries, usually in low numbers. Detrimental effects on hosts rarely are produced. However, accidental ingestion by deer of large numbers of these tapeworms' eggs can result in detrimental effects, ultimately leading to death from an acute hemorrhagic hepatitis and possibly complicated by peritonitis (Gregson 1937; Severinghaus and Cheatum 1956; Davies and Spraker, n.d.). Davies and Spraker observed acute hepatitis caused by larval tapeworms in one free-ranging and one captive-reared fawn in Colorado. Both fawns had extremely heavy infections and were terminal cases.

Echinococcus granulosus uses members of the family Canidae as definitive hosts and ruminants—except cattle—as intermediate hosts. The parasite is widely distributed among moose, caribou, and wolves in western Canada and Alaska but is not found as commonly in the contiguous United States. Most important, man also acts as an intermediate host for this species of tapeworm. Human infections have been reported in Alaska, Canada, Arizona, New Mexico, and Utah.

The adult parasite is extremely small, measuring 2–9 millimeters (0.08–0.35 inch) in length, and usually has no more than four segments. The larval stage, called a "hydatid cyst," occurs in mesenteries, on the surface of the liver, and in the lungs of the intermediate host. This larval stage differs considerably from those in the genus *Taenia* in that it has an inner germinative membrane that buds off small vesicles called "brood capsules." These small brood capsules are filled with numerous tapeworm heads called "hydatid sand" (species in the genus *Taenia* have only one tapeworm head within the bladder). As hydatid cysts develop, brood capsules and "daughter cysts" that develop from this germinative membrane give the "mother cyst" the appearance of compartmentalization. Small brood capsules appear to the unaided eye as small white spots. It is not unusual for members of Canidae—especially dogs, coyotes, and wolves—to sustain infections with several hundred or even thousand of these adult parasites. Also, it is not unusual for an intermediate host to have multiple infections, with several hundred hydatid cysts occupying the forenamed visceral organs.

Unfortunately, two foci of infection exist in the contiguous United States: one including southern Utah, northern Arizona, and western New Mexico, the other in northern California. Sylvatic cycles exist among deer and coyotes in northern California (Romano et al. 1974) and among man, domestic sheep, and dogs in Utah and Arizona (F. A. Anderson, pers. comm., May 1972). Although feral dogs and coyotes have been examined in southern Utah, examination of the mule deer population has not been conducted. Thus, the role of mule deer as a reservoir host is not known. However, considering current sheep management practices, it is a question of time until hydatid disease is found in deer in southern Utah, northern Arizona, and western New Mexico.

Brunetti and Rosen (1970) surveyed deer over a twenty-five-year period in California and found that *Echinococcus granulosus* was present in 26 of 2,049 deer (1.3 percent). However, 8 of 33 deer (24 percent) in western Glenn County and 6 of 25 deer (24 percent) in western Tehama County were infected.

Although *E. granulosus* poses no health threat to free-ranging deer populations in western North America, it is a zoonosis of considerable significance to man, primarily because hydatid cysts present in viscera of ruminants frequently are available to local dog populations. When adult parasites establish themselves in dogs, the eggs pass out with fecal material. Eggs sometimes stick to the perianal region or the hair coat of dogs, and man then becomes infected by contamination.

Trematodes

Two species of trematodes have been reported in cervids of western North America: *Fasciola hepatica,* the "common liver fluke" or "sheep liver fluke"; and *Fascioloides magna,* the large American liver fluke.

Fasciola hepatica can be dispensed with rather quickly, because, though this trematode is rather ubiquitous (although distributed discontinuously across the North American continent), natural infections in cervids are rare (Presidente et al. 1974). Despite the fact that white-tailed deer frequently occupy enzootic areas of this parasite (Kistner and Koller 1975), and despite popular belief that cervids act as reservoirs, it has been reported only three times from white-tailed deer, once from elk, and rarely from mule and black-tailed deer.

Fascioloides magna uses cervids as normal definitive hosts and domesticated ruminants as abnormal definitive hosts. Adult *F. magna* are flat, gray to greenish, leaflike trematodes that measure 3–10 centimeters (1.2–3.9 inches) in length by 2–3 centimeters (0.8–1.2 inches) in width. In normal definitive hosts (deer, elk, moose, and caribou), the parasite occupies a fibrous cyst in the liver parenchyma. This cyst opens to a bile duct, providing a means of escape for eggs. Little or no damage is associated with infection in cervids. However, the liver may be judged unfit for human consumption, at least from an aesthetic point of view.

Distribution and prevalence of this parasite pose a potential economic threat to the livestock industry. In bovids, cyst formation generally gives way to calcification, resulting in no access to the bile duct. Thus, eggs accumulate in the liver. Infection in cattle generally causes condemnation of liver at slaughter, usually as a result of cysts containing parasites. Red blood cell destruction and the release of porphyrin give liver tissue the appearance of having been injected with India ink. In domestic sheep, encapsulation of the parasite rarely occurs, so it wanders unchecked throughout the parenchyma of the liver, initiating massive damage, and frequently killing the sheep.

The parasite is distributed throughout eastern Canada, the Great Lakes region, the southeastern United States, and the coastal plains of Texas. It also is widespread, but not extremely prevalent, among cervids in Alberta, Washington, Oregon, and northern California (Stelfox 1962; Knapp and Shaw 1962; Cowan 1946b). I have not found the parasite in cervids examined in Arizona, Colorado, and New Mexico. For a discussion of *F. magna* and a description of its life history, see Cowan (1951) and Davis and Libke (1970).

Sarocystis

Species of *Sarocystis* were considered innocuous parasites of uncertain status until Fayer (1972) and Rommel et al. (1972) demonstrated that the species had a coccidia type of life cycle. This ostensibly harmless parasite became extremely important when it was shown that three species of *Sarocystis* were highly pathogenic in cattle. Parasitologists are just beginning to identify its biological cycles and its pathogenicity for intermediate hosts. Dubey (1976) said that the surface has barely been scratched.

As a result of Fayer's (1972) work, it is known that *Sarcocystis* has a typical coccidialike life cycle, but with alternation of hosts. Members of Felidae and Canidae act as definitive hosts in which sexual (gametogenous) stages occur. Asexual (schizogenous) stages occur in various intermediate hosts. When sarcocysts—small, thin, whitish streaks in the striated and cardiac musculature, and sometimes the smooth musculature—from an intermediate host are ingested by a specific carnivore, sexual stages develop in the small intestine, with no detrimental effects. From 11 to 15 days postingestion, small, naked sporocysts pass into the environment with fecal matter. These sporocysts are infective to intermediate (alternate) hosts. Once these small sporocysts are ingested, naked, banana-shaped organisms (zooites) are released (probably in the small intestine) that penetrate a blood vessel and circulate until they arrive in the musculature, at which time they develop into sarcocysts. When the sarcocyst ruptures, zooites produced then circulate and eventually lodge to produce other sarcocysts. This process continues until the intermediate (alternate) host develops sufficient immunity to prevent further development. Readers interested in *Sarcocystis* in domestic and wild animals should refer to Dubey (1976).

Very little work has been done on *Sarcocystis* in wild ruminants. I have noted that, if federal meat inspection regulations were used, up to 40 percent of elk carcasses in parts of Arizona and New Mexico would be judged unfit for human consumption, based on macroscopic evidence of sarcosporidiosis.

At present, research on the pathogenicity of *Sarcocystis* infection in mule and Columbian black-tailed deer indicates that one species (and possibly several) is extremely pathogenic to fawns (Hudkins and Kistner 1977). Hudkins and Kistner surveyed mule deer in Oregon and found prevalent infections by a species of *Sarcocystis* they named *S. hemionilatrantis*. The investigators bottle-reared 11 fawns and inoculated them with dosage levels of 5.0×10^4 to 1.0×10^5 sporocysts obtained from experimentally infected coyotes. All 11 of the inoculated fawns became clinically ill, and 9 died 27–63 days postinoculation. Clinical signs of anorexia, weight loss, pyrexia, and weakness were evident before death. Control fawns remained quite healthy. While this initial research indicates that *Sarcocystis* can be pathogenic to fawns, ultimate proof will be obtained when naturally occurring disease is demonstrated in a free-ranging population.

Research on *Sarcocystis* spp. currently is under way to discover what species of birds and mammals act as intermediate hosts. Results of these investigations and ultimate proof of pathogenicity (morbidity, mortality, or both) in free-ranging populations undoubtedly will be a long time coming. It is safe to say, considering the experience of various investigators, that all adult deer in western North America probably are infected with *Sarcocystis*.

Sarcocystis in deer, unlike that in elk, usually does not produce macroscopically visible cysts. Therefore, infection is based on microscopic examination of tissues. It is not unusual to find one or more sarcocysts per low power field during examination of striated, cardiac, or smooth muscle.

Toxoplasmosis

Toxoplasma gondii probably is one of the most prevalent parasites known to man. The host list includes many species of rodents, lagomorphs, insectivores, carnivores, herbivores, marsupials, and primates, including man. Many species of birds also are infected. Toxoplasmosis may vary from an inapparent infection to one that is acutely fatal, but the asymptomatic infection is most common. The disease is similar in man and in domestic and wild animals. Clinical signs include fever, coughing, anorexia, weakness, depression, ocular and nasal discharges, pale mucous membranes, dyspnea, and abortion. In addition to these signs, in man there are some additional manifestations of the disease, especially in the congenital type found in newborns (see Levine 1973).

Most of the information about toxoplasmosis and its various hosts has been documented for man, dogs, cats, swine, cattle, and domestic sheep. Undoubtedly, wild species closely related to the domestics would show similar clinical signs and comparable postmortem changes.

Elucidation of the biological cycle of *T. gondii* required the concerted efforts of a number of dedicated investigators. As Levine (1973, p. 288) aptly stated, "the life cycle of *T. gondii* has both extended and complicated our concept of the epidemiology of toxoplasmosis." However, to understand the disease, one must understand the biologic cycle.

The life cycle of this protozoan is essentially the same as the life cycle of intestinal coccidia, with the exception that there is alteration of hosts for the sexual and asexual phases. The only final host known to be suitable for development of the sexual stages (production of oocysts) is the domestic cat. When domestic cats ingest sporulated oocysts from contaminated environs, the sporozoites are released in the small intestine, where they undergo sexual and asexual development, resulting in the production of new oocysts 21–24 days later. If, however, these sporulated oocysts should be eaten by a mouse, for example, the sporozoites are released and enter many tissues of the body, where they multiply asexually and produce cysts. This generally results in an acute infection. If, for example, this animal in turn should die or become ill as a result of the infection and be eaten by another mouse, the organisms from the cyst are released in the intestine of the new host, whereupon they penetrate the body tissues to produce additional cysts by asexual multiplication. This generally results in a chronic type of infection. This mouse can congenitally infect an entire litter of its offspring. As indicated, if a cat eats oocysts, the life cycle requires 21–24 days. If the cat should eat an acutely infected mouse (in which one of the asexual stages already has occurred) completion of the cycle in the cat to the production of oocysts requires only 9–11 days. If the cat should eat a mouse supporting a chronic infection, oocyst production in the cat requires only 3 to 5 days, because organisms in the chronically infected mouse are ready to go into the sexual stage of reproduction in the cat. Although the cat/mouse cycle has been used as an example, a similar cycle occurs in the cat after ingestion of flesh from other animals.

Although isolation of the organism (cyst) is the most reliable means of diagnosing infection with *Toxoplasma,* most information about the prevalence and distribution of this parasite among its various hosts has been based on serology. Serologic surveys indicate previous or current infection with the organism, depending on the titer. Since both carnivorism and congenital infection are means of transmission, it is not surprising to find a rather high prevalence of infection among wild species. Although serologic evidence of experience with *T. gondii* is available for most of the host animals, very little information is available on mule and Columbian black-tailed deer. In a serologic survey of wildlife in California, Franti et al. (1975) found that 77 of 382 deer had serologic evidence of experience with this protozoan. About half of the deer had antibody titers in the lower range, and about 30 percent had antibody titers in the high range, indicative of recent exposure or challenge.

Diptera

There are few data on the subject of wildlife harassment by various Diptera in western North America. Therefore I will draw on personal observations and other unpublished observations on the effects of these insect pests. Since my experience has been limited to work with deer and elk in Arizona, Colorado, and New Mexico, discussion will relate to this geographic region.

All wild ruminants are subject to harassment by blood-sucking Diptera during summer months, and this harassment sometimes can be extremely severe. In New Mexico and Arizona, horseflies *(Hybomitra* and *Tabanus* spp.) emerge in mountainous regions about 1 June, and reach maximum population by mid- or late June. I have estimated conservatively that, at the time of maximum population, female horseflies feed on mule deer and elk at the rate of 100 per hour for approximately ten hours every day. Since horseflies prefer to feed about the forehead and face of mule deer and elk, skin in this region becomes raw, covered by a serous exudate, and is at least three to five times (15–25 millimeters: 0.6–1.0 inch) thicker than normal.

In these same mountainous regions, early morning and late evening examination of deer and elk has revealed their ears to be literally "packed" with black flies (*Simulium* spp.). During the day, the deer and elk are continuously harassed by small blood-sucking species of *Symphoromyia* (morphologically very similar to houseflies) and various deerflies (*Chrysops* spp.). In late afternoon in some areas, mule deer and elk are harassed by mosquitoes (*Aedes* sp.), and at night they are fed on by species of mosquitoes in the genera *Culex* and *Culiseta*. To make matters worse, the so-called black bodega gnat (*Leptoconops* sp.) is prevalent in parts of the Gila National Forest, New Mexico, during June. These small blood-sucking gnats attack about sundown and are very numerous in some years. This is accompanied by almost continual harassment by sundry houseflies, blowflies, eye gnats, and, in some areas, stable flies—especially near domesticated animals. It has been noted by Bergstrom (pers. comm., August 1970) that annual migration of elk in Yellowstone Park, Wyoming, to high country during summer months actually may be an effort to escape horseflies rather than to seek high mountain meadows.

Myiasis

The only botflies infesting mule and Columbian black-tailed deer in western North America are *Cephenemyia jellisoni* and *C. apicata*. These are rather large, beelike larviparous flies that use cervids as hosts for larval stages.

The adult female fly alights on the external nares and deposits first-stage larvae. These migrate to the posterior nasal passages and develop, in a period of about 6 months, to the second stage. Second-stage larvae migrate to the retropharyngeal pouches and develop, in about 5 months, to the third stage. When third-stage larvae are mature, they reenter the nasal passages and are blown or fall out of nostrils (Cowan 1943).

Mature, third-stage larvae or nasal bot of botflies (*Cephenemyia* sp.) emerging from the nostril. Note also the eyeworm. Photograph by Guy E. Connolly.

Activity of adult flies and the number of generations per year depend on climatic conditions. In southern Arizona and southern New Mexico, for example, there appear to be about three generations of throat bots present in deer populations any time of the year. In California, adult flies are most active from June to late September.

Infestation with throat bots generally initiates some inflammation in the host's retropharyngeal pouches. The degree of inflammation and subsequent edema usually is determined by the number of larval stages present.

C. jellisoni is a very common ectoparasite throughout western North America. It is not unusual to encounter 90 percent infestation in a deer population. Reports from Wyoming (Honess and Winter 1956), Arizona (Swank 1958), California (Taber and Dasmann 1958), and New Mexico (Hibler, pers. files) indicate that the parasite is widespread. Prevalence in deer populations varies from 25 to 95 percent, depending on time of year and environmental conditions.

A number of reports have indicated that throat bots are injurious to their hosts (Walker 1929; Linduska and Lindquist 1952). Like most other parasites, throat bots create an additional problem for hosts debilitated owing to inadequate nutrition. And, although they may play a role in morbidity and mortality, interpretation is subjective. In fact, it has been shown that this parasite does not play the role in starvation for which it has been blamed (Whitlock 1939). It is not unusual to find heavy infestations in healthy as well as starved deer.

Louse Flies

Louse flies commonly occur on mule and Columbian black-tailed deer throughout western North America. The two species usually found are *Lipoptena depressa* and *Neolipoptena ferrisi.* Both species are members of the Dip-

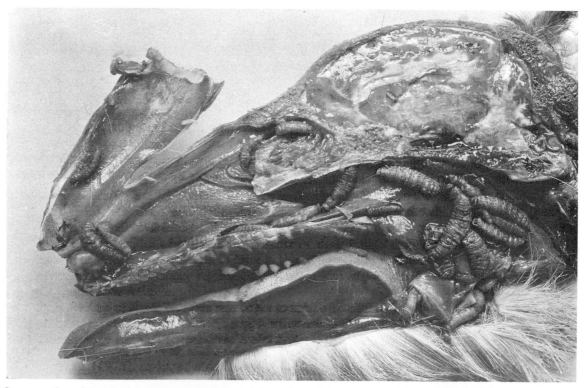

Cross-sectioned head of a deer reveals heavy infestation of throat and nasal bots. A Wildlife Management Institute photograph; by Miles D. Pirne.

An entomology student, studying the life cycle of the louse fly parasite, examines a fresh deer carcass and records skin temperatures. Photograph by Guy E. Connolly.

tera. For a short period during their life-spans, they possess wings that enable them to travel between hosts. Once on a new host, they lose their wings and begin a sedentary, blood-sucking existence. Light infestations are the rule. Hunters often confuse these flies with ticks or lice. A few reports of louse fly infestation occur in the literature (Cowan 1943; Dixon and Herman 1945; Hare 1945; Herman 1945*a*; Senger and Capelle 1959; Spencer 1939).

Lice

Native lice found on deer in western North America belong to the order Anoplura. These include species in the genera *Haematopinus, Linognathus, Tricholipeuris,* and *Cervophthirus.* Westrom et al. (1976) reported that *Bovicola tibialis,* a mallophagan louse imported

with European fallow deer, was found on three Columbian blacktails in California. Lice commonly are found on mule deer and Columbian black-tailed deer, especially during winter months. However, these ectoparasites are not detrimental provided the host is well nourished. I have found that deer generally suffer from pediculosis when malnourished or maintained in captive and crowded conditions.

Mites

Although most wild and domestic ruminants suffer from the debilitating effect of mite infestation, deer apparently are an exception, with only two or three vague and unverified references to discovery of "mites" on deer. I found that 2 of 16 hunter-killed mule deer from the Bloody Basin area in southeastern Arizona had ulcerative dermatitis about the forehead and face. Both had severe infestation with a species of *Demodex*.

Ticks

Ticks are one of the most common parasites of mule and black-tailed deer throughout their ranges. Most cervids in the Rocky Mountain region suffer infestation with the spinose ear tick *(Otobius megnini)*. It is unusual to find a wild or domestic ruminant that is not infested with this parasite. This soft tick attaches in the ear as a larva. Here it grows, molts to a nymph, and continues to grow and feed, eventually developing to adult stage. After leaving its host, the spinose ear tick deposits eggs and dies.

Another common tick in western North America is the winter tick or elk tick, *Dermacentor albipictus*. It is a one-host tick, and larval stages attach in autumn. Development on the host proceeds from larva through nymph and finally to adult stage. When the adult tick has mated and taken a large blood meal in late winter or early spring, it leaves the host, oviposits, and dies. Larval ticks emerge shortly thereafter and estivate until the following autumn. These ticks frequently infest cervids throughout western North America.

In the Rocky Mountain region, from the New Mexico/Colorado border northward, a very common parasite of cervids is the Rocky Mountain wood tick or Rocky Mountain spotted fever tick *(D. andersoni)*. This three-host tick uses smaller animals (rodents, rabbits, etc.) as hosts for larval and nymphal stages and large wild ruminants, canids, and man as hosts for adult parasites. Adult ticks attach from mid-April to mid-July. Thereafter, environmental temperatures generally are prohibitive and, if the ticks have not attached, mated, and oviposited, they must wait until the next year to attach. Generally, three years are required for *D. andersoni* to complete its life cycle.

Mule and black-tailed deer inhabiting the coastal regions of western North America frequently are heavily infested with *Ixodes scapularis, I. pacificus,* and *Ornithodoros coriaceus*. Species of *Ixodes* are three-host

ticks, some of which use reptiles for early developmental stages (Jellison 1934). *O. coriaceus* commonly is found in deer bedding areas in California (Cooley and Kohlus 1944).

Ticks are extremely debilitating when present in large numbers. Also, they are quite capable of acting as extremely efficient biologic vectors for relapsing fever, anaplasmosis (Herms and Wheeler 1935), Rocky Mountain spotted fever, and Colorado tick fever. In addition, *Dermacentor andersoni* and, quite possibly, some of the species of *Ixodes* may produce tick paralysis by injecting a neuroparalytic toxin present in the salivary glands of the gravid female tick. Tick paralysis, caused by *D. andersoni,* commonly occurs in dogs allowed to roam in mountainous regions of parts of Colorado. Only one tick is necessary to produce this paralysis. Logically, deer should be as susceptible to tick paralysis as other animals. There are some unsubstantiated reports from California of tick paralysis in deer.

Fleas

The only flea reported on deer is *Pulex irritans,* a relatively nonspecific flea that also infests humans (Longhurst et al. 1952; Taber and Dasmann 1958). This flea occurs on black-tailed deer in California. Reportedly, infestation is most common in late summer, but fleas have been found as early as April.

Anaplasmosis

Anaplasma marginale is an infectious, noncontagious rickettsial parasite found in erythrocytes of wild and domestic ruminants. It can be transmitted mechanically (as by surgical equipment and hypodermic needles) or by blood-sucking arthropods, such as horseflies, stable flies, and mosquitoes. However, the parasite usually is transmitted by ticks in the family Ixodidae. Ticks act as biological vectors, and a considerable number of species may be involved. The two most efficient vectors in the western United States are *Dermacentor occidentalis* and *D. andersoni*. Both are three-host ticks and are capable of transmitting organisms between developmental stages as well as through eggs. Since *Anaplasma* is a parasite of erythrocytes, clinical signs of anaplasmosis generally are associated with their destruction. Initially there is febrile response, depression, and loss of appetite in the host. After destruction of erythrocytes, clinical signs of anemia are most evident. These signs include pale mucous membranes, increased respiratory rate, rapid pulse, weakness, dehydration, thirst, and constipation. Eventually, icterus and marked loss of weight are evident in severe cases (Howe 1970). Postmortem changes resulting from anaplasmosis are related to massive destruction of erythrocytes and resulting anemia. Mucous membranes are pale; icterus often is evident; blood is thin and watery; and the spleen may be enlarged more than 2.5 times normal size. Hemorrhages may occur on the heart, and lymph nodes may be enlarged and edematous. Petechial hemorrhages sometimes occur on visceral and parietal pleurae. Final confirmation of disease depends on demonstration of *Anaplasma* in erythrocytes or on disease resulting from inoculation of erythrocytes into a susceptible host.

According to Howe (1970), there are no documented reports of naturally occurring acute anaplasmosis of wild ruminants. This may be due to lack of observation, but more likely it is due to natural immunity or host adaptation to the parasite over a long association. Mule and black-tailed deer are susceptible to anaplasmosis (Boynton and Woods 1940). Infection apparently is prevalent among black-tailed deer in California (Christensen et al. 1958; Osebold et al. 1959). Howarth et al. (1969), using susceptible bovine calves as test animals for experimental inoculation, showed that 31 percent of Columbian black-tailed deer fawns, 47 percent of yearlings, and 92 percent of the adults were latent carriers of *Anaplasma*. They suggested that, once infected, deer remained carriers for life. Howe and Hepworth (1965) reported infection of mule deer in Wyoming with *A. marginale*, but prevalence

apparently is much lower than in California. A number of other species—including pronghorn, Rocky Mountain bighorn sheep, elk, and white-tailed deer—also are susceptible to infection.

While the importance of anaplasmosis in wild ruminants is debatable, the obvious fact that mule and black-tailed deer frequently are latent carriers of the disease is of considerable importance to the livestock industry. As biological vectors, ticks are extremely numerous in mountainous regions of western North America. Their ability to perpetuate stage-to-stage as well as transovarially can constitute a hazard to livestock.

Experimental infections have shown that a number of wild ruminants—pronghorn, Rocky Mountain bighorn sheep, and elk—are susceptible to *A. marginale* (Howe et al. 1964). Roberts and Lancaster (1963) have demonstrated susceptibility in the white-tailed deer. Splitter et al. (1955) were the first to report *A. ovis* in North America. It has not been reported from wild ruminants, but Kreier and Ristic (1963) produced anaplasmosis in splenectomized white-tailed deer by inoculation of this species.

CONGENITAL ANOMALIES

Congenital anomalies occur among all species of plants and animals. The frequency of anomalies in mule and black-tailed deer probably is comparable to that found among man and domestic animals. However, reports of such anomalies in free-ranging wild populations are fewer, primarily because malformed individuals generally are incapable of long-term survival. Ryel (1963) presented an excellent review of certain congenital anomalies in white-tailed deer in Michigan, plus an excellent bibliography.

Although anomalies in mule and black-tailed deer may be as common as among white-tailed deer, little published information is available. Cowan (1946b) published one of few thorough studies on anomalies in Columbian black-tailed deer. He reported a case of hemimelus in an adult buck in British Columbia, plus a case of amelus in a fawn and two cases of micromelic dwarfism. Cowan noted that variations in teeth numbers are rare: he observed only one instance of a supernumerary incisiform tooth. He also commented on malplacement of one or more teeth in 6 of 38 deer taken at random in British Columbia.

NEOPLASTIC DISEASE OR TUMORS

Neoplastic disease probably occurs in deer with about the same frequency as in other animals. However, wild animals so affected frequently do not survive long enough to be found, examined, and documented. The most common tumors—or at least those most frequently reported—in mule and Columbian black-tailed deer throughout their ranges are papillomas and fibromas. Cowan (1946*b*) reported 3 Columbian black-tailed deer with papillomas and 4 with fibromasa, but he did

not know the prevalence. Longhurst et al. (1952) and Taber and Dasmann (1958) reported that papillomas are fairly common on black-tailed deer in California. It is not at all unusual to encounter a small percentage of fibromas or papillomas in hunter-killed deer in New Mexico, Arizona, and Colorado (Hibler, pers. files). Moreover, an occasional animal will have one of these types of tumors involving much of its body.

These "warts" are caused by a filterable virus and are not malignant. As with most warts, animals frequently develop an immunity to the infection, and the growth disappears. Transmission is generally by contact with an infected animal. They are not known to be transmissible to man, nor do they affect the infected animal's meat (Longhurst et al. 1952).

TESTICULAR ATROPHY

Antler anomaly, characterized by abnormal conformation and velvet retention, frequently is reported in mule and Columbian black-tailed

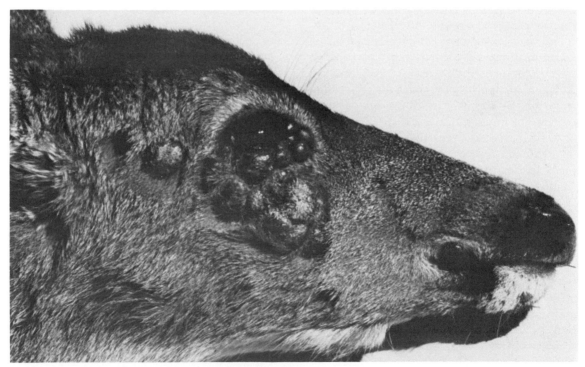

Papillomas—wartlike skin growths caused by filterable virus—have been reported to be fairly common in Columbian black-tailed deer in California. Photograph by Guy E. Connolly.

deer throughout western North America. It also is common in white-tailed deer (DeMartini and Connolly 1975; Murphy and Clugston 1971). Hunter-killed mule deer with antler anomalies are seen commonly in Arizona, New Mexico, Colorado, and Wyoming (Hibler, pers. files). Antler anomalies now are known to result from lack of testosterone. Testicular lesions have been characterized as tubular atrophy with aspermatogenesis and a decrease of interstitial cells. In the single case documented from Colorado, Murphy and Clugston (1971) also noted focal eosinophilia and plasma cell infiltration, but the cause of the condition was not discovered. DeMartini and Connolly (1975) examined testes from 6 similarly affected deer. They noted that lesions ranged from hypocellularity of seminiferous tubules and degeneration of interstitial cells to complete connective tissue replacement of the testicular parenchyma. They also noted chronic vascular changes in several testes. Although DeMartini and Connolly did not determine the etiology and pathogenesis of these lesions, they did discuss the possibility that atrophy could have resulted from an unknown toxic substance, vascular obstruction, or congenital hypoplasia. They indicated that these were more likely to be the cause than was an infectious process, owing primarily to lack of consistent inflammatory cell infiltrate. They also pointed out that viral or bacterial causes could not be excluded, considering chronicity (duration) of the lesions observed. Several mule deer I examined in the southwestern United States had testicular atrophy, grossly comparable with that reported by DeMartini and Connolly (1975).

Chapter 5

BEHAVIOR: ADAPTIVE STRATEGIES IN MULE DEER

Valerius Geist
Professor of Environmental Science
The University of Calgary
Calgary, Alberta

Understanding the behavior of deer is a very practical matter. Habitat selection, food habits, reproduction, and population dynamics all are basic interests of management, accomplished by deer through behavior or closely linked to behavioral adaptations. Today we know that behavior is the first and most common way individual organisms adjust to their environments. In the evolution of adaptations, change by an organism usually begins with behavioral modifications, followed by physiological and morphological adjustments. It is not possible to understand fully the performance of a population or the adequacy of its environment if there is no understanding of the behavior of individuals within that population. That mule deer bound when they run, for example, is not simply a matter of casual curiosity; it indicates something about the way these deer use habitat for security and therefore about their habitat requirements.

This chapter has several aims. First, it will permit the reader to identify the actions of deer and thus to begin to understand their behavior. To this end, a detailed description of behavior patterns and the situations in which they normally occur is essential. A second aim is to acquaint the reader with at least some of the principles that shape the behavior as well as the biology of mule deer. This necessitates a comparison of the ecology and behavior of different subspecies of mule deer, plus those of the closely related white-tailed deer species. Also, certain principles that shape the biology of ungulates—as they pertain to mule deer behavior—will be identified and discussed throughout the chapter. By referring to these principles I will sythesize knowledge from different biological disciplines in an attempt to show how various aspects of mule deer biology relate to each other.

In this chapter, the general term "mule deer" will refer only to the largest and most highly evolved of the subspecies—the Rocky Mountain mule deer. Other mule deer subspecies will be contrasted with Rocky Mountain mule deer and identified by name.

To understand mule deer, it is necessary to sketch some of their attributes that are due to phylogenetic inertia, since they are New World deer. Mule deer are so different from the Old World deer of Eurasia and North Africa that the species have little in common. The paleontological record unfortunately is not good, but if Scott (1937) was correct, Old and New World deer split in the early Tertiary period of the Cenozoic era and evolved antlers independently. New World deer have a foot structure different from that of Old World deer. The former retain long lower splinters of the second and fifth metacarpals, which results in well-developed and firmly anchored dewclaws, ideally suited for moving over soft ground. The culmination of this morphological adaptation is found in caribou, which can walk on crusted snow. The hoof is well suited for climbing, since it spreads widely and can almost grasp, but it is not good for fast running on hard ground. Soft ground usually is found in forests, bogs, and sandy deserts. Plant communities in those areas are more amenable to browsing than to grazing. Therefore, all New World deer tend to subsist on relatively soft, easily digestible forage and have retained relatively primitive teeth along with their primitive legs.

New World deer have relatively large brains (Kruska 1970), not a primitive characteristic. In contrast to Old World deer, they tend to carry less antler mass, and they have shorter gestation periods and therefore rut somewhat later in the year than do Old World deer of the same body size.

In the adaptive radiation of New World deer, the most extreme and specialized forms are caribou and several subspecies of North American moose. The extinct *Navahoceros,* a western mountain deer, and *Sangamona,* apparently a plains deer from central and eastern North America, probably also were specialized endforms (Kurtén 1975). The New World deer radiation is somewhat smaller than that of Old World deer. Their biology is so different that any similarity is likely to be analogous, not homologous. For this reason the literature on Old World deer—such as the elk, red deer, sika, or fallow deer—is not a good guide to the biology of white-tailed, black-tailed, and mule deer.

The fossil record of deer in America is rather sketchy and remains to be studied in depth. According to Kurtén (1975; pers. comm., February 1978), the genus *Odocoileus* dates back to the upper Pliocene epoch of the Tertiary period (approximately 13 million to 2.5 million years B.P.). Judging from fossils, physical characteristics of white-tailed deer present in the Blancan (the lowermost age of the continental Pleistocene sequence in North America)

were similar to those of whitetails of the late Pleistocene epoch and the Recent. Mule and black-tailed deer appeared very late in the Pleistocene epoch. Evolutionary radiation of mule deer and blacktails may have been precluded by the larger, mountain-adapted *Navahoceros* until the latter's extinction. In any case, deer of the *Odocoileus* genus have been present in California at least since the Pliocene epoch (Downs and White 1968). In contrast to other Blancan and Pleistocene New World deer genera, such as *Sangamona* and *Navahoceros, Odocoileus* is an old, primitive genus. Species of the latter have had relatively low-crowned teeth. Since the Blancan age, or the beginning of the Ice Age in North America, deer of the *Odocoileus* genus have been distributed widely throughout America.

In the absence of a good fossil record, it is necessary to rely on other means to study the history of deer. One such means is zoogeography, since geographic distribution is closely linked to the evolution of mammals (Geist 1971a,b, 1978b). By contrasting *Odocoileus* species to other ungulates with acceptable fossil records, it is possible to list criteria that segregate primitive from advanced forms. In general, more highly evolved forms are larger and have longer and heavier hornlike organs, a more strikingly patterned hair coat, a larger rump patch, and a shorter tail. The trend has involved adaptations from forest to open landscape, from low latitudes and altitudes to higher ones, and from old glacial refugia into more recently glaciated zones. Also, social adaptations tend to run ahead of or parallel to ecological ones.

By these criteria, the most primitive subspecies of *Odocoileus hemionus* is the coastal black-tailed deer of Alaska, or Sitka deer, and the most advanced is the Rocky Mountain mule deer. In southern California there are closely connected subspecies of intermediate character, evidenced by subtle differences in tail and rump-patch characteristics (Cowan 1936, 1956b). This suggests that coastal California is the ancestral home of mule and black-tailed deer. However, the habitat along California's coastline, particularly in the north, probably resembled that of coastal Alaska today, wherever glaciations were at a maximum. Sitka black-tailed deer live in a temperate/marine rain forest with nearly continuous rainfall. These are small-bodied, stocky deer with large tails, dense coats, rather small antlers, and a number of behavioral characteristics that can be linked to that habitat.

This view of mammalian evolution identifies differences among subspecies of deer not necessarily as adaptations to local environmental conditions, but as products of the subspecies' dispersal history. It is no surprise, therefore, that mule deer of different subspecies can exploit the same habitats equally well, as was discussed in chapter 1.

By looking at the landscape occupied by mule and black-tailed deer subspecies, one can identify the adaptive trend that gave rise to mule deer: they are blacktails that adapted progressively to mountainous topography of higher elevations. That, however, preadapts mule deer to spread to biomes of higher latitudes, since these deer have adapted to temperate/cold climates at higher elevations. This accounts for the broad range of Rocky Mountain mule deer, from the high Sierras of southern California to the borders of Alaska. Moreover, adaptation of mule deer to hot/dry mountains preadapts for hot deserts. Here probably lies the evolutionary origin of desert mule deer.

The origin of the mule deer is suspected to be the black-tailed deer, which illustrates its ancestral adaptations. The black-tailed deer and the mule deer are treated here as extremes in the adaptive syndrome; subspecies intermediate between these extremes in external appearance also will be intermediate in their behavior.

As we move from lower to higher elevations, the productivity of landscape declines, vegetational growing seasons are shorter, and ecosystems are less mature. Immature ecosystems, compared with climax ones, produce a greater amount of young, exploitable plant tissue per unit area. Difference between carrying capacities of winter and summer habitats increases; the pulse of productivity increases in amplitude. This in turn results in larger body size of individual deer (Margalef 1963), hence, the greater body size of mule deer as well as that of migratory subspecies of black-tailed deer (Taber 1961). Low productivity and spotty distribution of resources, as well as the occurrence of snowfalls (Geist 1974a,b), preclude territoriality of deer because, in such circumstances, they cannot defend their resources. Roaming to seek favorable habitat results in large home ranges, and migration is selected for. Also, forest and shrub cover occur irregularly in mountains; so there is selection by deer for greater diversity in antipredator adaptations, for gregariousness, against territoriality, and for a shift from olfactory to visual communication (Geist 1974a). In general, seasonality causes selection for shorter mating and fawning seasons. It enhances selection for combat ability and better combat organs, resulting in a greater range of combat tactics or specialization in combat, as well as for larger and more complex antlers. It also selects increasingly for relatively larger males and greater ability to fatten (Geist 1974b). Thus, the more highly evolved mule deer not only grow faster but also fluctuate more in body weight by season than do Columbian blacktails (Wood et al. 1962).

Therefore black-tailed deer colonizing dry mountains of California gave rise to larger, showier, noisier, more gregarious, roaming, adaptable mule deer with a preference for the ecotone between forest and openings and an ability to thrive in greater extremes of temperature, water availability, and biological productivity. Mule deer are expected to do everything the blacktails do and more, just as such changes are expected of any ungulate moving from forested lowlands to open mountains.

Black-tailed deer in temperate rain forests also experience a seasonal climate, but temperature fluctuations probably are not greater than those experienced by black-tailed deer in California. Although Sitka deer exploit hemlock/spruce forests from sea level to the alpine, they have access only to the lower part of the vegetational layer and thus can capitalize on only a very small fraction of the meristematic or fruiting parts of the plant layer. Moreover, rain leaches minerals. Whereas in dry mountains mule deer often have total access to the vegetational layer as well as to fine-fibered forage rich in proteins and minerals during the growing season, this may not be so for Sitka deer. The small body size and diminutive antlers of the latter may reflect such a restriction. If this is so, it remains to be investigated. What cannot be determined from general rules of how ungulates evolve is phlyogenetic inertia, for it is quite specific to each lineage.

Through repeated daily observations of individual mule deer, an observer is likely to notice a great diversity in coat markings and body configuration. In addition, there are noticeable individual variations in expressions of social signals and in the relative frequency of those signals. Individual deer vary in body color from dark brown gray, dark and light ash gray, to brown and even reddish (see chap. 2). The rump patch may be yellow or white. Some deer have one white throat patch, many have two distinct patches. Most tails terminate in a tuft of black hair. On some mule deer the tail terminates in a thin tuft of white hairs, while others have the barest admixture of black hairs. On other mule deer there is a dark dorsal line running from the back, down the top of the tail, to the black tail tip. Facial markings, body color, and leg, rump, and tail markings vary considerably among individuals but remain constant from year to year. Shape of antlers and presence of browpoints or supernumerary points vary among bucks and also are reasonably constant from year to year. For this reason individual mule deer can be readily identified.

When, by human observation, two bucks are very similar in appearance, other mule deer are also likely to have difficulty distinguishing between the two individuals. This can be deduced from the extended periods of examination given to one of these bucks by other deer, and the mistakes made in identification, before they engage in social encounters. Although not demonstrated experimentally, field observations indicate that, in daylight, deer can iden-

tify one another visually but have difficulty distinguishing among very similar individuals. In snowstorms, when visibility is obscured and conspecifics may be encrusted with snow, deer also make identification mistakes.

Mule deer do not live in an anonymous society. Individual recognition is, of course, a prerequisite for clan formation and group resource defenses, as will be discussed later.

Another means of investigating evolution of *Odocoileus* species and subspecies is blood serum protein analysis. This method showed that all black-tailed and white-tailed deer tested were related closely (Cowan and Johnston 1962). This also is indicated by hybridization. Mule and white-tailed deer hybrids usually, if not always, are sterile. Fertile crosses of black-tailed and mule deer show the black-tail's rump patch and tail configuration (Cowan 1962). Sterility of mule deer/whitetail hybrids suggests contact among these species and selection for isolation mechanisms. Krämer (1973) concluded that differences in social behavior and scent accounted for such a segregation. Thus it can be expected that white-tailed deer and mule deer will differ most in social behavior where they are sympatric. Whether this is so remains to be verified.

Another prediction remains to be tested: If indeed the mule deer is adapted to greater environmental extremes, uses more motor patterns, and has greater ability to adjust behaviorally than the black-tailed deer, then it ought to have a larger brain per unit of active body mass. Phenotypically, brain size is a product of the diversity of cognitive and motor abilities.

Behavior of an organism also is a product of individual adjustment to its environment. Studies on a variety of organisms have made it eminently clear that the whole environment mirrors itself in an individual phenotype, even the prenatal environment. In mountain sheep, for instance, it can be recognized from the morphology and behavior of individuals whether they developed under conditions of resource abundance or scarcity (Geist 1971*a*; Shackleton 1973; Horejsi 1976). Small body and horn size, delayed maturation, slow growth, sparse reproduction, short suckling duration, early feeding on vegetation by young sheep, lethargic behavior, emphasis on overt aggression, few dominance displays, and little play characterize individuals from populations in marginal habitats. Inspecting individuals to evaluate the quality of the environment they inhabit is a potentially powerful management tool because it permits assessment of a population without disturbing or reducing it. In the study of mule deer behavior, researchers must be aware of this parameter of variation. It has not yet been studied, but Dasmann and Taber (1956a) were very much aware of it in their pioneering work on black-tailed deer.

Variation in behavior is quantitative, not qualitative, in nature. Thus behavior patterns will remain the same between populations, but the frequency with which they are exhibited will vary. Not surprisingly, the basic behavior patterns are very conservative in evolution, because a genetic change in the performer must have a corresponding genetic change in the receiver (cf. Hofer 1972). Synchronous changes in a biological coding and decoding system are difficult to achieve. Not surprisingly, there are great similarities in basic behavior patterns of mule and white-tailed deer. But where, when, to whom, how often, and at what intensity these patterns are exhibited not only varies greatly between these species, but also is expected to vary among populations.

Fundamental to studies of behavior are precise descriptions of behavior patterns as well as their classification. Review of the literature shows that some observers consistently failed to note diagnostic body positions, motions, orientations, and patterns of movement over the ground. They also failed to note the initiation, conclusion, and, often, changes of signals between these actions. Another error is confusion of observations and conclusions: recording a priori that two bucks in antler contact are fighting is confusing a conclusion with an observation. Lack of attention to detail results in statements such as the following: Chasing of does by bucks increases during the rut. This statement is not particularly informative, since there are four entirely different types of chases

of does by mule deer bucks, and none have the same function. To some extent, haste toward quantification has been the cause of inadequate or inaccurate observations.

Some earlier studies suffered from taxonomic problems. For any science to be effective, including behavioral research, it must establish and employ universal systems of nomenclature. Without them, knowledgeable observers cannot organize, quantify, and explain observations in a manner immediately useful to others. Deficiencies were not uncommon in early pioneering studies, but some pioneer researchers bridged nomenclature gaps by careful observation and detailed description. Dasmann and Taber (1956a), for example, disclosed an important behavioral parameter when they noted that black-tailed deer in good habitat behave quite differently from blacktails in poor-quality habitat. Regrettably, that parameter has been largely ignored in subsequent behavior studies.

How to speak about behavior, how to organize it, and in part how to quantify it are problems that largely are solved. Progress in understanding ungulate biology and behavior was rapid in the late 1960s and early 1970s. There has been a shift from ethological conceptions to more ecologically based work—a shift that, in turn, spurred search for principles that could be predictors of biology. In behavior studies, computer simulation has played a small but significant part. It also has raised one still unsolved difficulty. Small and simple models have great heuristic value in that constructing them is an intellectual stimulant, and that is their chief value. There is no point in publishing them; yet some insights derived are valuable and should be disseminated for scrutiny and experimental testing. How to report these insights legitimately—without cluttering the literature with admittedly simplistic, unrealistic models—remains a problem.

Another problem, only partially solved, is the lack of good documentary films on behavior that serve scientific inquiry. The cost, time, and skills required to make documentary films for scientific purposes are very great. Yet such films ought to be made. (Two films on the social behavior of mule deer are being edited and will be available from the University of Calgary, Audiovisual Services.)

My personal experience is limited largely to free-living mule deer and whitetails. I studied the former in the Alberta foothills and Rockies during seven field seasons in autumn in Waterton National Park and three summers in Banff National Park. I studied white-tailed deer at the Aransas Wildlife Refuge during autumn and, as opportunity permitted, during my mule deer studies. I made incidental observations on mule deer in northern British Columbia and the Yukon Territory. I also have observed mule, black-tailed, and white-tailed deer in captivity. There is little behavioral literature to draw on for desert mule deer (see Kucera 1978) and Sitka blacktails, and I have no personal experience with free-roaming animals of these subspecies. This is a regrettable gap. Finally, my own studies have been done primarily with animals living in national parks, in unhunted populations thoroughly habituated to man.

To cover adequately the range of variation in behavior, it is important not only to spend a long time close to deer, but also to see, hear, and smell the significant details from close proximity. Habituation is very easy with mule deer and very difficult with white-tailed deer. All attempts must be made to get subject animals to accept an observer as an inconsequential part of the environment. If this is successful, no changes will be introduced in the social behavior of deer, provided the observer uses tact and common sense. If there is legitimate question about observer effect on the subject population's behavior, observations at close range and at long range by a hidden observer can be compared. I have detected no differences.

BEHAVIOR PATTERNS

Behavior patterns are distinct and recognizable postures and actions of individual animals. They occur within broader types of activities, such as predator avoidance, courtship, aggres-

sion, and feeding. Their division and classification are to some extent a matter of subjective judgment, much as is found in taxonomy. Most, but not all, behavior patterns are signals that are quickly recognized by experienced students of animal behavior. If properly described, they can be recognized just as easily by others.

Feeding

The body size of mule deer is reflected in manner of feeding. The smaller an ungulate, the more selectively it must feed, increasing its intake of soft, high-protein, easily digested vegetation (Bell 1971; Geist 1974*a*; see also chap. 3). However, the absolute amount of food required drops with body size. Therefore a smaller individual has more time to feed and can be more selective than a larger one. This is exemplified by white-tailed deer fawns, whose activity per unit of food eaten is higher than of adults (Ozoga and Verme 1970). In a climate with a year-round vegetational growing season, a herbivore can specialize by feeding on a few species of plants. Where the growing season is discontinuous and where food quality and availability vary greatly within the span of a few weeks or even a few days, plasticity of food habits is expected.

Feeding behavior of mule deer reflects those seasonal principles. Mule deer move distinctly from bite to bite, usually select small bites, may examine them, and eat a broad spectrum of food items. To stereotype the mule deer as a browser is a gross mistake. It may be a browser in some areas but not in others. Moreover, its food habits change not only seasonally but geographically (Leach 1956), with population density (Nellis and Ross 1969), and with major weather changes such as drought (Anthony 1976). This adaptability is emphasized in chapter 3. We do not know the extent to which food preference changes within an activity period, or whether deer first "fill up" and then select bits of highly preferred food items, as mountain goats appear to do (Geist 1971*b*).

On a study area in the Alberta foothills, mule deer fed heavily in autumn and winter on fallen leaves of balsam poplars, picking leaves off the ground or pawing for them in snow. The deer preferred leaf hay or dried leaves still clinging to poplar branches broken off by summer storms. However, they avoided fallen leaves or leaf hay of quaking aspen. Deer selected dried leaves and shriveled fruit of snowberry. With the first killing frost, the mule deer turned to thistles. An unexpected but highly preferred food source during autumn, winter, and even spring was natural ensilage. Ensilage ferments from frost-killed forbs that dry, fall to the ground, and become infected by fungi, turning into a brown, fragile, rotting mass. In particular, silaged false hellebore and cow parsnip were preferred. These plants contain toxins in the green stage and are avoided at that time. In essence, deer then feed on detritus. In prairie patches, dried leaves of balsamorrhiza were eaten, but only after snow had covered them. Discolored, dried, and wilted leaves were preferred, particularly those still on the stalk; a great variety of species were

A mule deer buck, in late autumn, feeds on ensilage, a decaying false hellebore. Photograph by Valerius Geist.

utilized. Deer deliberately entered Douglas fir forests after storms and picked broken annual tips of branches off the snow surface, which periodically was an abundant food source. Crowns of toppled balsam poplars and Douglas firs were browsed even when the needles of the firs were yellow. Regularly and often in all seasons, deer cropped green grasses along trails, clipping off short young shoots. Browsing on twigs of willows, red osier dogwood, aspen, chokecherry, saskatoon bush, or balsam poplar was confined mainly to periods of deep snow. In spring, however, catkins were a favorite food, and deer would readily climb tall, hard snowdrifts and feed on the tops of aspen trees, a food source normally some 4–8 meters (13–26 feet) above ground level. A rare food was pondweed. Saskatoon berries were consumed in season. In summer, deer fed extensively on forbs and growing leaves of a diversity of shrub species as well as on the inflorescence of many herbs. The literature on mule deer food habits reveals a taste so catholic that what a deer eats appears to be a function of habitat preference, not of forage preference. In this respect it is noteworthy that mule deer will feed readily in open areas, sometimes far away from cover, and thus significantly exploit these types of habitats.

It is important to know that a mule deer may feed without leaving a trace of its feeding activity. This happens when it feeds on fallen leaves, fruit, and twigs, leaf hay, or ensilage lying on the ground, or when it pulls fescue blades from the bunch. The latter can be pulled free leaving no trace that additional blades grew there. It is not always easy to discern what a deer is eating, even when an observer kneels directly beside the animal. Deer sometimes keep their muzzles in the vegetation, obviously eating but not readily observable. The assumption that a deer's food habits can be studied from a distance with a spotting scope is tenuous even under the most favorable conditions, such as when deer feed above snow. Wallmo et al. (1973) showed that, from a distance, observers can make significant errors in identification.

Mule deer thus select food from about a 1.5 meter (5 foot) vertical layer of vegetation and

Mule deer feeding habits and preferences are difficult to discern even by close observation. Photograph by O. C. Wallmo.

only rarely rise on their hind legs to reach higher. They remove snow with their muzzles and by pawing it away with a front hoof. However, this is not seen frequently because it occurs within rather narrow limits of snow hardness, and because deer prefer to feed where there is no snow.

Therefore in spring, when snow is melted from the prairie hills, mule deer move there to feed, away from aspen bluffs and conifers where snow still is deep and hard. In early winter they move to the cover of conifers where snow is lowest and softest (Bouckhout 1972). Conifers also act as a radiation shield on clear, cold winter nights (Moen 1968) and offer excellent protection during blizzards and chinook storms. Where deer feed and rest is very much a function of weather. During periods of strong wind, mule deer are found with greatest regularity in pockets of calm air

below the crests of hills and in densely crowned forests. Sudden changes in snow hardness or depth make them shift to different localities.

Actual feeding actions of mule deer are not particularly distinct from those of other deer. Twigs or fibrous stalks are chewed off with premolars. Shoots, buds, and leaves are plucked off either against the cutting edge of the lower incisors or simply by tearing. The latter action could result in a leaf or twig's coming off with a thin strip of bark attached, a nutritious and easily digestible addition. Twigs tend to be chewed down base first, as are thistles and ensilage. Much food simply is picked off the ground. Each piece of coarse food picked up is chewed down separately; deer apparently do not collect several bites before chewing (see also chap. 2). Study in Colorado has shown that mule deer pick up and chew small pieces of plant matter almost continually and that the mean amount taken is only 0.1 gram (0.0035 ounce) per bite (Carpenter 1975). From summer observations, Wallmo (pers. comm., October 1977) noted that the median number of bites taken before completing mastication and swallowing was about ten.

The total amount of activity budgeted for feeding by deer is expected to vary with individual metabolic demands, excluding other variables. During periods of growth, lactation, hair coat renewal, and fattening, more feeding activity can be expected than during seasons in which the animal is not growing. The resting metabolic rate of deer reflects seasonal demands, being highest in summer and lowest in winter (Silver et al. 1968). Ozoga and Verme (1970) showed that feeding activity of white-tailed deer has the same pattern of seasonal fluctuation.

Resting

The normal resting position of mule deer is on the brisket and belly, with legs tucked under. The front legs may be extended, probably to thermoregulate. It is probable, but has not yet been investigated, that inside the front

A yearling buck paws a crater in approximately 46 centimeters (18 inches) of snow to reach and feed on green grass that is a valuable but scarce winter forage. Photograph by Valerius Geist.

The typical alert, resting position of mule deer. Photograph taken in 1915 by Vernon Bailey; courtesy of the United States National Archives.

legs is an area where rapid heat loss may occur, similar to heat loss experienced by wild sheep. A deer occasionally extends its neck, rests its head on the ground, closes its eyes, and appears to sleep for short periods. During rest, deer normally are alert and generally minimize their own noise and movement. Other deer, such as searching bucks, easily miss resting companions and walk past without detecting them at distances as short as ten paces.

Most rumination is done while resting. The food bolus can be clearly seen moving up and down the throat when it is regurgitated or swallowed.

Comfort Movements

After resting, a deer normally performs a variety of comfort movements. It stretches, arches its back and then depresses it, extends its tail, and stretches its body and neck while stepping forward. Deer scratch with teeth and hind legs and may void and occasionally urine-rub (a marking behavior to be described later). Bucks with growing antlers rub the growing stumps against the inside of raised haunches and legs. Antler-rubbing movements cease with the shedding of velvet. Voiding and comfort movements are clustered at the beginning and end of activity periods. Rubbing the body against trees or rocks, common in bighorn sheep, has not been observed in mule deer. The exception is neck-rubbing on tree trunks by bucks during the rutting season, although that is not a comfort movement.

Etiquette, Submission, and Appeasement

When deer are resting or feeding, they are not randomly oriented to each other, nor are their body postures devoid of social significance. Deer observe a rather rigid set of rules when they mingle—similar to, if not ultimately homologous with, what people consider "courtesy."

When resting, individuals bed down so as not to look into each other's faces. This has been found in all ruminants that have been observed for the specific purpose of detecting it (Walther 1958, 1966). Such etiquette persists in all social behavior of mule deer as well: they normally avert their eyes from each other. Closer investigation shows that, while resting, the dominant deer may look anywhere; others adjust so as not to look at him. When deer are feeding, the same basic rule holds. This behavior, with the tendency of deer to follow each other, results in deer grazing in much the same direction when close to each other in the open. The matter of eye aversion between dominant and subordinate deer will be discussed later; in social interactions, one deer may "stare" at another in specific situations.

As in other ungulates, the grazing posture also serves as a signal of submission or nonaggression. This is explicitly demonstrated by deer in groups. When close together or moving past each other, they keep their heads low and ears back. They may crouch slightly, depress their backs, and press their tails close between their haunches. This is the posture of both submission and appeasement (Barrette 1977). It is a common courtesy posture, used even by dominants toward subordinates on specific occasions. Such behavior is seen most often in groups of white-tailed deer, which have much more exaggerated or expressive mannerisms than do mule deer. Crouching as they move past each other while feeding, for example, is far more pronounced.

Fully-fledged submissive or appeasement behavior normally is confined to clear-cut social interactions, yet it is occasionally seen in other situations. A fawn surprised by a larger animal may scamper away in a crouched and back-depressed posture with head raised, very much as a female scampers from a courting buck. On infrequent occasions, disturbance can lead to exaggerated appeasement behavior, as the following incident illustrates. Some 40 females, fawns, and yearlings appeared in full flight. They stopped in a tight bunch, with necks erect, ears forward, looking back along their path of flight. Seconds passed as the deer stood rigid. Slight movement occurred when individuals began to relax. Suddenly all abandoned the intense alarm posture and obviously found themselves too close to one another. Immediately, all members of the group slunk around and away from each other in intense appeasement posture. As individuals gained distance from others, they abandoned the appeasement crouch and returned to normal walking and feeding.

As with the courtesy behavior, the submissive or appeasement posture is never as strikingly expressed in mule deer as in whitetails. White-tailed deer may slink on their bellies, heads and necks extended flat over the ground, with snakelike movements. A white-tailed doe witnessed moving through a group of mule deer does exhibited this posture—a good indication of relative rank of individuals of these species. In addition, white-tailed deer may perform turning motions with the head. Neither mule nor white-tailed deer perform exaggerated chewing motions or distinct calls during submission, as do many Old World deer. However, exaggerated grazing or "sham grazing" is part and parcel of submissive or appeasement behavior of mule deer. For instance, a subordinate mule deer approached by a dominant may move off with head lowered, pluck a few mouthfuls of grasses, then begin grazing while watching the dominant from that position.

Appeasement postures were used very frequently by an old doe observed for several years. She led the way in appeasement posture while fawns crowded in behind and mounted her, which she tolerated. Other females centered their activity on her. She and her followers were identified as a home range group (Bouckhout 1972). When the doe disappeared, the home range group dissolved. In the area where the group often grazed and rested when she was present, no other deer have taken up permanent residence since.

Alarm and Predator-Avoidance Strategies: Security Measures

Normal feeding activities, rumination, resting, and conspicuous comfort movements have no discernable signal value. They appear to serve as necessary background against which signals or social significance are contrasted. Thus a sudden deviation from feeding, a cessation of calm relaxed movements and normal feeding noises, causes alarm. Normal circumstances are characterized by a number of actions, such as flicking of the tail and ears; slow, head-depressed walking; sounds of chewing and plucking; distinctly spaced steps, and rustling in leaves. All these denote a temporary absence of danger.

Followed by fawns and an adult buck, an old doe assumes a courtesy posture, with her head held low and ears pulled back. Photograph by Valerius Geist.

Before discussing the antipredator strategies of deer, let me note that mammals are very good at learning. They adjust themselves on the basis of experience. The best way to avoid predators is to go where there are none. Deer are highly sensitive to disturbance, as is seen in the studies on white-tailed deer by Hood and Inglis (1974) and Dorrance et al. (1975). It is striking how mule deer cluster around human settlements in national parks, where predators are rarely seen. The same was noted by Hoskinson and Mech (1976) for yarded white-tailed deer. Hoskinson and Mech introduced the intriguing idea that white-tailed deer gravitate to areas that lie at the territory edges of two (or more) wolf packs and that they gain some safety by staying in that boundary zone, a zone of insecurity to wolves.

Hornocker (1970) observed that mule deer vacate a drainage once mountain lions make a kill there. The observation that deer sneaked away from areas where a mountain lion ap-peared, as detected by radiotelemetry (Seiden-stricker et al. 1973), also is in accord with the hypothesis that deer avoid areas frequented by predators.

A second antipredator strategy of mule deer is to restrict movement to areas close to escape terrain or cover (Sweeney et al. 1971). Reflections of this are the tendencies of wintering mule deer to stay close to steep slopes, river-banks, and cover. Whitetails, on the other hand, use quite different escape strategies and may form large wintering herds on open, un-obstructed prairie (Krämer 1972).

The presence of a predator in the distance changes the actions of mule deer abruptly. Individuals assume the attention posture; body and extremities become rigid; the tarsal hair may be flared; metatarsal gland scent—an alarm scent—may be released, as reported by Müller-Schwarze (1971); ears are put forward; and nose is pointed toward the disturbance.

Black-tailed deer do not habituate readily to

A rigid, leg-raised alarm posture, exhibited by a mule deer fawn. Photo by Starr Jenkins; courtesy of the United States Forest Service.

scent of the metatarsal gland, but they do habituate to alarm odor from the metartarsal glands of white-tailed deer (Müller-Schwarze 1977). Müller-Schwarze (1971) stated that release of tarsal gland odor by blacktail fawns serves as a distress signal. Müller-Schwarze (1972) showed that young black-tailed deer responded, apparently instinctively, to predator odor, particularly that of coyote and mountain lion, and less so to the odors of predators these deer do not encounter in their normal range.

If the disturbance passes, just before deer drop their heads or commence normal activities, they suddenly wag their tails. This appears to signal a return to normal circumstances. If the disturbance does not pass, a variety of responses are possible. A mule deer, on rare occasions, just lies down behind a bush and continues watching through a screen of branches. If danger is seen or heard while it is still some distance away, the deer may move off. Escape often is triggered not by the appearance of a predator, but by its disappearance, as was also noted by Linsdale and Tomich (1953). When a group of deer seek to escape, one will turn suddenly and trot off. The others will follow, more or less in single file. This measured flight—usually uphill—is punctuated by a few stops when the deer look about and listen. This appears to be the common mode of moving away from danger. Such moves are made early, not in haste, and with orientation pauses to correct the retreat. In open landscapes, disturbed mule deer may move as much as several miles. When deer are in dense shrubbery, their retreat may not be far, and the animals remain alert when they stop. When pursued, mule deer do not always bolt. Usually they move with slow measured steps around the source of potential danger, always attempting to keep it located.

Mule deer also may bolt from a disturbance by making a sudden right turn and bounding off. Just before bolting, a deer is likely to perform the extreme alarm posture, where the hair on rump patch and tail is flared, the tail is held out horizontally, a small ridge of hair rises on the middorsal line close to the tail base, tarsal glands are flared, and the deer stands very erect. It may lift a front leg and stamp it down. It also may move its head laterally with ears extended and even turn in small circles. Infrequently, it may blow sharply through the nostrils, a sound more commonly emitted by alarmed black-tailed and white-tailed deer. Such extreme alarm behaviors may not lead to bolting; they appear to be associated with uncertainty about the disturbance. The deer then may calm down and continue feeding at the same site.

When a deer bolts, it may or may not stott (a bounding gait). Stotting is a highly developed form of locomotion in mule deer and, to some extent, in Columbian black-tailed deer. In Sitka blacktails, stotting apparently is not frequently seen (O. C. Wallmo, pers. comm., October 1977). At first, stotting appears to be an alarm behavior that alerts deer. Its sound also unmistakably identifies a mule deer screened by branches or foliage. Eslinger (1976) showed this bound to be a highly modified gallop. It is the most common form of

Trotting, as shown by this black-tailed buck, is a common form of locomotion by mule deer and blacktails when not alarmed. Photograph courtesy of the Oregon Department of Fish and Wildlife.

locomotion seen by observers, but not the fastest. Mule deer gallop quite similarly to white-led deer, though they lack the smooth-flowing elegance and, probably, the speed of whitetails. The gallop is employed by mule deer when chasing conspecifics, such as when bucks chase does in rush courtship, guarding or cutting the doe from other bucks, chasing a defeated rival or escaping attack, and during play by adults and among fawns.

Bounding occurs primarily when mule deer are alarmed and is particularly intense when they have been surprised. The evolutionary significance of mule deer's bounding gait or strotting is a matter of uncertainty. A common notion is that it is an adaptation to rough terrain (Eslinger 1976). Seton (1929) found that dogs could catch mule deer on open plains but not in broken terrain. For black-tailed deer, it is a logical mode of movement through low, dense, and impenetrable shrubs on steep slopes (Dasmann and Taber 1956*a*). In such habitat, bounding may well be a faster means of locomotion than galloping; it has been reported that bounding black-tailed deer do get ahead of chasing dogs (Linsdale and Tomich 1953).

Another explanation of bounding by mule deer is that it permits rapid vertical ascent on steep hillsides. In open country, mule deer often escape by bounding uphill and over ridgetops. In these areas, such as the Porcupine Hills in the foothills of the Alberta Rockies, white-tailed deer inevitably bolt down and along hillsides. Energy cost of vertical locomotion is a little more than twelve times the cost of horizontal locomotion (Moen 1973). Thus a mule deer bounding rapidly and directly uphill imposes a heavy cost on a predator chasing it. Consequently, steep, long hillsides act as escape terrain and as an obstacle to a predator's rapid ascent.

Why should a deer have recourse to bounding or slotting, a relatively slow form of locomotion, when escaping from danger? A number of observations suggest the following reasons.

Compared to the lateral gallop of white-tailed deer, the bound of mule deer has a compressed foot-fall pattern or steep angle of ascent, a long period of suspension, and thus a high trajectory. Eslinger (1976) emphasized that mule deer sacrifice speed for height. However, mule deer or black-tailed deer gain more than the ability to clear obstacles or land on a small spot of level ground; bounding also permits unpredictable changes of direction. Stotting therefore is part of a complex system of predator avoidance, and this is where its real significance may lie. It permits the deer to foil a predator's calculations by suddenly moving in an unpredicted direction, escaping upward from the predator's lunge, and rapidly placing obstacles between itself and the predator. To be effective as a form of escape, stotting must be combined with exact timing and take place in a landscape of the deer's choice, full of low obstacles such as brush, boulders, deadfalls, rock clefts, and sleep slopes. At present this is no more than a hypothesis based on circumstantial evidence; the actual escape of mule deer from a chasing predator, such as a wolf, has yet to be described.

Despite the uncertainties, stotting or bounding can work as an escape mechanism as follows: a chasing predator catches up with a stotting deer. The deer must go on, awaiting the lunge. At the moment of the predator's horizontal lunge, the deer accelerates upward and away. However, where the deer will land cannot be predicted. Not only may the deer depart at right angles from its former line of travel, it actually may bounce away backward. This can force the predator to reorient with each of the deer's bounds. In addition, the deer may have put an obstacle between itself and the predator. Each lunge by the predator is met with a change of direction. Furthermore, a predator catching up with a group of deer is likely to be confused by the sudden "explosion" of the group, with bodies and white rump patches moving in all directions.

In executing its escape, a mule deer must depend on timing. This is crucial. A deer must perform an unpredictable bound no earlier than the moment when the predator is committed to a lunge. If the deer jumps sooner, the predator can correct its lunge; if it jumps too

In many habitats, bounding is a faster means of locomotion than galloping. In open areas it is an important behavior for eluding pursuing predators. Photograph by Dave Daughtry; courtesy of the Arizona Game and Fish Department.

late, it gets caught. Therefore, this type of escape would select, in mule deer, for calm, relatively unexcitable individuals. One needs to postulate here a general increase in the threshold of excitation. This is a very important postulate, for it explains a surprisingly large amount of mule deer biology in contrast to that of whitetails, as will be discussed later.

Adult mule deer thus have several distinct strategies for avoiding predators:

1. They specialize in detecting danger at very long range by means of large ears and excellent vision—bucks can quickly detect and visually track another animal as far away as 600 meters (1,970 feet).

2. Once danger is detected, mule deer may opt to hide, probably much as black-tailed deer normally do (Dasmann and Taber 19563a).

3. Mule deer may move into cover and cautiously outmaneuver a predator.

4. They may depart while danger is still a long way off and move several miles to another area. This strategy may be new to the Rocky Mountain mule deer and absent from the more primitive black-tailed deer, to judge from the account by Leopold et al. (1951) of difficulties encountered when trying to chase California mule deer off small seasonal ranges. Observations by Dasmann and Taber (1956a) confirm this.

5. Mule deer may stott rapidly uphill, imposing on pursuing predators an unacceptably high cost per unit time of locomotion.

6. A deer may bound off and then trot away, stopping frequently to gain information on the disturbance. Initial stotting, combined with release of metatarsal scent that inhibits feeding (Müller-Schwarze 1971), is highly advantageous in that, by alarming others, it causes other deer/to bound off as well, reducing the conspicuousness of the deer who bounded off first. It also would trigger group formation.

7. In escaping, a deer may join others, which in itself is a form of protection against predators as long as it avoids being at the rear of the escaping group (Wilson 1975).

8. Finally, circumstantial evidence suggests that, when a predator closes in, a mule deer can initiate evasive maneuvers based on sudden unpredictable changes in direction and on placing obstacles between itself and the predator. This evasion probably would not succeed if the deer

was greatly weakened, since coordination and strength are both a function of nutrition, as shown in studies on humans (Berg 1973; Cravioto and De Licardie 1973). It also would fail against group-hunting predators. In that regard, mule deer are a favorite prey of wolves, which are highly effective in their predation on this species (Carbyn 1975) as well as on black-tailed deer (Klein and Olson 1960). Susceptibility of deer to predation is discussed in chapter 7.

In addition to these strategies and tactics, a mule deer adds a certain amount of unpredictability to its whereabouts from day to day. Although individuals occupy home ranges less than 1.6 kilometers (1.0 mile) across, and though it is possible to learn all the favorite places deer are likely to be, it is not possible to predict accurately from day to day, or even from hour to hour, where a given group of deer or an individual deer will go. This is particularly evident when one follows a rutting buck in search of does. A searching buck makes many changes in direction, is easily distracted, oscillates between feeding, investigating signs by other deer, horning, and listening for other deer, and at times it engages in random running. Similarly, a group of grazing females tends to shift locations so that no predictable routine develops. To find a specific individual from day to day, an investigator simply is forced to check, routinely, all the spots where the deer is likely to be on its home range, with success by no means assured. Mule deer thus shift between and within favorite localities in an unpredictable manner, reducing a predator's chances of meeting deer should it revisit sites where it previously met them.

A mule deer's frequent calm scanning of the area around it during feeding is a necessary correlate of its somewhat random movements. It cannot know from which direction danger is likely to come. Therefore, keen and continual scanning is needed. Since a mule deer does not bolt when it detects possible danger, but calmly investigates it, there appears to be no need for a highly diagnostic noise to be emitted by conspecifics like the hoof-click of caribou or elk. Only in a calm animal that loses few precious calories getting excited over potential danger is the presence of the hoof-click redundant.

In contrast to whitetails, mule deer do not often hide from predators and are showy, noisy, and smelly. When in groups, fawns call frequently and loudly, and bucks horn noisily for minutes on end. In daylight, mule deer readily move into the open, where they are easily seen. They urinate copiously on their hocks and have large glands on their hind legs and between the digits of the hooves. However, when population density is low, mule deer revert to hiding and can be very difficult to find.

A discussion of predator-escape techniques of adult white-tailed deer provides additional understanding of techniques used by mule deer and of how these techniques have influenced mule deer biology. Four strategies of white-tailed deer are to hide, to outrun the predator so that their scent evaporates, to cast their scent, by going into water, and to confuse the predator by crossing the trails of other deer. These have been discerned from studies of white-tailed deer hunted by dogs (Sweeney et al. 1971). Whitetails also form compact herds in open country, very likely as an antipredator behavior. Such behaviors are all logical correlates of tall but easily penetrable grasslands subject to fires, as well as of swamps and patches of thick shrub in subtropics and tropics—the evolutionary home ranges of white-tailed deer.

The hiding strategy is far better developed in whitetails than in mule deer. Its success depends on the deer's remaining rigid and silent. It also requires a quick getaway when the deer is surprised, hence the explosive eruption from hiding, the very fast gallop low over the ground, and the avoidance of obstructions. To maximize time for decision-making while escaping and thus maximize distance between itself and the predator (as well as diffusing its scent), the white-tailed deer requires a trail system. In tall grass and thickets, as well as in snow, a trail system is a necessity. Unlike the mule deer, the whitetail minimizes contact with obstructions to running. Once some distance is gained, the whitetail stops, normally in cover. Two reasons for this can be discerned. First, the deer can reorient to the source of danger. Second, by suddenly stopping, it can deprive the predator of information on its whereabouts. To "lose" the predator, the deer then may move to where there are other deer, and the pursuing predator may be in for a relay run. Dogs do run relays on whitetails (Sweeney et al. 1971). Some differences between sexes in escape from predators are described by Sweeney et al. (1971) and by Hood and Inglis (1974). For example, bucks tend to hide, then bolt and run long distances away from their home ranges, whereas does and fawns tend to circle back and use confusion tactics. Bucks become less active when hunted, and does become even more active (Roseberg and Klimstra 1974); bucks also move into cover earlier in the morning than do does (Zagata and Haughen 1974).

The significance of white-tailed deer's escape methods is that they select for a nervous, shy animal—one with a low threshold of excitement. It is an integral part of a whitetail's adaptations to conceal itself in thickets during the day, venture into open field under cover of night, and form large, secure groups if forced to winter on open prairie. It follows, therefore, that the excitable whitetail is expressive in its social signals, whereas the calm and plodding mule deer is not. The whitetail ought to require less stimulation for successful communication and therefore emit less odor and be less showy and noisy in social behavior. It follows that an excitable deer is less likely to habituate to humans and will be less readily tamed than an unexcitable one.

Consequently, characteristics of the mule deer's high threshold of excitement (compared with that of whitetails) are calm disposition, underexpressed signals, redundancy in communication, and tolerance of disturbance (Krämer 1973) and open space with little cover. Also, mule deer are readily tamed. And courting mule deer bucks and does remain rather fixed in space, compared with courting whitetails, which run in big circles or exhibit wide dispersal (see Krämer 1972). These characteristics, in turn, are necessary consequences of mule deer's antipredator strategies.

In other words, many differences between mule and white-tailed deer result from different antipredator strategies.

Mule deer also may escape danger by running into water, as whitetails are likely to do (see Sweeney et al. 1971). Mule deer and Columbian and Sitka blacktails are excellent swimmers, the latter crossing wide stretches of ocean to reach coastal islands. However, whereas creeks, swamps, and open water can be considered escape terrain for white-tailed deer, mule deer only rarely avail themselves of

Mule and black-tailed deer are excellent swimmers, but they rarely move to water as a means of escaping predators. Photograph by Edward P. Cliff; courtesy of the United States Forest Service.

these opportunities. For mule deer, broken terrain—not wet lowlands—is escape terrain.

Deer also may turn on predators. Black-tailed and mule deer may attack coyotes and bobcats. Linsdale and Tomich (1953) saw a buck, wounded by dogs, lunge with deep roars at his tormentors, attempting to gore them. Dasmann and Taber (1956a) indicated that black-tailed bucks may stay in thickets and fight dogs rather than flee. Normally, however, deer avoid even small predators.

The antipredator strategies of black-tailed deer described by Linsdale and Tomich (1953) are similar to those of mule deer. However, the black-tailed deer appears to be more of a "hider." If so, then it ought to be the more active, nervous animal that Müller-Schwarze (1971) and Cowan and Geist (1961) found it to be. Whether it is more expressive in its social signals than the mule deer remains to be seen. Certainly, blacktails' dominance display—the rut snort and the crouch—as observed among captive bucks, is more extreme than that of mule deer (Cowan and Geist 1961). Blacktails in captivity tend to interact more than mule deer (Quay and Müller-Schwarze 1971), and they certainly are more nervous and irritable than the placid mule deer. This is consistent with the hypothesis that black-tailed deer tend to hide more than do mule deer.

Urination, Marking, and Defecation

Urination and defecation postures in mammals, as well as urine and fecal matter themselves, are frequently of social significance. In mule deer, the defecation posture and fecal pellets carry no apparent social message, as they do in many bovids and in the pronghorn (Walther 1966, 1974; Kitchen and Bromley 1974; Kitchen 1974). Most defecation occurs shortly after an animal rises from its bed or changes activities, but deer also defecate while grazing or moving in an almost random manner. Defecation rarely disrupts ongoing activies. It is different with urination.

Whereas both sexes of white-tailed deer urinate in different body positions, as do most un-

gulates, male and female mule deer do not. The mule deer buck normally urinates in a low crouch, in female fashion. Only when urine-marking does the buck depart from the female posture, but female mule deer also urine-mark in this fashion. Normal urination posture of mule deer of both sexes is virtually identical to that of females of other deer and bovids, hence the justification for calling the bucks' posture a "female posture." The only noticeable difference between urinating mule deer is that the buck moves his tail up and down. This behavior can be helpful in sexing fawns, but it is not always consistent, at least not in Rocky Mountain mule deer. It may be more predictive in black-tailed deer, to judge from comments of Müller-Schwarze (1971).

The crouched urination posture of males appears to denote "femaleness" and submission in social encounters. Thus older bucks with hard antlers use it in the presence of dominants. In the absence of dominants, they tend to eliminate urine by rub-urinating. This behavioral strategy, weakly developed in mule deer, is very marked in mountain sheep society; a subordinate acts "female" in the presence of a dominant (Geist 1968b, 1971a).

A conspicuous urination posture by females must be to their advantage. The aim of courtship is to make the female urinate so that the male can test her urine to determine whether she is approaching estrus. Females do not part readily with their urine. Clearly, it is to a buck's advantage to let the female urinate undisturbed when she finally concedes, but this requires a signal by the female about her intentions. Males normally stand back and wait patiently while the female urinates. Therefore a female's urination posture appears to offer some protection from harassment—hence its value to a subordinate in the presence of a dominant male. Weak female minicry by mule deer bucks is a logical consequence of greater gregariousness and of the fact that only female mimicry—not juvenile mimicry—can be practiced in species in which males do not care for their own young (Geist 1971a).

A second way of voiding urine is by urine-marking or rub-urinating. In this activity the

Typical posture of urinating bucks outside the rut. This urination posture also is typical of does year-round and is assumed by subordinate bucks during the rut when a dominant buck is nearby. Photograph by Valerius Geist.

deer brings its hind legs forward and puts its hooves close together, pinching the hocks so that the long hairs of the tarsal glands press together. The hocks in both males and females are positoned directly under the orifice from which urine flows. In the male, therefore, hind legs tend to be a little more forward relative to front legs than in the female. While a deer urinates, it rubs the hocks together so that the tarsal glands rub against each other. This in turn imparts a gentle rhythmic, lateral movement to the rump. Rub-urination tends to be lengthy when done outside the rut by bucks, or anytime by does. During the rut, large bucks tend to rub-urinate very frequently but briefly, with little urine voided. Whereas older bucks normally simply rise from this posture after urinating and go on with courting, feeding, or agonistic behavior, females, fawns, and, less frequently, young bucks begin to lick the tarsal glands and hind legs. Apparently the latter deer lick off the urine, because they do not exhibit the urine-matted hind legs so typical of large rutting bucks.

All sex and age classes of mule deer urine-rub. During the rut, it is done most frequently by large bucks and less frequently by small bucks. Females and fawns do it relatively rarely during the rut, but females urine-rub frequently during winter (L. W. Bouckhout, pers. comm., 1972). During the rut, rub-urination is the principal elimination posture of males. When large bucks begin to void in female fashion, they have finished rutting for the year. The urine-rub is a major dominance display of mule deer—the principal olfactory message about the dominance position of individuals. As is true of other ungulates, the most dominant male in a group marks most frequently, presumably exudes the greatest amount of odor (Ralls 1971; Shank 1972; Barrette 1977), and thereby signals his status. Large bucks rub-urinate spontaneously after spotting a rival, after horning shrubs, poles, or trees, and when escorting a defeated rival from the female ranges.

Complementary to this urine-marking behavior is a great interest by individual deer in

A large buck displays scent-marking behavior in rub-urination posture. Photograph by Valerius Geist.

A doe licks her tarsal gland after rub-urinating. Photograph by Valerius Geist.

the tarsal glands of other deer. Fawns temporarily lost and running from deer to deer in apparent search of their dams sniff the tarsal glands of the deer they inspect. On first meeting a large unfamiliar buck, subordinate males try to sneak behind him and sniff his hocks. A strange buck coming to a female group may cause a female to sneak quickly around him on her belly, sniff his tarsals, and bound off. On rare occasions, a fawn noses the tarsals of urine-rubbing female and may be slapped for it. Tarsal gland hairs are widely flared by alarmed deer, occasionally by a suckling fawn, and by bucks and does during intense dominance displays.

There is some significant information about structure and secretions of tarsal, metatarsal, preorbital, caudal, and interdigital glands of mule deer and Columbian black-tailed deer, as well as relevant observations on social behaviors of the two subspecies (Müller-Schwarze 1971, 1977; Quay and Müller-Schwarze 1970, 1971; Brownlee et al. 1969). The active olfactory components of tarsal gland scent, or pheromones, are lactones. Male and female deer differ in the composition of complex lactone mixtures, as do young and old deer. Pheromones are adsorbed from the urine onto lipid-covered central hairs of the tarsal glands. These hairs are termed "osmetrichia" (Müller-Schwarze et al. 1977). Osmetrichia are specialized scent hairs that, in black-tailed deer, have large chambers between cuticular scales and comblike features on the scales. Osmetrichia hold lipids that, in turn, trap volatile lactones. Rub-urination by fawns was found to alert and attract the fawns' dams and other deer. Females were particularly interested in the tarsal scent of males. This is understandable, since its intensity and perhaps its composition ought to give direct evidence about a male's dominance status. Black-tailed deer rub-urinated and inspected others' hocks more frequently than did mule deer. This is a logical consequence of blacktails' life in dense shrubs and forest, in contrast to open country and ecotone adpatations of mule deer. During hours of darkness, black-tailed deer nosed each other's tarsals about five times more often than in daylight hours. Also, most rub-urination was done in the dark. Tarsal organs are not only sniffed, but also licked by other deer, although licking may be to remove tarsal scent—as it is most likely when tarsals of fawns are licked or when a deer licks its own tarsals. Large bucks, by contrast, rarely licked their tarsals. Müller-

Schwarze and Müller-Schwarze (1975) showed that mule and black-tailed deer each preferred the scent of their own subspecies.

Besides mule deer, black-tailed deer, and white-tailed deer, caribou (Espmark 1964; Lent 1965; Geist 1966*a*; Bergerud 1974) and moose (Geist 1963, 1966*a*) also urine-rub. In caribou this is well developed; in moose it is not. Caribou have small, smelly, but short-haired tarsal glands; moose have only hair whorls. After urine-rubbing, a caribou bull may draw his hind leg (and gland) over the bridge of his nose. This forms a wet, glistening patch on the nose, one way to disperse the scent. According to Müller-Schwarze (1977), urine hits the hooves and augments interdigital gland odors in caribou.

Aggression: The Threats

Aggression is behavior by which individuals create and maintain access to scarce resources against the actions of conspecific competitors. It is active competition in which one individual, in some fashion, displaces another. Aggressive behavior includes overt aggression or combat, which in turn is divided into tactics of attack and defense. Strategies of resource exploitation dictate specific weapon systems, and these in turn dictate tactics of attack and defense and their morphological counterparts (Geist 1978*a*).

A signal used by an animal to indicate a specific weapon system is termed a *threat*. Sometimes only a signal denoting impending violence is given, such as the rush threat. Therefore there are weapon threats and rush threats.

Since fighting, and even preparation for fighting, generally is very expensive in calories and nutrients and may be costly to both winner and loser, most animals have opted for more subtle forms of aggression. These forms of aggression aim at the same results as overt aggression but without the same costs and are known as *dominance displays*. In contrast to threats, dominance displays are not readily "understood" across species lines; they are subtle, indirect threats in which a great range of psychological principles, attention-gathering

mechanisms, and even optical illusions are used to intimidate opponents. It is these indirect threats that ultimately pattern the exterior of animals so markedly. In addition to intimidation, dominance displays also may function to advertise an individual's rank and thereby to attract females or incidentally challenge an opponent to combat. For a detailed discussion of aggression, principles of dominance displays, weapon evolution, and ecological determinants that dictate strategies of aggression, see Geist (1978*a*, 1971*b*, 1966*b*) and Walther (1974, 1966). These authors take issue with conventional ethological conceptions of aggression, in particular with the concept of "ritualized aggression."

The mule deer has two weapons: sharp front hooves used by all sex and age classes, and hard, polished antlers used by bucks. Unlike moose, mule deer do not kick with the hind legs; and, unlike so many Old World deer, they do not bite. In full-fledged fighting with the front hooves, mule deer rise on their hind legs and push or jab the front legs hard into an opponent's body or slash the hooves down-

Flail fights or displays are not unusual among females and juveniles. In this instance, one doe strikes at another in an apparent conflict over browse. Photograph by William V. Reeves; courtesy of the Texas Parks and Wildlife Division.

ward. Such fights are not common, and they are preceded by dominance displays, threats, and occasionally by threats alone.

The major threat is an intention movement to rise on hind legs and slash with front legs. It consists of the head-up threat posture, in which the aggressor is oriented toward an opponent. The aggressor faces its opponent, drops its ears, and tips its chin upward, while crouching slightly in the rear and thereby elevating its front quarters (fig. 18). This threat posture is very similar in all deer that fight with front legs. During the threat, preorbital glands may be open, eyes open wide, and nostrils flared.

During intense social interactions, elements of dominance display may be mixed with elements of threat. Opponents circle each other, heads slightly raised (in the broadside dominance display, the head is lowered), hairs on the body erect, tails raised, tail hairs flared, and tarsal glands sometimes flared. The animals' movements become tense. As in the display, antagonists may avert their eyes and, on rare occasions, rut-snort. Such elaborate display and threat behavior preceding a fight with front legs is rare; it can be expected among females and among bucks that have shed their antlers. Fights erupt quite quickly among females, between females and juveniles, and among juveniles. The loser in such a flail fight runs off, occasionally pursued briefly by the winner for a few bounds, during which time the winner strikes the ground hard with its front hooves and utters several short, harsh, deep grunts.

Dominant individuals tend to assume a head-high threat without raising body hair or showing any slow, stiff movements. They act quickly and decisively. They may raise a front leg and either strike it downward on the sides or haunches of a subordinate or simply strike the ground. Sometimes an upward stroke with one front leg is used, hitting the belly of the subordinate. This act is superfically similar to the front kick used in courtship by many bovids. Much of the time, a glance with elements of the head-up threat (such as dropping of the ears) suffices to make a subordinate run off.

Figure 18. The head-high threat postures of mule deer—graphically depicted by the three does on the left—represent intention to rise (characterized by the doe at right) and flail at an opponent. Drawing by author.

A completely dominant mule deer may forego the threat, rush directly at a smaller opponent, and hit it with one front leg. If the subordinate departs, the dominant may strike the ground with both front legs in quick succession and utter two or three sharp, exhaling, coughlike sounds before stopping. During the rut, large bucks rush at smaller ones. The greater the difference in size and dominance between the bucks, the greater the likelihood of a rush.

Unlike does, bucks use antlers as weapons in culminating the rush and can inflict serious wounds if successful in catching up with or surprising a subordinate. Miller (1974) observed that even bucks with antlers in velvet rushed conspecifics and attempted to gore with their soft antlers. Although a sharp inclination of antlers at other deer is recognized as a threat, this is not a particularly common behavior pattern except within the rush threat.

No biting intention in the form of snapping has been observed in mule deer, but it occurs occasionally in white-tailed deer and very seldom in blacktails (Miller 1974). Unlike mule deer, a surprisingly large percentage of individual whitetails in some populations still carry vestigial canines (Brokx 1972). Also, during the scrape ceremony (see Moore and Marchinton 1974), white-tailed bucks grasp branches with their mouths, tug at them, and then may rake a branch with their antlers or begin raking while actually holding onto the branch with the mouth. This was noted by Pruitt (1954) and confirmed by Hirth (1977) and by my observations. Biting in aggression, like the presence of canine teeth, is a mere vestige in white-tailed and black-tailed deer. It apparently is lost completely in mule deer, caribou, and moose.

The primary method of gaining access to scarce resources by displacing deer of the same species is the attack with weapons inflicting surface damage, thereby maximizing pain (Geist 1978a). In mule deer and many other deer, these weapons are front hooves for flail-

A large female-tending buck rushes a yearling male whose rump patch is flared. Photograph by Valerius Geist.

ing, with its iconic—that is, intention-signaling—threat derivative. This is most likely to occur in contest over resources and apparently increases in frequency as the condition of deer deteriorates; hungry individuals are more likely to be aggressive. This is implied by Ozoga's (1972) study on white-tailed deer, by Petocz's (1973) study of mountain sheep and goats, and by Dasmann and Taber's (1956*a*) observations that, at high density, black-tailed deer were more sensitive and aggressive than at low density. Totally debilitated deer, however, lose any tendency to be aggressive. The use of front hooves thus is a means of removing other deer from a contested resource, not simply of dominating them.

Dominance Displays and Indirect Threats

The expression of dominance displays is highly situationally dependent, as evidenced by such displays in the most common of interactions among bucks, namely, between a large and a medium-sized buck in the prerut during autumn. At the appearance of an unfamiliar, medium-sized buck, a large one fixes him with his eyes while still at a distance. Only at this time will the dominant look directly at the smaller male. At a distance of some hundred paces, the large buck will begin his advance. His head will be held low, with neck in line with the body, ears back and folded out, hair erect, tail held horizontally and whipping up and down with each step, and back slightly arched. His movements will be stiff and somewhat slow. At a distance, owing to the erectorpili effect, the displaying dominant looks very dark. Periodically the tongue will lick over the lips and nose. At first approach will be directly at the smaller buck, but within thirty paces the dominant will swing outward and approach at a tangent, averting his head slightly. The tarsal and preorbital glands are not likely to be flared.

A dominant buck *(foreground)* shows a low-intensity dominance display, while a subordinate buck exhibits typical avoidance behavior. Note the concave back and lowered tail position of the subordinate. Photograph by Valerius Geist.

During the approach phase, the smaller male, in all likelihood, will watch the larger buck while standing alert, slightly splay-footed, tail pinched in and back caved downward. His hair will be appressed, and therefore he will look lighter in color than the approaching dominant. As the dominant approaches tangentially, the subordinate is likely to evade by circling to the former's rear. The subordinate may attempt to get downwind of the dominant while looking directly at him; this is an unmistakable behavior of the subordinate. If they are in shrubbery, the bucks inevitably will have some bushes between them. In such circumstances, attempts by the subordinate to come from the rear and sniff the dominant's tarsal glands can be most pronounced. As the dominant buck continues his advance, the smaller buck avoids him by moving away, head erect, back depressed, and so forth, showing the submissive behavior of the species. The dominant keeps his head averted, and the subordinate continues to look at the dominant—

with either raised or lowered head—as he sneaks past. Glancing up from a lowered head is infrequent in mule deer but very common in the white-tailed deer. In whitetail encounters the subordinate may crawl on its belly around the dominant with neck extended and, from a crouched position, look upward at the larger deer.

Soon after reaching the vicinity of the small male, a dominant mule deer buck is likely to rut-snort (Cowan and Geist 1961). The dominant will quickly throw head and neck upward until his nose points upward at about a 45-degree angle. Simultaneously, he will inhale with a piglike snort and pull his head down toward the ground, averting it slightly, arch his back, extend his tail, and rise on stiltlike legs, while exhaling hard against closely appressed nostrils, which produces a hissing sound of 5–10 seconds duration. During the snort, the buck strains hard, his neck bulges, his flanks are drawn in, and his tail quivers. Invariably, the response of the smaller buck is to bolt away

A dominant buck rut-snorting at a rival. Photograph by Valerius Geist.

a few paces, then stop and look at the dominant. White-tailed deer also rut-snort, but not as loudly as mule deer. In captivity as well as in the wild, white-tailed bucks only rarely perform the rut-snort (Cowan and Geist 1961). Black-tailed deer not only rut-snort more loudly than mule deer, they also add a distinctive series of loud grunts after the snort.

The dominant mule deer buck will continue following, relaxing his display posture somewhat and rut-snorting periodically. He may stop and horn some shrubbery or overhanging branches of trees and may urine-rub thereafter. The small buck will evade the dominant, show signs of submission, urinate in crouched female posture in the dominant's presence, feed, and watch the larger buck closely. He too may horn shrubs whenever the dominant does so. This engagement may terminate with the dominant beginning to feed and the subordinate leaving; or it may be prelude to a sparring match, as will be described later.

If the meeting is with older and more closely matched bucks, display components in the interaction increase, as does the chance of reciprocal behavior and a full-blown dominance fight. However, the chances for a sparring match decline. In such a meeting, the dominant buck may move to a shrub and begin horning it vigorously before initiating his advance. He will urine-rub thereafter while looking toward the still-distant stranger. During the approach, the dominant's display posture and movement will become more extreme. After an initial approach, movements of both bucks become slow, deliberate, and stiff. Tarsal glands are widely flared and appear black; preorbital slits are opened, and body hair is erected to its fullest extent. As the opponents come close and begin circling, they begin to crouch lower and lower, moving about slowly on bent hind legs. A rut-snort by one may cause the other to bolt, or at least it will cause the opponent to jump laterally a little and continue displaying. The probable loser of this engagement often can be foretold; it will be the buck that, during display, tends to tilt his antlers at the opponent or glances at the opponent most frequently, as if preparing to meet the onslaught. At times one antagonist may suddenly incline his antlers, causing the other mule deer to jump away, crouch, also tilt antlers, and then bolt away. The dominant follows, rut-snorts, horns shrubbery, urinates, and walks after the defeated buck. This phase has only one aim—to escort the defeated buck out of the general area used by does with whom the dominant breeds. The defeated buck, head held low, stopping periodically to look back, may attempt to circle back. The dominant will intercept him on every

A dominant buck *(left)* presents a strong dominance display as he escorts a rival from the dominant's general rutting area. Photograph by Valerius Geist.

try, however, and continue to show display components until the defeated buck is well on his way. Such "escorting" can exceed 2 kilometers (about 1.2 miles) in distance. When the defeated buck finally is left unescorted, he invariably will horn shrubbery. This horning is done hesitantly at first, with periods when the buck merely stands and listens. However, he is likely to work himself into a frenzy, in which he smashes his antlers forcefully into a bush with all signs of high excitement.

Horning—quite rare in the white-tailed deer and of short duration—is performed frequently by mule deer and for very long periods of time. It acts as an auditory signal of male dominance. For mule deer, horning is almost what bugling is to elk. Pauses during horning, when a buck stops and listens, are for a good reason: another buck is likely to reply. One technique I used for gaining information was to follow a rutting buck by some 10–50 paces. Wandering bucks would stop at 50–200-pace intervals, horn, look and listen, then move on. They quickly pinpointed replies by other bucks and often moved to investigate. A social interaction could follow.

Horning by mule deer is not only extensive, but also intensive. There are several components to it, depending on the object horned. Small bushes, poles, hanging branches, and tree trunks may be horned. Tree trunks and poles often are gouged deeply and shredded with the short browpoint. A buck often grasps shreds of bark hanging from a horned tree or pole, pulls them off, and eats them. Quite frequently the buck rubs his face and occasionally his neck in the wound of the tree, a behavior very common in Old World deer. Horning and bark-pulling are focused on one or two branches rather than distributed over many. Sometimes a buck thrashes hard with fast rotary movements of the head or with nodding motions. More commonly, he deliberately rubs one antler against a twig, sapling, or branch. Infrequently a buck rises on his hind legs and thrashes some branches with his antlers. This

A buck horns red osier dogwood shrub with the basal parts of his antlers. Photograph by Valerius Geist.

behavior, called *preaching,* is common in some primitive Old World deer, such as axis and sambar deer (Schaller 1967). Head rubbing—reportedly common in the more olfactorily oriented black-tailed deer (Müller-Schwarze 1971)—is rare in mule deer. Some head rubbing by mule deer occurs incidental to horning by bucks, but forehead skin of mule and black-tailed deer is not as well endowed with glands as that of their distant relative, the roe deer (Quay and Müller-Schwarze 1970, 1971). A roe deer buck uses his forehead extensively in marking his territory (Kurt 1970).

Mule deer do not form "scrapes" as do white-tailed bucks (Moore and Marchinton 1974; Hirth 1977). Only once did I see a mule deer buck scrape the ground with a front leg three times while horning an overhanging branch. There are no reports of black-tailed deer forming scrapes.

There are a few minor differences between dominance displays of black-tailed deer bucks and those of mule deer bucks. In blacktails, the rut-snort is louder and contains loud grunts, as previously described. Horning appears to be less common in black-tailed deer than in mule deer, judging from description by Miller (1974). Broadside display of blacktails is more expressive in that the back is arched strongly upward and the tail is held well above the horizontal. In a mule deer buck, the back is weakly arched and the tail, though erected, tends to droop. In black-tailed deer the tail quivers; in mule deer it nods. The black-tailed deer tail may exude a more powerful odor during this display than does that of the mule deer (Quay and Müller-Schwarze 1971). In mule deer, erection of the tail and its black tip probably function as attention-catching adaptations during display, just as do tail-raising and tail-flicking in other broadside-displaying ungulates. Markings of the mule deer buck function to frame the animal during display and enhance its apparent size and mass. The theory of attention-catching organs—the biological basis of art—is discussed by Geist (1975, 1978*a,b*).

Displays in mule and black-tailed deer are subject to maturation; yearling and even 2-year-old bucks are less expressive in their displays than are older males. This was documented for captive deer by Cowan and Geist (1961) and is very noticeable in the field. Social maturation appears to continue in mule deer well past sexual maturation, although not in as pronounced a form as in mountain sheep (Geist 1968*b*, 1971*a*).

A rival buck bolts away from a dominant female-tending buck that turned and was ready to rush and gore him. The dominant buck's attention was drawn first to the larger of the two rival bucks shown, but it is only a matter of a short time before the yearling male at right receives equally abrupt and serious treatment. At the height of the rut, dominant bucks tend to discard dominance displays and preliminary threats in favor of immediate action, except toward rivals nearly their own size. Note, too, the neck enlargement of the rutting bucks. It is a highly visible secondary sexual characteristic of mule and black-tailed deer that has received little scientific attention. Photograph courtesy of the Wyoming Department of Game and Fish.

The Sparring Match

Interaction of two mature bucks of distinctly unequal body size and dominance rank frequently leads to a sparring match. In mule and white-tailed deer this behavior has nothing in common with fighting or the settling of dominance rank. In Old World deer it does. Except among yearlings and an occasional pair of 2.5-year-old bucks, sparring takes place only among bucks of distinctly different dominance ranks, usually reflected by difference in body sizes. In mule deer, quite unlike mountain sheep, dominance in mature bucks cannot readily be predicted from antler size. Even when sparring bucks are nearly equal in size, they are of distinctly different ranks, and sparring takes place only if their respective ranks are solidly established. The most uncommon sparring matches are among old bucks. Those I observed, all took place well before the rut, when the bucks were still placid and fat.

Sparring is solicited by the dominant, but it is commenced and terminated by the subordinate—except among bucks that have frequently sparred with each other and know one another well. There are no "winners" or "losers" in sparring matches. Sparring matches are greatly protracted and occasionally last more than an hour. They occur primarily before and after the peak of the rut, but yearling bucks spar throughout the rut. Small bucks, on sparring terms with a large buck, may parasitize his dominance and displace superior bucks in the dominant's presence. Some observations indicate that, even during the peak of the rutting season, dominant breeding bucks chase off former sparring partners less frequently and less intensely than they chase off strange bucks of similar size. From the foregoing points, it is evident that sparring is a kind of agonistic behavior distinct from fighting (Geist 1974c) and should not be confused with fighting.

The following is a probable scenario of an engagement of two greatly unequal mule deer bucks. After a larger buck has displayed and a smaller has evaded the dominant and looked at him, the dominant begins grazing, acting as if he is ignoring the subordinate. At this stage the smaller buck may follow the dominant, particularly if the smaller deer is a yearling or 2-year-old male. The smaller deer approaches cautiously from the rear, sniffs the dominant's tail and hocks, alertly watches the grazing buck's head, steps back, looks the dominant over again, and perhaps begins grazing. As an alternative, the smaller buck may begin to move off, in which case the larger deer follows, commencing to feed whenever the smaller animal feeds. At first the dominant may do no more than follow the smaller buck at a distance, feed, and rest in his vicinity, all the while acting as if he is ignoring the subordinate, yet looking in his direction every so often. In bucks of similar size but unequal status, the period of following may be very long, perhaps a day or two. In bucks of greatly different size, the period is brief, sometimes only a few minutes.

While grazing in the vicinity of the subordinate, the larger buck not only may forego all signs of the dominance display, but may occasionally show weak but recognizable appeasement behavior. He may crouch somewhat while grazing close to the smaller buck, then move slowly in a semicircle in front of the feeding subordinate, blocking his path some three to five paces away. At this point the subordinate may quit feeding, move several paces away from the dominant, and commence feeding again. Slow semicircling by the dominant, while grazing and even crouching slightly (with depressed back), may continue several more times. Then, while grazing with his body at right angles to the feeding subordinate, the dominant may turn his head so that his antlers point at the subordinate. He then stops feeding, raises his head slightly, and waits for the subordinate's response. By offering his antlers to the smaller deer and waiting, the dominant buck solicits a sparring match. Soliciting may be repeated a number of times before the smaller buck responds. When the subordinate responds, he steps forward and places his antlers into those of the dominant, and sparring is on.

If the antler sizes of two sparring bucks are very unequal, the buck with larger antlers may tilt his head in a way that offers only one antler for sparring. It is then engaged by the subordi-

A large buck advances for a sparring match with a yearling buck. Typically, the subordinate watches the dominant male as the latter exhibits components of dominance display. Photograph by Valerius Geist.

A large, dominant buck solicits a sparring match by holding his antlers toward a yearling buck. At this point the yearling averts his head in a display of courtesy. Photograph by Valerius Geist.

A small buck engages the antlers of a larger male, after the dominant has repeatedly solicited the sparring match. Photograph by Valerius Geist.

nate. This is common in sparring matches of a yearling buck and a large male. The smaller buck also may first sniff the antlers of the dominant, but this is rare. Among white-tailed deer—whose sparring matches are similar to those of mule deer—it is common for the subordinate to crawl in appeasement posture to the dominant, lick his face, and then engage antlers. In mule deer antler engagement is almost immediate, with both bucks standing.

Head and neck movements of sparring deer follow quite recognizable patterns. Most commonly, bucks hook antlers, then twist their heads around the sagittal plane. This type of sparring is akin to "Indian wrestling." Bucks also may hook the right antler of one buck into the right antler of the other and then push. Circling by both bucks results. Pushing frontally is not common. At first both bucks are very careful and apparently inhibited in their sparring, and disengagement is quite likely after a few seconds, usually initiated by the subordinate, who suddenly jumps backward, well away

from the larger buck. Both raise their heads and avert their eyes. This is a courtesy posture, not a display of antlers. This position is held for a few seconds, then the subordinate steps forward and inclines his head. Next the dominant buck inclines his head, offering his antlers again. The subordinate engages and a new bout of sparring begins.

As one sparring bout follows another, a number of changes become apparent. Both bucks appear to become less cautious, and their motions may gain an element of exuberance. Neck-twisting becomes more forceful, as does circling; eye aversion is less rigid. The time finally comes when even the dominant commences a sparring match—without the smaller buck's bolting. In pauses between bouts, the dominant may urine-rub, while the smaller— true to rank—urinates like a female. Eventually the larger buck may move vigorously to the smaller and directly engage the antlers of the smaller animal. Such a stage, however, is not likely to be reached before half an hour has

In sparring matches among bucks of very unequal size, the larger buck may extend and use only one antler. Photograph by Valerius Geist.

Neck twisting is the most common action during a sparring match. Photograph by Valerius Geist.

Disengagement during a sparring match usually is initiated by the subordinate buck. It often is accomplished by a backward jump. Photograph by Valerius Geist.

passed. The smaller buck may begin to graze after disengaging, and the dominant is likely to walk around him and engage his antlers. If the subordinate moves back, turns, and walks off, the dominant will stop, avert his eyes, and, after a few seconds, follow to try again. If the smaller buck declines these advances, the larger buck invariably stops and averts his eyes. Eventually both bucks feed—larger following smaller—and rest together; the pair may remain together for a day or two.

When sparring, the larger buck freely engages the smaller, and vice versa. The subordinate picks localities where sparring is to take place on highly advantageous terms; this may be the top of a steep bank. Here he can push the larger buck downward, preventing him from climbing up. As long as the dominant is close by, the smaller buck may approach larger bucks (but smaller than his sparring partner) in full dominance display. Bucks that rush and chase the subordinate are rushed and chased in turn by the larger sparring partner. However, this behavior is rarely seen; I saw it in only eight interactions in seven rutting seasons. A parallel to these sparring observations of mule deer has been noted in captive blacktails (Müller-Schwarze, pers. comm., November 1977). Fawns may chase large bucks after the latter have lost their antlers and once other adult bucks and does have chased the antlerless male. Although primates are known to form social bonds in which individuals parasitize the rank of a dominant, such have not been observed in any ungulate except mule deer.

Among yearling and 2-year-old mule deer bucks, sparring is very common; it tends to decline in frequency with age. In only one case, I witnessed an antlerless male fawn sparring with a yearling buck. Both performed the behaviors expected of subordinate and dominant just as if they were adults. In sparring, yearling bucks may poke each other's bodies with their antlers. A dominant, in particular, is affected when a

In the presence of a larger sparring partner, a subordinate buck may urinate in female fashion. Photograph by Valerius Geist.

During a sparring match, dominant and subordinate bucks usually can be identified by their tail positions. Dominants raise their tails; subordinates pull their tails in. Photograph by Valerius Geist.

Sparring among yearlings and 2-year-olds, as shown here by spike black-tailed bucks, is quite common. Photograph by Len Rue, Jr.

subordinate disengages, circles, and then pokes him in the haunches.

I once observed a very unusual interaction during a sparring match between mule deer. Two yearling bucks met, and the larger began a stiff display. The smaller buck circled to his rear, then calmly sniffed and licked the larger buck's tarsal glands. The larger yearling stood stiffly but glanced backward. The smaller yearling moved directly behind the larger buck, which remained in stiff display. The smaller buck then mounted the larger animal for several seconds before the latter circled and hooked its antlers into the smaller buck's side. Homosexual mounting is seen very rarely in free-living mule, black-tailed, and white-tailed deer. Although Hirth (1977) observed it twice in whitetails, the circumstances of these mountings were not reported. In the situation I witnessed, the small yearling responded to the rigidity of the other male—a rigidity typically assumed by does before breeding. Captive black-tailed does in estrus were seen to mount other does; and male fawns, when first brought together, mounted each other (Müller-Schwarze, pers. comm., November 1977).

As I indicated, sparring matches of white-tailed deer follow the very same principle as

those of mule deer; it is interaction of unequals in all observed instances. Hirth's (1977) data on sparring frequencies support that conclusion. The match differs from that of mule deer by being of shorter duration and in the manner of initial engagement. Small males approach dominants in distinct, low-crouched submissive posture, and they lick the faces of the dominants before engaging antlers. On rare occasions a small mule deer buck may lick his rhinarium (the hairless area at the end of the nose) a number of times before engaging, but I never saw one lick the face of a dominant before engagement.

Linsdale and Tomich (1953) confused sparring and fighting, and little can be extracted from their notations about sparring in black-tailed deer. The study by Wachtel et al. (1978) of sparring in a very small natural population of mule deer provides some valuable quantitative data. It supports, in large part, the preceding description based on my as yet unpublished quantitative studies. Some of their results, however, are an artifact of the small population as well as of their methods. Unfortunately, they lumped all sparring bouts irrespective of their sequence in a sparring match and did not study individual bucks to establish their relative ranks, but used antler-point differences for comparisons. Their finding that large bucks rather than small ones initiate most sparring matches can be duplicated easily by quantifying sparring bouts of bucks highly familiar with each other, as well as by lumping "soliciting" with "commencing." Moreover, bucks that know each other well may not follow the normal rules of conduct closely. This was found by Shackleton (1973) when comparing the behavior of bighorn rams from a small, relict population with those from large populations.

To date, rules of sparring have not been discerned for caribou or moose; in Old World deer the rules differ (Geist, in press).

Dominance Fights

Dominance fights differ entirely from sparring matches. Dominance fights occur among matched bucks and almost entirely among the mature older bucks. They are exceedingly rare and are initiated from intense dominance displays. They usually are very short in duration and are most common during peak of the rut, when sparring matches are not frequent. Dominance fights tend to be so violent and fast that detailed offensive and defensive tactics are almost undiscernible to an observer. These fights lead to wounding and tend to attract the attention of other bucks (which sparring matches do not), leading to disruption of the fight by a dominant male. They also lead to segregation of a dominant from a subordinate, not to social bonding as in the sparring match. In sparring matches there are no losers or winners; in dominance fights there are.

Dominance fighters need not be strangers. Such fighting may occur during the rut among bucks closely matched in size but of different dominance ranks. These serious fights are so rare that, in the time I collected data on social behavior, I recorded some 718 interactions among bucks but not a single dominance fight. Those seen were observed incidental to gathering data on aspects other than social behavior or while filming. I have seen only ten dominance fights among mule deer over the course of seven

rutting seasons.

All fights were preceded by intense dominance displays by both bucks. The opponents ducked so low that they were almost crouched on the ground; their hind legs were somewhat spread and kept crooked. This is a defensive tactic that reduces the target area for attack and holds the buck's body ready for the opponent's onslaught. From the broadside display, with antlers tilted toward the opponent, attack is initiated by a sudden powerful lunge low over the ground from a distance of about 2 meters (6 feet). Antlers meet with a clash. Bucks push against each other, keeping their bodies close to the ground. For seconds they may freeze into immobility, pressing hard against each other. In the next moment one may lock his antler into the other's, suddenly pull the opponent backward, then swing him sideways. Antlers are twisted forcefully about the sagittal plane. Bucks with antlers locked may swing around each other, pushing one moment, giving way the next. Such actions are surprisingly fast and violent, in complete contrast to the otherwise slow, plodding ways of mule deer.

Opponents may move back and forth quickly, with antlers locked and heads close to the ground. The erectorpili effect is strong, tarsal and orbital glands are flared, and breathing may be heavy. Combat consists of rapid forward thrusts and complex, forceful, rotating of heads, as well as sudden pulling of the opponent. Miller (1974) saw a blacktail buck hurl another buck over his head in a fight; and I saw a mule deer buck stand on his head, apparently pulled completely off balance by the eventual victor of the fight. Thus the major objective of the dominance fight as practiced by mule deer is to impose movement on the opponent and force him to lose control over his body.

A fight is terminated when one of the bucks suddenly turns and bolts. The winner attempts to thrust his antlers quickly into the loser's body and push him as he departs. Bounding after the loser, the dominant utters two to four barking coughs and strikes the ground forcefully with his hooves. Thereafter he falls into a trot after the subordinate, escorting him beyond the home range of the female group.

Two bucks in dominance display just before a dominance fight. The buck on the left—the eventual winner—averts his head. The eventual loser displays "insecurity" by depressing his tail and turning his antlers toward the approaching rival. Photograph by C. C. Shank.

The dark buck has been thrown off balance and is about to be defeated in a dominance fight. The light-colored buck's antlers have slipped past his opponent's defenses and may have pierced the body; this usually ends the fight. Photograph by C. C. Shank.

Intraspecific combat consists of tactics of attack and defense, plus deceptive moves probably meant to provoke mistakes by the opponent. The latter are difficult to identify with certainty and require rather extensive cinematography documentation for accurate analysis. Unfortunately, current documentation is not adequate.

The defensive strategy of a fighting buck is easier to discern. Unlike some ungulates (Geist 1966*b*, 1971*b*, 1978*b*), mule deer rely for protection less on skin armor than on speedy parrying of opponents' thrusts. For this purpose they use their antlers. By catching onto an opponent's antlers, an attack is foiled; by locking onto them, the next attack is prevented. This secondarily permits the defender to twist, push, or pull his opponent off balance. This type of combat correlates in mule deer with the wide occipital condyles by means of which the skull articulates with the vertebral column. (Axis deer, for example, have a very small set of occipital condyles and do not use twisting and pulling in fights.) Defensive tactics of mule deer therefore include body positions that not only reduce the target area open to attack and enhance opportunity to parry or catch an opponent's antler thrusts, but also prevent loss of balance. The low-crouch, spread, forward position of legs prevents the defensive buck from being pulled forward suddenly. Lateral circling is used to counter neck-twisting.

Again, little is known about dominance fights among black-tailed deer and among whitetails. I saw only two fights by the latter, neither clear of obstructing vegetation. Hirth (1977) witnessed a number of fights between white-tailed bucks, and his accounts agree with my limited observations. Essentially they are similar to those of mule deer, but they may be initiated from a slightly greater distance. The bucks hurled themselves into a clash from as much as 3 meters (10 feet) apart. Hirth noted little twisting of heads. Therefore we can hypothesize that whitetails do not twist and jerk backward as mule deer may do. Instead, they probably push more and wrestle less. Future documentation is needed to determine if this is true. Although neither species carries massive dermal shields, some thickening of skin on the head and neck does occur in large bucks during the rut.

These mule deer apparently were sparring or fighting when their antlers locked—a rare occurrence—and are shown to be near exhaustion. Both animals have been injured, probably from having fallen or been pulled to the ground and dragged, as evidenced by the scraped and disheveled condition of their coats. Photograph courtesy of the Smithsonian Institution, Natural History Museum, Division of Mammalogy.

The extent of wounding during fighting is not readily discernible. Only large gashes in the body can be detected easily. Small punctures are not visible, and some punctures may be visible one day and not the next. Still, wounds are seen, mainly on the face, neck, haunches, and occasionally the ribcage. Ears may be cut and bleed. Some bucks leave a trail of blood in their tracks, and some carry fresh or frozen blood on their antler tines. Wounds vary from punctures to deep gashes to superficial cuts by antler points that mainly shave a streak of hair off the dermis. An estimate of surface damage sustained can be obtained by examining freshly tanned hides. A large, mature mule deer buck about 5 years of age carried a total of forty-seven cuts that had penetrated the skin. A large white-tailed buck of similar age carried thirty-nine penetrations that were more severe than those on the mule deer. Distribution of wounds in the two bucks was mainly on the neck and the rump, with a lesser number on the flanks and shoulders. An 18-month-old mule deer buck carried no visible penetrations, nor did a yearling white-tailed deer. A 6.5-year-old mule deer doe, however, had six cuts that penetrated the skin. Some wounds of this female could have been caused by hooves, while several others may have been caused by barbed wire.

Courtship

Unlike other ungulates whose courtship behaviors have been studied, including the closely related white-tailed deer, mule deer have not one but two courtship strategies. In both instances, courtship aims at stimulating females to urinate, after which bucks perform urine-testing behavior called *lip-curling*.

Since females are courted frequently, they must ration their urine, because bucks will pursue them until urine is voided. Females urinate to avoid harassment, even though they may not be at all ready to part with their limited urine. An extended courtship pursuit plus various tricks, then, are used by bucks to make females void.

The reason that, of the two sexes of mule deer, bucks court so extensively lies with the basic difference in courtship between New World and Old World deer. Most of the latter have a breeding system based on male advertisement and a necessary consequent harem formation. In advertisement systems, females move to males and stay close to them. The greatest amount of a male's time, then, is devoted to advertising—that is, displaying its dominance—and to the consequences. Little time need be devoted to courtship by males because females are likely to remain in the vicinity anyway. This is discussed in some detail for elk (Geist, in press). No New World deer studied to date use an advertisement system; all use a tending bond whereby a male stays with a female until she is bred. This constitutes serial polygyny, not harem formation. The latter is characterized by a dominant male herding anestrous females back into a compact group. It is not a harem when female mule deer voluntarily cluster around a big male.

The gathering of females around a large buck is not considered to be harem formation. Photograph courtesy of the Wyoming Department of Game and Fish.

In an advertisement system, displays of a dominant male not only attract females but also mark and give away his position. However, to a male tending females serially, there is no advantage whatever in giving away his position to potential competitors. On the contrary, the less noise, and the less visual or olfactory evidence of his presence, the less likely his chances of being discovered by competitors. This appears to be the basic reason that mule deer, whitetails, and even moose are so inconspicuous during the rutting season, whereas elk, red deer, fallow deer, axis deer, and sika deer are so noisy and conspicuous.

When tending, it is in a male's interest to be inconspicuous, even to hide with a female and to treat this doe so as not to disturb her. However, this is not in the tended female's interest. To maximize reproductive fitness, a doe must be bred by the most dominant male so as to maximize her chances of producing equally competent sons, to minimize the chances of accepting deleterious genes, and to pass on to her children the physiological efficiency of the dominant. Therefore the doe must possess a mechanism whereby as many males as possible are attracted—whereby they can compete and be sorted out so that only the most dominant remains by the time the female is receptive. That mechanism is a conspicuous estrus combined with wide roving and noisiness to attract males. Ozoga and Verme (1975), working with captive whitetails, recorded a twenty-eight-fold increase in activity of estrous does compared with anestrous does. Thus a male must use every means to prevent a female from roaming, running, or leaving a hiding place. Compared with elk, mule deer face entirely different problems in courtship.

The problem for a mule deer buck is to identify, as early as possible, a doe approaching estrus and then to stay with and breed her. Estrus apparently can be identified by males through urine-testing (see Estes 1972). A male, however, cannot spend all his time with a female waiting for that one doe to urinate. He must canvass as many females as possible and therefore prompt females into urinating early. A male also must ensure that a female does not run from courtship, particularly once tending has begun, because that increases the likelihood of attracting competitors and increases his costs of tending.

For a buck, the solution to exciting a female and then preventing her from running appears to be the use of juvenile mimicry in courtship. In essence, bucks parasitize females' maternal responses. The most common courtship sound uttered by the mule deer buck is a deep, soft, low-volume version of a fawn's distress call. On rare occasions a buck will utter a very high, soft, long-lasting bleat while looking directly at a courted female. In the very few instances when I noted this, the sound was followed by a rush courtship. In addition, sexually dimorphic markings of a male's face appear to be an enhanced version of the markings on the face of a newborn fawn. In ethology, this phenomenon is termed a *superstimulus*. Therefore a mule deer buck, in such a situation, carries a "super baby face."

During courtship approach, a male approaches a female from the rear, with head held low. The buck flicks his tongue, buzzes softly, then stops and quickly pushes his nose at the female, licks her, bobs his head up, and averts his eyes. From the female's perspective, then, there appear behind her a large baby face and a fawn's distress call, together with a threatening male body. She is addressed directly by the male pointing his nose at her, signaling intention to lick her or even touch her with his muzzle. Instantly, though, the address is replaced by a white throat flash and the head points away from her; the sign of danger is averted. The address probably is an excitatory stimulus; the exaggerated eye aversion (the head bob) then would be a relief from it.

Confronted with such a courtship approach, a female normally advances a few steps, with her back depressed, feeds at once, and continues to watch the male. There is weak attempt or no attempt by females to avoid this low-stretch courtship behavior. The buck tends to stand for long periods with head held even with his back or lower, level with the line of the brisket. His eyes may be closed to narrow slits or periodically opened a little. He buzzes

The classical low-stretch approach of a courting buck. Photograph by Valerius Geist.

softly, then swings his muzzle toward the female. His tongue flicks against the female, then he quickly swings his head away and up and averts his eyes, looking away from the female. He may follow the female with head lowered, buzzing, flicking his tongue in and out or licking his rhinarium. Tongue-flicking in this instance appears to be a signal of intent. The female generally avoids the buck by circling to his rear with a few steps, as she continues grazing and watching the male. Here submissive behavior is barely apparent, except for grazing. In line with the generally calm disposition of mule deer, this courtship procedure is drawn out and tedious to observe. The buck patiently courts as the female grazes until she urinates. When a female finally urinates, a large buck will wait patiently with eyes averted until she has finished before he moves to inspect the urine. A small buck may creep forward, push his nose under the urinating female's tail, and lap at the urine.

Urine inspection is carried out by a buck mouthing litter, vegetation, or snow doused with urine. Then he suddenly raises his head high, opens his mouth, draws his upper lip up

A courting buck may point an ear at a courted doe and close his eye on the side toward that female. Photograph by Valerius Geist.

Head and eye aversion is most pronounced when a courted female turns toward a courting male. Photograph by Valerius Geist.

During courtship, typical behaviors include a low-stretch approach by the buck, who oscillates between facing the doe and averting his head. The doe grazes in a close circle around the courting buck and continues to watch his movements. Photograph by William S. Keller; courtesy of the United States National Park Service.

Courtship ends with urination by the female, done here in deep submissive crouch. The buck patiently waits until the female has finished. Note the buck's left ear hanging down. It was injured in a dominance fight. Photograph by Valerius Geist.

When a doe urinates toward the conclusion of a courtship ritual, the courting buck may crawl forward to sample urine even before the female finishes urinating. Photograph by Valerius Geist.

and backward, and slowly waves his head from side to side. Saliva can be seen dripping from his open mouth. Within 20 seconds to one minute, the buck lowers his head, his lip slips back to a normal position, and he then licks the tip of his nose extensively and resumes a relaxed stance. It is believed that the lip-curl is a behavior that exposes urine to the Jacobson's organ at the top of the palate, and signals from the Jacobson's organ inform the male whether the female is in heat (Estes 1972).

The patient, slow, fawn-mimicking courtship—not found in the white-tailed deer—is not the only courting behavior used by mule deer bucks. To extract urine from females, mule deer bucks may employ an entirely different method, known as "rush courtship." A courting buck may begin to tense noticeably,

A buck lip-curls female urine to determine her receptivity to being bred. Photograph by Valerius Geist.

his nose lifted and his head well above the level of his back. He faces in the direction of the female and his upper lip begins to twitch, made conspicuous by white patches below the nostrils. The courted female is likely to duck at this and continue feeding but, while feeding, to glance more frequently to the rear. The buck grows rigid and may emit a very low, very long drawn-out bleat. He suddenly leaps at the female with his head and antlers lowered. He strikes the ground with his front hooves, utters a short, harsh, loud, coughing roar, and gallops across the ground after the fast-escaping female. With each lunge, he roars. "Roar" is the only word to describe adequately the vocalization of a massive old buck in this situation. The chase covers ground at great speed until the buck suddenly stops and assumes a rigid low-stretch posture. The female stops, head high and alert. In the next moment she urinates, then runs on at least a few paces or starts back to where the courtship display began. The buck trots to where the female urinated and lip-curls. On rare occasions this rush courtship fails to make a female urinate, and it may be repeated at least once.

The rush courtship appears to achieve its objective by severely exciting the female. As I noted earlier, given the high threshold of excitation in mule deer, such a massive emission of excitatory signals may be needed to excite the female to urinate. An excitable whitetail buck does not need such a display in his rush courtship, which is his basic courtship style. This buck merely utters a few weak coughs or grunts, strikes the ground with his front legs once or twice, then gallops silently after the departing female in an extended but not necessarily crouched posture.

White-tailed bucks do not use juvenile mimicry in courtship. However, at the beginning of a courtship approach, a white-tailed buck sometimes briefly assumes the body posture of a fawn initiating a suckling run. In this the buck raises his tail, just as fawns do, but quickly drops it and runs at the female with head low and ears usually forward, utters a few coughs on reaching her vicinity, strikes the ground with his hooves, then runs after her.

The rush courtship. Photograph by Valerius Geist.

The rush courtship, rarely used by mule deer, thus appears to be the phylogenetically original or primitive one. Courtship appears to be an exciting affair to whitetail bucks, because they flare their tarsals at least at some time during courtship and lip-curling. I have not seen this in mule deer. Only when courting an estrous female does the whitetail buck use a crouched, low-stretched courtship minus the rush component. When so doing, the excited male—belly almost to the ground, head extended, tail pinched in, and with hackneyed-paced steps—moves at a fast trot to the rear of the female. The conspicuous upward bob of the head that terminates approach—so typical of mule deer—is absent or barely discernible in white-tailed deer.

In mule deer there is a large amount of situation-dependent and individual variation in courtship. Young bucks tend to be less cautious in low-stretch courtship. Their signal patterns are less distinct than old bucks', and they are more likely to touch the females and make them run. When they do rush-court females, they vocalize less, acting much like white-tailed deer. Occasionally they may approach the female in a plodding, slightly crouched, low-stretch posture.

As the rut progresses, a very excited buck may begin to chase a female using the low-stretch courtship, ignoring her urination, following her wherever she goes, pursuing until she flops on the ground and lies flat in an at-tempt to avoid attention. When pursued, females can crawl deliberately round and round through tangled thickets, where large antlered bucks have difficulty following. In all cases such pursuits are circular, with periodic escape attempts by the female, after which more circling follows. These circles vary from about 3 to 50 meters (10–164 feet) in diameter. If a buck catches up with a female, he does not touch her but continues his low-stretch courtship.

As courting activity of mule deer bucks increases, females tend to cluster around large bucks. A large buck may be tending a female, but other females are close by, with lesser males around them in a circle. A lesser buck periodically picks up a female at the periphery and courts her, but the female quickly turns back to the group and the large tending buck, at which time the younger buck terminates pursuit. Thus the presence of large bucks appears to protect females and, indirectly, young males from excessive exercise and wasteful energy expenditure. A large tending buck occasionally must chase off smaller bucks, but he does not herd the females. When females are widely scattered on the open prairie, a large buck may run out rather often and rush at courting subordinates.

A buck tending a female may resort to herding her, but he herds only that female. The point of herding is to keep the female from moving away. For example, as a courted female feeds (and is very alert), a buck stands close by, tense, erect, and facing the female with his head and muzzle raised. Without provocation, the male—while some ten or twenty paces away—may make a little pounce in the female's direction, slap the ground and utter two or three soft coughs, and immediately resume his rigid posture. The female may jump forward a little and continue grazing. The male infrequently utters a protracted, very low-volume bleat, and on occasion the female attempts to bolt past the buck. When that occurs the buck instantly gallops to intercept her, slapping the ground and at times coughing. Although it is rare, a buck trying to intercept a female may attempt to gore her with his antlers. If the bolting female stops, so does the male. This guarding with intermittent chases may serve the female by attracting competiton for the male. It also may excite the female into an earlier estrus and, hence, to a readiness to mate, shortening the energy-expensive guarding and tending phase for the buck.

Roaming, Hyperactive Bucks, and Vacuoejaculations

It is widely recognized that mule deer, black-tailed, and white-tailed bucks roam during the rutting seasons. It is instructive to tag along with such a roaming buck, staying some ten to one hundred paces behind, depending on the situation and individual. Where deer are not hunted, this is a very feasible method of gaining information—even with an occasional white-tailed buck (Moore and Marchinton 1974).

In various sections of this chapter, I have noted some of the observations and insights derived by following roaming bucks. Bucks went from "hot spot" to "hot spot"—that is, to localities that, from my observations, were highly preferred by does. It was not possible, however, to predict the sequence in which a buck would visit these localities, as I indicated earlier, nor could one predict whether the buck would continue roaming or suddenly terminate

it to lie down or feed. The bucks were clearly superior to me in locating active deer in cover, but they did not detect resting deer as readily as I did. They were able to detect other deer visually to distances of at least 600 meters (1,970 feet). However, I never noticed any of the bucks move to high hills and stand there scanning. If this occurred, it was incidental to crossing a ridge. Black-tailed bucks, on the other hand, were observed to do so in chaparral-covered, dissected country of coastal California (Dasmann and Taber 1956a). Owing to the precipitous terrain and the high density of deer on these areas, the blacktails opted for a behavior (scanning from pinnacles) that would not have been profitable in the Alberta foothills.

Large, roaming bucks horned and listened frequently, and occasionally they were answered in kind. This invariably led to an interaction. By far the majority of bucks declined to respond to horning or to investigate its source. Bucks could be made to pause and look about if I imitated the soft buzzing sound of a courting buck, but once they identified the (human) source of noise they ignored it thereafter.

Bucks were attracted to the general commotion of a large buck stopping lesser bucks from courting a doe about to enter estrus. Although courtship by one buck might attract another, nearby bucks do not necessarily come running at the sound of a courtship bleat. They do, however, occasionally come running to the sound of a dominance fight. In the few cases observed, bucks either trotted or stotted in. In the latter case they moved in with tail and rump patch flared and watched the action at close range in obvious excitement. Only some dominance fights draw bucks for an audience; others are ignored.

On rare occasions a buck enters a state of hyperactivity. He trots rapidly along, mouth open, panting, sniffing the ground here and there, and performing unpredictable turns in his running. He may attempt to court females, but they often escape. Some bucks vocalize in deep, loud grunts during these runs. Because of their speed, they are easily lost from view, and their total behavior remains to be investigated.

Compared with Old World deer, New World deer appear rarely to erect the phallus. Such erections in mule deer bucks can be predicted by the up-and-down pumping motions of the tail of a quietly standing buck. Erections in dominant bucks tend to occur during the horning of shrubs. The buck may lick its briefly erected phallus. Unpredictable and rare are the sudden ejaculations in vacuo by bucks. A buck—alone or in company, after resting or while moving—suddenly bunches up. The haunches are moved down and forward, the tail is raised steeply, the head and neck are extended forward, ears are folded back, and the erected phallus protrudes horizontally toward the front legs (fig. 19). For a few steps the buck staggers forward on stiff legs, then he relaxes into a normal stance.

Tending Disruptions, Estrus, and Breeding

As the period of breeding approaches during the rutting season, males have sorted themselves into groups of unequal bucks that stay continuously within the home range of a female group. In addition, there are wandering bucks of all ages. Large bucks are dispersed over the female home ranges, distributed so that each finds a locality where it can defend itself against others. Only when population density is low are bucks and does found in hiding during the tending phase. Although bucks initially return to the same female home range in successive years, they need not rut with the same females every year. A large male may defend his alpha position successfully one year and be displaced the following year, yet be able to maintain himself with another home range group. Then, unable to maintain himself the third year, he becomes an opportunistic wanderer. Barring this kind of displacement, bucks return year after year to much the same rutting area.

Intense antagonism of matched bucks older than three years ensures that those that tolerate each other more or less are bucks of unequal size and rank. These bucks may be seen feeding within the female groups during the rut. Mule deer bucks continue to feed through-

Figure 19. Vacuoejaculation by a mule deer buck. The phallus often is pressed against the belly and is not always easy to see. Drawing by author.

out the rut, circumstances permitting. However, older bucks in particular feed noticeably less than usual at this time. Dasmann and Taber (1956*a*) made the same point about black-tailed deer.

External changes in females from the anestrous to the estrous state occur rather quickly. Some three days before the event, a doe experiencing such change may be tended by a dominant male. He follows her, watches for other bucks, feeds and rests close by, courts her periodically with a low-stretch posture and soft buzzing, and now and again leaves her to chase a smaller buck away from another female the smaller male is courting.

A dominant buck approaches a smaller buck rapidly in a weak dominance display, then

During height of the rut, does may cluster about the largest bucks. A dominant buck breeds each estrous female in turn. Large bucks feed during the rut, although often hastily. Photograph by Valerius Geist.

rushes him. But subordinates are not easily discouraged. They avoid the dominant but continue courting, sometimes barely escaping serious injury, but seldom suffering severe wounds. On rare occasions a small buck succeeds in breeding a female temporarily abandoned by the larger buck in favor of a second female coming into heat or abandoned while the large buck confronts a potential rival.

Behavior of a guarding mule deer buck toward a doe nearing estrus is not particularly expressive—quite contrary to that observed in white-tailed bucks. When a mule deer buck courts a doe, he is in a normal, low-intensity, low-stretch posture with tongue-flicking and eye-aversion—which results in the head-bob so noticeable in mule deer courtship—accompanied by soft, low buzzing. He averts his eyes from the female, but this is not exaggerated, as it is in whitetail bucks. Hirth (1977) emphasized that a white-tailed buck acts so as not to disturb the doe. Given the low threshold of excitation in white-tailed deer, the cautious behavior of a guarding buck is not surprising. A standing mule deer buck buzzes softly when vocalizing; a white-tailed grunts. Thus, both use the sounds most often heard in courtship.

A tended mule deer doe holds her tail steady and angled away from her body rather than hanging down. This is a reasonably certain sign that estrus is soon to take place. The vulva of the female changes to light pink and appears slightly swollen. Although not restless, she seems to feed a little less. As soon as she permits a buck to lick below her tail a few times before she moves forward, breeding is very likely to occur within the next half hour. On subsequent approaches by the buck, the female permits increasing body contact. At first she permits him to lick the vulva. Next, she permits him to rest his chin on her croup for a moment, then she permits him to slide his chin and neck on her back before breaking contact. During body contact the female stands rigid, tail averted, looking forward or slightly sideways. She breaks contact by suddenly jumping forward and running several paces to the front or making a semicircle, stopping a few paces from the buck. The moment the female performs this

A large buck weakly courts a tended female. Photograph by Valerius Geist.

coquette jump, the buck averts his eyes, with head held very high and body rigid. He stands still for a moment, then drops into a low stretch while running toward the female to continue the action he was performing just before broken contact. Although noticeably excited and very expressive in his low stretch, the mule deer buck never drops into the low-crouch posture typical of a white-tailed buck. The latter runs to an estrous female almost on his belly.

After two or three successful attempts by a mule deer buck to place his chin on an estrous doe, the first precopulatory mount follows. In these the buck appears to rest on the female, with front legs extended stiffly downward and his neck along her back and withers. At the same time, the unsheathed phallus moves in the sagittal plane. During the precopulatory mounts, the buck carries his weight on his hind legs, and probably very little weight rests on the female, to judge from personal observation of human-imprinted mule deer bucks in zoos. Precopulatory mounts may be quite long, 15 seconds or more. The buck may dismount voluntarily, at which time the female again pounces forward and circles. The female also may be the one to break contact and then pounce forward. During such precopulatory activities and approaches, mule and white-tailed deer bucks may carry the phallus unsheathed. The number of precopulatory mounts varies. Usually there are more than five. The maximum number I have counted is forty-three, between each of which the estrous doe made long runs, followed at heel by the buck. Younger bucks may remain in the vicinity of a mating pair, watching their actions at-

A receptive estrous doe will permit a tending buck to touch her vulval region. Photograph by Valerius Geist.

Eye aversion is practiced by intensely courting males, even if the female is in heat. Just before mounting, the buck is highly excited and tense but maintains proper etiquette. Photograph courtesy of the Oregon Department of Fish and Wildlife.

tentively but not interfering.

Copulation follows from the mount. This occurs when a buck suddenly bounds upward with his haunches. His hind hooves leave the ground, and he simultaneously arches his back and throws his head up and back. The female bounds forward and stops with her back arched and tail erect. She suddenly presses her belly upward convulsively and, with head extended, strains hard in these contractions. In about one-third of females at this time, some blood flows or drips from the vulva and may be seen on the white rump patch. The female contracts her belly, strains every few seconds, and may urinate in the process. Her contractions continue with increasing pauses, sometimes for as long as an hour after copulation. Even during rest—common behavior by the bred doe—these contractions continue. Such conspicuous postcopulatory behavior is apparently unique among cervids. Morrison (1960) saw a similar straining in a few captive elk. C. Barrette (pers. comm., October 1978) never saw it in some sixty copulations by muntjacs and fifteen by axis deer. I have not seen it in any red, fallow, sika, sambar, or axis deer, nor in three copulations of white-tailed deer I observed in the wild. Hirth (1977) did not observe it in the white-tailed deer he studied.

In contrast to the more excitable white-tailed deer, mule deer have long foreplay before copulation, and females have long-lasting postcopulatory behavior. In three copulations of white-tailed deer I observed, two were preceded by one precopulatory mount. Hirth (1977) observed five estrous does that were mounted; he noted four copulations and only two precopulatory mounts. Also, there is no noticeable prelude in whitetails between the first sign of receptivity and copulation. Thus, vulval licking by mule deer bucks may be quite extensive, but it is of short duration in white-tailed deer, as observed by Hirth and by me. Female white-tailed deer do not exhibit a coquette run, which mule deer females use regularly before copulation. To date, no observations have been reported of female white-tailed deer courting bucks. Female whitetails in heat before copulation, which I observed, ran from the courting buck in small circles in crouched submissive posture, then stopped, crouched, looked back, and waited for the male to catch up. They performed a deep lordosis (exaggerated forward curvature of the spine) with widely spread hind legs, and crouched deeply downward when touched on the croup by bucks. Such behavior is not seen as such in mule deer does. I saw female whitetails lick their flanks, front legs, and tarsal glands after copulation—behaviors that also are rare or absent in female mule deer. The upward tail position after copulation is common in females of both species, but the white-tailed doe in estrus flicks her tail horizontally quite often, whereas the mule deer doe holds hers rather stiffly. Both may urinate shortly after copulation.

In the mule deer buck, copulation may be followed by an outburst of aggressive activity.

Several preliminary mounts by a buck precede copulation. Photograph by Valerius Geist.

Arched back, raised tail, and depressed head characterize the postcopulatory posture of a doe. She strains periodically and pulls in her belly as if attempting to expel a foreign object. Photograph by Valerius Geist.

A buck may lick his penis, then fix briefly on several bucks and move to rush-chase them. I have noticed similar postcopulatory aggression in captive red deer stags. At the other extreme, a mule deer buck may simply lie down after copulation. Postcopulatory aggression was seen only when other bucks were available on which the dominant could vent his aggression.

After copulation the buck continues tending, and another copulation may follow some three hours after the first. The courting pair feeds and rests together until the next round of copulatory activity. A dominant watches for smaller bucks and periodically horns shrubbery when they approach or meets them in a display walk or rushes them, causing the smaller bucks to bolt.

There are several variations of the copulatory behavior previously described. In what appears to be his first opportunity in the rut to copulate, a mule deer buck may grow progressively excited but fail to mount a perfectly re-ceptive doe. The doe may be standing in lordosis, tail averted, glancing back at the buck who, after approach in low stretch and touching the doe, suddenly bolts rigidly upright and averts without any sign of mounting.

At the other extremes are bucks who have bred extensively and, despite the opportunity, fail to mount a receptive female and simply remain close by, the very image of exhaustion. In these circumstances it is possible to observe the rare courtship behavior of a female.

Female Courtship

In principle, a courting female performs acts that normally startle or arouse a buck or cause aggression. These acts are a sudden bolting followed by a series of quick turns, and running around the male in small circles. Simultaneously, the female may twist her head, buck, and strike the ground with her front hooves. She may move behind the male and brush her foreleg against his side, or rub her head on his rump and croup. She also may attempt to mount the male, but this is exceptional. The male continues to stand rigid, averting his eyes, until he drops into a low-stretch courtship and copulatory behavior finally gets under way.

If two females are in estrus simultaneously in the vicinity of a dominant buck, he will move back and forth between them, with the next largest male taking over the vacated position. Both bucks tend to breed, although the dominant may interfere if he sees actual mounting take place. In that case the dominant leaves the female he is tending, rushes over (perhaps several hundred meters), and, if opportunity avails, attempts to gore the rival off the receptive female.

No exact data are available on how often a receptive doe is bred during her estrous period; I estimate four to six times in about 1.5 days, mostly at the beginning of major activity periods.

In female courtship, the female often runs in tight circles around the buck, shaking her head. Photograph by Valerius Geist.

A buck stands rigidly, while a courting female makes frolicking jumps with quick changes of direction. Courting females perform this activity to startle a buck or attract his attention. Photograph by Valerius Geist.

When a doe strikes a buck from behind with her front leg, she is taking the initiative in triggering courtship. Photograph by Valerius Geist.

Tending Disruptions by Subordinates

Although a tending buck with a receptive doe may find himself where there are no other bucks and have a respite from guarding, such respite will not last long. Bucks constantly rove over the range and learn very well the localities where other deer are likely to be. Only rarely do mule deer bucks travel nose to the ground, following a track. If interdigital scent is of any significance, this remains unknown. Bucks lip-curl over any female urine they find. Invariably, a roaming buck will come across a tending pair, even if the pair is in thick shrubbery.

When such an intruder appears, a dominant buck tends to rise in display posture, march out, stop and horn a bush, urine-rub, approach in display, then rush the rival. When, he returns to the doe, he stands beside her, alert to further intrusion. Occasionally several males gather, each watching the dominant. Yearlings may spar with each other, but larger bucks keep a distance from each other, all glancing periodically at the pair.

What may happen next apparently is unique to mule deer. One of the bucks suddenly blows a sharp alarm. In the next moment, he jumps directly at the mating pair in high bounds, rump hair flared, tail erect, blowing sharply with each bound. The tended doe bolts, and the intruding buck sprints after her. A fast chase ensues, led by the doe. Behind her, following each dodge, is the subordinate intruder, and behind him is the large breeding male or a string of bucks. Sometimes the exhausted breeding buck merely brings up the rear. The subordinate bucks interfere with each other. Then the doe circles back, and the dominant may catch up. Larger bucks turn to chase small bucks, and these chase other bucks in turn. If one comes near the dominant, he is rushed, contributing to the commotion. After this the bucks watch the dominant again and rush at each other less often. The dominant meets each rival's advance toward the doe, and finally all is reasonably quiet again.

On some occasions a young buck cuts out a receptive doe from the guarding buck, for these chases can be long and far. I lost track of a few breeding pairs and their attendant subordinate bucks when they disappeared after a chase of more than 0.8 kilometer (0.5 mile). In cutting out a doe, the rival—usually a small buck— uses alarm behavior to cause the receptive doe to bolt. In essence, a fake alarm is performed. Muntjacs also may use fake alarms (Barrette 1977), albeit for different purposes.

Conclusion of the Rut

Toward the end of the breeding season, bucks become noticeably less aggressive. Some small and medium-sized bucks begin to feed and rest together. Sparring matches begin to take place among even young medium-sized bucks, as well as among yearlings. All bucks have lost condition, but this is especially apparent in larger ones. Hind legs, from the hocks downward, are matted from frequent urination on the legs during marking. The fur looks scruffy, and there may be streaks on the body where an antler point has raked it. About 10 percent of bucks carry visible wounds, some serious. Antler points are broken off and, very rarely, most of an antler. Bucks may still display, rush subordinates, and even fight, but their courtship is of noticeably lower intensity. Then, from one day to the next, a dominant buck leaves the females. He stops rub-urinating and starts urinating in female fashion in a low crouch; for him, rutting is over for that season.

Large bucks then enter a stage of protracted rest and hiding. Quite apathetically, they rest in thickets, and occasionally they temporarily join small males and even solicit listless sparring matches. Bucks begin to disappear from female ranges, and the apparent ratio of males to females drops. It climbs to a peak again in late winter, when deer crowd the open areas where snow has melted (Bouckhout 1972). About

one month after the rutting season, bucks begin to lose their antlers. As in other New World deer, but not Old World deer, growth of new antlers does not commence immediately after shedding. Rather, an antler scar forms and no growth of antler tissue takes place for the duration of winter. As is true of all deer, old bucks shed antlers earlier than do young bucks. I have not found descriptions of bucks' behavior after antler loss.

RESOURCE TENURE: FACULTATIVE TERRITORIALITY AND ADAPTIVE STRATEGIES

It is not enough to describe what mule deer do; it is necessary to know why they do it. For this reason, it is helpful to focus on some principles through which we can gain the desired understanding. One of the main conclusions emerging from study of animal behavior is that most activities ultimately can be related to the way an animal acquires sustenance. Behavior, grouping characteristics, and so forth, are functions of the economic system. Constraints put on individuals are, in the first order, those dictated directly from reproductive fitness— that is, the requirement to maximize the number of offspring relative to those of other individuals of the same species. These constraints are: (1) to maintain physiological homeostasis; (2) to minimize energy expenditure on maintenance; (3) to acquire and retain access to scarce resources essential to reproduction; (4) to reduce reproductive fitness of others; (5) to use unutilized resources; (6) to support related individuals with shared genomes; and (7) to choose equal or superior partners for mating in following the preceding rules (Geist 1978b).

It follows that energy expenditures on maintenance should be minimized and that individuals will gravitate to localities where forage resources are of high density and quality. Clearly, less activity is required there to ingest food, so that cost of foraging relative to intake is low. Of course, if costs of maintaining homeostasis are high (for example, if the individual is subjected to excessive heat, cold, disease or predator activity), then the individual is better off feeding elsewhere, where total energy expenditures and benefits are more favorably balanced.

Where resources per unit of area are abundant, the possibility develops that the resources may become defendable (Brown 1964). An individual or a group of related individuals in such areas may begin to exclude others forcibly from an area chosen for its highly favorable mix of resources. The consequence is territoriality. Territoriality is feasible only where resource density is high, where virtually all requisites for life exist within a defendable area, and where exploitation of resources is not frequently disrupted by deep snowfalls or other factors that make tenure of a territory impossible (Geist 1974a). Of course, territories may be held seasonally and vacated annually owing to changes in requirements or in seasons.

For productive coastal ranges of California, with blacktail densities of 41–65 deer per square kilometer (90–144 deer per square mile), Dasmann and Taber (1956a) and Taber (1961) noted that deer had small, stable, well-dispersed home ranges akin to territories. They also noted considerable antagonism among does, and they identified this antagonism as responsible for the spacing of individuals. To clarify what was occurring, a year-round study of known, identifiable individual black-tailed deer was performed in Oregon by Miller (1974). His observations showed that individuals not only exclude others from large portions of the individuals' home ranges, but that they may unite in groups which exclude other groups from their areas of habitual use. Bouckhout (1972) noted that individuals were seasonally loyal to specific localities, that distinct female groups occupied distinct areas and did not mix with other groups, and that aggression within such female groups was low, whereas between individuals of different female groups it was high. This leads to the conclusion that, given favorable circumstances, black-tailed and mule deer become resource defenders and therefore may compete for resources actively (contest) or passively (scramble).

In regions of high resource productivity—such as coastal California, Oregon, and Washington—black-tailed deer are more likely to gravitate toward territoriality; this is less true where productivity is low, spotty, and seasonally restricted, as it is in regions normally exploited by mule deer.

In the foothills, badlands, and open prairie habitats of Montana, mule deer reach densities of only 10–15, 3.5–11, and 1–5 per square kilometer (25–40, 10–18, and 2.5–13 per square mile), respectively (Mackie, in press). These habitat types are characterized by progressively decreasing complexity, diversity, and climatic stability. As expected, the home ranges of mule deer increase in size along the same habitat gradient (Severson and Carter 1978). Clearly, the more productive and benign the habitat, the smaller the area exploited by each deer and the greater the chance for resource defense or territoriality.

Where there is high density of resources in open landscapes and defense is impossible because there are too many competitors, and where group cohesion is required to minimize predation, then individuals abandon active competition in favor of passive competition. Resource defense therefore is facultative in mule deer and blacktails, arising only where feasible.

Frequent marking of objects by black-tailed deer, but not by mule deer, as noted by Müller-Schwarze (1971), is a logical corollary to their tendency to claim and defend localities. The smaller home ranges occupied by black-tailed deer, compared with those of mule deer (see Robinette 1966), also is a logical consequence.

A mandatory consequence of resource defense is the possession of weapons—front hooves—that maximize surface damage and pain, as is shown in Geist (1978a,b). A mandatory consequence of group cohesion, if individuals live in an open society, is the evolution of weapons—complex antlers of bucks—that permit an animal to impose movement on the other without necessarily inflicting pain.

The adaptation that black-tailed deer form groups that, as a unit, enter into fighting with other groups (Miller 1974) could not have arisen, as evolutionary theory dictates, unless individuals of close relationship normally support each other against those of distant relationship—that is, unless black-tailed deer normally form demes (local groups of closely related individuals). Miller (1974) observed individuals that were trapped and brought together in a large enclosure. They formed social bonds and acted as a group despite being distantly related. Unfortunately, there is no study to indicate whether black-tailed and mule deer normally live in groups that are closely related genetically. However, a study of closely related white-tailed deer showed clearly that females tend to move in units closely related by maternal descent, whereas bucks form groups of unrelated individuals (Hawkins and Klimstra 1970). Supporting the contention that related individuals normally associate are reports by Hawkins and Montgomery (1969) and Dasmann and Taber (1955). That deer tagged together tend to stay together was reported by Hoskinson and Mech (1976). It is suspected, therefore, that mule and black-tailed deer have the same basic social system—female clans related by maternal descent that are facultative resource defenders, and bucks dispersed as individuals or in groups of unrelated individuals. A somewhat similar situation in the roe deer, also of New World descent, was analyzed by Kurt (1968, 1970) and others.

That territoriality in female mule and black-tailed deer is facultative, rather than obligatory as in some African antelope (see Walther 1974; Estes 1974), and that it may be shown by individuals or by clans, increases the diversity of behaviors, adds complexity to life histories, and, frankly, can be confusing. The view that deer may live a more complex life than do bovids fits very nicely with the findings of Kruska (1970), who noted that deer, as a group, have larger brains than bovids do. Brain size is a function of diversity of intellectual and motor tasks—a conclusion based on experimental studies on the effect of environment on brain size, histology, and chemistry (see Greenough 1975).

If facultative resource defense is to occur, then clearly it will arise over areas of particular

significance to the reproductive success of individuals. In mule deer, these may be the areas that permit does to recover adequately from the strain of lactation and to store sufficient resources to subsidize inadequate forage intake in winter, as well as to pay the cost of gestation in late winter and spring. Thus, does move in early autumn to a given range. They abandon this range if forced to do so by snow conditions, as observed by Bouckhout (1972). Clans then mix, with little strife, on habitats offering shelter and some food, such as conifer forests with soft, shallow snow. Thereafter, during snowmelt, individuals band together on open areas, which they exploit passively, while snow is deep and hard in forested areas. As soon as circumstances permit, individuals again occupy the areas they used in autumn, and does remain there until close to parturition.

Of course, if deep snow does not force individuals to abandon areas they occupied in autumn, and if open areas such as clearings seasonally produce an abundance of high-quality food, then deer will stay on one home range all winter and defend it, as observed by Miller (1974). If receding snow and sprouting vegetation on mountain slopes create a shifting altitudinal zone of superabundant high-quality forage, individuals would violate the roles of reproductive fitness if they did not avail themselves of this forage. Clearly, then, given the high and complex montane environments, migratory behavior can develop and, following the lines of thought of Waddington (1957, 1975), be "canalized"—that is, enhanced through genetic selection. Conversely, where such opportunity is negligible, territorial behavior will be canalized. Migration tends to contravene adaptations conducive to territoriality.

The peaks of mobility in mule deer are expected once during the rutting season in autumn and again in spring after snow cover begins to recede. In autumn the rut necessitates high energy expenditure, and coming snow conditions dictate deer concentrations on winter ranges with little snow. In spring, metabolic demands of growth, gestation, and coat-shedding demand increased searching for food. Ozoga and Verme (1970) showed that such peaks of activity for white-tailed deer apparently are obligatory, in that penned deer exhibit them as much as do free-roaming whitetails. There was no environmental correlate in penned deer to these activity peaks; the behavior appeared to represent an indigenous "wanderlust." Also, endocrine glands involved in metabolism showed minimal development between these peaks of activity. To what extent black-tailed and mule deer show the same behavior is not known, but relatively less obligatory "wanderlust" is expected in territorial blacktails.

If black-tailed deer and mule deer are facultatively territorial and, in particular, if females are aggressive to other deer—as reported by Linsdale and Tomich (1953), Dasmann and Taber (1956a), and Miller (1974)—they evidently can expel youngsters. In addition, young deer then ought to roam and settle wherever they can. Given greater irritability of deer in poor physical condition, the exodus of young ought to be directly related to population density, as Robinette (1966) indicated. As a result, dispersal to vacant habitat can be expected to be a continuous process even at low population density, as observed by Hungerford (1970).

Male mule deer tend to exploit habitat somewhat differently than do females. If heterosis contributes to reproductive fitness, a buck ought to breed does other than those of the maternal clan. In reindeer, sires from more distantly related herds produced a relatively larger number of offspring, with heavier neonatal weight and higher survivorship, than did sires from within a herd (Preobrazhenskii 1961). For female mule deer to disperse male offspring is more advantageous than for them to disperse female offspring. By dispersing a female offspring, a mother forces that yearling to quickly find, explore, and occupy a home range, which is then required to support the reproductive effort of the soon-to-be-bred yearling. The yearling female would be forced in her first year of pregnancy to find a suitable winter range and could suffer reproductive wastage, in essence depressing the reproductive fitness of her mother. Male yearlings, by contrast, have several years to find and occupy a productive home range, since they will breed only when they are adults, 4 years of age or older.

Does tend to be antagonistic to all yearlings, but moreso to males than to females of that age class. In mule deer (Robinette 1966) and white-tailed deer (Hawkins and Klimstra 1970), male yearlings tend to leave maternal bands, while female yearlings more often remain behind.

Once a buck joins a doe group and breeds the females, he will reduce his own reproductive fitness by staying with the does and consuming resources that the does require to live through the winter and that fawns need for growth (see Geist and Petocz 1977). Males, particularly breeding bucks, therefore are expected to vacate female ranges after the rut. This is exemplified by black-tailed and mule deer bucks' moving to higher elevations (Cowan 1956b; Miller 1974; Dasmann and Taber 1956a), as well as choosing relatively rough, precipitous terrain with openings that allow for longer views (I. M. Cowan, pers. comm., January 1979). White-tailed bucks were reported to cluster at the edge of wintering yards, leaving does and fawns to exploit central areas (Laramie and White 1964). The requirement of bucks to avoid females, however, is not stringent, unless the bucks have bred or will breed with a specific doe group only. Therefore smaller males need not vacate a female range and suffer a loss of reproductive fitness if their chance of breeding does is limited. As previously noted, a buck who breeds successfully one year with one home-range group of does may be displaced to another group the following year or may drop in rank to become an opportunistically breeding buck. Clearly, this mitigates against segregation of sexes, quite unlike the situation with mountain sheep, as discussed by Geist and Petocz (1977). Consequently, sexual segregation in mule deer should be of relatively low order. Therefore there is impetus for does to remove males from the females' ranges. After the rut, when bucks lose their antlers, females tend to dominate male yearlings and are even successful in driving off adult males, as observed for blacktails by

Miller (1974) and for white-tailed deer by Ozoga (1972). In mule deer herds, however, large males remained dominant (Bouckhout 1972).

After the rut, large bucks go into seclusion and rest, still on female ranges. Then they drift off, probably to peripheral patches of winter habitat, which results in the well-known phenomenon of bucks' wintering at higher elevations in deeper snow. They also roam farther than does, with resultant larger home ranges (see Robinette 1966). When deep snow drastically reduces available habitat, which might be as little as 10 percent of the area occupied by deer in seasons without snow (Gilbert et al. 1970), large bucks mingle with females in areas of light snow. The bucks then move with the does to open prairie patches or slopes once snowmelt begins, forming large bisexual herds. In these herds, as in the rut, contact between the sexes is maximal (Bouckhout 1972). This, however, leads to problems for the males.

Since they carry antlers, are less abundant, and grow larger with age than females, males in general—and large bucks in particular—stand out in female groups. If, for some reason, going into female company is mandatory for bucks, it would be advantageous for them to do so inconspicuously, to avoid becoming focal points for predators. It is in large bucks' interest to shed antlers early so that, when mingling with females, they blend into the group and are neither avoided by other deer nor conspicuous to predators. Avoidance would tend to leave the buck on the periphery of a group, where the risk of being caught by predators is high. If for some reason a buck is the focus of predators' attention, he is likely to be chased often and rapidly drained of energy resources. This may account for the relatively early shedding of antlers by mule, black-tailed, and white-tailed deer—a possibility first suggested for pronghorn by Bromley (1977); similar hypotheses were advanced earlier by ornithologists (Moynihan 1968; Marler 1956). Antler-casting in Old World deer follows the same principles, yet results in different patterns of casting from those of New World deer (Geist, in press). Regrowth of antlers ought not to occur until bucks segregate from does before the fawning season, when the need to group on limited areas for foraging has expired. It is then that bucks unite in male-only groups and move to montane habitats, usually distant from areas used by females and at higher elevations. Unisexual groups also ought to be prevalent among unexhausted young bucks shortly after the rut, and limited data indicate that this is so. Debilitated old bucks, ready targets for predators, hide until they have recovered somewhat from strain of the rut. Clearly, it is in the interest of debilitated males to shed antlers as early as possible, so they can utilize does as camouflage. This fits with empirical findings that debilitated or sick males shed antlers earlier than do healthy bucks (Long et al. 1959; Robinette et al. 1973). For further discussion of antler casting in deer, see Geist and Bromley (1978).

Early casting of antlers, seasonal grouping of sexes, maternal clan formation, options of facultative resource defense or passive competition in social groups, and other behaviors can be seen as a consequence of life in habitats where seasons and particularly wildfires create instability and opportunity. This consequence can lead to animals that have a diversity of adaptive strategies at their disposal. In the chaparral habitat of black-tailed deer and in the subtropical plains of tallgrass swamps, shrubs, and tree groves occupied by whitetails, wildfires frequently but unpredictably create open areas that can be exploited only by social grouping—selecting against obligatory territoriality. Mule deer, moving into areas of shorter, spotty, and highly seasonal vegetational productivity, as well as snowfalls and blizzards, reduce facultative territoriality even more and shift to still greater opportunism and a more highly developed social system in more open landscapes.

Segregation of mule and white-tailed deer is comprehensible wherever these species occur together. Krämer (1971, 1972, 1973) explored this phenomenon in detail. From his work it appears that the only significant difference in behavior of these species is the trend among whitetails either to go into cover and occupy valley bottoms or to move in larger herds to gently rolling open prairie in winter, whereas mule deer prefer slopes, broken terrain, and forest edge. There is overlap, however. This difference, I suggest, is not one of resource exploitation, but a reflection of differing antipredator strategies.

If white-tailed deer depend more on hiding than do mule deer, clearly the former will select thickets. If moving into water is a tactic to lose pursuing predators, clearly the deer will select wet valley bottoms with swamps, lakes, or running water. If deer depend on getting away from pursing predators by rapidly running ahead so that scent evaporates and becomes undetectable (see Sweeney et al. 1971), then they must choose areas where good footing will permit this escape tactic. Therefore, in some areas of winter, white-tailed deer move to open, flat, or rolling prairie with few obstructions, with hard, wind-packed snow for good footing when running, and with open areas for foraging. Here gregariousness is an effective antipredation strategy, and whitetails may form large herds. Krämer (1971) found an exodus of whitetails to open, windblown prairie from hilly regions with low snow-covered shrubs where rapid running could not be accomplished in winter owing to uncertain footing. Without the option of a rapid getaway, hiding is a useless antipredator tactic.

Yarding by white-tailed deer, but not by mule deer, also is explainable as an antipredator adaptation. In deep snow, many deer create a complex trail system that permits a pursued deer not only to develop full speed in running, but also to take advantage of the maze effect of multiple runways as well as the scent of other deer. By crossing the scent trail of another deer, they may cause the predator to veer off and chase the other deer. If white-tailed bucks winter peripherally to does in areas of low deer density—although does winter at higher density in the center of yarding areas (Laramie and White 1964)—that the bucks are better off running rapidly for long distances to shed pursuing predators. Does are better off taking advantage of the confusion effect of many deer by circling back toward their home range soon after they have begun to flee (Sweeney et al. 1971; Hood and Inglis 1974). Given the broad food habits of white-tailed and mule deer, the differences in the food habits of these species are more likely to be a function of the escape terrain chosen than of taste. Dominance of security over forage preference can be explained if a species is very much subject to predation (see chap. 7). Mule deer are expected to be less of browsers than the cover-dependent white-tailed deer. This, indeed, has been found by Krausman (1978).

BEHAVIOR AND HABITAT

Mule deer, and other ungulates for that matter, manifest daily activities that minimize energy expenditure and maximize energy gain.

It is not surprising, therefore, that one finds a great similarity among mule deer, black-tailed deer, white-tailed deer, mountain sheep, elk, and pronghorn in how they respond to winter weather. Such responses are superimposed on activities dictated by security and resource tenure. Differences among species in reactions to habitat conditions are likely to be primarily factors of body size, coat insulation, food habits, and antipredator strategy. It is important here to know the principles of variation, because in the field they explain the almost infinite variety of situations faced and activities demonstrated by individual animals and populations.

Since ungulates, by and large, live off forage that is difficult to digest and at best provides a modest surplus of energy above daily maintenance requirements, they are not only miserly in expressions of costly social interactions, but also very sensitive to climatic vagaries. Ungulates avoid costly climatic extremes such as unusually high or low temperatures and may depend more on shelter or escape terrain to conserve acquired resources than on areas of excellent forage that could be too costly in energy use to exploit. Computer simulations with simple models indicate, for example, that the higher the latitude or altitude, the less important forage resources become and the more important microclimates become as a factor in balancing energy and nutrient budgets. Ozoga and Verme (1970) reported observations of white-tailed deer that led them to a similar conclusion. With increasing latitude and altitude, species diversity and productivity decline, resulting in fewer competitors, predators, parasites, and pathogens and in seasonal concentrations of all these limiting factors. Therefore the prerequisite for exploitation of rich forage resources is access to localities that provide shelter from harsh weather and permit escape from predators. The greater the climatic extremes of an area, the greater the requirement of accessibility becomes. Moreover, escape and shelter localities must possess a sufficient supply of forage, particularly if individuals are forced to stay there for long periods, such as during blizzards.

I have observed mule deer during a number of blizzards. Although they tolerate very low temperatures and withstand buffeting by powerful winds, a combination of both conditions forces them to respond. These deer sought pockets of serenely calm air, for instance, in dense, mature Douglas fir forest. Here the only evidence of the blizzard was the violently shaking crowns, a drizzle of snow crystals, the periodic loud plopping of snow masses detaching from lower branches and hitting the snow blanket on the ground, the splintering of a branch, and the scraping of small annual twigs broken and sent tumbling to the ground. Outside the forest, blowing snow obscured vision; wind gusts on exposed hills exceeded 145 kilometers per hour (90 miles per hour).

The deer were nervous, particularly when a snow mass fell nearby. Unfamiliar noises generally are frightening to animals. They fed on the fallen twigs of Douglas firs, an abundant food source. They also took some cured forbs, especially dried leaves of Siberian aster firmly attached to stalks above the snow and false Solomon's seal from below the snow.

Other deer were in pine forests, in localities where the lay of the land already reduced wind speed. These deer fed on what happened to be available, including cured forbs, red osier dog-wood, evergreen leaves of Oregon grape, and annual twigs blown off a few Douglas firs.

Some deer were far away from conifer forests, feeding and resting in calm air just below the top of a hill, where vortices normally cause snowdrifts to form. Cattle favor the same localities on bare prairie hills during blizzards. Aspen invariably grows in these spots in the Canadian foothills, and deer find here a rich source of cured forbs, such as cow parsnip, false hellebore, nettles, various composites, and also some willows, rose, serviceberry, dogwood, and chokecherry.

I have seen only one buck leave shelter and cross gale-swept open space to reach other cover. He paused briefly while still in shelter, then moved at a gallop (not in bounds), minimizing the time of exposure to high winds.

Deer move over the landscape in this fashion so as to minimize convective heat loss, not only during blizzards but on cold, windy winter days as well. A study of whitetails by Ozoga and Gysel (1972) supports this observation. However, it is expected that deer will brave chilling winds if forage is scarce and will move into exposed areas to feed. They also may brave exposure if they are on a high-plane diet (see Ozoga and Verme 1970).

Like all ungulates, deer feed where snow is soft and at minimum depth, because costs of moving and foraging in deep snow are high (see Mattfeld 1973). In early winter, feeding may occur in thick conifer forests, on hillsides, behind big tree trunks, boulders, or upturned tree roots where vortices have cleared the snow, or on open prairie in spring. Snow depths in excess of 45 centimeters (17.7 inches) tend to preclude use of range by mule deer (Gilbert et al. 1970). Mule deer paw in soft snow for forage but consume food protruding above it when the snow is hard. They also climb hard snowbanks to feed on treetops. However, they avoid moving about in crumbly, hard snow, which is one reason deer, as well as wild sheep, tend to be active late in the day in late winter, when temperatures are high enough to soften snow. The late winter activity peak during noon and afternoon hours has been ascribed to warm temperatures (Geist 1971a; Miller 1970; Ozoga and Verme 1970), but it

A mule deer doe has pawed out a crater in soft snow in order to feed. Photograph courtesy of the Wyoming Department of Game and Fish.

may also have something to do with the animals' footing in snow. In crumbly snow, movement is difficult, and crusts may cut the legs.

Mule deer are expected to seek a radiation shield on cold winter nights with a clear sky, as whitetails do (Moen 1968). Deer also are expected to abandon cold air and frost pockets in favor of sun-warmed hillsides or to select warm inversion layers in mountains. They are expected to avoid direct sunshine during hot days and to gravitate to areas with few biting insects. They are expected to restore insulation of their fur coats after a downpour if the sun shines and to avoid getting their coats wet unnecessarily. And deer are expected to move seasonally between areas of favorable microclimates and forage resources so as to maximize gain or

minimize maintenance costs. In Oregon, spring and autumn migrations of black-tailed deer coincided with minimum relative humidity (McCullough 1964). Such movements may well be habitual, as in mountain sheep, but they may be accelerated or delayed by unseasonal snowfalls or melts of the snow blanket. Warm spells are a stimulus in moose for uphill movements toward distant summer ranges (Edwards and Ritcey 1956). Mule deer drifted gradually to and from subalpine summer ranges in Banff National Park, British Columbia (Geist 1966*a*), in a manner that McCullough (1964) earlier suggested was the more common mode of movement.

In general, deer are expected only exceptionally to act in such a fashion as to lose heat excessively when conservation is called for, gain heat loads when heat is difficult to remove, or generally impair a favorable energy and nutrient balance. That opportunities to safeguard invested resources will differ in the desert from those in the Rockies—or in foothills, Badlands, coastal ranges, boreal forest, or the Rocky Mountain trench close to the Yukon—is self-evident.

MOTHER AND YOUNG

Interactions among female mule, black-tailed, and white-tailed deer and their young are known only generally—not specifically enough to detect how black-tailed deer differ in this respect from mule deer or whitetails. We also do not know how deer reproductive strategies differ in different populations. For roe deer, such a picture is now emerging (Kurt 1977).

The "hider" syndrome invariably is present in ungulates that live in vegetational cover and are too small to drive off major predators. All syndromes of juvenile adaptation aim at minimizing contact with predators. Fawns are particularly vulnerable to predation, as reported by Cook et al. (1971), White et al. (1972), and Van Ballenberghe et al. (1975) for white-tailed deer. In the hider syndrome, adaptation is achieved by neonates through cryptic coloration, a tendency to hide and remain motionless, reduced scent output, and voiding of urine and feces only in the presence of the dam, who ingests what the fawn voids.

Dams also assist by ingesting the placenta and the substrate soaked with birth fluids, by early removal of fawns from birth sites, by segregation from conspecifices before birth, and by movement into escape terrain where possible. Furthermore, they visit neonates infrequently and only for brief periods. Consequently, suckling periods are few but lengthy relative to those of other wild ungulates. Also, it is adaptive for hiders to give birth at a different time from other females. This maximizes spacing of neonates over time within the population and reduces the risk of predators' forming search patterns to hunt for more neo-

nates. Consequently, where climate permits and forage is available, the birth season extends maximally; in tropical environments it extends over the whole year. Conversely, in cold or dry climates birth and rutting seasons tend to be of relatively short duration. For detail on adaptive syndromes of ungulate neonates, see Lent (1974) and Geist (1974*d*).

Mule deer are classic hiders; little is seen of fawns in their first six to eight weeks. A neonate hider must not show strong attachment to the doe, lest it begin following prematurely, which could result in fawns' following strange deer and becoming lost. To prevent this where deer live at high density, does should chase conspecifics away from the vicinity of bedded fawns. This behavior is pronounced in black-tailed deer (Linsdale and Tomich 1953; Dasmann and Taber 1956*a*; Miller 1974). It is not pronounced in mule deer because, unlike blacktails, they live on large home ranges at lower density. In fact, there is no indication that adult female mule deer are hostile to each other at fawning (see Krämer 1973), although they are hostile to yearlings. However, a definitive study is needed. It is expected, however, that even mule deer females expel others from favorable birth sites if the population density rises, as has been shown for roe deer (see Kurt 1977).

If deer live in a largely open, grassy landscape, females will band together when not attending to fawns, because gregariousness is an antipredator adaptation in these areas. Also, attacking conspecifics close to sites where fawns are hidden is incompatible behavior on such landscape, because attacks of this kind destroy the cohesiveness and gregariousness essential to maximum security. White et al. (1972) and Hirth (1977) reported that female whitetails on the Welder Wildlife Research Area, Texas, may band together in groups while their fawns are 50–1,600 meters (0.31–1.0 mile) away. However, Hirth (1977) found a threefold increase in aggression among these does around fawning time.

Intolerance of other does diminishes as fawns develop to the point where they regularly follow their dams. Yearlings again may be accepted by fawn-leading does. By early autumn, clans form again, not to be dispersed until the following fawning season (Miller 1974). According to Miller's (1974) observations, dominant individuals unite first, accepting yearlings only later. I observed considerable antagonism by mule deer does toward female yearlings, even during autumn. Miller (1974) reported that pregnant does become restless about one month before fawning. They are irritable and very antagonistic to other deer, leading to a disbanding of winter groups and, finally, to chasing off of the yearlings. Miller observed that, among black-tailed deer, it resulted in a more even distribution of individuals over the area.

Births in black-tailed and white-tailed deer are described by Haugen and Davenport (1950), Michael (1964), Severinghaus and Cheatum (1956), and Miller (1965). For a detailed treatment of the subject, see Lent (1974).

Play is a significant activity of fawns and appears to serve two major functions. First, it provides exercise essential to body growth and development. Second, it is a way to gain information by which the individual is "programmed" to function as an adult.

Play is associated closely with growth: (1) individuals play progressively less as they mature; (2) play is most common in the early vegetational growing season: (3) playlike behavior in adults is more likely to occur under good forage conditions, as the work of Petocz (1973) on mountain sheep indicates; and (4) young animals from productive populations—with high growth rates during ontogeny—in high-quality habitat play more than do those from poorer habitats. The last association was detected in black-tailed deer by Dasmann and Taber (1956a) and in mountain sheep by Geist (1971a). It has since been investigated by Shackleton (1973) and Horejsi (1976) in bighorn sheep.

A fawn mounts its feeding dam. This play usually is tolerated at least briefly by does. Photograph by Valerius Geist.

If play is experimentally thwarted, a weak compensatory increase in activity results. If physical activity preceding play bouts is increased, then running during play tends to decrease (Müller-Schwarze 1968; Müller-Schwarze and Müller-Schwarze 1969). The way deer play was described by Linsdale and Tomich (1953) and especially by Müller-Schwarze (1968). Play therefore is a useful indicator of environmental conditions experienced by individuals.

Müller-Schwarze and Müller-Schwarze (1971) also experimentally imprinted a black-tailed fawn with the scent of pronghorn, with the result that, when given a choice, the fawn stayed closer to pronghorn than to conspecifics. Olfactory imprinting may be one way that fawns avoid confusion in areas where both mule deer and white-tailed deer occur. In addition, facial markings of fawns of these two species are quite different, with mule deer fawns exhibiting black bars above the eyes, giving them a "buck" face. Where the two species are sympatric, it is unknown whether or how does and fawns behave to minimize fawns' self-disclosure or investigation of the wrong mothers.

A female must maximize flow of milk to her fawn, because its growth rate, and therefore body size at any point in time is likely to be a function of milk intake, as it is in other ruminants. Therefore females must select habitats not only with adequate cover but especially with a food supply to allow maximum milk production. Moreover, females are expected to subsidize from body stores any shortages in nutrients of ingested forage. Yet they also grow a new summer coat while lactating, which requires additional sulfur amino acids for the growth of hair. Whether a doe raids her body tissues for nutrients to support gestation or lactation, as reindeer apparently do (Nikolaevski 1961; Preobrazhenskii 1961), or as males may do to support antler growth (Bubenik 1966; Goss 1963), is not yet known.

Observations of mountain sheep and goats, and the detailed work of Hebert and Cowan (1971) on mountain goats, show that these ruminants visit mineral licks primarily during the period of lactation and hair growth. The work of Hanson and Jones (1976) indicates that ruminants are able to use their rumen microflora to generate sulfur amino acids from inorganic sulfur, and that the minerals sought at licks may be sulfur salts, not table salt. Therefore mineral licks may be of considerable significance to fawn production, in that they provide a source of sulfur to form sulfur amino acids, which may be deficient in available forage . The subject deserves further investigation.

Granted facultative territoriality in mule, black-tailed, and white-tailed deer, it is not at all unreasonable that females at fawning in areas of high productivity form temporary territories from which all other conspecifics are excluded, as suggested by Dasmann and Taber (1956a). If a female shifts to another exploitable and defendable area, it is not unreasonable for her to defend two or more areas of high productivity during her fawn's early development. This leads to observations of intolerant black-tailed deer females defending areas within a home range, as reported by Miller (1974). Defense of an area, then, would be due to its resource value, not to fawn movements. Whether this is so remains to be investigated, because blacktail does simply may chase deer away from the vicinity of bedded fawns (Miller 1974), something mule deer females need not do (see Krämer 1973). If a doe exploits scattered patches of resources, defense may be a losing strategy compared with a scramble strategy.

As plants mature during summer and the available volume of highly digestible forage decreases, so does the value of a contest compared with scramble strategy. Female black-tailed deer become less antagonistic and clans re-form (Miller 1974). In mule deer, does, fawns, and juveniles congregate some two months after fawning. In dense populations of white-tailed deer, females also congregate (Hirth 1977).

Compared with white-tailed fawns, mule deer fawns in larger congregations are noisy. They bleat often, but not as often as do elk calves with their dams. Black-tailed does with fawns are more aggressive than females without fawns (Miller 1974). Mutual grooming is common between does and fawns and not uncommon among adult does in home range groups. It continues among does and their fawns throughout winter up to dispersal of the fawns as yearlings before the next fawning season. Müller-Schwarze (pers. comm., November 1977) has found that captive black-tailed deer fawns that are raised together continue to lick each other, whereas fawns not raised together do not lick each other even if kept together in the same pen for three years. Grooming may be an expression as well as a means to secure social bonds (Miller 1971b).

Mule deer fawns wander, particularly during the rutting season. In general, young males wander more than young females. The extent to which fawns benefit from the presence of dams after ceasing to nurse frequently is problematic. I have seen nursing in mule deer extend into the rutting season, but there have been no studies of nursing frequency and duration in mule deer. On the basis of work with mountain sheep (Geist 1971a; Shackleton 1973; Horejsi 1976), nursing frequency and duration in mule deer are believed to be influenced by quantity of the habitat.

SOME PROBLEMS

This chapter has been a broad-brush sketch of mule deer behavior—not a detailed review, but an attempt to set their behavior within their overall biological context. Mule deer have many peculiarities, as I have shown, yet much remains to be learned. Why deer grow red summer coats, then shed them in favor of new winter coats is puzzling. It is not known if, in a subtle manner, dominant females throttle reproductive output of subordinates when resources are scarce. Actual encounters of mule deer and their major predators is another area of limited insight, though some knowledge is gained from indirect evidence (see Hornocker 1970). How mule deer deal with mountain lions, a major predator, is not well known, nor is there much information about how deer minimize predation by bears, wolves, coyotes, lynx, or bobcats. Comparative population

ecology, such as European biologists have begun to practice for roe deer (see Kurt 1977), has yet to be explored with regard to mule, black-tailed, and white-tailed deer. However, as European work suggests, there will be some surprises as North American deer become better known.

Learning, as a factor in deer ecology, has not yet received much attention. But there is little doubt that learning behavior of deer is and will be an important area of psychological research. Understanding of how ecology translates into phenotypic adjustment by mule deer is in its infancy. It promises to become a powerful tool in evaluating the status of deer populations in relation to their environments. However, exploitation strategies of deer living in different populations and the consequent differences in body structure, social behavior, physiology, and demography require investigation.

Detailed studies of the antipredator strategies of our native deer are needed to predict localities chosen under varying habitat conditions. To small-bodied animals, security must be far more vital than to large-bodied animals that, by sheer body size and power, reduce threats of predators. Mule deer and whitetails are preyed on heavily, and it would be valuable to know the security measures employed by these species. Studies relating deer to forage resources without reference to antipredator behavior or security measures are in principle not of great predictive value.

It would be useful to investigate in detail the paleontology of mule, black-tailed, and white-tailed deer. The absence of paleontological studies is a gap in current understanding of North American deer. For instance, it appears that the mule deer is a very recent adaptive radiation of coastal California blacktails, made possible by the extinction of the highly specialized mountain deer, *Navahoceros*. If so, a date can be placed on the "birth" of the "mule deer" proper, and mule deer can be appreciated as a relatively "unperfected" species in its northern fringes of distribution. Also, I hope that functional anatomists will attempt to explain differences in the morphologies of mule, black-tailed, and white-tailed deer.

Combat, as a factor shaping adaptation, needs study, and that requires first-rate film footage of actual combats among deer, which is difficult to obtain.

In summary, some progress has been made in understanding the complex behavior of mule deer, but the total results of that progress are insufficient. I hope that, through further insight and increased research efforts, current interpretations of mule deer behavior can soon be expanded and improved.

Chapter 6

TRENDS IN POPULATIONS AND HARVESTS

Guy E. Connolly
Wildlife Research Biologist
United States Fish and Wildlife Service
Denver Wildlife Research Center
Twin Falls, Idaho

Once upon a time, wildlife managers and biologists thought there were too many mule deer. From scarcity at the turn of the century to overabundance by midcentury, deer management needs changed more quickly than public attitudes or management philosophies. In the 1950s, the spreading phenomena of over-browsed winter ranges and starving deer created more and more pressure for doe hunts to reduce populations and thereby to keep the deer from destroying themselves and their ranges. During this era of overpopulation, some biologists dedicated their careers to promoting ever greater harvests. Usually they were opposed by sportsmen who felt there could never be too many deer. Politics often prevailed over biological expertise, so that the level of harvest sought by wildlife managers rarely was achieved.

This imbroglio continued into the 1960s, when the high populations began to dwindle. Suddenly, bewildered wildlife managers throughout the West confronted the specter of steadily declining deer herds. By the mid-1970s, decline was gloomily acknowledged as a general but unexplained phenomenon. The mule deer problem was a prominent subject at three meetings of wildlife biologists and managers in 1976: the Sixth Western States Mule Deer Workshop at Boise, Idaho, in February; a symposium, Mule Deer Decline in the West, at

Logan, Utah, in April; and the annual meeting of the Western Association of State Game and Fish Commissioners in Sun Valley, Idaho, in July. These meetings accomplished little for the deer, but they did reinforce the recognition that the decline was real and widespread.

Regardless of differing management approaches in various states, whether conservative or exploitative, mule deer population trends followed essentially the same pattern throughout the West: a gradual buildup of herds beginning in the 1920s, with peaks in the late 1940s to early 1960s, then a general decline during the 1960s, continuing to 1976 (Denney 1976). Because of the importance of the mule deer decline in current management thinking, it is important in this book to review recent population and harvest trends in some detail. I have drawn mainly on three sources of information: personal correspondence from wildlife managers or biologists within each western state and province and in federal land management agencies; proceedings of recent symposia on the mule deer decline; and annual big game population and harvest summaries compiled by the United States Forest Service, Fish and Wildlife Service, and Bureau of Land Management. The latter compilations rely primarily on data furnished by state wildlife management agencies.

From these sources, estimates of deer numbers and harvests from 1950 through 1976 were tabulated for both mule and black-tailed deer in each state. An overview of current deer population trends in Canada and the United States was prepared as well. This review was intended to cover the entire range of mule and black-tailed deer, but I was unable to obtain current information from Mexico.

STATE AND PROVINCIAL DEER STATUS REPORTS

One session of the 1976 meeting of the Western Association of Game and Fish Commissioners was devoted to mule deer population trends. The proceedings of this meeting included reports from each of the major mule deer states and provinces. From these reports and other sources, I prepared a synopsis of recent mule and black-tailed deer population trends (table 20). This summary represents mid-1976 opinions of wildlife biologists and administrators who are responsible for deer management in the respective states and provinces.

From reports abstracted in table 20, it is obvious that the major mule deer states (those from which most mule deer are harvested) were concerned about the status of their deer herds. More or less substantial declines in deer numbers were reported in Arizona, British Columbia, California, Colorado, Idaho, Montana, Nevada, New Mexico, Oregon, South Dakota, Texas, Utah, and Wyoming. Numerous causes of decline were cited, including poor fawn survival, severe winters, habitat deterioration or loss, overhunting, droughts, and others.

Mule deer populations were considered to be stable or increasing in Alberta, Kansas, Nebraska, North Dakota, Saskatchewan, and Washington. An increase from 1975 to 1976 was reported in Oregon. Black-tailed deer were believed to be increasing in Alaska. Most upward trends were attributed to the recovery of herds that had been reduced by severe winters.

DEER POPULATION ESTIMATES

No reliable estimate of mule or black-tailed deer numbers exists for any entire state or province. The only available estimates are speculative, and often they are no more than guesses by the best-qualified persons. Rather than making annual estimates, most states rely on various trend indicators such as aerial or ground counts on key areas, herd composition counts, or fecal pellet counts on selected parts of winter ranges. Harvest data are used as an index of population trends in some states. All of these approaches are attended by numerous potential sources of error (Gill 1976; Wolfe 1976).

Since wildlife managers have invested a great deal of time and money to count deer and measure population trends, it is disappointing to find that accurate and precise estimates generally have not been achieved. Wolfe (1976) suggested that naive acceptance of the results of browse-utilization and winter range occupancy measures, without appreciation of their limitations, may account in part for the failure of some states to recognize declining herds as early as they should have; the result was excessive harvest that contributed to the decline. Gill (1976) also was critical of management's approach to the enumeration problem, pointing out that conclusive evidence of the deer decline did not exist because there are no reliable estimates of deer numbers in the western United States. Methods of estimating deer numbers are discussed in detail in chapter 8.

For many years, the United States Fish and Wildlife Service (1952–71) solicited big game population estimates from state wildlife agencies and published annual summaries of these estimates. For this book I compiled the mule and black-tailed deer figures from 1950 onward (table 21) and sent them to state and provincial biologists or managers for review and revision. In my opinion, table 21 represents the most authoritative population estimates available for mule deer and black-tailed deer in the United States from 1950 to 1976. Nevertheless, most values shown are speculative and not supported by systematic measurements. The states are understandably reluctant to release population estimates of questionable accuracy, even when they are to be used only as indicators of general trends. Some state officials questioned the value of these figures even as trend indicators. How-

Table 20. Reported Population Trends of Mule and Black-tailed Deer in the United States and Canada

State or Province	Reported Trend	Explanation	Source
Alaska	Populations are increasing following very severe winter losses in 1968–69, 1970–71, and 1971–72.	Severity of winter weather controls deer numbers. Recovery has been slow in areas with wolves. Hunter harvest has essentially no impact.	D. E. McKnight (pers. comm., May 1976)
Alberta	Most herds have increased since 1968–69. Density increases for specific herds range from 6 percent to 300 percent.	Low densities followed the severe winters of 1964–65, 1968–69, and 1973–74. Recent increases are due to mild winters and restricted hunting.	E. H. Bruns (pers. comm., July 1976)
Arizona	A dramatic decline occurred in early and mid-1960s. Fawn survival remained low despite abolition of most either-sex hunts.	Low fawn survival is the basic problem. Predators take many fawns on some areas but are of secondary importance to forage conditions, which vary with precipitation.	Smith (1976b)
British Columbia	Mule deer are decreasing; black-tailed deer are stable. Resident hunter harvest of all deer species declined from about 65,000 in 1970 to 36,000 in 1974 (about 55 percent). License sales during the same period declined 12 percent.	Effects of severe winters are compounded by habitat deterioration or losses due to forest-fire suppression, livestock competition, farming, housing developments, reservoir construction and changes in logging practices.	Halladay (1976), P. F. Haley (pers. comm., July 1976)
California	Not all herds have declined, but the overall trend is downward. The buck kill declined 45 percent from 1973 through 1975. Deer tag sales during this period dropped 14 percent.	Poor fawn survival (low fawn-doe ratios in fall) is the problem. Winter losses are not excessive. Quality and quantity of habitat have declined owing to adverse weather, fire suppression, adverse silvicultural practices, successional changes, and overuse by deer and livestock.	MacGregor (1976)
Colorado	Deer herds or portions of herds have declined drastically for the past ten years. The buck harvest averaged 63,679 during 1960–64 and 44,273 during 1971–75, a drop of 30 percent.	The decline was the accumulative result of low reproduction, winter kill, overharvest, land use, and predation.	Rogers (1976)
Idaho	Nearly every mule deer population in Idaho declined between 1968 and 1972. Total mule deer population was down an estimated 35 percent at the end of 1974.	Overhunting is the main problem. Undesirable environmental changes have occurred, but deer populations currently are well below carrying capacity.	Thiessen (1976)
Kansas	Mule deer populations increased rapidly in the 1960s but now are nearly stable.	Available habitat is the limiting factor.	L. D. Peabody (pers. comm., March 1977)

(Table 20.)

State or Province	Reported Trend	Explanation	Source
Montana	A decline began about 1970–71. Approximately 83,000 deer were harvested in 1970 compared with 46,000 in 1975. Hunter success during these years dropped from 81 percent to 44 percent, while the average time required to take a deer increased from 1.5 to 13.6 days.	Competition for deer habitat by other forms of land use is severe. Sagebrush eradication, climax range management, hunting, and predation all contributed to the decline.	Freeman (1976)
Nebraska	Mule deer have declined but are nearly stable at present.	Deer are regulated by hunting (legal and illegal), predators, and habitat loss.	K. Menzel (pers. comm., April 1976)
Nevada	Deer declined about 68 percent between 1961 and 1976, from approximately 260,000 to 82,000. The hunter harvest averaged 34,000 deer during 1959–63 but was only 7,253 in 1975.	Harvest has exceeded recruitment in some areas. Recruitment is limited by habitat conditions.	Christensen (1976), G. K. Tsukamoto (pers. comm., July 1976)
New Mexico	Mule deer declined approximately 32 percent between 1967 and 1975, from about 405,000 to 276,000 animals. However, a 25 percent increase occurred during this time in three major management units. Most of the decline occurred in northern New Mexico.	Increased hunting pressure has had a detrimental effect on populations, owing to increased illegal harvest. However, the most drastic declines occurred on private lands with limited hunting pressure.	Snyder (1976)
North Dakota	Based on aerial censuses of established study areas, the observed mule deer density in 1975 was the highest recorded since 1956 when counts began.	The causes of population increase were not reported. Potential problems include loss of habitat due to reservoir construction and plowing of native grassland, and habitat deterioration due to livestock grazing.	Samuelson (1975), J. V. McKenzie (pers. comm., January 1977)
Oregon	Mule deer declined 37 percent from 1967 to 1972, remained stable until 1975, and increased in 1976 to within 17 percent of the 1967 base year.	Poor fawn survival is the basic problem. Causes include predators, severe weather, vegetation changes on summer and winter ranges, road development, human harassment, and poaching.	Ebert (1976)
Saskatchewan	Mule deer have been stable with little fluctuation over past five years.	The most limiting influence is severe environmental conditions. Some habitat is being lost to agriculture.	R. R. MacLennan (pers. comm., July 1976)
South Dakota	Stable or decreasing, with definite decrease in 1976.	Recent decrease was due to weather. Long term trend reflects quantity and quality of available habitat.	R. Fowler (pers. comm., March 1977)

(Table 20.)

State or Province	Reported Trend	Explanation	Source
Texas	Trans-Pecos mule deer population estimates were approximately 157,000 in 1965, 158,000 in 1974, and 125,000 in 1975.	Limiting factors include hunting (legal and illegal), predation, and livestock grazing practices.	C. K. Winkler (pers. comm., August 1976)
Utah	Deer numbers have declined since 1972. Pellet counts showed the 1975–76 winter population to be 34 percent lower than that of 1971–72. The 1975 harvest was 58 percent below the 1972 level.	The recent decline was primarily due to extreme weather conditions (droughts and severe winters). Antlerless harvest reduced recruitment in some areas. Habitat loss and degradation is a long-term problem.	John (1976)
Washington	Mule deer have been increasing since 1972. Population highs occurred in 1949, 1955, 1963, and 1968; lows occurred in 1952, 1957, 1965, and 1972.	Winter range and weather are the decisive factors. Fencing to exclude deer from orchards has eliminated winter range, as has increased recreational subdivision.	Parsons (1976)
Wyoming	Deer have declined since the late 1960s. The harvest (including white-tailed deer) was approximately 60,000 in 1975, compared with 87,000 in 1970.	Range management practices, extreme winters, and over-harvest may have contributed to decline. Survival has been good during recent mild winters.	Corsi (1976)

ever, I feel that it is necessary to review at least the overall trends, keeping in mind the reservations expressed.

Relative to the period 1965–70, the estimates in table 21 suggest the following trends in the 1970s:

1. Mule deer have declined in Arizona, Idaho, Montana, Nevada, New Mexico, Oregon, Texas, and Wyoming.

2. Mule deer have remained stable in North Dakota, South Dakota, and Washington.

3. Mule deer have increased in Kansas.

4. Black-tailed deer have remained stable in Alaska and Washington and may have increased in Oregon.

5. The data are insufficient to indicate recent trends for mule deer in California, Colorado, Nebraska, or Utah, or for black-tailed deer in California.

Deer population estimates for the Canadian provinces are not adequate to indicate trends.

Mule deer estimates for 1974–75 are 100,000 each in Alberta and British Columbia and 15,000 in Saskatchewan. British Columbia reported on the order of 500,000 black-tailed deer in 1975 (W. MacGregor, pers. comm., April 1977).

In addition to these estimates by state and provincial authorities, both the United States Forest Service and the Bureau of Land Management make annual estimates of big game populations on public lands under their jurisdictions. Since these lands include many important mule deer ranges, the estimates of federal agencies are valuable for comparison with state estimates.

Forest Service and Bureau of Land Management statistics are compiled from annual district estimates submitted by rangers, biologists, or district managers. The figures are primarily guesses, though they incorporate any systematic estimates that may be available. Estimates at

Table 21. Estimated Numbers of Mule and Black-tailed Deer in the United States, Expressed in Thousands of Animals

Year	Mule Deer[a]																Black-tailed Deer[b]			
	Arizona	California	Colorado	Idaho	Kansas	Montana	Nebraska	Nevada	New Mexico	North Dakota	Oregon	South Dakota	Texas	Utah	Washington	Wyoming	Alaska	California	Oregon	Washington
1950	225	600	275	70	—	145	14	80	124	2.5	200	22	6.5	300	100	99[c]		450	200	160
1951	S	625	299	120	—	172	13	90	124	3.5	375	23	6.0	350	105	139[c]		475	240	165
1952	L	500	292	129	—	177	18	90	129	5.5	325	27	5.0	350	120	176[c]		586	250	170
1953	225	540	300	130	—	202	13	90	200	7.7	350	35	5.0	350	130	200[c]		580	400	160
1954	215	590	330	240	0.1	195	12	100	272	4.0	400	33	5.0	375	170	200[c]		610	360	190
1955	195	575	325	260	M	238	60[c]	100	248	6.0	425	33	5.0	375	160	222[c]		625	440	180
1956	184	520	M	260	M	296	75[c]	150	275	10	475	40	15	375	110	166[c]		580	400	150
1957	185	520	L	260	M	299	75[c]	150	300	M	425	40	75	375	115	282[c]		580	350	180
1958	185	520	L	315	M	M	75[c]	175	318	S	425	30	75	375	135	272[c]		580	450	215
1959	185	520	M	M	M	M	75[c]	200	318	15	425	85	75	375	150	262[c]	120	580	560	245
1960	185	520	M	325	0.9	M	60[c]	246	318	20	400	35	77	375	155	336[c]	250	580	610	250
1961	190	520	M	L	1.2	M	75[c]	245	318	20	450	40	80	375	175	368[c]	M	580	650	250
1962	203	L	S	L	1.4	M	45	225	293	18	480	20	82	325	175	386[c]	250	L	630	250
1963	190	M	S	L	1.8	M	50	200	303	23	460	23	84	325	185	311[c]	225	M	530	253
1964	175	M	S	L	2.4	M	45	200	301	25	530	33	100	325	175	298[c]		M	580	230
1965	190	S	L	320	3.0	M	43	180	M	S	510	41	157	300	160	277[c]	S/M	S	480	210
1966	195	M	L	S	3.4	M	29	180	M	18	515	17	163	300	165	280[c]		M	590	215
1967	210	L	M	M	3.6	M	27	150	405	15	570	44	167	300	175	312[c]	200	L	550	225
1968	220	L	M	S	4.0	M/S	30	160	L	20	510	85	167	M	185	290	250	L	560	245
1969	23		S	L	4.5	S	28	170	M	17	500	100	167	M	120	333	100	L	480	195
1970	127	L	S	300	5.0	S	28	150	M	M	430	95	155	325	130	378	110	L	600	215
1971	128		S	L	5.4	L		150	L	20	416	70	163	L	120	298	105		650	230
1972	128		S	L	5.9	L		150	L	20	400	75	168	L	120	248	100		634	230
1973	132		S	L	6.7	L		144	L	20	404	90	169	L	150	244	110		686	240
1974	130		L	S	7.3	L		122	L	20	387	90	163	L	150	262	120		566	240
1975	120		365	210	7.6	L		82	276	20	383	90	130	S	150	280	140		635	240
1976	115		M	M	8.0	L			276		400		151	M			150		650	

Note: Compiled from U.S. Fish and Wildlife Service (1952–71) and personal correspondence with state wildlife agencies. Letters indicate population trend from previous year: L = Less; S = same; M = more. Data were obtained from and/or reviewed by E. H. Bruns, L. H. Carpenter, D. L. Eaton, P. N. Ebert, J. L. Egan, M. Egbert, R. Fowler, P. F. Haley, F. H. Jacot, R. T. John, J. F. Johnson, W. MacGregor, R. R. MacLennan, K. Menzel, J. V. McKenzie, D. E. McKnight, C. H. Nellis, L. D. Parsons, W. C. Peabody, V. C. Simpson, R. H. Smith, D. Strickland, D. Strode, T. C. Telfer, J. Thiessen, G. K. Tsukamoto, R. H. Wauer, P. M. Webb, E. R. Wiltse, and C. K. Winkler.
[a]Iowa, Minnesota, and Oklahoma also reported small numbers of mule deer.
[b]Hawaii also reported small numbers of black-tailed deer.
[c]Includes white-tailed deer.

the ranger or district manager level often are derived in consultation with local personnel of the state wildlife agencies.

Estimated numbers of mule and black-tailed deer on national forests within each state from 1950 through 1976 (table 22) were tabulated from United States Forest Service *Annual Wildlife Reports* (1950–76) that summarize figures for various national forests into regional totals. Most Forest Service regions include more than one state, so the regional tabulations were reworked as necessary to obtain state totals for comparison with the estimates of state agencies (table 21).

Because there are no gaps in the numbers, the Forest Service estimates (table 22) offer a more complete historical record of population trends than do state figures. The totals show that mule deer numbers on national forests increased from 1950 through 1962, remained near peak

Table 22. Estimated Numbers of Mule and Black-tailed Deer on National Forests in the United States, Expressed in Thousands of Deer as of 30 April Each Year.

	Mule Deer														Black-tailed Deer				
Year	Arizona	California	Colorado	Idaho	Montana	Nebraska	Nevada	New Mexico	Oregon	South Dakota	Utah	Washington	Wyoming	Total[a]	Alaska	California	Oregon	Washington	Total[a]
1950	57	279	228	135	98	0.4	67	53	141	16	184	44	47	1,349	29	166	36	23	254
1951	62	290	243	141	110	0.4	78	53	160	16	195	60	51	1,459	31	169	41	22	263
1952	63	275	221	140	128	0.4	80	52	155	17	199	55	52	1,437	39	169	41	24	273
1953	70	328	227	140	135	0.5	84	54	164	27	213	62	53	1,558	36	191	41	24	292
1954	75	355	245	135	141	0.4	93	56	172	26	221	64	55	1,638	48	207	49	27	331
1955	87	366	259	138	146	0.4	94	67	185	26	240	66	56	1,730	54	211	54	26	345
1956	89	384	261	137	164	0.6	104	73	186	11	252	57	57	1,776	69	220	56	26	371
1957	82	397	271	139	166	0.4	102	87	183	13	275	62	67	1,844	73	232	58	29	392
1958	94	398	238	149	170	0.4	105	99	227	14	277	63	71	1,905	98	242	76	30	446
1959	102	417	254	157	181	0.2	90	113	281	13	283	70	77	2,038	130	256	93	41	520
1960	116	413	272	164	184	2.4	89	115	325	15	299	67	88	2,149	125	258	136	40	559
1961	109	413	284	175	188	2.3	83	126	424	16	311	77	99	2,307	150	272	143	55	620
1962	123	394	302	190	202	2.4	99	120	444	23	307	80	113	2,399	163	279	171	57	670
1963	124	365	312	198	204	2.7	99	113	444	15	290	84	110	2,361	172	269	181	66	688
1964	105	362	331	202	202	2.7	101	116	403	15	288	93	114	2,335	174	295	175	70	714
1965	102	407	319	208	215	3.2	117	135	362	21	287	82	109	2,367	175	308	174	62	719
1966	101	367	294	206	197	3.6	113	122	345	15	251	85	104	2,204	195	300	166	58	719
1967	104	351	298	212	202	5.5	117	118	386	16	249	86	107	2,252	235	359	175	47	816
1968	84	316	262	207	202	5.1	114	116	367	28	245	93	107	2,146	218	318	177	52	765
1969	80	324	259	209	199	4.4	119	116	365	30	239	85	109	2,138	188	296	140	42	666
1970	75	309	247	212	195	5.1	122	118	345	26	251	82	102	2,089	191	284	141	43	659
1971	82	290	232	200	175	5.0	123	131	326	19	266	68	95	2,012	187	260	156	41	644
1972	85	249	234	174	179	5.2	134	131	244	21	253	52	90	1,851	198	241	148	43	630
1973	76	263	221	170	163	5.0	137	131	218	20	230	52	84	1,770	128	195	152	42	517
1974	75	231	215	145	152	4.9	126	131	246	16	189	57	74	1,662	144	174	147	42	507
1975	72	172	193	149	152	6.8	74	121	225	14	183	56	75	1,493	150	163	145	46	504
1976	64	157	180	138	121	6.8	53	111	246	14	164	64	76	1,395	150	179	146	44	519

Note: Compiled from U.S. Forest Service (1950–76). Estimates as of 30 June from 1950 through 1955.
[a]Totals are rounded to the nearest 1,000.

levels through 1965, declined slightly from 1966 through 1971, then dropped more rapidly after 1971. The 1976 total was down 42 percent from the peak of 2,399,000 mule deer reported in 1962. As might be expected, trends varied from state to state. Except in Nebraska, where the highest numbers were reported in 1975 and 1976, declines were recorded on national forests in all states. The largest reductions occurred in California and Nevada, whereas relatively modest declines were shown in New Mexico, Idaho, and Montana. In Oregon and Washington, mule deer numbers on national

forests reportedly increased from 1975 to 1976.

Forest Service estimates for black-tailed deer show a pattern similar to that recorded for mule deer, although the peak occurred later. Estimated numbers of black-tailed deer on national forests increased steadily from 1950 to a peak of 816,000 in 1967 and subsequently dropped about 38 percent by 1975. An increase of blacktails was reported in California between 1975 and 1976.

Big game estimates published by the United States Bureau of Land Management (1962–77) do not distinguish among various forms of

Odocoileus, but most lands administered by the BLM are inhabited by mule deer or blacktails; relatively few white-tailed deer are included. Before 1961, BLM records showed deer numbers only within grazing districts, but since that date all public domain lands—now called National Resource Lands—both inside and outside grazing districts have been represented. Because the pre-1961 data are not comparable with later figures, BLM statistics shown in table 23´begin with 1961.

The general pattern in Bureau of Land Management deer estimates (table 23) is similar to that shown by Forest Service data for mule deer. Both sets of estimates indicate a peak in 1962 and a slow decline in the late 1960s. However, BLM records showed an abrupt drop from 1974 to 1975, whereas Forest Service estimates reflect a gradual decline from 1970 on. The BLM figures show an overall decline of about 36 percent from 1962 to 1976, while Forest Service totals for mule deer plus black-tailed deer dropped 38 percent over the same period. The coincidence between Forest Service and BLM figures probably reflects their common source—state wildlife agencies.

Trends shown by Forest Service (table 22) and Bureau of Land Management (table 23) records do not coincide exactly with those in

estimates from state wildlife agencies (table 21). The differences reflect the imprecise nature of estimates, as well as the fact that the federal agencies deal with different fractions of the deer range within each state. Nevertheless, the three sets of figures collectively support the premise that deer numbers have declined in most mule deer states, as reported in narrative form in table 20.

Because of wide concern with overhunting as the possible cause of the deer decline, I tried to evaluate recent mule deer population trends in unhunted areas. Within the range of mule and black-tailed deer, the largest unhunted areas lie within national parks and monuments. Unfortunately, reliable deer population estimates for these areas are not available. From a resume prepared by F. H. Jacot (pers. comm.; November 1976), it seems that no generalizations can be made about deer population trends in national parks, at least in Arizona and California. Deer seemed to be increasing in some parks, decreasing in others, and stable in still others. Deer inhabit some parks only in summer and become vulnerable to hunting when they migrate to winter ranges outside park boundaries. Such complications, combined with the lack of reliable estimates, militate against any meaningful assessment of deer population

Table 23. Estimated Numbers of Deer on National Resource Lands in the United States, Expressed in Thousands of Deer

Year	Arizona	California	Colorado	Idaho	Montana	Nevada	New Mexico	Oregon	Utah	Wyoming	Total
1961	52	165	365	132	90	162	40	293	282	88	1,669
1962	51	162	467	161	97	183	41	286	257	92	1,797
1963	36	201	394	174	140	185	40	255	239	61	1,689
1964	36	246	369	170	112	186	40	249	238	84	1,730
1965	33	246	313	170	124	173	43	257	237	83	1,679
1966	28	220	289	113	162	186	34	275	237	97	1,641
1967	34	159	233	122	141	106	36	276	198	90	1,395
1968	35	245	227	122	141	107	38	278	198	120	1,511
1969	35	240	181	120	125	93	33	277	236	122	1,462
1970	35	211	167	120	125	109	35	289	220	119	1,430
1971	35	223	155	108	127	220	35	280	221	101	1,505
1972	35	223	155	108	127	220	35	280	221	101	1,505
1973	12	261	150	79	94	220	38	283	176	123	1,436
1974	33	216	236	68	110	184	38	275	165	135	1,460
1975	20	105	239	62	90	121	38	120	163	134	1,092
1976	10	126	162	52	79	146	35	272	108	167	1,157

Note: Compiled from U.S. Bureau of Land Management (1962–77).

trends in the unhunted national parks. The influence of hunting on deer populations is considered in chapter 7.

DEER HARVEST ESTIMATES

In most states and provinces, a concerted effort is made to determine the number of deer hunters take each year. Field checks and mail surveys commonly are used, and in some states each deer tag includes a report form to be mailed in by the hunter. Harvest estimation methods are discussed further in chapter 8; here it only is necessary to note that existing harvest estimates are much more reliable than total population estimates, because harvest is easier to measure.

The United States Fish and Wildlife Service (1952–71) annual big game inventories, cited previously as a source of deer population estimates (table 21), also give harvest data furnished by the states. For this book, harvest estimates were compiled from these inventories and sent to state and provincial deer biologists for review. The resulting updated estimates (table 24) are as current and correct as possible. Because some of the figures include whitetails as well as mule and black-tailed deer, no totals are shown.

The predominant pattern in mule deer harvests (table 24) over the past twenty-five years is one of increase through the 1950s to a peak in the early 1960s, followed by a slow decline into the 1970s. Data from Arizona, California, Colorado, Idaho, Montana, Nevada, New Mexico, Oregon, Utah, Washington, and Wyoming all show this sequence. Except in California, Idaho, and Washington, peak mule deer harvests in these states occurred from 1960 through 1963. In Montana and New Mexico, little decline in the harvest occurred until 1975. The harvest decline in Wyoming was minor, but Nevada recorded a 59 percent drop from 1974 to 1975. This was due in part to more restrictive hunting regulations in 1975. In Washington, the lowest mule deer harvest was recorded in 1972; from this low point, an increase of 138 percent occurred by 1975.

In those prairie states where mule deer are

hunted, peak harvests generally occurred later than in more westerly states. Kansas and South Dakota recorded all-time high harvests in 1974. Texas and Nebraska have experienced only moderate declines from peak harvests in the late 1960s. Mule deer harvests in North Dakota have fluctuated irregularly below peaks reached in 1956 and 1961.

Black-tailed deer harvest trends shown in table 24 are generally similar to those for mule deer, in that peaks occurred in the early 1960s (1956 in California). The figures from Alaska may be less indicative than those from other states, since most deer taken in Alaska—largely by native peoples—are not reported. Among other states, only in California has the blacktail harvest declined perceptibly since 1970.

In British Columbia, mule, black-tailed, and white-tailed deer are hunted. Provincial records show the total harvest but not the numbers of each subspecies taken. However, about 80 percent of the deer in the province are blacktails. The total harvest was approximately 18,000 in 1950, 78,000 in 1964, and 27,000 in both 1972 and 1975 (W. MacGregor, pers. comm., April 1977), indicating the same general increase and subsequent decrease seen in most states. I was unable to acquire enough data to define harvest trends in other provinces. However, the average annual mule deer harvest during 1971–75 was estimated to be 4,600 in Alberta and 2,100 in Saskatchewan.

United States Forest Service *Annual Wildlife Reports* (1950–76) contain annual estimates of big game harvested from national forests. Mule and black-tailed deer harvest figures from these reports are shown in table 25. Even though these data cover only part of the deer range in each state, it will be seen that overall trends parallel those shown by state wildlife agencies (table 24). The reason for this, of course, is that state agencies are the primary source of Forest Service figures. Judging from totals shown in table 25, the number of mule deer harvested from national forests increased through the 1950s to a peak of 455,000 in 1961 and declined steadily thereafter to only 173,000 in 1975. This represents an overall drop of 62 percent. Harvests declined in all states except Nebraska.

Harvest trends for black-tailed deer on na-

Table 24. Estimated Numbers of Mule and Black-tailed Deer Harvested by Hunters in the United States, Expressed in Thousands of Deer

Year	Arizona	California	Colorado	Idaho	Kansas	Montana	Nebraska	Nevada	New Mexico	North Dakota	Oregon	South Dakota	Texas	Utah	Washington	Wyoming	Alaska	California	Oregon	Washington
	Mule Deer[a]																Black-tailed Deer			
1950	11	35	65	23[b]		29	0.7	11	12[b]	1.6	27	1.5	0.2	73	21	23[b]	4.6	16	18	32
1951	11	47	75	33[b]		29	0.7	20	14[b]	NOS[c]	38	2.7	0.2	102	9.5	32[b]	4.2	21	20	17
1952	13	23	73	30[b]		41	1.9	23	15[b]	5.0	53	4.6	0.2	90	13	40[b]	3.3	27	25	34
1953	17	26	72	47[b]		62	3.7	20	18[b]	NOS	65	10	0.3	96	27	46[b]	5.1	35	41	32
1954	20	40	73	51[b]	NOS[c]	62	2.5	28	32[b]	6.7	77	7.0	0.4	108	29	50[b]	4.6	38	36	35
1955	21	36	70	65[b]	NOS	78	4.1	34	28[b]	4.7	90	4.3	0.4	112	39	51[b]	5.9	44	44	38
1956	25	54	85	71[b]	NOS	83	6.2	32	36[b]	7.7	85	6.4	2.0	123	15	38[b]	7.8	57	40	35
1957	20	31	115	67[b]	NOS	101	8.2	27	37[b]	2.9	82	3.3	1.9	106	14	65[b]	8	37	35	28
1958	28	28	84	71[b]	NOS	87	5.6	26	38[b]	3.8	71	4.6	2.4	117	18	62[b]	13	34	45	35
1959	26	37	107	70[b]	NOS	94	5.4	33	45[b]	5.7	88	7.0	5.0	126	22	60[b]	12	39	57	38
1960	28	36	110	75[b]	NOS	103	4.1	31	55[b]	6.0	96	5.0	5.5	131	22	77[b]	13	47	61	39
1961	31	27	147	76[b]	NOS	102	4.1	35	40[b]	6.1	98	7.2	6.0	132	27	85[b]	12	47	66	45
1962	24	21	143	66[b]	NOS	104	5.7	36	29[b]	4.6	77	7.5	5.5	131	22	89[b]	12	39	63	40
1963	21	20	148	63[b]	NOS	95	7.0	34	34[b]	2.6	65	7.0	6.5	109	29	72[b]	12	40	53	48
1964	15	29	119	67[b]	NOS	85	8.4	29	27[b]	3.7	85	4.4	8.2	116	27	68[b]	10	43	58	41
1965	13	27	103	56[b]	0.6	68	10	24	28[b]	4.6	72	3.8	9.3	88	16	64[b]	12	41	48	32
1966	14	29	79	65[b]	0.7	72	10	20	27[b]	4.7	89	0.4	9.0	93	18	64[b]	14	49	59	32
1967	14	19	78[b]	66[b]	0.5	66	9.1	19	26[b]	4.4	87	10	9.9	90	28	72[b]	10	28	55	32
1968	13	17	83[b]	78[b]	0.5	72	7.0	20	26[b]	1.6	89	12	13	95	36	67	14	35	62	43
1969	13	15	87[b]	67[b]	0.6	79	8.3	18	26[b]	4.0	69	13	10	82	12	77	10	34	32	19
1970	14	14	70[b]	77[b]	0.9	85	8.5	22	33[b]	3.8	72	7.1	11	103	14	87	12	25	29	26
1971	10	16	41[b]	55[b]	0.8	86	7.3	23	31[b]	4.3	47	7.5	12	99	15	69	6.8	26	41	31
1972	10	15	67[b]	48[b]	0.6	85	6.5	24	31[b]	4.2	29	9.9	12	108	8.4	57	4.5	24	44	27
1973	12	11	77[b]	54[b]	0.9	99	7.9	20	31[b]	2.1	41	12	10	87	19	56	9.7	21	62	31
1974	12	9.0	55[b]	42[b]	1.3	74	8.5	18	28[b]	2.5	31	13	9.4	55	17	49	11	13	45	25
1975	13	9.7	40[b]	33	1.1	46	8.0	7.3	21[b]	4.0	24	11	10	45	20	61	16	17	31	32
1976	11			21	1.1		6.9		19[b]		44		7.5			65	5.0		39	

Notes: Compiled from U.S. Fish and Wildlife Service (1952–71) and personal correspondence with state wildlife agencies. Avoid summing all totals, as some figures include mixtures of different types of deer.

[a]Oklahoma also reported a few mule deer.

[b]Includes white-tailed deer.

[c]NOS = no open season.

tional forests (table 25) also resemble those reported by state agencies (table 24) except that peak harvest on national forests occurred later than peaks recorded for whole states. This lag may reflect only a reporting delay for data that the Forest Service acquired from state agencies. Based on national forest totals, the peak harvest of 52,000 in 1966 was followed by a drop to 31,000 in 1971. From 1971 to 1975 it was essentially stable; decreases in California during this period were countered by increases in other states.

The data in tables 24 and 25 establish that total deer harvests have declined substantially since the early 1960s. In many states the kill has dropped 30 percent or more since 1970, and further declines are possible. But these reduced harvests cannot be cited as unqualified evidence of declining populations, because most state wildlife agencies have deliberately restricted

Table 25. Estimated Numbers of Mule and Black-tailed Deer Harvested by Hunters on National Forests in the United States, Expressed in Thousands of Deer Taken in Autumn Each Year

Year	Mule Deer														Black-tailed Deer				
	Arizona	California	Colorado	Idaho	Montana	Nebraska	Nevada	New Mexico	Oregon	South Dakota	Utah	Washington	Wyoming	Total[a]	Alaska	California	Oregon	Washington	Total[a]
1950	7.6	18	44	17	10	0	6.9	3.7	19	1.2	47	18	12	204	2.9	11	5.5	4.6	24
1951	7.4	21	45	23	15	0	8.6	4.7	32	1.9	64	6.7	13	242	3.5	11	4.8	3.1	22
1952	8.8	17	40	22	17	0	10	5.3	34	2.9	64	6.2	15	242	4.0	11	4.2	1.9	21
1953	11	18	36	20	20	0	9.3	6.4	38	10	69	9.2	16	263	5.5	11	8.9	2.2	28
1954	18	22	40	25	23	0	9.8	18	48	3.9	76	10	18	312	4.8	13	9.0	1.8	29
1955	16	24	34	25	31	0	13	15	55	2.8	81	16	20	333	5.5	13	9.2	2.2	30
1956	20	35	43	27	34	0.2	14	17	52	1.8	90	6.5	17	358	6.2	18	7.2	2.0	33
1957	17	23	54	26	37	0.1	14	25	54	1.6	81	7.7	25	365	9.4	16	9.0	2.1	36
1958	23	21	46	31	41	0	13	25	55	1.4	88	9.3	21	375	14	13	7.8	2.7	38
1959	20	27	63	30	40	0.8	12	28	58	2.1	92	9.7	23	406	11	14	7.8	2.9	36
1960	22	25	59	35	43	0.5	13	32	62	2.2	96	10	26	426	13	17	11	6.0	47
1961	22	21	79	38	47	0.4	14	20	70	2.4	96	13	32	455	12	15	12	5.6	45
1962	17	15	82	41	46	0.3	14	15	54	4.0	95	12	28	423	12	12	12	5.2	41
1963	13	14	81	41	44	0.3	14	15	43	2.1	88	16	30	401	12	14	12	8.4	46
1964	12	15	71	44	39	0.6	16	16	58	2.6	83	12	25	394	11	17	13	7.6	49
1965	11	14	62	38	32	0.6	13	16	50	2.8	66	11	23	339	12	16	14	5.3	47
1966	12	16	52	43	35	1.0	15	16	62	1.7	64	14	21	353	14	19	14	4.5	52
1967	8.7	9.2	59	44	34	1.0	11	16	60	3.7	66	16	21	350	13	10	14	4.5	42
1968	7.5	11	56	50	37	1.0	12	16	68	3.2	73	18	22	375	14	13	14	6.7	48
1969	7.0	9.6	58	49	34	1.0	9.9	16	53	3.3	55	8.0	25	329	7.7	13	11	3.2	35
1970	7.7	7.5	43	48	32	1.0	12	19	50	2.3	70	8.4	24	325	9.1	9.7	10	3.6	32
1971	6.2	6.7	23	38	32	0.9	11	19	35	2.4	67	5.4	23	270	7.1	10	9.1	4.4	31
1972	6.0	8.1	30	30	28	0.9	9.7	18	24	2.2	70	3.7	18	249	3.8	9.2	9.0	3.6	26
1973	6.3	6.4	39	31	29	0.9	7.9	18	28	3.0	47	4.9	16	238	8.7	8.7	12	4.6	34
1974	6.3	5.3	33	26	25	1.3	7.3	16	23	1.6	36	5.9	15	202	7.0	6.0	11	5.4	29
1975	7.0	5.9	22	24	20	1.3	2.9	11	19	1.5	32	11	15	173	11	7.4	10	4.7	33

Note: Compiled from U.S. Forest Service (1950–76).
[a]Totals are rounded to the nearest 1,000.

hunting opportunities to curtail harvests. The reader will be spared an exhaustive review of changes in hunting regulations; it will suffice to point out that nearly every mule deer state has adopted some combination of shorter hunting seasons, reduced numbers of antlerless tags, reduced bag limits, higher license fees, or other restrictions that reduce either hunter numbers or hunter success, or both. In Nevada, serious consideration was given to an absolute closure in 1976, but a restrictive permit allocation system finally was adopted instead (Christensen 1976).

RELATIONSHIP OF HUNTING PRESSURE AND HARVEST

Because declining mule deer harvests in the 1970s were accompanied by increasingly restrictive hunting regulations, one might ask if the reduced harvests simply reflect reduced hunting opportunity rather than declining deer herds. Most wildlife biologists and managers, however, seem to believe that populations, and therefore harvests, declined. In British Columbia, for example, license sales dropped only 12 percent from 1970 to 1974, but the deer harvest declined 55 percent (Halladay 1976). In California, a 14 percent reduction in deer tag sales from 1973 through 1975 was paralleled by a 45 percent decline in buck kill even though hunting regulations remained constant (MacGregor 1976). In Montana, from 1970 through 1975, the mule deer harvest dropped approximately 45 percent; hunter success during these years fell from 81 percent to 44 percent, while the average time required to take a deer increased from 1.5 to 13.6 days (Freeman 1976).

An overview of recent trends in hunting pressure on western deer ranges may be obtained from United States Forest Service estimates of the time spent in national forests each year by big game hunters. Table 26 summarizes records of big game hunter use since 1965 in those national forest regions that encompass the range of mule and black-tailed deer. Forest Service records expressed public use in numbers of visits before 1965, and in visitor-days thereafter. A visit might have lasted several days, whereas a hunting visitor-day means 1 person hunting for 12 hours or 12 persons hunting for 1 hour each. Therefore the data before 1965 are not directly comparable with more recent figures. The early data indicated a steady increase in big game hunter visits from 1950–64.

Table 26. Estimated Use of National Forests in the Western United States by Big Game Hunters, Expressed in Thousands of Hunter Days

Year	United States Forest Service Regions[a]							Total
	1	2	3	4	5	6	10	
1965	1,093	1,154	568	1,192	1,352	1,631	92	7,082
1966	1,093	999	563	1,176	1,497	1,391	75	6,794
1967	1,019	930	614	1,162	1,301	1,717	88	6,831
1968	1,145	1,027	602	1,269	1,395	1,829	102	7,369
1969	1,174	1,001	578	1,319	1,424	1,799	107	7,402
1970	1,168	903	687	1,348	1,398	1,649	102	7,255
1971	1,068	786	585	1,348	1,301	1,346	43	6,477
1972	1,034	805	686	1,487	1,232	1,370	34	6,648
1973	1,036	901	774	1,394	1,195	1,641	67	7,008
1974	1,008	1,075	701	1,318	1,153	1,594	72	6,921
1975	910	970	650	1,147	1,047	1,640	66	6,430

Note: Compiled from U.S. Forest Service (1950–76).
[a]Region 1: Montana, northern Idaho.
Region 2: Colorado, South Dakota, Nebraska, eastern Wyoming.
Region 3: Arizona, New Mexico.
Region 4: Utah, Nevada, southern Idaho, western Wyoming.
Region 5: California.
Region 6: Oregon, Washington.
Region 10: Alaska.

As shown in table 26, big game hunting pressure on western national forests was relatively constant from 1965 through 1975. The 6.43 million hunter-days recorded in 1975 was only 13 percent lower than the peak of 7.40 million hunter-days in 1969. However, the estimated deer harvest (blacktails plus mule deer) from national forests declined 44 percent during that period (table 25). These statistics support findings of state and provincial wildlife agencies that the declining harvest was due to causes other than reduced hunting pressure. (It should be noted that estimates of recreational visitor-days on national forests, like deer populations or harvests, generally are not obtained in a manner that permits definition of sampling precision or judgment of accuracy.)

The critical reader may point out that a change from either-sex to bucks-only hunting would reduce harvests even if the numbers of deer and hunters remained constant. Several states, in fact, have reduced the number of either-sex permits specifically to restrict harvests. Therefore it might seem that increasingly restrictive regulations could combine with reduced hunting pressure to produce declining harvests from stable deer herds, but this cannot be seen in the data at hand. What can be seen, in states such as California where hunting regulations have been relatively constant over time, is that harvest declined much more than hunter numbers. The most straightforward explanation for this result is that deer numbers declined. I conclude that, in the West as a whole, the decline in deer harvest was too great to be explained solely by declining hunting pressure or restricted hunting opportunity.

SUMMARY OF POPULATION AND HARVEST TRENDS

If available records and opinions are taken at face value, the only possible conclusion is that mule deer populations declined over most of the species' range from the early 1960s to 1976. More or less substantial declines have been reported in Arizona, British Columbia, California, Colorado, Idaho, Montana, Nevada, New

Mexico, Oregon, South Dakota, Texas, Utah, and Wyoming. In Alberta, Kansas, Nebraska, North Dakota, Washington, and Saskatchewan, mule deer populations appeared to be stable or increasing in the mid-1970s. Black-tailed deer populations also may have declined in the late 1960s and early 1970s.

The conclusion that mule deer have declined over large areas is not supported by precise population measurements, and the magnitude of the decline—either geographically or numerically—may never be known. No state or province makes statistically valid, annual estimates of the total deer population within its boundaries. Mule deer harvests have declined in most states, but harvests do not necessarily reflect population trends where hunting regulations were made more restrictive to intentionally curtail harvests.

CAUSES OF THE DEER DECLINE

If mule deer populations have declined generally, it is reasonable to seek some general, rangewide phenomenon to account for it. So far, no single overwhelming problem has been identified. With or without factual basis for their belief, many people blame the decline on overshooting. In Idaho and several other states, knowledgeable authorities cited excessive hunter harvest as a major or contributing cause of decline (table 20). At the April 1976 symposium, Mule Deer Decline in the West, Pengelly (1976) noted that no speaker had considered the population impact of legal hunting, which had removed about 6 million deer over the previous ten years. Denney (1976), however, had pointed out that states in which both sexes of mule deer were harvested reported only about half as much decline as other states, such as California, Oregon and Arizona, where, with few exceptions, only bucks were hunted. If the decline was due to overhunting, the states that harvested most intensively should have shown the greatest decline. Population and harvest estimates in tables 21–25 do not reveal any general relationship between harvest intensity and population trend. One suspects that legal harvests had little to do with the deer decline, and

that the harvestable surplus merely was lost wherever it was not taken by hunters.

One interesting feature of the decline, and another indication that overhunting was not the cause, is that the declining herds were characterized by poor fawn survival. For example, Salwasser (1976) pointed out that, in the Devil's Garden of California, the proportion of yearlings in the spring population dropped from 38 percent during 1955–59 to 20 percent during 1970–76. The herd declined about 70 percent in the interim. MacGregor (1976) reported that fawn-doe ratios in stable mule deer herds in California were higher than those in declining herds. Likewise, in eastern Montana, deer population trends were found to vary with fawn-doe ratios. Mackie (1976b) showed that fawn crops of 30–33 percent of the early winter population were required to maintain a stable population from one year to the next. Increases in this population were associated with ratios above 55–66 fawns per 100 does, and declines with ratios below 40 fawns per 100 does. The general principle probably applies to all deer herds, although the fawn-doe ratio required for stability or increase will vary with hunter harvest and other mortality factors.

Poor fawn survival might well be anticipated in declining deer herds, because fawns are more susceptible than adults to most causes of mortality (hunting is a notable exception). Also, it is obvious that, whenever fawn survival is inadequate to replace the adults lost from a population, the population must decline. But, if the fact of poor fawn survival is clear, the course of corrective management is not. Malnutrition and possibly predation are the most probable causes; these influences are discussed at length elsewhere in this book.

Disease must always be considered a potential factor, whether primary or secondary, in the decline of any deer population. Some of the many possibilities are discussed by Hibler in chapter 4. So far, disease has not been implicated in the mule deer decline.

Though wildlife biologists and managers are unable to attribute the deer decline specifically to any single major cause such as overhunting or disease, a long list of factors detrimental to deer or deer ranges in various states and provinces has been developed (table 20). These postulated causal factors fall into two general categories: overhunting and predation; and environmental problems such as severe winters, droughts, conflicting uses of deer ranges, loss of habitat through preemption for other uses, and unfavorable plant successional trends on deer ranges.

Longhurst et al. (1976) concluded that the decline in California resulted primarily from diminishing food supplies and loss of habitat, which in turn were caused by changes in burning, logging, and grazing patterns, unfavorable weather, excessive use by deer of overstocked ranges, and other land-use factors. In its deer recovery plan, the California Department of Fish and Game (1976) reiterated most of the problems cited by Longhurst et al. (1976) and,

in addition, identified farming, suburban developments, and reservoir and freeway construction as major causes of habitat loss. Peek (1976) and Pengelly (1976), in summarizing different meetings on the deer decline, listed similar arrays of suspected problems. In addition to climatic variables, it seems that nearly every action of man on deer ranges theoretically could affect the deer.

In my view, the only generalization needed to account for the mule deer decline throughout the West is that practically every identified trend in land use and plant succession on the deer ranges is detrimental to deer. Hunting pressure and predators might be controlled, and favorable weather could permit temporary recovery, but deer numbers ultimately are limited by habitat quantity and quality.

Logging is one of the most widespread influences of man on mule and black-tailed deer ranges. Resulting habitat changes—such as opening up old-growth forests—can be beneficial to deer and other wildlife. Photograph by Leland J. Prater; courtesy of the United States Forest Service.

These deer will be displaced from their winter range near Salmon, Idaho, by future subdivision development. A subdivision road is visible behind the deer. Photograph by Stu Murrell; courtesy of the Idaho Department of Fish and Game.

Woven wire fences are especially detrimental when they cross mule deer migration corridors. Note the large reservoir in the background. Photograph by Stu Murrell; courtesy of the Idaho Department of Fish and Game.

In 1870, members of the (Ferdinand V.) Hayden Expedition—first of the "Great Surveys" of western territories, authorized by the U.S. Department of Interior—gather for a meal of venison. The deer's head (antlers in velvet) and carcass are in lower right corner of the photograph, which was taken at the confluence of the Sweetwater and North Platte rivers. Photo reportedly taken by W. H. Jackson (although Jackson is standing at far right); courtesy of the U.S. Geological Survey.

PROSPECTS FOR RECOVERY

Many state wildlife management agencies seem to desire the largest possible deer populations. This is perhaps understandable, since their most vocal constituents are hunters who want more deer (at little or no cost to themselves). But, in view of the reported habitat destruction, starvation, and die-offs that accompanied peak populations, and given that deer production is only one of many uses of western range and forest lands, one may ask whether a return to maximum numbers is desirable. Smaller and more heavily cropped herds might be preferable; it has been shown that maximum harvest and maximum population size are biologically incompatible management goals (Gross 1969; F. M. Anderson et al. 1974).

In terms of deer population dynamics, the manager who wishes to reverse a population decline must accomplish some combination of the following: increase the proportion of females; increase life expectancy; increase natality (Giles et al. 1969). To achieve these things on a broad scale, however, a formidable array of ecological and economic obstacles must be

The grassland site where the Hayden Expedition bivouacked in 1870 (previous photo) now is inundated by the Pathfinder Reservoir in Wyoming (above). Although such reservoirs serve to provide needed water for human and wildlife resources in arid and semiarid areas, they sometimes preempt valuable big game habitat. Photo courtesy of the Wyoming Game and Fish Department.

overcome. Many ranges reportedly are declining in their ability to support deer (Schneegas and Bumstead 1977), because of successional trends related to fire control, reduced grazing, accelerated reforestation after logging, or climax management goals on rangelands. Other deer ranges are being preempted by reservoirs, agricultural or suburban development, off-road vehicles, or other incompatible uses.

On the economic front, deer managers either must continue to accept deer as a fortuitous by-product of other land uses or spend money to enhance deer ranges. But money for habitat improvement has never been plentiful, and future budgets may be even tighter owing to declining deer tag sales and inflation. In the United States, the best prospect for increased habitat management funds probably lies with the federal land management agencies. United States Forest Service biologists have suggested prescribed burning, logging, and grazing to rejuvenate stagnating deer habitat (Schneegas and Bumstead 1977), but I question whether any agency, or all agencies combined, can restore deer habitat on the massive scale needed to reverse present trends. Even with unlimited funds for habitat improvement, it is not certain that the peak deer populations of the early 1960s could be restored.

One potential source of deer management funds and talent that so far has not been tapped significantly is the private landowner. Many ranchers could and probably would expend money and effort on behalf of deer if they were able to profit from increased deer production. Economic exploitation of native ungulates is an accepted practice in most parts of the world, though it is discouraged in the United States. In western North America, such exploitation probably will continue to be vigorously opposed by sportsmen who are accustomed to "free" hunting.

A remarkable feature of the current mule deer situation, in my experience, is that every interested person visualizes the problem, and its solution, in terms of his own interest or expertise. Range men, for example, point to range deterioration, while conservation officers cite illegal hunting as a major problem. Sportsmen are worried about excessive hunting pressure, especially from nonresidents, and predator experts point out the detrimental influence of unchecked numbers of coyotes. Research workers decry the lack of knowledge and prophesy that the decline cannot be reversed without vigorous new research. Some or all of these things may be true, and all will receive consideration. New information and new approaches to management will be developed, but some important limiting factors will remain beyond the control of wildlife managers.

HISTORICAL PERSPECTIVE

In view of the present wave of concern for mule deer, it may be appropriate to recollect that such concern is not new. At the 1964 meeting of the Western Association of Game and Fish Commissioners, reports were heard of mule deer declines in Arizona, California, Nevada, Oregon, and Utah, though the data in tables 21–23 certainly do not support that concern generally. Mohler (1964) prognosticated that the days of fantastic hunter success were

gone. Jantzen (1964), MacGregor (1964), and McKean and Luman (1964) described contemporary political efforts to strip the game commissions in Arizona, California, and Oregon of deer management authority because of declining harvests. Similar voices were raised in 1968 and again in 1973. The chorus swelled to record volume in 1976, and additional replays of this theme are anticipated for future years.

Perhaps the greatest deer decline in the history of western North America occurred late in the nineteenth century. The cause generally was assumed to be overhunting, and there is no factual basis now to dispute that assumption. Herds that were near extirpation at the turn of the century subsequently increased to the point of overpopulation on many ranges by the 1940s or even earlier. "Too many deer" was the predominant management problem by 1950. Several biologists in the 1950s tried to draw attention to the temporary nature of deer abundance, attributing the increase to transient and unplanned improvements in deer habitat through extensive and frequently abusive logging, grazing, and burning practices. Leopold (1950a) pointed out that many deer ranges were created at exorbitant costs in timber and soil, as the fertility and biotic energy stored through eons of forest growth were released all at once through logging and burning, to produce a one-time bumper crop of deer forage. He forecast that wildlife managers could not produce deer indefinitely on this basis. Longhurst et al. (1952) found that nearly all California deer ranges were fully stocked or overstocked in the early 1950s, and half were deteriorating from overuse. They predicted a gradual decrease in deer numbers unless hunter harvests were increased to balance the deer herds with available forage. Similar warnings came from other areas.

Thus the record shows that forces beyond the control of wildlife managers caused larger deer populations than the ranges could support indefinitely, and that many biologists recognized the overpopulations for what they were. Given ample and repeated warnings, we should not be surprised that the forecasts of decline came true. And if deer were too numerous in the 1950s and 1960s, should we lament that they may be less abundant now? Could we really expect to have record high numbers of deer forever? I submit that we could not.

Author's note: The preceding discussion of deer population and harvest trends was written in 1977, at the depth of despair and hand-wringing over the mule deer decline. As this book goes to press in 1980, however, the outlook is much improved. At the Seventh Western States Mule Deer Workshop at Logan, Utah, in February 1978, most states reported significant deer increases since 1976. For at least some herds, the decline appeared to be over.

Rather than update this discussion of population and harvest trends to reflect the possible reversal of the mule deer decline, the editors of this book have elected to let it stand as one biologist's assessment of the state of mule deer management in 1976–77. Dated it may be, yet it reveals how little control biologists and managers have over the deer they purport to manage. Just as they were powerless to halt the decline, the biologists and managers now are unable to show in any scientifically acceptable way that improved management put the herds on the road to recovery. Nor can they assure the public that mule deer are now secure. It is not pessimistic, but merely realistic to note that society does not put high priority on mule deer management. It has opted for more rural subdivisions, more reservoirs and freeways, and many incompatible uses of deer ranges, to the detriment of deer habitat and the deer themselves.

Chapter 7

LIMITING FACTORS AND POPULATION REGULATION

Guy E. Connolly
Wildlife Research Biologist
United States Fish and Wildlife Service
Denver Wildlife Research Center
Twin Falls, Idaho

Deer numbers everywhere are limited by some combination of influences such as weather, food supplies, predation (including hunting), parasites, diseases, and human activities on deer ranges. A deer population at any given time and place reflects the composite effect of all regulating influences, so that it rarely is possible to measure or quantify the effect of any single factor. Nevertheless, wildlife biologists and managers frequently need to judge the relative importance of various factors even if such judgment can be made only speculatively. The shortcomings of existing knowledge on this subject will be all too apparent in the ensuing discussion, which emphasizes the significance of limiting factors in deer management.

Important to any discussion of mule deer population dynamics, and of population regulation in particular, are the concepts of "carrying capacity" and "limiting factors." Carrying capacity of a range for deer, according to Leopold (1933), is the maximum density of deer that a range can support. Later workers have added the concept of animal condition to the definition, since the number of deer that can be supported in good condition may be well below maximum possible numbers. Dasmann (1971), for example, distinguished between "maximum carrying capacity" and "optimum carrying capacity." Maximum carrying capacity—the greatest number of animals that can be supported on a strictly maintenance basis—rises during favorable years and falls in poor years. Many deer die-offs result from such fluctuations; a herd will increase during a succession of favorable years, as when forage production is above average or winters are particularly mild, only to face severe readjustment when changing conditions cause a rapid drop in carrying capacity. Optimum carrying capacity, in contrast, involves a relatively stable number of animals that can be supported in good condition on a sustained basis; that is, without damage to or depletion of the range. In a classic paper on this topic, Edwards and Fowle (1955) suggested that carrying capacity is not a stable property of a range, but the expression of continuing interactions among organisms and their environment.

One of the cherished ideals of big game management is that deer can be cropped or harvested at some specified rate that will maintain herds at optimum carrying capacity. But managers have had little success in measuring or forecasting optimum carrying capacity of deer ranges (see "Balancing Deer Populations with the Habitat" in chap. 8). It should be possible to estimate carrying capacity from various habitat measurements, but so far no one has accomplished this on mule or black-tailed deer ranges.

In view of the technical difficulties involved, perhaps one should not be surprised at the lack of progress in estimating carrying capacities of deer ranges. But livestock managers have determined carrying capacities of the same ranges for domestic livestock. Since the principles of ungulate nutrition apply to wild species as well as domestic ones, it seems reasonable to propose that carrying capacity of mule deer range is defined by the supply of usable forage (Giles and Snyder 1970; Raleigh 1970). Progress toward comprehension of range carrying capacity will require assessment of all available forage in terms of its potential to contribute to the animals' nutrition (Robbins 1973; Stewart et al. 1977; Wallmo et al. 1977). Chapter 3 provides background for this concept and explains why no adequate appraisal of carrying capacity can come from a superficial survey of the growth and use of twigs of a few "key" browse species.

Although application of carrying capacity concepts to deer population management remains a nebulous goal in western North America, research on this subject currently is under way in Colorado. Workers in Europe, meanwhile, have known that functionally adequate judgment of deer-habitat relationships can be developed empirically (de Nahlik 1974; Mutch et al. 1976). Development of such skill may be difficult under the superficial approach that characterizes current mule deer management on many ranges, but it should not be considered impossible.

At the present state of the art, the wildlife biologist or manager who tries to manage mule deer in relation to range capacity faces formidable obstacles. If he cannot determine optimum carrying capacity objectively, how is he to know when the herd is at optimum density? If carrying capacity fluctuates over time, how can a herd decline caused by reduced carrying capacity be distinguished from one caused by predation or hunting? Right now these answers can be answered only generally, and the notion of carrying capacity provides little guidance for mule deer management.

As a corollary to the idea of carrying capacity, it follows that deer cannot increase indefinitely. Deer numbers are regulated by various limiting factors. Some, such as food supplies and weather, are integral components of the environment, whereas others, such as mechanized recreational hunters, are not.

Whenever some one factor restricts the size of a deer herd—snow depth, food supplies, or predation, for example—that constraint may be described as the limiting factor; that is, the factor that at least temporarily sets the upper bound on size of a particular population. From a research standpoint, it is hard to assess the relative importance of various individual factors that may be limiting. There are two reasons for this.

1. No one factor operates independently of the others. A single influence may be chiefly responsible for an observed trend in deer numbers, but rarely is it possible to conclude that this factor alone caused the trend. Even if, in theory, the effects of various influences could be segregated, in practice interactions are too complex to be separated by existing research methods.

2. Most regulating influences affect deer populations in basically similar ways; they change birthrate, death rate, or both. Although the timing or magnitude of these effects may differ with the cause, deer managers often can see only the end product in the field. Thus, the biologist or manager who is confronted with poor fawn crops or declining herds, for example, may be unable to ascertain whether the fault lies with poor nutrition, predators, unfavorable weather, or some combination of these and other influences.

To evaluate the importance of any factor, one should identify its immediate demographic effects explicitly and characterize its effect on population density. In addition, it is necessary to compare the factor's impact with that of other factors and to describe its interactions with other factors in terms of additive, compensatory, or modifying effects (Keith 1974). Such detailed analysis rarely has been accomplished for factors that regulate mule deer populations, so the true roles of various limiting factors are obscure on most deer ranges.

HABITAT AS A LIMITING FACTOR

Habitat management for mule and black-tailed deer is discussed at several other places in this book, but it should be reemphasized here that certain aspects of habitat, especially food supplies, are widely believed to be the predominant constraint on size of most mule deer herds. In most deer management studies the relationships are described only subjectively, but there is good reason to believe that seasonal forage deficits limit the size of many herds. On most ranges the deficit occurs in winter, but some herds in southern California (Longhurst et al. 1952) and on the Kaibab Plateau (Russo 1964) appear to be limited by quality or size of their summer ranges. Nonmigratory populations of black-tailed deer whose environments lack heavy snows also may be limited by forage conditions in late summer (Taber and Dasmann 1958). Regardless of the timing of nutritional bottlenecks, however, the deficiencies are qualitative rather

than quantitative. There is always vegetation available, but most of it is too unpalatable or too indigestible to be used as forage. This is especially true for mule deer in winter when even the "preferred" browse species may fail to provide an adequate maintenance ration (Wallmo et al. 1977).

Responses of deer to nutritional conditions have been documented or identified speculatively in many studies. In general, good nutrition is reflected in deer by (1) good physical condition and above-average body weights; (2) high reproductive rates (breeding success of young does is thought to be an especially sensitive indicator of forage conditions); (3) high survival rates, especially for fawns; and (4) increasing populations.

Poor nutrition would cause the opposite of these conditions. Klein (1969) and Dasmann (1971) provided revealing discussions about relationships of deer populations and their ranges.

If deer herds reflect the quality of their ranges, it seems practicable from various measures of the health of the deer to draw inferences about range quality. This can be done to some extent (see "Indicators of Animal

Scarcity of good-quality forage frequently leads to malnutrition on many mule deer winter ranges. Note the browse line. Photograph courtesy of the United States Forest Service.

Condition" in chap. 8), but the indicators can be confounded by other variables. Poor condition can result from severe winter weather rather than food shortage; that is, deep snow can prevent access to forage that would be adequate if available. Low fawn survival could result from predation, or possibly from disease or parasite burdens, even when nutrition is adequate. Likewise, deer herds may decline owing to overhunting or predation when food is abundant. For these reasons there is urgent need for better methods to measure those aspects of habitat that govern its capacity to support mule and black-tailed deer.

WEATHER AS A LIMITING FACTOR

Weather has both direct and indirect effects on deer herds. On most mule deer ranges, indirect effects on forage production probably are more important than direct effects.

An example of indirect weather effects on deer population dynamics was given by Smith and LeCount (1976) for the Three Bar Wildlife Area in Arizona, where survival of mule deer fawns each year varied with total rainfall during the previous winter. This relationship appeared to result mainly from the influence of precipitation on production of winter-growing forbs. Variations in forb production accounted for about 75 percent of the total variation in fawn survival during the eight-year study. It can be presumed that random climatic variations cause similar fluctuations in forage production on most, if not all, deer ranges.

In addition to indirect effects of precipitation on forage production, water shortages on desert ranges may limit deer numbers directly. A year-long drought in southeastern Arizona, for example, caused an apparent decline in local deer populations (Anthony 1976). There are numerous accounts of mule deer subsisting and bearing fawns without access to free water (see Leopold 1933), but deer density in these arid ranges might increase if more water was available.

The direct limiting effects of weather are particularly apparent on northern deer ranges. Starvation losses and malnutrition due to deep and prolonged snow cover have been reported in southeastern Alaska (Ballard and Merriam 1975), Alberta (Burgess 1973), British Columbia (Edwards 1956; Smith 1969), western Oregon (Hines 1975), western Washington (Brown 1961), Wyoming (Strickland 1975), and elsewhere. Even when weather is not severe enough to cause catastrophic losses, snow

Deep snow covers many mule deer ranges in winter, making most forage inaccessible. Photograph by Ted Chu; courtesy of the Idaho Department of Fish and Game.

depth may govern the distribution of deer on winter ranges (Gilbert et al. 1970). In southeastern Wyoming, the presence of crusted snow more than 0.3 meter (1.0 foot) deep caused mule deer to move to other ranges with less snow (Strickland 1975). Deep snow not only interferes with deer's ability to find food, but also may increase their vulnerability to predation.

Snow depth on winter ranges usually is regarded as a problem over which wildlife managers have little control. Recent work on mule deer winter range in Colorado, however, indicates that snow fences can be used to reduce snow depth enough so that deer can occupy shrub stands that would otherwise be inaccessible (Regelin 1976a). On blacktail winter range in southeastern Alaska, forest managers also can minimize snow depth by preserving heavily stocked, old-growth timber stands that are frequented by deer in late winter. Clearcut logging of these areas increases snow accumulation and reduces carrying capacity for deer (Bloom 1978).

Except for the obvious die-offs in exceptionally severe winters, the influence of winter weather on deer population dynamics is indistinguishable from that of food shortage in general. Overwinter survival usually is high in dry winters with below-normal snowfall, regardless of other weather factors. In contrast, survival is low and condition of survivors is poor after winters of heavy snowfall, because deep snow covers much of the forage and makes it unavailable.

Weather conditions that are favorable to deer from the standpoint of forage conditions may also be favorable to certain parasites, especially roundworms that infest the lungs or gastrointestinal tracts of deer. In northern California, for example, warm, moist winters are conducive to forage production, but also may facilitate harmful infestations of stomach and intestinal worms (Longhurst and Douglas 1953). The forage relationships may be more important, but it seems desirable to consider parasites as well in assessing net impact of local, short-term deviations from normal weather patterns.

Because weather fluctuations are unpredictable and unmanageable, wildlife managers have no choice but to tolerate and allow for their effects. Any action that can improve the condition of deer before onset of winter, however, would be desirable. In this connection, it often is said that shooting surplus deer in autumn reduces winter losses by cutting down competition for limited winter forage. According to Dasmann (1971), removal of sizable numbers of deer by hunters each autumn permits survival of deer that otherwise would have perished. Even though this idea frequently is advanced as a justification for increased hunter harvests, it depends on the unproved premise that winter losses are density-dependent. I have been unable to find any documented example of reduced winter mortality due to increased hunter harvest before winter. If, on the other hand, winter losses are density-independent, mortality would be determined by the duration of deep snow or food deprivation regardless of the number of deer present. Under this concept, the appropriate strategy would be to enter winter with as many deer as possible, so as to maximize the number that survive until spring. On the basis of present knowledge, one probably should not characterize winter losses generally as either density-dependent or density-independent.

POPULATION REGULATION BY HUNTING

The Harvestable Surplus

Recreational hunting of deer is predicated on the notion of a harvestable surplus; that is, an annual crop that can be harvested without detriment to the breeding stock. Many hunters, biologists, and wildlife managers seem to believe that man is obliged to hunt in order to restrict deer herds to carrying capacity of their ranges, to maximize herd productivity, or even to prevent range damage. Dasmann (1971), for example, stated that the only way to maintain balance between deer and their habitat is to remove surplus animals each year, and that hunting benefits both the deer herd and the range by removing animals that otherwise would be lost and wasted.

Many similar statements by other authors can be found in recent literature, and they represent the traditional view of deer harvest management in North America. Studies throughout the range of mule and black-tailed deer, as well as many years of hunting experience, have shown that there is indeed a harvestable surplus in most deer herds, and deer that are not taken by hunters may die of other causes. The proposition that deer must be reduced to prevent range damage due to over-browsing or overgrazing by deer is less certain. Brown (1961) suggested that, in Douglas fir forests of western Washington, overpopulations of black-tailed deer tend to retard natural plant succession and may actually prolong the productive period of a range for deer. The same may be true of chaparral ranges in California, where heavy deer use holds down some shrubs that, in the absence of browsing, would soon grow beyond the reach of deer. At Oak Creek, Utah, on the other hand, low productivity of mule deer was attributed by Robinette et al. (1977) to range depletion from excessive deer use. Robinette believed that the deleterious effects of overpopulation were more pronounced in unhunted than in hunted herds, and that mule deer are capable of destroying their habitat.

Taken at face value, these opinions indicate that heavy deer use is detrimental to some habitat types but not others. The potential for range damage through overuse probably is greatest where deer concentrate seasonally. Whenever managers believe that deer are destroying their habitat, they have a professional obligation to preserve the habitat by any means available. But, where overpopulation of deer does not appear to cause range damage, managers can choose either to use or lose the harvestable surplus.

Size of harvestable surplus for a given deer herd usually can be determined only by experience with that herd. The biologist or manager will monitor harvest and then, from some combination of population measurements and

intuition, infer whether that harvest was excessive, conservative, or about right. Hunting regulations for the coming year then can be adjusted accordingly. In a confined, unhunted blacktail herd, Hines (1975) was able to estimate harvestable surplus by defining it as the number of deer that should have been removed each autumn to avoid excessive winter mortality. From analysis of known deer densities and known mortalities, he found that an autumn population of 29 deer per square kilometer (75 deer per square mile) could have been maintained without excessive winter losses. To bring the herd down to this level each autumn, it would have been necessary to harvest 9 deer per square kilometer (23 deer per square mile) each year.

Harvestable surplus varies with the age and sex classes harvested. Maximum numerical yield, for example, probably would result from heavy cropping of fawns and bucks combined with light culling of does (table 27). If the reader cannot conceptualize managing deer in this manner, it may help to consider domestic sheep production practices, in which most lambs and some cull ewes are sold each year.

Few if any mule deer herds are managed for maximum numerical yield, because hunters prefer to shoot bucks rather than fawns. Therefore the management goal—if one exists—often is maximum production and harvest of adult bucks, contrary to the beliefs of many sportsmen, maximum buck production is achieved not by hunting bucks only, but by taking both bucks and does. In Utah and Montana, for example, both buck kill and hunter success increased after statewide hunting was changed from buck-only to either-sex (Reynolds 1960; Egan 1971).

Computer simulation experiments also have shown that buck production is enhanced by taking some does as well. In the model of F. M. Anderson et al. (1974), an annual removal of 25 percent of legal bucks, 15 percent of does, and 5 percent of fawns and spike bucks resulted in average harvests of 23,000 deer (table 27). Approximately 7,400 of these deer were legal bucks, compared with a total take of only 6,400 when 25 percent of the legal bucks and

Table 27. Computer-Simulated Effects of Various Harvests on Black-tailed Deer in Mendocino County, California

	Harvest Strategy: Percentage Harvested Each Year						
Legal bucks	0	25	25	50	50	50	0
Spike bucks	0	0	5	0	5	50	0
Does	0	0	15	0	15	15	25
Fawns	0	0	5	0	5	60	0

	Effects of Harvest Strategy: Annual Population Statistics[a]						
Total deer (1 November)	192,000	195,000	169,000	198,000	170,000	135,000	151,000
Annual natural losses	94,000	100,000	52,000	105,000	54,000	18,000	29,000
Annual hunting kill	0	6,400	23,000[b]	8,400	27,000[c]	54,000	12,000
Hunting mortality rate[d]	0	0.03	0.12	0.04	0.14	0.37	0.08
Natural mortality rate[d]	0.46	0.46	0.28	0.47	0.28	0.12	0.18
Fawns born per doe[e]	1.16	1.17	1.16	1.18	1.17	1.32	1.26
Fawns per doe (1 November)	0.57	0.57	0.62	0.58	0.62	0.93	0.67
Fawns per doe (1 May)	0.36	0.37	0.54	0.37	0.55	0.40	0.75[f]
Fraction of fawns surviving first year	0.30	0.30	0.45	0.30	0.45	NA[g]	0.60
Legal bucks per doe (1 November)	0.48	0.18	0.29	0.09	0.15	0.08	1.32
Spike bucks per doe (1 November)	0.13	0.12	0.17	0.11	0.16	0.07	0.23
Mean age (years) of bucks (1 November)	4.9	3.1	3.4	2.3	2.5	2.6	6.1
Mean age (years) of does (1 November)	4.8	4.8	4.1	4.8	4.0	4.8	3.5

Source: F. M. Anderson et al. (1974).

[a] Values are averages from thirty-year computer runs.
[b] About 7,400 were legal bucks.
[c] About 9,800 were legal bucks.
[d] Mortality as fraction of total deer numbers on 1 July.
[e] "Does" include all females 12 months of age or older.
[f] Fawn-doe ratio increased from November to May because does (but not fawns) were harvested in the interim.
[g] Not calculated. Fawn survival was low owing to large harvest of fawns.

no does were killed. Aside from the issue of maximum buck production, it is not possible to use a harvestable surplus fully when only bucks are hunted.

An important aspect of harvestable surplus, from the standpoint of wildlife managers, is that its size may vary uncontrollably and perhaps unpredictably from one year to the next. Such variations are not often documented, but an example is available from the National Bison Range in Montana (table 28). On this United States Fish and Wildlife Service refuge, seven native North American species of ungulates are maintained at rigidly controlled stocking rates. Surplus animals are either re-moved alive or shot by the refuge staff. There is no public hunting. The 7,500 hectare (18,540 acre) refuge is surrounded by a high woven-wire fence that is not absolutely deer-tight, but mule deer within can be managed as a discrete population.

The management plan for mule deer on the National Bison Range calls for a winter population of 200–250 animals. In September and October each year, a count is made to determine how many animals should be removed before winter. Harvest quotas are established, and culling normally is completed by December. A few animals also are taken at other times of year for research purposes.

Table 28. Population Statistics for Mule Deer on the National Bison Range, Moiese, Montana, 1966–76

Year	Total Deer (October)	October Herd Ratios		Number of Deer Harvested	Percentage of October Herd Harvested
		Fawns per 100 Does[a]	Bucks per 100 Does		
1966	258	55	79	58	22
1967	312	78	80	84	27
1968	291	53	100	66	23
1969	306	84	105	80	26
1970	319	62	82	90	28
1971	261	50	90	50	19
1972	186	22	72	10	5
1973	204	46	67	2	1
1974	223	44	60	0	0
1975	262	57	74	0	0
1976	305	56	57	16	5
Means (1966–71)	291	64	89	71	24
(1972–76)	236	45	66	5	2

Source: Compiled from unpublished U.S. Fish and Wildlife Service records on file at the National Bison Range.

[a] These values may seem low, but many of the does are yearlings.

For many years, mule deer on the National Bison Range were heavily cropped. In the early 1960s, about 30–35 percent of the herd was removed annually (Nellis 1968) and, from 1966 through 1971, an average of 24 percent of the October herd was shot each year (table 28). Harvest from 1966 through 1971 consisted of 36 percent bucks, 53 percent does, and 11 percent fawns.

A significant feature of this deer herd, from the standpoint of harvestable surplus, is that the surplus vanished in 1972. The prehunt count that year revealed that no harvest was needed, but 10 deer were taken to fulfill a prior commitment for research. From 1972 through 1976, only small numbers of deer were shot, yet the herd did not increase beyond the desired size of 200–250 animals. A parallel decline in productivity occurred among white-tailed deer and elk on the refuge, and these populations also recovered by 1976.

It also is significant that the reasons for abrupt loss of harvestable surplus in this mule deer herd are not known, even though the refuge is attended full time by experienced wildlife technicians and managers. Lack of harvestable surplus mule deer in 1972 was accompanied by a low fawn-doe ratio, and low ratios also were recorded in 1973 and 1974 (table 28). The low fawn survival was thought by the refuge staff to be due to coyote predation, but

herd recovery in 1975–76 occurred when coyote numbers were higher than at the low point of mule deer production (Reichel 1976). Thus, causes of the sudden lack of harvestable surplus in 1972–75 may never be determined with certainty.

This example from the National Bison Range has at least three implications for mule deer management in general.

1. Even in herds that have sustained heavy annual harvests for many years, the harvestable surplus may vanish or decrease suddenly from one year to the next. Hunting regulations often are set six months or more before hunting season, and most herds are not monitored in the interim. At the Bison Range, the lack of harvestable surplus was discovered in time to adjust the cull appropriately, but in herds that are not monitored before hunting season, it is possible that population crises might not be detected in time to prevent excessive harvests.

2. Low fawn-doe ratios before hunting season may indicate that harvestable surplus is low (see "Effects of Hunting on Fawn Production and Survival," below).

3. When causes of poor fawn survival on a small area like the National Bison Range cannot be established with certainty, even by experienced people who work with the deer year-round, one begins to understand why the biologists of state agencies found it difficult, in

the early 1970s, to explain deer population declines over larger areas. With hundreds or thousands of square kilometers of deer range per biologist, intensive monitoring is not feasible.

Hunting as Compensatory Mortality

Along with the substantial body of research and management experience that verifies the existence of a harvestable surplus in most mule deer herds, there also is a more general, theoretical justification for deer hunting. It is the principle of compensatory mortality, developed in the 1940s by Paul Errington. Perhaps the clearest expression of his ideas is found in a book published posthumously (Errington 1967, p. 229): "In a resilient population, severe loss rates may in effect substitute for each other without mounting up excessively high in total. Extraordinary losses through one agency may automatically protect from losses through many other agencies. The death of one individual may mean little more than improving the chances for living of another one. Furthermore, in some species, extraordinary losses may be compensated by accelerated reproduction, more young being produced in consequence of more being destroyed."

In applying the idea of compensatory mortality to deer management, biologists point out that both hunted and unhunted herds lose many deer each year. If a herd is near the carrying capacity of its range, losses each year must equal gains (births) unless carrying capacity is increasing. Surplus deer will be lost from other causes if they are not taken by hunters. The theory of compensatory mortality holds that large losses due to hunting will result in smaller losses from other causes. One specific example of this concept is the previously mentioned argument that winter losses can be reduced by harvesting surplus deer in autumn.

Errington and other supporters of the compensatory mortality principle believed that hunters or other predators simply take animals that otherwise would die of other causes. This idea is endorsed by many biologists, but it has been challenged by some. Huffaker (1970) pointed out that Errington defined surplus animals as those above the "threshold of vulnerability" yet determined the threshold only after he knew how many "surplus" animals had died. This is, of course, a completely circular argument. Keith (1974) criticized the extrapolation of Errington's ideas to ungulates, since the prey species (muskrat and bobwhite quail) Errington studied may be self-limiting, whereas deer are not. In particular, Keith doubted whether significant compensatory increases in ungulate reproduction could occur in response to predation, since reproductive changes among ungulates in general tend to be related to level of nutrition rather than to density per se.

In summary, most if not all deer herds can produce a harvestable surplus, but the extent to which hunting can be substituted for other causes of mortality is not well known. Experience with mule deer on the National Bison Range shows that high mortality due to other causes can occur even when mortality due to hunting is high—in other words, that hunting can be a noncompensatory mortality factor. Harvestable surplus may be large in some years and small in others, and it seems that hunting could be either a compensatory or a noncompensatory form of mortality depending on the circumstances. In my opinion, hunting is a noncompensatory mortality factor for any deer population that is below the carrying capacity of its range.

Effects of Hunting on Deer Numbers

Regardless of whether the harvestable surplus of deer is harvested fully, hunting may affect population size, turnover rates, herd composition ratios, and other vital statistics of deer herds. These effects are considered here.

The effects of hunting logically could be studied by comparing hunted populations with unhunted ones. But, because no two deer ranges are alike, one could not assume that observed differences between hunted and unhunted herds were due entirely to hunting.

Some biologists have approached this problem by using computer simulation models in which every variable is controlled. Use of such models avoids the problem of comparing different ranges, but only at the cost of some uncertainty about the validity of the models themselves. Both field studies and modeling exercises have contributed information on the effects of hunting, and both are considered here.

Hunting can affect the following attributes of deer populations: numbers of animals; fawn production and survival; rates of mortality due to causes other than hunting; population turnover and age composition; and relative proportions of bucks, does, and fawns. These population characteristics, of course, are interrelated and subject to influence by many factors in addition to hunting. Because the nonhunting influences can be highly variable in their effects, any given level of hunting may affect two deer herds quite differently. For this reason, few broad generalizations about the effects of hunting are possible. In management, judgments about the impact of hunting should be made separately for each management unit.

A few authors have suggested that hunting increases deer numbers. In the Jawbone (California) deer study, for example, Leopold et al. (1951) found that hunted segments of the population had higher densities than unhunted segments. However, it was not shown that these higher densities actually were due to hunting. Results of computer simulations (table 27) intimate that hunting of bucks only may stimulate a small increase in population size in contrast to no hunting at all, because it theoretically increases potential productivity and maximizes the rate at which the population may increase (Longhurst et al. 1952; Robinette 1956; Giles et al. 1969). Because hunting (in models) does not change carrying capacity of habitat, the actual number of does increases whenever buck numbers are reduced by selective hunting pressure. In table 27 this is expressed in the buck-doe ratios that decrease as intensity of buck removal increases. As the number of does in a population increases, the number of births each year rises as well. And,

as the number of births increases relative to size of the breeding population, the potential rate of increase also rises. These relationships are demonstrated most easily with computer models, but there is good reason to believe that they take place in some real deer herds as well.

In contrast to hunting of bucks only, taking even a small percentage of does appears to cause some reduction in population size (table 27). This idea is basic to the premise that deer of both sexes should be taken to keep a population at optimum density (Dasmann 1971). The relationship of optimum density and maximum density already has been discussed in connection with carrying capacity.

Many deer populations have remained stable over time despite substantial annual removals of both bucks and does. An example is the heavily harvested mule deer herd at the National Bison Range (table 28). From 1966 through 1972, about 24 percent of the animals in this herd were shot each year, and in earlier years the harvest was even greater (Nellis 1968).

Mule deer numbers at Oak Creek, Utah, also remained stable during many years of substantial annual hunter harvests (see table 33). From 1947 through 1956, the reported hunting kill averaged about 16 percent of the prehunt population. Adding estimated wounding loss and illegal kill, about 23 percent of the herd present at the beginning of hunting season was removed annually by hunters. Yet this herd was stable; it contained an estimated 2,276 deer in January 1947 and 2,274 deer in January 1957. Few mule deer herds have provided higher sustained yields, but Robinette et al. (1977) believed that actual productivity of the Oak Creek herd was substantially below potential owing to range deterioration as a result of overuse by deer.

There is some question whether desert mule deer can yield hunter harvests as large as those recorded for many herds of Rocky Mountain mule deer. On the Three Bar Wildlife Area in Arizona, mule deer declined approximately 36 percent from 1961 through 1967, and hunting was identified as the main cause. Total hunting mortality, including crippling loss, accounted for about 11 percent of the deer present before each annual hunting season. The average kill for the last three years was only 5.5 percent. Even though only 9.4 percent, on the average, of does in the herd before hunting season were killed, calculations showed that the population could not remain stable if more than 4–7 percent of the does were harvested. The crux of the problem was poor fawn survival; the number of fawns per 100 does in January ranged from 11 to 49 during the seven-year study (Smith et al. 1969).

From 1969 through 1972, only bucks were hunted at Three Bar, with about 4 percent of the prehunt herd harvested each year. Deer numbers remained stable during this period (LeCount 1974*a*), even though they had declined during the previous eight years when both bucks and does were hunted. From 1972 to 1976, the Three Bar Wildlife Area was closed to all deer hunting, and the deer herd increased significantly (Smith and LeCount 1976).

Effects of hunting on desert mule deer also have been studied on the Black Gap Wildlife Management Area in west Texas (Brownlee 1975). From 1958 through 1969, deer of both sexes were harvested; an average of 9.1 percent of the population was taken yearly. The harvest consisted of 54 percent bucks and 46 percent does. During these years, the deer herd increased from an estimated 2,000 animals in 1958 to 3,540 in 1966, then declined to about 1,400 deer by 1969. After 1969, hunting was either closed or limited to bucks only, and the population increased to about 2,700 by 1974.

Although Brownlee (1975) attributed decline at Black Gap to heavy hunting pressure, harvest intensity during the decline was virtually identical to that during the period of increase. Deer numbers increased about 250 percent from 1958 through 1966, then declined 60 percent by 1969. The average annual harvest was 9.3 percent during the years of increase and 9.7 percent during the decline. In view of this nearly constant harvest, other factors must have been involved in the decline. Observed fawn-doe ratios in this herd averaged 49:100 during the years of increase, 21:100

during the decline, and 40:100 during the period of recovery (1970–74). Such apparent variations in fawn survival could have had more influence on observed population trends than did hunting. Nevertheless, at Black Gap, as on the Three Bar, investigators concluded that at times deer numbers were lower than they would have been in the absence of hunting.

There are few documented examples of the reduction of Rocky Mountain mule deer populations by hunting. However, Gill et al. (1975) cited hunting as the main cause of a deer decline in Middle Park, Colorado. Substantial harvests also probably checked, if not decreased, size of the Cassia deer herd in Idaho (McConnell and Dalke 1960). On this range, herd reduction was the management goal.

I have been unable to find any recent published example of a Columbian black-tailed deer herd reduced by hunting. On the other hand, a number of blacktail herds have maintained their numbers despite substantial annual harvests of both bucks and does. One of the most heavily hunted blacktail herds in the 1950s was on Whidby Island in Puget Sound, Washington, where deer numbers remained high despite an annual kill of about 30 percent (Cowan 1956*a*).

A lighter harvest of blacktails was recorded at the Hopland Field Station in Mendocino County, California (Connolly and Longhurst 1975). The deer on this University of California research station were subject to both recreational hunting and scientific collection. An average of about 11 percent of maximum (1 June) population was removed annually for twenty-three years. This harvest amounted to 4.6 deer per square kilometer (12 deer per square mile) of range each year, compared with fewer than 0.8 deer per square kilometer (2 deer per square mile) for the remainder of Mendocino County, where only adult bucks (at least two points on one antler) were legal game. The higher rate of harvest at Hopland Field Station had no apparent adverse impact on deer density, and the potential harvest was thought to be 50–100 percent larger than that actually achieved.

Deer numbers and harvestable surpluses fluctuate from year to year. Therefore sustained-yield harvest goals for each management unit must be tailored to the status of the deer population and hunting demand. Photograph courtesy of the Nebraska Game and Parks Commission.

Another example of high, sustained harvest from a blacktail population was given by Sturgis (1977) for McDonald Forest near Corvallis, Oregon. From 1954 through 1974, an annual average of about 5.7 deer per square kilometer (15 deer per square mile) was taken by hunters. Female deer constituted 43 percent of the harvest. Estimates of deer density were not available, but there was no indication that harvests exceeded the productive capacity of the herd. Over the years, however, there was a significant decline in hunting success, from an average of one deer taken per five hunter-days in 1954–59 to thirteen hunter-days per deer harvested in 1970–74.

In summary, some deer herds can sustain higher rates of harvest than others. Hunting only bucks tends to increase or maximize deer population size, but doe harvests can reduce deer herds in proportion to the percentage of does killed each year. Hunting can reduce or even eliminate deer herds, but there is no evidence that hunting has been the sole cause of population decline over any large area within the past fifty years. Hunting probably has depressed populations in which nonhunting mortality was nearly equal to annual fawn production. Effects of hunting on deer numbers should be evaluated separately for each deer herd management unit.

Effects of Hunting on Fawn Production and Survival

College-trained biologists traditionally believe that hunting stimulates higher rates of fawn production and survival than would otherwise occur. In keeping with the idea of compensatory mortality, Errington (1967) theorized that some species of animals compensate for extraordinary losses by accelerated reproduction, with more young being produced in consequence of more being destroyed. Among mule and black-tailed deer, it is hard to accept the idea that heavy harvest could directly cause increased fawn production (Keith 1974). Instead, most biologists explain the relationship as an indirect effect due to improved nutrition. The removal of some deer reduces intraspecific competition for food, thereby raising the general level of nutrition among those deer that survive the hunting season. Improved nutrition results in higher ovulation and birthrates, healthier fawns, and thus higher rates of fawn survival (Dasmann 1971).

This concept of improved reproduction as a consequence of hunting is at present widely accepted by wildlife biologists and managers. In fact, the reader will be hard pressed to find any conflicting theory in the recent literature on deer management. In applying these ideas to management, it has become axiomatic that heavily hunted deer herds are vigorous and healthy, with high production and survival of fawns. Unhunted or underhunted herds, in contrast, are unproductive because the animals are up against the carrying capacity of their environment. There is no room for more deer, so fawn survival is limited and fawn-doe ratios are low. It follows that, in hunted herds, high fawn-doe ratios are more desirable than low ratios, and that herds with low fawn-doe ratios need heavier hunting pressure to reduce the deer to a more nearly optimum stocking rate where fawn production and survival will be higher.

An impressive body of research, in fact, has shown fawn survival to increase with hunting pressure. A study of California deer herds disclosed that the most heavily hunted herds had highest fawn survival (Longhurst et al. 1952). Hunted parts of the Jawbone deer herd in California had higher fawn-doe ratios than unhunted parts, and hunting was believed to stimulate higher fawn production (Leopold et al. 1951). Black-tailed deer in the coastal chaparral ranges of California also produced more fawns under substantial cropping (Taber and Dasmann 1958). In the same region, Connolly and Longhurst (1975) found higher rates of fawn production and survival on the Hopland Field Station than on adjacent ranges where only adult bucks were legal game. Hunter harvest on Hopland Field Station was six times that on the adjacent ranges.

The relationships between harvest rates and fawn production have also been studied in computer simulation models. The work of F. M. Anderson et al. (1974), for example, showed both production and survival of fawns to be higher with either-sex hunting than with no hunting or buck-only hunting (table 27). However, the modelers assumed that both birth and fawn survival would increase if deer density was decreased. With these assumptions programmed into the model, it is a foregone conclusion that any reduction in deer density would be followed by increased fawn production and survival. In the real world, unfortunately, the relationship of fawn survival to deer density is not so simple.

Most published examples of improved fawn production due to hunting have come from herds whose numbers were believed to be in excess of carrying capacity. On the Cassia unit

in southern Idaho, for example, fawn production increased after deer and livestock numbers were balanced with range capacity (McConnell et al. 1975). In deer herds that already are below the point of optimum carrying capacity, however, it seems doubtful that hunting could produce any improvement in fawn production. In fact, removal of productive middle-aged does might reduce the potential number of births. Parsons (1975) suggested that doe hunting on the Black Gap Wildlife Management Area in Texas could have reduced fawn production by reducing the average age of breeding does.

On other areas, too, fawn production has declined in herds subjected to either-sex hunting. Examples include the Three Bar Wildlife Area (Arizona) herd from 1961 through 1968 (Smith et al. 1969) and the deer population in northern New Mexico from 1964 through 1973 (Rickman 1975). In these examples one might argue that hunting was not heavy enough to produce compensatory increases in reproductive success, but it seems likely that predation, poor range conditions, or other factors unrelated to hunting actually were responsible for poor fawn crops. Wherever predation is the main cause of fawn mortality, shooting does could reduce fawn production still further. It is worth reiterating that, on the Three Bar Wildlife Area in Arizona, the combination of light either-sex hunting and mortality from other causes was sufficient to cause a deer population decline (Smith et al. 1969). In this situation, then, either-sex hunting obviously did not enhance fawn production.

A good example of the difficulties a biologist might face in trying to account for reproductive performance of a deer herd is given by mule deer on the National Bison Range in Montana. This herd has shown wide fluctuations in fawn production in the face of sustained, heavy hunting pressure (table 28).

In the early 1960s, mule deer on the National Bison Range were controlled by shooting more than half the adults each year. Even though most does were yearlings, the birthrate was about 150 fawns per 100 does. Low postnatal fawn mortality was indicated by a ratio of

143 fawns per 100 does in autumn. Few deer died of any cause but hunting (Nellis 1968).

This high productivity did not continue. In the late 1960s, annual harvests from this herd were lower than those reported by Nellis, and fawn-doe ratios also were lower (table 28). In October 1972 there were only 22 fawns per 100 does, and there was no harvestable surplus that year or in the three years following. It now appears that this once-classic example of high fawn production in response to heavy cropping contradicted itself in the early 1970s and demonstrated instead that, at times, fawn production can be low even when hunting mortality is high. The obvious lesson here is that predictions of increased fawn survival due to heavy hunting pressure can be wrong if some factor other than food supply or quality is limiting deer numbers.

In retrospect, it appears that the mule deer herd on the National Bison Range was most capable of sustaining high harvests when fawn-doe ratios were highest, whereas low fawn-doe ratios signaled the disappearance of harvestable surplus. If this herd had been managed solely on the basis of fawn-doe ratios, the proper strategy would have been to harvest heavily when ratios were high and lightly or not at all when ratios were low. Thus it seems that a low fawn-doe ratio is not an infallible indicator that hunting pressure should be increased. What is important here is the reason for the low ratio. If the problem is one of food shortage, increased harvest may help fawn production by raising the average plane of nutrition in herds thinned by hunting. But, if the chief constraint on fawn survival is predation or weather, a heavier harvest may only compound the problem.

Here one should recognize that fawn survival can appear to have increased when, in fact, it has not. The standard measure of fawn survival—fawn-doe ratio—varies not only with the number of fawns in a population, but with the number of does as well. Whenever hunters remove more does than fawns, the fawn-doe ratio will be higher after the hunt than before. It is important to consider this effect of doe removals whenever fawn-doe ratios are to be used as a basis for decisions about either-sex hunting regulations.

Relationships of Hunting and Other Mortality Factors

A common, though poorly substantiated, belief of wildlife managers is that hunting can be substituted for other causes of mortality. This undoubtedly is true in the sense that a deer killed by a hunter cannot die of any other cause, but it is not well documented that nonhunting mortality in unhunted herds exceeds that in hunted ones. This subject has received little investigation and rarely is addressed in scientific literature. The point frequently is raised in popular articles, usually in the context of justifying recreational hunting. From a practical standpoint, relationships of hunting and other mortality are hard to study under field conditions. Not only is it difficult to measure or estimate losses from natural causes, disease, or predation, but, even if all those losses were measured in a hunted population, one could never be sure what might have happened had there been no hunting.

Although there is little information on compensatory mortality from field studies, simulation models have been used to investigate this subject. F. M. Anderson et al. (1974) used a computer to study both hunting and nonhunting mortality under a variety of harvest strategies (table 27). Their model defined all nonhunting mortality as natural losses and suggested the following general conclusions about the relationships between hunting and natural losses.

1. In deer herds at maximum density—that is, herds whose numbers are as high as the habitat can support—hunting only bucks produces more natural losses than would occur with no hunting at all. When only bucks are hunted, the sex ratio of the breeding population shifts toward fewer bucks and more does. With more does, more fawns are born. But, if carrying capacity of the habitat does not increase, the number of deaths each year must rise to keep pace with the number of births.

2. Natural losses are much lower when does are shot than when no deer or only bucks are shot. Doe hunting reduced the number of breeding does and thus the number of births as well. And, because doe hunting reduced the population below carrying capacity, it stimulated a higher rate of fawn survival. In addition, the annual harvest of does reduced the number of does subjected to natural mortality. These factors collectively accounted for the simulated reduction in natural losses due to doe hunting.

3. Total mortality, in absolute numbers, increased with intensity (percentage taken annually) of buck harvest and decreased with intensity of doe harvest.

4. The overall mortality rate was high, in the range of 40–50 percent annually, regardless of whether there was no hunting, hunting of bucks only, or hunting of both bucks and does.

If these results apply to real populations, they have a number of management implications. For example, they indicate that, if the management goal is to minimize natural losses, hunting should be restricted to adult females. Any reasonable level of doe hunting will produce substantial reduction in natural mortality, in comparison with no hunting or buck-only hunting, but the trade-off between hunting and natural losses is only partial. Comparing the various harvest strategies in table 27, one can see that harvest increased and natural losses decreased with change from buck-only hunting to either-sex or doe hunting. But natural losses decreased more than harvest increased. This means that it is impossible to convert all natural losses to hunter harvest. In view of these findings, the argument that hunting can be substituted for natural losses is only partly correct, and holds only when does are hunted. Buck hunting, on the contrary, actually may increase natural losses over what would occur with no hunting at all.

The reader should bear in mind that these conclusions are predicated on certain assumptions that are built into the model. The most important assumptions for the F. M. Anderson et al. (1974) model were that natural loss rates decline and birthrates increase as deer numbers are reduced below carrying capacity, either by hunting or by any other cause. If these assumptions are incorrect, or if carrying capacity declines, the assumed compensatory changes in birthrates and death rates may not occur. And, if they do not occur, any hunting losses simply will be additive to losses from other causes (and subtractive from population size). For these reasons, the model of F. M. Anderson et al. (1974), and perhaps other models, should be regarded as numerical exposition of traditional deer management theories, rather than as proof of those theories.

Even though few field studies have yielded clear examples of the relationship of hunting to nonhunting mortality, there is enough information to induce caution about generalizations on this subject. The mule deer herd on the National Bison Range has given contrary indications at various times. As discussed previously, hunting appeared to have been almost the sole cause of mortality in this population in the early 1960s (Nellis 1968). But, under continued heavy harvests, fawn production and survival declined so that harvests were virtually suspended from 1972 through 1976 (table 28). During these years, hunting presumably would have been an additive rather than a compensatory form of loss. Therefore it must be concluded that hunting might be substituted for other mortality factors under some circumstances but not others, and that the relationship of hunting to other losses can be determined only by continued local study of mortality from all causes. Again, deer harvests and their effects should be monitored and evaluated separately for each herd management unit.

Effects of Hunting on Population Turnover and Average Age

According to classical game management theory, unhunted deer herds contain a preponderance of old animals. Since average longevity is high, population turnover and survival of fawns to adulthood are low. Heavily hunted herds, by contrast, consist of younger, healthier animals, with high recruitment of yearlings to replace animals taken by hunters. Both field studies and modeling exercises have shown these ideas to be generally correct.

According to the simulation experiments of F. M. Anderson et al. (1974), average age of deer in the population declines as the intensity of hunting increases (table 27). Hunting only bucks causes average age of bucks to drop but has no effect on average age of does. The converse is true if only does are hunted. In these studies, age composition of the hunting kill reflected that of the population, since each age class was subjected to the same harvest rate. Annual turnover rates of both bucks and does increased as their respective average ages decreased.

These findings seem to be consistent with field studies in which age composition and turnover rates have been measured. In the mule deer herd at Oak Creek, Utah, for example, about half the adult bucks (including yearlings) in the population before hunting season were killed by hunters each year. Average age of the bucks killed was 1.9 years, and annual turnover rate was 52 percent. Does, in contrast, sustained a lighter rate of harvest; fewer than 20 percent were shot each year. Mean age of does taken was 3.8 years, and annual turnover was 27 percent. In this population, hunting kill (including cripples and illegal kills) accounted for about 93 percent of the total buck mortality; the comparable figure for does was 77 percent (see table 33).

On the Black Gap Wildlife Management Area in Texas, increased hunting pressure reduced average age of the hunting kill among both bucks and does. In 1957, when hunting pressure was low, 44 percent of the buck kill were under 4 years of age. After several years of more intensive hunting, 76 percent of the bucks taken in 1969 were under 4 years old. Does were first hunted on this area in 1958. In that year, 57 percent of the does taken were under 4 years of age, compared with 74 percent in 1969. This study also showed average age of bucks to increase during two years of no hunting (Brownlee 1975). In another study in Montana, the turnover rate among does decreased more than 50 percent when the area was closed to doe hunting (Mackie 1976b).

The observation that average age of animals killed by hunters decreases as harvest intensity increases has led several workers to suggest that age composition of kill might be used as an index of harvest intensity. However, I have been unable to locate any specific deer herd for which this has been successfully done. One suspects that normal variations and sampling problems would mask all but very large changes in age composition of the kill. Also, it might be difficult to show that observed changes were due to hunting rather than to some other cause.

The fact that average age of animals killed is related inversely to size of the harvest has one important implication for mule deer hunters: trophy quality declines as buck harvest numbers increase. This observation will come as no surprise to experienced hunters; nevertheless, it is appropriate here to provide documentation.

Decline in trophy quality with increasing harvest was shown in both computer modeling (Gross 1973; F. M. Anderson et al. 1974) and field studies (Brownlee 1975). Brownlee showed that both antler spread and buck weights declined on the Black Gap Wildlife Management Area in Texas as hunting pressure increased. From 1958 to 1969, mean antler spread dropped from 43 to 36 centimeters (17.0 to 14.3 inches), while mean buck weights declined from 50 to 39 kilograms (111 to 86 pounds).

From these findings it is obvious that maximum trophy quality as a management goal is incompatible with maximum numerical harvest of adult deer, or even with maximum buck harvest. To achieve maximum trophy quality, harvests (and presumably hunting opportunity) must be restricted to a small fraction of their potential under maximum-yield or optimum-yield objectives.

Effects of Hunting on Herd Composition

If hunting can affect longevity and fawn survival rates in deer herds, as discussed previously, it follows that hunting also can influence relative proportions of bucks, does, and fawns. Changes in herd composition ratios due to hunting, in fact, are the basis of the "Kelker index" method of estimating numbers (see "Methods for Estimating Deer Numbers" in chap. 8). Such change-in-ratio methods exploit the obvious fact that selective harvests from one sex class will reduce the number of animals in that class. When both bucks and does are harvested, bucks usually are cropped more heavily than does, so that the buck-doe ratio is lower after hunting season than before.

In most mule deer and blacktail herds, hunting is more or less selective for bucks. Therefore it is commonly accepted that buck-doe ratios are lower in hunted herds than in unhunted ones. Computer simulation experiments suggest that buck-doe ratios decline as buck harvests increase (table 27), and there is corroborating evidence from the field as well. For example, Robinette (1956) reported buck-doe ratios as wide as 1:14 from herds in Oregon and Washington where heavy hunting pressure was directed against bucks only. However, buck-doe ratios are not universally low wherever only bucks are hunted; the observed ratios vary with other factors in addition to hunting.

If buck hunting tends to depress buck-doe ratios, one may ask what ratio would be expected in the absence of hunting. Because nutritional constraints may cause sex differential mortality, the sex ratio still probably would not be equal. The simulation model of F. M. Anderson et al. (1974), for example, estimated that the buck-doe ratio in Mendocino County, California, would be about 61:100 in the absence of hunting (table 27). This was dictated largely by observation (and incorporation in the model) of sex differential losses among fawns during their first year of life, before they became subject to hunting. Other studies have shown proportionately higher mortality of bucks during their second year of life (Hines 1975) or as adults (Klein 1965). Klein suggested that adult bucks are more susceptible than does to winter mortality because they enter winter in poor physical condition after the rut.

Even though buck-doe ratios seldom are as high among adult deer as among fawns at birth, even in unhunted herds, one exception has been reported for white-tailed deer. On the Aransas National Wildlife Refuge in Texas, White (1973) found that both the fetal and adult sex ratios approximated 1:1. Such a high adult sex ratio has not been reported, to my knowledge, for any sizable blacktail or mule deer population. In an unhunted blacktail herd in western Oregon, Hines (1975) found an average of 45 bucks per 100 does. Other unhunted herds showed buck-doe ratios of 83:100 on the Three Bar Wildlife Area in Arizona (Swank 1958) and 74:100 in Sequoia National Park, California (Longhurst et al. 1952). If these values are representative, unhunted mule deer herds may tend to exhibit higher buck-doe ratios than do hunted ones, even though the ratios can be highly variable among both hunted and unhunted herds.

Aside from obvious and expected changes in herd composition ratios due to selective removals of particular age and sex classes, such as adult bucks, one other influence of hunting on herd composition remains to be considered: the possible increase in fawn production or survival due to removal of adults from the populations, as discussed previously. Here it is only necessary to reiterate that, if the adult cohorts do not change, increased fawn production or survival must result in increased fawn-doe and fawn-adult ratios. However, fawn-doe ratios also can rise when fawn production does not, if does are harvested more intensively than fawns. These facts must be incorporated into the interpretation of fawn-doe ratios from herds subject to either-sex hunting.

Summary of the Effects of Hunting

Hunting can affect nearly every measurable trait of deer populations. This is not to say that hunting invariably produces certain effects, or that hunting is the only influence that can produce such effects. The following principles are offered with the caveat that they are only generally correct. Documented exceptions to most of these rules have been presented elsewhere in this book.

Most deer herds can produce an annual harvestable crop of deer. The size of harvestable surplus varies from one herd to another. Within any one herd, surplus or potential harvest may be high in some years and low in others.

Size of harvestable surplus varies with the age and sex classes harvested. Maximum numerical yield would result from heavy cropping of fawns and adult bucks combined with light culling of does. Maximum production of adult bucks, on the other hand, would require substantial harvests of does as well as bucks, with no hunting of male fawns. Maximum yield of trophy bucks is not compatible with maximum buck production.

Unrestricted hunting can limit deer numbers, but controlled recreational hunting is unlikely to do so because hunting regulations in the mule deer states tend to be conservative. Some deer population declines have been attributed partly to hunting, in the sense that hunting combined with losses from other causes exceeded recruitment.

Hunting only bucks tends to produce increasing deer herds on ranges that are not fully stocked and to maximize impact of excessive deer numbers on ranges stocked to capacity. Doe hunting, on the other hand, tends to reduce deer densities.

Biologists traditionally believe that hunting stimulates higher rates of fawn production and survival than would otherwise occur; most published evidence supports this view. Improved fawn production results from reduced competition for forage and hence improved nutrition among deer herds thinned by hunting. There are herds, however, in which fawn production has declined in the face of heavy hunting. Increased fawn-doe ratios do not necessarily mean that fawn production or survival has increased; the ratio can rise whenever more does than fawns are harvested. Because fawn production does not invariably increase with intensity of hunting, observed fawn-doe ratios by themselves are not very useful for indicating whether hunting pressure should be increased or decreased. Proper interpretation of such ratios requires additional information or judgment about the size of a population relative to the carrying capacity of its range.

Relationships and possible trade-offs among hunting and other mortality factors have not been well documented under field conditions. Computer simulations have been constructed to show that populations at maximum carrying capacity of their habitat have high mortality rates regardless of whether they are hunted or not. In these circumstances, hunting only bucks tends to produce more natural losses than would occur with no hunting at all. Doe hunting reduces natural losses, but not all natural mortality can be converted to hunter harvest. Total mortality, from all causes, tends to increase with intensity of buck harvest and decrease with intensity of doe harvest. The limited field data on this subject imply that hunting does not always reduce nonhunting mortality.

In hunted herds, average age of deer declines as harvest increases. If only bucks are hunted, average age of bucks will be affected, but that of does will not. As average age of bucks decreases, trophy quality declines as well. Annual rates of population turnover increase as average age decreases.

Herd composition ratios are affected by any hunting that is selective for particular age and sex classes. Hunting bucks only, for example, tends to reduce the buck-doe ratio. Hunting may raise fawn-doe ratios either by selectively removing does at a greater rate than fawns or by stimulating increased production and survival of fawns. Unhunted mule deer herds tend to have higher buck-doe ratios than do hunted herds, because most hunting is selective for bucks.

MANAGING THE HARVEST

Other sections of this book have identified many kinds of biological information that are relevant to management of mule deer. Here an attempt is made to show how such information relates to the decision-making process that governs annual harvests. In limiting this synthesis to management of harvest, I do not mean to imply that other aspects of management are unimportant. But, as long as law enforcement, habitat maintenance and improvement, and other enhancement measures are financed largely from hunting license revenues, harvest will be a cornerstone of the management program.

Before discussing the management process itself, a few words are in order about the role of wildlife professionals (biologists, managers, and law enforcement officers) in the "biopolitical" system, which commonly includes more political than biological entities (Connolly 1974). Wildlife management decisions were being made long before trained, professional wildlifers became available in the 1930s and 1940s. Decisions could still be made without the involvement of professional expertise, but in the past four to five decades, state and provincial management agencies have moved toward biological facts and expert opinion as the firm base for wildlife management decisions.

Public pressure continues to be exerted at several political levels as well as on state and federal wildlife management agencies, so that current management programs are influenced by both public opinion and biological information. In all mule deer states, important decisions are made by elected or appointed officials, while biologists and managers serve research, technical, and advisory roles. For better or worse, this arrangement ensures that the influence of biological concepts and information in management is no greater than what the public will support. Public support, in turn, reflects the effectiveness of information and public relations efforts by professional wildlife workers.

The Annual Cycle of Harvest Management

Management of deer harvest involves an annual cycle of monitoring and decision-making processes, culminating each year in prescribed hunting seasons. Actual procedures differ from one state or province to the next but usually will resemble the model shown in figure 20.

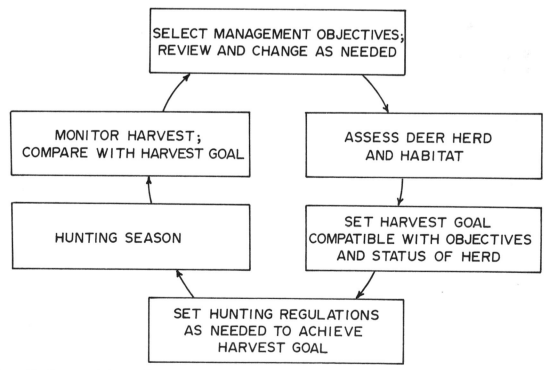

Figure 20. Deer population and harvest management—an annual process.

The key ingredients in harvest management are management objectives; harvest goals; information about deer herds, their habitat, and the annual harvest; hunting regulations; and the hunting season. Management objectives, harvest goals, and monitoring are best accomplished separately for each management unit, but hunting regulations usually apply to larger areas.

Management Objectives

In our diverse society, there are frequent differences of opinion about how deer should be managed. For each deer management unit, therefore, management objectives must be formulated and established through the biopolitical process. The role of the wildlife professional in this process is to identify the options that are biologically feasible and recommend those harvest regulations that are most compatible with the management objectives as he or she understands them. The objectives should be stated as specifically as possible, so that both professionals and laymen can assess the effectiveness of past management as a guide to improved management in the future. If objectives are vague or lacking, there is unlikely to be any consensus or majority view on what kind of harvest is preferred. The result is lack of management or, in some cases, mismanagement. Mismanagement occurs when public opinion or political considerations prevent management in the best, long-range interest of the resource; an example would be failure to harvest enough deer to prevent overuse and consequent destruction of winter ranges (see Leopold et al. 1947; Petrides 1961).

The first step toward actual management, then, is determining objectives for each recognizable management unit. The objectives must be specific enough to enable all interested parties to judge whether they are being met by current management, and whether new management proposals are consistent with them.

On most ranges where mule deer are hunted, the overall goal should be to maintain or improve productivity of the deer and their habitat. In adhering to this principle, management might seek to increase or reduce deer numbers, produce as many bucks as possible, or maintain deer numbers between specified maximum and minimum levels, to name but a few possible objectives. In national parks or other areas closed to hunting, the assumed deer management objective is to allow "natural" regulation of numbers. However, this discussion is oriented toward hunted populations.

Assessment of Population and Habitat

Regardless of management objectives and other political considerations, decisions about harvest must be realistic in relation to deer numbers and habitat conditions in each herd management unit. As is shown elsewhere in this book, monitoring of deer herds and ranges is a formidable task. Nevertheless, information is needed on both deer and their habitat if management is to be effective. Some important considerations are changes in population size, fawn production and survival, population density relative to carrying capacity, levels of deer damage to crops, forest regeneration, or other conflicting land uses that must receive priority over deer production, observed or expected changes in range carrying capacity, and numbers of deer harvested in previous years.

Even after decades of research on methods of assessing deer herds and ranges, foolproof procedures for collecting information needed in management still are not available and may never be. Yet management decisions must be made; professional judgment will always be needed no matter how much field information is available. Deer management, like most important human enterprises, requires that decisions be made under conditions of uncertainty. In wildlife management or elsewhere, it is a rare decision-maker who has statistically reliable data on each of the elements he must consider in reaching decisions.

Wildlife managers and biologists certainly should strive for better methods of evaluating deer population and habitat and for better information; but at any given time and place, they must do the best they can with what is

The "show-me" trip gives wildlife managers, biologists, sportsmen, ranchers, and others a chance to exchange opinions and information on the management of deer and their ranges. This group in northern California is inspecting habitat that was converted from chaparral brush to a mixture of grasses and legumes. Photograph by Guy E. Connolly.

available. Other citizens (including decision-makers), in turn, should realize that biologists and managers cannot produce perfect data—certainly not with limited funds and manpower and under complex field conditions.

Harvest Goals

Once information is available on the deer herds and their habitats, it must be reviewed in light of management objectives to determine what sort of harvest should be taken. If deer numbers seem excessive, as was typically true in the 1950s (Petrides 1961), a significant removal of does is indicated. But, if deer numbers appear to be below range capacity and fawn survival is poor, a harvest of bucks only may be in order.

By considering the deer herd and its habitat in relation to objectives for the management unit, managers can decide how many animals of each age and sex should be removed by hunters. The resulting harvest goal or quota is the level of harvest that, if achieved, will most nearly fulfill management objectives. The harvest goal must allow for crippling losses and illegal kills.

In Colorado, computer simulation models are used to help set harvest goals. Models help organize all available information on the status of herds, and objectives act as constraints in the model (Pojar 1977). Experiments with the computer help determine how many animals should be harvested from each age and sex class, and hunting regulations then are set to achieve that harvest. The simulations are repeated annually for each of thirty-three deer, thirty-three elk, and thirteen pronghorn management units. But, regardless of whether a computer model is used, harvest goals must be set before hunting regulations can be prescribed.

Hunting Success

It is customary to define hunter success as the ratio of number of animals killed to number of hunters afield, or number of licenses sold. Success in terms of hunter satisfaction, of course, depends on many other factors. In planning hunting regulations, it is essential to be able to predict the relationship between harvest and number of licenses sold.

Hunter success can be highly variable from one area to another, or even from year to year in the same area, and some variations are unpredictable. In general, though, hunting success is inversely proportional to hunting pressure and size of the harvest (in terms of the fraction of legal animals harvested each year). Hunting regulations often are intended to keep hunting success low, so as to provide hunting opportunities for as many people as possible. In such instances, the goals of management conflict with the goals of individuals; each hunter wants to bag a deer even when hunters are more abundant than deer.

With increasing numbers of hunters or decreasing numbers of deer, it has become more and more necessary to restrict the number of hunters, hunter success, or both. In Arizona, the number of hunters in various management units is restricted by issuing limited numbers of permits. Most areas of California, in contrast, are open to unlimited numbers of hunters, who legally may take only bucks with at least two points on one antler. The latter approach offers more people an opportunity to hunt but virtually guarantees that hunter success will be low.

One of the more obvious truths about harvest management is that deer numbers are limited. Therefore, high rates of success cannot be expected for unlimited numbers of hunters. In fact, Einarsen (1956) stated that not more than 5–15 percent of hunters can expect to bag game if sustained yields are the goal. However, most mule deer states have done better than this (table 29). Only in California has success been as low as that suggested by Einarsen. From 1971 through 1975, an annual average of 537,560 mule deer was taken by 1,746,703 hunters in the eleven contiguous western states, for an overall success rate of 31 percent. Average success for the eleven states dropped from 40 percent in 1971 to 29 percent in 1975.

Table 29. Mule Deer Harvests and Hunting Success in Eleven Western States, 1971–75

State[a]	Average Mule Deer Harvest, 1971–75[b]	Average Number of Hunters, 1971–75	Percentage of Hunter Success		
			1971–75[c]	1971	1975
Oregon	79,210	264,972	30	32	21
Utah	78,759	189,154	42	53	26
Montana	78,732	110,336[d]	71[d]	80[d]	52[d]
Wyoming	60,283	100,029[d]	60[d]	70[d]	64[d]
Colorado	56,156	142,291	39	40	29
Idaho	47,737	144,297	33	35	30
Washington	45,202	214,470[d]	21[d]	23[d]	24[d]
California	32,503	362,883	9	11	9
New Mexico[e]	28,749	106,291	27	32	21
Nevada	18,542	44,470	42	49	21
Arizona	11,777	67,510[d]	17[d]	14[d]	23[d]
Total	537,560	1,746,703			
Average			36	40	29

Source: Compiled by R. T. John, Utah Division of Wildlife Resources.

[a] Ranked from highest to lowest average harvest.

[b] These figures include 44,702 black-tailed deer in Oregon, 29,216 black-tailed deer in Washington, and an unknown number of blacktails in California.

[c] Expressed as average percentage for the period 1971–75.

[d] Some hunters could take either mule deer or whitetails. The hunter success rate would be higher if white-tailed deer were included in harvest totals.

[e] Figures include both white-tailed and mule deer.

Hunting regulations became more restrictive in most states during this period owing to an apparent general decline in deer numbers (see chap. 6).

Because hunting success is influenced by so many factors other than hunting regulations, it often is difficult to predict what harvest will result from a given set of regulations. Both hunter distribution and deer distribution affect hunting success, and on many mule deer ranges both may be influenced by unpredictable weather during the hunting season. Heavy snowfall can move deer from summer range to winter range (from high to low elevations), where they may be more accessible to hunters. But the same storms may cause hunters to vacate hunting grounds. Depending on their severity and timing in relation to the hunting season, storms can cause harvests to be either much smaller or much larger than expected (Mohler 1964). In Middle Park, Colorado, Freddy (1975) measured weather, deer distribution, and hunter distribution, participation, and success for several years. He concluded that these factors were so variable that predetermined harvest objectives could not be achieved within desired limits. On the Kaibab Plateau in Arizona, Russo (1964) also reported difficulty in achieving the desired harvest. Not only did adverse weather reduce hunter participation, but some hunting permits could not be sold.

Such practical problems obviously can make it impossible to control a harvest precisely, but this does not invalidate the concept of harvest goals. It only shows that more flexible means of controlling harvest are needed. With contemporary methods of communication, for example, it is feasible to close a season on short notice if the desired harvest is being approached or exceeded. Another option would be a series of short seasons separated by closed periods, with the later openings abolished if necessary. And, if bag limits of one or two deer per hunter are too low, they can be increased to four or five or more deer per hunter, as proposed in Montana by Egan (1971). Larger bag limits have been used to increase hunting pressure in given situations. In any event, good

management requires the best possible control over a harvest.

Hunting on Ranges Shared by Mule and White-tailed Deer

Where mule and white-tailed deer occur within the same management unit, it generally is agreed that mule deer are more vulnerable to harvest. Thus it may be difficult to secure adequate harvests of whitetails without overharvesting mule deer. Burgess (1973) reported that, in parts of Alberta, ratios of whitetails to mule deer were increasing. He theorized that whitetails gradually were taking over former mule deer habitat because of whitetails' ability to recover from severe winter losses, fill available whitetail habitat, and expand into mule deer habitat before the mule deer could recover.

When white-tailed deer seem to be increasing at the expense of mule deer, it may be desirable to increase hunting pressure selectively for whitetails. In one part of British Columbia, for example, the hunting season on white-tailed deer was extended two weeks beyond the season on mule deer, to curtail a buildup of whitetails (Spalding 1968). In the Southwest, different seasons or bag limits sometimes are set for desert mule deer and Coues white-tailed deer.

Doe Hunting

No aspect of harvest management is as controversial as shooting does. Because wildlife biologists in the 1950s and 1960s perceived the predominant deer management problem to be too many deer for available range, the research literature from that period emphasized the need for population reduction, which could be achieved only by shooting does. The reader is directed to Leopold et al. (1951), Longhurst et al. (1952), Taber and Dasmann (1958), Swank (1958), Taber (1961), Dasmann (1971), and Robinette et al. (1977) for some of the classic arguments on this subject.

In my opinion, doe hunting is essential whenever deer are found to be destroying or about to destroy their habitat. Does also should be shot wherever goals are to reduce deer numbers, maximize hunting kill, or minimize natural mortality. But, on ranges where deer numbers are stable and not excessive in relation to available habitat, managers may choose either to have does taken by hunters or to allow them to die of natural causes.

Even though most recent literature on harvest management portrays doe hunting as right and proper, or even as a responsibility of hunters, there are circumstances in which does should not be shot. In particular, does should be protected wherever an increase in deer numbers is desired, if available habitat will support more deer. A conservative approach to doe harvests also is warranted whenever mortality from nonhunting causes approaches annual recruitment—again, providing that deer numbers do not exceed carrying capacity of habitat.

Some people object to doe hunting on sentimental or philosophical grounds even though they recognize the propriety of antlerless hunts in certain circumstances. Still others flatly oppose doe hunting under any conditions. Because these persons often are active in politics, doe hunts may not be politically feasible in some areas regardless of sound biological bases for them.

Monitoring the Harvest

Measurements of harvest, including crippling losses and illegal kills, provide data needed to determine how closely a harvest goal has been met. Techniques for measuring harvest are discussed in chapter 8. If actual harvest turns out to be much larger or smaller than expected, some judgment usually can be made about the reasons, and corrective measures then can be planned for the next year.

In conclusion, a system that includes objectives, harvest goals, hunting regulations, and monitoring of deer herds and ranges in each management unit offers a systematic and

politically acceptable way to improve deer management. Lacking any of these ingredients, biopolitical systems cannot expect to manage deer harvests properly.

NONHUMAN PREDATORS

Because man preys on mule deer for recreation or for food, he traditionally has resented and killed other predators that compete with him. Early in this century, deer numbers were low, and predator control was an accepted game-restoration tool. As deer herds increased through the 1930s and 1940s, often to the point of overpopulation (Leopold et al. 1947), more and more wildlife biologists and managers came to believe that predator control was no longer necessary once the deer herds had been restored. Through the 1950s and 1960s, most wildlife biologists opposed predator control as counterproductive in deer management, but the United States Bureau of Sport Fisheries and Wildlife, Branch of Predator and Rodent Control (now Animal Damage Control Program, United States Fish and Wildlife Service), continued to control predators on many deer ranges for the protection of livestock that also used those ranges.

During the 1960s, preservationist groups became increasingly critical of the governmental predator control program and, through political channels, sought restrictions and reductions in predator control activities. In 1972, use of poisons for predator control on federal land or by federal agents was banned altogether. The ban later was relaxed to permit limited use of one toxicant, but wholesale reduction of coyote populations with poison bait stations is no longer legally possible. Before the ban, more coyotes were killed with toxicants than with any other single technique used by predator control workers. For more details on predator control programs and methods, see Cain et al. (1972), Connolly (1978), and United States Fish and Wildlife Service (1978).

On the deer ranges, meanwhile, a general decline of mule deer populations in the early 1970s (see chap. 6) stimulated new research to identify factors that were limiting deer numbers. By 1977, state wildlife agencies in Arizona, Colorado, Idaho, Montana, New Mexico, Oregon, Utah, Wyoming, and possibly other states had studied or were studying effects of predation on mule deer by coyotes or mountain lions.

In North America, predator control is a highly controversial political issue. Although this review deals only with factual aspects of predation and predator control in mule deer management, one must recognize that some of the most important questions are political. For example, should hunters receive preference over other predators in being allowed to use the harvestable surplus from deer populations? Is the control (killing) of coyotes, mountain lions, or wolves an acceptable means of increasing the number of deer available to hunters? Who should pay the costs of predator control to increase deer populations?

Wildlife biologists can best contribute to the resolution of such issues by developing factual information. Central to this theme are two

questions: Under what conditions do predators limit deer numbers? And can predator control increase the number of deer available for harvest by hunters? These and related questions are addressed here.

Identification of Predator Kills

In studies of deer mortality, it is important to identify the cause of death when deer carcasses are found. Investigators should skin the remains of possible predation victims, since puncture wounds inflicted by predators often are not detected in superficial examinations. Mule deer killed by coyotes frequently have fang (canine tooth) punctures and tissue damage in the neck, particularly at the junction of head and neck and in the nasopharyngeal region. Head wounds also are common, particularly on small fawns. Nielsen (1975) and Bowns (1976), who presented color photographs of typical wounds, believed that coyotes usually killed deer by collapsing the trachea so

The head of a healthy, male blacktail fawn killed by a coyote that was flushed from the carcass only minutes after the kill occurred. Note the puncture wound in the neck made by the coyote's canine tooth. Photograph by Guy E. Connolly.

that the animals suffocated. A similar technique is used by coyotes to kill domestic sheep (Connolly et al. 1976; Timm and Connolly 1977).

Mountain lions also kill deer with bites to the neck. However, they most frequently bite from above; seven of eight lion kills examined by Robinette et al. (1959) each had a single set of tooth marks on the nape of the neck. Lion kills examined by McBride (1976) showed similar wounds. For detailed descriptions of several lion-killed deer, see Robinette et al. (1959).

It is common knowledge that lions frequently cover their deer kills with grass, leaves, soil, or other debris. I have seen blacktail fawns killed by bobcats similarly covered. Steel traps set at a fresh, covered carcass frequently catch the cat when it returns to feed.

Frequently a biologist must decide whether a dead deer was killed by a predator or merely was scavenged after it died of other causes. If the carcass is fresh and reasonably intact, predation may be indicated by subcutaneous bleeding around tooth or claw marks; animals that have been dead for several hours or longer do not bleed extensively when scavengers feed on them. Deer killed by coyotes may be dismembered, scattered, or even obliterated, whereas deer that die of starvation or disease are more likely to be intact and may have the limbs folded beneath the body, indicating that they died in a resting or recumbent posture.

A greater obstacle in studies of predation is that predator victims often are devoured before they can be found. This is especially true of small fawns, but even adult deer may disappear completely within twenty-four hours (Knowles 1976b). Robinson (1952) pointed out that big game animals dying of malnutrition, disease, or old age are more likely to be

Starved or disease-killed deer frequently succumb in a resting or recumbent position, with limbs folded back or beneath the body. Photograph by Jim Weiss; courtesy of the Utah Division of Wildlife Resources.

Wildlife biologists usually try to determine the cause of death whenever a deer carcass is found. This fawn was still warm when it was discovered on winter range in southern Idaho. It appeared to have been killed by golden eagles. Photograph by Stu Murrell; courtesy of the Idaho Department of Fish and Game.

found by an observer because they may lie for hours or days before being located by scavengers, whereas predator kills may vanish with amazing speed. Since predator kills are less likely to be tabulated than deaths from other causes, Robinson suggested that predation should be suspected if animals seemingly disappear and leave no trace.

Do Predators Select Weak, Sick or Crippled Deer?

Of all the myths surrounding predators and predation, none is more persistent than the notion that predators deliberately cull weak, crippled, or inferior individuals from prey populations. The idea that coyotes prey only on sick or weak mule deer can be traced to Murie's (1940) study on overpopulated deer ranges in Yellowstone Park. Murie found that coyotes there took weak fawns in winter, but that healthy adult deer were not killed. He stated that a mule deer can readily cope with the coyote under normal circumstances, falling victim only when its abilities of defense are diminished by crippling injuries, old age, malnutrition, disease, or perhaps extreme snow conditions. Leopold et al. (1947) also suggested that the coyote was an ineffective deer predator, but other investigators disagree. Horn (1941) described a study that found coyotes to prey heavily on newborn fawns (see case 2 below) and pointed out that coyotes could kill either weak or strong newborn fawns with ease. Such predation, he believed, was not selective for weak or inferior fawns. Several more recent studies have found coyotes to kill healthy adult mule deer quite effectively (Nielsen 1975; Trainer 1975; Knowles 1976b).

Regarding the mountain lion, too, there are conflicting reports about relative fitness of animals taken as prey. Hibben (1936) suggested that most deer killed by lions in New Mexico were diseased or abnormal. By "abnormal" he meant that certain skeletal measurements departed from usual or expected values. It was not shown that these abnormalities would have caused weakness or physical disability, but Hibben concluded that lions caught whatever deer they could and that the least able-bodied prey were most likely to be caught.

Of the various published accounts of mountain lion studies, Hornocker (1970) presented the most data on selection of ungulate prey by lions. For both elk and mule deer, he found that the relative frequency of various age and sex classes killed by lions differed from that in the total population; significantly more young (calves and fawns) and mature males, but fewer females, were taken than would have been expected in purely random selection. Hornocker (1970, p. 33) ruled out malnutrition as a factor of vulnerability of calves and fawns, stating that "physical condition was not a significant factor in determining the makeup of the total kill of either elk or deer. Poor animals were not selected but were taken proportionally to their occurrence in the population." However, he did believe that the most vulnerable animals were killed, and that vulnerability was determined by various physical, biological, and ecological factors.

It is noteworthy that professional hunters and trappers almost unanimously reject the contention that predators take sick or inferior individuals selectively. Many, in fact, espouse the contrary view that predators select the healthiest prey. For example, a professional lion hunter in Texas described several field experiences that collectively portray the mountain lion as an exceedingly skilled and selective deer hunter, killing healthy deer at will and avoiding cripples (McBride 1976). Some people might dispute McBride's conclusions, but few have comparable firsthand experience.

In conclusion, no brief review can resolve the long-standing differences of opinion regarding the relative fitness of deer killed by predators.

The preponderance of evidence shows that deer taken by predators are not selected at random, but one cannot argue that prey individuals are necessarily inferior. If fawns are acknowledged as being more vulnerable to predation than adult deer, this does not necessarily mean that the fawns are unfit. The real question, of course, is whether the deer killed by predators would otherwise have died before they could reproduce or be taken by a hunter. Only when the death of a deer is imminent, from some other cause if not by predation, can predation on that deer be dismissed as insignificant in deer management.

Indirect Effects of Predation

Even though this review deals mainly with direct effects of predation, it is worth pointing out that predators also can affect mule deer adversely by perpetuating certain forms of para-

The mountain lion is a highly skilled predator of mule deer, and throughout most of its range the lion feeds primarily on mule deer. However, there is much conjecture about the age and sex class of mule deer that lions select, or whether they select at all. Photograph courtesy of the Wyoming Department of Game and Fish.

sites. In particular, some tapeworms must infest both deer and carnivores to complete their life cycles and thus could not persist in the absence of predators. Most of these parasites probably have little or no debilitating effect, but at least one coccidian form has been shown to be directly fatal to mule deer. When *Sarcocystis hemionilatrans* from Steens Mountain, Oregon, was experimentally transmitted from coyotes to 11 healthy fawns, 9 of the fawns died within 63 days of inoculation (Hudkins and Kistner 1977). This parasite occurs on many mule deer ranges, with the coyote as the definitive (adult) host and deer as intermediate host, but its role in mule deer population dynamics is unknown.

PREDATION ON MULE AND BLACK-TAILED DEER: CASE HISTORIES

Following are nineteen brief accounts of predation studies that involved mule or black-tailed deer. These include all the genuine field studies I could find in the literature. Other publications that gave casual speculations about predation, with no original data, were excluded from this review.

One of the most widely publicized accounts of the supposed effects of predation, or the lack thereof, is that of mule deer on the Kaibab Plateau in Arizona during the first three to four decades of this century. The Kaibab story has been told and retold countless times (see Connolly 1978), but, because actual data are remarkably poor, this incident is not recounted here.

Case 1: Coyotes and Mule Deer in Yellowstone National Park (Murie 1940).

In Yellowstone Park, it was believed for many years that control of coyotes and other predators was necessary to preserve pronghorn, bighorn sheep, mule deer, and other ungulates. Park records show that 121 mountain lions, 132 wolves, and 4,352 coyotes were killed for this purpose from 1904 to 1935. In 1935 predator control was stopped in accordance with National Park Service policy that no native predator should be destroyed because of

A coyote and magpies feed on the carcass of an adult mule deer doe in Yellowstone National Park. Photograph courtesy of the United States National Park Service.

its normal utilization of any other park animal, unless the prey species was in danger of immediate extinction. By 1937, however, sentiment for coyote control became so strong that a thorough scientific study of the coyote was authorized. The resulting study was conducted from May 1937 to March 1939.

Murie (1940) analyzed more than 5,000 coyote scats from the park and found that rodents—especially field mice and pocket gophers—constituted the bulk of the coyote diet during spring, summer, and autumn. Therefore he concluded that coyotes were not harmful to other park fauna in these seasons. In winter, big game herds furnished most of the coyotes' food. This was said to consist mostly of carrion and, in the case of deer, of weakened animals fated to succumb before spring. Mule deer, like other ungulate species, appeared to be limited not by predation, but by extent and quality of winter range.

Relationships of coyotes and mule deer in Yellowstone were studied most intensively during the winter of 1937–38. Deer that were killed seemed to be in poor condition; Murie himself ran down and captured a fawn. Coyote predation reportedly was heaviest where range conditions were poorest, and fawn-doe ratios also were lowest on the poor ranges. Thus Murie concluded that the coyote was merely the agent rather than the actual cause of deer mortality. As added evidence that coyotes were not detrimental to the deer, Murie pointed out that deer had increased steadily since coyote control was stopped in 1935. Official counts in that year revealed 610 mule deer; in 1938, 850 deer were counted. Assuming that Murie's assessment of range conditions was accurate, more rather than less predation might have been desirable in those unhunted deer herds.

Case 2: Coyotes and Deer in the Los Padres National Forest, California (Horn 1941)

One of the earliest documented efforts to increase fawn survival by coyote control began near Santa Barbara, California, in 1937. Horn and ten other workers collected and analyzed approximately 6,700 coyote scats and found

that deer remains constituted 30 percent or more of the scats in each month of the year (Young and Jackson 1951). Deer remains were found in about 60 percent of the scats, and the remains of rodents and rabbits in only 23 percent. Thus it appeared that deer constituted the major part of the coyote diet.

Horn reported that removal of coyotes from 414 square kilometers (160 square miles) of the Los Padres National Forest resulted in increased fawn survival and that coyotes in the area were holding deer numbers in check. He also pointed out that, if coyote control was to become a part of deer management on the area, it would be necessary in herd regulation to increase hunter take of deer. "If increased hunting cannot be allowed, the amount of coyote control should be limited to what will favor the proper size of the deer herd" (Horn 1941, p. 286).

In the wisdom of hindsight, it may be regretted that Horn's published report did not provide more data. He failed to state how much coyote densities were reduced through control, and how much fawn survival increased following control. Consequently, later workers have challenged his conclusions. Longhurst et al. (1952) suggested that fawn survival did not increase in the area where Horn and his colleagues trapped coyotes heavily, but that fawns actually were more numerous on the area where coyotes were not controlled. Robinette et al. (1977) pointed out that Horn's successor on the project, James Ashley, did not find consistently higher fawn crops on the coyote-control area and so concluded that coyotes were taking a cross section of all age classes in the herd. As reported by Robinette et al., Ashley did not determine the net effect of coyote predation on herd productivity, owing to the difficulty of censusing the deer.

Case 3: Coyotes, Black Bears and the Jawbone Mule Deer Herd, California (Leopold et al. 1951)

The Jawbone deer herd occupies approximately 692 square kilometers (267 square miles) of summer range and 96 square kilometers (37 square miles) of winter range along the north and west boundaries of Yosemite National Park. From 1947 to 1950, this herd was the object of a general ecological study. Predation was not assessed quantitatively, but nevertheless it was considered one of several influences that controlled deer numbers. Although five species of deer predators were present, only coyote and black bear were regarded as potentially important.

Examinations of bear and coyote scats in summer showed that both species consumed substantial quantities of deer. Even allowing that many of the deer eaten were carrion, there was no doubt that significant numbers of fawns were killed.

According to the local state trapper, coyote numbers doubled during the course of this study. Yet the deer population fluctuated irregularly and did not seem to be adversely influenced by predation. Leopold and his coworkers recognized that earlier predator control may have hastened recovery of depleted deer herds. "Once the ranges were saturated, however, continued control has simply permitted more rapid increases in the deer which have led to more frequent and more violent die-offs than if predators were uncontrolled. Until such time as full utilization is being made of deer crops produced annually, predator control is more of a hindrance than a help in deer management" (Leopold et al. 1951, p. 130).

Case 4: Coyotes and Mule Deer at Duck Creek, Nevada (Robinette et al. 1977)

The history of mule deer on the 363 square kilometer (140 square mile) Duck Creek area near McGill, Nevada, was evaluated in relation to the achievement of significant coyote reduction with "1080" (sodium monofluoroacetate) beginning in 1947. This deer herd had irrupted in the late 1930s and early 1940s. Herd classifications indicated fawn crops of 90–100 or more fawns per 100 does (after hunting season) from 1942 through 1946. In 1947, however, the fawn crop dropped to 78 per 100 does, and fawn-doe ratios remained low

through 1952, when the study was terminated. The average for 1948 and 1950–52—omitting 1949 because of its severe winter—was 78 fawns per 100 does.

In autumn 1947, 1080 poison stations were placed in the Duck Creek area for the first time (Robinson 1948). Coyotes were substantially reduced that winter and were held at a low level for the duration of the study. Still, fawn crops remained low. In this case it appeared that fawn survival was declining before the introduction of 1080, and any subsequent reduction of predation was masked by the counterbalancing influence of deteriorating range. It seemed reasonable to conclude that declines in deer population due to habitat deterioration or overuse cannot be reversed by predator control.

Case 5: Coyotes and Mule deer in the Pahvant Range, Fishlake National Forest, Utah (Robinette et al. 1977)

As at Duck Creek, Nevada, the poison 1080 was used to reduce coyote populations on many sheep ranges in Utah, including the Pahvant Range. Fawn crops on this range were high (82–90 fawns per 100 does in prehunt counts) in 1939 and 1940. At about this time, the herd reached its peak; deer numbers declined in 1941 and remained generally low thereafter. No classifications were made during 1943–45, but counts in 1941, 1942, and 1946 averaged 60.1 fawns per 100 does.

After the introduction of 1080 in 1947, fawn crops from 1950 through 1957 averaged 69.9 fawns per 100 does. No count was made in 1948, and the 1949 value of 60 fawns per 100 does was deleted from the comparison because of the preceding winter's deleterious effects on fawn survival. Statistical tests indicated that the fawn crops after 1947 were significantly higher than those in the early 1940s, consistent with the hypothesis that coyote predation on fawns was substantial before the introduction of 1080. Unfortunately, no check area without 1080 was available, so it is not certain that differences in the fawn counts were due solely to predation.

Case 6: Coyotes and Mule Deer in Oak Creek, Fishlake National Forest, Utah (Robinette et al. 1977)

An intensive coyote control program was begun in 1955 on a 137 square kilometer (53 square mile) study area to determine if coyotes were partly responsible for low fawn crops there. Before that time, limited numbers of coyotes were taken, and an estimated 25–30 coyotes were present. From 1949 to 1955, deer herd composition counts in early autumn showed an average of 64 fawns per 100 does.

In autumn 1955, about thirty cyanide guns (Robinson 1943) and two 1080 stations were placed on the area, and trapping efforts were stepped up. At least 5 coyotes were killed with the cyanide guns, 2 others were trapped, and 3 more were shot. Three litters of pups, totaling 15 animals, were taken in spring 1956. There is no way of knowing how many coyotes were killed with 1080, but these combined efforts appeared to have reduced coyote numbers by approximately 76 percent.

After this removal of coyotes, herd composition counts in 1956 and 1957 averaged 70 fawns per 100 does, an increase of 9 percent over the precontrol value of 64 fawns per 100 does. On a nearby range where predator control was constant, fawn-doe ratios for comparable years did not change. By relating herd composition data to estimates of deer numbers in Oak Creek, Robinette et al. (1977) estimated that 83 fawns were saved by the coyote control described above, and tag returns showed that at least part of the increased fawn survival might have been passed on to hunters. However, predator control failed to restore the high fawn crops that apparently prevailed as late as 1939. In comparison with other possibilities for increasing deer production, the potential of predator control seemed marginal.

Case 7: Coyotes and Black-tailed Deer in Western Washington (Brown 1961)

In December 1954, the 324 square kilometer (125 square mile) Capital State Forest was

A biologist examines the carcass of a Columbian black-tailed deer that was fed on by coyotes and bobcats in Washington; it was not known whether the deer was a victim of predation. Photograph by V. Scheffer; courtesy of the National Archives.

saturated with poison stations to determine whether an intensive coyote control program on a logged-off area would significantly increase fawn survival. Insofar as was practical, one poison station—consisting of horsemeat impregnated with 1080—was placed in each 2.59 square kilometers (1 square mile) of the study area. This was truly a saturation poisoning program; standard practice calls for only one 1080 station per 93 square kilometers (36 square miles) (Anonymous 1976). The experiment was evaluated by comparing observed fawn-doe ratios on the poisoned area with those on the nearby Clemons Tree Farm, where no predator control was practiced.

During the two years before the poisoning program, autumn counts showed no significant difference between fawn-doe ratios on the experimental and check areas. Averages were 47 fawns per 100 does on the Capital Forest and 49.5 per 100 on Clemons Tree Farm. In the two years following the 1080 program, however, counts averaged 50.5 fawns per 100 does on the Capital Forest and only 29.5 fawns per 100 does on the Clemons property. Similar differences appeared in ratios of fawns to does in the hunting kill.

Although these figures indicated that coyotes may have been an important cause of fawn mortality in western Washington, Brown felt more information was needed before any definite conclusions could be reached.

Case 8: Coyotes and Mule deer in Arizona (McMichael 1970)

In the late 1960s, 1080 poison stations were used on some Arizona ranges for the protection of livestock. On game management units where 1080 was used, the mule deer fawn crop averaged 58.9 fawns per 100 does, with 50.7 fawns per 100 does on other units where coyotes had not been controlled for two years. Fawn counts on all areas were similar before the coyote control program, so it appeared that predator control raised fawn survival by about 16 percent—(58.9–50.7)/50.7.

Case 9: Coyotes and Mule Deer on the Three Bar Wildlife Area, Arizona (Smith and LeCount 1976; LeCount 1974*b*)

Because of low fawn survival in many mule deer herds in Arizona during the 1960s, a study of factors affecting fawn survival was conducted from 1968 to 1976 on the Three Bar Wildlife Area. Approximately 104 square kilometers (40 square miles) of this 168 square kilometer (65 square mile) area were occupied by mule deer. A comparison of fawn survival rates inside and outside a predator-free enclosure disclosed that coyotes and other large predators took at least one-third of the fawns born where predators were not controlled. However, fawn survival in different years varied with winter rainfall as well as with forage production by winter-growing forbs (forage herbs). During eight years of measurements, variations in production of winter forbs accounted for about 76 percent of the total variation in fawn survival.

Even though Smith and LeCount were reluctant to offer firm conclusions about the relationships of fawns, forage, and predators, they hypothesized that in poor forage years fawns would be malnourished and thus especially vulnerable to predation. At the same time, a shortage of fawning and escape cover could facilitate predation on the fawns. Also, it seemed that the variety and quantity of alternate foods available to coyotes would rise and fall with forage production so that in poor forage years predators would have been especially dependent on fawns for food. These factors collectively could have intensified predation on fawns during poor years. If this analysis was correct, it seems unlikely that removing coyotes would have yielded permanent increases in deer numbers.

Case 10: Coyotes and Mule deer in Northeastern Utah (Austin et al. 1977)

From 1973 to 1976, mule deer were studied on two piñon/juniper winter ranges. The deer on these ranges occupied a common summer range in the Blue Mountain Plateau. In autumn, one herd migrated south into Miners Draw while the other herd went west into the Cub Creek drainage. The wintering herds were discrete, although they were only about 11 kilometers (7 miles) apart. Winter ranges were comparable in elevation, climate, and major browse species. Browse utilization transects and field observations indicated that deer numbers were well below carrying capacity on both ranges.

Although the two areas were similar in most respects, predator control was more intensive in the Cub Creek drainage than in Miners Draw. Professional hunter-trappers of the United States Fish and Wildlife Service took approximately 80 coyotes in Cub Creek during winters from 1973 to 1976, compared with only 45 in Miners Draw during the same period. Amateur predator hunters also were more active in the Cub Creek drainage.

Field observations in the two study areas revealed that there were more coyotes and fewer deer in Miners Draw than in Cub Creek. With approximately the same amount of effort in both areas, only 1 coyote was seen in Cub Creek compared with 9 in Miners Draw. Mean deer densities for two winters were 19 deer per square kilometer (7 per square mile) in Cub Creek and 6 deer per square kilometer (2 per square mile) in Miners Draw. Deer classification counts after hunting season revealed no genuine difference between the fawn-adult ratios, but by spring the fawn-adult ratio for three years (1974–76) was 59:100 in Cub Creek and only 29:100 in Miners Draw.

These comparisons show that a significantly higher proportion of fawns entering the winter period survived in the Cub Creek drainage, and that this higher fawn survival could have resulted from lower incidence of predation owing to more intensive predator control there.

Case 11: Coyotes and Deer in the Missouri River Breaks, Montana (Knowles 1976b; Schladweiler 1976)

Fawn production by mule and white-tailed deer populations in the Missouri River breaks of north-central Montana was poor from 1971 to 1975. Poor fawn crops could not be readily explained, but there was evidence of coyote predation. Therefore in 1975 a study was initiated to investigate coyote predation further as a possible cause of low fawn survival.

Helicopter surveys in early December 1975 revealed only 19.1 fawns per 100 adult mule deer on one study area and 36.9 fawns per 100 adults on another. By late March 1976 the ratios had dropped to 5.5 and 11.0 fawns per 100 adults on the two areas. Meanwhile, elk calf production was excellent; 58 calves per 100 adults were observed in late March 1976. The most likely explanation for differing survival between elk and mule deer is that coyotes preyed on deer fawns but not on elk calves. Forage conditions appeared to be excellent.

Causes of fawn mortality during summer were not determined. In the winter of 1975–76, however, 66 probable coyote kills (45 mule deer, 10 whitetails, 1 species undetermined) were found. Most kills were located from aircraft, and 52 were on ice on the Missouri River or in cultivated fields. Kills were almost completely consumed within twenty-four hours. Four coyote-deer confrontations were witnessed, and three of these resulted in death of the deer.

This study provided impressive and dramatic evidence of coyote predation on both adult deer and fawns. It appeared that coyotes took almost all fawns born in 1975. This finding was confirmed in summer, autumn, and winter of 1976–77, when coyote numbers declined on the study area and predation on deer also declined. Coyote pregnancy rates, litter sizes, and pup survival all were substantially lower than in the previous year, and fawn survival was much improved. Fawns born in 1977 also survived at high rates, with ratios in excess of 100 fawns per 100 does in autumn 1977 (E. O. Allen, pers. comm., April 1978).

Because of the observed drop in reproductive success of coyotes in 1976, and because predator control was less intensive than in previous years, it seems that the coyote decline on this study area was due to factors other than predator control. The Montana Fish and Game Department had planned to control coyotes in the study area during the winter of 1976–77, but these plans were dropped when it became apparent before winter that the level of predation on deer had decreased.

These observations show that it would be possible to monitor deer and coyote populations, on this study area at least, so that predator control could be applied as needed for deer management.

Case 12: Coyotes and Mule deer on Steens Mountain, Oregon (Trainer 1975; Trainer et al. 1978b; Lemos et al. 1978b)

Because of declining hunter harvests and low fawn-doe ratios in Oregon mule deer herds in the early 1960s, the Oregon Department of Fish and Wildlife began a study in 1968 to identify the cause or causes of low production or survival of fawns on Steens Mountain. The fertility of does in this herd was high, with an overall birthrate of 133 fawns per 100 does, but nearly 80 percent of fawns born were lost in their first nine months of life.

Radio monitoring of fawns with transmitter collars revealed that predation, mostly by coyotes, accounted for about 75 percent of fawn losses. Most predation losses were confined to two periods: June to mid-July (when fawns were 1–45 days old), and November to March (when fawns were 5 to 9 months of age).

Following up the finding that coyote predation was the major cause of fawn mortality in this herd, researchers initiated coyote control in 1976 to investigate the effect of reduced coyote numbers on fawn survival. From January through March 1976, 104 coyotes were taken from 194 square kilometers (75 square miles) of winter range. Herd composition counts in March revealed 31 fawns per 100 does, compared with only 15 fawns per 100

"Newborn fawns may vanish quickly after they have been killed by predators. On Steens Mountain, Oregon, the radio collar led biologists to the remains of this mule deer fawn killed by a coyote no more than 48 hours before the picture was taken. In other instances, only some hair and a blood spot have been found with the transmitters" (Connolly 1978, p. 380). Photograph by Walt Van Dyke; courtesy of the Oregon Department of Fish and Wildlife.

does on a nearby winter range where few coyotes had been killed.

Coyote control was continued during the next winter, with 164 coyotes removed from the 194 square kilometer control area between November 1976 and March 1977. Again, fawn survival was higher on the control area than on the nearby range without predator control.

From November 1977 to April 1978, 138 coyotes were shot on the study area. Herd composition counts in March 1978 showed 33 fawns per 100 does on the coyote removal area, compared with 27 fawns per 100 does on the check or nonremoval area. Through the period of coyote removals, periodic observations on the ground showed that coyotes remained abundant, and coyote predation continued to be the main cause of mule deer mortality. Therefore it appeared that more intensive coyote removal would have been needed to reduce predation on deer significantly.

Overall, the results of the Steens Mountain study document that poor fawn survival in this herd was due to predation. Fawn survival was increased by predator control, but it remains to be seen whether aerial shooting of coyotes on this area can reduce coyote densities enough to give the deer significant relief from predation. Likewise, it is uncertain whether such predator control can increase numbers of deer available to hunters, or whether such increase would be sufficient to justify the costs of control.

Case 13: Wolves and Black-tailed Deer in Southeast Alaska (Klein and Olson 1960)

Some islands of southeastern Alaska have wolves and others do not. During 1952–56, deer populations on wolf-free islands were found to be stable or slowly increasing, with numbers in excess of range carrying capacity and with heavy winter mortality and severely deteriorated winter ranges. Ranges supporting both deer and wolves, by contrast, were characterized by rapidly increasing deer populations, light winter mortality from starvation, and winter ranges in fair to good condition. In general, wolf-populated ranges supported a greater annual hunter harvest of deer per unit of area under comparable hunting pressure.

These observations implied that the impact of wolves was more beneficial than harmful to deer during this study. More recently, however, a somewhat different picture has emerged. On the same islands, it now appears that wolves may have hampered recovery of some deer herds that were reduced by a series of severe winters.

In 1968 deer populations throughout southeastern Alaska were at extremely high levels after four years of mild winters. The winter of 1968–69 was one of the worst on record in terms of total snowfall and duration of ground snow cover; 50–60 percent of the deer died. The following winter was mild, but the winters of 1970–71 and 1971–72 were at least as severe as that of 1968–69. A succession of mild winters since 1972 has resulted in a return of deer abundance on wolf-free islands, but on islands occupied by wolves recovery of deer has been variable. Recovery was fairly good on the more southerly islands, where the impact of winter weather had been least severe, but on the northernmost islands occupied by wolves, deer were still scarce or rare in 1976 (D. E. McKnight, pers. comm., January 1977). These observations verify that wolf predation on deer can be a serious limiting factor under certain conditions.

Case 14: Wolves and Black-tailed Deer on Coronation Island, Alaska (Merriam 1964)

In 1960 four captive timber wolves were deliberately released on Coronation Island, Alaska, to test the impact of wolves on the deer population. At the time of the release, deer were not abundant on the island, but the herd was thought to have been stable for many years. Despite the low deer density, utilization of food species had been so complete that available forest understory was almost completely gone. The deer, especially males, were about 20 percent smaller than deer of equivalent age on better ranges.

Healthy mule and black-tailed deer are fairly successful at eluding pursuing wolves, even in deep snow, but recent studies have found that coyotes are able to kill healthy mule deer. The deer's bounding gait (see chap. 5), speed, and ability to detect predators at a distance are important defense mechanisms. Photograph by Tom W. Hall.

By 1964 there were 9–13 wolves on the 83 square kilometer (32 square mile) island. Incidence of deer remains in wolf scats increased from 78 percent in 1961 to 95 percent in 1964. Deer numbers were much reduced; deer sightings per man-day in the field declined from 8.2 per day in 1959 to 0.1 per day in 1964. A dramatic recovery of the vegetation used by deer was apparent.

Even though wolves on Coronation Island almost eliminated the resident deer herd, the effect was not permanent. The wolves apparently increased to about 15 pairs and then declined—wolves eating wolves—until only one was left (Klein 1969). In the mid-1970s the wolves were gone, and deer were repopulating the island (Rausch and Hinman 1977).

Case 15: Mountain Lions and Mule Deer in the Oak City Deer Herd Area, Utah
(Robinette et al. 1977)

During the winters of 1947–48 and 1948–49, W. L. Robinette and J. S. Gashwiler tried to estimate mountain lion numbers on the 670 square kilometer (260 square mile) Oak City Deer Herd Area, which surrounds the Oak Creek Deer Study Area of Robinette et al. (1977). This is the same area where coyote control was tried experimentally in 1955 (see case 6). Although the Oak City herd unit proved too large for effective census, at least 5 lions were found at one time on a 137 square kilometer (53 square mile) deer study area.

Through the winter of 1949–50, lion hunting was intensified, and the lion population was reduced by 50 percent or more. During 1950–57, the number of lion sightings each year was 70 percent lower than in the two years preceding intensified control, and the number of tracks seen was 46 percent lower. However, the proportion of definite lion kills among deer carcasses found did not decline; it was 2.5 percent before intensified control and 2.9 percent afterward.

Because of manpower reduction and other problems, Robinette and his co-workers were unable to evaluate fully the impact of lion predation on the Oak Creek deer herd. Nevertheless, they speculated that a 50 percent reduction of lions could have saved 30–90 deer per year on the study area. Based on an annual hunting kill of about 20 percent of the herd, therefore, lion reduction could have increased hunter harvest by 6–18 deer per year, or ap-

proximately 1–4 percent of the average legal harvest of 447 deer per year. Thus the intensified lion control probably made only a trivial contribution to hunter harvest. As another indication that lion reduction had little effect on deer numbers, annual population estimates showed deer numbers in Oak Creek to be quite stable through the entire study (1947–57).

Case 16: Predators and Mule deer in Daggett County, Utah (Richens 1967)

In deer herds that wintered in Daggett County, Utah, during 1958–60, predation accounted for 54 percent of observed losses. Of 89 deer found dead, 26 had been killed by mountain lions, 19 by coyotes, and 3 by bob-

This mule deer fawn, badly mauled by a bobcat, was found by a rodent control crew in Utah. Its wounds were treated, and after several weeks it was able to stand. It subsequently recovered and became very tame. Photograph by P. J. Fair; courtesy of the United States Forest Service.

cats. Domestic dogs were seen chasing deer, but were not known to have killed any.

More deer were killed by predators than by other natural causes during this study, but the number killed constituted only a small fraction of the population. The range was used heavily both by deer and by livestock, with preferred browse species severely hedged or highlined. Under these conditions, Richens concluded that predators on the Daggett range were more beneficial than harmful to the deer herds.

Case 17: Mountain Lions and Deer in the Idaho Primitive Area (Hornocker 1970)

Because it featured fairly abundant lion and ungulate populations, few livestock, and not too much hunting, the Idaho Primitive Area was selected as the best site to study lion population impact on big game animals. The evaluation took place during winter and spring of each year from 1964–65 to 1967–68, primarily on the Big Creek drainage of the Middle Fork of the Salmon River.

Mule deer and elk made up 70 percent of the prey item occurrences in lion droppings. Forty-six mule deer killed by lions were examined, and 40 percent of these were fawns, even though frequency of fawns in the population was only 22 percent. Selection for adult males also was noted. Malnutrition did not seem to be a factor in the vulnerability of fawns. Poor animals were not selected by lions but were taken proportionately to their occurrence in the total deer population.

During this study, the density of lions remained constant while that of elk and deer increased. The numerical ratio of lions to deer fell from 1:135 in 1964–65 to 1:201 in 1967–68. Thus lion predation was not controlling deer numbers during this study. In fact, Hornocker speculated that lion predation was beneficial in several ways. It damped and protracted severe prey oscillations, culled individuals possessing undesirable behavioral or physical traits, and redistributed animals on winter range. However, these effects were not demonstrated in this study.

Case 18: Mountain Lions, Mule Deer and Cattle in Northwestern Arizona (Shaw 1977)

Between 1971 and 1975, 16 adult mountain lions were captured, marked, and released on a 407 square kilometer (157 square mile) study area northwest of Prescott, Arizona. Through radiolocations, recaptures, and tracks, the study area was estimated to contain at least 24 lions (1 lion per 16.9 square kilometers: 6.5 square miles). Sixty-two lion kills were found, including 37 mule deer, 23 cattle, 1 pronghorn, and 1 cottontail. Contents of 50 lion scats were similar: 27 contained only deer, 13 contained only cattle, 4 contained both cattle and deer, and 6 contained neither deer nor cattle. Lions selected calves over other prey. Depending on the method of estimation, researchers determined that lions killed 77–193 deer and 21–97 cattle each year in the study area.

During the four years of this research, the mule deer population apparently was stable at a density (in January) of about 2.5 deer per square kilometer (6.5 square mile). Total mortality was about 500 deer per year. Hunters took about 75 bucks annually, with wounding loss and illegal kill unknown. Lions apparently took more deer than did hunters, and a high proportion of the remaining losses were attributed to other predators and to early postnatal mortality. Shaw concluded that lions were a major cause of mortality contributing to the relatively low deer population but that lion predation alone would not have prevented the deer from increasing if other losses had been significantly reduced. Nevertheless, general observation of range and forage conditions led Shaw to believe that the area could have supported many more deer than actually were present.

Shaw (pers. comm., February 1977) speculated that the seasonal availability of calves as lion prey may have maintained this mountain lion population at a higher density than would have been supported by native prey alone. If so, the artificially high lion population could have had a greater depressing influence on deer than would have occurred in the absence of cattle.

Case 19: Mountain Lions and Mule Deer in the Cassia Unit, Idaho (Nellis 1977a)

In the early 1970s it appeared to wildlife managers that the size of the Cassia deer herd in south-central Idaho was controlled by mortality rather than by habitat limitations. Accordingly, research was undertaken in 1975–76 to identify causes of mortality. Of 38 newborn fawns marked with radio transmitters, 21 died within six months. At least 15 and probably 20 of these deaths resulted from predation, primarily by mountain lions.

Deer numbers in the 1,540 square kilometer (594 square mile) Cassia Unit during 1975–76 were speculated to be about 7,500 before the hunting season. The annual kill by mountain lions was estimated at 800 deer per year (20 lions killing 40 deer each), with coyotes, bobcats, and golden eagles taking perhaps 200 more. Legal hunter harvest in 1976 was approximately 750 deer plus an estimated 20 percent crippling loss. Therefore it appeared that nonhuman predators and legal hunters removed roughly equal numbers of deer from this herd in 1976. To reduce herd mortality, deer hunting regulations were made more restrictive, and cougar seasons were liberalized.

PRINCIPLES FOR PREDATOR CONTROL IN DEER MANAGEMENT

From the foregoing case histories, together with other information in the literature, it is possible to advance several conclusions and principles about predator control as a deer management tool.

1. Predators on many ranges kill substantial numbers of mule and black-tailed deer, but only by careful local study can it be determined whether such predation causes the deer to be less numerous than they would be in the absence of predation.

2. In no case has predation by coyotes or mountain lions been documented as the principal cause of a mule deer population decline. But, because of difficulties in obtaining unequivocal proof of the effects of predation, lack of documentation does not necessarily mean that the impact of predation is insignificant.

3. In one case—Coronation Island (Merriam 1964)—wolves were shown virtually to extirpate a blacktail population. Wolves also literally killed off the white-tailed deer population in part of the Superior National Forest in Minnesota (Mech and Karns 1977).

4. The most frequently offered evidence of predation's impact on mule deer is low fawn survival. But low fawn survival can result from causes other than predation, and many reports have failed to show positively that the poor fawn survival was due to predation. By the same token, there are several accounts of apparent increases in fawn survival due to predator control. But only in one Utah study (Robinette et al. 1977) was it shown that predator control increased the number of deer taken by hunters, and in that case the increase was marginal.

5. In many studies in which predator control was attempted for the benefit of deer, one may question whether effective predator control actually was achieved. Some individual coyotes are more likely than others to kill domestic sheep (Connolly et al. 1976), and this may be true of coyote predation on deer as well. If certain coyotes have a special predilection or learned ability to prey on deer, these coyotes must be removed to reduce deer predation significantly. One suspects that experienced resident coyotes may be more effective deer predators than younger individuals and also may be less vulnerable to predator control. If so, general reduction of coyote populations may not reduce predation rates in proportion to numbers of coyotes killed. This subject needs further study.

6. Predator control costs money. There is no published cost analysis of predator control as a mule deer management practice. However, Beasom (1974) suggested that predator control in southern Texas could be justified by increased production of turkeys and white-tailed deer, provided that the game so produced was sold to hunters.

7. Mule deer numbers ultimately are limited by quality and quantity of habitat. Predator control may produce measurable population

gains where deer are below the carrying capacity of their range, but deer population declines due to habitat deterioration or overuse cannot be reversed by predator control. The practical value of such generalizations, however, is limited because it is hard to determine carrying capacity of ranges for deer.

8. In general, predator control is justified in mule deer management only when it will produce substantial increases of deer at reasonable cost, when extra deer production offsets the value of the predators to be destroyed, and when the increased production will be used. For more detailed discussion of the justification of predator control in big game management, see Connolly (1978).

D.R. BARRICK

Chapter 8

ASSESSING POPULATIONS

Guy E. Connolly
Wildlife Research Biologist
United States Fish and Wildlife Service
Denver Wildlife Research Center
Twin Falls, Idaho

To manage deer populations, managers must have information about them. To establish realistic management goals, and to assess progress toward those goals, management must measure harvests and evaluate their probable effect on populations. The state of the art in measuring and predicting the dynamics of mule and black-tailed deer populations, and in applying such knowledge to management, is reviewed here.

ESTIMATION OF AGE

One of the most frequently gathered bits of information at hunter check stations and in deer research projects is the age of each deer examined. The age of any one deer means little, except perhaps to the hunter who killed it, but the ages of a representative sample of harvested animals can yield useful vital statistics about the entire population. Age data are essential to the calculation of birthrates and death rates and may give a rough indication of harvest rate. In general, average age of the kill decreases as rate of harvest increases.

Because age information is basic to work in deer population dynamics, biologists have devoted considerable effort to development of age-estimation techniques. Three methods have received most attention.

Tooth Replacement and Wear

Eruption and replacement of deer teeth follow a regular chronological schedule. Adult dentition is complete at about 2–2.5 years of age, and younger deer are aged with certainty by anyone who can distinguish deciduous from permanent teeth. In older deer, the estimate must be based on judgments of relative tooth wear. This usually is done by comparison with jaws from deer of known age. "Jaw boards" (displays of known-age jaws) are standard equipment for this purpose at check stations.

Rate of tooth wear is quite regular within most deer poulations, although substantial differences may occur between one herd and another. It is standard practice to use known-age jaws from the same locality as unknown-age jaws wherever possible. On Vancouver Island, British Columbia, teeth of male deer seem to wear faster than those of females (Thomas and Bandy 1975). Locally, fluorosis (Robinette et al. 1957*b*) and possibly other unusual conditions may disrupt the normal patterns of tooth eruption or wear, making accurate age determinations from tooth examinations impossible.

For mule and black-tailed deer, the dental-aging standards in general use are those developed by Cowan (1936), Robinette et al. (1957*b*), Rees et al. (1966*a*), and others. Each half of the normal deer mandible (lower jaw) contains four incisor teeth (the outer one technically is a canine), three premolars, and three molars. Anomalous extra teeth occur infrequently. Incisors and premolars that are present at birth are deciduous "milk teeth" and are replaced later by permanent teeth. The molars, when they appear, are permanent. The tooth eruption schedule is given in table 30.

Although dental examinations are fast and inexpensive, they are subject to errors that increase with age of the deer. In a test of observer error, Brown (1961) presented a set of fifty jaws to fourteen biologists and found that only 43 percent of the resulting seven hundred estimates were correct. Yearlings were aged correctly 90 percent of the time; the errors with this age class were obviously due to carelessness or inexperience on the part of observers. Another test showed that permanent, experienced employees of the Nevada Fish and Game Department correctly aged 88 percent of a sample of known-age jaws, while temporary employees were 54 percent correct. Permanent personnel aged all the yearlings correctly, but temporaries scored only 79 percent correct (Papez 1976).

One might expect errors in dental inspections to be compensating, so that age distribution from a series of jaws would be accurate even though some individual specimens were aged incorrectly. Unfortunately, this does not seem to be the case. Brown (1961) found observers to overestimate ages of young deer and to underestimate ages of older deer. Only one of fourteen observers had an age structure for fifty jaws that closely approximated the known age composition.

The dental examination method is most often used on jaws that have been removed from dead animals, but it is possible to make plaster casts of teeth of live deer (Barnes and Longhurst 1960). After several years of experience with this method on wild trapped deer, however, it is my opinion that the results are no better than those obtained through visual inspection using a jaw spreader and flashlight.

In an attempt to remove subjectivity from age estimates based on tooth wear, Robinette et al. (1957b) proposed a system of measuring widths and heights of molariform teeth (molars and premolars). The molar tooth ratio was the sum of occlusal widths of seven buccal crowns divided by the sum of the corresponding lingual crown heights. Measurements were taken with a vernier caliper to the nearest 0.1 millimeter (0.004 inch). Despite such painstaking measurements, however, sixty-two of one hundred age estimates made by Erickson et al. (1970) with this method were incorrect—thirty-seven were overestimated and twenty-five underestimated. Robinette et al. (1977) also reevaluated this technique and found it to be of limited use; only 43 percent of the deer more than 36 months old were aged correctly.

Despite limitations of age determinations based on visual assessment of tooth replacement and wear, this method is likely to remain

Table 30. Tooth Eruption in the Lower Jaw of Mule Deer

Age	Incisors			Canine[a]	Premolars			Molars		
	1	2	3	1	2	3	4	1	2	3
1–3 weeks	D	D	D	D	D	D	D	—	—	—
2–3 months	D	D	D	D	D	D	D	(P)	—	—
6 months	D	D	D	D	D	D	D	(P)	(P)	—
12 months	(P)	D(P)	D	D	D	D	D	P	(P)	—
18 months	P	P	P	D	D	D	D	P	P	(P)
24 months	P	P	P	P	(P)	(P)	(P)	P	P	(P)
30 months	P	P	P	P	P	P	P	P	P	P

Source: Taber (1971).

Note: D, milk or deciduous tooth; P, adult or permanent tooth. Parentheses indicate that the tooth is in the process of eruption at that particular time.

[a] Resembles incisors.

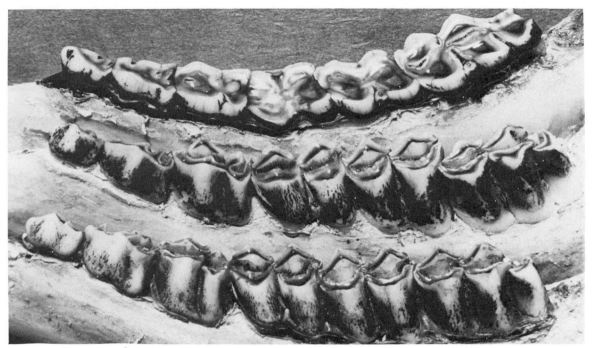

Premolar and molar teeth of adult deer show progressively greater wear with increasing age. These teeth are from black-tailed deer of known ages: 2 years *(bottom);* 3 years *(middle);* and 14 years *(top).* To distinguish between 2- and 3-year-old deer, particular attention should be paid to the fourth premolar (third tooth from left) and the last cusp of the third molar *(far right).* Photograph by Guy E. Connolly.

the standard aging technique for the foreseeable future. Not only is the accuracy sufficient for most purposes, but the only alternatives are more expensive laboratory methods.

Eye Lens Weights

In many species of mammals, the eye lens gains weight continuously throughout an animal's life. This apparently is true for mule and black-tailed deer, but the rate of lens growth in adult deer is too slow and too variable to permit accurate age determination from lens weights.

Longhurst (1964) proposed that lens weights could provide accurate age estimates of deer up to about 5 years, provided that sex-specific regression models were used. Improved statistical treatment of his data, however, showed that the age/lens weight relationship was less precise, and that lens weights did not differ between male and female deer of comparable

ages. Confidence limits indicated that the probability of placing a 24-month-old deer in the correct year class was 80 percent; for 36-month-old deer, it was only about 50 percent (Connolly et al. 1969). However, the method may be useful for aging fetuses and young fawns.

Counts of Annuli in Dental Cementum

In many kinds of mammals, dental cementum is deposited at a rate that varies seasonally. This results in annuli that can be counted in microscopic examination of stained sections of decalcified teeth. The work of Erickson et al. (1970) shows this to be the most reliable of methods available for estimating age of deer. The first incisor is the tooth most frequently used. For details of the laboratory procedure, see Erickson and Seliger (1969), Low and Cowan (1963), and Thomas and Bandy (1973).

Despite its purported accuracy, not all workers have been successful with this method. The annulations may be too indistinct to permit an exact judgment of the tooth's age. For this reason, most age estimates of incisors from California black-tailed deer that were sectioned and examined by experienced technicians in British Columbia and Colorado were in error by one year or more (Connolly et al. 1969).

Such errors may not seriously bias estimates of a population's age structure, however. In a sample of 166 mule deer incisors from Utah, 49 percent were aged incorrectly, but the errors were compensating and would not have impaired conclusions regarding age structure or mortality rates (Robinette et al. 1977). Furthermore, as pointed out in that work, only older animals need to be aged by this technique since gross inspection of teeth can be used for deer less than 2 years old.

DETERMINATION OF SEX OF DEER CARCASSES

Because life expectancy of bucks differs from that of does in most deer populations, it often is necessary to differentiate between sexes in evaluating deer population dynamics. This presents no problem as long as whole animals can be examined. When skulls and external organs are missing, the sex of adult deer can readily be determined by examination of the pelvic girdle; suspensory tuberosities for the attachment of penis ligaments are lacking in the female (Taber 1971).

REPRODUCTION

Reproduction in deer begins with production of ova by the ovaries of the doe. These eggs pass into oviducts, where they are fertilized by sperm from the buck. After fertilization, eggs implant on the uterine wall and develop into fetuses. The ruptured ovarian follicles fill with pink or yellow cells to become the yellow bodies, or corpora lutea, of pregnancy. These can be seen easily with the naked eye; if a fresh ovary is sliced with a razor blade, each corpus

luteum of pregnancy appears as a solid yellow ball. After fawns are born, the maternal corpora lutea begin to degenerate and are called corpora albicantia of corpora lutea of pregnancy. They remain visible for at least eight months after parturition and therefore may reveal the number of fawns produced long after fawns have been born. For additional information on the ovarian cycle in deer, see Cheatum (1949*b*) and Taber and Dasmann (1958).

Birthrates in deer can be estimated by counting either corpora lutea (or corpora albicantia) or the fetuses themselves. Better estimates come from fetal counts, but often it is not possible to examine pregnant does. When fetuses cannot be counted, as is usually true during autumn hunting seasons, reproduction still can be monitored by examining the ovaries.

Ovarian Analysis

In many deer herds, wildlife biologists can study reproductive performance only by examining ovaries from does taken in autumn hunting seasons; substantial numbers of does cannot be examined at any other time of year. In analyzing autumn collections of ovaries, the largest corpora albicantia are assumed to reflect the most recent reproductive cycle, which culminated in births four to five months earlier. Also it is assumed that corpora albicantia of corpora lutea from the most recent pregnancy can be distinguished from other corpora albicantia that may be found. Cheatum (1949*b*) stated that corpora albicantia resulting from ovulation without ensuing pregnancy do not become pigmented, whereas the corpora albicantia of corpora lutea of pregnancy are pigmented. Also, the corpora albicantia of corpora lutea of pregnancy are larger than corpora albicantia of luteinized, nonovulated follicles.

Because not all eggs released from the ovaries become fertilized, and because there is some intrauterine loss of embryos, the number of corpora lutea (or corpora albicantia) is greater than the number of fawns actually born. Therefore a correction factor is needed to estimate birthrate from counts of corpora lutea or corpora albicantia. As is shown in table 31, the number of viable fetuses may range from 85 to 95 percent of the number of corpora lutea observed.

Several workers have reported difficulties in interpreting results of ovarian analyses. Accessory or false corpora lutea sometimes may be confused with genuine corpora lutea of pregnancy (Golley 1957a; Gill 1972a). Also, corpora albicantia—as corpora lutea are called after fawns are born—may persist longer than one year. Robinette et al. (1977) found in Utah that ovulation rates increased with age, but total counts of corpora albicantia increased more than ovulation rates. Contrary to the findings of Cheatum (1949b) for white-tailed deer, it seems that corpora albicantia in mule and black-tailed deer may be formed from sources other than corpora lutea of pregnancy. Golley (1957a) reported an example of this from a captive, 18-year-old doe that had never been bred. After this animal died, its ovaries were found to contain two large, bright, pigmented spots and ten smaller pigmented spots. These corpora albicantia must have been formed from corpora lutea of estrus that did not persist but degenerated shortly after formation. Brown (1961) found that ovaries collected during the breeding season showed a higher corpora lutea count than those collected later in gestation. Brown surmised that this might result from biologists' inability to distinguish between corpora lutea of estrus and corpora lutea of pregnancy.

In a study of black-tailed deer in Washington, Golley (1957a) overestimated the rate of ovulation by 18 percent, owing to inaccurate identification of corpora albicantia of corpora lutea of pregnancy in does taken during the autumn hunting season. For pregnant does during gestation, however, Golley found that corpora lutea of pregnancy could be reliably identified.

Counts of Embryos

Because of the difficulties reported with ovarian analyses, it is preferable to estimate birthrates directly from fetal counts whenever possible. Examples of fetal counts are given in table 32. The number of fetuses per doe, and presumably the birthrate, varies with the age of the doe. Therefore, age structure of the breeding does, as well as age-specific pregnancy rates, must be considered in determining overall birthrate for any deer population.

Black-tailed deer and mule deer may breed as fawns (Thomas and Smith 1973; Nellis et al. 1976), but pregnant fawns are so rare that their role in reproduction can be ignored. Yearlings, especially among black-tailed deer, are less productive than older deer. Middle-aged does exhibit the highest pregnancy rates. The incidence of breeding in some populations seems

Table 31. Relationship of Corpora Lutea and Fetal Counts in Several Mule and Black-tailed Deer Populations

Location of Study	Age of Doe[a]	Number of			Fetuses as Percentage of Corpora Lutea	Reference
		Does Examined	Corpora Lutea	Live Fetuses		
Northern California	All	26	39	36	92	Taber (1953)
Western Washington	All	49	69	61	88	Brown (1961)
Middle Park, Colorado	Yearlings	26	36	33	92	Gill (1972a)
	Adults	147	285	270	95	
Utah	Yearlings	218	282	263	93	Robinette et al. (1977)
	2 years	102	189	175	93	
	3–7 years	287	567	524	92	
	8+ years	139	291	247	85	

[a] Yearlings are approximately 17 months old at breeding.

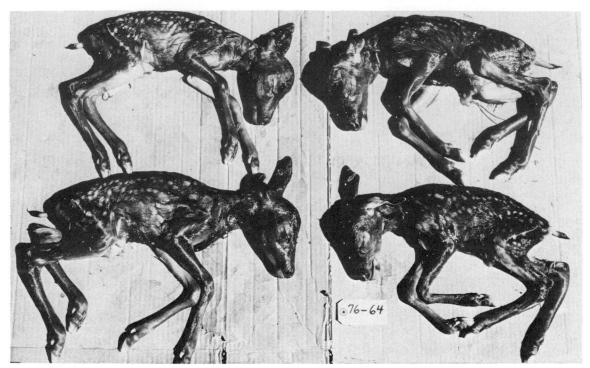

Most mule deer does produce one or two fawns each year. Triplets are unusual and quadruplets are rare. This litter of quadruplets—three males and one female—was taken from a 6-year-old doe on Steens Mountain, Oregon, 5 May 1976. Photograph by Charles E. Trainer; courtesy of the Oregon Department of Fish and Wildlife.

to decline in old does (table 32), though fetal counts remain high for those old does that do breed. Pregnancy rates for blacktail does are slightly lower than those for mule deer does of comparable age.

Fetal Sex Ratios

Biologists traditionally assume that the sex ratio among deer at birth is unbalanced in favor of males, but the possibility that fetal sex ratios vary with maternal age (Robinette et al. 1957a) has received less attention. In five of six populations for which I compiled data on fetal sex ratios (table 32), there was a preponderance of male fetuses and a higher male-female ratio in young and old does than in middle-aged does. The sixth population, on Steens Mountain, Oregon, showed just the reverse—young and old does produced a lower proportion of males

than did middle-aged does. I am unable to explain this difference.

In addition to apparent variations with maternal age, fetal sex ratios may vary from year to year. The proportion of males in samples of fetuses from Middle Park, Colorado, was 52 percent in 1972 and 67 percent in 1970, with intermediate values in 1969 and 1971 (Gill 1972a). On Steens Mountain, Oregon, males constituted 29–61 percent of fetuses examined in various years (Trainer et al. 1976). Because of the small yearly sample sizes in most field studies, however, it is not clear whether observed year-to-year variations are genuine or merely artifacts due to sampling variations.

If it is true that fetal sex ratios in blacktail and mule deer herds vary with maternal age, and from year to year, how and why such variations occur should be of interest to managers. Nutrition is one of the likely causal factors. Information on its effect on fetal sex ratios is available

Table 32. Age-Specific Pregnancy Rates and Fetal Sex Ratios in Selected Mule and Black-tailed Deer Populations

Location of Study	Age Class[a] (Years)	Number Examined	Percentage Pregnant	Number of Live Fetuses	Fetuses per Doe Examined	Fetal Sex Ratio— Males: 100 Females	Reference
Western	1	22	45	10	0.45	233	Brown (1961)
Washington	2–6	73	92	100	1.37	104	
	7+	15	67	16	1.07	300	
Hopland,	1	36	36	15	0.42	217	F. M. Anderson
California	2	35	91	36	1.03	75	et al. (1974);
	3–6	132	98	195	1.48	105	Longhurst and
	7+	90	93	127	1.41	153	Connolly (n.d.)
Middle Park,	1	26	92	33	1.27	137	Gill (1972a, n.d.)
Colorado	2	18	100	38	2.11	274	
	3–7	88	99	163	1.85	110	
	8+	40	98	69	1.72	213	
Black Gap,	1	19	47	11	0.58	300	Parsons (1975),
Texas	2	17	88	21	1.24	112	Brownlee (n.d.)
	3–7	39	97	64	1.64	128	
	8+	3	67	4	1.33	300	
Utah	1[b]	156	53	87	0.56		Robinette et al.
	1[c]	232	83	245	1.06	115[d]	(1977, 1957a)
	2	160	98	264	1.65	104	
	3–7	422	95	727	1.72	108	
	8+	252	90	396	1.57	115	
Steens	1	21	62	15	0.71	25	Trainer et al.
Mountain,	2	13	85	15	1.15	56	(1976); Trainer
Oregon	3	32	97	55	1.72	108	(n.d.)
	4–10	106	99	191	1.80	101	
	11+	9	100	16	1.78	78	

[a] Yearlings are approximately 1.5 years old at breeding and 2 years old at parturition.

[b] Yearlings that died of malnutrition.

[c] Yearlings that died of causes other than malnutrition.

[d] Numbers of fetuses sexed were 277, 208, 597, and 333, from yearling, 2-year-old, 3–7-year-old, and older does, respectively (Robinette et al. 1957a).

for some species, but not for mule and black-tailed deer.

Effects of Nutrition on Reproduction

Numerous studies have shown that does on good range have higher rates of ovulation, conception, and pregnancy than does on poor range. Effects of nutrition are especially apparent in yearling does, whose reproductive rates under normal conditions are far below their potential. In Utah, Robinette et al. (1977) found pregnancy rates in yearling does that died of malnutrition to be only about half those in yearlings that were shot or that died suddenly (table 32).

Nutrition also affects prenatal mortality. In Utah, the computed prenatal loss after the first month and until midpregnancy was 4.0 percent among does dying from malnutrition, compared with only 2.8 percent among does dying of other causes. Most prenatal mortality occurred during the first two months of pregnancy. Similar evidence from Middle Park, Colorado, likewise showed prenatal mortality to increase when does were poorly nourished (Robinette et al. 1977).

It seems possible that some age-related variations in pregnancy rates (table 32) could be explained by body condition of does in various age groups. One might conjecture that the lower productivity of young and old does is not a direct function of age but an indication that they may be less healthy, on the average, than does of prime age. Likewise, differing fetal sex ratios among does of various ages might be a function of nutrition rather than age. In white-tailed deer, sex ratios at birth seem to vary with the nutritional plane of the doe—males constituted 70 percent of births from does on a poor diet at breeding, compared with 47 percent from does on a good diet (Verme 1969). This concept might be expected to apply equally well to mule and black-tailed deer. In Utah, Robinette et al. (1977) found a fetal sex ratio of 79 males per 100 females for does on good range, while on poor range the fetal sex ratio was 192 males per 100 females. For a detailed discussion of the influence of nutrition on fetal sex ratios, see Robinette et al. (1957*a*).

Because of documented relationships among nutrition and reproductive success, it seems appropriate to generalize that, in any deer herd where fawn production is suboptimal, the first priority of management should be to consider the nutritional status of does at breeding and during pregnancy. Sportsmen frequently question whether there are enough bucks to breed the does, but no reproductive failure due to shortage of bucks has ever been documented in any wild blacktail or mule deer population.

HERD COMPOSITION COUNTS

General Principles and Assumptions

Composition or classification counts are a routine part of deer management in many states and often are used in research projects as well. Their usual objective is to determine proportions of bucks, does, and fawns in a population. In late winter, after bucks have dropped their antlers, the animals usually are classified either as fawns or as adults. Dasmann and Taber (1956*b*) proposed use of five age and sex categories—fawns, yearling bucks, yearling does, adult bucks, and adult does—but this system has not been widely used because of the difficulty of distinguishing yearlings from adult deer under field conditions.

Herd composition counts usually are made over standardized routes at predetermined seasons each year so that results from different years can be compared. Counting is most often done by persons on foot, on horseback, or in motor vehicles, although Riordan (1948) believed that herd composition ratios could be estimated as accurately from the air as from the ground, and at lower cost. Aerial counts are used routinely in North Dakota to estimate buck-doe and fawn-doe ratios each autumn (Samuelson 1975).

Results of herd composition counts may be expressed either in ratios or in percentages. Thus, a herd with 65 fawns and 45 bucks per 100 does also may be said to contain 31 percent fawns, 21 percent bucks, and 48 percent does. The more common procedure is to use ratios.

If classification counts are to estimate accurately the relative abundance of deer in various age and sex classes, each deer in the population must be equally likely to be classified. This assumption is implicit in all herd classification counts even though there is no direct way to determine whether it is true. Often, it obviously is not. Prehunt buck-doe ratios recorded by Longhurst and Connolly (n.d.) at the Hopland Field Station (California) usually were lower than posthunt ratios, even though substantial numbers of bucks were removed in the interim. I believe these prehunt counts underestimated the true buck-doe ratios because at that time of year (July) bucks moved less than does during daylight hours. In a Utah study area, Robinette et al. (1977) concluded that both bucks and fawns were less visible than does during prehunt counts. The true numbers of fawns and bucks were believed to have been 3.5 and 2.8 percent higher, respectively, than observed numbers. (This conclusion was based in part on the assumption that observed posthunt ratios were accurate.) Such observational biases may be particularly serious if observed changes in ratios are to be used for estimation of numbers. This subject is discussed at length elsewhere in this chapter (see "Methods for Estimating Deer Numbers: Change-in-Ratio Estimates," below). There is little an investigator can do about the problem of differential observability of deer in various age and sex classes other than to make counts at the season when such bias is lowest. For many herds the best season appears to be autumn. Regardless of how much observability bias may be present, however, herd classifications also are subject to sampling error.

Sample Sizes for Herd Composition Ratios

The usual procedure in herd composition sampling is to classify as many animals as possible, on the premise that accuracy (the probability that observed ratios approximate true ratios in the population) increases with sample size. This assumption intuitively seems correct, but sampling variability in herd classifications has received remarkably little attention in the literature (Wallmo 1964). One possible reason is that the sampling distribution is complicated by variations in both the numerator and denominator of the ratio (Cochran 1977), and appropriate procedures for calculating variance

and confidence limits are not taught in the college statistics courses usually taken by wildlife students.

Although their statistical procedure was not given, Leopold et al. (1951) stated that only small samples were needed to estimate herd ratios. Their study showed that ratios based on careful classification of 50 deer erred by only 5 percent in comparison with ratios from a much larger sample, and that more than 200 deer would need to be classified to reduce the probable error below 2 percent.

Robinette et al. (1977) forecast much greater sampling requirements, based on analysis of pre- and posthunt herd classifications made annually for many years at Oak Creek, Utah. The samples in various years were estimated to contain 12–50 percent of the entire population (approximately 2,200 deer after hunting season). From the variation in ratios in 25-animal samples taken consecutively from field record sheets, sample sizes needed to provide sex and age ratios within a 10 percent sampling error and a 95 percent confidence interval were estimated as follows:

Herd composition counts on many deer ranges are made by observers on foot, from ridgetops, and from selected vantage points. Using binoculars and a spotting scope, all deer seen within one-half mile can be identified as buck, doe, or fawn. From this spot on the Hopland Field Station near Hopland, California, fifty or more black-tailed deer sometimes were classified within two hours. Photograph by Guy E. Connolly.

1. Buck-doe ratio (prehunt—15,000 deer; posthunt—3,750);
2. Doe-fawn ratio (prehunt—975; posthunt—1,600);
3. Adult-fawn ratio (prehunt—750; posthunt—700).

Possible explanations for the differing conclusions of Robinette et al. (1977) and Leopold et al. (1951) are that the ratios were more variable in the population studied by Robinette et al. or that faulty statistical procedures were used by one or both research groups. Unfortunately for those who dislike fieldwork, the sampling projections by Robinette et al. (1977) probably are most realistic.

A statistical comparison of two herd-composition sampling plans (route counts and quadrat counts) was made by Anderson and Bowden (1977). Deer were counted by a two-person team on the ground using binoculars and spotting scopes. Route counts consisted of dawn-to-dusk, mainly circular routes designed to classify the maximum number of deer. Quadrat counts consisted of classifying deer within randomly selected 0.65 square kilometer (0.25 square mile) quadrats stratified by subjective estimates of high and low deer densities and proportionally allocated within topographic quadrangles. The two plans yielded nearly identical fawn-doe and buck-doe ratios during 1975–76; but to estimate fawn-doe ratios within 10 percent of the true value at the 95 percent confidence level would have required either six routes or 103 quadrats. Six route counts could have been completed in six days, compared with twenty-six days needed to count 103 quadrats, so the route sampling plan was clearly superior. Buck-doe ratios, to be estimated with comparable precision, would have required impractically large sample sizes for either plan. The authors stated that these preliminary results might apply only to Cache la Poudre (Colorado) deer.

Although statistical work on herd composition sampling has been very limited to date, one general conclusion can be drawn. If buck-doe and fawn-doe ratios are to be estimated with comparable precision, much more sampling will be required for the buck-doe ratio. Put another way, a classification of any given number of deer will estimate the fawn-doe ratio more precisely than the buck-doe ratio. Fawn-adult ratios may be even less variable than fawn-doe ratios.

Interpretation of Herd Composition Ratios

Despite sampling problems and biases inherent in herd composition data, fawn-adult or fawn-doe ratios observed in autumn or spring are widely used indexes of fawn production and survival. In the Boundary deer herd of British Columbia, for example, "good" survival is considered to have occurred if the spring population contains 35–45 percent fawns (54–82 fawns per 100 adults). A spring ratio below 33 fawns per 100 adults connotes low fawn survival (Spalding 1968). Several studies have shown a relationship between fawn-doe ratios and trends in deer numbers, as discussed in chapter 6. Low ratios were characteristic of declining herds in California (MacGregor 1976; Salwasser 1976), Oregon (Ebert 1976), eastern Montana (Mackie 1976b), Texas (Brownlee 1975), and elsewhere.

Some biologists estimate fawn mortality from changes over time in fawn-doe ratios, assuming that drops in observed ratios result solely from fawn mortality. On Steens Mountain, Oregon, for example, herd classifications in August 1977, December 1977, and March 1978 showed ratios of 99, 53, and 32 fawns per 100 does. From these data, Trainer et al. (1978b) estimated fawn mortality at 46.5 percent ([99 − 53]/99) between August and December 1977, and 39.6 percent ([53 − 32]/53) between December 1977 and March 1978. The estimated birthrate in June 1977, adjusted to allow for nonbreeding fawns that became yearling does in June, was 136 fetuses per 100 does. Since only 32 fawns per 100 does remained by March 1978, it was concluded that 77 [*sic*] percent ([136 − 32]/136) of the fawns born in 1977 were lost in the first ten months of life. These herd composition studies were paralleled by radiotelemetry observations of instrumented fawns, which indicated an almost identical rate of fawn loss (McInnis et al. 1978). Nevertheless, such calculations from herd composition data underestimate the fawn mortality rate if any does are lost between the counts.

The relationships between herd composition ratios and mortality can be seen best in populations for which both herd count ratios and seasonal estimates of deer numbers are available. One such population of black-tailed deer on the Hopland Field Station (California) showed average ratios of 67 fawns per 100 does in October and 48 per 100 in April during 1964–66. Following the rationale of Trainer et al. (1978*b*), the average fawn loss between October and April would have been about 28 percent ([67−48]/67). Estimates of actual numbers, however, indicated that does declined from 300 to 270 between October and April, or 10 percent, while fawn numbers dropped from 200 in October to 130 in April, or 35 percent (Connolly 1970; F. M. Anderson et al. 1974). These results illustrate that the actual fawn mortality rate exceeds that indicated by seasonal declines in fawn-doe ratios if both fawns and does die, as is usually, if not always, true of mule and black-tailed deer populations during winter. An overwinter drop in the fawn-doe ratio indicates only that fawns died at a higher rate than does. From changes in herd composition ratios, however, it would have been correct to conclude that overwinter fawn mortality at Hopland Field Station exceeded 28 percent, or that on Steens Mountain at least 76 percent of the fawns were lost between birth and 10 months of age. Such conclusions, of course, assume that birthrate and herd composition ratios were accurately estimated.

Despite widespread use of herd classifications as indexes of fawn production and survival, at least one biologist has questioned the utility of age ratios. Caughley (1974*a*, p. 557) noted that most papers on wildlife populations provide age ratios but fail to interpret them: "One's curiosity over why these data were collected or what they reveal about the population is usually left unsatisfied by the author. Occasionally he confides that the reported ratio indicates that the population is in good heart, or that the ratio gives cause for concern, but never have I seen spelled out the logical steps by which these judgements are reached." Caughley pointed out that a sudden rise or fall in mortality rate that affects all age classes equally has no effect on age ratio; and, even when the ratio responds to a change in rate of increase, there are circumstances in which its trend is the same for two populations, one of which is erupting and the other plunging to extinction. These facts, based on computer simulations rather than on field observations, suggested to Caughley that age ratios may provide ambiguous information and that their facile interpretation can lead to serious management blunders. He concluded that age ratios cannot be interpreted without a knowledge of the rate of increase, but if the rate of increase is known, age ratios become superfluous.

This challenge of such a widely used practice might have been expected to provoke a response from management practitioners. Instead, herd counting has proceeded as usual, with no indication that wildlife managers anywhere in western North America have reevaluated their basic assumptions or, indeed, have even been aware of Caughley's views. In retrospect, it seems that the points raised by Caughley do not necessarily invalidate the use of age ratios in deer management. He showed that massive increases or decreases in numbers could occur without change in age ratios if changes in survival rates were equal for all age classes, and also that the juvenile-adult ratio could rise while the population declined if the decline resulted from lowered survival among mature animals. However, these conditions have not been demonstrated in blacktail or mule deer populations. There is no documented example of a decline or die-off in which the relationship among adult and fawn mortality rates remained constant. Under normal conditions, fawns have a higher rate of mortality than do adults; the disparity between fawn and adult mortality rates increases with adversity, whereas under the best environmental conditions, fawn mortality rate may approximate that of adults. Therefore it seems that fawn-adult ratios should be higher in increasing populations than in decreasing ones under conditions prevailing on mule and black-tailed deer ranges.

A number of studies cited earlier have shown this to be the case.

PRODUCTIVITY AND RATE OF INCREASE

Definitions of Productivity

In wildlife ecology, the word "productivity" refers to reproduction and early survivorship in relation to the breeding stock or population. Many different measures and definitions of productivity appear in the literature on deer management. Productivity was defined by Leopold (1933) as the rate at which mature breeding stock produces other mature stock, or mature removable crop. In keeping with the first part of this definition, later workers defined productivity as the ratio of animals reaching adulthood to the mature animals in the herd or, in other words, the ratio of sub-adult to adult animals (Swank 1958; Hanson 1963). This definition is especially useful to deer managers because it translates to the fawn-adult ratio in late winter as measured by herd composition counts; in many states and provinces, herd count data are used in this way. Various workers also have found it feasible to determine productivity (the ratio of subadults to adults) from the ratio of yearlings to older deer in the hunting kill, or by dividing the fawn-doe ratio in half (Kelker 1947; Leopold et al. 1951; Richens 1967). In some cases the resulting values have been incorrectly described as net increase or rate of increase. Distinction between productivity and rate of increase is discussed later.

Examples of Productivity Measures

Aldo Leopold's (1933) definition of productivity implies at least two concepts: augmentation or replacement of breeding stock, and allowable harvest. Other views of productivity also have arisen. A few productivity measures are illustrated in table 33.

Productivity may be expressed as the ratio of yearlings to older deer, as noted previously. In table 33, productivity measures 1–5 were calculated from various age ratios according to procedures taken from the literature. Computed values range from 0.27 to 0.55. There is little basis for deciding which may be most nearly correct, because all are abstract measures having little value in management. They indicate neither the trend in deer numbers nor actual or potential harvest. Age ratios, as an indicator of fawn survival, already have been discussed in the section "Herd Composition Counts." No new information is gained by changing the name from "fawn-adult ratio" to "productivity."

In table 33, the reader will notice that the proportion of yearlings in the doe kill (0.27) was much different from that in the buck kill (0.52). Such difference would be expected whenever life expectancy differs between bucks and does, and it creates a dilemma for those who would measure productivity as the percentage of yearlings in the hunting kill. For the deer herd at Oak Creek, which of these values (0.27 or 0.52) is the correct estimate of productivity? Actually, the most valuable information in these statistics is that the turnover rate of bucks was higher than that of does.

Productivity might be defined as the allowable kill, expressed as a percentage of the base herd. There are two problems with this concept. First, there is no consensus on what constitutes the base herd. Some define it as the population present at start of hunting season, others as the number surviving winter, and still others use the postfawning or posthunt values. Second, the allowable harvest—in the sense of "the ratio or percent which can be removed yearly without diminishing the capital" (Leopold 1933, p. 71)—cannot be determined except by experimentation with variable harvest rates in populations whose sizes can be monitored annually. (Computer simulation models can be used for this purpose, as discussed later in this chapter.) All that can be done with most deer populations is to estimate actual harvest and, from observed responses of the population, infer whether maximum or optimum allowable kill might be higher or lower.

Table 33. Population Statistics and Productivity Measures for Mule Deer at Oak Creek, Utah

Population statistics[a]

A. Percentage fawns in late winter population	35.4
B. Percentage adults in late winter population	64.6
C. Percentage fawns in posthunt population	38.0
D. Percentage does in posthunt population	50.8
E. Estimated buck kill (including yearlings)	245
F. Percentage yearlings in buck kill	52.0
G. Estimated doe kill (including yearlings)	149
H. Percentage yearlings in doe kill	27.0
I. Minimum (postwinter, prefawning) number of deer	2,053
J. Maximum (postfawning) number of deer (I + P)	3,444
K. Average posthunt number of deer	2,198
L. Legal hunting kill (E + G + fawns)	445
M. Crippling loss and illegal kill	202
N. Range area	137 km² (53 mi²)
O. Average dressed carcass weight	32.1 kg (70.8 lb)
P. Number of fawns born annually	1,391
Q. Average legal kill from each fawn cohort	442
R. Population size, 1947 (posthunt)	2.706
S. Population size, 1956 (posthunt)	2,274

Productivity measures

1. Fawns per adult in late winter (A/B)	0.55
2. One-half of fawns per doe in autumn (posthunt) ((C/D)/2)	0.37
3. Proportion of yearlings in buck kill (F)	0.52
4. Proportion of yearlings in doe kill (H)	0.27
5. Proportion of yearlings in adult hunting kill (((E × F) + (H × G))/(E + G))	0.43
6. Legal kill as fraction of minimum (prefawning) population (L / I)	0.22
7. Legal kill as fraction of maximum (postfawning) population (L / J)	0.13
8. Legal kill as fraction of posthunt population (L / K)	0.20
9. Total hunting kill as fraction of posthunt population ((L + M)/K)	0.29
10. Legal hunting kill in deer per unit area (L / N)	3.2 per km² (8.4 per mi²)
11. Legal hunting kill in biomass per unit area ((L × O)/N)	104 kg per km² (594 lbs per mi²)
12. Proportion of each fawn cohort taken by hunters (Q / P)	0.32
13. Annual rate of population turnover, assuming population was stable ((J − I)/J)	0.40
14. Net increase, 1947–56 ((S − R)/R)	−0.160 or −16.0 percent
15. Average annual rate of increase, 1947–56 ((S/R)$^{1/9}$)	0.98086[b]
16. Rate of increase as an interest value compounded annually (((S/R)$^{1/9}$) − 1)	−0.01914 or −1.914 percent

Source: Values shown were either given by Robinette et al. (1977) or calculated from their data.
[a] Unless otherwise indicated, each value is the annual average, 1947 through 1956.
[b] Rate of increase is not a productivity measure, but it is included here for purposes of comparison.

Productivity measures 6–11 are expressions of the actual harvest recorded at Oak Creek, Utah (table 33). Measures 6–8 illustrate variations that result when a given harvest is expressed as a proportion of different base herds. There is little theoretical advantage to one percentage base over another, but Robinette et al. (1977) pointed out that better estimates of deer numbers could be made at some seasons of the year than at others. In Oak Creek, the posthunt estimate was considered to be most reliable and therefore the posthunt population was preferred as the base herd. The most important consideration is that the base must be the same when harvest percentages from different herds are being compared.

Crippling losses usually are not considered part of the hunter harvest, since these animals are unretrieved rather than bagged. In terms of population dynamics, however, deer that are illegally killed or crippled and lost are removed from the population just as effectively as if hunters had taken them legally. To evaluate fully the impact of hunting on the population, crippling losses and illegal kills must be considered as hunting mortality. In Oak Creek, estimated crippling loss and illegal kill amounted to 45 percent of the legal harvest. Thus, the legal hunting kill equaled 20 percent of the posthunt population, but total legal and illegal shooting mortality was 29 percent (table 33, productivity measures 8–9).

Hunter harvests sometimes are expressed in terms of animals or biomass per unit of range area. Biomass estimates are particularly useful for comparisons with livestock production from ranges occupied jointly by deer and domestic livestock. In Oak Creek, the annual harvest averaged 3.2 deer or 104 kilograms of meat per square kilometer (8.4 deer or 594 pounds of deer meat per square mile of range).

Robinette et al. (1977) pointed out that productivity could be defined as the percentage of the fawns born that ultimately is harvested by hunters. Estimation of this quantity requires not only annual estimates of numbers of births, but also serial records of the annual kill from each cohort. The average value of this statistic in Oak Creek was 32 percent (table 33, productivity measure 12).

Yet another possible expression of productivity is annual turnover rate (table 33, measure 13). This rate generally might be expected to increase with harvest percentage, even though by definition it includes mortality from all causes. Annual turnover rate is most meaningful in stable populations; that is, herds in which numbers of births and deaths are equal. Management implications of this rate cannot be assessed without information on the various causes of mortality.

Net increase and rate of increase are not measures of productivity, but they are included in table 33 (measures 14–16) for purposes of comparison. The deer herd at Oak Creek was quite stable and had a negligible rate of increase from 1947 to 1956, yet it was very productive in terms of hunter harvest.

The word "productivity" has so many possible meanings that it cannot be considered to describe any specific deer population statistic. If "productivity" means the ratio of yearlings to adults, this definition must be given, and the word "productivity" then becomes superfluous.

Rates of Increase

Rates of increase express changes in absolute numbers over time. Three such rates are shown in table 33 (measures 14 through 16) for the Oak Creek deer herd. The net increase from 1947 to 1956 was −16.0 percent; in other words, the population decreased 16 percent during this nine-year interval. (Actually, the Oak Creek herd appeared very stable during these years. The 1947 estimate was substantially higher than that for any other year and is purposely taken out of context here to illustrate computation of rates of increase.) One might think the net increase of −16.0 percent in nine years could be divided by nine to obtain −1.778 as the annual rate of change. However, the reader may verify that reducing the 1947 estimate by 1.778 percent annually for nine years will not yield the 1956 estimate. Instead, it is necessary to resort to geometric formulas, as used by Kelker (1947), to determine annual rate of increase. This rate, r, may be found from the relationship $P_2 P_1(r)^t$ in which P_1 is the population size at time 1, P_2 is the population size at time 2, and the exponent t is the number of years between time 1 and time 2. In table 33 (measure 15), $P_1 = 2{,}706$ deer, $P_2 = 2{,}274$ deer, and $t =$ nine years. The rate of increase r is equal to the ninth root of (P_2/P_1). If one desires to express rate of increase in a form analagous to interest rates used by bankers, this expression (table 33, measure 16) is equal to $r - 1$. The chief advantage of the latter statistic is that it is negative for decreasing populations and positive for increasing ones, and therefore it expresses trends in readily comprehensible form.

These calculations may seem complex to persons unfamiliar with compound-interest calculations, but they are easily performed on any electronic calculator that has exponential functions, or with paper and pencil if logarithm tables are available.

One can see that the rate of increase in stable populations is 1.00, while in increasing herds it is larger than 1.00. The rate of 0.98086 at Oak Creek means that this herd was declining at a rate of 1.914 percent per year, compounded annually. This is an extremely low rate of decline, and for all practical purposes the population was stable. The point to be made here is that rate of increase in the Oak Creek deer herd was very low, yet the herd produced many deer and had a high rate of turnover.

In my opinion, the rate of increase is more useful to wildlife managers than any productivity measure because it tells whether a population is increasing, decreasing, or stable. Unfortunately, the annual population estimates needed to determine rate of increase often are not available.

The Difference between "Rate of Increase" and "Productivity"

One point of confusion in the deer literature over the past thirty years or so is that the terms "rate of increase," "net increase," or "annual

increase" sometimes were used in ways that were misleading or incorrect. Of the Jawbone deer herd in California, for example, one can read that "the yearly fawn crop successfully raised and led to the winter range was enough to account for an annual 32 percent increase in the herd" (Leopold et al. 1951, p. 61), but elsewhere the same report states that the number of deer declined from 7,000 in 1947 to 6,000 in 1950. Actually, then, the rate of increase was −5 percent per year (computed as in table 33). The 32 percent figure was the fawn production thought to have been necessary to compensate for estimated losses during the last two years of the study.

Even though "productivity" is a general concept, many deer managers and biologists have used the word to describe specific statistics of deer populations. Several examples were illustrated in table 33. The statistic most often defined as "productivity" is the ratio of subadults to adults in a population (Swank 1958; Hanson 1963). This same statistic is sometimes called "annual increase" or "rate of increase." But, if productivity is the ratio of subadults to adults, and rate of increase describes changes over time in population size, the two expressions should not be used synonymously. Rate of increase reflects either increase or decrease in deer numbers, depending on whether the herd is increasing or decreasing, though increasing herds generally would be expected to exhibit higher yearling-adult ratios than decreasing ones. (This subject was addressed in the section "Herd Composition Counts," above.) In any event, the proportion of subadults in the spring population cannot equal the rate of increase except in special circumstances. A productive herd might have a high or low rate of increase depending on what happens to the production. In a stable herd the rate of increase would be 1.00, regardless of the rate of hunter harvest.

Some of the confusion between rate of increase and yearling-adult population ratios may have resulted from Kelker's (1947) theoretical work on rate of increase in deer. He showed that white-tailed deer on the George Reserve in Michigan increased for six years at an average annual rate of 1.651, and he theorized that the annual rate of fawn survival per doe was twice the interest rate of 65.1 percent compounded annually, or 1.302 fawns per doe. This relationship assumed a 50:50 sex ratio among adult deer and was not checked against fawn-doe ratios in the field. Nevertheless, Kelker proposed that wildlife workers could convert annual rate of increase into the number of fawns per doe existing in winter herds. This rule of thumb was widely adopted but was reversed in practice, with fawn-doe ratios measured as an indicator of rate of increase. Wide application of this concept without critical reexamination is hard to understand in light of Kelker's statement that the relationship applied only to increasing populations. It is now clear that the simplistic assumptions involved in this practice rarely are met in blacktail or mule deer populations, and therefore the practice of describing age ratios as rates of increase should be discontinued.

MORTALITY

Fawn Mortality

In nearly all blacktail and mule deer populations, the mortality rate of fawns is greater than that of adults. Poor fawn survival was identified as a common feature of declining mule deer populations in many states during the early 1970s, as was discussed in chapter 6. But, among stable or even increasing herds, poor fawn survival is commonplace. Deer numbers at Oak Creek, Utah, for example, were stable from 1947 to 1956 even though the annual either-sex hunting kill (including crippling losses) equaled 29 percent of the posthunt population. Fawn mortality in this herd averaged 48 percent per year—33 percent natural losses in summer, 7 percent hunting mortality, and 8 percent natural losses during winter. Even higher fawn losses were reported from an unhunted blacktail population in the Tillamook Burn, Oregon: 70 percent were lost between birth and 12 months of age (Hines 1975). A similarly high rate of fawn mortality was reported from Mendocino County, California, where only bucks were hunted (F. M. Anderson et al. 1974).

Many more examples could be offered to show that high fawn losses were common in mule and blacktail deer herds in the 1960s and early 1970s, in both hunted and unhunted herds. One of few recent documented examples of low fawn mortality comes from the National Bison Range, Montana, where 58 percent of the adult mule deer were cropped annually to keep deer numbers within prescribed limits. The observed herd composition ratio of 1.43 fawns per doe in autumn was only 5 percent below the

Unless deer are found soon after they die, biologists often can only speculate about the cause of death. This month-old blacktail fawn had been dead about a week before it was examined by research workers at the Hopland Field Station in northern California. Because the carcass was not dismembered and had no broken bones, death was attributed to some natural cause other than predation. Photograph by Guy E. Connolly.

fetal rate of 1.50 fawns per doe, indicating very low postnatal fawn mortality (Nellis 1968). Since Nellis' study, however, fawn production or survival, or both, has decreased in this population, and the high rate of harvest has not been needed to limit deer numbers. From 1972 through 1975, the population stayed within desired limits even though few deer were shot. This herd was discussed further in chapter 7.

In many deer herds there appears to be substantial loss of fawns soon after birth. Such loss is extraordinarily hard to measure. Carcasses often cannot be found, so the magnitude of early fawn losses must be determined by indirect means. Robinette et al. (1977) defined early fawn mortality as that between birth and the hunting season, when surviving fawns were 4 to 5 months old. These workers used three methods to appraise early fawn mortality: (1) comparison of estimated fawn-doe ratio at birth with the ratio observed in mid-September classification counts (correction was made for nonproductive yearlings); (2) comparison of estimated numbers of fawns at birth and in the prehunt population; and (3) prehunt carcass survey using line transect methods.

Best results, from the second method, showed an average prehunt loss of 32 percent of the fawns born. Estimates for different years ranged between 11 and 45 percent. More than half of this prehunt fawn loss occurred in the first week after birth. Mortality of fawns from birth until the hunt was a major herd drain, equaling the legal kill of all deer (Robinette et al. 1977).

Study of a confined, unhunted blacktail population in the Tillamook Burn, Oregon, also showed high fawn loss soon after birth (Hines 1975). The proportion of summer fawn loss occurring within a week after birth ranged from 71 percent after severe winters down to 29 percent under more mild conditions.

Fawn Mortality Related to Litter Size

It stands to reason that fawn mortality would increase with litter size, because birth weights and presumably energy reserves tend to decrease as the number of fawns per litter increases. This premise has received little study, but it has been verified in one mule deer herd. At Oak Creek, Utah, Robinette et al. (1977) found that tag returns from fawns marked soon after birth were 33.5 percent for single fawns, 26.7 percent for twins, and 9 percent for triplets. Twin litters were most prevalent and produced the greatest number of survivors, even though a greater percentage of twins than of single fawns was lost.

Mortality of Older Fawns and Adult Deer

Mortality among adult deer and fawns during their first winter can be estimated in several ways.

1. Calculation of numbers of deer present in various sex and age classes at different seasons, such as autumn and spring, with mortality inferred from differences between seasonal estimates. For example, a blacktail herd in California contained an estimated 100 bucks, 300 does, and 200 fawns in October. Through natural mortality and other causes, the population decreased during the winter so that in April an estimated 80 bucks, 270 does, and 130 fawns were left. These figures imply that, on the average, 20 percent of the bucks, 10 percent of the does, and 35 percent of the fawns present in October died before April (Connolly 1970). Similar population estimates were available for the months of May and July. Assuming that the population was stable, annual mortality rates for bucks, does, and fawns, respectively, were 47, 18, and 50 percent. The annual turnover rate for this herd was 37 percent. The feasibility of calculating mortality from such population estimates depends entirely on the quality of the estimates.

2. Calculation from life tables, which usually are derived from age composition of hunting kill (see table 37 and the section "Population Analysis and Modeling," below).

3. Direct estimation from the number of carcasses found in systematic searches, usually

by means of strip censuses or line transects. A common procedure is for persons on foot or on horseback to travel across country on pre-determined compass bearings. Each observer watches the ground on both sides of the line of travel as well as in front. When he spots a carcass, he measures either the right-angle distance from the line of travel to the carcass or the actual sighting distance from observer to carcass, depending on the method. Total number of carcasses on an area can be calculated from mean sighting distance or mean perpendicular distance, number of carcasses seen, length of transect lines, and size of area censused.

Whether actual sighting distances or right-angle distances from line of travel are to be used depends on the formula chosen by the investigator. Robinette et al. (1974) evaluated ten strip census methods and recommended two methods based on perpendicular or right-angle distance for level, open ground. In rough terrain where compass line courses were difficult to follow, however, methods based on sighting distance were more practical. Four such methods were evaluated, and best results were achieved with the King procedure. The King formula is $N = (nA)/(2L\bar{R})$, where N = total estimated number of carcasses, n = number of carcasses seen, A = area to be censused, L = length of census line, and $\bar{R}$ = mean sighting distance.

As an example of the King method, consider a 259 hectare (640 acre) area on which 31.5 carcasses were sighted in 97 kilometers (60 miles) of census lines. If the mean sighting distance was 11.70 meters (38.39 feet), the estimated number of carcasses (N) was $(31.5 \times 27,878,400)/(2 \times 316,800 \times 38.39)$, or 36.1 carcasses. Note that the same unit of measure must be used throughout; in this example, area was expressed in square feet and distances were expressed in linear feet.

In the above example, drawn from Robinette et al. (1974), the true number of carcasses was 38.4. The reader is referred to that paper for other examples of the King procedure, as well as for comparisons of the King method with other strip census procedures.

Perhaps the largest single body of published line transect data related to deer mortality is that of Robinette et al. (1977), who recorded 907 carcasses along 4,535 kilometers (2,818 miles) of transect lines in a twelve-year study at Oak Creek, Utah. Summer deaths were distinguished from winter deaths on the basis of hair color (red in summer; gray in winter). Mean sighting distance for fawn carcasses was 81–84 percent of that for adults. This study concluded that line transects yielded reasonable estimates of adult mortality but underestimated early fawn mortality. The latter result was attributed to sampling variations or obliteration of some fawn carcasses by predators or scavengers.

Although Robinette et al. (1977) preferred the King procedure for estimating the density of deer carcasses, other investigators have found this method to possess an inherent negative bias related to angle of observation. For this reason, Welch (1974) and Kovner and Patil (1974) preferred the Gates et al. (1968) estimator, which is said to be "unbiased."

The formula for the Gates et al. (1968) procedure may be given as $N = [(n-1)A]/(2L\bar{Y})$, where $\bar{Y}$ = mean perpendicular distance, and the other quantities are as previously defined for the King method. If this equation is applied to the previously cited example from Robinette et al. (1974), in which the mean perpendicular distance was 6.72 meters (22.06 feet), the estimated number of carcasses(N) equals (30.5 × 27,878,400) / 2 × 316,800 × 22.06), or 60.8. Unbiased or not, this is a substantial overestimate compared with the true number of carcasses (38.4). The result obtained with the King procedure was 36.1 carcasses.

It is not possible to review line transect methods in detail here. Anyone considering the use of such methods should consult the literature before proceeding. When it is not clear which method may be best, the safest practice may be to record the data in such a manner that they can be evaluated by several line transect procedures. For this purpose, the comparisons of Robinette et al. (1974) will be especially useful.

Although line transects are the predominant tool for direct estimates of deer mortality, it sometimes is possible to determine density of carcasses by other means. In western Washington, for example, Brown (1961) reported that forestry crews discovered 26 carcasses of winter-killed deer while planting trees on 635 hectares (1,570 acres). This recorded loss of 4.1 deer per square kilometer (10.6 per square mile) equaled 29 percent of the estimated autumn population.

SEX DIFFERENTIAL MORTALITY

In nearly all blacktail and mule deer herds, there are many more does than bucks. This could result from at least four possible causes: an unbalanced sex ratio at birth; sex-differential mortality among fawns; selective hunting of bucks; or sex-differential mortality among adults.

Unbalanced Sex Ratio at Birth

It already has been shown that sex ratio at birth varies with the age and nutritional state of the doe during pregnancy (see "Reproduction: Fetal Sex Ratios," above). The proportion of females at birth increases with the level of nutrition. But it seems that, on the average, the sex ratio at birth is unbalanced in favor of males. Among black-tailed deer in western Washington, for example, the sex ratio among embryos was 128 males:100 females (Brown 1961). Records for 2,299 blacktail and mule deer fetuses from six states gave a male-female ratio of 111:100 (Robinette et al. 1957a).

If males predominate at birth, this unbalanced sex ratio obviously cannot account for the observed preponderance of females among adult deer. Males must suffer proportionately heavier mortality between birth and adulthood.

Sex Differential Losses among Fawns

Several researchers have theorized that poor nutrition accentuates mortality among male fawns (Taber and Dasmann 1954; Klein 1965),

and it is widely believed that male fawns have a higher mortality rate than do females. As evidence of this, Brown (1961) showed that the sex ratio among black-tailed deer embryos was 128 males:100 females, but the ratio among fawns caught for tagging was only 112:100. Brown suggested that disproportionate losses of male fawns immediately after birth caused the disparity between these two ratios. In a computer simulation study of black-tailed deer, F. M. Anderson et al. (1974) found it necessary to assume that 40 percent of the deer that reached 12 months of age were males. When a 50:50 sex ratio was tried in the model, the simulation results showed a higher buck-doe ratio than actually existed in the population. But, with a yearling sex ratio of 40 males:60 females, simulated buck-doe ratios agreed with field data.

Although there is good reason to suspect proportionately greater mortality of male fawns in many deer herds, not all the evidence points in this direction. In an unhunted population of black-tailed deer in Oregon, no sex-differential mortality occurred until the deer were approximately 20 months old. The male-female ratio at birth was 103:100; at one year of age, it was 106:100. During their second winter, however, 38 percent of the males and only 8 percent of the females died. The result was an unbalanced sex ratio that favored does among deer 2 years old and older (Hines 1975).

The largest published body of data on sex ratios of mule deer fetuses and fawns failed to show conclusively that differential losses of male fawns occurred. Observed sex ratio of 2,299 fetuses was 111 males:100 females. The male-female ratio for 808 newborn fawns was 121:100; and among 13,046 fawns killed by hunters, it was 114:100 (Robinette et al. 1957a). In later work, however, Robinette et al. (1977) found that the sex ratio among fawns in the reported hunting kill probably was not representative of the population. The number of fawns shot and abandoned by hunters at Oak Creek, Utah, was nearly equal to the number taken out, and there was reason to believe that males were more likely to be kept than females. From other calculations, the prehunt sex ratio among fawns at Oak Creek was found to be 87 males per 100 females. Thus it was concluded that proportionately more male than female fawns died.

As is discussed later in this chapter (see "Change-in-Ratio Estimates") the average sex ratio among yearling black-tailed deer at Hopland Field Station (California) for a five-year period was estimated to be 83 males per 100 females. The average fetal sex ratio for the same five fawn cohorts was 104 males per 100 females (Longhurst and Connolly, n.d.). In this population, therefore, it appears that males suffered greater mortality than females during their first twelve months of life. Every study of this subject in mule or black-tailed deer has shown a sex-differential loss of males in either their first or second year of life.

Selective Hunting of Males

Buck-doe ratios in mule and black-tailed deer populations appear to vary inversely with hunting pressure, especially when only bucks are hunted (Leopold et al. 1951). Computer simulation has verified this. The model of F. M. Anderson et al. (1974) showed that an annual kill of 25 percent of the legal bucks (forked-horn or better) would result in an average ratio of 18 legal bucks per 100 does in the posthunt population. With no hunting, the ratio was 48 legal bucks per 100 does; but, when 50 percent of the legal bucks were shot annually, the ratio was only 9:100. Therefore it seems that selective buck hunting causes lower buck-doe ratios than would be found in the absence of hunting. However, even unhunted populations usually exhibit unbalanced sex ratios. For additional discussion of this subject, see "Effects of Hunting on Herd Composition" in chapter 7.

Sex Differential Mortality among Adult Deer

In addition to selective buck hunting, other sex-differential losses among adult deer seem to occur. Throughout their lives, bucks apparently have a higher mortality rate than do does. Bucks are said to have greater growth requirements when young, greater activity, and therefore greater propensity for accidents. Bucks draw heavily on their fat reserves during the rut, causing them to enter the winter in poor condition and thus contributing to their higher mortality rate (Taber and Dasmann 1954). Does, by contrast, experience greatest nutritional demands during spring and early summer, when forage quality is at its peak. Because of these differences between sexes, Klein (1969) generalized that the poorer the feed, the lower the buck-doe ratio.

DETERMINING THE HARVEST

Of all deer population statistics, annual harvest is perhaps most important to wildlife managers. It may no longer be fashionable to equate management effectiveness with the number of animals killed, but the harvest each year is an important consideration in setting regulations for the following year. Therefore, in most western states, a concerted effort is made to measure harvests.

If the number of deer killed each year is important information, one may ask why states do not require mandatory kill reports from hunters. The answer is that mandatory reports have proved unworkable. California, in theory, requires each deer to be "validated"; that is, the tag must be countersigned by a game warden, deputy sheriff, forest ranger, or other authority, and the attached postcard is to be mailed promptly to the Fish and Game Department. In fact, however, only about half the bucks killed are so reported (MacGregor 1976).

South Dakota also distributes hunters' report cards with deer licenses. The completed cards are to be returned to the Department of Game, Fish, and Parks no more than ten days after the end of the hunting season. The reporting rate ranges between one-third and two-thirds of the licensed hunters. Through follow-up contacts in 1972, it was determined that nonreporting hunters in East River and

West River districts were 70–75 percent as successful as hunters who returned their cards. Using this correction factor, it was possible to calculate actual hunting success (Richardson and Petersen 1974).

Because mandatory tag returns fail to provide a complete tally of the hunting kill, most mule deer states collect this information through mail surveys (Aney 1974). Mail surveys are subject to two sources of bias: response bias, introduced by respondents who incorrectly report their hunting activity; and nonresponse bias, or differences in hunting activity and success between those who respond to mail questionnaires and those who do not. It is possible to measure the extent of such biases and make corrections for them. Thus, in a three-year survey of New Mexico deer hunters whose performance was known, the net error in estimating total deer harvest was 7.6 percent; 9.1 percent of the unsuccessful hunters reported a kill, while 4.5 percent of the successful hunters reported no kill. A significant nonresponse bias, toward overestimation, was found for resident big game hunters. With appropriate corrections, mail surveys can provide reasonable estimates of total deer harvest (MacDonald and Dillman 1968).

Although mail surveys are the predominant tool for measuring harvests of mule and black-tailed deer, several other methods are used as well. Most states issue report forms with the tags or hunting licenses. Check stations are found in selected areas of most states; Nebraska has a compulsory check station system. In addition to information collected on the kill, hunting pressure, and hunter success, check stations have public relations value in that they allow professional employees of state wildlife agencies to make many personal contacts in a short time. Feedback from hunters can be particularly valuable when major changes in hunting regulations have been made or are contemplated.

Hunter check stations give wildlife managers opportunities to make personal contacts with many hunters in a short time and also to collect information needed to manage future deer harvests. Most check stations are for data collection rather than law enforcement. Photograph by Stu Murrell; courtesy of the Idaho Department of Fish and Game.

The main objective of mail surveys and other hunter checks is to determine the number of deer killed, but other kinds of information usually are gathered at the same time. The ratio of successful to unsuccessful hunters, sex and age composition of the kill, distribution of hunting pressure, and harvest by management areas all have application in management. For a discussion of these measures, see Hunter and Yeager (1956).

To compare the effects of hunting in different herds, it is useful to express the harvest as a percentage of the deer population. This normally requires separate estimates of population size and hunter harvest. In Washington, hunter kill is used as a direct indicator of population size. Buck harvest there is believed to be the best available measure of deer numbers; it is assumed that there are approximately 10 deer in the population for every buck harvested (Parsons 1976) or, in other words, that the buck kill each year equals 10 percent of the posthunt population. That assumption was put forward by Lauckhart (1950), who prepared a graph to estimate the number of deer left per buck killed. The graph showed that the posthunt population could contain 7–20 deer for each buck killed, depending on the fawn-doe and buck-doe ratios. Anyone looking back at this work will find it hard to interpret because the X-axis on the graph is not labeled. Lauckhart's concepts have received limited use outside the state of Washington, possibly because of the simplistic assumptions involved. Yet it is well to remember that all estimation methods contain assumptions that often are violated. Lauckhart's model is well worth using when data limitations preclude more sophisticated calculations.

Another way to evaluate hunter harvest is to express it as a percentage of a herd's annual increase. The Kaibab North deer herd in Arizona, for example, contained an estimated 958 yearling bucks in 1955, and the buck kill that year was 1,086. Therefore, it was calculated that hunters removed 113 percent ([1,086/958] × 100) of the annual increase to the buck population in that year (Swank 1958). In this case, use of the term "annual increase" is misleading; it implies an increase when, in fact, the estimated number of bucks decreased 63 percent from 1954 to 1955. Nevertheless, it would be desirable to express hunting kill as a fraction of allowable harvest wherever possible.

CRIPPLING LOSS AND ILLEGAL KILL

Some biologists define "crippling loss" to include both the wounding loss of legal game and illegal kills during hunting season. Others make a distinction between crippling loss and illegal kill, as follows. Crippling or wounding loss consists of legally shot animals that are not recovered and subsequently die of those wounds. Illegal kills include deer that are shot outside the legal hunting season; illegal deer shot during hunting season; and legal deer shot during hunting season but not tagged. The latter category includes both untagged deer that are taken out and deer abandoned in the field by hunters who hope to bag more desirable animals. Tagging consists of affixing hunter identification to the carcass; a paper or metal identification tag accompanies the hunting license in most North American states and provinces.

At check stations, hunters frequently are queried about cripples lost or illegal kills witnessed. Most hunters will volunteer information about crippling losses but not about illegal kills, unless the guilty party is someone else. Because those responsible for illegal kills usually avoid detection, it is hard to measure the extent of mortality due to this cause. Few, if any, real estimates of out-of-season kill exist, but a number of estimates have been made of both crippling loss and illegal kills during hunting season.

Crippling Loss and Illegal Kill during Hunting Season

At least five published studies of crippling loss and illegal kill of mule deer have depended on intensive ground searches to locate deer carcasses and paunches or entrails. In each study, entrails or paunches were believed to represent legally killed deer, while carcasses were tallied as illegal kills or cripples. One project attempted complete coverage of 2,036 hectares (5,030 acres) with large crews of men (Costley 1948), but the others used strip census or line-transect sampling methods to estimate carcass density. Line transect procedures already have been described (see "Mortality"), so the present discussion is limited to line transect surveys aimed specifically at estimating crippling loss and illegal kill.

In each of the four line-transect surveys, visibility of deer carcasses differed from that of entrails. Average sighting distance for dead deer ranged from 0.91 (Welch 1974) to 2.95 (Stapley 1971) times as far as that for entrails. On two areas surveyed in Utah, mean sighting distance for carcasses was 1.81 and 2.02 times that for entrails (Robinette et al. 1977). In addition to the differential visibility of deer carcasses and paunches, it might seem that whole carcasses would persist on the range longer than entrails, especially where scavengers are abundant. If some entrails were oblit-erated before surveys took place, the results would tend to inflate estimates of illegal kills. Costley (1948) and Welch (1974) recognized the possibility of this bias but did not believe it occurred in their studies. Robinette (pers. comm., December 1978) found no indication that paunches were obliterated. Stapley (1971) recognized that such an error may have occurred and concluded that, for this reason, his survey may have overestimated the true losses. However, Stapley's estimates were lower than all the others.

The five intensive field surveys yielded estimates of crippling loss and illegal kill ranging from 8 to 92 percent of the legal kill (table 34). Three of these studies compared losses in buck-only hunts and any-deer hunts, and all three showed much lower losses in the any-deer hunts. However, the highest crippling and illegal loss was reported from an area where some hunters had any-deer permits and others had buck-only permits.

Two surveys attempted to differentiate between genuine cripple losses and illegal kills. Stapley (1971) found the illegal kill to be more

Table 34. Estimates of Crippling Loss and Illegal Kill in Mule and Black-tailed Deer Herds

Subspecies	Study Area	Type of Hunt	Illegal Kill and Cripple Loss as Percentage of Legal Harvest	Reference
Mule deer	Utah	Bucks only	26[a]	Stapley (1971)
	Utah	Any deer	8[a]	Stapley (1971)
	Utah	Bucks only	72[a]	Costley (1948)
	Utah	Any deer	33[a]	Costley (1948)
	Oak Creek, Utah	Bucks only[b]	60[a]	Robinette et al. (1977)
	Oak Creek, Utah	Any deer	35[a]	Robinette et al. (1977)
	Fishlake, Utah	Any deer	19[a]	Robinette et al. (1977)
	Guadalupe Mountains, New Mexico	Mixed[c]	92[a]	Welch (1974)
	California	Bucks only[d]	30[e]	Longhurst et al. (1952)
	Nebraska	All hunts	15–20[e]	Menzel (1975)
	Ruby Butte, Nevada	Any deer	Less than 35[e]	Papez (1976)
Black-tailed deer	Lake County, California	Bucks only[d]	Over 40[e]	Taber and Dasmann (1957, 1958)
	Hopland Field Station, California	Bucks only[d]	21[f]	Connolly and Longhurst (1975)

[a] Estimates from intensive field surveys.

[b] A few special-permit holders could take either sex.

[c] Some hunters had either-sex tags; others could hunt bucks only.

[d] Legal bucks require at least two points on one antler.

[e] Estimates from sources other than intensive field surveys.

[f] Minimum estimate based on voluntary hunters reports plus fresh carcasses examined by research workers.

Crippling losses result when wounded legal deer escape from hunters. At the Hopland Field Station in northern California, the carcasses of lost cripples frequently were found by other hunters or research workers investigating concentrations of scavenger birds. Hunters reported losing one crippled buck for every five bucks brought through the check station—a 20 percent crippling loss. Photograph by Guy E. Connolly.

than double the wounding loss in buck-only hunts, and Welch (1974) reported that 92–93 percent of deer left in the field were illegal kills. At Oak Creek, Utah, Robinette et al. (1977) did not estimate crippling loss separately from illegal kill, but in "any-deer" hunts they found 35 deer left in the field for every 100 that were checked out legally. They suspected that hunters often abandoned fawns because of their small size, and does because of poor condition, usually due to lactation.

Perhaps the most detailed published study of crippling and illegal hunting mortality is that of Robinette et al. (1977) in Oak Creek, Utah. These workers used three methods to measure losses:

1. *Lincoln index.* Hunters en route to the study area were asked to cut off an upper ear from each current crippling loss they encountered while hunting and to turn in the ears at a check station as they left. A horseback and foot survey was subsequently conducted, and the proportion of dead deer with missing ears was noted. In twelve years, 214 ears were received at the check station. On the twelve surveys, 70 dead deer were encountered, and 10 of these lacked an ear. If 214 ears represented one-seventh (10/70) of the dead deer, estimated crippling and abandonment loss for the twelve-year period was 1,498, or an average of 125 per year. Correcting for additional ears turned in during the last two days of hunting season (surveys were made late in the season), the average estimated crippling and abandonment loss by this method was 132 deer per year.

2. *King's strip census method.* This procedure already has been described (see "Mortality"). It yielded an estimated mean annual wastage of 174 deer.

3. *Ratio of dead deer to entrails,* as previously described. This method gave an average annual crippling and illegal kill of 183 deer. Estimates from Oak Creek shown in table 34 were derived by this method.

Of the three methods tested at Oak Creek, Utah, the dead deer/entrail approach gave the best results. Other studies (Robinette et al. 1974) showed that King's method gave slight underestimates, and the Lincoln index gave a significantly lower result than the other two methods.

In New Mexico, a recent attempt was made to estimate crippling losses and illegal kills by means of change-in-ratio calculations (see "Methods for Estimating Deer Numbers: Change-in-ratio Methods," below), using estimates of legal kill and of herd composition before and after the hunting season as determined by aerial surveys. Resulting population estimates were so inconsistent that crippling losses could not be determined from them (Johnson 1975).

Even though most of the reports cited in table 34 showed high illegal kills of antlerless mule deer, especially where only bucks were legal game, some studies have reached a contrary conclusion. Taber and Dasmann (1958) found that few antlerless deer were killed on a blacktail range in California, even though crippling loss of adult bucks was at least 40 percent of the reported kill. In this area, only bucks with at least two points on one antler were legal game, and large numbers of spike bucks were shot and abandoned. At the Hopland Field Station, near the study area of Taber and Dasmann, Longhurst and Connolly (n.d.) also found that hunters killed very few does or fawns.

A comprehensive review of crippling losses and illegal kills of both mule and white-tailed deer was made by Losch and Samuel (1976). They found it hard to compare various estimates because most studies were not systematic or extensive, and methods of collecting and analyzing data were highly variable. However, their compilation for mule deer showed an average cripple loss equal to 23 percent of the reported kill during either-sex hunts (based on 15 studies) and 27 percent during buck-only hunts (11 studies). In addition to crippling losses, five studies showed an average illegal kill of 79 percent during buck-only hunts. Because of the sampling inconsistencies noted above, Losch and Samuel urged caution in extrapolating these statistics to large areas. However, it is obvious that crippling loss and illegal kill can be a substantial drain on deer populations and must be considered when harvest regulations are established.

Both crippling loss and illegal kill seem to vary from place to place and are hard to measure. Given present constraints on methodology and manpower, it seems unlikely that reliable estimates will ever be available for most deer populations. However, one management implication can be drawn from the information on hand: crippling loss and illegal kill in mule deer herds seem to be higher when only bucks are hunted than when any deer is legal game. Therefore, on ranges where the kill must be restricted, limited numbers of hunters with any-deer permits may be preferable to larger numbers of hunters allowed to take only bucks.

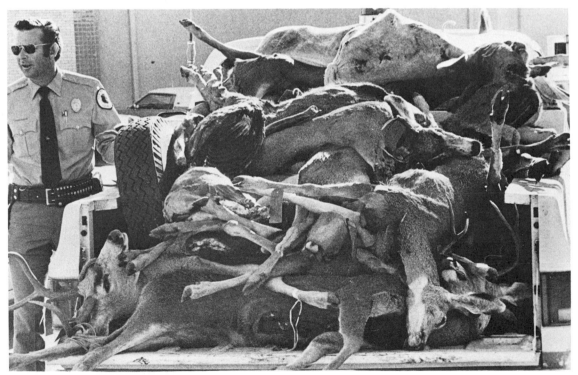

A truckload of confiscated desert mule deer—the result of in-season hunting violations. Most of these animals either were illegal (does, fawns, and spike bucks) or were not properly tagged. Photograph courtesy of the New Mexico Department of Game and Fish.

Out-of-Season Kills

Because illegal activities are particularly hard to measure and study objectively, little is known about the out-of-season kill of mule and black-tailed deer. Wildlife law enforcement officials frequently express their suspicion that only a small fraction of violations are detected, but objective support for this contention has only recently become available.

Three poaching simulation studies—one each in Idaho, New Mexico, and California—have attempted to estimate the magnitude of the out-of-season big game kill. In each state, one or more undercover agents committed some violations and simulated others by leaving deer hides, legs, hair, viscera, or other evidence at various sites. Knowledge of each research project was restricted to a few top fish-and-game administrators, with most enforcement officers in the field unaware of the studies until after they had been completed. From the number of violations simulated in each study and the fraction detected by enforcement officers or reported to them, the total number of violations in each state was estimated.

The first poaching study was part of a larger project to determine characteristics of big game law violators, public attitudes toward poaching and poachers, and magnitude of the out-of-season big game kill in Idaho. Vilkitis (1968) shot 31 big game animals, mostly mule deer, during January–June 1967. Three more animals were crippled and lost. Some of these violations were witnessed, but none was reported to enforcement officers. Vilkitis also simulated 62 additional violations by leaving parts of big game animals in various locations. Four of these incidents were discovered by enforcement personnel, but Vilkitis was not identified as the violator. While committing his simulations, he found evidence of 7 other violations by unknown persons. Enforcement agents reported a total of 82 incidents during the study period. From these and other data, Vilkitis estimated the maximum out-of-season big game kill in Idaho during 1967 at about 8,000 animals. The legal harvest in Idaho that year included about 66,000 mule and white-tailed deer (table 24).

A similar study took place in New Mexico in 1975, when a research poacher killed 19 animals and simulated 125 more kills. While committing these 144 violations, he was observed by the public at least 43 times but was reported to authorities only once. From the data developed in this study, Pursley (1977) calculated that New Mexico poachers might be taking about 34,000 deer during the closed season each year; this approximates the annual legal harvest. However, the 34,000 figure was not a very precise estimate. Statistical evaluation (95 percent confidence intervals) indicated that the actual poaching loss was somewhere between 2,400 and 662,000 deer per year.

The California Fish and Game Department carried out a poaching study in the winter of 1975–76 (V. C. Simpson, pers. comm., May 1978). Two two-man poaching teams killed 21 deer and combined them with parts of additional animals to simulate a total of 134 kills. Three of these simulations were reported to game wardens. Both poaching teams (veteran wardens) were observed by members of the public during actual kills or immediately after when their purpose must have been obvious, yet wardens received no eyewitness report that could be tied to the simulated violations. In this study it was concluded that the out-of-season deer kill might be nearly twice the legal harvest.

In each of these studies, the researchers recognized that out-of-season kill could not be estimated reliably from the limited information that was collected. Nevertheless, very few of the violations came to the attention of game wardens. Vilkitis (1968) believed that, for each violation, a poacher had a 99.5 percent chance of escaping detection and arrest. In his study, he was reported once to an enforcement officer by third parties, but only after deliberately flagrant violations; he hung and butchered nine deer and two elk in his garage in town.

Despite the sparse statistical evidence, these studies collectively verify that poaching may be a significant source of loss from many mule deer herds.

Spotlighting or "shining" deer at night is a common method used by illegal hunters. Illegal shooting results in significant loss of deer from certain ranges. Not only are these losses significant in number, but they make it difficult for managers to compute total hunting mortality, an important variable affecting management decisions associated with future harvests. Photograph courtesy of the New Mexico Department of Game and Fish.

METHODS FOR ESTIMATING DEER NUMBERS

It seems appropriate to begin this discussion by pointing out that wildlife biologists disagree over the basic issue of whether population estimates are needed in deer management. Which is more important to know—the trend in deer numbers or the trend in habitat condition? Will the public support a management program that refuses to give estimates of deer numbers and population trends? How much of limited wildlife management funds can be afforded for population estimates? There are differences of opinion on these issues.

Lauckhart (1950, p. 648) believed that "hunter management or public relations make population figures a virtual necessity. The public does not trust managers who do not profess to know how many animals are available and how many should be killed." Similarly, Leopold et al. (1938, p. 47) counseled that "any wildlife management worthy of the name will be difficult or impossible until we develop satisfactory methods of inventory." This view was reiterated by Gill (1976).

Leopold apparently changed his mind on this subject, since he later wrote that "a common error is to try to appraise by census, rather than by browse conditions. The public can dispute endlessly about censuses, but it cannot dispute dead browse plants" (Leopold et al. 1947, p. 175). This contention was supported by Egan (1971, p. 57): "It is impossible to accurately count deer numbers, but it is possible to measure the habitat and the effects of good habitat in terms of deer health." Thus some respected authorities believe that deer densities need not be known for satisfactory management of harvests. As pointed out by Eberhardt (1978b), however, this is not true if the harvest is measured quantitatively. From comparisons of absolute numbers (harvests) with trend indexes, one cannot make the kind of analysis needed; that is, determination of the fraction of the population that was harvested.

The philosophical conflict among opponents and proponents of numerical population estimates is nearly as old as deer management itself. The real issue is not whether population estimates are useful, but whether deer numbers or habitat conditions should be the focal point of management. The shortcomings of both habitat and population measures have become increasingly apparent in the 1960s and 1970s, as wildlife managers in most mule deer states have sought explanations for an apparent general decline in mule deer populations (see chap. 6). At a symposium on this subject, Gill (1976) described the decline as a myth, not because it did not occur, but because there were no real estimates of deer numbers. Wolfe (1976) continued in this vein by pointing out that staggering amounts of resources and effort were expended annually, yet real accuracy and precision in the enumeration of deer remained elusive. Gill and Wolfe also questioned the value of habitat measures such as browse-utilization transects, since some deer herds had declined substantially without commensurate changes in the indexes of vegetation use.

It appears that the general mule deer decline of the 1960s and 1970s affected most major mule deer states irrespective of local management philosophies as to the relative value of deer population and habitat measures. We may assume that there are causal relationships among habitat conditions and population performance, but there is great need for improvement in census techniques and habitat assessments alike if those relationships are to be understood.

Most population estimation techniques in use today were developed in the 1940s or earlier. The reader who compares current methods with those listed by McCain and Taylor (1956) will be impressed by the apparent lack of progress since that time. However, a great deal of experience has been gained with the old methods, and wildlife biologists and managers are not as optimistic about estimating deer numbers as they used to be.

Distinction should be made here between population estimates and trend counts. The terms "population estimate" and "census" refer to the number of deer in a specific area at a specific time. Trend counts, in contrast, purport to monitor changes in deer numbers over time without actually enumerating entire populations. Certain field procedures are adaptable to either trend counts or population estimates, but this review considers trend counts separately.

Methods for estimating deer numbers may be grouped into four general categories: direct counts; ratios of marked to unmarked animals; measurements of signs left by deer, such as feces or tracks; and calculations based on kill statistics and herd-composition ratios.

Direct Counts

Sample Area Counts (From the Ground)

Except for herds within small enclosures, it rarely is possible to make accurate total counts of blacktail or mule deer populations. Therefore direct counts usually are restricted to small sample areas. Observed deer density on these sample areas then may be projected to larger areas, assuming that deer density on the sample areas is representative of the unit as a whole. But in many cases this assumption cannot be made because deer are not distributed randomly over the range. In winter, for example, most mule deer herds concentrate on traditional winter ranges, and even within these ranges their densities vary with topography, snow depth, cover, and other factors.

Though it may be impractical for use in most mule deer herds, the sample area count was considered the best of four census methods tested on resident black-tailed deer by Dasmann and Taber (1955). Their study took place in hilly country where large expanses of deer range could be watched from selected vantage points during morning and evening feeding periods. They noted that the method had limited application elsewhere because it required relatively open areas of hill or mountain country and sedentary deer herds.

Aerial Counts

Visual counts from aircraft. Aerial counts of mule deer are made routinely in a number of states and provinces. Both helicopters and fixed-winged craft are used, and counts ordinarily are made in winter when visibility is enhanced by snow cover. Most of these surveys are regarded as trend counts, though Mackie (1976*b*) used aerial counts during early winter to estimate total mule deer numbers in part of the Missouri River Breaks of eastern Montana. Deer numbers in the Idaho primitive area were estimated by adding one-third to the highest figure obtained in aerial and ground counts (Hornocker 1970).

The accuracy, speed, and cost of aerial counts are affected by numerous variables, including weather, light, snow cover, terrain, vegetation, and flight techniques. A most important factor is the skill of the pilot (Riordan 1948).

Gill (1969) described a procedure in which all deer seen on randomly selected, square-mile sampling units are counted from a helicopter. The quadrats are stratified into three general deer-density levels. Since the deer are confined by snow to a known area from which the sample is drawn, the total winter population can be estimated with definable sampling error. Caughley (1977), however, stated that transect sampling usually is more efficient than quadrat sampling.

Aerial surveys often provide gross underestimates of animal density, because observers fail to see some of the animals. There is reason to believe that biases inherent in aerial surveys cannot be eliminated, but that they can be measured and estimates corrected accordingly. A regression technique has been proposed to estimate density from series of counts taken at various cruising speeds and altitudes (Caughley and Goddard 1972; Caughley 1974*a*; Caughley et al. 1976). Other sampling designs are given by Caughley (1977). These approaches have obvious potential for enumeration of mule deer. Black-tailed deer generally live in denser vegetation types where aerial counts are impractical.

Infrared scanning. Since the advent of the space age, wildlife managers have been hoping for a technological panacea to solve the deer census problem. No such solution has yet appeared, but infrared scanning is perhaps the closest thing to it. Infrared sensors detect electromagnetic radiations of certain wavelengths, and visibility of deer in infrared images depends on differences in the emission of thermal radiation between deer and their backgrounds. These differences apparently are greater during night or very early morning than at midday (Graves et al. 1972). Training and experience are necessary for accurate identification of deer

Aerial counts usually are made in winter when snow enhances visibility of deer. Photograph by Dec Hibbert; courtesy of the Idaho Department of Fish and Game.

on infrared images. The optimum wavelength band for infrared detection of deer has been variously reported as 8–14 microns (Croon et al. 1968) and 3–5 microns (Graves et al. 1972).

A test of infrared scanning at the George Reserve in Michigan yielded a count of 93 positive white-tailed deer plus 5 probables. The estimate by other methods was 101 (Croon et al. 1968). White-tailed deer in Pennsylvania shrublands were detected at altitudes of 30, 76, and 152 meters (100, 250, and 500 feet) during nighttime summer flights (Graves et al. 1972). Penned mule deer were visible in infrared images from 91 and 152 meters (300 and 500 feet), but not from 305 meters (1,000 feet), and they could not be reliably distinguished from pronghorn (Parker and Driscoll 1972).

Some of the problems that prevent wide-scale use of the technique at present include the inability of infrared to penetrate green leaf canopy, variability of animal and background temperatures depending on weather and other factors, difficulty in distinguishing between species of animals, and high initial cost of the scanning device. Under the right conditions, however, infrared scanning with present technology gives good counts. Biologists who have worked with the technique state that continued improvement in methodology is likely.

Strip Census

Strip censuses, or line transects, already have been discussed in connection with mortality and crippling loss estimates. This technique also has been applied to live deer.

In Oak Creek, Utah, Robinette et al. (1977) recorded sighting or flushing distances of mule deer over about 80 kilometers (50 miles) of census lines each year from 1948 through 1957. An average of 937 deer per year was observed, and the average sighting distance was about 244 meters (800 feet). Resulting population estimates, calculated according to King's method, were unrealistically low. One possible reason for this was that the census lines followed ridgetops. This permitted observation of deer on opposite slopes, but many

closer deer could not be seen. Thus the method probably overestimated mean sighting distance and underestimated deer density.

Anyone planning to use line transects for estimating deer numbers will find it helpful to review the literature before proceeding. In particular, the publications of Robinette et al. (1974), Anderson et al. (1976), and Eberhardt (1978a) are recommended.

The Petersen or Lincoln Index

One of the oldest techniques for estimating animal numbers is the Petersen (1896) or Lincoln (1930) index. The basic concept is straightforward—animals are captured, marked, and released back into the population. A survey then is made to record the number of marked and unmarked animals seen. From the number of marked deer known to be present and the numbers of marked and unmarked deer seen in the survey, population size can be calculated. If, for example, a tally of 200 deer included 16 of 52 marked deer known to be present, the estimated population would be $16/52 = 200/x$, or 650 deer.

Despite the attractive simplicity of this method, in practice it is subject to a number of pitfalls. One problem is immigration or loss of some marked animals between marking and follow-up, so that the actual number of marked animals present during the survey is not known. The method assumes that all marked animals will be recognized as such, and that marked individuals are just as likely to be included in follow-up surveys as are unmarked animals. There is an indication that a high proportion of the population must be marked to obtain a reliable measure of population size. Strandgaard (1967) found it necessary to mark two-thirds of his roe deer in order to get good results with the Lincoln index, but he stated that this proportion may not apply to other species. Comparable values have not been developed for mule or black-tailed deer.

One example of the Lincoln index, as applied to mule deer, was given by Robinette et al. (1977). From numbers of ear-tagged deer

A mule deer bounds away after having been tagged and collared on the Kaibab Plateau in Arizona. Deer were driven by helicopter into a 458 meter (1,500 foot) net strung up in 30.5 meter sections. This method—first adopted by the New Mexico Department of Game and Fish—enabled the capture of 36 deer in two days, after box-trapping produced only 2 deer in two months. Tranquilizers were not necessary to control the deer, and none of the animals were injured. Photograph by Steve Gallizioli; courtesy of the Arizona Game and Fish Department.

An ear-tagged mule deer doe is recaptured in a nylon-mesh clover trap (Clover 1956) during a migration study in Utah. Photograph by Kay Boulter; courtesy of the Utah Division of Wildlife Resources.

This box trap was used to capture deer for tagging and collaring to study migration of a herd that moved seasonally between Wyoming and Colorado. The study was a cooperative effort of the Colorado Division of Wildlife and the Wyoming Department of Game and Fish. Photograph courtesy of the Wyoming Department of Game and Fish.

individually identified during prehunt classification counts, and the proportion of these animals killed in the subsequent hunt, Lincoln index calculations were made separately for fawns, does, and bucks at Oak Creek, Utah. Because too few tagged individuals were recovered to permit annual estimates, the data were pooled for a ten-year period, during which 6 of 93 marked fawns, 10 of 21 marked bucks, and 4 of 51 marked does were taken by hunters. These figures, combined with the hunting kill and other data, yielded estimates of 1,816, 2,071, and 3,230 deer in the posthunt herd, based on recoveries of marked fawns, bucks, and does, respectively. Variations among these three independent estimates were attributed primarily to small sample sizes. However, the mean of the estimates agreed quite well with results of pellet group counts and change-in-ratio calculations.

The Lincoln index also was used on Steens Mountain, Oregon, to estimate mule deer numbers on two study areas. About 1 percent of the deer on one area and 4 percent on the other were marked. In three replicate counts by helicopter on each area, the fraction of marked deer that was observed averaged 48 percent (range 39–72 percent). The resulting population estimates were 1,800–2,800 deer for one area and 900–1,100 for the other (Lemos et al. 1978a).

Examples of the Lincoln index applied to black-tailed deer are given by Dasmann and Taber (1955) and by Brown (1961). Dasmann and Taber (1955) did not give the number of marked deer present, but in Brown's (1961) work the tagged animals constituted approximately 3 percent of the estimated population.

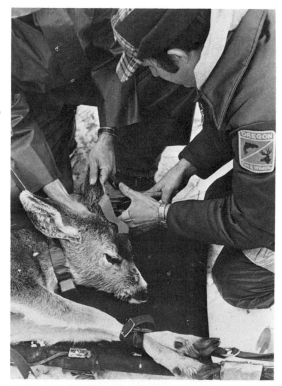

A radio-collared mule deer doe from the Steens Mountain area of southeastern Oregon is fitted with an ear tag. The radio collar will send a constant signal, enabling researchers to follow her movements. Photograph courtesy of the Oregon Department of Fish and Wildlife.

A fawn is released after being given ear tags and a radio collar. The fluorescent ear tags will aid in resighting the animal in sagebrush habitat. Photograph courtesy of the Oregon Department of Fish and Wildlife.

Resulting estimates agreed reasonably well with those from other methods.

Methods Based on Signs Left by Deer

Track Counts

For deer herds whose travel routes between summer and winter ranges are well defined, track counts may give an indication of population size. As applied to mule deer, counts ordinarily are made in spring as the animals move from winter range toward summer range. Tracks usually are counted where they cross secluded roads that lie perpendicular to the direction of travel. Counters travel these routes daily or every other day during migration, towing a drag or spring-tooth harrow behind their vehicle to obliterate tracks after they are recorded.

An assumed advantage of track counts is that they provide an unassailable minimum estimate of deer numbers. This assumption might be disputed on several grounds. Disadvantages are many: track counts are time-consuming; roadbed preparation may be difficult; frozen ground may prevent track registration; snow, sleet, rain, wind, or livestock may obliterate tracks; some deer migrate before and after the counts; track routes may not include all migration routes; and some deer do not migrate.

One widely publicized example of the use of track counts to estimate mule deer numbers was the Devil's Garden deer herd, which wintered in northern California and summered in Oregon. Deer tracks crossing the California/Oregon stateline road were counted each spring from 1947 through 1973. Manpower constraints caused the work to be abandoned in 1974. Salwasser (1976) found that track count records gave the best available estimate of the size of this population, even though its winter range was shared with two other deer herds.

There is no record of the degree of precision achieved in estimates of mule deer numbers by means of track counts. For white-tailed deer in Texas, however, Daniel and Frels (1971) suggested that annual fluctuations of more than 15 percent could be detected by track counts.

Precision was best when deer populations were high, so that the number of tracks exceeded 28 per kilometer (45 per mile) of road.

Fecal Pellet Counts

Pellet group counts have long been used to estimate deer numbers. Problems of designing, establishing, and operating pellet group sampling systems have been thoroughly explored by many workers for a variety of habitats. No insuperable difficulties have been encountered, but there are many potential sources of error.

Estimates of deer numbers from counts of fecal pellet groups are based on density or total number of deer pellet groups on the area occupied by a subject population; length of time over which the pellets were deposited; and average number of pellet groups produced daily by each deer. Each of these variables will be considered in turn.

Determining the density of pellet groups. The greatest problem in censusing deer by pellet counts lies in determining the density or number of groups present on a study area. Except for specialized research applications on small plots, total counts are impractical, and therefore some type of sampling procedure must be used. The investigator not only must decide whether to use temporary or permanent plots, but also must select the size, shape, number, and distribution of plots that best suit his needs. Data-processing and calculation procedures must be established before he starts fieldwork. A voluminous literature exists on pellet group sampling; the review of Neff (1968) is especially recommended.

Several workers have shown that circular plots of different sizes give varying estimates of pellet group density that, in turn, yield varying estimates of deer numbers. Small plots generally give the highest estimates (Neff 1968; Batcheler 1975). The usual explanation for this is that observers fail to see some pellet groups, and the fraction of groups missed increases with plot size. However, Batcheler (1975) suggested that differences result less from observer error than from the problem of defining pellet groups. By analysis of mule deer pellet count data, Batcheler showed that varying estimates due to plot size could be explained by the specific "edge effect" problem of defining groups. Counts were influenced by groups outside the plots, and this influence was proportional to plot size and area over which pellet groups were scattered.

If this interpretation is correct, there probably is no such thing as an ideal plot size. Likewise, it is incorrect to propose that the smallest plots are best merely because they yield the highest counts. In fact, Batcheler showed that the high estimates from very small plots (0.00004 hectare: 0.0001 acre) were even more biased than the low estimates from 0.004 hectare (0.01 acre) plots.

Given the apparently intractable problems associated with bounded plots, Batcheler suggested that a plotless, distance method be used instead. With this technique the observer selects temporary sample points at fixed distances along cross-country routes. Distance from each sample point to the center of the nearest pellet group is measured, along with the distance from that group to the next nearest group. To avoid endless searches about points with no nearby groups, the search distance is limited to a radius that includes groups at more than 50 percent of the sample points. Batcheler (1975) described calculation of deer density from these point distances and nearest group distances. In addition to the point distances, he used slope measurements in hilly terrain to correct the estimates to map area. An estimate of the rate of pellet group disappearance also is needed, along with daily defecation rate and the time interval between surveys.

Practical advantages of the point distance method, as used by Batcheler (1975) in New Zealand, were that it permitted the observer to assess the validity and position of a group without the artificial constraint of searching within a plot boundary, and that it enabled observers to make quick measurements in areas of high group density so that more time could be spent recording relative scarcity of groups in low-density areas. The main disadvantage was the need for a particularly accurate measure of the pellet disappearance rate. Also, users of this method might find it hard to establish the midpoints of strewn-out or scattered groups.

Returning to more traditional pellet count methods, it has been customary to use permanently marked plots or transects from which pellets are periodically cleared. An amazing variety of sampling schemes has been employed (Neff 1968). In general, sampling intensity should be related inversely to group density; that is, the number of plots needed to estimate the number of pellet groups with comparable precision increases as group density decreases. At any given density of pellet groups, the required sampling intensity varies directly with the degree of precision desired. Robinette et al. (1958) suggested that it was of doubtful value, in terms of manpower, time, and economics, to attempt greater precision than ±10 percent sampling error with 70 percent confidence limits. Even this standard of precision likely will be out of reason on areas with fewer than 247 pellet groups per hectare (100 groups per acre). Note that this estimate of precision pertains only to pellet group density. Additional error is introduced in calculating deer numbers from pellet group density.

It is common knowledge that fecal pellet groups are not distributed randomly on deer ranges, but few biologists have concerned themselves with theoretical aspects of pellet distribution. Nevertheless, use of an appropriate mathematical model is essential to calculation of reliable confidence intervals and standard errors for pellet count estimates. Several theoretical frequency distributions have been shown to fit pellet group data equally well, but the negative binomial model was preferred for computational ease (Bowden et al. 1969; McConnell and Smith 1970).

A frequent complication in pellet count estimates is that other ruminant species may be present on mule deer or blacktail ranges. In such cases it may be hard to distinguish deer fecal pellets from those of other species. On ranges shared by deer and domestic sheep, one might count all groups and then subtract a fraction to allow for the sheep, whose number and duration of range occupancy are known.

However, such deductions introduce a new possibility for error. One correction of this kind, at the Hopland Field Station, California (Longhurst, n.d.), left a negative value for the number of deer pellet groups on an 85 hectare (210 acre) area, even though 25–40 deer were known to be present. Robinette (pers. comm., December 1978) also unsuccessfully attempted to correct deer pellet counts for known numbers of sheep. He surmised that the very uneven distribution of sheep pellet groups, especially owing to accumulations on bedgrounds, precluded such corrections.

A more direct means of differentiating between pellets of deer and those of other herbivores is pH analysis. On ranges shared by mule deer and other species, the pH of mule deer pellets differed significantly from that of pronghorn (Howard 1967), domestic sheep (Nagy and Gilbert 1968), white-tailed deer (Krausman et al. 1974), Iranian ibex, and desert bighorn sheep (Howard and DeLorenzo 1974). Hansen (1978) found that fecal pH values for any herbivore may vary seasonally and from one area to another. His observed mean pH values for mule deer dung were significantly higher than those reported by other workers. Hansen's data showed that droppings of mule deer and wild horses could not be differentiated by pH analysis. This will cause little concern among skilled wildlife biologists, who usually can distinguish horse dung from mule deer dung by the difference in particle size.

Defining the time interval for deposition of pellet groups. Perhaps the most reliable way to define the period of pellet group deposition is to use permanently marked plots that are cleared periodically. Temporary, uncleared plots sometimes are used where the deposition period can be dated by reference to leaf fall, deformation of pellets owing to emergence of succulent feed, or estimation of the period of occupancy of seasonal range. Such dating schemes, however, introduce additional sources of error.

Although periodic clearing of plots may be the most reliable means of defining the period of pellet group deposition, removing old pellets can be time-consuming. Kufeld (1968) suggested that laborious clearing of plots could be avoided by marking pellets with paint instead of removing them.

The plotless distance method of pellet group sampling proposed by Batcheler (1975) poses special problems in defining the sample period. This method required two estimates of pellet density separated by time. A fraction of the groups present at sample x disappeared before sample y, and some groups deposited after sample x also vanished before sample y. Batcheler assumed that the decay rate was exponential and pointed out that a particularly accurate assessment of disappearance rate was required for successful use of his method.

Daily defecation rate. Most estimates of deer numbers from pellet counts treat defecation rate as a constant—the most frequent values being 12.7–13 groups per deer per day. However, defecation rates vary with age, diet, and other factors. A comprehensive list of published defecation rates is given by Neff (1968).

The diverse sources of error in pellet group counting, not all of which are covered here, have produced results ranging from excellent to poor. Pellet counts in Nebraska were highly variable and showed little relation to other population indexes (Menzel 1975). Nine tests of the pellet count technique in enclosures containing known numbers of white-tailed deer in Michigan gave estimates ranging from 47 to 167 percent of the known populations (Neff 1968). Neff also cited a number of comparisons of pellet group counts with estimates made by other techniques.

At Oak Creek, Utah, Robinette et al. (1977) compared results from pellet group counts and from Kelker and Lincoln indexes over a ten-year period. The ten-year averages agreed closely, but only pellet group counts gave annual estimates that were even close to being realistic. The pellet count also required less effort than the other methods.

Because pellet group sampling is most efficient in areas of high pellet group density, Neff (1968, p. 602) recommended that "winter ranges or other deer concentration areas should be chosen for herd census or trend studies whenever possible." However, Strickland (1975) found that year-to-year fluctuations in observed pellet group density on Wyoming winter ranges probably were due to differences in deer distribution rather than to differences in deer numbers. Strickland's sampling sites on marginal winter range failed to include critical areas. But, regardless of the location of pellet plots on winter range, differential weather severity may greatly influence animal occupancy of key areas. Annual variations in pellet group counts on such areas therefore will reflect some composite of population and weather fluctuations. The value of such counts as population estimates is questionable.

Pellet counts frequently are used to compare occupancy or use of range areas or experimental plots by deer. To give but a few examples, pellet counts have been employed: to document changes in deer use after logging (Edgerton 1972) and wildfire (Kruse 1972); to determine deer use on crested wheatgrass plantations (Tueller and Monroe 1974); and to compare deer use on fertilized versus unfertilized Douglas fir trees (Oh et al. 1970).

Whenever pellet counts are used as an index of relative deer use, it is assumed that the most pellets are deposited where the deer spend the most time. This premise may seem reasonable, but it has not been verified. An attempt to relate pellet count data to shrub utilization on a mule deer winter range in Colorado was inconclusive (Anderson et al. 1972*c*).

Calculations Based on Kill Statistics and Herd Composition Ratios

Number of Deer Left for Each Buck Killed

In any deer herd, it takes a certain minimum number of animals to sustain any given level of hunting harvest. Several equations, graphs, and tables were developed in the early 1950s to estimate such minimum population sizes. Lauckhart (1950) suggested that the number of deer remaining for each buck killed ranged from 7 to 20 depending on buck-doe and fawn-doe ratios in posthunt populations. For practical management purposes, Lauckhart proposed that any deer herd in Washington would have at least 10 deer left for each buck killed.

Lauckhart's work was reinforced by calculations of Longhurst et al. (1952) showing that if all adult bucks (2 years old and older) were killed each year, the yield would stabilize at 9.5 percent. These calculations incorporated assumptions that yearling bucks would breed the does and that each doe would raise one fawn. The 9.5 percent figure is maximum, and no herd in California sustained such a high buck kill. Based on actual kill in various herds, the number of deer left for each buck killed was estimated to vary between 8 and 30. For California as a whole, it appeared that, on the average, there were 24 deer on the range for each buck reportedly killed, or at least 15 deer for each buck actually killed. These calculations were reiterated by Dasmann (1952) in a simple model that permitted the number of deer left for each buck killed to be read directly if buck-doe and fawn-doe ratios were available (table 35).

Dasmann's table is reproduced here because, in my opinion, it offers a very useful guide to deer densities when only hunter kill and herd composition data are available. Dasmann allowed for an illegal kill of does equal to 20 percent of the total buck kill and assumed that yearlings as well as adult bucks would be harvested. The method works best for herds with relatively constant hunting pressure and herd composition ratios, and use of a single year's data may give misleading results.

As an example, I applied this method to data for deer at Hopland Field Station, California, for 1964–66. Detailed reconstruction of this population, using all available information on population dynamics, had given an estimate of 600 deer in autumn (Connolly 1970). Average herd composition ratios were 33 bucks and 67 fawns per 100 does in autumn and 48 fawns per

Table 35. Estimated Number of Deer Remaining in Autumn Population for Each Buck Killed during Hunting Season

Winter Ratio—Bucks: 100 Does	Average Late Winter Ratio—Fawns: 100 Does									Average Early Winter Ratio—Fawns: 100 Does
	100	90	80	70	60	50	40	30	20	
20	8	8	9	10	11	13	15	19	29	100
20			8	9	10	12	14	18	26	80
20					9	10	12	17	24	60
20							11	14	21	40
30	9	10	10	12	13	15	18	22	33	100
30			9	11	12	14	16	21	31	80
30					11	13	15	19	28	60
30							13	17	25	40
40	11	12	12	14	15	17	22	30	43	100
40			11	12	14	16	20	25	36	80
40					13	15	18	23	33	60
40							16	21	30	40
50	13	14	16	17	20	22	27	36	49	100
50			14	16	18	20	25	31	45	80
50					16	18	23	29	42	60
50							20	26	38	40
60	17	18	20	21	24	27	34	48	50+	100
60			18	20	22	25	32	41	50+	80
60					20	24	29	37	50+	60
60							26	34	49	40

Source: Dasmann (1952).

100 does in early spring. Rounding to the nearest comparable values, table 35 was entered at 30 bucks and 50 fawns (late winter), and 60 fawns (early winter) per 100 does, to read an estimated 13 deer in the autumn population for each buck killed during hunting season. The known annual take of yearlings plus older bucks, including hunter kills, crippling losses, illegal kills, and scientific collections, averaged 50 bucks. Thus the autumn population estimate, using Dasmann's table, was 50 x 13 = 650 deer. This agrees well with the estimate of 600 deer that was based on more detailed calculations.

Dasmann's (1952) method, like that of Lauckhart (1950), contained some obvious sources of error. Both assume that nonhunting loss rates are equal for fawns, does, and bucks; that fawns survive to yearling age in an approximately equal sex ratio; that there are no sex-differential losses of either fawns or adults (except due to hunting); and that no changes in sex ratio are introduced by deer movements into or out of the area. In addition, both methods are based on the recorded or known buck kill, which usually is lower than the total kill. Dasmann (1952) believed that any errors resulting from these assumptions caused his method to underestimate the true population size.

As I noted earlier (see "Determining the Harvest"), Lauckhart's (1950) generalization that each deer herd will have at least 10 deer left for each buck killed is still used in Washington as an index to population size. Such rules of thumb ignore the fact that harvests vary in response to many factors other than deer density. Some of the more obvious influences are weather, season length, type of hunt (antlerless, buck-only, etc.), timing of the hunt with respect to breeding season, bag limits, numbers of hunters, and hunter access to deer. Because of these influences, it is unreasonable to propose that harvest trends correlate exactly with population trends. Yet Ziegler (1978) found buck harvest to be the best indicator of population trends in the Okanogan (Washington) deer herd, because numbers of hunters, season lengths, and bag limits had changed little in the past twenty years.

Change-in-Ratio (CIR) Estimates

Any estimation technique that takes advantage of changes in observed sex or age ratios is a CIR method. Such estimators have long been used under a variety of names. To wildlife biologists, perhaps the most familiar name is the Kelker index, which is misleading because CIR procedures yield population estimates, not indexes, and many persons other than Kelker have contributed to the development of CIR techniques. For a comprehensive history, a list of references, and formulas for CIR procedures, see Hanson (1963).

The basic concept of CIR estimates is that, if one sex or age class (such as bucks) is hunted more heavily than another, selective removal will be reflected in differences between prehunt and posthunt sex or age ratios. If prehunt and posthunt ratios can be estimated along with the number of animals killed, both the prehunt and the posthunt populations can be calculated. This concept is applicable both to buck-only and to either-sex hunts, but it will work only if one sex incurs a higher rate of hunting mortality than the other. When bucks, does, and fawns all are hunted, CIR methods usually would be applied to two of those classes, with the third calculated later from herd composition ratios. CIR calculations are illustrated here with two examples—one buck-only and one either-sex hunt.

First it is necessary to define some terms and symbols. Various workers have used different notation and terminology, so that the same formulas appear in numerous forms (Hanson 1963). My definitions and examples (table 36) are expressed in Hanson's notation. The basic CIR formulas are as follows:

When only bucks are hunted,

$$E_{Gb} = \frac{F_{Gb}F_{Gc}A_{Gd}}{M_{Gb}F_{Gc} - M_{Gc}F_{Gb}}.$$

When both bucks and does are hunted,

$$E_{Gb} = \frac{F_{Gb}(F_{Gc}A_{Gd} - M_{Gc}E_{Gd})}{F_{Gc}M_{Gb} - F_{Gb}M_{Gc}}.$$

Once the number of does before hunting sea-

Table 36. Definitions, Symbols, and Examples of Change-in-Ratio (CIR) Estimates for Mule Deer Populations

Definition	Symbol[a]	Sample Data	
		Buck-Only Hunt[b]	Either-Sex Hunt[c]
Adult does in prehunt count	F_{Gb}	100	3.06
Adult bucks in prehunt count	M_{Gb}	40	1
Adult does in posthunt count	F_{Gc}	100	4.93
Adult bucks in posthunt count	M_{Gc}	25	1
Adult bucks killed during the hunt	A_{Gd}	150	282.6
Adult does killed during the hunt	E_{Gd}	0	267.2
Adult does present before hunt[d]	E_{Gb}	1,000	1,843
Adult does present after hunt $(E_{Gb} - E_{Gd})$	E_{Gc}	1,000	1,575
Adult bucks present before hunt $(E_{Gb}[M_{Gb}/F_{Gb}])$	A_{Gb}	400	602
Adult bucks present after hunt $(A_{Gb} - A_{Gd})$	A_{Gc}	250	320

[a] From Hanson (1963).
[b] Data from Rasmussen and Doman (1943).
[c] Data from Robinette et al. (1977).
[d] See text for formula.

son (E_{Gb}) has been calculated, the number of bucks before (A_{Gb}) and after (A_{Gc}) hunting season and the number of does after hunting season (E_{Gc}) can be obtained with simple arithmetic, as shown in table 36.

Hanson's formulas are designed for use with raw sample data. A prehunt classification, for example, might show 153 does and 50 bucks. These values would be entered in the formulas as $F_{Gb} = 153$ and $M_{Gb} = 50$, but the corresponding ratio (306 does per 100 bucks) could just as well be used. The formulas can be simplified if ratios are expressed as number of does per buck, as in the either-sex example of table 36. When this is done the CIR formula—when both does and bucks are hunted—reduces to

$$E_{Gb} = \frac{(F_{Gb}[F_{Gc}A_{Gd} - E_{Gd}])}{F_{Gc} - F_{Gb}},$$

because the quantities M_{Gb} and M_{Gc} can be deleted when they equal 1.

The CIR estimation concept is ingenious, but its effectiveness depends on a high degree of accuracy in both kill and herd classification data. Several workers have reported special difficulty in estimating prehunt buck-doe ratios. One might expect that a small error in the prehunt ratio would be inconsequential, but such errors are magnified by the CIR formulas. An example of this was given by Robinette et al. (1977), whose prehunt counts underrepresented fawns by about 3.5 percent. This seemingly insignificant error resulted in a population estimate of 1,574, about 29 percent lower than the expected value of 2,229. Parallel calculations using buck-doe ratios yielded an estimate that was equally biased in the opposite direction. A third estimate based on fawn-adult ratios was considered very accurate.

Computer analysis of CIR methods currently used to determine mule deer population trends in Nevada also showed estimates to be very sensitive to small errors in determining either pre- or posthunt buck-doe ratios. Estimates also were sensitive to changes in the buck kill but were relatively unaffected by changes in the doe kill (Alldredge et al. 1977).

In addition to problems introduced by even minor biases in herd composition and kill data, CIR estimates assume that nonhunting mortality between the prehunt and posthunt counts affects all age and sex classes equally and that the herd count data are from precisely the same population from which the hunting kill is removed. Often these assumptions are not valid.

Herd composition data needed for CIR estimates normally are collected by observers on the ground (see "Herd Composition Counts," above). Riordan (1948) gave an example of CIR calculations based on aerial herd counts; he believed the results were as accurate as those based on ground counts. However, a more recent attempt at CIR estimates based on herd composition data from aerial surveys gave unusable results (Johnson 1975). CIR estimates also have been made with herd composition data gathered in spotlight counts (Hines 1975).

Although CIR methods are applied most often to pre- and posthunt herd classifications, together with harvest data, to estimate deer numbers before and after the hunting season, they can be used for many other estimation problems. Two special applications to research on deer population dynamics are illustrated here.

Calculation of deer numbers in spring, using autumn population estimate and winter loss and spring herd composition ratios. Consider these values for black-tailed deer on the Hopland Field Station, California, 1964–66:

Number of does in autumn (E_{Gb}) 300
Number of fawns in autumn (U_{Jb}) 200
Fawns per doe in winter mortality
   (N_{Jd}/F_{Gd}) 2.00
Fawns per doe in spring population
   (N_{Jc}/F_{Gc}) 0.48

Numbers of does and fawns in autumn were estimated by Connolly (1970). The ratio of fawns to does in winter loss is based on carcass examinations during the three winter periods (1964–66), and the spring fawn-doe ratio is from herd composition counts (Longhurst and Connolly, n.d.).

From these data, the number of does in spring can be calculated as:

$$E_{Gc} = \frac{U_{Jb} - E_{Gb}(N_{Jd}/F_{Gd})}{(N_{Jc}/F_{Gc}) - (N_{Jd}/F_{Gd})},$$

or $\dfrac{200 - 300(2.00)}{0.48 - 2.00} = 263$ does.

The number of fawns in spring (U_{Jc}) equals $E_{Gc}(N_{Jc}/F_{Gc})$, or $263 \times 0.48 = 126$ fawns. Numbers of fawns and does lost during winter are given by the differences between autumn and spring estimates; that is, $300 - 263 = 37$ does lost, and $200 - 126 = 74$ fawns lost.

Calculation of sex ratio among yearlings (11–14 months old), using herd composition data. At the Hopland Field Station, California, herd composition counts were made each April and July (Longhurst and Connolly, n.d.). In April the male and female fawns (approximately 11 months old) could not be reliably differentiated, and all were classified as fawns. As shown below, the number of fawns per doe in April *(F)* ranged between 0.34 and 0.91 during 1966–70. By the time these fawns were 14 months old (now yearlings), antler growth permitted males to be identified and classified separately in July herd counts. The number of yearling bucks per doe in July *(Y)* varied between 0.10 and 0.27 in different years. The does in July included the April does plus yearling females that had been classified as fawns in April. There was little mortality of either does or fawn-yearlings between April and July.

If the male fraction of the yearlings is arbitrarily designated as B, the female fraction is $(1 - B)$. The ratio of yearling bucks to does in July was $(Y/1)$, or simply (Y), but in April it was $BF/(1 + [1 - B])$. The numerator of this expression contains the male fraction of the yearlings, and the denominator includes adult does (1) plus the female fraction of the yerlings $(1 - B)$. Since these quantities for July and April represent different expressions of the same value, they can be equated:

$$Y = \frac{BF}{1 + (1 - B)}.$$

The only unknown in this equation is B. By algebraic manipulation,

$$B = \frac{Y + FY}{F + FY} = \frac{Y(1 + F)}{F(1 + Y)}.$$

Estimates of B for different years, as shown below, were calculated from this expression

Year	April Fawns/Doe (F)	July Yearling Bucks/Doe (Y)	Yearling Bucks as Proportion of All Yearlings (B)	Yearling Sex Ratio (Males/Female) (B/[1 − B])
1966	0.48	0.10	0.28	0.39
1967	0.34	0.18	0.60	1.50
1968	0.65	0.27	0.54	1.17
1969	0.91	0.16	0.29	0.41
1970	0.70	0.20	0.40	0.67
Averages	0.62	0.18	0.42	0.83

using the herd count estimates F and Y for each year. Thus the proportion of males among the yearlings appeared to vary between 0.28 and 0.60 in different years, with corresponding sex ratios of 0.39–1.50 males per female. The average yearling sex ratio for the five years was 0.83 males per female.

These calculations, of course, are subject to the same assumptions and biases that apply to traditional CIR estimates. Therefore it is uncertain how much of the indicated variation among years in yearling sex ratio is real and how much is due to observational error or bias in herd composition ratios. However, fetal sex ratios from these same fawn cohorts showed a similar range of variation from year to year (Longhurst and Connolly, n.d.). In any event, the yearling sex ratio is a valuable statistic, and every possible means of estimating it deserves consideration.

One subject that almost everyone has ignored in applying CIR methods to deer is sample variance. Most workers treat prehunt and posthunt sex ratios and harvest data as fixed quantities, but each of these values actually is an estimate with a sample variance. To determine the validity or precision of a CIR estimate, it is necessary to consider the variability associated with each parameter. Paulik and Robson (1969) provided a cogent discussion of experimental bias in CIR estimates, together with procedures for detecting and correcting such bias. These workers also outlined techniques for calculating the variance and confidence limits for CIR estimates. Such information has obvious utility in planning CIR experiments; it can predict the level of precision likely to be achieved with any given expenditure of sampling effort.

Estimates Based on Survival or Mortality Rates

From age composition of animals killed by hunters, it is possible to compute survival or mortality rates that can be used along with other data to estimate deer numbers. This approach is considered in detail here because, in my opinion, it is one of the more useful estimation methods for many deer herds. The following data are needed: an age breakdown of legally killed bucks (fawns excluded) from which a mortality rate can be derived; an estimate of total legal buck kill; a classification of the posthunt herd to give proportions of bucks, does, and fawns; and the percentage of adult buck mortality attributable to legal kills. Sample data are presented in table 37. Wherever both bucks and does are hunted, separate estimates can be calculated from the buck and doe data; results then can be averaged to give the best estimate.

From these data, size of the posthunt population may be estimated by the following steps: (1) calculate mortality rate of adult bucks; (2) calculate percentage of adult buck mortality attributable to legal kills; (3) calculate prehunt number of adult bucks; (4) subtract legal kill plus any other known buck losses to determine the posthunt number of bucks; (5) calculate posthunt numbers of does and fawns from the estimated number of bucks, using proportions shown in herd composition data; and (6) sum numbers of does, fawns, and bucks to get the total posthunt population estimate.

Step 1. The mortality rate of adult bucks can be calculated in several ways. Two methods are illustrated here.

Table 37. Adult Buck Mortality and Herd Composition Data from Oak Creek, Utah, 1947–56

	Legal Buck Kills													
Age (years)	1	2	3	4	5	6	7	8	9	10	11	12	13	14
Number [a]	1,045	596	141	104	47	39	22	13	6	1	0	1	1	2

Source: Robinette et al. (1977).

Note: Average composition of posthunt population: bucks = 11.2 percent; does = 50.75 percent; fawns = 38.05 percent.

[a] Total kill = 2,018; average annual legal buck kill = 246.4; average crippling and summer loss of adult bucks = 54.8; average winter loss of adult bucks = 4.1; total adult buck mortality per year = 305.3.

a. Kill data may be arranged into a conventional life table (table 38). From that analysis, the overall mortality rate for adult bucks at Oak Creek, Utah, was 51.5 percent.

b. The Chapman-Robson method of estimating survival can be used. The calculations, after the example of Eberhardt (1971), require that the youngest age class be coded as 0, the next as 1, and so on, as in table 39. The Chapman-Robson equation for estimating survival is:

$$S = \frac{T}{n + T - 1},$$

where n = total number examined (2,018) and $T = N_1 + 2N_2 + 3N_3 + \ldots + 13N_{13}$. From

table 39, $T = 596 + 2(141) + 3(104) + 4(47) + 5(39) + 6(22) + 7(13) + 8(6) + 9(1) + 11(1) + 12(1) + 13(2) = 1,902$. $S = 1,902/(2,108 + 1,902 - 1) = 0.485$. If survival rate equals 0.485, the mortality rate would be $1 - 0.485 = 0.515$, or 51.5 percent. In this case the result obtained with the Chapman-Robson method agreed with that from life table analysis (table 38), and therefore it may seem that one method is as good as the other. However, Eberhardt (1971) strongly recommended that the Chapman-Robson method be used in preference to life tables, for the following reasons.

Both the Chapman-Robson method and the life table method assume constant survival rates among all age classes. For many deer herds, it will be questionable whether this is true. A statistical test of the validity of this as-

Table 38. Mortality Rates for Adult Bucks at Oak Creek, Utah, 1947–56, as Derived by Dynamic Life Table from Composition of the Legal Kill

Age Class in Years (x)	Deaths (d_x)	Alive at Start (l_x)	Mortality Rate in Percent (q_x)
1	1,045	2,018	51.8
2	596	973	61.3
3	141	377	37.4
4	104	236	44.1
5	47	132	
6	39	85	
7	22	46	
8	13	24	
9	6	11	41.8
10	1	5	
11	0	4	
12	1	4	
13	1	3	
14	2	2	
Totals	2,018	3,920	
Mean			51.5[a]

Source: Robinette et al. (1977).

[a] Based on totals.

Table 39. Buck Kill Data from Oak Creek, Utah, 1947–56, Coded for Calculation of Survival Rate According to the Method of Chapman and Robson

Age	Coded Age	Number Examined	
1	0	$N_0 =$	1,045
2	1	$N_1 =$	596
3	2	$N_2 =$	141
4	3	$N_3 =$	104
5	4	$N_4 =$	47
6	5	$N_5 =$	39
7	6	$N_6 =$	22
8	7	$N_7 =$	13
9	8	$N_8 =$	6
10	9	$N_9 =$	1
11	10	$N_{10} =$	0
12	11	$N_{11} =$	1
13	12	$N_{12} =$	1
14	13	$N_{13} =$	2
Total			2,018

Source: Data of Robinette et al. (1977) arranged for calculation of survival rate (Eberhardt 1971).

sumption, for a particular set of data, can be made if the Chapman-Robson method is used. By comparing a computed Q value with a tabular chi-square value, one can judge whether the number of yearlings in the kill is compatible with the assumption of constant survival rates (Eberhardt 1971). For the data in table 39, $Q = 0.15$. Since this is much lower than the tabular chi-square value of 3.84 ($p = 0.05$; 1 degree of freedom), the data do not contradict the assumption of constant survival rates.

Another possible concern with both methods is the questionable accuracy of age estimates for older deer. The Chapman-Robson method permits one to circumvent this source of possible error by calculating survival on the basis of grouped ages. If we suspected, for example, that the ages of older deer from Oak Creek had not been reliably estimated, the data in table 39 could be regrouped as follows:

Age	Coded Age	Number Examined
1	0	$N_0 = 1,045$
2	1	$N_1 = 596$
3	2	$N_2 = 141$
4+	—	$m = 236$
Total		2,018

T then would equal $596 + 2(141) + 3(236) = 1,586$, and the estimate of survival rate $S = T/(n - m + t) = 1,586/(2,018 - 236 + 1,586) = 0.471$. This is very close to the previous estimate of 0.485, indicating that little information is lost by pooling the older age classes. Persons considering the use of this method should consult Eberhardt (1971) before proceeding.

Step 2. Table 37 shows that the average legal kill at Oak Creek was 246.4 bucks per year. Average annual crippling and other summer loss was 54.8, and the average winter loss was 4.1 bucks. Thus, the fraction of adult buck mortality represented in the legal kill was $246.4/305.3 = 0.807$.

Step 3. If mean annual mortality rate for bucks was 51.5 percent (step 1) and 80.7 percent of all buck mortality was attributable to legal kills (step 2), it follows that the legal kill constituted 41.6 percent (0.807 x 0.515) of all bucks present before losses occurred; that is,

before the hunting season. If the mean legal kill of 246.4 equaled 41.6 percent of the prehunt buck population, the number of bucks before hunting season was approximately $246.4/0.416 = 592$.

Step 4. Deducting legal kill (246.4) plus crippling and other summer losses (54.8) from the prehunt buck population (592), the number of bucks present after hunting season was approximately 291.

Step 5. Since the posthunt population contained 50.75 percent does and 11.2 percent bucks (table 37), the total number of does was approximately $291(50.75/11.20) = 1,319$. Similarly, the number of fawns was about $291(38.05/11.20) = 989$.

Step 6. The total posthunt population contained approximately 291 bucks, 1,319 does, and 989 fawns, for a total of 2,599 deer. Average estimate of this posthunt population by three other methods (pellet count, Kelker index, and Lincoln index) was 2,263 deer.

In step 1 the survival rate was calculated as 0.471 when kill data for age classes above 3 years were pooled. If the corresponding mortality rate of $1 - 0.471 = 0.529$ is used in place of the value from the standard Chapman-Robson method (0.515), the resulting population estimate would be 2,464 rather than 2,599. Thus this method is sensitive to minor errors in estimation of buck mortality rate.

Note that this method can be applied only to stable populations. From other data given by Robinette et al. (1977), it seems valid to assume stability for the population used here as an example.

Comparisons of Deer Census Methods

As has been shown on previous pages, deer numbers can be estimated by many different methods. Each method can be accurate if required assumptions are met. In practice, however, some assumptions almost always are violated. Because the raw data are subject to both sampling error and biases, the precision of the resulting population estimates can never be conclusively proved. One might seek reassurance by applying two or more different methods to the same herd. If the results are not too dissimilar, the average can be taken as the best available estimate. What, the reader may ask, is meant by "not too dissimilar"? This is a completely subjective decision to be made by each investigator. My arbitrary standard is that the largest estimate should be no more than double the smallest one; if the discrepancy is greater, the most questionable estimate should be rejected. But, regardless of how many estimates are available and how closely they agree, some degree of judgment will be needed in their interpretation and use.

There are many published accounts of two or more census methods applied concurrently to blacktail or mule deer populations. A few of these comparisons are summarized in table 40. Sometimes various methods yielded comparable results but differed in efficiency. The experience of Robinette et al. (1977) is particularly instructive in this regard—only pellet counts provided realistic annual estimates during their ten-year study, and they did so with substantially less effort than other methods required. Twelve man-days per year were spent on pellet counts, compared with twenty man-days on King's strip census, fifty-eight man-days on the Kelker index, and eighty-two man-days on the Lincoln index. These workers found that winter counts failed to measure herd trends reliably.

TREND COUNTS

Few wildlife management agencies try to estimate numbers of mule or black-tailed deer each year, but many try to assess population trends with such measures as browse-utilization transects, pellet group transects on critical or key areas, aerial or ground "trend counts," trends in hunting pressure, harvest and hunter success, or herd composition surveys.

Table 40. Comparisons of Various Census Methods as Applied to Mule or Black-tailed Deer

Methods Compared	Results	Location of Study and Reference
Ground count, airplane count, strip census, roadside counts, winter spot counts, Lincoln index, CIR estimates, pellet group count, forage utilization	Indirect methods gave better results than direct counts. Sample area counts were recommended to determine population trends.	Utah (Rasmussen and Doman 1943)
Total and sample area counts, Lincoln index, pellet count	Sample area count was most useful. Pellet counts suggested seasonal variations in defecation rate.	California (Dasmann and Taber 1955)
Pellet count, Lauckhart (1950) curve	Results of the two methods agreed satisfactorily.	California (Leopold et al. 1951)
Pellet count, Lincoln index	Results were close enough to establish confidence in the estimates.	Washington (Brown 1961)
CIR method, strip census	CIR estimates were 1.9–5.5 times as high as strip census results.	Wyoming (Strickland 1975)
CIR methods, Lincoln index	Lincoln index results were 1.2–1.6 times as high as CIR estimates. CIR estimates were believed to be most accurate.	Nevada (Papez 1976)
Pellet count, Lincoln index, Kelker index, King's strip census, and winter spot counts	Ten-year averages from pellet count, Lincoln index, and Kelker index agreed; King's estimates were 20 percent low. Winter counts were useless as population indicators. Pellet count was most efficient.	Utah (Robinette et al. 1977)

The greater popularity of trend counts, relative to population estimates, may be traced to the convictions of early workers such as Rasmussen and Doman (1943), who concluded that determination of trends was much more feasible than estimation of numbers, and that trend data were of nearly equal value in management. They suggested that counting deer on sample areas in winter was the most practical, direct method of assessing mule deer population trends.

In interpreting trend count data, it is presumed that fluctuations in observed numbers of deer on key areas reflect fluctuations of similar magnitude over larger areas. Even though the validity of this premise never has been documented, trend counts have been accepted uncritically as a management tool in many states. An intensive study of deer census techniques in Utah revealed that trend counts were unreliable, because a higher percentage of the population was seen in severe winters than in mild winters when deer were more widely scattered. For this reason, late winter trend counts have been discarded as a management technique in Utah (Robinette et al. 1977).

Measurements of the degree of browse plant utilization on key winter ranges also have been used to indicate population trends. The goal of such measurements is to determine the intensity of browsing on important species of shrubs on critical ranges. Intensity of use is assumed to reflect deer numbers, and, in particular, excessive use is interpreted to mean that too many deer are present.

Such information and logic was commonly used through the 1950s to justify more liberal harvest regulations, even though the major premises were disputed by at least some biologists. Edwards (1956) argued that overuse of key areas did not necessarily mean that the range as a whole was overstocked. More recently, Wallmo et al. (1977) questioned the value of browse as deer forage; their experiments showed that supposedly preferred browse species were inadequate to meet the nutritional needs of wintering mule deer in Colorado. Gill (1976) suggested that browse twigs are not preferred winter forage but are contingency survival food. But, if browse is only survival food, does this mean it is unimportant? It seems to me that browse could make the difference between life and death when all other food is covered by snow. Nutritionally inadequate food may be better than no food at all.

Recent research on deer nutrition and metabolism indicates that winter forage is not the only factor that governs winter survival of deer. Perhaps equally important is the supply of body fat that each animal accrues before winter. Consequently, late summer and autumn foods are receiving increased attention because these provide the energy to be stored as fat reserves (Mautz 1978).

Apart from the question of how valuable browse may be to wintering deer, it is now clear that, as an indicator of deer population trends, browse utilization measurements leave much to be desired. The intensity of deer use on critical winter ranges can change independent of deer numbers, and browse transects can continue to show heavy use after deer numbers have declined significantly. A theoretical account of how this might happen was presented by Wolfe (1976), who suggested that utilization of key areas by deer is not necessarily proportional to population size. At low population levels, practically all animals may be found in the preferred areas. As population density reaches a saturation point in key areas (where transects are located), no more animals can use them, even though the population continues to increase. If deer density rises further, more and more animals will use marginal and less preferred areas. These relationships may be diagnostic of what has happened to some mule deer herds over the past twenty-five years. Deer numbers on many ranges were excessive during the late 1940s, 1950s, and perhaps into the 1960s. Some herds were reduced by continuing liberal harvests, but commensurate changes in occupancy and vegetation-use indexes were not evident. Consequently, deer populations in some areas may have been overharvested.

Another reason for the apparent failure of browse measurements to reflect declining deer populations is that such surveys provide hindsight rather than foresight. They reflect cumulative past events more adequately than contemporary conditions.

In view of the many factors that may influence deer use of browse at a given time and place, it is perhaps not surprising that Anderson et al. (1972c) found no consistent relationship between shrub use and levels of range occupancy as indicated by pellet group counts. This is additional evidence that browse utilization measurements are not very good indicators of deer density. Such findings, however, do not mean that browse is unimportant to deer, or that managers should be unconcerned about overuse of critical browse stands. It seems logical that chronic overuse of key winter ranges eventually would lead to reduced carrying capacity for the herd unit as a whole, but some key areas are bound to sustain heavy use if surrounding areas are used at all. Therefore it seems that locally heavy browsing on key areas is not, of itself, proof that deer numbers are excessive.

Some workers have gone beyond the prospect of browse utilization measurements to indicate deer population trends and have suggested that deer numbers could be estimated directly from such measurements. Rasmussen and Doman (1943, p. 377) stated that "recent range investigations have shown methods of determining forage production and utilization by weight, and . . . that the weight of forage taken by deer is a relatively constant factor. Use of these factors can supply information on numbers." Other authors (McCain and Taylor 1956) have proposed more specifically that deer numbers could be estimated from the percentage consumption of key forage species such as bitterbrush. However, I have been unable to find any study in which this has been done. Such use of browse measurements would require determination of the mean daily intake of browse—both for the range as a whole and by the average deer—together with the assumption that daily consumption of browse was

Annual measurements of browse production on "key" shrub species, such as bitterbrush on this winter range in southern Idaho, have been a traditional feature of mule deer management in many western states. In recent years the value of browse measurements in deer management has been increasingly challenged by wildlife biologists and managers. Photograph by Stu Murrell; courtesy of the Idaho Department of Fish and Game.

constant during the period of measurements. However, it would be unrealistic to assume such constancy over any appreciable length of time; both percentage and species of browse in the diet fluctuate widely (Leach 1956). Use of browse tends to be inversely proportional to the availability of other forage (see chap. 2).

INDICATORS OF ANIMAL CONDITION

Because deer are a product of their environment, it seems reasonable that their health and physical condition should reflect habitat quality. Accordingly, wildlife biologists have devoted much effort to study of animal characteristics that might be measured as indicators of condition. A remarkably long list of factors and parameters have been shown to relate in some way to animal condition. Body weight, carcass weight, carcass density, percentage of carcass fat, depth of back fat, kidney fat index, femur marrow fat, length of jaw, and numerous blood parameters are only a few possibilities. For mule and black-tailed deer, most attention has centered on measures of body depot fat in dead animals, such as hunter kills or deer shot for scientific study. For a detailed discussion of fat metabolism in mule deer, see chapter 2.

Ever since the landmark papers by Cheatum (1949a) on bone marrow as an index of malnutrition in deer and by Riney (1955) describing the kidney fat index, wildlife biologists have tested, assessed, and refined these measures. Kidney fat index is the weight of fat surrounding the kidney expressed as a percentage of kidney weight. There are many possible kidney fat indexes, and, regardless of the method chosen, the results will show high variability (Anderson et al. 1972b).

Bone marrow, usually from the femur, is assessed in terms of its fat content. The most accurate measures of marrow fat content come from somewhat cumbersome laboratory methods. Because of the time, expense, and equipment involved, much effort has gone into developing faster and cheaper procedures. Cheatum (1949a) proposed that bone marrow could be assessed visually, since marrow of deer in good condition is white and solid,

whereas that of undernourished deer is gelatinous and yellow or red. His subjective method has been used widely, but its primary value is to distinguish extremely high from extremely low marrow fat levels. A more objective compression method was developed by Greer (1968), but still more precise results can be obtained simply by determining dry matter content, which correlates directly with fat content. Marrow samples are weighed before and after drying to determine the percentage of dry matter. Drying can be accomplished either in a controlled-temperature oven (Nieland 1970) or by dehydrating the sample with a chloroform/methanol solution and allowing the moisture to evaporate (Verme and Holland 1973). Mansfield et al. (1975) found an acid digestion method faster than conventional solvent extraction and equally accurate, but both methods required laboratory facilities.

Neither kidney fat index (KFI) nor femur marrow fat (FMF) measures have been com-

Fat content of bone marrow correlates with general health of deer. Marrow is easily removed, either for fat analysis or dry matter determination. Photograph courtesy of the Oregon Department of Fish and Wildlife.

pletely satisfactory as condition indicators for deer. The metabolism of depot fat varies from one storage site to another, so that no one site provides a good index to the entire range of possible body conditions. As a deer declines in condition, it uses subcutaneous fat first, followed by visceral fat and, finally, femur marrow fat (Pojar and Reed 1974). Kidney fat index is apparently not a reliable indicator of physical condition during mobilization of femur marrow fat, so Ransom (1965) suggested a method that combined the two measures. Such a method, called CONINDEX, is currently in use on the Steens Mountain mule deer population study in Oregon. CONINDEX is expressed as follows: for KFI equal to or above 20, CONINDEX = (KFI - 20) + FMF; for KFI below 20, CONINDEX = FMF. CONINDEX is a positive index; that is, the larger the fat deposits, the higher the index and the better the physical condition of the deer.

Average CONINDEX ratings for mule deer fawns from Steens Mountain were relatively high in September (74.1) and December (65.7), with a substantial drop to 29.0 in March. Adult does in March yielded higher scores. The indexes increased with age for does 21–45 months old, then decreased. Does 93+ months of age had the lowest scores observed for adult does. Through use of this condition index, it was concluded that the high fawn mortality rate in this population was not due to inadequate nutritional reserves of does during late pregnancy (Trainer et al. 1978*a,b*).

Kistner (1976) has developed a condition scheme in which the carcass is rated (1) emaciated, (2) poor, (3) fair or thrifty, (4) good, or (5) excellent, based on fullness of body musculature and relative amounts of fat present in each of the indicator depot sites— heart, pericardium, omentum, kidney, and subcutaneous areas. Visual estimates of fat are rated from 0 to 3, as follows:

Estimate of Fat	Rating	Contribution to Score
No visible fat	0	0 points
Slight quantities of fat	1	5 points
Moderate quantities of fat	2	10 points
Heavy quantities of fat	3	15 points

In addition, full body musculature contributes 5 points to the total score, but bony musculature contributes 0 points. The numerical rating of each indicator site will contribute 0 to 15 points, and total score will fall between 0 and 100. These scores relate to condition classes as follows:

Score	Condition Class
0–6	(1) Emaciated
7–15	(2) Poor
16–50	(3) Fair
51–70	(4) Good
Over 70	(5) Excellent

Kistner has found this technique applicable to white-tailed deer in the southeastern United States as well as to mule and black-tailed deer in Oregon. The method is similar to carcass grading as applied to most domestic livestock meat sold in the United States.

Various condition indicators were applied to Colorado mule deer by Anderson et al. (1972*b*), who found most indexes of fat to be significantly interrelated. During winter, all fat indexes were significantly higher for females than for males. From 1962 to 1964, there was a significant annual decrease in femur marrow fat for females, and also in the mean percentage of carcass fat for both males and females. Total annual precipitation and mean browse yields were decreasing during this period.

In a study of black-tailed deer at Hopland Field Station, California, Mansfield et al. (1975) used a variety of measures to compare the physical condition of fawns from oak/woodland and chaparral habitat types. Fawns from oak/woodland appeared to be in better condition than those from chaparral, as shown by significantly higher femur marrow fat and muscle tissue fat. Several other measures also appeared to differ in favor of the oak/woodland animals, but the differences were not statistically significant. Measurements of volatile fatty acids (VFA) in rumen contents indicated higher concentrations of VFA energy and higher propionic–acetic acid ratios in oak/woodland than in chaparral fawns, indicating that forage quality probably was superior in the oak/woodland. In keeping with this assessment, blood urea nitrogen levels also were higher in fawns from oak/woodland.

Even in this cursory review, it is obvious that useful condition indicators exist for mule and black-tailed deer. In view of the amount of effort invested, it is surprising that such indicators have found so little application in management.

BALANCING DEER POPULATIONS WITH THE HABITAT

One of the oldest deer management principles is that harvests should be set and adjusted as needed to keep deer herds in balance with the available habitat. Wildlife managers, in theory, should make annual assessments of both the deer and their range, then set hunting regulations to achieve either increase or decrease in deer numbers, depending on whether the range is understocked or overstocked. As logical and desirable as this approach may seem, however, mule deer managers have had little success in implementing it. In this review of techniques for measuring and analyzing populations, therefore, I am unable to present any established set of procedures by which mule deer harvests can be tailored to habitat conditions.

The lack of appropriate and feasible methods to assess the relationships between deer and deer ranges was discussed at length by wildlife managers and biologists at the Seventh Western States Mule Deer Workshop in Logan, Utah, in February 1978. One participant in this meeting was Jerold Thiessen, state big game manager for the Idaho Department of Fish and Game, who expressed his views as follows:

> The problem of relating environmental conditions to mule deer welfare is just as difficult in Idaho as in other states. We do not understand how to rehabilitate ranges to some predictable end or how mule deer are precisely affected by habitat variables. We do not know how to determine carrying capacity by looking at plants or other indicators as purported in the past. We do not know how to evaluate ranges to determine when they are as optimum as they can be, or which habitat components are causing reduced deer productivity or survival. We are anxiously awaiting a usable explanation of the inter-relationships between range plants or habitat parts and mule deer welfare that will allow us to take a real step forward in management. We have all but given up running utilization transects, pellet group transects, and using range methods which give us some nebulous rating to range status but little else.
>
> Until a habitat evaluation program is developed that has predictive value as it relates to mule deer, Idaho biologists will probably spend their time looking at deer themselves and measuring their performance. We will probably harvest liberally when the survival of young is good and be conservative when survival is poor.
>
> I challenge this group, the most powerful working group presently involved in mule deer management, to chart a course with great determination toward developing meaningful habitat management guidelines and recommending essential ecological research for the states . . . to collectively or individually pursue. The progress of mule deer and mule deer habitat management will be impeded until we do.

This statement is reproduced here because it is a clear and cogent summation of the challenge that confronts deer managers. It is too soon to judge whether the Mule Deer working group will progress in the direction urged by Thiessen.

In Scotland, meanwhile, a management study on red deer (Mutch et al. 1976) provided formal checklists to be used there for annual adjustments to the cull (harvest). There are, of course, fundamental differences between British and North American deer management practices, but the guidelines of Mutch and his colleagues are described here in the hope that they might find catalytic application to mule deer management. Mutch's system requires herd classifications and harvest data much like those recorded by many mule deer biologists. Subjective appraisals of habitat conditions are included as well. In establishing the hind (doe) cull each year, each deer clan (natural herd unit) is to be rated separately against this checklist:

Indicators to *Reduce* the hind cull:

(Check if applicable)

1. Rainfall at Aschnashellach last year in June to September inclusive was more than 28 inches (711mm). If less than 28 inches, no action. ____

2. Calf survival observed last April averaged less than 30 percent. ____

3. Hinds were found dead last winter and this spring (ignore calves). Do deaths exceed average of previous three years in mortality index areas? ⸻
   (Deduct dead hind number from this year's cull.)
4. Red Deer Commission census this year or last year reported a decrease of 10 percent or more in the hind population. ⸻
5. There has been a reduction in deer wintering areas in the last year amounting to 2 percent or more. ⸻

Indicators to *Increase* the hind cull:
6. Calf survival observed in April last year averaged more than 40 percent and there has been no evidence of unusual calf mortality since then. ⸻
7. R.D.C. census this year or last year reported an increase of 10 percent or more in the hind population. ⸻
8. On the wintering areas in late April
   a) Greens look mossy   Yes/No
   b) Heather is "buttoned" or "cushioned"   Yes/No
   c) Less palatable plants are being eaten   Yes/No
   d) Most birch seedlings eaten (lack of birch thickets in/near birch woods)   Yes/No
   (If 3 "yes" above, check here.) ⸻
9. Kidney fat index in milk (lactating) hinds culled last December/January was 1.5 or less. ⸻
10. Increase in winter nutrition by substantial hind feeding or in improved pasture used by hinds (i.e., by 5+ percent of hinds in this deer clan). ⸻

If the indicators for reducing the cull (1–5) are equal in number to those for increasing the cull (6–10), or if there is a difference of only one either way, keep the hind cull as it was in the previous year. If the difference is two, then increase (or reduce) the cull by about 5 percent in the coming season. If the difference is three or more, then increase (or reduce) the cull by about 10 percent in the coming season, subject to the rule that the cull should not be changed in one direction by more than 22 percent in all in any three consecutive seasons. Thus, an important objective is to maintain relative stability over time, both in deer numbers and the annual cull.

Those guidelines were proposed for application in spring each year. In midsummer, a slightly different checklist was given to assess the stag cull. As in North America, the cull in Scotland is taken in autumn.

In proposing these guidelines, Mutch and his colleagues noted that they were not new, but only a formalization of existing practice on many deer estates. The guidelines apply only where the primary land-use objective is deer production. On lands devoted to forestry, deer would be controlled as needed to keep forest damage within acceptable bounds.

North American biologists will find nothing new in the data required for this system, and the management significance of each piece of information is obvious. But the synthesis of separate bits of information on both the habitat and the animals into an overall, decision-making framework is an innovation that could well be emulated in the management of mule and black-tailed deer. One could, of course, program such a system for computer analysis, as is fashionable nowadays, but the system of Mutch et al. is simple enough that computer analysis would perhaps be more hindrance than help. A number of computer models for deer management already exist in the United States and Canada (see "Population Analysis and Modeling," below), but in my opinion none are as relevant to harvest management at the local level as is the model of Mutch et al. (1976). Similar systems can and should be developed for use in the management of mule and black-tailed deer.

POPULATION ANALYSIS AND MODELING

Population analysis is the process of attempting to determine changes over time in age and sex composition, reproduction, mortality, survival, or numbers of animals in a population. The basic ingredients for such analysis are birth rates and death rates, observed age and sex ratios, and time-specific estimates of deer numbers. Given good estimates of these essentials, few complications of mathematics, logic, or terminology are involved in understanding population behavior. For a detailed introduction to this subject, see Eberhardt (1971).

Life Tables

Life tables are a well-known means of summarizing survival and mortality data about animal populations. For wildlife biologists, the primary value of life tables is that they can be used under certain conditions to estimate survival and mortality rates.

Life tables for deer herds usually are based on age composition of animals removed from the population, often by hunters. In making life table calculations, the investigator assumes that the age composition of his sample mirrors that of the population and also that the population is stable over time; that is, births exactly balance deaths, and survival rates are constant from year to year. But rarely, if ever, are these assumptions true for deer populations. The value of life tables is further limited by the fact that they give no information on reproduction.

Use of life tables to estimate survival rates has been discussed previously (see "Methods for Estimating Deer Numbers: Estimates Based on Survival or Mortality Rates"). As indicated there, other techniques are preferred for calculation of survival rates.

Survival and turnover rates often differ between bucks and does in the same deer herd. Life tables offer a good way of comparing mortality patterns of bucks and does, as illustrated by Taber and Dasmann (1957) for black-tailed deer and by Robinette et al. (1977) for mule deer. Both of these studies showed higher survival and life expectancy for does than for bucks. Taber and Dasmann (1957) contrasted survivorship curves for black-tailed deer with those for roe deer, red deer, and Dall's sheep and concluded that observed differences between various ungulate populations were not inherent in the species but rather were imposed by environmental conditions.

There are two kinds of life tables. "Cohort" or "dynamic" tables are based on the fate of a group of animals all born at the same time. Such tables are hard to construct for deer because they require that each fawn born be accounted for throughout its life so that its date of death is known. The more commonly used "current" or "time-specific" life table, in contrast, is based on mortality of each age class within a year's time. The reader is referred to Eberhardt (1971) for discussion of the relative merits of these two kinds of life tables.

Both "dynamic" and "time-specific" life tables were prepared by Robinette et al. (1977) for mule deer at Oak Creek, Utah. Resulting estimates of mortality rates from the two types of tables were virtually identical. However, Eberhardt (1971) strongly recommended against use of "dynamic" calculations on grounds that "time-specific" calculations are likely to be freer of bias.

Reconstructions of Populations

Numerous authors have "reconstructed" deer populations to show births, deaths, and other aspects of population dynamics over time. In contrast to the well-defined life table procedures, population reconstruction is an ad hoc process in which all available data are assembled as necessary to get the required information with maximum accuracy and expediency. Because both the investigator's goals and available information are unique in each case, no two reconstructions are alike. Some reconstructions of fluctuating and of stable deer herds are cited in tables 41 and 42.

The number of statistics that can be calculated from population reconstructions is large; for a partial list, see table 33. Different investigators may be interested in different kinds of information, and a comprehensive listing of all possible statistics that could come from reconstructions is not feasible here. For each reconstruction, a few sample values are given in tables 41 and 42, and readers should consult the original papers for additional information.

Table 41 includes reconstructions of both increasing and decreasing deer herds. The work of Hines (1975) is particularly valuable because it is based on known numbers of deer. All other examples in tables 41 and 42 are from wild populations, and in each case data were subject to normal sampling errors.

For stable deer herds, it becomes meaningful to express population dynamics in terms of

Table 41. Reconstructions of Some Fluctuating Mule and Black-tailed Deer Populations

Study Area	Number of Years Reconstructed (*t*)	Total Deer Numbers		Mean Annual Rate of Increase[a], in Percent	Reference
		Start (*B*)	End (*E*)		
Interstate deer herd, California/Oregon	2	20,000	13,599	− 17.5	Cronemiller (1951)
Lake County, California	4[b]	2,901	3,384	+ 3.9[c]	Taber and Dasmann (1957)
Western Washington	8	2,690	1,441	− 7.5	Brown (1961)
North Kaibab, Arizona	6	9,569	12,739	+ 4.9	Russo (1964)
Three-Bar, Arizona	6	1,200	773	− 7.1	Smith et al. (1969)
Cedar Creek, Oregon[d]	5	30	60	+14.9	Hines (1975)
Missouri River Breaks, Montana	15	1,100	400	− 6.5	Mackie (1976*b*)
Middle Park, Colorado	1	10,000	11,617	+16.2	Freddy and Gill (1977)
Okanogan deer herd, Washington	1	180	230	+27.8	Ziegler (1978)

[a] Expressed as an interest rate compounded annually, the rate of increase equals $(E/B)^{1/t} - 1$. Negative values indicate decreasing populations.

[b] Dynamics of black-tailed deer for four years after wildfire in chaparral.

[c] Population nearly tripled during first year after fire but decreased thereafter.

[d] Enclosed population with known numbers of deer.

turnover and mortality rates. (This could be done with fluctuating populations, too, but the information would be less useful.) It may be significant that turnover and mortality rates for various stable deer herds (table 42) fall within a relatively restricted range, in comparison with what is theoretically possible. Such similarity may reflect the fact that each population was believed to be limited by nutritional constraints. Deer at Oak Creek, Utah, and the Hopland Field Station, California, were subject to either-sex hunting, but in the other herds only bucks with two or more points on at least one antler were legal game.

Population reconstruction frequently serves to furnish input data for computerized models; for example, see F. M. Anderson et al. (1974).

Development of Modeling Concepts

It is assumed that most readers of this book will have had little or no firsthand experience with computer models or simulation of deer

Table 42. Reconstructions of Some Stable Mule and Black-tailed Deer Populations

Study Area	Total Deer Numbers		Annual Turnover Rate ([B−A]/B), in Percentage	Annual Mortality Rates in Percentage			Reference
	Minimum (*A*)	Maximum (*B*)[a]		Bucks	Does	Fawns	
Chaparral, Lake County, California	2,498	3,448	28	27	17	45	Taber and Dasmann (1957)
Shrubland, Lake County, California	5,154	9,005	43	34	25	63	Taber and Dasmann (1957)
Hopland Field Station, California	480	740	35	47	18	50	Connolly (1970); F. M. Anderson et al (1974)
Mendocino County, California	142,000	240,000	41	22	23	69	F. M. Anderson et al. (1974)
Oak Creek, Utah	2,053	3,444	40	53	19	48	Robinette et al. (1977)[b]

[a] Maximum population equals minimum (prefawning) population plus fawn crop.

[b] Additional data on this population are given elsewhere in this chapter (see "Productivity and Rate of Increase" and table 33).

populations. Therefore this section is intended as a general introduction to modeling and simulation as applied to deer management. A guide to some relevant literature (table 43) is included for those who wish to explore the subject further.

Ever since the origin of wildlife management as a science, biologists have struggled with the quantitative aspects of deer numbers, limiting factors, and harvests. Managers have always tried to abstract mentally the most important features governing deer populations and have made management decisions based on their intuitive notions about how these important features relate to one another. Whenever a biologist tries to anticipate or predict the behavior or response of a deer herd from past or current information, he is applying his mental model of that deer herd. It is important to realize that modeling is taking place, regardless of whether the model is written down or whether a computer is involved. But by writing out or programming his model a biologist or manager makes it more useful to other persons who may be interested in the same deer herd.

In writing or programming his model, the modeler must clarify his thinking and make it specific. Inconsistencies and vague concepts that may have existed in the mental model must be resolved and clarified. The written model offers a base from which to experiment as well as a framework for evaluating both the data and the assumptions that went into it. Most important, written or programmed models lend themselves to criticism and use by other people, whereas mental models do not. To be useful in wildlife management, a written model does not necessarily have to be programmed on a computer. For examples of written, unprogrammed models, see tables 41 and 42.

To formulate a written or programmed model, one must select the most important features of the population or ecosystem being modeled, then specify how they relate to one another. After each process and relationship has been expressed mathematically, the pieces must be put together to see if the whole model operates logically. Computers are not essential to this process, but they are very useful because of their tremendous capability for information storage and retrieval. However, the computer is simply an accounting and calculating tool. It contributes no insights or truths except those written into its program. That a model runs on a computer confers no extra credibility on its assumptions or input data, nor on the conclusions drawn from experiments with the model.

From the foregoing discussion, it will be apparent that construction and use of simulation models is accomplished in a series of steps.

1. Establish boundaries, purpose, and time scale.

2. Determine what information to include and what to exclude from the model; that is, which variables about the population of interest are to be included and which are to be excluded.

3. State how various quantities in the model are related to one another. This usually is accomplished by block diagrams or flow charts, with lines connecting the boxes that influence one another. It is helpful to write down the assumptions that are incorporated in the diagram.

4. Describe or program relationships in mathematical terms for processing on a calculator or computer.

5. Evaluate, verify, and modify the running model.

6. Make simulation experiments.

7. Assess the results in light of all assumptions made.

8. Present the data and the model in such a way that other persons can comprehend them.

These steps can be accomplished without advanced mathematical techniques, although sophisticated procedures may be used for efficiency in the computer program. Most useful simulations are based on simple, tedious arithmetic.

Simulation Models of Deer Populations

Simulation models can differ widely in scope and content depending on their intended use. Most models developed to date for blacktail and mule deer populations deal with the effects of

Table 43. Selected References on Simulation Models in Deer Research and Management

Reference	Contents
F. M. Anderson et al. (1974)	Shows effects of various hunting strategies on a simulated black-tailed deer population and on benefits and costs associated with that population.
Black et al. (1975)	Describes a model to evaluate the effect of timber management decisions on elk and deer habitat. By considering these effects in advance, there is opportunity to lessen negative impact or to enhance habitat.
Bunnell (1974)	Exposition of the modeling approach, including fundamental procedures, reasons for building models, and applications to management.
Cooperrider and Behrend (1974)	Describes a model to account for effects of winter weather, forest management practices, and harvest pressure on whitetail populations; also simulates impact of deer on forest regeneration.
Davis (1967)	Describes a linear programming model for deer management planning.
Giles et al. (1969)	Presents a topographic, three-dimensional model of population stability and a discussion of management problems related to population stability.
Giles and Snyder (1970)	Describes a model that simulates production of deer and elk forage on national forests in northern Idaho. The model allows simulated manipulation of habitat to achieve predetermined objectives.
Gross (1969)	Defines optimum yield management of deer as that intensity of harvest that will maximize annual production of young.
Gross (1972)	Suggests that computer models can be used to reduce intuitive errors in big game management planning.
Gross (1973)	Discusses how computerized information systems might improve decision-making by wildlife management agencies.
Gross et al. (1973)	Describes "Program ONEPOP," which has been used to model mule deer and other big game herds in several states. This report details development and validation of the model and gives the computer program.
Hayne (1969)	General discussion of modeling concepts. Suggests a comprehensive modeling scheme for white-tailed deer management in the southeastern United States.
Henny et al. (1970)	Presents a method for calculating parameters necessary to maintain stable populations.
Lipscomb (1974)	Presents a three-stage method of analysis for annually determining desired harvest levels of big game populations.
Medin (1976)	Detailed description of a model that simulates dynamics of a hunted mule deer population; computer program is included. Gives a good general discussion on strengths and weaknesses of simulation models.
Pojar (1977)	Describes the use of program ONEPOP in big game management in Colorado, where 79 simulations have been established for annual use. Gives examples of modeling to establish harvest goals for pronghorn and elk.

(Table 43.)

Reference	Contents
Pospahala (1969)	Literature review on use of computers in wildlife biology.
Walters and Bandy (1972)	Gives a theoretical argument that total yield from big game herds can be maximized through periodic (once in every several years) rather than annual harvests.
Walters and Gross (1972)	Illustrates use of model to determine priorities for collection of deer population data. Consequences of increased harvest and population catastrophes (such as complete loss of one year's fawn crop) are shown, along with optimum yield under various constraints.

either harvests or habitat modifications. Simulation experiments with various kinds of harvests have been described by Davis (1967), Gross (1969, 1972, 1973), Walters and Gross (1972), Walters and Bandy (1972), F. M. Anderson et al. (1974), Medin (1976), and Pojar (1977). Space does not permit a detailed discussion of these studies, but examples of their findings are given in table 44. Experienced wildlife managers will realize that the general conclusions are more or less common knowledge. The models do not give much new information but tend to organize, quantify, and reinforce the knowledge that experienced wildlife managers and biologists already have. Modelers are fond of saying that their work identifies gaps in existing data, but often these gaps were apparent before modeling took place.

In table 44, the conclusions listed under "Economics" show how one can apply simulation models to political and economic aspects of deer management. As demonstrated by F. M. Anderson et al. (1974), models can provide "best" management solutions only when arbitrary values are assigned to intangible benefits and costs. For this reason it is unlikely that computer models will supplant professional judgment in formulating decisions on controversial deer management issues.

Although computerized deer management models have been rather successful in elucidating or providing numerical support for important management principles (table 44), the use of computer models to aid harvest management decisions for specific mule deer herds

has been very limited to date. In Colorado, however, separate simulation models have been established for each of thirty-three deer, thirty-three elk, and thirteen pronghorn populations (data analysis units). The simulations are used to experiment with harvest options and are believed to aid in long-range planning and goal-oriented management. For a very readable description of the application of these simulations to specific big game harvest decisions, see Pojar (1977). The Colorado simulations, and similar ones in Wyoming and other states, are based on the ONEPOP program of Gross et al. (1973).

While Colorado and some other states have found computer simulations useful in planning big game harvests, Oregon has abandoned the ONEPOP model after preliminary trials with four big game herds. The leader of the Oregon modeling project concluded that deficiencies in the model, available data, and knowledge of animal-environment interactions prevented effective use of this model to predict allowable harvests for specific big game populations (Hall 1978). However, simulation was said to have been useful in identifying research needs in Oregon.

An example of the use of the ONEPOP model to assess mule deer harvest strategies was given by Gross (1973) for the Uncompahgre deer herd in Colorado. The first option considered was maximum possible production of trophy bucks, which turned out to be realized with an annual harvest of about 2,550 bucks along with about 450 antlerless deer. A

Table 44. Some General Conclusions from Deer Population Simulation and Modeling Studies

Subject	Conclusions	References[a]
Maintaining population stability	Population stability can be maintained under extremely variable sex ratios, natalities, and life expectancies.	(1)
	The likelihood that a population will decrease becomes less as the proportion of females increases.	(1)
	As hunting reduces life expectancy in a stable population, natality and/or the proportion of females must increase to maintain stability.	(1)
	To reverse a declining population, a manager must: increase the proportion of females; increase life expectancy; increase birthrates; or achieve some combination of these. The converse is true for increasing herds in need of reduction.	(1)
Effects of harvest on population dynamics	High harvest rates tend to lower average age of animals in the hunted population. If only bucks are hunted, average age will drop for bucks but not for does.	(2, 3)
	Selective hunting of bucks increases the proportion and actual number of does in a population and thereby increases the number of fawns born.	(1, 2)
	Compared with hunting of bucks only, either-sex hunts result in a smaller, more productive deer herd.	(2)
	Compared with unhunted herds, hunting of bucks only has little effect on total deer numbers but does reduce the number of bucks and increase the number of does in a population.	(2)
Managing the harvest	When only bucks are hunted, both hunter success and trophy quality decline as hunting pressure increases.	(2)
	Where deer numbers must be reduced, this can best (most efficiently) be achieved by taking does only.	(2)
	Increased yields might be obtained from some big game populations by harvesting only once every several years, rather than by harvesting annually.	(4)
	Maximum production of adult bucks can be achieved only when does as well as bucks are harvested.	(2)
	Maximum harvest and maximum population size are biologically incompatible management goals.	(2, 5, 6)
	Maximum harvest and maximum reproductive rate are biologically incompatible management goals.	(6)
	Maximum numerical yield requires heavy harvest of fawns.	(2, 3)

(Table 44.)

Subject	Conclusions	References[a]
	There is no uniquely best long-term harvest strategy in an environment that fluctuates annually.	(3)
Economics	Dynamic programming offers a way to determine minimum dollar value of harvested deer needed to justify deer management on different timber sites.	(7)
	Output from simulation models can be used to determine which hunting strategy will maximize economic value of a deer herd. However, this requires arbitrary definition of dollar values for intangible benefits and costs.	(2)

[a] (1) Giles et al. (1969).
(2) F. M. Anderson et al. (1974).
(3) Medin (1976).
(4) Walters and Bandy (1972).
(5) Gross (1969).
(6) Gross (1972).
(7) Davis (1967).

constraint then was introduced into the model; to satisfy hunter demand, it was necessary to harvest at least 4,600 animals each year. Simulation of maximum trophy production under this constraint showed that the desired 4,600 animals could be achieved, but only at a cost of about a 50 percent reduction in trophy value of the annual harvest. The number of bucks produced under option 2 was greater than in option 1, but average trophy value (based on age and size of bucks) was lower. If the decision-maker for this deer herd was satisfied with the harvest of 4,600 animals, subject to the stated loss in trophy value, then his objective for this population was achieved by option 2. According to the model, this strategy would have produced a preharvest population of about 31,000 deer with a sex ratio of 56 males per 100 females. The strategy would have provided about 30,000 recreation-days each year. Assumptions and relationships on which the conclusions are based appear in another report (Gross et al. 1973) that the reader will need in order to evaluate the model critically.

In presenting the above example, Gross (1973) used some innovative visual displays. One planning device, which he called a "ouija board," consisted of response surfaces or contour maps that graphically represented all possible values that could occur for selected variables under all possible harvest strategies. Six variables were shown for the Uncompahgre deer herd: total annual harvest, antlered harvest, annual trophy harvest, preharvest population, preharvest sex ratio, and number of recreation-days. Gross also illustrated a "critical path plotter" that was intended to help the planner establish five-year management plans. The critical path plotter provided alternative ways to move from an established, or current, harvest program to the new program suggested by the model. These visual aids merit careful study by persons who contemplate use of simulation models in management, since the best possible communication aids are needed to convey model output to decision-makers, sportsmen, and other interested parties.

By changing input data to reflect the biological characteristics of the species involved, the model of Gross et al. (1973) can be used on many species of wild ungulates. Such simulations are undergoing continuous development and refinement, and therefore their utility in big game management is likely to increase.

Evaluating the Validity of Simulation Models

No one can accept or use results from a model without first accepting the premise that the model is valid. In modeling, "validation" refers to the process of developing an acceptable level of confidence that the model adequately represents the actual process and field situation being simulated. Validity might be assessed by judging whether the assumptions and data are rational and reasonable, or by showing that the simulated population behaves like the real one. The latter course contains an element of circular logic whenever the validation is based on the same data used as input; agreement between input and output may demonstrate only that the model reproduces what is fed into it. Gross et al. (1973) made a distinction between validation of the model and validation of test data but stated that the two usually proceeded simultaneously. When discrepancies occurred between simulated results and measured real-world values, either the models or the test data were changed as needed to secure acceptable agreement among simulated and known results.

Regardless of what is done in the name of validation, acceptance of a model as valid comes down to pure judgment, by someone, that the data are correct and the assumptions are valid. In the final analysis, validity of the model is a function of the knowledge, experience, and integrity of the modelers (McLeod 1973). A model can be valid for one application but invalid for another.

In discussing the validity of his mule deer simulation model, Medin (1976) identified three reasons why it could not be expected to provide accurate numerical predictions for a real population: uncertainty in estimates of the model's essential parameters, including the initial conditions; possible omission of some important relationships and incorrect modeling of others; and unpredictable fluctuations in environmental conditions that influence the dynamics of mule deer populations. Such constraints probably apply to most big game simulation models, but they do not prevent exploration of broader questions of management policy and population dynamics, nor do they preclude conditional predictions.

Simulation modeling of wildlife populations often is a joint enterprise of biologists and modelers. The former must provide realistic data on the population and its life processes so the latter can construct realistic mathematical representations of those processes. The modeler must comprehend the limitations of field data, and the biologist must not expect the output to be any more reliable or precise than the input. Constraints and weaknesses of the model must be explained fully to potential users of the output. Otherwise some users may overestimate the capabilities of the model or draw inappropriate conclusions from its output. Dissatisfied users may criticize modelers, and modeling in general, for interpretation errors that actually resulted from their own failure to comprehend limitations of the model.

Constraints on the Use of Computer Models in Deer Management

To date, only a small percentage of wildlife biologists in North America has been involved with the development or application of simulation models. Other biologists, as well as legislators, administrators, and the public, must see that models are truly useful before their use can become widespread. This is a substantial educational challenge that faces modeling advocates. Not only are models attended by various limitations on their use that must be appreciated by all parties, but even the simplest models contain enough detail that to understand them requires formidable study.

Suitable computers for simulation modeling of deer ecosystems are widely available for nominal use charges, but competent systems analysts are no more or less recognizable than competent biologists. Some agencies may be discouraged from using this technology by the difficulty of securing appropriate expertise or by the high initial costs of data collection and model development. Cooperrider and Behrend (1974) suggested that these costs would delay adoption of simulation modeling by wildlife managers, but modifications of existing models may save a substantial part of development costs. Data collection is another matter.

Models can identify which variables need to be sampled most precisely in the field, but one would not expect modeling to replace field data collection. As it turns out, data requirements for deer simulation models are similar to those for deer management in general: the better the data, the better will be management decisions and the more realistic will be the model. Modeling should be regarded not as a possible substitute for field data but as a technique to get the greatest possible amount of information from data that will (or should) be gathered regardless of whether modeling is to be done. Once the data are at hand, the cost of modeling is relatively trivial. In Colorado in 1976, for example, the computer time to model seventy-nine big game populations cost less than the helicopter time expended to get herd-structure data on a single elk herd (T. M. Pojar, pers. comm., July 1978).

Although Pospahala (1969) suggested that the greatest constraint on increased use of models is the difficulty of programming functional relationships to represent the complex systems that exist in nature, I suggest that getting really good field data is a more difficult problem than the programming. A more immediate limitation may be the lack of enthusiasm among influential persons to whom simulation modeling is an unknown and therefore suspect discipline. Some officials who make management decisions (based on their own mental models) may resist the intrusion of modelers into their domain. Granted, there is ample reason for skepticism about models, but the only purpose of the modeler should be to provide better understanding of the population or resource to be managed. Output from present models leaves ample leeway for decision-makers to weigh implications of simulation results against political and socioeconomic considerations that are beyond the purview of the models and yet are as important as biological information in many management decisions.

Often, the politically feasible management options are very limited in comparison with what might be biologically feasible. When political rather than biological constraints prevent progress toward management goals, models offer little help toward improved management. Models might be useful, however, in information and education programs aimed at relieving political constraints. For readers who wish to pursue the differences between the theory and practice of management decisions, Lindblom (1959) is recommended.

Conclusions

Computerized models are useful tools for both research and management, but they do not offer instant and painless solutions to complex management problems. Following is a list of things that, in my opinion, models can and cannot do for mule deer management.

Models *can:*

1. Organize piecemeal bits of information into a unified and logical framework to help guide research or management decisions.

2. Help managers develop realistic, specific management objectives.

3. Show what kinds of data are most useful in management and what information is lacking.

4. Help managers define the range of possible management options from which one must be chosen.

5. Estimate, in general terms, the effects of various hunting strategies on deer herds.

6. Make conditional forecasts of potential harvests or other variables of interest.

7. Stimulate critical and constructive thought about assumptions on which deer management decisions are based.

8. Help biologists, sportsmen, and others reevaluate intuitive notions about deer population dynamics and the effects of hunting.

Models *cannot:*

1. Produce correct and precise predictions from fragmentary input data of questionable accuracy, combined with assumptions of unwarranted simplicity.

2. Spare the wildlife biologist or manager the need to collect field data.

3. Free wildlife managers from the need for careful study and reflection about management problems as they exist in the field.

4. Circumvent political realities or the need for good information and education programs.

DESERT AND CHAPARRAL HABITATS

Part 1. Food Habits and Nutrition

Philip J. Urness
Associate Professor of Range Science
Utah State University
Logan, Utah

Drought is the dominant feature affecting mule and black-tailed deer occupying desert and chaparral habitats. Annual drought in these types is a function of normally high temperatures and low rainfall or uneven distribution of effective precipitation. Variations in these factors dictate the seasonal march of forage availability, quality, and selection. The sequence or timing of precipitation over extended periods is important; often two or more relatively wet seasons in a row are necessary to produce abundant forage and fawn crops (Martin 1975; Shaw 1965). Indeed, the reproductive cycle appears attuned to variations in annual drought periods across the Southwest (Wallmo 1973). Fawning coincides most favorably with new plant growth to promote lactation in postpartum does in Arizona, New Mexico, and Texas—all of which are areas of summer rainfall (fig. 21). In California, with long summer drought, fawning is highly variable, but resident deer populations in chaparral habitat generally peak in May, toward the end of the growing season (Bischoff 1957). At this time of year, does in these areas approach maximum body condition, and late spring growth of nutritious forage sustains lactation.

Soils of most desert and chaparral sites are poorly developed, frequently shallow and stony, and moderately fertile at best (Buol 1966; Sampson and Jespersen 1963). Many are calcareous and are low in phosphorus and nitrogen (Vlamis et al. 1954). Despite these limitations, many browse and forb species on such sites are of fair to good nutritional quality for deer, and supply adequate dietary nutrients most of the year. This is especially true where management or natural disturbance factors have increased diversity in vegetational communities that tend to be dominated by one or a few species. Greater diversity provides deer a wider array of forage choices and permits them to shift dietary composition to avoid certain types of forage that decline in quality as they mature. Fruits of various woody plants and succulents are particularly valuable in this regard.

Vegetational management also can affect deer diets and nutrition through rejuvenated shrub growth, improved water distribution, and balance of forage classes. For example, once chaparral shrubs are established, leachates from their foliage may suppress germination and growth of herbaceous plants (Muller and

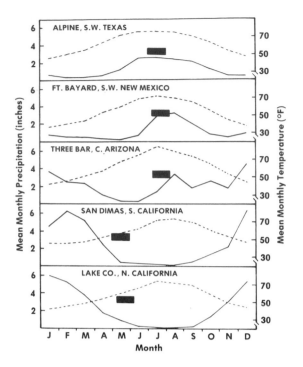

Figure 21. Relation of peak fawning period *(bar)* of nonmigratory mule deer to precipitation *(solid line)* and temperature *(dashed line)* patterns over a broad geographical range of desert and chaparral habitats in the Southwest.

Chou 1972). Reduction of shrub density can greatly increase growth of high-quality forbs and cool-season grasses, which are important deer forage. Warm-season grasses are of little value.

Successional changes since European settlement, and particularly in the past hundred years, have had both beneficial and detrimental effects on mule deer habitat in the Southwest. Through increased cover and forage values, encroachment of woody plants onto areas formerly dominated by grasses has compensated in part for areas lost to intensive cultivation and other economic developments (Hastings and Turner 1965; Taber 1963; Leopold 1924; Humphrey 1958b; Sampson 1944; Martin 1975). These changes have resulted from livestock grazing practices, alterations in fire patterns, and possibly subtle climatic shifts (Longhurst et al. 1952, 1976; Taber and Dasmann 1958; Urness 1976). Differences in climate, soils, vegetation, and land-use patterns make generalities among regions of doubtful utility,

despite some gross similarities. Therefore, broad geographic subunits will be discussed separately in this part of the chapter.

CALIFORNIA CHAPARRAL

The term "chaparral" is applied rather broadly here to brushland communities west of the Sierra Nevada Summit, including elements extending upward into coniferous forest and down into woodland/grass types (Sampson and Jespersen 1963). Nonmigratory Columbian black-tailed deer and Southern mule deer occupy intermediate and lower-elevation chaparral in a belt between 300 and 1,200 meters (1,100–4,000 feet). Above this zone, chaparral is used for the most part as winter range by migratory California mule deer that summer in the Sierra Nevada (Longhurst et al. 1952; Dixon 1934).

Composition of California chaparral varies from extensive, nearly monospecific communities dominated by chamise, manzanita, or ceanothus to highly complex mixtures with oak and many other shrubs. Typically, chaparral dominants are sclerophyllous, deep-rooted, and drought-tolerant; many sprout vigorously from root crowns when burned.

Food habits of resident and migratory deer in California chaparral have been studied by many workers at various locations. But relatively few studies have been quantitative, and the nutritional value of species or classes of forage seldom has been discussed in any but general terms. Cronemiller and Bartholomew (1950) found that leaves of scrub oak and toyon constituted 95 percent of summer and autumn diets of deer at San Dimas. Herbaceous material, green grasses, and numerous forbs were most abundant in rumens collected in winter and spring. Dixon (1934) vaguely described the winter diet of a migratory mule deer population that summered in Yosemite National Park and wintered in west-slope chaparral as consisting mainly of browse, heavily supplemented in some years with green annual grasses that developed after autumn rains.

The average winter diet of the migratory Jawbone herd was described by Ferrel and Leach (1950) as 89 percent browse, 9 percent green grass, and about 2 percent forbs (table 45). On the Tehama winter range—a mixture of annual grassland, oak woodland, and chaparral—the average winter diet consisted of 54 percent browse, 20 percent forbs, and 26

Table 45. Principal Foods of Three California Deer Herds (Species or Classes Constituting 3 Percent or More of the Volume of Seasonal Diets)

Herd Location (type)	Season	Food	Percentage of Volume	Source
Tehama (migratory)	Winter	Manzanita	4.9	Leach and Hiehle (1957)
		Buckbrush ceanothus	3.7	
		Deer brush ceanothus	3.2	
		Birchleaf mountain mahogany	4.0	
		Oak (acorns)	11.1	
		Blue oak	9.1	
		Scrub oak	8.9	
		Oregon white oak	3.0	
		Black oak	13.6	
		Total forbs	10.8	
		Total grass	19.3	
		Total	91.6	
Jawbone (migratory)	Winter	Manzanita	11.2 (9.0)	Ferrell and Leach (1950)—rumen contents;[a] Leopold et al. (1951)—sight records[b]
		Buckbrush ceanothus	12.3 (51.0)	
		Sierra mountain misery	37.3 (25.0)	
		Incense cedar	3.0	
		Toyon	4.0	
		Oak	14.3 (13.0)	
		Stonecrop	3.1	
		Green grass	9.1	
		Total	94.2 (98.0)	
Lake County (resident)	Yearlong	Chamise	31.6	Bissell and Strong (1955)
		Scrub oak	9.4	
		Interior oak	11.7	
		Poison oak	3.5	
		Forbs	10.9	
		Grass	9.0	
		Total	74.1	
Lake County (resident)	Yearlong	Chamise	40.2 (21.5) [38.1]	Taber and Dasmann (1958)[c]
		California buckeye	(3.0)	
		Deer brush ceanothus	4.6	
		Mountain mahogany	[3.6]	
		Fremont silk tassel	9.9	
		Chaparral pea	3.5	
		Oak (acorns)	6.5	
		Scrub oak	15.0 (13.1) [23.1]	
		Interior oak	9.3 (5.6) [7.0]	
		Poison oak	(5.0) [5.4]	
		California wild grape	3.7	
		Forbs	(16.8) [9.3]	
		Grass	(14.6) [4.2]	
		Total	92.7 (74.6) [90.7]	

[a] List not in parentheses is from Ferrell and Leach (1950).

[b] List in parentheses is from Leopold et al. (1951).

[c] List not in parentheses or brackets represents study of herd in chaparral; list in parentheses represents herd in shrubland; list in brackets represents herd in wildfire burn. All from Taber and Dasmann (1958).

percent grasses (Leach and Hiehle 1957). The summer range of these deer—open mixed-conifer forest with a brushland understory—provided a diet with less herbaceous forage: 72 percent browse; 25 percent forbs; and 3 percent grass.

It can be concluded that diets of deer in chaparral are dominated by mature browse during the hot-dry summer and autumn when herbaceous species have matured, or by browse in dense, mature stands with poor understories (Taber 1956*b*; Taber and Dasmann 1958). Browse also is important in winter and spring when new growth appears. In all situations, grasses and forbs are used in winter and spring to the extent that they are available, but they are the predominant forage class wherever they are abundant, as in manipulated shrublands (fig. 22). Thus, heavy use of low-quality browse reflects the scarcity of other forage (Hagen 1953; Biswell et al. 1952; also see table 45).

Of course, regional averages obscure local variations. For example, in habitats that include irrigated valley lands, deer may consume

appreciable amounts of agricultural crops in summer and autumn after natural feeds mature (Taber 1963; Longhurst et al. 1952). Mis-

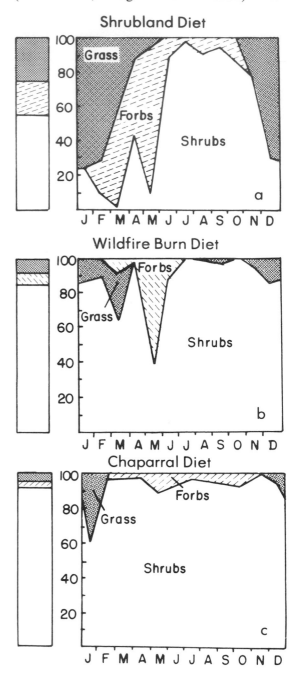

Figure 22. Composition (percentages) of the annual black-tailed deer diet in three kinds of chaparral habitats in northern California, showing increased use of herbaceous forage as the chaparral community is opened up by fire or other means (from Taber and Dasmann 1958).

A Columbian black-tailed doe in California chaparral. Both the chamise buckbrush *(top right)* and scrub oak *(lower left)* have been heavily browsed by deer. Photograph by Guy E. Connolly.

tletoe, fungi, and mast, especially acorns, are eaten avidly when available (Biswell 1959). Such foods are of greatest value in late summer and autumn when deer are at the lowest levels of the annual nutritional cycle, before autumn rains and new plant growth.

Most nutritional studies of deer have focused on selected forage species, not on entire diets, so it is difficult to generalize on overall nutrient intake. Crude protein has been given the most attention. In general, crude protein levels in browse decline from late summer through winter (Hagen 1953; Taber 1956b; Sampson 1944; Dasmann and Dasmann 1963a; Bissell and Strong 1955). Also, crude protein content of regrowth browse is high immediately after a fire but declines rapidly in the second and third years (Reynolds and Sampson 1943; Taber and Dasmann 1958; Sampson 1944). In autumn and winter, crude protein content of most browse species approaches minimum requirements for deer, and protein digestibility of those species also is low (Bissell and Weir 1957; Bissell et al. 1955; Hagen 1953). Nevertheless, total diets appear to be deficient

in crude protein only during summer and autumn in dense stands of chaparral with little understory vegetation. On managed stands or recently burned areas, dietary crude protein levels are good yearlong (fig. 23). Evaluations of the nutritional potential of "hardened" browse suggest that other foods are necessary to prevent serious nutritional deficiencies during periods of shrub dormancy, or that methods of analysis have underestimated browse values.

There have been few studies on the digestibility of individual forage species, and none on entire diets of deer in California chaparral. Most have involved a single browse species or simple mixtures. In a study by Hagen (1953), total digestible nutrient (TDN) coefficients for buckbrush were about 50 percent, the same level as for alfalfa. The deer used in these tests lost 11–13 percent of their body weight over 8–12 days, but this was attributed to low feed intake rather than forage quality. The material offered was dried, ground, and apparently unpalatable. In similar trials, Bissell et al. (1955) obtained lower TDN coefficients for live oak (34 percent) and higher coefficients for chamise (59 percent). Again, daily intake was low. Later, Bissell and Weir (1957) pelleted live oak and chamise mixed with alfalfa to improve intake. They obtained TDN values of 38 percent for live oak and 48 percent for chamise.

Longhurst et al. (1952) reasoned that, if populations remain at excessively high levels for long periods, the supply of nutrients on the range will be depleted. As plant species of higher quality are utilized heavily and continuously, their vigor and relative abundance decline, and the animals have progressively less opportunity for selection. According to Dasmann (1956), the result is increased nutrition-related mortality. The implication is that controlling deer populations and purposely managing chaparral stands to increase forage diversity are conducive to healthier and more productive deer herds. Although deer numbers seem to have decreased generally in California, population controls have not been applied specifically for this purpose. Research on nutritional aspects of deer management has progressed little there since 1960.

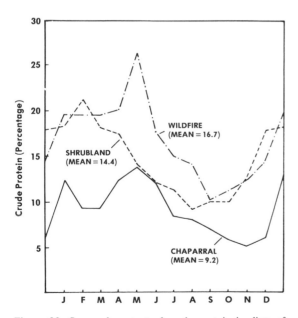

Figure 23. Seasonal content of crude protein in diets of black-tailed deer in dense, mature chaparral and manipulated stands; the latter show marked improvement in nutritional quality of winter and spring forage (from Taber and Dasmann 1958).

MOJAVE DESERT

There is little quantitative information on food habits or nutrition of desert mule deer in the Mojave and "Colorado" desert areas of California. For the most part, deer occur as sparse populations in isolated mountain ranges and along the Colorado River. McLean (1930) observed deer eating paloverde and ironwood browse in drainages and uplands. During dry seasons they concentrated near seep springs or "tanks" and, in the phreatophyte belt along the Colorado River, particularly in willow and screwbean thickets. Dixon (1934) reported them eating paloverde, ironwood, cat's-claw, and mesquite mistletoe in late December. Honey mesquite leaves and pods were important early autumn foods. Longhurst and Chattin (1941) found deer along desert washes lined with paloverde, ironwood, and creosote brush in early January, but the deer were eating mostly green big galleta.

ARIZONA CHAPARRAL

Arizona chaparral extends across the state as a narrow belt, mostly between about 900 and 1,800 meters (3,000–6,000 feet) elevation above sea level, from northwest to southeast below piñon/juniper or ponderosa pine vegetal zones and above desert shrub or desert grassland. Some characteristic plant species extend into southwestern New Mexico and Utah as understory elements in piñon/juniper or oak-woodland types (Nichol 1937). Estimates of the area occupied by chaparral vary from about 1.2 to 2.4 million hectares (3–6 million acres) depending on the criteria used to identify the type (Hibbert et al. 1974). Major dominants are shrub live oak, mountain mahogany, and manzanita. Although many other shrubs occur, sometimes as local dominants, the type is less complex than California chaparral. Herbaceous understories usually are sparse except for a short period after fire (Pase 1966; Pase and Pond 1964; Cable 1975).

In the western sector, in the general vicinity of Prescott, desert mule deer are yearlong residents of chaparral (Hoffmeister 1962). Data on diets and nutritional plane of these deer are limited. As determined from inspection of feeding sites and a few rumens collected near Tonto Springs, west of Prescott, the major browse species are desert ceanothus, hairy mountain mahogany, and cliffrose. Shrub live oak, skunkbush, and manzanita are much more abundant than those species but are relatively unpalatable (Hanson and McCulloch 1955). Neff (1963) reported that deer at Doce, near Tonto Springs, used desert ceanothus heavily and mountain mahogany lightly. Analyses of rumens from other areas near Prescott showed considerable local variation in the relative importance of various species (table 46). Species in the April 1969 rumen were digested in vitro with inoculum from that rumen; estimated dietary digestibility was 55 percent. New leaves of skunkbush dominated the sample and were unexpectedly high in digestibility.

Crude protein and phosphorus contents of most browse species of the Arizona chaparral decline from nutritious levels during active growth to poor levels in dormancy (Swank 1956, 1958). Even crown sprouts exhibit this pattern (Reynolds 1967). Although Swank did no diet analyses, he accepted low nutritional values of dormant shrubs as evidence that forage quality controlled mule deer populations in this area at an average of about 10 deer per section (2.59 square kilometers). However, given the tendency of deer to eat a wide range of forage species, that view cannot be evaluated without data on complete seasonal diets.

Distribution of water is another potential nutritional factor for deer in Arizona chaparral. At Whitespar, near Prescott, an intermittent stream became a permanent watercourse after trees and shrubs along its channel were removed (Ingebo 1971). Over a three-year period, significantly more deer use was recorded in this watershed than in an untreated "control" watershed. In some areas where water is not available year-round, the management practice of providing for permanent water sources might be expected to relieve seasonal concentrations of deer and thereby increase the animals' opportunity for selective foraging.

Table 46. Mean Percentage of Volume of Identified Mule Deer foods in Western Chaparral Areas of Arizona

Species	Prescott	Bloody Basin		Prescott	Tonto Springs	Bloody Basin
	Jan. 1953 (6)[a]	Feb.–Mar. 1953 (7)[a]	Feb.–Mar. 1963 (3)[a]	Apr. 1953 (5)[a]	Apr. 1969 (1)[a]	May 1953 (5)[a]
Birchleaf mountain mahogany	16.2		11.9	48.2		
Silk tassel	11.0			3.0		
Juniper	2.0	40.0		1.4		
Desert ceanothus	1.7	7.1	11.9			22.4
Shrub live oak	51.3				18.0	
Pointleaf manzanita	17.5					
Unclassified forbs		7.6	1.0	5.0		
Louisiana wormwood		21.4	1.5	2.0		16.0
Hollyleaf buckthorn		16.7	45.7			15.4
Unclassified grass			3.7			
Buckwheat			4.8			
Green rabbitbrush		5.0				
Sugar sumac			16.1			
Skunkbush				36.2	61.0	
Hairy (and true?) mountain mahogany					15.0	
Globe mallow					4.0	
Euphorbia						29.0
Eriastrum						15.0
Totals	99.7	98.8	96.6	95.8	98.0	97.8

Source: Data from McCulloch (pers. comm., 1978).

[a] Sample size.

Artificial sources of water in desert and chaparral habitats are important management devices for influencing concentrations of deer during certain seasons of forage scarcity or abundance. Photograph by Ned Smith; courtesy of the Arizona Department of Game and Fish.

In dense brushfields with sparse understory vegetation, openings permit development of semipermanent herbaceous communities and increase availability of forbs (Pase et al. 1967; Urness 1974). Openings are especially attractive to deer when green forage is present. The generally high nutritional quality of actively growing forbs available on these sites suggests the potential value to deer of such management. Urness et al. (1971) reported that forbs in diets at Three Bar Wildlife Area from January to April contributed considerably more to deer nutrition than their percentage composition indicated.

SONORAN DESERT

Southern desert shrub occupies a general elevational zone of about 300–900 meters (1,100–3,000 feet) above sea level in southern Arizona (Nichol 1937). It is dominated by bur sage, mesquite, cat's-claw, paloverde, and numerous cacti and other shrubs. Desert grassland is generally at higher elevations, between 900 and 1,525 meters (3,000–5,000 feet), and its prominent species are mesquite, Emory oak, grama grasses, curly mesquite, and tobosa grass. Invasion of woody plants, mostly leguminous shrubs and cacti typical of the desert shrub zone, has created mule deer habitat where little existed before in large areas of southern Arizona (Martin 1975).

Mule deer occur most abundantly on upper bajadas in desert shrub near or in ecotones of desert shrub and chaparral, grassland, or woodland. Consequently, their food selection and nutrition frequently reflect ecotonal diversity in the eastern sector. They are marginally sympatric with Coues white-tailed deer, which are more common in the chaparral and oak woodland (McCulloch 1972; Wallmo 1973). In this zone at the Three Bar Wildlife Area in central Arizona, diets of mule deer and white-tailed deer were studied for more than ten years (McCulloch 1967a, 1973), followed by exhaustive studies of the potential contribution of various forage species to deer nutrition (Urness 1973; Urness and McCulloch 1973).

Diet composition was shown to vary greatly from season to season within years and from year to year as a result of phenological development and climatic influences on relative availability of different types of forage (McCulloch 1973; figs. 24 and 25). While a few forage species stand out in seasonal diets, as at other locations and in other vegetal types, it is

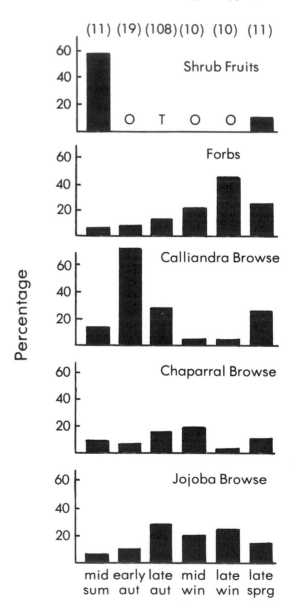

Figure 24. Seasonal variation in diet composition of desert mule deer on the Three Bar Wildlife Area, Arizona (from McCulloch 1973). () = number of stomachs sampled.

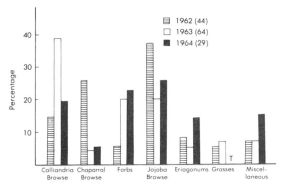

Desert mule deer in the Sonoran Desert. Photograph courtesy of the United States Forest Service.

Figure 25. Yearly variations in late autumn composition (volume) of mule deer stomach contents, Three Bar Wildlife Area, Arizona (from McCulloch 1973). () = number of stomachs. Summer 1962 was dry; stomachs were collected before frosts. Summer 1963 was wet; stomachs were collected before frosts. Summer 1964 was wet; stomachs were collected after frosts.

apparent that vegetal diversity provides ample choices for deer to be highly opportunistic feeders. In some seasons and years, for example, fruit appears prominently in diets. In years of poor fruit production, other forage is substituted, mediated by fluctuations in the bimodal precipitation pattern, periodic extended drought and other climatic events, such as late frosts and erratic, locally intense convectional storms.

Forage species that contribute large percentages to seasonal mule deer diets at the Three Bar Wildlife Area are: fairy duster browse in early and late autumn; jojoba browse from late autumn through late winter; buckwheat—mostly Wright buckwheat—in mid and late winter; and mesquite beans, shrub live oak acorns, and cat's-claw beans in midsummer. In late autumn and winter, forbs are important as a class, especially bluedicks, filaree, and Louisiana wormwood. In all, 106 forage species were identified in 285 mule deer rumen samples over all seasons.

Analyses of individual forages and total diets indicated moderately good levels of most nutrients yearlong (Urness and McCulloch 1973; Urness et al. 1971). Through shifts in diet composition, average crude protein content of seasonal diets was maintained at a consistent level of about 12 percent (range 10–14 percent), and phosphorus-calcium ratios remained below 1:5

except in November-December (table 47; figs. 26 and 27). In vitro digestibility of seasonal diets varied from 34 to 51 percent, but later comparisons with in vivo data indicated that the in vitro method underestimated in vivo values, especially for browse (Urness et al. 1977).

Urness et al. (1971) concluded that the nutritional status of adult mule deer in the Sonoran Desert is adequate or better than adequate for maintenance and reasonable production. Definitive knowledge of energy metabolism is lacking, however, and the nutritional status of fawns in this area is unknown. Low fawn recruitment into the adult population resulted in a decline in mule deer at the Three Bar Wildlife Area in the early 1960s (Shaw 1965; Smith et al. 1969; Smith and LeCount 1976), yet nearly all deer collected for diet composition studies were in good body condition (C. Y. McCulloch, pers. comm., 1977).

The Santa Rita Experiment Station, about 50 kilometers (30 miles) south of Tucson, was the site of early deer-feeding experiments (Nichol

Table 47. Estimated Nutrient Consumption by Mule Deer on the Three Bar Wildlife Area, Arizona

	Percentage in Diet						
Nutrient Factor	Feb.–Mar. (10)[a]	May–June (11)[a]	July–Sept. (11)[a]	Oct. (19)[a]	Nov.–Dec. (137)[a]	Jan. (10)[a]	Mean
Crude protein	13	12	14	12	10	11	12
Acid-detergent fiber	29	36	34	38	40	38	36
Dry matter	33	38	41	56	48	49	44
In vitro digestibility	51	43	42	35	34	40	41
Phosphorus	0.29	0.25	0.23	0.26	0.16	0.21	0.23
Calcium	1.26	0.88	0.84	1.22	1.56	1.00	1.13
Average seasonal diet constituted by plants tested	96	94	83	98	92	92	92
Phosphorus-calcium ratio	1 : 4.3	1 : 3.5	1 : 3.7	1 : 4.7	1 : 9.8	1 : 4.8	1 : 4.9

Source: Urness et al. (1971).

[a] Rumen sample size.

1938). This is a desert shrub or desert grassland type below oak woodland. Penned mule deer were fed numerous types of forage to determine relative palatability and forage requirements. In all, 168 native species were tested. The important woody plants from southern Arizona were mistletoe, kidney-wood, Fendler ceanothus, cat's-claw, wait-a-minute, fairy duster, cliff fendlera bush, indigobush, wild grape, and Wright buckwheat. Of these, buckwheat was

considered one of the most important deer foods because of its widespread distribution and yearlong use. Mistletoe exceeded all other browse forage in palatability, and broad-leaved forms of mistletoe were more palatable than

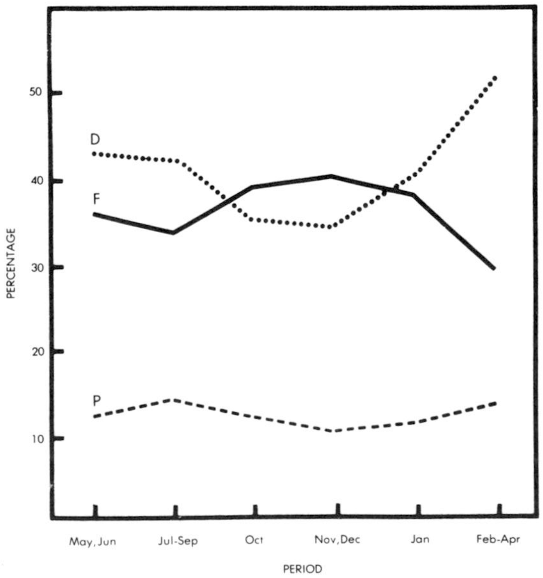

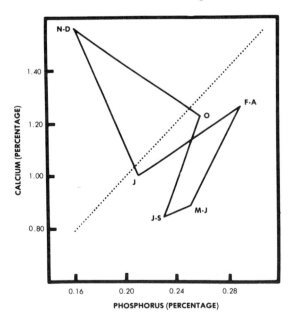

Figure 26. Annual cycle of in vitro digestibility (D), acid-detergent fiber content (F), and crude protein content (P) for diets of desert mule deer on the Three Bar Wildlife Area, Arizona (from Urness and McCulloch 1973).

Figure 27. Annual cycle of mean dietary phosphorus and calcium levels for desert mule deer on the Three Bar Wildlife Area, Arizona (from Urness and McCulloch 1973). The dotted line indicates the 1:5 P-Ca ratio (Dietz et al. 1962) which, if exceeded, is considered undesirable on a sustained basis. J = January, F–A = February–April, M–J = May–June, J–S = July–September, O = October, N–D = November–December.

Table 48. Principal Plant Species and Parts Selected by Mule Deer on the Santa Rita Experimental Range

Species	Percentage of Plant Parts in Diet[a]			
	Spring (21)[b]	Summer (20)[b]	Autumn (58)[b]	Winter (49)[b]
Cacti				
Jumping cholla	19.9 (F)		7.7 (F)	
Engelmann prickly pear		10.2 (F)		
Cane cholla				10.3 (F)
Barrel cactus	5.4 (F)		35.6 (F)	42.5 (F)
Trees				
Honey mesquite		24.0 (F)		
Shrubs				
Cat's-claw	17.9 (L)		11.2 (L)	
Fairy duster	9.5 (L)	31.5 (L)	31.1 (L)	21.6 (L)
Forbs				
Eriastrum	9.2 (P)			
Euphorbia	4.8 (P)	16.5 (P)		
Total	66.7	82.2	86.6	74.4

Source: Short (1977).
[a] (F) = fruit; (L) = leaves; (P) = whole plant.
[b] Sample size.

leafless types. The latter species were collected from conifers and leguminous shrubs. Mistletoes were shown to be highly digestible, with leaves averaging 74 percent (range 71–79 percent) digestibility yearlong (Urness 1969).

A later study of diet composition of free-ranging mule deer at Santa Rita was reported by Short (1977). Analyses of rumens collected throughout the year (table 48) indicated that spring (April–June, N=21) diets were dominated by cactus fruits (especially jumping cholla), cat's-claw leaves, fairy duster leaves, and several forbs (especially eriastrum and euphorbias). Summer (July–September, N=20) diets contained half as much cactus fruit (mainly prickly pear). Mesquite beans, fairy duster leaves and spurge were the major diet components. Barrel cactus fruit dominated autumn diets (October–December, N=58), with fairy duster leaves second. Jumping cholla fruit and cat's-claw leaves also were prominent in autumn diets. Winter diets (January–March; N=49) were similar to those in autumn, except that barrel cactus fruit increased and fairy duster leaves declined in importance. Those two, plus fruit of cane cholla, constituted about three-fourths of the total winter diet.

That the bulk of the diet comprised only a few types of forage in all seasons might be taken as evidence of more restricted choices at Santa Rita than at the Three Bar Wildlife Area. Nutrient analyses of diets at the two locations bear this out. Mean protein and phosphorus levels in seasonal diets at the Santa Rita Experimental Range (table 49) were well below those at the Three Bar Wildlife Area (table 47), though mean digestibility was somewhat higher. Higher

Table 49. Selected Nutrients in Seasonal Diets of Mule Deer on the Santa Rita Experimental Range

Season	Percentage of Dry Matter					
	Percentage of Diet Tested	Digesti-bility	Crude Protein	Phos-phorus	Calcium	P-Ca Ratio
Spring	87.0	51.8	10.3	0.23	1.55	1 : 6.7
Summer	93.7	48.2	9.6	0.16	1.09	1 : 6.8
Autumn	93.4	45.3	10.4	0.15	1.17	1 : 7.8
Winter	91.0	53.5	9.8	0.15	1.33	1 : 8.8

Source: Short (1977).

average digestibility is attributable in part to the large content of cactus fruits; no other study has reported so high a level in deer diets. As with many similar foods, fruits should be expected to provide more soluble carbohydrates and therefore higher digestibility but correspondingly lower protein content. Short's (1977) findings at Santa Rita point out the need for more complete information on the potential contribution of cactus fruits to the nutrition of desert mule deer.

The effect of drought on mule deer diets and population levels from a desert grassland type in south-central Arizona was reported by Anthony (1976). Sharp differences were noted in the composition of March–July diets in 1970 and 1971. In early 1970, conditions for plant growth were near normal, but effective precipitation failed to occur later that summer, thus severely restricting plant development in 1971. Deciduous browse species—such as kidneywood, fairy duster, range ratany, and desert honeysuckle—are important spring and early summer forage, but they did not leaf out on upland sites in 1971 (table 50). Evergreen browse and coarse herbaceous species, presumably of poor quality, were consumed in greater amounts during the drought. Nutritional analyses of the contrasting diets were not made,

Table 50. Diets of Mule Deer in the San Cayetano Mountains, Arizona, March–July 1970 and 1971, as Indicated by Feces Contents

	Percentage of Volume	
Forage Species	1970	1971
Kidney-wood	19.5	5.7
Fairy duster	17.6	2.2
Range ratany	23.0	11.8
Desert honeysuckle	5.6	1.5
Ocotillo	4.2	2.1
Buckwheat	4.6	4.4
Netleaf hackberry	3.9	14.3
Cat's-claw	2.1	12.3
Stickweed	2.1	11.5
Bear-grass	tr.	9.3
Cliff fendlera bush	2.7	8.3
Honey mesquite	2.2	7.5
One-seeded juniper	1.8	4.2
Mexican blue oak	tr.	3.2
Grama grasses	4.0	4.6

Source: Anthony (1976).

but deer populations declined either through mortality or emigration in 1971 and remained at low levels in 1972.

Generally, desert deer face more frequent and more severe restrictions on forage quality than do those with access to other vegetational types, and their reproductive rates tend to be lower. Summer rains are not effective in producing usable forb growth, and a long autumn to late winter drought is normal over much of the area with rather minimal winter forb growth. Consequently, desert shrub/grassland habitats tend to be marginal for deer, and wide oscillations in population density can be expected, with low maximum densities compared with those in other habitats.

CHIHUAHUAN DESERT

The Chihuahuan Desert in the United States includes only a small portion of south-central New Mexico and a narrow strip along the Rio Grande in Texas (Shreve 1942). However, much of the desert/grassland transition surrounding this area has woody plant elements that, for purposes of this chapter, are considered part of the Chihuahuan Desert. The desert shrub vegetation of this region—in southeastern Arizona, southern New Mexico, southwestern Texas, and north-central Mexico—is much less diverse than that of the Sonoran Desert (McGinnies 1972). Desert mule deer have a scattered distribution throughout the region (Beltran 1953; Wallmo 1973).

Elevation varies from less than 900 meters (3,000 feet) to more than 1,800 meters (6,000 feet) above sea level. Summer precipitation accounts for 65–80 percent of the annual total, which ranges from 75 to 635 millimeters (3–25 inches). Normally, little plant growth occurs in winter, but as in the Sonoran Desert, winter precipitation stimulates abundant growth of forbs in occasional years. Of the twelve most common plants in the Sonoran and the Chihuahuan deserts, only creosote bush, ocotillo, and mesquite occur in both (Shreve 1942). On areas most frequently inhabited by mule deer, the dominant shrubs are acacias,

Desert mule deer does and fawns in the Chihuahuan Desert. Photograph courtesy of the United States National Park Service.

honey mesquite, sandpaper bush, and tarbush. Taller cacti are less abundant, except locally, than in the Sonoran Desert, but short species are very common, as are yucca, bear-grass, and sotol.

Data on food habits of mule deer in the Chihuahuan Desert proper are not available from Mexico or the state of New Mexico. Rather, studies have been made of populations occupying vegetational complexes of succulent/shrub, shortgrass/shrub, juniper/piñon woodland, and in some areas, peripheral chaparral. Anderson et al. (1965) found that four forage species constituted 54 percent of the volume of 93 rumens sampled from the Guadalupe Mountains. These were wavyleaf oak (mostly green leaves), juniper, yucca, and hairy mountain mahogany. Fifty-three food items occurred in volumes of 1 percent or more per individual sample; forty-four other foods occurred in less than 1 percent volume. The more important forage species are listed in

table 51. The four years of study encompassed variable growing conditions; browse dominated diets in dry years, and forbs dominated in wet years. Body condition also reflected this difference, with deer weights significantly higher in 1958–59, a wet year of high forb production.

Some of the forage material collected in the Anderson et al. (1965) study was analyzed and reported separately by Snyder (1961). The composition of 56 rumen samples of mule deer collected from 1956 to 1958 was somewhat different from the composition reported by Anderson et al. (1965), but order of importance of the first four species remained the same. Protein content was moderate to low for the thirteen species tested, except for leaves of hairy mountain mahogany, which were above 12 percent for most of the year (range 10–16 percent). From May to October, protein content of leaves of wavyleaf oak varied from 11 to 14 percent, and that of skunkbush leaves

Table 51. Composition of Rumen Contents of Desert Mule Deer from the Guadalupe Mountains, New Mexico

Food Item	Percentage of Volume				
	Jan.–Mar. (30)[a]	Apr.–June (21)[a]	July–Sept. (23)[a]	Oct.–Dec. (19)[a]	Total (93)[a]
Wavyleaf oak	2.5	27.2	27.1	23.9	17.7
Juniper	27.1	1.7	8.0	11.7	13.9
Hairy mountain mahogany	13.3	11.3	3.7	20.7	11.9
Yucca	17.3	17.6	1.1	3.2	10.5
Skunkbush	0.0	3.6	9.1	9.0	4.9
Silk tassel	7.7	0.9	0.1	0.2	2.7
Louisiana wormwood	tr.[b]	0.2	6.1	tr.	1.6
Broom snakeweed	3.6	tr.	tr.	tr.	1.2
Unidentified forbs	6.0	13.7	13.2	8.0	9.9
Flax	4.7	tr.	0.0	13.7	4.3
Euphorbia	0.0	3.3	5.1	tr.	2.0
Fetid marigold	0.0	0.0	6.3	0.0	1.5
Acanthus (Acanthaceae)	0.0	4.3	tr.	0.0	0.9
Globe mallow	tr.	3.1	tr.	tr.	0.7
Grasses (Gramineae)	3.1	tr.	tr.	tr.	1.0
Total	85.3	86.9	79.8	90.4	84.7

Source: Anderson et al. (1965).

[a] Rumen sample size.

[b] tr. = trace.

varied from 10 to 16 percent. As in other areas of the Southwest, phosphorus tended to be low and calcium high in all forages, resulting in wide phosphorus-calcium ratios. In winter samples, when consumption of juniper and yucca was high, levels of apparent digestible protein and phosphorus in the diet were low. Otherwise, nutritient levels were adequate or better than adequate for requirements of domestic sheep (table 52); requirements for mule deer are assumed to be similar.

Table 52. Dietary Nutrients in Sample Rations Based on Contents of Five Mule Deer Rumens from the Guadalupe Mountains, New Mexico, Compared with Requirements for Domestic Sheep

Month of Rumen Sample Collection	Composition of Sample Ration		Nutrients per 1.5 Kilograms (3.3 lbs) of Dry Matter			
	Species	Percentage of Volume	Digestible Protein (lbs)	TDN (lbs)	Calcium (g)	Phosphorus (g)
November	Hairy mountain mahogany	75				
	Alligator juniper	20	0.13	1.7	15.8	2.9
	Wavyleaf oak	5				
December	Hairy mountain mahogany	73				
	Wavyleaf oak	25	0.12	1.5	12.2	2.5
	Apache plume	5				
January	Hairy mountain mahogany	95				
	Alligator juniper	5	0.15	1.6	11.1	2.1
February	Alligator juniper	92				
	Soaptree yucca	8	0.05	1.9	17.5	2.5
March	Soaptree yucca	50				
	Alligator juniper	40				
	Wavyleaf oak	6	0.09	1.8	17.9	2.5
	Apache plume	2				
	Hairy mountain mahogany	2				
			0.14[a]	1.7[a]	4.1[a]	3.2[a]

Source: Snyder (1961).

[a] Requirements for domestic ewe.

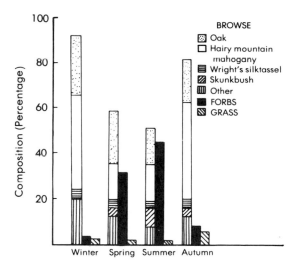

Figure 28. Seasonal diets of mule deer on the Fort Bayard area, New Mexico, ascertained from analyses of 77 rumens (from Boeker et al. 1972).

A study of food habits and nutrition of mule deer conducted at Fort Bayard in southwestern New Mexico (Boeker et al. 1972) is marginally applicable to the Chihuahuan Desert even though the area is more typical of juniper/piñon woodland. The New Mexico Department of Game and Fish classifies the deer there as desert mule deer, and therefore the data are included. Forage types constituting 1 percent or more of the mean total volume of 77 rumens are presented in table 53. Seasonal variation in major food items is shown in figure 28. In many respects, deer diets from the Fort Bayard and Guadalupe Mountains studies are similar.

Table 53. Major Foods of Mule Deer at Fort Bayard, New Mexico, Based on the Contents of Seventy-seven Rumens

Plant Species	Percentage of Volume
Shrubs and trees	
Hairy mountain mahogany	33
Oaks	24
Junipers	5
Wright's silk tassel	4
Skunkbush	3
Cacti	2
Mistletoe	2
Yucca	1
Fairy duster	1
Forbs	
Dalea	3
Prairie mimosa	3
Dayflower	3
Pinnate tansy mustard	2
Tansy mustard	2
Missouri (buffalo) gourd	1
White sweetclover	1
Grasses	2
Total	92

Source: Boeker et al. (1972).

The Fort Bayard results provide conservative estimates of diet quality because they covered only 73–95 percent of seasonal diets (table 54). Protein levels were moderate; phosphorus levels and digestibility (in vitro) were rather low. Values approximate those obtained at Santa Rita (table 49) more closely than those from Three Bar Wildlife Area (table 47), both in the Sonoran Desert.

Table 54. Nutrients in Seasonal Diets of Mule Deer on the Fort Bayard Area, New Mexico

Nutrient Component	Percentage				
	Winter (14)[a]	Spring (17)[a]	Summer (14)[a]	Autumn (32)[a]	Total (77)[a]
Portion of total diet tested	95	87	73	89	86
Protein	12	11	9	9	10
Crude fiber	44	25	24	29	31
Digestibility (in vitro)	23	45	37	43	37
Phosphorus	0.19	0.26	0.17	0.18	0.20
Calcium	1.16	0.78	0.59	0.92	0.86
Phosphorus-calcium ratio	1 : 6.0	1 : 3.0	1 : 3.5	1 : 5.1	1 : 4.6

Source: Boeker et al. (1972).

[a] Rumen sample size.

Food habits of desert mule deer in the Trans-Pecos region of southwestern Texas have been extensively studied (Anderson 1949; Brownlee 1971, 1973; Keller 1975; Krausman 1978; Uzzell 1958). The vegetation of this region is generally more representative of Chihuahuan Desert than the Fort Bayard area, particularly to the south and west. But, at higher elevations and toward the east, juniper/piñon or juniper/piñon/oak vegetation is common.

Krausman (1978) compared diets of desert mule deer on exclusive ranges with those of desert mule deer whose range overlapped with Carmine Mountain white-tailed deer, both in Big Bend National Park, Texas. Only slight differences in diet composition by forage class occurred (fig. 29); browse use was somewhat higher on overlapping ranges. Succulents dominated mean annual diets and were represented most heavily in winter and spring. Browse was somewhat more important in summer and autumn (table 55). The five most important species yearlong were, in descending order, lechuguilla, euphorbia, Engelmann prickly pear, acacia, and guayacan. No nutritional analyses were run, but in an earlier paper

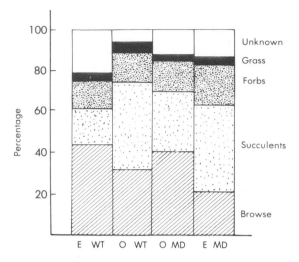

Figure 29. Proportions of browse, succulents, forbs, and grasses in the diets of white-tailed (WT) and mule deer (MD) on exclusive (E) and overlapping (O) ranges, Big Bend National Park, Texas (from Krausman 1978).

by Krausman and Bissonette (1977), observations were reported of mule deer consuming deer bones. This was attributed speculatively to mineral deficiencies, possibly of phosphorus or some trace mineral, in desert vegetation.

Table 55. Composition, in Percentage of Volume, of Mule Deer Rumens Collected from June 1972 to April 1974 in Big Bend National Park, Texas

Species	Summer (6)[a]	Late Summer (13)[a]	Winter (5)[a]	Spring (5)[a]	Exclusive (19)[a]	Overlapping with White-tailed Deer (10)[a]	Total (29)[a]
Browse							
Cat's-claw	7.7	7.5		0.2	3.2	8.5	5.0
Evergreen sumac	0.2		9.4	6.2	1.1	5.8	2.7
Guaycan		9.0	4.8	0.6	2.8	9.1	5.0
Littleleaf sumac	11.7	2.1	0.8		2.7	4.9	3.5
Honey mesquite	0.3	4.5			0.1	5.9	2.1
Dalea	9.3	6.2	1.2		7.1	0.8	4.9
Forbs							
Euphorbia	15.3	23.8	5.4	2.0	15.3	14.8	15.1
Mendora	0.3	0.2	9.6		2.7	0.1	1.8
Succulents							
Lechuguilla	3.3	17.1	41.6	48.0	28.6	14.7	23.8
Engelmann prickly pear	18.7	8.9	13.4	22.6	13.5	15.1	14.0
Grasses							
(Gramineae)	8.5	1.5		1.4	3.2	1.7	2.7
Total	75.3	80.8	86.2	81.0	80.3	81.4	80.6

Source: Krausman (1978).

[a] Rumen sample size.

Uzzell (1958) studied desert mule deer food habits in southwest Texas from 1956 to 1957, near the end of a sustained drought. From the Black Gap Wildlife Management Area, varying in elevation from about 760 to 1,220 meters (2,500–4,000 feet), with true desert shrub vegetation, 23 rumens were collected. Of these, 18 were taken in winter, so only those data are considered here and in table 56. Lechuguilla, candelilla, and sotol were the main browse species, in descending order of importance. Torrey yucca fruit occurred in high volume in 2 rumens. Seventeen rumens were collected during winter from the Sierra Diablo, and 7 were collected during winter from the Del Norte Mountains. Both areas are characterized by juniper/piñon/oak woodland with significant areas of chaparrallike mountain shrub. Some differences in relative importance occurred among the two areas, but the four most prominent forage types were essentially the same species: oak; Ashe juniper; prickly pear; and agave. Of the contents of all of those rumens combined, browse constituted 84 percent, forbs 8 percent, and grasses 8 percent. No nutritional analyses were made, but dominance of fibrous browse leads one to speculate that dietary quality is rather low during protracted droughts. These ranges were not grazed by domestic live-stock, so interspecific competition was not a factor.

Later investigations at the Black Gap Wildlife Management Area were conducted during a period of normal rainfall (Brownlee 1971). It was anticipated that diet composition would differ markedly from that obtained by Uzzell (1958), but representation of forage classes was very similar: 89 percent browse; 7 percent forbs; and 2 percent grasses. However, there was above-normal precipitation in 1971, and the importance of forbs increased. They composed 24 percent of rumen contents, browse composed 75, and grass 1 percent.

A few species occurred in abundance in all of these samples (table 57). Lechuguilla (with tough, sclerophyllous, daggerlike leaves) and candelilla (with perennial, leafless, wax-covered green stems) retain appreciable succulence even during drought and have greater moisture content when precipitation is normal. Prickly pear manifests similar variations in moisture content. Guayacan is a woody shrub whose leaves and twigs are very palatable to deer, but production of these parts is extremely low during drought, though prolific when soil moisture is available. The euphorbias listed last in table 57 are succulent annuals that occur abundantly when there is adequate rainfall, and

Table 56. Major Foods, in Percentage of Volume, in Winter Diets of Desert Mule Deer in Southwest Texas, Based on Rumen Samples from Woodland (Sierra Diablo and Del Norte Mountains) and Desert Shrub (Black Gap Wildlife Management Area) Habitats during an Extended Drought, 1956–57

Species	Sierra Diablo (17)[a]	Del Norte Mountains (7)[a]	Black Gap (18)[a]
Lechuguilla	13.9	8.9	70.7
Mohr oak		55.4	
Wavyleaf oak and sandpaper oak	31.7		
Ashe juniper	10.4	17.3	
Engelmann prickly pear	22.1	8.9	0.2
Cane cholla	8.4	3.7	
Candelilla			13.7
Sotol			9.5
Torrey yucca			3.9
Blue yucca	2.7		
Mexican piñon	4.2		
Unidentified forbs		2.8	
Total	93.4	97.0	98.0

Source: Uzzell (1958).

[a] Rumen sample size.

Table 57. Rank Order of Several Important Types of Forage of Desert Mule Deer in Years of Subnormal, Normal, and Above-Normal Precipitation on the Black Gap Wildlife Management Area in Southwestern Texas

Species	Rank Order in Volume		
	1956 (Drought)	1969 (Normal Precipitation)	1971 (Above-Normal Precipitation)
Lechuguilla	1	1	1
Sotol	2	6	
Candelilla	3	4	5
Torrey yucca	4	3	
Engelmann prickly pear	5	2	2
Guayacan		5	3
Euphorbias			4

Source: Uzzell (1958); Brownlee (1971, 1973).

are grazed heavily by deer at such times. Sotol and yucca have tough, hard, fibrous leaves at all times and probably should be ranked as lower-quality deer foods, except when flowering structures are consumed. These observations are based largely on personal communications from O. C. Wallmo (1977). Need for nutritional analyses to aid interpretation of food habits data from the Trans-Pecos region was recognized by Brownlee (1973), and will be carried out in future investigations.

Keller (1975) analyzed rumen contents of desert mule deer collected in Pecos County, Texas. These collections were made on private lands grazed by cattle (livestock are excluded from Big Bend National Park and Black Gap

Table 58. Seasonal Occurrence of the Ten Most Important Foods in the Annual Diet of Desert Mule Deer in Pecos County, Texas

Species	Percentage of Volume of Rumen Contents				
	Spring (Mar.–May)	Summer (June–Aug.)	Autumn (Sept.–Nov.)	Winter (Dec.–Feb.)	Annual Total
Daleas	5.8	15.2	23.4	10.7	13.1
Emory oak	13.4	2.8	12.6	10.0	9.5
Euphorbias	9.9	5.9	9.3	2.2	6.7
Littleleaf sumac		13.8	6.3		5.7
Honey mesquite		19.8			5.3
Acacias	14.9	3.9	2.1		4.9
Bladderpod				12.3	3.5
Goldeneye	2.8	5.3	4.8		3.4
Grasses (Poaceae)	1.3	3.2	4.0	5.0	3.4
Redberry juniper	8.6			10.0	3.1
Bluet	3.3			5.9	
Feather dalea	2.7	6.8			
Mariola		4.4	2.9		
Cuneate-leaved draba			3.0	6.4	
Broom snakeweed				12.4	
Wild onion	2.5				
Wild mercury			2.6		
Cloak fern				2.3	
Unidentified material	7.1	11.5	9.2	9.0	9.2
Total	72.3	92.6	80.2	86.2	67.8

Source: Keller (1975).

Wildlife Management Area). The vegetational mosaic was very complex, however, and deer had access to six major vegetal types. Browse constituted 45 percent, forbs 42 percent, grasses 3 percent, and unidentified material 9 percent of the total year-round sample. That the ten most important plants in seasonal diets (table 58) appear in such low percentages indicates a greater array of choices than at the Sierra Diablo, Del Norte, and Black Gap areas (tables 56 and 57).

This review indicates that it is not yet possible to generalize on nutritional regimes of mule deer in desert and semidesert habitats of the Southwest. Some data suggest that their nutritional plane seldom falls as low as that of most Rocky Mountain mule deer in winter and that it does not rise as high in summer (see chap. 10, part 1). This may protect mule deer in the Southwest from the mass starvation often suffered by northern deer. But does it also suppress their productivity? More extensive research will be required for wildlife biologists and managers to understand the implications of nutrition for population dynamics of desert mule deer (Short 1979).

Part 2. Habitat Evaluation and Management

Olof C. Wallmo
Principal Wildlife Biologist
United States Forest Service
Pacific Northwest Forest and
Range Experiment Station
Juneau, Alaska

Albert LeCount
Wildlife Research Biologist
Arizona Game and Fish Department
Phoenix, Arizona

Sam L. Brownlee
Wildlife Biologist
Texas Parks and Wildlife Department
Alpine, Texas

CHAPARRAL

Chaparral vegetation, represented distinctly in California and in modified form in Arizona, is a product of Mediterranean climate. Climatically intermediate between desert and forest, or grassland and forest, chaparral has various delineations that are either broad—occurring in semiarid portions of most of the western United States and scattered areas of Mexico (Leopold 1950*b;* Weaver and Clements 1938)—or narrow, consisting only of certain brushlands in California and northern Baja California, Mexico (Plummer 1911). The latter delineation is curious, since "chaparral" was derived from the Spanish *chaparro,* referring specifically to evergreen scrub oaks. But, in California, chaparral is dominated by chamise, and most other areas are dominated by oaks, though not always evergreen oaks. In fact, Stoddart and Smith (1943) mapped as chaparral all of the Gambel oak/mountain mahogany type in Colorado and Utah (mountain mahogany/oak scrub of Küchler 1964), plus an area of oak "shinnery" in southeastern New Mexico.

Although no consensus seems to have been reached by plant ecologists, the question of what chaparral is and where it occurs has been settled by range and wildlife biologists and managers in North America (fig. 30). They apply the term to plant communities dominated by broad-leaved evergreen shrubs with rather leathery leaves ("broad sclerophylls"), occurring in extensive areas of central Arizona, along the length of California, and for some distance into Baja California. These areas are similar climatically, having moist seasons with mild temperatures and dry seasons with warm or hot temperatures. There are two moist seasons— winter and late summer—in Arizona, and there is one—winter to spring—in California. Mean annual precipitation can range from well below 51 centimeters (20 inches) in southern Califor-

Figure 30. Approximate distribution of chaparral in the United States (after Küchler 1964; Lowe and Brown 1973).

nia and parts of Arizona to 127–152 centimeters (50–60 inches) in northern California and southwestern Oregon, but comparable moisture and physiological regimes result from the equaling out of insolation and evaporation conditions (Weaver and Clements 1938).

These climatic patterns determine the vegetation. The shrubs are deep-rooted xerophytes, capitalizing on seasonal moisture and enduring long drought. Forbs and annual grasses are characterized by species with short life cycles correlated with moist periods rather than with periods of drought. Between these extremes there are numerous half-shrubs, some of which provide important forage but are never dominant. Climax condition, however, is typified by a dense canopy of shrubs usually 1.5–4.6 meters (5–15 feet) in height, with little understory vegetation. Except for its minimal value for grazing livestock, such vegetation was held in low esteem by early settlers, who learned—from its extreme flammability in dry periods—that an appreciable increase in usable forage resulted from wildfires. But it was a two-sided coin, for the fires often were uncontrollable, destructive, and followed by massive erosion and downstream damage.

Purposeful research to regulate vegetation of the chaparral zone was instituted in California in the 1940s and Arizona in the 1950s. It has resulted in management practices that have been applied to large areas of those states. Before we review that subject, it is important for the reader to recognize that chaparral, as treated here, is a climax formation. It is believed to have existed in the late Miocene and early Pliocene epochs (approximately 12–25 million years before the present) as a continuous belt from California to Oklahoma and Texas, but divided by geologic and climatic changes into a California segment and a southwestern segment—the two dwindling over time to their present distribution (Cable 1975). Its evolution and persistence required adaptation to fire. Many of the shrub species are vigorous root-sprouters, and others produce seeds that are responsive to heat scarification and the zone's unique weather conditions for germination and survival. However, mature stands can maintain themselves as a climatic climax without fires, and, as a whole, the formation would consist naturally of a perpetually varying admixture of climax and disclimax communities. The postfire successional stage is brief—less than twenty years—and succession cannot be halted and maintained at some arbitrary stage without intensive and costly management.

Manipulation of chaparral to provide favorable deer habitat is based on the premise that climax stands offer less available forage than do early successional stages. However, mature stands provide essential cover and forage at least during some portions of the year. The biomass of live plant material in climax stands may average about 20,000–25,000 kilograms per hectare (17,820–22,275 pounds per acre) (Olson 1975). Although no actual measurements seem to have been made, based on work with other shrub types, the live plant material potentially edible and available to deer probably is less than 10 percent, and the standing crop of forbs and grasses perhaps only one-tenth of that. For a few years after removal of shrub canopy, available forage in the form of

An anchor chain and ball are used to crush the vegetation before burning during a chaparral clearing project in California. Photograph by Guy E. Connolly.

grasses and forbs and of shrub sprouts and seedlings is increased manyfold.

Methods used purposefully to achieve this state have been reviewed by Cable (1975). Primarily, they include prescribed burning, mechanical destruction of brush (by cabling, chaining, railing, flailing, mowing, root-plowing, or bulldozing), and chemical control with foliar or soil-applied herbicides (mainly 2,4,5-T, silvex, picloram, and fenuron). Initial treatment commonly is followed by seeding with nonnative grasses and legumes to increase forage supplies and enhance watershed stabilization. Thereafter, pyric, mechanical, or chemical treatments may be used to maintain the area in a subclimax state.

Arizona Chaparral

The chaparral type in Arizona is delineated by Hibbert et al. (1974) as a discontinuous band of vegetation occupying some 1.2–1.6 million hectares (3–4 million acres) of mostly rough, broken terrain running southeast to northwest

A rangeland drill is used to plant grasses and legumes on rough ground in the area *(previous photograph)* of recently chained and burned California chaparral. Photograph by Guy E. Connolly.

across the center of the state at an elevation of 900–1,800 meters (3,000–6,000 feet) between desert and woodland or forest zones. Shrub live oak is the most widespread dominant, and skunkbush sumac is the only common deciduous shrub. Community structure of Arizona chaparral has not been well defined. Swank (1958) described diverse manifestations varying from shrub live oak/skunkbush to these species mixed with many other shrubs to small areas with nearly pure stands of mountain mahogany or manzanita.

Mule deer are the more common occupants of Arizona chaparral, but Coues white-tailed deer may be more abundant locally, relegating mule deer to lower elevations (McCulloch 1972). The northern edge of this chaparral roughly coincides with the northern edge of the Coues whitetails' range and with the demarcation between ranges of desert mule deer and Rocky Mountain mule deer (Hoffmeister 1962). In the early 1950s, population densities of about 4–5 desert mule deer per square kilometer (10–12 per square mile) were considered by Hanson and McCulloch (1955) to be approximately at carrying capacity. In the same general period, as many as 25–30 deer were observed at one time on areas of approximately 2.6 square kilometers (1 square mile) (Swank 1958), so much higher densities apparently have prevailed in many areas. These estimates indicate that the chaparral was inhabited by 50,000 to 100,000 deer—a resource of considerable importance.

Of the fourteen major shrub species in the Arizona chaparral listed by Cable (1975), all but perhaps one, Pringle manzanita, have been reported in one publication or another to be significant contributors to deer diets. The value to deer of these shrubs relative to that of other forage species whose abundance increases after shrub removal is discussed in part 1 of this chapter. McCulloch (1972) believed that moderate brush control could enrich the food supply for deer by providing additional herbaceous forage while retaining adequate evergreen browse and mast.

Quantitative effects of brush suppression on forage supplies per se have not been reported, but there is some information on vegetation responses in general. After an effective fire, rapid development of forbs and grasses can be expected for three or four years, followed by an abrupt drop to preburn levels in two or three more years, with forbs dropping out more rapidly than grasses. On a portion of the Mingus Mountain area, the crop of forbs peaked at an estimated 315 kilograms per hectare (281 pounds per acre) in the third growing season after a fire, and grasses peaked at 239 kilograms per hectare (213 pounds per acre) in the fifth year (Pase and Pond 1964). On the Three Bar Wildlife Area, the yield of forbs and grasses on a watershed with no postfire treatment was about 244–365 kilograms per hectare (217–325 pounds per acre) in the fifth and sixth growing seasons after burning, and 122–24 kilograms per hectare (109–10 pounds per acre) in the seventh to tenth growing seasons. An adjacent area seeded the year after burning with lovegrasses (weeping lovegrass, Boer lovegrass and Lehmann lovegrass) and yellow sweetclover, and treated with 2,4,5-T herbicides annually for four years after the burn, yielded an average of 1,500 kilograms per hectare (1,336 pounds per acre) of grasses and forbs in the fifth through tenth growing seasons (Hibbert et al. 1974). These responses are represented schematically in figure 31.

Comparable estimates of shrub biomass are not available, but crown-cover measurements indicate that, without postfire treatment, shrubs recover rapidly to dominate the site within perhaps five years and regain preburn levels sometime after eleven years. Follow-up treatments, of course, can suppress the recovery (Cable 1975; Hibbert et al. 1974). A generalized interpretation of shrub response is presented in figure 32.

An obvious conclusion to be drawn from these dynamics is that there is no one-phase technique for achieving and maintaining optimum deer habitat. If, for example, the management goal is to maintain one-third of a 608-hectare (1,500-acre) area in 10-hectare (25-acre) blocks less than five years old by burning alone, it would be necessary to treat twenty such blocks initially. Twenty more would be treated

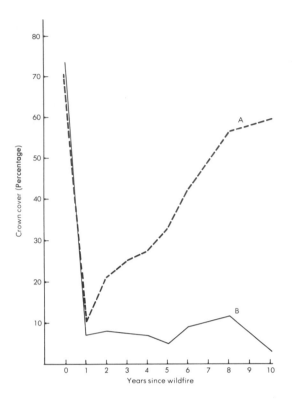

Figure 31. Shrub development after burning Arizona chaparral: A, with no postfire treatment; B, treated with herbicides in years 1–5 and 9 (after Hibbert et al. 1974).

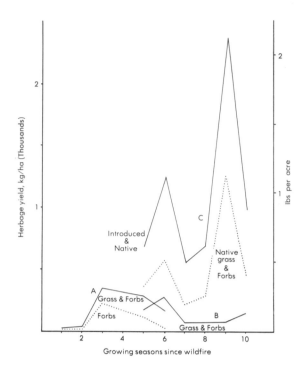

Figure 32. Herbage yield on Arizona chaparral areas after burning: A, Upper Mingus Mountain; B, Three Bar Wildlife Area without postfire treatment; C, Three Bar Wildlife Area seeded with lovegrass in Year 2 and treated with herbicides in years 2–6 and 8 (after Cable 1975; Hibbert et al. 1974).

after five years and the remaining blocks at ten years, returning to the first twenty in the fifteenth year. At the average cost of $27.18 per hectare ($11.00 per acre) for prescribed burning in 1972 (Brown et al. 1974), this would amount to an outlay of $16,500 for each fifteen years. Current prices would place the cost at more than $20,000. Assuming that carrying capacity of mature chaparral was 4.6 deer per square kilometer (12 per square mile), or 1 deer per 21.5 hectares (1 per 53 acres)—the questionable estimate of Hanson and McCulloch (1955)—and that carrying capacity of the portion of the area then five years old was doubled, the prescription would result in a net increase in carrying capacity from 28 to 33 deer on the 607 hectares (1,500 acres). The habitat management cost would be $220 per additional deer (closer to $300 at current prices). However, other forage and watershed values would also be realized.

That prescription is an example, not a recommendation. More detailed total cost estimates for treating a representative area—burning, seeding, and herbicide application—over a fifty-year period were outlined by Brown et al. (1974). Their estimates came to approximately $20.25 per hectare ($50 per acre).

The following guidelines (reworded) were developed by the Arizona Game and Fish Department and the United States Rocky Mountain Forest and Range Experiment Station, and listed as applicable to its Southwestern Region (U.S. Forest Service 1970):

1. Strip clearings provide more edge between cover and feeding areas than do block clearings.

2. Optimum opening size is 12–14 hectares (30–35 acres).

3. Optimum width of standing brush is 400 meters (0.25 mile); a 200-meter width (0.125

mile) is adequate with tall, dense brush.

4. Isolated patches of brush openings should be at least 8 hectares (20 acres) in size with dense brush and 16 hectares (40 acres) with sparse brush.

5. Large trees—riparian woodland, oak islands, or isolated pine or juniper stands—should be left for bedding and resting areas.

6. Brush should be left around watering areas as security for deer.

7. Shrub live oaks should be left for food.

8. Extremely dense chaparral should be thinned.

9. In reseeding, legumes and forbs should be included in seed mixtures.

Urness (1974) offered the following recommendations:

1. Regardless of acreage treated, control areas should not exceed about 274–366 meters (300–400 yards) in width.

2. No more than 50 percent of any area should be treated.

3. Specifying that only certain slopes be treated is not advisable; data indicate that deer shift seasonally in the habitat segment they select, using north slopes more extensively in spring and summer and south-facing slopes in autumn and winter.

4. Irregular strips and small patches should be root-plowed in unobtrusive patterns that treat and retain some areas on all types of slope.

5. Large treated blocks are objectionable from almost any aesthetic criterion and are not compatible with optimum diversity of habitat.

6. "Properly done, treatments should not reduce overall populations if sufficient cover is retained. The creation of a high-quality forage resource in treated pastures no doubt increases the value of adjacent chaparral, but it is not certain that this resource affects deer population levels materially" (Urness 1974, p. 7).

It is important to note that Urness was concerned less with potential benefits to deer habitat than with possible detriment. In Arizona, wildlife habitat improvement customarily has been used as a secondary selling point to help justify the cost of chaparral management for other purposes, mainly water yield and livestock forage production. Even with

those benefits, economic returns must be viewed with caution. Using some loose assumptions (rather than measurements) of benefits to be expected from a large number of potentially treatable areas, Brown et al. (1974) concluded that one set of management practices would yield benefit-cost ratios greater than 1.0 on two-thirds of the treated areas over a fifty-year period, and an alternative set of practices would yield such benefits on half the treated areas. That is, depending on feasible alternative management practices, one-third to one-half of the areas would not yield returns of all resources combined to justify the cost. However, 47 percent of the total chaparral area considered (344,250 hectares; 850,000 acres) already had been excluded because of steep slopes, low brush densities, inability to achieve desirable conversion patterns, prior management designations, or for other reasons. So, in truth, only about 11–14 percent of the area might have yielded a break-even return or better.

Wildlife biologists in Arizona have been singularly reticent about expressing quantitatively the improvement in deer habitat that may be brought about by chaparral management. Although the amount of area treated has increased greatly over the past twenty-five years, the deer population generally has decreased. This cannot be attributed to brush control, but it also is not encouraging testimony to the effectiveness of chaparral manipulation for deer habitat improvement.

California Chaparral

About 3 million hectares (7.4 million acres) in California are considered to be in the chaparral vegetation type (Sampson 1944). The area extends discontinuously along the Coast Range from southeastern Oregon into northern Baja California, Mexico, with isolated units along the Sierra Nevada. In contrast to Arizona, virtually all annual precipitation occurs between September and April. Where there are less than 36 centimeters (14 inches) of annual rainfall, chaparral becomes open and more suggestive of desert shrub vegetation.

Where there is more than 102 centimeters (40 inches) of rainfall per year, the chaparral blends into forest.

The most common shrubs, in descending order of abundance over the type as a whole, are chamise, photinia, buckbrush ceanothus, California scrub oak, leatheroak, birchleaf mountain mahogany, interior live oak, California buckthorn, and canyon live oak (Cooper 1922).

Chaparral in California is inhabited by Columbian black-tailed deer in the central and northern Coast Range, California mule deer in the south-central Coast Range and the Sierra Nevada foothills, and Southern mule deer along the southern Coast Range extending into Baja California. Because of their numbers, black-tailed deer and their habitat in the North Coast Range have been given the most management attention.

California chaparral has been notorious for its large, destructive wildfires. Total fire protection proved to be a frustrating management expedient because it permitted brush stands to develop large volumes of dead, highly flammable fuel. Within a decade or so after a burn, though stands become impenetrably dense and of full stature, they are relatively fire-resistant. A management rationale evolved from the premise that, in early stages of succession, herbaceous vegetation might be burned repeatedly (Biswell et al. 1952). It involved increasing herbaceous ground cover by seeding with grasses and legumes to minimize erosion and provide forage and a fuel source for repeat burning. Grass, increased grazing, and repeated fires all tended to favor root-sprouting shrubs, however, and to discourage several other important forage shrubs. Elimination of brush cover was not desired, so patterns of interspersed successional stages were developed, with fire applied according to prescription. This necessitated maintaining firebreaks to control both prescribed and natural fires. General principles considered applicable to North Coastal Range chaparral were proposed by Biswell et al. (1952) and Taber and Dasmann (1954). Their recommendations are synthesized as follows:

1. Burn in spring (before March) or late autumn. Summer burning involves excessive fire-control costs.

2. Spot burn areas of about 2 hectares (5 acres) each, evenly scattered and amounting to two-thirds of the total area on south slopes, but only one-third on north slopes, which deer use in periods of most harassment.

3. Leave "adequate" cover between cleared areas.

4. Mechanical treatment is optional when feasible but normally is more costly and is reserved for ridgeline firebreaks.

5. Seed shortly before autumn rains with such species as soft chess, domestic ryegrass, smilo, tall fescue, orchardgrass, rose clover, and burnet.

6. Reburn before brush becomes dense and crowds out grass, or use "selective" herbicides in spring.

More specific variations of these generalities have been developed by the United States Forest Service, which manages much of the land in chaparral type. Continuation of this management would be expected to result in

Prescribed burning is used to open California chaparral to improve deer habitat. Note the firebreaks on ridges. Photograph by Guy E. Connolly.

three types of habitat that Taber and Dasmann (1958) referred to as wildfire (recently burned), open brushland, and chaparral, each offering certain seasonal benefits of forage or cover, or both. Taber and Dasmann reported highest densities of deer use in recently burned areas (more than 46 deer per square kilometer in midsummer; 120 per square mile), with use diminishing over several years. On an area burned in 1948, the population density was estimated at one deer per 2.2 hectares (5.4 acres) in 1949, and one deer per 5.9 hectares (14.6 acres) in 1952. In 1952 ridgetops were disked, spot burns were applied, and both treatment areas were seeded. Use level of the treated areas increased to one deer per 2.4 hectares (5.9 acres) by 1955.

From the same set of data, Biswell (1961) inferred that populations increased as a result of brush-cover manipulation. Actually, all that was observed, according to reports including that of Taber and Dasmann (1958), was intensity of use as estimated by pellet group sampling and "sample area" counts. However, Biswell's (1961, p. 143) generalization on use of opened brush ("small burned patches here and there, seeded to suitable herbaceous species") and large wildfire burns versus heavy untreated brush (each sample area about 405 hectares: 1,000 acres) suggests an immediate quadrupling of use that rapidly declines to preburn levels (fig. 33) If these data indicate what is generally to be expected, chaparral control may be a more fruitful habitat management enterprise in California than in Arizona.

Maintenance of firebreaks is an important aspect of chaparral management, whether for deer habitat, water yield, or fire control. Repeated chemical or mechanical control is costly. Recently, domestic goats were used experimentally in the Cleveland National Forest in southwestern California to suppress shrubs by intensive grazing on "fuelbreaks" (Hughes 1976). While this requires more intensive management than normal goat grazing, it may provide fire control benefits while yielding goats for market. Under such control, negligible damage to deer habitat was anticipated; the consequences have not yet been seen.

Results of predictable magnitude with a given

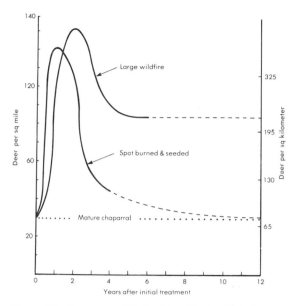

Figure 33. Response of Columbian black-tailed deer to chaparral manipulation (after Biswell 1961).

level of management effort are not likely to be claimed unequivocally. Natural amplitude of climatic and vegetational dynamics in the chaparral zone can have a profound influence on productivity of deer populations (Shaw

Chemical control of brush sprouts with a backpack mist-blower in California chaparral. Photograph by Ted Plumb; courtesy of the United States Forest Service.

1965). Furthermore, in neither California nor Arizona does chaparral occur as an endless, unbroken, uniform, dense thicket of tall shrubs. Rather, it normally is interspersed with relatively or largely open shrub stands and a variety of other vegetational situations to diversify available habitat. Consequently it is unlikely that the effect on deer populations of chaparral manipulation can be detected with certainty. In the meantime, confidence in the practice will have to be based on improved knowledge of the kinds of factors changed, the degree of change, and assumptions regarding the influence of change on deer.

DESERT

According to the criteria of Köppen, deserts are regions of the biosphere with relatively high temperatures and less than 25 centimeters (10 inches) annual rainfall (Strahler 1966). On this basis, four major desert areas occur in North America: the Great Basin, Mojave, Sonoran, and Chihuahuan (Leopold 1962) (see fig. 34).

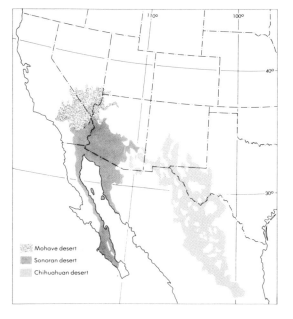

Figure 34. Distribution of the Chihuahuan, Sonoran, and Mojave deserts (from Brown et al. 1977; Küchler 1964; Leopold 1950*b*).

Much of the Great Basin Desert is transitional with steppe. Its small mountain ranges with juniper-piñon woodland, mountain mahogany/oak scrub or pine forest (see Küchler 1964) give it quite a different character from the other deserts. It is inhabited by Rocky Mountain mule deer. The Mojave Desert of southeastern California, southwestern Arizona, and extreme southern Nevada is the hottest, driest, most barren, and most topographically unrelieved of the deserts. Peripherally, it supports some Southern and desert mule deer, largely because habitat conditions are transitional to other vegetation zones. However, it is devoid of deer over large areas. Consequently, this part of chapter 9 is concerned with the Sonoran and Chihuahuan deserts. Desert mule deer inhabit most of both deserts. Southern and peninsula mule deer occur in Sonoran Desert habitat in Baja California, and Cedros Island and Tiburon Island mule deer—if these truly are distinct subspecies—exist on adjacent islands.

Lexical definitions of "desert"—suggesting hot, barren, desolate, foreboding landscapes incapable of supporting much life—tend to shape popular misconceptions of what these areas are like. Deserts can be biotically complex and dynamic. They are no more harsh and forbidding to animals adapted there than are the environments of organisms adapted elsewhere.

The most extreme desert areas in North America support only widely scattered, stunted shrubs such as creosote bush and bur sage and often only a sprinkling of big galleta grass on extensive intervening areas of "desert pavement." Shallow washes and occasional arroyos provide some topographic relief and a few larger shrubs. Cover is inadequate to meet the needs of deer for shade, concealment, or escape, and usable forage normally is too poor in nutritional quality to sustain even one deer. But upland desert areas offer a large array of shrubs, half-shrubs, cacti, and perennial forbs and grasses as well as a rich, seasonal flora of succulent ephemeral forbs in most years.

Desert scrub sites on the Three Bar Wildlife Area in Arizona had average annual crops, over an eight-year period, of 702 kilograms per

Mule deer habitat at the northern edge of Mojave Desert habitat in the extreme southern tip of Nevada. Photograph courtesy of the United States Bureau of Land Management.

hectare (626 pounds per acre) of forbs and grasses in spring and 421 kilograms per hectare (376 pounds per acre) in autumn (Smith and LeCount 1976). These herbage yields were divided about evenly between forbs and grasses; browse yield was not estimated. By comparison, on subalpine summer range sites in Colorado, biomass of deer forage at the end of the growing season averaged 386 kilograms per hectare (346 pounds per acre) in forest and 570 kilograms per hectare (509 pounds per acre) in clear-cuts (Wallmo et al. 1972). On sagebrush winter range used by the same deer population, the end-of-summer crop of forbs and grasses ranged from about 400–700 kilograms per hectare (357–625 pounds per acre) annually over five years of measurement (Carpenter 1976). About 57 percent of that yield was composed of grasses. There were an additional 400–650 kilograms per hectare (357–580 pounds per acre) of shrub leaves and current growth twigs, but most of this was big sagebrush, which has limited value as deer forage.

Thus, in terms of herbage biomass, desert can be as productive as other habitats. Annual variations in productivity may be greater, however. In eight years of measurement on the Three Bar Wildlife Area in Arizona, annual spring grass yields ranged from 24 to 713 kilograms per hectare (21–637 pounds per acre), spring forb yields from 9 to 840 kilograms per hectare (8–750 pounds per acre), autumn grass yields from 36 to 392 kilograms per hectare (35–350 pounds per acre), and autumn forb yields from 125 to 308 kilograms per hectare (112–275 pounds per acre) (Smith and LeCount 1976).

Vegetation of the Sonoran and Chihuahuan deserts includes three distinct kinds of plants from which deer can derive their nutritional needs: (1) drought-tolerant perennials, such as shrubs, cacti, yuccas, and agaves, with some "armor" that protects against grazing; (2) winter annuals; and (3) summer annuals that have specific photosynthetic capabilities to withstand summer temperatures and that rely on rapid, prolific growth and early maturation

Mule deer habitat in the Sonoran Desert near Hermosilla, Sonora, Mexico. Photograph by L. C. Fierro.

to accomplish life cycles and regeneration. Few of the annuals have special antigrazing characteristics. A variety of photosynthetic strategies has evolved in plants in the process of adapting to different environments (see Hatch et al. 1971). The C^3 photosynthesis exhibited commonly by winter annuals is more efficient in moderate temperatures. Many species begin growth as rosettes occupying a warm microenvironment close to the ground between September and mid-December and burst forth with upright stems and leaves as winter moisture and rising late winter temperatures permit. Summer annuals exhibit C^4 photosynthesis. Their seeds germinate abruptly after summer showers, and they grow and mature rapidly; but, if moisture is too limited, many may not mature (Mulroy and Rundel 1977). Mulroy and Rundel revealed that the Arizona upland subdivision of the Sonoran Desert has three to four times as many species of winter annuals, and nine to ten times as many summer annuals as the more westerly and more xeric Lower Colorado subdivision.

Much of what is referred to as deer habitat in deserts really is climatically semiarid, on the average. On the Three Bar Wildlife Area in Arizona, average annual precipitation from 1968 to 1975 was 38 centimeters (15 inches)

(Smith and LeCount 1976). Much of the "desert" habitat there is transitional with chaparral. Truly desert climates may be experienced for periods of years, however. On the Black Gap Wildlife Area of Texas, in the Chihuahuan Desert, average annual precipitation from 1952 through 1976 was 28 centimeters (11 inches), but from 1951 through 1957, less than 15 centimeters (6 inches) was received annually (Brownlee, pers. files).

In both the Sonoran and Chihuahuan desert regions, there normally are summer and winter rainy seasons, separated by drought in autumn and spring. Summer rains are quite dependable, though their frequency and total amount are highly variable. Winter rains are less dependable. At the Three Bar Wildlife Area, 68 percent of the precipitation from 1968 through 1975 occurred from October through April. In 1970–71, 22 percent occurred in winter, and in 1972–73, 92 percent occurred in winter. However, on the Black Gap Wildlife Area, 70 percent of the precipitation from 1952 through 1976 occurred from May through September.

Precipitation patterns are discussed at length here because of their conspicuous influence on productivity of desert and semidesert ranges of mule deer.

Sonoran Desert

Delineations of the Sonoran Desert are highly variable, so arbitrary boundaries are drawn here to clarify the following discussion. On the west, the Sonoran Desert grades into the Mojave Desert over a wide portion of southwestern Arizona. There is a fairly distinct northeast boundary extending from northwestern Arizona, at the southern tip of Nevada, in a southeasterly direction where desert grades into chaparral (mainly) in central Arizona and into semidesert grassland in south-central Arizona. From there the eastern boundary extends through Sonora west of the Sierra Madre Occidental to the Gulf of California in the vicinity of Guaymas (Küchler 1964; Leopold 1950*b;* Lowe and Brown 1973). All but the northwest corner and southern tip of Baja California are included, as delineated by Leopold (1950*b*).

Lowe and Brown (1973) lumped all vegetational manifestations of the Sonoran Desert in Arizona into two "communities"—the Lower Colorado division and the Arizona Upland division. Although they are widely intermixed, elements of the latter become progressively less common to the west. The Lower Colorado division is dominated by sparse creosote bush/bur sage communities, with saltbush/desert-thorn/mesquite communities in floodplains and undrained areas. This division, by itself, is marginal mule deer habitat at best.

The Arizona Upland division has received more attention from deer ecologists because it supports significant populations of deer. "Magnificent, beautiful, majestic, picturesque, bizarre, are words that have been used to describe this highly diverse and arborescent subtropical desertscrub community in southern Arizona and adjacent northern Sonora, Mexico. . . . This is the most structurally diverse vegetation in the entire United States" (Lowe and Brown 1973, pp. 35–36, 37). It includes numerous species of subtropical desert trees, a diverse array of cacti—several of tree size—and a large number of shrubs (sixteen common species are listed by Lowe and Brown), plus an extremely complex herbaceous flora.

Research by the Arizona Game and Fish Department and the United States Forest Service Rocky Mountain Forest and Range Experiment Station on the Three Bar Wildlife Area in central Arizona has contributed much to the understanding of mule deer habitat in the Sonoran Desert. There, desert mule deer occur principally in the desert scrub zone, and Coues white-tailed deer occur in higher chaparral and woodland zones.

The Three Bar Wildlife Area was closed to livestock grazing in 1947. Deer hunting was prohibited from the late 1940s to 1961. Limited permits then were issued for either-sex hunting until 1968 and for buck-only hunting until 1972. In that period, the mule deer population declined radically. Estimates of crops of fawns surviving until winter in 1969, 1970, and 1971 suggested that recruitment was too low for the population to tolerate any significant amount of hunting in addition to other adverse factors (Smith and LeCount 1976).

What were these adversities? For one thing, there was a significant downward trend in summer precipitation in southern Arizona during 1954–66 (Cable and Martin 1975). Anthony (1976) reported an abrupt decline of mule deer in the San Cayetano Mountains, southeastern Arizona, after a drought period from late 1969 to mid-1971.

Eight years of measurements of weather, forage yields, and fawn-doe ratios on the Three Bar Wildlife Area revealed significant linear relationships among: (1) winter fawn-doe ratios (the fawn crop) and October–June precipitation the preceding year; (2) fawn crop and the combined winter and summer yield of forbs and half-shrubs the preceding year; and (3) October–April precipitation and the winter crop of forbs and half-shrubs (Smith and LeCount 1976). Forb crops accounted for more than 75 percent of the variation in fawn production.

Although a central hypothesis in the Three Bar Wildlife Area study was that the nutritional state of does during pregnancy and lactation has a pronounced effect on the viability of their fawns (as shown in whitetails by Verme 1963*b*), predation was considered as a factor potentially interacting with forage production. The hypothesis was that, in dry years, the food base for coyotes is reduced, especially mast, so they direct more effort to hunting fawns. And, at the same time, herbaceous cover for fawns to hide in is reduced, and fawns are weaker and more easily caught.

An important corollary of the Three Bar Wildlife Area findings was that, during 1971–75, fawn-doe ratios were 33 percent higher there than on surrounding range, most of which was grazed by livestock, yet densities of coyotes and bobcats were believed to be higher on the Three Bar Wildlife Area (Gallizioli 1976*a*).

In recent years there has been growing concern that livestock grazing is continuing to degrade southwestern ranges, even on public lands where responsible agencies are mandated to regulate grazing so as to maintain or improve range condition. Although there is no extensive measurement documentation of the relative condition of these rangelands over time, analyses by both the United States Bureau of Land Management and the United States Forest Service seem to support this belief (Gallizioli 1976*b*).

An interesting by-product of the study reported by Smith and LeCount (1976) was the discovery of a negative relationship among forbs produced in winter and grasses produced the following summer, suggesting that ground cover produced in winter might somehow inhibit the growth and vigor of perennial grasses. This speculation is supported by studies on the Santa Rita Experimental Range in the semidesert grass/shrub type south of Tucson, Arizona. Here, seasonal precipitation components with the greatest effect on year-to-year changes in grass production were current August rainfall, and current August rainfall multiplied by June–September rainfall of the previous year (Cable and Martin 1975).

In view of those findings, and with respect to planning livestock grazing, Cable and Martin (1975, p. 1) said: "Management decisions should be made with the thought in mind that it takes at least two years to recover from a one-year drought." Heavy use (52–59 percent) by

livestock of perennial grass production greatly restricted gains in grass production in wet years following a dry year; gains were highest where use was lowest (21–25 percent). Alternate-year summer deferment did not improve the range condition, because there was too little time for recovery between grazing periods. It is important to add that the precautions suggested by Cable and Martin rarely, if ever, are applied in operational grazing on either public or private lands in the Southwest.

Range managers have expended much effort to improve carrying capacity of range or to restore it after destructive grazing. Half a century ago, such possibilities were viewed optimistically. Today they appear considerably less promising.

Judd and Judd (1976) reviewed the condition of several sites in Arizona—on semidesert shrub, chaparral, semidesert grassland, and piñon/juniper range—thirty years after the sites had been subjected to "revegetation" operations. Treatments of semidesert shrub sites in 1945 and 1946 included broadcast seeding alone and with various combinations of disking, cultipacking, harrowing, and mulching. Seeds of nineteen grass and shrub species were used, most of which were not native to those particular locations. A few species germinated and established stands. Plains bristle grass, hooded windmill grass, Lehmann lovegrass, Boer lovegrass, and bush muhly still were growing on mulched plots in 1949. The first two of these disappeared before 1954, and the latter three disappeared sometime between 1962 and 1965. Judd and Judd (1976, p. 248) did not describe the grazing to which these sites were subjected, but they said, "Several plots protected from grazing had [in 1946] approximately four times the plant density and double the plant height of those in grazed plots." Slight reassurance comes from that fact—considering that all treatments essentially failed within five years, with or without grazing pressure.

One strategy in arid land "renovation" is to retain precipitation in the soil rather than to allow it to run off. Tromble (1976) reported that pitting and root-plowing desert shrub range in southeastern Arizona significantly reduced

Cattle are introduced to an area of semidesert grassland in the Santa Rita Mountains in southern Arizona. Photograph taken in 1903 by D. Griffiths; courtesy of the United States Forest Service.

This is the same area and approximate vantage point as shown in the previous photograph, but thirty-eight years later. The type conversion from grassland to grassland/scrub was the result of persistent livestock grazing, even during a succession of dry years. Such conversions to mesquite may provide shade and cover for deer, but this does not offset the loss of forage quality and diversity. Photograph by Matt Culley; courtesy of the United States Forest Service.

runoff in two years of posttreatment observation; root-plowing was most effective. In the third year, overgrazing overcame the moisture-retaining effect of root-plowing and caused an increase in runoff compared with untreated range. Runoff was correlated negatively and strongly with the amount of plant cover and was correlated positively and more strongly with the amount of bare soil.

Tromble (1976, p. 254) cautioned that "range restoration can leave treated portions of watersheds largely denuded of vegetation until replacement vegetation is established." Considering that replacement vegetation may never become established (see Judd and Judd 1976), it can be questioned whether these practices should be considered "renovations" or another of man's delusions that he can manage the biosphere better than nature does—simultaneously with misusing it.

It seems obvious that desert ranges cannot be maintained in or restored to optimal conditions in the presence of heavy livestock grazing. Occasionally, or even for a series of good years, there may be a surplus of forage that can be used without degrading the productivity of range. However, no proved management strategy has been offered that will sustain an economically viable livestock industry on desert rangelands without destroying them.

Though they feel assured that additional management will permit significant profits from livestock grazing on their own deserts, Americans are appalled at the complete desecration of the Sahel Desert in Africa. Desert vegetations have evolved with herbivores, but the mutual adaptation requires that each yield before destroying the other. To survive, the livestock industry must make the same concession. In western New Mexico, the simple expedient of keeping cattle off semidesert grassland range from May through November, when the most and best cattle forage was available, permitted ground cover to increase dramatically (Hickey and Garcia 1964). If desert range is used in such a way that it will not support desert mule deer, which are adapted to it, it cannot be expected to support domesticated livestock, which are not similarly adapted.

Anthony and Smith (1977) added up several

A butane gas burner is used to kill juniper during a revegetation project in an area of semidesert shrub, following a period of extended drought and overgrazing by livestock. Photograph by Joseph F. Arnold; courtesy of the United States Forest Service.

ecological interpretations of the trend of arid vegetation zones in southern Arizona and concluded that the zones have expanded as a consequence of climatic change, overgrazing, and protection from fire. Humphrey (1958*b*) inferred that, if fires had been allowed to run uncontained, this would not have occurred, and unrestricted grazing practices could have continued without altering the vegetation. This interpretation seems presumptuous and unlikely.

Chihuahuan Desert

The Chihuahuan Desert is an even less discrete climate-vegetation region than the Sonoran Desert. Much of it, as recognized by plant ecologists, is classified as semiarid rather than arid by climatologists (Critchfield 1966). Furthermore, much of it is considered by some ecologists as being in a grassland or steppe climate rather than a desert climate where vegetational conditions represent grazing, fire, or recent weather disclimax (Gardner 1951; Hastings and Turner 1965; Humphrey 1953). This distinction has considerable significance to desert mule deer but only an obscure relationship to where the boundaries of the Chihuahuan Desert are drawn.

Lowe and Brown (1973) showed the Chihuahuan desert scrub extending into southeastern Arizona along the Gila and San Simon valleys from New Mexico and crossing the border from Chihuahua and Sonora, Mexico, into extreme southeastern Arizona. Leopold (1950*b*) extended the western boundary southeastward to southern San Luis Potosí and the eastern boundary northward along the Sierra Madre Oriental to the Rio Grande. Desert-scrub vegetation continues into southeastern New Mexico as tarbush/creosote bush savanna and, some distance up the Rio Grande, tarbush/creosote bush type (Küchler 1964). In Texas the Pecos River constitutes an arbitrary eastern boundary (Webster 1950; Rowell 1970). There, on the Stockton Plateau, junipers become more common, and the Trans-Pecos tarbush/creosote bush savanna grades into mesquite savanna and juniper/oak savanna (Küchler 1964).

Little is known of the ecology and population status of desert mule deer in the Mexican states of Chihuahua and Coahuila except that their numbers have been dwindling. Studies have been conducted and management programs implemented in Trans-Pecos Texas, southern New Mexico, and southeastern Arizona. Throughout these areas the landscape is broken by mountains of various magnitudes, chaparrallike shrub communities, and woodland. In most places higher zones are inhabited by Coues white-tailed deer, while desert mule deer occupy desert-scrub and grassland zones, with considerable overlap in some areas (Anthony and Smith 1977).

The ecology and population responses of mule deer in the Chihuahuan Desert are similar to those in the Sonoran Desert. Research on desert mule deer habitat has been conducted continuously since the early 1950s on the Black Gap Wildlife Management Area, within the Big Bend of the Rio Grande. The original 11,000 hectares (27,000 acres) of the Black Gap Area were purchased by the state of Texas in 1948; it was finally expanded to about 37,000 hectares (91,000 acres). Most of the original area was severely degraded by indiscriminate grazing of goats, cattle, and horses; but, because it was so remote from human population centers, hunting pressure on deer was light. In 1948 it was closed to hunting until 1954, and predator control was intensified. Mountain lions, the major predator, were rigorously controlled but by no means eliminated thereafter. By 1952 all livestock had been removed.

Previous overgrazing, coupled with extreme drought from 1951 through 1957, resulted in severely impoverished range conditions and apparent, but unmeasured, low deer densities. Nevertheless, nominal hunting—largely to initiate a program of regulated experimental harvesting—was allowed in 1955. Fifty buck-only permits were issued, and twenty-five hunters killed five deer. The drought broke in 1958 when more rain fell on the area than in any year since 1948. Several relatively good

Mule deer feeding on lechuguilla in the Texas Big Bend area of the Chihuahuan Desert. Photograph by William V. Reaves; courtesy of the Texas Parks and Wildlife Department.

years followed, and there were appreciable increases in areal coverage of shrubs, forbs, and grasses between 1956 and 1961 (Wallmo 1961).

In 1960 the ovulation rate of yearling and older does was 2.02, based on counts of corpora lutea of pregnancy. In October–November of 1958, 1959, and 1960, fawn-antlerless deer ratios were estimated at 42 : 100, 74 : 100, and 76 : 100, respectively (Wallmo 1961). Ratios of fawns to adult does in the harvests from 1958 through 1965 were 68, 95, 94, 56, 39, 38, 48, and 51:100 (Brownlee 1966).

At the end of the drought in 1957, the mule deer population on the Black Gap Wildlife Area was estimated at approximately 1,000 and, in 1967, at approximately 3,600, though annual harvests increased from 5 in 1955 to 444 in 1963 and 372 in 1964. Thereafter, hunting permits were reduced, but by 1969 the population had declined to levels experienced at the end of the drought. Hunting was discontinued in 1972, and in 1973 the population was estimated to be nearly 3,000. Above-average precipitation occurred from 1970 through 1974 (Brownlee 1976).

Despite extreme fluctuations in annual precipitation on the Black Gap Area, in the absence of livestock grazing there has been a progressive increase in perennial plant cover (table 59). Experience there demonstrates that, without excessive livestock competition, perhaps aided necessarily by predator control, Chihuahuan Desert habitat can support rather large and highly productive mule deer populations. It also is clear that deer there were very sensitive to the effects of drought. This, of course, prevents them from overusing the forage resource and preserves that resource for deer use when the climate improves and deer populations recover.

Anthony (1976) reported an abrupt decline in mule deer numbers in southeastern Arizona

Table 59. Percentage Change in Plant Cover, Relative to 1956, on the Black Gap Wildlife Area

| Year | Spatial Coverage | | | Density |
	Shrubs	Ground Cover Plants[a]	Grasses[b]	Forbs[c]
1961	37	32	49	87
1967	116	42	100	82
1972	260	61	131	122
1977	278	126	210	−17

Source: Russ (1978).

[a] Ground cover plants include grasses, certain cacti, and other succulents.
[b] Also included in ground cover plants.
[c] Includes some woody perennials whose aboveground parts are mostly herbaceous.

(Chihuahuan desert shrub-desert grassland habitat) in one year of severe drought and observed a pronounced change in deer diets from succulent forage to drought-resistant evergreen species. That study also suggested that competition from livestock may accentuate effects of drought on deer diets, as revealed in the following observations (Anthony and Smith 1977): in the San Cayetano Mountains, there was heavier livestock grazing in mule deer habitats than in whitetail habitats, and grasses and herbs made up a smaller percentage of mule deer diets; in the Dos Cabezos Mountains, all the range was overused by livestock, and there were no significant differences in the percentage of grasses and herbs in mule deer and whitetail diets.

Anthony and Smith (1977) theorized that the range of mule deer in southeastern Arizona has expanded upward over the past century, at the expense of whitetail habitat, as a result of a trend toward hotter and drier climates, fire suppression, and overgrazing by livestock. This was construed as favorable to mule deer, but it does not consider the corollary probability that mule deer habitat at lower elevations was simultaneously deteriorating. Anthony and Smith remarked that mule deer were dominant over whitetails in all observed behavioral interactions. It seems reasonable to infer from their report that zones from which mule deer were ousting whitetails also were being degraded, as is suggested by the apparent effect of livestock competition on deer food habits.

Chihuahuan Desert habitat in Texas almost universally shows the scars of excessive livestock use. Leithead (1959) rated only 2 percent (5,540 hectares: 13,689 acres) in the Terlingua Creek Drainage in the Big Bend region as in good range condition and considered 53 percent (146,810 hectares: 362,768 acres) in poor condition. Range sites in good condition absorbed moisture five to six times as fast as did similar sites in poor condition or worse. Evaporational loss from the first 30 centimeters (12 inches) of soil was three times as great on closely grazed, poor-condition range as on good-condition range. Reduced moisture retention compounds the problem, of course.

There may be little difference in total runoff from good- and poor-condition watersheds, but much of the rainfall from minor storms is retained for plant growth on good-condition ranges, whereas on poor range it runs off to be absorbed in the drainage channels. Heavy storms significantly increase erosion and accelerate range deterioration.

As discussed with regard to the Sonoran Desert, and from experience on the Black Gap Wildlife Area, ranges will recover in time after livestock use ceases. To overcome results of overgrazing and drought, range managers have experimented with a variety of practices for brush control and range restoration. To date, results have not been encouraging. Improvement usually is of short duration at best and normally is quickly overcome by drought and resumption of grazing.

Studies of desert mule deer movements were conducted on the Black Gap and the Sierra Diablo Wildlife Management areas (Brownlee 1963). The latter is northwest of Van Horn in western Trans-Pecos, Texas. The mean distances that marked deer were observed from trap sites, over a four-year period, were 1.8 and 1.2 kilometers (1.1 and 0.7 miles) on those two areas, respectively. It also was discovered that deer would not regularly travel more than 2.4 kilometers (1.5 miles) to water.

Since water is scarce and poorly distributed on these arid ranges, large areas are essentially uninhabitable during extensive dry periods. During wet periods, when water was widely available in potholes or drainage channels, deer used the range more generally. It was apparent from these studies that year-round utilization of otherwise suitable habitat depended on adequately distributed, permanent water.

Support for these conclusions is found in a study at the Fort Stanton Cooperative Range Research Station in southern New Mexico (Wood et al. 1970). Use of the range by mule deer decreased with distance from water. Deer densities increased where permanent water sources were developed in formerly unwatered areas. In one area deer use increased from less than 1 to more than 5 deer per square kilometer (1.6–13 per square mile) in five years. In another area, use increased from 5.5 to 7.4 deer per square kilometer (14.2–19.2 per square mile) in one year, then dropped to 3.6 per square kilometer (9.4 per square mile) in the fourth year when the water sources deteriorated. It rose again to 8.5 deer per square kilometer (22.1 per square mile) in the fifth year when water was again available.

Wood et al. (1970) concluded that a desirable distance between water sources at Fort Stanton would be 4–5 kilometers (2.5–3 miles). This agrees with data from the Black Gap and Sierra Diablo areas. If none of the range is more than 1.6–2.4 kilometers (1–1.5 miles) from permanent water, all of it can be used by mule deer.

In some areas, windmills can be installed or springs developed, but over much of the desert, rainwater collectors ("guzzlers") have been the only practical device. Roberts (1977) and Bonn (1976) explained various designs, all of which involve an impervious collecting apron that feeds rainwater into a storage cistern.

Elder (1954) calculated that desert mule deer near Tucson, Arizona, drank an average of about 24 liters (6.3 gallons) of water per visit at watering sites in summer. This is liberal compared with Bonn's (1976) estimate of 3 liters (0.8 gallon) per deer visit in southeastern Oregon. Bonn recorded 834 deer visits to water in eleven days of round-the-clock observations of one guzzler, yielding a total of more 2,526 liters (667 gallons) of water drunk in that period.

Guzzlers can and do influence distribution of mule deer, as is evidenced by the Oregon Fish and Wildlife Commission's use of them to reduce highway mortality of deer. In an area where deer crossed a highway to obtain water from the Deschutes River west of the highway, a series of guzzlers was installed in a line 1.6–3.2 kilometers (1–2 miles) east of the highway. This succeeded in reducing traffic mortality more than two-thirds by the second summer after installation (Bonn 1976).

A helicopter lowers one of two 4,826 liter (1,275 gallon) tanks into an excavated hole during the construction of a wildlife guzzler in Mojave Desert habitat used by desert and Southern mule deer. Photograph courtesy of the United States National Park Service.

A wildlife "guzzler" in the Chihuahuan Desert at the Black Gap Wildlife Management Area, Texas. Photograph by Sam Brownlee; courtesy of the Texas Parks and Wildlife Department.

HABITAT EVALUATION

Standardized habitat evaluation procedures for desert habitats have not been generally adopted. The key browse-survey method commonly used in the North (see chap. 10, part 2) clearly is not applicable to desert range, even though browse may be used extensively and, in drought periods, heavily by desert mule deer.

Research reviewed in this part suggests that quality of range is determined by supplies of succulent forage, including deciduous shrubs, and its use by deer is governed by the availability of drinking water. The adequacy of water supplies should be easy to evaluate, but determining adequacy of forage supplies requires development of a rationale that is relevant to the kinds and amounts of forage needed by deer.

The review of nutrition and metabolism of mule deer in chapter 3 clarifies that wildlife biologists and managers first must consider available forage in terms of nutritional parameters—most important, its digestibility and its usable nitrogen (protein) content. In part 1 of this chapter, Urness gives results of analyses of seasonal dietary nutritional planes of mule deer on arid and semiarid ranges. Crude protein content of seasonal diets ranged from 10 to 14 percent, at Three Bar Wildlife Area (Arizona), 9.6 to 10.4 percent at Santa Rita Experimental Range (Arizona), and 9 to 12 percent at Fort Bayard (New Mexico). In vitro digestibility was 34–51, 45–54, and 23–45 percent, respectively. The 34 percent digestibility level in November–December at the Three Bar Wildlife Area (Urness et al. 1971) and the 23 percent level in winter at Fort Bayard (Boeker et al. 1972) are far below that required for deer to obtain sufficient metabolizable energy for maintenance. Although the indicated crude protein levels were never as extremely low as in winter on some other ranges (see chap. 10, part

1), neither were they as high in summer, when needs for lactation and growth are greatest.

Granting that the methods used probably underestimated both protein content and digestibility of the forage that deer actually selected, it still seems that one of the first needs, in evaluating the supply of forage nutrients, is confidence in judging whether the kinds of forage present are qualitatively adequate to meet the nutritional needs of deer. Thereafter, quantitative estimates of available forage are in order.

If forage intake averaged 1 kilogram (2.2 pounds) per deer per day (Alldredge et al. 1974; Nichol 1938), 1 square kilometer (0.4 square mile) of range should supply 365 kilograms (805 pounds) for 1 deer, or 3,650 kilograms (8,050 pounds) for 10 deer over one year. The latter represents an average of less than 40 kilograms per hectare (35.7 pounds per acre). Smith and LeCount (1976) estimated the average winter crop of forbs and grasses, over eight years, at 702 kilograms per hectare (626 pounds per acre) and the summer crop at 421 kilograms per hectare (376 pounds per acre). In one year the winter crop was only 35 kilograms per hectare (31.2 pounds per acre). In the absence of livestock grazing, forage production was regulated by seasonal precipitation.

In the absence of other deleterious factors, weather will continue to govern transient variability in the condition of mule deer habitat in deserts. In light of the history of other deserts of the world, it can be expected that Sonoran and Chihuahuan desert habitats will deteriorate. With some experience, it is not difficult to distinguish a "beat-up" desert range from one that is able to respond prolifically when weather conditions permit. Furthermore, experience suggests that meddling with "range improvement" practices will not overcome the inherent limitations of desert.

ROCKY MOUNTAIN AND INTERMOUNTAIN HABITATS

Part 1. Food Habits and Nutrition

Olof C. Wallmo
Principal Wildlife Biologist
United States Forest Service
Pacific Northwest Forest and
Range Experiment Station
Juneau, Alaska

Wayne L. Regelin
Range Scientist
United States Fish and
Wildlife Service
Kenai, Alaska

The heart of Rocky Mountain mule deer range is the Rocky Mountain/Intermountain region, an area more than 2,500 kilometers (1,553 miles) in length, extending from central Arizona and New Mexico to northern Alberta and British Columbia (fig. 35). The region is about 1,500 kilometers (932 miles) in width from the eastern slope of the Rockies to the Sierra Nevada and Cascade-Coast ranges. Adaptability of mule deer to this vast geographic expanse suggests remarkable climatic tolerance (Cowan 1956b), but the area as a whole is characterized by common climatic features, as are the ranges of other subspecies. Most significant are the relatively warm, mesic summers and the cold, relatively dry winters. Although average winter precipitation is not high, in the form of snow it has a pronounced influence on forage availability. In general the "growing season" (period between the last and first killing frosts) averages about half the length of that in ranges of subspecies to the south and west. The impediment of snow, added to a prolonged period of poor forage, accounts for large-scale winter die-offs, frequently in the North (Edwards 1956) and occasionally in the South (Rasmussen 1941).

Throughout the Rocky Mountain/Intermountain region, most mule deer are migratory, spending a brief summer in the mountains and in autumn being driven downward by snow to foothills and valleys. (Some deer live at low elevations year-round. In the absence of snow, most migratory deer remain at high elevations during winter.) Their summer ranges commonly consist of a diverse mixture of coniferous forest, meadows, aspen woodlands, and often alpine tundra, together providing a rich, herbaceous flora for deer forage. Montane forest serves as winter range in many areas, but juniper-piñon pygmy forest, northern desert shrub, or shrub/grass communities are more typical winter range. Most of the shrub species are leafless in winter, and

Much of the Rocky Mountain/Intermountain region offers a complex variety of summer and winter ranges for mule deer. Photograph by Len Rue, Jr.

Most mule deer spend brief summers in the mountains and winter at lower elevations where forage supplies are somewhat more accessible. Summer range photograph on left by M. S. Benedict; courtesy of the United States Forest Service. Winter range photograph on right courtesy of the Wyoming Department of Game and Fish.

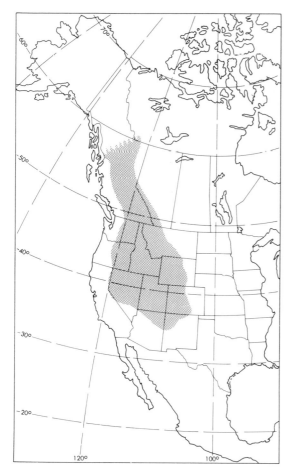

Figure 35. The Rocky Mountain and Intermountain region.

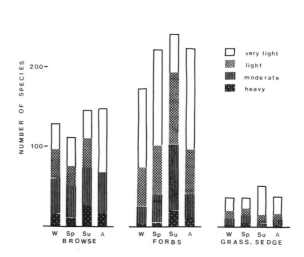

Figure 36. Numbers of forage species reported as receiving heavy, moderate, light, and very light seasonal use by Rocky Mountain mule deer throughout their range (after Kufeld et al. 1973).

those that retain their leaves—such as sagebrush, juniper, pine, and other conifers—have limited value as forage. Grasses generally are conspicuous on winter ranges, and, though their summer growth has ended, the "cool season" species that predominate put out new basal growth in winter. Forbs flourish in spring and early summer, but they mature early and include few species that provide significant amounts of succulent forage in winter.

FOOD HABITS

The compilation by Kufeld et al. (1973) of available information on food habits of Rocky Mountain mule deer provides some basis for generalizing on foods of the entire subspecies.

Of at least 788 kinds of plants reported eaten (the total is inexact because some were listed only by genus), 484 were forbs, 202 were shrubs and trees, 84 were grasses, sedges, and rushes, and 18 were "lower" plants. In all seasons, more kinds of forbs were reported used than shrubs and grasses (fig. 36). The greatest number of browse species reported were used in summer and autumn, and the smallest number in spring. This does not reveal relative quantitative use, nor are seasonal categories phenologically identical throughout the range. However, the data permit some speculation about relative preference by deer for life form classes. Browse plants tend to be available throughout the year, especially during winter, but the greatest variety were used in summer and autumn, when the plants presumably were in leaf.

In the review by Kufeld et al. (1973), approximate levels of use were assigned to species on the basis of their composition in sample data of reported studies. Those levels do not represent quantifications of relative use, but, by weighting species used with level-of-use factors, they provide a speculative construction of composite seasonal "diets" of Rocky Mountain mule deer (fig. 37). This suggests relative use of forbs and browse by seasons as

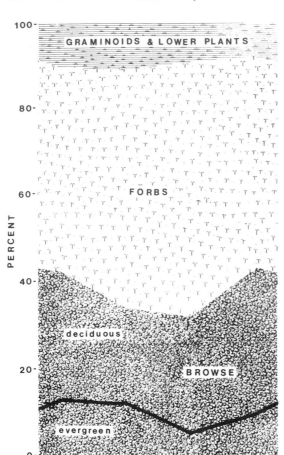

Figure 37. The hypothetical sum diet of all Rocky Mountain mule deer derived by giving weights of 1, 2, 3, and 4 to very light, light, moderate, and heavy use ratings, respectively, as reported by Kufeld et al. (1973; see fig. 36).

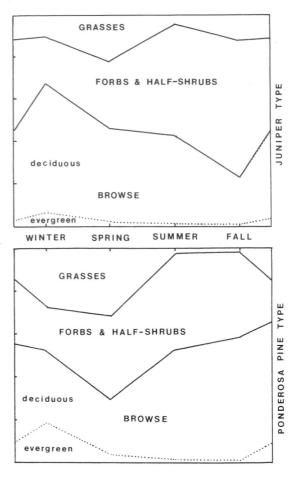

Figure 38. Seasonal diets of mule deer in north-central Arizona (after Neff 1974).

follows: spring—1.5 : 1, summer—1.9 : 1, autumn—1.1 : 1, and winter—1.2 : 1. Ratios of deciduous browse to evergreen browse were: spring—1.9 : 1, summer—5.9 : 1, autumn—3.5 : 1, and winter—2.3 : 1. Manipulation of data not designed for this purpose should be viewed cautiously. Here it is intended only to stimulate thought about the phenology of forage selection. For the range of the subspecies as a whole, the data suggest that, when available, succulent forbs tend to be selected over browse, and that deciduous browse species are favored when in leaf rather than in winter, when they are of greatest importance.

More defensible portrayals of seasonal composition of diets are available from studies of

Rocky Mountain mule deer in Arizona and Colorado (figs. 38 and 39). These data were obtained from observations of tame deer, but they suggest that leafless browse twigs are taken in quantity only when there is a deficiency of other forage. Leach (1956) concluded that winter use of browse by Rocky Mountain and Inyo mule deer was related to the severity of winter (see "Seasonal Nutrition," below). Although Ashcroft (1973, p. 4) considered browse important to sustain deer populations in winters of extended snow cover on Great Basin ranges in California, he felt that it could provide only a maintenance diet and that herbaceous forage was the "key to high productivity."

Readers interested in what plant species constitute potential forage for Rocky Mountain

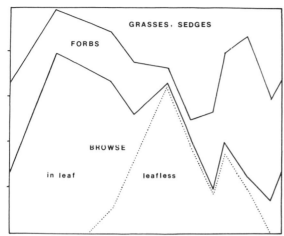

Figure 39. Seasonal pattern of mule deer diets in north-central Colorado.

mule deer are referred to table 60 and to Kufeld et al. (1973).

SEASONAL QUALITY AND AVAILABILITY OF FORAGE

In many areas, topographic and spatial distinctions among summer and winter ranges are vague. Moreover, areas used in winter vary annually depending on weather and snow cover. Still, there are conspicuous differences in seasonal forage quality that apply generally. Succulent forage high in cell contents (protein and soluble carbohydrates) and low in fiber (hemicellulose, cellulose, lignin, and cutin)—and consequently with high digestibility—is abundant in summer. The opposite is true in winter, and deficiency of protein and soluble carbohydrates is compounded by slow and incomplete digestion of plant fiber.

Among major forage species used by mule deer in northern Colorado, the cell wall content of browse was low in summer and high in autumn and winter, and that of forbs was low throughout the year (fig. 40). An intriguing feature is that cell contents (the inverse of cell wall constituents in fig. 40) increased during plant growth until the end of the growing season. This may be attributed to synthesis of soluble carbohydrates before translocation to the root system for overwinter storage. If true, the synthesis provides an extra energy boost to

Table 60. Most Frequently Cited Forages of Rocky Mountain Mule Deer

Type of Forage	Number of Citations
Browse	
Snowberry	69
Big sagebrush	67
Rose	67
Black chokecherry	64
Antelope bitterbrush	52
Quaking aspen	49
Oregon grape	47
Willow	45
Saskatoon serviceberry	41
Curl-leaf mountain mahogany	39
Rubber rabbitbrush	37
Ponderosa pine	32
Rocky Mountain juniper	28
Tobacco brush	26
Skunkbush	24
True mountain mahogany	23
Gambel oak	21
Grasses and sedges	
Bluegrass	31
Wheatgrass	29
Chess	22
Sedge	22
Fescue	10
Squirreltail	7
Forbs	
Buckwheat	63
Aster	50
Lupine	49
Phlox	46
Beardtongue	38
Fleabane	35
Balsamorrhiza	33
Sagebrush	32
Cinquefoil	30
Yarrow	27
Fringed sagebrush	27
Alfalfa	26
Thistle	25
Dandelion	25
Pussytoe	22
Vetch	22
Clover	21

Source: Kufeld et al. (1973).

deer even though protein supplies may wane during this period. The lignin-cutin fraction of fiber in browse species was high throughout the year and was low in forbs during spring and summer (fig. 40).

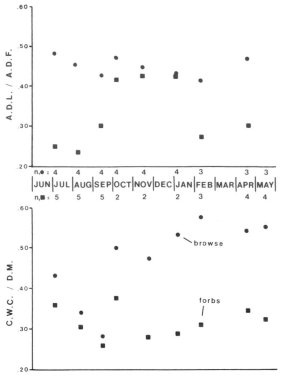

Figure 40. Mean ratios of acid-detergent lignin:fiber *(upper)* and cell wall constituents:total dry matter *(lower)* in forbs and browse used by mule deer in winter in north-central Colorado. The number of species in each sample is indicated above the months for browse and below for forbs.

In southwestern Idaho, crude protein content of major types of deer forage was reported as 24.5 percent in June, 13.7 percent in September, and 7.5 percent in November (Trout and Thiessen 1973). In north-central Colorado, principal deer forage species contained 19.7 percent crude protein in July, 9.5 percent in September, 5.9 percent in October, and 5.1 percent in February (Regelin et al. 1974; Gill and Wallmo 1973). In the Colorado work, mean dry-matter digestibility (in vitro) of major forage species in mule deer diets varied from a high of 59.4 percent in August, with half the forage species exceeding 65 percent, to a low of 36.4 in February and 34.8 percent in April. In February only big sagebrush exceeded 50 percent digestibility, and in April only grasses (all species combined) exceeded 50 percent digestibility. Ammann et al. (1973) estimated that dry-matter digestibility below

50 percent would not provide sufficient energy for maintenance. Somewhat higher digestion coefficients for winter browse were obtained, in vivo, by Dietz et al. (1962): mountain mahogany—52.7 percent; bitterbrush—52.5 percent.

Reduction of usable range and forage availability by snow severely compounds the forage-quality dilemma. On a mule deer range in northern Colorado, proportional areas of summer, early winter, and late winter range were reported as 125 : 25 : 1 (Wallmo et al. 1977). Deer can remain in areas with up to about 45 centimeters (18 inches) of snow, but the amount of forage available is drastically reduced, particularly herbaceous species. Moen and Evans (1971) estimated that 30 centimeters (12 inches) of snow rendered 97 percent of potential food unavailable to whitetails in hardwood forests in New York. Snow of high density, almost regardless of depth, eliminates the availability of herbaceous forage.

In addition to limiting energy intake, snow increases energy expenditure. Studies by Mattfeld (1973) suggest that a 45-kilogram (100-pound) deer would expend four to five times as much energy walking in 40 centimeters (16 inches) of snow, and seven to eight times as much energy in 50 centimeters (20 inches) of snow, as walking on bare ground. At an ambient temperature of -20 degrees Celsius (-4 degrees Fahrenheit), a deer's daily energy expenditure without walking would exceed 2,000 kilocalories (Holter et al. 1975). Winter forage cannot be expected to meet that demand (Wallmo et al. 1977), much less the additional energy cost of grazing in deep snow for a poorer forage supply.

On 40–50 million hectares (99–124 million acres) of mule deer winter range, sagebrush, juniper, or both are dominant or conspicuous components of the vegetation. Both have long been considered important winter forage because they frequently compose a large part of the deer diet, but many questions have arisen regarding their nutritional value. Bissell et al. (1955) speculated that essential oils of sagebrush might adversely affect rumen microbes. Further study suggested that deer could toler-

Rocky Mountain mule deer buck on winter range, in poor physical condition as a result of nutritional deficiency on a high-percentage sagebrush diet. Photograph by Arthur Buckingham; courtesy of the United States Forest Service.

ate something in the range of 15–30 percent sagebrush in the diet without incurring significant inhibition of bacterial activity in the rumen (Nagy et al. 1964; Nagy and Tengerdy 1967). At about that level of intake, physical deterioration became apparent in tame deer in an experiment in Colorado (Carpenter 1976; Carpenter, pers. files).

Essential oils of Douglas fir (Oh et al. 1970) and juniper (Schwartz et al. 1979*a, b*) have the same effect on rumen microbes as do oils of sagebrush. Given equal choice, deer preferred juniper species with the lowest oil content. Based on composition and amount of the various oil fractions and their effect on rumen microorganisms, it was estimated that deer could tolerate Rocky Mountain or Utah juniper only up to about 20 percent of their diet. Deer can compensate to a degree by selecting plants with less oil, at least in sagebrush (Carpenter 1976),

but this would permit only a minor increase in diet composition.

Results of feeding experiments by Nichol (1938) suggest that deer also may compensate by cyclically varying the amount of juniper in their diets. Daily variations in the consumption of big sagebrush by tame deer in a native-range pasture in Colorado may have been a similar phenomenon (Carpenter et al. 1979). In northeastern California, western juniper received considerable use in all winters in the Devil's Garden area and was considered an important emergency food in severe winters; but, for unexplained reasons, western juniper was used very lightly in the Lassen-Washoe area (Leach 1956). Continued research on factors associated with forage selection might add measurably to explanations of such apparently inconsistent or irregular uses of certain forages.

Association of heavy deer mortality with excessive use of sagebrush (Longhurst et al. 1968*a*) suggests that the compensations previously mentioned sometimes are inadequate. Therefore it also suggests that thought should be given to diversifying the forage complex. On many Rocky Mountain and Great Basin ranges, sagebrush or juniper forage, or both, approaches or exceeds 1,000 kilograms per hectare (892 pounds per acre) (Anderson 1969; Carpenter 1976; Robinette et al. 1952). Intensity of use of these ranges often reaches 250 or more deer-days per hectare (101 or more deer-days per acre). If average daily forage intake was 1.5 kilograms (3.3 pounds) per deer (Alldredge et al. 1974), deer could eat less than half that amount of sagebrush. At 20 percent of the daily diet, or 0.3 kilograms (0.66 pounds) per deer per day, only 75 kilograms (165 pounds)—less than 1 percent of the available sagebrush forage—would be consumed.

Some genotypes or ecotypes of big sagebrush apparently are more palatable and physiologically tolerable than others. A cooperative program of the Utah Division of Wildlife Resources and the United States Forest Service Intermountain Forest and Range Experiment Station has focused on this subject (McArthur et al. 1974). Studies by Jobman (1972) and

A mule deer doe, feeding on sagebrush, is instrumented for nighttime observation of feeding habits and other behavior on winter range in Colorado. Photograph by O. C. Wallmo.

Paintner (1971) suggest that one-seeded and alligator juniper are more suitable as deer forage than Utah and Rocky Mountain juniper. Rabbitbrushes also appear to be variable in their value as deer forage. Genetics and chemical composition of rubber rabbitbrushes are being studied from this standpoint in the cooperative program in Utah (Hanks et al. 1975).

Assays of the apparent nutritional quality of plants with high levels of essential oils can be misleading. Gross energy and apparent digestible energy may be high. However, metabolizable energy may be low because essential oils are absorbed but not metabolized, and potential energy is lost in urine. Unless care is taken to minimize volatilization of essential oils in drying and grinding samples for analysis, in vitro digestion coefficients may be higher than would be expected on the basis of bacterial inhibition by the oils.

The importance of grasses in the mule deer diet generally has been discounted in the past. However, as was discussed in chapter 3, the potential value of grasses should not be ignored. Studies show use of grass to be heaviest in spring, when succulent new growth is available (Kufeld et al. 1973). Leach (1956) considered grass consumption in winter in northeastern California to be proportional to its availability—the inference being that it was desirable forage. In studies of tame deer grazing on native ranges in northern Colorado, cured grasses constituted 16, 19, and 34 percent of mule deer diets in three successive midwinter samples in one area, and 70 and 73 percent in two successive midwinter samples on another area (Carpenter 1976). Grass constituted 52 percent of the year-round diet of mule deer in a study in the eastern foothills of the Front Range in Colorado (A. W. Alldredge and W. J. Arthur, III, pers. comm., February 1977).

Digestibility of grasses during winter is high compared with that of shrubs, owing to low levels of lignin in grasses. Bluebunch wheatgrass—the grass most heavily used by deer in the Colorado study (Carpenter 1976)—had a midwinter cellulose-lignin ratio

Grasses are a valuable and preferred component of mule deer winter diet, but their availability often is limited by deep snow in Rocky Mountain habitats. Photograph courtesy of the Wyoming Department of Game and Fish.

of 8.3 : 1, while the three most heavily used browse species—bitterbrush, mountain snowberry, and saskatoon serviceberry—had ratios of 0.8 : 1, 1.5 : 1, and 1.5 : 1, respectively (Wallmo, pers. files; Regelin, pers. files). In vitro dry matter digestibility for grass was 45 percent, and values for current annual growth twigs of the three shrub species were 31, 33, and 37 percent, respectively. Perhaps the availability of cellulose in grasses provides some benefit when other forage is of extremely low digestibility.

Digestibility of high-roughage forage has been increased in domestic livestock by adding nonprotein nitrogen to the diet. Similar synergistic effects were observed, in vitro, for deer forage by Milchunas (1977). He found that digestibility of high-fiber species was increased by adding high-quality alfalfa or urea to forage samples. However, no synergistic effect was observed unless large amounts of cellulose were available for synthesis of amino acids. Though much more research needs to be done

on this complex phenomenon, we may speculate that grasses—with high cellulose, high digestibility, and low protein—are not only important for high energy value but may increase digestibility of shrubs with low digestibility but higher protein levels. If, in fact, such roughage-to-roughage synergistic effects do occur, in vivo, the significance of diet diversity is increased.

Unfortunately, assays of forage quality do not always coincide with the choices made by deer. In studies of Rocky Mountain and desert mule deer, Wright buckwheat (Urness 1973) and sulfur buckwheat (Gill and Wallmo 1973), respectively, were very low in apparent nutritional quality but highly preferred. The lignin content of sulfur buckwheat was unusually high. Milchunas (1977) pointed out that lignin sometimes makes forage "brittle" so that it breaks down to smaller particle size and passes more rapidly. Thus net digestible and metabolizable energy may increase. It does not imply that plants with lignin are ideal forage, but it suggests that lignin may enhance the opportunity for deer to obtain maximum benefit from forage of otherwise limited digestibility.

SEASONAL NUTRITION

The annual nutritional cycle of Rocky Mountain mule deer may be demonstrated most clearly by the annual cycle of fat storage and depletion, as depicted by Anderson et al. (1972*a*). It reveals a buildup of fat stores from spring (March–April) to a peak for males in September and for females in November–December, followed by a decline to spring. Diet digestibility and protein content are high enough in spring and summer to permit growth but are inadequate for maintenance in winter. Estimates of deer diets in northern Colorado suggest a high intake of metabolizable energy in summer and a large deficit in winter (Wallmo et al. 1977). The graphic model of these relationships presented in figure 41 is hypothetical, but it illustrates the value of understanding the effect of seasonal diet quality on condition of deer.

Chemical and structural attributes of plants that contribute to or detract from their nutritional potential are discussed in chapter 3, which makes it clear that succulent forage is required for optimum nutrition of deer. Carrying this concept to an extreme, Robinette et al. (1973) markedly increased growth and productivity of penned mule deer by sup-

plementing their ration with hydroponically grown oat and barley sprouts. Reduced to the simplest terms, the nutritional plane of wild deer also is governed by the seasonal supply of succulent forage, because live cell contents provide the principal nutrients. Accordingly, it is reasonable to assume that the phenology of physical condition of deer will vary with factors such as climate, latitude, and elevation, which govern the phenology of plant growth. More extensive data are needed to confirm this, but the pattern is suggested by differences in the timing of forage quality between northern Colorado and northern Arizona (*e* and *f* in fig. 42).

Perhaps with exeptions, which are not well documented as yet, deer in the Rocky Mountain/Intermountain region consistently experience a good plane of nutrition in sum-

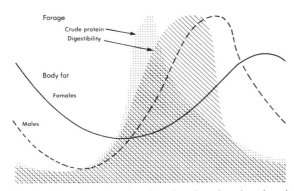

Figure 41. Hypothetical model of the annual cycle of forage quality and fat storage and depletion in northern Colorado mule deer.

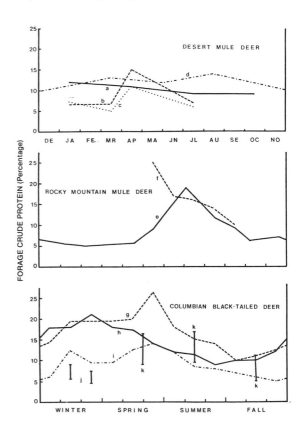

Figure 42. Geographic variations in seasonal levels of crude protein in the diets of mule and black-tailed deer (from Wallmo 1978). Sources: a, Boeker et al. (1972); b, c, Swank (1958); d, Urness and McCulloch (1973); e, Wallmo et al. (1977); f, Urness et al. (1975); g, h, i, Taber and Dasmann (1958); j, Brown (1961); k, Hines (1973).

mer. In some years "Indian summer" weather may last until December so that the nutritional plane declines slowly. In other years it may drop abruptly in October. Likewise, spring relief of nutritional stress conditions can vary from late February to May.

As a result of such climatic variations, autumn-winter-spring diets of deer can vary greatly from year to year, as is exemplified by extensive food habit studies in northeastern California (fig. 43). In the cold and dry winter of 1946–47, little green grass was available in northeastern California, but the diet contained a large percentage of dry grass and forbs and a decreasing percentage of browse throughout the winter. No starvation mortality was observed. In the mild and wet winter of 1950–51, rainfall was heavy in November and December, and in January and February there were heavy snows that rapidly melted. Green grass was available throughout the winter and constituted 45–55 percent of November–March diet samples and 100 percent of the April sample. The deer wintered in good condition, and the spring population estimate was 28 percent higher than the previous year. In the winter of 1951–52, heavy snowfalls occurred in December, January, and February. In the January and February samples, browse—mostly juniper and sagebrush—composed nearly the entire diet. Deer deteriorated rapidly, and large numbers of carcasses were seen by the middle of February. It was estimated that approximately 32 percent of the Devil's Garden herd succumbed during winter (Leach 1956).

The effects of winter malnutrition in deer populations may be expressed in reduced fawn crops even without extensive winter starvation. As reflected by the percentage of yearling does in the harvest the following year, food shortages occasioned by early and prolonged snow cover have a measurable effect on herd productivity in the central Rockies (Wallmo and Gill 1971). Productivity may be further reduced by late snowstorms, causing heat loss

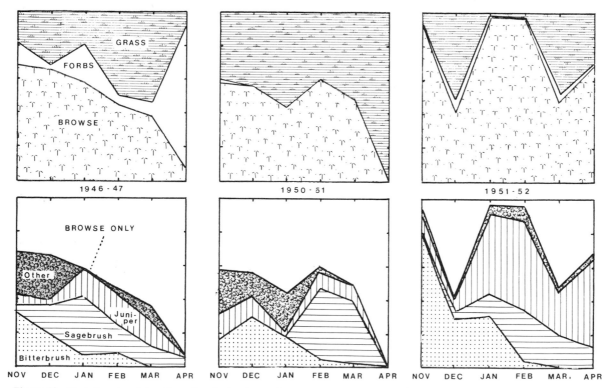

Figure 43. Variations in winter diets of mule deer in northeastern California, as inferred from contents of stomachs collected in a cold and dry winter (1946–47), a mild and wet winter (1950–51), and a winter (1951–52) with deep snow from December through February (from Leach 1956).

Weakened by starvation to the point of being unable to find shelter, this fawn nearly froze to death. It was retrieved and ultimately recovered. Photograph courtesy of the Wyoming Department of Game and Fish.

that exceeds the thermoregulatory capacity of newborn fawns. While not directly related to forage quality, expected mortality would be higher among fawns of low vitality from does that had suffered excessive nutritional stress during winter.

Although maintaining winter range in "good condition" is an unquestioned principle in the Rocky Mountain/Intermountain region, the available literature suggests that kind of winter rather than range condition is the major determinant of the winter nutritional plane of deer. As emphasized by Leach (1956, p. 258), deer die-offs "cannot be attributed entirely to inanition or lack of food, quantitatively speaking." The kinds of foods available are more important. Range condition surveys traditionally are directed to foods that deer consume

most heavily while starving to death. Heavy use of sagebrush and juniper, for example, may even accelerate their demise. On the other hand, as the only foods available, sagebrush and juniper might help prevent starvation. But, here again, only speculation is possible on conflicting theories.

While there is much more to learn of the nutritional regimes of Rocky Mountain mule deer throughout their range, it is safe to say that they are more likely to experience prolonged nutritional stress than are blacktails in California or desert mule deer in Arizona (fig. 42). Rocky Mountain mule deer obviously have adapted successfully to this environmental limitation, but it is a fundamental constraint that must be considered in management aimed at designated population goals.

Part 2. Habitat Evaluation and Management

Len H. Carpenter
Wildlife Researcher
Colorado Division of Wildlife
Kremmling, Colorado

Olof C. Wallmo
Principal Wildlife Biologist
United States Forest Service
Pacific Northwest Forest and
Range Experiment Station
Juneau, Alaska

The general aspect of the Rocky Mountain and Intermountain regions is one of arid or semiarid lowlands, shrub-covered or wooded foothills, and forested mountains capped with alpine tundra. Higher elevations have moister growing conditions and support a greater biomass of vegetation. Owing to variable slope, aspect, and elevation, there is a great diversity of habitat types. Mule deer tend to use higher elevations in preference to lower elevations when possible, but snow usually forces them downward in winter onto mountain shrub, juniper/piñon woodland, sagebrush-steppe, or desert scrub ranges.

This is, of course, an overgeneralization. In most areas some deer live in lower habitat zones all year, and in some areas most of the deer population may be restricted to lower habitat zones year-round. Also, the intermediate montane forest—below the elevation of the subalpine forest zone—constitutes year-round habitat for mule deer in some areas and winter range of migratory mule deer in other areas. However, most mule deer habitat management in the Rocky Mountain and Inter-

mountain regions is focused generally on winter ranges. For additional information on forest life zones, see Costello (1954), Cronquist et al. (1972), Küchler (1964), and Nelson (1969).

Weather—most importantly snow—is a major factor influencing population dynamics (Edwards 1956; Gilbert et al. 1970; Leach 1956; Robinette et al. 1952; Strickland and Diem 1975; Wallmo and Gill 1971). In some areas of small isolated plateaus or mountains surrounded by arid lowlands, summer range may be limiting in forage quality, especially in the availability of forb species (Julander et al. 1961; Pederson 1970; Russo 1964), but this is more a local than a general phenomenon. Therefore this part of chapter 10 deals primarily with practices employed or advocated for management of winter range and with the concepts on which they are based.

Sagebrush-steppe, juniper/piñon woodland, and mountain mahogany/oak scrub are the most extensive winter range types, in that order, and the most-studied from the standpoint of deer habitat management. The

following discussion focuses on these vegetation types.

SAGEBRUSH-STEPPE

Of all winter range vegetation types in the Rocky Mountain and Intermountain regions, sagebrush-steppe is the largest in area (Plummer 1973). Because mule deer commonly use big sagebrush heavily, wildlife managers have tended to consider it important to maintain it as a dominant species in the vegetational community. Ranchers and range managers, on the other hand, have preferred to encourage grasses as forage for livestock. Largely in the interest of the latter view, fire, mechanical manipulation, and herbicides have been employed to control and eradicate sagebrush. Sagebrush suppression commonly is followed by seeding with perennial grasses and legumes. Opposing attitudes toward the desirability of these practices have engendered considerable dissension among resources management personnel (see Trout 1968), as well as protests from sportsmen and conservationists (see Milek 1968; Reavley 1974; Trueblood 1967).

Management with Herbicides

Herbicidal chemicals became generally available in the mid-1940s. The most attractive for sagebrush ranges were 2,4-D and 2,4,5-T, which had the advantage of killing broad-leaved plants but not grasses. Large areas could be treated rapidly by spraying the chemical from low-flying aircraft. By the mid-1960s more than 2 million hectares (4.9 million acres) (Pechanec et al. 1965) of the 35–39 million hectares (86.5–96.4 million acres) (Platte 1959; Pechanec et al. 1965) of big sagebrush range had been treated.

It soon was found that 2,4-D was lethal to fewer species than was 2,4,5-T, and that it had brief residual effects and no known toxic breakdown products (Sheets and Harris 1965; Sneva and Hyder 1966). However, selectivity of 2,4-D still is relative; at the phenological stage when sagebrush is most susceptible, some

In the 1960s, several million hectares of sagebrush rangeland in the West were treated with chemical herbicides to eliminate sagebrush and release understory grasses. Such use of herbicides—to increase forage quality and quantity for both livestock and deer—has since become extremely selective in terms of chemicals used and time and method of application. Photograph by John L. Rogers; courtesy of the United States Forest Service.

other broad-leaved species are only less susceptible (Carpenter 1975; Sneva and Hyder 1966). In the process of spraying sagebrush, many kinds of forbs and browse that are valuable to deer can be damaged (Blaisdell and Mueggler 1956; Carpenter 1976; Laycock and Phillips 1968; Tabler 1968; Turner 1969), though some may recover as a result of reduced competition or regrowth after the pruning effect of the original setback.

Whatever benefits might accrue to deer from sagebrush control, they should result from stimulating the growth of other kinds of forage in lieu of the lost sagebrush. Although the point was discussed in part 1, let us repeat that available knowledge indicates that mule deer cannot

long endure a diet composed exclusively of big sagebrush. For extended periods, maximum consumption of big sagebrush by deer may be 15–20 percent of the diet.

Whatever the useful level of consumption might be, the wildlife manager or land manager would want to retain sufficient sagebrush to provide a sustained yield of that amount of forage. Forage intake by mule deer in winter is on the order of 1.5 kilograms (3.3 pounds) dry weight per deer per day (Alldredge et al. 1974; Wallmo et al. 1977). If sagebrush could constitute 50 percent of the diet, 77.2 deer per square kilometer (200 deer per square mile), for 120 days (93 deer-days per hectare: 37.5 deer-days per acre) would require 70 kilograms of sagebrush forage per hectare (62.5 pounds per acre). Such high deer densities for such long periods have not yet been documented.

Where sagebrush density is great enough to justify treatment, however, the crop of sagebrush forage usually far exceeds 70 kilograms per hectare (62.5 pounds per acre) before and after treatment. Thus in many cases, even with herbicide treatments, more than enough sagebrush remains to support existing numbers of mule deer. On high elevation sagebrush range in southwestern Colorado, it was estimated there were 419–536 kilograms per hectare (373–478 pounds per acre), dry weight, of sagebrush forage on untreated sample areas, and 217–542 kilograms per hectare (193–484 pounds per acre) on areas treated with 2,4-D (Anderson 1960). For lower-elevation winter range in north-central Colorado, Carpenter (1976) estimated there were 453–688 kilograms per hectare (404–614 pounds per acre), dry weight, of shrub forage on untreated plots and 279–435 kilograms per hectare (249–388 pounds per acre) on plots sprayed with 2,4-D. Carpenter's estimate included small amounts of other shrubs. For winter ranges in Utah where cliffrose, mountain mahogany, Gambel oak, or all three, also were abundant, Robinette et al. (1952) estimated there were 135, 193, and 399 kilograms per hectare (120, 172, and 356 pounds per acre), green weight, of big sagebrush on three study areas.

At such levels of abundance, removal of some sagebrush seems justified, particularly if yields of other kinds of forage could be increased as a result. Carpenter (1976) recorded a significant increase in the abundance and use by mule deer of bluebunch wheatgrass and green rabbitbrush after the number of big sagebrush plants on study areas were reduced 40 percent with 2,4-D. Sagebrush in the diet actually increased, too, but only from 0.8 percent before treatment to 1.7 percent afterward. Other browse species in the diet were not influenced by treatment, but, as the yield of forbs decreased 38 percent owing to treatment, forbs dropped from about 23 percent to about 5 percent of the diet. However, part of the decreased use of forbs was attributed to snow conditions.

Individual plants and species vary phenologically in their susceptibility to 2,4-D. In two studies, this principle has been used to see if damage to other forage species could be minimized while achieving satisfactory reduction of big sagebrush. Sneva and Hyder (1966) treated study plots in eastern Oregon at two-week intervals from the beginning of May to the end of June. Early May and mid-May treatments killed about 95 percent of the sagebrush and only 10 percent of the bitterbrush. They concluded that, in phenological terms, treatment should precede bitterbrush flowering, but only when growing conditions are sufficiently advanced for sagebrush to be susceptible. In Colorado, Carpenter (1975) treated big sagebrush range at two-week intervals from early April to mid-June. Early May treatments most nearly accomplished the objective of reducing sagebrush with minimal effect on forbs. Again, it was cautioned that phenological stages rather than calendar dates should determine application time.

Other Control Methods

With the advent of herbicides, use of fire and mechanical techniques for controlling sagebrush diminished until public opposition—on the grounds of potential undesirable side

Big sagebrush is chained preparatory to aerial seeding on winter range of mule deer. About 70 percent of the sagebrush is removed. Serviceberry, bitterbrush and rubber rabbitbrush are not appreciably damaged during chaining, and their subsequent growth is stimulated by reduced competition with sage. Photograph by Perry Plummer; courtesy of the United States Forest Service.

effects—limited resources agencies' freedom to use herbicides. Consequently, the use of fire and mechanical techniques has since increased. As described by Koehler (1975) and Plummer et al. (1968), other effective techniques include burning, plowing, railing (dragging heavy rails behind bulldozers), harrowing, disking, rotary-cutting and shredding, chaining and cabling (dragging heavy chains or cables with two bulldozers), and root-plowing (cutting roots below the soil surface with V-shaped blades). There has been little research on the relative advantages or disadvantages to deer of these alternative control procedures, so methodologies and effects will not be discussed here.

Life Expectancy of Sagebrush Control

Studies by Johnson (1969) in central Wyoming revealed that, seventeen years after herbicidal treatment and in the absence of livestock grazing, the density of big sagebrush plants was as great as that on untreated range.

With grazing, density of sagebrush on treated areas exceeded that on untreated areas within fourteen years. For ten to twelve years after big sagebrush range was burned in Idaho, sagebrush density remained low, grasses continued to increase, and the production of forbs—after peaking in three years—was constant. Horsebrush and green rabbitbrush increased steadily for twelve years. Thereafter, sagebrush began to increase, and grasses, forbs, horsebrush and rabbitbrush began to decrease rapidly. In thirty years the vegetation approximated pretreatment conditions, but the biomass of forbs, grasses, and shrubs was somewhat below pretreatment levels (Harniss and Murray 1973).

Many factors—including grazing, fire, weather, erosion, and the particular complex of competitive plants present—will influence posttreatment succession. In any case, though, repeated control efforts will be necessary to maintain the vegetation in some stage desirable to man. In using such procedures on big game habitat, wildlife biologists and managers should not be deceived into thinking that a one-shot panacea is available, or that the ecological conditions with which they are coping are permanent. Rather, these conditions are ever-changing.

Fertilizing Sagebrush Habitat

There is ample documentation that fertilizers can significantly increase the yield of range forage and, to some degree, its quality. In an experiment in Utah to determine potential yields on big game range, Bayoumi and Smith (1976) found that beardless wheatgrass, prairie june grass, Pacific aster, and the twig growth of bitterbrush and big sagebrush increased significantly with increasing levels of nitrogen fertilizer (from 33.6 to 168.0 kilograms of nitrogen per hectare: 30 to 150 pounds per acre). Crude protein content of bitterbrush and big sagebrush also increased. Phosphorus, however, had no measurable effect. Although elk and deer responded positively to nitrogen-treated areas, the authors concluded that results did not justify costs. They calculated, at 1974 rates, that the cost per additional elk-day would range from $0.94 to $1.97 depending on rate of nitrogen applied.

Carpenter (1976) applied nitrogen with and without 2,4-D to sagebrush winter range in Colorado. For three years after treatment, total herbage yields and total yields of shrub twigs and leaves increased significantly, with higher fertilizer applications resulting in higher yields. Application rates ranged from 33.6 to 134.4 kilograms of nitrogen per hectare (30–120 pounds per acre). After six years, however, plots treated only with nitrogen yielded less total herbage than did the control plots, and fertilizer-herbicide plots still produced 18.6 percent more total herbage than did control plots (Carpenter 1977).

Based on increased forage yields, changes in vegetative composition, and forage selections by mule deer, Carpenter concluded that the combination of fertilizer and herbicide was superior to either applied alone in improving mule deer winter range. The highest application level (134.4 kilograms of nitrogen per hectare: 120 pounds per acre) was most effi-

cient from the standpoint of increased herbage yield per unit of nitrogen.

Nevertheless, because of the rapidly increasing cost of petrochemical fertilizer and the growing demand for and decreasing abundance of petroleum, it behooves wildlife managers to consider use of fertilizers and herbicides in a larger social context.

Reseeding after Sagebrush Control

Most often, the principal justification of sagebrush control is to improve range for livestock grazing. Accordingly, it is common practice to seed with forage species useful to livestock. This usually requires some kind of tillage. Numerous species and mixtures that have been used were reviewed by Koehler (1975).

Plummer et al. (1955, 1968) did not consider reseeding to be economically justified on ranges in sufficiently good condition to recover with improved grazing management. To avoid overuse by big game, it was suggested that planted areas should be more than 200 hectares (494 acres) in size (Plummer et al. 1968).

Reseeding bitterbrush on mule deer winter range in Idaho. Photograph courtesy of the Idaho Fish and Game Department.

Competition among deer and livestock introduces other problems. If browse is to become established, livestock should be grazed early in summer rather than in late summer or autumn (Smith and Doell 1968); but early grazing must be regulated to avoid overuse of young herbaceous plants.

Urness (1966) considered the provision of good crops of winter-active grasses to be one of the important potential benefits of sagebrush control and reseeding. One of the most commonly planted species, crested wheatgrass, is highly palatable to deer in winter and spring.

Although reseeding with various grasses and legumes has been considered justifiable on livestock range, the results of seeding or planting browse have been considerably less encouraging (Plummer et al. 1968). Regelin (1975) inferred that the most successful efforts with bitterbrush—amortized over the time required to attain full production—would provide too little deer forage to justify the cost.

JUNIPER/PIÑON WOODLAND

More popularly known as the piñon/juniper type, this pygmy forest or woodland association occurs on some 36 million hectares (89 million acres) in the western United States (Plummer 1973), mainly in Nevada, Utah, Colorado, Arizona, and New Mexico. Over the past century, the area occupied by the type and density of piñon/juniper tree stands reportedly has increased greatly (Barney and Frischknecht 1974), dominating rangelands at the expense of more useful understory vegetation (Ffolliott and Clary 1972). The spread has been attributed variously to grazing, protection from fire and climatic shifts (Burkhart and Tisdale 1976).

Management Methods

Partial or complete removal of the trees can result in marked increases in production of grasses, forbs, and shrubs, demonstrable increases in livestock carrying capacity, and at least theoretical improvement of deer habitat (Clary et al. 1974). Methods used to remove or suppress the trees include fire, individual tree felling, pushing trees over with bulldozers, chaining, and herbicides (Alden and Springfield 1972).

Inferred benefits to deer habitat of piñon/juniper removal or suppression remain theoretical because of the lack of unequivocal proof that deer actually do benefit. Terrell and Spillett (1975, p. 105) said, "A summary conclusion for the several million acres of treated P-J is one of no overall impact [on deer] . . . either positive or negative." Results of a major long-term research program in Arizona led Clary et al. (1974, p. 24) to express a similar opinion: "The response by deer to the pinyon-juniper . . . treatments was, on the average, neutral."

In synthesizing results of fourteen years of study of the effects of juniper/piñon control on deer habitat in Arizona, McCulloch (1973) saw as many potential detriments as benefits, and his recommendations were largely precautionary. He suggested confining the clearing to areas of dense, extensive woodland in which former openings had been invaded by trees, and keeping the clearings 30–200 meters (98–656 feet) wide, with leave strips of juniper/piñon at least as wide as the clearings. A somewhat ambiguous recommendation was that the total area cleared should be "less than one-third of the home range of each individual deer in the vicinity" (McCulloch 1973, p. ii). But the important point is that habitat manipulation to benefit a particular deer population must be based on the movement patterns and needs of the individuals making up that population.

Recent evidence further suggests that factors other than amount of forage produced should be evaluated in any piñon/juniper treatment of mule deer habitat. In a study area in New Mexico, Short et al. (1977) found that, before piñon/juniper overstory, was cleared, 23 percent of their plots received abundant deer use (10 or more deer per square kilometer per year: 26 or more per square mile per year). After clearing, only 12 percent of the plots had

A bulldozer pushes juniper into windrows during a clearing and reseeding project. Photograph by Leland J. Prater; courtesy of the United States Forest Service.

abundant use. Since food quantity actually increased on the areas after clearing, Short et al. concluded that the absence of cover apparently reduced habitat quality enough to limit use by deer.

The optimum treatment prescription for deer, according to McCulloch (1973), would require some financial concessions and, for deer habitat improvement alone, juniper/piñon control would not be economically justifiable. Clary et al. (1974, p. 24) concluded that "under 1972 economic conditions the most successful projects just about break even from a benefit-cost standpoint. Projects that are less successful than the best will produce a negative net return." The benefits, in the Clary et al. analyses, included water yield and quality, livestock range improvement and wildlife habitat improvement. They essentially dismissed the practicality of mechanical treatment and suggested that further research consider the feasibility of fire and herbicides as control agents.

Life Expectancy of Juniper/Piñon Control

Studies by Barney and Frischknecht (1974) in west-central Utah indicated that the posttreatment increase in yield of forbs and grasses would diminish to pretreatment levels in less than twenty years. They also indicated that sagebrush, snakeweed, and green rabbitbrush would increase for up to forty years, as black sagebrush, bitterbrush, and Utah snowberry slowly established in limited areas. In forty years, juniper and piñon again would dominate the site.

Tausch and Tueller (1977) drew the following successional picture for eastern Nevada: annual and perennial forbs dominate for 1–2 years after clearing; perennial grasses achieve dominance in the second year and reach maximum abundance in the fourth year; shrubs follow closely behind grasses and reach a peak 1–3 years later; and trees again dominate study sites in less than fifteen years. As with other winter habitat types in the Rocky Mountain and Intermountain regions, if real benefits accrue to deer from type conversion, it is apparent that they can be maintained only with continual management. If so, wildlife biologists and managers need to consider more seriously the returns in relation to efforts required to maintain the habitat complex achieved.

In the face of all of these reservations, it should be emphasized that the cooperative program of the Utah Division of Wildlife Resources and the United States Forest Service has resulted in many persuasive examples of deer habitat improvement associated with juniper/piñon control.

MOUNTAIN MAHOGANY/OAK SCRUB

What Küchler (1964) referred to as the mountain mahogany/oak scrub type also is known as "mountain brush," "mountain shrub," and sometimes "chaparral"—the latter being quite inappropriate. By whatever name, it is a discrete type dominating more than 6 million hectares (14.8 million acres) (Plummer 1973) in Colorado, Utah, and to some extent

Nevada. Gambel oak, the most conspicuous species in the mountain mahogany/oak scrub type, often develops into tall, dense thickets of little value to either livestock or big game. In Utah, bigtooth maple and black chokecherry often form similar stands. Many other shrubs, including mountain mahogany, occur throughout the type as subdominants and often are crowded out by the aforementioned dominants.

Management Methods

Plummer et al. (1968) recommended anchor-chaining or burning to break down shrub thickets and permit establishment of herbaceous species in order to provide better game forage. According to Marquiss (1972), spraying Gambel oak stands in Colorado with the herbicide 2,4,5-TP doubled livestock forage yields, nearly doubled steer weight gains per acre, and significantly increased summer soil moisture.

In a cooperative study by the Colorado Division of Wildlife and the United States Forest Service, dense Gambel oak stands were sprayed with 2,4,5-TP to determine its potential for use in improving deer and elk habitat (Kufeld 1977a). Two years after treatment, the abundance of grasses had increased 44 percent over pretreatment levels, while shrubs had decreased 29 percent and forbs 15 percent. After five years, grasses were 17 percent below pretreatment abundance, and shrubs had decreased 7 percent. Consequently, the treatment was considered beneficial and attractive to deer and, more clearly, elk. However, repeated treatments at three-year intervals were considered necessary to maintain this improved condition.

Mountain mahogany/oak scrub is vigorous and aggressive on sites to which it is best adapted, and any attempt to manage it must be a continuing effort. Moreover, Anderson (1969) considered such oak-dominated range in Colorado to be important mule deer habitat and, for that reason, cautioned against oak control as a general policy.

BROWSING TOLERANCE AND BROWSE REJUVENATION

Woody plant species that are palatable to large herbivores have many adaptive strategies for survival. Annual proliferation of excessive vegetational tissue is one, and the ability to regenerate vigorously after severe setbacks is another. Range and wildlife habitat managers have studied these phenomena in several species browsed by mule deer to obtain information on the levels of use the species can tolerate and still maintain good productivity, and to determine potential for stimulating vegetational growth or reproduction with occasional severe pruning or burning.

Bitterbrush

The twig yield (leaves and twigs) of bitterbrush plants in eastern Oregon was described by McConnell and Smith (1977) as increasing to a maximum at the age of sixty to seventy years and decreasing rapidly thereafter. Plants in study populations that were heavily grazed by cattle in spring and early summer for fifteen to twenty years had low, compact, tightly hedged crowns. Level of use was approximately 80–90 percent of the annual twig production. Plants that received moderate use (30–50 percent) in late summer and autumn were taller and had open-growing crowns. Individual plants subjected to early, heavy use produced an appreciably larger crop of twigs and leaves annually than did plants of the same age subjected to late, moderate use, but very few survived to the age of maximum yield. There were similar numbers of plants per unit area under the two kinds of use, but under heavy early grazing most of the population was less than twenty-five years old, whereas there was a relatively even distribution of age classes from one to one hundred years under moderate late summer and autumn grazing.

In a study in Idaho, topping overmature bitterbrush caused a marked increase in twig yield (Ferguson 1972). Shrubs 1.5–2.1 meters (5–7 feet) tall were cut to 0.9–1.2 meters (3–4 feet);

A Rocky Mountain mule deer fawn browses on nearly snow-covered bitterbrush. Photograph by Paul F. Gilbert.

smaller shrubs were cut so as to remove about half the crown volume. On three study areas, the increase in twig production ranged from 62 to 128 kilograms per hectare (55–114 pounds per acre) in the first year, 34 to 379 kilograms per hectare (30–338 pounds per acre) in the second year, 16 to 49 kilograms per hectare (14–44 pounds per acre) in the third year, and 2 to 45 kilograms per hectare (1.8–40 pounds per acre) in the fourth year. There was no appreciable mortality in this period, but long-term consequences were not measured. Ferguson's calculations suggested that, at that time, the cost would be about 4–8 cents per kilogram (1.8–3.6 cents per pound) of increased browse production over four years. However, such practices obviously require maintaining a precarious balance between stimulated growth and accelerated deterioration.

In Colorado, Shepherd (1971) annually removed 20, 40, 60, 80, and 100 percent of current annual growth (CAG) of all stems of mature bitterbrush plants on plots in late summer for eleven years. He found that 80 percent "use" damaged or killed many plants, and he suggested 50 percent as an acceptable level. This agreed with Garrison's (1953) recommendation of a maximum of 50–65 percent use of bitterbrush on winter range. In Shepherd's (1971) study, 20 and 40 percent use stimulated vigor of the plants. An additional "destructive" treatment consisted of removing all current and previous year's growth in the first clipping and cutting all twigs back to 3 millimeter (0.12 inch) diameter the next year. This destructive clipping resulted in a doubled yield by the second year, but all plants died within four years.

In some areas of montane forests, bitterbrush is a conspicuous understory component. Logging may destroy many of the larger shrubs but stimulate productivity of residual plants (Edgerton et al. 1975; Struth and Winward 1976).

Sagebrush

Shepherd's (1971) low clipping levels did not stimulate growth and yield of big sagebrush plants, but the plants were able to maintain high levels of production with up to 80 percent removal of current growth. Summer-autumn use of 20–40 percent or winter use of 50–60 percent seemed reasonable levels for sustained production. This is in approximate agreement with the findings of Cook and Stoddart (1963) and of Wright (1970).

Destructive clipping and clipping 100 percent of current annual growth quickly killed all of Shepherd's (1971) sagebrush plants. He predicted that destructive use of individual branches unprotected by snow in winter would progressively kill plants.

Serviceberry

Of several browse species studied by Shepherd (1971), saskatoon serviceberry was most resistant to clipping. Growth was stimulated at clipping levels of up to 60 percent of current annual growth. The results led him to conclude that sustained use of more than 80 percent would kill the plants. Young and Payne

(1948) recommended a maximum use level of 60–65 percent for serviceberry.

From research on the autecology of serviceberry in Montana, Hemmer (1975) suggested that, in some sites, burning or mechanically setting back serviceberry plants can stimulate production or improve availability of the growth that is produced. But on harsh sites with low densities these practices were expected to reduce long-term production and kill many plants. Hemmer saw serviceberry as a seral species whose productivity eventually would begin to decline, regardless of management. If practices are employed to stimulate vigor, such mature stands of serviceberry should be avoided.

Gambel Oak

Under light use, Gambel oak tends to grow into tall, dense, tree-size stands providing relatively little available browse; it responds to

A Rocky Mountain mule deer fawn browses on serviceberry. Photograph by Paul F. Gilbert.

heavy use by sprouting. Accordingly, Shepherd (1971) considered normal use of 60 percent of current annual growth and occasional use of 80–100 percent to be desirable on big game range, although greatest twig yields resulted from 20–60 percent use. Although destructive clipping did not completely kill Gambel oaks more than eleven years old, it drastically reduced their twig production.

Shepherd thought that such extreme use was unlikely to occur on deer range because of the low palatability of Gambel oak. In contrast, Neff (1974) found this species to be quite palatable to mule deer in northern Arizona and considered it one of the most important year-round foods. Robinette et al. (1977, p. 136) exhibited a photograph of a stand of dead Gambel oak in Utah whose condition was "attributed entirely to deer" browsing.

Mountain mahogany

Optimum level of use for true mountain mahogany appeared to Shepherd (1971) to be about 70 percent of current annual growth. It was resistant to clipping, extremely productive under annual clipping rates of 60–80 percent, and maintained good production at the 100 percent rate. After eleven years, the browse yield of 100 percent clipped plants was fifteen times as great as base-year yields. The destructively clipped plants produced well through the second year, then rapidly declined in production; all were dead after the sixth year. The use level suggested by Shepherd for true mountain mahogany is similar to that proposed for curl-leaf mountain mahogany in Oregon and Washington by Garrison (1953) and for hairy mountain mahogany in Arizona by Neff (1970).

Summary

Results from these studies suggest levels of use that browse plants can tolerate and still maintain satisfactory forage production for deer. However, the studies do not adequately consider successional dynamics of browse populations and the influence of such factors as

A biologist measures growth and vigor of a mountain mahogany plant in an area cleared of juniper/piñon overstory. Photograph by Don Domenick; courtesy of the Colorado Division of Wildlife.

climatic variations, insects, and pathogens on their productivity and longevity. Much more knowledge of the autecology of each species is needed to make the information on clipping, burning, and poisoning applicable to reliable management prescriptions.

THE ROLE OF SNOW IN HABITAT MANAGEMENT

In mountainous terrain in the North, snow is the primary factor governing the amount of range seasonally available to mule deer and, in some areas, blacktails. Available range expands in spring with the recession of snow and shrinks in autumn with expansion of snow cover. In Middle Park, Colorado, because of snow, usable winter range for mule deer often is less than 1 percent of summer range area (Wallmo et al. 1977).

Furthermore, usable areas generally are those that receive most sunlight, are driest in summer, and therefore support the least vegetation. The microclimate there may favor winter sprouting of some forbs and grasses, but the bulk of vegetation dies or becomes dormant in autumn. Other usable areas, such as wind-scoured ridges, have similar limitations.

In areas such as Middle Park, Colorado, the quantity of good-quality forage during winter is insufficient for large concentrations of deer, and so the animals are forced to use forage of poorer quality. Deep snow can cause significant changes in diet composition. Deer continue to eat, and the large amount of ingesta in their stomachs—the often-observed phenomenon of starving deer with full stomachs—can be symptomatic of consumption of less palatable and less digestible browse (Gasaway and Coady 1974). These problems are covered elsewhere in this chapter (see part 1) and chapter 14, and are mentioned here only to emphasize that they are influenced directly by snow.

Elevation, slope, and aspect, wind in relation to topography and vegetation, and vegetation cover itself are salient factors governing the local depth and character of snow. In general, snow depth increases with elevation in the Rocky Mountain and Intermountain regions. Usually snow accumulation is inversely proportional to the angle of incidence of solar radiation. Steep southerly slopes accumulate the least snow. Furthermore, these slopes are more conducive to formation of melt-freeze crusts, whereas steep northerly slopes accumulate snow that remains soft and relatively trafficable for deer for longer periods. Level areas, including valley bottoms, lack the insolation advantage of southerly slopes and are subject to both melt-freeze and wind crusting.

Newly fallen snow is redistributed even by light winds, beginning at about 19 kilometers per hour (12 miles per hour), and older, metamorphosed snow is redistributed by stronger winds. The average transport distance of blowing snow particles in southeastern Wyoming was about 1 kilometer (0.6 mile) (Tabler 1973). If the wind is interrupted within that distance by topography or vegetation, the particle can be deposited in a snowdrift. But these blowing particles also are in the process

of sublimation and will disappear beyond that distance. All these phenomena have a pronounced influence on deer habitat.

Snow Accumulation in Relation to Vegetation

Even low, shrubby vegetation affects snow accumulation. In Wyoming a sagebrush stand averaging 50 centimeters (19.6 inches) in height accumulated 2.5 centimeters (1 inch) more water in the form of snow than did an adjacent grassland, until the snowpack completely covered the sagebrush; thereafter there was no difference in accumulation (Hutchison 1965). Once low vegetation is covered, distribution of ensuing snow is a function of prevailing wind and other topographic or vegetational features of the landscape (Sturges 1975, 1977).

The more irregular the canopy of partially covered low shrub stands, the more complex will be the mixture of surface snow densities and depth as a result of irregular formation of wind crusts and greater variety of microclimates. Carpenter (1976) observed that mule deer avoided herbicide-treated sagebrush areas where there were more uniform and continuous snow crusts. They preferred to graze on untreated areas or those treated only with fertilizer, where the sagebrush canopy tended to disrupt wind crusting and provide melted open spots on the south side of large sagebrush plants. This was most pronounced on more or less level areas with soil and moisture conditions that supported larger shrubs. On south-facing slopes that had been treated with herbicides or herbicide plus fertilizer, and that were more generally snow-free, deer capitalized on the greater availability of winter-growing forbs. Deer use of south-facing slopes treated with herbicides and fertilizer was most apparent in a winter with wind and snow conditions less conducive to crusting. These observations suggest that the effects of sagebrush control on snow cover warrant further study.

Major snowdrift areas on the leeward side of ridges, rolls, and incised drainages often support heavier stands of mature shrubs, such as serviceberry, snowberry, mountain mahogany, bitterbrush, and chokecherry, partly because of increased soil moisture—apparently a minor factor (see Regelin 1976*b*)—and partly because the snowdrift confers protection from repeated heavy use. There is little advantage for wintering deer in treating these areas to rejuvenate shrubs or establish other kinds of forage. In periods when the areas can be used, forage should be amply available elsewhere if the range is otherwise well managed. The potential of managing snow in such areas will be discussed later.

Stands of deciduous trees, such as aspen and cottonwood, accumulate drifting snow plus most snow that falls in place, but the snow tends to form a loose, soft pack on the woodland floor. Tree stems interrupt solar radiation and reduce melt-freeze crusting. Low snow density is favorable to deer for a while, but leafless canopies intercept little snow, and snow depth usually exceeds the tolerance of deer early in winter. In midwinter, aspen stands are more often the province of elk than of deer.

The canopy of coniferous forests intercepts much falling snow (see chap. 11, part 2). And much of the snow that is deposited on the canopy ultimately sublimates or is moved along to some downwind deposition area (Hoover 1971). Isolated stands of conifers within mule deer winter range—commonly Douglas fir in the central Rocky Mountain and Intermountain region—provide important refuge from the inclement weather and untrafficable snow conditions that deer often encounter on the open range (see chap. 5).

Managing Snowdrifts

The multitude of purposes for which snow fences are used led wildlife managers in Colorado to consider the potential of using them to

Conifer stands are an important source of winter shelter for mule deer in the central Rocky Mountain and Intermountain region. Photograph courtesy of the United States National Archives, Bureau of Biological Survey Collection.

expose stands of browse that normally are covered with snowdrifts for much of the winter. An experiment conducted by Regelin (1976*b*) demonstrated that drifting snow could be deposited upwind of a browse stand, freeing it for use by deer. In stands protected by snow fences, snow that fell in place remained soft, powdery, and well within depths that deer could negotiate. Unprotected stands paired with the fence-protected stands had deep, wind-crusted drifts that deer could not enter. In addition, sites of relocated snowdrifts were seeded with palatable forage species. New snowdrifts protected these stands from winter use during the period of establishment. Incidentally, the seeded and protected sites did not show increased soil moisture in spring. This was attributed speculatively to the strong evaporative power of air from large dry areas moving across small moist areas.

Economical snow fences designed for five-year durability were constructed at a cost of $3.28 per linear meter ($3.00 per yard) at 1972 prices, including labor. From estimates of forage biomass freed for deer use, and assuming a five-year rotation of snow fences with their original cost amortized over that period, it was calculated that it would cost about 20 cents per kilogram (9.1 cents per pound) of forage made available (Regelin et al. 1977). Cost could be reduced on a second site by the savings in reusable materials.

Accelerating Snowmelt

The melting rate of snow can be increased by darkening its surface and thereby increasing absorption of shortwave radiation. This technique has been used to accelerate spring snowmelt on airport landing strips and to increase summer water runoff from glaciers (Slaughter 1966). In Finland, soot was applied to black grouse habitat to improve early nesting conditions (Rakkolainen 1971).

On mule deer winter range in Colorado, carbon black was applied on 30 January to experimental plots with gentle southerly and easterly slopes and sagebrush/mixed-shrub-grass vegetation (Regelin and Wallmo 1975). In two days, snow depth decreased an average of about 14 centimeters (5.5 inches) on southerly aspects and 3 centimeters (1.2 inches) on easterly aspects despite day and night temperatures well below freezing. On the second day, 2–3 centimeters (0.8–1.2 inches) of new snow fell. Snowmelt continued at a slower rate on southerly aspects, while snow depth increased slightly on easterly aspects.

Carbon black was applied again on the fifth day, and 7–8 centimeters (2.8–3.1 inches) of snow fell that evening. Snow depth increased about 3 centimeters (1.2 inches) on easterly aspects and decreased slightly to the ninth day on southerly aspects. A third treatment was applied on the tenth day. By the seventeenth day, the mean snow depth on treated plots with southerly aspect was 3.5 centimeters (1.4 inches), compared with 37.6 centimeters (14.8 inches) on paired control plots. On easterly aspects, mean depth was 26.4 centimeters (10.4 inches) on treated plots and 53.3 centimeters (21 inches) on control plots. There was no significant difference in density or crusting of snow on treated and control plots until the end of the measurement period, when the remaining shallow snow on treated plots became slushy in the daytime and froze at night.

Throughout that experiment, snow melting was accelerated while daily temperatures remained below freezing. Treated plots were completely bare of snow, with green vegetation appearing, a month before the control plots were bare. By midsummer, little residual carbon black could be detected on treated plots. It was estimated that aerial application would cost about $12 per hectare ($4.86 per acre) at 1975 prices. It was suggested that carbon black might be combined with nitrogen fertilizer for the added advantage of increasing herbage yields and protein content of forage, at little increase in application cost.

More extensive research is necessary to evaluate the operational feasibility of such practices and the long-term effect of a darkened soil surface on soil moisture and temperature. But, before rejecting them out of hand, consideration should be given to the fact that they are directed at the heart of the major winter problem for deer, whereas improvement of the forage supply may miss the mark completely because snow prevents access to forage.

LAND OWNERSHIP AND USE

Throughout the Rocky Mountain and Intermountain regions, problems of mule deer in winter have intensified because important winter range areas have been usurped for other purposes (see chap. 14). Wildlife management efforts are futile if managers have no control over the way habitat is used. To maintain necessary control, many state wildlife management agencies have purchased critical winter ranges to be managed primarily for the benefit of big game. Attention is given in this section to the economic justification of such measures and to several aspects of habitat use that should be considered in determining what kinds of areas are important to control.

While the value of deer cannot be adequately expressed in monetary terms, public use and enjoyment of them involve expenditure of money, so "economic" value of deer-related human activities can be calculated in dollars just as legitimately as it can be for other recreational activities. Various estimates place the average expenditure per deer hunter at $100–$300 per year for equipment, supplies, food, and a miscellany of services (Nobe and Gilbert 1970; Prenzlow et al. 1974; Ross et al. 1975), excluding hunting license costs and not deducting the value of the meat (venison). Over a five-year period, 1971–75, the average successes of mule deer hunters in Colorado, Idaho, Montana, Utah, and Wyoming were 40, 33, 71, 42, and 60 percent, respectively (see chap. 6). Thus, some $140–$900 may have been spent for each mule deer harvested.

In periods of extreme winter concentrations, many deer on a single winter range may die of starvation, highway and railroad collisions, and other causes related to man's uses of the range. Annual winter losses on a narrow strip of winter range (10 square kilometers: 3.9 square miles) flanked by a railroad and a highway in

Middle Park, Colorado, averaged about 8 deer per square kilometer (21 deer per square mile) over a six-year period from 1973 to 1978 (Colorado Division of Wildlife, n.d.). If, instead, those same deer had been harvested by hunters, at a value of $400 per animal, they might have represented a dollar flow in the local economy of more than $3,200 per square kilometer ($8,288 per square mile), or about $32 per hectare ($13 per acre).

Economics often is less a science than it is a mechanism to rationalize monetary gain or personal gratification. Potential hunters could spend money on other pastimes if they lost opportunities to hunt deer. But, to sustain deer populations in the Rocky Mountain and Intermountain regions, winter range of mule deer cannot be sacrificed without sacrificing deer, whatever their value may be.

In mountainous regions, valleys are the primary sites of human occupation and activity, and southerly exposures have the same importance for people as they do for deer. So, if these limited areas that are necessary winter range of mule deer continue to be preempted for human uses, the effect on mule deer numbers obviously will be adverse. Even where artificial structures and human activities occur on only a small percentage of deer habitat, they often interfere with the access of deer to needed habitat, particularly when the deer are in or confronted with stress conditions.

But wildlife managers cannot focus entirely on "critical" winter range. If deer are divested of intermediate winter range areas, where they concentrate when first driven from summer range by early snows and to which they return as snow recedes in spring, stresses of severe winters will be increased. Pockets of aspen woodland and coniferous forest interspersed in mountain shrub and sagebrush habitat can provide forage and shelter vital to deer in early winter and give respite from an impoverished winter diet during "green-up" in spring.

Understanding of the ways snow, in particular, dictates distribution of deer is essential to planning patterns of land use on deer range. Although wildlife managers, to date, seldom have had any significant influence on uses to which private lands are put, they must force-fully impress upon administrators of public lands the need for allocating certain habitats primarily for wildlife.

SUPPLEMENTAL FEEDING

Deer can be nourished with "artificial" feed as well as or better than with natural forages. This well-established fact makes it reasonable to suppose that supplemental feeding can pre-vent deer starvation in periods of winter stress. However, innumerable emergency feeding programs that have been conducted on mule deer winter range have yet to document meas-urable benefits to deer.

In many cases deer have continued to die for days or weeks after feed was distributed (Carhart 1943; Doman and Rasmussen 1944). This can be attributed to many factors. The unfamiliar food may be unpalatable initially. It may be distributed in a way that makes it un-available to a sufficient number of deer in the population. A dominance hierarchy in the deer population might prevent individuals in great-est need from gaining access to the feed. Perhaps too little feed is made available, or the feed may be supplied too late, when many deer already have starved beyond help.

The last possibility often is a critical likeli-hood. Because of cost and logistical problems of supplemental feeding, it rarely is undertaken until there is an obvious emergency, when many deer already are in advanced stages of malnutrition. The experience of deCalesta et al. (1975) suggests that adult deer—originally in good condition and not subjected to severe weather conditions—can be starved totally for as long as two months during spring (March and April) and still be successfully refed. How-ever, the deer were confined in small pens when refed and were given feed to which they were accustomed. Free-roaming deer, in con-trast, can be expected to be on a progressively deteriorating diet beginning in autumn (Wallmo et al. 1977). Furthermore, some period of time will be required for them to learn where supplemental feed is and, perhaps, to recognize it as feed. Deer with exhausted

energy reserves—particularly fawns (deCalesta et al. 1975) and bucks that have drained their reserves during the rut (Bandy et al. 1970)—cannot be expected to meet these challenges.

Although rumen microbes in starving deer may allow them to adapt to richer sup-plemental feed (deCalesta et al. 1975), previ-ous natural diet can influence that capacity. Rumen fluid from deer previously fed pelleted sagebrush was less capable of digesting alfalfa hay, in vitro, than were rumen fluids of deer previously fed other natural browse (Nagy et al. 1967). Any radical change in deer diet re-quires adjustment by the rumen microflora before optimal use can be made of the new diet. But there also are "mechanical" problems to consider.

Deer can starve while they continue to eat, as witnessed by many reports of dead deer found with full stomachs. A large amount of ingesta may in itself be symptomatic of poor forage quality (Gasaway and Coady 1974). After coarse, fibrous food is chewed and swal-lowed, the small, easily digested particles sink in the rumen fluid, where they can be attacked by rumen microbes. But the larger fibrous par-ticles float on the surface of the rumen fluid and periodically are withdrawn into the diver-ticulum, regurgitated, rechewed, and swal-lowed again. This process must continue until particles are broken down enough for all of their usable substance to be extracted by rumen microbes and for the remnant to be suf-ficiently reduced in size to pass on to the omasum (Bell 1971). If the diet is too high in fiber, a "traffic jam" develops, food intake falls, and the deer continues to starve while the stomach continues to be filled to capacity. Pro-viding better-quality supplemental feed might tend to relieve the problem, but it may take many days to get deer back to a significantly improved nutritional plane and additional days for them to regain strength and health. Thus, many deer already on the verge of death can be expected to die even if they do begin to use supplemental feed as soon as it is available.

Ullrey et al. (1975) suggested a different ap-proach to supplemental feeding. In their ex-periment, some groups of white-tailed deer were fed winter browse alone, and some groups

Radical change in diet of deer already under severe nutritional stress from winter conditions often leads to starvation. These two deer invaded a rancher's haystack and died of rumen impaction. Photograph by Don Domenick; courtesy of the Colorado Division of Wildlife.

were fed browse plus a high energy/high protein feed in blocks. Although deer in both treatments lost weight, the latter lost significantly less, even when the supplement constituted as little as 10 percent of total dry matter intake. While not so stated by Ullrey et al., the inference was that providing an energy- and protein-rich supplement before starvation is far advanced might be more effective than crash programs initiated after deer are in the process of starving. From a logistical standpoint, however, this might be difficult to accomplish for reasons previously cited.

It is implicit in results of the aforementioned studies that supplemental feeding should be considered in terms of the condition deer have attained while consuming available range forage, and in recognition of the practicality of making fullest use of that poor-quality forage. Ullrey et al. (1975) tried a supplement that was rich in both energy and protein. Cook and Harris (1968) found that a protein supplement (cottonseed and soybean meal) was more effec-

tive than an energy supplement (corn and barley) in helping domestic sheep utilize poor-quality forage on winter range. Supplements such as corn and barley tend to reduce digestibility of cellulose and other carbohydrates of range forage, and thus supplements do not significantly increase the overall energy intake. Metabolic interactions of energy deficiency and protein deficiency in mule deer in winter are receiving increasing attention (see Baker 1976), but there is much to learn before supplemental feed can be prescribed appropriate to needs of mule deer on different winter ranges and under a variety of stress conditions.

If the proper kind of feed is identified, there still is the problem of making it available to deer and getting them to eat it. Nagy et al. (1974) recognized that deer were attracted more readily to scattered alfalfa hay than to pelleted rations placed in feed bunkers, so alfalfa was used as "bait." It still took two to four days for deer to discover and use the feed bunkers, and the time was not measurably reduced by baiting with alfalfa. During the study by Nagy et al., many deer aggressively dominated others in feeding, but there was no clear pattern of age or sex classes of dominant individuals.

In Idaho an experiment was conducted to test the feasibility of irrigation on mule deer and elk winter range (Nellis 1977*b*). The rationale was that, since most winter ranges are on exposures that are hot and dry in summer and therefore relatively unproductive naturally, cultivation and irrigation might increase their productivity. The experiment led to the conclusion that it would be more efficient to grow and harvest forage on agricultural land for subsequent feeding to deer. Nellis did not broach the subject of the cost effectiveness of the latter practice. Nagy et al. (1974) calculated hypothetically that it would cost nearly $34,000 (1974 prices) for feed, manpower, and equipment to feed 2,500 deer a pelleted concentrate ration for twenty-one days. The hypothetical situation assumed that one-fourth of 10,000 deer wintering in Middle Park, Colorado, could be fed.

Despite extensive research on the subject, wildlife biologists and managers remain unenthusiastic about emergency feeding of deer, but public sentiment and consequent political pressures still force them to undertake such programs. On one hand, biologists and managers cherish the concept of unfettered wild populations of deer roaming vast areas of essentially unmanaged wild land. On the other hand, they must attempt unnatural kinds of management intervention to protect deer from the devastating adversities that deer occasionally experience and, by virtue of habitat restrictions imposed by human activities, cannot avoid.

Experiences in Europe offer incontrovertible evidence that, under feedlot conditions, some big game populations can be sustained through periods of forage scarcity with many kinds of hay, cut browse, human food vegetables, live-

A mule deer doe flails at and strikes a fawn in a display of dominance during an artificial feeding operation. Such aggressive behavior can further complicate attempts to make artificial feed available to all members of a deer population, particularly the young, nondominant component. Photograph courtesy of the Oregon Department of Fish and Wildlife.

stock grains, and ground and pelleted feed mixtures. There is reason to believe that similar success with emergency feeding of mule deer, in terms of making a significant contribution to the diet of a large percentage of deer in a population, can be achieved only under somewhat similar conditions.

HABITAT EVALUATION

Whenever the quotient of an area of mule and black-tailed deer habitat is divided by the number of persons who actually conduct routine habitat evaluation procedures on the ground, it is enormously large. Also, consider that area-per-person ratio in terms of the small percentage of the year devoted to habitat evaluation. Typically, one wildlife biologist or manager is joined by one or two public land management officers for a week or two in autumn and spring to survey conditions on hundreds or thousands of square kilometers of deer habitat. It is understandable why Connolly (see chap. 6) was forced to conclude that managers have failed to demonstrate that habitat quality can be reliably measured in either absolute or relative terms.

Evans and O'Regan (1962, p. 60) said: "We conclude . . . that there is . . . a distinct unhappiness with the status of range surveys, and that there is a tacit indictment of the methods produced by 30-odd years of research. There is also a certain awareness that the problem is a universal one, not unique to range and wildlife research." Evans and O'Regan (1962, p. 55) further noted: "We know also that in the real world we do not have all the time, all the money, nor all the manpower, and therefore will have to settle for less, and usually considerably less than a complete census [*sic*: success]."

The last statement implies that failure is due, in part, to the fact that wildlife biologists and managers have not applied and perhaps cannot afford to apply enough time and money to expect to succeed. If so, it may suggest that the range survey methods previously indicted were inadequate precisely because they were short-cut methods devised as substitutes for actually learning about the total forage resource.

Another indictment of range and wildlife habitat surveys is that they often are initiated with a flush of enthusiasm that is not followed by a continuing commitment of field personnel to do the work. In Montana the number of established "key browse survey" transects that were measured decreased by about 20 percent from 1966 to 1971 (Mackie 1975). Kufeld (1977*b*) discussed the outcome of a program in Colorado to evaluate all habitat modification projects two, five, and ten years after treatment. So many of the scheduled evaluations were omitted or delayed that Kufeld recommended the evaluation program be dropped less than ten years after it was begun.

Nevertheless, most state and provincial wildlife management and national land management agencies continue to consider habitat evaluation an important part of their responsibilities, and professors of wildlife management continue to teach that it is essential to effective management. Thus it is appropriate to ask if the evaluation procedures used are capable of accomplishing their intended purpose. Or, if they are not capable, is it reasonable to believe that meaningful evaluations can be achieved by other methods?

The Key Browse Survey Method

Settling for something less than a complete inventory of forage resources, agencies responsible for wildlife habitat management on public land in the West came up with "condition and trend" surveys involving some or all of the elements of what Cole (1959) called the "key browse survey method," or variations thereof. That method consists of measuring or estimating length and utilization of current annual growth of twigs on a sample of plants of selected "key" browse species on "key" areas. These areas usually are where deer repeatedly concentrate in winter. Cole's method also included subjective judgments of the age and form classes—as presumed to result from past history of use—of sample plants.

The rationale for these procedures was that they would indicate the trend of forage components most important to maintenance of a deer population on particular ranges. After a decade or two of more or less complete records had accumulated, there developed an undercurrent of disillusion. Mackie (1975, p. 3) said of the Montana efforts: "By the mid-1960s, game managers and biologists began to express concern about the adequacy of the surveys. They pointed to possible deficiencies in basic techniques, variation and inconsistencies in application of the techniques, and an apparent lack of consistent correlation between utilization and plant condition as well as between these parameters and deer population trends and productivity as indicative of a need for critical evaluation of the program."

Reconsidering the information on food habits and seasonal nutrition reviewed in several chapters in this book, particularly chapter 3, should provide some clues to why Cole's method, no matter how assiduously applied, cannot be expected to provide a very complete picture of the performance of deer populations relative to forage resources. Even assuming that measured forage characteristics might be indicative of what is happening to the total forage resource, sampling procedures and data analyses rarely, if ever, are planned so as to provide assurance that temporal or spatial differences in the parameters measured can be detected at some artibrary level of confidence. But examining the major elements of this type of range survey will help to identify its utility and limitations.

Key Winter Range

It seems unreasonable to argue that any range area where deer repeatedly concentrate is unimportant to them. But is it possible that such concentrations reveal only where they end up and what they subsist on under desperate conditions? The migratory behavior of mule and black-tailed deer is not stereotyped. In Alaska or Arizona, Washington or Wyoming, they move downward in mountainous areas in autumn only as far as necessitated by snow depth. They make little use of "critical" winter range areas in years with light snow accumulations. In such mild winters they fare well, whereas, in severe winters, the longer deer are restricted to concentration areas the more they and the range deteriorate.

This line of reasoning suggests that the level of nutrition that deer are at before being forced to the poorest portions of their range is more relevant to their survival than is last-resort forage available to them there. There is only theory now—but a substantial body of it—to justify pursuit of this possibility. If other range areas or other seasonal nutritional levels are equally important or more important to survival and reproduction of a deer population, they will not be discovered by observations made only on winter concentration areas.

The longer that deer are forced by winter conditions to concentrate and remain in a given area, the greater the deterioration of the range condition in that area, and the greater the rate and degree of stress on the animals. Photograph by Don Domenick; courtesy of the Colorado Division of Wildlife.

Key Browse Species

Because quantitative information on food habits is ipso facto not a part of this simplified evaluation procedure, evidence of what deer eat can be obtained only from those plants that most clearly are used. Generally, twigs of deciduous browse plants reveal use most clearly. Equivalent volume removal from evergreen species, such as sagebrush or juniper, is more difficult to measure. Removal of the same amount of forage from bluebunch wheatgrass, for example, will go completely undetected if the procedure ignores grasses. And consumption of many species of forbs will be missed because the entire plant is consumed.

Before attributing exceptional importance to any one or few browse species, consideration should be given to the contradictory knowledge that winter browse twigs alone cannot maintain deer for long (Ammann et al. 1973; Mautz et al. 1976; Wallmo et al. 1977; see chap. 3), even though certain characteristics of such foodstuffs might enable them to contribute significantly to the overall diet (Milchunas et al. 1978). Reconsideration also should be given to the inference by Leach (1956) that high mortality of mule deer often is associated with a winter diet consisting of a high percentage of browse, and low mortality is associated with a diversified winter diet. This suggests that changing supplies or availability of other kinds of forage might provide a better key to the condition of the range.

Age and Form Classes

Since individual browse plants have a finite life-span and eventually decline in vigor and productivity, knowledge of the browse population's age structure theoretically should provide an indication of its potential to continue producing forage. The age of individual plants and the age composition of populations of some browse species can be determined with appropriate methods, but not just by looking at them (Roughton 1962). Plants and populations of similar age can appear quite different as a result of differences in site, genotype, climate, disease, parasitism, browsing history, and so on.

Accordingly, similar levels of browsing can have different effects, and different levels of browsing can have similar effects on the form of plants of similar ages but different backgrounds. Subjective judgments of age and form classes are likely to be hopelessly confounded by these factors. Moreover, individual observers vary widely in placing plants in age and form classes (Mackie 1975). Unless realistic and universal methods are used to measure age and uniform methods are used to describe form, the result is likely to be an accumulation of years of records that defy interpretation.

Growth and Use Measurements

These phases of the key browse survey method consist of actual measurements and therefore are potentially amenable to uniform interpretation. It is unnecessary here to review extensive documentation that twig growth and use can be quantified as precisely as the purpose justifies. For the reader's guidance, the following studies of method are cited: Basile and Hutchings (1966), Ferguson and Marsden (1977), Jensen and Scotter (1977), Lyon (1970), and Smith and Urness (1962).

In general, the methods advocated rely on predictive equations derived from intensive measurements to permit estimation of length or mass of growth or length or mass of use from more extensive measurements. In all cases the purpose is to increase efficiency, but in all cases the sample still must be sufficiently large, stratified, and well distributed to provide estimates of the precision needed for detecting temporal or spatial differences in parameters of interest. Few agencies have applied such rigorous requirements to survey procedures, so data obtained often contribute more confusion than enlightenment.

In summary, if wildlife biologists and managers expect to resolve the problem of deer habitat evaluation, they must recognize that "quick and dirty" condition-and-trend or key browse surveys have not fulfilled their promise. Other critiques have arrived at the same general conclusion. Gill (1976) saw two basic faults. One fault was that, no matter how measured, browse alone cannot provide adequate indication of habitat quality. The other fault was that it was impossible to extrapolate from the key area transects to general populations of browse plants with the sample methods used. Wolfe (1976) pointed out that variations in utilization indexes may reflect variations in winter weather rather than changes in deer numbers, thus misdirecting harvest management. Wolfe also noted that measurements obtained in browse surveys reflect past rather than current conditions. He recommended annual estimates of deer population levels and periodic, more refined vegetation measurements to evaluate long-term trends in range condition, productivity, and species composition.

Other Vegetational Sampling Methods

If traditional habitat condition-and-trend surveys have fallen short of their intended purpose, are there any practical alternatives? There are innumerable ways to estimate all sorts of vegetation parameters. The literature in quantitative plant ecology and range biometry is far too vast to synthesize here, but it certainly suggests that many measurement and sampling techniques are available once one decides what to measure. For some reason, wildlife ecologists have ignored knowledge and technology pertinent to their interests developed in livestock range ecology.

Estimating forage biomass on large areas is an expensive undertaking, but it can be done. If frequency of measurements and precision of estimates have to be rather low because of budgetary constraints, "ball park" estimates at long intervals still might give some notion of the magnitude of forage supplies relative to deer, other wildlife, and domestic livestock population levels, existing or desired. Most research on biomass estimating methods has resulted in advocating some kind of "double-sampling" procedure in which a relationship is first developed among a simple, fast measurement or estimate and actual weight of vegetation. Thereafter the simple, fast measurement is used on a large sample of plots. Studies describing numerous variations of this technique and their advantages and disadvantages are many, including Anderson (1969), Carpenter (1976), Carpenter et al. (1973), Neal and Neal (1973), Payne (1973), Pechanec and Pickford (1937), Reppert et al. (1963), Robel et al. (1970), and Shoop and McIlvain (1963).

Payne (1973) showed that cover can provide a usable index to herbage production of most herbaceous species. Anderson (1969), Bentley et al. (1970), and Rittenhouse and Sneva (1977) demonstrated that there is a similar relationship for many browse species. It was the opinion of Morris (1973, p. 1) that "plant cover—[the] percent [of] area occupied by shrubs, forbs, and grasses—is the best single measure of . . . impacts upon understory vegetation." Morris proposed a rapid, precise procedure for estimating cover that, with further simplification, was found to be useful for estimating the composition of all plant cover—including shrubs, forbs, and grasses—on deer winter range (Carpenter 1974). The procedure involves plots so small—12.7 by 25.4 millimeters (0.5 by 1.0 inch) or 25.4 by 50.8 millimeters (1.0 by 2.0 inches)—that errors or bias in judgment of the percentage of the plot covered by the plant species present are negligible.

Relationships of plant cover and biomass established by other researchers justify further study of the potential of Morris's "rated microplot" concept to estimate biomass of an entire forage complex by a double-sampling procedure.

These developments clearly suggest that it is possible to learn a great deal more about forage resources on deer ranges than the standard browse surveys can possibly tell, and to do it without sacrificing any useful knowledge that those surveys might provide. Minor, subtle changes in the condition of large areas of rangeland are not likely to be detected, so it is unnecessary to conduct inventories annually. And, within vegetation types, variability does not increase with size of area, so sample size need not increase proportionally to the area

Recent research has shown that an electronic capacitance meter—incorporating a double-sampling method—is effective in estimating yields of vegetation on sagebrush rangelands. Photograph by Len H. Carpenter.

involved. Consequently, stratification of a sample can keep sampling intensity within reasonable limits.

However, quantitative evaluations of forage are meaningless without knowledge of the quality of the kinds of forage—that is, their ability to contribute to year-round nutritional needs of deer. Raleigh (1970) stated that an inventory of forage nutrients—that is, a quantitative and qualitative inventory of forage resources—is essential to development of a range livestock and forage management program. That logic was applied by Wallmo et al. (1977) to evaluation of mule deer range. Stewart et al. (1977) showed convincingly that knowledge of seasonal quality of moose forage was imperative in understanding the relationship of forage quantity to range carrying capacity. They revealed that simple measurements of weather could provide indexes to annual and seasonal variations in forage quality.

Once data are acquired to quantify and qualify the total forage resources, wildlife biologists and managers should not be deceived into thinking they can predict how a deer population will perform. Biologists and managers then are in a position only to estimate the point at which forage is likely to be a limiting factor. Without the data, however, they are in no position to estimate how many deer might exist on a given management unit if other limiting factors were to be regulated.

CONIFEROUS FOREST HABITATS
Part 1. Food Habits and Nutrition

Glenn L. Crouch
Research Wildlife Biologist
United States Forest Service
Fort Collins, Colorado

Columbian black-tailed deer occupy forests along the northern Pacific coast of North America from south-central California to northern British Columbia, including Vancouver Island. They intergrade with California mule deer in the south of this range, with Rocky Mountain mule deer in the eastern part, and with Sitka blacktails to the north (Cowan 1956*a*). Inadequate information on Sitka black-tailed deer precludes their consideration in this chapter. Research is needed on the food habits of this subspecies.

Food habits of blacktails are limited by availability of plants, both overall and seasonally. Availability varies greatly from north to south within the blacktail range (fig. 44).

The climate of the north coastal region grades from primarily winter precipitation (mostly rainfall) at the southern end of the California range to year-round moisture (summer rain and winter snow) farther north into British Columbia. Annual precipitation ranges from less than 51 centimeters (20 inches) to more than 330 centimeters (130 inches). A similar gradient also exists from lower to higher elevations, such as in western Washington, where it ranges from beaches at sea level to the middle slopes of 4,267-meter (14,000-foot) Mount Rainier in little more than 81 kilometers (50 miles).

Many blacktails spend summer high in the mountains, but they must move downward in winter to avoid deep snow. In much of the steep northwest country, deer may not migrate far because snow-free areas often are nearby. Where mild winters produce little snow, many deer do not migrate, occupying the same general range all year (Dasmann 1953; Hines 1975; McCullough 1964). The latter areas usually are farther south and almost always at lower elevations.

Seasonal availability of blacktail forage varies greatly with latitude and elevation. In much of the region, plant growth cycles follow usual patterns of spring-summer growth and autumn-winter dormancy. But, on some California ranges, growth of forage species may be regulated by summer dryness, not winter cold (Taber 1956*b*). In these areas, succulent forage is abundant during spring, autumn, and winter, and is relatively scarce during summer. Areas also exist where green forage is available all year (Crouch 1968*a*).

Most of the Douglas fir region of the Pacific Northwest is blacktail habitat. It is characterized by dense, highly productive conifer forests broken at lower elevations by oak woodlands and grasslands, especially in Oregon and northwestern California. Except for oaks, broadleaf trees generally occur only as stands in riparian habitats or as seral species following wildfire or logging. The understories of conifer forests often are dominated by ferns and

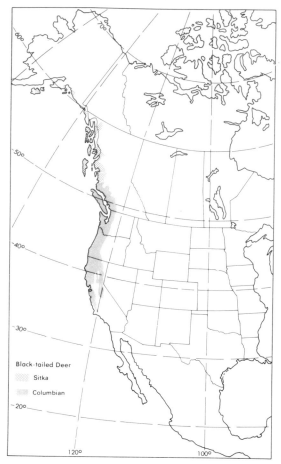

Figure 44. Coastal range of Sitka and Columbian black-tailed deer (from Dasmann 1958 [updated by W. MacGregor in 1975]; Cowan 1936; Cowan and Guiguet 1975; Alaska Department of Fish and Game 1973).

ericaceous shrubs, some of which are evergreen (Franklin and Dyrness 1969). Natural openings, including oak woodlands and grasslands, are dominated by many species of perennial and annual grasses and forbs. Extensive stands of sclerophylous shrubs are common on more southerly habitats in the Coast Range and at lower elevations in the Cascade Mountains where fire or logging has destroyed the conifers (Franklin and Dyrness 1969).

Availability of forage is generally low within forests. Usually dense conifer overstories allow little light or growing space for most plants favored by deer. This is a major reason why deer primarily frequent the forest edge (Leopold 1950a; Mitchell 1950). Vast, unbroken expanses of timber seldom support large numbers of deer year-round. However, most stands have occasional openings caused by windthrow, insect damage, or old age, where deer can feed. Thus, small numbers of deer inhabit even densely timbered lands.

Deer numbers increase after deforestation, when replacement plant communities are in early successional stages. Early successional plant communities usually provide more deer forage than closed-canopy, old-growth timber (Cowan 1945b). Because black-tailed deer numbers are regulated largely by changes in forest cover, populations have changed over time as a function of forest dynamics. Except in

A Columbian black-tailed buck on summer range near the base of Mount Rainier in Washington. Photograph taken in 1919 by J. B. Flett; courtesy of the United States National Archives.

relatively few permanent natural openings, river bottoms, and oak woodlands, these deer have been dependent on catastrophic natural disasters to provide opportunities for population growth. Wildfire periodically has caused heavily timbered areas to revert to early successional stages of vegetation favored by deer. Unlike most western deer ranges, especially winter ranges, blacktail habitat is mostly transitory, suitable from deforestation through reforestation (Robinson 1958).

Logging and associated activities have had the greatest effect on black-tailed deer numbers. Few totally undisturbed areas of nonmigratory blacktail habitat still exist. Road construction, timber harvest, logging slash disposal, and man-caused fires all modify forest-land vegetation and, during the past century, have affected much of the north Pacific region. All these activities continue to produce growing conditions favorable to deer forage (R. F. Dasmann and W. P. Dasmann 1963).

Opening of old-growth forests has benefited many black-tailed deer populations in north coastal habitats. Photograph by Leland J. Prater; courtesy of the United States Forest Service.

FOOD HABITS

Most of few published studies on food habits of black-tailed deer on forest lands have dealt mainly with winter feeding. Reports by Cowan (1945b) on Vancouver Island and by Brown (1961) in western Washington provide the most comprehensive information. Other data are available from Browning and Lauppe (1964) for coastal California and from Crouch (1968a) for the northern Oregon Coast Range. Additional information from Chatelain (1947) in Oregon, Gates (1968) on Vancouver Island, the California Wildlife Investigations Laboratory (n.d.), and Crouch (pers. files) has been utilized here to describe the annual foraging in coastal habitats.

Unfortunately, no definitive information is available from higher elevations in the Cascade Range, which constitute much of the intermediate and summer ranges of migratory deer. Lack of data on food habits and nutritional status has necessitated considerable interpretation and extrapolation.

Blacktail forage is most abundant during the growing season and declines progressively in quantity, variety, and quality after annual growth ceases (Brown 1961; Cowan 1945b; Crouch 1968a). In treeless openings, shrub and herbage growth is characteristically luxuriant and, barring complete domination by one or more shrub or fern species, provides many potential forage plants.

Blacktails are as selective as other deer in their choice of plant species, plants within species, and parts of individual plants. Also, their relative preferences for individual species and plants usually vary from season to season (Brown 1961; Browning and Lauppe 1964; Cowan 1945b). These deer eat a wide variety of vegetation. Cowan (1945b) examined 223 species of plants on Vancouver Island and noted deer feeding on 71 percent of those examined. I monitored deer use on 92 species in Oregon and also recorded feeding on 71 percent.

Deer usually eat a little of many plants of several species rather than completely consuming all available forage from a few plants. Their selectivity is limited only by the plants available. Although some species are preferred over others, few are completely ignored. Also, species that are highly preferred in one season or area may be unattractive at other times and places.

Studies of deer food habits usually attempt to rank preferences among species and relate preference ranking to amounts of forage available. This is important because preference for species and plants within species may vary depending on relative abundance. A given species may be highly preferred when scarce and rarely eaten where common. Similarly, species may not be eaten frequently in one season or growth stage but may be eagerly sought at other times.

In general, blacktails prefer green leafage in all seasons. Obviously, then, the greatest amount of feed is available to them during the growing season when most plants have leaves and succulent stems. Browse—feed produced by woody plants—provides the plant parts most eaten throughout the range (Brown 1961; Browning and Lauppe 1964; Cowan 1945*b*; Crouch, pers. files). Deer eat leaves of deciduous species when available, but buds and twigs of most deciduous species rank low as forage during dormant periods. Acorns also are preferred deer food, but distribution of oaks is limited in the Pacific Northwest.

Evergreen shrubs, such as salal, and semi-evergreen species, such as Pacific blackberry, that retain green leaves during much of the winter are characteristic of the region and provide leafage all year in many locations. Conifers also offer year-round green feed when small trees are within reach of deer or when snow or wind breaks limbs from larger trees.

Forbs are important blacktail food plants. With few exceptions, forage from forbs is available only during growing seasons, which become progressively shorter as latitude and altitude increase. Some forbs—such as cat's-ear—retain their leaves through the winter, and others—such as montia and phacelia—grow in autumn and winter, and offer fresh forage when supplies are low.

Grasses have been recognized as important feed for blacktails (Brown 1961; Cowan 1945*b*). In more southerly ranges and at lower elevations, grasses begin growing after autumn rains and provide succulent green feed throughout winter where snowfall is minimal. Otherwise the only fresh feed consists of residual leaves of evergreen trees and shrubs and winter-active forbs. Feeding by deer on grasses gradually declines as seed stalks form, and it virtually ceases after seed heads appear.

Blacktails usually have abundant forage in some seasons and face shortages in others. In most areas, more forage is available than can be utilized by reasonable deer population levels in the late spring, summer, and autumn. In winter and early spring, feed may be severely restricted because of low residual supplies, poor early growth, or inaccessibility due to snow cover.

REGIONAL FEEDING PATTERNS

California

North coastal ranges of California generally are the driest black-tailed deer habitat and are least affected by winter snows. Forests grade into chaparral, oak woodlands, and grasslands.

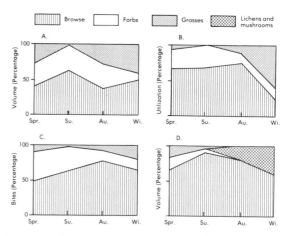

Figure 45. Seasonal forage use by black-tailed deer in four north-central habitats.

A, California—rumen analyses (California Wildlife Investigations Laboratory, n.d.).

B, Oregon—observations of marked plants (Crouch, pers. files).

C, Washington—observations of tame deer (Brown 1961).

D, Vancouver Island—rumen analyses (Cowan 1945*b*).

Table 61. Major Seasonal Forage Plants of Black-tailed Deer in a California Coastal Habitat

Spring	Summer	Autumn	Winter
Pacific madrone	Pacific madrone	Grasses	Grasses
Douglas fir	Coast whitethorn	Acorns	Tobacco brush
Whipplea	Evergreen huckleberry	Canyon live oak	Horsetail
Horsetail	Tobacco brush	Phacelia	Pacific madrone
Grasses	Starflower	Salal	Tan oak

Source: California Wildlife Investigations Laboratory (n.d.).

The more coastal areas are carpeted with redwood and Douglas fir, with the latter dominant inland and at higher elevations. Workers from the California Wildlife Investigations Laboratory collected deer year-round on cutover land in a coastal area and determined feeding habits from stomach analyses (fig. 45A). Their findings indicated that browse, including acorns, was eaten consistently throughout the year, composing about 48 percent of the forage consumed annually. Forbs made up about 28 percent of the diet and were eaten mostly in the summer when most abundant. Grasses and grasslike plants were important food in cooler months and amounted to about 24 percent of the annual intake. Major seasonal forage plants in this coastal area are shown in table 61.

Oregon

Blacktail habitats in southwestern Oregon are similar to those found in northern California, and, though no studies of food habits have been conducted there, it seems reasonable that seasonal foraging patterns and species preferences also are similar.

Farther northward in Oregon, summers are cooler and winters more severe. The vegetation changes gradually, with deciduous and ericaceous woody plants replacing sclerophyllous shrubs as major browse producers. Snowfall is common during winter, but amount and duration of snow cover are highly variable. Warm rains may occur almost anytime and can melt considerable accumulation of snow in a short period (Crouch 1964).

I monitored vegetation for evidence of feeding by deer over a one-year period on clear-cut blocks of Douglas fir one to ten years old, west of Corvallis, Oregon. Browse was the forage most frequently utilized, with leaves of woody plants providing about 59 percent of the annual food supply (fig. 45B). Forbs were eaten readily during spring and summer, but at no season did they constitute the largest proportion of plants eaten. Green grasses were eaten consistently in winter in this area, where relatively mild weather permitted their growth and availability at most times. Seasonally important species in the central Coast Range of Oregon are listed in table 62.

Washington

Brown (1961) compiled results of several food-habit studies in the lowlands of western

Table 62. Major Seasonal Forage Plants of Black-tailed Deer in a Central Oregon Coastal Habitat

Spring	Summer	Autumn	Winter
Cat's-ear	Western thimbleberry	Blackcap	Grasses
Ocean spray	Vine maple	Pacific blackberry	Blackcap
Bitter cherry	Bitter cherry	Bitter cherry	Pacific blackberry
Blackcap	Beaked hazel	Grasses	Iris
Douglas fir	Cat's-ear	Big deervetch	Salal

Source: Crouch (pers. files).

Table 63. Major Seasonal Forage Plants of Black-tailed Deer in a Washington Coastal Habitat

Spring	Summer	Autumn	Winter
Grasses	Pacific blackberry	Pacific blackberry	Pacific blackberry
Pacific blackberry	Cat's-ear	Vine maple	Grasses
Cat's-ear	Plantain	Red alder	Salal
Plantain	Vine maple	Huckleberry	Huckleberry
Evergreen huckleberry	Clover	Plantain	Plantain

Source: Brown (1961).

Washington. This area contains some of the most productive timberlands in the Northwest and has been logged extensively over the past one hundred years. Precipitation is high, and growing seasons are relatively long, resulting in luxuriant growth of many plant species after logging or wildfires.

Based on observations of tame blacktail deer, browse was by far their most important food in Washington, amounting to 65 percent of the yearly diet (fig. 45C). Forbs accounted for 25 percent and grasses 10 percent of food eaten by deer throughout the year. Seasonally preferred plants are shown in table 63.

Vancouver Island, British Columbia

Cowan (1945b) studied deer food habits over a wide range of habitats on southern Vancouver Island. He worked in the northern part of this area, but blacktails are found considerably farther northward and possibly have different food habits there. Cowan found that deer fed on 92, 64, and 56 percent, respectively, of the browse, forb, and grass species, and 73 percent of twenty-six species of lichens, mushrooms, and aquatic plants.

Rumen analyses showed that browse—constituting 71 percent of identifiable stomach

contents—was the major source of food year-round. Lichens and mushrooms made up 22 percent, ferns and horsetails 5 percent, and grasses 2 percent of the annual diet (fig. 45D). No forbs appeared in the listing of food plants, but these may have been included in a miscellaneous, unidentified category. Major seasonal forage plants, based on rumen analyses, are shown in table 64.

Gates (1968) worked on another area on southeastern Vancouver Island about twenty years after Cowan (1945b) did, and found a somewhat different feeding pattern (table 65). He reported that browse made up only 17 percent of identifiable rumen contents during the spring-summer period and that forbs, grasses, and lichens, respectively, constituted 59, 15, and 7 percent of the diet. In contrast to Cowan's results, Gates indicated less browse and more herbage in deer diets at all seasons, but especially in spring and summer.

Seasonal Influences

Available evidence from all areas indicates that green leafage is available and contributes virtually all the plant material eaten by blacktails during most of the year. Even in winter, when succulent forage traditionally is

Table 64. Major Seasonal Forage Plants of Black-tailed Deer on Southern Vancouver Island

Spring	Summer	Autumn	Winter
Douglas fir	Salal	Salal	Douglas fir
Willow	Red alder	Red alder	Lichens
Horsetail	Blackcap	Mushrooms	Salal
Bracken	Willow	Douglas fir	Mushrooms
Salal	Grasses	Willow	Red cedar

Source: Cowan (1945b).

Table 65. Major Seasonal Forage Plants of Black-tailed Deer on Southeastern Vancouver Island

Spring–Summer Transition	Autumn	Winter
Pearly everlasting	Salal	Salal
Grasses	Pacific blackberry	red cedar
Cat's-ear	Red alder	Lichens
Lichens	Mushrooms	Grasses
		Bearberry

Source: Gates (1968).

scarce, blacktails still depend primarily on residual green leaves from the previous growing season, or on grasses and forbs that grow during winter. In the tables, nearly all plants shown to be used in winter provide leaves during that season. Huckleberry in Washington is a notable exception, but in many instances, even huckleberry twigs retain a characteristic green coloration from the growing season. Furthermore, most secondary winter forage also is leafage.

Residual twigs of woody plants such as bitterbrush—supposedly vital for wintering deer on other western ranges—are far less important to blacktails, especially in Coast Range habitats. On a regionwide basis, only huckleberry and several species of ceanothus can be considered important deciduous shrubs that provide substantial amounts of winter feed. Locally, a few other woody plants also contribute acceptable twigs.

Most winter feeding occurs in openings—mainly cutover or burned areas. However, several of the more common winter forage plants, including salal, also grow abundantly as forest understory. This is fortunate because, at more northerly latitudes, snow is prevalent on winter ranges, and blacktails characteristically depend on timbered areas for both food and cover at certain times (Gates 1968; Jones 1974). Even farther south, in Oregon, snow occasionally accumulates, even at sea level, to depths that preclude foraging on low-growing plants in the open. When this occurs, deer are forced to feed under the timber or eat twigs of low-preference woody plants where timber stands are absent or conifer regeneration is not available.

In Oregon's Tillamook Burn, with no timber present, it was estimated that 30 centimeters (12 inches) of snow cover would reduce available forage from about 224 to 34 kilograms per hectare (200 to 30 pounds per acre) fresh weight in midwinter (Crouch 1968a). Assuming that the average-weight (45 kilograms: 100 pounds) deer eats 0.9–1.4 kilograms (2–3 pounds) of air-dry feed per day (Brown 1961), it can be predicted that prolonged, continuous snow cover could result in substantial mortality in a dense population of deer. Such a die-off occurred in 1969–70, after snow covered the Tillamook Burn area for more than fifty consecutive days (Hines 1975).

FORAGE AVAILABILITY, PREFERENCE, AND IMPORTANCE

Availability of various plant species determines the forage base for deer. To a large extent, availability also controls the relative preferences deer show for various forage species. Rumen or fecal analyses, or observations of feeding deer, can reveal preferences among forage species eaten, but may not indicate relative availability of these plants unless accompanied by some measure of species abundance.

High preference may mean little to the forage needs of blacktails if preferred species are rare and if high preference ranking occurs because deer eat every existing plant. Therefore, relative importance of a plant species as deer forage depends on the degree of preference for it as well as the amount of feed the species can provide. Often, moderately preferred species may be far more important if abundant and readily available to deer. Such plants usually are the most significant forage resources on blacktail ranges.

In some areas of the Oregon Coast Range,

Green leafage generally is the most abundant and preferred year-round forage of Columbian blacktails. Photograph courtesy of the United States National Park Service.

red-stem ceanothus is highly preferred browse. Virtually every available leaf or twig on these plants may be browsed at some time during the year. However, the species rarely is found and thus contributes little to the forage supply. On the other hand, salal is common over much of the same area, but, on the basis of percentage browsed, it ranks low in preference even though much more salal than red-stem is eaten. Consequently, in this area, salal is more important to deer than red-stem.

Some species are very abundant and yet little used by blacktails. Examples from western Oregon include woodland groundsel, tansy ragwort, bracken, sword fern, and Oregon grape. Collectively, these five species covered 32 and 28 percent of the ground in two areas I studied. Although tansy and bracken are considered toxic to some classes of livestock (see Kingsbury 1964), no instances of deer poisoning by these plants have been reported. Moreover, bracken is an important food plant on Vancouver Island (Cowan 1945*b*). Several other species listed as poisonous to domestic livestock are common on

blacktail ranges, including horsetail, red elderberry, and bleeding heart (Kingsbury 1964). They apparently are harmless to deer, since blacktails eat them readily (California Wildlife Investigations Laboratory, n.d.; Brown 1961; Crouch, pers. files).

Some plants are common foods of blacktails in one area and seldom utilized in other areas. Starflower, a forb, was highly preferred in California (California Wildlife Investigations Laboratory, n.d.) but was virtually untouched in Oregon (Crouch, pers. files), though it was common there. Cowan (1945*b*) reported large amounts of bracken consumed by blacktails on Vancouver Island, but, as I stated earlier, it rarely was eaten in Oregon. Without doubt, such different food habits are related to the diversity of available forage among areas, and probably to the fact that local subspecies and even individual plants within the same species are considerably different in chemical composition (Dimock et al. 1976; Longhurst et al. 1968*a*; Radwan 1972).

Seasonal differences in relative acceptability

to deer of the same plant or species are well known. Some causes for this are obvious, but others are much more subtle. A major reason—the preference of blacktails for green leaves—has already been discussed and probably explains satisfactorily why large amounts of deciduous tree and shrub foliage and forbs are consumed in the growing season. It also suggests why semievergreen and evergreen species, such as Pacific blackberry and salal, increase in importance in winter when leaves are in short supply. Still unanswered is the apparent reluctance of most blacktails to feed on plants, such as sword fern, that retain fronds through most winters. The apparent within-season changes in preference for grasses and some woody and forb species very likely are due to physiological and structural changes occurring in the plants (Crouch 1964; Heady 1964; Longhurst et al. 1968a; Oh et al. 1970). Examples are the declining acceptance of grasses as flower stalks

appear and the abrupt increase in acceptability of red alder leaves and big deervetch in autumn.

NUTRITION

Brown (1961) fed natural forage to captive blacktails in western Washington, and controlled feeding experiments were carried out in British Columbia (Bandy 1965; Cowan and Wood 1955a). Other researchers have determined the chemical composition of selected forages at various seasons and places (Brown 1961; Crouch 1964; Gates 1968; Radwan and Crouch 1974), but no comprehensive nutritional studies have been conducted on blacktailed deer in north coastal habitats.

Even though nutritional capabilities have not been assessed, it is clear that most north coastal range can support large numbers of blacktails within certain mixes of successional stages of vegetation. Estimates of deer numbers from

A Columbian black-tailed buck in velvet strips leaves of red alder. Photograph by Leonard Lee Rue III.

representative areas throughout the range leave no doubt that the habitat can support and the deer can produce large numbers of animals (table 66).

The probable sequence of blacktail response to forage improvement by wildfire or logging has been outlined, but documentation of this process is sorely lacking (Brown 1961; Cowan 1945*b*; R. F. Dasmann and W. P. Dasmann 1963; Lawrence 1969; Mitchell 1950). Researchers agree that deer numbers increase soon after deforestation in response to increasing quantities and nutritive quality of available forage. Deer numbers increase for ten years or so, but weight per deer begins to decline as production of high-quality forage fails to keep pace with the increasing deer population (Robinson 1958). Deer numbers may continue to remain high or even increase after ten years, but average body weight continues to decline. Finally, numbers decline due to decreased fawn production and survival (Klein 1969). The length of the cycle depends on the type of range, and on the method and rate of deforestation and reforestation applied to it.

Although many areas of deforested blacktail habitat provide enough nutritious forage to maintain large numbers of deer, the weights of those deer seldom approach the weights that have been attained experimentally or where great amounts of high-quality forage have been available to relatively few deer (Bandy 1965; Brown 1961; Einarsen 1946; Robinson 1958).

Also in these areas, antler growth—known to be influenced by forage quality—indicated that the nutrient supply to high populations of blacktails is less than optimal (Cowan and Wood 1955*a*; French et al. 1955; Robinson 1958).

Where black-tailed deer numbers are high—about 19 deer per square kilometer (50 per square mile) or more—feeding pressure is apparently too great to permit individual animals to approach maximum growth potential in terms of weight and antler development. Although data about weights of blacktails over the entire range are not available, virtually nowhere are wild deer comparable in size to captive animals fed high-quality experimental diets. Robinson (1958) reported captive yearlings weighing 73–77 kilograms (160–170 pounds) with three- to four-point antlers. Cowan and Wood (1955*a*) raised male fawns that weighed 32 kilograms (70 pounds) at 135 days and bucks that had three- to four-point antlers at 15 months. Nordan et al. (1968) produced 68-kilogram (150-pound) bucks and 50-kilogram (110-pound) does at 15 months.

In 1964, yearling bucks in the Tillamook Burn, Oregon, had average live weights of about 41 kilograms (90 pounds) and only spike antlers (Crouch 1964). At the time, deer numbers probably averaged 19–23 per square kilometer (50–60 per square mile), and forage availability had long passed its peak. Einarsen (1946) reported hog-dressed 2-year-old bucks weighing more than 59 kilograms (130 pounds)

Table 66. Numbers of Black-tailed Deer in Cut-over Coastal Habitats

Location	Number of Deer		Reference
	Per Square Mile	Per Square Kilometer	
Mendocino County, California	45–80	17–31	F. M. Anderson et al. (1974)
Humboldt County, California	95	37	Bonn (1967)
Tillamook Burn, Oregon	54	21	Hines (1975)
Washington	48	19	Brown (1961)
Southeast Vancouver Island, British Columbia	50–60	19–23	Robinson (1958)
Northern Vancouver Island, British Columbia	51	20	Willms (1971)

Table 67. Hog-Dressed Weights of Hunter-Killed Yearling Black-tailed Bucks from Coastal Habitats

Location	Weight		Reference
	Pounds	Kilograms	
Hopland, California[a]	51	23	Taber (1956*a*)
Harlan, Oregon	66	30	Vohs (pers. comm., February 1972)
Corvallis, Oregon	76	35	Vohs (pers. comm., February 1972)
Gray Harbor County, Washington	86	39	Brown (1961)
Whidbey Island, Washington	72	33	Brown (1961)
Vancouver Island, British Columbia	70	32	Smith (1961)

[a] Chaparral habitats adjacent to forested ranges; hunting season about six weeks earlier than in other areas.

in the Tillamook Burn in 1943, when numbers of animals were estimated at 12 per square kilometer (30 per square mile) and forage availability was about optimal. Although variable because of different carcass-handling procedures, weights of hog-dressed deer may give some indication of the nutritive status of forage on certain ranges. Table 67 shows weights of hunter-killed yearling bucks from widely separated blacktail habitats.

Throughout the coastal mountains of their range, blacktails generally exhibit characteristics of large number and small size. Constant logging of different tracts maintains forage resources at fairly uniform levels of abundance and nutritional quality from year to year, and the deer population is subject to ultraconservative harvest regulations. These combined, stabilizing influences on the aforementioned blacktail characteristics operate satisfactorily except during severe winters when heavy, persistent snowfall buries the low-growing vegetation on which the deer depend. Then large populations of small blacktails often sustain catastrophic losses (R. F. Dasmann and W. P. Dasmann 1963; Hines 1975). The deer cannot obtain sufficient forage to survive, except where mature timber with adequate understory is available for shelter and food (Crouch 1968*a*; Jones 1974). Otherwise they must subsist on conifers or twigs of taller woody plants that usually are in limited supply and of relatively poor nutritional quality (Brown 1961; Crouch 1964).

Periodic winterkills that decimate blacktail herds have little long-term effect. Where forage is abundant, the herds can recover and increase very quickly. Hines (1975) reported that a captive, self-regulating herd of blacktails in Oregon's Tillamook Burn expanded from 22 to 49 animals per square kilometer (56–126 per square mile) in a twenty-one-month period, including two reproductive seasons. Forage resources to support similar rates of deer production are common over much of the blacktail range.

Part 2. Forest Management for Deer

Olof C. Wallmo
Principal Wildlife Biologist
United States Forest Service
Pacific Northwest Forest and
Range Experiment Station
Juneau, Alaska

John W. Schoen
Game Research Biologist
Alaska Department of Fish and Game
Juneau, Alaska

Every forest type in western North America is used by mule deer or blacktails in one or more seasons of the year, and deer can be considered a natural component of those forest ecosystems. However, there are appreciable differences among those ecosystems with regard to their potential to meet the requirements of deer and, consequently, in how they can best be managed for that purpose. In some areas, early stages of secondary succession provide highly productive deer habitat. In other areas, climax forest appears to be the most important of the available or potential habitat types for maintaining high year-round carrying capacity.

Deer tend to prosper at certain stages of forest succession, but the forest cannot be held in one stage of development if it also is managed for timber production. Although it is possible to produce timber and deer on the same land, management for the greatest long-term yield of one is not likely to permit the greatest long-term yield of the other. But the art and science of multipurpose forest management still are being learned, and we can hope for improvement in the technology of managing jointly for deer and timber production. This part of the chapter is concerned primarily with what is now known about managing forests to produce deer; part 3 deals with managing deer to accommodate production of trees.

As Short (1972) observed, yields of various products of forest ecosystems depend on how much energy in the ecosystem is directed to each product. A century ago, the supply of trees and deer in Canada and the United States seemed practically inexhaustible. Today we realize that, without responsible planning and management, trees and deer can be rapidly depleted. And, as responsible planning and management progress, we must face the difficult decisions of how to apportion energy among the resources.

Although cover is important to deer, habitat quality on potentially or currently forested lands usually is considered in terms of forage. Most edible portions of forest trees are above the reach of terrestrial grazers, and the trees usurp sunlight, moisture, and soil nutrients at the expense of understory vegetation. In mature coniferous forests of the central Rocky Mountains, more than 99 percent of the total aboveground vegetational biomass may be tied up in trees. Less than 10 percent of that biomass is in foliage that is not only inaccessible but largely unpalatable to deer. Less than 1 percent of the total vegetational biomass consists of shrubs and herbaceous plants (Gary 1974; Landis and Mogren 1975; Wallmo et al. 1972). In climax Douglas fir forest in the western Cascades of Oregon, 99.1 percent of the aboveground biomass consisted of trees, 0.9 percent of shrubs, and less than 0.004 percent of herbs (Grier and Logan 1977).

Multiple uses and stockpiling of wood on an early homestead in Washington were indications of a seemingly limitless supply of forest resources in the Pacific Northwest. This misconception and the land-use practices it engendered threatened the productivity of both timber and deer. Modern forestry management practices seek to balance timber production with the habitat needs of wildlife, including deer. Photograph courtesy of the United States Bureau of Land Management.

It is well documented that, in forest habitat, forage supply for ruminant grazers is inversely related to the amount of tree overstory (Ffolliott and Clary 1972), as diagrammed in figure 46. This suggests a general principle with respect to managing forest habitat for deer: removing trees should improve deer habitat. But, as will be discussed later, this may not be entirely true.

It is apparent that total aboveground biomass of the climax forest, at one moment in time, may be many orders of magnitude greater than that of an early seral stage on a similar site. But the former represents the culmination of perhaps a century or more of growth, after which the turnover rate of energy and matter is slow relative to the total biomass involved. The latter, on the other hand, is extremely dynamic, with a relative turnover rate several times that of the mature forest. From the standpoint of multiple-use forest management, decisions as to which of these stages or which compromise is most desirable must be based on social as well as ecological considerations.

Additional significance to deer of disclimax forest vegetation was suggested by Gates and Orians (1975). They hypothesized that plants of late successional or climax stages tend to have more chemical defenses (secondary products of metabolism) against herbivores than do plants of early successional stages. According to their theoretical approach, plants of early successional stage persist as a result of prodigious reproduction, large numbers of individuals, and rapid maturation. The long-lived climax species—which ultimately gain a foothold and dominance—lack such advantages.

The conifers that dominate most western forests contain chemical substances that make them less than optimally nutritious for deer (Schwartz et al. 1979a; Oh et al. 1970). Deer and other herbivores may have some capacity to detoxify such secondary chemical compounds

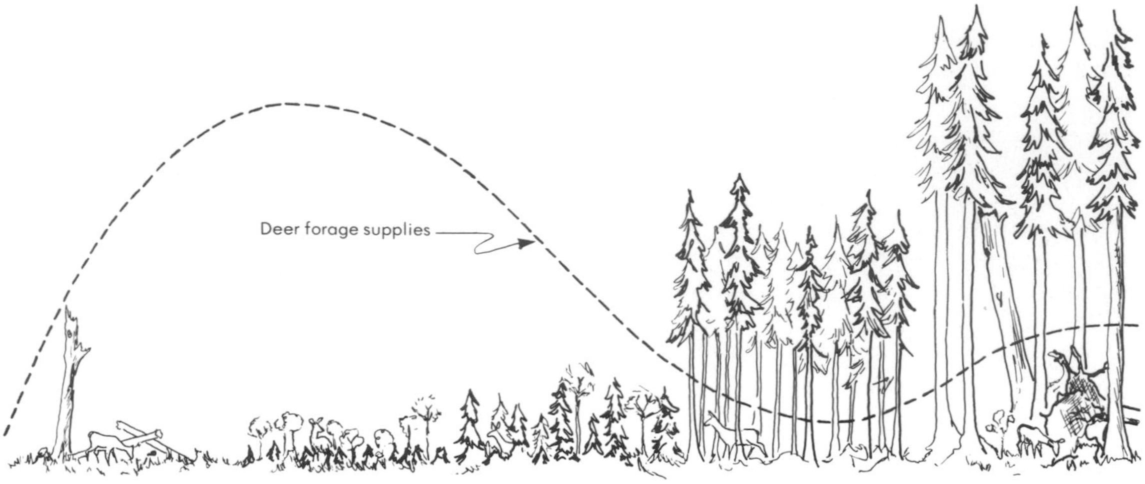

New clearcut	Seedling conifer	Advanced regeneration	Second growth timber	Old growth forest
Forb - grass - sedge	Shrub - herb	Young tree - shrub	Minimum undergrowth	Moderate undergrowth
1-5 years	6-10	10-20	20-200	200 +

Figure 46. Generalized schematic concept of deer forage supplies during secondary succession in coniferous forest habitat. Age spans shown are rough averages for western hemlock/Sitka spruce forests of the northern Pacific Coast.

(Freeland and Janzen 1974), but, regardless, the benefits of living among an abundance of palatable forage rather than among small supplies of relatively unpalatable forage are obvious.

The present discussion is not restricted to potentially harvestable or actually harvested forest. On many forested areas in the West, logging is economically impractical. Wildlife managers are concerned with quality of forest habitat whether or not it is commercial forest land, and they are obliged to plan its management for wildlife with consideration for other resources present. Most principles for enhancing deer habitat in forests have evolved from results achieved through silvicultural practices and timber harvesting on commercial forest lands, but they also are applicable to deer habitat in areas where timber management is not a primary goal.

FOREST AS COVER

The general term "cover" refers to various animal-environment relationships that have been widely discussed but seldom measured.

Here it refers to vegetational and topographic features that conceal or protect organisms from adverse conditions (such as severe weather) or circumstances (such as predation).

Climatic and structural characteristics of forest environments probably have some logical relationship to the habitat selection of deer. So far, however, inferences that deer actually do select for the situations that would be presumed to enhance their comfort (see Ozoga and Gysel 1972; Black et al. 1976) are not supported by hard evidence. Mule deer's ability to tolerate, with apparent comfort, climates as extreme as Alberta winters and Chihuahua summers suggests thermoregulatory capacity great enough to make the minor microclimate modification provided by forest cover seem rather insignificant.

After considering how well mule deer adapt to desert and prairie as well as to shrubland and forest habitats, the same might be said of concealment and escape cover provided by forest. This is not to suggest that deer are insensitive and unresponsive to more comfortable environments, or that the cover that permits choice is unimportant. It does suggest, however, that wildlife biologists and managers do not understand the relationship of concealment cover and comfort movements well enough to describe forest structure in those terms. Consequently, one can argue only that, at this time, provision of cover for mule and black-tailed deer—as an important aspect of forested habitat—must be based largely on broad principle rather than on precise prescriptions. Geist (see chapt. 5) discussed theoretical use of forest cover for energy conservation. However, there still are no useful prescriptions to structure managed forests in this respect for mule and black-tailed deer.

Reduction of snow depth by forest canopy, however, is a tangible and well-documented cover effect. Mule deer, blacktails, and white-tails can cope with snow depths up to about 50–60 centimeters (20–24 inches) if the snow is not excessively dense or crusted (Gilbert et al. 1970); but any depth of very dense, crusted snow may be intolerable. There is an inverse

linear relationship between vertical crown-cover density and snow accumulation on the forest floor (Meiman 1968). On northern Vancouver Island, British Columbia, observations by Jones (1975) indicated that, when snow in old-growth forest is 15 centimeters (6 inches) deep near sea level and 60 centimeters (24 inches) deep at 300 meters (984 feet) above sea level, the snow in clearings will be about 75 and 100 centimeters (30 and 39 inches) deep at those elevations. In southeast Alaska, Merriam (1971) found snow to average about twice as deep in clear-cuts as in mature timber stands. Except during unusually snow-free winters, clear-cuts and other openings are completely unusable in these areas.

The reduction of snow accumulation as forest regenerates has not been described, so it is not known how long clear-cutting eliminates winter habitat in deep snow regions. Density, uni-

In all habitats, deer can cope with deep snow if it is not excessively dense or crusted. Reduction of snow depth by hemlock/spruce canopy is important to the well-being and winter survival of Sitka black-tailed deer in Alaska, as it is to all deer in north coastal habitats. Photograph by David R. Klein; courtesy of the Alaska Cooperative Wildlife Research Unit.

formity, and height of the regrowth stand, plus topography, are influential factors. As progressively larger areas of northern coastal forests are put under management, hastening maturation of regrowth forests becomes a common interest of silviculturists and wildlife biologists. Also, it is important to understand attributes of old-growth stands that contribute to the suitability of winter habitat. Research being conducted in British Columbia and Alaska will help provide that understanding.

MANAGEMENT PRACTICES

Cutting Systems

Deer are attracted to forest openings by the great variety and abundance of forage. They make little use of the centers of large openings because of the distance from cover. Use is concentrated near the edges of openings, where both food and nearby cover are readily accessible. These statements are widely accepted as true, though supported by very few and often equivocal studies.

In three cases reported by Reynolds (1966a,c), data showed average use of openings to be less than, or at least no greater than, use of the forest. In one case there was no increase in sign of use near the edge in either forest or opening. In the other two cases there was increased sign 30–91 meters (100–300 feet) and 61–122 meters (200–400 feet) within the forest. Deer sign (fecal pellets) fell off to zero at 183, 305, and 366 meters (600, 1,000, and 1,200 feet) into the openings, where sampling terminated in the three studies.

Although Reynolds' studies may have been misinterpreted, several other researchers indicated that mule deer and blacktails do respond positively to openings created by logging. Patton (1974) reported a two- to tenfold increase in use by mule deer of patch clear-cut ponderosa pine forest in Arizona in the first six years after logging. Use of clear-cut strips in subalpine conifer forest in Colorado decreased during the first two years after logging. But eight years later it was three times as high as in adjacent

Openings in the forest can provide abundant food close to shelter and escape cover. Photograph by James D. Yoakum.

uncut strips (Wallmo 1969). Increased deer use of ponderosa pine clear-cuts in Arizona was measured by Pearson (1968), and that of mixed conifer clear-cuts in Oregon by Edgerton (1972).

As suggested by work in Arizona (Kruse 1972), British Columbia (Gates 1968), and Oregon (Hines 1973), openings created by wildfire can result in increased deer use. In parks and wilderness areas—where logging is not permitted—the United States Forest Service and National Park Service have management programs that involve both prescribed and natural fires to maintain more natural ecosystems and better habitat diversity for wildlife.

Thus, concepts of forest management to benefit mule deer and blacktails are largely built around the hypothesis that small openings with early successional vegetation are desirable in late successional or climax timber stands. From that principle, numerous management prescriptions have been offered, of which the following are examples:

1. Arizona—one-fifth of the area should be in openings of 0.4–4.0 hectares (1–10 acres) (Clary 1972), less than 488 meters (1,600 feet) across (Reynolds 1966a).

2. Arizona and New Mexico—clear-cuts should be less than 8.1 hectares (20 acres) in spruce/fir and less than 18.2 hectares (45 acres) in ponderosa pine (Reynolds 1969a).

3. Central and southern Rockies—one-sixth of a cutting block should be cut every twenty years, in openings about four or five times tree height (Alexander 1974).

4. Northern Rockies—small, scattered clear-cuts followed by fire in the Douglas fir type; larger blocks in grand fir, also followed by burning, with scattered islands of timber left for restocking and as cover (Pengelly 1963).

5. Oregon—staggered, clear-cut logging of 12.1–24.3 hectares (30–60 acres) is a sound practice for western Oregon north of the Rogue River (Hooven 1973).

6. Eastern Oregon and Washington—see Black et al. (1976) for a complex set of guidelines.

Of the many recommendations of this sort, some are based on speculation only, others on indirect measures of relative use by deer, and none on demonstrations of changes in the condition of deer or a deer population. Moreover, they are contradicted by widespread belief that major increases in deer populations have resulted from removal of extremely large areas of forest by fire and logging.

Benefits of forest openings to deer generally are attributed to increased abundance and variety of forage. In one study in Colorado, the end-of-growth standing crop of the edible portions of known species of deer forage, fifteen years after logging, was 47 percent greater than in adjacent overmature forest (Wallmo et al. 1972). With equal areas of cut and uncut forest available, free-ranging tame deer used to sample food habits obtained nearly 70 percent of their forage from clear-cuts.

Theoretically, partial cutting (removal of individual trees or groups of trees from the stand) can confer similar benefits by opening forest canopy and stimulating understory vegetation. An inverse, usually curvilinear relationship between overstory and understory seems to apply to most forest types (Ffolliott and Clary 1972). However, mule deer in northern Arizona failed to show a clear response to areas of ponderosa pine thinned to various basal area levels (Pearson 1968). In mixed conifer forest of northeastern Oregon, removing 30 percent of the basal area resulted in a decrease in understory vegetation and no material change in deer use, whereas clear-cutting significantly increased both. Moreover, partial cutting was believed to have eliminated hiding cover for deer (Edgerton 1972).

In short, the limited knowledge available about overstory-understory relationships, and generalizations drawn from them, suggest that timber management practices commonly used in the West are beneficial to mule deer and blacktails except, perhaps, in the northern part of the western hemlock/Sitka spruce type. If partial cutting is not entirely beneficial, this should not be a great concern, because it apparently is not very harmful. At any rate, regeneration requirements and harvesting economics may limit the adoption of uneven-age timber management. Whether or not large clear-cuts or unmanaged wildfires are conducive to good deer habitat seems irrelevant, because the former are no longer tolerated on public lands and the latter are prevented when possible. More and more, multiple-use silviculture is the order of the day, and management prescriptions can be expected to result in diversified forest environments. However, neither dramatic nor even detectable returns in deer production should be anticipated from a multiple-use forest management scheme.

As example of a potential management plan for the subalpine spruce/fir type of the central and southern Rockies is Alexander's (1974) prescription: clear-cut one-sixth of the management unit every twenty years in openings four to five times tree height; that is, about 100–150 meters (328–492 feet) wide. If these clear-cuts are more or less square to maximize snow-catch and water yield, and somewhat irregular for aesthetic purposes, they might aver-

Large clear-cut blocks in black-tailed deer habitat provide a poorer mixture of food and cover resources than do small clear-cutting units. Photograph courtesy of the United States Forest Service.

Compared with the previous photograph, these clear-cuts in blacktail habitat still may be too large for optimal deer use, but they eventually will produce smaller areas of even-aged timber than will the clear-cut block of land shown in the previous photograph. Photograph courtesy of the United States Forest Service.

age about two hectares (five acres). In a management unit of 600 hectares (1,483 acres), 100 hectares (247 acres) would be cut every twenty years. Of course, habitat improvement following clear-cutting would last only a fraction of the rotation period if satisfactory forest regeneration was achieved. In subalpine forest clear-cuts in Colorado, deer forage began to decrease after twenty years (Regelin and Wallmo 1978); it was expected to decrease more rapidly thereafter.

From fragmentary bits of information on the subject, a model of changes in forage supplies is hypothesized for the above plan, cutting one-sixth of the area every twenty years (fig. 47). For this hypothetical situation, it will be assumed that logging operations and slash will reduce the supply of available forage below that in mature forest, by an average of 60 percent over the first

five years. Before the end of that period, herbage and browse will develop rapidly, and slash will settle and decompose. In the sixth through tenth years, forage biomass will average 60 percent above that in mature forest. Then, at 11–15, 16–20, 21–25, 26–30, 31–35, and 36–40 years, it will average 72, 48, 31, 12, 6, and 9 percent above mature forest levels for those respective five-year periods. There are some data to support the above estimates for the central Rockies, but forage yields in middle-aged second-growth forests there and elsewhere may be expected to fall below that of climax forests (Schoen and Wallmo 1979). This concept is not well understood because few studies of overstory-understory relationships have considered the opening up of the stand during the process of silvicultural overmaturation.

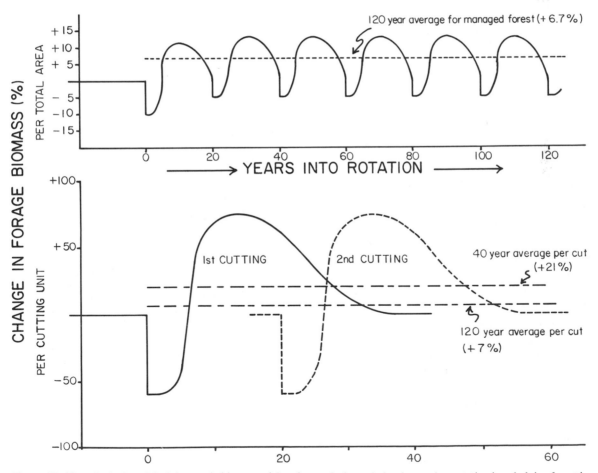

Figure 47. Hypothetical model of changes in biomass of deer forage during a timber harvesting rotation in subalpine forest in the central Rocky Mountains.

For each tract cut, this would represent an average annual increase in forage supplies of 21 percent over forty years. Cutting one-sixth of the entire management unit would result in a 3.5 percent increase in forage. Successive cuttings would overlap in time to cause periodic reductions and increases in forage supplies. After the first twenty years, when the cycle becomes regular, there is an average net forage increase above levels in old-growth forests of 7 percent over forty years or 6.7 percent for the entire 120-year rotation, including the first twenty years.

Summer carrying capacity of subalpine forest habitat in Colorado was calculated theoretically to be about 70 deer per square kilometer (27 per square mile) (Wallmo et al. 1977), which amounts to 420 deer on this imaginary management unit. If herd size responded proportionately to the average increase in forage, it might be expected to increase to 450.

We should emphasize that this hypothetical model applies to Colorado subalpine forests, not to all western forest types. Brown (1961) presents a somewhat different seral picture for western Washington. Preliminary results of investigations by Schoen and Wallmo (1979) of the hemlock/spruce type of southeastern Alaska suggest that, while there is an enormous increase in deer forage for a few years after clearcutting, regrowth of shrubs and trees becomes so dense as to be virtually impenetrable to deer within fifteen years and remains in that condition for at least another decade. Thereafter, conifers achieve dominance and the stand slowly begins to open up, but the understory vegetation remains impoverished for perhaps two centuries. Furthermore, the understory is composed of annuals and stunted deciduous shrubs that are not of significant value to deer in winter, whereas the understory of overmature forest yields a much larger crop of nondeciduous subshrubs and perennial forbs and fully developed deciduous browse plants. Under these conditions, a management system involving a 100- to 150-year rotation would be expected to reduce carrying capacity well below that of overmature forest. Knowledge of the total forage supply in regrowth forest—including wind-clipped foliage, windthrown trees, and fallen lichens—is incomplete, but available data from pellet group counts indicate that deer make little use of regrowth stands up to 150 years old compared with old-growth stands with dominant trees more than 300 years old.

Among many weaknesses in the assumption that logging in most western forest regions will improve deer production is that the extent and diversity of summer habitat and the supplies and quality of summer forage normally exceed the needs of the number of deer that can be supported through winter. Actual deer densities in the preceding Colorado example were estimated at about 2–4 deer per square kilometer (0.8–1.5 per square mile). Population levels were governed by winter conditions (Wallmo et al. 1977). In such circumstances, logging expressly to improve deer habitat would be futile.

Feasible timber management practices in most forest types of western North America might be expected to improve deer habitat, but

Clear-cutting of the hemlock/spruce type forest in southeastern Alaska generates a great increase in deer forage. In approximately fifteen years, second-growth shrubs and trees in many areas can become so dense that Sitka blacktails are unable to move throughout these areas and utilize the vegetation fully. Photograph courtesy of the United States Forest Service.

they may not result in measurable changes in deer populations. In central Alberta, Stelfox et al. (1976) observed actual deer densities of one deer per 16.2 hectares (40 acres) where calculated carrying capacity was increased to one per 0.3 hectare (0.7 acre) after logging. Clary and Larson (1971) reported that, under extremely low deer densities (fewer than 5.2 deer per square kilometer: 2 per square mile) in Arizona ponderosa pine, their distribution was essentially random and unrelated to forage availability or tree density. This might be attributed to an excess of food and cover for the small number of deer. The concept that timber harvesting at least will not degrade habitat significantly is not applicable to some areas in the northern Rocky Mountains and coastal British Columbia and Alaska where deer must winter in forest, and where openings accumulate more snow than deer can tolerate (G. W. Jones 1975; Merriam 1971; Mundinger 1976). These openings may provide more summer forage, but

they can be recommended for that purpose only in climatic areas and topographic situations where they will not magnify the problem of inadequate winter range.

Slash Disposal

Disposal of slash—the residue of branches and unusable felled trees—is another aspect of silviculture that can be influential to deer. With some species—such as Engelmann spruce, whose seedlings cannot tolerate much sunlight—it can be effective to leave considerable slash for shade in order to get satisfactory regeneration (Ronco 1970). However, excessive amounts of slash can limit deer use of the site at least for a few years. On the other hand, residual slash in some areas may provide cover conditions that are more attractive to deer than are slash-cleared sites (Reynolds 1966*b*).

In forests of the north Pacific Coast region, logging slash can improve regeneration of some woody plant species and provide attractive cover conditions for deer. However, excessive slash can preclude deer access to second-growth forage resources. Photograph by W. L. Sheridan; courtesy of the United States Forest Service.

In an Oregon study, clear-cut logging of lodgepole pine, followed by piling and burning slash, caused extensive soil disturbance and damage to bitterbrush. But the net effect after the initial forage setback was stimulated growth of browse, forbs, and grasses (Edgerton et al. 1975). Slightly different floral associations develop if slash is not burned. Higher soil stability often results, benefiting both trees and wildlife (Robinson 1958).

Policy on slash disposal is dictated largely by compromises among cost, regeneration goals, erosion, water yields, insect control, and aesthetics. Better guidelines are needed for deer habitat goals if they are to be included in the compromise.

Regrowth Management

As "virgin" timber supplies near depletion, an increasing percentage of forest will come under some form of sustained-yield management, and an increasing percentage of the landscape will be in intermediate stages of regrowth—the most impoverished condition as deer habitat. And more and more regrowth stands will be subjected to various management practices to accelerate timber growth rate and yield. As yet, the impact of these procedures on deer habitat has received little attention.

Some information is available from northern Arizona, where the yield of herbs and browse was related to intensity of thinning of pole-sized regrowth stands of ponderosa pine (Reynolds 1962). This is diagramed in figure 48. The yields of sedges, grasses, forbs, and aspen reproduction all were related inversely to density of the second-growth pine as measured by basal area. (Basal area is the sum of the cross-sectional areas, at breast height, of the trunks of all the trees in the stand.) Sanitation logging of mixed conifer forest in northeastern Oregon, to remove diseased trees and encourage regeneration, resulted in a range of crown-cover densities (Young et al. 1967). Cover, current annual growth, and weight of understory shrubs (all of them deer forage species) three to four years after logging were greatest under intermediate crown-cover densities (fig. 49).

Forage improvements from thinning will vary, of course, with the original and final tree densities, which also may be expected to vary with forest type and climate. In Arizona it was necessary to thin ponderosa pine from high

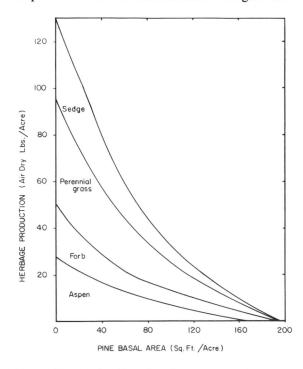

Figure 48. Relationship of understory vegetation and basal area of pole-sized ponderosa pine, northern Arizona (after Reynolds 1962).

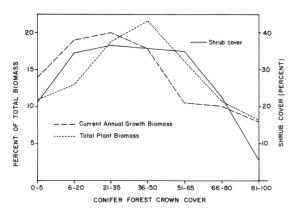

Figure 49. Relationship of shrub biomass and cover to mixed-conifer canopy cover three to four years after sanitation logging, northwestern Oregon (after Young et al. 1967). The shrubs were mainly ninebark, ocean spray, snowberry, rose, and huckleberry.

densities to less than 6.5 square meters (70 square feet) of basal area to get appreciable increases in herbage (Clary and Ffolliott 1966). Currie et al. (1977), Edgerton (1972), and Pearson (1968) also treated relationships between forest thinning and deer habitat. It remains a rather ambiguous subject, however.

Insect and Disease Control

Increasingly intensive timber management also will involve more intensive control of insect, parasite, and disease infestations. Stands decimated by insects or disease may result in conditions transiently favorable to deer (Yeager and Riordan 1953). On the other hand, windthrow in dead stands can create a tangle that may be impenetrable to deer for decades. Prevention of epidemics, and salvage sales to clean up such sites and prepare for reforestation, seem to be preferable alternatives for deer habitat.

Broad application of insecticides generally is the most efficient, if not politically feasible, means of insect control in forest. Potential effects of insecticides on deer have not been studied in any depth. Although DDT, for example, would be expected to concentrate in deer body fat and possibly be transmitted farther along the food chain, levels required to affect deer directly are much higher than those used in field applications (Schwartz et al. 1973).

Forest Fertilization

That silviculturists are more than tree farmers is apparent as one reads the proceedings of the symposium Forest Fertilization (Northeastern Forest and Range Experiment Station 1973). The subjects covered included limnological effects, stream flow, urban forestry, recreational developments, general environmental effects, and wildlife habitat as well as growing timber. On that occasion Behrend (1973) reviewed much of the scant literature pertaining to deer habitat.

So far, nitrogen has proved the most effective elemental fertilizer in stimulating growth and increasing protein content and palatability of deer forage. Other researchers—including Abell and Gilbert (1974), Curlin (1962), and Dressler and Wood (1976)—have extended those findings. Application of nitrogen seems to have been conceptualized in two ways: improving the nutrition of deer, and attracting deer away from areas where they threaten tree crops. As for the first, the effect is diluted by the fact that improved nutrition occurs during the growing season, when there already is an abundance of palatable and nutritious forage. The second application has not proved effective (see chap. 11, part 3). However, the potential value of nitrogen fertilizers in forest management has not been studied exhaustively. If the cost of wildlife habitat fertilization can be rationalized when there is a shortage of fertilizer for human food crops, the subject might be pursued. However, human wastes appear to have a significant potential as forest fertilizers (Gagnon 1973; Dressler and Wood 1976). If, in future intensive forest management, fertilization is a common practice, the major effect on deer probably will be through the effect on timber-stand development, because it can be economically effective for that purpose if not for improvement of the nutritional welfare of deer. Without additional management practices such as thinning, however, the effect may only be the acceleration of growth of even-aged stands with inherently low carrying capacity for deer.

SILVICULTURE FOR WILDLIFE

Silviculture has often been practiced for purposes other than growing timber. For centuries, private forests in Europe have been managed primarily for game animals. In western North America, knowledge of management of non-commercial forests or tree species is developing slowly.

McCulloch et al. (1965) and Reynolds et al. (1970) recommended ways to manage Gambel oak for the benefit of deer and other wildlife in the Southwest. Management of spruce/birch forest on the Kenai Moose Range in Alaska is designed specifically to benefit moose. Numerous methods have been proposed for managing aspen stands to enhance deer habitat in the West (Gruell and Loope 1974; J. R. Jones 1975; Hilton and Bailey 1974; Patton and Avant 1970; Reynolds 1969*b*); for the most part, fire and cutting are used to stimulate sprouting and increase the volume of available browse. The extensive technology for managing juniper/piñon pygmy forests (see chap. 10, part 2) for watershed, livestock, and wildlife also qualifies as silviculture.

Both prescribed burns and unregulated wildfires are becoming standard tools for obtaining a more natural admixture of habitat types in western national forests and parks in the United States (Barney 1975). To accelerate

Creation of openings by prescribed burning is a widely used method of manipulating habitat for wildlife in United States national parks and forests. Photograph by R. D. Daigle; courtesy of the United States Forest Service.

development of open, parklike forests of giant sequoia in the University of California's Whitaker's Forest, which was logged in the 1870s, thickets of competing vegetation were cut, piled, and burned. This reduced the hazard of destructive wildfires and increased the abundance, nutritional quality, and use of deer forage (Lawrence and Biswell 1972).

On some sites it may be economically practical to convert from forest to another vegetational type. In the Black Hills of South Dakota, an unproductive ponderosa pine site was converted to grass/forb/shrub vegetation, creating more productive deer and livestock range and capitalizing on the small amount of poor-quality timber available in the process (Thompson and Gartner 1971).

FUTURE FOREST MANAGEMENT

Multiple-use forest management is becoming more prevalent on public lands, but if demand for wood products continues to increase along with the demand for all other commodity resources, intensive timber management also can be expected to increase. Intensive culture of industrial forest lands in the United States was estimated to be capable of increasing annual roundwood supplies by 2.6 million cubic meters (28 million cubic feet) in the North, 17.1 million cubic meters (184 million cubic feet) in the South, 1.8 million cubic meters (19 million cubic feet) in the Rocky Mountain region, and 27.3 million cubic meters (294 million cubic feet) on the Pacific Coast. By 1985 this would represent an average of 14 percent above the 1970 level (DeBell et al. 1977). If applied on public lands, too, the payoff in timber yield would be of great economic significance.

However, in the Multiple Use–Sustained Yield Act of 1960, the Congress of the United States directed that the national forests be administered for a sustained yield of timber, range forage, water, fish, wildlife, and outdoor recreation, making it implicit that not all of the land would be managed for a maximum yield of one product. In the Forest and Rangeland Renewable Resources Planning Act of 1974 and its amendment, the National Forest Management Act of 1976, the Congress put greater emphasis on maintaining a high level of timber production in perpetuity, but still with the caveat that soil, watershed, fish, wildlife, recreation, and aesthetic resources be protected in the process.

The latter two acts did not abrogate the charge of the Multiple Use–Sustained Yield Act for management to "best meet the needs of the American people" by providing that "some land will be used for less than all of the resources" and "not necessarily [for] the combination of uses that will give the greatest dollar return or the greatest unit output" (PL 86–515, 74 Stat. 215, 16 USC [Sec. 4(a)]:528–31).

Certainly, in many forested areas, deer will be a secondary resource priority. If timber yield is to be maximized, available sunlight, soil, water, and nutrients cannot be used most efficiently for growing herbs and shrubs for deer at the expense of tree growth. Heavy stocking during early stages of regeneration

may permit trees to overcome competition from other vegetation more readily. But, as the stocked trees develop, their growth will be slowed by competition among themselves. Thinning can stimulate growth of remaining trees and result in a larger increment of wood per unit of time, earlier attainment of harvestable size, and, at the proper level, maximum volume yield per unit area per rotation. In single-purpose "timber forestry," this ideal leaves little space for deer forage at any time during the rotation.

Overmature natural stands do not fit that ideal. Growth declines or stops, and death results in scattered openings from disease, insect and mammal attacks, windthrow, and old age. Herbs and shrubs can capitalize on these opportunities, resulting in more forage and, presumably, a more favorable complex of cover for deer, but decreased timber yield. Likewise, holding a regenerating stand in an early stage of succession may be beneficial to deer but is contrary to efficient timber production. If

Uneven-aged climax forest is an important element of Sitka black-tailed deer habitat. Photograph courtesy of the United States Forest Service.

Even-aged regrowth stands in north coastal rain forests produce impoverished deer habitat, even when the trees are mature from the standpoint of timber yield. Photograph by Ian McTaggart Cowan.

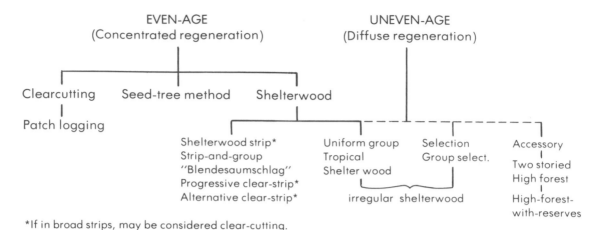

Figure 50. Terminology for high-forest silvicultural systems (after Ford-Robertson 1971).

compromises are to be made for deer, they must be justified by predictable and quantifiable results.

In a few decades, all commercial-quality timber lands in North America, except those specifically reserved, will have been subjected to at least their first harvest. Most will be in a stage of regrowth under some form of management. Under the clear-cutting system (clear-cutting and initiating regeneration at one time), the customary plan is to remove timber from more or less equal fractions of a management unit at the same fractions of the rotation time—for example, one-tenth of the total timber volume every ten years. Ultimately, under perpetual management, this would result in ten age classes and ten tree-deer habitat situations, which must be considered in adjusting timber management objectives to achieve deer habitat management objectives. There is theoretical flexibility in the use of clear-cutting, however. Areas can be cut smaller and more frequently, or the rotation periods can be adjusted.

Even-age management by the shelterwood system (removal of trees throughout a stand to open it for reproduction while waiting to harvest the residual mature trees), or uneven-age management by selection cutting (single trees or small groups of trees selected here and there, leaving small spots for reproduction) offer prospects for compromise. However, their potential is not yet known. Compromises among deer and timber resource management priorities and practices in most cases require knowledge not yet acquired and social decisions not yet faced.

It behooves the wildlife manager to understand the language of forest management so as to help the forest manager become an all-purpose silviculturist. A good place to start is with the terminology for silvicultural systems reviewed by Ford-Robertson (1971) and summarized for high-forest systems in figure 50. One should keep in mind that potential benefits to deer of harvesting systems, silvicultural systems, and site treatment practices may differ considerably among climates and forest types. The expertise of the silviculturist can be used to produce deer habitat as well as to grow timber. Today, with responsibility for multiple-use forest management, he seeks guidance and must obtain more precise information and increased assistance from wildlife managers. Wildlife biologists are contributing to the development of management guidelines for many of the forest communities of Canada and the United States, but much empirical testing is necessary to demonstrate whether these guidelines meet the desired goals.

Part 3. Effects of Deer on Forest Vegetation

Glenn L. Crouch
Research Wildlife Biologist
United States Forest Service
Fort Collins, Colorado

CONIFERS AS DEER FORAGE

As a class, conifers have been considered unimportant deer foods because in many areas they are browsed to noticeable extent only during periods of forage scarcity. Yet, wherever they occur in blacktail or mule deer ranges, conifers are common components of deer diets. The list of species known to be used by mule and black-tailed deer is extensive (table 68). In certain seasons and areas, some are preferred foods even when there is an abundance of other forage. This is especially true of Douglas fir.

Essential oils in conifer needles inhibit overall microbial fermentation in the rumen of deer and may be the major factor causing low palatability and digestibility (Oh et al. 1970). Nevertheless, deer can ingest moderate quantities safely when the intake is mixed with other forage. In addition, variations in chemical composition among conifer genotypes can account for differences in palatability and use by deer (Dimock et al. 1976; Radwan 1972).

Two western conifers—Douglas fir and ponderosa pine—currently are of major economic importance for commercial timber. They can be browsed heavily by deer. Browsing of other tree species seldom is considered a silvicultural problem.

Browsing damage to trees occurs throughout the West, in all seasons. However, where browsing damage is severe enough to affect reforestation economically, browsing usually is seasonal (Brown 1961; Browning and Lauppe 1964; Crouch 1968a, b; Hines 1973). Browsing of this magnitude in interior forests normally occurs in autumn and winter. In the Douglas fir region, deer browse on trees during both dormant and growing seasons (Crouch 1969b).

In interior forests, heavy use in the dormant season often is associated with food shortages. Such use is most apparent in severe winters when deer are concentrated on limited areas, but it is not a widespread problem. Mule deer generally winter below elevations of good timber productivity, in areas where reforestation efforts are minimal. However, browsing in the dormant season also occurs during autumn and spring migrations, when deer pass through tree plantations. In central Oregon, efforts to reestablish forests in brushlands have been impeded by deer moving from summer range in the Cascade Mountains to wintering areas on the desert fringe (Crouch 1969a; Frewing 1968). A similar pattern has been observed on migration routes of deer that summer in southern Oregon and winter on shrub ranges in northern California (Salwasser 1976). This problem may become more widespread as timber management intensifies in interior forests of the West.

The seasonal deer distribution pattern is more complicated in the Douglas fir region, where some black-tailed deer are migratory

Table 68. Conifers Known to Be Used as Food by Mule and Black-tailed Deer

Species and Subspecies	Source
Cedar	
incense[a]	6, 7
western red[a]	2, 4
Douglas fir[a]	2, 3, 4, 6
Fir	
grand[a]	2, 4
subalpine[a]	6
white[a]	6, 7
Hemlock, western[a]	2, 4
Juniper	
alligator	6, 9
California	7
common	6
creeping	6
one-seeded	8
Rocky Mountain	4
Utah	9
western	6
Larch, western[a]	5
Pine	
Digger	7
jack	6
limber	6
lodgepole	4, 7
piñon	1, 9
ponderosa[a]	7, 9
scotch	6
western white[a]	4
whitebark	6
Redwood	3
Spruce	
Engelmann[a]	6
Sitka[a]	2
Yew, Pacific	2, 4

Sources: 1, Anderson et al. (1965); 2, Brown (1961); 3, Browning and Lauppe (1964); 4, Cowan (1945b); 5, Crouch (pers. observations); 6, Kufeld et al. (1973); 7, Leach and Hiehle (1957); 8, McCulloch (1973); 9, Neff (1974).
[a] Important western timber species or subspecies.

and others are nonmigratory. Many spend summer high in mountains and move downward in autumn to middle and lower elevations, where regenerating clear-cuts become favored wintering grounds. There, deer may browse young trees throughout winter. However, this browsing intensifies just after budburst, before and during migration back to summer range (Crouch 1968*a,b;* 1969*a*). Other blacktail populations do not migrate but spend their entire lives on small home ranges in Douglas fir forests. Though conifers are available to them year-round, use usually is limited to the period of new growth in spring, or in winter when green feed is scarce (Browning and Lauppe 1964; Crouch 1968*a,b*).

Because all forest management practices influence the composition and abundance of vegetation, each affects deer use of regenerating trees in some way. Practices that encourage growth of deer populations also can encourage deer damage.

Although seasonal patterns of use appear to be stable throughout most of the Douglas fir region (table 69), the amount of browsing may not be consistent from year to year. As discussed by Hines (1973), several environmental factors—including number of deer, forage availability, and amount and persistence of snow cover—can cause variations in deer use of Douglas fir.

Seasonal use of ponderosa pine is less well documented. In Colorado, the number of bites taken by tame deer in April and October exceeded the number taken in summer; other periods were not sampled (Currie et al. 1977). In Arizona, ponderosa pine was browsed predominately in winter, with mostly incidental use at other times (Neff 1974). Ponderosa pine

Table 69. Seasons of Greatest Use of Douglas Fir Browse by Black-tailed Deer

Area	Season(s)	Reference
California	Spring	California Wildlife Investigations Laboratory (n.d.)
Oregon Coast Range	Spring and winter	Crouch (1969*a*)
Oregon Coast Range	Winter	Hines (1973)
Washington	Midwinter and spring	Brown (1961)
Vancouver Island, British Columbia	Autumn, winter, and spring	Cowan (1945*b*); Gates (1968)

Douglas fir may be either seasonally important browse or a valuable crop that is damaged by black-tailed deer, depending on management objectives in particular forests. Photograph by Guy E. Connolly.

appears prominently in mule deer diets in many areas (see Kufeld et al. 1973), and, though such use has resulted in forest damage in some localities, it is not a widespread economic problem (Heidmann 1972).

EFFECTS OF BROWSING

Tree Damage

Deer browsing may kill trees, but more often it slows tree growth. When enough trees are killed to bring stocking rates and distribution below established silvicultural standards, or when growth of a stand falls below these standards, the stand is considered damaged. Most mortality of planted seedlings occurs within one or two years after planting (Black et al. 1969; Hines 1973; Crouch, pers. observations). Except on sites that are difficult to reforest even without interference from deer, direct mortality seldom is extensive.

Growth retardation is a more general and serious effect, particularly when shoots are browsed year after year. In some stands it may

extend the rotation age. Even one or two years of this terminal browsing is detrimental where trees can be overtopped or otherwise overwhelmed by competing vegetation. Repeated browsing also may keep leaders within reach of small mammals so that deer use, although not important by itself, is the initial cause of severe damage. Adverse effects on individual seedlings usually are less severe in coastal forests than in the interior, where conditions for seedling survival and growth are less favorable.

Although degree of damage to young Douglas fir may not be closely related to the amounts eaten, retardation of seedling growth and in some cases mortality of young trees from terminal browsing is well documented (Black et al. 1969; Browning and Lauppe 1964; Crouch 1966a; Crouch and Paulsen 1968; Hines 1973; Roy 1960). On the other hand, removing one or two lateral shoots from a vigorously growing tree, transplant, or larger seedling probably has little effect on its survival and growth. While there is considerable information on short-term effects of browsing on Douglas fir, virtually nothing is known about the consequences of browsing at an early age to

Black-tailed deer on a cutover portion of a Douglas fir tree farm. The primary effect of deer browsing on conifers is retardation of the trees' growth, and the most extensive damage is caused to first- and second-year seedlings. Photograph courtesy of the Weyerhaueser Company.

the condition of the same tree forty, sixty, or one hundred years later, or about the effect on its ultimate timber yield.

Economic Effects

Deer damage to forest stands in the West since the early 1900s has been documented. Munger (1943) included deer as a damage factor on Douglas fir plantations installed in 1915 in Oregon and Washington. Stahelin (1941) mentioned deer damage in a summary of thirty-five years of tree planting in Colorado, and Bates (1927) noted deer damage to ponderosa pine in that state.

Interior Forests

From Arizona there are reports of browse damage to ponderosa pine (Pearson 1950; Schubert et al. 1970), Douglas fir, and corkbark fir and of slight damage to Engelmann spruce or blue spruce (Jones 1967). Heidmann (1972) surveyed national forests in the Southwest and obtained reports of damage by deer and elk on 243 hectares (600 acres) in Arizona and 80,940 hectares (200,000 acres) in New Mexico. He concluded that it was not a matter of economic concern.

Heavy damage to ponderosa pine and Douglas fir by white-tailed deer on winter ranges in northern Montana was reported (Adams 1949; Neils et al. 1955), but no mention was made of damage by mule deer. Foiles and Curtis (1973), Halls (1970), and Shearer and Schmidt (1970) briefly described deer browsing on Douglas fir and ponderosa pine in the northern Rockies. Boldt and Van Deusen (1974) discounted deer browsing as having a serious effect on ponderosa pine in the Black Hills of South Dakota.

There was an early report of deer damage to planted conifers from one area in southern California (True 1932). Since then, damage has been observed in nearly every forested area of the state, with the major species affected being ponderosa pine and white fir. In eastern Oregon and Washington, damage to ponderosa pine is fairly common (Black et al. 1969; Crouch 1969*b*; Driscoll 1963). Although damage to other species is not recorded, I have observed it on grand fir and western larch in the Blue Mountains of Oregon and Washington, and on white fir and lodgepole pine in central Oregon.

Coastal Forests

Forests dominated by Douglas fir, extending along and west of the crest of the Cascade Range from northern California into British Columbia, constitute the most productive timber region of the West. Douglas fir is the most important timber species and the species for which deer damage is the greatest cause of concern. Much of the timberland is privately owned and is intensively managed for maximum yield. Public forests are extensive and also are subjected to increasingly intensive timber management.

Douglas fir is harvested mainly by clear-cutting and is regenerated by planting with nursery-grown stock. Deer are attracted to clear-cuts, and Douglas fir is an acceptable and sometimes preferred forage species. This situation invites browsing of sufficient intensity to influence forest regeneration in many areas.

Relatively few acres are managed by systems that rely on natural regeneration, and even shelterwood cuttings may be underplanted to assure reforestation. In California, damage by animals—primarily deer—reportedly was most extensive in partially cut stands (Dimock and Black 1969). Some lands still are seeded, but this practice is being discontinued because of the uncertainty of success, slowness of early growth, and lack of stocking control. There are tens of thousands of hectares of unstocked lands resulting from past wildfires or reforestation failures. Efforts to restock these lands are accelerating rapidly.

The extent of damage by all kinds of animals on public and private lands in West Coast states, summarized by Dimock and Black (1969), ranged from a high in California of 56 percent of stocked areas on industrial lands and 61 percent on national forest lands to a low of 10 percent of plantations on state lands in Oregon. Deer were major causes of this damage.

Although many researchers have discussed the adverse effect of deer on reforestation in the West, assessments have not been substantiated by convincing quantification. Likewise, the quality of estimates of potential economic impact needs improvement if deer damage is as serious as suggested. These deficiencies probably are attributable to diverse ownership of the land, varying management objectives, public ownership of deer regardless of land ownership, and the resulting multiplicity of goals. Similar on-the-ground inspections, or even the same set of measurements, often result in different conclusions by different investigators.

It is certain, however, that deer in the West materially impede reforestation in some localities, especially blacktails in the Douglas fir region. It is equally apparent that complex, thorough, and costly data—needed to estimate realistically the significance of the damage either locally or generally—still are lacking. Considering other environmental factors that affect final yield of forests—most of them quite unpredictable—it seems unlikely that effects of any but the severest deer browsing ever will be accurately predicted.

DAMAGE CONTROL

European foresters struggled with problems of deer damage long before it became a concern in North America, but the problems remain far from solved. Despite the benefit of the European experiences, plus intensive research in North America over twenty to thirty years, there still is a lack of practical solutions.

Among the many animal species that inflict forest damage in North America, deer and elk are unique in that they have great aesthetic and recreational value to the public and generate appreciable economic activity. Some animals that damage forest crops, such as rodents and insects, may have to be controlled when their populations reach pest levels. But, because of economic benefits and public sentiment, it is difficult to maintain deer populations appropriate to range carrying capacities and economic tolerance ceilings.

Consequently, control efforts have concentrated on five general methods: mechanical barriers; nontoxic chemical repellents; silvicultural methods; habitat modification; and deer population control. Barriers and repellents currently are in use, but the others are only theoretical or, at best, in trial stages.

Mechanical Barriers

The kinds of cages and fences that have been used throughout the West to protect trees from deer vary widely from devices that protect only tree terminals to wire-net fences enclosing large areas. Design criteria are reviewed here only in terms of general effectiveness and cost.

Many types of fences have been used to protect forest plantings from deer. Construction methods and costs of exclosures were reported by Grisez (1959) in Pennsylvania, Blaisdell and Hubbard (1956) in California, and Halls et al. (1965) in Texas. Longhurst et al. (1962) described several types of wire fences that could be used against deer in California, but they provided no results on the effectiveness of these structures. Tierson (1969) experimented with an electric fence in the Adirondack Mountains, but he rejected its use because the control achieved was marginal and the cost was too high.

Frewing (1968) reported that fencing gave protection to eastern Oregon plantations, but installation (as much as $1,553 per kilometer: $2,500 per mile) and maintenance were costly. Mealy (1969) described the use of nylon-net fencing to bar deer from Douglas fir plantations in western Oregon. He cited costs of more than $247 per hectare ($100 per acre) to enclose a 16.2 hectare (40 acre) clear-cut where construction was relatively easy. Benefits seldom have been evaluated, and cost has proved prohibitive, so fencing rarely is used today to protect plantations. However, it still is used to exclude deer from tree nurseries, seed-production plantings, and other high-value areas.

Various forms of individual-tree barriers largely have replaced fencing to control damage by deer and other mammals. Single-tree exclosures have advantages over fences. Depending on mesh size, they can protect against several damaging animal species and do not exclude deer from the other forage available in plantations. Wire cages have been widely used (Longhurst et al. 1962; Mealy 1969; Talich and Inman 1968), but they also are expensive, often are deformed by snow, and must be removed to avoid damage as enclosed trees grow. In recent years plastic-net tubing has proved effective in protecting seedlings (Campbell 1969; Campbell and Evans 1975). These devices can be installed so that tree leaders can grow freely through the tubes until 0.9 meter (3 feet) or more in height. They can be designed to protect terminal shoots of existing trees, allowing them to grow quickly beyond the reach of deer, and to disintegrate after a given period. Net tubes have been tested

widely, and some public and private foresters currently are using them on plantations in the Pacific Northwest. Whatever method is used, enclosing individual small trees adds to the cost of timber production.

Other variations of mechanical barriers include piling logging slash or brush on and around seedlings (Grisez 1960; Talich and Inman 1968). Planting behind logs, rocks, and stumps also has been advocated (U.S. Forest Service 1968).

Repellents

A wide variety of compounds have been placed on trees to repel deer. Unfortunately, the repellency claimed for many compounds has not been substantiated by subsequent testing. The major effort to develop deer repellents in the United States was begun by the United States Fish and Wildlife Service after World War II (Besser and Welch 1959; Welch 1967). Initially, the large number of candidate chemicals submitted to the service's Denver laboratory taxed the testing facilities (Spencer 1958). By the 1970s the program was curtailed for a number of reasons, including mounting public apprehension about pesticides, more stringent requirements for registration (Evans 1974), lack of promising candidate chemicals, and costs of development versus marketing potential.

Literally thousands of chemicals were screened at the Denver laboratory during the twenty-year period (Kverno et al. 1965), with the most promising candidates tested further in cooperation with the United States Forest Service at its Olympia, Washington, laboratory (Dodge 1969). The primary focus of research was to identify an effective, environmentally acceptable, translocatable or systemic repellent that would provide year-round protection to trees by a single application.

No acceptable systemic chemicals were found, and only two relatively short-lived contact repellents emerged from the program. The two compounds, currently in limited use on western forests, are TMTD (tetramethylthiuram disulfide), originally developed as a rabbit repellent (Hildreth and Brown 1955) but also effective against deer (Dodge 1969; Evans 1974), and ZAC (zinc dimethyldithiocarbamate cyclohexylamine), used in a commercial formulation known as ZIP. Both currently are registered for use on seedlings in nurseries and for application to trees in the field (Evans 1974). A new repellent, developed by the United States Fish and Wildlife Service and Weyerhaeuser (Campbell and Bullard 1972; Rochelle et al. 1974) and commercially marketed as BGR, currently is registered with the federal government and used by some landowners. (Mention of trade names does not imply endorsement by the United States Fish and Wildlife Service or Forest Service or Department of Agriculture.)

Other repellents also may be effective, registered for use, and available, but only those discussed have been applied recently in operational programs. In general, operational repellent applications have ranged from totally ineffective to moderately protective. Effectiveness depends on many factors including timing, rate and method of application, season and length of exposure to deer, and, perhaps most important, the interest of deer in feeding on seedlings compared with feeding on other forage.

Silvicultural Practices

In the West, economic damage by deer occurs primarily in the Douglas fir region, where, except for wildfires, logging is the major forerunner of deer damage. Clear-cutting is the practice most often associated with subsequent browse damage (Crouch 1969b; Mitchell 1950), though heavy selection logging in northern California also has resulted in severe browsing problems on regenerating trees (California Pest Control Action Council 1964).

There are indications that deer use of openings decreases with distance from cover (see chap. 11, part 2). If this is correct then clear-cutting larger areas might be useful in alleviating browsing on seedlings. Cutting in circular blocks also should be beneficial because less "edge" would be created per unit area of commercial forest lands, minimizing the area considered most attractive to deer (Leopold 1933; Patton 1975).

Adequate natural regeneration after shelterwood harvesting of Douglas fir and associated species has been observed in upper slope stands in the Oregon Cascades (Franklin 1963; Williamson 1973). Although these stands were not

Minute amounts of chemical repellents being screened by means of a choice-preference apparatus. Photograph by Dan Campbell; courtesy of the United States Fish and Wildlife Service.

subjected to deer browsing because of location, the restocking success suggests that similar results might be attained on Cascade and Coast Range sites at lower elevations. The advantage, theoretically, would be that overstory is not opened sufficiently to attract deer.

Reforesting immediately after harvest might help alleviate browsing damage in some situations, because deer use often is low initially and increases a few years after logging (Crouch 1974; Dasmann and Hines, n.d.; Gates 1968; Willms 1971). Thus seedlings would have opportunity to become well established before appreciable browsing occurred.

Cowan (1945b) showed that percentages of trees browsed decreased as numbers of trees per unit area increased on southern Vancouver Island, British Columbia. I have made similar observations in Oregon and Washington. Perhaps by initially planting more than the 988 trees per hectare (400 per acre) currently prescribed by many landowners, enough undamaged trees would remain to meet stocking requirements.

Oversized planting stock, up to 1.5 meters (5 feet) in height, may be browsed less than small seedlings (Hartwell 1973; Hines 1973), and large seedlings can withstand damage better than small stock (Newton 1973). Such findings suggest that large stock may be useful on sites that allow maximum growth potential and where damage by deer is expected.

Cowan (1945b) proposed reforesting with western hemlock in areas on Vancouver Island where deer damage Douglas fir. Others have made similar suggestions on the assumption that deer prefer Douglas fir to hemlock. However, this assumption has not been tested where equal numbers and sizes of both species were offered to deer. Moreover, Brown (1961) reported that hemlock was preferred over Douglas fir. Experiences with hemlock planting programs underway in Oregon and Washington may provide better understanding.

Natural resistance of conifers to feeding by deer was observed by Bates (1927) and by Squillace and Silen (1962). Pen tests showed that Douglas fir genotype affects feeding selection by black-tailed deer (Dimock 1974) and that properties of resistance are inherited (Dimock et al. 1976). These findings suggested that

Deer browsing on Douglas firs can be remarkably selective. Trees on either side of the biologist were of approximately the same age and appeared to be equally accessible to deer. However, the tree on the right was hedged by browsing deer and was 0.9 meter (36 inches) tall. The tree at the left was not browsed and had reached a height of 2.7 meters (106 inches). Research to permit genetic selection of browse-resistant trees for planting is in its infancy. Photograph by Guy E. Connolly.

production of inherently resistant planting stock may be possible, though not without considerable research and development.

Finally, leaving logging slash unburned may decrease browsing damage to live trees (Gockerell 1966). This also may be true for plantings in areas with greater logging debris (Crouch 1968a).

Habitat Modification

Many attempts have been made to lure deer away from young trees by providing alternate foodstuffs (Baron et al. 1966; Campbell 1974; Dasmann et al. 1967). This procedure has been tried repeatedly in Europe, but results seem to be about as variable as the number of trials reported. In the Pacific Northwest, grasses and legumes have been seeded, fertilizers and molasses applied, and browse seed sown in attempts to reduce use of young trees by deer. No reliable evaluations have come from these trials. Also, herbicide-induced vegetational changes have not reduced browsing damage by deer (Borrecco et al. 1972).

Population Reduction

Because intensity of young tree browsing by deer is closely related to number of deer per unit area (Crouch 1966b; Hines 1973), the most realistic way to alleviate deer damage may be to reduce the number of deer. Hunting has been advocated as a means of lessening damage (Mitchell 1950; Crouch 1976), but the effectiveness of deer population reduction in the West for this purpose has not been adequately evaluated. In Oregon, hunting regulations were periodically liberalized in the 1950s and early 1960s for areas where deer browsing damage was acute (Hines 1973). Long-term effects of hunts in these areas were not evaluated. More intensive measures were tried in California. There, hunting at night removed relatively large numbers of deer from small areas. Results were encouraging but inconclusive (Agrons 1964).

At present there appears to be little interest in designing and implementing hunting regulations that will protect young trees and at the same time optimize or maximize harvest of the deer production that logging promotes. Although special or extended hunting seasons are employed to protect agricultural lands in some states, little consideration is given to expanding such programs to benefit forest crops.

Justification of Damage Control

In any crop damage control program, benefits must outweigh costs. Most forest managers currently lack the field data needed to assess the economic magnitude of deer browsing losses. Also not available is information needed to differentiate deer-caused losses from those resulting from other agents. Complicating this is the fact that many areas incur damage from several animal species (Black et al. 1969; Crouch 1969b), and measures to control one can increase problems from others. Consequently, present decisions to apply controls are largely subjective, and their effectiveness seldom is appraised.

To evaluate the need for controls in a given management unit, the following information is required:

1. Data from periodic field examinations of valid samples of marked trees, from time of planting through the period when damage can occur;

2. Accurate recording of all injuries to each marked tree and correct identification of causative agents;

3. Some method to measure response of trees protected from deer but subjected to damage from other animals and environmental factors;

4. Realistic stocking and growth standards;

5. An accurate method of predicting the impact of early damage on productivity of the stand at harvest.

Each of these informational requirements is subject to great variation in interpretation. Even with identical or similar field data on browsing, stocking, and growth, the choice of assumptions and method of economic analysis can produce vastly different estimates of actual or potential losses. Flora (1968) provided an interesting and useful commentary on the intricacies of damage appraisal.

In summary, deer browse many conifers throughout the West. In some locations this causes economic losses—particularly to Douglas fir and ponderosa pine. Also, in some areas reductions in height growth of conifers are sufficient to warrant controls on deer damage. However, conclusions about the extent and ultimate effect of damage on timber crops have been influenced more by the viewpoint of landowners and appraisers than by objective interpretations of thorough data. Before the situation can be understood fully and—if a serious problem exists—deer damage to conifers must receive more than the superficial attention it has been given to date.

Chapter 12

PLAINS HABITATS

Kieth E. Severson
Research Wildlife Biologist
United States Forest Service
Tempe, Arizona

The Great Plains—a term used to describe mixed and shortgrass prairies inclusively—constitute the largest grassland ecosystem in North America, extending from southern portions of the Texas panhandle northward into central portions of Alberta, Saskatchewan, and southwestern Manitoba. Their western edge is marked by the Rocky Mountains, and their eastern edge is delineated rather ambiguously by the True (tallgrass) Prairie (approximately 98 degrees longitude) (fig. 51).

The mention of Plains connotes, in the minds of many people, a flat, grass-covered prairie. This aspect has been reinforced by stories of Indians and bison, cowboys and cattle. The Plains are predominately a grassland, but one that includes a variety of vegetational types dominated by species other than grasses. The entire region is dissected by streams. First-order drainages, sometimes no more than gentle swales, contain thickets of low-growing shrubs such as snowberry. The riparian type of vegetation in these stream bottoms increases in dominance as the moisture regime becomes more favorable. Farther downstream, both deciduous trees and taller shrubs can be found. On the mainstream floodplains, such as the Yellowstone River in Montana and the Niobrara River in Nebraska, extensive cottonwood stands are interspersed with willows.

Erosion patterns created by these drainages also have developed habitat types characterized by very steep, rough, and irregular topography, or "breaks." This has resulted in a complex of vegetational types, characteristic of the Little Missouri River in North Dakota and the Cheyenne and White rivers in South Dakota.

Geologic features (escarpments and buttes) also are scattered throughout the Great Plains. The rough topography of these features provides excellent mule deer habitat. Many areas are capped by open stands of ponderosa pine, such as the Long Pine Hills in southeastern Montana and the Pine Ridge Escarpment in eastern Wyoming and northwestern Nebraska.

Mule deer are not characteristic of the open grasslands, at least not as much as bison and pronghorn are. Instead, mule deer depend on these interspersed habitat types. Therefore, discussion of prairie and Plains mule deer habitats will delve into the not-so-obvious types in the Great Plains, while making relatively brief reference to extensive grassland associations.

HISTORICAL SKETCH
OF GREAT PLAINS DEER

Mule deer generally are not thought of as animals associated with the Great Plains. This probably is because deer were virtually absent from this region for about fifty years. During the early nineteenth century, deer apparently were very common. The journals of the Lewis and Clark expedition of 1804–06 contain many

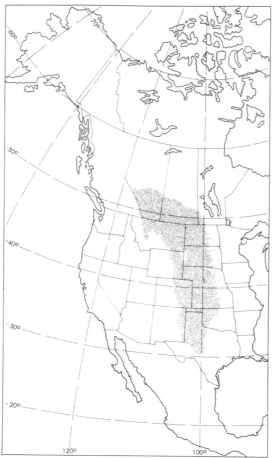

Figure 51. The Great Plains (adopted from a description by Weaver and Albertson 1956, and modifications of Küchler 1964).

grounds and are seldom found in the woodlands near the river; when they are met with in the woodlands or river bottoms and are pursued, they invariably run into the hills or open country as the Elk do. The contrary happens with the common white-tailed deer" (Cutright 1969, pp. 83–84). Cutright further elaborated that the tendency of mule deer to frequent rough country explained why explorers crossing the Dakotas did not kill many of them. He also noted that mule deer were more abundant than the journals indicate.

The history of Plains deer is not as well documented as that of bison. The few references available, however, indicate there were substantial numbers of black-tailed deer on the prairies of both Dakotas. While crossing the prairies in North Dakota with the Custer expedition to the Black Hills in 1874, naturalist George Bird Grinnell noted that "about many of the bluffs and tall buttes which we passed there were great numbers of black-tailed deer. . . . The company never suffered for lack of fresh meat" (Reiger 1972, p. 89). However, a 1914 report from the same region stated that "black-tailed mule deer were formerly found in the breaks along the Little Missouri River . . . and in the rough country north of the East Short Pines. . . . They were exterminated by 1900" (Visher 1914, p. 88). Another report stated that deer east of the Missouri River disappeared between 1875 and 1880 and that west of the Missouri, excluding the Black Hills, the deer population was near zero by 1900 (Richardson and Peterson 1974).

The latter nineteenth century apparently marked a decline in number of deer throughout the Great Plains. Low populations have been described for Alberta, Saskatchewan, North Dakota, South Dakota, and Nebraska by Krämer (1972). Mackie (1970) reported that, in the Missouri River breaks of north-central and eastern Montana, deer were abundant in 1869–80, declined in the early 1900s, and were extremely scarce in the 1920s and early 1930s. In 1955 the once-common mule deer no longer existed in Kansas. However, in 1965 they were well established in the West and expanding eastward (Krämer 1972).

The decline of Plains deer followed extirpa-

references to white-tailed or "common" deer (Cutright 1969). Similar indications of many whitetails were noted by the Astoria party in 1811 (Irving 1961) and by Audubon's expedition in 1843 (McDermott 1951).

Lewis, Clark, and Audubon saw mule deer for the first time in the vicinity of South Dakota's Big Bend country, just north of the present city of Chamberlain. However, the routes of the explorers were confined to the Missouri River, along which timbered floodplains and rough breaks were common. One of the reasons fewer mule deer were sighted was the animals' habitat preference. Lewis observed that they rarely found mule deer "in any except a rough country; they prefer the open

As seen in the 1870s, this portion of shortgrass/shrub Plains habitat (in what now is eastern Wyoming) was almost entirely covered by grama grasses and the plant winterfat. Dense stands of boxelders and cottonwood trees lined the riverbank. The site now is dominated by sagebrush. Photograph by W. H. Jackson; courtesy of the United States Soil Conservation Service.

tion of bison, which had disappeared from the northern Great Plains by 1883, and it closely paralleled the decline of pronghorn. The period 1880 to 1909 also marked settlement of the region. Once the Indian Reserve Lands between the Missouri River and the Black Hills were opened to settlement, domestic livestock was brought in. Cattle numbers in the western Dakotas reached a peak in 1884 but decreased sharply in a series of blizzards during the winter of 1886–87. There had been a severe drought the previous year, and ranges were heavily overstocked. An estimated 80–90 percent of the cattle in eastern Wyoming and eastern Montana were lost during the blizzards. Such losses were only slightly lower in the western Dakotas and Nebraska. These ranges were restocked in 1887 (Lee and Williams 1964).

Although no one is sure why deer disappeared from the prairies, it is logical to suppose that their decline started with habitat change caused by drought and overgrazing by domestic livestock. Blizzards merely hastened the decline. Ranges apparently continued to be overgrazed after the winter of 1886–87.

Homesteaders, encouraged by the Homestead Act of 1862, also began moving into the northern Great Plains in increasing numbers after 1880 and during the early 1900s. The 65 hectare (160 acre) tracts allotted by this act were not enough to sustain most families in dry regions west of the Missouri River. This was not common knowledge at the time, and the result was further habitat destruction induced by plowing of nonarable lands and intensive livestock grazing on small acreages. Disregarding John Wesley Powell's 1879 report on arid lands of the United States (Box 1978), Congress made only feeble and ineffective efforts to halt the damage. They increased the number of acres per landholder (Homestead Act of 1909 and the Stock-Raising Homestead Act of 1919), but individual property units remained inadequate (Stoddart and Smith 1943), far below the 1,036 hectares (2,560 acres) suggested by Powell. Plowing and overgrazing were not the only damaging influences to deer habitat. Early settlers also used wood wherever it was available. Although the sod shanty has captured contemporary imaginations as the typical "home on the range," many dwellings, outbuildings, corrals, and other structures were constructed of logs, which often were skidded considerable distances. "Cedar" trees (actually

Homesteaders and speculators line up in 1893 for a land rush that opened the 2.6 million hectare (6.5 million acre) Cherokee Outlet in Oklahoma. Promises of free land led to a mass invasion of the Plains and to considerable hardship and frequent failure, but not before severe damage was done to wildlife habitats and populations. Photograph courtesy of the United States Bureau of Land Management.

A farm couple in central Nebraska, 1886. Homesteaders on the Plains were forced to utilize their land to the fullest extent simply to endure from one harsh, unpredictable season to the next. Note the sod house and outbuilding, and the uses of wood undoubtedly hauled from some distance away. Photograph from the Solomon D. Butcher Collection; courtesy of the Nebraska State Historical Society.

juniper) were used as fenceposts and were so resistant to weathering that many still are cut for this purpose.

These hard-pressed settlers probably subsisted, to a large extent, on wild game. Market hunting—well documented in the case of bison—was less evident in the case of deer. However, Young (1956, p. 19) pointed out that "as the buffalo hunter was hired to supply railroad construction camps with buffalo meat, so the deer hunter was employed by steamboat companies on the upper Missouri River. . . . The carcasses were brought to the river banks where they were picked up by the steamer's tenders." Cook (1945) concluded that white-tailed deer populations on the Great Plains were greatly restricted by habitat destruction and overhunting.

The period from 1900 to the drought of the 1930s probably marked the low point for deer populations on the Great Plains. Not until the late 1930s did deer populations begin to increase to the high densities of the late 1960s and early 1970s. There is no single explanation for the increase. Mackie (1970) suggested one

of the reasons was "human depopulation." This idea is reinforced by the fact that South Dakota's population dropped by more than 50,000 persons during the drought years (Lee and Williams 1964).

Predator control increased greatly during World War II, and this probably relieved some pressure on remaining deer populations. Enactment of game laws and increased law enforcement activities certainly accounted for some increase. Development of livestock watering impoundments on the prairies was important because it allowed deer to occupy previously uninhabitable areas.

Another possibility that must be considered is that the Plains have experienced relatively favorable and stable environmental conditions since the 1930s. After "depopulation," cattle and farming operations adjusted to environmental constraints of the Great Plains. Stocking rates stabilized somewhat when private landholdings enabled subsistence or better living. Weather conditions also became and have remained favorable, with only a few short-term droughts since that time. Range conditions

With settlement of the Northern Great Plains spurred by construction of the Northern Pacific and Great Northern railroads, and with the once-vast bison herds virtually depleted by the 1880s, market hunters turned their attention to other game to supply ready markets. This market hunting camp was on the Yellowstone River near Miles City, Montana. Photograph by L. A. Huffman; courtesy of Coffrin's Old West Gallery.

therefore improved. Range condition—determined by the intensity of domestic livestock use and by drought—can be one of the most important factors affecting Plains wildlife habitats.

HABITAT TYPES

Plains habitats of mule deer are very diverse. For simplification, they are grouped here into the three major categories used by the United States Soil Conservation Service to classify range sites of the Great Plains. Each site is a unique combination of soils and climate (including microclimate) that has the potential to produce a different combination or amount of vegetation. The classification is based on topography and soils as they influence a site's ability to use rainfall to produce vegetation. The three groups are run-in sites, runoff sites, and normal sites. Because of topography and/or soil characteristics, run-in sites receive more moisture than normally falls on the site. The added moisture may run into these areas on the surface or through the soil. They generally are at the bottom of slopes, in swales, or near major streams that provide additional moisture through subirrigation. Runoff sites have slopes or soil characteristics that limit infiltration. Precipitation is lost to evaporation or by runoff, usually to run-in sites, and is not available for vegetational growth. Normal sites have fairly deep, well-developed soils and are on relatively level ground. Precipitation that falls on normal sites is available directly for plant growth. Normal sites are the typical grassland areas of the Great Plains, and they are subdivided by soil texture.

Run-in Sites

Shrubby Draws

Extreme upper ends of Great Plains streams, the first-order drainages, may be nothing more than shallow depressions in nearly level grasslands. Clones of western snowberry characterize such draws. As second-order drainages

form and a more favorable moisture regime develops, other shrubs—such as silvery buffaloberry, common chokecherry, common snowberry, golden currant, and several species of rose—become prevalent and form dense thickets that serve as a summer shrub cover type for both mule and white-tailed deer. This pattern is noticeable from north-central Montana (Dusek 1971) and the southern portions of Alberta and Saskatchewan south to Oklahoma. Silvery buffaloberry often is the sole dominant, and its distribution is so extensive that Carpenter (1940) considered it ecologically important in his analysis of the grassland biome in the Dakotas, Nebraska, and Kansas. Its distribution, however, becomes negligible in Oklahoma and western Texas. Even though these "brushy" draws may be miles from a major stream, they also are favored by mule deer in Kansas (W. C. Peabody, pers. comm., 1976).

Hardwood Draws

When moisture conditions are optimal, one of the mainstay habitat types in the Plains develops. Described as "woody" or "hardwood" draws, these are characterized by an overstory of trees common to the eastern deciduous forest ecosystem, primarily green ash, American elm, boxelder, and hackberry.

Hardwood draws exhibit considerable local variability in species composition (Nelson 1961) and even greater variability over their regional distribution from North Dakota to Oklahoma. In north-central Montana, both Mackie (1970) and Dusek (1971), working in the Missouri River breaks and in the Milk River area, respectively, described deciduous shrub draws similar to those previously mentioned, but neither mentioned draws dominated by deciduous trees. Mackie (1970) described an evergreen ponderosa pine/Rocky Mountain juniper type that apparently supplants the deciduous type on wet footslopes and in draws. Also, the hardwood draw is virtually absent in eastern portions of Wyoming and Colorado. In eastern Montana, the western Dakotas, Nebraska, and Kansas, however, this habitat type is extremely important to both mule and white-tailed deer.

In eastern Montana and western North Dakota, green ash generally is the dominant tree. American elm, bur oak, quaking aspen, and paper birch also are found. Farther south, oak, aspen, and birch disappear, leaving green ash as the primary dominant, with scattered elms and boxelders. Draws in southeastern Montana also contain occasional stands of ponderosa pine (Jonas 1966).

Bur oak is abundant in draws bordering the Black Hills in South Dakota and the Bear Lodge Mountains in Wyoming. Although it is scarce immediately east of this region, bur oak again becomes abundant in the west-central Dakotas and Nebraska. Eastward into prairie regions of the Dakotas, Nebraska, and Kansas, American elm increases in proportionate density. In woody stands leading into the Cheyenne River in South Dakota, some hardwood draws are completely dominated by American elm, whereas others in the same vicinity are almost entirely green ash. Most draws contain about equal mixtures of these species (Severson, pers. files). Boxelder and hackberry predominate farther east. Draws in western Nebraska have species compositions similar to those in South Dakota (Nixson 1967). Green ash dominates in comparable sites in west-central Kansas, though American elm and hackberry generally are larger (Griswold 1942). All three species become less abundant farther west (Gesink et al. 1968).

Hardwood trees may pinch out entirely down a draw and then reappear as a thin band in the middle and on the north sides of the drainage. A True Prairie type dominated by big bluestem, prairie cordgrass, or a shrub community may occupy the opening.

Density of trees varies within such draws. Nelson (1961) found mature tree densities to be from 351 to 855 stems per hectare (142–346 per acre) in North Dakota. South Dakota draws contained from 59 to 603 mature trees per hectare (24–244 per acre) (Severson, pers. files). The trees generally are smaller than their eastern counterparts. Mature green ash, forty to eighty years old, seldom are higher than 10.7 meters (35 feet) and are dense and shrubby,

A draw in western South Dakota dominated by deciduous trees and shrubs. Note the first-order drainages and swales dominated by western snowberry *(A)*; farther downstream the bottoms contain buffaloberry *(B)*; and still farther downstream are deciduous trees, primarily green ash and American elm *(C)*. Photograph by Kieth E. Severson; courtesy of the United States Forest Service.

forming rather compact crowns (Nelson 1961).

Herbaceous components of the understory are complex because they contain species from the eastern deciduous forest as well as from surrounding prairies. Grasses include big bluestem and switchgrass—elements of the True Prairie—as well as introduced Kentucky bluegrass, which provides green growth in early spring. Important forbs include asters, bluebell, scarlet gaura, wild licorice, several fleabanes, introduced sweetclover, and several violets.

Shrub understory includes previously described species occurring on the shrub-dominated sites. Western snowberry is generally most abundant in northern areas where, because of its clonal form of growth, it may reach densities of more than 94,000 stems per hectare (38,000 per acre). Woods rose, another low-growing shrub, often is mixed with snowberry and reaches densities of 24,700–27,200 stems per hectare (10,000–11,000 per acre). Taller-growing shrubs such as chokecherry, serviceberry, American plum, and hawthorn, although far less abundant, provide better cover for deer (Nelson 1961; Severson, pers. files). Silvery buffaloberry more often dominates at the edges of the hardwood draws rather than within them (Nelson 1961; Hladek 1971). Sumacs, such as skunkbush sumac, poison ivy, and smooth sumac, are well represented in Kansas draws. Clove currant and prairie rose also are abundant (Hubbard 1968).

Floodplains

Many of the larger streams within the Great Plains have developed extensive floodplains that are remarkably similar, from the Canadian provinces to Kansas. The dominant tree is eastern cottonwood. There may be some confusion about the name of this subspecies because many investigators refer to it as plains cottonwood. However, Stephens (1973) considered the western variety of eastern cottonwood to be the same as plains cottonwood.

Floodplains of many Great Plains streams and rivers are geologically unstable. Water channels change constantly because of erosion on the downstream side of meanders and deposition on the upstream side. This creates a unique successional change involving eastern cottonwood. This species reproduces only on sunny, moist, and bare areas, such as those created by recent alluvial deposits (Nelson 1961). Dense thickets of seedlings and saplings can be found on sandbars. In areas of older alluvium, thin stands of large cottonwoods can be found, sometimes arranged along the line of deposition so precisely that they appear to have been planted. Farther back from the river, very old cottonwoods (80–150 years) reach heights of 21.3 meters (70 feet). No reproduction is evident in such older stands and, with the death of older trees, dominance of eastern cottonwood declines (Nelson 1961).

In the eastern and central Great Plains, green ash, American elm, hackberry, and boxelder are common associates of cottonwood. The number of native woody trees decreases farther west. In northeastern Colorado, along the South Platte River, only cottonwood, peachleaf willow, and a few small, scattered boxelders occur (Crouch 1961). Farther south, on the Arkansas River in southwestern Kansas, cottonwood was reported to be dominant on the floodplain but decreased to the west (Gesink et al. 1968). Cottonwood was the only tree found in western portions of the study area, on the Colorado/Kansas line.

Several willow species are common associates of eastern cottonwood on floodplains, particularly on more recent alluvium. Allen (1968) reported peachleaf willow, sandbar willow, Mackenzie willow, and Bebb willow to be common in Montana. The most common species on floodplains in North Dakota were peachleaf willow, heart-leaved willow, and sandbar willow (Nelson 1961). Peachleaf willow occurs as a tree, whereas the others form dense brush thickets.

Although there are species changes from north to south and east to west, willows are found consistently throughout the Great Plains. Peachleaf willow was reported to persist from the Canadian provinces southward into Kansas (Stephens 1973).

Salt cedar—a willowlike shrub—was introduced to North America from Eurasia in the mid-1800s and has spread along stream courses in semiarid and arid portions of the continent. Salt cedar is very rare on the northern Great Plains, occurring only sparsely in Nebraska and northeastern Colorado, but it becomes the predominant shrub along floodplains in Kansas, Oklahoma, southern Colorado, Texas, and New Mexico. In Kansas, salt cedar becomes more abundant along the Arkansas River from east to west, composing about 94 percent of vegetational cover in the western portions (Gesink et al. 1968).

A shrub type dominated by silver sagebrush occurs on older terraces in floodplains. Western snowberry is abundant, particularly in the Dakotas and northwestern Nebraska. Skunk and rubber rabbitbrush are common associates. Nelson (1961) reported that many silver sagebrush types contained evidence of previous cottonwood domination.

Floodplains in the Texas Panhandle and eastern New Mexico contain plants from the desert grasslands as well as from the Great Plains. Canyon bottom flats with intermittent streams contain mesquite, four-winged saltbush, forestiera, soapberry, and many other shrubs. Forbs and grasses also are common. Along permanent streams, eastern cottonwood still is dominant. Hackberry, salt cedar, four-winged saltbush, and soapberry also occur (Riskind 1976).

Runoff Sites

The physiography of runoff sites varies considerably. Some are dominated by grasses, others by shrubs, and others by trees. Runoff sites generally are associated with rough topography of varying steepness and with shallow or impervious soils. In the "river breaks" country of the Great Plains, a great variety of runoff sites can be found within a relatively small area.

North-facing Slopes

North-facing slopes provide some of the best cover for mule deer in the Plains. The dominant vegetation varies from Canada to Texas, but the aspect is generally a coniferous or evergreen type. North slopes, although identified as runoff sites due to steep topography, maintain vegetational types characteristic of wetter areas because of their exposure. Even though precipitation is lost via runoff, cooler temperatures resulting from the northern exposure reduce evapotranspiration.

In the Missouri River breaks of north-central Montana, north-facing slopes are dominated by Douglas fir and Rocky Mountain juniper. Ponderosa pine may be present in several stages but is gradually replaced by Douglas fir. Western snowberry is a common understory associate. Chokecherry, silver sagebrush, and green rabbitbrush frequently occur in more open or burned stands (Mackie 1970).

Douglas fir becomes less important farther east. Ponderosa pine and Rocky Mountain juniper, however, maintain dominance on these sites in the western Dakotas, eastern Wyoming, and western Nebraska.

The Long Pine Hills of southeastern Montana rise 366 meters (1,200 feet) above the surrounding plains. Ponderosa pine covers about 40 percent of the area and is best represented on north- and east-facing slopes, although gallery forests may extend into prairies as far as 1.6 kilometers (1 mile) along drainageways (Jonas 1966), occupying the same kinds of sites as hardwood types farther east. Other ridges or relict geological tables that are similar include the Cave Hills and Slim Buttes in South Dakota and the Pine Bluffs region of southeastern Wyoming.

The Pine Ridge Escarpment is most conspicuous in northwestern Nebraska. This north-facing escarpment extends from eastern Wyoming through northwestern Nebraska, then northeastward into South Dakota, but it soon turns east, paralleling the White River but some distance south of it. Ponderosa pine is dominant on these slopes (Weaver and Albertson 1956). Chokecherry and serviceberry are the predominant shrubs in the understory (Nixson 1967).

Rocky Mountain juniper is the most prevalent evergreen found on north-facing slopes in the northern half of the Great Plains. Eastern red cedar also occurs throughout the Plains. Van Haverbeke (1968) concluded that the entire population within the Missouri River basin is of hybrid origin (Rocky Mountain juniper × eastern red cedar), with neither parental type found. This hybrid will be referred to as Rocky Mountain juniper unless otherwise stated.

Rocky Mountain juniper can be found on open, exposed bluffs, rocky points, and southern exposures, but it does best along ravines and in sheltered canyons and other protected areas (Van Haverbeke 1968). In the Great Plains it occurs primarily on moderate to steep north-facing slopes with little soil development (Ralston 1960; Nelson 1961). In the northern areas (north-central Montana) it can be found mixed with ponderosa pine on south-facing slopes.

Rocky Mountain juniper on north slopes, and skunkbush sumac plus yucca on south-facing slopes—Cheyenne River breaks, South Dakota. Photograph by Kieth E. Severson; courtesy of the United States Forest Service.

Ridges and knolls often protrude from these north-facing slopes, breaking the stand into several facets. Stands in South Dakota generally are thin near the tops of the slopes, with trees confined to surface microdrainages. Downslope, juniper forms a dense, continuous stand that borders a hardwood or shrub draw. Nelson (1961) described this as the most heterogeneous type of woody vegetation in the North Dakota badlands. In that area, density of juniper was 1,216 to 4,485 trees per hectare (492–1,815 per acre) (Ralston 1960; Nelson 1961). Juniper stands in South Dakota exhibited densities of 1,690–2,152 trees per hectare (684–871 per acre) (Severson, pers. files).

Ralston (1960) and Nelson (1961) reported the most common shrubs in juniper understory to be chokecherry, skunkbush sumac, common juniper, western snowberry, and Woods rose. In South Dakota, western snowberry is the dominant shrub, and common associates are skunkbush sumac, poison ivy, chokecherry, and Woods rose.

Herbaceous vegetation is related inversely to juniper densities. Thick juniper stands contain very few grasses and forbs, whereas other less dense stands contain a variety of herbaceous species, notably western wheatgrass, little bluestem, and side oats grama.

Sanford (1970) described a skunkbush sumac type on north slopes in the Little Missouri River breaks that he considered a possible transition to juniper types described by Nelson (1961). Skunkbush sumac densities were highest at midslope and lowest at the top and bottom of slopes. Herbaceous species were similar to those reported from juniper stands.

In the northern parts of its range, silvery buffaloberry often will form scattered clumps on northern exposures with gradual slopes. These clumps generally are surrounded by mixed prairie grasslands dominated by little bluestem (Hladek 1971).

In the southern Plains (Texas and New Mexico), Rocky Mountain juniper is abundant locally but is replaced in other areas by one-seeded juniper. Associate species in this area include mountain mahogany, hop tree, and Havard oak (Riskind 1976).

South-facing Slopes

South-facing slopes are the drier sites in the Great Plains because of moisture loss through runoff and increased insolation. Farther north, however, a relatively dry type may be dominated by trees. As described by Mackie (1970), the Missouri River breaks in north-central Montana have south- and west-facing slopes dominated by ponderosa pine and Rocky Mountain juniper. Near the ridgetops, bluebunch wheatgrass replaces juniper. Stands of pine are never very dense, and at higher elevations there may be only scattered pines, giving a savannalike appearance. Rocky Mountain juniper forms dense thickets on lower west-facing slopes, but more open stands characterize southern exposures. To the southeast, tree densities diminish on south-slope habitats, although occasional scattered Rocky Mountain junipers may be found on small, isolated run-in sites and perched water tables.

Skunkbush sumac is distributed throughout the Plains. It is found particularly on sites with shallow or coarse-textured soils. Although this species occurs as a subdominant or only occa-sionally on other sites, it is the primary shrub on steep south-facing slopes from North Dakota southward.

Martin (1972) and Sanford (1970) reported lower densities of skunkbush on south-facing slopes than on north-facing exposures in Montana and North Dakota. Silver sagebrush and western snowberry were common associate shrubs.

Little soapweed and leadplant amorpha often are abundant on south-facing slopes throughout the Great Plains, particularly on sandy soils and in association with prairie sand reed.

Dry exposures in the Texas Panhandle are characterized by deciduous chaparral and include many species from the more southern desert grasslands. Skunkbush sumac is present, and among many other species are mesquite, dalea, and littleleaf sumac (Riskind 1976).

Badlands

Badlands are locally common throughout the region, characterized by steeply sloping, rough, broken areas that are devoid of plant cover or

Badlands in western South Dakota. Barren areas are indicated by *(A)*, grassed benches *(B)*, and little bluestem-dominated alluvium *(C)*. Photo by Kieth E. Severson; courtesy of the United States Forest Service.

only sparsely vegetated. Badland soils consist of soft shales, sandstones, or chalkrock with no profile development. Surface erosion is active and virtually uncontrollable in many areas. Clay slopes may have scattered shrubs consisting primarily of rabbitbrush, saltbush, and broom snakeweed.

Flat, tablelike benches dominated by grasses are common in the badlands. Western wheatgrass, blue grama, buffalograss, and prickly pear are the most common species. Stabilized alluvium at the base of such benches supports little bluestem and a great variety of forbs.

The most extensive badland areas in the Great Plains occur along the Little Missouri River in North Dakota and along the White River in northwestern Nebraska and South Dakota. Smaller badland types are associated with escarpments and buttes scattered throughout the Plains.

Normal Sites

Normal sites are those dominated by grasses and forbs that are perpetuated by the prevailing climate and give a grassland aspect to Great Plains. Uplands in the northwestern portions (southern Alberta, southwestern Saskatchewan, eastern Montana, and eastern Wyoming) are dominated by cool-season midgrasses, such as western wheatgrass, bluebunch wheatgrass, green needlegrass, and needle and thread grass, and a warm season shortgrass—blue grama—is predominant in some understories. Big sagebrush and fringed sagewort are shrub components. In south-central Saskatchewan and the western Dakotas, western wheatgrass is found on all sites, but it dominates, along with green needlegrass, on soils with high clay content. Blue grama and buffalograss form a second layer under the taller grasses. Needle and thread grass and prairie sand reed are characteristic species on coarser-textured soils. Fringed sagewort is the only shrublike species found consistently. Green rabbitbrush and broom snakeweed become abundant on overgrazed pastures. Southward into Nebraska, Kansas, and particularly the Nebraska Sand Hills, warm season tallgrasses—such as sand bluestem, little bluestem, and prairie sand reed—are most common. In central Kansas, little bluestem, side oats grama, and blue grama share dominance. Westward into eastern Colorado and southward into northwestern New Mexico and the Texas Panhandle, most of the midgrasses and tallgrasses drop out, leaving warm season shortgrasses—such as blue grama, buffalograss, side oats grama, and hairy grama—as dominants, resulting in a dense but very short grassland habitat.

Forbs are important components of upland sites throughout the Great Plains. However, species composition is so variable that it would be pointless to list them.

Shelterbelts, established primarily to protect homesteads and fields from wind, also are valuable wildlife habitats. Shelterbelts owe their origin to the drought of the 1930s. Such plantings—made with many different species, mostly introduced—generally are found on uplands. Shelterbelts alone are not discrete habitats for deer. Their use by deer depends greatly on the presence of other habitat units within the animals' home range, especially natural wetlands or other woody types. White-tailed deer utilize shelterbelts extensively in eastern portions of the Great Plains, but less so farther west. Mule deer seldom are found in shelterbelts unless they are situated on or near rough terrain.

A unique vegetational type—aspen parklands—occurs across central Alberta and Saskatchewan. This is dominated by varying proportions of aspen groves and grasslands that form a belt 64.3–96.5 kilometers (40–60 miles) wide between the northern boreal forest and the grasslands of the Plains. The proportion of grassland decreases from south to north. In the north, aspen cover is broken by occasional small patches of grassland, while in the southern part of the zone, aspen groves are restricted to depressions (run-in sites). Common aspen understory plants include prostrate juniper, serviceberry, common snowberry, and kinnikinnick (J. W. Skene, pers. comm., April 1976). Grasslands of aspen parklands are dominated by rough fescue, slender wheatgrass, and shrubby cinquefoil.

Mule deer in the aspen parklands of Alberta, which form a belt between the northern boreal forest and Plains grassland. Photo by Valerius Geist.

USE OF PLAINS HABITATS

Use of Plains habitats by mule deer often appears to center on cover requirements rather than on food. However, forage could become critical under certain conditions, such as drought, unusually heavy snows, or intensive livestock use. Cover is considered in this chapter only in terms of security—an important factor on the Plains. The role it plays in energy and thermoregulatory responses for deer in these habitats appears to be important, but specific measurements are lacking.

By virtue of the cover they afford, run-in and runoff sites are utilized much more heavily by deer than are normal sites. Mackie (1970) found that the pine/juniper type received maximum use in summer and concluded that it was the most important habitat for that season. The Douglas fir/juniper type was used primarily for bedding and escape cover. Mackie also commented that dense timber made observations difficult; and these types may have received much greater use than was recorded.

Observations of deer in South Dakota indicated that the most important habitat types were the hardwood and shrubby draws and associated grass-dominated bottoms. The second most important vegetational type in summer was north-facing slopes covered with Rocky Mountain juniper (Severson and Carter 1978).

Both Mackie's studies in Montana and Severson and Carter's work in South Dakota showed that normal sites were important feeding areas for mule deer. The big sagebrush/bluebunch and western wheatgrass type in Montana, and the western wheatgrass/blue grama/green needlegrass type in South Dakota are important only where they occur in close association with cover. Grass-dominated bottoms also are important feeding sites in South Dakota. Mule deer were observed feeding early and late in the day in small openings in juniper stands. Production of important deer foods in such stands, plus the cover these stands provide, led Nelson (1961) to state that the Rocky Mountain juniper type was the most important summer habitat for deer in North Dakota.

Away from major river breaks, where there are no extensive stands of juniper, mule deer almost exclusively utilize hardwood and shrubby draws (Severson and Carter 1978). Buffaloberry, American plum, and chokecherry thickets, as well as hardwood draws dominated by green ash and American elm, assume the same importance and function as do north-slope juniper stands within the breaks.

During autumn, mule deer tend to abandon heavily wooded north slopes and make greater use of hardwood and shrubby draws as well as cottonwood flats along the larger drainages. Mackie (1970) noted increased use of the sagebrush-wheatgrass type in Montana. Mule deer tend to feed farther from cover as cooler weather approaches.

Although a tendency of mule deer for increased movement away from cover during autumn was documented in South Dakota (Severson, pers. files), the reasons for this are not well understood. It is assumed that mule deer prefer cooler north-facing slopes during hot summer days, but this preference becomes less acute during autumn.

Cottonwood habitat is of varying importance to mule deer, depending on its physiographic location. Nelson (1961) and Allen (1968) indicated that wider floodplains associated with major drainages—the Little Missouri and Missouri rivers—are not used extensively by mule deer during summer. Smaller drainages with narrower floodplains receive proportionately higher use by mule deer. This presumably is related to the distance from rougher terrain leading into the floodplains. The less mule deer have to travel from such terrain, the more they will use the floodplain. Mule deer preference for rough terrain was documented by Krämer (1972) and Hudson et al. (1976). On Saskatchewan prairies, mule deer are selective for both topographic variation and tree cover (J. W. Skene, pers. comm., April 1976).

During winter, mule deer use more open habitats. In Montana, Mackie (1970) reported the primary habitat to be big sagebrush-wheatgrass. He stated that this reflected mule deer dependence on big sagebrush and rubber rabbitbrush when forage availability decreased in other habitat types. In South Dakota and Nebraska, snow cover usually is not continuous

South-facing slopes—where snow cover is relatively light and lasts for relatively short periods—are important winter foraging areas for mule deer. Photograph courtesy of the Wyoming Department of Game and Fish.

throughout winter. South-facing slopes are covered with snow only for relatively short periods, making them extremely important feeding areas. Cottonwoods and associated shrub species—such as silver sagebrush, rubber rabbitbrush, and western snowberry—also receive greater use. Agricultural crops, particularly alfalfa, may be utilized heavily during winter.

Winter cover types frequented by mule deer are characterized more commonly by rough terrain than by particular vegetation. Because of their northern exposure, juniper stands retain snow longer, thereby reducing deer use. However, during years of scant snowfall, this type still is used, particularly on higher slopes.

Use of hardwood and shrubby draws in winter depends on the configuration of the draw as well as on exposure to prevailing winds. The relatively narrow but shallow, steep-sided draws that lie perpendicular to prevailing wind direction tend to fill with drifting snow. Even during years of scant snowfall, these areas may be inaccessible to deer. In wider or very deep, steep-sided draws, however, snowdrifts accumulate on the upper sides, leaving wooded bottoms relatively snow-free. These draws, plus those that orient parallel to prevailing wind direction, are very important winter habitats for both mule and white-tailed deer.

During spring, deer feed on south-facing slopes. Cool-season grasses and forbs tend to start growing earlier on these warmer sites. In late spring, deer seek out developing flower buds of little soapweed, which is quite common on the upper sides of south-facing slopes and on ridgetops. Mackie (1970) indicated that mule deer tended to remain on the big sagebrush-wheatgrass type during late March and early April. Continued deer use of this type also was due to the early appearance of green plants, especially bluegrass. Use of this habitat declined after mid-April, when deer moved into the timbered pine-juniper type. Fields of winter wheat are used quite heavily in the spring, especially if they are next to rough terrain.

Although data are limited, studies in South Dakota indicate mule deer's strong preference for deciduous thickets as fawning sites—particularly buffaloberry, American plum, chokecherry, and hawthorn. Some use is made of the lower edges of the juniper type in close association with brushy areas. Upper edges of juniper stands also are used, particularly if skunkbush sumac is present.

FACTORS INFLUENCING HABITAT QUALITY

Fire

Fire is a significant factor in grassland environments (Daubenmire 1968). Jackson (1965) discussed the prevalence and magnitude of fire on the southern Great Plains before and during settlement by European man. Lewis and Clark mentioned the prevalence of fires on northern grasslands and indicated that most were set by Indians for signals, warnings, and to hide their trails or attract wildlife (Cutright 1969), although many certainly were caused by lightning. Lewis also thought that these frequent fires explained the absence of trees on the Plains. Sauer (1950) and Stewart (1956) are more recent advocates of this theory. Fire does play a role in suppression of woody vegetation in the True Prairie (Humphrey 1962; Tester and Marshall 1962; Kirsch and Kruse 1972) and on the periphery of ponderosa pine–dominated Black Hills (Gartner and Thompson 1972). However, it is doubtful that woody species ever dominated normal sites or most runoff sites on the Great Plains because of erratic precipitation, emphasized by periodic severe droughts (Weaver and Albertson 1956; Humphrey 1962).

Most research concerning fire on the Great Plains has centered on the response of grasses and forbs to seasonal burning (Launchbaugh 1972; Wolfe 1972). Generally, only brief mention is made of the response of woody vegetation, such as Weaver and Albertson's (1956, p. 161) statement that "fire is less destructive to grasses than to woody vegetation." Thus very little is known about the specific effects of fire on cottonwood floodplains, hardwood or brushy draws, and north-slope juniper types. The following is based mostly on personal conjecture from the few facts available.

Historically, fire was very common in the Rocky Mountain juniper type. However, burns generally were restricted to small areas because of many natural firebreaks, such as the barren ridge spurs common to rough breaks. Ralston (1960) determined that most fires in juniper stands of North Dakota varied from 0.4 to 4.0 hectares (1–10 acres) and occurred between 1910 and 1920, although others had burned as early as 1850. Fire intensity was of major importance in determining stand structure; density of recovered stands increased as intensity of burns increased. The "importance values" of

George Catlin—"dean of the American Indian painters"—documented this scene he witnessed along the bluffs of the Upper Missouri River in 1832. Catlin noted that, though many fires were the result of natural phenomena, some were started by the Indians to improve the grasses for horses and wildlife grazers and to make their own movement easier. Photograph courtesy of the National Gallery of Fine Art; Smithsonian Institution.

shrubs were highest in juniper stands in which fires caused damage only to the lower limbs of trees.

It is doubtful that natural fire has an adverse effect on the value of the juniper type to mule deer; it even may be beneficial. Although these evergreens probably are the most combustible woody plant on the Plains, topography tends to restrict fires. Small burns of variable intensity can improve deer habitat by creating temporary openings, improving shrub growth, and generally creating more diversity by changing the age class structure of stands.

Fires in deciduous types (brushy and hardwood draws and cottonwood/willow-dominated floodplains) may create an entirely different situation. I have already mentioned that fire was instrumental in controlling the spread of deciduous forest components into the True Prairie, and it is certain that fire limited deciduous growth in many draws farther west. Attempts to determine the extent of such limitations would be purely speculative. There are several compensating factors that appear to allow some deciduous growth even under favorable burning conditions. First, not all draws are susceptible to fire. Some are so deep and steep-sided that rapidly moving grass fires tend to skip over them. Second, the more favorable moisture conditions afforded by these drainage patterns tend to ensure longer green growth periods in the understory. This, coupled with green foilage of the overstory, would make these areas somewhat less vulnerable to fire during late summer and early autumn—a time when the grasslands are most apt to burn. Third, many of the shrubs and trees found in grassland environment are adapted to fire, as are the grasses. The trees—green ash, boxelder and American elm—crown-sprout prolifically when the main stem is damaged, whereas bur oak not only crown-sprouts but also has bark that is highly fire-resistant. The major shrubs—buffaloberry, chokecherry, American plum, western snowberry, and skunkbush sumac—will sprout from rhizomes or crowns if burned. Stands of many of these species, however, can be reduced by spring fires, particularly if burned just when the plants leaf out and start to grow. Western snowberry is particularly susceptible to such fires (Kirsch and Kruse 1972; Smith and Owensby 1972).

On floodplains, the dominant tree—eastern cottonwood—tends to root-sprout and crown-sprout if the main stem is damaged. Larger, older trees are somewhat fire-resistant because of their thick bark. Many older trees have fire scars, indicating that the areas were burned without killing the trees. Dominant shrubs in the floodplains also will respond to fire. Western snowberry, willows, and silver sagebrush will sprout when burned in late summer or autumn, but all may be damaged by spring fires. Rubber rabbitbrush also will crown-sprout, but perhaps not as readily or as vigorously as other shrubs.

Drought

The Great Plains are characterized as a land of climatic extremes. They commonly are described by residents and visitors alike as being either too hot or too cold, too wet or too dry. Because weather extremes do occur, the characteristics of average precipitation and temperature do not adequately describe the climate. Drought is recurrently a dominant influence on plant life. The effects of drought usually are compounded by high temperatures, low relative humidity, and strong winds that increase evapotranspiration, making scarce soil moisture even less available to plants.

Since security cover is a limiting factor for Plains mule deer, the primary interest here is the effects of drought on woody vegetation. It must be emphasized that all Plains plants are affected adversely by drought, and during such periods food and free water can also become limiting factors.

Albertson and Weaver (1945) found that mortality of trees on the Great Plains resulting from the drought of the 1930s was greatest in what they described as dry ravines or what I consider first- and second-order drainages (hardwood draws). Cottonwoods on floodplains associated with intermittent streams also were severely affected by drought. Many willows on the same sites died. On floodplains associated with continuously flowing streams, considerably fewer trees died.

Mortality of eastern red cedar usually was less than in any of the deciduous forms. Red cedars continued to replace their losses throughout the drought and in some cases extended their area of occupation (Albertson and Weaver 1945).

Shrub damage by drought differed according to exposure and depth of the water table. Much skunkbush sumac, American plum, snowberry, and smooth sumac died. Shrubs on north-facing slopes had fewer losses, whereas all shrubs on many south-facing slopes were killed. Although chokecherry and buffaloberry were not mentioned specifically, one can assume that mortality of these species was even greater, considering the relatively moist nature of their settings.

Floodplain shrubs probably responded, as did the trees, according to the frequency with which the stream carried free water. On floodplains of intermittent streams, more silver sagebrush and rubber rabbitbrush died than on permanent streams.

Loss of drinking water prevented deer from using many areas. Stockponds were not numerous. When free water sources—such as natural ponds, springs, and streams—dried up, the few deer present were restricted to favorable habitats near permanent water, which was a rarity on the Plains at that time.

Man

Indians living on the Great Plains had little effect on vegetation except through their use of fire. Low populations coupled with a nomadic existence would indicate a low degree of disturbance. Movements were controlled by availability of water, which also means they were restricted, at least partially, to Plains forest types. Although they made use of wood for many purposes, their impact on woody vegetation probably was minimal because of their periodic movements. The introduction of the horse into North America (by the Spanish conquistadores in the mid-1500s) also may have increased the frequency and length of travel, decreasing the time spent in one area.

More sedentary tribes, such as the Mandan, Hidatsa and Arikara of the Dakotas, significantly affected floodplain vegetation along the Missouri River. Lewis and Clark reported that the Arikaras used cottonwoods extensively (Cutright 1969). They used bark to feed their horses in winter, and in the vicinity of their winter camps all trees were cut. Lewis and Clark described the area as a "treeless land" and noted that Indians obtained what wood they needed by roping and dragging trees that were floating down the river.

The arrival of Europeans signaled the beginning of a change in the vegetation of the Great Plains. In addition to the impact of their domestic livestock, as discussed later in this chapter (see also chap. 13), settlers used wood wherever it was available. Their influence, in this respect, was greatest in the late 1880s when homesteading was at a peak. The uses they made of wood probably were similar to those of the Indians. On the other hand, the settlers were much more sedentary and soon outnumbered the Indians. Wood was used for heating, cooking, buildings, corrals, and fencing. As I previously noted, juniper was especially popular for use as fenceposts. Ralston (1960) attempted to study uncut juniper stands in North Dakota but found that all stands had been cut for posts at one time or another, especially during the early part of the century.

Construction of stock ponds appears to have benefited deer and other wildlife by providing a free water source. However, stock dams placed in certain habitats concentrated livestock that, consequently, damaged habitat. Also, stock dams may have produced a long-term detri-

Railroad construction across the Great Plains was accomplished only by the use of wood, exploited wherever it was found. This habitat destruction was the first but by no means the least significant impact of railroads on mule and white-tailed deer, bison, and pronghorn populations on the Plains. Photograph courtesy of the United States Bureau of Land Management.

The key to success of wild ungulate populations on the Great Plains was water. It also governed the rate, distribution, and survival of settlement in the late 1800s and early 1900s. Photograph from the E. E. Smith Collection; courtesy of the United States Library of Congress.

mental effect on habitats that depend on run-in moisture. No one has yet addressed the possible effects of several such dams on moisture relationships within a draw.

Grazing

Bison

Factual knowledge of the effects of bison on woody vegetation of the Plains is scarce. Seton (1929) estimated that 40–60 million bison roamed North America just before discovery and settlement of the continent by whites. By 1850, 12–50 million bison existed, almost exclusively on the Great Plains. Given the magnitude of these population estimates—empirically substantiated by numerous accounts of astounded visitors to the Plains in the mid-1800s—there is little doubt that the grass-eating, ever-roving bison had a tremendous impact on vegetation. Like trees, shrubs, Indians, and early settlers of the Plains, bison also were associated with available water. The effects of a herd of many thousands of animals trailing down deciduous-dominated ravines leading to floodplains of the Cheyenne, Platte,

and Cimarron rivers must have been devastating. The combined influences of bison grazing, rubbing, and trampling, and the tendency for rutting bulls to gore and strip bark from large trees undoubtedly damaged and destroyed many existing shrubs and trees.

England and DeVos (1969) presented an excellent discussion of the influence of bison on the pristine conditions of Canadian grasslands. They cited from the journals of early explorers who described damage done to woody vegetation by bison. One, from the travels of Alexander Henry, who visited Manitoba and North Dakota in 1801, described the following experience in North Dakota: "This afternoon I rode a few miles up Park river. The few spots of wood along it have been ravaged by buffaloes; none but the large trees are standing, the bark of which is rubbed perfectly smooth, and heaps of wool and hair lie at the foot of the trees. The small wood and brush are entirely destroyed, and even the grass is not permitted to grow in the points of the wood. The bare ground is more trampled by these cattle than the gate of a farmyard" (England and DeVos 1969, p. 89).

Moss (1932) felt that bison may have had significant impact on aspen parklands by hin-

The great bison herds of the mid-1800s undoubtedly had an extreme impact on the grass and woody vegetation of the Plains. The extent to which this impact influenced mule deer distribution may never be known. Photograph by E. W. Jenkins; courtesy of the United States Soil Conservation Service.

dering southward expansion of aspen forests. Roe (1939), however, concluded that these animals had little or no significance in extending grasslands or deforesting areas, but he did recognize that bison were "enemies of regeneration." Because bison were always on the move, the contentions of both Moss and Roe seem quite reasonable. If grassland areas were visited repeatedly by immense bison herds, it is logical to assume that their impact on the woody vegetation had long-lasting effects. In some cases they may have kept trees from invading grasslands as Moss (1932) suggested. If, however, the nomadic herds roamed through wooded areas less frequently, their immediate effect may have been great; but through root- and crown-sprouting, many woody plants may have become reestablished and, by tillering, even spread to larger areas than before. The trampling and cutting action of thousands of hooves would have eliminated competing grasses and created excellent seedbed conditions for tree and shrub seedlings. Thus Roe's (1939) seemingly contradictory contention could be equally valid. Although bison were "enemies of regeneration," at least in terms of immediate effect, this does not imply widespread elimination of woody species.

Although overall effects of fire, Indians, and bison on the hardwood vegetation of the Great Plains will never be known in quantitative terms, it seems logical to assume that the extent of hardwood communities was less then than it is today. How did this affect mule deer? This too is an unanswerable question. Mule deer distribution on the Plains probably was more restricted than it is at present, although populations in good habitats then may have been somewhat larger. It also is possible that mule deer populations on the pristine Plains fluctuated more dramatically than those of recent times, because of frequent, temporary habitat modification by fire, Indians, and bison.

Livestock

Effects of domestic cattle on vegetation differed from those of bison. Whereas bison were nomadic—not only from season to season but also from day to day—cattle were restricted to a general area year-round, and their impact was

Introduction of livestock on the Plains had a severe impact on mule deer habitat. In this turn-of-the-century scene, a trail herd is driven down a ravine to water. The upland is gullied, trampled, and almost totally denuded of vegetation. Photograph from the E. E. Smith Collection; courtesy of the United States Library of Congress.

continuous. During the late 1880s, much of the Plains was open range, with too much livestock. It can be assumed that wooded draws suffered accordingly.

The homesteader's plow and barbed wire also had great impact on Plains vegetation. Plowing was predominant on normal uplands, though floodplains were cleared and cultivated as well. In the long run, plowing floodplains proved beneficial to deer, especially whitetails. Fencing farmland to protect it from grazing livestock put an end to open range. Fenced fields often included parts of shrubby or woody draws. However, other potential deer habitat probably received excessive use because it was fenced to confine livestock. This variable treatment of woody habitats continued until the drought of the 1930s, when many farmers were forced out of the Great Plains area. The drought, combined with overgrazed conditions, marked a low for wildlife habitat on the Plains.

During this drought, however, the sciences of rangeland management, soils, and wildlife management began. With the latter there developed a new consideration for habitat and wildlife population management and the need for game

A ranch hand "riding fence" on a ranch in Texas. Fencing put an end to open range, a mixed blessing for mule deer. Photograph from the E. E. Smith Collection; courtesy of the United States Library of Congress.

laws. Range management programs emphasized proper stocking based on range carrying capacity, the importance of livestock distribution, and grazing in proper seasons. The United States Department of Agriculture provided technical and financial assistance for soil stabilization, stockpond construction, shelterbelt plantings, and other range improvement practices. Government-funded programs, such as the Civilian Conservation Corps, provided manpower that enabled many of these practices to be initiated immediately.

Range conditions, including the woody vegetation types, improved steadily but slowly for the next thirty years. Many permanently marked areas were photographed from 1908 to about 1930, and were rephotographed from 1958 to 1960. Most of the latter photos document an increase in woody habitats, but a few show decreases (Phillips 1963).

Emphasis on meat production and other economic considerations have renewed a concern about the future of hardwood and shrubby draws, particularly on the northern Plains.

Numerous theories have been suggested to explain why many hardwood (shrubby) draws are deteriorating today (Dakota Planning Team 1974). The explanations include natural plant succession, geologic evolution, climatic change, insects, and disease. In hardwood draws in the western Dakotas, the most common cause of deterioration appears to be mismanagement of domestic livestock, in the form of season-long summer grazing. Nelson (1961, p. 58) stated: "It would be difficult to judge which factor, grazing, injuring the vegetation by trampling and rubbing, or soil compaction, has the greatest effect upon the woody and herbaceous vegetation in these stands, but there is little doubt that the combined effect has changed the shrub and herb composition in the green ash [hardwood draw] type."

Plains woodlands exist under extreme conditions at the very edges of their range. Any environmental change, even a minor drought, can weaken and kill trees. Overgrazing induces what is best described as "microclimatic drought." Soil compaction reduces water infil-

A decrease over time of woody vegetation on the Plains.

tration, and constant herbage removal destroys the insulating effects of cover and litter, allowing soil to increase in temperature. Such conditions put additional stress on trees and shrubs needing continuous or abundant moisture.

When trees and shrubs common to hardwood draws are stressed—through micro- or macroclimatic drought, breakage, or rubbing—they become more vulnerable to attacks by disease and insects. Thus, in many cases where damage by such organisms is evident, it often is a symptom of hardwood deterioration rather than the primary cause. In some cases, however, insects and disease can cause serious damage to hardwoods regardless of the trees' general condition. A good example is Dutch elm disease, which has decimated American elms from southern South Dakota southward.

Hardwood draws are susceptible to summer use by cattle because they offer shade and a relatively long "green" season of herbaceous forage, both of which are attractive to domestic livestock. Because of their moisture "run-in" characteristic, such draws also are the sites

selected for stockpond construction. Therefore, even if a pasture is properly stocked or even slightly understocked, the shade, green vegetation, and water in its draw or draws tend to attract cattle—resulting in overgrazed draws and lightly used uplands.

Winter use of hardwood draws by cattle, on the other hand, does not appear to damage these areas as much as during summer. Reasons for this may include: cattle need less shade in this season; frozen ground prevents soil compaction; vegetation is dormant and less susceptible to damage; and other sites, such as south-facing slopes, may be more favorable for loitering in winter.

Floodplain vegetation is similarly affected by grazing. This type is preferred by domestic livestock because it occurs on flat terrain with relatively abundant supplies of water, shade, and forage. Studies in Montana by Allen (1968) and Dusek (1971) indicated high grazing use of bottomlands during all seasons. Crouch (1961, p. 119) concluded that "livestock grazing, of the intensity encountered [in Colorado], had

An increase over time of woody vegetation on the northern Great Plains. Photographs on left were taken in 1924 by H. L. Shantz, and the contrast photos *(right)* on this and the previous page were taken in 1959 by Walter S. Phillips; all courtesy of the Department of Botany, University of Arizona, Tucson.

one dominant effect on the bottom lands with respect to wildlife, and that was the removal of vegetation which served as cover for most species and as food for many."

North-facing coniferous types, particularly Rocky Mountain juniper, suffer relatively less damage from grazing livestock because of steep slopes and dense stands of trees. Use of these slopes, however, can vary greatly depending on degree of slope, time of year, weather conditions, and class of livestock. Localized damage can occur when cattle trails on slopes destroy binding vegetation, accelerating erosion. Livestock use of south-facing slopes also is relatively light but varies according to the circumstances that, as previously noted, affect use of north-facing slopes.

In summary, cattle compete with deer primarily by destroying cover, not necessarily by utilizing the same foods. Mackie (1970), Knapp (1972), Dusek (1975), Knowles (1975), and Komberec (1976), all working in Montana, observed and reported very little overlap in forage use by mule deer and cattle during most periods of the year (see also chap. 13).

The primary effect of cattle on deer habitat on the Great Plains is the decrease in abundance of almost all woody species when a site is overgrazed. On most other grasslands in western North America, many shrubs increase during the early stages of overgrazing.

HABITAT MANAGEMENT

Key habitat types of mule deer on the Great Plains are draws dominated by hardwoods and shrubs and narrow floodplains dominated by cottonwoods, both associated with rough terrain. These habitats, as discussed, are susceptible to damage by drought, uncontrolled fire, and overgrazing by domestic livestock. There is a tremendous potential for increasing deer habitat on the Plains by improving hardwood cover types. Other types, such as grasslands on normal uplands, are not as critical because they are used relatively little by mule deer. Runoff sites, south-facing slopes, and conifer-domi-

nated north slopes, though important to deer, are not as vulnerable to damaging agents.

At present, summer-long use by cattle appears to be the most common cause of deterioration of hardwood and shrubby draws. What can be done to arrest this situation? First, we must note that woody species on the Plains evolved under rather sporadic but sometimes heavy use by bison and other large wild ungulates. Second, most of the Great Plains is privately owned, and the principal use is livestock grazing. Therefore it would not be practicable or feasible to fence off large areas for exclusive use by wildlife. One factor in favor of wildlife habitat, however, is that many Plains ranchers are concerned about deterioration of woody draws because draws are valuable shelter for livestock from storms in winter and provide shade in summer. In many cases a viable solution to the problem of overgrazing of hardwood and shrubby draws is more careful regulation of livestock distributions, season of use, and stocking rates.

Controlling livestock distribution often is very complex. One consideration is the proportion of hardwood and shrubby draws in a pasture. Nelson (1961) noted that, in pastures with relatively higher proportions of wooded ravines, the green ash type suffered less damage than did areas with low proportions. Thus, where there is a high proportion of hardwood types, judicious placement of salt or water sources on uplands may relieve grazing pressure so that woody vegetation can maintain itself. Relocating water on uplands is a problem, though it has been done by constructing dugouts or laying plastic pipelines to watering tanks.

Although fencing is expensive, it may be the only alternative on units with a low proportion of woody draws. Fencing does not necessarily imply livestock exclusion but, rather, suggests a grazing system tailored to meet the need of that particular management unit. If a fenced hardwood draw is large enough, it could be opened to managed grazing during the hottest time of the year and closed when utilization of the draw reached a predetermined point or as weather permitted. In this manner, shade

On many areas of the Plains, installation of plastic pipelines has proved to be a feasible method of relocating water supplies for domestic livestock. Photograph courtesy of the United States Soil Conservation Service.

would be available to the livestock when it was needed most, and vegetation in the draw could be protected from grazing during the period of most active growth (spring and early summer).

Grazing systems geared to the growth of grasses have been promoted by range managers for many years. The responses of woody species important for wildlife, however, have been largely ignored. Under standard grazing systems, such as deferred grazing or rest-rotation, pastures are grazed intensively when used. Although subsequent seasonal or periodic rest may be long enough for grasses to recover, it is not long enough for shrubs or young trees. Heavy short-duration grazing also appears to promote soil compaction in draws because of the distribution factors discussed previously.

So little is known about the effects of grazing systems on shrubs and trees that it is difficult to determine how such a system should be designed, much less the practicality of its installation or its acceptability by a private landowner. Standard grazing systems may not be appropriate for such purposes for a variety of reasons, including heterogeneity of the range complex

owing to draws; proportion of draws in a pasture; condition of vegetation; and requirements of different woody species occupying a particular pasture or draw. Therefore it is more likely that a grazing system must be designed specifically for each management unit. Whatever the design, the physiological and ecological requirements of shrubs and trees, as well as of the grasses, must be considered if mule deer habitats on the Plains are to be improved and maintained.

One possibility to consider when designing a grazing system is to rotate pasture use not only within a season but also among seasons. Although this may permit woody vegetation to recover in areas previously grazed only in summer, it must be implemented so that healthy draws in winter pastures are not degraded when switched to summer use. Not all pastures can be used in winter, however. In addition to having rather specific cover requirements for livestock, winter pastures also must be readily accessible for emergency or supplemental feeding.

If damage to deciduous woody vegetation in a draw is nominal—that is, where overbrowsing

Hardwood draws are a vital habitat element of mule deer on the Great Plains. This draw has been fenced to prevent use by cattle. Photograph by Don Domenick; courtesy of the Colorado Division of Wildlife.

has occurred, but not to the extent that shrub densities have declined—the vegetation may be improved by adjusting livestock distribution. If, however, the vegetational composition has changed significantly, other techniques may be necessary in addition to livestock management.

In some cases complete protection from livestock may be required, perhaps for several years. Complete protection may suffice if remnant plants of such species as chokecherry, American plum, and buffaloberry are present, and if some tree reproduction is occurring. In this situation, controlled burning also can be used to stimulate reproduction of these root- or crown-sprouting species. Such fires should be controlled so mature trees are not damaged, but allowed to burn hot enough to destroy existing ground vegetation in order to stimulate growth of woody plants and encourage them to tiller and spread.

Seriously damaged hardwood or cottonwood areas—without woody understory and only remnant, dead or dying, mature trees—require intensive improvement. Soil compaction in these areas generally is a problem, and protection, even if used with fire, is unlikely to result in natural regeneration of woody species within a reasonable time. Many of these areas have a dense grass cover—buffalograss and blue grama on relatively dry areas, or Kentucky bluegrass on wet sites—that can outcompete shrub or tree seedlings. In this case seedbed preparation and planting seeds or nursery stock may be necessary. Plantings may require the same care and attention that is devoted to shelterbelt establishment. Cultivation can be abandoned as planted trees and shrubs become established, if native species that can maintain themselves have been used. To improve such habitat for mule deer, randomized or clumping patterns are preferable to row plantings.

There also appears to be a use for fire in stimulating growth of certain large, clonal shrubs that have not been subjected to over-

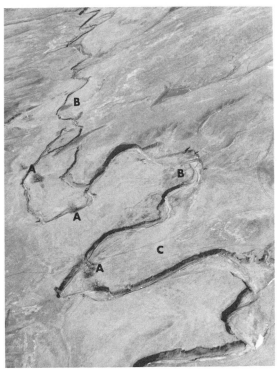

This draw on the northern Great Plains of western South Dakota has been overgrazed by livestock to the point where only scattered trees *(A)* are present with a few isolated clones of western snowberry *(B)*. Note the trails caused by cattle *(C)*. Photograph by Kieth E. Severson; courtesy of the United States Forest Service.

grazing, such as buffaloberry, western snowberry, and prairie rose. These species, particularly buffaloberry and rose, often produce large

but relatively senescent clumps that can provide some cover but do not appear to be expanding. These clones may be revitalized and expanded by prescribed burning. Many large, clonal shrub species evolved under periodic, irregular burning, and it is possible that complete protection from fire may be just as damaging as too much fire. If fire is used in management of hardwood draws, complete protection from grazing must be given to the burned areas for an undefined period, depending on season and intensity of the burn. Ungulates—domestic and wild—are attracted to burned areas, and the resulting concentrations may erase the beneficial effects of burning.

Very little is known about how fire or grazing management can be used specifically to increase mule deer woody habitats on the Great Plains. Knowledge of the ecology of hardwood draws is deplorably limited. However, as awareness of the value of this resource increases, so do research efforts and mule deer management implications.

Drought cannot be managed or prevented, at least with present technology, and it will continue to occur in the Great Plains. Effects of drought, however, can be minimized by ensuring that vegetation—woody and herbaceous—is in a healthy, vigorous condition at the onset of a dry period. Some damage and mortality will occur, depending on the length of the dry cycle. But such damage and loss will be significantly less in a healthy stand than in a mismanaged stand in poor condition.

Chapter 13

INTERSPECIFIC RELATIONSHIPS

Richard J. Mackie
Professor of Wildlife Management
Montana State University
Bozeman, Montana

The geographic range of mule deer encompasses the most ecologically diverse region of North America in terms of number and distribution of large herbivorous mammals. In most areas and at least seasonally, mule deer may share rangelands with one or more of at least eight species of native wild ungulates, a number of wild exotic ungulate species, and seven species of domestic "grazers." The native wild ungulates include white-tailed deer, elk, moose, bighorn sheep, mountain goat, pronghorn, bison, and collared peccary. Exotics known to occur locally within the range of mule deer include Barbary sheep, fallow deer, sambar deer, tahr, gemsbok × Kalahari oryx, Siberian ibex, and wild boar (Decker 1978). Most western American rangelands are grazed by domestic livestock, including cattle, sheep, horses, and occasionally mules, burros, goats, and hogs. Feral or "wild" populations of domestic species, especially horses and burros, also occur in a number of areas inhabited by mule deer.

In many respects, all these herbivorous species make similar use of the rangeland ecosystem. Where they occur individually, they tend to be of major influence on the biotic community. Where species overlap, they often utilize many of the same range resources. The wild species frequently react to and are affected by many of the same environmental factors and conditions, have common predators, serve as hosts of the same or similar parasites, and are afflicted by the same or similar diseases. Consequently, the probability of interaction is high whenever and wherever they occupy common rangeland.

Historically, interactions between mule deer and other native ungulates probably played a significant role in determining distribution and abundance of mule deer, as well as in the evolution of habitat-use patterns and requirements. During the past century, with development of the livestock industry and major reductions in many native ungulate populations, interspecific relationships with domestic animals have been viewed variously as both beneficial and detrimental to mule deer populations. Today, with increasing use and intensified management of rangeland resources, the matter of interspecific competition is important to resource managers charged with planning and evaluating management actions on millions of hectares of mule deer range throughout western North America. This, plus the fact that all the potentially interacting ungulate forms are highly valued economic or aesthetic resources on western rangelands, has made competitive interaction one of the most controversial aspects of mule deer management.

Although wildlife biologists and managers have been vitally concerned about interspecific relationships of mule deer and other ungulates, the exact nature and importance of interaction in rangeland ecosystems is not well understood. Remarkably few conclusions of general appli-

487

cation can be drawn from existing literature, and much current thinking appears to be rooted largely in inference and speculation (Mackie 1976a). Moreover, little has been done as yet to establish a basic theoretical framework defining patterns and processes of interaction—including competition—between larger herbivores from an ecosystem perspective. Such problems, together with a lack of quantitative information on many aspects of interspecific interactions between mule deer and other ungulate species, continue to hamper effective evaluation of interrelationships in both management and research situations.

PATTERNS OF INTERSPECIFIC INTERACTIONS

In all natural systems, the occurrence and well-being of any animal species or population is governed by a complex of environmental factors and biological and ecological processes that are linked dynamically in an "ecosystem." Within these systems, each animal and population of a particular species become part of another's environment, and interactions automatically become part of the total dynamic process of population regulation. Moreover, natural environments are never static. Basic animal resources (food, space, cover or shelter, etc.) are changing almost constantly in response to many factors, including the activities of the animals themselves. Climate and weather, and the occurrence and actions of other animals and man, also vary. In this context, the nature, intensity, and importance of interaction between any two animals or populations or between species is almost certain to vary in time and space. Similarly, interactions may take many forms, involve a number of different elements, and have numerous direct and indirect effects. Because of this, many aspects of interspecific relationships can be defined and evaluated effectively only in terms of their role in the system as a whole. This certainly appears to be the case among large herbivores, all of which are capable of exerting some influence on range resources.

Wildlife biologists and managers now recognize that association of two animal populations, including mule deer and other ungulates whose ecological roles (or niches) are similar, does not automatically imply that either population will be adversely affected. Associations may occur in which either population or both may benefit in some manner, and the interaction can be viewed as cooperative. There also are instances in which interactions may be competitive in one respect and cooperative in another. Or, because the nature and effects of interactions often are related to animal density or activity, they may be basically cooperative at one level or time, neutral at another, and competitive at still another (Mather 1961). In some cases, interrelationships also may change directly or vary from competitive to cooperative above and below certain thresholds of density or activity.

Interspecific Competition

Odum (1971) referred to competition as two-species interactions in which each population adversely affects the other in a struggle for food, nutrients, living space, or other common need. It is limited to interactions that adversely affect growth and survival in both populations and that ultimately result in the elimination of one, as defined by the competitive exclusion principle (Hardin 1960), or in ecological separation. Interactions in which only one species is affected adversely are not considered competitive. On the other hand, Miller (1967, p. 6) held that competition is "the active demand by two or more individuals of the same species population (intraspecies competition) or members of two or more species at the same trophic level (interspecies competition) for a common resource or requirement that is actually or potentially limiting." He left open the questions whether exclusion or ecological separation is inevitable and whether both species are necessarily affected in interspecies competition. Miller's view generally has been followed in ungulate ecology, although competition commonly is applied rather loosely to almost any interaction with a negative outcome, including those in which the welfare of only one species may be affected.

The extent to which two species graze and prefer the same forage generally has been considered the main factor determining interspecific competition (Julander 1958). However, it also may be important that resources used in common are in limited supply and overutilized or deteriorating as a result of combined use (Cole 1958). Here it is important to recognize that, whereas (1) distribution, range-use patterns, and food habitats of the animals and (2) abundance, degree of utilization, and condition trends of preferred forage plants all may be important to the occurrence of interspecific competition, similarities or differences in the former and relatively high or low levels of the latter are not evidence a priori for or against a competitive relationship (Mackie 1976a). Severson et al. (1968) also questioned the necessity of having a resource in limited supply for competition to occur. The importance of food, especially preferred species, may be exaggerated in interspecific interaction; competition can occur even where food is superabundant (Mayr 1963). Specific population densities always are extremely important. They determine not only the occurrence of competition, but much of its nature, intensity, and mode of effect. Behavioral characteristics and adaptations, mobility, and nutrient and energy requirements all are known to be extremely important in patterns of resource utilization and thus in the competitive process as well.

Many animals such as wild ungulates are broadly adaptable as species in their choice of food and habitat requirements, but individuals may be strongly limited by behavioral mechanisms to certain areas, habitats, and food plants (Beament 1961). Competitive selection for certain behavioral patterns may lead to greater specialization and separation in selection of food and habitat. Because of this, food and range-use habits observed where two or more animal species have been associated for a long time may be more indicative of the individual species' responses to each other's presence in that environment over time than of the potential for competition between those species generally

or where they come newly into contact with each other.

Competition can involve elements of interference as well as exploitation (Park 1954; Milne 1961; Miller 1967). "Interference" refers to any activity or behavioral phenomenon that directly or indirectly limits a competitor's access to a necessary resource, usually in a spatial context. "Exploitation" refers to utilization of a resource once access has been achieved, usually in the sense that two individuals or species with unlimited access to a common source of food or nutrients will have different abilities or opportunities to use the available supply. Odum (1971) recognized these two modes of competition in differentiating interference competition and resource-use competition. The element of interference also is implicit in the disturbance competition concept of Denniston (1956) and others. It refers to an animal's movement from or avoidance of areas used by another, at least to the extent that alternative areas or habitats are available (Schladweiler 1974), and could result in more intensive use of all parts of an animal's normal home range, larger home ranges, or use of inferior habitats. It also seems that Smith and Julander (1953) recognized the involvement of factors other than supply and use of food in differentiating both forage competition and land-use competition among large herbivores on rangeland. Smith and Julander associated forage competition with common use of preferred forage plants in short supply or at levels above those considered proper for sustained productivity and yield. They associated land-use competition with common use of a forage supply that is adequate to meet the requirements of both animals, but where removing one would permit greater numbers of the other.

Interspecific competition may be indirect or more or less direct in process and effect. Direct competition does not require that both species populations or all members of the populations use the same areas or resources at the same time (Cole 1958). Use of food resources by one animal or population during one season may preclude subsequent use of that area or food by another. Different resource values also may be involved. What is food for one species may be cover or shelter for another; in the process of foraging, one species can reduce or eliminate important cover resources for the other. Or different activities may be involved, such as where exploitation by trampling or other nonconsumptive activity by one population reduces or denies another the use of a resource for food or cover.

The processes and effects of indirect competition often are subtle, and they can be observed and measured only in long-term changes or trends in the supply or some other attribute of resources or in the behavior, distribution, or dynamics of one or more of the associated species populations. Included are: (1) gradual reductions in the vigor of plants, and in the amount and quality of forage produced or available for animal use; (2) elimination or reduction of reproductive parts or vigor of plants or of germination, growth, and survival of young plants such that future forage supplies are diminished; (3) reduction or elimination of locally important cover types and replacement by less favorable types or communities, either by direct actions over time or by setting back or increasing the rate of natural succession; and (4) general alterations and reduction in the kinds, quality, and amounts of preferred or otherwise important plants through selective grazing or browsing or other activities. In some cases, where grazing or browsing is uniform or becomes uniform over large areas, vegetational diversity also may be decreased.

Beament (1961) indicated that behavioral modifications through competition ultimately may lead resource utilization patterns away from what might be considered optimal in a physiological sense. Similarly, specialization—tying a species to relatively few kinds of food or habitats through long-term competitive selection—may have a marked influence on genetic variability within a population and can result in a loss of resiliency and stability in that population should any of these resources fail or change dramatically in supply (Wynn-Edwards 1962).

Dice (1952) believed that competition al-

ways is an interaction among individuals. However, individual interaction and response in terms of growth, survival, and reproduction also can be viewed as merely a part of the overall population consequence.

Interspecific Cooperation

Cooperative aspects of interspecific interaction, although widely observed and reported, as yet are even less defined than are competitive aspects. While various terms have been applied, Mather's (1961) use of "cooperation" to describe collectively all beneficial interactions, in contrast to those that are basically competitive (detrimental to one or both species), seems closest to practical use. Thus, in the ecology of large herbivores, interspecific cooperation essentially would describe all situations in which basic resource and population benefits accrue to a species' population as a result of either the occurrence and activities of one or more species or populations with which it shares some of the same resources, or the combined activity and resource use of both populations. A relationship that is competitive in one respect or at one level of animal density or activity may be cooperative in another respect or at another level. For example, dual use of certain plants and foraging areas may be sufficient to have an immediate competitive effect. On the other hand, combined grazing or browsing may promote diversity in habitat or forage production or greater availability of some kinds of plants, hence providing a floristic complex more favorable to one species or both. Or, just as important, it may serve to maintain existing conditions and resources needed by one or both animals, populations, or species.

Cooperative interactions also may be more or less direct. Examples include cases in which (1) grazing or browsing by one species increases the availability of plants or plant parts selected by another species (Bell 1971); (2) dispersionary patterns are altered to affect more complete use of all resources; (3) the effects of some other regulating factor (predation, hunting, etc.) may be spread over two or more species populations.

Elk and mule deer starving on winter range. More deer than elk died from malnutrition, perhaps due to direct competition for forage. Where management favors elk, such that large numbers of these animals occur on deer winter ranges, they may out-compete deer or cause the deer to use marginal areas and forage plants. Photograph by Don Domenick; courtesy of the Colorado Division of Wildlife.

INTERSPECIFIC RELATIONSHIPS OF MULE DEER AND OTHER WILD UNGULATES

The coexistence of native wild ungulate species in North America for perhaps thousands of years—together with broad differences in their habitat selection and use, food habits, and behavioral characteristics—testifies that, in the process of sharing resources, most came to occupy fairly divergent ecological niches. Thus, even the closely related deer species show rather distinct differences in habitat preference, although food habits are fairly similar (Krämer 1972). Through the ages, interspecific interaction and competition undoubtedly fostered ecological separations that preclude, or at least limit, opportunities for severe competition among most wild ungulate species under natural conditions. This does not mean that competition cannot or does not occur. To the contrary, as wild ungulate numbers rise in periodic population fluctuations and occupy new or more marginal habitats, or if supplies of important habitat resources change dramatically, either naturally or in response to the actions and activities of man, it seems likely that ecologically important interaction and competition can occur even between species of broadly divergent habits. However, it also follows that environmental forces and ecological processes other than interspecific competition usually will be the overriding means of population regulation, at least over large areas.

Most studies of interspecific relationships of mule deer and other wild ungulates have been based largely on comparisons of seasonal distributions, food habits, and uses of various habitat or vegetational types. As later discussion of relationships of species will show, there is much information to suggest that mule deer compete with each of these other species. However, there is as yet no substantial documentation to indicate that competition necessarily regulates mule deer and other wild ungulate populations in any area. There may be many reasons for this.

Opportunity to compete and similarity

among wild ungulate species in various aspects of resource use do not automatically imply that competition is occurring or—if it is—that it is important in the regulation of numbers of coexisting species. If two species with generally similar habits occur in an area, some overlap must be expected in uses of food, water, and cover resources. Many biological and behavioral adaptations probably have occurred to accommodate or even provide benefits from such dual use. Thus, in many instances, what is perceived by comparative study to indicate the occurrence or absence of "competition" today actually may reflect accommodation to dual use in the past.

Means of adequately measuring the biological and ecological effects of interaction between two populations are lacking. So, too, are methods of distinguishing these effects from those of other population-regulating mechanisms that are expressed in much the same way.

Mule deer appear to be fairly adaptable to a variety of habitats and foods. Under natural conditions, they normally occupy a rather wide range of habitats in which carrying capacities and population densities vary in relation to the available kinds, quality, and amounts of food and cover or other requirements. In typical rangeland situations in which the densities of either competitor or both competitors are near carrying capacity, it is difficult to distinguish effects of interspecific and intraspecific competition. It also is difficult to distinguish effects of interspecies interactions from those of various other environmental factors. Normal fluctuations in weather and snow conditions, forage production, predation, hunting, and other factors may elicit changes in carrying capacities, species responses, and population consequences that are essentially indistinguishable from both intraspecific and interspecific interactions. In many cases of long-term interspecific coexistence, these other environmental factors and forces may be the primary or overriding means of population regulation.

Competition occurs between species with similar habitat needs and habits when the ratio of their population to environmental resources

reaches a certain value (Crombie 1947) or threshold level. Below certain minimal densities or distributional limits, ecologically significant interaction may never occur. Above certain maxima it may always occur, at least within zones of greatest overlap. Generally, among ecological equivalents, the species present in greatest numbers or having the highest sustained reproductive and recruitment rates will be more effective in competitive situations than a smaller and less productive population. Also, a less numerous but more productive species population that is more specialized in its selection of food may be an effective competitor in the presence of a less productive and more generalized wild herbivore population. All these factors probably have been important in interspecific relationships of mule deer with other wild ungulates.

That populations of mule deer, as well as other ungulates, declined drastically and became quite localized in the late 1800s and early 1900s probably precluded serious competition during this period. A rapid increase in mule deer throughout the West, between 1920 and the 1940s and extending through the 1950s and 1960s, undoubtedly changed this. In many if not most portions of the West, high mule deer populations were marked not only by locally high densities but also by occurrence of deer in nearly all suitable habitats. This probably included many areas of marginal quality.

The population increase also included intrusion of mule deer into areas and habitats occupied by other wild ungulates, themselves in various stages of recovery from turn-of-the-century lows in both numbers and distributions. Management—including vigorous protection from predation and hunting, transplants and reintroductions, and acquisition and protection of important winter ranges—encouraged recovery of several ungulate species. In some areas, particularly in the North, pronghorn populations aided by transplants, increased and spread, during the 1940s and 1950s to fill most suitable habitats. Elk numbers and distribution increased greatly, also with the help of widespread transplants. Moose populations increased in many northern Rocky Mountain areas and in Canada. Small populations of bison were established or fostered on a few refuges and national parks in the United States and Canada, and in scattered private herds. Several exotic ungulate species were introduced (Teer 1971; Decker 1978). In recent years, both bighorn sheep and Rocky Mountain goats have been transplanted widely and reintroduced in former or potential habitats. These changes served to increase zones of overlap with mule deer or to increase local densities of potential competitors.

Since the mid-1960s and early 1970s, mule deer populations generally have declined throughout western North America. In many areas this has meant a shrinkage in zones of overlap or reductions in mule deer densities within these zones.

Because of these population changes, interspecific relationships of mule deer and all other wild ungulates have varied greatly in time and space over the past century, especially since about 1900. There is nothing in the literature to indicate that interspecific interactions with wild ungulates were a factor in any of the mule deer population changes. Nor is there evidence that further change or growth in some species' populations was precluded by interspecific competition. Even though maximum opportunity for competition between other wild ungulates and mule deer generally was coincidental with the decline of deer, it is not possible to conclude that competition was of singular or widespread importance (Mackie 1976a). This does not mean that interspecific relationships and competition were not important locally or even generally; it is said only to emphasize that the causes of population change have not been adequately assessed.

Management policies and practices applied to wild ungulate populations and domestic livestock grazing have been important variables in the population ecology of all wild herbivores in North America. They have had a confounding influence on both the occurrence and the assessment of interspecific relationships of mule deer. Management of wild ungulates and their habitats varies among states and provinces from total protection of populations to general

exploitation, and from passive or indirect management of habitats to aggressive protection and development programs. During the past twenty-five to fifty years, however, management of mule deer in most areas was directed either passively or actively at manipulating populations, while at the same time most other wild ungulates generally were encouraged.

Domestic animal husbandry and range management also vary in time and space, under the control of both private individuals and public agencies. During the past twenty-five to fifty years, livestock and range management has intensified greatly and moved toward increased use of pasturing and grazing systems, additional fencing, water development, different seasons of use, different breeds or classes of livestock, supplementary feeding on the range, and habitat improvement such as brush control, reseeding, and fertilization. On some ranges, livestock grazing has been reduced greatly or eliminated. On others, especially private lands, grazing pressures have increased in many areas. And on still other ranges in grazing systems, livestock grazing patterns and intensities are varied among seasons and years.

Together, wildlife, livestock, and range management practices of the past quarter-century have served to increase both the complexity and the variability of interspecific relations in time and space. They also have complicated the inherently difficult task of evaluating these interrelationships. More important, however, they probably have had and continue to have the effect of reducing both the quantity and quality of mule deer habitat and the distribution and numbers of mule deer on western North American rangelands.

DISTRIBUTIONAL AND HABITAT RELATIONSHIPS OF MULE DEER AND OTHER WILD UNGULATES

The following is a broad overview of the distributional and habitat relationships of mule deer and other wild ungulates, as these relationships might influence opportunities for interspecific interaction and competition generally. Assessment of interspecific relationships for any given areas must be left to detailed evaluations, given conditions at the time of assessment.

Mule Deer/Whitetails

The geographic range of white-tailed deer overlaps that of mule deer in southern Canada from western Manitoba to Alberta and southeastern British Columbia, across the northern United States from the western Dakotas to eastern Washington, in northeastern Wyoming, western portions of Nebraska, Kansas, Oklahoma, and Texas, and in parts of Colorado, New Mexico, and Arizona. Interspecific relationships of mule deer and whitetails have been studied in several areas, including Alberta (Krämer 1971, 1973), Montana (Allen 1968; Martinka 1968; Kamps 1969), Nebraska (Mensel and Havel 1969), southeastern Arizona (Anthony 1972), and southeastern British Columbia (Hudson et al. 1976). Krämer (1972) evaluated ecological relationships of the two species in detail.

Within the zone of overlap, habitat preferences and some aspects of behavior of mule and white-tailed deer seem to be significantly different, while food habits are fairly similar (Krämer 1972). In general, whitetails tend to be associated with more mesic brush types and transitional habitats and agricultural lands of relatively low elevation, along river and stream drainage systems, or on rolling uplands and foothills. Mule deer tend to occupy drier, more open rangelands of somewhat higher elevation, characterized by rough, broken terrain and open montane forest. However, white-tailed deer occur extensively in dense coniferous forest types throughout northwestern Montana, northern Idaho, and northeastern Washington, as well as in conifer-dominated habitat types of the Black Hills of South Dakota and northeastern Wyoming and the Long Pines area of eastern Montana. At the same time, mule deer at least seasonally occupy riparian habitats and agricultural lands associated with mountain valleys, foothills, and river and stream drainage

systems over much of the northern Great Plains. In the southwestern United States, mule deer tend to be associated more with dry forest, foothill, chaparral, and desert shrub types, whereas whitetails tend to be found in montane habitats, desert grassland, and areas of denser vegetation, including woodlands.

That food habits of whitetails and mule deer are similar and that there is some overlap in habitat use where the two species occur together indicate possible competition in local areas. However, Krämer (1972) concluded that these species occupy fairly divergent ecological niches, so that interspecific competition probably is not an important factor, either generally or in recent extensions of white-tailed deer range in northern areas where mule deer have declined.

Mule Deer/Elk

Elk occur generally across much of the range of mule deer. Wherever studies have been conducted, patterns of habitat use by elk appear quite similar to those of mule deer. Elk, however, appear to move more widely and discriminate less than do mule deer in selection of habitat types.

In mountainous areas, both species winter at lower elevations and distribute themselves upward during spring to spend summer and autumn scattered across their range. In most areas and except during calving, elk tend to aggregate and move more extensively than do mule deer.

Food habits of elk frequently overlap those of mule deer; elk food habits generally appear to be broader and more flexible. On prairie/montane forest ranges, both species eat similar grasses and forbs during spring and appear to prefer similar forbs during summer. During summer, both apparently use some of the same browse species as well. However, if forbs are not available, elk may switch to greater use of grasses, whereas mule deer browse more intensively. In autumn and winter, elk prefer grasses where available but utilize some forbs and may browse intensively during periods of snow cover or when crusting limits access to grass. Although mule deer tend to browse most extensively during winter in most areas, they may depend heavily on forbs or grasses or both, in areas where they are available and shrubs are limited. On heavily forested ranges of western Montana and northern Idaho, both mule deer and elk may browse extensively throughout the year and may prefer similar species.

In general this suggests considerable opportunity for competition between mule deer and elk where they occupy the same range. Because elk appear to be capable of adapting successfully to a wide range of environments and are more flexible than deer in their choice of habitats and forage preferences, they seem to be the more efficient competitors, having the advantage over mule deer in competitive situations (Mackie 1970). However, as yet, there is little quantitative support for the idea that competition between the two species is an important factor in regulating populations of either. It may be that the nature, extent, and effects of interaction between mule deer and elk vary widely depending on the type of habitat and other local environmental conditions. Cliff (1939) ascribed heavy deer mortality in Idaho during the severe winter of 1931 to heavy use by elk of important mule deer forage plants. Similarly, Cowan (1947) believed that elk competed seriously with mule deer by heavy use of browse on winter range in Jasper Park, Alberta. However, at the time of Cowan's study, the worst conflict had subsided because elk already had destroyed that part of the highly palatable browse supply formerly available to deer and had forced deer to utilize alternative foods, including less palatable browse and forbs. Cowan also noted that trampling of snow by large herds of elk on some winter range areas caused crusting that reduced the amount of forage available to deer.

Waldrip (1977) reported that white-tailed deer appear to avoid elk and are not regularly seen in areas containing dense elk populations. His data suggested that competition with elk may have been forcing whitetails into marginal habitat for fawning, thus predisposing fawns to predation. Avoidance of elk by mule deer has not been documented, although Bayoumi and Smith (1976) indicated that dominance by elk may have been responsible for the low abundance of mule deer in the vicinity of the Hardware Ranch, an elk winter range, in Utah.

Mule deer and elk compete for scarce forage during a long winter with deep snow. Being larger, elk can tolerate deeper snows and a wider array of forage plants than can deer and, thus, may be better "competitors" where conditions such as shown limit the mobility of deer and the amount of food available. Photograph courtesy of the Wyoming Department of Game and Fish.

Mule Deer/Bighorn Sheep

Although the distribution of mule deer almost completely overlaps that of bighorn sheep in the western United States and Canada, bighorn ranges constitute a very small proportion of the total range of mule deer. Studies of local populations indicate that, in many areas, these two species may occupy similar habitats and prefer much the same forage. In other areas their habitats and food habits are unrelated except in terms of general proximity. In general, bighorn sheep appear to be more selective and restricted in their use of habitats than are mule deer. Bighorn prefer rocky, inaccessible terrain (Capp 1968) or small, rather specific areas (Constan 1972; Hudson et al. 1976).

Comparisons of food habits (Capp 1968) indicate that bighorn generally utilize grasses to a much greater extent throughout the year and browse to a lesser extent than do mule deer in most areas. However, there is enough overlap in use of browse species to suggest local competition, especially on winter range. Capp (1968) thus noted that, in almost every area where they occur, during winter bighorn sheep appear to compete for forage with other wild ungulates. Competition also may occur during early spring when both mule deer and bighorn are feeding on limited supplies of new growth of grasses (Sheppard 1960; Lauer and Peek 1976). As yet, however, there seems to be no evidence that competition between bighorn sheep and mule deer has been a major limiting factor on either species.

Mule Deer/Moose

Moose occur within the range of mule deer along the southern edge of the boreal forest in Canada from Manitoba to British Columbia and in the Rocky Mountains of Montana, Idaho, Wyoming, and northeastern Utah. According to Prescott (1974), the moose is classified generally as a boreal/coniferous forest species, and the mule deer is classified as an occupant of more open range. Therefore the area of overlap may be marginal. In mountainous areas, however, moose and deer occur together seasonally in all major habitat types, from transitional foothills and wet bottomland to subalpine ranges. Moose seldom occur in large groups. This, plus the circumstance that moose can tolerate much greater snow depths than deer can, tends to distribute moose throughout the year to a greater extent than mule deer, which often concentrate in high densities on winter ranges.

Although food preferences of moose and mule deer may be very similar during winter, with both utilizing large amounts of the same browse species, the widespread distribution of moose may spread out browsing pressures (Prescott 1974). However, with persistent deep snow, moose may be forced into areas used by deer, and direct competition for forage may occur (Prescott 1974; Schladweiler 1974). Schladweiler believed competition probably would affect mule deer more drastically than it would affect moose. Prescott, on the other hand, suggested that the higher reproductive potential of deer would give deer the advantage in situations of initial invasions of new habitats or when recovering from low populations. Competition between mule deer and moose is not well documented, particularly on the basis of population consequences to either species.

Mule Deer/Pronghorn

Pronghorn may occur in association with mule deer on prairie and on mountain valley or basin grass and shrublands in many areas of western North America. They may utilize some of the same habitats and prefer many of the same forage plants throughout the year, but broad differences in food and cover requirements as well as in behavior probably minimize opportunities for interspecific interaction in most areas. Competition could occur in areas where high mule deer densities occur on open or broken prairie lands or along drainages that provide mule deer with cover and are used seasonally by pronghorn. It also could occur locally in rough uplands or foothills used seasonally by both species. Comparative studies, however, are lacking. This in itself might suggest that competition between the two has not been recognized as an important problem in any area.

Mule Deer/Mountain Goat

Mountain goats occur locally within the range of mule deer in many areas of the northern Rocky Mountain region in Alberta, British Columbia, Idaho, Montana, Oregon, Washington, and Wyoming. Introduced populations also occur in the Black Hills of South Dakota and northeastern Wyoming and in several areas of Colorado (Hibbs 1966). Habitat preferences and food habits of mountain goats seem to vary widely among local populations. Available data suggest that mountain goats and mule deer may overlap seasonally on many areas, and that there are similarities in habitat usage and forage selection. Interspecific competition generally has not been considered an important factor in the ecology of mountain goats in North America (Hibbs 1966). However, there are few comparative ecological studies with other wild ungulates, and general interrelationships with mule deer remain uncertain.

Mule Deer/Other Wild Ungulates

Bison may occur locally in association with mule deer, such as on the National Bison Range in western Montana. In the Southwest, collared peccary, Barbary sheep, and, locally, Siberian ibex, gemsbok × Kalahari oryx, and wild boar may occur on mule deer ranges. Wild boar also occur in California and Oklahoma, fallow deer may be found in north-central Nebraska, California, and British Columbia, and sambar deer and tahr both occur in San Luis Obispo County, California (Decker 1978). Ramsey (1970) listed twenty-six species of hoofed mammals that were introduced into Texas, of which eight have become established in large herds on private rangeland. Little in-

formation is available by which to judge possible interactions and competition between mule deer and any of these species. Knipe (1957) believed that competition is keen between peccaries and desert mule deer for herbs, especially in areas where these plants are scarce or in years of low forage production. Ogren (1962) indicated that Barbary sheep eat some of the same foods as mule deer, but that field observations showed that apparent competition may not be real because the sheep frequented and concentrated their feeding along the steepest canyon walls and on other sites that were little used by mule deer.

INTERSPECIFIC RELATIONSHIPS OF MULE DEER AND DOMESTIC LIVESTOCK

The relationships of mule deer with livestock have been very different from their relations with wild ungulates. There is no long history of cohabitation and adaptation. Except in the vicinity of Spanish settlements in the Southwest (especially in Texas, New Mexico, Arizona, and California), where livestock grazing dates back to the 1700s (Stewart 1936), livestock did not become a significant element on western rangelands generally until 1860–80. Also, livestock range use has been much more variable than that of wild ungulates. Seasonal patterns and intensities of use, stocking rates, and breeds or classes of livestock have changed almost constantly through time in most areas. Consequently, mule deer have had much less opportunity to adapt to livestock and livestock grazing patterns than to the more or less "fixed" patterns of use by wild ungulate species.

The ecology and behavior of domestic animals are entirely different from those of deer and other wild ungulates, and the responses of domestic animals to wild species are entirely different from the responses of deer to other wild animals (Mackie 1978). Centuries of domestication, husbandry, and selective breeding have made the domestic herbivore little more than a machine for converting vegetation to animal protein or other goods for people. Indeed, the major purpose for livestock is to make a profit from range forage (Raleigh and Lesperance 1972). Grazing, habitat use, and behavioral patterns of livestock often are highly stereotyped and controlled by man, so that they tend to be little influenced by the occurrence of other animals on rangelands. Also, the well-being of domestic animals generally rests with the livestock operator and depends on the husbandry employed. The prevalence of livestock has been enhanced by man's predation on wild herbivores and by protection from diseases, predation, and nutritional ailments through management efforts (Rice et al. 1971). From this perspective, livestock grazing may be viewed more as an environmental impact on mule deer than as a stage or setting for interspecific interaction and competition.

Once established in western North America, the livestock industry spread rapidly during the late 1800s. By the turn of the century, grazing had become a dominant factor in the ecology of mule deer throughout the West. The vast majority of mule deer range has been or is grazed at least seasonally by domestic stock. According to Wagner (1978), sheep (excluding lambs) numbered nearly 20 million by 1895, then varied from 20 to 30 million in the eleven westernmost United States until about 1945, when they declined by two-thirds to three-fourths until the present. Numbers of cattle rose more slowly, but continuously, from before the time of the great boom in range cattle, 1880–85 (Stewart 1936), to an all-time high of more than 20 million since the late 1960s.

Abusive rangeland use was most severe from 1880 to 1930 (Urness 1976). Unrestricted and selective grazing by livestock led to widespread alteration of original vegetation and soils. In some cases abuses have continued. Nearly one-third of public rangelands in the western United States currently are rated in poor or bad condition, and only 17 percent are considered good or excellent (U.S. Bureau of Land Management 1962–77 [1975]).

As I mentioned previously, the effects of heavy grazing probably contributed to the decline of mule deer populations during the late 1800s and early 1900s (see also chap. 12). Later the conversion of much western rangeland, by livestock grazing, from perennial grassland to a diverse array of shrub or annual grass forb types is believed to have favored mule deer in many areas. Many of the shrubs and other plant species that invaded or increased on disturbed rangeland were more palatable and digestible for deer than were perennial forage species (Longhurst et al. 1968*a*, 1976). Whatever the relationship, it is notable that the mule deer increase from the 1920s through the 1950s occurred in the presence of livestock and continued heavy grazing.

Today, approximately 70 percent of the eleven westernmost states remains subject to grazing (Council for Agricultural Science and Technology 1974), and forage demand for western livestock is at an all-time high as a result of growth in cattle numbers (Wagner 1978). The 23 million cattle, sheep, and lambs that grazed 238 million hectares (588 million acres) in 1970 represents an average stocking rate of about one animal per 10 hectares (25 acres). In contrast, fewer than 4 million mule deer were estimated to occur in the same area (Wagner 1978).

While local stocking rates and mule deer densities vary considerably, numbers of domestic animals frequently, if not usually, exceed those of deer, and total herbage removal by livestock grazing is much greater than that by mule deer. Beef cattle require 7.4–12.7 kilograms (16.3–28.0 pounds) dry weight forage per animal per day, and sheep need 1.5–2.3 kilograms (3.3–5.1 pounds) (Halls 1970). Nichol (1938) estimated the daily dry weight forage requirement of mule deer in southern Arizona at 1.1 kilogram (2.4 pounds), and Alldredge et al. (1974) obtained a similar estimate in Colorado. In Texas, Davis (1952) determined that, on the average, a 454 kilogram (1,000 pound) steer eats as much as do 13 white-tailed deer. Also, direct herbage consumption may account for only 36–47 percent of the total herbage removed or lost on rangelands where cattle are grazed (Pearson 1975), the remainder being lost to trampling and other factors. Laycock et al. (1972) estimated trampling losses due to cattle grazing at 17–23 percent of available herbage, and Quinn and Hervey (1970) estimated the loss at 1–5 percent. That diets of mule deer and livestock often overlap by only 1–10 percent is not sufficient basis for dismissing competition as insignificant when consumption and total herbage removal rates differ greatly (Hamlin 1978). Thus, whether reviewed in terms of distribution and numbers of livestock or of herbage removal and other vegetational influences, livestock grazing has to rate as one of the most important land-use or environmental variables affecting mule deer on rangelands.

There are no documented instances of mule deer directly influencing the numbers, distribution, or general well-being of any domestic species on rangeland, though range forage consumption and possible disease transmission occasionally have caused concern among stockmen and others (see chap. 4). McKean and Bartmann (1971) found that daily weight gains of livestock were not affected by moderate grazing by mule deer of controlled pastures during winter. However, there may be indirect operational effects as a result of deer damage to haystacks, crops, and fences. Thus changes in deer numbers, distribution, and behavior often are associated with livestock grazing and grazing management practices, but not the reverse. Tueller and Monroe (1974, pp. 6–7) noted that "throughout Nevada, deer did not compete with livestock for 'traditional' livestock forage (grass), nor, by virtue of low grass preference did they consume very large amounts, even at great deer populations. Livestock, however, consumed not only most of the 'traditional' livestock forage but . . . ate heavily of the best deer forages as well."

All large herbivores, both domestic and wild, are specialized to some degree in their nutritional requirements and in the kinds of plants or plant tissues they select (Bell 1971). The structure of their digestive systems differ, and so do the kinds of microorganisms that inhabit those systems and are an essential part of the digestive process in ruminants. Large herbivores also differ in their ability to tolerate or break down secondary plant compounds that may be toxic to

the animal or to microorganisms of the gastrointestinal tract (Longhurst et al. 1968a; Freeland and Janzen 1974). This may limit physiologically the kinds and amounts of food ingested (Smith 1959; Longhurst et al. 1968a) or may require simultaneous consumption of other kinds of plants to offset or neutralize the toxicity. Thus each species often is restricted in feeding to a particular portion of the total vegetation available. At the same time, certain available plants or plants utilized in only small amounts may be extremely important, and a variety of interspersed habitat types or plant communities—composed of different plant species—also may be important in satisfying requirements.

Low numbers of livestock may not infringe greatly on the dietary needs or other resource uses of mule deer because of differences between the two species in food and other requirements. However, some disturbance or interference types of impact may occur. Studies in north-central Montana indicated that radio-marked mule deer in rotationally grazed pastures either moved from the area or moved farther and used all parts of their home range more frequently after cattle were turned into pastures in which the deer occurred (Knowles 1975, 1976a; Komberec 1976). Other studies also have suggested that livestock may interfere with deer use of all available habitats and may preclude deer use of some (McMahan 1966; Ellisor 1969; Firebaugh 1969; Dusek 1971; Hood and Inglis 1974).

Wherever deer and livestock share a range, some overlap in uses of food and other resources is inevitable. And, as livestock numbers and forage utilization increase, the probability of overlap in the use of basic resources and the likelihood of impact on deer also increases. When forage supplies on primary range areas become depleted, livestock are forced to move farther and to use less-preferred plants and range sites more important to the deer. This also may occur in important mule deer habitats where other means are employed to distribute livestock grazing uniformly. On ranges heavily stocked or overstocked for long periods, direct and severe grazing impact is almost certain.

McKean and Bartmann (1971) found that mortality of mule deer was two to three times greater in areas where controlled study pastures were stocked and grazed heavily with livestock than in areas where pastures were grazed moderately by livestock. Similarly, with white-tailed deer in Texas, studies showed that heavy livestock use of pastures under controlled grazing either greatly reduced or eliminated deer use (Merrill et al. 1957; McMahan 1964; McMahan and Ramsey 1965). McMahan (1964) and McMahan and Ramsey (1965) reported satisfactory deer survival and reproduction only in areas where there was little or no competition from livestock; no fawns survived

Overgrazing is detrimental to the livestock industry as well as to wildlife. Before overgrazing, this range supported both deer and cattle, but the combination of too many cattle and drought in consecutive years eliminated the deer, and the cattle shown have no market value. Photograph by John McConnell.

in pastures heavily stocked by livestock.

Where mule deer continue to occur in areas grazed heavily by livestock, food habits may be greatly altered. McMahan (1964) noted that tame white-tailed deer used significantly more browse, greater amounts of grass, and less forbs during spring, summer, and autumn on pastures grazed by livestock, compared with forage use by whitetails on an ungrazed area. In Montana, Knowles (1976a) found much greater use of forbs, primarily yellow sweetclover, by mule deer in an ungrazed pasture than by mule deer on an adjacent pasture where cattle were grazed and browse was used to a greater extent. The difference was attributed to more intensive use by cattle of the latter pasture due to grazing treatments during the previous two years. In this respect one must recognize that most existing information on mule deer food habits and habitat selection has been collected in places where livestock grazing occurred and some impact was implicit. Therefore data used to determine whether competition is occurring or likely to occur usually reflect the effects of grazing. Indeed, heavy use and the apparent "preference" by mule deer for browse conceivably may be caused by use of other forage by domestic livestock. Use of certain habitat types, steeper slopes, or particular forage plants may reflect the presence and activities of prior foraging by livestock rather than an inherent requirement or preference of deer.

Changing stocking practices or breeds or classes of livestock may alter deer/livestock relationships greatly. Again, depending on stocking rates and primary distributional factors, the wider the range of vegetational types used by a domestic animal, the greater its potential impact on habitat.

Larger, more generalized herbivores can use a forage resource more completely than smaller, more specialized ones. This relates to both the structure of digestive tracts, and impediments imposed on passage of food through the gut, and to the absolute and relative maintenance requirements for protein and energy as determined by relative body size (Bell 1971). Large nonruminants, such as the horse and burro, have no mechanism in the digestive system that imposes a limit on how quickly food materials pass through the gut. Because of this, nonruminants use succulent grasses and forbs to their advantage but also can use coarse, fibrous forage more effectively than can ruminants such as cattle, sheep, and deer. The more elaborate ruminant digestive system emphasizes high efficiency of extraction and utilization of protein at the expense of a high rate of intake and processing of food; these animals must select for higher-protein plants or plant components. However, because of differences in metabolic rates associated with body size, smaller animals require more protein and energy per unit weight per day than do larger animals, though the absolute amount of forage required is less. The larger an animal, the greater is its tolerance for plants and plant tissue containing fibrous materials. Therefore cattle can use a wider range of plants and plant parts than sheep, which use grass and high-quality browse but apparently have a general preference for forbs. Goats, with a potential for increasing intake and turnover rate of fibrous forage in the gut, can consume more browse.

Mule deer require succulent forage for optimum growth and productivity (see chap. 3). Their relatively small digestive organs (see Nagy and Regelin 1975) and the limitations imposed by "fill" and turnover rate (see Ammann et al. 1973; Thornton and Minson 1972) make them incapable of deriving enough nutrients for maintenance from woody browse, though they browse woody stems extensively if necessary. Wallmo (1978) classed mule deer as "intermediate feeders," adaptable to a wide array of forage types.

A study in Texas revealed that, during drought and a scarcity of forbs, white-tailed deer preferred to forage with cattle and sheep, in that order, rather than with goats, with whom the deer competed for browse (Merrill et al. 1957). In periods of normal or above-normal moisture, the whitetails preferred to forage with cattle, then goats, and avoided sheep pastures, where the forbs were overused. According to Smith and Julander (1953, p. 112), food habits of domestic sheep generally overlap those of mule deer more closely than

those of cattle, such that "the similarity . . . is sure to cause conflict wherever the supply of preferred species is inadequate to meet the requirements of both animals."

Different breeds of cattle have different forage requirements and ways of utilizing range. Angus cattle typically tend to range more widely and use more (all) habitat types and steeper slopes than do Herefords. Also, yearlings, steers, and cows without calves have lower food requirements (Halls 1970) and are likely to range differently and use different plants than cows with young calves.

The diets of mule deer and domestic animals often are very similar in early spring, when they tend to seek out new, rapidly growing grasses and forbs on similar range sites. Substantial overlap in diets and range use may occur with very early grazing on many spring ranges where regrowth is not advanced, if temperatures and water requirements do not limit the distribution and movements of livestock. During this period, the nutritional needs of deer—especially pregnant does—are very high, and substantial quantities of new green plants are required. On some migratory ranges, early spring distribution of mule deer may be as limited as at any other time of the year, or more limited. Also, heavy grazing throughout spring may reduce fawning cover or fawn bedding cover significantly and be important in terms of newborn fawn security and survival.

Defoliation of many plants at any time during the green period may reduce their ability to regrow the next year, and close defoliation year after year ultimately results in loss of plants and depletion of food reserves for deer (Hormay 1970). Early spring browsing by livestock, especially sheep, tends to depress browse production (McKean and Bartmann 1971). Conversely, light use of some browse species by livestock in late spring and early summer may increase plant vigor and production for winter use by mule deer (Jensen et al. 1972).

Many comparative studies have recognized that range use and food habits of livestock and mule deer tend to become similar after midsummer, as grasses and forbs mature or are used more heavily than at other times. Under these conditions, livestock readily turn to palatable browse plants and distribute themselves more widely across the range. Autumn range may be very limited for many migratory mule deer populations, and autumn nutrition may be extremely important for growth and survival of fawns through winter and for production of a new fawn crop the following year (Wallmo and Gill 1971). The critical nature of winter range and forage for mule deer is universally recognized. Almost any livestock use of these ranges after annual plant growth has ended may have an adverse effect on deer.

The long-term influences of livestock grazing on vegetational characteristics of rangelands have been widely and intensively studied in western North America, especially with respect to successional changes. The net effect on mule deer and their habitat—including the kinds, quality, and amount of available food and cover—is poorly understood, but both beneficial and adverse effects occur (Urness 1976).

The possible beneficial effects on mule deer of early conversions of perennial grassland to shrub or annual grass forb types were noted previously. Whether continuation of historical grazing patterns is necessary in order to maintain mule deer habitat values has been a matter of debate. Longhurst et al. (1976) reasoned that recent declines in mule deer populations may be attributed to the long-term decline in domestic sheep grazing, which has resulted in plant succession toward species less palatable and digestible for deer, at least on annual grass forb ranges of California. In the same light, many range biologists and managers adhere to the concept that "sound grazing practices play an important role in maintaining adequate browse stands essential for big game" (Clawson and Lesperance 1973, p. 38). Also, Smith (1949) reported that removal of livestock grazing during the growing season on foothill winter range in Utah was followed by rapid recovery of perennial bunchgrasses and forbs and a reduction in shrub cover including palatable winter browse plants for mule deer.

Others believe that heavy grazing or overgrazing is inherently detrimental to mule deer

Intensive management of livestock can encourage certain practices—such as fencing and rest-rotational grazing of pastures—that may be beneficial or detrimental to deer, depending on when, where, and how they are applied. Photograph by Leonard Lee Rue III.

habitats. This view is supported by numerous examples where persistently heavy livestock grazing has led or contributed to widespread degradation of browse and other forage and cover plants important or essential to mule deer, as well as to reduction in other habitat values. Severson (see chap. 12) noted that livestock grazing on the northern Great Plains has extensively reduced or eliminated deciduous trees and shrub cover along drainageways. Cover, for security, is an important factor in mule deer use of Plains habitats, and its absence due to grazing has limited the occurrence of deer in many areas. In the Southwest, some biologists feel that livestock grazing continues to be destructive to wildlife habitats, including those of mule deer (Gallizioli 1977). McCulloch (1955) and Gallizioli (1977) both cited higher deer populations on the ungrazed Three Bar Range in Arizona—compared with similar adjacent vegetational types where cattle were grazed—as evidence that cattle compete with deer and limit their numbers. It also is contended that livestock grazing is the major factor influencing the quality of mule deer on ranges in the Chihuahuan Desert (see chap. 9, part 2).

Perhaps such divergent views should be expected. Climate and weather, vegetational types and successional relationships, grazing intensities and patterns, and the kinds and degrees of management employed all vary regionally. Patterns of habitat use and food habits of mule deer also vary, so that what is preferred and heavily used in one area may be avoided or of minimal value in another. In some areas, critical habitat elements for mule deer may be neither winter range nor browse supplies. A particular browse species can be a climax plant in one area or habitat and be successional in another. And it may vary genetically and physiologically from one habitat to another, so that its degree of use and its response to browsing also differ in various portions of mule deer range.

Often, the impact on mule deer of livestock grazing may be not so much a factor of the presence and activities of livestock, per se, as an effect of the range and grazing management practices employed in the livestock operation. As noted earlier, fencing, water development, alteration of vegetation through brush control, fertilization, and other vegetational management, the use of pesticides in range or cropland insect control, and the type of grazing management system employed may cause new effects or alter the nature of basic effects of livestock on mule deer. In addition there may be impact due to disturbance, alteration of predator-prey relationships, disease transmission, and changed relationships of mule deer and other wild ungulates.

Fencing—depending on the type and on when, where, and how it is used—can have an indirect effect on deer by interfering with migration or access to necessary seasonal habitat (Urness 1976). Direct mortality of animals crossing fences also may occur. In a Nevada study, fence kills accounted for 13 percent of 144 mule deer deaths caused by factors other than hunting and winterkill (Papez 1976). More important, perhaps, fencing controls livestock distribution and range use and thus indirectly influences the nature and extent of overlapping use of range resources by livestock and wild ungulates, including deer, with either beneficial or adverse effects.

In the same respect, water developments—depending on where, when, and how used—may influence livestock and mule deer distributions and uses of range. On some arid ranges, development and better distribution of water sources for livestock can benefit deer by permitting year-round or seasonal use of ranges from which they may have been excluded by a lack of free water (Wright 1959; Dasmann 1971). On other ranges, however, water development for livestock may have little or no beneficial effect on mule deer, or it may be detrimental. In recent years, water development has been used extensively on rangelands occupied by mule deer and other wild ungulates to obtain more uniform distribution of livestock in certain areas and, ostensibly, to reduce opportunities for interspecific competition. Frequently, successful redistribution of livestock in this manner infringes on areas and habitat resources previously used

Mule deer usually are adept at negotiating fences. Crawling *(top left)* is a common method when the deer are not hurried (photograph by Valerius Geist), as is leaping *(top right)* when they are startled or chased (photograph by Don Domenick; courtesy of the Colorado Division of Wildlife). Deep, soft snow *(bottom left)* and high, woven-wire fences *(bottom right)* can prove insurmountable for some mule deer, particularly fawns and animals in weakened condition (both photographs courtesy of the Wyoming Department of Game and Fish).

primarily or solely by mule deer or other wild ungulates. The result is further overlap of habitat use and increased opportunity for competition harmful to local mule deer populations. This is especially true on ranges grazed continuously over many years. It also is true on seasonally grazed ranges, particularly deer wintering areas, where stocking rates are high. Uniform livestock grazing patterns on some rangeland can have the additional adverse effect on mule deer of decreasing vegetational diversity of an area. Hamlin (1978) reported that almost all of the thirteen new stock water reservoirs, developed on his 259 square kilometer (100 square mile) study area in the Missouri River breaks, Montana, during the late 1960s and 1970s, were placed in primary mule deer habitat. This resulted in redistribution of more cattle into deer habitat, subsequent forage depletion around the reservoirs, and increased competition between deer and livestock on this area where high and medium mule deer densities occurred in places of least overlap with other ungulates.

Brush control and other vegetational management practices—to increase livestock use of rangeland, increase livestock forage production, or meet other range objectives—have been applied in varying degrees of intensity on public and private rangelands throughout the West. Effects on mule deer differ greatly, depending on the particular practices employed, the area and its habitat characteristics, time of year, size of the treated area, posttreatment management, and other factors. Potential or real conflicts arising from the loss of food or cover either directly (see Quimby 1966; Short et al. 1977) or through increased livestock use of treated areas concentrating deer in untreated areas, have been reported or suggested. In some areas, however, especially on chaparral-dominated southwestern range areas, brush control may create new openings and increase the diversity and quality of forage resources (see chap. 9, part 2).

It is possible that some chemical pesticides used in control of grasshoppers and other insects on rangelands or croplands may affect mule deer directly or indirectly. Although the toxicity to deer of some of these chemicals has

Construction of stockponds for livestock can benefit mule deer on some areas; on others it may lead to increased competition of livestock with deer by increasing the amount of overlap in areas grazed by the two animals. Top photograph taken in 1927 by Homer L. Shantz; bottom photograph from same vantage, taken in 1958 by Walter S. Phillips; both photographs courtesy of the Department of Botany, University of Arizona, Tucson.

been tested, with no evidence of pathogenicity at field application levels, additional study is needed. Schwartz et al. (1973) determined experimentally that high concentrations (1,000 parts per million) of several common pesticides (bordeaux mixture, toxaphene, Mema RM, DDT, ENP, Zeetran, dieldrin, parathion, Mobam, and aldrin) reduced in vitro dry matter and cell wall constituent digestibility of forage fed to domestic goats.

Rotation of livestock among pastures or deferment of grazing on portions of range are grazing systems being adopted increasingly on public lands in the West. They usually include increased fencing and water development and less continuous grazing from season to season than previously permitted. The basic objective is improvement of vegetation. The basic approach is rotational grazing of designated portions of a specific range management unit.

To date, very few studies have attempted to evaluate the effects of grazing systems on mule deer populations and habitat values. Skovlin et al. (1968) found that, in Oregon, mule deer preferred sites of rotational grazing over sites of year-round grazing, apparently owing to greater abundance of forage in the former system's deferred units. From studies in the Missouri River breaks of Montana, Knowles (1975) and Komberec (1976) reported little difference in forage plant selection and range use habits of mule deer on rest-rotational pastures as compared with continuously grazed range. However, Knowles observed differences in availability and use of forbs on rotationally grazed pastures. He attributed this to livestock grazing treatments and intensities during previous years, which influenced the occurrence of some forbs—especially yellow sweetclover, a biennial preferred by deer.

A mule deer fawn is unable to get out of a water tank installed exclusively for cattle. Deer mortality from artificial water sources is uncommon, but the concentration of livestock in areas that otherwise might be important deer habitat may be a significant limiting factor. Photograph courtesy of the Arizona Department of Game and Fish.

Merrill et al. (1957) found that, in Texas, white-tailed deer made greater use of pastures in a rest-rotational system than of those grazed year-round at lighter rates. Although mule deer distribution and movements appeared to be somewhat influenced by grazing treatments, and fawn production and survival may be depressed on ranges where pastures are subject to heavy livestock grazing, the results of Knowles's (1976*a*) study still are largely inconclusive with respect to the ultimate effects of rest-rotation grazing on mule deer.

Possible disturbance effects stemming from the highly variable nature of livestock grazing and many grazing management practices have not been studied widely in wildlife/livestock relationships. Mayr (1963) observed that dramatic competition occurs only where populations of two or more species come newly into contact, or where radical environmental change upsets a previous existing dynamic balance among habitat conditions and the cohabiting species. Also, what is known about the effects of disturbance on animal behavior, with repercussions on the physiology, population dynamics, and ecology of the animal (see Geist 1971*a*), is cause for concern and additional research. Also pertinent to future investigation are Beament's (1961) conclusions that (1) an animal's environment is what it selects through its behavior mechanisms, and (2) behavioral effects of competition or other environmental factors can lead away from what might be considered optimal with respect to the physiological adaptations and needs of at least one of the competing animals.

Choice and use of habitats and forage by mule deer, as with other wild animals, are governed closely by behavioral mechanisms, including innate response, preference, and population or group tradition that can be learned. Each animal strives to live and functions best in a thoroughly familiar (predictable and stable) physical and social environment (Geist 1971*a*). In this context, any environmental change that is unknown to the animal becomes a disturbance. The more severe or unpredictable the disturbance, the more likely it is to be detrimental to the physiology and ecology of the animal through stress alterations of behavior.

Predator control on rangelands has always been vigorously pursued by livestock grazing interests, especially sheepmen. As a result, benefits may accrue to mule deer, at least on local areas. On the other hand, the way livestock are grazed may indirectly influence the predator-prey relationship of coyotes and deer by altering rodent numbers. Where livestock grazing leaves little residual vegetation, populations of some rodent species may be reduced, forcing coyotes to seek alternative food sources, including deer. In other cases, some rodent species may be encouraged by certain grazing practices and pressures.

Possible disease transmissions between domestic livestock and mule deer periodically have concerned wildlife managers and stockmen alike. This concern occasionally is justified by serious effects, such as the mass reduction of the Stanislaus deer herd in California during an outbreak of foot-and-mouth disease that was introduced to cattle in the area by a naval vessel and subsequently transmitted to mule deer (Leopold et al. 1951). The potential for disease transmission is reviewed in chapter 4.

Mule deer frequently occur on rangelands in association with one or more other species of wild ungulates as well as with domestic livestock. Because each wild species may respond differently to the presence of livestock and the effects of livestock grazing or livestock management practices, interspecific relationships may differ from those observed when only one species or the other is present. For example, range use and food habits of elk are similar to and in many respects overlap with those of both mule deer and cattle. However, elk tend to avoid cattle or areas grazed by cattle whenever possible (Skovlin et al. 1968; Mackie 1970; Lonner 1975; Knowles 1975; Komberec 1976). Areas to which elk move to avoid cattle or cattle-grazed land often are important habitats for mule deer. Thus the presence of cattle can bring about or intensify competition between elk and mule deer.

Chapter 14

CONFLICTS WITH CIVILIZATION

Dale F. Reed
Wildlife Researcher
Colorado Division of Wildlife
Wheat Ridge, Colorado

Anthropologists are quite certain that man first occupied the North American continent as a result of invasion rather than evolution. They are less certain about the specific time of this invasion, but it is widely believed among these scientists that the general period was 27,000 to 17,000 years ago. The immigration undoubtedly centered on a land bridge crossing what is now the Bering Strait between the Chukotski Peninsula, Soviet Union, and the Seward Peninsula, Alaska. There may have been other routes or corridors, but their existence and use are a matter of speculation, since there is no hard evidence. Nevertheless, prehistoric invasion of North America by man was a gradual and sporadic process over the course of many thousands of years.

When European man "discovered" and first occupied North America within the past millennium, the total human population of the continent probably numbered less than 300,000. But the earliest invaders—the "native Americans"—were hardy and self-sufficient people who survived by living in relative harmony with the landscape. Because of the natives' small numbers, primitive life-styles, and cultural kinship with their environment, the Europeans found a land of pristine, if somewhat desolate, wilderness.

European man's invasion of North America coincided generally with the inception of the industrial and medical revolutions. Firearms were becoming widely available. Machines and "power" tools were replacing hand tools. The causative agents of disease were discovered, and methods for their control were soon to follow. Human life expectancy and proliferation increased greatly. Each of the multiplying individuals had the potential to modify his surroundings more rapidly than could an entire community of aboriginals. Collectively, the influence of the "new" North Americans grew exponentially.

If it were possible to obtain comparative satellite views for the years 1480 and 1980, our perspective of the magnitude of changes on the surface of North America might be improved. Instead, imagination must substitute. There is a reason to believe that, in some respects and for some periods, the changes were beneficial to deer. In other respects they were detrimental. Any generalization, however, must consider that deer are conceptualized as "wild" life, dependent for maintenance of populations on suitable expanses of wildlands and sufficient freedom from man-related sources of harassment and mortality. If a current satellite view of North America were to be accompanied by a series of ground level transects across biomes that are or were inhabited by deer—bisecting cities, suburbs, farms, factories, highways, fences, fields, pastures, strip mines, sawmills, airports, dams, reservoirs, canals, and campgrounds and including the growing masses of living resources—it no longer would be germane to ask how closely that conceptualized ideal is approximated.

If our society's sense of values includes wildlife, the most pertinent questions include: How far have we departed from the ideal? How fast are we losing ground? And can processes of change be slowed or reversed? Because answers involve the complexities of our entire social and economic system as well as the ecology of deer, they cannot be answered fully in a single chapter or even a book. Nevertheless, the relationship of deer ecology to the social trends and capabilities of human society must be identified and given serious consideration if deer are to retain their value as a resource of the future.

The earliest economic ventures by Europeans in much of the West were fur trapping and mining. The former had a miniscule effect on the native landscape. The latter created cities, justified railroads, denuded forests locally, and focused attention on deer as a source of food. The next economic waves were agriculture and livestock, which transformed the Great Plains and the mountain valleys to the west. Where there was insufficient water, rivers were impounded and the water rechanneled to create arable land. Throughout this period of the late 1800s and early 1900s, logging and lumbering grew in step with demand of local markets until transportation facilities were adequate for an export market. Still, the human population was small relative to similar land areas in the eastern United States. After constraints were imposed on hunting and extensive areas were inadvertently converted to more productive deer habitat, the populations of deer mushroomed.

During the 1940s and 1950s, there may have been more mule deer and blacktails than ever before in history. The management prescription was simple: keep deer populations within the carrying capacities of their habitats through liberal hunting. In the 1960s, however, not all deer populations were responding as anticipated. By the mid-1970s, wildlife management agencies throughout the West concluded that the prescription was not working. Its premise still seemed sound, so other factors obviously were involved. In several conferences and symposia on the subject (see chap. 6), many factors were considered.

The United States Department of Agriculture (1974) projected that the amount of land devoted to urban, industrial, and related uses in the United States in 1949 would double by the year 2000. Meanwhile, the area of rangeland and pasture was projected to remain essentially unchanged, and forest woodland acreage was expected to decline slightly. A disproportionate amount of the urban-related growth was anticipated in the West. The human population clustered along the Front Range of the Rocky Mountains in Colorado quadrupled between 1950 and 1970, while the population of the United States as a whole increased 34 percent. In 1950 mule deer and whitetails occupied gaps between communities at the base of the Colorado Front Range. Today there are few gaps.

Human population growth in the West since the 1860s, particularly in recent decades, has been prompted to a considerable extent by congestion in the East. In any case, the effect on mule deer habitat of human population growth and movements toward open spaces in the West may be more significant than habitat losses to urban expansion. For example, in 1940 the nation's roads and highways received some 486 billion kilometers (302 billion miles) of vehicle use. By 1970, annual vehicle use was 1,804 billion kilometers (1,121 billion miles)—an increase of 371 percent in a thirty-year period when roads and highways increased 28 percent and the national population increased 54 percent (U.S. Department of Commerce 1972).

As the habitat base for mule deer has shrunk because of human population growth and movement, it also has been preempted in many areas by the demand for recreation space. From 1950 to 1977, for example, the use of national forests in the United States, expressed as "visitor-days," increased nearly 1,000 percent. In addition to transient visits to outdoor recreational areas, many people have built permanent or part-time residences in the country to more fully enjoy the amenities of open space. Incursions of this sort certainly affect the suitability of habitat for deer, but there are cases to demonstrate that a harmonious relationship of deer and people can exist (Geist 1966a, 1971a). Whether deer still qualify as "wildlife" after they have become habituated to people, however, is sometimes debated.

Other kinds of human intrusions into wild

land can irreversibly eliminate deer habitat. Urban sprawl and certain industrial developments are in this category. Still other intrusions only modify the habitat—sometimes only temporarily—such as strip mining followed by reclamation. Effects of agriculture can range from beneficial—if the farming practices allow for patches of deer cover and include crops used by deer—to destructive—if cropland is extensive, unbroken by shelter and surface water resources, and if crops are of insufficient diversity or quality to supplement natural forage.

Because mule deer of one subspecies or another have occupied nearly every ecosystem of the West, though not in equal densities or in all seasons, every activity of man on any part of the landscape has had an impact on mule deer. This chapter examines the influences of several conspicuous activities of man and their byproducts. It also reviews measures that have been proposed or tested to mitigate adverse effects on deer.

AGRICULTURE

Cropland

Interactions of mule deer and agriculture on the Plains were discussed in chapter 12. In this chapter, mule deer/agriculture relationships in the area from the Rocky Mountains westward—approximately one-third of the United States and portions of Canada and Mexico—will be presented. West of the Rocky Mountains, farming has become established wherever topography and soils permit. Water has been made available in most places where topography and soils are conducive to agriculture. West of the Rocky Mountain chain, about 80 million hectares (198 million acres) of land are devoted to agriculture (Statistics Canada 1973; U.S. Department of Commerce 1972). This constitutes nearly one-fifth of the total land area within the range of mule deer from the Rockies westward. However, the extent to which agriculture excludes deer varies with its local continuity.

Extensive agricultural land is concentrated in several areas in the West: (1) a belt between the Coast Range and the Cascades from British Columbia to west-central Oregon; (2) the southeastern quarter of Washington and adjacent Oregon and Idaho; (3) the Sacramento, San Joaquin, and Imperial valleys of California; (4) south-central Idaho to south-central Utah; (5) the Salt and Gila river valleys of Arizona; and (6) a strip along the Rio Grande from northern New Mexico into Texas. Although mule deer and blacktails have not been entirely eliminated in these areas, they remain in small numbers only in pockets of marginal habitat or on peripheral terrain that permits them to make occasional use of farmland. Where agriculture is continuous and extensive, there no longer is a conflict between mule deer and farming because, for the most part, deer have been excluded. Where agriculture is interspersed with otherwise normal habitat, the presence of deer may result in measurable or contended damage to crops. On the other hand, agriculture interspersed with deer habitat can provide benefits to deer, as is the case for blacktails in the chaparral zone of northern California (see chap. 9, parts 1 and 2).

Historical records offer little information useful for interpreting the effect of agricultural development on numbers and distribution of mule deer. However, if relationships of topography, cover preferences, and seasonal distributions of mule deer are understood correctly, we can assume that agriculture has influenced deer in areas where they were widely dispersed before agriculture was introduced. This assumption is not valid with respect to the many areas where tillable lowlands constituted deer winter range.

In montane regions, high precipitation and, consequently, deep snow are the cause of mule deer migration to areas of lower precipitation in the valleys. Were it not for irrigation, much of the lowland would be unsuitable for agriculture. But development of irrigation has been one of the major factors in the economic development of the West. In 1964 the seventeen western states of the United States accounted for more than 13.4 million hectares

Early agricultural practices in the West probably had limited impact on mule and black-tailed deer. But, as farms—such as this homestead in the state of Washington—grew larger and more abundant, deer tended to be excluded from areas of preferred habitat that were converted to cropland. Photograph by C. H. Park; courtesy of the United States National Archives.

(33.1 million acres) of 15 million hectares (37.1 million acres) under irrigation nationwide (National Research Council 1970). Much of this land was cultivated first as dryland, but large areas of "new" cropland have been created by irrigation. In the most arid states—New Mexico, Arizona, Utah, and Nevada—121,403 hectares (299,987 acres) of new farmland have been added as a result of irrigation.

The National Research Council (1970) reported that 51 percent of irrigated cropland in the West was used to grow livestock feed—much of it in pasture, hayfields, and unharvested crops. From these practices, deer may realize some benefits not possible if these same lands were used for grain production or other harvested crops. As is discussed later, even though deer benefit from certain agricultural practices, and even though deer may be tolerated or enjoyed in one way or another by farmers, the farmers' primary interest is managing land for the crops that are their livelihood.

Considering the long-standing interest in mule and black-tailed deer by the public and

within the wildlife profession, it is remarkable that there is so little information about the encroachment of civilization on deer habitat. An effort to obtain such information with regard to agriculture in Colorado resulted in an estimate that, from the Front Range of the Rockies westward, 5.8 percent of the mule deer range was in irrigated cropland and 1.1 percent in nonirrigated cropland (Wallmo et al. 1976). That amount of cropland was construed as a negligible influence on deer populations. But, more important, the fragmentary sources from which the estimates were derived revealed the deplorable state of land resources inventories. Implementation of the Forest and Rangeland Renewable Resources Planning Act of 1974 may improve this situation in the United States.

Rangeland

" 'The forty-niner,' on his way overland to the Pacific Coast, found a vast, unspoiled natural reservoir of forage extending from the Mississippi River to the Pacific Ocean and from

By 1886 the number of cattle grazing western rangelands was more than 7.6 million, which then probably was greater than the total of all big game animals in what is now the lower forty-eight United States. Photograph by E. E. Smith; courtesy of the United States Library of Congress.

Canada to Mexico. . . . How could they have guessed that this land would produce five times more wealth for the Nation through the pasturage of livestock than all the gold they would dig out of the earth with their picks and shovels" (McArdle and Costello 1936, p. 71). In the mid-1800s this seemingly endless "wasteland" was the domain of Indians and wildlife. By 1886 more than 7.6 million cattle were grazing rangelands of the eleven westernmost states, as were large numbers of sheep between 1880 and 1910 (Stewart 1936).

In the late 1800s sheep caused extensive damage to western rangelands, particularly to areas already grazed by cattle—which the sheep outnumbered. Photograph courtesy of the United States Library of Congress, Wittemann Collection.

The range cattle industry, operating on a narrow profit margin because of the cost of shipping to eastern markets, was forced to gouge the forage resource to its limit in order to survive. Blizzards and droughts of the late 1880s nearly wrecked it. On rangeland where cattle could no longer subsist, sheep and goats took over to strip what was left of a depleted resource. The nation had not learned to avoid overgrazing before the next great drought in the 1930s, which nearly completed the devastation of western range.

An epochal publication, *The Western Range* (U.S. Congress, Senate 1936), documented the resource destruction and set the first guidelines for its restoration. But extensive changes in the virgin plant cover already had occurred. According to McArdle et al. (1936) sagebrush/grass range had expanded by some 2.4 million hectares (6 million acres). Woodland/chaparral vegetation increased by 1.4 million hectares (3.4 million acres) in California alone. Much of the Pacific bunchgrass range had given way to shrubland. Nearly half of the shortgrass plains had suffered severe depletion, and most of the remainder experienced substantial depletion. Vast areas of semidesert grassland had been degraded to desert scrub and noxious weeds. While the piñon/juniper vegetational type had changed little in total area, tree stands generally had thickened, and useful forage plants commonly associated with piñon/juniper had "practically vanished" from much of it (McArdle et al. 1936, p. 102). It is presumed that these changes were not conducive to efficient livestock production, but they provided food and cover benefits to mule deer.

Since the 1950s, nearly 2 million hectares (4.9 million acres) of sagebrush lands, 1 million hectares (2.5 million acres) of piñon/juniper woodland, and perhaps a like area of chaparral have been treated mechanically, chemically, or with fire in the United States to improve their carrying capacity for livestock (Biswell et al. 1952; Cable 1975; Terrell and Spillet 1975; Vale 1974). At first this continued manipulation of vegetation was received inhospitably by wildlife managers. Lately they have taken a more favorable attitude and, due in part to federal policy of multiple-use management, have participated in such efforts for the benefit of both deer and livestock.

In 1918, rangeland of the eleven westernmost states was grazed by livestock to the extent of about 210 million animal unit months (Chapline 1936). In general, an "animal unit month" (AUM) is defined as the amount of forage eaten by one cow, one horse, one mule, five sheep, five swine, or five goats for one month. According to carrying capacity of a given range in a given year, animal unit months are calculated in terms of grazing space and allotted for a designated period of time. The United States Department of Agriculture (1972) noted that estimated use of rangeland in the lower forty-eight states by cattle and sheep in 1970 was 213 million animal unit months. It also indicated that future use would have to increase to 320 million and 394 million animal unit months to meet beef needs by the year 2000 and mutton needs by 2020.

The geographic range of mule deer overlaps about 60 percent of the "forest-range" ecosystems of the lower forty-eight states. About 83 percent of the area within the geographic range of mule deer is classified as "rangeland." Of western rangeland, about 93.2 million hectares (230.4 million acres) out of 169.4 million hectares (418.6 million acres), or 55 percent, is in federal ownership. Of western forestland, about 40 million hectares (99 million acres) out of 65 million hectares (160.6 million acres), or 62 percent, is in federal ownership. And, of Great Plains "forest-range" about 4.5 million hectares (11 million acres) out of 92.6 million hectares (228.9 million acres), or 5 percent, is federally owned (U.S. Department of Agriculture 1972).

It is on those 140 million hectares (346 million acres) or so of government land that effective pressure is most likely to be exerted for preservation of mule deer habitat. The economic incentive for raising livestock on rangeland is the opportunity to exploit natural forage at nominal cost. Thus, rangeland may be expected to remain more nearly in the original habitat types than will any lands other than parks, wilderness areas, and similar preserves.

Damage by Deer

Crop depredation by mule deer has been a problem at least since pioneer times (Young 1956). Since then, demand for increased food and fiber production has accelerated agriculture in many areas of the West, especially in mountainous areas where irrigation has been developed. If, as suggested by Harder (1968), mule deer populations increased from the 1930s through the 1960s, the extent of crop damage by deer probably also increased during the period.

McDowell and Pillsbury (1959) found that four western states—Colorado, Utah, Washington, and Wyoming—compensated farmers and ranchers for crop damage caused by some game species. Damage was caused primarily by mule deer, the most abundant and widespread big game species in the western states. Deer damage of economic importance often occurs during winter when migratory herds are concentrated at low elevations on range adjacent to ranches, hayfields, stackyards, and orchards. As might be expected, crop damage and claims can vary widely from year to year depending on weather and other factors, such as deer population levels and range conditions.

Mule deer in Colorado typically respond to new growth on pasture and hayland meadows in early spring (April–May) (Bartmann 1974). Crested wheatgrass is noted for its early growth and use by deer. Other species, including alfalfa, are grazed as new growth, or "green up," occurs. Despite abundant complaints of damage, little attention has been given to quantifying the net economic impact of forage eaten by mule deer. The absence of such documentation works in favor of the public agencies responsible for compensating the losses. For example, under Colorado laws, the state is liable for damage to orchards and to crops under cultivation or harvested, but only moderate numbers of deer damage claims have been filed and paid. Whether these public funds are well spent is arguable, because the extent of deer dependence on this forage—in relation to the benefits that accrue to a particular area as a result of croplands maintaining a productive deer population—remains unknown.

In some areas of the West, mule deer damage to crops is an economic burden on some ranchers and farmers. In many instances, deer feeding at stockyards during periods of nutritional stress do considerable damage to themselves as well. Photograph courtesy of the Wyoming Department of Game and Fish.

In a literature review of orchard damage by deer, Harder (1968) reported that Colorado expended $7,585.73 for deer and elk damage to orchards during 1964–65. From 1966 to 1977, individual claims for damage by deer ranged from $157 to $12,366 and averaged $4,652. If payment of claims actually approximates the value of crops lost, the damage cannot be considered a significant cost either to the taxpayer or in terms of crop production.

Various methods have been used to control deer damage to crops. Emergency feeding programs, in general, continue to be viewed unfavorably. Hunter and Yeager (1956) discussed the cost and consequences of artificial and emergency feeding and indicated that many animals have died from impaction and related problems during such programs. Some states practice artificial feeding over longer periods. Other control measures involve use of scare devices, chemical repellents, fencing, removal by shooting or trapping, and population control through recreational hunting. Removable or permanent stackyards, when properly installed, have been relatively effective in lessening depredation on hay in Colorado and Wyoming. Harder (1968) reviewed methods for preventing damage to orchards and concluded that population control through recreational hunting offered the best and most economical solution. However, complex social, institutional, and political obstacles commonly preclude applying this solution precisely when and where the damage occurs. Therefore a plaintiff's best resort—usually with full cooperation of the local wildlife management agency—is a combination of control methods.

Fencing is a costly method to control deer damage, but it is effective. To offset costs, some state wildlife agencies have instituted cost-sharing arrangements with landowners whose property or crops are repeatedly subject to deer depredation. Photograph courtesy of the Oregon Department of Fish and Wildlife.

Blood meal in a cloth bag has been used as a deer repellent to protect orchards. Photograph courtesy of the Oregon Department of Fish and Wildlife.

One method of preventing deer damage to crops is to use scare devices, such as a butane-fed cannon that goes off at timed intervals. Photograph courtesy of the Oregon Department of Fish and Wildlife.

MINING

"Gold!" That mineral turned the invasion of the West from a trickle to a stampede. Although gold eventually turned out to be of less importance than numerous other mineral resources of the continent, it was a significant factor in the origin and growth of the West's mining industry. Antimony, borax, copper, lead, molybdenum, silver, tungsten, zinc, and many other minerals also played a part. Large mining and processing centers developed throughout the range of mule deer, from the Black Hills to the west coast, from Alaska to Chihuahua, Mexico. Population centers grew, then stabilized to a degree, in the vicinity of mines, and mule deer served as a major food and recreational resource.

Coal, oil, oil shale, and uranium also occurred in vast quantities, but their exploitation was minimal at first. Strip mining of coal on western ranges abruptly accelerated after 1973, with the recognition of impending energy shortages. Government programs were instituted to stimulate and regulate the mining activity.

The potential of surface mining to wreak environmental damage is a major contemporary dilemma. About 21 percent of the United States west of the 100th meridian is underlain by coal, but only a small portion of it can be strip mined (fig. 52). The National Academy of

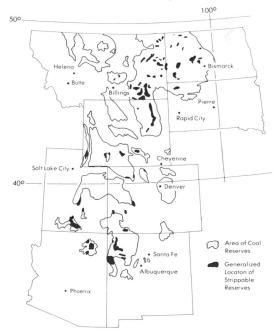

Figure 52. Major coal reserves west of the 100th meridian in the United States (after National Academy of Sciences 1974).

Mining attracted settlement to some areas in the West that then would not support other types of human occupation. Mule deer and other wildlife were exploited as a major source of food. Photograph of Bisbee, Arizona, taken in 1895; courtesy of the United States Soil Conservation Service.

Early mining practices that influenced habitat were not necessarily confined to the immediate site. As is shown in this early photograph, an area of Colorado was logged excessively to provide timber for mine props. Photograph by A. C. Verela; courtesy of the United States Forest Service.

Sciences (1974) estimated that the land area disturbed by surface mining as of 1 January 1972, plus projected disturbance from 1972 to 2000, would constitute only about 0.03 percent of the total area within the seven states where it will occur (table 70). Although this seems to represent a small portion of the total landscape, all of it is within the range of mule deer, and much of it occurs in critical or limited winter range.

Three of the six general vegetational types on the seven strippable areas in Colorado are important for mule deer (fig. 52). These three—sagebrush, mountain mahogany/oak, and piñon/juniper—made up an average of 18.3, 20.7, and 19.7 percent, respectively, of vegetation in the seven areas. Mapping done by the Colorado Division of Wildlife indicates that most of the seven reserves are under important mule deer ranges (Colorado Division of Wildlife/U.S. Fish and Wildlife Service 1978). Thus, about 2,075–3,535 hectares (5,127–8,735 acres) of important mule deer range are projected to be disturbed by coal surface mining in Colorado by the year 2000. Montana has more than 455,144 hectares (1,124,686 acres) of important mule deer range underlain by coal that can be strip-mined (Martinka 1974).

Oil shale extraction has high potential for disturbing ranges of mule deer in Colorado (Kilburn 1976), Utah, and Wyoming. Six tracts

of National Resource Land have been set aside or leased for prototype oil shale development in major oil shale reserve areas (fig. 53). Two of the tracts in western Colorado, C-a and C-b,

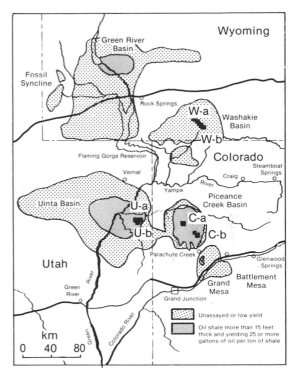

Figure 53. Major oil shale deposits in the United States. Most of the high-grade ore is found in the Piceance Creek Basin in western Colorado. Black areas indicate the tracts of federal land leased for private development (after Metz 1974).

Table 70. Estimation of Land Disturbances from Surface Coal Mining in Selected Western States

State	Total Area		Area Underlain by Coal		Estimated Area of Disturbance as of 1 January 1972		Projected Area of Disturbance, 1972–2000	
	Hectares	Acres	Hectares	Acres	Hectares	Acres	Hectares	Acres
Arizona	29,502,296	72,901,760	787,356	1,945,600	40	100	15,716	38,836
Colorado	26,999,849	66,718,080	7,666,365	18,944,000	1,214	3,000	3,535	8,736
Montana	38,108,567	94,168,320	13,286,639	32,832,000	850	2,100	17,071	42,182
New Mexico	31,511,349	77,866,240	3,794,333	9,376,000	1,174	2,900	13,285	32,829
Utah	21,993,143	54,346,240	3,884,982	9,600,000	Negligible	Negligible	3,351	8,280
Washington	17,661,647	43,642,880	297,849	736,000	81	200	4,257	10,520
Wyoming	25,359,610	62,664,960	10,374,197	25,635,200	728	1,800	9,547	23,592
Total	191,136,461	472,308,480	40,091,721	99,068,800	4,087	10,100	66,762	164,975

Source: National Academy of Sciences (1974).

[a] The Colorado Division of Mine Land Reclamation listed 5,608 hectares (13,857 acres) of land to be reclaimed by forty-two surface coal mines as of December 1978.

involve approximately 4,145 hectares (10,242 acres) of mule deer range in the Piceance Creek Basin. Besides these tracts, additional areas—such as the Colony Development Plant in the Parachute Creek drainage—may be expanded if favorable economic conditions develop.

Greatest disturbance is likely at the lease and disposal sites of tract C-a, where surface mining techniques may be used (U.S. Department of the Interior 1973). Rogers (1974) speculated that production of 119,246,471 liters (1 million barrels) of oil per day would result in the removal of several wildlife species, including deer, from approximately 60,699 hectares (149,990 acres). Four management units of the Colorado Division of Wildlife in the area of oil shale activity had the highest total deer kill of any four contiguous units in Colorado, with a mean annual harvest of 11,209 deer on 733,984 hectares (1,813,714 acres) (Colorado Division of Wildlife 1963–76).

Uranium mining and sand and gravel mining also disturb significant expanses of wildlife habitat (Copeland 1973). Cook (1976) delineated five large areas where uranium could be surface-mined in Arizona, Colorado, New Mexico, Utah, and Wyoming. The Colorado Division of Mine Land Reclamation (pers. comm., December 1978) reported 12,556 hectares (31,027 acres) of land in 851 different sand and gravel operations that required reclamation to comply with the Colorado Mine Land Act. Most involved only a few hectares, but each radically modified the site on which it was situated. All other surface and underground mine disturbances in Colorado totaled 8,685 hectares (21,461 acres).

It has been suggested that prompt revegetation of mined lands may solve problems associated with loss of deer winter range (Special Committee of the Governor's Oil Shale Advisory Committee 1971). But revegetation of mined lands is a lengthy process when woody species are involved and may not be successful in many areas of the West (National Academy of Sciences 1974). A formidable research effort was launched to devise methods for effective revegetation of areas disturbed by surface mining (Brown et al. 1976; Farmer et al. 1974, 1976; Packer 1974). Surface Environment and Mining (SEAM) is a major program organized by the United States Forest Service to research, develop, and apply technology to help maintain surface values and a quality environment while helping meet the nation's mineral needs. Many other state and federal agencies and universities are involved in that program or in other research directed at those objectives. Among them are the United States Environmental Protection Agency, Bureau of Land Management, Agricultural Research Service, Soil Conservation Service, Intermountain and Rocky Mountain Forest and Range Experiment Stations of the Forest Service, Colorado State University, and the University of Wyoming. In Montana, the Department of Natural Resources, the Bureau of Mines and Technology, and the Fish and Game Department also are involved. This list is not all-inclusive; several mining companies also are involved in the research.

It may be fortunate, as expressed by Packer (1974, p. 43), that "those portions of the Northern Great Plains that present the most difficult rehabilitation problems are also the smallest areas that will be disturbed for a given amount of extracted coal. Conversely, the easiest rehabilitation problems exist in those portions of the Northern Great Plains where the largest areas will be disturbed per unit of extracted coal." Packer conceded, however, that expeditious, effective, and economical rehabilitation depends on considerable knowledge that has not yet been acquired. There is growing confidence that areas affected by acid mining wastes from mineral ore production also can be revegetated, but the cost of the effort and the time required may be appreciable (Brown and Johnston 1976; Farmer et al. 1976).

The potential effect on wildlife, direct or indirect via habitat degeneration, has not yet been qualified or quantified, but some evidence suggests that it may not and need not be absolute. Mule deer and, more frequently, pronghorn continued to occupy areas of the Bell Ayre coal mine, south of Gillette, Wyo-

Strip mining in the West is entirely within the range of mule deer, and much of it occurs on critical or limited deer winter range. Extraction of fossil fuels is a foregone conclusion in many areas; the major concern, with respect to wildlife, is how strip-mined areas can best and most expeditiously be reclaimed as viable habitat. Photograph by D. J. Feeling; courtesy of the United States Soil Conservation Service.

ming, in the midst of mining activity (J. Thilenius, pers. comm., December 1977). A nonharassment policy was enforced at Bell Ayre that may have made the area something of a sanctuary. Thilenius also observed pronghorn resting within the factory area of a uranium processing plant in the Gas Hills of Wyoming. The few strip-mined areas that had the overburden replaced and then were revegetated suggest that it is possible to restore a site to a reasonable semblance of natural terrain and vegetation.

It seems unlikely that preservation of wildlife habitat will take precedence over mineral or fossil fuel exploitation. After mineral exploitation of an area is completed, scars eventually

may be healed by natural processes, but human ingenuity, creativity, and commitment will be needed to hasten the recovery.

RESERVOIRS AND WATER DEVELOPMENT

Demand for water for agricultural, domestic, and industrial uses, including hydroelectric power, has resulted in a substantial increase in the number of reservoirs and water development projects in recent years. While small bodies of water in selected areas of the semiarid West may increase the availability of water and therefore improve the habitat of mule deer, large bodies of water can result in habitat loss and may act as barriers to daily or seasonal movements. The extent to which habitat is lost is indicated by the fact that about 87 percent of surface water area in the eleven westernmost states is composed of bodies of water larger than 16.2 hectares (40 acres) (table 71). Considering the locale and terrain selected for large impoundments, it is safe to say that most have flooded areas once inhabited by mule deer. Whether the water, in specific cases, improves the peripheral habitat or impedes its use by deer is a question that arises in planning and in subsequent evaluation of a project's effect.

Piñon-juniper woodland, mountain brush, northern desert shrub, salt desert shrub, and southern desert shrub are major habitat types for mule deer in the Upper Colorado region of Arizona, Colorado, New Mexico, and Utah (fig. 54). Within this region, the total area covered by these vegetation types is 8,694,123 hectares (21,483,647 acres), or 29.6 percent of the gross area. Nineteen reservoir or irrigation projects will cover 80,725 hectares (199,476 acres) of land in these vegetation types, providing a total of 107,191 hectares (264,874 acres) of water surface area (S. McCall, pers. comm., March 1977). The land surface lost will be less than 1 percent of the gross area.

Other disturbances accompany reservoir construction. For example, the Dallas Creek Project in southwestern Colorado resulted in relocation of United States Highway 550 and

Table 71. Water Surface Area in Eleven Western States

State	Total Area of Water Surfaces Less Than 16.2 Hectares (40 Acres) in Size		Total Area of Water Surfaces More Than 16.2 Hectares (40 Acres) in Size		Total	
	Hectares	Acres	Hectares	Acres	Hectares	Acres
Arizona	5,261	13,000	86,603	214,000	91,864	227,000
California	81,342	201,000	467,817	1,156,000	549,158	1,357,000
Colorado	29,137	72,000	103,600	256,000	132,737	328,000
Idaho	16,187	40,000	226,624	560,000	242,811	600,000
Montana	80,128	198,000	374,739	926,000	454,867	1,124,000
Nevada	6,070	15,000	168,754	417,000	174,824	432,000
New Mexico	809	2,000	61,108	151,000	61,917	153,000
Oregon	87,412	216,000	215,697	533,000	303,110	749,000
Utah	15,378	38,000	655,995	1,621,000	671,373	1,659,000
Washington	53,823	133,000	277,614	686,000	331,438	819,000
Wyoming	44,111	109,000	182,918	452,000	227,029	561,000
Totals	419,658	1,037,000	2,821,469	6,972,000	3,241,128	8,009,000

Source: U.S. Department of the Interior (1975).

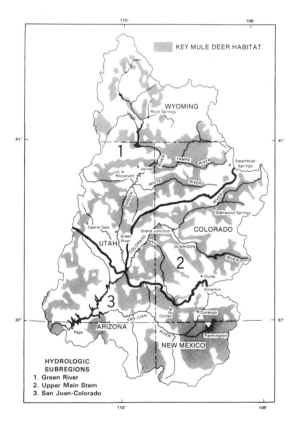

Figure 54. Important mule deer habitat *(shaded)* in the hydrologic subregion of the Upper Colorado River drainage (after Upper Colorado Region State–Federal Inter-Agency Group 1971).

the development of recreational sites. Barrier fencing was used in an attempt to exclude mule deer from 11.6 kilometers (7.2 miles) of the highway along one side of the reservoir, thereby precluding their use of an additional amount of habitat. To determine the effects of such projects with any precision, the agencies involved must monitor deer movements, migration patterns, mortality, and other factors both before and after construction.

Lewke and Buss (1977) documented the impact of an impoundment at the Lower Granite Dam on the Snake River in Washington. They reported 1,319 hectares (3,260 acres) of wildlife habitat inundated. More generally, in Washington, ninety-four hydroelectric power development projects (forty-six completed and forty-eight authorized) were expected to inundate about 172,392 hectares (425,991 acres) of land, or about 1 percent of the total land area of the state (Oliver 1974). It was estimated that about 4,780 deer either utilized or were supported by the impoundment areas of eight of those reservoirs. In most cases, compensation or mitigation permitted the acquisition or management of additional wildlife habitat, but not necessarily habitat of equivalent quality or size. Also, in most cases, the additional habitat was already "wildlife habitat" before such acquisition or management was initiated. Hence the concept of compensation or mitigation becomes an absurdity as wildlife habitat continues to be whittled away.

In addition to inundating habitat, reservoirs often disrupt deer migration routes and daily movement areas. Drowning may occur, particularly when deer attempt to cross ice-covered reservoirs. In arid regions, deer evicted from their normal range by reservoir projects may be forced to occupy less suitable habitat. On the other hand, as often is contended in benefit-cost calculations, a reservoir may make otherwise dry habitat more usable.

ROADS AND HIGHWAYS

Although deer can adapt to and exist in the proximity of roads and highways, that association is not ideal. Highways usurp habitat, including forage, water, and cover, and often intersect normal migratory and daily travel routes. They present auditory and visual stimuli, though deer readily habituate to them. And in some seasons, roadways offer attractive forage along shoulders or on medians, thereby inviting vehicle-deer collisions. Except for hunting of mule deer, road kill probably is the most frequent cause of death among deer examined by wildlife personnel.

Loss of Habitat

From data on the number, length, and average right-of-way width of roads and highways in the occupied range of mule deer, it is possible to calculate the total amount of former habitat that roadways have usurped directly. So many qualifications necessarily follow such calculations that results would be too equivocal to be useful. Needless to say, however, the amount of area involved is large and increasing. Interstate, rural, and county highways, as defined in the western United States, occupy about 11, 3, and 2 hectares of land per kilometer (45, 12, and 7 acres per mile), respectively. Therefore just two interstate highways traversing the geographic range of mule

deer—Interstate 80, more than 2,000 kilometers (1,243 miles) from east to west, and Interstate 15, more than 2,700 kilometers (1,678 miles) from north to southwest—will preempt more than 53,014 hectares (131,000 acres) of land.

In Colorado, the area encompassed by interstate, rural, and county highways increased 42.7, 7.5, and 4.8 percent, respectively, between 1960 and 1974. Nationwide, there was little change in the total miles of rural roads between 1960 and 1970, but the Federal-Aid Highway System increased about 7 percent (U.S. Department of Commerce 1972). Compared with the eastern United States, the West is experiencing a disproportionate share of this increase. Superhighways will proliferate as long as people continue to indulge themselves in unrestricted travel.

The degree to which highways alter deer habitat is a factor of their length, right-of-way width, traffic volume, and the structures and developments associated with them. High traffic volume requires long, space-consuming curves and expansive entrance and exit ramps. Location on the terrain also is important, but economics, safety, and convenience of vehicular travel normally take precedence over most environmental considerations. In mountainous areas, highways commonly follow river valleys, frequently on south-facing slopes for ease of winter maintenance, precisely the locations where they bisect deer winter range and interfere with migration routes.

Still, there is ample evidence that deer and other wild ungulates do habituate to well-traveled highways and maintain viable populations in their presence. Caribou (Johnson and Todd 1977), reindeer (Klein 1971), moose (Grenier 1974; Almkvist et al. 1976), elk (Altmann 1952; Ward et al. 1973), white-tailed deer (Carbaugh et al. 1975), and mule deer (Ward et al. 1976) all appear to adapt to roadways and remain within their auditory and visual range. Observations near a deer underpass on Interstate 70 in western Colorado revealed that, within 15–30 meters (49–98 feet) of westbound traffic, mule deer reacted with flight or escape behavior to only 103 of 1,021

Highways and rights-of-way not only pose formidable obstacles to mule deer daily and seasonal movements, but also usurp a considerable amount of land, particularly in mountainous areas where they often are constructed in river valleys that are critical deer winter habitat. Photograph by Don Domenick; courtesy of the Colorado Division of Wildlife.

westbound vehicles (Reed, pers. files). Similarly, along Interstate 80 in Wyoming, mule deer frequently were observed feeding within 10 meters (33 feet) of the highway, where noise levels generated by high speed traffic exceeded 70 decibels (A-scale). Some resident deer lived within 0.8 kilometer (0.5 mile) of the highway (Ward et al. 1976).

Behrend and Lubeck (1968) provided evidence that white-tailed deer are more sensitive to disturbance along roads than they are in the more removed areas. In two of three habitat types—mountain shrub and ponderosa pine—studied in Colorado, deer densities, as indicated by feces counts, decreased with increasing proximity to roads (Rost 1975). In juniper type, the decrease did not occur to the same extent.

Adaptation of wild ungulates to roadways may be more a matter of necessity than of choice. Highways are an issue on mule deer ranges simply because they cause problems. Regardless of how well deer may adapt in some areas, a certain amount of habitat is lost or degraded by the existence of a highway. Examining the loss or degradation of habitat because of roadways and their effects on local mule deer populations or the total population is a challenge remaining to wildlife biologists and managers.

Highway Mortality

No technological development has played a more pervasive role in styling the lives of North Americans than the automobile. Perhaps no development has so profoundly influenced, directly or indirectly, the continent's environment. Who could have foreseen that a sputtering curiosity of 1900 would spawn about 20 million registered motor vehicles in North America within a quarter of a century, 50 mil-

Accessible forage along roads may encourage deer to habituate to vehicles and remain close to roadways. Photograph courtesy of the Wyoming Department of Game and Fish.

lion by midcentury, and 125 million by 1975? Certainly it was not foreseen by the deer that bounded safely out of the path of the 1900 vintage Phaeton bouncing over the rocks and ruts of wagon roads. But by the 1930s, when roads were built for cars and most cars could cover 50 meters (164 feet) in two or three seconds, the toll of wildlife taken by motor vehicles was becoming something to reckon with (Dickerson 1939; Knobloch 1939; Warren 1936*a*, *b*). By the 1960s, deer-vehicle collisions, and the consequent damage to vehicles, people, and deer, had become a serious problem to wildlife management agencies even in the West (Myers 1969; Nevada Department of Fish and Game 1967; Ross 1963; Williams 1964; Zimmerman 1971).

Although some states do not record the number of deer killed by motor vehicles, tabulations of reported road kills in other states provide a perspective on the overall magnitude and seriousness of the problem. In 1967, 8,387 deer reportedly were killed by vehicle collisions in California (Thompson 1968). By 1974 the

Roadkills exact a significant and increasing toll from many deer herds in the West. This mule deer doe and her unborn twin fawns were killed when struck by a vehicle on a six-lane highway that intersected heavily used deer winter range. Photograph courtesy of the Utah Division of Wildlife Resources.

Not all incidents involving deer and vehicles result in losses of deer, but some are costly in terms of human life and property. In this remarkable sequence, the black-tailed deer apparently were attracted, or at least halted on the highway, by salt used to reduce icing. Photographs by Tom W. Hall.

number of road-killed deer in that state had risen to an estimated 20,000 annually (Longhurst et al. 1976), which represented 60 percent of annual deer harvests in California for 1970–75 (Wolfe 1978). In Pennsylvania, deer-vehicle collisions increased 218 percent from 1960 to 1967 (Puglisi et al. 1974) and in 1976 more deer reportedly were killed by vehicles (24,183) in that state than were harvested by recreational hunting in thirty-five other states (Woolf 1978). The number of reported road-killed deer in Wisconsin rose steadily from 790 in 1953 to 14,109 in 1975 (Fred Bear Sports Club 1978), an increase of 1,786 percent in a span of twenty-three years. A survey by the Fred Bear Sports Club (1975) revealed that, in thirty-six states, approximately 146,229 deer were killed in collisions with vehicles in 1974. Among some of the states with mule or black-tailed deer populations, or both, reported or estimated road kills numbered 1,000 in Arizona, 20,000 in California, 5,862 in Colorado, 1,654 in Montana, 4,000 in Texas, 1,040 in Nebraska, 1,211 in Kansas, 1,270 in South Dakota, 941 in Utah, and 1,537 in Wyoming. These latter data do not differentiate among mule and white-tailed deer, but, in states where the two species are present, both undoubtedly are well represented.

Fences that bar deer from roadways are the most obvious means of reducing the problem of deer-vehicle accidents. Barrier fences sufficient (in height, mesh, basal closure, strength, and permanency) to stop approximately 90 percent of approaching deer from crossing or passing through are costly to construct. Deer fencing specifications—including a height of 2.4 meters (8 feet)—were developed and are being utilized by the Colorado Division of Highways (1973). Of about 27.8 kilometers (17.3 miles) of deer fencing contracted for by the Colorado Division of Highways in 1978, the average accepted bid was $26,969.07 per kilometer ($43,438.02 per mile) (E. Huff. pers. comm., February 1979). Financial constraints normally dictate compromises. Fences 2.1 meters (7 feet) in height along the New York Thruway reduced deer-vehicle collisions by 44.3–83.9 percent in fenced areas and by 12.9–24.7 percent beyond the ends of the fences (Free and Severinghaus,

n.d.) Liberalized hunting (an antlerless deer season) was an additional control measure adjacent to the area with the 24.7 percent collision reduction. More recently, slightly higher fences (2.4 meters: 8 feet) of various lengths on one or both sides of a highway were evaluated in Colorado in terms of reducing road kills (Woodard and Reed 1974). Kill reduction ranged from 67.8 to 86.5 percent, but it was unrelated to length of fence or to fencing one or both sides of the right-of-way (table 72). Some deer were killed in collisions with vehicles after they had penetrated or jumped over fences, moved around their ends, or approached from an unfenced side.

A disadvantage of barrier fences is that they also prevent deer from leaving a right-of-way. To permit deer to escape from fenced roadways, researchers installed one-way gates in four of six fences (Reed et al. 1974) (table 72). Again, the relative amount of use of the gates was unrelated to reduction in deer kill, but the fact that the gates were used, in some cases quite heavily, is an argument in their favor. The experience from this study suggests, however, that proper location of such gates is of utmost importance.

Since most deer-vehicle collisions occur at night, it is plausible that a variety of lighting techniques could be employed to discourage deer from approaching the rights-of-way and to permit motorists to see deer that do. The effect of high-intensity lighting was tested on a section of Highway 82, near Glenwood Springs, Colorado, during 1974, 1975, 1978, and 1979. The lighting was turned on or off during alternate weeks. There was no significant difference in the crossings-per-kill ratios with lights on or off. However, there was considerable variability in lighting levels during lights-on periods. Gallagher and Meguire (1974) provided data on lighting contrast requirements in terms of the perceptions and reactions of urban drivers.

Roadway signs identifying deer-crossing sites and areas are used widely to alert motorists to the increased probability of sighting animals and the need to react. Where the effectiveness of such warning signs has been evaluated, the results have not been en-

Table 72. Effect of One-Way Gates and Fencing on Highway Deer Kills in Colorado

Location	Fence Length		Mean Annual Preinstallation Kill[a]	Mean Annual Postinstallation Kill[b]	Percentage of Kill Reduction	Mean Annual One-Way Gate Use[c]
	Kilometers	Miles				
Vail—both sides Interstate 70 (I-70)	2.4	1.5	36.0 (1)	11.6 (10)	67.8	36.3 (8)[d]
Avon—one side I-70	3.5	2.2	28.0 (1)	3.9 (7)	86.1	81.7 (6)
Edwards—one side I-70	3.5	2.2	27.0 (1)	5.7 (7)	78.9	7.5 (7)[e]
Eagle—one side I-70	7.7	4.8	167.0 (1)	22.5 (6)	86.5	14.4 (10)
Carbondale N.W.—one side Hwy 82	1.8	1.1	10.0 (3)	1.8 (8)	82.0	
Carbondale S.E.—one side Hwy 82	1.8	1.1	14.0 (5)	4.2 (5)	70.0	
Average					78.5	

Source: Reed et al. (1974).
Note: Fences were 2.44 meters (8.0 feet) in height.
[a] Numbers of preinstallation years are in parentheses.
[b] Numbers of postinstallation years are in parentheses.
[c] Numbers of one-way gates are in parentheses.
[d] The number of gates was reduced to seven in autumn of the fourth year and to six in spring of the seventh year, then increased back to seven in autumn of the eighth year after installation.
[e] The number of gates was reduced to six in spring of the third year and to five in the fifth year after installation.

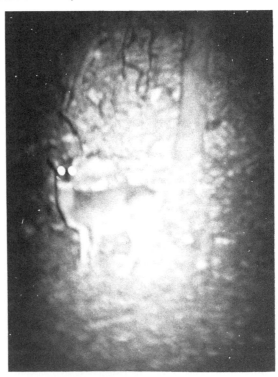

When deer fences are used along highways, one-way gates can enable deer that move around the ends of the fences or approach from an unfenced side of the roadway to escape through the fence rather than be trapped on or along the highway and possibly killed. Photograph by Dale F. Reed.

Additional research is needed to determine lighting techniques and intensities to (1) discourage deer from approaching vehicular thoroughfares and (2) improve the capability of motorists to see deer on or along roadways. Photograph courtesy of the Wyoming Department of Game and Fish.

Mule deer move along a 2.44-meter (8-foot) fence toward a highway underpass. Photograph by Dale F. Reed.

couraging. In a study of a symbol type of (deer silhouette) warning signs in California eleven of nineteen signed areas showed reductions in deer mortality, but in only two cases were they statistically significant ($p < 0.05$) (Mansfield and Miller 1975). However, the number of deer avoided and, accordingly, the property damage and personal injury prevented because drivers were alerted by such signs were not fully examined. Lighted, animated signs were tested in Colorado. They were lighted or unlighted during alternate weeks in the winters of 1972 and 1973. There was no statistical difference in crossings-per-kill ratios between on and off periods in either year of study (Pojar et al. 1975).

A more realistic "warning" was tested one evening in March of 1975, in the same area as described by Pojar et al. (1975). A transverse section of a full taxidermy mount of a female mule deer was placed on the emergency lane and shoulder of a lighted portion of the highway. During the three-hour test, the speed of passing vehicles decreased by a mean of 13.7 kilometers per hour (8.5 miles per hour). Of eighty-five vehicles observed during a thirty-

minute period, 51 percent braked (as evidenced by brake lights), and 5–10 percent slowed down enough to cause a traffic hazard (Reed, pers. files). Because of the danger caused by these few vehicles, this experiment was abruptly terminated, but it suggests that any measures extreme enough to alter the behavior of most motorists may cause a few to overreact.

In some areas, underpasses are constructed to help deer cross where highways intersect major deer travel corridors. Mansfield and Miller (1975) reported negligible use of nineteen underpasses in California. However, studies in Colorado indicate that many factors—such as adjacent deer numbers and their motivation to move or migrate—must be considered in designing and siting underpasses if they are to be effective. Over a period of four years, a mean of 345.1 ± 133.0 (S.D.) mule deer per year passed through a concrete box underpass under Interstate 70 near Vail, Colorado (Reed et al. 1975). A barrier fence was constructed on both sides of the highway to channel deer to the entrance. Certain responses, such as look-up and tail-up behaviors,

A collared mule deer emerges from a highway underpass. Photograph by Dale F. Reed.

indicated that deer were reluctant to enter the structure; about 61 percent of the local deer population have continued to migrate through the underpass.

Characteristics of this and several other underpasses used by deer in Colorado are listed in table 73. From studies of the relative effectiveness of these structures, a number of general recommendations can be made. Underpasses should be at least 4.3 meters (14 feet) wide and high, of minimal length, and situated where crossing has been shown to occur or is likely, and should include barrier fencing that channels deer to the underpass and prevents their crossing over the highway surface. Such structures can be expected to cost about $100,000 to $150,000 (1978 U.S. dollar value).

Overpasses have been studied less extensively, but there is some evidence that they can be effectively used. In the autumn-to-spring

Table 73. Dimensions of Highway Underpasses and Use of Underpasses by Deer

Underpass	Height × Width[a]		Number of Deer Passages per Year	Openness[b]	Highway Fencing	Adjacent Deer Activity
	Meters	Feet				
Vail, I-70 [c]	3.0 × 3.0	10 × 10	345.1 [d]	0.3	Both sides	Heavy
Arch, West Durango [c]	3.1 × 6.1	10 × 20	66.5	0.7	Both sides	Light
Eagle, I-70 no. 1	4.3 × 4.3	14 × 14	3.0	0.4	One side	Moderate
Eagle, I-70 no. 2	2.4 × 2.4	8 × 8	1.5	0.1	One side	Moderate
Salida East no. 1	5.5 × 14.6	18 × 48[e]	124.0	5.2	None	Heavy in May
Salida East no. 2	7.3 × 14.6	24 × 48[e]	35.0	5.4	None	Moderate

[a] Width measured parallel to direction of traffic.
[b] Openness is expressed as follows: $\dfrac{height \times width \ (or \ open\text{-}end \ surface \ area)}{length}$.
[c] Designed specifically for deer.
[d] Seasonal mean, from a four-year study (Reed et al. 1975).
[e] Adjusted for irregular inside topography.

periods of 1974–75 and 1975–76, approximately 258 mule deer crossed a creek by an unused bridge near Vail, Colorado. This was estimated by track counts and a video time-lapse surveillance system (Reed et al. 1973). The video imagery of 329 crossings revealed that the deer were less reluctant to cross at this overpass than at underpasses generally. Highway overpasses have yet to be tested for use as deer crossings.

FREE-ROAMING DOGS

Free-roaming or feral dogs are an increasingly serious hazard to wild animals and to deer in particular. Beck (1973) found that about one-third to one-half of the people who own dogs permit them to run free. Estimates of the total number of uncontrolled, free-roaming dogs in the United States range from 12 to 30 million (Denney 1974).

Despite thousands of years of domestication, the hunting and chasing instincts are still latent in most dogs (Fox 1969, 1973). In fact, specialization for chasing, catching, and retrieving has been the goal of selective breeding in many breeds of dogs. These inherent or latent behaviors are reinforced when dogs are allowed to roam freely.

Interactions of white-tailed deer with free-running dogs have been studied rather extensively (Corbett et al. 1971; Gavitt 1973; Kreeger 1977; Marchinton et al. 1970; Perry and Giles 1970; Progulske and Baskett 1958; Scott and Causey 1973). Much of the research has been directed at identifying the escape tactics of deer. Few studies have focused on the potential effect of feral dog predation on deer populations, perhaps because most of the few studies have suggested that the influence is minimal. On the other hand, considerable interest has arisen in the use of dogs for deer hunting in the East. In the West, use of dogs for deer hunting is legal only in California (Marchinton et al. 1970).

Predation by dogs is considered a serious problem in many areas of the West where deer are forced to concentrate on winter ranges with deep snow that restricts their mobility (Boyles

Although feral dogs are a threat to deer year-round, they are a particular menace during winter on ranges where deer cannot tolerate the energy-depleting stresses of harassment. Photograph by Allen F. Whitaker; courtesy of the Colorado Division of Wildlife.

1976; Houston 1968; Moser 1975; Washington State Game Department 1974). Linsdale and Tomich (1953) documented cases of mule deer mortality from dog attacks in California. Dasmann and Taber (1956a) mentioned the effect of dogs in restricting access of black-tailed deer to areas with adequate escape cover. However, Cowan (1956a) minimized the overall influence of harassment and attack by dogs on blacktails but conceded that evidence for the conclusion was meager. More recently, Lowry and McArthur (1978) stated that it was essential to learn more about this predator-prey relationship.

There are few data concerning dog/deer interactions in the West. A questionnaire on the subject yielded data from only three of ten western states: Colorado, New Mexico, and

Chased by dogs into the Colorado River, an exhausted fawn is trapped by an ice shelf and unable to return to shore. Hypothermia was evidenced by the animal's violent shaking. Photograph by Dale F. Reed.

Utah recorded 314, 3, and 48 deer reportedly killed by dogs in 1973 (Denney 1974). There is no reason to believe that this even remotely approximates true relative or total figures for those states. Data obtained from several wildlife conservation districts in the western two-thirds of Colorado (table 74) suggest much greater interaction. If estimates obtained from those districts (a mean of approximately 71 deer harassed and 24 killed by dogs annually in 1973, 1974, and 1975) were extrapolated to include the entire western two-thirds of Colorado, the total would be 1,077 deer harassed and 359 killed annually. However, such extrapolation is not reliable. It is likely that many, if not most, dog/deer interactions occur without being observed or reported.

Table 74. Recorded Incidents of Dog Predation on Deer Reported by Selected Wildlife Conservation Districts in Colorado

Year	Number of Recorded Incidents	Number of Deer		
		Killed	Injured	Harassed
1973	51[a]	40	11	71
1974	35	19	1	102
1975	18	12		40
Totals	104	71	12	213

Note: Most Colorado Division of Wildlife districts do not maintain records on dog deer conflicts. Ten districts are represented in 1973 and only four in 1974 and 1975.

[a] Incomplete data; should be considered a minimum estimate.

The incidents of harassment reported in table 74 occurred largely during the winter stress period when deer were concentrated on winter ranges, close to human habitation. The winter of 1976–77 was very mild, and few dog/deer interactions were noted. It seems reasonable to speculate that harassment by dogs can constitute an intolerable added stress to deer in severe winters.

RESIDENTIAL DEVELOPMENTS

Rural land is being converted to urban and transportation uses in the United States at a rate of approximately 299,993 hectares (741,300 acres) per year (Bormann 1976). Solid waste disposal, gravel pits, land disturbance by heavy construction equipment, air pollution, increased recreational use, and greater incidence of forest fires are a few of the by-products. Bormann saw no way to measure accurately or even adequately the collective impact of these stresses on wildlands. However, he indicated that the effect of urban, residential, or recreational developments, with their accompanying human activities and by-products, extends well beyond their actual boundaries. Likewise, the cumulative effect of human growth and activity on deer habitat is more extensive than is indicated solely by the amount of area directly affected.

Wallmo et al. (1976) estimated that about 279,454 hectares (690,546 acres), or 1.7 percent, of former mule deer range in Colorado were in rural housing developments, including only those areas that had been platted and offered for sale. This may seem to be a comfortably low percentage, but distribution of privately owned rural land in the West is such that mountain home developments frequently preempt critical deer migration routes and wintering areas.

An example of a situation in which critical mule deer habitat nearly was lost to development was the area of the Upper Eagle River Valley and Gore Creek Valley of Eagle County in western Colorado. The area—noted for recreational skiing and housing development—is relatively small (417 hectares: 1,030 acres). However, it has been used historically as a deer migration route, providing a corridor between summer and winter ranges. This migration corridor was blocked by Interstate 70, which was completed in 1970, except for one passageway under the highway. In addition, a planned housing development near the passageway threatened to sever the migration corridor. Considerable effort was expended over several years to negotiate a land exchange between the developers and the United States Bureau of Land Management. The exchange was unsuccessful for a multitude of reasons, including differences in market and appraisal values. To solve this problem and provide reasonable assurance that the migration corridor would not be severed by a street and houses, in 1976 the Colorado Division of Wildlife purchased 41.6 hectares (102.8 acres) of land in the corridor for $292,126. Despite an additional purchase of 1.4 hectares (3.5 acres) by the Nature Conservancy with a private donation of $41,000, some residential units have been planned within about 300 meters (984 feet) of the underpass.

Observations of influences on deer (high- to low-level harassment) were recorded in this area from 1970 through 1976. The number of instances of human, dog, and horse interference recorded were 150, 63, and 7, respectively. Interference was defined as human, dog, or horse activity in areas that were closed (posted) to use by humans or domestic animals. Six sites where most of the interference was detected were 100–800 meters (328–2,625

feet) from the nearest residential units. Human or dog interference in the posted area during the migration periods took place almost daily.

Generally, such residential and recreational developments affect only limited areas of mule and black-tailed deer range in western states. The amount of deer habitat involved would not be expected to result in widespread decline of deer populations. Locally, however, residential, recreational, and associated developments may eliminate deer from limited areas. And the composite effect of these local developments throughout mule deer range may exact a significant toll on the number and distribution of deer.

Recreation

It has been said that the behavior of deer toward people is determined largely by the behavior of people toward deer (Geist 1971a). Certainly there is ample evidence that deer can habituate readily to human presence when customary behaviors of man—primarily hunting—are considerably constrained. Over most of the joint "range" of man and deer, such constraints do not exist. People have preyed on deer throughout history, so it seems unlikely that deer, in their sensory evolution, have failed to identify man as a predator. To people who have raised fawns from infancy, it is clear that fear of man is instilled early, within twenty-four hours of birth. Although deer may adapt to man, they remain sensitive to and apprehensive of man-related disturbance; sensitivity varies temporally with a number of factors. Altmann (1958) indicated that factors influencing flight reaction in elk and moose had a seasonally changing threshold of sensitivity due to reproduction and nutritional status, type of habitat, and specific experiences of individuals or groups. Altmann also indicated that mule deer, like moose, appeared to be more tolerant of human intruders at dusk and dawn, and that groups in close formation often show less flight tendency than do solitary animals.

On the basis of continuing trends, Brockman (1959) estimated that the average workweek would decrease by more than 20 percent between 1930 and 1975, affording the average worker more than twenty-four hours a week of leisure time. Granting that inflation is whittling it away, mean disposable income also has increased significantly since the 1930s. With increased leisure time and the wherewithal to enjoy it, the American public took quick advantage. "Practically overnight, recreational journeys consisting of one-day trips to a picnic ground near the end of a streetcar line were broadened to weekends spent . . . many miles distant" (Brockman 1959 pp. 19–20).

A significant amount of the potential to travel and visit more distant places was satisfied through wildland recreation. From 1965 to 1978, recreational use of national forests of the western United States increased from 124.8 million visitor-days to 162.7 million visitor-days (U.S. Department of Agriculture 1978). Given the location of the national forests, nearly all of these visits occurred in the range of mule or black-tailed deer.

This phenomenal growth of outdoor recreational activity has greatly increased the number of and opportunity for people/deer encounters. It has been compounded by man's propensity to build machines for every activity, including recreation on wildlands. Off-the-road vehicles have significantly extended the radius of human influence. In summer, when most mule deer are widely dispersed in good cover, encounters with people probably are of minor consequence. In winter, when deer are concentrated in areas with sparse cover, under physiological stress because of poor forage, harsh weather, or both and restricted in mobility by deep snow, encounters with people can be a serious matter.

Some think snowmobiles pose a significant threat to a wide range of wild species (Young and Boyce 1971; Newmann and Merriam 1972). Wanek (1974) reported their effects on trees, shrubs, herbs, and soil microbes. Jarvinen and Schmid (1971) studied snowmobile use and winter mortality of burrowing mammals. Klein (1971) and Thomson (1972) reported that reindeer were disturbed by "snow scooter" use in Scandinavia. And, though there is increasing concern about the impact of snowmobiles on ungulates in North America (Malaher 1967; Baldwin 1968; Shields 1968; Doan 1970; Mace 1974; Severinghaus and Tullar 1975), there has been only limited research on specific effects.

Lavigne (1976) found that white-tailed deer became habituated to snowmobile disturbance in Maine. Eckstein and Rongstad (1973) compared movements of radio-collared white-tailed deer in northern Wisconsin during periods with and without snowmobile operation. There were no significant changes in the home range size or rate of movement when snowmobiles were used, though 3 of 5 deer were significantly farther from the nearest snowmobile trail when snowmobiles were in operation.

Dorrance et al. (1975) reported on the effects of snowmobiles on white-tailed deer in Minnesota. Home range size, movement, and distance of radio-collared deer from the nearest trail increased with snowmobile activity in one study area but remained unchanged in another. In one of the areas, light snowmobile traffic displaced deer from locations immediately adjacent to trails, but increased snowmobile traffic caused no additional response. In the same area, deer returned to locations along trails within hours after snowmobiling stopped. Dorrance et al. hypothesized that, during severe winters and on poor ranges, displacement of deer from even small segments of their home range is detrimental.

In severe winters, mule deer suffer a pronounced energy deficit and can tolerate little additional energy cost if they are to survive. For white-tailed deer the cost of running, especially in deep snow, is many times that of walking on bare ground (Mattfeld 1973). More subtle is the possibility that energy use increases even in the absence of overt behavior. Preliminary studies indicate that harassment causes changes in the heart rate of mule deer even without strong overt reactions (Freddy 1978). Repeated disturbance by snowmobiles may not drive deer entirely out of their established home ranges if there is no other range they can retreat to, but, at least theoretically, it can exact an intolerable energy toll.

Ski touring is another form of winter recre-

North Americans have long valued mule and black-tailed deer as a source of food and a trophy recreational opportunity. Featured here on the Kaibab Plateau in Arizona in 1892 is a hunting party led by the famous pony express rider, hunter, scout, and showman William F. "Buffalo Bill" Cody, seated at right. Photograph courtesy of the Union Pacific Railroad Museum.

ation that has burgeoned in recent decades. Skiers are quieter and less mobile than snowmobilers, and the sphere of disturbance each generates is relatively low. On the other hand, the skier—seen by deer in bipedal form—might be perceived more readily as a familiar predator than is the driver of a snowmobile. How deer perceives man in the various forms of intrusion is a question for future behavioral research. Needless to say, deer no longer endure the rigors of winter in solitude.

As with other types of outdoor recreation, the number of people who participate in deer hunting has increased. In Colorado, for example, slightly more than 15,000 deer hunting licenses were sold in 1903, the first year of legally restricted hunting; in 1977 more than 155,000 licenses were sold (Colorado Division of Wildlife 1978).

In this recreation, interaction with deer is intentional rather than incidental and accidental.

Deer behavior obviously is influenced by the activities of hunters. It is documented in whitetails (Marshall and Whittington 1968; Sparrowe and Springer 1970; Tester and Heezen 1965), and similar reactions can be expected of mule deer (see chap. 5).

A high value is placed on deer as game animals, and much of the general concern over the inroads of other human activities on deer is motivated by a desire to maintain deer and deer habitat for the recreation of hunting. Meanwhile, a growing faction opts for preserving them for aesthetic purposes. There is much information on the effects of hunting as a direct mortality factor (see chap. 6), but few data are available on indirect effects on deer populations of hunting or any other kind of recreational pursuit. It seems likely that, in any case, considerable forbearance will be required to ensure that deer survive for the enjoyment of future generations of North Americans.

Chapter 15

MANAGEMENT CHALLENGES AND OPPORTUNITIES

Guy E. Connolly
Wildlife Research Biologist
United States Fish and Wildlife Service
Denver Wildlife Research Center
Twin Falls, Idaho

Olof C. Wallmo
Principal Wildlife Biologist
United States Forest Service
Pacific Northwest Forest and
Range Experiment Station
Juneau, Alaska

This final chapter focuses on some important problems and issues that will affect wildlife managers' ability to serve public interests concerning mule deer and black-tailed deer in coming years. We have attempted to address these problems and issues from the perspective of the managers who must deal with them. Many management problems are accompanied by research needs that also are identified or reiterated here. Because some important deer management issues cannot be solved simply by applying more biological expertise, this chapter touches on sociopolitical considerations as well. However, the emphasis is on biological knowledge of mule and black-tailed deer, their habitats and deer/habitat interactions, and the applicability of this knowledge to management.

In attempting to understand and regulate selected aspects of the deer-environment-man system, we must recognize that this system is extremely complex. Many variables are uncontrollable, and others are deliberately uncontrolled; all are dynamic. For the most part, wildlife managers can exert only limited regulation on more or less wild systems. The degree and extent of wildness vary with the resource management philosophies and land-use priorities that society applies to habitats where deer live.

To clarify this point, six levels of management intensity can be identified. First is the zoo, in which everything is artificial and controlled. Second is the wildlife park, an expansion of the zoo. Third is the game preserve or game ranch, where management concentrates on economically efficient production of animals that are kept as wild as possible.

The fourth level may be called the "forest and rangeland" management philosophy. It applies to the largest acreage of mule and black-tailed deer range, most of which is publicly owned. Significant areas of semiwild private lands are included as well. Most of these lands in Canada, the United States, and, to a lesser extent, Mexico are devoted to such uses as timber production, livestock grazing, mining, and various kinds of recreation. Even though these uses may entail or result in manipulation of the landscape, the land remains essentially uncultivated. Since deer production is not the predominant use on most of these ranges, management for deer must be coordinated and integrated with other uses. Most efforts of federal, provincial, and state wildlife management agencies in western North America are applied within this management framework. Deliberate management efforts on behalf of wildlife species such as deer often are frustrated by constraints imposed by other interests. Also, most deer hunters say they want to hunt in a wildernesslike setting.

The least intensive levels of management are found on "wilderness areas" and "national parks." In the former, some regulation of certain components and processes of ecosystems is permitted. In the latter, all natural processes ideally are allowed to operate without human interference. Actually, wildlife populations in many large and popular national parks may be influenced by high-density human use and consequent management practices, so that few, if any, mule or black-tailed deer exist there under pristine conditions. Also, some parks—though considered large—are too small or are otherwise unsuitable to accommodate deer year round. When the deer migrate or move beyond park boundaries, they invariably become subject to a higher level of management intensity.

Early in this century, big game hunting and wildlife management in western North America occurred mostly in de facto wilderness. As this wilderness was eroded by a multiplicity of encroachments, public interest developed to preserve what remained. Wilderness areas and wildlife sanctuaries have become significant to wildlife biologists and managers for at least two reasons. First, deer management must recognize and accommodate public desires and demands for large preserves in which deer are protected from hunting. Second, some wilderness areas and national parks should support relatively unmanaged or unhunted deer populations as comparative references for managed or hunted populations. However, the value of these reference populations is only theoretical unless their numbers and trends are documented (see chap. 6).

Although much of this chapter pertains to the most prevalent level of management intensity—"forest and rangeland"—the principles presented here should be of interest to anyone concerned with mule deer or black-tailed deer. We take a pragmatic view of management, recognizing that implementation of improved technical information in North America will continue to be influenced by egalitarian traditions and political processes. Both are frequent sources of frustration to wildlife biologists and managers, in that they often prevent clear definition of wildlife management goals or prohibit biologists and managers from pursuing the expressed goals of the public they serve.

Despite such constraints, however, wildlife professionals can take pride in the progress evidenced throughout this book. Skeptics of current management expertise will do well to compare the present status of mule deer with that existing around 1900, before concerned citizens and wildlife workers began the conservation and restoration work that continues to this day. But pride in past accomplishments must be tempered by a realization that deer management is and probably will continue to be a dynamic blend of biological facts, professional opinion and expertise, and political concerns. As a field of professional endeavor, deer management probably has never been more challenging, and there is small probability that present problems will disappear soon.

KNOWLEDGE OF THE SPECIES

Though *Odocoileus hemionus* is a discrete kind of animal, the genetic identity of the variations that compose the species remains essentially unknown. The practical significance of that fact is suggested by a reminder from Valerius Geist (pers. comm. to R. E. McCabe, 16 November 1979) that the degree to which environment may influence phenotype is poorly understood. That it does so, however, is clearly suggested by work at the University of British Columbia (Bandy et al. 1970).

Concepts of genecology, or race ecology, in botany could be useful in understanding the extent to which deer, locally or regionally, are products of their genes or their environment. Nutritional regimes and energy budgets, reviewed in chapter 3, are clear examples of phenotypic influence. Many natural and man-imposed factors can impede deer's ability to achieve optimal growth and physiological performance.

Before we can judge the importance of these factors, however, there must be adequate data on the morphology and physiology of the animal over a range of habitat conditions. After compiling what was available, Allen Anderson (see chap. 2) concluded that relevant data are fragmentary or totally lacking in many areas and, at best, usually are too limited for reliable interpretation. Nevertheless, it is clear that some animal features, such as fat deposits, can be related to forage or habitat quality. The application of such measures to deer management is in its infancy.

Knowledge of endemic and epidemic diseases also is vital to interpretation of deer populations. As Charles Hibler emphasized in chapter 4, acquiring such knowledge is not simple. Qualified deer clinicians are needed, yet few are available to wildlife managers. Even where they exist, the cases they deal with tend to be complex and require more extensive evaluation than merely the examination of a carcass in a clinic. If management is to include an effective response to problems of disease, much more effort must be applied much more generally to detection, diagnosis, and treatment.

Assessments of deer and deer habitats also require realistic understanding of the animal's innate and adaptive behavior in different places and under a full range of ecological conditions. For example, because migrational patterns between winter and summer ranges appear to be learned, it may be possible to transplant deer and "teach" them new territorial and migratory traditions. Results of rigorous behavioral research are conspicuously lacking in the literature on mule and black-tailed deer. The pioneering investigations of Rocky Mountain mule deer by Geist (see chap. 5) are most enlightening. No comparable studies of other subspecies exist. Herein lie challenging and practical problems for ambitious ungulate behaviorists.

Assessing Populations

To determine population trends, effects of harvests, and responses to habitat modifications, or to understand the influence of any environmental factor on deer numbers, wildlife managers must be able to estimate population size with sufficient accuracy for the purpose at hand.

As was explained in chapter 6, estimates of deer numbers for large areas, such as provinces, states, and large national forests and parks, continue to be essentially speculative. Some agencies are attempting to overcome this management deficiency. The Texas Parks and Wildlife Department now uses systematic, though varied, procedures to estimate total numbers of mule deer, as well as whitetails, by area, by region, and statewide. The Colorado Division of Wildlife is experimenting with procedures for estimating total populations and sex and age composition in four major regions of that state. Such information is essential to the simulation modeling that now is used to test and guide management programs in Colorado.

As Lauckhart (1950, p. 648) said: "Hunter management or public relations make population figures a virtual necessity. The public does not trust managers who do not profess to know how many animals are available and how many should be killed." Wildlife managers must be careful, however, of professing to know when they do not.

The story of the Kaibab deer herd is a celebrated example of embarrassment owing to lack of population data. The reported eruption and decline of that mule deer population in northern Arizona (Rasmussen 1941) and its presumed causes become gospel to American deer managers and college biology teachers until Caughley (1970) revealed that, among the many conflicting "estimates" of the population by persons who professed to know, not one was based on any kind of systematic census method. As Caughley emphasized, one cannot credibly infer causes if an effect has not been reliably demonstrated. For a review of the Kaibab legend as portrayed by wildlife instructors, see Burk (1973).

Although much effort has been spent on developing methods for estimating deer numbers, there is clear need for further research toward efficient strategies that will be reliable enough to meet management requirements, at costs wildlife management agencies can afford. Such strategies will not necessarily require totally new census techniques, but they will have to recognize that, regardless of the method used, sampling will be involved, and the reliability of an estimate depends on its precision. Improved sample design and increased sample size can increase precision—at a cost.

With present estimation technology, wildlife managers often cannot commit sufficient time and money to obtain trustworthy estimates of deer numbers. Moreover, each method in current use contains limitations and sources of error, so several procedures may have to be applied to acquire the information needed. But it would be a mistake to wait for an ideal census method when existing ones can be applied to deer populations whose sizes are only a matter of speculation.

BALANCING DEER POPULATIONS WITH THEIR HABITATS

A fundamental principle in deer management is that population levels should be maintained at or somewhat below the carrying capacities of their ranges in order to achieve optimal development of individuals and optimum productivity of populations. Several definitions of carrying capacity are possible, as was shown in chapter 7. When wildlife managers think of balancing deer numbers with range capacity, they usually desire an optimum stocking rate somewhat below the largest possible number of deer that can survive the greatest period of annual stress. In theory, the logic of maintaining deer at optimum density seems indisputable. In practice, however, it is extremely difficult to produce objective evidence to show whether a particular deer herd is above, below, or at optimum density.

Some people might expect wildlife managers to measure both carrying capacity and deer numbers periodically and, through hunting, to adjust deer numbers to achieve proper balance. But few if any mule or black-tailed deer populations are managed so intensively that the desired optimum density is demonstrably achieved. Nevertheless, many state wildlife management agencies make the effort. In so doing, they not only encounter political constraints (see chap. 7), but also deal with limited

or inadequate estimates of both carrying capacity and population size.

There is, however, an increasing conviction among researchers that the habitat ingredients that contribute to range carrying capacity can be identified and measured. The information on desired characteristics of forage—presented in chapter 3 (nutrition and metabolism), chapters 9–12 (regional habitat complexes), chapter 13 (interspecific competition), and chapter 5 (behavior)—reveals that significant progress has been made in understanding the interaction of deer and forage supplies.

Contemporary researchers are developing the technology to make useful quantitative and qualitative estimates of deer forage supplies and their fluctuations. As was discussed in chapter 10, part 2, this technology must involve more than superficial sampling of deer use of a few plant species that are presumed to be "key" indicators for entire vegetational complexes.

It is encouraging that tangible progress has been made in associating data on climate and edaphic factors with dynamics of the vegetation and deer population. An example comes from Arizona (Smith and LeCount 1979; see also chap. 9), where long-term research made it possible to predict forage yields and desert mule deer fawn crops from precipitation in the preceding winter.

Another instructive example comes from work on moose in Saskatchewan (Stewart et al. 1977). It was found that the combination of autumn and spring weather, plus winter snow depth, determined subsequent energy requirements of moose and necessary supplies of digestible nutrients in forage, which governed the physical condition of individual moose and the productivity of the population.

Other examples of such integrated research on mule deer and their habitats lie in programs on the Wasatch Front in Utah, the Bridger Mountains and Missouri River breaks in Montana, in Middle Park and the Piceance Basin in Colorado, and in the Big Bend region of Texas.

As stated by Len Carpenter (pers. comm. to R. E. McCabe, 14 November 1979): "It is feasible to make meaningful measurements on various parameters of deer habitat that relate to carrying capacity. . . . What is needed is a positive approach to the problem . . . [and] continued research on improving sampling intensities and on methods for implementation into management systems." The authors of chapter 9, part 2, assert that the job consists of determining the nutritional quality of available forage and then estimating how much of it is present. Obviously these tasks need to be done in the appropriate time and space frames.

Habitat evaluation, at whatever intensity, is a form of carrying capacity assessment. It should be a basic function in management of mule deer and blacktails in every state and province that has significant populations of the species. Chapter 10, part 2, offers some explanations for failures in the process and some suggestions for overcoming them. Until practical techniques for measuring forage quality and quantity become cost effective for routine field application, wildlife managers may have to be content with empirical approaches. Guidelines such as those recently developed in Scotland to adjust red deer culls according to animal and habitat conditions (see chap. 8) might be modified for application to mule and black-tailed deer.

For now, such guidelines certainly are preferable to none. Meanwhile, many universities and management agencies in Canada and the United States are working to develop more objective bases for evaluating habitat. These efforts—involving integration of virtually all the kinds of knowledge of deer and environmental relationships that are reviewed in this book—offer exciting challenges to contemporary and future researchers, as well as to managers who can pilot test the results.

HABITAT MANAGEMENT

As long as human populations continue to increase in western North America, we can expect continued pressure for diversion of deer ranges to other uses. All federal, state, and provincial land and wildlife management agen-

cies recognize the fundamental need to maintain deer ranges and keep them habitable for deer. In chapter 14, Dale Reed reviewed the magnitude of encroachment by other uses, such as agricultural developments, rangeland conversion, mining, roads and highways, housing tracts, and a miscellany of recreational activities.

To counter this trend, many states and provinces have purchased critical areas, especially winter ranges, to maintain as big game habitat. But, because of political opposition to government acquisition of privately owned lands, plus a scarcity of funds for this purpose, only a small fraction of the big game range in private ownership is likely to be so acquired.

Western North America has much wild land in public ownership, compared with many other parts of the world, but the amount of publicly owned mule or black-tailed deer range is unlikely to increase. The prognosis must be a gradual reduction in land area managed primarily or partially for deer.

The effects of reduced or lost deer ranges can be mitigated by better management of the remaining lands to maximize their productivity for deer. Many kinds of habitat management are discussed in the text of this book, including manipulation of livestock grazing, various cultivative and vegetational communities that are most beneficial to deer in particular areas and during particular seasons. For many mule and black-tailed deer ranges, the "right" successional stages are subclimax plant communities that can be perpetuated only through the periodic or continuous influence of man. But for black-tailed deer in some coastal habitats of the Pacific Northwest, and for some mule deer populations occupying desert habitats, climax stages appear to be best.

In addition to technical difficulties, each effort to improve deer habitat normally is confronted with political, economic, and institutional obstacles. Extensive funds are needed to influence any significant area of deer range, and negotiating for such funds requires deft maneuvering among diverse political factions. This problem is complicated in most of western North America by the fact that no one agency manages both the animals and their habitat. State and provincial wildlife management agencies are responsible for managing deer harvests, but most of the habitat is controlled by private landowners or public land management agencies that have little or no authority to regulate deer numbers. Since deer production is not the primary management goal on most private or public lands, deer habitat improvement programs typically involve a complex process of coordination among bureaucracies with missions that are not always compatible.

It no doubt is because of such economic, political, and institutional roadblocks that deer habitat improvement projects large enough to contribute substantially to hunter harvests are difficult, if not impossible, to identify. Cost and controversy both seem to be increasing and perhaps will limit the future of such programs. Still, as long as significant numbers of people have an interest in deer hunting and, through their taxes, employ wildlife managers to attempt to fulfill their wishes, habitat improvement probably will remain one of the management strategies.

Although recreational values usually are difficult or impossible to express in dollar terms, wildlife managers may find it necessary to develop benefit-cost assessments to justify deer habitat improvement projects. It was estimated, for example, that the cost of a chaparral management program in northern California would come to $234 (1970 values) for each Columbian black-tailed deer potentially added to the harvest (Longhurst and Connolly 1970). Similar analysis showed chaparral management in Arizona to cost $220 (1972 values) per additional desert mule deer potentially added to the population (see chapter 9, part 2). Estimates of hunting success and hunter expenditure in the Rocky Mountain states yield an approximation of $200 to $600 (mid-1970s values) spent for each mule deer harvested (see chapter 10, part 2).

If the object of habitat improvement is to increase the number of deer available to hunters, it seems logical that full harvest of present deer production should precede expenditures to create more deer. But, even where full harvest is being achieved, it may take some artful

persuasion to convince hunters that additional costs—which they will bear directly or indirectly as taxpayers—are tolerable. Often, however, wildlife habitat improvement is one of several land management goals, such as water yields, increased livestock forage, wildfire control, and others. Then the full cost of management need not be justified solely on the basis of increased wildlife production. Coordination of goals and activities to provide multiple benefits, including maintenance and enhancement of deer habitat, seems to be one of the most promising management opportunities for the future.

DEER HABITAT IN MULTIPLE-USE LAND MANAGEMENT

A project conducted in California in 1976, referred to as "large scale deer habitat improvement," involved fewer than 405 hectares (1,000 acres) (California Department of Fish and Game 1977). Matched against the 20.2 million hectares (50 million acres) occupied by deer in California (Longhurst et al. 1952), the project is not very impressive. By comparison, 40,500–121,400 hectares (100,000–300,000 acres) are burned annually by wildfires, more than 200,000 hectares (500,000 acres) are logged annually to some degree, and 12.6–16.2 million hectares (30–40 million acres) are grazed by livestock (W. M. Longhurst, pers. comm., July 1979). If fire, timber, and livestock management programs could be tailored to include benefits for deer, the results might far surpass those that are likely to be achieved by token deer-habitat improvement projects.

Indeed, on most public lands in western Canada and the United States, except parks and wilderness areas, multiple-resource management considerations are required by law or regulations, though they are executed to various degrees of satisfaction in the views of different public factions. State and provincial wildlife management agencies have a say in the process, but so do other interests. And the acreage approved for habitat improvement may be offset by other acreage dedicated to uses that are detrimental to deer.

There has been tangible progress for deer, however. In the Rocky Mountain region of the United States National Forest System, a current planning objective is to take approximately one-third of timber harvests from sales designed specifically to benefit wildlife (W. B. Gallaher, pers. comm., July 1979). The timber and wildlife managers' problem there is to "design" logging operations to benefit wildlife. There is as yet little documentation that such management has produced the desired result—namely, increased deer populations. Current knowledge on this subject is discussed in chapter 11.

It should become apparent from chapter 11 that the "designs" still must be rather conjectural. To quote John Schoen (pers. comm. to R. E. McCabe, 14 November 1979): "We must beware of falling into the old trap of implementing our hypotheses before they are tested and thus contributing to new and unfounded generalities." Unfortunately, many of the old generalizations about deer-timber management relationships remain largely hypothetical or, in some areas, demonstrably inapplicable.

Similar limitations apply to the subject of livestock grazing as a tool for deer habitat improvement. Theory abounds, but supportive documentation of effective results is in short supply. Livestock use probably is beneficial to deer in some circumstances, but intentional manipulation of livestock to enhance deer range is another matter. In this area much remains to be learned. Examples of progress are seen in reports by Jensen et al. (1976) and Smith et al. (1979) on the manipulation of sheep grazing to benefit deer. However, we are unaware of measured responses in numbers of mule and black-tailed deer such as have been shown for elk as a result of cattle grazing systems (Anderson and Scherzinger 1975) and for white-tailed deer to sheep-goat-cattle grazing (Merrill et al. 1957).

Foraging interactions of deer and livestock are discussed in chapter 13 and, to a lesser extent, in chapters 9 and 12 as well. From these reviews, it is obvious that much more needs to be done to assess the potential of livestock management for deer range enhancement.

To summarize, it is easy to list research needs for multiple-use management, but more difficult to advise managers what to do right now. As Thomas et al. (1976, p. 453) said about planning logging to benefit deer and elk, "The need is critical. The time is now." Clearly, the manager must do the best he or she can with the information at hand. The task can be alleviated by appropriate guidelines, such as those developed by Thomas et al. (1976) and Black et al. (1976). If the outcome is uncertain, there should be comfort in the knowledge that managing wildlife habitat on an extensive scale is a relatively recent objective. Best efforts will have to suffice while we are acquiring better knowledge and empirical experience.

EFFECTS OF HUNTING ON DEER POPULATIONS

The extensive discussion of relationships of deer harvests and population dynamics in chapter 7 reveals several research and management needs, including better estimates of both deer populations and harvests. These technical and managerial problems, however difficult, may be more solvable than several philosophical and political problems related to hunting.

One problem is the concept, held by one faction, that hunting is immoral, uncivilized, and incompatible with the goal of maintaining deer populations. Others, including hunters, believe that hunting is not only an honorable and spiritually healthy pursuit, but even essential for the maintenance of vigorous, healthy deer herds. Still others have rendered eloquent value judgments for and against hunting. It should be the function of wildlife biologists and managers to offer factual understanding of particular deer populations in specified habitats, as a source of objectivity in the debate. Wildlife biologists and managers would be well advised to view hunting/antihunting issues dispassionately, since hunting is neither moral or immoral. To approach this subject otherwise may bias and distort the ecological information that must serve as a basis for making biopolitical decisions.

The evidence is irrefutable that mule and black-tailed deer populations can be maintained despite heavy, *regulated* hunting year after year for decades. Populations that are large enough to support hunting during two or three weeks in autumn offer countless recreational opportunities for public enjoyment through the remainder of the year.

On the other hand, mule deer and blacktail populations have persisted in many places without benefit of cropping by man. Although unhunted populations obviously are subject to checks and balances that regulate their numbers, the dynamics of unhunted mule deer or blacktail herds have received little study. There is no evidence that such unhunted herds have any attributes that are more appropriate to the desires of antihunters, unless tame deer begging at the picnic table is one.

Crippling and illegal killing of deer is a special cause of concern to hunters and wildlife managers, as well as to nonhunters and antihunters. In the practical view of wildlife managers, who are confronted with too many obstacles to efficient production, crippling losses are an intolerable waste. The problem and its magnitude are discussed in chapter 8. For many deer populations, the greatest potential for increasing legal harvest may lie in reducing illegal kill and crippling losses. In the Oak Creek mule deer herd in Utah, for example, Robinette et al. (1977) found that crippling loss and illegal kill amounted to 45 percent of the legal, reported kill. These authors suggested that many deer might be saved if hunter attitudes and conduct could be changed.

Under current laws and traditions in North America, wildlife managers have little control over hunter conduct, but they can promote improved hunting skill and responsible behavior through education. Sportsmen, likewise, can minimize adverse public attitudes toward hunters and hunting by initiating or supporting such efforts.

More rigorous law enforcement often is advocated as an additional need, but adequate intensification of enforcement may be prohibitively expensive. If conservation officers currently detect no more than 2 percent of big game law violations, as estimated in several studies (see chap. 8), then even a fivefold increase in their efforts still might leave 90 percent of violations undetected.

Another frequent obstacle to maximum legal harvests of deer is hunting regulations that restrict harvests to bucks only. Not only are crippling loss and illegal kills higher in buck-only hunts than in any-deer hunts (see chap. 8), but buck-only hunting also assures that harvestable antlerless deer will be wasted rather than used by hunters. This does not mean that every deer herd should be managed for maximum harvest, but where this is the goal it usually can be accomplished only by harvesting does as well as bucks. Analysis of this problem in Mendocino County, California, indicated that if hunters were allowed to take both antlered and antlerless deer, rather than only bucks with at least one forked antler, the legal harvest could be increased 200–300 percent, and the ratio of natural to hunting losses reduced from 12–16:1 down to 2:1 (F. M. Anderson et al. 1974).

PREDATORS AND PREDATOR CONTROL

Predator management or nonmanagement is another highly charged social and political issue associated with the regulation of deer populations. A quarter of a century ago, when *The Deer of North America* (Taylor 1956) was being written, wholesale reduction of predator populations was the goal of governmental control programs in much of the western United States.

Cowan (1956*a*, p. 596) wrote then: "Despite the hundreds of thousands of dollars that have been expended in attempts to control the animals known to prey upon deer, there are as yet no published accounts of careful, scientific experiments designed to measure the effects of predation upon a coast deer population; on the success of control programs in terms of proportion of the predators removed; or of increased productivity of the deer populations resulting from the control . . . there is urgent need for controlled experiments to determine: (1) the influence of different levels of predator populations on deer herds living under various conditions; (2) the efficacy of different control techniques; and (3) the results that can be anticipated from different levels of control."

These questions still have not been addressed adequately for either mule deer or black-tailed deer, and the need for facts remains acute because of keen public interest in predator management. Since the 1950s, social and political pressures have forced government predator control programs to curtail or stop wholesale reductions in favor of more selective efforts to take only individual animals or local populations that are damaging livestock. Some predator species clearly have increased in many areas, and the impact of predation on mule and black-tailed deer may be greater now than in the 1950s.

Research on predator-ungulate relationships was greatly accelerated in the 1970s (see chap. 7), but such relationships are complex and will require continuing effort to provide the information needed for management decisions. Regarding the question whether predator control is a feasible way to increase deer numbers, the most informative studies will be those in which both predator and prey populations are monitored while predator control is in effect.

CONCLUSION

Deer management consists of habitat management and population management. Enough experience with both has been acquired over the past half century to show that mule and black-tailed deer can be managed professionally, provided that opportunities to refine and apply biological knowledge are not excessively restricted. The dismay and frustration felt by wildlife professionals over political interference, or court challenges to wildlife management, arise partly because nothing in their training or experience prepares them to accept legal expertise or maneuvering as taking precedence over biological and ecological considerations in the practice of wildlife management.

Politics and resource management policy certainly are germane to the practice of deer management. It is not the function of this book, however, to advise how they can be bent to that purpose. Rather, this book has synthesized the available biological and ecological knowledge, together with relevant management experience.

As is evidenced by the wealth of literature reviewed here, few wildlife species have been researched so extensively, or subjected to so much management effort, as mule and black-tailed deer. Much is known about deer, their environmental relations, and their management, but much remains to be learned.

We assert that, little by little, wildlife biologists and managers are learning to do a better job of deer management. Although there is plenty of room to develop and apply improved techniques and concepts, the level of management that ultimately is achieved will be defined by the priorities of our modern society.

ALPHABETICAL LIST OF ANIMALS CITED IN THE TEXT

bear, American black	*Ursus americanus*
bison	*Bison bison*
boar, wild (feral hog)	*Sus scrofa*
bobcat	*Lynx rufus*
caribou	*Rangifer tarandus*
coyote	*Canis latrans*
deer, axis	*Axis axis*
deer, burro	*Odocoileus hemionus eremicus*
deer, California mule	*O. h. californicus*
deer, Carmine Mountains white-tailed	*O. virginianus carminis*
deer, Cedros Island	*O. hemionus cerrosensis*
deer, Columbian black-tailed	*O. h. columbianus*
deer, Columbian white-tailed	*O. virginianus leucurus*
deer, Coues white-tailed	*O. v. couesi*
deer, Dakota white-tailed	*O. v. dacotensis*
deer, desert mule	*O. hemionus crooki*
deer, fallow	*Dama dama*
deer, Northwest white-tailed	*Odocoileus virginianus ochrourus*
deer, peninsula mule	*O. hemionus peninsulae*
deer, red	*Cervus elaphus*
deer, Rocky Mountain mule	*Odocoileus hemionus hemionus*
deer, roe	*Capreolus capreolus*
deer, sambar	*Cervus unicolor*
deer, sika	*Cervus nippon*
deer, Sitka black-tailed	*Odocoileus hemionus sitkensis*
deer, Southern mule	*O. h. fuliginatus*
deer, Texas white-tailed	*O. virginianus texanus*
deer, Tiburon Island mule	*O. hemionus sheldoni*
eagle, golden	*Aquila chrysaetos*
elk	*Cervus canadensis*
gemsbok × Kalahari oryx	*Oryx gazella*
goat, Rocky Mountain	*Oreamnus americanus americanus*
grouse, black	*Lyrurus tetrix*
ibex, Iranian	*Capra aegagrus*
ibex, Siberian	*C. siberica*
lion, mountain	*Felis concolor*
lynx, Canadian	*Lynx canadensis*
moose	*Alces alces*
muntjac	*Muntiacus reevsi*
musk-ox	*Ovibus mochatus*
peccary, collared	*Dicotyles tajacu*
pronghorn	*Antilocapra americana*
reindeer	*Rangifer tarandus*
sheep, Barbary (aoudad)	*Ammotragus lervia*

sheep, bighorn	*Ovis canadensis*
sheep, Dall's	*O. dalli*
sheep, desert bighorn	*O. canadensis*
tahr	*Hemitragus jemlahicus*
wolf	*Canis lupus*

ALPHABETICAL LIST OF PLANTS CITED IN THE TEXT

acacia (cat's-claw)	*Acacia* spp.
agave	*Agave* spp.
alder, red	*Alnus rubra*
alfalfa	*Medicago sativa*
amorpha, leadplant	*Amorpha canescens*
apache plume	*Fallugia paradoxa*
ash, green	*Fraxinus pennsylvanica*
aspen	*Populus tremuloides*
aspen, quaking	*P. tremuloides*
aspen, trembling	*P. tremuloides*
aster	*Aster* sp.
aster, Pacific	*A. chilensis*
aster, Siberian	*A. sibiricus*
balsamorrhiza	*Balsamorrhiza sagittata*
bearberry	*Arctostaphylos uva-ursi*
beardtongue	*Penstemon* spp.
bear-grass	*Nolina microcarpa*
birch, Alaska	*Betula neoalaskana*
birch, paper	*B. papyrifera*
birch, white	*B. papyrifera*
bitterbrush	*Purshia tridentata*
bitterbrush, antelope	*P. tridentata*
bitter cherry	*Prunus emarginata*
blackberry, Pacific	*Rubus ursinus*
blackcap	*R. leucodermis*
bladderpod	*Lesquerella* spp.
bleeding heart	*Dicentra formosa*
bluebell	*Campanula rotundifolia*
bluedicks (grassnut)	*Dichelostemma pulchellum*
bluegrass	*Poa* spp.
Bluegrass, Kentucky	*P. pratensis*
bluestem, big	*Andropogon gerardi*
bluestem, little	*A. scoparius*
bluestem, sand	*A. hallii*
bluet	*Hedyotis (Houstonia) acerosa*
boxelder	*Acer negundo*
bracken	*Pteridium aquilinum*
bristle grass, plains	*Setaria macrostachya*
buckeye, California	*Aesculus californica*
buckthorn, California	*Rhamnus californica*
buckthorn, hollyleaf	*R. crocea*
buckwheat, sulfur	*Eriogonum umbellatum*
buckwheat, Wright	*E. wrightii*
buffaloberry, silvery	*Shepherdia argentea*
buffalograss	*Buchloë dactyloides*

burnet	*Sanguisorba* sp.
bur sage	*Franseria* sp.
bur sage, white	*F. dumosa*
cactus, barrel	*Ferocactus wislizeni*
candelilla	*Euphorbia antisyphilitica*
cat's-claw	*Acacia greggii*
cat's-ear	*Hypochaeris radicata*
ceanothus, buckbrush (deer brush)	*Geanothus cuneatus*
ceanothus, desert	*C. greggii*
ceanothus, Fendler	*C. fendleri*
ceanothus, red-stem	*C. sanguineus*
cedar, incense	*Libocedrus decurrens*
cedar, western red	*Thuja plicata*
chamise	*Adenostema fasciculatum*
chess	*Bromus* spp.
chess, soft	*B. mollis*
chokecherry	*Prunus* sp.
chokecherry, black	*P. virginiana* var. *melanocarpa*
chokecherry, common	*P. virginiana*
cholla, cane	*Opuntia spinosior* var. *imbricata*
cholla, jumping	*O. fulgida*
cinquefoil, shrubby	*Potentilla fruticosa*
cliffrose	*Cowania mexicana*
clover	*Trifolium* sp.
clover, rose	*T. pratense*
cordgrass, prairie	*Spartina pectinata*
cottonwood	*Populus* spp.
cottonwood, eastern	*P. deltoides* var. *occidentalis*
cottonwood, plains	*P. sargentii*
cow parsnip	*Heracleum lanatum*
creosote bush	*Larrea divaricata*
creosote bush	*L. tridentata*
currant, clove	*Ribes odoratum*
currant, golden	*R. aureum*
dalea, feather	*Dalea formosa*
dandelion	*Taraxacum officinalis*
dayflower	*Commelina diathifolia*
deervetch, big	*Lotus crassifolius*
desert honeysuckle	*Anisacanthus thurberi*
desertthorn	*Lycium andersoni*
dogwood	*Cornus* sp.
dogwood, red osier	*C. stolonifera*
Douglas fir	*Pseudotsuga menziesii*
draba, cuneate-leaved	*Draba cunefolium*
elderberry, red	*Sambucus racemosa*
elm, American	*Ulmus americana*
eriastrum	*Eriastrum* sp.
euphorbia	*Euphorbia serrula*
fairy duster	*Calliandra eriophylla*
feathergrass	*Stipa* spp.
fendlera bush, cliff	*Fendlera rupicola*
fern, cloak	*Notholanae sinuta*
fern, sword	*Polystichum munitum*
fescue, Idaho	*Festuca idahoensis*
fescue, rough	*F. scabrella*
fescue, tall	*F. arundinacea*
filaree (storksbill)	*Erodium cicutarium*

fir, balsam	*Abies balsamea*
fir, cork-bark	*A. lasiocarpa* var. *arizonica*
fir, grand	*A. grandis*
fir, red	*A. magnifica*
fir, silver	*A. amabilis*
fir, subalpine	*A. lasiocarpa*
fir, white	*A. concolor*
flax	*Linum* sp.
fleabane	*Erigeron* sp.
forestiera	*Forestiera pubescens*
galleta, big	*Hilaria rigida*
gaura, scarlet	*Gaura coccinea*
globe mallow	*Sphaeralcea* sp.
goldeneye	*Viguiera stenoloba*
gourd, Missouri (buffalo)	*Curcibita foetidissima*
grama, blue	*Bouteloua gracilis*
grama, chino	*B. breviseta*
grama, hairy	*B. hirsuta*
grama, side oats	*B. curtipendula*
grape, California wild	*Vitis californica*
grape, wild	*V. arizonica*
grass, needle and thread	*Stipa comata*
greasewood	*Sarcobatus vermiculatus*
groundsel, woodland	*Senecio sylvaticus*
guayacan	*Porlieria angustifolia*
hackberry	*Celtis occidentalis*
hackberry, netleaf	*C. reticulata*
hawthorn	*Crataegus rotundifolia*
hazel, beaked	*Corylus cornuta*
hellebore, false	*Veratrum viride*
hemlock, mountain	*Tsuga mertensiana*
hemlock, western	*T. heterophylla*
hop tree	*Ptelea trifoliata*
horsebrush	*Tetradymia canescens*
horsetail	*Equisetum* sp.
huckleberry	*Vaccinium parvifolum*
huckleberry, evergreen	*V. ovatum*
indigobush	*Amorpha californica*
iris	*Iris tenax*
ironwood	*Olneya tesota*
ivy, poison	*Rhus radicans*
jojoba	*Simmondsia chinensis*
june grass	*Koeleria cristata*
juniper, alligator	*Juniperus deppeana*
juniper Ashe	*J. ashei*
juniper, California	*J. californica*
juniper, common	*J. communis*
juniper, one-seeded	*J. monosperma*
juniper, prostrate, creeping	*J. horizontalis*
juniper, redberry	*J. pinchotii*
juniper, Rocky Mountain	*J. scopulorum*
juniper, Utah	*J. osteosperma*
juniper, western	*J. occidentalis*
kidney-wood	*Eysenhardtia orthocarpa*
kinnikinnick	*Arctostaphylos uva-ursi*
larch, western	*Larix occidentalis*
leatheroak	*Quercus durata*

lechuguilla	*Agave lechuguilla*
licorice, wild	*Glycorrhiza lepidota*
lovegrass	*Eragrostis* spp.
lovegrass, Boer	*E. chloromelis*
lovegrass, Lehmann	*E. lehmanniana*
lovegrass, weeping	*E. curvula*
lupine	*Lupinus* spp.
madrone, Pacific	*Arbutus menziesii*
manzanita	*Arctostaphylos* spp.
manzanita, pointleaf	*A. pungens*
manzanita, Pringle	*A. pringlei*
maple, bigtooth	*Acer grandidentatum*
maple, vine	*A. circinatum*
marigold, fetid	*Dyssodia papposa*
mariola	*Parthenium incanum*
matrimony vine	*Lycium* sp.
mendora	*Mendora* spp.
mercury, wild	*Argythamnia neomexicana*
mesquite	*Prosopis* sp.
mesquite, curly	*Hilaria belangeri*
mesquite, honey	*Prosopis juliflora*
mistletoe	*Phoradendron* spp.
mistletoe	*P. villosum*
mistletoe, mesquite	*P. californicum*
montia	*Montia* spp.
mountain mahogany	*Cercocarpus* spp.
mountain mahogany, birchleaf	*C. betuloides*
mountain mahogany, curl-leaf	*C. ledifolius*
mountain mahogany, hairy	*C. breviflorus*
mountain mahogany, true	*C. montanus*
mountain misery, Sierra	*Chamaebatia foliolosa*
muhly, bush	*Muhlenbergia porteri*
needlegrass, green	*Stipa viridula*
nettle	*Urtica* sp.
ninebark	*Physocarpus malvaceus*
oak	*Quercus* spp.
oak, black	*Q. kelloggii*
oak, blue	*Q. douglasii*
oak, bur	*Q. macrocarpa*
oak, California scrub	*Q. dumosa*
oak, canyon live	*Q. chrysolepis*
oak, coast live	*Q. agrifolia*
oak, Emory	*Q. emoryi*
oak, Gambel	*Q. gambelli*
oak, Harvard	*Q. harvardii*
oak, interior live	*Q. wislizenii frutescens*
oak, Mexican blue	*Q. oblongifolia*
oak Mohr	*Q. mohriana*
oak, Oregon white	*Q. garryana*
oak, sandpaper	*Q. pungens*
oak, scrub	*Q. dumosa*
oak, shrub live	*Q. turbinella*
oak, valley	*Q. lobata*
oak, wavyleaf	*Q. undulata*
ocean spray	*Holodiscus discolor*
ocotillo	*Fouquieria splendens*
onion, wild	*Allium* spp.

orchardgrass	*Dactylis glomerata*
Oregon grape	*Berberis nervosa, B. repens*
paloverde	*Cercidium floridum*
pea, chaparral	*Pickeringia montana*
pearly everlasting	*Anaphalis margaritacea*
phacelia	*Phacelia* spp.
phacelia, Bolander	*P. bolanderi*
phlox	*Phlox* spp.
photinia	*Heteromeles arbutifolia*
pine, bristlecone	*Pinus aristata*
pine, Coulter	*P. coulteri*
pine, Digger	*P. sabiniana*
pine, foxtail	*P. balfouriana*
pine, jack	*P. banksiana*
pine, limber	*P. flexilis*
pine, lodgepole	*P. contorta*
pine, piñon	*P. edulis, P. monophylla*
pine, ponderosa	*P. ponderosa*
pine, scotch	*P. sylvestris*
pine, sugar	*P. lambertiana*
pine, western white	*P. monticola*
pine, whitebark	*P. albicaulis*
piñon, Mexican	*P. cembroides*
plantain	*Plantago* sp.
plum, American	*Prunus americana*
poison oak	*Rhus diversiloba*
poplar, balsam	*Populus balsamifera*
pondweed	*Potamogeton* sp.
prairie mimosa	*Desmanthus cooleyi*
prickly pear	*Opuntia polyacantha*
prickly pear, Engelmann	*O. engelmannii*
pussytoe	*Antennaria* spp.
rabbitbrush	*Chrysothamnus* spp.
rabbitbrush, green	*C. viscidiflorus*
rabbitbrush, little	*C. viscidiflorus*
rabbitbrush, rubber	*C. nauseosus*
ragwort, tansy	*Senecio jacobaea*
ratany, range	*Krameria parvifolia*
red cedar, eastern	*Juniperus virginiana*
redwood	*Sequoia sempervirens*
ricegrass, Indian	*Oryzopsis hymenoides*
rose	*Rosa* sp.
rose, Nootka	*R. nutkana*
rose, prairie	*R. suffulta*
rose, Woods	*R. woodsii*
ryegrass, domestic	*Lolium multiflorum*
sagebrush	*Artemisia* spp.
sagebrush, big	*A. tridentata*
sagebrush, black	*A. arbuscula*
sagebrush, fringed	*A. frigida*
sagebrush, silver	*A. cana*
sagebrush, small	*A. nova*
sagewort, fringed	*A. frigida*
salal	*Gaultheria shallon*
saltbush	*Atriplex* spp.
saltbush	*A. confertifolia*
saltbush, four-winged	*A. canescens*

salt cedar	*Tamarix ramasissima*
sandpaper bush	*Mortonia scabrella*
sand reed, prairie	*Calamovilfa longifolia*
screwbean	*Prosopis pubescens*
sedge	*Carex* spp.
sequoia, giant	*Sequoiadendron giganteum*
serviceberry	*Amelanchier*
serviceberry, saskatoon (saskatoon bush)	*A. alnifolia*
silk tassel, Fremont	*Garrya fremontii*
silk tassel, Wright	*G. wrightii*
skunkbush	*Rhus trilobata*
smilo	*Oryzopsis miliacea*
snakeweed, broom	*Xanthocephalum sarothrae*
snowberry	*Symphoricarpos* spp.
snowberry, common	*S. albus*
snowberry, mountain	*S. oreophilus*
snowberry, Utah	*S. utahensis-vaccinoides*
snowberry, western	*S. occidentalis*
soapberry	*Sapindus saponaria*
soapweed, little	*Yucca glauca*
Solomon's seal, false	*Smilacina* sp.
sotol	*Dasylirion leiophyllum*
spruce, black	*Picea mariana*
spruce, blue	*P. pungens*
spruce, Engelmann	*P. engelmanni*
spruce, Sitka	*P. sitchensis*
spruce, white	*P. glauca*
squirreltail	*Sitanion hystrix*
starflower	*Trientalis latifolia*
stickweed	*Stephenomeria panciflora*
stonecrop	*Sedum spathulifolium*
sumac, evergreen	*Rhus virens*
sumac, littleleaf	*R. microphylla*
sumac, skunkbush	*R. trilobata*
sumac, smooth	*R. glabra*
sumac, sugar	*R. ovata*
sweetclover	*Melilotus* spp.
sweetclover, yellow	*M. officinalis*
sweetclover, white	*M. alba*
switchgrass	*Panicum virgatum*
tan oak	*Lithocarpus densiflora*
tansy mustard	*Descurainia obtusa*
tansy mustard, pinnate	*D. pinnata*
tarbush	*Flourensia cernua*
thimbleberry, western	*Rubus parviflorus*
thistle	*Cirsium* sp.
tobacco brush	*Ceanothus velutina*
tobosa grass	*Hilaria berlangeri*
toyon	*Photinia arbutifolia*
vetch	*Vicia* spp.
violet	*Viola* sp.
wait-a-minute	*Mimosa biuncifera*
wheatgrass, beardless	*Agropyron inerme*
wheatgrass, bluebunch	*A. spicatum*
wheatgrass, crested	*A. desertorum*
wheatgrass, slender	*A. trachycaulum*

wheatgrass, western	*A. smithii*
Whipplea	*Whipplea modesta*
whitethorn, coast	*Ceanothus incanua*
wild rye, Virginia	*Elymus virginicus*
willow	*Salix* spp.
willow, Bebb	*S. bebbiana*
willow, heart-leaved	*S. cordata*
willow, Mackenzie	*S. mackenziana*
willow, peachleaf	*S. amygdaloides*
willow, sandbar	*S. interior*
windmill grass, hooded	*Chloris cuculata*
winterfat	*Eurotia lanata*
wormwood, Louisiana	*Artemesia ludoviciana*
yarrow	*Achillea millefolium*
yew, Pacific	*Taxus brevifolia*
yucca	*Yucca* spp.
yucca, blue	*Y. baccata*
yucca, soaptree	*Y. elata*
yucca, Torrey	*Y. torreyi*

Names listed are those used by the various authors or as given in the literature cited. For the spelling of most common plant names, *Webster's Third New International Dictionary* was used as reference. The names are not verified here for taxonomic accuracy.

REFERENCES

Abell, D. H., and Gilbert, F. F. 1974. Nutrient content of fertilized deer browse in Maine. *J. Wildl. Manage.* 38:517–24.

Adams, L. 1949. The effects of deer on conifer reproduction in northwestern Montana. *J. For.* 47:909–13.

Adcock, J. L. 1967. Neuro-opthalmic pathology of elaeophorosis. Ph.D. thesis, Colorado State University, Fort Collins.

Adcock, J. L.; Hibler, C. P.; Abdelbaki, Y. Z.; and Davis, R. W. 1965. Elaeophoriasis in elk (*Cervus canadensis*). *Bull. Wildl. Dis. Assoc.* 1:48.

Agrons, B. Z. 1964. *Analysis of effects of 1963 deer depredation hunt.* Multilith. Westport, Calif. Rockport Redwood Company. 10 pp.

Alaska Department of Fish and Game. 1973. *Alaska's wildlife and habitat.* Juneau: Alaska Department of Fish and Game. 121 pp., ca. 620 maps.

Albertson, F. W., and Weaver, J. E. 1945. Injury and death or recovery of trees in prairie climate. *Ecol. Monogr.* 15:393–433.

Alden, E. F., and Springfield, H. W. 1972. *Southwestern pinyon-juniper ecosystems: A Bibliography.* Fort Collins, Colo.: USDA Forest Service, Rocky Mountain Forest and Range Experiment Station. 66 pp.

Alexander, R. R. 1974. *Silviculture of subalpine forests in the central and southern Rocky Mountains: The Status of our knowledge.* USDA Forest Service Research Paper RM-121. 88 pp.

Alldredge, J. R.; Tueller, P. T.; and Dean, S. 1977. *Evaluation of methods used in determining deer population trends.* Job Performance Report, P-R Project W-48-8, Study R I-A, Job 1. Reno: Nevada Department of Fish and Game. 8 pp.

Alldredge, W. A.; Lipscomb, J. F.; and Whicker, F. W. 1974. Forage intake rates of mule deer estimated with fallout cesium-137. *J. Wildl. Manage.* 38:508–16.

Allen, E. O. 1968. Range use, foods, condition and productivity of white-tailed deer in Montana. *J. Wildl. Manage.* 32:130–41.

Allen, W. V. 1976. Biochemical aspects of lipid storage and utilization in animals. *Amer. Zool.* 16:631–47.

Allred, W. J.; Brown, R. C.; and Murie, O. J. 1944. Disease kills feedground elk. *Wyo. Wildl.* 9:1–8, 27.

Almkvist, B.; André, T.; Ekblom, S.; Holm, S.; Persson, O.; and Rempler, S. A. 1976. *Research on wildlife accidents on roads (VIOL).* Progress report. Stockholm: National Swedish Road Administration. 11 pp.

Altmann, M. 1952. Social behavior of elk, *Cervus canadensis nelsoni*, in the Jackson Hole area of Wyoming. *Behaviour* 4:116–43.

———. 1958. The flight distance in free-ranging big game. *J. Wildl. Manage.* 22:207–9.

Ammann, A. P.; Cowan, R. L.; Mothershead, C. L.; and Baumgardt, B. R. 1973. Dry matter and energy intake in relation to digestibility in white-tailed deer. *J. Wildl. Manage.* 37:195–201.

Anderson, A. E. 1960. *Effects of sagebrush eradication by chemical means on deer and related wildlife.* Completion Report, P-R Project W-78-R-13, WP7, J1, Denver: Colorado Game and Fish Department. 72 pp.

———. 1969. *2-4-D, sagebrush, and mule deer-cattle use of upper winter range.* Special Report no. 21. Denver: Colorado Division of Game, Fish, and Parks. 21 pp.

———. 1976. Evaluation of radio telemetry. In *Game research report, July 1976*, part 2, pp. 463–503. Denver: Colorado Division of Wildlife. 561 pp.

Anderson, A. E., and Bowden, D. C. 1977. Age and sex ratios and deer densities. In *Colorado game research review, 1975–1976*, ed. O. B. Cope, p. 16. Fort Collins: Colorado Division of Wildlife, Game Research Section. 73 pp.

Anderson, A. E.; Frary, L. G.; and Stewart, R. H. 1964. A comparison of three morphological attributes of mule deer from the Guadalupe and Sacramento Mountains, New Mexico. *J. Mammal.* 45:48–53.

Anderson, A. E., and Medin, D. E. 1964. Reproductive studies. Job Completion Report, P-R Project W-105-R-3. In *Game research report, January 1964*, pp. 239–69. Denver: Colorado Game and Fish Department. 325 pp.

———. 1965. Reproductive studies. Job Completion Report, P-R Project W-105-R-5. In *Game research report, January 1965*, part 4, pp. 531–52. Denver: Colorado Game, Fish and Parks Department. 618 pp.

———. 1967. *The breeding season in migratory mule deer.* Information Leaflet 60. Denver: Colorado Division of Game, Fish and Parks. 4 pp.

———. 1969. Antler morphometry in a Colorado mule deer population. *J. Wildl. Manage.* 33:520–33.

———. 1971. Antler phenology in a Colorado mule deer population. *Southwest. Natur.* 15:485–94.

Anderson, A. E.; Medin, D. E.; and Bowden, D. C. 1970. Erythrocytes and leukocytes in a Colorado mule deer population. *J. Wildl. Manage.* 34:389–406.

———. 1971. Adrenal weight in a Colorado mule deer population. *J. Wildl. Manage.* 35:689–97.

———. 1972a. Indices of carcass fat in a Colorado mule deer population. *J. Wildl. Manage.* 36:579–94.

———. 1972b. Total serum protein in a population of mule deer. *J. Mammal.* 53:384–87.

———. 1972c. Blood serum electrolytes in a Colorado mule deer population. *J. Wildl. Dis.* 8:183–90.

———. 1972d. Carotene and vitamin A in the liver and blood serum of a Rocky Mountain mule deer (*Odocoileus hemionus hemionus*) population. *Comp. Biochem. Physiol.* 41B:745–58.

———. 1972e. Mule deer numbers and shrub yield-utilization on winter range. *J. Wildl. Manage.* 36:571–78.

———. 1974. Growth and morphometry of the carcass, selected bones, organs, and glands of mule deer. *Wildl. Monogr.* no. 39. 122 pp.

———. 1975. Growth of the mule deer stomach. *New Mexico Acad. Sci. Bull.* 15:49 (abstract).

Anderson, A. E.; Medin, D. E.; and Ochs, D. P. 1969. Relationships of carcass fat indices in 18 wintering mule deer. *Proc. West. Assoc. Game and Fish Commissioners* 49:329–40.

Anderson, A. E.; Snyder, W. A.; and Brown, G. W. 1965. Stomach content analyses related to condition in mule deer, Guadalupe Mountains, New Mexico. *J. Wildl. Manage.* 29:352–66.

———. 1970. Indices of reproduction and survival in female mule deer, Guadalupe Mountains, New Mexico. *Southwest. Natur.* 15:29–36.

Anderson, A. W. 1949. Early summer foods and movements of the mule deer (*Odocoileus hemionus*) in the Sierra Vieja range of southwestern Texas. *Texas J. Sci.* 1:45–50.

Anderson, D. R.; Laake, J. L.; Crain, B. R.; and Burnham, K. P. 1976. *Guidelines for line transect sampling of biological populations.* Logan: Utah Cooperative Wildlife Research Unit, Utah State University. 28 pp.

Anderson, E. W., and Scherzinger, R. J. 1975. Improving quality of winter forage for elk by cattle grazing. *J. Range Manage.* 28:120–25.

Anderson, F. M.; Connolly, G. E.; Halter, A. N.; and Longhurst, W. M. 1974. *A computer simulation study of deer in Mendocino County, California.* Agricultural Experiment Station Technical Bulletin 130. Corvallis: Oregon State University. 72 pp.

Anderson, R. C. 1972. The ecological relationships of meningeal worm and native cervids in North America. *J. Wildl. Dis.* 8:304–10.

Aney, W. W. 1974. Estimating fish and wildlife harvest: A survey of methods used. *Proc. West. Assoc. Game and Fish Commissioners* 54:70–99.

Annison, E. F., and Lewis, D. 1959. *Metabolism in the rumen.* New York: John Wiley. 184 pp.

[Anonymous.] 1924. Modoc deer disease. *Calif. Fish and Game* 11:27–28.

[Anonymous.] 1976. *Standard guideline for the use and development of sodium monofluoroacetate (Compound 1080) as a predacide.* Subcommittee E. 35.17 on Vertebrate Control Agents. Philadelphia: American Society for Testing and Materials. 15 pp.

Anthony, R. G. 1972. Ecological relationships between mule deer and white-tailed deer in southeastern Arizona. Ph.D. thesis, University of Arizona, Tucson, 123 pp.

———. 1976. Influence of drought on diets and numbers of desert deer. *J. Wildl. Manage.* 40:140–44.

Anthony, R. G., and Smith, N. S. 1977. Ecological relationships between mule deer and white-tailed deer in southeastern Arizona. *Ecol. Monogr.* 47:255–77.

Armstrong, H. L., and MacNamee, J. K. 1950. Blackleg in deer. *J. Amer. Vet. Med. Assoc.* 117:212.

Armstrong, R. A. 1950. Fetal development of the northern white-tailed deer (*Odocoileus virginianus borealis* Miller). *Amer. Midl. Natur.* 43:650–66.

Arthur, W. J., III. 1977. Plutonium intake by mule deer at Rocky Flats, Colorado. M.S. thesis, Colorado State University, Fort Collins. 123 pp.

Asdell, S. A. 1964. *Patterns of mammalian reproduction.* 2d ed. Ithaca; Comstock Publishing Associates. 670 pp.

Ashcroft, G. C., Jr. 1973. *Formulation of big game habitat manipulation projects.* Job Progress Report, P-R Project W-51-R-8, Job II-3, Sacramento: California Fish and Game Department. 14 pp.

Aughey, E. 1969. Histology and histochemistry of the male accessory glands of the red deer (*Cervus elaphus* L.). *J. Reprod. Fertility* 18:399–407.

Austin, D. D.; Urness, P. J.; and Wolfe, M. L. 1977. The influence of predator control on two adjacent wintering deer herds. *Great Basin Natur.* 37:101–2.

Bailey, E. D. 1960. Behavior of the Rattlesnake mule deer on their winter range. M.S. thesis, Montana State University, Bozeman. 110 pp.

Baker, D. L. 1976. Energy requirements of mule deer fawns in winter. M.S. thesis, Colorado State University, Fort Collins. 76 pp.

Baker, M. F., and Leuth, F. X. 1967. Mandibular cavity tissue as a possible indicator of condition in deer. *Proc. Annu. Conf. SE Assoc. Game and Fish Commissioners* 20:69–74.

Baker, R. H. 1956. Mammals of Coahuila, Mexico. *Univ. Kansas Mus. Natur. Hist. Publ.* 9:125–335.

Baldwin, M. R. 1968. The snowmobile and environmental quality. *Living Wilderness* 32(104):14–17.

Ballard, W., and Merriam, H. 1975. The deer dilemma. *Alaska Fish Tales and Game Trails*, January–February 1975, pp. 4–5, 20–21.

Bandy, P. J. 1965. A study of comparative growth in four races of black-tailed deer. Ph.D. diss., University of British Columbia, Vancouver. 189 pp.

Bandy, P.J.; Cowan, I. McT.; and Wood, A. J. 1956. A method for assessment of the nutritional status of wild ungulates. *Can. J. Zool.* 34:48–52.

———. 1970. Comparative growth in four races of black-tailed deer (*Odocoileus hemionus*). Part I. Growth in body weight. *Can. J. Zool.* 48:1401–10.

Bandy, P. J.; Kitts, W. D.; Wood, A. J.; and Cowan, I. McT. 1957. The effect of age and the plane of nutrition on the blood chemistry of the Columbian black-tailed deer (*Odocoileus hemionus columbianus*). B. Blood glucose, non-protein nitrogen, total plasma protein, plasma albumen, globulin, and fibrinogen. *Can. J. Zool.* 35:283–89.

Banfield, A. W. F. 1960. The use of caribou antler pedicles

for age determination. *J. Wildl. Manage.* 24:99–102.

Banks, W. J. 1974*a*. *Histology and comparative organology: A Text-atlas.* Baltimore: Williams and Wilkins. 285 pp.

———. 1974*b*. The ossification process of the developing antler in the white-tailed deer *(Odocoileus virginianus). Calcified Tissue Res.* 14:257–74.

Banks, W. J.; Epling; G. P.; Kainer, R. A.; and Davis, R. W. 1968*a*. Antler growth and osteoporosis. I. Morphological and morphometric changes in the costa compacta during the antler growth cycle. *Anat. Rec.* 162:387–98.

———. 1968*b*. Antler growth and osteoporosis. II. Gravimetric and chemical changes in the costa compacta during the antler growth cycle. *Anat. Rec.* 162:399–406.

Barnes, R. D., and Longhurst, W. M. 1960. Techniques for dental impressions, restraining and embedding markers in live-trapped deer. *J. Wildl. Manage.* 24:224–26.

Barney, M. A., and Frischknecht, N. C. 1974. Vegetation changes following fire in the pinyon-juniper type of west-central Utah. *J. Range Manage.* 27:91–96.

Barney, R. J. 1975. Fire Management. A definition. *J. For.* 73:498, 519.

Baron, F. J.; Nord, E. C.; Evanko, A. B.; and Makel, W. J. 1966. *Seeding conifers and buffer crops to reduce deer depredations.* USDA Forest Service Research Note PSW-100. 8 pp.

Barrette, C. 1977. The social behavior of captive muntjacs *(Muntjacus recusi* Ogilby 1839). *Z. Tierpsychol.* 43:188–213.

Barsch, R. C.; McConnell, E. E.; Innes, G. D.; and Schmidt, J. M. 1977. A review of exertional rhobdmyolysis in wild and domestic animals and man. *Vet. pathol.* 14:314–24.

Bartmann, R. M. 1974. *Guidelines for estimating deer numbers in connection with claims of damage to growing crops.* Game Information Leaflet 97. Denver: Colorado Division of Wildlife. 3 pp.

Basile, J. V., and Hutchings, S. S. 1966. Twig-diameter-length relationships of bitterbrush. *J. Range Manage.* 19:34–38.

Batcheler, C. L. 1975. Development of a distance method for deer census from pellet groups. *J. Wildl. Manage.* 39:641–52.

Batcheler, C. L., and Clarke, C. M. H. 1970. Note on kidney weights and the kidney fat index. *New Zeal. J. Sci.* 13:663–68.

Bates, C. G. 1927. Varietal differences. *J. For.* 25:610.

Baxter, D.; Harmel, D.; Armstrong, W. E.; and Butts, G. 1977. Spikes vs. forked-antlered bucks. *Texas Parks and Wildl.* 35(3):6–9.

Bayoumi, M. A., and Smith, A. D. 1976. Response of big game winter range to fertilization. *J. Range Manage.* 29:44–48.

Beament, J. W. L. 1961. The role of physiology in adaptation and competition between animals. In *Symposium of the Society for Experimental Biology,* no. 15, pp.

62–71. Cambridge: Cambridge University Press. 365 pp.

Beasom, S. L. 1974. Intensive short term predator removal as a game management tool. *Trans. N. Amer. Wildl. and Natur. Resour. Conf.* 39:230–40.

Beck, A. M. 1973. *The ecology of stray dogs: A study of free-ranging urban animals.* Baltimore: York Press. 98 pp.

Behnke, A. R. 1961. Comment on the determination of whole body density and a resume of body composition data. In *Techniques for measuring body composition,* ed. J. Brožek and A. Henschel, pp. 118–33. Washington, D.C.: National Academy of Sciences, Natural Resources Council. 300 pp.

Behrend, D. F. 1973. Wildlife management–forest fertilization relations. In *Forest fertilization symposium proceedings,* pp. 108–10. USDA Forest Service General Technical Report NE-3. 246 pp.

Behrend, D. F., and Lubeck, R. A. 1968. Summer flight behavior of white-tailed deer in two Adirondack forests. *J. Wildl. Manage.* 32:615–18.

Behrend, D. F., and McDowell, R. D. 1967. Antler shedding among white-tailed deer in Connecticut. *J. Wildl. Manage.* 31:588–91.

Bell, G. H.; Davidson, J. N.; and Scarborough, H. 1959. *Textbook of physiology and biochemistry.* Baltimore: Williams and Wilkins. 1,065 pp.

Bell, R. H. V. 1971. A grazing ecosystem in the Serengeti. *Sci. Amer.* 225:86–93.

Beltran, E. 1953. *Vida silvestre y recursos naturales a lo largo de la carretera panamericana.* Mexico City: Instituto Mexicano de Recursos Naturales Renovables, A. C. 228 pp.

Benjamin, M. M. 1961. *Outline of veterinary clinical pathology.* 2d ed. Ames: Iowa State University Press. 186 pp.

Bentley, J. R.; Seegrist, D. W.; and Blakeman, D. A. 1970. *A technique for sampling low shrub vegetation by crown volume classes.* USDA Forest Service Research Note PSW-215. 11 pp.

Berg, A. 1973. *The nutritional factor.* Washington, D.C.: Brookings Institution.

Bergerud, A. T. 1974. Rutting behaviour of Newfoundland caribou. In *The behaviour of ungulates and its relation to management,* ed. V. Geist and F. Walther, 1:395–435. IUCN New Series Publication 24. Morges, Switzerland: IUCN. 511 pp.

Bernard, R. 1963. Specific gravity, ash, calcium and phosphorus content of antlers of Cervidae. *Can. Natur.* 90:310–22.

Berry, L. J. 1932. A "horned" blacktail doe with fawn. *J. Mammal.* 13:282–83.

Besser, J. F., and Welch, J. F. 1959. Chemical repellents for the control of mammal damage to plants. *Trans. N. Amer. Wildl. Conf.* 24:166–73.

Bianca, W. 1968. Thermoregulation. In *Adaptation of domestic animals,* ed. E. S. E. Hafez, pp. 97–118. Philadelphia: Lea and Febiger. 415 pp.

Billingham, R. E. 1958. A reconsideration of the

phenomenon of hair neogenesis with particular reference to the healing of cutaneous wounds in adult mammals. In *The biology of hair growth,* ed. W. Montagna and R. A. Ellis, pp. 451–68. New York: Academic Press. 520 pp.

Billingham, R. E.; Mangold, R.; and Silvers, W. K. 1959. The neogenesis of skin in the antlers of deer. *New York Acad. Sci. Annals* 83:491–98.

Bischoff, A. I. 1954. Limitations on the bone marrow technique in determining malnutrition in deer. *Proc. West. Assoc. Game and Fish Commissioners* 34:205–10.

———. 1957. The breeding season of some California deer herds. *Calif. Fish and Game* 43:91–96.

———. 1958. Productivity in some California deer herds. *Calif. Fish and Game* 44:253–59.

Bissell, H. D.; Harris, B.; Strong, H.; and James, F. 1955. The digestibility of certain natural and artificial foods eaten by deer in California. *Calif. Fish and Game* 41:57–78.

Bissell, H. D., and Strong, H. 1955. The crude protein variations in the browse diet of California deer. *Calif. Fish and Game* 41:145–55.

Bissell, H. D., and Weir, W. C. 1957. The digestibilities of interior live oak and chamise by deer and sheep. *J. Anim. Sci.* 16:476–80.

Biswell, H. H. 1959. Deer forage from common mistletoe. *Calif. Fish and Game* 45:218–19.

———. 1961. Manipulation of chamise brush for deer range improvement. *Calif. Fish and Game* 47:125–44.

Biswell, H. H.; Taber, R. D.; Hedrick, D. W.; and Schultz, A. M. 1952. Management of chamise brushlands for game in the North Coast region of California. *Calif. Fish and Game* 38:453–84.

Black, H.; Scherzinger, R. J.; and Thomas, J. W. 1975. Relationships of Rocky Mountain elk and Rocky Mountain mule deer habitat to timber management in the Blue Mountains of Oregon and Washington. In *Elk-logging-roads symposium proceedings,* pp. 11–31. Moscow: Forest, Wildlife and Range Experiment Station, University of Idaho. 142 pp.

Black, H. D.; Dimock E. J., II; Dodge, W. E.; and Lawrence, W. H. 1969. Survey of animal damage on forest plantations in Oregon and Washington. *Trans. N. Amer. Wildl. and Natur. Resour. Conf.* 34:388–408.

Blaisdell, J. A., and Hubbard, R. L. 1956. *An "outrigger" type deer fence.* USDA Forest Service California Forest and Range Experiment Station Research Note 108. 3 pp.

Blaisdell, J. P., and Mueggler, W. F. 1956. Effect of 2,4-D on forbs and shrubs associated with bog sagebrush. *J. Range Manage.* 9:38–41.

Blaxter, K. L. 1962. *The energy metabolism of ruminants.* London: *Hutchinson Scientific and Technical.* 329 pp.

Bloom, A. M. 1978. Sitka black-tailed deer winter range in the Kadashan Bay area, southeast Alaska. *J. Wildl. Manage.* 42(1):108–12.

Boeker, E. L.; Scott, V. E.; Reynolds, H. G.; and Donaldson, B. A. 1972. Seasonal food habits of mule deer in southwestern New Mexico. *J. Wildl. Manage.* 36:56–63.

Boldt, C. E., and Van Deusen, J. L. 1974. *Silviculture of ponderosa pine in Black Hills.* USDA Forest Service Research Paper RM-124. 45 pp.

Bonn, P. J. 1976. Deer guzzlers. *Oregon Wildl.* 31(8):6–7.

Bonn, R. L. 1967. Deer-soil-vegetation relationships in the forest and grasslands. M.S. thesis, Humboldt State College, Arcata, Calif. 86 pp.

Book, S. A.; Connolly, G. E.; and Longhurst, W. M. 1972. Fallout cesium-137 accumulation in two adjacent populations of northern California deer. *Health Phys.* 22:379–85.

Boone and Crockett Club, Committee on Records of North American Big Game (R. S. Waters, chairman). 1964. *Records of North American big game.* New York: Holt, Rinehart and Winston. 398 pp.

Bormann, F. H. 1976. An inseparable linkage: Conservation of natural ecosystems and the conservation of fossil energy. *Bioscience* 26:754–60.

Borrecco, J. E.; Black, H. C.; and Hoover, E. J. 1972. Response of black-tailed deer to herbicide induced habitat changes. *Proc. West. Assoc. Game and Fish Commissioners* 52:437–51.

Bouckhout, L. W. 1972. The behavior of mule deer (*Odocoileus hemionus hemionus* Rafinesque) in winter in relation to the social and physical environment. M.S. thesis, University of Calgary, Alberta. 124 pp.

Bourne, G. H., and Jayne, E. P. 1961. The adrenal gland. In *Structural aspects of ageing,* ed. E. H. Bourne and E. M. H. Wilson, pp. 303–24. New York: Hafner. 419 pp.

Bowden, D. C.; Anderson, A. E.; and Medin, D. E. 1969. Frequency distributions of mule deer fecal group counts. *J. Wildl. Manage.* 33:895–905.

Bowers, D. E. 1956. Methods of color determination. *Syst. Zool.* 5:147–60, 182.

Bowne, J. G.; Luedke, A. J.; Foster, N. M.; and Jochim, M. M. 1966. Current aspects of bluetongue in cattle. *J. Amer. Vet. Med. Assoc.* 148:1177.

Bowns, J. E. 1976. Field criteria for predator damage assessment. *Utah Sci.* 37(1):26–30.

Box, T. W. 1978. The arid lands revisited 100 years after John Wesley Powell. 57th Annual Faculty Honors Lecture, Utah State University, Logan. 30 pp.

Boyles, D. E. 1976. Dogs and deer don't mix. *Colo. Outdoors* 25(2):12–13.

Boynton, W. H., and Woods, G. M. 1933. Deer as carriers of anaplasmosis. *Science* 78:559.

———. 1940. Anaplasmosis among deer in the natural state. *Science* 91:168.

Brockman, C. F. 1959. *Recreational use of wild lands.* New York: McGraw-Hill. 346 pp.

Brody, S. 1945. *Bioenergetics and growth.* New York: Reinhold. 1,023 pp.

Brody, S., and Kibler, H. H. 1941. Growth and development with special reference to domestic animals. III. Relations between organ weight and body weight in growing and mature animals. *Mo. Agric. Exp. Sta. Bull.* 328:1–41.

Brokx, P. A. 1972. The superior canines of *Odocoileus* and other deer. *J. Mammal.* 53:359–66.

Bromley, P. T. 1977. Aspects of the behavioural ecology and sociobiology of the pronghorn *(Antilocapra americana)*. Ph.D. thesis, University of Calgary, Alberta. 370 pp.

Browman, L. G. 1957. Seasonal variations in the mule deer thyroid. *Anat. Rec.* 128:528 (abstract).

Browman, L. G., and Sears, H. S. 1955. Erythrocyte values, and alimentary canal pH values in the mule deer. *J. Mammal.* 36:474–76.

———. 1956. Cyclic variation in the mule deer thymus. *Proc. Soc. Exp. Biol. Med.* 93:161–62.

Brown, D. F.; Lowe, C. H.; and Pase, C. P. 1977. *Biotic communities of the Southwest.* USDA Forest Service General Technical Report RM-41. 2 pp. plus map and slides.

Brown, E. R. 1961. *The black-tailed deer of western Washington.* Biological Bulletin 13. Olympia: Washington Department of Game. 124 pp.

Brown, J. L. 1964. The evolution of diversity in avian territorial systems. *Wilson Bull.* 76:160–69.

Brown, R. W., and Johnston, R. S. 1976. *Revegetation of alpine mine disturbance: Beartooth Plateau, Montana.* USDA Forest Service Research Note INT-206. 8 pp.

Brown, R. W.; Johnston, R. S.; Richardson, B. Z.; and Farmer, E. E. 1976. Rehabilitation of alpine disturbances: Beartooth Plateau, Montana. In *High-altitude revegetation workshop no. 2,* ed. R. H. Zuck and L. F. Brown, pp. 58–73. Environmental Resource Information Series no. 21, Fort Collins: Colorado State University. 128 pp.

Brown, T. C.; O'Connell, P. F.; and Hibbert, A. R. 1974. *Chaparral conversion potential in Arizona.* II. *An economic analysis.* USDA Forest Service Research Paper RM-127. 28 pp.

Browning, B. M., and Lauppe, E. M. 1964. A deer study in a redwood–Douglas-fir forest type. *Calif. Fish and Game* 50:132–45.

Brownlee, R. G.; Silverstein, R. M.; Müller-Schwarze, D.; and Singer, A. G. 1969. Isolation, identification and function of the chief component of the male tarsal scent in black-tailed deer. *Nature* 221:284–85.

Brownlee, S. 1963. *Trans-Pecos game management survey.* P-R Project W-57-R-11, Job 8. Austin: Texas Parks and Wildlife Department. 6 pp.

———. 1966. *Big Bend ecological survey.* Progress Report, P-R Project W-57-R-14, Job 9. Austin: Texas Parks and Wildlife Department. 6 pp.

———. 1971. *Composition and usage of plants by desert mule deer through rumen samples.* P-R Project W-28-D, Job 3, Plan II. Austin: Texas Parks and Wildlife Department, 45 pp.

———. 1973. *Composition and usage of plants by desert mule deer through rumen samples.* P-R Project W-48-D, Job 3, Plan II. Austin: Texas Parks and Wildlife Department. 25 pp.

———. 1975. The effects of hunting pressure on population dynamics of desert mule deer. Unpublished. On file at Texas Parks and Wildlife Department, Alpine. 10 pp.

———. 1976. *Black Gap Wildlife Management Area development: Fawn mortality.* Performance Report, P-R Project W-48-D-25, Objective 1, Job 1, Plan II. Austin: Texas Parks and Wildlife Department. 8 pp.

———. N.d. Records of deer studies on Black Gap Wildlife Management Area. Unpublished. On file at Texas Parks and Wildlife Department, Alpine.

Brunetti, O. A. 1952. Apparent personal communication cited in *A survey of California deer herds,* ed. W. Longhurst, A. S. Leopold, and R. F. Dasmann, p. 108. Game Bulletin 6. Sacramento: California Department of Fish and Game. 136 pp.

———. 1969. Redescription of *Paralaphostrongylus* (Boev and Schulz, 1950) in California deer, with studies on its life history and pathology. *Calif. Fish and Game* 55:307–16.

Brunetti, O. A., and Rosen, M. N. 1970. The prevalence of *Echinococcus granulosus* hydatid in California deer. *J. Parasitol.* 56:1138–40.

Bruns, E. 1976. Recent changes in Alberta's mule deer populations and management. *Proc. West. Assoc. Game and Fish Commissioners* 56:364–66.

Bubenik, A. B. 1966. *Das Geweih* [Antlers]. Hamburg and Berlin: Paul Parey. 214 pp.

———. 1968. The significance of the antlers in the social life of the Cervidae. *Deer* 1:208–14.

———. 1971. Geweihe und ihre biologische Funktion [Antlers and their biological function]. *Naturwissenschaft und Medizin* 8(36):33–51.

Bubenik, A. B.; Tachezy, R.; and Bubenik, G. A. 1976. The role of the pituitary-adrenal axis in the regulation of antler growth processes. *Säugetierkundliche Mitteilungen* 24:1–5.

Buechner, H. K. 1957. Three additional records of antlered female deer. *J. Mammal.* 38:277–78.

Bullard, F. A. 1926. A horned doe. *Calif. Fish and Game* 12:47.

Bunnell, F. L. 1974. Computer simulation of forest-wildlife relations. In *Wildlife and forest management in the Pacific Northwest,* ed. H. C. Black, pp. 39–50. Corvallis: Oregon State University. 236 pp.

Buol, S. W. 1966. *Soils of Arizona.* Technical Bulletin 171. Tucson: University of Arizona Agricultural Experiment Station. 25 pp. and map.

Burgess, T. E. 1973. Alberta mule deer: Present status and management considerations. Unpublished. On file at Alberta Recreation, Parks and Wildlife Department, Red Deer. 52 pp.

Burk, C. J. 1973. The Kaibab deer incident: A long persisting myth. *Bioscience* 28:113–14.

Burkhardt, J. W., and Tisdale, E. W. 1976. Causes of juniper invasion in southwestern Idaho. *Ecology* 57:472–84.

Buss, I. O. 1959. Another antlered female deer. *J. Mammal.* 40:252–53.

Cable, D. R. 1975. *Range management in the chaparral type and its ecological basis: The status of our knowl-*

edge. USDA Forest Service Research Paper RM-155, 30 pp.

Cable, D. R., and Martin, S. C. 1975. *Vegetation responses to grazing, rainfall, site condition, and mesquite control on semidesert range.* USDA Forest Service Research Paper RM-149. 24 pp.

Cain, S. A., Kadlec, J. A.; Allen, D. L.; Cooley, R. A.; Hornocker, M. G.; Leopold, A. S.; and Wagner, F. H. 1972. *Predator control: 1971.* Report to the Council on Environmental Quality and Department of Interior, by the Advisory Committee on Predator Control. Ann Arbor: University of Michigan Press. 207 pp.

California Department of Fish and Game. 1976. *A plan for California deer.* Sacramento: California Fish and Game Commission. 15 pp.

———. 1977. *Annual wildlife management unit reports and recommendations for antlerless deer hunts.* Sacramento: California Fish and Game Commission. 65 pp.

California Pest Control Action Council. 1964. Animal damage survey—1962. California Pest Control Action Council Report. Multilith. 13 pp.

California Wildlife Investigations Laboratory. N.d. *Report on special deer collection, 1961–1962, Rockport, Mendocino County, California.* Sacramento: California Department of Fish and Game. 8 pp.

Campbell, D. L. 1969. Plastic fabric to protect seedlings from animal damage. In *Proceedings: Wildlife and reforestation in the Pacific Northwest symposium, 1968,* ed. H. C. Black, pp. 87–88. Corvallis: Oregon State University. 92 pp.

———. 1974. Establishing preferred browse to reduce damage to Douglas-fir seedlings by deer and elk. In *Proceedings: Wildlife and forest management in the Pacific Northwest symposium, 1973,* pp. 187–92. Corvallis: Oregon State University. 236 pp.

Campbell, D. L., and Bullard, R. W. 1972. A preference testing system for evaluating repellents for black-tailed deer. *Proc. Vert. Pest Conf.* 5:56–63.

Campbell, D. L., and Evans, J. 1975. *"Vexar" seedling protectors to reduce wildlife damage to Douglas-fir.* U.S. Fish and Wildlife Service Wildlife Leaflet 508. 11 pp.

Capp, J. C. 1968. *Bighorn sheep, elk, mule deer range relationships: A review of literature.* Fort Collins: Rocky Mountain Nature Association and Colorado State University. 75 pp.

Capps, B. 1973. *The Indians.* New York: Time-Life Books. 240 pp.

Carbaugh, B.; Vaughan, J. P.; Bellis, E. D.; and Graves, H. B. 1975. Distribution and activity of white-tailed deer along an interstate highway. *J. Wildl. Manage.* 39:570–81.

Carbyn, L. N. 1975. Wolf predation and behavioural interactions with elk and other ungulates in an area of high prey density. Ph.D. thesis, University of Alberta, Edmonton. 234 pp.

Carhart, A. H. 1943. Fallacies in winter feeding of deer. *Trans. N. Amer. Wildl. Conf.* 8:333–37.

Carpenter, J. R. 1940. The grassland biome. *Ecol. Monogr.* 10:617–84.

Carpenter, L. H. 1974. Middle Park deer study: Range fertilization. In *Game research report, July 1974,* part 2, pp. 183–95. Denver: Colorado Division of Wildlife. 398 pp.

———. 1975. Middle Park deer study: Experimental range fertilization. In *Game research report, July 1975,* part 2, pp. 199–207. Denver: Colorado Division of Wildlife. 504 pp.

———. 1976. Nitrogen-herbicide effects on sagebrush deer range. Ph.D. thesis, Colorado State University, Fort Collins. 159 pp.

———. 1977. Middle Park cooperative deer study: Experimental range fertilization. In *Game research report, July 1977,* part 1, pp. 43–60. Denver: Colorado Division of Wildlife. 123 pp.

Carpenter, L. H.; Wallmo, O. C.; and Gill, R. B. 1979. Forage diversity and dietary selection by wintering mule deer. *J. Range Manage.* 32(3):226–29.

Carpenter, L. H.; Wallmo, O. C.; and Morris, M. J. 1973. Effect of woody stems on estimating herbage weights with a capacitance meter. *J. Range Manage.* 26:151–52.

Carter, G. R., and Bain, R. V. S. 1960. Pasteurellosis (*Pasteurella multocida*): A review stressing recent developments. *Vet. Rev. Annotations* 6:105–28.

Caughley, G. 1970. Eruption of ungulate populations with emphasis on the Himalayan thar in New Zealand. *Ecology* 51:53–72.

———. 1974a. Bias in aerial survey. *J. Wildl. Manage.* 38:921–33.

———. 1974b. Interpretation of age ratios. *J. Wildl. Manage.* 38:557–62.

———. 1977. Sampling in aerial survey. *J. Wildl. Manage.* 41:605–15.

Caughley, G., and Goddard, J. 1972. Improving the estimates from inaccurate censuses. *J. Wildl. Manage.* 36:135–40.

Caughley, G.; Sinclair, R.; and Scott-Kemmis, D. 1976. Experiments in aerial survey. *J. Wildl. Manage.* 40:290–300.

Chalmers, C. A.; Vance, H. N.; and Mitchell, G. J. 1964. An outbreak of epizootic hemorrhagic disease in wild ungulates in Alberta. *J. Wildl. Dis.,* no. 42. 6 pp.

Chapline, W. R. 1936. Excessive stocking. In *The Western Range,* pp. 151–71. U.S. Senate Doc. no. 199, 74th Cong., 2d sess. Washington, D.C.: GPO. 620 pp.

Chapman, D. I. 1975. Antlers: Bones of contention. *Mammal Rev.* 5:122–72.

Chatelain, E. F. 1947. Food preferences of the Columbian black-tailed deer, *Odocoileus hemionus columbianus* (Richardson), on the Tillamook Burn, Oregon. M.S. thesis, Oregon State University, Corvallis. 64 pp.

Chattin, J. E. 1948. Breeding season and productivity in the Interstate deer herd. *Calif. Fish and Game* 34:25–31.

Cheatum, E. L. 1949a. The use of corpora lutea for determining ovulation incidence and variations in the fertility of white-tailed deer. *Cornell Vet.* 39:282–91.

———. 1949*b*. Bone marrow as an index of malnutrition. *New York State Conservationist* 3:19–22.

Cheatum, E. L., and Morton, G. H. 1946. Breeding season of white-tailed deer in New York. *J. Wildl. Manage* 10:249–63.

Choquette, L. P. E. 1970. Anthrax. In *Infectious diseases of wild mammals,* ed. J. W. Davis, L. H. Karstad, and D. O. Trainer, pp. 256–66. Ames: Iowa State University Press. 421 pp.

Christensen, G. C. 1976. Recent changes in Nevada's mule deer populations and management. *Proc. West. Assoc. Game and Fish Commissioners* 56:401–3.

Christensen, J. F.; Osebold, J. F.; and Rosen, M. N. 1958. The incidence of latent *Anaplasma marginale* infection in wild deer in an area where anaplasmosis is enzootic in cattle. *Proc. Ann. Meet. U.S. Livestock Sanit. Assoc.* 62:59.

Christian, J. J. 1964. Potassium deficiency: A factor in mass mortality of sika (*Cervus nippon*). Microfiche. *Wildl. Dis.* no. 37, pp. 1–11.

Christian, J. J., and Davis, D. E. 1964. Endocrines, behavior and population. *Science* 146:1550–60.

Christian, J. J.; Flyger, V.; and Davis, D. E. 1960. Factors in the mass mortality of sika deer, *Cervus nippon. Chesapeake Sci.* 1:79–95.

Christian, K. R., and Williams, V. J. 1960. Attempts to produce hypomagnesalmia in dry non-pregnant sheep. *New Zeal. J. Agric. Res.* 3:389–98.

Church, D. C. 1969. *Digestive physiology and nutrition of ruminants.* Vol. 1. Corvallis: Oregon State University. 316 pp.

———, ed. 1971. *Digestive physiology and nutrition of ruminants.* Vol. 2. *Nutrition.* Corvallis: Oregon State University. 400 pp.

Church, W. L. 1979. *Private lands and public recreation.* Washington, D.C.: National Association of Conservation Districts. 36 pp.

Clary, W. P. 1972. A treatment prescription for improving big game habitat in ponderosa pine forests. In *Proceedings of the 16th annual Arizona watershed symposium.* Report no. 2, pp. 25–28. Phoenix: Arizona Water Commission. 43 pp.

Clary, W. P.; Baker, M. B., Jr.; O'Connell, P. F.; Johnsen, T. N., Jr.; and Campbell, R. E. 1974. *Effects of pinyon-juniper removal on natural resource products and uses in Arizona.* USDA Forest Service Research Paper RM-128. 28 pp.

Clary, W. P., and Ffolliott, P. F. 1966. *Differences in herbage-timber relationships between thinned and unthinned ponderosa pine stands.* USDA Forest Service Research Note RM-74. 4 pp.

Clary, W. P., and Larson, F. R. 1971. Elk and deer use related to food sources in Arizona ponderosa pine. USDA Forest Service Research Note RM-202. 4 pp.

Clawson, W. J., and Lesperance, A. L. 1973. The environmental role of range livestock. *Proc. West. Sect., Amer. Soc. of Anim. Sci.* 24:38–41.

Cliff, E. P. 1939. Relationship between elk and mule deer in the Blue Mountains of Oregon. *Trans. N. Amer.* *Wildl. Conf.* 4:560–69.

Clover, M. R. 1956. Single-gate deer trap. *Calif. Fish and Game* 42 (3):199–201.

Coblentz, B. E. 1975. Serum cholesterol level changes in George Reserve deer. *J. Wildl. Manage.* 39 (2):342–45.

Cochran, W. G. 1977. *Sampling techniques.* 3d ed. New York: John Wiley. 428 pp.

Cole, G. 1958. Big game-livestock competition on Montana's mountain rangelands. *Montana Wildl. April* 1958:24–30.

Cole, G. F. 1959. Key browse survey method. *Proc. West. Assoc. Game and Fish Commissioners* 39:181–86.

Colorado Division of Highways. 1973. *Deer fence and gate standard.* M-607-E. Denver: Colorado Division of Highways. 2 pp.

Colorado Division of Wildlife. 1963–76. *1962–1975 Colorado big game harvest.* Denver: Department of Natural Resources, Colorado Division of Wildlife. 14 vols.

———. 1977. *Colorado big game harvest.* Denver: Department of Natural Resources, Colorado Division of Wildlife. 268 pp.

———. 1978. *1977 Colorado big game harvest.* Denver: Department of Natural Resources, Colorado Division of Wildlife. 268 pp.

———. N.d. Unpublished data on winter losses on a strip of winter range in Middle Park, Colorado. Denver: Colorado Division of Wildlife.

Colorado Division of Wildlife/U.S. Fish and Wildlife Service. 1978. *Ranking of wildlife on federal coal lands, Colorado.* Vol. 1. Denver: Colorado Division of Wildlife. 177 pp.

Connolly, G. E. 1970. A population model for deer on the Hopland Field Station, Mendocino County, California. M. A. thesis, Sonoma State College, Rohnert Park, Calif. 54 pp.

———. 1974. The politics of wildlife management in California. *Trans. 1974 Meet. West. Sec. Wildl. Soc., Amer. Fish. Soc.*:101–5.

———. 1978. Predators and predator control. In *Big game of North America: Ecology and management,* ed. J. L. Schmidt and D. L. Gilbert, pp. 369–94. Harrisburg, Pa.: Stackpole Books. 494 pp.

Connolly, G. E.; Dudziński, M. L.; and Longhurst, W. M. 1969. An improved age-lens weight regression for black-tailed deer and mule deer. *J. Wildl. Manage.* 33:701–4.

Connolly, G. E., and Longhurst, W. M. 1975. Deer production at Hopland Field Station. *Calif. Agric.* 29(6):8–9.

Connolly, G. E.; Timm, R. M.; Howard, W. E.; and Longhurst, W. M. 1976. Sheep killing behavior of captive coyotes. *J. Wildl. Manage.* 40:400–407.

Constan, K. 1972. Winter foods and range use of three species of ungulates. *J. Wildl. Manage.* 36:1068–76.

Cook, B. B.; Witham, L. E.; Olmstead, M.; and Morgan, A. F. 1949. Influence of seasonal and other factors on the acceptability and food value of the meat of two subspecies of California deer and of antelope. *Hilgardia* 19:265–84.

Cook, C. W. 1976. Surface-mine rehabilitation in the American West. *Environ. Conserv.* 3:179–83.

Cook, C. W., and Harris, L. E. 1968. *Effect of supplementation on intake and digestibility of range forage.* Bulletin 475, Utah Agricultural Experiment Station. Logan: Utah State University. 38 pp.

Cook, C. W., and Stoddart, L. A. 1963. Effect of season and intensity of use on the vigor of desert range plants. *J. Range Manage.* 16:315–17.

Cook, F. W. 1945. White-tailed deer in the Great Plains region. *J. Wildl. Manage.* 9:237–42.

Cook, R. S.; White, M.; Trainer, D. O.; and Glazener, W. C. 1971. Mortality of young white-tailed deer fawns in south Texas. *J. Wildl. Manage.* 35:47–56.

Cooley, R. A., and Kohlus, G. M. 1944. The Argasidae of North America, Central America and Cuba. *Amer. Midl. Natur. Monogr.* 1:1–152.

Cooper, W. S. 1922. *The broad-sclerophyll vegetation of California: An ecological study of the chaparral and its related communities.* Carnegie Institute of Washington Publication 319. Washington, D.C.: Carnegie Institute. 124 pp.

Cooperrider, A. Y., and Behrend, D. F. 1974. Monitoring forest deer population through simulation modeling. In *Monitoring forest environment through successive sampling: Proceedings of a symposium,* ed. T. Cunia, pp. 373–83. Syracuse: State University of New York. 390 pp.

Copeland, O. L. 1973. Mining impacts and resource management. *Trans. N. Amer. Wildl. and Natur. Resour. Conf.* 38:111–20.

Corbett, R. L.; Marchinton, R. L.; and Hill, C. E. 1971. Preliminary study of the effects of dogs on radio-equipped deer in a mountainous habitat. *Proc. Ann. Conf. SE Assoc. Game and Fish Commissioners* 25:69–77.

Cornelius, C. E., and Kaneko, J., eds. 1963. *Clinical biochemistry of domestic animals.* New York and London: Academic Press. 678 pp.

Corsi, R. M. 1976. Recent changes in Wyoming's mule deer population management. *Proc. West. Assoc. Game and Fish Commissioners* 56:434–36.

Costello, D. F. 1954. Vegetation zones in Colorado. In *Manual of the plants of Colorado,* ed. H. D. Harrington. Denver: Sage Books.

Costley, R. J. 1948. Crippling losses among mule deer in Utah. *Trans. N. Amer. Wildl. Conf.* 13:451–58.

Council for Agricultural Science and Technology. 1974. Livestock grazing on federal lands in the 11 western states. *J. Range Manage.* 27:174–81.

Cowan, I. McT. 1936. Distribution and variation in deer (Genus *Odocoileus*) of the Pacific Coast region of North America. *Calif. Fish and Game* 22:155–246.

———. 1943. Notes on the life history and morphology of *Cephenemyia jellisoni* Townsend and *Lipoptena depressa* Say, two dipterous parasites of the Columbian black-tailed deer (*Odocoileus hemionus columbianus* Richardson). *Can. J. Res. Zool.* 21:171–87.

———. 1945a. The ecological relationships of the food of the Columbian black-tailed deer (*Odocoileus*

hemionus columbianus Richardson) in British Columbia. *Can. J. Res.,* sec. D (3):71–103.

———. 1945b. The ecological relationships of the food of the Columbian black-tailed deer (*Odocoileus hemionus columbianus* Richardson) in the coast forest region of southern Vancouver Island, British Columbia. *Ecol. Monogr.* 15:109–39.

———. 1946a. Antlered doe mule deer. *Can. Field Natur.* 60:11–12.

———. 1946b. Parasites, diseases, injuries and anomalies of the Columbian black-tailed deer, *Odocoileus hemionus columbianus* (Richardson) in British Columbia. *Can. J. Res.* 24:71–103.

———. 1947. Range competition between mule deer, bighorn sheep and elk in Jasper Park, Alberta. *Trans. N. Amer. Wildl. Conf.* 12:223–27.

———. 1951. Diseases and parasites of big game animals of western Canada. *Rep. Proc. Ann. B.C. Game Conv.* 5:37–64.

———. 1956a. Life and times of the coast black-tailed deer. In *The deer of North America,* ed. W. P. Taylor, pp. 523–617. Harrisburg, Pa.: Stackpole. 668 pp.

———. 1956b. What and where are the mule and black-tailed deer? In *The deer of North America,* ed. W. P. Taylor, pp. 334–59. Harrisburg, Pa.: Stackpole. 668 pp.

———. 1962. Hybridization between the black-tailed deer and the white-tailed deer. *J. Mammal.* 43:539–41.

Cowan, I. McT., and Bandy, P. J. 1969. Observations on the haematology of several races of black-tailed deer. *Can. J. Zool.* 47:1021–24.

Cowan, I. McT., and Geist, V. 1961. Aggressive behavior in deer of genus *Odocoileus. J. Mammal.* 42:522–26.

Cowan, I. McT., and Guiguet, C. J. 1975. *The mammals of British Columbia.* Handbook no. 11. Victoria: British Columbia Provincial Museum. 414 pp.

Cowan, I. McT., and Holloway, C. W. 1978. Geographical location and current conservation status of the threatened deer of the world. In *Threatened deer: Proceedings of a working meeting of the Deer Specialist Group of the Survival Service Commission,* pp. 11–12. Morges, Switzerland: IUCN. 434 pp.

Cowan, I. McT., and Johnston, P. A. 1962. Blood serum protein variations at the species and subspecies level in deer of the genus *Odocoileus. Syst. Zool.* 11:131–38.

Cowan, I. McT., and Raddi, A. G. 1972. Pelage and molt in the black-tailed deer (*Odocoileus hemionus* [Rafinesque]). *Can. J. Zool.* 50:639–47.

Cowan, I. McT., and Wood, A. J. 1955a. The growth rate of the black-tailed deer (*Odocoileus hemionus columbianus*). *J. Wildl. Manage.* 19:331–36.

———. 1955b. The normal temperature of the Columbian black-tailed deer. *J. Wildl. Manage.* 19:154–55.

Cowan, R. L.; Hartsook, E. W.; and Whelan, J. B. 1968. Calcium-strontium metabolism in white-tailed deer as related to age and antler growth. *Proc. Soc. Exp. Biol. Med.* 129:733–37.

Cravioto, J., and De Licardie, E. R. 1973. Nutrition and behaviour and learning. In *World review of nutrition and dietetics,* 16:81–96. New York: S. Karger.

Crispens, C. G., Jr., and Doutt, J. K. 1973. Sex chromatin in antlered female deer. *J. Wildl. Manage.* 37:422–23.

Critchfield, H. J. 1966. *General climatology.* 2d ed. Englewood Cliffs, N.J.: Prentice-Hall. 420 pp.

Crombie, A. C. 1947. Interspecific competition. *J. Anim. Ecol.* 16:44–73.

Cronemiller, F. P. 1932. Does have antlers. *Calif. Fish and Game* 18:83.

———. 1951. Some dynamics of a mule deer population. *J. Wildl. Manage.* 15:206–8.

Cronemiller, F. P., and Bartholomew, P. S. 1950. The California mule deer in chaparral forests. *Calif. Fish and Game* 36:343–65.

Cronquist, A.; Holmgren, A. H.; Holmgren, N. H.; and Reveal, J. L. 1972. *Intermountain flora.* Vol. 1. New York and London: Hafner. 270 pp.

Croon, G. W.; McCullough, D. R.; Olson, C. E., Jr.; and Queal, L. M. 1968. Infrared scanning techniques for big game censusing. *J. Wildl. Manage.* 32:751–59.

Crouch, G. L. 1961. Wildlife populations and habitat conditions on grazed and ungrazed bottomlands in Logan County, Colorado. M.S. thesis, Colorado State University, Fort Collins. 144 pp.

———. 1964. Forage production and utilization in relation to deer browsing of Douglas-fir in the Tillamook Burn, Oregon. Ph.D. thesis, Oregon State University, Corvallis. 162 pp.

———. 1966a. Effects of simulated deer browsing on Douglas-fir seedlings. *J. For.* 64:323–26.

———. 1966b. Preferences of black-tailed deer for native forage and Douglas-fir seedlings. *J. Wildl. Manage.* 30:471–75.

———. 1968a. Forage availability in relation to deer browsing of Douglas-fir seedlings by black-tailed deer. *J. Wildl. Manage.* 32:542–53.

———. 1968b. *Spring-season deer browsing of Douglas-fir on the Capitol Forest in western Washington.* USDA Forest Service Research Note PNW-84. 8 pp.

———. 1969a. *Animal damage on national forests in the Pacific Northwest region.* USDA Forest Service Resource Bulletin PNW-28. 13 pp.

———. 1969b. Deer and reforestation in the Pacific Northwest. In *Proceedings: Wildlife and reforestation in the Pacific Northwest symposium, 1968,* ed., H. C. Black, pp. 63–66. Corvallis: Oregon State University. 92 pp.

———. 1974. Interactions of deer and forest succession on clear-cutting in the Coast Range of Oregon. In *Proceedings: Wildlife and forest management in the Pacific Northwest symposium, 1973,* pp. 133–38. Corvallis: Oregon State University. 236 pp.

———. 1976. Deer and reforestation in the Pacific Northwest. *Proc. Vert. Pest Conf.* 7:298–301.

Crouch, G. L., and Paulson, N. R. 1968. *Effects of protection from deer on survival and growth of Douglas-fir seedlings.* USDA Forest Service Research Note PNW-94. 6 pp.

Cupal, J. J.; Ward, A. L.; and Weeks, R. L. 1974. A repeater type biotelemetry system for use on wild big game animals. *Biomed. Sci. Instrument.* 10:145–52.

Curlin, J. W. 1962. Dogwood responds to nitrogen fertilization. *J. For.* 60:718–19.

Currie, P. O.; Reichert, D. W.; Malechek, J. C.; and Wallmo, O. C. 1977. Forage selection comparisons of mule deer and cattle under managed ponderosa pine. *J. Range Manage.* 30:252–56.

Cutright, P. R. 1969. *Lewis and Clark: Pioneering naturalists.* Urbana: University of Illinois Press. 506 pp.

Dakota Planning Team. 1974. Wildlife in the badlands. Badlands planning unit. Unpublished report. On file at USDA Forest Service, Custer National Forest, Billings, Mont. 84 pp.

Daniel, W. S., and Frels, D. B. 1971. *A track-count method for censusing white-tailed deer.* Texas Parks and Wildlife Department, Technical Series no. 7. 18 pp.

Darling, F. F. 1937. *A herd of red deer: A study in animal behaviour.* London: Oxford University Press. 215 pp.

Dasmann, R. F. 1952. Methods for estimating deer populations from fill data. *Calif. Fish and Game* 38:225–33.

———. 1953. Factors influencing movement of non-migratory deer. *Proc. West. Assoc. of Game and Fish Commissioners* 33:112–16.

———. 1956. Fluctuations in a deer population in California chaparral. *Trans. N. Amer. Wildl. Conf.* 21:487–99.

Dasmann, R. F., and Dasmann, W. P. 1963. Mule deer in relation to a climatic gradient. *J. Wildl. Manage.* 27:196–202.

Dasmann, R. F., and Hines, W. W. N.d. Logging, plant succession, and black-tailed deer in the redwood region. Unpublished. On file at Humboldt State College, Arcata, Calif. 12 pp.

Dasmann, R. F.; Hubbard, R. L.; Longhurst, W. M.; Ramstead, G. I.; Harn, J. H.; and Calvert, E. 1967. Deer attractants: An approach to the deer damage problem. *J. For.* 65:564–67.

Dasmann, R. F., and Taber, R. D. 1955. A comparison of 4 deer census methods. *Calif. Fish and Game* 41:225–28.

———. 1956a. Behavior of Columbian black-tailed deer with reference to population ecology. *J. Mammal.* 37:143–64.

———. 1956b. Determining structure in Columbian black-tailed deer populations. *J. Wildl. Manage.* 20:78–83.

Dasmann, W. P. 1958. *Big game of California.* Revised in 1975 by Wallace MacGregor. Sacramento: California Department of Fish and Game. 58 pp.

———. 1971. *If deer are to survive.* Harrisburg, Pa.: Stackpole Books. 128 pp.

Dasmann, W. P., and Dasmann, R. F. 1963. Abundance and scarcity in California deer. *Calif. Fish and Game* 49:4–15.

Daubenmire, R. 1968. Ecology of fire in grasslands. *Ecol. Res.* 5:209–66.

Dauphine, T. C. 1975. Kidney weight fluctuations affecting the kidney fat index in caribou. *J. Wildl. Manage.* 39:379–86.

Davies, R. B. N.d. 1976 necropsy reports. Unpublished. On file at Wild Animal Disease Center, Colorado State University, Fort Collins.

Davies, R. B., and Spraker, T. L. N.d. 1975 necropsy reports. Unpublished. On file at Wild Animal Disease Center, Colorado State University, Fort Collins.

Davis, J. W.; Karstad, L. H.; and Trainer, D. O., eds. 1970. *Infectious diseases of wild mammals.* Ames: Iowa State University Press. 421 pp.

Davis, J. W., and Libke, K. G. 1970. Trematodes. In *Parasitic diseases of wild mammals,* ed. J. B. Davis and R. C. Anderson, pp. 235–67. Ames: Iowa State University Press. 364 pp.

Davis, L. S. 1967. Dynamic programming for deer management planning. *J. Wildl. Manage.* 31:667–79.

Davis, R. B. 1952. The use of rumen contents data in a study of deer-cattle competition and "animal equivalence." *Trans. N. Amer. Wildl. Conf.* 17:448–58.

Davis, R. W. 1962. Studies on antler growth in mule deer (*Odocoileus hemionus hemionus,* Rafinesque). In *Proceedings: First national white-tailed deer disease symposium,* pp. 61–64. Athens: University of Georgia. 202 pp.

Davis, W. B. 1960. *The mammals of Texas.* Bulletin no. 41. Austin: Texas Game and Fish Commission. 252 pp.

DeBell, D. S.; Brunette, A. P.; and Schweitzer, D. L. 1977. Expectations from intensive culture on industrial forest lands. *J. For.* 75:10–13.

deCalesta, D. S.; Nagy, J. G.; and Bailey, J. A. 1974. Some effects of starvation on mule deer rumen bacteria. *J. Wildl. Manage.* 38:815–22.

———. 1975. Starving and refeeding mule deer. *J. Wildl. Manage.* 39:663–69.

Decker, E. 1978. Exotics. In *Big game of North America: Ecology and Management,* ed. J. L. Schmidt and D. L. Gilbert, pp. 249–56. Harrisburg, Pa.: Stackpole Books. 494 pp.

DeMartini, J. C., and Connolly, G. E. 1975. Testicular atrophy in Columbian black-tailed deer in California. *J. Wildl. Dis.* 11:101–6.

de Nahlik, A. J. 1974. *Deer management: Improved herds for greater profit.* North Pomfret, Vt.: David and Charles. 250 pp.

Denney, R. N. 1974. The impact of uncontrolled dogs on wildlife and livestock. *Trans. N. Amer. Wildl. and Natur. Resour. Conf.* 39:257–91.

———. 1976. Regulations and the mule deer harvest: Political and biological management. In *Mule deer decline in the west: A symposium,* ed. G. W. Workman and J. B. Low, pp. 85–90. Logan: Utah State University College of Natural Resources and Agricultural Experiment Station. 134 pp.

Denniston, R. H. 1956. Ecology, behavior and population dynamics of the Wyoming or Rocky Mountain moose, *Alces alces shirasi.* Zoologica 41:105–18.

Dhindsa, S.; Cochran, T. H.; Costro, A.; Swanson, J. R.; and Metcalfe, J. 1975. Serum biochemical and electrophoretic values from four deer species and from pronghorn antelope. *Amer. J. Vet. Res.* 36:1455–57.

Dice, L. R. 1952. *Natural communities.* Ann Arbor: University of Michigan Press. 547 pp.

Dickerson, L. M. 1939. The problem of wildlife destruction by automobile traffic. *J. Wildl. Manage.* 3:104–16.

Diem, K. L. 1958. Fertile antlered mule deer doe. *J. Wildl. Manage.* 22:449.

Dietz, D. R.; Udall, R. H.; and Yeager, L. E. 1962. *Chemical composition and digestibility by mule deer of selected forage species, Cache la Poudre range, Colorado.* Technical Bulletin no. 14. Denver: Colorado Game and Fish Department. 89 pp.

Dimock, E. J., II. 1974. Animal-resistant Douglas-fir: How likely and how soon? In *Proceedings: Wildlife and forest management in the Pacific Northwest symposium, 1973,* pp. 133–38. Corvallis: Oregon State University. 236 pp.

Dimock, E. J., II, and Black, H. C. 1969. Scope and economic aspects of animal damage in California, Oregon, and Washington. In *Proceedings: Wildlife and reforestation in the Pacific Northwest symposium, 1968,* ed. H. C. Black, pp. 10–14. Corvallis: Oregon State University. 92 pp.

Dimock, E. J.; Silen, R. R.; and Allen, V. E. 1976. Genetic resistance in Douglas-fir to damage by snowshoe hare and black-tailed deer. *For. Sci.* 22:106–21.

Dixon, J. S. 1927. Horned does. *J. Mammal.* 8:289–91.

———. 1934. A study of the life history and food habits of mule deer in California. *Calif. Fish and Game* 20:1–146.

Dixon, J. S., and Herman, C. M. 1945. Studies on the condition of California mule deer at Sequoia National Park. *Calif. Fish and Game* 31:3–11.

Doan, K. H. 1970. Effect of snowmobiles on fish and wildlife resources. *Proc. Int. Assoc. Game, Fish and Conserv. Commissioners* 60:97–104.

Dodge, W. E. 1969. Protective measures: A review of chemical, mechanical, and other means of controlling damage by animals. In *Proceedings: Wildlife and reforestation in the Pacific Northwest symposium, 1968,* ed. H. C. Black, pp. 63–66. Corvallis: Oregon State University. 92 pp.

Doman, E. R., and Rasmussen, D. I. 1944. Supplemental winter feeding of mule deer in northern Utah. *J. Wildl. Manage.* 8:317–38.

Donaldson, J. C., and Doutt, J. K. 1965. Antlers in female white-tailed deer: A 4-year study. *J. Wildl. Manage.* 29:699–705.

Dorrance, M. J.; Savage, P. J.; and Huff, D. E. 1975. Effects of snowmobiles on white-tailed deer. *J. Wildl. Manage.* 39:563–69.

Douglas, J. R. 1939. The domestic cat, a new host for *Thelazia californiensis* Price, 1930 (Nematoda; Thelaziidae). *Proc. Helm. Soc. Wash.* 6:104.

Downs, T., and White, J. A. 1968. A vertebrate faunal succession in superimposed sediments from late Pliocene to middle Pleistocene in California. *Intern. Geol. Congr.* 10:4147.

Dressler, R. L., and Wood, G. W. 1976. Deer habitat response to irrigation with municipal waste water. *J. Wildl. Manage.* 40:639–41.

Driscoll, R. S. 1963. *Repellents reduce deer browsing on ponderosa pine seedlings.* USDA Forest Service Research Note PNW-5. 8 pp.

Dubey, J. P. 1976. A review of *Sarcocystis* of domestic animals and of other coccidia of dogs and cats. *J. Amer. Vet. Med. Assoc.* 169:1061–78.

Dukes, H. H. 1955. *The physiology of domestic animals.* Ithaca, N.Y.: Comstock. 1,020 pp.

Dunn, A. M. 1969. The wild ruminant as a reservoir host of helmintha infection. *Symposia Zool. Soc. London.* 24:221–48.

Dusek, G. L. 1971. Range relationships of mule deer in the prairie habitat, northcentral Montana. M.S. thesis, Montana State University, Bozeman. 63 pp.

———. 1975. Range relations of mule deer and cattle in prairie habitat. *J. Wildl. Manage.* 39:605–16.

Eberhardt, L. L. 1968. A preliminary appraisal of line transects. *J. Wildl. Manage.* 32:82–88.

———. 1971. Population analysis. In *Wildlife management techniques,* ed. R. H. Giles, Jr., pp. 457–95. Washington, D.C.: Wildlife Society. 633 pp.

———. 1978*a*. Transect methods for population studies. *J. Wildl. Manage.* 42(1):1–31.

———. 1978*b*. Appraising variability in population studies. *J. Wildl. Manage.* 42:207–38.

Ebert, P. N. 1976. Recent changes in Oregon's mule deer population and management. *Proc. West. Assoc. Game and Fish Commissioners* 56:408–14.

Eckroades, R. J.; Zurhein, G. M.; and Foreyt, W. 1970. Meningeal worm invasion of the brain of a naturally-infected white-tailed deer. *J. Wildl. Dis.* 6:430–36.

Eckstein, R. G., and Rongstad, O. J. 1973. Effects of snowmobiles on the movements of white-tailed deer in northern Wisconsin. *Proc. Midwest Fish and Wildl. Conf.* 35:39 (abstract).

Edgerton, P. J. 1972. Big game use and habitat changes in a recently logged mixed conifer forest in northeastern Oregon. *Proc. West. Assoc. Game and Fish Commissioners* 52:239–46.

Edgerton, P.J.; McConnell, B. R.; and Smith, J. G. 1975. Initial response of bitterbrush to disturbance by logging and slash disposal in a lodgepole pine forest. *J. Range Manage.* 28:112–14.

Edwards, R. Y. 1956. Snow depths and ungulate abundance in western Canada. *J. Wildl. Manage.* 20:159–68.

Edwards, R. Y., and Fowle, C. D. 1955. The concept of carrying capacity. *Trans. N. Amer. Wildl. Conf.* 20:589–602.

Edwards, R. Y., and Ritcey, R. W. 1956. The migrations of a moose herd. *J. Mammal.* 37(4):486–94.

Egan, J. 1971. Mule deer. In *Game management in Montana,* ed. T. W. Mussehl and F. W. Howell, pp. 53–67. Helena: Montana Fish and Game Department. 238 pp.

Einarsen, A. S. 1946. Management of black-tailed deer. *J. Wildl. Manage.* 10:54–59.

———. 1956. Life of the mule deer. In *The deer of North America,* ed. W. P. Taylor, pp. 363–90. Harrisburg, Pa.: Stackpole. 668 pp.

Elder, J. B. 1954. Notes on summer water consumption by desert mule deer. *J. Wildl. Manage.* 18:540–41.

Elkins, W. A., and Nelson, U. C. 1954. Wildlife introductions and transplants in Alaska. Paper presented at Fifth Alaska Science Conference, Anchorage, Alaska, 7–10 September 1954. On file at U.S. Fish and Wildlife Service, Juneau, Alaska. 21 pp.

Ellisor, J. E. 1969. Mobility of white-tailed deer in south Texas. *J. Wildl. Manage.* 33:221–22.

Ellsworth, R. S. 1930. Female deer has antlers. *Calif. Fish and Game* 16:82–83.

Elyakov, G. B.; Chetyrina, N. S.; and Dobryakov, Y. I. 1971. Lipids from antlers of punctate deer. *Khim-Farm Zh.* 5:21–24.

Emlen, J. M. 1973. *Ecology: An evolutionary approach.* Reading, Mass.: Addison-Wesley. 493 pp.

England, R. E., and DeVos, A. 1969. Influence of animals on pristine conditions on the Canadian grasslands. *J. Range Manage.* 22:87–94.

Ensminger, M. E. 1969. *Horses and horsemanship.* Danville, Ill.: Interstate Printers and Publishers. 907 pp.

Erickson, A. B.; Gunvalson, V. E.; Stenlund, M. H.; Burculon, D. W.; and Blankenship, L. H. 1961. *The white-tailed deer of Minnesota.* Technical Bulletin 5. St. Paul: Minnesota Department of Conservation. 64 pp.

Erickson, J. A. 1967. Estimating ages of mule deer. M.S. thesis, Colorado State University, Fort Collins. 93 pp.

Erickson, J. A.; Anderson, A. E.; Medin, D. E.; and Bowden, D. C. 1970. Estimating ages of mule deer: An evaluation of technique accuracy. *J. Wildl. Manage.* 34:523–31.

Erickson, J. A., and Seliger, W. G. 1969. Efficient sectioning of incisors for estimating ages of mule deer. *J. Wildl. Manage.* 33:384–88.

Errington, P. L. 1967. *Of predation and life.* Ames: Iowa State University Press. 277 pp.

Eslinger, D. H. 1976. Form, function and biological role in the locomotory apparatus of the genus *Odocoileus* in Alberta. M.S. thesis, University of Calgary, Alberta. 137 pp.

Espmark, J. 1964. Rutting behaviour in reindeer (*Rangifer tarandus* L.). *Anim. Behav.* 12:159–63.

Estes, R. D. 1972. The role of the vomeronasal organ in mammalian reproduction. *Mammalia* 36:315–41.

———. 1974. Social organization of the African Bovidae. In *The behaviour of ungulates and its relation to management,* ed. V. Geist and F. R. Walther, 1:166–205. IUCN New Series Publication 24. Morges, Switzerland: IUCN. 511 pp.

Evans, J. 1974. Pesticides and forest wildlife in the Pacific Northwest. In *Proceedings: Wildlife and forest management in the Pacific Northwest symposium, 1973,* pp. 205–19. Corvallis: Oregon State University. 236 pp.

Evans, T. C., and O'Regan, W. G. 1962. Sampling problems in the measurement of range vegetation. In *Range research methods: A symposium,* pp. 54–60. USDA Miscellaneous Publication no. 940. 172 pp.

Faber, R. D., and Dasmann, R. F. 1958. *The black-tailed deer of the chaparral.* Game Bulletin 8. Sacramento: California Department of Fish and Game. 163 pp.

Farb, P. 1967. *The land and wildlife of North America.* New York: Time. 200 pp.

Farmer, E. E.; Brown, R. W.; Richardson, B. Z.; and Packer, P. E. 1974. *Revegetation research on the Decker coal mine in southeastern Montana.* USDA Forest Service Research Paper INT-162. 12 pp.

Farmer, E. E.; Richardson, B. Z.; and Brown, R. W. 1976. *Revegetation of acid mining wastes in central Idaho.* USDA Forest Service Research Paper INT-178. 17 pp.

Farrell, D. J.; Corbett, L.; and Leng, R. A. 1970. Automatic sampling of blood and ruminal fluid of grazing sheep. *Res. Vet. Sci.* 11:217–20.

Farris, G. C.; Whicker, F. W.; and Dahl, A. H. 1967. Effect of age on radioactive and stable strontium accumulation in mule deer bone. In *Strontium metabolism,* ed. J. M. A. Leniham, J. F. Louitt, and J. H. Martin, pp. 93–102. London: Academic Press. 354 pp.

———. 1969. Strontium-90 levels in mule deer and forage plants. In *Symposium on radioecology,* ed. D. J. Nelson and F. C. Evans, pp. 602–8. Extension Conference 67503. Oak Ridge, Tenn.: U.S. Atomic Energy Commission, Division of Technical Information. 774 pp.

Fayer, R. 1972. Gametogony of *Sarcocystis* sp. in cell culture. *Science* 175:65–67.

Fenstermacher, R.; Olsen, O. W.; and Pomeroy, B. S. 1943. Some diseases of white-tailed deer of Minnesota. *Cornell Vet.* 33:323–32.

Ferguson, R. B. 1972. *Bitterbrush topping: Shrub response and cost factors.* USDA Forest Service Research Paper INT-125. 11 pp.

Ferguson, R. B., and Marsden, M. A. 1977. Estimating overwinter bitterbrush utilization from twig diameter-length-weight relationships. *J. Range Manage.* 30:231–36.

Ferrel, C. M., and Leach, H. R. 1950. Food habits of a California deer herd. *Calif. Fish and Game* 36:235–40.

Ffolliott, P. F., and Clary, W. P. 1972. *A selected and annotated bibliography of understory-overstory vegetation relationships.* Technical Bulletin 198. Tucson: Agricultural Experiment Station University of Arizona. 33 pp.

Firebaugh, J. E. 1969. Relationships of mule deer to livestock on summer range in the Pryor Mountains, Montana. M.S. thesis, Montana State University, Bozeman. 55 pp.

Fletch, A. L. 1970. Foot-and-mouth disease. In *Infectious diseases of wild mammals,* ed. J. W. Davis, L. H. Karstad, and D. O. Trainer, pp. 68–75. Ames: Iowa State University Press. 421 pp.

Flook, D. R. 1970. *Causes and implications of an observed sex differential in the survival of wapiti.* Canadian Wildlife Service Report, ser. 11. 71 pp.

Flora, D. F. 1968. POOH on damage appraisal. *J. For.* 66:12–16.

Foiles, M. W., and Curtis, J. D. 1973. *Regeneration of ponderosa pine in the northern Rocky Mountain–Intermountain region.* USDA Forest Service Research Paper INT-145. 44 pp.

Folk, G. E., Jr. 1966. *Introduction to environmental physiology: Environmental extremes and mammalian survival.* Philadelphia: Lea and Febiger. 308 pp.

———. 1968. Measurement of physiological responses to environmental stimuli. In *Adaptation of domestic animals,* ed. E. S. E. Hafez, pp. 338–51. Philadelphia: Lea and Febiger. 415 pp.

Fontenot, J. P. 1971. Nitrogen metabolism and nutrition in ruminants. In *Digestive physiology and nutrition of ruminants.* Vol. 2. *Nutrition,* ed. D. C. Church, pp. 575–99. Corvallis: Oregon State University. 801 pp.

Ford-Robertson, F. C., ed. 1971. *Terminology of forest science, technology, practice, and products.* Multilingual Forest Terminology, ser. no. 1. Washington, D.C.: Society of American Foresters. 349 pp.

Fowle, K. F., and Church, D. C. 1969. Effects of starvation and refeeding in goats. *Proc. West. Sec. Amer. Soc. Anim. Sci.* 20:157–62.

Fox, M. W. 1969. Ontogeny of prey-killing behavior in Canidae. *Behaviour* 35:259–72.

———. 1973. Origin of the dog and effects of domestication. *Amer. Kennel Gazette* 90:33–35.

Franklin, J. F. 1963. *Natural regeneration of Douglas-fir and associated species using modified clearcutting systems in the Oregon Cascades.* USDA Forest Service Research Paper PNW-3. 14 pp.

Franklin, J. F., and Dyrness, C. T. 1969. *Vegetation of Oregon and Washington.* USDA Forest Service Research Paper PNW-80. 216 pp.

Franti, C. E.; Connolly, G. E.; Riemann, H. P.; Behymer, D. E.; Ruppanner, R.; Willadsen, C. M.; and Longhurst, W. 1975. A survey for *Toxoplasma gondii* antibodies in deer and other wildlife of a sheep range. *J. Amer. Vet. Med. Assoc.* 167:565–68.

Franzmann, A. W. 1972. Environmental sources of variation of bighorn sheep physiologic values. *J. Wildl. Manage.* 36:924–32.

Franzmann, A. W., and Arneson, P. D. 1976. Marrow fat in Alaskan moose femurs in relation to mortality factors. *J. Wildl. Manage.* 40:336–39.

Franzmann, A. W.; Flynn, A.; and Arneson, P. D. 1975. Serum corticoid levels relative to handling stress in Alaskan moose. *Can. J. Zool.* 53:1424–26.

Franzmann, A. W.; LeResche, R. E.; Arneson P. D.; and David, J. L. 1976. *Moose productivity and physiology.* Final Report, P-R Project W-17-R, Job no. 1.1R. Juneau: Alaska Department of Fish and Game. 87 pp.

Franzmann, A. W., and Thorne, E. T. 1970. Physiologic values in wild bighorn sheep (*Ovis canadensis canadensis*) at capture, after handling, and after captivity. *J. Amer. Vet. Med. Assoc.* 157:647–50.

Frasier, M. B.; Banks, W. J.; and Newbrey, J. W. 1975. Characterization of developing antler matrix. I. Selected histochemical and enzymatic assessment. *Calcified Tissue Res.* 17:273–88.

Fred Bear Sports Club. 1975. Highway deer kills versus game taken by bowhunters. In *1974 Bowhunting survey.* Grayling, Mich.: Fred Bear Sports Club. Multilith. 22 pp.

———. 1978. The American bowhunter. *Big Sky,* vol. 6, no. 4. 6 pp.

Freddy, D. J. 1975. Middle Park deer study: Experimental harvest regulations. In *Game research report, July 1975,* part 2, pp. 209–40. Denver: Colorado Division of Wildlife. 504 pp.

———. 1978. Snowmobile harassment of mule deer on cold winter ranges. In *Game research report, July 1978,* part 2, pp. 137–44. Denver: Colorado Division of Wildlife. 298 pp.

Freddy, D. J., and Gill, R. B. 1977. *A life-table for managing deer populations.* Game Information Leaflet no. 104. Fort Collins: Colorado Division of Wildlife. 2 pp.

Free, S. L., and Severinghaus, C. W. N.d. *Report on the effectiveness of a "deer proof" fence on the New York State Thruway.* Special Report P-R Proj. W-89-R-3. Albany: New York Department Environmental Conservation. 22 pp.

Freeland, W. J., and Janzen, D. H. 1974. Strategies in herbivory by mammals: The role of plant secondary compounds. *Amer. Natur.* 108:269–89.

Freeman, W. G. 1976. Changes in Montana mule deer populations and management. *Proc. West. Assoc. Game and Fish Commissioners* 56:395–400.

French, C. E.; McEwen, L. C.; Magruder, N. D.; Ingram, R. H.; and Swift, R. W. 1955. *Nutritional requirements of white-tailed deer for growth and antler development.* Bulletin 600. University Park: Pennsylvania Agricultural Experiment Station. 50 pp.

———. 1956. Nutrient requirement for growth and antler development in the white-tailed deer. *J. Wildl. Manage.* 20:221–32.

French, C. E.; McEwen, L. C.; Magruder, N. D.; Rader, T.; Long, T. A.; and Swift, R. W. 1960. Responses of white-tailed bucks to added artificial light. *J. Mammal.* 41:23–29.

Fretwell, S.D. 1972. *Populations in a seasonal environment.* Monographs in Population Biology 5. Princeton: Princeton University Press. 217 pp.

Frewing, D. K. 1968. The field use of ZIP and TMTD on the Fremont National Forest. In *Proceedings: First reforestation workshop, 1968,* pp. 218–19. Portland: USDA Forest Service, Region 6. 293 pp.

Fry, W. E., and Gustafson E. P. 1974. Cervids from the Pliocene and Pleistocene of central Washington, *J. Paleontol.* 48:375–86.

Fuller, M. F. 1969. Climate and growth. In *Animal growth and nutrition,* ed. E. S. E. Hafez and I. A. Dyer, pp. 82–105. Philadelphia: Lea and Febiger. 402 pp.

Gagnon, J. D. 1973. Environmental aspects of sewage-derived fertilizers. In *Forest fertilization symposium proceedings,* pp. 101–7. USDA Forest Service General Technical Report NE-3. 246 pp.

Gallagher, V. P., and Meguire, P. G. 1974. *Contrast requirements of urban drivers.* U.S. Department of Transportation, Federal Highway Administration Report FHWA-RD-74-76. 72 pp.

Gallizioli, S. 1976a. Livestock vs. wildlife. Paper presented at a seminar on improving fish and wildlife benefits in range management, Washington, D.C. 11 pp.

———. 1976b. Wildlife and overgrazed ranges. Paper presented at annual meeting of Arizona Section, Society for Range Management, 1976, Globe, Ariz. 7 pp.

———. 1977. Statement. In *Improving fish and wildlife benefits in range management, proceedings of a seminar,* pp. 90–96. U.S. Department of Interior, Fish and Wildlife Service FWS/ OBS-77/1. 118 pp.

Gardner, J. L. 1951. Vegetation of the creosotebush area of the Rio Grande Valley in New Mexico. *Ecol. Monogr.* 21:379–403.

Garrison, G. A. 1953. Effects of clipping on some range shrubs. *J. Range Manage.* 6:309–17.

Gartner, F. R., and Thompson, W. W. 1972. Fire in the Black Hills forest-grass ecotone. *Proc. Tall Timbers Fire Ecol. Conf.* 12:37–68.

Gartner, R. J. W.; Ryley, J. W.; and Beattie, W. A. 1965. The influence of degree of excitation on certain blood constituents in beef cattle. *Aust. J. Exp. Biol. Med. Sci.* 43:713–24.

Garton, G. A.; Duncan, W. R. H.; and McEwan, E. H. 1971. Composition of adipose tissue triglycerides of the elk (*Cervus canadensis*), caribou (*Rangifer tarandus groenlandicus*), moose (*Alces alces*), and white-tailed deer (*Odocoileus virginianus*). *Can. J. Zool.* 49:1159–62.

Gary, H. L. 1974. Canopy weight distribution affects windspeed and temperature in lodgepole pine forest. *For. Sci.* 20:369–71.

Gasaway, W. C., and Coady, J. W. 1974. Review of energy requirements and rumen fermentation in moose and other ruminants. *Can. Natur.* 101:227–62.

Gates, B. R. 1968. Deer food production in certain seral stages of the coast forest. M.S. thesis, University of British Columbia, Vancouver. 101 pp.

Gates, C. E.; Marshall, W. H.; and Olson, D. P. 1968. Line transect method of estimating grouse population densities. *Biometrics* 24:135–45.

Gates, D. M. 1969. Infrared measurement of plant and animal surface temperature and their interpretation. In *Remote sensing in ecology,* ed. P. A. Johnson, pp. 95–107. Athens: University of Georgia Press. 244 pp.

Gates, R. G., and Orians, G. H. 1975. Successional status and the palatability of plants to generalized herbivores. *Ecology* 56:410–18.

Gavitt, J. D. 1973. Disturbance effect of free-running dogs on deer reproduction. M.S. thesis, Virginia Polytechnical Institute, Blacksburg, Va. 52 pp.

Geilmann, W. 1968. Age determination of deer antlers. *Fresenius' Z. Anal. Chemie* 235:172–76.

Geist, V. 1963. On the behaviour of the North American moose *(Alces alces andersoni* Peterson 1950) in British Columbia. *Behaviour* 20:377–416.

———. 1966a. Ethological observations on some North American cervids. *Zool. Beiträge* 12 (N.S.):219–50.

———. 1966b. The evolution of horn-like organs. *Behaviour* 27:175–214.

———. 1968a. Horn-like structures as rank symbols, guards and weapons. *Nature* 220:813–14.

———. 1968b. On the interrelation of external appearance, social behaviour and social structure of mountain sheep. *Z. Tierpsychol.* 25:194–215.

———. 1971a. A behavioural approach to the management of wild ungulates. In *The scientific management of animal and plant communities for conservation,* ed. E. Duffey and A. S. Watt, pp. 413–24. The 11th symposium of the British Ecological Society. Oxford: Blackwell Scientific Publications. 652 pp.

———. 1971b. *Mountain sheep: A study in behaviour and evolution.* Chicago: University of Chicago Press. 432 pp.

———. 1971c. On the relation of social evolution and dispersal in ungulates during the Pleistocene with emphasis on the Old World deer and the genus *Bison. Quat. Res.* 1:283–315.

———. 1971d. Is big game harassment harmful? *Oil Week* 22(17):12–13.

———. 1974a. On fighting strategies in animal combat. *Nature* 250:354.

———. 1974b. On the evolution of reproductive potential in moose. *Can. Natur.* 101:527–37.

———. 1974c. On the relationship of ecology and behaviour in the evolution of ungulates: Theoretical considerations. In *The behaviour of ungulates and its relation to management,* ed. V. Geist and F. Walther, 1:235–46. IUCN New Series Publication 24. Morges, Switzerland: IUCN. 511 pp.

———. 1974d. On the relationship of social evolution and ecology in ungulates. *Amer. Zool.* 14:205–20.

———. 1975. On the management of mountain sheep: Theoretical considerations. In *The wild sheep in modern North America,* ed. J. B. Trefethen, pp. 77–98. New York: Boone and Crockett Club. 302 pp.

———. 1977. A comparison of social adaptations in relation to ecology in gallinaceous bird and ungulate societies. In *Annual review of ecology and systematics 8,* ed. R. J. Johnston, pp. 193–207. Palo Alto, Calif.: Annual Reviews.

———. 1978a. On weapons, combat and ecology. In *Aggression, dominance and individual spacing,* ed. L. Krames, pp. 1–30. Vol. 4 of *Advances in the study of communication and effect.* New York: Plenum.

———. 1978b. *Life strategies, human adaptations, environmental design.* New York: Springer. 480 pp.

———. In press. Adaptive behavioral strategies. In *The ecology and management of the North American elk,* ed. J. W. Thomas and D. E. Toweill. Washington, D.C.: Wildlife Management Institute.

Geist, V., and Bromley, P. T. 1978. Why deer shed antlers.

Z. Saügetierkunde 43(4):223–32.

Geist, V., and Petocz, R. 1977. Bighorn sheep in winter: Do rams maximize reproductive fitness by spatial and habitat segregation from ewes? *Can. J. Zool.* 55(1):1802–10.

Gesink, R. W.; Tomanek, G. W.; and Huelett, G. K. 1968. *A descriptive survey of the woody phreatophytes on the Arkansas River in Kansas.* Hays, Kans. Division of Biological Science, Fort Hays Kansas State College. 87 pp.

Gilbert, P. F.; Wallmo, O.C.; and Gill, R. B. 1970. Effect of snow depth on mule deer in Middle Park, Colorado. *J. Wildl. Manage.* 34:15–23.

Giles, R. H., Jr.; Buffington, C. D.; and Davis, J. A. 1969. A topographic model of population stability. *J. Wildl. Manage.* 33:1042–45.

Giles, R. H., and Snyder, N. 1970. Simulation techniques in wildlife habitat management. In *Modelling and systems analysis in range science,* ed. D. A. Jameson, pp. 23–49. Science Series 5. Fort Collins: Range Science Department, Colorado State University. 134 pp.

Gill, R. B. 1969. Middle Park deer study: Population density and structure. In *Game research report, July 1969,* part 1, pp. 105–22. Denver: Colorado Division of Wildlife. 140 pp.

———. 1972a. Middle Park deer study: Productivity and mortality. In *Game research report, July 1972,* part 2, pp. 179–98. Denver: Colorado Division of Wildlife.

———. 1972b. Productivity studies of mule deer in Middle Park, Colorado. Paper presented at Annual Mule Deer Workshop, Elko, Nev. 12 pp.

———. 1976. Mule deer management myths and the mule deer population decline. In *Mule deer decline in the west: A symposium,* ed. G. W. Workman and J. B. Low, pp. 99–106. Logan: Utah State University College of Natural Resources and Agricultural Experiment Station. 134 pp.

———. N.d. Records of Middle Park deer studies. Unpublished. Colorado Division of Wildlife, Fort Collins.

Gill, R. B.; Roper, L. A.; Driscoll, R. S.; Wallmo, O. C.; and Nagy, J. G. 1975. Middle Park cooperative deer study. In *Colorado game research review, 1972–1974,* ed. O. B. Cope, pp. 2–8. Fort Collins: Colorado Division of Wildlife. 76 pp.

Gill, R. B., and Wallmo, O. C. 1973. Middle Park deer study: Physical characteristics and food habits. In *Game research report, July 1973,* part 2, pp. 81–103. Denver: Colorado Division of Wildlife. 275 pp.

Gist, C. S., and Whicker, F. W. 1971. Radioiodine uptake and retention by the mule deer thyroid. *J. Wildl. Manage.* 35:461–68.

Gochenour, W. S. 1924. Hemorrhagic septicemia studies. *J. Amer. Vet. Med. Assoc.* 65:433–41.

Gockerell, E. C. 1966. Plantations on burned and unburned areas. *J. For.* 64:392–94.

Goering, H. K., and Van Soest, P. J. 1970. *Forage fiber analyses (apparatus, reagents, procedures and some applications).* USDA Agricultural Handbook no. 379. 20 pp.

Goldman, R. F., and Buskirk, E. R. 1961. Body volume measurement by underwater weighing: Description of method. In *Techniques for measuring body composition,* ed. J. Brožek and A. Henschel, pp. 78–79. Washington, D.C.: National Academy of Sciences, Natural Resource Council. 300 pp.

Golley, F. B. 1957*a*. An appraisal of ovarian analyses in determining reproductive performance of black-tailed deer. *J. Wildl. Manage.* 21:62–65.

———. 1957*b*. Gestation period, breeding and fawning behavior of Columbian black-tailed deer. *J. Mammal.* 38:116–20.

Good, G. H. 1956. Anthrax in the Wyoming mountains. *J. Amer. Vet. Med. Assoc.* 129:470–71.

Gorbman, A., and Bern, H. A. 1962. *A textbook of comparative endocrinology.* New York: John Wiley. 468 pp.

Goss, R. J. 1963. The deciduous nature of deer antlers. In *Mechanisms of hard tissue destruction,* ed. P. Sognnaes, pp. 339–69. Publ. no. 75. Washington, D.C.: American Association for the Advancement of Science. 764 pp.

———. 1969*a*. Photoperiodic control of antler cycles in deer: I. Phase shift frequency changes. *J. Exp. Zool.* 170:311–24.

———. 1969*b*. Photoperiodic control of antler cycles in deer: II. Alterations in amplitude. *J. Exp. Zool.* 171:224–34.

Goss, R. J.; Severinghaus, C. W.; and Free, S. 1964. Tissue relationships in the development of pedicles and antlers in the Virginia deer. *J. Mammal.* 45:61–68.

Gove, P. B., ed. 1961. *Webster's third new international dictionary of the English language, unabridged.* Springfield, Mass.: G. and C. Merriam. 2,662 pp.

Graf, W. 1956. Territorialism in deer. *J. Mammal.* 37:165–70.

Graves, H. B.; Bellis, E. D.; and Knuth, W. M. 1972. Censusing white-tailed deer by airborne thermal infrared imagery. *J. Wildl. Manage.* 36:875–84.

Greenough, W. T. 1975. Experimental modification of the developing brain. *Amer. Sci.* 63:37–46.

Greer, K. R. 1968. A compression method indicates fat content of elk (wapiti) femur marrows. *J. Wildl. Manage.* 32:747–51.

Gregson, J. D. 1937. Cycticerocis in deer. *Parasitology* 29:409.

Grenier, P. A. 1974. Originaux túes sur la route dans le Parc des Laurentides, Québec, de 1962 à 1972. *Can. Natur.* 101:737–54.

Grier, C. C., and Logan, R. S. 1977. Old-growth *Pseudotsuga menziesii* communities of a western Oregon watershed: Biomass distribution and production budgets. *Ecol. Monogr.* 47:373–400.

Grieser, K. C., and Browman, L. G. 1956. Total gonadotrophic potency of mule deer pituitaries. *Endocrinology* 58:206–11.

Grinnell, G. B. 1928. Mountain sheep. *J. Mammal.* 9:1–9.

Grisez, T. J. 1959. A low cost deer fence. *J. For.* 57:42–43.

———. 1960. Slash helps protect seedlings from deer browsing. *J. For.* 58:385–87.

Griswold, S. B. 1942. A study of the woody plants along streams which cross Ellis County, Kansas. *Trans. Kansas Acad. Sci.* 45:98–106.

Gross, J. E. 1969. Optimum yield in deer and elk populations. *Trans. N. Amer. Wildl. and Natur. Resour. Conf.* 34:372–86.

———. 1972. Criteria for big game planning: Performance measures vs. intuition. *Trans. N. Amer. Wildl. and Natur. Resour. Conf.* 37:246–59.

———. 1973. Push-button deer management: Boon or boondoggle? *Proc. West. Assoc. Game and Fish Commissioners* 53:157–73.

Gross, J. E.; Roelle, J. E.; and Williams, G. L. 1973. *Program Onepop and information processor: A system modeling and communications project.* Progress Report. Fort Collins: Colorado Cooperative Wildlife Research Unit, Colorado State University. 327 pp.

Gruell, G. E., and Loope, L. L. 1974. *Relationships among aspen, fire, and ungulate browsing in Jackson Hole, Wyoming.* Ogden, Utah: USDA Forest Service, Intermountain Region. 33 pp.

Hafez, E. S. E. 1968*a*. Environmental effects on animal productivity. In *Adaptation of domestic animals,* ed. E. S. E. Hafez, pp. 74–93. Philadelphia: Lea and Febiger. 415 pp.

———. 1968*b*. Female reproductive organs. In *Reproduction in farm animals,* 2d ed, ed. E. S. E. Hafez, pp. 61–80. Philadelphia: Lea and Febiger. 440 pp.

Hagen, H. L. 1953. Nutritive value for deer of some forage plants in the Sierra Nevada. *Calif. Fish and Game* 39:163–75.

Hakonson, T. E., and Whicker, F. W. 1971*a*. The contribution of various tissues and organs to total body mass in mule deer. *J. Mammal.* 52:628–30.

———. 1971*b*. Tissue distribution of radiocesium in the mule deer. *Health Physics* 21:864–66.

Halford, D. K. 1974. A method for artificially raising mule deer fawns. M.S. thesis, Colorado State University, Fort Collins. 21 pp.

Hall, D. O. 1971. *Ponderosa pine planting techniques, survival, and height growth in Idaho Batholith.* USDA Forest Service Research Paper INT-104. 28 pp.

Hall, K. R. 1978. *Evaluation of modeling as a big game management tool for Oregon.* Job Final Report, P-R Project W-70-R, Subproject F, Study VIII, Job 1. Portland: Oregon Department of Fish and Wildlife. 7 pp.

Hall, M. C. 1925. Parasites in deer, *Odocoileus* sp. *J. Parasit.* 12:105.

Hall, T. C.; Ganong, W. F.; and Taft, E. B. 1966. Hypophysectomy in the Virginia deer: Technique and physiologic consequences. *Growth* 30:383–92.

Halladay, D. R. 1976. Recent changes in British Columbia mule deer populations and management. *Proc. West. Assoc. Game and Fish Commissioners* 56:370–72.

Halls, L. K. 1970. Nutrient requirements of livestock and game. In *Range and wildlife habitat evaluation: A research symposium,* pp. 10–18. USDA Forest Service

Miscellaneous Publication no. 1147. 220 pp.

Halls, L. K.; Boyd, C. E.; Lay, D. W.; and Goodrum, P. C. 1965. Deer fence construction and costs. *J. Wildl. Manage.* 29:885–88.

Hamlin, K. L. 1976. Population ecology and habitat relationships of mule deer and white-tailed deer in prairie-agricultural habitats of eastern Montana. In Progress Report, P-R Project W-120-R for period 1 July 1975–30 June 1976. pp. 139–56. Helena: Montana Department of Fish and Game. 170 pp.

———. 1978. Mule deer population ecology, habitat relationships and relations to livestock grazing management and elk in the Missouri River breaks, Montana. In *Montana deer studies,* pp. 141–76. Job Completion Report, P-R Project W-120-R-9, Study BG-1.00, J3. Helena: Montana Department of Fish and Game. 217 pp.

Hammersland, H., and Joneschild, E. M. 1937. Pseudo-tuberculosis of deer. *J. Amer. Vet. Med. Assoc.* 91:180–92.

Hanks, D. L.; McArthur, E. D.; Plummer, A. P.; Guinta, B. C.; and Blauer, A. C. 1975. Chromatographic recognition of some palatable and unpalatable subspecies of rubber rabbitbrush in and around Utah. *J. Range Manage.* 28:144–48.

Hansen, R. M. 1978. Use of dung pH to differentiate herbivore species. *J. Wildl. Manage.* 42:441–44.

Hanson, H. C., and Jones, R. L. 1976. *The biochemistry of blue, snow and Ross' geese.* Appendix 2. Special Publication no. 1. Urbana: Illinois Natural History Survey.

Hanson, W. C.; Whicker, F. W.; and Dahl, A. H. 1963. Iodine-131 in the thyroids of North American deer and caribou: Comparison after nuclear tests. *Science* 140:801–2.

Hanson, W. R. 1963. Calculation of productivity, survival, and abundance of selected vertebrates from sex and age ratios. *Wildl. Monogr.* no. 9. 60 pp.

Hanson, W. R., and McCulloch, C. Y. 1955. Factors influencing mule deer on Arizona brushlands. *Trans. N. Amer. Wildl. Conf.* 20:568–88.

Harder, J. D. 1968. A literature review on orchard damage by deer. Special Report 12. Denver: Colorado Department of Game, Fish and Parks. 22 pp.

Harder, J. D., and Woolf, A. 1976. Changes in plasma levels of oestrone and oestradiol during pregnancy and parturition in white-tailed deer. *J. Reprod. Fert.* 47:161–63.

Hardin, G. 1960. The competitive exclusion principle. *Science* 131:1292–97.

Hare, J. E. 1945. Flying stage of the deer lousefly, *Lipoptena depressa* (Say), in California (Diptera: Hippoboscidae). *Pan-Pacific Ent.* 21:48–57.

Harniss, R. O., and Murray, R. B. 1973. 30 years of vegetal change following burning of sagebrush-grass range. *J. Range Manage.* 26:322–25.

Harrah, V. J. 1971. Colorado corkscrew. *Colo. Outdoors* 20(6):46.

Harris, D. 1945. Symptoms of malnutrition in deer. *J. Wildl. Manage.* 9:319–22.

Harrow, B., and Mazur, A. 1958. *Textbook of biochemistry.* 7th ed. Philadelphia and London: W. B. Saunders. 557 pp.

Harthoorn, A. M. 1965. Application of pharmacological and physiological principles in restraint of wild animals. *Wildl. Monogr.* no. 14. 78 pp.

Hartwell, H. D. 1973. *A comparison of large and small Douglas-fir nursery stock outplanted in potential wildlife damage areas.* State of Washington Natural Resource Note 6. Forest and Land Management. Division Contract 173. 5 pp.

Hastings, J. R., and Turner, R. M. 1965. *The changing mile: An ecological study of vegetation change with time in the lower mile of an arid and semiarid region.* Tucson: University of Arizona Press. 317 pp.

Hatch, M. D.; Osmond, C. B.; and Slatyer, R. O. 1971. *Photosynthesis and photo respiration.* New York: Interscience.

Haugen, A. O., and Davenport, L. A. 1950. Breeding records of white-tailed deer in the Upper Peninsula of Michigan. *J. Wildl. Manage.* 14:290–95.

Haugen, A. O., and Speake, D. W. 1958. Determining age of young fawn white-tailed deer. *J. Wildl. Manage.* 22:319–21.

Hawkins, R. E., and Klimstra, W. D. 1970. A preliminary study of the social organization of white-tailed deer. *J. Wildl. Manage.* 34:407–19.

Hawkins, R. E., and Montgomery, G. G. 1969. Movements of translocated deer as determined by telemetry. *J. Wildl. Manage.* 33:196–203.

Hawkins, R. E.; Schwegman, J. E.; Autry, D. C.; and Klimstra, W. D. 1968. Antler development and loss for southern Illinois white-tailed deer. *J. mammal.* 49:522–23.

Hayne, D. W. 1969. The use of models in resource management. In *White-tailed deer in the southern forest habitat,* pp. 119–22. Nacogdoches, Tex.: USDA Forest Service Southern Forest Experiment Station. 130 pp.

Heady, H. F. 1964. Palatability of herbage and animal preference. *J. Range Manage.* 17:76–82.

Hebert, D. and Cowan, I. McT. 1971. Natural salt licks as a part of the ecology of the mountain goat. *Can. J. Zool.* 49:605–10.

Heidmann, L. J. 1972. *An initial assessment of mammal damage in the forests of the Southwest.* USDA Forest Service Research Note RM-219. 7 pp.

Hemmer, D. M. 1975. *Serviceberry: Ecology, distribution, and relationships to big game.* Job Final Report, P-R Project W-120-R-5, 6, Work Plan II, Study 28.01, Job BG-202, Subjob 3. Helena: Montana Department of Fish and Game. 76 pp.

Hemmer, H. 1964. Zur Frage genetischer Grundlagen bei Geweihmissbildungen des Rehes *(Capreolus capreolus).* Z. Jagdwiss. 10:176–82.

Henny, C. J.; Overton, W. S.; and Wight, H. M. 1970. Determining parameters for populations by using structural models. *J. Wildl. Manage.* 34:690–703.

Hensel, H. 1968. Adaptation to cold. In *Adaptation of*

domestic animals, ed. E. S. E. Hafez, pp. 183–93. Philadelphia: Lea and Febiger. 415 pp.

Herman, C. M. 1944. Eyeworm (Thelazia californiensis) infection in deer in California. Calif. Fish and Game 30:58–60.

———. 1945a. Hippoboscid flies as parasites of game animals in California. Calif. Fish and Game 31:16–25.

———. 1945b. Some parasites of deer in California. Calif. Fish and Game 31:201.

———. 1949. A new host for the eyeworm (Thelazia californiensis). Calif. Fish and Game 35:139.

Herman, C. M., and Bischoff, A. I. 1946. The foot worm parasite of deer. Calif. Fish and Game 32:182.

Herman, C. M., and Rosen, M. N. 1949. Disease investigations on mammals and birds by the California Division of Fish and Game. Calif. Fish and Game 35:193–201.

Herms, W. B., and Wheeler, C. M. 1935. Tick transmission of California relapsing fever. J. Econ. Ent. 28:846–55.

Hiatt, G. S. 1977. Plutonium dispersal by mule deer at Rocky Flats, Colorado. M.S. thesis, Colorado State University, Fort Collins. 143 pp.

Hibben, F. C. 1936. A preliminary study of the mountain lion (Felis cougar). M. S. thesis, University of New Mexico, Albuquerque. 89 pp.

Hibbert, A. R.; Davis, E. A.; and Scholl, D. G. 1974. Chaparral conversion potential in Arizona. Part 1. Water yield response and effects on other resources. USDA Forest Service Research Paper RM-126. 36 pp.

Hibbs, L. D. 1966. A literature review on mountain goat ecology. Special Report no. 8. Fort Collins: Colorado Department of Game, Fish, and Parks and Colorado State University Cooperative Wildlife Research Unit. 23 pp.

Hibler, C. P. 1965. Description of the microfilaria of Wehrdikmansia cervipedis (Wehr and Dikmans, 1935) and observations on its location in Arizona deer. Bull. Wildl. Dis. Assoc. 1:48.

———. N.d. 1970–1978 necropsy reports. Unpublished. On file at Wild Animal Disease Center, Colorado State University, Fort Collins.

Hibler, C. P., and Adcock, J. L. 1970. Elaeophorosis. In Parasitic diseases of wild mammals, ed. J. W. Davis and R. C. Anderson, pp. 263–78. Ames: Iowa State University Press. 364 pp.

Hickey, W. C., and Garcia, G. 1964. Changes in perennial grass cover following conversion from yearlong to summer-deferred grazing in west central New Mexico. USDA Forest Service Research Note RM-33. 3 pp.

Hildreth, A. C., and Brown, G. B. 1955. Repellents to protect trees and shrubs from damage by rabbits. USDA Technical Bulletin no. 1134. 31 pp.

Hillman, J. R.; Davis, R. W.; and Abdelbaki, Y. Z. 1973. Cyclic bone remodeling in deer. Calcified Tissue Res. 12:323–30.

Hilton, J. E., and Bailey, A. W. 1974. Forage production and utilization in a sprayed aspen forest in Alberta. J. Range Manage. 27:375–80.

Hines, W. W. 1973. Black-tailed deer populations and Douglas-fir reforestation in the Tillamook Burn, Oregon. Game Research Report no. 3. Portland: Oregon State Game Commission. 59 pp.

———. 1975. Black-tailed deer behavior and population dynamics in the Tillamook Burn, Oregon. Oregon Wildlife Commission Wildlife Research Report no. 5. 31 pp.

Hirth, D. H. 1977. Social behaviour of white-tailed deer in relation to habitat. Wildl. Monogr. no. 53. 55 pp.

Hitchcock, A. S. 1950. Manual of grasses of the United States. Miscellaneous Publication no. 200. Washington, D.C.: USDA. 1,051 pp.

Hitchcock, C. L., and Cronquist, A. 1973. Flora of the Pacific Northwest. Seattle: University of Washington Press. 597 pp.

Hladek, K. L. 1971. Growth characteristics and utilization of buffaloberry (Shepherdia argentea Nutt.) in the Little Missouri River badlands of North Dakota. Ph.D. thesis, North Dakota State University, Fargo. 115 pp.

Hofer, H. 1972. Prolegomena primatologiae. In Die Sonderstellung des Menschen, ed. H. Hofer and G. Altner, pp. 3–146. Stuttgart: Fischer.

Hoffman, R. A., and Robinson, P. F. 1966. Changes in some endocrine glands of white-tailed deer as affected by season, sex, and age. J. Mammal. 47:266–80.

Hoffmeister, D. F. 1962. The kinds of deer, Odocoileus, in Arizona. Amer. Midl. Natur. 67:45–64.

Holter, J. B.; Urban, W. E., Jr.; and Hayes, H. H. 1977. Nutrition of northern white-tailed deer throughout the year. J. Anim. Sci. 45:365–76.

Holter, J. B.; Urban, W. E.; Hayes, H. H.; and Silver, H. 1976. Predicting metabolic rate from telemetered heart rate. J. Wildl. Manage. 40:626–29.

Holter, J. B.; Urban, W. E.; Hayes, H. H.; Silver, H.; and Skutt, H. R. 1975. Ambient temperature effects on physiological traits of white-tailed deer. Can. J. Zool. 53:679–85.

Honess, R. F., and Frost, N. M. 1942. A Wyoming bighorn sheep study. Bulletin 1. Cheyenne: Wyoming Game and Fish Department. 127 pp.

Honess, R. F., and Winter, K. 1956. Diseases of wildlife in Wyoming. Bulletin 9. Cheyenne: Wyoming Game and Fish Department. 279 pp.

Hood, R. E., and Inglis, J. M. 1974. Behavioral responses of white-tailed deer to intensive ranching operations. J. Wildl. Manage. 38:488–98.

Hooven, E. F. 1973. A wildlife brief for the clearcut logging of Douglas-fir. J. For. 71:210–14.

Hoover, M. D. 1971. Snow interception and redistribution in the forest. Proc. Int. Semin. Hydrol. Prof. (West Lafayette, Ind. July 1971) 3:114–22.

Horejsi, B. L. 1976. Suckling and feeding behaviour in relation to lamb survival in bighorn sheep (Ovis canadensis canadensis Shaw). Ph.D. thesis, University of Calgary, Alberta, 265 pp.

Hormay, A. L. 1970. Principles of rest-rotation grazing and multiple use land management. Washington, D.C.: GPO. 26 pp.

Horn, E. E. 1941. Some coyote-wildlife relationships. *Trans. N. Amer. Wildl. Conf.* 6:283–87.

Hornocker, M. G. 1970. An analysis of mountain lion predation upon mule deer and elk in the Idaho primitive area. *Wildl. Monogr.* no. 21. 39 pp.

Hoskinson, R. C., and Mech, L. D. 1976. White-tailed deer migration and its role in wolf predation. *J. Wildl. Manage.* 40:429–41.

Houston, J. 1968. Dogs vs. deer. *Colo. Outdoors* 17(1):22–23.

Howard, V. W., Jr. 1967. Identifying fecal groups by pH analysis. *J. Wildl. Manage.* 31:190–91.

Howard, V. W., Jr., and DeLorenzo, D. G. 1974. Specific differentiation of herbivore pellet groups by pH. *J. Wildl. Manage.* 38:948–49.

Howarth, J. A.; Roby, T. O.; Amerault, T. E.; and McNeal, D. W. 1969. Prevalence of Anaplasma marginale in California deer as measured by calf inoculation and serologic techniques. *U.S. Anim. Health Assoc.* 73:136–44.

Howe, D. L. 1966. *Annual report federal aid in wildlife restoration.* Project FW3-R-13. Cheyenne: Wyoming Game and Fish Department. 16 pp.

———. 1970. Anaplasmosis. In *Infectious diseases of wild animals,* ed. J. W. Davis, L. H. Karstad, and D. O. Trainer, pp. 363–71. Ames: Iowa State University Press. 421 pp.

Howe, D. L.; Hepworth, W. G.; Blunt, F.; and Thomas, G. M. 1964. Anaplasmosis in big game animals: Experimental transmission and reevaluation of serologic tests. *Amer. J. Vet. Res.* 25:1271.

Howe, D. L., and Hepworth, W. G. 1965. Anaplasmosis in big game animals: Tests of wild populations in Wyoming. *Amer. J. Vet. Res.* 26:1114.

Howell, T. G. 1963. Bluetongue. In *Emerging diseases of animals,* pp. 111–53. Food and Agriculture Organization of the United Nations, Department of Veterinary Service, no. 61. Onderstepoort, South Africa: FAO.

Hubbard, J. J. 1968. A study of the woody vegetation on remnant grasslands in western Kansas. M.S. thesis, Fort Hays Kansas State College, Hays. 32 pp.

Hudkins, G., and Kistner, T. 1977. *Sarcocystis hemionilatrantis* sp. n.: Life cycle in mule deer and coyotes. *J. Wildl. Dis.* 13:80–84.

Hudson, P. 1959. Fetal recoveries in mule deer. *J. Wildl. Manage.* 23:234–35.

Hudson, P., and Browman, L. G. 1959. Embryonic and fetal development of the mule deer. *J. Wildl. Manage.* 23:295–304.

Hudson, R. J.; Hebert, D. M.; and Brink, V. C. 1976. Occupational patterns of wildlife on a major East Kootenay winter-spring range. *J. Range Manage.* 29:38–43.

Huffaker, C. B. 1970. The phenomenon of predation and its roles in nature. In *Dynamics of populations,* ed. P. J. den Boer and G. R. Gradwell, pp. 327–43. Netherlands: Oosterbeek. 611 pp.

Huggett, A. St. G., and Widdas, W. F. 1951. The relationship between mammalian foetal weight and concep-

tion age. *J. Physiol.* 114:306–17.

Hughes, C. L. 1976. *Environmental analysis report: Use of goats to control brush regrowth, Descanso Ranger District.* USDA Forest Service, Cleveland National Forest. 27 pp.

Humphrey, R. R. 1953. The desert grassland, past and present. *J. Range Manage.* 6:159–64.

———. 1958a. *The desert grassland.* Bulletin 299. Tucson: Arizona Agricultural Experiment Station. 62 pp.

———. 1958b. The desert grassland: A history of vegetational change and an analysis of causes. *Bot. Rev.* 24:193–252.

———. 1962. *Range ecology.* New York: Ronald Press. 234 pp.

Humphreys, F. A., and Gibbons, R. J. 1942. Some observations on corynebacterial infections with particular reference to their occurrence in mule deer, *Odocoileus hemionus,* in British Columbia. *Can. J. Comp. Med.* 6:35–45.

Hungerford, C. R. 1970. Responses of Kaibab mule deer to management of summer range. *J. Wildl. Manage.* 34:852–62.

Hunter, G. N. 1947. *Physical characteristics of Colorado mule deer in relation to their age class.* Denver: Colorado Game and Fish Department. 38 pp.

Hunter, G. N., and Yeager, L. E. 1956. Management of the mule deer. In *The deer of North America,* ed. W. P. Taylor, pp. 449–82. Harrisburg, Pa.: Stackpole. 668 pp.

Hunter, J. W. 1924. Deer hunting in California. *Calif. Fish and Game* 10:18–24.

Hunter, V. E. 1973. Comparison of blood components of Nevada mule deer in relation to age, sex, and location. M.S. thesis, University of Nevada, Reno. 56 pp.

Hunter, V. E.; Lesperance, A. L.; and Papez, N. J. 1972. Plasma inorganic phosphorus levels in Nevada mule deer. *J. Anim. Sci.* 35:230 (abstract).

Hutchison, B. A. 1965. *Snow accumulation and disappearance influenced by big sagebrush.* USDA Forest Service Research Note RM-46. 7 pp.

Hyder, D. N. 1970. Water intake by cattle as a measure of forage intake and quality. In *Range and wildlife habitat evaluation: A research symposium,* pp. 120–26. USDA Miscellaneous Publication no. 1147. 220 pp.

Hyder, D. N.; Bement, R. E.; and Norris, J. J. 1968. Sampling requirements of the water-intake method of estimating forage intake by grazing cattle. *J. Range Manage.* 21:392–97.

Illige, D. 1951. An analysis of the reproductive pattern of whitetail deer in south Texas. *J. Mammal.* 32:411–21.

Ingebo, P. A. 1971. Suppression of channel-side chaparral cover increases streamflow. *J. Soil and Water Cons.* 26:79–81.

Irving, W. 1961. *Astoria; or, Anecdote of an enterprise beyond the Rocky Mountains.* Philadelphia: Lippincott. 461 pp.

Isaković, I. 1969. Antler morphology in the red deer from Belje. *Jelen* 8:5–59.

Jackson, A. S. 1965. Wildfires in the Great Plains grassland. *Proc. Tall Timbers Fire Ecol. Conf.* 4:261–75.

Jackson, G. F. 1971. Energy transfer potential of velvet-stage deer antlers. *Bull. Ecol. Soc. Amer.* 52:39 (abstract).

Jacobsen, N. L. K. 1973. Physiology, behavior, and thermal transactions of white-tailed deer. Ph.D. thesis, Cornell University, Ithaca, N.Y. 346 pp.

Jaczewski, Z.; Zurowski, W.; and Zaniewski, L. 1962. Regulation of blood pressure in the growing antlers of red deer *(Cervus elaphus L.). Int. Congr. Game Biol.* 5:115–39.

James, E. 1823. *Account of an expedition from Pittsburgh to the Rocky Mountains.* Vol. 2. Philadelphia: Carey and Lea. 442 pp.

Jantzen, R. A. 1964. Population declines of mule deer in northern Arizona. *Proc. West. Assoc. Game and Fish Commissioners* 44:158–66.

Jarvinen, J. A., and Schmid, W. D. 1971. Snowmobile use and winter mortality of small mammals. In *Proceedings 1971 snowmobile and off the road vehicle research symposium,* pp. 131–41. Technical Report 8. East Lansing: Michigan State University. 196 pp.

Jellison, W. L. 1934. The parasitism of lizards by *Ixodes ricinus californicus* Banks. *J. Parasit.* 20:243.

Jenkins, J. H., and Fendley, T. T. 1968. The extent of contamination, defection, and health significance of high accumulations of radioactivity in southeastern game populations. *Proc. Ann. Conf. SE Assoc. Game and Fish Commissioners* 22:89–95.

Jenness, R., and Sloan, R. E. 1970. The composition of milks of various species: A review. *Dairy Sci. Abstr.* 32:599–612.

Jensen, C. H., and Scotter, G. W. 1977. A comparison of twig-length and browsed-twig methods of determining browse utilization. *J. Range Manage.* 30:64–67.

Jensen, C. H.; Smith, A. D.; and Scotter, G. W. 1972. Guidelines for grazing sheep on rangelands used by big game in winter. *J. Range Manage.* 25:346–52.

Jensen, C. H.; Urness, P. J.; and Smith, A. D. 1976. Productivity of big game winter forage can be enhanced by grazing with domestic sheep. *Proc. Ann. Meeting Soc. Range Manage.* 29:17 (abstract).

Jensen, R., and Seghetti, L. 1955. Eleophoriasis in sheep. *J. Amer. Vet. Med. Assoc.* 127:499.

Jensen, W., and Robinette, W. L. 1955. A high reproductive rate for Rocky Mountain mule deer. *J. Wildl. Manage.* 19:503.

Jobman, W. G. 1972. Consumption of juniper by deer and inhibition of rumen microorganisms by volatile oils of juniper. M.S. thesis, Colorado State University, Fort Collins. 51 pp.

John, R. T. 1976. Recent changes in Utah's mule deer populations and management. *Proc. West. Assoc. Game and Fish Commissioners* 56:415–23.

Johnson, D. R., and Todd, M. C. 1977. Summer use of a highway crossing by mountain caribou. *Can. Field-Natur.* 91:312–14.

Johnson, J. F. 1975. *Illegal kill and crippling loss of deer during regulated hunting seasons.* Performance Report, P-R Project no. W-93-17, WP 2, J 7. Santa Fe: New Mexico Game and Fish Department. 4 pp.

Johnson, W. M. 1969. Life expectancy of sagebrush control in central Wyoming. *J. Range Manage.* 22:177–82.

Jonas, R. 1966. *Merriam's turkey in southeastern Montana.* Technical Bulletin no. 3. Helena: Montana Fish and Game Department. 36 pp.

Jones, F. L. 1954. Ageing the Inyo mule deer. *Proc. West. Assoc. Game and Fish Commissioners* 33:209–19.

Jones, G. 1974. Influence of forest development on black-tailed deer winter range on Vancouver Island. In *Proceedings: Wildlife and forest management in the Pacific Northwest symposium,* ed. H. C. Black, pp. 139–48. Corvallis: Oregon State University. 236 pp.

Jones, G. W. 1975. Aspects of winter ecology of black-tailed deer *(Odocoileus hemionus columbianus* Richardson) on northern Vancouver Island. M.S. thesis, University of British Columbia, Vancouver, 80 pp.

Jones, J. R. 1967. *Regeneration of mixed conifer clearcuttings on the Apache National Forest–Arizona.* USDA Forest Service Research Note RM-79. 8 pp.

———. 1975. *Regeneration on an aspen clearcut in Arizona.* USDA Forest Service Research Note RM-285. 8 pp.

Jones, M. B., and Longhurst, W. M. 1958. Overhanging deer fences. *J. Wildl. Manage.* 22:325–26.

Jones, R. H.; Roughton, R. D.; Foster, N. M.; and Bando, B. M. 1977. *Culicoides,* the vector of epizootic hemorrhagic disease in white-tailed deer in Kentucky in 1971. *J. Wildl. Dis.* 13:2–9.

Jones, S. D. M.; Price, M. A.; and Berg, R. T. 1978. A review of carcass density, its measurement and relationship with bovine carcass fatness. *J. Anim. Sci.* 46:1151–58.

Jordan, J. W., and Vohs, P. A., Jr. 1976. Natality of black-tailed deer in McDonald State Forest, Oregon. *Northwest Sci.* 50:108–13.

Judd, I. B., and Judd, L. W. 1976. Plant survival in the arid Southwest 30 years after seeding. *J. Range Manage.* 29:248–51.

Julander, O. 1958. Techniques in studying competition between big game and livestock. *J. Range Manage.* 11:18–21.

Julander, O.; Robinette, W. L.; and Jones, D. A. 1961. Relation of summer range condition to mule deer herd productivity. *J. Wildl. Manage.* 25:54–60.

Kamps, G. F. 1969. Whitetail and mule deer relationships in the Snowy Mountains of central Montana. M.S. thesis, Montana State University, Bozeman. 59 pp.

Karstad, L. H. 1970. Miscellaneous viral diseases. In *Infectious diseases of wild mammals,* ed. J. W. Davis, L. H. Karstad, and D. O. Trainer, pp. 166–72. Ames: Iowa State University Press. 421 pp.

Karstad, L. H.; Winter, A.; and Trainer, D. O. 1961. Pathology of epizootic hemorrhagic disease of deer. *Amer. J. Vet. Res.* 22:227–35.

Kayser, C. 1965. Hibernators. In *Physiological mammal-*

ogy, ed. W. Mayer and R. Van Gelder. Vol. 2. *Mammalian reactions to stressful environments*, pp. 179–296. New York and London: Academic Press. 326 pp.

Kearney, T. H., and Peebles, R. H. 1969. *Arizona flora*. Berkeley: University of California Press.

Keith, L. B. 1974. Some features of population dynamics in mammals. *Trans. Int. Congr. Game Biol.* 11:17–58.

Kelker, G. H. 1947. Computing the rate of increase for deer. *J. Wildl. Manage.* 11:117–83.

———. 1952. Yield tables for big game herds. *J. For.* 50:206–17.

Keller, G. L. 1975. Seasonal food habits of desert mule deer *(Odocoileus hemionus crooki)* on a specific mule deer-cattle range in Pecos County, Texas. M.S. thesis, Sul Ross State University, Alpine, Tex. 80 pp.

Kellogg, R. 1956. What and where are the whitetails? In *The deer of North America*, ed. W. P. Taylor, pp. 31–55. Harrisburg, Pa.: Stackpole.

Kemper, H. E. 1938. Filarial dermatosis of sheep. *N. Amer. Vet.* 19:36.

Kilburn, P. D. 1976. Environmental implications of oil-shale development. *Environ. Conserv.* 3:101–15.

King, J. A. 1963. Disease survey trips among the caribou herds in Alaska. *J. Amer. Vet. Med. Assoc.* 143:887–88.

Kingsbury, J. M. 1964. Poisonous plants of the United States and Canada. Englewood Cliffs, N.J.: Prentice-Hall. 626 pp.

Kirsch, L. M., and Kruse, A. D. 1972. Prairie fires and wildlife. *Proc. Tall Timbers Fire Ecol. Conf.* 12:289–303.

Kistner, T. P. 1976. *Evaluating physical condition in deer.* Job Progress Report, P-R Project W-70-R-6, Subproject F, Study VI, Job 4, Objective E. Portland: Oregon Department of Fish and Wildlife. 11 pp.

Kistner, T. P.; Johnson, G. R.; and Rilling, G. A. 1977. Naturally occurring neurologic disease in a fallow deer. *J. Wildl. Dis.* 13:55–59.

Kistner, T. P., and Koller, L. D. 1975. Experimentally induced Fasciola hepatica infections in black-tailed deer. *J. Wildl. Dis.* 11:214–21.

Kitchen, D. W. 1974. Social behaviour and ecology of the pronghorn. *Wildl. Monogr.* no. 38. 96 pp.

Kitchen, D. W., and Bromley, P. T. 1974. Agonistic behaviour of territorial pronghorn bucks. In *The behaviour of ungulates and its relation to management*, ed. V. Geist and F. R. Walther, 1:365–81. IUCN New Series Publication 24. Morges, Switzerland: IUCN.

Kitts, W. D.; Bandy, P. J.; Wood, A. J.; and Cowan, I. McT. 1956a. Effect of age and plane of nutrition on the blood chemistry of the Columbian black-tailed deer *(Odocoileus hemionus columbianus).* A. Packed-cell volume, sedimentation rate, and hemoglobin. *Can. J. Zool.* 34:477–84.

Kitts, W. D.; Cowan, I. McT.; Bandy, J.; and Wood, A. J. 1956b. The immediate post-natal growth in the Columbian black-tailed deer in relation to the composition of the milk of the doe. *J. Wildl. Manage.* 20:212–14.

Klein, D. R. 1964. Range-related differences in growth of deer reflected in skeletal ratios. *J. Mammal.* 45:226–35.

———. 1965. Ecology of deer range in Alaska. *Ecol. Monogr.* 35:259–84.

———. 1969. Food selection by North American deer and their response to over-utilization of preferred plant species. In *Animal populations in relation to their food resources*, ed. A. Watson, pp. 25–44. Oxford: Blackwell Scientific Publications. 477 pp.

———. 1971. Reaction of reindeer to obstructions and disturbances. *Science* 173:393–98.

Klein, D. R., and Olson, S. T. 1960. Natural mortality patterns of deer in southeast Alaska. *J. Wildl. Manage.* 24:80–88.

Knapp, S. E., and Shaw, J. N. 1962. Occurrence of *Fascioloides magna* (Bassi) in Oregon cattle and deer. *J. Parasit.* 49:339.

Knapp, S. J. 1972. Range use of mule deer prior to initiation of rest rotation grazing for cattle on the Ft. Howes Ranger District, Custer National Forest, Montana. M.S. thesis, Montana State University, Bozeman. 50 pp.

Knipe, T. 1957. *The javelina in Arizona.* Wildlife Bulletin 2. Phoenix: Arizona Game and Fish Department. 96 pp.

Knobloch, I. W. 1939. Death on the highway. *J. Mammal.* 20:508–9.

Knowles, C. J. 1975. Range relationships of mule deer, elk and cattle in a rest-rotation grazing system during summer and fall. M.S. thesis, Montana State University, Bozeman. 111 pp.

———. 1976a. Mule deer population ecology, habitat relationships, and relations to livestock grazing management in the Missouri River breaks, Montana—Nichol's Coulee RCA. In *Montana deer studies*, pp. 95–106. Progress Report P-R Project W-120-R-7. Helena: Montana Fish and Game Department. 170 pp.

———. 1976b. Observations of coyote predation on mule deer and white-tailed deer in the Missouri River breaks, 1975–1976. In *Montana deer studies*, pp. 117–38. Progress Report, P-R Project W-120-R-7. Helena: Montana Fish and Game Department. 170 pp.

Knox, K. L.; Nagy, J. G.; and Brown, R. D. 1969. Water turnover in mule deer. *J. Wildl. Manage.* 33:389–93.

Koehler, D. A. 1975. *A review of the literature on reseeding sagebrush-bunchgrass ranges in semi-arid western United States.* Wildlife Research Report no. 4. Corvallis: Oregon Wildlife Commission. 47 pp.

Kolenosky, G. B. 1972. Wolf predation on wintering deer in east central Ontario. *J. Wildl. Manage.* 36:357–69.

Komberec, T. J. 1976. Range relationships of mule deer, elk and cattle in a rest-rotation grazing system during winter and spring. M. S. thesis, Montana State University, Bozeman. 79 pp.

Kovner, J. L., and Patil, S. A. 1974. Properties of estimators of wildlife population density for the line transect method. *Biometrics* 30:225–30.

Krämer, A. 1971. Notes on the winter ecology of mule and white-tailed deer in the Cypress Hills, Alberta, Canada. *Can. Field Natur.* 85:141–45.

———. 1972. *A review of the ecological relationships between mule and white-tailed deer.* Occasional Paper no. 3. Edmonton: Alberta Fish and Wildlife Division, Wildlife Section. 48 pp.

———. 1973. Interspecific behavior and dispersion of two sympatric deer species. *J. Wildl. Manage.* 37:288–300.

Krausman, P. R. 1978. Forage relationships between two deer species in Big Bend National Park, Texas. *J. Wildl. Manage.* 42:101–7.

Krausman, P. R.; Ables, E. D.; and McGinnis, D. M. 1974. Deer identification through pellet pH. *J. Wildl. Manage.* 38:572–73.

Krausman, P. R., and Bissonette, J. A. 1977. Bone-chewing behavior of desert mule deer. *Southwest. Natur.* 22:149–50.

Kreeger, T. J. 1977. Impact of dog predation on Minnesota whitetail deer. *J. Minn. Acad. Sci.* 43(2):8–13.

Kreier, J. P., and Ristic, M. 1963. Anaplasmosis. VII. Experimental *Anaplasma ovis* infection in white-tailed deer (*Dama virginiana*). *Amer. J. Vet. Res.* 24:567.

Kruse, W. H. 1972. *Effects of wildfire on elk and deer use of a ponderosa pine forest.* USDA Forest Service Research Note RM-226. 4 pp.

Kruska, D. 1970. Über die Evolution des Gehirns in der Ordnung Artiodactyla Owen 1848, ins besondere der Teilordnung Suina Gray 1868. *Z. Säugetierk.* 35:214–38.

Kucera, T. E. 1978. Social behavior and breeding system of the desert mule deer. *J. Mammal.* 59:463–76.

Küchler, A. W. 1964. Potential natural vegetation of the conterminous United States. Special Publication no. 36. New York: American Geographical Society. 116 pp.

Kufeld, R. C. 1968. Use of paint for marking deer pellet groups. *J. Wildl. Manage.* 32:592–96.

———. 1977a. Improving Gambel oak ranges for elk and mule deer by spraying with 2,4,5,-TP. *J. Range Manage.* 30:53–57.

———. 1977b. Inventory of range manipulation projects in Colorado. In *Game research report, July 1977,* part 1, pp. 1–6. Denver: Colorado Division of Wildlife. 123 pp.

Kufeld, R. C.; Wallmo, O. C.; and Feddema, C. 1973. *Foods of the Rocky Mountain mule deer.* USDA Forest Service Research Paper. RM-111. 31 pp.

Kurt, F. 1968. Das sozialverhalten des rehes (*Capreolus capreolus* L.). In *Mammalia depicta,* Hamburg: Parey. 102 pp.

———. 1970. *Rehwild.* Munich: BLV Jagdbiologie. 174 pp.

———. 1977. *Wildtiere in der kulturlandschaft.* Erlenback-Zurich: Rentsch. 175 pp.

Kurtén, B. 1975. A new pleistocene genus of American mountain deer. *J. Mammal.* 57:507–8.

Kverno, N. B.; Hood, G. A.; and Dodge, W. E. 1965. Development of chemicals to control forest wildlife damage. *Proc. Soc. Amer. Foresters Ann. Meet.* 1965:222–26.

Lamb, S. H. 1975. *Woody plants of the Southwest.* Santa Fe: Sunstone Press.

Landis, T. D., and Mogren, E. W. 1975. Tree strata biomass of subalpine spruce-fir stands in southwestern Colorado. *For. Sci.* 21:9–12.

Lang, E. M. 1957. *Deer of New Mexico.* Bulletin no. 5. Santa Fe: New Mexico Department Game and Fish. 41 pp.

Lange, N. A., and Forker, G. M., eds. 1956. *Handbook of chemistry,* 9th ed. Sandusky, Ohio: Handbook Publishers. 1,969 pp.

Laramie, H. A., Jr., and White, D. L. 1964. *Some observations concerning hunting pressure and harvest on white-tailed deer.* Technical Publication 20. Concord: New Hampshire Fish and Game Department. 55 pp.

Laron, Z., and Kowaldo, A. 1963. Fat-mobilizing effect of testosterone. *Metabolism* 12:588–91.

Lassen, R. W.; Ferrel, C. M.; and Leach, H. 1952. Food habits, productivity and condition of the Doyle mule deer herd. *Calif. Fish and Game* 38:211–24.

Lauckhart, J. B. 1948. Black-tailed deer in western Washington. *Proc. West. Assoc. Game and Fish Commissioners.* 28:153–61.

———. 1950. Determining the big-game population from the kill. *Trans. N. Amer. Wildl. Conf.* 15:644–50.

Lauer, J. L., and Peek, J. M. 1976. Big game relationships on the bighorn sheep winter range, East Fork of the Salmon River, Idaho. Forest Wildlife and Range Experiment Station Bulletin no. 12. Moscow: University of Idaho. 44 pp.

Launchbaugh, J. L. 1972. Effect of fire on shortgrass and mixed prairie species. *Proc. Tall Timbers Fire Ecol. Conf.* 12:129–51.

Lavigne, G. R. 1976. Winter response of deer to snowmobiles and selected natural factors. M.S. thesis, University of Maine, Orono. 70 pp.

Lawrence, G., and Biswell, H. 1972. Effect of forest manipulation on deer habitat in giant sequoia. *J. Wildl. Manage.* 36:595–605.

Lawrence, W. L. 1969. The impact of intensive forest management on wildlife populations. In *Proceedings: wildlife and reforestation in the Pacific Northwest symposium, 1968,* ed. H. C. Black, pp. 72–74. Corvallis: Oregon State University. 92 pp.

Laycock, W. A.; Buchanan, H.; and Kruger, W. C. 1972. Three methods of determining diet, utilization, and trampling damage on sheep ranges. *J. Range Manage.* 25:352–56.

Laycock, W. A., and Phillips, T. A. 1968. Long-term effects of 2,4-D on lanceleaf rabbitbrush and associated species. *J. Range. Manage.* 21:71–73.

Leach, R. H. 1956. Food habits of the Great Basin deer herds of California. *Calif. Fish and Game* 42:243–308.

Leach, R. H., and Hiehle, J. L. 1957. Food habits of the Tehama deer herd. *Calif. Fish and Game* 43:161–78.

Leathem, J. H. 1961. Nutritional effects on endocrine secretions. In *Sex and internal secretions*, 3d ed., ed. W. C. Young, 1:666–704. Baltimore: Williams and Wilkins. 704 pp.

LeCount, A. 1974*a*. Effects of hunting on a desert mule deer population. In *Wildlife research in Arizona*, pp. 21–30. Phoenix: Arizona Game and Fish Department. 124 pp.

———. 1974*b*. Causes of fawn mortality. In *Wildlife research in Arizona*, pp. 55–60. Phoenix: Arizona Game and Fish Department. 124 pp.

LeDune, E. K., and Volkmar, F. 1934. Malignant edema in deer. *Vet. Med.* 29:276.

Lee, B., and Williams, D. 1964. *The last grass frontier: The South Dakota stockgrower heritage*. Sturgis, S.D.: Black Hills Publications. 456 pp.

Leithead, H. L. 1959. Runoff in relation to range condition in the Big Bend–Davis Mountain section of Texas. *J. Range Manage.* 12:83–87.

Lemos, J. C.; McInnis, M. L.; Castillo, W. J.; and Anglin, R. E. 1978*a*. *Steens Mountain deer population study: Aerial deer census on winter range*. Job Progress Report, P-R Project W-70-R-8, Subproject F, Study XI, Job 2-R. Portland: Oregon Department of Fish and Wildlife. 6 pp.

Lemos, J. C.; McInnis, M. L.; Trainer, C. E.; Castillo, W. J.; and Anglin, R. E. 1978*b*. *Steens Mountain mule deer population study: Coyote population evaluation*. Job Progress Report, P-R Project W-70-R-8, Subproject F, Study VII, Job 5. Portland: Oregon Department of Fish and Wildlife. 5 pp.

Lent, P. C. 1965. Rutting behaviour in a barren-ground caribou population. *Anim. Behav.* 13:259–64.

———. 1974. Mother-infant relationships in ungulates. In *The behaviour of ungulates and its relation to management*, ed. V. Geist and F. R. Walther, 1:14–55. IUCN New Series Publication 24. Morges, Switzerland: IUCN.

Leopold, A. 1924. Grass, brush, timber, and fire in southern Arizona. *J. For.* 22:1–10.

———. 1933. *Game management*. New York: Charles Scribner's Sons. 481 pp.

Leopold, A.; Sowls, L. K.; and Spencer, D. L. 1947. A survey of overpopulated deer ranges in the United States. *J. Wildl. Manage.* 11:162–77.

Leopold, A.; Taylor, W. P.; Bennett, R.; and Chapman, H. H. 1938. Wildlife research: Is it a practical and necessary basis for management? *Trans. N. Amer. Wildl. Conf.* 3:42–55.

Leopold, A. S. 1950*a*. Deer in relation to plant succession. *Trans. N. Amer. Wildl. Conf.* 15:571–79.

———. 1950*b*. Vegetation zones of Mexico. *Ecology* 31:507–18.

———. 1959. *Wildlife of Mexico: The game birds and mammals*. Berkeley: University of California Press. 568 pp.

———. 1962. *The desert*. Life Nature Library. New York: Time. 192 pp.

Leopold, A. S.; Riney, T.; McCain, R.; and Tevis, L., Jr. 1951. *The Jawbone deer herd*. Bull. no. 4. Sacramento: California Department of Fish and Game. 139 pp.

Levine, N. D. 1973. *Sarcocystis, Toxoplasma* and related protozoa. In *Protozoan parasites of domestic animals and man*, 2d ed. p. 288. Minneapolis: Burgess. 406 pp.

Lewall, E. F., and Cowan, I. McT. 1963. Age determination in black-tailed deer by degree of ossification of the spiphyseal plate in the long bones. *Can. J. Zool.* 41:629–36.

Lewke, R. E., and Buss, I. O. 1977. Impacts of impoundments to vertebrate animals and their habitats in the Snake River Canyon, Washington. *Northwest Sci.* 51:219–70.

Lincoln, F. C. 1930. *Calculating waterfowl abundance on the basis of banding returns*. USDA Circular no. 118, Bureau of Biological Survey. Washington, D.C.: USDA.

Lincoln, G. A. 1971. The seasonal reproductive changes in the red deer stag (*Cervus elaphus*). *J. Zool.* [London] 163:105–23.

Lincoln, G. A.; Guiness, F.; and Short, R. V. 1972. The way in which testosterone controls the social and sexual behavior of the red deer stag (*Cervus elaphus*). *Hormon. Behav.* 3:375–96.

Lindblom, C. E. 1959. The science of "muddling through." *Pub. Admin. Rev.* 19:79–88.

Lindsdale, J. M., and Tomich, P. Q. 1953. *A herd of mule deer: A record of observations made on the Hastings Natural History Reservation*. Berkeley: University of California Press. 567 pp.

Linduska, J. P., and Lindquist, A. W. 1952. Some insect pests of wildlife. In *Insects: The yearbook of agriculture 1952*, pp. 708–24. Washington, D.C.: USDA. 780 pp.

Lipscomb, J. F. 1974. A modeling approach to harvest and trend data analysis. *Proc. West. Assoc. Game and Fish Commissioners* 54:56–61.

Lisk, R. D. 1969. Estrogen: Direct effects on hypothalamus or pituitary in relation to pituitary weight changes. *Neuroendocrinology* 4:368–73.

Long, T. A.; Cowan, R. L.; Wolfe, G. W.; Rader, T.; and Swift, R. W. 1959. *Effect of seasonal feed restriction on antler development of white-tailed deer*. Pennsylvania State University Agricultural Experiment Program Report 209. 11 pp.

Longhurst, W. M. 1964. Evaluation of the eye lens technique for aging Columbian black-tailed deer. *J. Wildl. Manage.* 28:773–84.

———. N.d. Records of deer investigations at Hopland Field Station, Mendocino Co., California, 1951–1962. Unpublished. On file at University of California, Davis.

Longhurst, W. M.; Baker, N. F.; Connolly, G. E.; and Fisk, R. A. 1970. Total body water and water turnover in sheep and deer. *Amer. J. Vet. Res.* 31:673–77.

Longhurst, W. M., and Chattin, J. E. 1941. The burro deer (*Odocoileus hemionus eremicus*). *Calif. Fish and Game* 27:2–12.

Longhurst, W. M., and Connolly, G. E. 1970. The effects

of brush burning on deer. *Cal-Neva Wildlife* 1970:134–55.

———. N.d. Records of deer investigations at Hopland Field Station, Mendocino Co., California, 1963–1975. Unpublished. On file at University of California, Davis.

Longhurst, W. M., and Douglas, J. R. 1953. Parasite inter-relationships of domestic sheep and Columbian black-tailed deer. *Trans. N. Amer. Wildl. Conf.* 18:168–88.

Longhurst, W. M.; Garton, E. O.; Heady, H. F.; and Connolly, G. E. 1976. The California deer decline and possibilities for restoration. *Annu. Meet. West. Sect. Wildlife Society (Fresno, Calif.)* 1976:74–103.

Longhurst, W. M.; Jones, M. B.; Parks, R. R.; Neubauer, L. W.; and Cummings, M. W. 1962. *Fences for controlling deer damage.* California Agricultural Experiment Station Extension Service Circular 514. 15 pp.

Longhurst, W. M.; Leopold, A. S.; and Dasmann, R. F. 1952. *A survey of California deer herds, their ranges and management problems.* Game Bulletin no. 6. Sacramento: California Department of Fish and Game. 136 pp.

Longhurst, W. M.; Oh, H. K.; Jones, M. B.; and Kepner, R. E. 1968a. A basis for the palatability of deer forage plants. *Trans. N. Amer. Wildl. and Natur. Resour. Conf.* 33:181–89.

Longhurst, W. M.; Schultz, V.; and Connolly, G. E. 1968b. Accumulation of strontium-90 in yearling Columbian black-tailed deer 1960–67. *J. Wildl. Manage.* 32:621–23.

Lonner, T. N. 1975. Long Tom Creek study. In *Montana cooperative elk-logging study,* pp. 60–72. Progress Report, P-R Project W-120-R, Helena: Montana Fish and Game Department. 146 pp.

Losch, T. A., and Samuel, D. E. 1976. Unretrieved deer left by hunters: A literature review. *Proc. Northeast Fish and Wildl. Conf.* 33:17–34.

Loveless, C. M. 1967. *Ecological characteristics of a mule deer winter range.* Technical Bulletin no. 20. Denver: Colorado Game, Fish and Parks Department. 124 pp.

Low, W. A., and Cowan, I. McT. 1963. Age determination of deer by annular structure of dental cementum. *J. Wildl. Manage.* 27:466–71.

Lowe, C. H., and Brown, D. E. 1973. *The natural vegetation of Arizona.* Cooperative Publication no. 2. Phoenix: Arizona Resources Information System. 53 pp.

Lowry, D. A., and McArthur, K. L. 1978. Domestic dogs as predators on deer. *Wildl. Soc. Bull.* 6:38–39.

Lund-Larsen, T. R. 1977. Relation between testosterone levels in serum and proteoloytic activity in the neck muscles of the Norwegian reindeer (*Rangifer tarandus tarandus*). *Acta Zool.* (Stockholm) 58:61–63.

Lyon, L. J. 1969. Wildlife habitat research and fire in the northern Rockies. *Proc. Tall Timbers Fire Ecol. Conf.* 9:213–27.

———. 1970. Length- and weight-diameter relations of serviceberry twigs. *J. Wildl. Manage.* 34:456–60.

McArdle, R. E., and Costello, D. F. 1936. The virgin range. In *The western range,* pp. 71–80. U.S. Senate Doc. no. 199, 74th Cong., 2d sess. Washington, D.C.: GPO. 620 pp.

McArdle, R. E.; Costello, D. F.; Birkmaier, E. E.; Ewing, C.; Hendricks, B. A.; Kutzleg, C. A.; Simpson, A. A.; and Standing, A. R. 1936. The whiteman's toll. In *The western range,* pp. 81–116. U.S. Senate Doc. no. 199, 74th Cong., 2d sess. Washington, D.C.: GPO. 620 pp.

McArthur, E. D.; Guinta, B. C.; and Plummer, A. P. 1974. *Shrubs for restoration of depleted ranges and disturbed areas.* Reprint from *Utah Science* for March 1974. 6 pp.

McBride, R. T. 1976. The status and ecology of the mountain lion (*Felis concolor stanleyana*) of the Texas-Mexico border. M.S. thesis, Sul Ross State University, Alpine, Tex. 160 pp.

McCain, R., and Taylor, W. P. 1956. Methods of estimating numbers of mule deer. In *The deer of North America,* ed. W. P. Taylor, pp. 431–88. Harrisburg, Pa.: Stackpole. 668 pp.

McCann, S. 1973. An occurrence of an antlered female mule deer in eastern Montana. *Proc. Mont. Acad. Sci.* 33:24–26.

McConnell, B. 1957. A productivity study of mule deer on the Cassia Division of the Sawtooth National Forest. M.S. thesis, University of Idaho, Boise. 76 pp.

McConnell, B., and Dalke, P. D. 1960. The Cassia deer herd of southern Idaho. *J. Wildl. Manage.* 24:265–71.

McConnell, B. R.; Davis, J. A.; and Dalke, P. D. 1975. The old "1-2-3." *Idaho Wildl. Rev.* 28(2):3–7.

McConnell, B. R., and Smith, J. G. 1970. Frequency distributions of deer and elk pellet groups. *J. Wildl. Manage.* 34:29–36.

———. 1977. Influence of grazing on age-yield interactions of bitterbrush. *J. Range Manage.* 30:91–93.

McCulloch, C. Y. 1955. *Arizona chaparral deer study: Field observations of deer in the Three Bar vicinity.* P-R Project. W-71-R-2, WP3, J 1. Phoenix: Arizona Game and Fish Department. 24 pp.

———. 1967a. Habitat manipulation in chaparral vegetation. In *Wildlife research in Arizona 1966,* pp. 63–123. Phoenix: Arizona Game and Fish Department. 177 pp.

———. 1967b. Measurements of two races of mule deer in Arizona. Paper presented at 47th annual meeting, American Society of Mammalogists, Nags Head, N.C., 10 June 1967. 6 pp.

———. 1972. Deer foods and brush control in southern Arizona. *Ariz. Acad. Sci.* 7:113–19.

———. 1973. Seasonal diets of mule and white-tailed deer. In *Deer nutrition in Arizona chaparral and desert habitats,* pp. 1–37. Special Report no. 3. Phoenix: Arizona Game and Fish Department. 68 pp.

———. 1974. *Control of pinyon-juniper as deer management measure in Arizona.* Final report P-R Project W-18-R, WP4, J 2 and 7. Phoenix: Arizona Game and Fish Department. 32 pp.

———. 1978. Statewide deer food preferences. P-R Project W-78-R, WP4, J 15. Phoenix: Arizona Game and Fish Department. 29 pp.

McCulloch, C. Y.; Wallmo, O. C.; and Ffolliott, P. F. 1965. *Acorn yield of Gambel oak in northern Arizona.* USDA Forest Service Research Note RM-48. 2 pp.

McCullough, D. R. 1964. Relationship of weather to migrating movements of black-tailed deer. *Ecology* 45:249–56.

———. 1965. Sex characteristics of black-tailed deer hooves. *J. Wildl. Manage.* 29:210–12.

McCullough, D. R.; Olson, C. E., Jr.; and Queal, L. H. 1969. Progress in large animal census by thermal mapping. In *Remote sensing in ecology,* ed. P. L. Johnson, pp. 138–47. Athens: University of Georgia Press. 244 pp.

McDermott, J. F., ed. 1951. *Up the Missouri with Audubon: The journal of Edward Harris.* Norman: University of Oklahoma Press. 222 pp.

MacDonald, D., and Dillman, E. G. 1968. Techniques for estimating nonstatistical bias in big game harvest surveys. *J. Wildl. Manage.* 32:119–29.

McDowell, R. D., and Pillsbury, H. W. 1959. Wildlife damage to crops in the United States. *J. Wildl. Manage.* 23:240–41.

Mace, R. U. 1974. Application of vehicle restrictions in wildlife management. *Proc. West. Assoc. Game and Fish Commissioners* 54:205–10.

McEwan, E. H. 1975. The adaptive significance of the growth patterns in cervid compared with other ungulate species. *Zoologichesky Zhurnal* 54:1221–32.

Mcfarlane, W. V. 1968. Comparative functions of ruminants in hot environments. In *Adaptation of domestic animals,* ed. E. S. E. Hafez, pp. 264–76. Philadelphia: Lea and Febiger. 415 pp.

McGinnies, W. G. 1972. Continental aspects of shrub distribution, utilization, and potentials: North America. Section I. In *Wildland shrubs—Their biology and utilization: A symposium,* pp. 55–66. Logan: Utah State University. 494 pp.

MacGregor, W. G. 1964. Analysis of Great Basin deer decline: California. *Proc. West. Assoc. Game and Fish Commissioners* 44:167–76.

———. 1976. Recent changes in California mule deer populations and management. *Proc. West. Assoc. Game and Fish Commissioners* 56:373–78.

McInnis, M. L.; Lemos, J. C.; Trainer, C. E.; Castillo, W. J.; and Anglin, R. E. 1978. *Steens Mountain mule deer population study: Radiotelemetry study of fawn mortality.* Job Progress Report, P-R Proj. W-7-R-8, Subproject F, Study VI, Job 3. Portland: Oregon Department of Fish and Wildlife. 7 pp.

McIntosh, J. E. 1969. A quantitative microradiographic study of cyclic morphological changes in trabecular bone of mule deer (*Odocoileus hemionus hemionus*). M.S. thesis, Colorado State University, Fort Collins. 45 pp.

McKean, J. W. 1947. Interstate deer herd study. *Proc. West. Assoc. Game and Fish Commissioners* 27:110–15.

McKean, J. W., and Luman, I. D. 1964. Oregon's 1962 decline in mule deer harvest. *Proc. West. Assoc. Game and Fish Commissioners* 44:177–80.

McKean, W. T., and Bartmann, R. M. 1971. *Deer-livestock relations on a pinon-juniper range in northwestern Colorado.* Final report, P-R Project W-101-R. Denver: Colorado Game, Fish and Parks Department. 132 pp.

Mackie, R. J. 1964. Montana deer weights. *Montana Wildl.* 1964 (winter):9–14.

———. 1970. Range ecology and relations of mule deer, elk and cattle in the Missouri River breaks, Montana. *Wildl. Monogr.* no. 20. 79 pp.

———. 1975. Evaluation of the key browse survey method. Paper presented at the Fifth Mule Deer Workshop, Boise, Idaho, February 1975. 17 pp. Available from author on request.

———. 1976a. Interspecific competition between mule deer, other game animals and livestock. In *Mule deer decline in the West: A symposium,* ed. G. W. Workman and J. B. Low, pp. 49–54. Logan: Utah State University College of Natural Resources and Agricultural Experiment Station. 134 pp.

———. 1976b. Mule deer population ecology, habitat relationships, and relations to livestock grazing management and elk in the Missouri River breaks, Montana. In *Montana deer studies,* pp. 67–94. Job Completion Report, P-R Project W-120-R, Study BG-1.4, J 1. Helena: Montana Fish and Game Department. 170 pp.

———. 1978. Impacts of livestock grazing on wild ungulates. *Trans. N. Amer. Wildl. and Nat. Resour. Conf.* 43:462–76.

———. In press. Natural regulation of mule deer populations. In *Natural regulation of wildlife,* ed. D. S. Eastman and F. L. Bunnell. New York and London: Academic Press.

McLean, D. D. 1930. The burro deer in California. *Calif. Fish and Game* 16:119–20.

———. 1936. The replacement of teeth in deer as a means of age determination. *Calif. Fish and Game* 22:43–44.

———. 1940. The deer of California with particular reference to the Rocky Mountain mule deer. *Calif. Fish and Game* 26:139–66.

McLeod, J. 1973. Simulation today: From fuzz to fact. *Stimulation Today* 3:9–12. In *Simulation* 20(3).

McMahan, C. A. 1964. Comparative food habits of deer and three classes of livestock. *J. Wildl. Manage.* 28:298–308.

———. 1966. Suitability of grazing enclosures for deer and livestock research on the Kerr Wildlife Management Area, Texas. *J. Wildl. Manage.* 30:151–62.

McMahan, C. A., and Ramsey, C. W. 1965. Response of deer and livestock to controlled grazing. *J. Range Manage.* 18:1–7.

McMichael, T. J. 1970. Rate of predation on deer fawn mortality. In *Wildlife research in Arizona, 1969–70,* pp. 77–83. Phoenix: Arizona Game and Fish Department.

McMillin, J. M.; Seal, U. S.; and Keenlyne, K. D.; Erickson, A. W.; and Jones, J. E. 1974. Annual testosterone rhythms in the adult white-tailed deer (*Odocoileus virginianus borealis*). *Endocrinology* 94:1034–40.

MacNeish, R. S. 1976. Early man in the New World. *Amer. Sci.* 64:316–27.

Magruder, N. D.; French, C. E.; McEwen, L. C.; and Swift, R. W. 1957. *Nutritional requirements of white-tailed deer for growth and antler development.* II. *Experimental results of the third year.* Bulletin 628. University Park: Pennsylvania Agricultural Experiment Station. 21 pp.

Malaher, G. W. 1967. Improper use of snow vehicles for hunting. *Trans. N. Amer. Wildl. and Natur. Resour. Conf.* 32:429–33.

Mankins, J. V., and Baker, G. A. 1956. Factor analysis of growth of California mule deer *Odocoileus hemionus californicus. Growth* 20:179–86.

Mansfield, T. M. 1974. A comparison of black-tailed deer fawns from oak woodland and chaparral vegetation types. M.S. thesis, University of California, Davis. 60 pp.

Mansfield, T. M.; Connolly, G. E.; and Longhurst, W. M. 1975. Condition of black-tailed deer fawns from oak woodland and chaparral habitat types. *Cal-Neva Wildl. Trans.* 1975 (Proc. Annual Meet., Calif-Nev. Sections, Wildl. Soc. and Amer. Fish. Soc.): 1–12.

Mansfield, T. M. and Miller, B. D. 1975. *Highway deer-kill District 02 regional study.* Sacramento, Calif.: Caltrans Environmental Branch. 49 pp.

Marburger, R. G.; Andregg, M. J.; and Clark, K. A. 1972. Antler malformation produced by leg injury in white-tailed deer. *J. Wildl. Dis.* 8:311–14.

Marburger, R. G.; Robinson, R. M.; and Thomas, J. W. 1967. Genital hypoplasia of white-tailed deer. *J. Mammal.* 48:674–76.

Marchinton, R. L.; Johnson, A. S.; Sweeney, J. R.; and Sweeney, J. M. 1970. Legal hunting of white-tailed deer with dogs: Biology, sociology and management. *Proc. Ann. Conf. SE Assoc. Game and Fish Commissioners* 24:74–89.

Marchinton, R. L.; Johnson, A. S.; Sweeney, J. R.; Sweeney, J. M.; and Moore, W. G. 1971. Auto-erotic behavior in male white-tailed deer. *J. Mammal.* 52:616–17.

Margalef, R. 1963. On certain unifying principles in ecology. *Amer. Natur.* 97:357–74.

Markwald, R. R. 1968. Histological and histochemical study of testicular periodicity in mule deer (*Odocoileus hemionus hemionus*). M.S. thesis, Colorado State University, Fort Collins. 165 pp.

Markwald, R. R.; Davis, R. W.; and Kainer, R. A. 1971. Histological and histochemical periodicity of service Leydig cells in relation to antler growth. *Gen. Comp. Endocr.* 16:268–80.

Marler, P. 1956. Studies of fighting in draft inches 3: Proximity as a cause for aggression. *Brit. J. Anim. Behav.* 4:23–30.

Marquiss, R. W. 1972. Soil moisture, forage, and beef production benefits from Gambel oak control in southwestern Colorado. *J. Range Manage.* 25:146–50.

Marsh, H. 1944. Necrobacillosis of the rumen in young lambs. *J. Amer. Vet. Med. Assoc.* 104:23–25.

Marshall, A. D., and Whittington, 1968. A telemetric study of deer ranges and behavior of deer during managed hunts. *Proc. Ann. Conf. SE Assoc. Game and Fish Commissioners* 22:30–46.

Martin, P. R. 1972. *Ecology of skunkbush sumac (Rhus trilobata Nutt.) in Montana with special reference to use by mule deer.* Final Report, P-R Project W-120-R-3, 4. Helena: Montana Department of Game and Fish. 97 pp.

Martin, P. S. 1970. Pleistocene niches for alien animals. *Bioscience* 20:218–21.

Martin, S. C. 1975. *Ecology and management of southwestern semidesert grass:shrub ranges: The status of our knowledge.* USDA Forest Service Research Paper RM-156. 39 pp.

Martinka, C. J. 1968. Habitat relationships of white-tailed and mule deer in northern Montana. *J. Wildl. Manage.* 32:558–65.

Martinka, R. R. 1974. Potential effects of coal and related industrial developments on wildlife in eastern Montana. *Proc. West. Assoc. Game and Fish Commissioners* 54:180–85.

Mather, K. 1961. Competition and cooperation. *Symp. Exp. Biol.* 15:264–81.

Mattfeld, G. F. 1973. The effect of snow on the energy expenditure of walking white-tailed deer. *Proc. NE Fish and Wildl. Conf.* 30:327–43.

Mautz, W. W. 1978. Nutrition and carrying capacity. In *Big game of North America: Ecology and management,* ed. J. L. Schmidt and D. L. Gilbert, pp. 321–48. Harrisburg, Pa.: Stackpole Books. 494 pp.

Mautz, W. W., and Petrides, G. A. 1971. Food passage rate in the white-tailed deer. *J. Wildl. Manage.* 35:723–31.

Mautz, W. W.; Silver, H.; Holter, J. B.; Hayes H. H.; and Urban, W. E., Jr. 1976. Digestibility and related nutritional data for seven northern deer browse species. *J. Wildl. Manage.* 40:630–38.

Maynard, L. A., and Loosli, J. K. 1956. *Animal nutrition.* New York: McGraw-Hill. 484 pp.

———. 1969. *Animal nutrition.* 6th ed. New York: McGraw-Hill. 613 pp.

Mayr, E. 1949. *Systematics and the origin of species from the viewpoint of a zoologist.* New York: Columbia University Press. 334 pp.

———. 1963. *Animal species and evolution.* Cambridge: Harvard University Press. 797 pp.

Mazur, P. E. 1973. Seasonal plasma androgen level and its relation to antler growth and seasonal feed consumption in male white-tailed deer (*Odocoileus virginianus*). Ph.D. thesis, Pennsylvania State University, University Park. 138 pp.

Mealy, R. H. 1969. Nylon fencing to protect forest plantations. In *Proceedings: Wildlife and reforestation in the*

Pacific Northwest symposium 1968, ed. H. C. Black, pp. 89–90. Corvallis: Oregon State University 92 pp.

Mech, L. D., and Karns, P. D. 1977. *Role of the wolf in a deer decline in the Superior National Forest.* USDA Forest Service Research Paper NC-148. 23 pp.

Medin, D. E. 1976. Modeling the dynamics of a Colorado mule deer population. Ph.D. thesis, Colorado State University, Fort Collins. 167 pp.

Meiman, J. R. 1968. Snow accumulation related to elevation, aspect and forest canopy. In *Snow hydrology,* pp. 35–47. Proceedings of a workshop seminar sponsored by Canadian National Commission for the International Hydrological Decade and the University of New Brunswick. 82 pp.

Meng, M.; West, G. C.; and Irving, L. 1969. Fatty acid composition of caribou bone marrow. *Comp. Biochem. Physiol.* 30:187–91.

Menzel, K. 1975. The deer of Nebraska. *Nebraskaland* 53:10–42.

Menzel, K., and Havel, R. 1969. Changes in relative abundance of white-tailed and mule deer in Nebraska. Paper presented to 31st Midwest Fish and Wildlife Conference, Minneapolis, Minn. 7 pp.

Merriam, H. R. 1964. The wolves of Coronation Island. *Proc. Alaska Sci. Conf.* 15:27–32.

———. 1971. *Deer report.* P-R Project W-17-1. Juneau: Alaska Department of Fish and Game. 21 pp.

Merrill, L. B.; Teer, J. G.; and Wallmo, O. C. 1957. Reaction of deer populations to grazing practices. *Texas Agric. Progr.* 3(5):10–12.

Metz, W. D. 1974. Oil shale: A huge resource of low-grade fuel. *Science* 184:1271–75.

Michael, A. 1975. The world of the brain. *Harper's* 251(1507):3–4.

Michael, E. D. 1964. Birth of white-tailed deer fawns. *J. Wildl. Manage.* 28:171–73.

Mierau, G. W. 1972. Studies on the biology of an antlered female mule deer. *J. Mammal.* 53:403–4.

Milchunas, D. G. 1977. *In vivo–in vitro* relationships of Colorado mule deer forages. M.S. thesis, Colorado State University, Fort Collins. 133 pp.

Milchunas, D. G.; Dyer, M. I.; Wallmo, O. C.; and Johnson, D. E. 1978. In vivo–in vitro *relationships of Colorado mule deer forages.* Special Report no. 43. Denver: Colorado Division of Wildlife. 44 pp.

Milek, B. 1968. They're spraying away your wildlife. *Sports Afield* 160(3):56, 57, 106, 107.

Miller, F. L. 1965. Behaviour associated with parturition in black-tailed deer. *J. Wildl. Manage.* 29:629–31.

———. 1970. Distribution patterns of black-tailed deer *(Odocoileus hemionus columbianus)* in relation to environment. *J. Mammal.* 51:248–60.

———. 1971a. Behaviour of maternal black-tailed deer *(Odocoileus hemionus columbianus)* associated with the death of fawns. *Z. Tierpsychol.* 28:527–33.

———. 1971b. Mutual grooming by black-tailed deer in northwestern Oregon. *Can. Field Natur.* 85:295–301.

———. 1974. Four types of territoriality observed in a herd of black-tailed deer. In *The behaviour of ungu-*

lates and its relation to management, ed. V. Geist and F. R. Walther, 2:644–60. IUCN New Series Publ. 24. Morges, Switzerland: IUCN.

Miller, R. S. 1958. The Munsell system of color notation. *J. Mammal.* 39:278–86.

———. 1967. Pattern and process in competition. *Adv. Ecol. Res.* 4:1–74.

Milne, A. 1961. Definition of competition among animals. *Symp. Soc. Exp. Biol. 15:40–61, no. 15* (Cambridge University Press). 365 pp.

Mitchell, B. 1971. Annual cycle of condition and body composition of red deer on the Island of Rhum. In *Range ecology research,* pp. 66–73. 1st Progress Report Edinburgh: Nature Conservancy. 93 pp.

Mitchell, G. E. 1950. Wildlife-forest relationships in the Pacific Northwest region. *J. For.* 48:26–30.

Modell, W. 1969. Horns and antlers. *Sci. Amer.* 220:114–22.

Moen, A. N. 1967. Hypothermia observed in water-chilled deer. *J. Mammal.* 48:655–56.

———. 1968. Energy exchange of white-tailed deer, western Minnesota. *Ecology* 49:676–82.

———. 1973. *Wildlife ecology: An analytical approach.* San Francisco: W. H. Freeman. 458 pp.

———. 1974. Radiant temperatures of hair surfaces. *J. Range Manage.* 27:401–3.

Moen, A. N., and Evans, K. E. 1971. The distribution of energy in relation to snow cover in wildlife habitat. In *Snow and ice in relation to wildlife and recreation symposium proceedings,* ed. A. O. Haugen, pp. 1–15. Ames: Iowa State University.

Moen, A. N., and Jacobsen, F. L. 1974. Changes in radiant temperature of animal surfaces with wind and radiation. *J. Wildl. Manage.* 38:366–68.

Moen, A. N., and Jacobsen, N. K. 1975. Thermal exchange, physiology, and behavior of white-tailed deer. In *Perspectives of biophysical ecology,* ed. D. M. Gates and R. B. Schmerl, pp. 509–24. New York: Springer Verlag. 609 pp.

Mohler, L. L. 1964. Deer harvest fluctuations in Idaho. *Proc. West. Assoc. Game and Fish Commissioners* 44:170–72.

Molello, J. A. 1960. Alkaline phosphatase and mucopolysaccharide study of the deer antler. M.S. thesis, Colorado State University, Fort Collins. 55 pp.

Moore, T. 1957. *Vitamin A.* Amsterdam: Elsevier. 645 pp.

Moore, W. G., and Marchinton, L. 1974. Marking behaviour and its social function in white-tailed deer. In *The behaviour of ungulates and its relation to management,* ed. V. Geist and F. R. Walther, 1:447–56. IUCN New Series Publication 24. Morges, Switzerland: IUCN.

Morales, M. F.; Rathbun, E. N.; Smith, R. E.; and Pace, N. 1945. Studies on body composition. II. Theoretical considerations regarding the major body components, with suggestions for application to man. *J. Viol. Chem.* 158:677–84.

Moreland, R. 1953. A technique for determining age in black-tailed deer. *Proc. West. Assoc. Game and Fish*

Commissioners 32:214–19.

Morris, M. J. 1973. *Estimating understory plant cover with rated microplots.* USDA Forest Service Research Paper RM-104. 12 pp.

Morrison, J. A. 1960. Characteristics of estrus in captive elk. *Behaviour,* 16:84–92.

Morrison-Scott, T. C. S. 1960. Antler anomalies. *J. Mammal.* 41:412.

Moser, K. 1975. Developments at Vail. *Colo. Outdoors* 24(1):14–17.

Moss, E. H. 1932. The vegetation of Alberta. IV. The poplar association and related vegetation of central Alberta. *J. Ecol.* 20:380–415.

Moynihan, M. 1968. Social mimicry: Character convergence versus character displacement. *Evolution* 22:315–31.

Mueller, C. C., and Sadleir, R. M. F. S. 1977. Changes in the nutrient composition of milk of black-tailed deer during lactation. J. Mammal. 58:421–23.

Muller, C. H., and Chou, C. H. 1972. Phytotoxins: An ecological phase of phytochemistry. In *Phytochemical ecology,* ed. J. B. Harborne, pp. 201–16. Proceedings of the Phytochemical Society Symposium, Royal Holloway College, Englefield Green, Surrey, England. New York and London: Academic Press. 272 pp.

Müller-Schwarze, D. 1967. Social odors in young mule deer. *Amer. Zool.* 7:807 (abstract).

———. 1968. Play deprivation in deer. *Behaviour* 31:144–62.

———. 1969. Pheromone function of deer urine. *Amer. Zool.* 9:570 (abstract).

———. 1971. Pheromones in black-tailed deer *(Odocoileus hemionus columbianus). Anim. Behav.* 19:141–52.

———. 1972. Responses of young black-tailed deer to predator odors. *J. Mammal.* 53:393–94.

———. 1977. Complex mammalian behavior and pheromone bioassay in the field. In *Chemical signals in vertebrates,* ed. D. Müller-Schwarze and M. M. Mozelli, pp. 413–33. New York: Plenum.

Müller-Schwarze, D., and Müller-Schwarze, C. 1969. Spielverhalten und allgemeine Aktivität bei Schwarzwedelhirschen. *Bonner Zool. Beiträge* 10:282–89.

———. 1971. Olfactory imprinting in a precocial mammal. *Nature* 229:55–56.

———. 1975. Subspecific specificity of response to a mammalian social odor. *J. Chem. Ecol.* 1:125–31.

Müller-Schwarze, D.; Volkman, N. J.; and Zemanek, K. F. 1977. Osmetrichia: Specialized scent hair in black-tailed deer. *J. Ultrastructure Res.* 59:223–30.

Mulroy, T. W., and Rundel, P. W. 1977. Annual plants: Adaptations to desert environments. *Bioscience* 27:109–14.

Mundinger, J. G. 1976. Population ecology and habitat relationships of white-tailed deer in coniferous forest habitat of northwestern Montana. In *Progress Report for period July 1, 1975 to June 30, 1976,* pp. 7–37.

P-R Project W-120-R. Helena: Montana Department Fish and Game. 170 pp.

Munger, T. T. 1943. Vital statistics for some Douglas-fir plantations. *J. For.* 41:53–56.

Murie, A. 1940. *Ecology of the coyote in the Yellowstone.* Fauna National Parks Bulletin no. 4. Washington, D.C.: GPO. 206 pp.

Murie, O. J. 1930. An epizootic disease of elk. *J. Mammal.* 11:214–22.

———. 1951. *The elk of North America.* Harrisburg, Pa.: Stackpole. 376 pp.

Murphy, B. D. 1969. The relationships of selected physiological factors to antler growth in mule deer. M.S. thesis, Colorado State University, Fort Collins. 60 pp.

Murphy, B. D., and Clugston, R. E. 1971. Bilateral testicular degeneration in a wild mule deer *(Odocoileus hemionus). J. Wildl. Dis.* 7:67–69.

Mutch, W. E. S.; Lockie, J. D.; and Cooper, A. B. 1976. *The red deer in South Ross: A report on wildlife management in the Scottish Highlands.* Edinburgh: Department of Forestry and Natural Resources, University of Edinburgh. 196 pp.

Myers, G. T. 1969. Deer-auto accidents: Serious business. *Colo. Outdoors* 18(3):38–40.

Nagy, J. G. 1970. Biological relations of rumen flora and fauna. In *Range and wildlife habitat evaluation: A research symposium,* pp. 159–63. USDA Miscellaneous Publication no. 1147. 220 pp.

Nagy, J. G.; Baker, D. L.; Bailey, J. A.; deCalesta, D. S.; Reeder, D. E.; and Schoonveld, G. G. 1974. *Middle Park cooperative deer study: Physiology and prevention of deer starvation.* Final Report, P-R Project W-38-R-28, WP14, J 6. Denver: Colorado Division of Wildlife. 156 pp.

Nagy, J. G., and Gilbert, J. G. 1968. Fecal pH values of mule deer and grazing domestic sheep. *J. Wildl. Manage.* 32:961–62.

Nagy, J. G., and Regelin, W. L. 1975. Comparison of digestive organ size of three deer species. *J. Wildl. Manage.* 39:621–24.

Nagy, J. G.; Steinhoff, H. W.; and Ward, G. M. 1964. Effects of essential oils of sagebrush on deer rumen microbial function. *J. Wildl. Manage.* 28:785–90.

Nagy, J. G., and Tengerdy, R. P. 1967. Antibacterial action of essential oils of *Artemisia* as an ecological factor. II. Antibacterial action of the volatile oils of *Artemisia tridentata* (big sagebrush) on bacteria from the rumen of mule deer. *Appl. Microbiol.* 16:441–44.

Nagy, J. G.; Vidacs, G.; and Ward, G. M. 1967. Previous diet of deer, cattle, and sheep and ability to digest alfalfa hay. *J. Wildl. Manage.* 31:443–47.

Nalbandov, A. V. 1964. *Reproductive physiology, comparative reproductive physiology of domestic animals, laboratory animals, and man.* 2d ed. San Francisco and London: W. H. Freeman. 316 pp.

National Academy of Sciences. 1974. *Rehabilitation potential of western coal lands.* Cambridge: Ballinger. 198 pp.

National Research Council. 1970. *Land use and wildlife*

resources. Washington, D.C.: National Academy of Sciences. 262 pp.

Neal, D. L., and Neal, J. L. 1973. Uses and capabilities of electronic capacitance instruments for estimating standing herbage. Part 1. History and development. *J. Br. Grassl. Soc.* 28:81–89.

Neff, D. J. 1963. *Deer population trend techniques.* P-R Project W-78-R-7, WP1, J 4. Phoenix: Arizona Game and Fish Department. 6 pp.

———. 1968. The pellet-group technique for big game trend, census, and distribution: A review. *J. Wildl. Manage.* 32:597–614.

———. 1970. Effect of simulated use on the vigor of browse plants. In *Wildlife research in Arizona, 1969–70,* pp. 121–74. Phoenix: Arizona Game and Fish Department.

———. 1974. *Forage preferences of trained mule deer on the Beaver Creek watersheds.* Special Report no. 4. Phoenix: Arizona Game and Fish Department. 61 pp.

Neiland, K. A. 1970. Weight of dried marrow as indicator of fat in caribou femurs. *J. Wildl. Manage.* 34:904–7.

Neiland, K. A.; King, J. A.; Huntley, B. E.; and Skoog, R. O. 1968. The diseases and parasites of Alaskan wildlife populations. Part I. Some observations on brucellosis in caribou. *Bull. Wildl. Dis. Assoc.* 4:27–36.

Neils, G.; Adams, L.; and Blair, R. M. 1955. Management of white-tailed deer and ponderosa pine. *Trans. N. Amer. Wildl. Conf.* 20:539–51.

Nellis, C. H. 1968. Productivity of mule deer on the National Bison Range, Montana. *J. Wildl. Manage.* 32:344–49.

———. 1977a. *Environmental influences upon deer.* Report, P-R Project W-160-R-4, Study VI, J 1-9. Jerome: Idaho Department of Fish and Game. 16 pp.

———. 1977b. *Evaluate response of forage species and evaluate response of deer to irrigation/fertilization.* Project Completion Report, P-R Project W-160-R-5, Study no. 5, J 2, 3, 4. Boise: Idaho Department Fish and Game. 5 pp.

Nellis, C. H., and Ross, R. L. 1969. Changes in mule deer food habits associated with herd reduction. *J. Wildl. Manage.* 33:191–95.

Nellis, C. H.; Thiessen, J. L. and Prentice, C. A. 1976. Pregnant fawn and quintuplet mule deer. *J. Wildl. Manage.* 40:795–96.

Nelson, D. 1974. Necrobacillosis in mule deer. M.S. thesis, Colorado State University, Fort Collins. 43 pp.

Nelson, J. R. 1961. Composition and structure of the principal woody vegetation types in the North Dakota Badlands. M.S. thesis, North Dakota State University, Fargo. 195 pp.

Nelson, R. A. 1969. *Handbook of Rocky Mountain plants.* Estes Park, Colo.: Skyland. 331 pp.

Nettles, V. F.; Prestwood, A. K.; and Nichols, R. G. 1977. Meningeal worm-induced neurologic disease in black-tailed deer. *J. Wildl. Dis.* 13:137–44.

Nevada Department of Fish and Game. 1967. Save a deer. *Nevada Outdoors* 1(13):17.

Newbrey, J. W., and Banks, W. J. 1975. Characterization of developing antler cartilage matrix. II. An ultrastructural study. *Calcified Tissue Res.* 17:289–302.

Newmann, P. W., and Merriam, H. G. 1972. Ecological effects of snowmobiles. *Can. Field Natur.* 86:207–12.

Newton, M. 1973. *Environmental management for seedling establishment.* Research Paper 16. Corvallis: Oregon State University Forest Research Laboratory. 5 pp.

Nichol, A. A. 1936. The experimental feeding of deer. *Trans. N. Amer. Wildl. Conf.* 1:403–10.

———. 1937. The natural vegetation of Arizona. In Technical Bulletin 68. Tucson: University of Arizona Agricultural Experiment Station (from reprint).

———. 1938. *Experimental feeding of deer.* Technical Bulletin 75. Tucson: University of Arizona Agricultural Experiment Station. 39 pp.

Nichols, R., and Murray, J. 1973. Blacktail deer–whitetail deer breeding study. Final Report, P-R Project W-46 (V-A, V-B). Nashville: Tennessee Game and Fish Commission. 13 pp.

Nickerson, D. 1946. *Color measurement and its application to the grading of agricultural products.* USDA Miscellaneous Publication 580. 62 pp.

Nicolls, K. E. 1969. Cytometry and volumetry of acidophil cells in the hypophysis cerebri, pars distalis, of Colorado mule deer, *Odocoileus hemionus hemionus,* relative to seasons of the photoperiod and antler cycles. Ph.D. thesis, Colorado State University, Fort Collins. 144 pp.

———. 1971. A light microscopic study of nuclear and cytoplasmic size of the aggregate acidophil population in the hypophysis cerebri, pars distalis, of adult male mule deer, *Odocoileus hemionus hemionus,* relative to seasons of the photoperiod and antler cycles. *Z. Zellforsch. Mikrs. Anat.* 115:314–26.

Nielsen, D. B. 1975. Coyotes and deer. *Utah Sci.* 36(3):807–90.

Nikolaevski, D. L. 1961. Diseases of reindeer. In *Reindeer husbandry,* ed. P. S. Zhigunov, pp. 230–93. Springfield: U.S. Department of Commerce. Translated from the Russian.

Nixson, E. S. 1967. A vegetational study of the pine ridge of northwestern Nebraska. *Southwest. Natur.* 12:134–45.

Nobe, K. C., and Gilbert, A. H. 1970. *A survey of sportsmen expenditures for hunting and fishing in Colorado, 1968.* Technical Publication no. 24. Denver: Colorado Division of Game, Fish and Parks. 83 pp.

Nordan, H. C.; Cowan, I. McT.; and Wood, A. J. 1968. Nutritional requirements and growth of black-tailed deer, *Odocoileus hemionus columbianus,* in captivity. In *Comparative nutrition of wild animals,* ed. M. A. Crawford, pp. 89–96. New York: Academic Press. 429 pp.

———. 1970. The feed intake and heat production of the young black-tailed deer (*Odocoileus hemionus columbianus*). *Can. J. Zool.* 48:275–82.

Northeastern Forest and Range Experiment Station. 1973. *Forest fertilization symposium proceedings.* USDA

Forest Service General Technical Report NE-3. 246 pp.

Novakowski, N. S.; Consineau, J. G.; Kolenosky, G. B.; Wilton, G. S.; and Choquette, L. P. E. 1963. Parasites and diseases of bison in Canada. II. Anthrax epizootic in the Northwest Territories. *Trans. N. Amer. Wildl. and Natur. Resour. Conf.* 28:233–39.

Odum, E. P. 1971. *Fundamentals of ecology.* Philadelphia: W. B. Saunders. 574 pp.

Ogren, H. A. 1962. *Barbary sheep of New Mexico.* Bulletin no. 11. Santa Fe: New Mexico Department of Game and Fish. 32 pp.

Oh, J. H.; Jones, M. B.; Longhurst, W. M.; and Connolly, G. E. 1970. Deer browsing and rumen microbial fermentation of Douglas-fir as affected by fertilization and growth stage. *For. Sci.* 16:21–27.

Oliver, W. H. 1974. Wildlife problems associated with reservoirs used for electrical power generation (with special emphasis on Wells Hydroelectric Project Wildlife Study). *Proc. West. Assoc. Game and Fish Commissioners* 54:146–55.

Olsen, O. W., and Williams, J. F. 1959. Cysticerci of *Taenia krabbei* in mule deer in Colorado. *J. Wildl. Manage.* 23:119–22.

Olson, J. S. 1975. Productivity of forest ecosystems. In *Productivity of world ecosystems,* pp. 33–43. Washington, D.C.: National Academy of Sciences. 166 pp.

Ommundsen, P., and Cowan, I. McT. 1970. Development of the Columbian black-tailed deer *(Odocoileus hemionus columbianus)* during the fetal period. *Can. J. Zool.* 48:123–32.

Opdyke, N. D.; Lindsay, E. H.; Johnson, N. M.; and Downs, T. 1977. The paleomagnetism and magnetic polar stratigraphy of the mammal-bearing section of Anza Borrego State Park, California. *Quater. Res.* 7:316–29.

Osebold, J. W.; Christensen, J. F.; Longhurst, W. M.; and Rosen, M. N. 1959. Latent *Anaplasma marginale* infections in wild deer demonstrated by calf inoculation. *Cornell Vet.* 49:97.

Oswald, E. T. and Senyk, J. P. 1977. *Ecoregions of Yukon Territory.* Victoria, B.C.: Canadian Forest Service, Pacific Forest Research Centre. 115 pp.

Ozoga, J. J. 1972. Aggressive behaviour of white-tailed deer to winter cuttings. *J. Wildl. Manage.* 36:861–68.

Ozoga, J. J., and Gysel, L. W. 1972. Response of white-tailed deer to winter weather. *J. Wildl. Manage.* 36:892–96.

Ozoga, J. J., and Verme, L. J. 1970. Winter feeding habits of penned white-tailed deer. *J. Wildl. Manage.* 34:431–39.

———. 1975. Activity patterns of white-tailed deer during estrus. *J. Wildl. Manage.* 39:679–83.

Packer, P. E. 1974. *Rehabilitation potentials and limitations of surface-mined lands in the northern Great Plains.* USDA Forest Service General Technical Report INT-14. 44 pp.

Paintner, W. W. 1971. Volatile oil content and composition of juniper and its effect on rumen microorganisms. M.S. thesis, Colorado State University, Fort Collins. 40 pp.

Pálsson, H. 1955. Conformation and body composition. In *Progress in the physiology of farm animals,* ed. J. Hammond, 2:430–542. London: Butterworth Scientific Publications. 740 pp.

Pantić, O. J., and Brna, J. 1967. The development of red deer skeleton during embryogenesis. *Int. Congr. Game Biol.* 7:105–12.

Papez, N. J. 1976. The Ruby-Butte deer herd. Biological Bulletin no. 5. Reno: Nevada Department Fish and Game. 61 pp.

Park, T. 1954. Experimental studies of interspecies competition. II. Temperature, humidity, and competition in two species of *Tribolium. Physiol. Zool.* 27:177–238.

Parker, H. D., Jr. 1972. Airborne infrared detection of deer. Ph.D. thesis, Colorado State University, Fort Collins. 186 pp.

Parker, H. D., and Driscoll, R. S. 1972. An experiment in deer detection by thermal scanning. *J. Range Manage.* 25:480–81.

Parker, H. D., and Harlan, J. C. 1972. *Solar radiation affects radiant temperatures of a deer surface.* USDA Forest Service Research Note RM-215. 4 pp.

Parkes, A. S. 1945. The adrenal-gonad relationship. *Physiol. Rev.* 25:203–54.

Parmelee, W. E.; Lee, R. D.; Wagner, E. D.; and Burnett, H. S. 1956. A survey of *Thelazia californiensis,* a mammalian eye worm, with new local records. *J. Amer. Vet. Med. Assoc.* 129:325–27.

Parsons, J. 1975. Status of desert mule deer research in Texas. Unpublished. On file at Texas Parks and Wildlife Department, Austin. 15 pp.

Parsons, L. D. 1976. The mule deer are back. *Proc. West. Assoc. Game and Fish Commissioners* 56:424–33.

Pase, C. P. 1966. Grazing and watershed value of native Arizona plants. *Amer. Assoc. Adv. Sci., Rocky Mtn. and SW Div. Contrib.* 8:31–40.

Pase, C. P.; Ingebo, P. A.; Davis, E. A.; and McCulloch, C. Y. 1967. Improving water yield and game habitat by chemical control of chaparral. *Int. Union For. Res. Org. Congr.* 14:463–86 (papers section 01–02–11).

Pase, C. P., and Pond, F. W. 1964. *Vegetation changes following the Mingus Mountain burn.* USDA Forest Service Research Note RM-18. 8 pp.

Patton, D. R. 1974. Patch cutting increases deer and elk use of a pine forest in Arizona. *J. For.* 72:764–66.

———. 1975. A diversity index for quantifying habitat "edge." *Wildl. Soc. Bull.* 3:171–73.

Patton, D. R., and Avant, H. D. 1970. *Fire-stimulated aspen sprouting in a spruce-fir forest in New Mexico.* USDA Forest Service Research Note RM-159. 3 pp.

Paulik, G. J., and Robson, D. S. 1969. Statistical calculations for change-in-ratios estimators of population parameters. *J. Wildl. Manage.* 33:1–27.

Payne, G. F. 1973. Cover-weight relationships. *J. Range Manage.* 27:403–4.

Pearson, G. A. 1950. *Management of ponderosa pine in the*

Southwest. USDA Agricultural Monograph 6. 618 pp.

Pearson, H. A. 1968. *Thinning, clearcutting, and reseeding affect deer and elk use of ponderosa pine forests in Arizona*. USDA Forest Service Research Note RM-119. 4 pp.

———. 1969. Rumen microbial ecology in mule deer. *Appl. Microbiol.* 17:819–24.

———. 1975. Herbage disappearance and grazing capacity determinations of southern pine bluestem range. *J. Range Manage.* 28:71–73.

Pechanec, J. F., and Pickford, G. D. 1937. A weight estimate method for the determination of range or pasture production. *J. Amer. Soc. Agron.* 29:894–904.

Pechanec, J. F.; Plummer, A. P.; Robertson, J. H.; and Hull, A. C. 1965. *Sagebrush control on rangelands*. USDA Handbook 277. 40 pp.

Pederson, J. C. 1970. *Productivity of mule deer on the La Sal and Henry Mountains in Utah*. Publication no. 70-2. Salt Lake City: Utah Division of Fish and Game. 133 pp.

Peek, J. M. 1976. Summary contents: Mule deer panel. *Proc. West. Assoc. Game and Fish Commissioners* 56:437–38.

Pengelly, W. L. 1963. Timberlands and deer in the northern Rockies. *J. For.* 61:734–40.

———. 1976. Probable causes of the recent decline of mule deer in western U.S.: A summary. In *Mule deer decline in the west: A symposium,* ed. G. W. Workman and J. B. Low, pp. 127–32. Logan: Utah State University College of Natural Resources and Agricultural Experiment Station. 134 pp.

Perry, M. C., and Giles, R. H., Jr. 1970. Studies of deer-related dog activity in Virginia. *Proc. Ann. Conf. SE Assoc. Game and Fish Commissioners* 24:64–73.

Petersen, C. G. J. 1896. The yearly immigration of young plaice in the Limfjord from the German Sea. *Rep. Danish Biol. Sta.* 6:1–48.

Petocz, R. G. 1973. The effect of snow cover on the social behaviour of bighorn rams and mountain goats. *Can. J. Zool.* 51:987–93.

Petrides, G. A. 1961. The management of wild hoofed animals in the United States in relation to land use. *Terre et Vie* 2:181–202.

Phillippo, M.; Lincoln, G. A.; and Lawrence, C. B. 1972. The relationship between thyroidal calcitonin and seasonal and reproductive changes in the stag (*Cervus elaphus* L.). *J. Endocrinol.* 53:xlviii–xlix.

Phillips, W. S. 1963. *Vegetational changes in the northern Great Plains*. Report 214. Tucson: Arizona Agricultural Experiment Station. 185 pp.

Pierson, R. E.; McChesney, J. S.; and Thake, D. 1974. Experimental transmission of malignant catarrhal fever. *Amer. J. Vet. Res.* 35:523–25.

Platte, K. B. 1959. Plant control: Some possibilities and limitations. I. The challenge to management. *J. Range Manage.* 12:64–68.

Plummer, A. P. 1973. Morphogenesis and management of woody perennials in the United States. In *Plant morphogenesis as a basis for scientific management of*

range resources, pp. 72–80. USDA Miscellaneous Publication 1271. 232 pp.

Plummer, A. P.; Christenson, D. R.; and Monsen, S. B. 1968. *Restoring big game range in Utah*. Publication no. 68–3. Salt Lake City: Utah Division of Fish and Game. 183 pp.

Plummer, A. P.; Hull, A. C., Jr.; Stewart, G.; and Robertson, J. H. 1955. *Seeding rangelands in Utah, Nevada, southern Idaho, and western Wyoming*. USDA Agricultural Handbook 71. 73 pp.

Plummer, F. G. 1911. *Chaparral studies in the dwarf forest, or elfinwood of southern California*. USDA Forest Service Bulletin 85. 48 pp.

Pojar, T. M. 1977. Use of a population model in big game management. *Proc. West. Assoc. Game and Fish Commissioners* 57:82–92.

Pojar, T. M.; Prosence, R. A.; Reed, D. F.; and Woodard, T. N. 1975. Effectiveness of a lighted, animated deer crossing sign. *J. Wildl. Manage.* 39:87–91.

Pojar, T. M., and Reed, D. F. 1974. *The relation of three physical condition indices of mule deer*. Game Information Leaflet no. 96. Fort Collins: Colorado Division of Game, Fish and Parks. 4 pp.

Pospahala, R. S. 1969. A literature review on computers in wildlife biology. Special Report no. 23. Denver: Colorado Division of Game, Fish and Parks. 15 pp.

Prenzlow, E. J.; Ashton, P. M.; and Wykstra, R. A. 1974. Identifying optimal wildlife resource supply quantities which maximize public use benefits. *Trans. N. Amer. Wildl. and Natur. Resour. Conf.* 39:195–207.

Preobrazhenskii, B. V. 1961. Management and breeding of the reindeer. In *Reindeer husbandry,* ed. P. S. Zhigunov, pp. 78–128. Springfield, Va.: U.S. Department of Commerce. Translated from the Russian.

Prescott, W. H. 1974. Interrelationships of moose and deer of the genus *Odocoileus*. *Can. Natur.* 101:493–504.

Presidente, P. J.; Lumsden, J. H.; Presnell, K. R.; Rapley, W. A.; and McCraw, B. M. 1973. Combination of etorphine and xylazine in captive white-tailed deer. II. Effects on hematologic, serum biochemical and blood gas values. *J. Wildl. Dis.* 9:342–48.

Presidente, P. J.; McCraw, B. M.; and Lumsden, J. H. 1974. Pathologic features of experimentally induced *Fasciola hepatica* infection in white-tailed deer. *J. Wildl. Dis.* 63:1–59.

Prestwood, A. K. 1970. Neurologic disease in a white-tailed deer massively infected with meningeal worm. *J. Wildl. Dis.* 6:84–86.

Prestwood, A. K.; Kistner, T. P.; Kellogg, F. E.; and Hayes, F. A. 1974. The 1971 outbreak of hemorrhagic disease among white-tailed deer of the southeastern United States. *J. Wildl. Dis.* 10:217–25.

Prestwood, A. K., and Pursglove, S. R. 1977. Prevalence and distribution of *Setaria yehi* in southeastern white-tailed deer. *J. Amer. Vet. Med. Assoc.* 171:933–35.

Prestwood, A. K., and Ridgeway, T. R. 1972. Elaeophorosis in white-tailed deer of the southeastern U.S.A.: Case report and distribution. *J. Wildl. Dis.*

8:233–36.

Progulske, D. R., and Baskett, T. S. 1958. Mobility of Missouri deer and their harassment by dogs. *J. Wildl. Manage.* 22:184–92.

Pruitt, W. O. 1954. Rutting behaviour of the whitetail deer (*Odocoileus virginianus*). *J. Mammal.* 35:129–30.

Puglisi, M. J.; Lindzey, J. S.; and Bellis, E. D. 1974. Factors associated with highway mortality of white-tailed deer. *J. Wildl. Manage.* 38:799–807.

Pursley, D. 1977. Illegal harvest of big game during closed season. *Proc. West. Assoc. Game and Fish Commissioners* 57:67–71.

Purves, H. D. 1961. Morphology of the hypophysis related to its function. In *Sex and internal secretions,* ed. W. C. Young, 3d ed., 1:161–239. Baltimore: Williams and Wilkins. 706 pp.

Quay, W. B., and Müller-Schwarze, D. 1970. Functional histology of integumentary glandular regions in black-tailed deer (*Odocoileus hemionus columbianus*). *J. Mammal.* 51:675–94.

———. 1971. Relations of age and sex to integumentary glandular regions in Rocky Mountain mule deer (*Odocoileus hemionus hemionus*). *J. Mammal.* 52:670–85.

Quimby, D. C. 1966. A review of literature relating to the effects and possible effects of sagebrush control on certain game species in Montana. *Proc. West. Assoc. Game and Fish Commissioners* 46:142–49.

Quinn, J. A., and Hervey, D. F. 1970. Trampling losses and travel by cattle on Sandhills range. *J. Range Manage.* 23:50–54.

Quortrup, E. R. 1942. Hemorrhagic septicemia in mule deer. *N. Amer. Vet.* 23:34–36.

Raddi, A. G. 1967. The pelage of Columbian blacktail deer *Odocoileus hemionus columbianus* (Richardson). Ph.D. thesis, University of British Columbia, Vancouver. 215 pp.

Radwan, M. A. 1972. Differences between Douglas-fir genotypes in relation to browsing preference by black-tailed deer. *Can. J. For. Res.* 2:250–55.

Radwan, M. A., and Crouch, G. L. 1974. Plant characteristics related to feeding preference by black-tailed deer. *J. Wildl. Manage.* 38:32–41.

Rakkolainen, P. 1971. Snow melting in spring tends to assemble grouse. *Suomen Riista* 23:65–71.

Raleigh, R. J. 1970. Manipulation of both livestock and forage management to give optimum production. *J. Anim. Sci.* 30:108–14.

Raleigh, R. J., and Lesperance, A. L. 1972. Range cattle nutrition. In *Digestive physiology and nutrition of ruminants,* vol. 3, *Practical nutrition,* ed. D. C. Church, pp. 185–99. Corvallis: Oregon State University. 350 pp.

Ralls, K. 1971. Mammalian scent marking. *Science* 171:443–49.

Ralston, R. D. 1960. The structure and ecology of the north slope juniper stands of the Little Missouri Badlands. M.S. thesis, University of Utah, Salt Lake City. 85 pp.

Ramsey, C. W. 1970. *Texotics.* Bulletin no. 49. Austin: Texas Parks and Wildlife Department. 46 pp.

Ransom, A. B. 1965. Kidney and marrow fat as indicators of white-tailed deer condition. *J. Wildl. Manage.* 29:397–98.

Rasmussen, D. I. 1941. Biotic communities of Kaibab Plateau, Arizona. *Ecol. Monogr.* 3:229–75.

Rasmussen, D. I., and Doman, E. R. 1943. Census methods and their application in the management of mule deer. *Trans. N. Amer. Wildl. Conf.* 8:369–79.

Rausch, R. 1950. Observations on histopathological changes associated with starvation in Wisconsin deer. *J. Wildl. Manage.* 14:156–61.

Rausch, R. A., and Hinman, R. A. 1977. Wolf management in Alaska: An exercise in futility? In *Proceedings of the 1975 predator symposium,* ed. R. L. Phillips and C. Jonkel, pp. 147–56. Missoula: Montana Forest and Conservation Experiment Station, University of Montana. 268 pp.

Reavley, B. 1974. How to destroy deer habitat at taxpayers' expense. *Conserv. News* 39(15):12–13.

Reed, D. F., and Pojar, T. M. 1977. Unpublished data, files of P-R Project W-38-R. On file at Colorado Division of Wildlife, Glenwood Springs.

Reed, D. F.; Pojar, T. M.; and Woodard, T. N. 1973. *A video timelapse system for wildlife surveillance.* Game Information Leaflet 94. Denver: Colorado Division of Wildlife. 3 pp.

———. 1974. Use of one-way gates by mule deer. *J. Wildl. Manage.* 38:9–15.

Reed, D. F.; Woodard, T. N.; and Pojar, T. M. 1975. Behavioral response of mule deer to a highway underpass. *J. Wildl. Manage.* 39:361–67.

Rees, J. W. 1971*a.* Discriminatory analysis of divergence in mandibular morphology of *Odocoileus. J. Mammal.* 52:724–31.

———. 1971*b.* Mandibular variation with sex and age in white-tailed deer in Canada. *J. Mammal.* 52:223–26.

Rees, J. W.; Kainer, R. A.; and Davis, R. W. 1966*a.* Histology, embryology, and gross morphology of the mandibular dentition in mule deer. *J. Mammal.* 47:640–54.

———. 1966*b.* Chronology of mineralization and eruption of mandibular teeth in mule deer. *J. Wildl. Manage.* 30:629–31.

Regelin, W. L. 175. Middle Park cooperative deer study: Junction Butte wildlife habitat improvement project. In *Game research report, July 1975,* part 2, pp. 265–94. Denver: Colorado Division of Wildlife. 314 pp.

———. 1976*a.* Snowdrift manipulation. In *Colorado game research review, 1975–1976,* ed. O. B. Cope, pp. 6–7. Fort Collins: Colorado Division of Wildlife. 73 pp.

———. 1976*b.* Effects of snow drifts on mountain shrub communities. Ph.D. thesis, Colorado State University, Fort Collins. 120 pp.

Regelin, W. L.; Nagy, J. C.; and Wallmo, O. C. 1977. Effects of snow drifts on mountain shrub communities. *Int. Congr. Game Biol.* 13:414–19.

Regelin, W. L., and Wallmo, O. C. 1975. *Carbon black increases snow melt and forage availability on deer winter range in Colorado.* USDA Forest Service Research Note RM-296. 4 pp.

———. 1978. *Duration of deer forage benefits after clearcut logging of subalpine forests in Colorado.* USDA Forest Service Research Note RM-356. 4 pp.

Regelin, W. L.; Wallmo, O. C.; Nagy, J., and Dietz, D. R. 1974. Effect of logging on forage values for deer in Colorado. *J. For.* 72:282–85.

Reichel, J. D. 1976. Coyote-prey relationships on the National Bison Range. M.S. thesis, University of Montana, Missoula. 94 pp.

Reiger, F. J., ed. 1972. *The passing of the great west: Selected papers of George Bird Grinnell.* New York: Winchester. 182 pp.

Reppert, J. N.; Hughes, R. H.; and Duncan, D. A. 1963. Herbage yield and its correlation with other plant measurements. In *Range research methods: A symposium,* pp. 15–21. USDA Miscellaneous Publication no. 940. 172 pp.

Řerábek, J., and Bubenik, A. 1963. *The metabolism of phosphorus and iodine in deer.* Translation Series AEC-tr-5631. U.S. Atomic Energy Commission, Division of Technical Information. 51 pp.

Reynolds, H. G. 1962. *Effect of logging on understory vegetation and deer use in a ponderosa pine forest of Arizona.* USDA Forest Service, Rocky Mountain Forest and Range Experiment Station Research Note 80. 7 pp.

———. 1966*a. Use of a ponderosa pine forest in Arizona by deer, elk, and cattle.* USDA Forest Service Research Note RM-63. 7 pp.

———. 1966*b. Slash cleanup in a ponderosa pine forest affects use by deer and cattle.* USDA Forest Service Research Note RM-64. 4 pp.

———. 1966*c. Use of openings in spruce-fir forests of Arizona by elk, deer, and cattle.* USDA Forest Service Research Note RM-66. 4 pp.

———. 1967. Chemical constituents and deer use of some crown sprouts in Arizona chaparral. *J. For.* 65:905–8.

———. 1969*a.* Improvement of deer habitat on southwestern forest lands. 67:803–5.

———. 1969*b.* Aspen grove use by deer, elk, and cattle in southwestern coniferous forests. USDA Forest Service Research Note RM-138. 4 pp.

Reynolds, H. G.; Clary, W. P.; and Ffolliott, P. 1970. Gambel oak for southwestern wildlife. *J. For.* 68:545–47.

Reynolds, H. G., and Sampson, A. W. 1943. Chaparral crown sprouts as browse for deer. *J. Wildl. Manage.* 7:119–23.

Reynolds, T. A. 1960. *The mule deer.* Publication no. 60–4. Salt Lake City: Utah State Department of Fish and Game. 32 pp.

Rice, R. W.; Nagy, J. G.; and Peden, D. G. 1971. Functional interaction of large herbivores on grasslands. In *Preliminary analysis of structure and function in grasslands,* ed. N. R. French, pp. 241–65. Range Sci-

ence Department, Science Series no. 10. Fort Collins: Colorado State University. 385 pp.

Richard, S. H.; Schipper, I. A.; Eveleth, D. F.; and Shumard, R. F. and 1956. Mucosal disease of deer. *Vet. Med.* 50:431–34.

Richardson, A. H., and Petersen, L. E. 1974. *History and management of South Dakota deer.* Bulletin no. 5. Pierre: South Dakota Department Game, Fish and Parks. 113 pp.

Richens, V. B. 1967. Characteristics of mule deer herds and their range in northeastern Utah. *J. Wildl. Manage.* 31:651–66.

Rickman, G. 1975. Mule deer in the north. *New Mexico Wildl.* 20(2):27–29.

Riney, T. 1951. Standard terminology for deer teeth. *J. Wildl. Manage.* 15:99–101.

———. 1955. Evaluating condition of free-ranging red deer (*Cervus elaphus*), with special reference to New Zealand. *New Zeal. J. Sci. and Technol.* 36 (section B):429–63.

Riordan, L. E. 1948. The sexing of deer and elk by airplane in Colorado. *Trans. N. Amer. Wildl. Conf.* 13:409–28.

Riskind, D. H. 1976. *Plant communities of Palo Duro Canyon State Park.* Austin: Research Management Section, Texas Parks and Wildlife Department. 2 pp.

Rittenhouse, L. R., and Sneva, F. A. 1977. A technique for estimating big sagebrush production. *J. Range Manage.* 30:68–70.

Robbins, C. T. 1973. The biological basis for the determination of carrying capacity. Ph.D. thesis, Cornell University, Ithaca, N.Y. 239 pp.

Robbins, C. T., and Moen, A. N. 1975. Uterine composition and growth in pregnant white-tailed deer. *J. Wildl. Manage.* 39:684–91.

Robbins, C. T.; Moen, A. N., and Rein, J. T. 1974. Body composition of white-tailed deer. *J. Anim. Sci.* 38:871–76.

Robel, R. J.; Briggs, J. N.; Dayton, A. D., and Hulbert, L. C. 1970. Relationships between visual obstruction measurements and weight of grassland vegetation. *J. Range Manage.* 23:295–97.

Roberts, H. H., and Lancaster, J. L., Jr. 1963. Determining susceptibility of white-tailed deer to anaplasmosis. *Arkansas Farm Res.* 12(1):12.

Roberts, R. F. 1977. Big game guzzlers. *Rangeman's J.* 4:80–82.

Robinette, W. L. 1956. Productivity: The annual crop of mule deer. In *The deer of North America,* ed. W. P. Taylor, pp. 415–29. Harrisburg, Pa.: Stackpole. 668 pp.

———. 1966. Mule deer home range and dispersal in Utah. *J. Wildl. Manage.* 30:335–49.

Robinette, W. L.; Baer, C. H.; Pillmore, R. E.; and Knittle, C. E. 1973. Effects of nutritional change on captive mule deer. *J. Wildl. Manage.* 37:312–26.

Robinette, W. L.; Ferguson, R. B.; and Gashwiler, J. S. 1958. Problems involved in the use of deer pellet group counts. *Trans. N. Amer. Wildl. Conf.*

23:411–25.

Robinette, W. L., and Gashwiler, J. S. 1950. Breeding season, productivity, and fawning period of the mule deer in Utah. *J. Wildl. Manage.* 14:457–69.

———. 1955. Antlerless mule deer bucks. *J. Mammal.* 36:202–5.

Robinette, W. L.; Gashwiler, J. S.; Jones, D. A.; and Crane, H. S. 1955. Fertility of mule deer in Utah. *J. Wildl. Manage.* 19:115–36.

Robinette, W. L.; Gashwiler, J. S.; Low, J. B.; and Jones, D. A. 1957a. Differential mortality by sex and age among mule deer. *J. Wildl. Manage.* 21:1–16.

Robinette, W. L.; Gashwiler, J. S.; and Morris, O. W. 1959. Food habits of the cougar in Utah and Nevada. *J. Wildl. Manage.* 23:261–73.

Robinette, W. L.; Hancock, N. V.; and Jones, D. A. 1977. *The Oak Creek mule deer herd in Utah.* Resource Publication 77–15. Salt Lake City: Utah Division of Wildlife. 148 pp.

Robinette, W. L., and Jensen, W. 1950. A simplified method for determining the age of mule deer. Information Bulletin 1. Salt Lake City: Utah State Department of Fish and Game. 5 pp.

Robinette, W. L., and Jones, D. A. 1959. Antler anomalies of mule deer. *J. Mammal.* 40:96–108.

Robinette, W. L.; Jones, D. A.; Rogers, G.; and Gashwiler, J. S. 1957b. Notes on tooth development and wear for Rocky Mountain mule deer. *J. Wildl. Manage.* 21:134–53.

Robinette, W. L.; Julander, O.; Gashwiler, J. S.; and Smith, J. G. 1952. Winter mortality of mule deer in Utah in relation to range condition. *J. Wildl. Manage.* 26:289–99.

Robinette, W. L.; Loveless, C. M.; and Jones, D. A. 1974. Field tests of strip census methods. *J. Wildl. Manage.* 38:81–96.

Robinette, W. L., and Olsen, O. A. 1944. Studies of the productivity of mule deer in central Utah. *Trans. N. Amer. Wildl. Conf.* 9:156–61.

Robinson, D. J. 1958. Forestry and wildlife relationships on Vancouver Island. *For. Chron.* 34:31–36.

Robinson, P. F. 1966. Organ:body weight relationships in the white-tailed deer, *Odocoileus virginianus*. *Chesapeake Sci.* 7:217–18.

Robinson, R. M., and Thomas, J. W. 1966. Comparative bioassay of pituitary function in normal and hypogonadal white-tailed deer. *Amer. J. Vet. Res.* 27:375–80.

Robinson, R. M.; Thomas, J. W.; and Marburger, R. G. 1965. The reproductive cycle of male white-tailed deer in central Texas. *J. Wildl. Manage.* 29:53–59.

Robinson, W. B. 1943. The "humane coyote-getter" vs. the steel trap in control of predatory animals. *J. Wildl. Manage.* 7:179–89.

———. 1948. Thallium and compound 1080 impregnated stations in coyote control. *J. Wildl. Manage.* 12:279–95.

———. 1952. Some observations on coyote predation in Yellowstone National Park. *J. Mammal.* 33:470–76.

Robinson, W. L. 1960. Test of shelter requirements of penned white-tailed deer. *J. Wildl. Manage.* 24:364–71.

Rochelle, J. A.; Gauditz, I.; Oita, K.; and Oh, J. H. K. 1974. New developments in big-game repellents. In *Proceedings: Wildlife and forest management in the Pacific Northwest symposium, 1973,* pp. 103–12. Corvallis: Oregon State University. 236 pp.

Roe, F. G. 1939. Buffalo as a possible influence in the development of prairie lands. *Can. Hist. Rev.* 20:275–87.

Rogers, G. E. 1974. Effects of oil shale development on wildlife. *Proc. West. Assoc. Game and Fish Commissioners* 54:165–79.

———. 1976. Recent changes in Colorado's mule deer population and management. *Proc. West. Assoc. Game and Fish Commissioners* 56:379–90.

Rohwer, G. L. 1970. Blood composition of wintering Nevada mule deer. (*Odocoileus hemionus hemionus*). M.S. thesis, University of Nevada, Reno. 56 pp.

Rohwer, G. L.; Lesperance, A. L.; and Papez, N. J. 1971. Plasma mineral indexes of northeast Nevada mule deer. *J. Anim. Sci.* 33:244 (abstract).

Romano, M. N. 1947. *Some parasites of Oregon wildlife.* Technical Bulletin 17. Corvallis: Oregon State College.

Romano, M. N.; Brunetti, O. A.; Schwake, C. W.; and Rosen, M. N. 1974. Probable transmission of *Echinococcus granulosus* between deer and coyotes in California. *J. Wildl. Dis.* 10:225–28.

Romano, M. N.; Simms, B. T.; and Muth, O. H. 1934. Some diseases of Oregon fish and game and identification of parts of game animals. *Oregon Agric. Exp. Sta. Bull.* 322:2–32.

Romer, A. S. 1966. *Vertebrate paleontology.* 3d ed. Chicago: University of Chicago Press. 468 pp.

Rommel, M.; Heydorn, A. O.; and Gruber, F. 1972. Beitrage zum lebenszyklus der sarkosporidien. I. Die sporozyste van *S. tenelle* in den fazes der katze. *Berl. Much. Tierarztzl. Wochenschr.* 85:101–5.

Ronco, F. 1970. *Shading and other factors affect survival of planted Engelmann spruce seedlings in central Rocky Mountains.* USDA Forest Service Research Note RM-163. 7 pp.

Rosen, M. N. 1951. A noticeable absence of bladder worms in Catalina deer. *Calif. Fish and Game* 37:217.

———. 1952. Apparent personal communication cited in *A survey of California deer herds,* ed. W. Longhurst, A. S. Leopold, and R. F. Dasmann, p. 11. Bulletin 6. Sacramento: California Department of Fish and Game. 136 pp.

———. 1970 Pasteurellosis. In *Infectious diseases of wild mammals, ed.* J. W. Davis, L. H. Karstad, and D. O. Trainer, pp. 214–23. Ames: Iowa State University Press. 421 pp.

Rosen, M. N., and Bischoff, A. I. 1952. The relation of hematology to condition in California deer. *Trans. N. Amer. Wildl. Conf.* 17:482–96.

Rosen, M. N.; Brunetti, O. A.; Bischoff, A. I.; and Azevedo, J. A., Jr. 1951. An epizootic of foot rot in California deer. *Trans. N. Amer. Wildl. Conf.*

16:164–77.

Rosen, M. N., and Holden, F. F. 1961. Multiple purulent abscess *(Corynebacterium pyogenes)* of deer. *Calif. Fish and Game* 47: 293–300.

Roseberry, J. L., and Klimstra, W. D. 1974. Differential vulnerability during a controlled deer harvest. *J. Wildl. Manage.* 38(3):499–507.

Ross, F. 1963. Deer vs. auto. *Outdoor California* 24(7–8):8–9.

Ross, L. A.; Blood, D. M.; and Nobe, K. C. 1975. *A survey of sportsmen expenditures for hunting and fishing in Colorado, 1973.* Report no. NRE-20. Fort Collins: Colorado State University, Department of Economics. 102 pp.

Rost, G. R. 1975. Response of deer and elk to roads. M.S. thesis, Colorado State University, Fort Collins. 51 pp.

Roughton, R. D. 1962. A review of literature on dendrochronology and age determination of woody plants. Technical Bulletin no. 15. Denver: Colorado Department of Game and Fish. 99 pp.

Rowe, J. S. 1972. *Forest regions of Canada.* Department of the Environment, Canadian Forest Service Publication no. 1300. Ottawa: Information Canada. 172 pp.

Rowell, C. M. 1970. The Chihuahuan Desert in Texas. Unpublished. On file at Angelo State University, San Angelo, Tex. 22 pp.

Roy, D. F. 1960. Deer browsing and Douglas-fir seedling growth in northwestern California. *J. For.* 58:518–22.

Russ, W. B. 1978. *Vegetation reconnaissance.* Performance Report, P-R Project W-109-R-1, Job no. 36. Austin: Texas Parks and Wildlife Department. 7 pp.

Russo, J. P. 1964. *The Kaibab North deer herd: Its history, problems and management.* Wildlife Bulletin no. 7. Phoenix: Arizona Game and Fish Department. 195 pp.

Ryder, M. L. 1977. Seasonal coat changes in grazing red deer *(Cervus elaphus). J. Zool.* (London) 181:137–43.

Ryder, M. L., and Kay, R. N. B. 1973. Structure of and seasonal change in the coat of red deer *(Cervus elaphus). J. Zool.* (London) 170:69–77.

Ryel, L. A. 1963. The occurrence of certain anomalies in Michigan white-tailed deer. *J. Mammal.* 44:70–98.

Sacher, G. 1970. Allometric and factorial analysis of metabolic and constitutional variables in mammals: Relation to longevity. *Amer. Zool.* 10:308 (abstract).

Salwasser, H. 1976. Man, deer and time on the Devil's Garden. *Proc. West. Assoc. Game and Fish Commissioners* 56:295–318.

Salwin, H.; Block, I. K.; and Mitchell, J. H., Jr. 1955. Rapid determination of fat in meat products. *J. Agric. Food Chem.* 3:588–93.

Sampson, A. W. 1944. *Plant succession on burned chaparral lands in northern California.* Bulletin 685. Berkeley: University of California Agricultural Experiment Station. 143 pp.

Sampson, A. W., and Jespersen, B. S. 1963. *California range brushlands and browse plants.* University of California Agricultural Experimentation Station. Berkeley: Manual 33. 162 pp.

Samuelson, J. 1975. *Deer population studies: 1975 mule deer census.* Annual Report, P-R Project W-67-R-15, Job C-I-12. Bismarck: North Dakota Game and Fish Department. 10 pp.

Sanford, R. C. 1970. Skunkbush *(Rhus trilobata* Nutt.) in the North Dakota Badlands: Ecology, phytosociology, browse production and utilization. Ph.D. thesis, North Dakota State University, Fargo. 165 pp.

Sauer, C. O. 1950. Grassland climax, fire and man. *J. Range Manage.* 3:16–21.

Sauer, P. R. 1971. Tooth sectioning versus tooth wear for assigning age to white-tailed deer. *Proc. NE Fish and Wildl. Conf.* 28:9–20.

Schad, G. A., and Raught, R. A. 1958. *Thelazia californiensis* from a mule deer, *Odocoileus hemionus crooki* (Mearns, 1879), in New Mexico. *J. Parasit.* 44:483.

Schaller, G. B. 1967. *The deer and the tiger.* Chicago: University of Chicago Press. 370 pp.

Schalm, O. W. 1965. *Veterinary hematology.* 2d ed. Philadelphia: Lea and Febiger. 664 pp.

Schladweiler, P. 1974. *Ecology of Shiras moose in Montana.* Final Report, P-R Projects W-98-R and W-120-R. Helena: Montana Department of Fish and Game. 100 pp.

———. 1976. *Effects of coyote predation of big game populations in Montana.* Report, P-R Project W-120-R-7, Study NG-47.1, 1 July 1975–30 June 1976. Helena: Montana Department of Fish and Game. 26 pp.

Schneegas, E. R., and Bumstead, R. S. 1977. Decline of western mule deer populations: Probable cause, tentative solution. *Proc. West. Assoc. Game and Fish Commissioners* 57:218–32.

Schoen, J. W., and Wallmo, O. C. 1979. Timber management and deer in southeast Alaska: Current problems and research direction. In *Proceedings: Sitka black-tailed deer conference* (Juneau, Alaska, 22–24 February 1978), ed. O. C. Wallmo and J. W. Schoen, pp. 69–85. USDA Forest Service, Region 10. 231 pp.

Schreckhise, R. G., and Whicker, F. W. 1976. A model for predicting strontium-90 levels in mule deer. In *Radioecology and energy resources,* ed. C. E. Cushing, Jr.; pp. 148–56. Ecology Society of America, Special Publication no. 1. Stroudsburg, Pa.: Dowden, Hutchinson and Ross. 401 pp.

Schubert, G. H.; Heidmann, L. J.; and Larson, M. 1970. *Artificial reforestation practices for the Southwest.* USDA Forest Service Agricultural Handbook 370. 25 pp.

Schultz, V. 1964. Sampling white-tailed deer antlers for strontium-90. *J. Wildl. Manage.* 28:45–49.

———. 1965. Comparison of strontium-90 levels between antler and mandible of white-tailed deer. *J. Wildl. Manage.* 29:33–38.

Schultz, V., and Flyger, V. 1965. Relationship of sex and age to strontium-90 accumulation in white-tailed deer mandibles. *J. Wildl. Manage.* 29:39–43.

Schultz, V., and Longhurst, W. M. 1963. Accumulation of strontium-90 in yearling Columbian black-tailed deer, 1950–1960. In *Radioecology,* ed. V. Schultz and A. W. Klement, Jr., pp. 73–76. New York: Reinhold.

746 pp.

Schwartz, C. C.; Nagy, J. G.; and Regelin, W. L. 1979*a*. Effects of volatile oils of juniper on mule deer. I. Volatile oil yield, terpenoid concentration and antimicrobial effects *in vitro*. *J. Wildl. Manage.* In press.

Schwartz, C. C.; Nagy, J. G.; and Streeter, C. L. 1973. Pesticide effect on rumen microbial function. *J. Anim. Sci.* 37:821–26.

Schwartz, C. C.; Regelin, W. L.; and Nagy, J. G. 1979*b*. Effects of volatile oils of juniper on mule deer. II. Deer preference for juniper forage and volatile oil-treated foods. *J. Wildl. Manage.* In press.

Scott, M. D., and Causey, K. 1973. Ecology of feral dogs in Alabama. *J. Wildl. Manage.* 37:253–65.

Scott, W. B. 1937. *A history of land mammals in the western hemisphere.* Rev. ed. New York: Hafner.

Scotto, K. C.; Bohman, V. R.; and Lesperance, A. L. 1971. Effect of oral potassium and sodium chloride on plasma composition of cattle: A grass tetany related study. *J. Anim. Sci.* 32:354–58.

Seal, U. S., and Erickson, A. W. 1969. Hematology, blood chemistry and protein polymorphisms in the white-tailed deer *(Odocoileus virginianus)*. *Comp. Biochem. Physiol.* 30:695–715.

Seal, U. S.; Ozoga, J. J.; Erickson, A. W.; and Verme, L. J. 1972*a*. Effects of immobilization on blood analyses of white-tailed deer. *J. Wildl. Manage.* 36:1034–40.

Seal, U. S.; Verme, L. J.; Ozoga, J. J.; and Erickson, A. W. 1972*b*. Nutritional effects on thyroid activity and blood of white-tailed deer. *J. Wildl. Manage.* 36:1041–52.

Sears, H. S. 1955. Certain aspects of the reproductive physiology of the female mule deer. M.S. thesis, Montana State University, Missoula. 82 pp.

Sears, H. S., and Browman, L. G. 1955. Quadruplets in mule deer. *Anat. Rec.* 122:335–40.

Seghetti, L., and McKenney, F. D. 1941. Caseous lymphadenitis of deer *(Odocoileus hemionus)* in Washington. *J. Amer. Vet. Med. Assoc.* 98:129–31.

Seidensticker, J. C.; Hornocker, M. G.; Wiles, W. B.; and Messick, J. P. 1973. Mountain lion social organization in the Idaho primitive area. *Wildl. Monogr.* no. 35. 60 pp.

Senger, C. M., and Capelle, K. J. 1959. Louse flies from mule and white-tailed deer in western Montana. *J. Parasit.* 45:sec 2:32 (abstract).

Seton, E. T. 1929. *Lives of game animals.* Vol. 3, part 2. New York: Doubleday, Doran. 368 pp.

Severinghaus, C. W. 1947. Relationships of winter weather to winter mortality and population levels among deer in the Adirondack region of New York. *Trans. N. Amer. Wildl. Conf.* 12:212–23.

Severinghaus, C. W., and Cheatum, E. L. 1956. Life and times of the white-tailed deer. In *The deer of North America,* ed. W. P. Taylor, pp. 57–186. Harrisburg, Pa.: Stackpole. 668 pp.

Severinghaus, C. W.; Maguire, H. F.; Cookingham, R. A.; and Tanck, J. E. 1950. Variations by age class in the antler beam diameters of white-tailed deer related to range conditions. *Trans. N. Amer. Wildl. Conf.*

15:551–70.

Severinghaus, C. W., and Tullar, B. F. 1975. Wintering deer versus snowmobiles. *New York Conservationist* 29(6):31.

Severson, K.; May, M.; and Hepworth, W. 1968. *Food preferences, carrying capacities, and forage competition between antelope and domestic sheep in Wyoming's Red Desert.* University of Wyoming Agricultural Experiment Station Science Monograph 10. 51 pp.

Severson, K. E., and Carter, A. V. 1978. Movements and habitat use by mule deer in the Northern Great Plains, South Dakota. In *Proceedings: First international rangelands congress,* ed. D. N. Hyder, pp. 466–68. Denver: Society for Range Management. 742 pp.

Shackleton, D. M. 1973. Population quality and bighorn sheep *(Ovis canadensis canadensis* Shaw). Ph.D. thesis, University of Calgary, Alberta. 227 pp.

Shank, C. C. 1972. Some aspects of social behaviour in a population of feral goats *(Capra hircus* L.). *Z. Tierpsychol.* 30:488–528.

Shaw, H. 1965. Investigation of factors influencing deer populations. In *Wildlife research in Arizona 1964,* pp. 125–45. Phoenix: Arizona Game and Fish Department. 251 pp.

Shaw, H. G. 1977. Impact of mountain lion *(Felis concolor azteca)* on mule deer and cattle in northwestern Arizona. In *Proceedings of the 1975 predator symposium,* ed. R. L. Phillips and C. Jonkel, pp. 17–32. Missoula: Montana Forest and Conservation Experiment Station, University of Montana. 268 pp.

Shaw, J. N. 1947. *Some parasites of Oregon wildlife.* Technical Bulletin 11, Corvallis: Oregon State College. 16 pp.

Shaw, J. N.; Simms, B. T.; and Muth, O. H. 1934. Some diseases of Oregon fish and game and identification of parts of game animals. *Oregon Agr. Exp. Sta. Bull.* 322:3–23.

Shearer, R. L., and Schmidt, W. C. 1970. *Natural regeneration in ponderosa pine forests of western Montana.* USDA Forest Service Research Paper INT-86. 19 pp.

Sheets, T. J., and Harris, C. I. 1965. Herbicide residues in soils and their phytotoxicities to crops grown in rotations. In *Residue reviews 11,* ed. F. A. Gunther, pp. 119–40. New York: Springer-Verlag. 164 pp.

Shepherd, H. R. 1971. *Effects of clipping key browse species in southwestern Colorado.* Technical Publication no. 28. Denver: Colorado Division of Game, Fish and Parks. 104 pp.

Sheppard, D. H. 1960. The ecology of the mule deer of the Sheep River region. M.S. thesis, University of Alberta, Edmonton. 123 pp.

Shields, T. 1968. The use and misuse of snowmobiles. *Colo. Outdoors* 17(1):26–28.

Shillinger, J. E. 1937. Disease relationship of domestic stock and wildlife. *Trans. N. Amer. Wildl. Conf.* 2:298–302.

Shock, N. 1962. The physiology of aging. *Sci. Amer.* 206:100–110.

Shoop, M. C., and McIlvain, E. H. 1963. The micro-unit forage inventory method. *J. Range Manage.*

16:172–79.

Shope, R. E.; MacNamara, L. G.; and Mangold, R. 1955. Report on the deer mortality; Epizootic hemorrhagic disease of deer. *New Jersey Outdoors* 6:15–21.

Short, C. 1970. Morphological development and aging of mule and white-tailed deer fetuses. *J. Wildl. Manage.* 34:383–88.

Short, H. L. 1964. Postnatal stomach development of white-tailed deer. *J. Wildl. Manage.* 28:445–58.

———. 1972. Ecological framework for deer management. *J. For.* 70:200–203.

———. 1977. Food habits of mule deer in a semi-desert grass-shrub habitat. *J. Range Manage.* 30:206–9.

———. 1979. Deer in Arizona and New Mexico: their ecology and a theory explaining recent population decreases. USDA Forest Service, Rocky Mountain Forest and Range Experiment Station Gen. Tech. Rept. RM-70. 25 pp.

Short, H. L.; Blair, R. M.; and Epps, E. A., Jr. 1975. *Composition and digestibility of deer browse in southern forests.* USDA Forest Service Research Paper SO-111. 10 pp.

Short, H. L.; Blair, R. M.; and Segelquist, C. A. 1974. Fiber composition and forage digestibility by small ruminants. *J. Wildl. Manage.* 38:197–209.

Short, H. L., and Epps, E. A., Jr. 1976. Nutrient quality and digestibility of seeds and fruits from southern forests. *J. Wildl. Manage.* 40:283–89.

Short, H. L.; Evans, W.; and Boeker, E. L. 1977. The use of natural and modified pinyon pine–juniper woodlands by deer and elk. *J. Wildl. Manage.* 41:543–59.

Short, H. L.; Medin, D. E.; and Anderson, A. E. 1965. Ruminoreticular characteristics of mule deer. *J. Mammal.* 46:196–99.

———. 1966. Seasonal variations in volatile fatty acids in the rumen of mule deer. *J. Wildl. Manage.* 30:466–70.

Short, H. L., and Reagor, J. C. 1970. Cell wall digestibility affects forage value of woody twigs. *J. Wildl. Manage.* 34:964–67.

Shreve, F. 1942. The desert vegetation of North America. *Bot. Rev.* 8:195–246.

Silberberg, M., and Silberberg, R. 1971. Steroid hormones and bone. In *The biochemistry and physiology of bone,* 2d ed., ed. G. Bourne, 3:401–79. New York: Academic Press. 584 pp.

Silver, H. 1961. Deer milk compared with substitute milk for fawns. *J. Wildl. Manage.* 25:66–70.

Silver, H., and Colovos, N. F. 1957. *Nutritive evaluation of some forage rations of deer.* Technical Circular no. 15. Concord: New Hampshire Fish and Game Department, 56 pp.

Silver, H.; Holter, J. B.; and Hayes, H. H. 1969. Fasting metabolism of white-tailed deer. *J. Wildl. Manage.* 33:490–98.

Silver, H.; Holter, J. B.; Colovos, N. F.; and Hayes, H. H. 1971. Effect of falling temperatures on heat production in fasting white-tailed deer. *J. Wildl. Manage.* 35:37–46.

Silver, H.; White, D. L.; and Laramie, H. A. 1968. The white-tailed deer of New Hampshire. Report 10. Concord: New Hampshire Fish and Game Survey. 256 pp.

Simpson, G. G.; Roe, A.; and Lewontin, R. C. 1960. *Quantitative zoology.* Rev. ed. New York: Harcourt, Brace. 440 pp.

Skinner, M. P. 1921. Horn shedding in Yellowstone Park. *J. Mammal.* 2:172–73.

Skovlin, J. M.; Edgerton, P. J.; and Harris, R. W. 1968. The influence of cattle management on deer and elk. *Trans. N. Amer. Wildl. and Natur. Resour. Conf.* 33:169–81.

Skutt, H. R.; Bock, F. M., IV; Haugstad, P., Holter, J. B.; Hayes, H. H.; and Silver, H. 1973. Low-power implantable transmitters for telemetry of heart rate and temperature from white-tailed deer. *J. Wildl. Manage.* 37:413–17.

Slaughter, C. W. 1966. *Snow albedo modification: A review of literature.* Technical Report 217. Hanover, New Hampshire: U.S. Army Cold Regions Research and Engineering Laboratory. 25 pp.

Smith, A. D. 1949. Effects of mule deer and livestock upon a foothill range in northern Utah. *J. Wildl. Manage.* 13:421–23.

———. 1959. Adequacy of some important browse species in overwintering mule deer. *J. Range Manage.* 12:8–13.

Smith, A. D., and Doell, D. E. 1968. *Guides to allocating forage between cattle and big game on big game winter ranges.* Publication no. 68-11, Salt Lake City: Utah Division of Fish and Game. 32 pp.

Smith, A. D., and Urness, P. J. 1962. Analyses of the twig-length method of determining utilization of browse. Bulletin 62-9. Salt Lake City: Utah Division of Fish and Game. 34 pp.

Smith, C. F., and Owensby, C. E. 1972. Effects of fire on True Prairie Grasslands. *Proc. Tall Timbers Fire Ecol. Conf.* 12:9–22.

Smith, I. 1969. Last winter hard on deer. *Brit. Col. Wildl. Rev.* 5(3):4–7.

Smith, J. G., and Julander, O. 1953. Deer and sheep competition in Utah. *J. Wildl. Manage.* 17:101–12.

Smith, L. D. 1961. The effects of hunting and seral succession upon Vancouver Island black-tailed deer. M.S. thesis, University of British Columbia, Vancouver. 140 pp.

Smith, M. A.; Malachek, J. C.; and Fulgham, K. O. 1979. Forage selection by mule deer on winter range grazed by sheep in spring. *J. Range Manage.* 32:40–45.

Smith, R. H. 1968. A comparison of several sites of circular plots for estimating deer pellet-group density. *J. Wildl. Manage.* 32:585–91.

———. 1976a. *Hematology of deer.* Final Report, P-R Project W-75-R-20, WP3, J 4. Phoenix: Arizona Game and Fish Department. 9 pp.

———. 1976b. Recent changes in Arizona mule deer populations and management. *Proc. West. Assoc. Game and Fish Commissioners* 56:367–69.

Smith, R. H., and LeCount, A. 1976. *Factors affecting survival of mule deer fawns.* Final Report, P-R Project W-78-R, WP2, J 4. Phoenix: Arizona Game and Fish Department. 15 pp.

———. 1979. Some factors affecting survival of mule deer fawns. *J. Wildl. Manage.* 43:657–65.

Smith, R. H.; McMichael, T. J.; and Shaw, H. G. 1969. Decline of a desert deer population. Abstract 3, *Wildlife Digest*. Phoenix: Arizona Game and Fish Department. 8 pp.

Sneva, F. A., and Hyder, D. N. 1966. Control of big sagebrush associated with bitterbrush in ponderosa pine. *J. For.* 64:677–80.

Snyder, W. A. 1959. *Deer harvest information.* Job Completion Report, P-R Project W-75-R-6, WP 14, J 3. Santa Fe: New Mexico Game and Fish Department. 14 pp.

———. 1961. A chemical analysis of thirteen major deer forage plants from the Guadalupe Mountains of New Mexico and their adequacy for maintaining deer. M.S. thesis, New Mexico State University, Las Cruces. 58 pp.

———. 1976. Changes in New Mexico's mule deer population and management. *Proc. West. Assoc. Game and Fish Commissioners* 56:404–7.

Song, S. K. 1970. Influence of deer horn on erythropoietin activity and radioactive iron uptake in rabbits. *J. Catholic Med. Coll.* 18:51–60.

Soper, J. D. 1964. *The mammals of Alberta.* Edmonton, Alberta: Hamly Press. 402 pp.

Spalding, D. J. 1968. *The Boundary deer herd.* Wildlife Management Publication no. 2. Victoria: Fish and Wildlife Branch, British Columbia Department of Recreation and Conservation. 54 pp.

Sparrowe, R. D., and Springer, P. F. 1970. Seasonal activity patterns of white-tailed deer in eastern South Dakota. *J. Wildl. Manage.* 34:420–31.

Spearman, C. 1904. The proof and measurement of associations between two things. *Amer. J. Psych.* 15:72–101, 102–3.

Special Committee of the Governor's Oil Shale Advisory Committee. 1971. *Report on the economics of environmental protection for a federal oil shale leasing program.* Denver: Director of Natural Resources, State of Colorado. 204 pp.

Spencer, D. A. 1958. Prevention of mammal damage in forest management. *Proc. Soc. Amer. Foresters Ann. Meet.* 1958:183–85.

Spencer, G. J. 1939. Ectoparasites of deer in British Columbia. *Ent. Soc. Brit. Col.* 35:15–19.

Splitter, E. J.; Irviehaus, M. J.; and Castron, E. R. 1955. Anaplasmosis in sheep in the United States. *J. Amer. Vet. Med. Assoc.* 127:244.

Spraker, T. L., and Hibler, C. P. In press. Verminous pneumonia in bighorn sheep.

Squillace, A. E., and Silen, R. R. 1962. *Racial variation in ponderosa pine.* Forest Science Monograph 2. 27 pp.

Stahelin, R. 1941. *Thirty-five years of planting on the National Forests of Colorado.* USDA Forest Service, Rocky Mountain Forest and Range Experiment Station. 82 pp.

Stair, E. L.; Robinson, R. M.; and Jones, L. P. 1968. Spontaneous bluetongue in Texas white-tailed deer. *Path. Vet.* 5:164.

Stapley, H. D. 1971. *Deer illegal kill and wounding loss.* Final Report, P-R Project no. W-65-R-18, J A-8. Salt Lake City: Utah Division of Wildlife Resources. 7 pp.

Statistics Canada. 1973. *Canada yearbook 1973.* Ottawa: Information Canada. 951 pp.

Stein, C. D. 1955. Anthrax. In *Diseases transmitted from animals to man,* 4th ed., ed. T. G. Hull. Springfield, Ill.: Charles C. Thomas.

Steinhoff, H. 1957. The buck with 2 points. *Colo. Outdoors* 6(5):28–29.

Stelfox, J. G. 1962. Liver, lungs and larvae/parasites and diseases in moose, deer and elk in Alberta. *Land-Forest-Wildlife* 5:5–12.

Stelfox, J. G.; Lynch, G. M.; and McGillis, J. R. 1976. Effects of clearcut logging on wild ungulates in the central Albertan foothills. *For. Chron.* 52:65–70.

Stephens, H. A. 1973. Woody plants of the north central plains. Lawrence: University of Kansas Press. 530 pp.

Stevens, D. S. 1972. Thermal energy exchange and the maintenance of homeothermy in white-tailed deer. Ph.D. thesis, Cornell University, Ithaca, N.Y. 231 pp.

Stewart, G. 1936. History of range use. In *The western range,* pp. 119–33. U.S. Senate Doc. no. 199, 74th Cong., 2d sess. Washington, D.C.: GPO. 620 pp.

Stewart, M. A. 1940. Ovine thelaziasis. *J. Amer. Vet. Med. Assoc.* 96:486–89.

Stewart, O. C. 1956. Fire as the first great force employed by man. In *Man's role in changing the face of the earth,* ed. W. L. Thomas, pp. 115–29. Chicago: University of Chicago Press. 1,193 pp.

Stewart, R. R.; MacLennan, R. R.; and Kinnear, J. D. 1977. *The relationship of plant phenology to moose.* Technical Bulletin no. 3. Regina: Saskatchewan Department of Tourism and Renewable Resources. 20 pp.

Stoddart, L. A., and Smith, A. D. 1943. *Range management.* New York: McGraw-Hill. 433 pp.

Stonehouse, B. 1968. Thermoregulatory function of growing antlers. *Nature* 218:870–72.

Strahler, A. N. 1966. *Introduction to physical geography.* New York: John Wiley. 455 pp.

Strandgaard, H. 1967. Reliability of the Peterson method tested on a roe-deer population. *J. Wildl. Manage.* 31:643–51.

Strickland, D. 1975. *Mule deer in the Medicine Bow mountains, southeastern Wyoming.* Wildlife Technical Report no. 2. Cheyenne: Wyoming Game and Fish Department. 103 pp.

Strickland, M. D., and Diem, K. 1975. The impact of snow on mule deer. In *The Medicine Bow ecology project,* final report, ed. D. H. Knight, pp. 135–74. Laramie: University of Wyoming. 397 pp.

Sturges, D. C. 1977. *Snow accumulation and melt in sprayed and undisturbed big sagebrush vegetation.* USDA Forest Service Research Note RM-348. 6 pp.

Sturges, D. L. 1975. *Hydrologic relations on undisturbed and converted big sagebrush lands: The status of our knowledge.* USDA Forest Service Research Paper RM-140. 23 pp.

Sturgis, H. 1977. Twenty years at McDonald Forest. *Ore-*

gon Wildl. 32(7):3–6.

Struth, J. W., and Winward, A. H. 1976. Logging impacts on bitterbrush in the lodgepole pine–pumice region of central Oregon. *J. Range Manage.* 29:453–56.

Suring, L. H., and Vohs, P. H., Jr. 1979. Habitat use by Columbian white-tailed deer. *J. Wildl. Manage.* 43(3):610–19.

Swank, W. G. 1956. Protein and phosphorus content of browse plants as an influence on southwestern deer herd levels. *Trans. N. Amer. Wildl. Conf.* 21:141–58.

———. 1958. *The mule deer in Arizona chaparral and an analysis of other important deer herds: A research and management study.* Wildlife Bulletin no. 3. Phoenix: Arizona Game and Fish Department. 109 pp.

Sweeney, J. R.; Marchinton, R. L.; and Sweeney, J. M. 1971. Responses of radio-monitored white-tailed deer chased by hunting dogs. *J. Wildl. Manage.* 35:707–16.

Taber, R. D. 1953. Studies of black-tailed deer reproduction on three chaparral cover types. *Calif. Fish and Game* 39:177–86.

———. 1956a. Characteristics of the pelvic girdle in relation to sex in black-tailed and white-tailed deer. *Calif. Fish and Game* 42:15–21.

———. 1956b. Deer nutrition and population dynamics in the North Coast range of California. *Trans. N. Amer. Wildl. Conf.* 21:159–72.

———. 1958. Development of the cervid antler as an index to late winter physical condition. *Proc. Mont. Acad. Sci.* 18:27–28.

———. 1961. The black-tailed deer: A review of ecology and management. *La Terre et la Vie* 2:221–45.

———. 1963. Land use and native cervid populations in America north of Mexico. *Proc. Int. Congr. Game Biol.* 6:201–25.

———. 1971. Criteria of sex and age. In *Wildlife management techniques,* ed. R. H. Giles, pp. 325–401. Washington, D.C.: Wildlife Society. 633 pp.

Taber, R. D., and Dasmann, R. F. 1954. A sex difference in mortality in young Columbian black-tailed deer. *J. Wildl. Manage.* 18:309–15.

———. 1957. The dynamics of three natural populations of the deer *Odocoileus hemionus columbianus. Ecology* 38:233–46.

———. 1958. *The black-tailed deer of the chaparral: Its life history and management in the North Coast Range of California.* Game Bulletin 8. Sacramento: California Department of Fish and Game. 163 pp.

Taber, R. D.; White, K. L.; and Smith, N. S. 1959. The annual cycle of condition in the Rattlesnake, Montana, deer. *Proc. Mont. Acad. Sci.* 19:72–79.

Tabler, R. D. 1968. Soil moisture response to spraying big sagebrush with 2, 4-D. *J. Range Manage.* 22:12–15.

———. 1973. Evaporation losses of windblown snow and the potential for recovery. *West. Snow Conf. Proc.* 41:75–79.

Talich, P., and Inman, J. 1968. Covering trees with brush on the Wallowa-Whitman National Forest. In *Proceedings: First reforestation workshop 1968,* pp. 246–51. Portland, Oreg.: USDA Forest Service Region 6. 293 pp.

Tausch, R. J., and Tueller, P. T. 1977. Plant succession following chaining of pinyon-juniper woodlands in eastern Nevada. *J. Range Manage.* 30:44–49.

Taylor, D. O. N.; Thomas, J. W.; and Marburger, R. G. 1964. Abnormal antler growth associated with hypogonadism in white-tailed deer in Texas. *Amer. J. Vet. Res.* 25:179–85.

Taylor, J. C. 1959. A relationship between weight of internal fat, "fill," and the herbage intake of grazing cattle. *Nature* 184:2021–22.

Taylor, W. P., ed. 1956. *The deer of North America.* Harrisburg, Pa.: Stackpole. 668 pp.

Teer, J. G. 1971. Introduction of exotic animals. In *A manual of wildlife conservation,* pp. 90–92. Washington, D.C.: Wildlife Society. 206 pp.

Terrell, T. L., and Spillett, J. J. 1975. Pinyon-juniper conversion: Its impact on mule deer and other wildlife. In *The pinyon-juniper ecosystem symposium, Logan, Utah, May 1975.* pp. 105–18. Logan: Utah State University. 194 pp.

Tester, J. R., and Heezen, K. L. 1965. Deer response to a drive census determined by radio tracking. *Bioscience* 15:100–104.

Tester, J. R., and Marshall, W. H. 1962. Minnesota prairie management techniques and their wildlife implications. *Trans. N. Amer. Wildl. and Natur. Resour. Conf.* 27:267–87.

Thiessen, J. 1976. Recent changes in Idaho mule deer populations and management. *Proc. West. Assoc. Game and Fish Commissioners* 56:391–94.

Thomas, D. C. 1970. The ovary, reproduction, and productivity of female Columbian black-tailed deer. Ph.D. thesis, University of British Columbia, Vancouver. 211 pp.

Thomas, D. C., and Bandy, P. J. 1973. Age determination of wild black-tailed deer from dental annulations. *J. Wildl. Manage.* 37:232–35.

———. 1975. Accuracy of dental-wear age estimates of black-tailed deer. *J. Wildl. Manage.* 39:674–78.

Thomas, D. C., and Cowan, I. McT. 1975. The pattern of reproduction in female Columbian black-tailed deer, *Odocoileus hemionus columbianus. J. Reprod. Fert.* 44:261–72.

Thomas, D. C., and Smith, I. D. 1973. Reproduction in a wild black-tailed deer fawn. *J. Mammal.* 54:302–3.

Thomas, J. W.; Miller, R. J.; Black, H.; Rodiek, J. E.; and Maser, C. 1976. Guidelines for maintaining and enhancing wildlife habitat in forest management in the Blue Mountains of Washington and Oregon. *Trans. N. Amer. Wildl. and Natur. Resour. Conf.* 41:452–76.

Thompson, F. A. 1968. *Deer on highways 1967, supplement.* Santa Fe: New Mexico Department of Game and Fish. 6 pp.

Thompson, P. D., and O'Brien, R. 1970. *Weather.* New York: Time-Life Books. 200 pp.

Thompson, W. W., and Gartner, F. R. 1971. Native forage response to clearing low quality ponderosa pine. *J. Range Manage.* 24:272–77.

Thomson, B. R. 1972. Reindeer disturbance. *Deer* (J. Brit. Deer Soc.) 2:882–83.

Thorne, E. T. 1975. Normal body temperature of pronghorn antelope and mule deer. *J. Mammal.* 56:697–98.

Thorne, E. T.; Morton, J. K.; and Thomas, G. M. 1978. Brucellosis in elk. I. Serologic and bacteriologic survey in Wyoming. *J. Wildl. Dis.* 14:74–81.

Thornton, R. F., and Minson, D. J. 1972. The relationship between voluntary intake and mean apparent retention time in the rumen. *Austr. J. Agric. Res.* 23:871–77.

Tierson, W. C. 1969. Controlling deer use of forest vegetation with electric fences. *J. Wildl. Manage.* 33:922–26.

Timm, R. M., and Connolly, G. E. 1977. How coyotes kill sheep. *Rangeman's J.* 4:106–7.

Tolman, C. D. 1950. Productivity of mule deer in Colorado. *Trans. N. Amer. Wildl. Conf.* 17:482–96.

Topinski, P. 1975. Abnormal antler cycles in deer as a result of stress inducing factors. *Acta Ther.* 20:267–79.

Trainer, C. E. 1975. Direct causes of mortality in mule deer fawns during summer and winter periods on Steens Mountain, Oregon. *Proc. West. Assoc. Game and Fish Commissioners* 55:163–70.

———. N.d. Field records of Steens Mountain mule deer population study. Unpublished. On file at Oregon Department of Fish and Wildlife, Hines.

Trainer, C. E.; Lemos, J. C.; McInnis, M. L.; Castillo, W. J.; and Anglin, R. 1978*a*. *Steens Mountain mule deer population study: Deer reproduction and condition.* Job Progress Report, P-R Project W-70-R-8, Subproject F, Study VI, Job 1. Portland: Oregon Department of Fish and Wildlife. 6 pp.

Trainer, C. E.; McInnis, M. L.; Lemos, J. C.; Castillo, W. J.; and Anglin, R. E. 1978*b*. *Steens Mountain mule deer population study: Fawn survival.* Job Progress Report, P-R Project W-70-R-8, Subproject F, Study VI, Job 2. Portland: Oregon Department of Fish and Wildlife. 11 pp.

Trainer, C. E.; Sheehy, D.; Garner, R.; and Ferry, B. 1976. *Aspects of fawn mortality: Deer reproduction and condition.* Job Progress Report, P-R Project W-70-R-6. Portland: Oregon Department of Fish and Wildlife. 7 pp.

Trainer, D. O. 1961. Diseases of the white-tailed deer (*Odocoileus virginianus*). Ph.D. thesis, University of Wisconsin, Madison.

———. 1970. Bluetongue. In *Infectious diseases of wild mammals,* ed. J. W. Davis, L. H. Karstad, and D. O. Trainer, pp. 55–59. Ames: Iowa State University Press. 421 pp.

Trainer, D. O., and Hanson, R. P. 1960. Leptospirosis and brucellosis serological reactions in Wisconsin deer, 1957–1958. *J. Wildl. Manage.* 24:44–52.

Trainer, D. O., and Karstad, L. H. 1970. Epizootic hemorrhagic disease. In *Infectious diseases of wild mammals,* ed. J. W. Davis, L. H. Karstad, and D. O. Trainer, pp. 50–54. Ames: Iowa State University Press. 421 pp.

Tromble, J. M. 1976. Semiarid rangeland treatment and surface runoff. *J. Range Manage.* 29:251–55.

Trout, L. 1968. Chemical sprays, plants and wildlife. *Idaho Wildl. Rev.* 21(1):9–11.

Trout, L., and Thiessen, J. L. 1968. Food habits and condition of mule deer in Owyhee County. *Proc. West. Assoc. Game and Fish Commissioners* 48:188–200.

———. 1973. *Physical condition and range relationships of the Owyhee deer herd.* Wildlife Bulletin no. 5. Boise: Idaho Fish and Game Department. 37 pp.

True, G. H. 1932. Damage by deer to crops in California. *Calif. Fish and Game* 18:136–47.

Trueblood, T. 1967. Look what they're doing to your land. *Field and Stream* 72(6):10, 12, 16, 20, 84.

Tsukamoto, G., and Wickersham, M. 1971. *Guzzler construction and rehabilitation.* Progress Report, P-R Project W-18-2, Study II, Job 19. Reno: Nevada Department of Fish and Game. 35 pp.

Tucker, J. M. 1963. Major Long's route from the Arkansas to the Canadian River, 1820. *New Mexico Hist. Rev.* 38(3):185–219.

Tueller, P. T., and Monroe, L. A. 1974. *Management guidelines for selected deer habitats in Nevada.* Nevada Agricultural Experiment Station Publication no. R 104. 185 pp.

Tunnicliff, E. A., and Marsh, H. 1935. Bang's diseases in bison and elk in the Yellowstone National Park and the National Bison Range. *J. Amer. Vet. Med. Assoc.* 86:745–62.

Turner, G. T. 1969. Responses of mountain grassland vegetation to gopher control, reduced grazing, and herbicide. *J. Range Manage.* 22:377–83.

Tyler, G. V. 1977. Experimental infection of mule deer (*Odocoileus hemionus*) with *Parelaphostrongylus tenuis*. M.S. thesis, Colorado State University, Fort Collins. 45 pp.

Ullrey, D. E.; Youatt, W. G.; Johnson, H. E.; Fay, L. D.; and Bradley, B. L. 1967. Protein requirement of white-tailed deer fawns. *J. Wildl. Manage.* 31:679–85.

Ullrey, D. E.; Youatt, W. G.; Johnson, H. E.; Fay, L. D.; Covert, R. L.; and Magee, W. T. 1975. Consumption of artificial browse supplements by white-tailed deer. *J. Wildl. Manage.* 39:699–704.

Ullrey, D. E.; Youatt, W. G.; Johnson, H. E.; Fay, L. D.; Schoepke, B. L.; and Magee, W. T. 1970. Digestible and metabolizable energy requirements for winter maintenance of Michigan white-tailed does. *J. Wildl. Manage.* 34:863–69.

Ullrey, D. E.; Youatt, W. G.; Johnson, H. E.; Fay, L. D.; Schoepke, B. L.; Magee, W. T.; and Keahey, K. K. 1973. Calcium requirements of weaned white-tailed deer fawns. *J. Wildl. Manage.* 37:187–94.

United States. 1974. *Statutes at large.* Vol. 215.

United States Bureau of Land Management. 1962–77. *Public land statistics.* Washington, D.C.: GPO. (Published annually.)

United States Congress. Senate. 1936. *The western range.* Senate Doc. no. 199. 74th Cong. 2d sess. 620 pp.

———. 1975. *Range condition report prepared for the Senate Committee on Appropriations.* Washington D.C.: GPO. 134 pp.

United States Department of Agriculture. 1972. *The nation's range resources.* USDA Forest Service, Forest Resource Report no. 19. 147 pp.

————. 1974. *Our land and water resources: Current and prospective supplies and uses.* USDA Economic Research Service Miscellaneous Publication 1290. 54 pp.

————. 1978. *State summary of national forest recreation use.* Washington, D.C.: USDA Forest Service. 5 pp.

United States Department of Commerce. 1972. *Statistical abstract of the United States.* 93d annual edition. Washington, D.C.: USDC, Bureau of the Census. 1,017 pp.

United States Department of the Interior. 1973. *Final environmental impact statement for a prototype oil shale leasing program.* 6 vols. Washington, D.C.: GPO.

————. 1975. *Westwide study report on critical water problems facing the eleven western states.* Washington, D.C.: GPO. 457 pp.

United States Fish and Wildlife Service. 1952–71. *Annual big game inventory.* Wildlife Leaflets 342, 348, 364, 376, 387, 395, 399, 411, 425, 437, 440, 446, 454, 461, 470, 473, 477, 481, 487, 492, and 497. Washington, D.C.: Division of Wildlife Research, USDI Fish and Wildlife Service.

————. 1978. *Predator damage in the West: A study of coyote management alternatives.* Washington, D.C.: U.S. Fish and Wildlife Service. 168 pp.

United States Forest Service. 1950–76. *Annual wildlife reports.* Washington, D.C.: Division of Wildlife Management, USDA Forest Service.

————. 1968. *Animal damage control handbook.* FSH 2609.26 R6. Portland: USDA Forest Service, Region 6. (Pagination by chapters)

————. 1970. *Chaparral vegetation type.* Albuquerque: Division of Range and Wildlife, Southwestern Region, USDA Forest Service. 48 pp.

Upper Colorado Region State–Federal Inter-Agency Group. 1971. *Upper Colorado region comprehensive framework study.* Appendix 13, *Fish and wildlife.* Denver: Upper Colorado Region State–Federal Inter-Agency Group. 108 pp.

Urbston, D. F. 1976. Descriptive aspects of two fawn populations as delineated by reproductive differences. Ph.D. thesis, Virginia Polytechnic Institute and State University, Blacksburg. 104 pp.

Urness, P. J. 1966. Influence of range improvement practices on composition, production and utilization of *Artemisia* deer winter range in Oregon. Ph.D. thesis, Oregon State University, Corvallis. 183 pp.

————. 1969. Nutritional analyses and *in vitro* digestibility of mistletoes browsed by deer in Arizona. *J. Wildl. Manage.* 33:499–505.

————. 1973. Chemical analyses and *in vitro* digestibility of seasonal deer forages. In *Deer nutrition in Arizona chaparral and desert habitats,* pp. 39–52. Special Report no. 3. Phoenix: Arizona Game and Fish Department. 68 pp.

————. 1974. *Deer use changes after root plowing in Arizona chaparral.* USDA Forest Service Research Note RM-255. 8 pp.

————. 1976. Mule deer habitat changes resulting from livestock practices. In *Mule deer decline in the West: A symposium,* ed. G. W. Workman and J. B. Low, pp.

21–35. Logan: Utah State University College of Natural Resources and Agricultural Experiment Station. 134 pp.

Urness, P. J.; Green, W.; and Watkins, R. K. 1971. Nutrient intake of deer in Arizona chaparral and desert habitats. *J. Wildl. Manage.* 35:469–75.

Urness, P. J., and McCulloch, C. Y. 1973. Nutritional value of seasonal deer diets. In *Deer nutrition in Arizona chaparral and desert habitats,* pp. 53–64. Special Report no. 3. Phoenix: Arizona Game and Fish Department. 68 pp.

Urness, P. J.; Neff, D. J.; and Vahle, J. R. 1975. Nutrient content of mule deer diets from ponderosa pine range. *J. Wildl. Manage.* 39:670–73.

Urness, P. J.; Smith, A. D.; and Watkins, R. K. 1977. Comparison of *in vivo* and *in vitro* dry matter digestibility of mule deer forages. *J. Range Manage.* 30:119–21.

Uzzell, P. B. 1958. *Deer food habits study: Trans-Pecos game management survey.* P-R Project W-57-R, Job 7. Austin: Texas Game and Fish Commission. 21 pp.

Vale, T. R. 1974. Sagebrush conversion projects: An element of contemporary environmental change in the western United States. *Biol. Conserv.* 6:274–84.

Van Ballenberghe, V.; Erickson, A. W.; and Byman, D. 1975. Ecology of the timber wolf in northeastern Minnesota. *Wildl. Monogr.* no. 43. 43 pp.

Van Haverbeke, D. R. 1968. *A population analysis of Juniperus in the Missouri River Basin.* University of Nebraska Studies, new series no. 38, Lincoln: University of Nebraska. 82 pp.

van Tets, P. A., and Cowan, I. McT. 1966. Some sources of variation in the blood sera of deer (*Odocoileus*) as revealed by starch gel electrophoresis. *Can. J. Zool.* 44:631–47.

————. 1967. The starch-gel electrophoretic serum lipid fraction of two species of deer in the genus *Odocoileus. Can. J. Zool.* 45:579–81.

van Zyll De Jong, C. G. 1967. Review of Das Geweih [Antlers], by A. B. Bubenik (Hamburg-Berlin: Paul Parey, 1966. 214 pp.). *J. Mammal.* 48:681–83.

Vaughan, T. A. 1972. *Mammalogy.* Philadelphia: W. B. Saunders. 463 pp.

Verme, L. J. 1962. Mortality of white-tailed deer fawns in relation to nutrition. In *Proceedings: First national white-tailed deer disease symposium,* pp. 15–28, 37–38. Athens: University of Georgia. 202 pp.

————. 1963a. Effect of nutrition on growth of white-tailed deer fawns. *Trans. N. Amer. Wildl. and Natur. Resour. Conf.* 28:431–43.

————. 1963b. Reproduction studies on penned white-tailed deer. *J. Wildl. Manage.* 29:74–79.

————. 1967. Influence of experimental diets on white-tailed deer reproduction. *Trans. N. Amer. Wildl. and Natur. Resour. Conf.* 32:405–20.

————. 1969. Reproductive patterns of white-tailed deer related to nutritional plane. *J. Wildl. Manage.* 33:881–87.

Verme, L. J., and Holland, J. C. 1973. Reagent-dry assay of marrow fat in white-tailed deer. *J. Wildl. Manage.*

37:103–5.

Verme, L. J., and Ullrey, D. E. 1972. Feeding and nutrition of deer. In *Digestive physiology and nutrition of ruminants,* vol. 3, *Practical nutrition,* ed. D. C. Church, pp. 275–91. Corvallis: Oregon State University. 350 pp.

Vilkitis, J. R. 1968. Characteristics of big game violators and extent of their activity in Idaho. M.S. thesis, University of Idaho, Moscow. 202 pp.

Villmo, L. 1975. The Scandanavian viewpoint. *Proc. Int. Reindeer and Caribou Symp.* 1:4–9.

Visher, S. S. 1914. *Biology of Harding County.* Bulletin no. 6. Pierre: South Dakota Geological Survey. 126 pp.

Vlamis, J.; Stone, E. C.; and Young, C. L. 1954. Nutrient status of brushland soils in southern California. *Soil Sci.* 78:51–55.

Vosdingh, R. A.; Trainer, D. O.; and Easterday, B. C. 1968. Experimental bluetongue disease in white-tailed deer. *Can. J. Vet. Sci.* 32:382.

Wachtel, M. A.; Bekoff, M.; and Feunzalida, C. E. 1978. Sparring by mule deer during rutting: Class participation seasonal changes and the nature of asymmetrical contests. *Biol. of Behaviour* 3(4):319–30.

Waddington, C. H. 1957. *The strategy of genes.* London: Allen and Unwin.

———. 1975. *The evolution of an evolutionist.* Ithaca: Cornell University Press.

Wagner, F. H. 1978. Livestock grazing and the livestock industry. In *Wildlife and America,* ed. H. P. Brokaw, pp. 121–45. Washington, D.C.: GPO. 532 pp.

Waldo, C. M.; Wislocki, G. B.; and Fawcett, D. W. 1949. Observations on the blood supply of growing antlers. *Amer. J. Anat.* 84:27–61.

Waldrip, G. P. 1977. Elk habitat use during calving season with possible effects on white-tailed deer at the Wichita Mountains National Wildlife Refuge. M.S. thesis, Oklahoma State University, Stillwater. 81 pp.

Walker, C. R. 1929. *Cephenomyia* killing deer. *Science* 69:646–47.

Walker, E. P. 1975. *Mammals of the world.* Vols. 1 and 2. 3d ed. Baltimore and London: Johns Hopkins University Press. 1,500 pp.

Wallace, L. R. 1948. The growth of lambs before and after birth in relation to the level of nutrition. *J. Agric. Sci.* 38:243–302.

Wallmo, O. C. 1960. *Big Bend ecological survey.* Job Completion Report, P-R Project W-57-R-8, J 9. Austin: Texas Game and Fish Commission. 43 pp.

———. 1961. *Big Bend ecological survey.* Job Completion Report, P-R Project W-57-R-9, J 9. Austin: Texas Game and Fish Commission. 29 pp.

———. 1964. Problems in the use of herd classification data. *Proc. Ann. Meet. New Mexico–Arizona Sec., Wildl. Soc.* 3:6–17.

———. 1969. *Response of deer to alternate-strip clearcutting of lodgepole pine and spruce-fir timber in Colorado.* USDA Forest Service Research Note RM-141. 4 pp.

———. 1973. Important game animals and related recreation in arid shrublands of the United States. *Proc.*

Workshop U.S. /Austral. Rangelands Panel 3:98–107.

———. 1978. Mule deer and black-tailed deer. In *Big game of North America: Ecology and management,* ed. J. L. Schmidt and D. L. Gilbert, pp. 31–41. Harrisburg, Pa.: Stackpole Books. 494 pp.

Wallmo, O. C.; Carpenter, L. H.; Regelin, W. L.; Gill, R. B.; and Baker, D. L. 1977. Evaluation of deer habitat on a nutritional basis. *J. Range Manage.* 30:122–27.

Wallmo, O. C., and Gill, R. B. 1971. Snow, winter distribution and population dynamics of mule deer in the central Rocky Mountains. In *Snow and ice in relation to wildlife and recreation symposium proceedings,* ed. A. O. Haugen, pp. 1–15. Ames: Iowa State University. 280 pp.

Wallmo, O. C.; Gill, R. B.; Carpenter, L. H.; and Reichert, D. W. 1973. Accuracy of field estimates of deer food habits. *J. Wildl. Manage.* 37:556–62.

Wallmo, O. C.; Reed, D. F.; and Carpenter, L. H. 1976. Alteration of mule deer habitat by wildfire, logging, highways, agriculture, and housing developments. In *Mule deer decline in the West: A symposium,* ed. G. W. Workman and J. B. Low, pp. 37–47. Logan: Utah State University College of Natural Resources and Agricultural Experiment Station. 134 pp.

Wallmo, O. C.; Regelin, W. L.; and Reichert, D. W. 1972. Forage use by mule deer relative to logging in Colorado. *J. Wildl. Manage.* 36:1025–33.

Walters, C. J., and Bandy, P. C. 1972. Periodic harvest as a method of increasing big game yields. *J. Wildl. Manage.* 36:128–34.

Walters, C. J., and Gross, J. E. 1972. Development of big game management plans through simulation modeling. *J. Wildl. Manage.* 36:119–23.

Walther, F. R. 1958. Zum Kampf und Paarungs verhalten einiger Antilopen. *Z. Tierpsychol.* 15:340–80.

———. 1966. *Mit Horn und Huf.* Berlin: Parey. 171 pp.

———. 1974. Some reflections on expressive behaviour in combat and courtship of certain horned ungulates. In *The behaviour of ungulates and its relation to management,* ed. V. Geist and F. R. Walther, 1:56–106. IUCN New Series Publication 24, Morges, Switzerland: IUCN. 511 pp.

Wanek, W. J. 1974. The ecological impact of snowmobiling in northern Minnesota. In *Proceedings: 1973 snowmobile and off the road vehicle research symposium,* pp. 57–76. Technical Report 9. East Lansing: Michigan State University. 202 pp.

Ward, A. L.; Cupal, J. J.; Goodwin, G. A.; and Morris, H. D. 1976. *Effects of highway construction and use on big game populations.* U.S. Department of Transportation, Federal Highway Administration Report. FHWA-RD-76-174. 92 pp.

Ward, A. L.; Cupal, J. J.; Lea, A. L.; Oakley, C. A.; and Weeks, R. W. 1973. Elk behavior in relation to cattle grazing, forest recreation, and traffic. *Trans. N. Amer. Wildl. and Natur. Resour. Conf.* 38:327–37.

Waring, R. H., and Franklin, J. F. 1979. Evergreen coniferous forest of the Pacific Northwest. *Science* 204:1380–86.

Warren, E. R. 1936a. Casualties among animals on

mountain roads. *Science* 83(2140):14.

———. 1936*b*. Mountain road casualties among animals in Colorado. *Science* 84(2187):485.

Washington State Game Department. 1974. Dogs and deer. *Wash. Wildl.* 26(2):11.

Watt, K. E. F. 1968. *Ecology and resource management.* New York: McGraw-Hill. 225 pp.

Weaver, J. E., and Albertson, F. W. 1956. *Grasslands of the Great Plains: Their nature and use.* Lincoln: Johnson. 395 pp.

Weaver, J. E., and Clements, F. E. 1938. *Plant ecology.* New York and London: McGraw-Hill. 601 pp.

Webster, G. L. 1950. Observations on the vegetation and summer flora of the Stockton Plateau in northeastern Terrell County, Texas. *Texas J. Sci.* 2:234–42.

Weinmann, C. J.; Anderson, J. R.; Longhurst, W. M.; and Connolly, G. 1973. Filarial worms of Colu   an black-tailed deer in California. I. Observations   the vertebrate host. *J. Wildl. Dis.* 9:213–20.

Weinmann, C. J.; Anderson, J. R.; Rubtzoff, P.; Connolly, G.; and Longhurst, W. M. 1974. Eyeworms and face flies. *Calif. Agric.* 28(11):4–5.

Welch, B. L. 1962. Adrenals of deer as indicators of population conditions for purposes of management. In *Proceedings: First national white-tailed deer disease symposium,* pp. 94–108. Athens: University of Georgia. 202 pp.

Welch, J. F. 1967. Review of animal repellents. *Proc. Vert. Pest Conf.* 3:36–40.

Welch, R. D. 1974. *Illegal kill and crippling loss of deer during regulated hunting seasons.* Final Report, P-R Project W-93-16. Santa Fe: New Mexico Department of Game and Fish. 14 pp.

West, N. O. 1968. The length of the estrous cycle in the Columbian black-tailed deer or Coast deer *(Odocoileus hemionus columbianus).* B.S. thesis, University of British Columbia, Vancouver. 31 pp.

West, N. O., and Nordan, H. C. 1976*a*. Hormonal regulation of reproduction and the antler cycle in the male Columbian black-tailed deer *(Odocoileus hemionus columbianus).* Part I. Seasonal changes in the histology of the reproductive organs, serum testosterone, sperm production, and the antler cycle. *Can. J. Zool.* 54:1617–36.

———. 1976*b*. Hormonal regulation of reproduction and the antler cycle in the male Columbian black-tailed deer *(Odocoileus hemionus columbianus).* Part II. The effects of methallibure and hormone treatment. *Can. J. Zool.* 54:1637–56.

———. 1976*c*. Cytology of the anterior pituitary at different times of the year in normal and methallibure-treated male Columbian black-tailed deer *(Odocoileus hemionus columbianus). Can. J. Zool.* 54:1969–78.

Westrom, D. R.; Nelson, B. C.; and Connolly, G. E. 1976. Transfer of *Bovicola tibialis* (Piaget) (Mallophaga: Trichodectidae) from the introduced fallow deer to the Columbian black-tailed deer in California. *J. Med. Ent.* 13:169–73.

Whicker, F. W. 1964. Density studies of mule deer body fat. *J. Mammal.* 45:252–59.

Whicker, F. W.; Farris, G. C.; and Dahl, A. H. 1966. Radioiodine in Colorado deer and elk thyroids during 1964–65. *J. Wildl. Manage.* 30:781–85.

———. 1967. Concentration patterns of ^{90}Sr, ^{137}Cs, and ^{131}I in a wild deer population and environment. In *Radioecological concentration processes,* ed. B. Aberg and F. P. Hungate, pp. 621–33. New York: Pergamon Press. 1,040 pp.

———. 1968. Wild deer as a source of radionuclide intake by humans and as indicators of fallout hazards. In *Radiation protection, proceedings: First international congress on radiation protection,* ed. W.S. Snyder, pp. 1105–10. New York: Pergamon Press. 1,623 pp.

Whicker, F. W.; Farris, G. C.; Dahl, A. H.; and Remmenga, E. E. 1965. Factors influencing the accumulation of fallout Cs-137 in Colorado mule deer. *Health Physics* 11:1407–14.

Whicker, F. W.; Walters, R. A.; and Dahl, A. H. 1967. Fallout radionuclides in Colorado deer liver. *Nature* 214:511–13.

White, K. L. 1958. The determination of cervid antler weight from linear measurements. *Proc. Mont. Acad. Sci.* 18:29–31.

White, M. 1973. The whitetail deer of the Arkansas National Wildlife Refuge. *Texas J. Sci.* 24:457–89.

White, M.; Knowlton, F. F.; and Glazener, W. C. 1972. Effect of dam-newborn fawn behaviour on capture and mortality. *J. Wildl. Manage.* 36:897–906.

Whitlock, S. C. 1939. The prevalence of disease and parasites in white-tailed deer. *Trans. N. Amer. Wildl. Conf.* 4:244–47.

Whittow, G. C. 1971. Ungulates. In *Comparative physiology of thermoregulation,* vol. 2, *Mammals,* ed. E. C. Whittow, pp. 191–279. New York and London: Academic Press. 410 pp.

Wika, M., and Krog, J. K. 1971. Surface temperatures and avenues of heat loss during summer conditions in reindeer with growing antlers. *Norwegian J. Zool.* 19:89–91.

Wilber, C. G., and Robinson, P. F. 1958. Aspects of blood chemistry in the white-tailed deer. *J. Mammal.* 39:309–11.

Williams, D. E., and Goetz, H. N.d. Growth, production and browse utilization characteristics of serviceberry *(Amelanchier alnifolia* Nutt.) in the badlands of southwestern North Dakota. Unpublished. On file at Department of Botany, North Dakota State University, Fargo. 20 pp.

Williams, J. E. 1964. Deer, death and destruction. *Colo. Outdoors* 13(2):1–3.

Williamson, R. E. 1973. *Results of shelterwood harvesting of Douglas-fir in the Cascades of western Oregon.* USDA Forest Service Research Paper PNW-161. 13 pp.

Willms, W. D. 1971. The influence of forest edge, elevation, aspect, site index, and roads on deer use of logged and mature forest, northern Vancouver Island. M.S. thesis, University of British Columbia, Vancouver. 184 pp.

Wilson, E. O. 1975. *Sociobiology: The new synthesis.*

Cambridge: Belknap Press of Harvard University Press. 697 pp.

Wilson, P. N., and Osbourn, D. F. 1960. Compensatory growth after undernutrition in mammals and birds. *Biol. Rev.* 35:324–63.

Wislocki, G. B. 1942. Studies on the growth of deer antlers. I. On the structure and histogenesis of the antlers of the Virginia deer *(Odocoileus virginianus borealis). Amer. J. Anat.* 71:371–415.

———. 1943. Studies on the growth of deer antlers. II. Seasonal changes in the male reproductive tract of the Virginia deer *(Odocoileus virginianus borealis),* with a discussion of the factors controlling the antler gonad periodicity. In *Essays in biology: In honor of Herbert M. Evans,* pp. 651–53. Berkeley and Los Angeles: University of California Press. 686 pp.

———. 1956. Further notes on antlers in female deer of the genus *Odocoileus. J. Mammal.* 37:231–35.

Wislocki, G. B., and Singer, M. 1946. The occurrence and function of nerves in the growing antlers of deer. *J. Comp. Neurol.* 85:1–19.

Wolfe, C. W. 1972. Effects of fire on a Sand Hills grassland environment. *Proc. Tall Timbers Fire Ecol. Conf.* 12:241–55.

Wolfe, J. N. 1963. Impact of atomic energy on the environment and environmental sciences. In *Radioecology,* ed. V. Schultz and A. W. Klement, Jr., pp. 1–2. New York: Reinhold. 746 pp.

Wolfe, M. L. 1976. Reliability of mule deer population measurements. In *Mule deer decline in the West: A symposium,* ed. G. W. Workman and J. B. Low, pp. 91–86. Logan: Utah State University College of Natural Resources and Agricultural Experiment Station. 134 pp.

———. 1978. Habitat changes and management. In *Big game of North America: Ecology and management,* ed. J. L. Schmidt and D. L. Gilbert, pp. 349–68. Harrisburg, Pa.: Stackpole Books. 494 pp.

Wood, A. J., and Cowan, I. McT. 1968. Post natal growth. In *A practical guide to the study of large herbivores,* ed. F. B. Golley and H. K. Buechner, pp. 106–13. I.B.P. Handbook 7, 1st ed. Oxford: Blackwell Scientific Publications. 308 pp.

Wood, A. J.; Cowan, I. McT.; and Nordan, H. C. 1962. Periodicity of growth in ungulates as shown by deer of the genus *Odocoileus. Can. J. Zool.* 40:593–603.

Wood, J. E.; Bickle, T. S.; Evans, W.; Germany, J. C.; and Howard, V. W., Jr. 1970. *The Fort Stanton mule deer herd (some ecological and life history characteristics with special emphasis on the use of water).* Bulletin 567. Las Cruces: New Mexico State University Agricultural Experiment Station. 32 pp.

Woodard, T. N., and Reed, D. F. 1974. Economic considerations in reduction of deer-vehicle accidents. *Trans. Central Mtn. Plains Sec., Wildl. Soc. Conf.* 19:18 (abstract).

Woolf, A. 1978. Pathology and necropsy techniques. In *Big game of North America: Ecology and management,* ed. J. L. Schmidt and D. L. Gilbert, pp. 425–36. Harrisburg, Pa.: Stackpole Books. 494 pp.

Woolf, A.; Mason, C. A.; and Kradel, D. 1977. Prevalence and effects of *Parelaphostrongylus tenuis* in a captive wapiti population. *J. Wildl. Dis.* 13:149–55.

Worley, D. E. 1975. Observations on epizootiology and distribution of *Elaeophora schneideri* in Montana ruminants. *J. Wildl. Dis.* 11:486–88.

Wright, H. A. 1970. Response of big sagebrush and three-tip sagebrush to season of clipping. *J. Range Manage.* 23:20–22.

Wright, J. T. 1959. *Desert wildlife.* Wildlife Bulletin no. 6. Phoenix: Arizona Game and Fish Department. 78 pp.

Wynn-Edwards, V. C. 1962. *Animal dispersion in relation to social behaviour.* Edinburgh: Oliver and Boyd. 653 pp.

Yeager, L. E., and Riordan, L. E. 1953. Effects of beetle-killed timber on range and wildlife in Colorado. *Trans. N. Amer. Wildl. Conf.* 18:596–616.

Young, J., and Boyce, A. 1971. Recreational uses of snow and ice in Michigan and some of its effects on wildlife and people. In *Proceedings: Snow and ice in relation to wildlife and recreation symposium,* ed. A. O. Haugen, pp. 193–96. Ames: Iowa State University. 280 pp.

Young, J. A.; Hedrick, D. W.; and Kenniston, R. F. 1967. Forest cover and logging: Herbage and browse production in the mixed conifer forest of northeastern Oregon. *J. For.* 65:807–13.

Young, R. A. 1976. Fat, energy and mammalian survival. *Amer. Zool.* 16:699–710.

Young, S. P. 1956. The deer, the Indians, and the American pioneers. In *The deer of North America,* ed. W. P. Taylor, pp. 1–27. Harrisburg, Pa.: Stackpole. 668 pp.

Young, S. P., and Goldman, E. A. 1946. *The puma, mysterious American cat.* Washington, D.C.: American Wildlife Institute. 358 pp.

Young, S. P., and Jackson, H. H. T. 1951. *The clever coyote.* Harrisburg, Pa.: Stackpole. 411 pp.

Young, V. A., and Payne, G. F. 1948. Utilization of "key" browse species in relation to proper grazing practices in cutover western white pine lands in northern Idaho. *J. For.* 46:35–40.

Yousef, M. K.; Hahn, L.; and Johnson, H. D. 1968. Adaptation of cattle. In *Adaptation of domestic animals,* ed. E. S. E. Hafez, pp. 233–45. Philadelphia: Lea and Febiger. 415 pp.

Yuill, T. M.; Low, J. B.; and Fitzgerald, P. R. 1961. The foot worm of northern Utah deer. *Wildl. Dis.* no. 10. 5 pp. (microfiche).

Zagata, M. D., and Haughen, A. D. 1974. Influence of light and weather on observability of Iowa deer. *J. Wildl. Manage.* 38:220–28.

Ziegler, D. L. 1978. *The Okanogan mule deer.* Biological Bulletin no. 15. Olympia: Washington Department of Game. 106 pp.

Zimmerman, W. B. 1971. How to drive in deer country. *Colo. Outdoors* 20(2):4–7.

Zwank, P. J. 1976. Mule deer productivity: Past and present. In *Mule deer decline in the West: A symposium,* ed. G. W. Workman and J. B. Low, pp. 79–86. Logan: Utah State University College of Natural Resources and Agricultural Experiment Station. 134 pp.

INDEX

Abomasum, 103
Actinomyces bovis, 135
Actinomycosis, 135
Adaptive strategies. *See* Behavior
Adrenal glands, 66–67
Aedes sierrensis, 140
Aerial counts, 314–16
Age estimation; by dental cementum annuli counts, 61, 289–90; by eye lens weight method, 289; by tooth replacement and wear method, 287–89; by tooth wear, 60–61; of twin fawns, 52
Aggression: and defensive strategy, 194; and direct threats, 178; and dominance displays, 178–79, 180–84; and flail fights, 177–80; and horning, 183–84; and intraspecific combat, 194; as related to testosterone, 78; and rut-snorting, 182; use of antlers in, 78; and weapons, 177–79
Agriculture and mule deer, 511–12
Alarm strategies, 167, 168
Alaska: deer population trend in, 227; distribution of deer in, 6; estimated deer harvest in, 234; estimated deer population in, 230
Alberta: deer population trend in, 227; distribution of deer in, 7
Albumen, 32
Anaplasma marginale, 152
Anaplasmosis, 152–53
Animal unit month, 514
Anthrax, 136–38
Antlers, 77–95; in aggression, 78; blood supply to, 81–83; and carcass weight, 89, 90; characteristics of, 78–79, 87–88; composition of, 83; deformities of, 91–92; development of, 79–80; and environment, 83, 88; evolution of, 77–78; in females, 92, 94–95; growth of, 79, 84–87; mineral trace elements in, 83; of mule deer subspecies, 87–88; ossification process of, 79, 80; and osteoporosis, 83–84; phenology of, 82; and radioactive fallout, 83; shedding of, 78, 80–81, 85; and social interaction, 78; symmetry of, 89; and testicular pathology and castration, 90–91; and testosterone, 79; and thermoregulation, 78; velvet stage of, 80, 81, 92; weights of, 84

Arizona: chaparral habitat of, 352, 354; deer population trend in, 227; distribution of deer in, 9; estimated deer harvest in, 234; estimated deer population in, 230; hunting success in, 266
Artificial feeding, 125, 126, 414–17
Aspen parklands, 470–71
Audubon, John J., 460
Axis deer, 194

Bacillus anthracis, 136
Bacterial diseases, 133–36
Badlands, 469–70
Barbary sheep, 487, 497
Behavior: alarm and security measures of, 167–74; in artificial feeding, 414–16; attempts to classify, 161; and comfort movements, 166; at conclusion of the rut, 211; constraints on, 211; in courtship, 195, 202; differences of, from white-tailed deer, 215–16; and dominance displays, 180–84; and escape strategies, 171, 173–74; and etiquette, submission, and appeasement, 166–67; and facultative territoriality, 212–14; and feeding, 162–64, 165; and female courtship, 208–9; habitat and, 159–60, 216–19; and "hider" syndrome, 219; in homosexual mounting, 191; and hyperactivity, 202; of mother and young, 219–22; and play, 220; in predator avoidance, 168–72; problems in assessing, 161–62; related to reproductive fitness, 211–12, 214; and resting, 164–66; and roaming, 202; in segregation from whitetails, 215–16; and sparring matches, 185–92; in swimming, 173–74; in tending disruptions, 203–8, 210–11; and threats, 177–80; in urination, marking, and defecation, 174–76, 187, 210; and vacuoejaculations, 203
Bighorn sheep, 35, 133, 137, 153, 160, 180, 184, 192, 220, 221, 222, 273, 487, 493, 496; and interspecific competition with mule deer, 496
Bilirubin, 33
Biopolitics, 262–63
Birthrates, methods of estimating, 290–91

Birth weights, 51
Bison, 133, 134, 138, 463, 477, 478, 482, 487, 493, 497; historical effects of, on Great Plains, 477–78; and interspecific relationship with mule deer, 497
Bitterbrush and browsing, 406–7
Black bears, 143, 222, 274–75
Black flies: as disease carriers, 143; parasitism by, 149
Blackleg, 135–36
Black-tailed deer: and chaparral manipulation, 373; computer simulation of harvests of, 251; effects of hunting on, 255–56; estimated population of, 230, 231; habitat provinces of, 13–14; harvests of, 234; historical distinction of, 2
Blood: cellular constituents of, 31; chemical constituents of, 31–35; as diagnostic aid, 31; as percentage of body weight, 30
Blood serum, 32
Blood urea nitrogen, 33
Bluetongue, 129–30
Bobcat, 174, 222, 270, 276, 282, 284, 378
Bobwhite quail, 253
Body composition, 27–35
Body fat: and taxonomy, 36; and annual storage depletion cycle, 396; biochemistry of storage of, 29; considerations in measuring, 73; estimation of, by carcass density, 71–72; femur marrow index of, 70–71; importance of, 70; kidney fat index of, 71; as percentage of body weight, 28–29; seasonal changes in, 73–74, 123, 125
Body temperature, 36–39, 118
Body weight: at birth, 50–51; of bled carcass, 56; bone as percentage of, 30; compared with captive deer, 432; general seasonal pattern of, 69; growth curve of, 54; hog-dressed, of yearling blacktail bucks, 433; increase rate of, in fawns, 42–54; pattern of, in coniferous forest habitats, 432–33; postpubertal fluctuations of, 54; seasonal fluctuations of, 54–55
Bone marrow index, 333–34
Boreal forest habitat, 20–22
Botflies, parasitism by, 149–50